Eighth Edition

Canadian
Democracy

Stephen Brooks

OXFORD
UNIVERSITY PRESS

OXFORD
UNIVERSITY PRESS

Oxford University Press is a department of the University of Oxford.
It furthers the University's objective of excellence in research, scholarship,
and education by publishing worldwide. Oxford is a registered trade mark of
Oxford University Press in the UK and in certain other countries.

Published in Canada by
Oxford University Press
8 Sampson Mews, Suite 204,
Don Mills, Ontario M3C 0H5 Canada

www.oupcanada.com

Copyright © Oxford University Press Canada 2015

First Edition published in 1993
Second Edition published in 1996
Third Edition published in 2000
Fourth Edition published in 2004
Fifth Edition published in 2007
Sixth Edition published in 2009
Seventh Edition published in 2012

Library and Archives Canada Cataloguing in Publication
Brooks, Stephen, 1956–, author
Canadian democracy / Stephen Brooks. — Updated eighth edition.

Includes bibliographical references and index.
ISBN 978-0-19-902876-4 (pbk.)

1. Canada—Politics and government—Textbooks.
2. Democracy—Canada—Textbooks. I. Title.

JL65.B76 2016   320.971   C2016-906944-3

Brief Contents

Contents

PART I   Introduction   1

1   An Introduction to Political Life   2

PART II   The Societal Context of Politics   31

2   Political Culture   32

3   The Social and Economic Setting   76

4   Diversity and Multiculturalism   104

PART III   The Structures of Governance   155

PART IV Participation in Politics   323

Figures and Tables

Figures

Tables

Boxes

Politics in Focus

The Social Fabric

Governing Realities

Media Spotlight

Preface

What is democracy? And what is the state of democracy in Canada today? The title of this book—*Canadian Democracy*—is not a judgement or a conclusion. It is, rather, a focus. Over the previous seven editions of this textbook, as in the present edition, I have tried to structure my treatment of the key components of Canada's political system around such themes as equality, freedoms, rights, and access. This approach is neither an uncritical celebration of Canadian politics nor a lopsided condemnation of its shortcomings and failures. In using the complex and contested concept of democracy as my touchstone I hope to encourage readers to think about Canadian government and politics in ways that will enable them to assess fairly and realistically the performance of Canada's political system.

Most readers of this book are university undergraduates, many in their first year. Working on this latest edition of *Canadian Democracy* has prompted me to reflect on what has changed and what has remained the same since I was a student in an Introduction to Canadian Politics and Government course in 1974! Several rather profound changes stand out in my mind. Aboriginal issues were almost entirely absent from the teaching of Canadian politics. Feminist perspectives were beginning to gain traction in Canadian universities, but the major accomplishments of the women's movement were yet to come. The term and idea of multiculturalism were barely known to most Canadians. The policies now associated with it and the central place that multiculturalism has come to occupy in relation to Canada's identity were still years away. Ontario was still Canada's wealthiest province and the undisputed leader among Canada's provincial governments. The significant westward shift in population and wealth would come later, particularly in the last couple of decades. The Liberal Party of Canada was frequently, and in some quarters only half-jokingly, referred to as the "Natural Governing Party." It dominated Canadian politics for most of the twentieth century. As incredible as it may seem, rights and freedoms were relatively marginal concerns among political scientists and politicians. There was much more talk about federalism and the powers of governments than about the limitations on those powers. Finally, globalization was not part of the political lexicon. Although there was quite a lot of discussion of multinational corporations and of various transnational economic and cultural trends, the phenomenon of globalization as we have come to know it—with a scale, forms, and consequences far beyond what existed 40 years ago—was just a dot on the horizon of some visionary thinkers.

At the same time, some things have remained recognizably the same. A Trudeau (Pierre) led the Liberal Party and was Prime Minister. A Trudeau (Justin) leads the party in 2014 and aspires to be Prime Minister. This is perhaps not so significant. More seriously, about one-third of Quebecers supported political independence for their province and roughly the same percentage express this preference 40 years later. Members of Parliament, once described by Prime Minister Pierre Trudeau as "nobodies," continue to express frustration over their role and what many of them see as their inability to break out of the straitjacket of party discipline. Canada is about as dependent on trade and investment with the United States as it was when Richard Nixon was leaving the White House. The Canada–United States relationship continues to overshadow all other aspects of Canada's engagement with the rest of the world. Canada continues to have an unelected head of state, Queen Elizabeth II, who resides in another country, and an unelected Senate. Most Canadians seem unconcerned about either of these facts and, indeed, many are quite unaware of them. Canada's political landscape is today recognizably the same as it was a couple of generations ago, but many of the borderlines, roads, and place names have changed. What has not changed, however, is the fact that all of the central issues in Canadian political life raise questions of fairness, freedom, representation, justice, and dignity. These are values we associate with democracy. We may not agree on the concrete meaning of these values or on the balance among them that best satisfies our ideal of democracy. But hardly anyone would disagree that whether what is at stake is the location of a landfill or revisions to the Constitution, these values and trade-offs are fundamental to democratic politics.

Canadian Democracy is organized into five parts. The first chapter, Part One, examines some basic concepts in the study of politics and government, including the central concept of democracy. Some readers will have been introduced to this material in a previous course, such as the Introduction to Politics course that is the necessary stepping stone to further political science courses at many universities. I have attempted to address these foundational concepts in ways that link them very directly to Canadian politics, so that even those students who already have taken a sort of "Political Science 101" course can gain something useful from what might otherwise be familiar territory.

Part Two, Chapters 2–5, focuses on the broad societal context of Canadian politics. Chapter 2 looks at the ideological roots of Canadian political institutions and controversies, highlighting in particular the similarities and differences between the political values and beliefs of Canadians and Americans. Chapter 3 surveys some of the politically significant social and economic characteristics of Canadian society, and is followed by a discussion of multiculturalism and diversity in Chapter 4. In Chapter 5, the nature and political impact of regionalism is examined. Part Three, Chapters 6–10, turns to the structures of governance. Here we examine the Constitution (Chapter6), rights and freedoms (Chapter 7), federalism (Chapter 8), the machinery of parliamentary government in Canada (Chapter 9), and the development of the administrative state and major features of the federal bureaucracy (Chapter 10). Part Four considers the main vehicles for individual and group participation in politics: Chapter 11 discusses the origins and contemporary character of Canada's political parties, their role in politics, and the nature and consequences of our electoral system, party finances, and voting; Chapter 12 looks at the characteristics and influence of interest groups; Chapter 13 examines the crucial place occupied by the mass media in modern democracies and the particular features of the media's role in Canadian politics.

Part Five, Chapters 14–17, focuses on four important issues in modern Canadian politics—language, women and politics, the status and treatment of Aboriginal Canadians, and Canada's role in the world—that illustrate well the complex interplay of values in democratic politics. Other issues are certainly deserving of attention and instructors may wish to supplement this material with an issue-oriented reader such as Mark Charlton and Paul Barker's *Crosscurrents: Contemporary Political Issues* (seventh edition, 2012).

Highlights of the Eighth Edition

While preparing this eighth edition of *Canadian Democracy*, one paramount goal was kept in mind: to produce the most accessible and interesting, yet comprehensive and authoritative introduction to Canadian politics available.

This edition builds on the strengths of the market-leading previous editions, using approachable content and dynamic pedagogy to explore the characteristics and controversies associated with Canadian politics. The following pages outline some of the most significant features of the new edition.

Comprehensive updates throughout bring readers the latest data, research, court rulings, and analysis of current events that come to bear on Canadian politics and society. Some specific changes to note:

✔ Chapter 1, "An Introduction to Political Life," includes a new discussion of Muslim democracy as well as updated examples illustrating what democracy means to people in Canada and elsewhere today.

✔ Chapter 3, "The Social and Economic Setting," contains new data and considerations of the long-term repercussions of the 2008 global economic crisis.

✔ Chapter 5, "Regionalism and Canadian Politics," incorporates new data on the changing relations between Canadian regions as well as new data comparing the political and social activities of these regions.

✔ Chapter 9, "The Machinery of Government," includes new statistics and content on visible minorities in the judiciary.

✔ Chapter 10, "The Administrative State," provides an expanded exploration of how issues of fair representation have played out in Canada in recent years.

✔ Chapter 17, "Canada in the World," includes significant new material on the Canada–United States relationship.

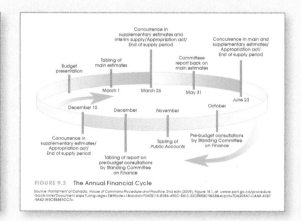

FIGURE 9.3   The Annual Financial Cycle

Updated feature boxes highlight current issues, show politics at work, and encourage students to think critically.

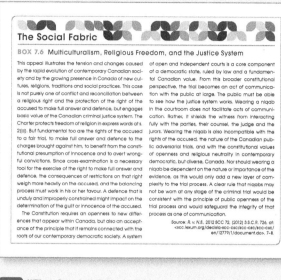

NEW! "The Social Fabric" boxes explore social issues that impact—and are impacted by—political developments and concerns.

"Governing Realities" boxes analyze examples of government at work as well as concepts related to the institutions and processes of government.

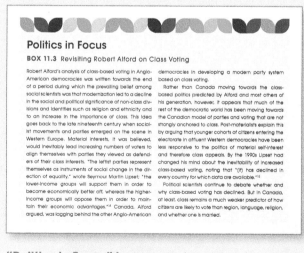

"Politics in Focus" boxes examine current issues and events through a critical lens.

"Media Spotlight" boxes highlight key media pieces and editorials and consider the media's role in politics.

Revised aids to student learning enhance students' engagement with the material, encouraging critical thinking and further exploration.

✔ **Chapter overviews** outline the main topics covered in each chapter and serve as a quick reference and study tool for students.

✔ **Lists of starting points for research** provide readings that serve as a jumping-off point for students looking to do further research for assignments and papers.

✔ **Review exercises** encourage students to apply what they have learned and use practical research skills.

✔ **A glossary of key terms** provides students with concise definitions for concepts that are, in many cases, unfamiliar and perhaps a bit specialized for most laypersons. These terms are important to an understanding of the material covered in this book.

✔ **An engaging photo and political cartoon program**—featuring an extensive selection of both contemporary and historic photos as well as insightful and thought-provoking editorial cartoons from renowned artists such as Roy Peterson and Len Norris—brings a visual dimension to the discussion of Canadian politics.

The reading of a new budget is a ceremonial affair in Ottawa, and though no one knows its origin, there is a long-standing tradition of the Finance Minister purchasing and wearing a new pair of shoes for the occasion. Finance Minister Jim Flaherty always wore new shoes.

In 2012, Canada celebrated the 200-year anniversary of the War of 1812, which has been characterized as a defining moment in Canadian history and, therefore, in the development of Canadian identity. In the cartoon above, what is the artist suggesting about the ways in which Canadians perceive this historical event?

A robust ancillary suite. The companion website for the eighth edition of *Canadian Democracy* can be found at www.oupcanada.com/Brooks8e. This site offers a wide variety of tools and resources designed to enhance the learning and teaching experiences.

✔ **A student study guide** offers short-answer study questions; self-testing quizzes; an expanded glossary; annotated lists of relevant websites; suggestions for books, articles, and media resources highlighting political issues in Canada; and RSS feeds from major news outlets.

✔ **A "Get Involved" section** for students features an overview of the history of Canadian political parties, interviews with and letters from leaders of Canada's major political parties, biographies of political science graduates who have put their degrees to work in exciting careers, and links to websites of interest, including those sponsored by Elections Canada and Democracy Watch.

✔ **Podcasts**—many new for this edition—provide students with mini-lectures that hone in on the issues of the day.

✔ **"Conversations on Canadian Politics" videos**—a number new for this edition—feature interviews with experts on various core concepts introduced in the text.

✔ **A test generator, an instructor's manual, and PowerPoint slides** for instructors offer a comprehensive array of teaching supports.

COMPANION WEBSITE	Stephen Brooks *Canadian Democracy* , Eighth Edition ISBN 13: 9780199011155

Inspection copy request

Ordering information

Contact & Comments

About the Book

While offering a thorough grounding in the institutions and processes of Canadian government, this book focuses on issues of individual, group, and regional equalities and freedoms while raising thought-provoking questions about the nature of Canadian democracy itself.

Readership : A core text for introduction to Canadian politics courses offered out of political science departments at the first- and second-year university levels.

Sample Material

Get Adobe PDF reader [US | UK]

Instructor Resources

You need a password to access these resources. Please contact your local Sales and Editorial Representative for more information.

Student Resources

Acknowledgements

Over the years I have been privileged to work with truly exceptional people at Oxford University Press, including Phyllis Wilson, Euan White, Katherine Skene, and Jodi Lewchuk. The reviewers for this edition—Cheryl Collier, University of Windsor; Holly Gibbs, University of Toronto Scarborough; Neil Hibbert, University of Saskatchewan; Wolfgang Koerner, University of Ottawa; J.P. Lewis, University of Guelph; David G. MacDonald, University of the Fraser Valley; and Jonathan Malloy, Carleton University—as well as anonymous reviewers for all seven previous editions provided thoughtful comments and suggestions that I sometimes followed, and perhaps should have more often. Richard Tallman's meticulous editing and advice on points of style and substance have transformed the manuscript for each edition of this book into a much better product. It is always a pleasure to work with him.

Over the years I have taught Canadian politics to several thousands of students in Canada, the United States, France, and Belgium. I have come to realize what a privilege and responsibility it is to be able to try to explain to others how politics works, and who it works for. This edition is dedicated to my students, past, present, and future.

Stephen Brooks
Windsor, Ontario, and Dearborn, Michigan

Part I
Introduction

We all have an idea of what politics involves. But the term *political science* may be less familiar and, in some ways, rather puzzling. The problem arises from the word "science." Science evokes images of laboratories, ideas of measurement, and the domain of hard facts on which depend the construction of bridges that do not collapse and medications that cure rather than kill us. The study and understanding of politics, as is true of all forms of human behaviour and organization, would seem to lack the hard edge and to rely on techniques quite different from those characteristic of physics and genetic biology. Can there be such a thing as political science?

The answer is, "within limits." "Political science" expresses the aspiration among those who study politics to do so in an objective way. It involves the attempt to understand why things are the way they are and therefore how they may be changed, rather than how they ought to be. Political science rests on a bedrock of empirical analysis—analysis that seeks to formulate laws about the world of politics and government based on verifiable observation and, in some cases, experimentation—and not on the ideological leanings and personal preferences of the person doing the observing and

explaining. But whereas genes may be spliced and the weight-bearing capacity of a bridge may be tested through a computer simulation, political scientists generally have to make do with observing behaviour and the functioning of institutions in less controlled circumstances. How they undertake their analysis of politics and the certitude of their observations may not look very much like the activities and results of those in the natural and applied sciences, but the aspiration to produce objective, empirical knowledge is the same.

Those who study Canadian politics and government rely on the same concepts and analytical methods used by those who wish to understand these subjects in France, China, Egypt, or any other society. Power, authority, identity, participation, bureaucracy, integration, stability, and equality are just some of the core concepts relevant to an understanding of politics in any country. In this first section of *Canadian Democracy* we will examine some of the concepts that are crucial to an understanding of politics and government in Canada. This will provide the basis for the subsequent chapters that focus on particular features of Canadian political life.

1 An Introduction to Political Life

To understand politics and government, one requires a tool kit consisting of the fundamental concepts and terms that are useful in analyzing political life. This chapter aims to equip the reader with these tools by examining the following topics:

- What is politics?
- Power.
- State and government.
- Democracy.
- Consent and legitimacy.
- Political identities.
- Political fault lines: old and new.
- Who gets heard and why?

This book aims to explain how the political system works in Canada, and to give you the tools needed to evaluate the processes and outcomes of Canadian politics. Whatever your conclusions, they should include the belief that politics does matter and that your thoughts and actions hold political significance. (©Rob Howard/Corbis)

If you want a job that earns you the trust and respect of your fellow citizens, then become a firefighter, pharmacist, pilot, or nurse. Do not become a politician. In fact, you would fare just about as well in the eyes of your fellow Canadians selling used cars as you would as a politician. This, at least, is the conclusion that emerges from a 2013 *Reader's Digest* poll conducted by the survey research firm Harris/Decima. Politicians came in thirtieth of the 31 professions that were ranked according to the trust that Canadians place in them, ahead of psychics but behind taxi drivers, lawyers, and real estate agents.[1] Politicians and their craft have what advertising people would call an image problem.

This image of politicians as untrustworthy, and of their calling as low and dishonest, is not entirely fair. There is no hard evidence that politicians are more likely to be dishonest or have low morals than those in other occupations. Indeed, many if not most people who run for and are elected to public office are motivated by a desire to serve and to improve the lives of those they represent. And popular perceptions notwithstanding, many politicians make significant financial and personal sacrifices by holding public office.

But Canadians do not trust them. To understand why, we need to think about the nature of the politician's craft in societies where not everyone shares the same opinions or has identical interests, and where the political system is such that the votes of about 40 per cent or more of those who bother to cast their ballots will be needed for a political party to win a federal election. In these circumstances, politicians and political parties—or at least those serious about winning elections—need to appeal to a range of interests and values. Once elected, they must do the same, balancing competing demands and points of view. On top of this, they may find that their ability to do certain things that may be popular or that they believe to be the right things to do, regardless of public opinion, is limited by circumstances beyond their control. The promises that they made cannot be kept, or perhaps not quite in the form they were made or according to the timetable that was expected. And perhaps they knew or suspected this all along, saying things and making promises with what some might

Most Canadians do not follow politics very closely. Surveys show that younger voters tend to be the least interested in politics and less likely to participate than middle-aged and older citizens. A contributing factor to Canadians' political apathy is their lack of trust in their politicians.

characterize as reckless disregard for their truth or prospects of achievement.

It is the messy activity of politics—including the compromises, the occasional evasiveness, the failure to deliver on promises made, and the resulting sense that those elected to public office do not faithfully represent those who put them there—that leads to cynicism about politicians and political parties. Canadians, however, are not alone in their negativity. In fact, in no established democracy do a majority of people say that they have a great deal or quite a lot of confidence in political parties.[2]

A healthy dose of cynicism about politics is probably a good thing, at least if it is cynicism fuelled by knowledge. Cynicism based on ignorance or coupled to apathy, however, can make no such claim. Whether you are a hardened cynic or an enthusiastic fan when it comes to Canadian politics—in fact, if you are like most Canadians your age, you probably do not follow politics very closely and therefore do not feel strongly one way or the other—no judgment about how well the political system works and in whose interests should be uninformed. This book aims to give you that information and the analytical tools needed to evaluate the processes and outcomes of Canadian politics. The conclusions you draw and the judgments you arrive at are, of course, up to you. Whatever your conclusions, they should not include the belief that politics does not matter in your life and that your thoughts and actions are somehow without political significance. The Polish poet and 1996 Nobel Prize laureate, Wislawa Szymborska, has this to say about such ideas:

> All affairs, day and night,
> yours, ours, theirs,
> are political affairs.
>
> Like it or not,
> your genes have a political past,
> your skin a political cast,
> your eyes a political aspect.
>
> What you say has a resonance;
> what you are silent about is telling.
> Either way, it's political.[3]

What Is Politics?

Politics arises from the fact of scarcity. In the real world it is not possible for all of us to satisfy all of our desires to the fullest extent. Limits on the stock of those things that people desire—wealth, privacy, clean air and water, social recognition—ensure that conflicts will take place between rival claimants. These conflicts explain why politics comes about. But politics is about more than the fact of conflict. It is also about how rival claims are settled. What distinguishes politics from the conflicts, struggles, and rivalries that take place in such settings as the family, the workplace, and the economic marketplace, and in social organizations like churches and labour unions, is the *public nature* of political disputes and the use of public authority—embodied in the state—to deal with them. **Politics**, then, is the activity by which rival claims are settled by public authorities. The boundaries of what is considered to be political are located where the state's authority reaches. Political philosophers sometimes call this the public realm. Beyond this line is the private realm, where the state's authority does not extend.

As Box 1.1 shows, this definition does not have the field all to itself. All of these contending definitions agree that politics is about the exercise of power. They disagree, however, about what power relations count as political ones. Foucault, Marx, and the feminist movement define politics in ways that would include the relations between bosses and workers in a corporation, between parents and children in a family, between teachers and students in schools, and between spiritual shepherd and flock in a church. And in a sense they are right. In the words of American political scientist Charles Merriam, "obviously there is governance everywhere—government in heaven; government in hell; government and law among outlaws; government in prison."[4] Locke and Easton both offer a more limited definition of politics, one that goes back to Aristotle's conception of the Greek *polis*. They argue that what is distinctive about politics is the association of this activity with a system of settling disputes that is both public and binding on the whole community. At the centre of this system is the state, or government, as those raised in the Anglo-American tradition are more likely to call it.

These definitions disagree in another important way. **Marxism**, postmodernism (Foucault), and feminism associate politics with a pervasive pattern of oppression. Politics is, for them, fundamentally about how inequalities are generated and reinforced through the power relations that exist between classes/gender groups at all levels of society.

Does it matter, in the end, how we define politics? Or is this mainly a harmless diversion for academic hair-splitters? We would argue that there is a very practical reason for rejecting those definitions of politics that confer on all power relations, wherever they may be located and however limited they may be, the title "political." If politics is viewed as being everywhere and in all social interactions, we lose the ability to see the boundary that separates the public and private realms. This boundary may not be very distinct, but it is crucial for understanding the politics of any society. Moreover, the existence of such a boundary is necessary in order to protect the freedoms that most of us believe to be important features of a democratic society. Political conflict is largely about where exactly this boundary between public and private should be drawn, what should be considered a proper matter for public life and decisions by the state, and what should remain private matters. We can agree that power relations are ubiquitous without going the next step to claim that politics, therefore, has no bounds.

Not everyone agrees. Political scientist Jill Vickers echoes many of her feminist colleagues when she argues that the public realm/private realm distinction is fundamentally sexist. It is based, she maintains, on a tradition of political thinking that accepted as natural the domination of the public realm by males and the limitation of woman to the private sphere. When women were finally admitted to the public realm it was on identical terms with men, a formal equality that failed to recognize the substantive inequalities in the typical life conditions of males and females.

But whatever sexist biases may have been embedded in the public-versus-private distinction in traditional Western political thought, is it not the case that its contemporary importance lies in the value it assigns to individual freedom? This, too, says Vickers, is fundamentally sexist. "The concept of *freedom*," she writes, "has become an almost totally masculinized idea in Western political thought, meaning *freedom from* constraints—an autonomy in which no dependence on another is required or recognized."[5] According to Vickers, this is a value with little appeal to most women, who have as their goal "interdependence among equals" rather than the freedom to act without constraint.

But there is, perhaps, another reason for adopting the more limited definition of politics that we have

Politics in Focus

BOX 1.1 Some Important Definitions of Politics and Power

"(A) political system can be designated as those interactions through which values are authoritatively allocated for a society."

David Easton, *A Systems Analysis of Political Life*

"Political power, then, I take to be a right of making laws with penalties of death and, consequently, all less penalties for the regulating and preserving of property, and of employing the force of the community in the execution of such laws and in the defense of the commonwealth from foreign injury; and all this only for the public good."

John Locke, *The Second Treatise of Government*

"Political power, properly so called, is merely the organized power of one class for oppressing another."

Karl Marx and Friedrich Engels, *The Communist Manifesto*

"Basically power is less a confrontation between two adversaries or the linking of one to the other than a question of government. This word must be allowed the very broad meaning which it had in the sixteenth century. 'Government' did not refer only to political structures or to the management of states; rather it designated the way in which the conduct of individuals or of groups might be directed: the government of children, of souls, of communities, of families, of the sick. It did not cover only the legitimately constituted forms of political or economic subjection, but also modes of action . . . which were destined to act upon the possibilities of action of other people. To govern, in this sense, is to structure the possible field of action of others."

Michel Foucault, *The Subject and Power*

"The personal is political."

Slogan of the 1960s feminist movement

put forward. Only those power relations that take place in the public realm can legitimately be associated with the use of force in its most naked, punitive forms. Compulsion, punishment, and violence do of course take place in all sorts of social settings. It is clear, however, that only the public authorities—those who wield the power of the state—have the legitimate right to back up their decisions with the full power of society. All other power relations are more limited than this. The reason for this difference is that the state is the only institution that can reasonably claim to speak and act on behalf of the entire community, and its unique function is to ensure the conditions for some degree of social order. This social order is a necessary condition for all other social activities. Without it there is no peaceful basis for reconciling conflicts in society.

Power

Power is the ability to influence what happens. It is found in all sorts of settings, not simply political ones. When Microsoft uses its dominant market position in computer operating systems to compel PC manufacturers to integrate its Internet browser into their computers, that is power. When the Vatican issues an official proclamation on same-sex marriage or the exclusion of women from the priesthood, elements within the Roman Catholic Church respond. The Vatican has power within the community of Roman Catholics. When a person is persuaded to give up his wallet at gunpoint, his attacker has power. Parents who are able to compel their children's obedience through the threat or fact of punishment, or through persuasive arguments, have power. A television network whose programs shape the issues that viewers are thinking about has power. And when a peaceful demonstration of citizens outside the headquarters of a corporation or in front of the legislature changes the behaviour of the targeted institution, that, too, is power. In each of these cases one party affects the behaviour of another, although the reasons for compliance differ.

Social scientists like to unpack the concept of power, breaking it down into species that are distinguished from one another according to the reason why the compliant party obeys. Compliance may result from the threat or use of force (**coercion**); from the ability of A to convince B that a particular action is reasonable or otherwise in B's best interests (**influence**); or from the recognition on the part of the compliant party that the person or organization issuing a command has the right to do so and should be obeyed (**authority**). Politics involves all of these faces of power—coercion, influence, and authority—at various times and in different circumstances. Democratic politics relies primarily on the two non-coercive species of power. But coercion is used, and no democracy is without its system of courts, police, and prisons.

How far coercion and democracy are compatible, however, is an open question. This is illustrated by a famous and timeless exchange between former Prime Minister Pierre Trudeau and CBC journalist Tim Ralfe in October 1970,[6] a few days after the Canadian government had suspended civil liberties by invoking the War Measures Act at the time of the FLQ Crisis in Quebec.

Ralfe: "Sir, what is it with all these men with guns around here?"

Trudeau: "Haven't you noticed?"

Ralfe: "Yes, I've noticed them. I wondered why you people decided to have them."

Trudeau: "What's your worry?"

Ralfe: "I'm not worried, but you seem to be."

Trudeau: "If you're not worried, I'm not worried."

Ralfe: "I'm worried about living in a town that's full of people with guns running around."

Trudeau: "Why? Have they done anything to you? Have they pushed you around or anything? . . . [T]here are a lot of bleeding hearts around who just don't like to see people with helmets and guns. All I can say is, go on and bleed, but it is more important to keep law and order in the society than to be worried about weak-kneed people. . . . I think the society must take every means at its disposal to defend itself against the emergence of a parallel power which defies the elected power in this country, and I think that goes to any distance."

Is Trudeau right? It is one of the great ironies of democracy that, unlike other political systems, it requires that dissenting points of view and opposition to those in power be respected. Arresting people suspected of terrorist acts is, most would agree, necessary to protect democratic government.

At some point, however, the protection of law and order may exact a high cost in terms of personal freedoms. In a democracy, those in power must justify their use of coercion as being necessary to maintain such values as freedom, equality, justice, and the rule of law. Inevitably, however, people will disagree over the meaning and relative importance of these values, and over how much coercion, in what circumstances, is acceptable. Whether the issue is the War Measures Act in 1970 or the measures taken to combat terrorism since 11 September 2001, the eternal trade-off is the same.

The practical difficulties that can arise in an *open society*—a society in which individuals are free to

CP Images/AP Photo/Christophe Ena

Police stand guard along a three-metre-high security fence circling the meeting site for G20 Summit leaders in Toronto in June 2010. Security measures, including a five-tier screening process, required accreditation for residents living inside the zone, and temporary extension of police powers, were criticized by some as an unnecessary infringement on personal freedoms during the gathering of world leaders to discuss the stability of the global economy.

speak their minds, associate with whom they wish, and move freely about without having to notify or justify their movements to the public authorities—was brought home to Canadians, and even more so to Americans, after the terrorist attacks on the World Trade Center and the Pentagon of 9/11. Access to public buildings became more restricted, border crossings became more time-consuming and stressful, airport security was tightened, and measures were taken to curb the rights of immigrants. Some of these changes proved to be temporary, but many—such as the air travel security tax that all Canadian travellers have been required to pay since 2002, the Anti-Terrorism Act, which came into effect in December 2001, and a general increase in legal surveillance, both public and private—have been enduring. Among the most significant consequences of 9/11 and subsequent terrorist plots exposed in Canada[7] has been the reflection and debate it has generated regarding the appropriate balance between individual rights and national security in a democratic society. Some believe that Canadian co-operation with the United States in the creation and maintenance of what officialdom calls a "common security perimeter" is necessary to protect the open society from enemies who would take advantage of the freedoms it affords to spread terror. Others see such a policy as being democracy's own "Iron Curtain," and thus a flagrant violation of the principles that the open society is supposed to embody and uphold.

State and Government

The existence of the state is, we argued earlier, a necessary condition for a social order that allows for the peaceful resolution of conflict. But what is the "state"? To this point we have used the terms "state" and "government" as though they meant the same thing. This failure to make a distinction between them is often harmless, but it can lead to serious confusion. For example, to argue that the government is corrupt or wasteful, or that its policies are undesirable or unjust, does not necessarily call into question the state's legitimacy. It does, however, challenge the authority of the particular people who control the levers of the governmental system. In an established and stable democracy, political activity is far more likely to be directed at influencing and changing the government than at reforming the state.

Canadian political scientist Leo Panitch provides this definition of the **state**:

> [The state is] a broad concept that includes government as the seat of legitimate authority in a territory but also includes bureaucracy, judiciary, the Armed Forces and internal police, structures of legislative assemblies and administration, public corporations, regulatory boards, and ideological apparatuses such as the education establishment and publicly owned media. The distinguishing characteristic of the state is its monopoly over the use of force in a given territory.[8]

Defined this way, the state has three main characteristics. First, it involves territorial boundaries. States have borders, beyond which their legal authority is either nil or strictly limited. Second, the state consists of a complex set of institutions that wield public authority. The courts, the police, and the educational system are outposts of the state's authority no less than are the elected legislature and the bureaucracy. Third, the state is defined in terms of power, what Weber (see Box 1.2) called its "monopoly of the legitimate use of physical force in the enforcement of its order." For what purposes and in whose interests this power is exercised are important questions.

Some definitions of the state offer answers to these questions. The Marxist definition in Box 1.2 characterizes the state as an instrument of class oppression. Marx argued that the end of class conflict would sound the death knell for the state. It would "wither away," no longer having any function to perform. Contemporary Marxists, except for a few diehards, no longer predict the state's demise. Feminists view the state as a patriarchal institution, reinforcing and perpetuating the social superiority of men over women. Many political scientists, and probably most economists, would argue that the state is responsive to any group with enough

Politics in Focus

BOX 1.2 Alternative Definitions of the State

"The executive of the modern State is but a committee for managing the common affairs of the whole bourgeoisie."

Marx and Engels, *The Communist Manifesto*

"The state is that fiction by which everyone seeks to live at the expense of everyone else."

French economist Frédéric Bastiat, *circa* 1840

"L'État, c'est moi." (I am the state.)

Louis XIV of France

"(The state is that institution which) successfully upholds a claim to the monopoly of the legitimate use of physical force in the enforcement of its order . . . within a given territorial area."

Max Weber, *The Theory of Social and Economic Organization*

"All state-based political systems are patriarchal—that is, in no country in the world are women equal participants in the institutions of the state or equal beneficiaries in its distribution of power or in the norms and values sanctioned in law and enforced by those institutions."

Jill Vickers, *Reinventing Political Science*

political clout to persuade policy-makers that it is in their interest to meet the group's demands for public actions on private wants.

An adequate explanation of the state must ask on whose behalf and in whose interests the state's authority is exercised. Contemporary political science offers four main answers to these questions: **pluralism**, **class analysis**, **feminism**, and **postmodernism**.

Pluralism. Those who see politics as being fundamentally a competition between different interests are likely to conclude that the state responds chiefly to the demands of those groups that are best organized, have superior financial resources, can credibly claim to speak on behalf of large numbers of voters or segments of the population that are influential for other reasons, and are successful in associating their special interests with the general interests of society. The pluralist model assumes various forms, some of which are society-centred. The *society-centred* variants emphasize the impact of groups in society on the state, while *state-centred* variants place greater emphasis on the ability of public officials to act on their own preferences and according to their own interests, rather than merely responding to the demands of voters and interest groups.

Pluralist models of the state do not assume that the competition among groups takes place on a level playing field. On the contrary, many of those who work within this perspective argue that business interests occupy a privileged position within this competition. Many pluralist thinkers argue that those who shape our perception of the world, especially those in the media, tend to lean in a particular ideological direction that favours certain interpretations, values, and interests over others.

Class analysis. Beginning with Karl Marx, class analysis has always seen the state in capitalist societies as an instrument through which the small minorities who control most of a society's wealth maintain their social and economic dominance. Precisely how this is done has been the subject of enormous debate, but the state's complicity in perpetuating inequalities rooted in the economic system is an article of faith shared by all variants of class analysis. Few of those who analyze politics from a class analysis perspective today would deny that the demands and interests of subordinate classes influence state decision-makers. But this influence, they argue, is sharply limited by the state's vulnerability to a decline in business confidence, the control that the dominant class has over the mass media and popular culture, and a lack of class consciousness among even the least privileged groups in society that stems from the widespread acceptance—what Marx called "false consciousness"—of capitalist and individualistic values as normal and inevitable.

Feminism. Feminists view the state as an inherently patriarchal institution. This means that the state, its structures, and its laws all serve to institutionalize male dominance. Increasing the representation of women in elected legislatures, the bureaucracy, and the courts, and creating governmental bodies and programs that recognize women as a group with interests and needs that are not identical to those of men can attenuate this male dominance. However, most of feminist political theory still insists that a state-centred political system will be patriarchal. "A feminist state that is a structure of authority," says R.W. Connell, "a means by which some persons rule over others, is self-contradictory."[9] It is the hierarchical nature of authority embodied in the state that makes it fundamentally patriarchal. Like Karl Marx's famous prediction that the state would "wither away" once classes were abolished, some feminists argue that if gender discrimination were to be eliminated the state, *as we know it*, would disappear.

Postmodernism. Postmodernism views the state as an essentially oppressive and even repressive institution. But unlike class analysis and feminism, postmodernism is much more eclectic in the forms of oppression that it associates with the state and public authority. That oppression may be targeted at groups based on their race, gender, ethnicity, sexual preference, or some other trait that places them outside the dominant group in control of the levers of state power and whose values and identity are reflected in the institutions, language, and mores of the society. Postmodernism views the state as a repressive institution in that the structures, laws, and activities that constitute the state repress the expression of some values at the same time as they legitimize and nurture others. Those who embrace this approach comprise what is sometimes called the New Left. The Old Left wished to see the overthrow of the capitalist state and its transformation into the vehicle whereby those without property,

money, and status would be able to reform society. Postmodernism is more dubious about the revolutionary visions associated with class analysis and the Old Left, believing that the problem of the state is not simply its relationship to economic power but to forms of oppression and repression more generally. This leads some postmodernists, such as the French philosopher Jean Baudrillard, to despair of the possibility of achieving justice and democracy through the state. Others, such as the American philosopher Richard Rorty, are more optimistic.

A distinction can be made between the state and government. **Government** is a term more usefully reserved for those who have been elected to power. It is more personal than the state, being associated with a particular group of people and, usually, with political parties. In democratic political systems governments are chosen and removed through elections. These elections—the rules and procedures by which governments are formed—are part of the state system. And like the rest of the state, they are much less likely to generate political controversy and to undergo change than are the government and its policies.

Underlying this distinction between state and government is an important practical difference in how each compels the obedience of citizens, corporations, and associations that fall within its jurisdiction. The willingness of individuals and groups to obey the decisions of government—decisions they may vigorously disagree with, and a government they may not have voted for—is based on their view that the state's authority is legitimate. By **legitimacy** we mean that the rules and institutions that comprise the state, and which determine how governments are chosen, are accepted by most people as being reasonable. The legitimacy of the state is, therefore, based on the *consent* of those who are governed. It does not depend on an ever-present fear of the penalties that follow from disobeying the law. It rests instead on what is usually an implicit acceptance of the rules of the political game. If the state's authority, and ultimately the ability of governments to govern, depended on a sort of constant referendum of the popular will, politics would be a brittle enterprise. In reality, this popular consent is not something that people regularly (if ever!) reflect on or consciously avow (the "Pledge of Allegiance" recited by American schoolchildren in all but a handful of states has no counterpart in most democracies, and certainly not in Canada).

Perhaps the best way to understand the importance of the state/government distinction in a democracy is to imagine what would happen if a government's ability to pass and implement laws depended on its popularity. Assume for a moment that a government's "approval rating" sinks to 20 per cent, according to public opinion polls, and that particular actions of the government are opposed by a clear majority of citizens. Should people simply choose to disobey the law and treat this unpopular government as one that has lost its right to govern? And if polls showed that the leader of another political party was clearly preferred by most voters, would this leader have a better moral claim to govern than the discredited leader of the government?

This is a scenario for chaos and anarchy. Democracy requires some measure of stability and respect for rules, including those rules that determine who has the right to govern and how and when that right ends. A particular government or prime minister may be deeply unpopular, but people continue to obey the law and refrain from storming the legislature (although they may organize protests and even throw some tomatoes) because of their implicit acceptance of the state's legitimacy. Government popularity and state legitimacy are not the same.

Government may be upheld by consent or by force. In fact, it is usually upheld by both. When anti-abortion protesters defy court injunctions against demonstrating near an abortion clinic and are arrested and charged for this act of civil disobedience, they are challenging the authority of the state. When Quebec nationalists demand political independence for their province they are registering their belief that the existing boundaries of the Canadian state, and its authority in Quebec society, are not legitimate. And when striking unions ignore back-to-work legislation, and in doing so run the risk of being fined or their leaders being imprisoned, this also goes beyond disagreement with government policy to challenge the legitimacy of the state. The state's authority is sometimes questioned by individuals or by organized interests. When this happens, the public authorities may resort to force in order to crush civil disobedience and maintain their ability to govern.

The question of when citizens may be justified in resisting the law, through either passive disobedience of public authority or violence, is an old one. Two of the world's greatest democracies, the United States and France, trace their modern origins

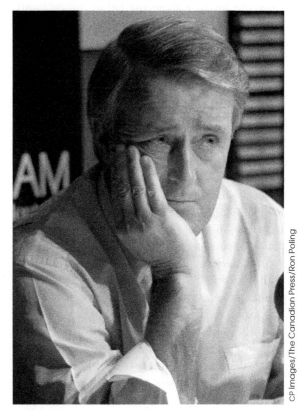

In a 1992 Gallup Poll, then Prime Minister Brian Mulroney earned an approval rating of just 11 per cent, making him one of the most unpopular Canadian leaders since the inception of opinion polling. His government's introduction of the Goods and Services Tax, a recession, and the failure of the Meech Lake Accord contributed to the decline in his popularity during his second term in office. It was through the processes of the state that Canadians made their dissent known: in the 1993 federal election, the Progressive Conservatives were reduced from 151 seats to a mere 2 in the House of Commons, losing their official party status.

to bloody revolutions undertaken in defence of principles that the revolutionaries believed warranted violence against the state. Some, such as the American writer and libertarian thinker Henry David Thoreau, India's Mahatma Gandhi, and the black civil rights leader Martin Luther King Jr, developed a philosophy of non-violent civil disobedience that has been influential across the world. Others, like some of the leaders of the American student movement of the 1960s, the French students whose actions paralyzed public authority in Paris and brought about the fall of the de Gaulle presidency in 1968, and Malcolm X, whose slogan "By any means necessary" encapsulates a philosophy of justifiable resistance to unjust treatment, have acted on the premise that violent opposition to the law and those who enforce it is consistent with democracy when it targets oppression and injustice.

The debate over civil disobedience—when it is justified and what forms it may take in a democracy—has resurfaced in recent years, principally around issues associated with globalization and income inequality. Since what the media dubbed the "Battle in Seattle" in 1999, when the meetings of the World Trade Organization were disrupted by thousands of protesters and scenes of violent confrontations with the police were broadcast live around the world, organized protest has become a standard and expected part of any meeting of policy-makers from the world's wealthiest countries. The experience of street tactics used at anti-globalization protests in Seattle, Genoa, Quebec City, Rostock, Toronto, and elsewhere has produced a globally oriented service industry that specializes in providing activist groups with advice and training on confrontations with the police, effective use of the media, and, more generally, strategies and tactics for influence through civil disobedience. Training for Change (www.trainingforchange.org) and the Ruckus Society (www.ruckus.org) are examples of such organizations.

It is, of course, perfectly lawful to provide information that one intends will disrupt the status quo. But what about advice or action that involves breaking the law? Here are three examples of actions that, strictly speaking, appear to involve violations of the law. Do you think that any or all of them can be justified in a democracy?

- On 7 December 2009, 20 activists with Greenpeace managed to elude security on Parliament Hill and unfurl banners high on the West Block building, proclaiming "Climate inaction costs lives." They remained for several hours on the roof of the building, some of them suspended in harnesses over onlookers and RCMP officers until they were all arrested and taken away in handcuffs. "They really care about these issues, and they're willing to put themselves on the line," said Greenpeace spokesperson Christy Ferguson. "They're willing to risk arrest and face those charges in order to do something that they feel is important."[10]

- On 13 February 2013, 48 people were arrested in front of the White House after refusing police orders to disperse. Some of them had chained themselves to the White House fence. They were protesting the proposed Keystone XL pipeline that would transport oil from Alberta's oil sands to refineries on the Gulf of Mexico. The protest was organized by the Sierra Club and was the first act of civil disobedience in the organization's 120-year history. Michael Brune, the Club's executive director, had this to say: "We look at this project, the tar sands pipeline, and it's a boondoggle. [I]t would contribute to such a climate disaster that we realize we have to use every single tool of democracy in order to fight this thing. We'll fight it in the courts. We'll fight it in statehouses and here in the Beltway, in the streets."[11]

- In January of 2013 an Ontario court judge publicly rebuked the province's police for failing to carry out the terms of two injunctions that he had issued concerning the blockade of the railway line near Kingston, running from Toronto to Montreal. Members of the Idle No More movement had erected the blockades in protest against federal Aboriginal policy. "We seem to be drifting into dangerous waters in the life of the public affairs of this province," Justice David Brown stated, "when courts cannot predict . . . whether police agencies will assist in enforcing court injunctions." He went on to say that "Just as 15 persons would not have the right to stand in the middle of the main line tracks blocking rail traffic in order to espouse a political cause close to their hearts, neither do 15 persons from a First Nation."[12]

Although public opinion in these cases and others like them was divided, there is no shortage of Canadians or of citizens in other countries who believe that such resistance is a justifiable reaction to a history of oppression and a political system and justice system believed by some to be heavily biased against the interests of those who have been marginalized. The oppression and violence that the state may inflict on members of the society, the argument goes, warrant self-defence on the part of victims of this oppression and violence.

Government that relies primarily on threats and violence to maintain its rule is generally unstable. Even the most repressive political authorities usually come to realize that popular consent is a firmer basis on which to govern. In some societies the popular consent that legitimizes political rule may appear to emerge more or less spontaneously from the unco-ordinated activities of the media, the schools, the family, governments: from the various social institutions that influence the values and beliefs of citizens. In other societies, the state's legitimacy is deliberately and assiduously cultivated through the organs of official propaganda. The calculated fostering of consent is a characteristic feature of totalitarian rule. **Totalitarianism** is a system of government that suppresses all dissent in the name of some supreme goal. This goal may be tied to the destiny of the "race," as it was in Nazi Germany, or to "class struggle," as it was in the Soviet Union under Stalin. It survives today in North Korea, where virtually every aspect of the lives of citizens is controlled by the state and where access to and information about the outside world is tightly restricted. Distinctions between the state, government, and society lose all meaning—indeed, they are considered to be subversive—under totalitarianism.

The active mobilization of society by the state, the deliberate manipulation of public attitudes, and the ruthless suppression of dissent by the public authorities are not features that most of us associate with democracy. The way in which legitimacy is generated in political democracies is more subtle than under totalitarian rule, depending primarily on social institutions that are not part of the state system. This gives legitimacy the appearance of being based on the free choice of individuals, an appearance that some argue is an illusion. Marxist critics use the term **cultural hegemony** to signify the ability of society's dominant class to get its values and beliefs accepted as the conventional wisdom in society at large.

Howard Zinn, a prominent American historian and social critic, long argued that Americans were duped into believing that theirs is a society of freedom and equal opportunities. "If those in charge of our society—politicians, corporate executives, and owners of press and television—can dominate our ideas," he wrote, "they will be secure in their power. They will not need soldiers patrolling the streets. We will control ourselves."[13] This was, Zinn maintained, the state of affairs under American capitalism. Noam Chomsky takes this same position in arguing that the privately owned mass media reinforce and perpetuate inequalities in wealth and power by presenting "facts," images, and interpretations that either justify or gloss over these inequalities.[14] Feminists make a similar case, arguing that sexist attitudes of male superiority are pervasive in social institutions—from the bedroom to the boardroom—so that the legitimacy of patriarchal power relations is reinforced on a daily basis. For both Marxists and feminists, government by "popular consent" is a sham that conceals the fundamentally undemocratic character of society and politics.

This may strike you as, at a minimum, an exaggeration of the disconnect that may be created between the reality of people's lives and their beliefs about how the world works and what possibilities exist for them. Or perhaps you find the cultural hegemony argument to be plausible. Either way, it directs our attention to something that is quite important in all societies. This is the role played by the various agents of learning. Families, schools, the mass media, governments, and organizations and groups, formal and informal, contribute to the information, ideas, and sentiments that we have about the world around us. Indeed, in many respects the system through which information, ideas, and interpretations are generated and disseminated deserves to be considered the cornerstone of democracy. If our ideas are manipulated, based on falsehoods, and at odds with important aspects of the reality in which we live, no constitution, elections, or grand speeches can turn this sow's ear into a silk purse.

Democracy

"Democracy is like pornography," says classical historian and political commentator Victor Davis Hanson, "we know it when we see it."[15] But as is also true of pornography, what one person may believe to be unredeemed smut, another may think is art. And yet a third may say that it is all a matter of personal judgment anyway, no one's standard being, a priori, superior to anyone else's. At the same time, however, Hanson's observation seems commonsensical. Most of us would agree that a country in which free elections are held is almost certainly more democratic than one where they are not. And where we see egregious and persistent violations of human rights or a serious lack of accountability on the part of those who govern, we are likely to be skeptical about claims that such a country is democratic.

But that does not stop leaders in political systems as different as those of Canada, the United States, the Democratic People's Republic of Korea, the People's Republic of China, and the Islamic Republic of Iran from all claiming to be democracies. Democracy is a label to which regimes throughout the world try to lay claim. Obviously they cannot all be democratic without our understanding of this concept being diluted to the point that it becomes meaningless.

In a book published at the height of the Cold War, Canadian political philosopher C.B. Macpherson argued that there are in fact three different types of democracy in the modern world.[16] Only one of these, *liberal* democracy, is characterized by competition between political parties. What Macpherson calls the *developmental* and *communist* versions of democracy do not have competitive elections, and probably would not be considered democratic by most Canadians. But they both claim to attach greater importance to the social and economic equality of individuals than does liberal democracy, in addition to recognizing the formal political equality of citizens. If democracy is about equality, Macpherson argues, the developmental and communist versions are at least as democratic as the liberal version that we in the capitalist world automatically assume to be the genuine article.

If we accept Macpherson's argument that there are three types of democracy, not one, each with a legitimate claim to the title, the world looks like a very democratic place. Leaving aside personal and military dictatorships, and the odd monarchy like Saudi Arabia and the Sultanate of Brunei, most of what is left would seem to qualify. While common sense suggests that democracy is not as widespread as this, Macpherson is challenging us to reflect on what makes politics and society democratic or not. Is democracy a system of government? Or does democracy connote a type of society? Was Canada "democratic" before the female half of the population received the vote? Do the persistence of poverty and the clear evidence of large inequalities in the economic condition and social status of different groups in Canada oblige us to qualify our description of Canadian society as "democratic"?

In recent times the debate over what is and is not democratic has become even more complicated. Some argue that in addition to the familiar Western model of democracy, there is a Muslim model that deserves to be called democratic. Turkey and Indonesia, whose populations are overwhelmingly Muslim, are said to demonstrate that there is no necessary incompatibility between Islam and democracy. "Muslim Democracy rests not on an abstract, carefully thought-out theological and ideological accommodation between Islam and democracy," writes Vali Nasr, "but rather on a practical synthesis that is emerging in much of the Muslim world in response to the opportunities and demands created by the ballot box."[17] A rather different argument is made by those who claim that faith in the public square, such as through laws inspired by religious texts and teachings, is not necessarily antithetical to democracy and who insist that the notion is false that only secular societies can be truly democratic.

In the final analysis about the only thing that everyone can agree on is that democracy is based on equality. Agreement breaks down over how much equality, in what spheres of life, is necessary for a society to qualify as democratic. Majority rule, government by popular consent, one person–one vote, and competitive elections are the political institutions usually associated with democratic government. But it has long been recognized that the operation of democratic political institutions can result in oppressive government. If, for example, a majority of Quebecers agree that legislative restrictions on the language rights of non-francophones are needed to preserve the French character of Quebec, is this democratic? In order to safeguard the rights and freedoms of individuals and minorities against what Alexis de Tocqueville called "democratic despotism," constitutional limits on the power of the state over its citizens may be set or the political status of particular social groups may be entrenched in the formal rules and informal procedures of politics. For example, the Canadian Constitution entrenches the coequal official status of the French and English languages at the national level, and the operation of federalism and the Canadian electoral system reinforce the political power of this country's French-speaking minority, 90 per cent of whom live in Quebec.

Perhaps even more important than constitutional guarantees and political practices are the social and cultural values of a society. Tocqueville argued that the best protection against the **tyranny of the majority** is the existence of multiple group identities in society. When individuals perceive themselves as being members of particular social groups—whether a religious denomination, an ethnic or language group, a regional community, or whatever the group identity happens to be—in addition to sharing with everyone else a common citizenship, the likelihood of the democratic state

being turned to oppressive ends is reduced. After all, everyone has a personal interest in the tolerance of social diversity because the rights and status of their own group depend on this.

Some twentieth-century writers argued that cultural values represented the main bulwark against the tyranny of the majority. Democratic government, they have suggested, depends on popular tolerance of diversity. In *The Civic Culture*, American political scientists Gabriel Almond and Sidney Verba make the argument that democratic government is sustained by cultural attitudes.[18] According to this political culture approach, the determination of how democratic a society is must be based on an examination of the politically relevant attitudes and beliefs of the population. This, and not the mere fact of apparently democratic political institutions, is argued to be the true test of democracy and the key to sustaining it.

The civic culture thesis has enjoyed a renaissance in recent years through work on what is called **social capital**. This refers to norms of interpersonal trust, a sense of civic duty, and a belief that one's involvement in politics and in the life of the community matters. Where levels of social trust are low, public authorities must invest more in institutions and policies that rely on repression and force to maintain social order. Social capital is argued to have an economic value, but the main argument made for policies, practices, and institutions that promote social capital is that citizens will be happier and their control over their own lives will be greater. Empirical studies of social capital show that all countries in which levels of social trust and cohesion are highest—a list that includes Canada—are well-established, stable democracies.[19] This may, however, just beg the question: does a high level of social capital contribute to successful democracy or does the experience of successful democratic politics encourage and reinforce high levels of social trust and cohesion? The causal arrows probably point in both directions.

Socialists argue that a society in which a large number of people are preoccupied with the problem of feeding and housing themselves decently cannot be described as democratic. This preoccupation effectively excludes the poor from full participation in political life, and in this way socio-economic inequality translates into political inequality. The formal equality of citizens that democratic government confers, and even the fact that most people subscribe to democratic values, does not alter the fundamental fact that social inequalities produce inequalities in political power. Some critics go even further in dismissing the democratic claims of capitalist societies (see Box 1.3). They argue that inequality results from the simple fact that a very small proportion of the population—the capitalist class—controls the vast majority of the means of economic production and distribution. This inequality in property ownership, Marxists have long argued, far outweighs the importance of "one person–one vote" and competitive elections in determining the real political influence of different classes in society.

Inequalities between bosses and workers, between parents and children, between men and women, between ethnic or language communities—the list could go on—are often claimed to undermine the democratic character of societies whose formal political institutions are based on the equality of citizens. Indeed, if we use any of the all-inclusive definitions of politics examined earlier in this chapter it is impossible to resist the logic of this argument. Inequalities confront us wherever we turn, and true democracy seems to be terribly elusive. Even if we define politics more narrowly to include only those activities that focus on the state, it is obvious that a small portion of all citizens actually dominates public life. This is true even in the most egalitarian societies. For most of us, participation in politics takes the form of short bursts of attention and going to the polls at election time. Is it reasonable to speak of democratic government when the levers of state power are in the hands of an elite?

The short answer is, "It depends on what we expect from democracy." If we expect that all citizens should have the opportunity to participate in the law-making process, we are bound to be disappointed. With some historical exceptions like the Greek *polis* and the township democracies of seventeenth- and eighteenth-century America, examples of direct government of the citizens by the citizens are scarce. Direct democracy survives in some tiny New England towns where citizens are given the chance to participate directly in local government[20] and in largely rural Swiss cantons where the *Landsgemeinde*—outdoor gatherings of citizens that take place each spring to vote on important public questions—still exist. Modern technology has, however, created the possibility of direct democracy from people's living rooms in all advanced industrial societies. Everyone who has watched an episode of *American Idol* or its Canadian spinoff knows how this brave new world of participatory

REASONS CANADIANS GIVE FOR NOT VOTING

REASONS SYRIANS GIVE FOR NOT VOTING

LINE-UP HERE

Unlike other forms of government, democracies do not depend primarily on coercion and violence. In Canada, the promotion of citizen engagement continues to be a challenge and citizen apathy continues to be high.

democracy could work. Whether over telephone lines or by clicking the mouse of your computer, there is no physical or technological reason why this method of popular choice could not be adapted to political decision-making. There may, however, be other reasons for rejecting what modern technology makes possible.

Perhaps the most commonly advanced reason for rejecting direct democracy via the Internet and for being skeptical about the value of public opinion polls is that many citizens are poorly informed about important public issues much of the time, and it occasionally happens that most citizens are grossly uninformed or misinformed about public issues. What sense does it make to ask citizens what the government's policy should be on a matter about which the majority of people know either little or nothing, and where what they think they know may be factually incorrect?

Thomas Jefferson provided a famous answer to this question. "Every government degenerates when trusted to the rulers of the people alone. The people themselves therefore are [democracy's] only safe depositories."[21] Members of the public, Jefferson acknowledged, are often poorly informed or wrong in their opinions on public matters. But the democratic solution to the problem of an ill-informed public is not to exclude it from the determination of public affairs; rather, it is to educate public opinion. Jefferson placed great stress on the role of the press and public education in producing an informed citizenry.

Governing Realities

BOX 1.3 Is Canada a Real Democracy?

Murray Dobbin is an activist, journalist, and author who is highly critical of the state of Canadian democracy. Here is some of what he had to say in a 24 June 2013 article entitled "Reinventing Progressive Politics," in Canadian Dimension.

We are so accustomed to the connection between political parties and democracy that to question the relationship between the two might seem absurd. But for those who recognize the multiple crises faced by humanity—the destruction of our environment, climate change, the ravages of unfettered finance capital, the undeniable limits to growth—the failure of our liberal, multi-party democracies seems increasingly obvious.

To many people, the millions who can't even be bothered to vote, they are simply irrelevant.

Of course for the elites and the corporations that feed off it, the current system is working fine. Deregulation, privatization, high-end tax cuts and the Orwellian security state now being exposed in the US all contribute to wealth and political power of the One per cent (actually more like the Ten per cent). While they still have to breathe the same polluted air as the rest of us, the elites believe they can somehow achieve immunity from the global forces now in play. Of course they are wrong. But so long as they believe they are right, the crises will continue to worsen and the rest of us will continue to suffer.

The tragic irony in all this is that in most democracies the majority of people actually share values that, if they drove government policy, would begin to address the crises. But there is a persistent disconnect between what people want and what the system can deliver. The multi-party system is designed to be dominated by money and increasingly sophisticated marketing, micro-targeting and data-mining. Disengaged citizens haven't a prayer in dealing with the modern election machine

Elections as we experience them are themselves apolitical. People are supposed to suddenly become informed citizens—for one month every four years. There is no substantive dialogue with the citizenry. The parties are like alien entities that suddenly arrive in your living room, not to engage you but to somehow coax you into voting for them.

Is Dobbin right? Do you agree with the claims that underpin this very negative judgment on Canadian democracy? The full text of the article may be read at: <canadiandimension.com/articles/5367/>.

Source: http://canadiandimension.com/articles/5367.
Reprinted with permission from Murray Dobbin.

We often hear that the information explosion generated by satellite communication, television, and the Internet has made us the best-informed generation of all time. But as Neil Postman observes, this conceit fails to address why most people are unable to explain even the most basic elements of issues that have received saturation coverage in the media. This ignorance does not prevent pollsters from asking people for their opinion on matters they may barely understand, and clearly deprives the results of polls of any meaning other than the signals they send to politicians looking for waves to ride. Postman blames modern education and especially the media for this ignorance. Television, the defining medium of the last half-century, is singled out for particular blame.

> What is happening here is that television is altering the meaning of "being informed" by creating a species of information that might properly be called *disinformation*. . . . Disinformation does not mean false information. It means misleading information—misplaced, irrelevant, fragmented or superficial information—information that creates the illusion of knowing something but which in fact leads one away from knowing. . . . [W]hen news is packaged as entertainment, that is the inevitable result.[22]

The pillars that Jefferson counted on to support democratic government have rotted, according to Postman. The irony is that this has happened in an age when more information from more corners of the world is available to the average person than ever before.

All modern democracies are **representative democracies**. Government is carried out by elected legislatures that represent the people. Citizens delegate law-making authority to their representatives, holding them responsible for their actions through periodic elections. Representative democracies sometimes include decision-making processes that provide opportunities for greater and more frequent citizen participation than simply voting every few years. *Plebiscites* and *referendums*—direct votes of citizens on important public questions—frequently held elections, choosing judges and some administrative officials through election, and formal procedures for removing an elected official before the end of his or her term, as through voter petitions and "recall" elections, are democratic institutions that appear to allow for widespread citizen participation in public affairs.

This appearance may be deceiving. In countries like the United States and Switzerland, where referendums are a normal part of the political process, voter turnout is usually very low. Partly because of this, and partly because vested interests are quick to spend money on advertising and mobilizing their supporters, critics charge that referendums may produce outcomes that are far from democratic. Indeed, one of the most common accusations levelled at referendums is that they are too easily used as tools of conservative political interests. This may once have been the case, but it has not been true, at least not in the United States, for many election cycles. In the 2012 American elections there were 176 state-wide ballot measures ranging from the legalization of same-sex marriage and the sale and use of marijuana to the requirement that a state referendum be held before approval of any new border crossing between Michigan and Ontario. Liberal-leaning causes won at least as often as they lost and were clearly more successful than conservative causes when it came to the high-profile and most controversial ballot items. Indeed, in recent years the referendum has become an important tool for progressive groups in the United States to achieve their political goals.[23]

Respect for rights and freedoms is generally considered a distinguishing feature of democratic government. Which rights and freedoms warrant protection, and in what circumstances they may legitimately be limited by government, are matters of dispute. Libertarians, many economists, and conservative philosophers argue that government that levies heavy taxes on citizens is undemocratic. Their reasoning is that individual choice is reduced when government, representing the collectivity, decides how a large share of people's income will be spent. Others argue that the same levels of taxation actually promote freedom by paying for policies that give less advantaged groups opportunities that they would not have in a "free" market. Even a value as central to democracy as freedom of speech is sometimes argued to have undemocratic side effects. For example, some believe that any person or organization should have the right to spend money on advertising a particular political point of view during an election campaign. Others argue that unlimited freedom of speech in these circumstances is undemocratic, because some individuals and groups are better endowed than others and, therefore, the points of view of the affluent will receive the greatest exposure.

Rights and freedoms are believed by most of us to be important in democracies, but everyone except extreme libertarians believes that protecting these rights or freedoms can sometimes produce undemocratic outcomes. No surefire test can tell us when democracy is promoted or impaired by protecting a right or freedom. Indeed, this is one of the greatest sources of conflict in modern democracy, sometimes portrayed as a struggle between the competing pulls of individualism (the private realm) and collectivism (the public realm). A private realm beyond the legitimate reach of the state is a necessary part of what is sometimes called a free society. "Legitimate" is the key word here. Recall Prime Minister Trudeau's exchange with a CBC journalist, discussed earlier in this chapter, in which he justified the use of extraordinary police and surveillance powers on the grounds that such infringements on individual rights are sometimes necessary to protect the greater good and the very fabric of democracy. The recent revelations from Edward Snowden of widespread collection of telephone records by the US government, justified by the White House on grounds of national security, is a more recent case of this same dilemma. How much interference with our rights, on what grounds, jeopardizes democracy?

So how democratic is Canada? According to the Freedom House's World Democracy Audit (www.worldaudit.org), Canada is one of the most democratic countries in the world. But it is not the most democratic country, trailing slightly behind some of the Scandinavian and Northern European democracies. In arriving at its ranking of countries, Freedom House **operationalizes** the concept of democracy, defining it in ways that can be measured so that scores can be assigned to each country. This methodology has the advantage of making explicit the criteria used in determining whether a country is more or less democratic. The criteria used in the Freedom House survey of the world's political systems combine measures of political rights, civil liberties, press freedom, public corruption, and the rule of law in arriving at a country's democracy ranking (see Box 1.4).

A country may have free elections, a constitution that protects rights and freedoms, and a media system that permits the expression of diverse points of view and criticism of the powerful. But if individuals and organizations are able to buy special treatment, or nepotism is rampant, or the law applies to different people in different ways, depending on who they are and who they know, this will undermine a society's claim to be democratic. Corruption, including bribery and special treatment based on friendship and family connections, can be found in any political system. In a democracy, however, such behaviour is considered to be unlawful or at least unethical, depending on how egregiously it violates the rule of law. The **rule of law** may truly be said to be the foundation of democratic government, on which all else rests. "It means," writes Eugene Forsey, one of Canada's foremost constitutionalists of the twentieth century, "that everyone is subject to the law; that no one, no matter how important or powerful, is above the law."[24] The rule of law means that no public official has the legitimate right to exercise any powers other than those assigned to his or her office by the law. And if someone in a position of public trust attempts to go beyond the authority that the law permits? Then it is up to the courts to check that abuse of power. An independent judiciary is, therefore, a necessary feature of democratic governance.

This is all fine theory. But consider the following two questions. The first asks what sorts of inequalities, in what circumstances, may undermine democratic values and processes. Are some voices and interests more likely to be heard and be taken seriously by policy-makers? The second highlights the always present

Listen to the "Political Corruption in Canada: It's Not as Bad as You Think!" podcast, available at: www.oupcanada.com/Brooks8e

tension between majoritarianism and competing visions of democracy. When should the will of the majority be decisive and in what circumstances should the rights of minorities be protected and trump majority opinion?

Who Gets Heard, and Why?

Access to political decision-makers and the ability to influence public opinion are not equally distributed in society. If the president of the Royal Bank of Canada places a telephone call to the federal Minister of Finance, this call will be returned. Your call or mine probably will not (try it!). For as long as elections have taken place in Canada, individuals and organizations have made financial contributions to political parties and their candidates. For the relatively modest sum of $1,200 per year—the maximum contribution an individual can make to a federal party or candidate—you can join the Liberal Party's Laurier Club. Among other things, this buys an invitation to party functions across the country, including the possibility of some face time with the party leader. Corporations are banned from buying memberships, but their CEOs, presidents, board members, and so on are not, and many of the individual members of the Laurier Club have corporate connections.

Between election campaigns, interest groups of all sorts are active in many ways, trying to influence the actions of government and the climate of public opinion. Much of this activity costs money, often a lot of money. The services of a high-powered, well-connected lobbying firm can easily run into hundreds of thousands of dollars. A public relations campaign that uses polling and focus groups, followed by some combination of electronic and print media advertising, may cost as much or more. Although spending money on such activities carries no guarantee of favourable political outcomes, a widespread and probably well-founded belief suggests that such an investment may yield impressive returns. Spending on such activities is quite unevenly distributed across groups in society. Some people conclude from this that having more money buys, at a minimum, greater access to those in positions of political

authority and the ability to get a wider and perhaps more sympathetic hearing for the issues and points of view that matter most to the group spending the money.

But it is not this simple. The issues that get onto the **public agenda**—the matters that have been identified by opinion leaders in the media and in government as ones that warrant some policy response, even if that response is a decision not to act—are not determined by the spending of self-interested groups alone. The American journalist H.L. Mencken once said that the proper role of his profession was to "bring comfort to the afflicted and afflict the comfortable." Some in the media, in Canada and elsewhere, take Mencken's counsel to heart. But whether what they report and how they report it "afflicts the comfortable" or not, it is undeniably the case that the values and beliefs of those who shape public opinion—including teachers, journalists, television and radio producers, researchers, and even, in their minor way, textbook writers!—influence the stories they tell and how they are told.

In Canada, as in other capitalist democracies, there is a long-standing and ongoing debate over whether those in the media—an important segment of the opinion-shaping class—do more to afflict or comfort the privileged and the powerful. On one point, however, the evidence is clear: interests and points of view that are not those of the wealthy and the well-connected do find their way into the public conversation. Getting heard is not only or always a matter of money.

Is Democracy a Process or an Outcome?

Tocqueville warned about the tyranny of the majority, that the multitude might show little concern for the rights and interests of minorities and see little wrong in imposing their force of superior numbers on those whose values and behaviour are different from those of the majority. Most people agree that majoritarianism needs to be tempered by protections for individual and group rights. That is why constitutions like Canada's include express guarantees for rights and freedoms.

Governing Realities

BOX 1.4 Measuring Freedom

In determining how well a particular country respects and protects civil liberties, an important component of its democracy index, Freedom House uses the following criteria:

- Are there free and independent media and other forms of cultural expressions?
- Are religious institutions and communities free to practice their faith and express themselves in private and public?
- Is there freedom of assembly, demonstration, and open public expression?
- Do the people have the right to organize in different political parties or other competitive political groupings of their choice, and is the system open to the rise and fall of these competing parties or groupings?
- Are there free trade unions and peasant organizations or equivalents, and is there effective collective bargaining? Are there free professional and other private organizations?
- Is there protection from political terror, unjustified imprisonment, exile, or torture, whether by groups that

support or oppose the system? Is there freedom from war and insurgencies?

- Is government free from pervasive corruption?
- Is there open and free private discussion?
- Do citizens enjoy freedom of travel or choice of residence, employment, or institution of higher education?
- Do citizens have the right to own property and establish private business? Is private business activity unduly influenced by government officials, the security forces, political parties/organizations, or organized crime?
- Are there personal social freedoms, including gender equality, choice of marriage partners, and size of family?
- Is there equality of opportunity and the absence of economic exploitation?

These criteria are part of a Political Rights Checklist, whose purpose is to measure several key components of democracy.

Source: Freedom House, *Freedom in the World 2012*, at: <www.freedomhouse.org/report/freedom-world -2012/checklist-questions>.

But it often happens that when the rights claims of a minority are upheld by the courts, in the face of unsympathetic or divided public opinion and in circumstances where elected officials have shown an unwillingness to legislate such protection, some will argue that this is undemocratic. What is undemocratic, these critics charge, is that unelected public officials—judges in this case— have usurped policy-making prerogatives that, in a democracy, should be exercised by the people's elected representatives. For example, when the Charter of Rights and Freedoms was agreed to in 1981 by Ottawa and the provincial governments, its equality section (s. 15) did not include sexual orientation among the banned grounds for discrimination. This omission was deliberate. The case for including a reference to sexual orientation had been made during the hearings on the

Charter, but had been rejected by the governments representing Canadians and the 10 provincial electorates. Several years later, however, the Supreme Court of Canada decided that discrimination under the law on the basis of sexual orientation was *analogous* to discrimination based on religion, race, or colour—forms of discrimination that are expressly prohibited by s. 15 of the Charter—and that sexual orientation should have the same constitutional status under the equality rights provision of the Charter as those forms of discrimination that were expressly mentioned by those who drafted and agreed to this important part of Canada's Constitution. Almost 20 years after the equality section came into effect, the Ontario Court of Appeal used it as the basis for its decision striking down the federal Marriage Act's definition of marriage as restricted to heterosexual couples. Reform of the law quickly followed. Public opinion was about evenly divided at the time.

You might agree that this was the right thing to do. Or you may not. The point is, however, that this case and many like it raise contentious issues about what processes are democratic. Is there a problem when unelected officials, who cannot be removed from office when they make unpopular decisions, determine such matters? Even if public opinion is divided, so that many people support the decisions of judges or other unelected officials, should some issues—by their nature or because of their importance—be resolved only by those who have been elected to govern? Does democracy involve a particular process, and if so what process? Or is it more about particular outcomes being produced—a destination rather than a journey—whether by politicians, bureaucrats, or judges?

On reflection, most of us would probably agree that democracy involves a bit of both. Throughout this book we will argue that formal institutions are only part of what makes a society's politics democratic or not. The activities of the media, interest groups, and political parties are at least as crucial to the quality of democracy. Likewise, the socio-economic and ideological backgrounds to democratic government have important effects on how the formal and informal features of the political system operate. Democracy, then, cannot be reduced to a simple constitutional formula or to some particular vision of social equality. Several complex elements come into play, so that defining the term "democracy" is a perilous task (see Box 1.5). Someone is bound to disagree, either with what is included in the definition or with what has been left out.

In full recognition of these hazards, we offer the following definition. **Democracy** is a political system based on the formal political equality of all citizens, in which there is a realistic possibility that voters can replace the government, and in which certain basic rights and freedoms are protected.

Media Spotlight

BOX 1.5 What Does Democracy Mean to Canadians?

As is true of so many questions, the answer that you get depends on who you ask. In 2012 the Environics Institute for Survey Research, a partner in the AmericasBarometer Project, asked a representative sample of Canadians to describe in their own words what democracy meant to them. It was an open-ended question with no prompts or pre-determined options from which respondents could choose. Some people were stumped or decided for some other reason not to respond, but three-quarters of those surveyed gave an answer to this question.

The single most popular response (30 per cent) involved the democratic right of citizens to participate in politics by voting, electing governments, or participating in elections. In second place was freedom or free speech, mentioned by 24 per cent of respondents. About one out of seven respondents (14 per cent) answered fair treatment, respect, or equality. Majority rule was mentioned by 5 per cent, followed by peace, safety and security (4 per cent) and then what might be called quality-of-life responses (right to a decent life, be Canadian: 4 per cent). Freedom of religion and values was mentioned by 1 per cent.

Does this surprise you? When politicians, pundits, and professors weigh in on this question they usually mention equality, tolerance, respect for diversity and difference, and group rights at the top of their list of democratic values in Canada. Most Canadians would agree that these are important aspects of democracy. But unprompted, they are more likely to mention the democratic rights and freedoms of individuals than aspects of democracy that have to do with minority and group rights.

The results of the survey may be read at: <www.vanderbilt.edu/lapop/canada/Canada-2012-Report.pdf>.

Political Identities

Identities are ideas that link individuals to larger groups. They are self-definitions, such as "I am a Canadian" or "Je suis québécois," that help us make sense of who we are and how we fit into the world around us. An identity is a state of mind, a sense of belonging to a community defined by its language, ethnic character, religion, history, regional location, gender experiences, belief system, or other factors (see Box 1.6).

Identities perform important psychological and emotional functions. They provide the moorings that connect us to places, beliefs, and other people. People who share an identity are more likely to feel comfortable together and understand one another than they are with those who are not part of their identity group. Often we only become aware of the importance of identity when we find ourselves in a very unfamiliar place or set of circumstances. Responses ranging from disorientation and longing for home—"home" understood both physically and culturally—to hostility and xenophobia are common when we become unmoored from our familiar identities.

By nature, identities are exclusive. If, for example, I think of myself as a member of the working class, I implicitly acknowledge the existence of other groups with which I do not identify. It is possible to identify with a number of groups without causing a sort of multiple personality disorder. There is, for example, no reason why a person could not think of himself or herself as a Canadian and a québécois(e) at the same time. And, indeed, the evidence shows that many do. Multiple identities are common, but some will be more significant in shaping a person's ideas and behaviour than others.

A shared identity is based on a perception of having common interests. But the fact of some number of people having interests in common does not necessarily generate a shared identity. Most of us have no difficulty in recognizing that corporations

The Social Fabric

BOX 1.6 Identity Politics

In Canada, as elsewhere, individuals have long thought of themselves as members of groups with specific traits that set them apart from others. After the French defeat on the Plains of Abraham in 1759 and the final terms of surrender in the 1763 Treaty of Paris, which ceded New France to the British, French-speaking *canadiens* thought of their language and the Catholic religion as defining features of who they were and who they were not. From the late 1800s until the middle of the 1900s, religion was an important marker of identity in Canadian society, separating Catholics from Protestants. Regional identities acquired political significance from the time of Confederation, when it became apparent that the greater population and economic influence of Ontario and Quebec would ensure that their voices would be louder and their values and interests more prominent in Canadian politics.

But since the 1960s the number of identities that matter in Canadian politics, as in other democracies, has proliferated enormously. Part of the reason for this proliferation has been the emergence of a culture of rights—group rights, but also individual rights—that gained irresistible momentum after World War II. Various social movements, involving women's rights, Aboriginal rights, gay and lesbian rights, environmentalism, and multiculturalism, have provided the intellectual architecture and the organizational impetus for this culture of group rights. Older identities tied to religion, language, territory, and values systems have not been washed away. But some have faded in significance and all must contend with the fact that newer identities have assumed a social and political importance far beyond what they had a couple of generations ago.

in the same industry, or consumers, municipal ratepayers, or university students, have identifiable interests in common. These interests are related to the conditions that promote or impair the material well-being of the members of these groups. They become political interests when they are organized under a collective association that claims to represent the members of the group and attempts to influence the actions of the state. Organization is expected to provide the group's members with more collective influence in politics than any individual member could hope to exercise alone. The number of possible political interests is virtually without limit. Of these, only a finite number actually become organized for collective political action, and an even smaller number achieve significant political clout.

A political interest brings together individuals who might otherwise have little in common in terms of their attitudes and beliefs. What they often have in common is a material stake in how some political conflict is resolved. Wheat farmers, automotive workers, university students, east-coast fishers, pulp and paper companies, and small business people are all examples of political interests. Their participation in politics as organized groups is based on considerations of material well-being. Indeed, the interests that the members of such groups have in common are primarily economic ones.

The desire to protect or promote one's material well-being, while an important basis for the political organization of interests, is certainly not the only one. Politically active interests may come together around ideas, issues, and values that have little or no immediate relationship to the incomes, living conditions, social status, or other self-interest of a group's members. Mothers Against Drunk Driving (MADD) is an example of a group whose political involvement is motivated by shared values rather than material self-interest. The Canadian Abortion Rights Action League and the Canadian Conference of Catholic Bishops are opposing groups whose political involvement on the abortion issue is motivated by values rather than material concerns.

Interests and identities are not inevitably political. One can be a French Canadian, an Albertan, a woman, or the member of some other social or cultural group, and be conscious of the fact, without this having any special political relevance. Identities such as these become politically relevant when those who share them make demands on the state—or when the state recognizes their group identity as a reason for treating them in a particular way. Some political identities emerge spontaneously in society, while others are forged and promoted by the state. Governments in Canada have come to play an increasingly active role in defining and promoting political identities in this country, a role that has generated much controversy.

The **nation** has been a particularly crucial political identity in Canadian politics. It is probably the single most powerful political identity in the world today—although religious identity surpasses it in some societies. The meaning of the term "nation" is a matter of dispute (see Box 1.7). These disputes are not merely academic. Most people would agree that a nation is a community with certain characteristics that distinguish it from other communities. The devil, however, is in the details. What traits are associated with nationhood? Are they racial, as in Hitler's "Aryan nation"? Are they sociological, including the sorts of "objective" and "subjective" attributes referred to in the first definition offered in Box 1.7? Is shared citizenship enough, as former Canadian Prime Minister Pierre Trudeau apparently believed? Or is a nation simply an imagined community—not the same as an *imaginary* community—as Rupert Emerson's definition suggests? Is nationalism a good and normal state of mind conferring dignity on those who believe themselves to be part of a nation and producing positive social and political consequences? Or is it, on the whole, a negative phenomenon, as Pierre Trudeau and George Orwell believed (see the definitions below)?

In *Blood and Belonging*, Michael Ignatieff describes the consequences that can follow from ideas about who does and does not belong to the nation. His book examines the rise of ethnic nationalism in the former Yugoslavia after the end of the Cold War, leading to the violent breakup of the country and to a long chain of events that ultimately produced several ethnic states—Bosnia, Croatia, Kosovo,

Macedonia, Montenegro, and Serbia—out of what had previously been a single country. Ignatieff, one of Canada's foremost intellectuals, reserves a chapter for Quebec and Québécois nationalism. He endeavours to explain how a society whose sons were Canada's prime ministers for over half of the twentieth century has produced a powerful nationalist movement whose goal is nothing less than the independence of Quebec.

Nationalism usually is accompanied by territorial claims. The nation is associated with some particular territory—"the homeland," "la patrie"—that is argued to belong to the members of the nation. Quebec nationalists have asserted such claims, but so, too, have organizations representing Aboriginal Canadians, many of which are grouped together under the Assembly of First Nations. The territorial demands of organizations that claim to represent nations boil down to a demand for self-government, a demand that those making it usually justify as the democratic right of any "people" to self-determination.

But a sense of place—a regional consciousness—may produce political demands that stop far short of independence and self-determination. A regional identity may be based on a variety of cultural, economic, institutional, and historical factors that distinguish the inhabitants of one region of a country from those of other regions. This identity may influence the political behaviour of those

Politics in Focus

BOX 1.7 What Is a Nation?

"A nation is a community of persons bound together by a sense of solidarity and wishing to perpetuate this solidarity through some political means. Contributing to this solidarity are common 'objective' factors such as history, territory, race, ethnicity, culture, language, religion and customs and common 'subjective' factors such as the consciousness of a distinct identity, an awareness of common interests and a consequent willingness to live together. Because of the existence of such factors, there is a special relationship among members of a nation which enables them to co-operate politically more easily among themselves than with outsiders."

Canada, *Report of the Task Force on Canadian Unity* (1979)

"A nation . . . is no more and no less than the entire population of a sovereign state."

Pierre Elliott Trudeau, "Federalism, Nationalism, and Reason" (1965)

"Nationalism is not to be confused with patriotism. Both words are normally used in so vague a way that any definition is liable to be challenged, but one must draw a distinction between them, since two different and even opposing ideas are involved. By 'patriotism' I mean devotion to a particular place and a particular way of life, which one believes to be the best in the world but has no wish to force upon other people. Patriotism is by its nature defensive, both militarily and culturally. Nationalism, on the other hand, is inseparable from the desire for power. The abiding purpose of every nationalist is to secure more power and more prestige, not for himself but for the nation or other unit in which he has chosen to sink his own individuality."

George Orwell, "Notes on Nationalism" (1945)

"The simplest statement that can be made about a nation is that it is a body of people who feel that they are a nation; and it may be that when all the fine-spun analysis is concluded this will be the ultimate statement as well."

Rupert Emerson, *From Empire to Nation* (1960)

"That this House recognize that the *québécois* form a nation within a united Canada."

Motion passed by the Canadian House of Commons by a vote of 266 to 16, on 27 November 2006 who share it, but their political demands generally will be less sweeping than those made by nationalist groups. When regionalism enters politics, it usually takes the form of demands for fairer treatment by the national government, better representation of the region in national political institutions, or more political autonomy for regional political authorities—all of which stop short of the usual catalogue of nationalist demands.

Cultural and social identities are not inherently political. The differences that exist between religious, ethnic, language, regional, or gender groups—to name only a few of the most important social-cultural divisions in the world today—may give rise to political conflicts when they are associated with inequalities in the economic status, social prestige, and political power of these groups. In other words, identities acquire political consequences when the members of a group, the "identity-bearers," believe they experience some deprivation or injustice because of their socio-cultural identity and when a "critical mass" of the group's membership can be persuaded to take political action based on their self-identification as women, French Canadians, westerners, or whatever the identity happens to be. Political identities may not be primarily economic, but they usually have an economic dimension. Even when the stakes appear to be mainly symbolic—for example, the long-standing political debate over special status for Quebec in Canadian federalism—material considerations generally lurk behind the demands that the representatives of a social or cultural group make on the state.

Why particular identities surface in politics, while others remain "pre-political," is a question that can only be answered by looking at the particular history and circumstances of any society. The persistence of regional, ethnolinguistic, and religious identities in the modern world and the emergence of gender inequality onto the political agendas of virtually all advanced industrial societies have confounded the earlier belief of many social scientists, and all socialists, that class divisions would come to dominate the politics of advanced capitalism. The term "class" (like most of the concepts discussed in this chapter) means different things to different people. When used as in the labels "upper class" or "middle class," it refers to a social status that is determined by such measures as the societal prestige of a person's occupation, an individual's income, or one's lifestyle. Since Karl Marx's time, many social scientists have defined class as being primarily an economic concept. According to this usage, a person's class membership is determined by one's relationship to the means of economic production—the main division in society being between those who control the means of production and those who must sell their labour in order to earn a livelihood.

No one seriously argues that modern-day capitalism is characterized by a simple division between the owners of capital—the *bourgeoisie*—and their workers—the *proletariat*—as Marx predicted would happen. Advanced industrial/post-industrial democracies like Canada all have very large middle-class components. Moreover, the growth of pension funds and other large institutional investors has given a significant share of the middle class a direct ownership stake in their national economy and the economies of other countries. The last several decades have also seen a proliferation in the number of jobs that, while they involve dependence in the sense of relying on an employer for a salary, also are characterized by considerable personal freedom in terms of how work is done and even the nature of the work. These people—university professors, engineers, consultants of various sorts, physicians, and lawyers, to name a few—cannot reasonably be squeezed into a definition of the working class.

In recent years, however, the concept of class has experienced a comeback. This comeback has been linked to the phenomenon of **globalization**, which refers to the unprecedented integration of the world's economies through trade, capital flows, and internationalized production, as well as cultural integration through mass media, marketing, satellite- and computer-based information technologies, and migration. Critics argue that globalization has produced greater polarization between the affluent and the poor, both within advanced industrial democracies like Canada and between the wealthy developed countries and the poor developing countries. "Globalization is creating, within our industrial democracies, a sort of under-class of the demoralized and impoverished," says a former United States Secretary of Labour, Robert Reich.[25] Moreover, critics argue that the ability of governments to protect the interests of society's poorest and most vulnerable groups, and to pursue policies that are unpopular with powerful corpor-ate interests and investors, has been diminished by globalization.

In some societies class identity is a powerful force in politics. Political parties make calculated appeals to class interests and draw on different classes for their electoral support. This is not par-ticularly true of Canada. The sense of belonging to a class is relatively weak in Canadian society. Other political identities, especially ethnolinguistic and regional identities, have overshadowed class in Canadian politics. Some commentators argue that this should be taken at face value—that the linguis-tic and regional interests of Canadians are simply more vital to them than is something as abstract as class. Others maintain that the consciousness of belonging to a class whose interests are at odds with those of other classes has been suppressed in various ways by political parties and elites who have vested interests in preventing the emergence of class awareness and action.

Political Fault Lines, Old and New

Some of the fault lines that shape the topography of Canadian politics extend back to the early years of this country, in some cases to the colonial era of Canada's history. The rift that separates French and English Canada is the oldest, going back to the mil-itary conquest of New France in 1759 and the subse-quent domination of the francophone population by an English-speaking minority. The demographic balance would soon shift in favour of the anglo-phone population, a shift that lent even greater urgency to the fundamental issues of whether and how the language and distinct society of French Canada would be recognized and protected. These

are fundamental questions, and they have not changed very much between the Conquest and the present-day possibility of Quebec separation.

A second fault line that reaches back to Canada's colonial past involves this country's relationship to the United States. The American Revolution and the victory of the Thirteen Colonies in the American War of Independence had a profound and enduring impact on Canada. At times this impact has been felt as a territorial threat from the United States. But for more than a century now, the economic, cul-tural, and political influences of the United States have replaced the fear of American troops and annexation. And over this entire period, from the Americans' Declaration of Independence in 1776 to the present day, a long shadow has been cast over Canadian politics and culture by the simple but primordially important fact of living alongside a much more powerful neighbour that resembles us in terms of historical origins, values, and dominant language but that, very clearly, is not us. David Bell argues that at the root of the identity dilemma in English Canada is a need—a need that goes back to 1776—to explain to ourselves who we are as Canadians and in what ways we are not Americans.

A third fault line of somewhat less ancient vintage than the French–English and Canada–United States ones involves regionalism. In a country as physic-ally vast and diverse as Canada it was unavoidable that the economic and social characteristics of the regions would develop differently. Moreover, the concentration of most of the country's population and wealth in Ontario and Quebec, not surpris-ingly, led Ottawa to be more sensitive to the needs and preferences of the centre over those of the "hin-terland" regions. Inter-regional conflict began to acquire a sharp edge in the late nineteenth century around such issues as high tariffs and railroads. This particular fault line quickly assumed an inter-governmental character, as provincial governments became the spokespersons for aggrieved regional interests in opposition to the federal government.

These three fault lines have been called by Donald Smiley the enduring axes of Canadian pol-itics. They are not, however, the only fault lines that mark the Canadian political landscape. Some his-torically prominent ones, such as religious conflict

artizans.com

Malcolm Mayes/Artizans.com

Regional identities and power dynamics are constantly shifting. Most of the country's population and wealth has traditionally been concentrated in Ontario and Quebec, but in recent years, some have perceived a shift in focus towards Alberta.

and division between agrarian-rural and urban-industrial interests, have receded in importance (in the former case because of the diminished force of religion in Canadian life, and in the second because the rural and farm populations are today vastly outnumbered by those who live in urban centres and work in non-farm sectors of the economy). But other issues, including gender equality, Aboriginal rights, environmental protection, and multiculturalism, have traced new lines in Canadian politics.

The evidence of this may be seen in the issues profiled by political parties and their leaders in recent elections. Climate change, social justice, human rights, and environmental protection have become more prominent issues for all of the parties. The older issues associated with language, region, and Canada–US relations are still on the agenda, but they must compete for time and attention with these newer issues, particularly among citizens who reached voting age towards the end of the 1960s and later. The baby boomers and the generations who have followed them are more likely than previous generations of voters to be interested in issues that have to do with the quality of life rather than the standard of living.

This is what Ronald Inglehart and his colleagues refer to as the post-materialist/materialist divide.[26] In recent decades it has emerged as an important political cleavage—social scientists' term for the important lines of political division in a society—in all affluent democracies.

Recent years also have seen the re-emergence of a political fault line that, while quite prominent in the politics of many societies, has generally assumed a rather muted form in Canada and the United States: class conflict and the politics of the distribution of wealth. It is today widely believed that the forces of globalization have widened the gap between the affluent and the poor in Canada and in other advanced industrial democracies. "A select group of wealthy Canadians are taking home fat pay cheques sweetened with bonuses and stock options. Meanwhile, a growing number of working people are seeing their incomes drop," says the Toronto-based Centre for Social Justice. "Economic inequality is fundamentally tied to our market system," the study continues. "This is why income inequality is at its largest spread . . . in the last generation. Additionally, when governments are in retreat . . . this bad dynamic gets even worse."[27]

Stories and analyses linking globalization to claims of growing income inequality, increasing poverty, unemployment and homelessness, and a shrinking middle class have been common since the 1990s. Some of these claims rest on stronger empirical foundations than others (we will revisit this issue in Chapter 3). Nevertheless, if they are believed to be true by large numbers of people, then we would expect to find some political fallout. In other words, the class fault line should become a more prominent feature of Canada's political landscape. To this point, however, the class polarization that many argue is taking place in Canadian society has not reached very deeply into the consciousness of most Canadians, nor has it affected very profoundly their political behaviour. Political parties that appeal to voters on class issues, notably the New Democratic Party, have not experienced a surge of support. The NDP's breakthrough in the 2011 federal election, which saw it win the second largest share of the popular vote and number of seats for the first time in its history, had more to do with leadership, the collapse of the Bloc Québécois, and the feckless Liberal campaign than with class politics. Political protest and activism by labour unions and social justice advocacy groups probably have increased since the 1990s, in response to issues like free trade, outsourcing, and the cutbacks to social spending that were front and centre in that decade. It is not clear, however, that such activism reflects an awakening sense of class consciousness on the part of the general population. A more plausible argument can probably be made that the main manifestations of the new politics of class include the explosion in books, articles, blogs, and other social media dealing with globalization, class polarization, and social activism. But if behaviour at the ballot box is the litmus test of how deeply this fault line has cut into Canada's political landscape, one would have to conclude that class inequality remains a comparatively unimportant issue for most Canadians.

Listen to the "Nouveau Politics" podcast on parties, branding, and political ideology, available at: www.oupcanada.com/ Brooks8e

Starting Points for Research

Bernard Crick, *Democracy: A Very Short Introduction* (Oxford: Oxford University Press, 2002). In barely more than 100 pages Crick provides a pithy and engaging exploration of some of the concepts and controversies discussed in this chapter.

George MacLean and Duncan Wood, *Politics: An Introduction*, 2nd edn (Toronto: Oxford University Press, 2014). Written by two outstanding teachers, this introduction to the discipline situates its key concepts and issues within a Canadian perspective.

Jill Vickers, *Reinventing Political Science: A Feminist Approach* (Halifax: Fernwood, 1997). Vickers invites readers to rethink conventional ways of understanding political life, viewed through a feminist lens.

World Values Survey (www.worldvaluessurvey. org). This ongoing cross-national project includes a number of online publications having to do with modernization and democratization, written by some of the world's foremost political scientists.

Review Exercises

1. Nationalism is a powerful force in the modern world. In 2014 Scotland held a referendum on national independence. Why would this relatively affluent society consider political separation from the United Kingdom? (You may want to start with the website of the Scottish National Party.) Compare the reasons motivating the Scottish independence movement to those offered by separatists for the independence of Quebec. (If you read French, see pq.org/souverainete/ for the Parti Québécois explanation of why independence is necessary.)

2. This chapter introduced some concepts and issues relevant to Canadian political life. An easy way to tell what political issues are current in Canada is to look at the political cartoons included in Canadian print journalism. Find a Canadian political cartoon that relates to a political issue with which you are familiar. One of the best sources is: <www.artizans .com>. Click on "Political toons—CDN." What message do you think the cartoonist is trying to communicate? Do you think the cartoonist's treatment of the subject is fair or biased? In what ways and why?

3. How does identity affect your political behaviour? If you were asked to describe who you are and what aspects of your self-image are most important to you, what would you list? When you see or hear a newsperson, a politician, or a professor do you notice his or her race, gender, signs of ethnicity, accent, or other features of the person? Do you think other people notice such traits?

4. Which country is more democratic, Canada or the United States? Canada or Sweden? You probably have an answer to the first comparison, but you may not be certain about the second. What criteria have you used in arriving at your conclusions and how would you set about measuring whether a society has more or less of the attributes that you associate with democracy? In order to guide your thinking about how the concept of democracy can be operationalized, go to the website for Freedom House: <www.freedomhouse.org>. Does Freedom House's ranking of Canada seem reasonable to you?

Part II
The Societal Context of Politics

In every society certain issues and divisions have a more prominent status and are more fundamental to an overall understanding of its politics and government than are others. In the United States, for example, the issue of race and the relations between white and black America are at the centre of that country's political history. In the case of France, the values of the French Revolution continue to shape the political conversation, influencing policies and ideas that concern the integration of the large black, Maghreban (North African) and Muslim minorities that now live in France. In Canada, the fact that English and French are spoken by large portions of the population, and that the French-speaking population is concentrated largely in one region of the country with a history that pre-dates the emergence of an anglophone majority, continues to influence Canadian political life. The arrival of millions of immigrants from countries outside of Europe has changed Canadian demography in important ways over the last several decades, having a significant impact on Canadian politics. The country's long-standing relationship to the United States, a relationship that involves a complex web of interconnections through trade, investment, population, culture, and foreign policy, has always been a major factor affecting Canadian politics and government. In short, the societal context within which political life unfolds is crucial to an understanding of the nature of any country's politics and of the distribution of power and influence.

Some argue, however, that the actions of the state and their impacts on society are at least as important as the effects that societal forces have on the policies and institutions of government, and that sometimes these actions of the state are more important. State actors, including key political leaders and bureaucrats, often have a determining influence on what happens in politics, shaping the contours of the political conversation, the interests and voices that are listened to, and the outcomes that ensue. But only rarely are elected and appointed officials able to ignore the pressure of ideas and interests from the society around them. These ideas and interests, including the significant **political identities** in a society, its economic structure, and the major fault lines that cut across its landscape, provide the broader context within which political behaviour and policy-making take place. These societal factors are the subject of this next section of the book.

Political Culture

Ideas constitute an important element of political life. This chapter surveys some of the key issues pertaining to the role of ideas in Canadian politics and discusses the political ideas of Canadians. The following topics are examined:

- Ideologies, values, and institutions.
- Fragment theory.
- Formative events.
- Economic structures and political ideas.
- The political ideas of Canadians.
- The nature of Canadian and American value differences.
- Community.
- Freedom.
- Equality.
- Citizen expectations for government.
- How different are Canadian and American values?

Families wave from the Canadian Filipino Association of Yukon float during a Canada Day parade. Many Canadians take pride in the values they feel distinguish them from other countries, including beliefs of multiculturalism, tolerance, compassion, and collectivity. (Ian Stewart/Yukon News)

There is no more Canadian pastime than reflecting on what it means to be a Canadian. Unlike the French, the English, the Chinese, the Russians, and the Americans, to name a handful of other peoples, Canadians have long obsessed over what it is in their values and beliefs that makes them distinctive, that sets them apart from others. In recent years some societies that have long been thought of as having quite confident self-identities seem to have acquired the Canadian penchant for introspection. The French government launched its Grand débat sur l'identité française in 2009. The issue of the consequences of multiculturalism for the American identity has roiled the waters of that country's politics and intellectual life for a generation. But in neither France nor the United States has the question of national identity been asked so urgently and often—and with answers seeming to be so elusive—as in Canada.

In fact, this perennial search for the cultural essence of the Canadian condition has most often been about identifying and explaining the ways in which the values and beliefs of Canadians are different from those of Americans. Various answers have been given over the years. Until the latter half of the twentieth century, these answers more or less boiled down to this: Canadians believe in a more orderly, less individualistic society than that of the United States, in which the state is expected to engage in activities that promote the welfare of society and the development of an independent Canada. The affective tie to Great Britain remained strong well into the middle of the last century, and indeed many Canadians thought of themselves as British and of their country as more British than American in its institutions, values, and heritage.

This answer to the question of what it means to be a Canadian seemed less plausible as immigration changed the ethnic profile of Canada in the latter half of the twentieth century. Even among those of British ancestry, the connection to Great Britain increasingly became a matter of history rather than part of their contemporary identity. Many still believe, however, that Canadian values continue to be less individualistic and less hostile to government than in the United States. Such words as "tolerant," "compassionate," and "caring"

are often used in comparisons between the two countries, always suggesting that Canadians have more of these qualities than Americans. And it is not just Canadians who make this claim. On the American left, Canada, for more than a generation now, has served the function of a sort of "Nirvana to the north," a place that shows what is possible in public policy and social relations and a model to be emulated.[1] As the bonds joining Canada to the United States economically and culturally have multiplied and deepened, the question of what it means to be a Canadian continues to be a sort of national obsession.

This is not true, however, in French-speaking Canada, whose centre of gravity is Quebec, where over 90 per cent of Canadian francophones live. Insulated from American cultural influences by language and for much of their history by the strongly Catholic character of their society, French Canadians have been much less likely than their English-speaking compatriots to define themselves and their history with reference to the United States. They have long worried about anglicizing influences on their language and culture, but they have tended to see the challenge as coming chiefly from within Canada, with its English-speaking majority, rather than from the United States. This perceived challenge has provided the basis for the rise of, first, French-Canadian nationalism and, more recently, Quebec nationalism. Over the last generation, as non-traditional sources of immigration became increasingly important in Quebec, the question of what it means to be Québécois received greater attention. But in answering it, few French-speaking Canadians would think of using as a starting point the United States and what are believed to be American values and beliefs.

Ideologies, Values, and Institutions

Ideas assume various forms in political life. When they take the form of a set of interrelated beliefs about how society is organized and how it ought to function—an interpretive map for understanding the world—this is an **ideology**. An ideology spills beyond the boundaries of politics to embrace beliefs and judgments about other social relationships, including economic ones. This holistic character of ideologies distinguishes them from more limited political value systems. Although most people are not aware of having ideological leanings, and might be puzzled or even startled at being labelled "conservative," "liberal," or "socialist," this does not mean that ideology is irrelevant to their political beliefs and actions. When the politics of a society is described as "pragmatic" and "non-ideological" this may simply indicate that a particular ideology dominates to such a degree that it has become the conventional wisdom.

Someone who regularly and consciously thinks about political matters and other social relationships in ideological terms is an ideologue, a person who is consciously committed to a particular interpretive map of society. Most people are not ideological in this sense of the word.

If ideology is the currency of the political activist, political culture is the medium of the general population. A political culture consists of the characteristic values, beliefs, and behaviours of a society's members in regard to politics. The very definition of what is considered by most people to be political and an appropriate subject for government action is an aspect of political culture. The relative weight that people assign to such values as personal freedom, equality, social order, and national prestige is another aspect of political culture. The expectations that citizens tend to hold for their participation in public life and the patterns of voter turnout, party activism, social movement activities, and other politically relevant forms of behaviour are part of political culture, as is the pattern of knowledge about political symbols, institutions, actors, and issues. Beliefs about whether government actions tend to be benign or malign, and towards whom, also are part of the political culture.

Obviously, people will not hold identical views on these matters, nor will their participation in politics conform to a single template. It is reasonable, nevertheless, to speak of a society as having certain core values or a belief system that is shared by most of its members. Political culture may be thought of as a cluster of typical orientations towards the political universe. The fact that in one society this cluster may be comparatively scattered and marked by division between different segments of society, while in another it is relatively compact, is in itself an observation about political culture.

In Canada, research on political culture has focused primarily on the differences that exist between the politically relevant attitudes and beliefs of French-speaking and English-speaking Canadians, and on the question of whether English-speaking Canada is characterized by regional political cultures. In recent years intergenerational differences in values and beliefs have become another focus of research on political culture. To determine whether significant and persistent differences exist, political scientists have attempted to measure such things as levels of political knowledge and participation, feelings of political efficacy (people's sense of whether their participation in politics matters) and alienation (variously defined as apathy, estrangement from the political system, or the belief that politics is systematically biased against one's interests and values), attitudes towards political authority and the different levels of government, and the sense of belonging to a particular regional or linguistic community.

A third way in which ideas are relevant for politics is through individual *personality*. Historically, one of the most often repeated claims about Canadians has been that they are less likely to question and challenge authority than are Americans. Canadians are said to be more deferential. We examine this claim later in the chapter. Several of the standard questions used in studies of political culture, such as those dealing with political efficacy, trust in public officials, and emotional feelings towards political authorities, tap politically relevant dimensions of personality. Much of the research on the political consequences of individual personality traits has focused on the relationship between a person's general attitudes towards authority and non-conformity, on the one hand, and, on the other, his or her political attitudes on such issues as the protection of civil liberties, toleration of political dissent, the group rights of minorities, and attitudes towards public authorities. The main conclusion of this research is that general personality traits show up in an individual's political ideas and action.

One way of categorizing political ideas—perhaps the most popular way—is to describe them as being *left-wing, right-wing,* or *centrist/moderate*. These labels are used to signify the broader ideological premises believed to lie behind an action, opinion, or statement. For example, a newspaper editorial slamming welfare fraud and calling for mandatory "workfare" would be called right-wing by some, as would a proposal to cut taxes for the affluent or to eliminate public funding for abortions. Proposals to increase the minimum wage, ban the use of replacement workers during a strike or lockout, or increase spending on assistance for developing countries are the sorts of measures likely to be described as left-wing. Centrist or moderate positions, as these terms suggest, fall between the right and left wings of the political spectrum. They attempt to achieve some middle ground between the arguments and principles of **left** and **right**. The **centre** is, virtually by definition, the mainstream of a society's politics, and those who occupy this location on the political spectrum are likely to view themselves as being non-ideological and pragmatic.

"Right" and "left" are shorthand labels for conflicting belief systems. These beliefs include basic notions about how society, the economy, and politics operate, as well as ideas about how these matters *should* be arranged. Generally speaking, to be on the right in Anglo-American societies means that one subscribes to an *individualistic* belief system. Such a person is likely to believe that what one achieves in life is due principally to his or her own efforts—that the welfare of society is best promoted by allowing individuals to pursue their own interests and that modern government is too expensive and too intrusive. To be on the left, however, is to prefer a set of beliefs that may be described as *collectivist*. A leftist is likely to attribute greater weight to social and economic circumstances as

Michael De Adder/Artizans.com

The right–left political spectrum is one way to map out the ideologies embedded in actions, opinion, and statements. Some would suggest, however, that the ideological gap between the principal "right" and "centre" parties in Canada, the Conservative Party and the Liberal Party, is quite small, and even the main party on the "left," the New Democratic Party, if it ever attained power at the federal level, would drift to the centre, as has most often been the case in recent years with NDP governments at the provincial level. In this political cartoon, former Liberal leader Michael Ignatieff is stopped for what looks like drunk driving—for "swerving," rather than settling at the centre as expected.

determinants of one's opportunities and achievements than does someone on the right. Moreover, those on the left have greater doubts about the economic efficiency and social fairness of free markets, and have greater faith in the ability of government to intervene in ways that promote the common good. Although those on the left may be critical of particular actions and institutions of government, they reject the claim that the size and scope of government need to be trimmed. Smaller government, they would argue, works to the advantage of the affluent and privileged, at the expense of the poor and disadvantaged.

In reality, the politics of left and right is more complicated than these simplified portraits suggest.

For example, while opposition to abortion, same-sex marriage, and assisted suicide generally is viewed as a right-wing position, many who subscribe to all the elements of right-wing politics listed above may support these policies. Such people, sometimes labelled **libertarians**, believe that individuals should be allowed the largest possible margin of freedom in all realms of life, including those that involve moral choices. The libertarian right is, however, smaller and less of a political force than the socially conservative right. Social conservatives are distinguished by such stands as opposition to abortion and same-sex marriage, support for capital punishment and stiffer jail sentences, and rejection of forms of pluralism, which they believe are corrosive of traditional values. The wellsprings of their conservatism are quite different from those of libertarianism, but their shared antipathy for certain aspects of the modern welfare state cause libertarians and social conservatives to be grouped together on the right. The fissures in this alliance, and the limitations of the right–left categorization of political ideas, become apparent when the issue is one of personal morality (e.g., abortion, homosexuality, religious teachings in public schools).

Left versus right may also be of limited use, and even misleading, when it comes to environmental issues. It is true that the modern environmental movement and "green" political parties are clearly on the left, as seen in their skepticism towards private enterprise and market forces, their support for state measures, from taxation and regulation to outright bans on certain behaviours, and their general opposition to military solutions to international conflicts. But support for protection of the environment and particularly for conservation of natural habitats and species may also be generated by values and beliefs that are usually thought of as conservative. Social conservatives, whose conservatism is linked to their religious beliefs, often believe that protection of the environment is a moral duty. They see human beings as the stewards of nature, entrusted with its use but also obliged to protect it and ensure that it is passed on to future generations in a state that enables those later generations to profit from nature's bounty. This sort of environmentalism derives from a very different source than that based on the premises that there are physical limits to economic and population growth and that capitalist economics is the road to guaranteed environmental catastrophe.

The waters separating the ideological categories of left and right are further muddied by the exigencies of governing and what is required for re-election. Different parties may claim to be quite different ideological animals and may be clearly distinguishable during the heat of an election campaign. But once in power the pragmatics attached to future electoral success and to successful governance mean that the governing party moves to the centre to meet the needs and demands of the broader society rather than merely those of their core constituency.

Despite various limitations, and the fact that labels like "right" and "left" are more often used to dismiss and discredit one's opponents in politics than to inform in a dispassionate way, the right–left spectrum taps a crucial and enduring truth of modern politics. This involves the issue of the character of the good society and how best to achieve it. We have said that the underlying struggle is essentially one between collectivist and individualist visions of the good society. These visions differ in how they view the conditions that promote human dignity and in their conceptions of social justice. For example, it is often said that one of the cultural characteristics distinguishing Canadians from Americans is the greater propensity of Canadians to sacrifice individual self-interest for the good of the community. In this connection Canada's health-care system is invoked whenever Canadian–American cultural differences are discussed, and when fears are expressed by Canadian nationalists that Canada is sliding down the slope towards American values and public policies (see Box 2.1). What the watchdogs of Canadian-style health care are really saying is that the more collectivist Canadian health-care model provides greater dignity for individuals and is fairer than the more individualistic American system.

Defenders of the American health-care system often retort that Canadian health policy is a form of socialism. **Socialism** is one of a trio of ideologies that have greatly influenced the politics of

Western societies since the American and French revolutions. The other two are **liberalism** and **conservatism**. The idea that Canada's health-care model both reflects and is vital to the protection of Canadian values has often found its way into election campaign advertising, particularly to attack parties and candidates who appear to favour significant reform of the system. They are portrayed as being un-Canadian and, worse, American in their sympathies and values.

The importance of these ideologies in defining the contours of political life is suggested by the fact that major and minor political parties in many Western democracies continue to use the names "liberal," "conservative," and "socialist." In Canada, the two parties that have dominated national politics for most of the country's history are the Liberal Party and the Conservative Party (the Conservative Party was renamed the Progressive Conservative Party in 1942; in December 2003, when it merged with the Canadian Alliance, the federal party dropped the "Progressive" moniker and is once again the Conservative Party of Canada). These two parties have their roots in the ideological divisions of the nineteenth century. Over time, however, the labels have lost much if not all of their informative value. Today, the ideological distance between a Liberal and a Conservative is far from insignificant, but it is narrower than that separating a Democrat from a Republican in the United States. Indeed, at the beginning of the twentieth century the astute French observer André Siegfried had already remarked that the Liberal and Conservative parties were virtually indistinguishable in terms of their

The Social Fabric

BOX 2.1 Health Care and Canadian Culture: Two Views

Our universal, public health-care system defines who we are . . .

"In their discussions with me, Canadians have been clear that they still strongly support the core values on which our health care system is premised—equity, fairness, and solidarity. These values are tied to their understanding of citizenship. Canadians consider equal and timely access to medically necessary health care services on the basis of need as a right of citizenship, not a privilege of status or wealth."

Roy Romanow, from the Commission on the Future of Health Care in Canada, Final Report (2002), xvi

"Medicare has become culturally and politically important to Canadians as a reflection of, and as a defining influence on, our national identity. Shared principles of equity, fairness and compassion are embodied in the health care system, and the services it provides are now regarded as a basic right."

From the website of the Alberta Physician Link: <www.albertaphysicianlink.ab.ca>.

Medicare does not define us . . .

"There is no greater fallacy than the idea that Canada's system of socialized medicine is essential to our system of national values. Without it, Roy Romanow and others tell us, we would not be Canadian.

"This is intellectual hogwash.

"Canada had existed as a distinct country for 101 years before the introduction of a form of socialized medicine in 1968. Millions upon millions of Canadians were born, flourished, received health care and died without giving a thought to the "core value" of a state monopoly on the provision of essential health care. They defined their country sometimes as a rugged northern land, sometimes as a British kingdom, sometimes as a bastion of personal freedom, sometimes as an improvement on the US. Canadian lumberjacks, farmers and their wives, hockey players, and the men who seized Vimy Ridge in 1917 had no interest in the idea of a nanny state, and for the most part believed deeply in notions of personal responsibility and freedom."

Michael Bliss, "Contrary History: Socialized Medicine and Canada's Decline", Canadian Medical Association Journal (July 2007).

ideological principles. They and their supporters shared in the dominant liberal tradition that pervaded Canada and the United States.

At the heart of this tradition was the primacy of individual freedom. *Classical liberalism*—liberalism as understood until the middle of the twentieth century—was associated with freedom of religious choice and practice, free enterprise and free trade in the realm of economics, and freedom of expression and association in politics. These liberal values constituted a sort of national ethos in the United States, where they were enshrined in the Declaration of Independence and in the American Bill of Rights. In the colonies of British North America, which would become Canada in the late nineteenth century, liberalism's dominance was somewhat more tentative than in the United States. This was due to the streak of conservatism kept alive by some of the elites in colonial society, notably the Catholic Church, the Church of England, and the British colonial authorities.

Classical conservatism was based on the importance of tradition. It accepted human inequality—social, political, and economic—as part of the natural order of things. Conservatives emphasized the importance of continuity with the past and the preservation of law and order. They were wary of innovation and opposed such basic liberal reforms as equal political rights for all men (even liberals did not come around to the idea of equal political rights for women until the twentieth century). Unlike liberals, who located the source of all just rule in the people, conservatives maintained that God and tradition were the true founts of political authority. Consequently, they supported an established church and were strong defenders of the Crown's traditional prerogatives against the rival claims of elected legislatures.

Although no party having the label "socialist" has ever achieved the status of even an important minor party in either Canada or the United States, socialist ideology has been influential in various ways. *Classical socialism* was based on the principle of equality of condition, a radical egalitarianism that distinguished socialist doctrine from liberalism's advocacy of equality of opportunity. Socialists supported a vastly greater role for the state in directing the economy, better working conditions and greater rights for workers vis-à-vis their employers, and reforms like public health care, unemployment insurance, income assistance for the indigent, public pensions, and universal access to public education that became the hallmarks of the twentieth-century welfare state.

The usefulness of these three "isms" as benchmarks for reading the political map is no longer very great. There are two main reasons for this. First, all three of these classical ideologies, but especially liberalism and conservatism, mean something quite different today from what they meant 100–200 years ago. For example, contemporary liberalism does not place individual freedom above all else. Instead, modern liberals are distinguished by their belief that governments can and should act to alleviate hardships experienced by the poor and the oppressed. They are more likely to worry about the problems of minority group rights than individual freedoms, or at any rate to see the improvement of the conditions of disadvantaged minorities as a necessary step towards the achievement of real freedom for the members of these groups. Modern liberalism also has become associated with support for multiculturalism and openness towards nontraditional lifestyles and social institutions.

The doctrine of classical conservatism has disappeared from the scene in contemporary democracies, leaving what has been called the conservative outlook or "conservative mind."[2] Modern conservatives tend to embrace the economic beliefs that once were characteristic of liberals. And like classical liberals they defend the principle of equality of opportunity. They are more likely to place the protection of personal freedoms before the advancement of minority rights. As in earlier times, conservatism is generally viewed as the ideology of the privileged in society. It is worth noting, however, that conservative politicians and political parties receive much of their support from middle-class voters whose hands are far from the levers of economic power and social influence.

Of the three classical ideologies, the meaning of socialism has changed the least. There is today, however, much less confidence among socialists that state ownership of the means of economic production and distribution is desirable. Modern socialists, or *social democrats* as they often call themselves, temper their advocacy of an egalitarian society with an acceptance of capitalism and the inequalities that inevitably are generated by free-market economies. The defence of the rights of society's least-well-off elements, which has always been a characteristic of socialism, is today carried out largely under the banner of other "isms," including feminism, multiculturalism, and environmentalism. In Canada and the United States these other collectivist–egalitarian belief systems have more of an impact on politics than does socialism.

A second reason why the traditional trio of "isms" is no longer a reliable guide to politics has to do with the character of political divisions in modern society. The aristocracy of land and title and the deferential social norms that nurtured classical conservatism belong to the past. They live on as the folklore of castles and estates in the once rigidly hierarchical societies of Europe, in the continuing pomp of hereditary royalty, and in Britain's House of Lords. Otherwise, classical conservatism has no legitimacy in the middle-class cultures of Western societies. In the United States the structures and values that supported classical conservatism never existed, and in Canada they achieved only a precarious and passing toehold.

The struggles of liberalism in the eighteenth and nineteenth centuries, and of socialism in the nineteenth and twentieth, have largely been won. Liberals fought for free-market reforms and the extension of political rights and freedoms, first to the new propertied classes created by the Industrial Revolution and then more widely to the (male) adult population. They fought against conservatives who dug in to protect the political privileges of a hereditary aristocracy and the economic dominance of the traditional land-owning classes. Socialists fought for more government control over the economy, for workers' rights like collective bargaining and limits on the hours of work, and for the welfare state. They fought against both the vestiges of conservatism and liberalism's emphasis on individualism.

The classical ideologies were formed and evolved in response to one another as well as to the social and economic conditions in which they were rooted. Today, Canadians, Americans, and Western Europeans live in affluent, middle-class societies that bear little resemblance to those of the nineteenth century, when Europe was a tilting ground for the rivalries between conservatism, liberalism, and socialism. As the character of Western societies has changed, so too have the ideologies that slug it out in their politics.

Does this mean, as some have argued, that the traditional ideologies are obsolete, unsuited to the realities of modern society? This is the **"end of ideology"** thesis that American sociologist Daniel Bell put forward in the 1960s. "In the western world," he argued, "there is today, a rough consensus among intellectuals on political issues: the acceptance of a Welfare State; the desirability of decentralized power; a system of mixed economy and of political pluralism."[3] Some commentators dismiss the traditional "isms" and the left–centre–right ideological grid as outmoded ways of thinking about politics.

It is a great mistake, however, to underestimate the continuing importance of ideology in politics. Although the traditional ideologies now must jostle with feminism, environmentalism, multiculturalism, and other "isms" on a more crowded playing field, and despite the changes that have taken place in the meanings of the classical ideologies, they continue to be useful, though certainly not infallible, guides to understanding political ideas. The right-versus-left or individualism-versus-collectivism dichotomy is probably the most useful. In the real world, however, we should seldom expect to find that the ideas of an individual, or those associated with a group or political party, can be neatly categorized as one or the other.

Those who would argue that the individualism/collectivism dichotomy has become obsolete and that politics has become largely a debate about means rather than ends underestimate the continuing vitality of the struggle between what we might call competing images of the moral order (see Box 2.2). Many of the most profoundly felt differences of opinion on issues of importance in contemporary public life, from abortion and same-sex marriage to issues of trade and taxation, are based on the different ideas that people have about what social, economic, and political arrangements are consistent with personal dignity, justice, social order, and the good society. By and large, those on the right of the modern ideological divide are less likely than those on the left to look to state action for the advancement and protection of the moral order that they prefer. This may be seen in the ongoing debate over the consequences of globalization—a debate in which moral considerations are seldom far from the surface.

Explaining Ideas and Institutions

Explanations of Canadians' political ideas, and of the institutions that embody them, can be grouped into three main camps. They include **fragment theory**, the role of formative events, and economic explanations. Each of these perspectives stresses a different set of causes in explaining the origins of Canadians' political ideas and institutions, and the forces that have shaped their development down to the present.

Fragment Theory: European Parents and Cultural Genes

Canada, along with other New World societies, was founded by immigrants from Europe. Aboriginal communities already existed, of course, but the sort of society that developed in Canada had its roots and inspiration in the values and practices of European civilization. Those who chose to immigrate to the New World—or who were forced to, as were the convicts sent from Britain to Australia—did not represent a cross-section of the European society from which they came. They were unrepresentative in terms of their social class (the privileged tended to remain in Europe, although primogeniture traditions forced many of the younger scions of privilege to emigrate), their occupations, and in some cases their religion. Moreover, immigration tended to occur in waves. New World societies were "fragments" of the European societies that

gave birth to them. They were fragment societies because they represented only a part of the socio-economic and cultural spectrum of the European society from which they originated, and also because their creation coincided with a particular ideological epoch in European development. The timing of settlement is crucial. Along with whatever material possessions immigrants brought with them, they also brought along their "cultural baggage": values and beliefs acquired in Europe and transplanted into the New World. As David Bell and Lorne Tepperman observe, "the 'fragment theory' sees the culture of founding groups as a kind of *genetic code* that does not determine but sets limits to later cultural developments."[4]

But why should the ideas of the founders carry such weight that they shape the political values and beliefs of subsequent generations? Fragment theory is rather weak on this point, arguing that the fragment's ideological system "congeals" at some point—the ideology of the founders becomes the dominant ideology—and that immigrants who arrive subsequently have little choice but to assimilate to the dominant values and beliefs already in place. The transmission of the fragment culture from generation to generation presumably depends on social structures and political institutions that date from the founding period, and embody the dominant ideas of the founding immigrants.

Canada has been characterized as a two-fragment society. French Canada was founded by immigrants from France who brought with them their Catholicism and *feudal* ideas about social and political relations. Feudal society is characterized by the existence of fairly rigid social classes, connected to one another by a web of mutual rights and duties based on tradition, and by the exclusion of most people from the full right to participate in politics. According to French-Canadian historian Fernand Ouellet, this was the ideological and social condition of New France when the colony was conquered by British forces in 1759.[5] Cut off from the social and political developments unleashed by the French Revolution (1789)—emigration from France, with the exception of some priests, virtually dried up—French Canada's ideological development was shaped by its origins as a feudal

Governing Realities

BOX 2.2 European vs American Models of Society?

The economic crisis that began in 2008 and pulled the global economy into recession was widely blamed on the American housing market. Years of very low interest rates and lending policies that allowed for the accumulation of enormous and ultimately unsustainable levels of private indebtedness collapsed like a house of cards once it became clear that the assets of many banks and investment firms were grossly overvalued. The crisis was seen as provoked by unbridled greed—CEO and other management compensation became a lightning rod for criticism—and a failure of governments to adequately regulate financial markets. The American model—individualistic, capitalistic, and anti-statist—came in for a pummelling in the United States and especially abroad.

Two years later the crisis morphed into something rather different. It began with Greece and the inability of that country's government to pay its debts. These debts, it was discovered, were rather formidable and had been made possible by the fact that as a member of the Eurozone—the 17 European Union (EU) countries who share a common currency—Greece had been able to borrow money for many years at rates of interest more favourable than its economic conditions warranted. This would not have been seen as calamitous if the only victims of default were expected to be some banks and other private investors. But the prospect of Greece defaulting on its loans had wider implications for the status of the euro, leading the other Eurozone countries, but especially Germany, and the IMF to put together a bailout plan for Greece and a contingency fund in the event that another Eurozone country also became incapable of paying its creditors. Spain, Italy, and Ireland were among the countries whose finances appeared to teeter on the brink.

This was a different crisis that had nothing to do with American housing markets and CEOs receiving gargantuan compensation packages. It was a crisis provoked by state spending, not private lending. By the late spring of 2010 the European story had acquired dimensions far beyond tiny Greece and its messy finances. It was, observers now said, the European model itself that was in question. That model was based on a more generous welfare state, shielding individuals and families from a greater number of risks that were experienced under the American model. Retirement ages in Western Europe came in for particular criticism. In some countries the average age of retirement was below 60. In France, the Socialist government of François Mitterand in the early 1980s had legislated 60 as the age at which one became eligible for a full public pension. But populations were aging across the EU, with proportionately fewer workers supporting proportionately more pensioners. The left dug in its heels in defence of existing retirement ages and benefits, while the European right argued that they were unrealistic and unsustainable.

Right versus left: the American model of smaller, less generous government versus the Western European welfare state. It was clear that what some had argued was an old and outdated way of viewing political conflict was still very much alive and relevant.

Where did Canada fit into this debate? It is usual to say that Canada falls somewhere between the American and Western European models, being somewhat more statist and collectivist in thinking and policies than the United States, but not as left-leaning as such societies as France, the Netherlands, the Scandinavian democracies, and others. Canada did not fare as badly as most capitalist democracies in the crisis that began in 2008, avoiding the housing collapse that afflicted the United States and the huge unemployment experienced in many EU countries. So the conversation about right versus left tended to be somewhat more muted in Canada than in these other societies, where the scale of economic hardship and its social costs focused attention more sharply on the ideological nature of the economic crisis and its solutions.

fragment of pre-revolutionary France. Institutions, chiefly the Catholic Church, the dominant social institution in French Canada until well into the twentieth century, operated to maintain this pre-liberal inheritance.

The "cultural genes" of English Canada are, according to fragment theory, very different. English Canada was originally populated mainly by immigrants from the United States. These were the so-called Loyalists; those who found themselves on the losing side of the American War of Independence (1776). They migrated north to British colonies that were overwhelmingly French-speaking.[6] The "cultural baggage" they carried with them has been the subject of much debate, but the general view seems to be that they held predominantly *liberal* political beliefs. The liberalism that emerged in the eighteenth century was built around the idea of individual freedom: freedom in politics, in religion, and in economic relations. One of its crucial political tenets was the idea that government was based on the consent of the people. So why did the Loyalists leave the United States, a society whose political independence was founded on liberal beliefs?

The defenders of fragment theory offer different answers to this question. Some argue that the liberalism of the Loyalists was diluted by *conservative* or *Tory* political beliefs: deference towards established authority and institutions, an acceptance of inequality between classes as the natural condition of society, and a greater stress on preserving social order than on protecting individual freedoms.[7] Others reject the view that Tory values were ever a legitimate part of English Canada's political culture, arguing that this belief system had no roots in the pre-revolutionary Thirteen Colonies and therefore could not have been exported to English Canada through the Loyalist migration.[8] The Loyalists were "anti-American Yankees" who had rejected American independence because of their loyalty to the British Empire and to the monarchy, and their dislike of republican government (or, as they were more likely to put it, "mob rule"). Their quarrel was not with liberal ideology, as shown by the fact that they immediately clamoured for elected assemblies and the political rights they had been used to in America. Bell and Tepperman thus argue that:

Forced to leave their country, the Tories, or Loyalists, suffered profound doubts. Expulsion kept the Loyalist from basing a fragment identity on the liberal principles of John Locke. Made to give up his real identity, the Canadian Loyalist invented a new one. As a substitute, it was not quite good enough, of course. How could it be, when he had continuously to deny its true nature, liberalism? "The typical Canadian," an Englishman observed a hundred years ago, "tells you that he is not, but he is a Yankee—a Yankee in the sense in which we use the term at home, as synonymous with everything that smacks of democracy." The Loyalist in Canada is thereafter always a paradox, an "anti-American Yankee." Only one path leads out of his dilemma: creating a myth that helps him survive. In this myth, he insists that he is British.[9]

The debate over how important non-liberal values were among the Loyalists is not merely academic. For most of Canada's history, analyses of English Canada as a more deferential and conservative society than the United States traced this alleged difference back to the original ideological mixtures of the two societies. A second reason why the debate matters involves the explanation for Canadian socialism. Some of those who contend that conservative values were an important and legitimate component of English Canada's original cultural inheritance go on to argue that the emergence of socialism in Canada was facilitated by, first, the fact that liberalism never achieved the status of an unchallenged national creed (as it did in the United States) and, second, the fact that social class was not a foreign concept in English Canada.[10] Conservatism and socialism, according to this view, are two varieties of collectivism.

Formative Events: Counter-Revolution and the Conquest

Societies, like human beings, are marked by certain major events at critical periods in their development. These events are "formative" in the sense that they make it more probable that a society will evolve

TABLE 2.1 Liberalism, Conservatism, and Socialism: Classical and Contemporary Versions

I.	CLASSICAL	Liberalism	Conservatism	Socialism
a.	Characteristics of the Good Society	Individual freedom is maximized; politics and economics are free and competitive; achievements and recognition are due to personal merit and effort; a capitalist economy will produce the greatest happiness for society and maximize material welfare; personal dignity depends on the individual's own actions.	The traditional social order is preserved; individuals are members of social groups that are linked together by a web of rights and obligations; those born in privileged circumstances have an obligation to those below them on the social ladder; there is a natural social hierarchy based on inherited status; personal dignity depends on one's conformity to the norms and behaviour of one's social group.	Social and economic equality are maximized; private ownership of property is replaced by its collective ownership and management; competition is replaced by co-operation; the welfare of society is maximized through economic and social planning; personal dignity depends on work and one's solidarity with the working class.
b.	Nature of Government	All just government rests on the consent of the governed; party system is competitive; the state is subordinate to society; government should be small and its scope limited; the elected legislature is the most powerful component of the state; separation between church and state.	The rights and responsibilities of those who govern derive from God and tradition; the state's fundamental role is to preserve social order; the state is superior to society and is owed obedience by all citizens and groups; the Crown is the most powerful component of the state; the size and scope of government are small by modern standards, but are not limited by liberalism's suspicion of the state; the state recognizes an official church.	All just government rests on the consent of the governed and the principles of social and economic equality; the state should control crucial sectors of the economy; government has a responsibility to redistribute wealth from the wealthy to the less fortunate social classes; government is large and its scope wide; a socialist state is the embodiment of the will and interest of the working class; no officially recognized religion.
c.	Chief Supporters	Industrialists, merchants, property-owning individuals.	Landed aristocracy, established church, military officers and agents of the Crown whose status and income depend on maintenance of the traditional social hierarchy.	Organized workers; intellectuals.

II.	CONTEMPORARY	Liberalism	Conservatism	Socialism
a.	Characteristics of the Good Society	Individual freedom is balanced by protection for disadvantaged elements in society and recognition of group rights; capitalism must be regulated by the state to ensure the social and economic well-being of the majority; social diversity should be recognized and promoted through public education, hiring, and the policies of governments; social entitlements are respected, including a certain standard of living and access to decent education, health care, and accommodation; personal dignity is based on freedom and social equality.	Individual freedom is more important than social equality and should not be sacrificed to the latter; state regulation of capitalism should be kept to a minimum and should not be used to promote any but economic goals; social diversity is a fact, but is not something that should be actively promoted by government; individuals should be responsible for their own lives and policies that encourage dependency on the state should be avoided; personal dignity depends on one's own efforts and is undermined by collectivist policies and too much emphasis on promoting social and economic equality.	Social and economic equality values; individual rights must be subordinated to collective goals; small-scale capitalism has its place, but state economic planning and active participation in the economy are still necessary to promote both economic competitiveness and social fairness; the environmental consequences of all public and private actions must be considered; systemic discrimination based on gender, race, and ethnicity is eliminated through government policies; personal dignity depends on social and economic equality.

continued

TABLE 2.1 continued

I.	CONTEMPORARY	Liberalism	Conservatism	Socialism
b.	Nature of Government	The state has a responsibility to protect and promote the welfare of the disadvantaged; the post-WWII welfare state is a necessary vehicle for ensuring social justice; government should reflect the diversity of society in its personnel and policies; the state should not be aligned with any religious group.	The state's primary function should be to maintain circumstances in which individuals can pursue their own goals and life plans; government should be small and the level of taxation low in order to minimize interference with individual choice; government should not remain neutral between different systems of morality, but should promote traditional values through the schools and through support for the traditional family.	The state should redistribute wealth in society and ensure the social and economic equality of its citizens; some modern socialists argue that political power should be decentralized to community-level groups as the best way to ensure democratic responsiveness and accountability; the state should reflect the society in its personnel and policies; traditional value systems are based on systemic discrimination and oppression, and government has a responsibility to eradicate these values.
c.	Chief Supporters	Many middle-of-the-road advocacy groups within the feminist, environmental, and multicultural movements; public-sector workers; middle-class intellectuals in the universities and the media; the national Liberal Party and much of the Bloc Québécois; think-tanks, including the Institute for Research on Public Policy and the Canada West Foundation.	Business groups; middle-class workers in the private sector; the mainstream of the Conservative Party of Canada; think-tanks, including the Fraser Institute, the Atlantic Institute for Market Studies, and the Manning Centre.	More extreme advocacy groups within the feminist, environmental, and multicultural movements; some elements in the NDP and within organized labour; the Green Party; think-tanks, including the Canadian Centre for Policy Alternatives, the Caledon Institute of Social Policy, and the Canadian Council on Social Development; some university-based intellectuals; the Council of Canadians.

along particular lines, instead of along others. In the world of politics, these formative events are associated both with ideas and with institutions. For example, the American Revolution was fought in the name of liberal values and was followed by the adoption of a constitution and structures of government that enshrined the victors' preference for dispersed political power, a weak executive, and guarantees for individual rights. The institutions put in place after the Revolution embodied eighteenth-century liberal values of individual freedom and limited government. They shaped the subsequent pattern of American politics by promoting and legitimizing behaviour and issues that conformed to these values.

The main exponent of the formative events theory of political culture is American sociologist Seymour Martin Lipset. He first introduced it by arguing that the political development of the United States has been shaped by its **revolutionary origins**, while that of English Canada has been shaped by its **counter-revolutionary origins**. Lipset writes:

Americans do not know but Canadians cannot forget that two nations, not one, came out of the American Revolution. The United States is the country of the revolution, Canada of the counterrevolution. These very different formative events set indelible marks on the two nations. One celebrates the overthrow of an oppressive state, the triumph of the people, a successful effort to create a type of government never seen before. The other commemorates a defeat and a long struggle to preserve a historical source of legitimacy: government's deriving its title-to-rule from a monarchy linked to church establishment. Government power is feared in the south; uninhibited popular sovereignty has been a concern in the north.[11]

Many of those who found themselves on the losing side of the American Revolution—the Loyalists—migrated north. They were the founders of an English-speaking society that originated in its rejection of the new American republic. This original rejection would be repeated several times: in the War of 1812; in the defeat of the American-style democratic reforms advocated by the losers in the 1837–8 rebellions in Lower and Upper Canada; in the 1867 decision to establish a new country with a system of government similar to that of Great Britain. The political history of Canada, including many of the major economic and cultural policies instituted by Canadian governments, reads largely as a series of refusals in the face of Americanizing pressures.

Is rejection of American political values and institutions proof of the greater strength of conservative values in English Canada? Some of those who agree with Lipset about the importance of formative events do not agree that counter-revolutionary gestures signify *ideological conservatism*. David Bell and Lorne Tepperman have argued that **Loyalism** concealed an underlying *ideological liberalism*. They acknowledge that the Loyalists were not anti-government, and that Canadians ever since appear to have been more willing to use the state for social, economic, and cultural purposes than have their American neighbours. But, they argue, a fondness for government is not inconsistent with liberal values. It is only in the United States, where the Revolution was directly about the tyranny of government, that liberalism acquired a strongly anti-government character.[12]

If Loyalism was not a conservative ideology, what was it? Bell and Tepperman argue that Loyalism was essentially a self-justification for not being American. Faced with the paradox of being cast out of a society whose political values they shared, the Loyalists had a serious identity crisis. They resolved it by insisting on their Britishness, and by constant criticisms of American values and institutions. This anti-Americanism is a component of Loyalism that endures even today. It explains, according to Bell and Tepperman, English Canada's centuries-old national identity puzzle.

What 1776 represents for English Canada's political development, the British Conquest of New France in 1759 represents for that of French Canada. The Conquest has always occupied a central place in French-Canadian nationalism, testifying to French Canadians' own awareness of its significance. The motto on Quebec licence plates, "Je me souviens" ("I remember"), is in fact an

In 2012, Canada celebrated the 200-year anniversary of the War of 1812, which has been characterized as a defining moment in Canadian history and, therefore, in the development of Canadian identity. In the cartoon above, what is the artist suggesting about the ways in which Canadians perceive this historical event?

Graeme MacKay/Artizans.com

oblique reference to the time before the Conquest, when French-speaking Canadians presumably were free from the oppression of Ottawa and English Canadians. Particularly under Parti Québécois governments in Quebec it has been common for the Conquest to be mentioned in official government documents on subjects ranging from language to the economy and constitutional reform.

There is no agreement as to how the Conquest has affected the ideological development of French Canada. Some, like historian Michel Brunet and sociologist Marcel Rioux, have argued that the Conquest cut off the development of a French-speaking bourgeoisie—francophones were rarely found in Canada's corporate elite until only a few decades ago—thereby depriving French Canada of the class that elsewhere was the main carrier of liberal political values. The mantle of social leadership, and the task of defining French-Canadian society, eventually fell on the Catholic Church and the ideologically conservative politicians who accepted the clerics' interpretation of that society as Catholic, French-speaking, non-liberal, and agrarian—in about that order of importance.

Others, like historian Fernand Ouellet and political scientist Louis Balthazar, maintain that there was no fledgling bourgeoisie, and therefore no catalyst for liberal political reform. French Canada, they argue, was essentially a feudal society at the time of the Conquest. It fixated at this pre-liberal/pre-capitalist stage because it was cut off from the future, not because French Canada was deprived of something it once possessed.

History did not, of course, stop at the Conquest. The crushed 1837 rebellion in Lower Canada (Quebec) signalled the defeat of the politically liberal *patriots* and consolidated the dominance of the conservative ideology in French Canada. This ideology would ultimately collapse by the end of the 1950s, finally brought down by the weight of the enormous social and economic transformations that the conservatives had ignored and even denied. Since then, conservative ideology has had little credibility in Quebec, but the memory of the Conquest continues to be a favourite starting point for Quebec nationalists. The protests generated in 2008 by plans (ultimately cancelled) to re-enact the 1759 Battle of the Plains of Abraham, as part of Quebec's 400th anniversary celebration, showed how raw this nerve remains.

Both the fragment theory and the formative events explanation for the development of Canadian political culture are **path dependency models**. This explanatory framework emphasizes the impact that key historical events and conditions have on the trajectory that will be followed by a society, a value system, or an economy. James Mahoney explains it this way:

> [P]ath dependence characterizes specifically those historical sequences in which contingent events set into motion institutional patterns or event chains that have deterministic properties. The identification of path dependence therefore involves both tracing a given outcome back to a particular set of historical events, and showing how these events are themselves contingent occurrences that cannot be explained on the basis of prior historical conditions.[13]

Economic Structures and Political Ideas

From a class analysis perspective, both fragment theory and the formative events explanation are "hopelessly idealistic."[14] This is because they locate the sources of political values and institutions primarily in ideas—the "cultural baggage" of fragment theory and the cultural mindset and symbols associated with the notion of formative events. An economic interpretation, by contrast, explains culture and the institutions that embody and perpetuate it as the products of class relations. These class relations are themselves rooted in the particular system of economic production and distribution—the *mode of production* as Marxists generally call it—that is found in a society at any point in time. Ideas and institutions change in response to transformations in the economic system and in the class relations associated with this system. The dominant ideas and existing political arrangements of a society are not, however, merely the shadows cast by economic phenomena. But what sets this approach apart from the other two we have examined is the belief that *culture and institutions are the embodiments of power relations whose sources lie in the economic system.*

How is political culture produced? By whom? For whom? With what effects? How do political institutions embody and reinforce the power relations that characterize society? These are the questions addressed by those who approach political values and institutions from the angle of economically determined class relations. They argue that the dominant ideas of a society are inevitably those of its most powerful class, i.e., those who control the system of economic production and distribution. After all, important means of forming and disseminating ideas and information, such as the privately owned mass media, are controlled by the dominant class. Others, including the schools, mainstream religious organizations, and the state, accept and propagate the values of this class for reasons more subtle than ownership. Chief among these reasons is their support for *social order*, and their rejection of tendencies and ideas that fundamentally challenge the status quo. None of these major institutions is in the business of overturning society. They depend on a stable social order to carry out their respective activities and to satisfy their particular organizational needs. But the social order they support, and whose values they accept, embodies a particular economic system and the power relations it produces. Defence of established institutions and values is not, therefore, a class-neutral stance.

Why would the members of subordinate classes embrace values and beliefs that, according to this class perspective, are basically justifications for the self-interest of the dominant class? The answer has two parts. First, those who are not part of the dominant class—and this would by definition include the majority of people—may be the victims of **false consciousness**. This concept, first used by Karl Marx, involves the inability of the subordinate classes to see where their real interests lie. For example, deference to established authority and belief in a hereditary aristocracy's "natural right to rule," ideas that defend the privileges of the dominant class in a feudal society, very clearly reinforce the subordinate social position of those who are not

fortunate enough to be born into the ruling aristocracy. In liberal societies, the widespread belief that opportunities to move up the socio-economic ladder are relatively open to those who are willing to work hard is argued by some to reinforce the dominant position of that small minority who control the economy and who account for most of society's wealth. After all, critics argue, abundant empirical evidence shows that significant barriers to socio-economic mobility exist, that a good deal of poverty is passed on from generation to generation, and that those at the top of the socio-economic pyramid constitute a largely self-perpetuating elite. And yet we learn in school, through the mass media, and in countless other ways that equality of opportunity, not systemic inequality, is a characteristic feature of our society.

The second reason why, according to this class perspective, members of subordinate classes accept the ideas of the dominant class as "common sense" is because these ideas conform, to some significant extent, to their personal experience. Democratic claims about the fundamental equality of all persons have a false ring in societies where some people are denied a share of this equality because they are black or female, for example. But in a society in which, under the constitution, there are no second-class citizens, and where everyone has the right to vote and participate in politics and enjoys equal protection under the law, claims about equality may appear to be valid. Or, consider the liberal belief, discussed earlier, that opportunities to acquire wealth and social standing are relatively open. There is, in Canada and in other liberal societies, enough evidence of this mobility to make the proposition appear true (see Chapter 3 on social mobility). The election of Barack Obama as President of the United States—the son of a Kenyan goatherd!—is evidence of mythic proportions. While some people never escape the socio-economic circumstances they are born into, many others do. There is enough proof that hard work and/or intelligence pays off in terms of material success to make liberalism's claim about what determines a person's socio-economic status a credible one. As Patricia Marchak observes, "the propagation of an ideology cannot occur in a vacuum of experience; there must be a fair amount of congruence between personal experience and ideological interpretation for the propaganda [read, 'dominant ideology'] to be successful."[15] Where this congruence is either weak or totally absent, the dominant class must rely on force to uphold its rule.

This idea is important: a certain degree of congruence must exist between the dominant values and beliefs of a society and the lived experience of most of its members, for otherwise the ideas of the dominant class will be exposed as pure self-interest. It means that what some have called "false consciousness" cannot be totally false. Ideological systems not anchored in the social and economic realities of those subject to them are just not viable. We can understand this better by looking at the case of Quebec and the ideological changes associated with that province's "Quiet Revolution" of the 1960s.

As recently as the 1950s, the dominant ideology in French-speaking Quebec was traditionally religious and politically conservative. It was an ideology based on the concept of *la survivance* (survival): conserving the religious and linguistic heritage of French Canada in the face of assimilationist pressures. While possessing the formal structures of political democracy, Quebec's political life was dominated by autocratic politicians, rampant patronage, and social institutions—notably the Church and conservative newspapers—that encouraged submission to established authority.[16] Functions like education and social services that, in virtually all industrial democracies, were already under state control, were still in the hands of the Church. Even the province's francophone labour unions were predominantly confessional, linked to a Church whose ideas about industrial relations were shaped largely by its concern for preserving social harmony. In short, the dominant ideology and the social institutions that embodied it were conservative.

This conservatism, linked as it was to the social dominance of the Church and to a sharply limited role for the provincial state, was increasingly out of step with the industrial society that had been evolving in Quebec throughout the twentieth century. Those who advocated reforms that entailed a more interventionist role for the Quebec state, such as public control over education and social assistance, and whose vision of Quebec was of a secular industrial society necessarily found themselves in conflict with the spokespersons for the conservative ideology. By the 1950s, however, as the reformist elements in Quebec politics were quick to point out, the typical Québécois was a city-dweller who worked in a factory, store, or office,[17] and a new middle class of university-educated francophone professionals was gaining numerical strength in the province.[18] This new middle class was the leading force behind the expansion of the Quebec state that took place in the early to mid-1960s. Ultimately, the lack of "congruence" between the values of the conservative ideology and the personal experience of most Québécois brought about the collapse of one dominant ideology and its replacement by one more in tune with those social groups—the new middle class and the growing francophone business community—who have dominated Quebec politics since the Quiet Revolution.

The Political Ideas of Canadians

What do Canadians believe about politics? Is it true that they value social order more, and individual freedom less, than their American counterparts? Does French Canada, and more particularly French-speaking Quebec, constitute a "distinct society" in terms of its values and beliefs? Is it reasonable to talk about the political ideas of English-speaking Canadians, or are the regional differences in political culture too great to warrant such an approach?

In the following pages we will organize our analysis of political culture under four themes: community, freedom, equality, and attitudes towards the state. These tap crucial dimensions of political culture and at the same time allow us to explore the differences and similarities between French- and English-speaking Canadians, between different regions of the country, and between Canadians and Americans. The evidence we will use is drawn from history, survey research data on attitudes, and measures of actual behaviour of individuals, groups, and governments from which values can be inferred.

Community

"Canadians," Margaret Atwood once wrote, "are forever taking the national pulse like doctors at a sickbed; the aim is not to see whether the patient will live well but simply whether he will live at all."[19] Canada's best-known writer made this observation at a time when Quebec separatism was on the rise and anxiety over American cultural domination was perhaps at its highest level. Forty years later Canada is still one country and fears about American culture seem to have abated, at least among the general public. Nevertheless, reflections on what it means to be Canadian and whether there is a Canadian identity that can survive the winds that buffet it from inside and outside the country continue to be part of the Canadian condition.

The roots of this preoccupation with national identity go back to the Conquest and the American War of Independence. In more recent years these two historical pillars of Canada's identity preoccupation have been joined by newer challenges to the political community. These have come from Aboriginal Canadians and from some ethnic minorities who reject what they argue is their marginalization within Canadian society. Lacking a robust unifying sense of national identity, Canadian society has been buffeted by identity politics and the often irreconcilable definitions of Canada—sometimes proposing the dismemberment of the country as we know it—advanced by various groups. At the same time we should not imagine that Canadians are alone in asking such questions and facing such challenges. "Identity politics throughout the West," argues Will Kymlicka, "have become routinized and domesticated as part of everyday processes of democratic deliberation and negotiation."[20]

The term "political community" implies, quite simply, a shared sense of belonging to a country whose national integrity is worth preserving. This is something less than nationalism, which defines a community by its language, ethnic origins, traditions, or unique history. And it is not quite the same as patriotism, which one associates with a more fervent and demonstrative love of country and its symbols than is usually considered seemly in Canada. Political community is, rather, what historian W.L. Morton once described as "a community of political allegiance alone."[21] National identity, in such a community, is free from cultural and racial associations. Instead, national identity is essentially political—a sense of common citizenship in a country whose members have more in common with one another than with the citizens of neighbouring states and who believe there are good reasons for continuing to live together as a single political nation. The term "political nationality" is used by Donald Smiley to refer to precisely this sort of non-ethnic, non-racial sense of political community.[22]

Canada's sense of community has often seemed terribly fragile, threatened by French–English tensions, western grievances against Ontario and Quebec, and, most recently, conflicts between the aspirations of Aboriginal Canadians and the policies of federal and provincial governments. This apparent fragility needs to be viewed alongside evidence suggesting that the country has been relatively successful in managing (repressing, critics would say) challenges to the idea and continuation of a united Canada. The existing Constitution dates from 1867, making it one of the oldest and most durable in the world. Moreover, the territorial integrity of the country has (so far) remained unshaken by either civil war or secession. This is not to understate the importance of the rifts in Canada's sense of community. But the problems of Canadian unity and identity should be viewed from a broader perspective.

In recent years, the Canadian political community has faced two major challenges: the management of French–English relations and Aboriginal demands for self-government. Some commentators would include regional conflict as a third challenge to the Canadian political community. Such conflict certainly has deep roots in Canadian history and has generated regionally based movements and parties of protest. But these regional grievances and conflicts have never threatened the territorial integrity of Canada. Westerners and, less stridently, eastern Canadians have long complained about policies and institutions that favour the interests of Ontario and Quebec. They also have complained about an idea of Canada that often has seemed to relegate their regional histories and realities to the margins. But their resentment has never boiled over to produce politically significant separatist movements in these regions, nor popular defection from the *idea* of Canada. The importance of regionalism will be discussed in Chapter 5.

For most of Canada's history, relations between the francophone and anglophone communities have not posed a threat to the political community. The differences and tensions between Canada's two major language groups were managed through political accommodations between their political elites. This practice arguably goes back to the Quebec Act of 1774. Official protection was extended to the Catholic Church and Quebec's civil law system just when the British authorities were worried about the prospect of political rebellion in the American colonies spreading north. The tradition of deal-making between French and English Canada acquired a rather different twist in the couple of decades prior to Confederation, when the current provinces of Ontario and Quebec were united with a common legislature. The practice of dual ministries, with a leader from both Canada East (Quebec) and Canada West (Ontario), quickly developed, as did the convention that a bill needed to be passed by majorities from both East and West in order to become law. The federal division of powers that formed the basis of the 1867 Confederation continued this deal-making

CP Images/ The Canadian Press/Chuck Mitchell

In Canada to attend Expo 67, then French President Charles de Gaulle roused—and stunned—a crowd assembled at Montreal's city hall on 24 July 1967 when he spoke from a small hotel balcony and exclaimed, "Vive Montréal! Vive le Québec! Vive le Québec libre!" ("Long live free Quebec!"). The slogan became a rallying cry for those organizing around a growing Quebec sovereignty movement at the time.

tradition. The assignment to the provinces of juris-diction over education, property, civil rights, and local matters was shaped by Quebec politicians' insistence on control over those matters involving cultural differences.

This tradition of elitist deal-making has con-tinued throughout Canada's history at two different levels. Nationally, the federal cabinet and national political parties, particularly the Liberal Party of Canada, have been important forums where the interests of Quebec could be represented. But with the rise of a more aggressive Quebec-centred nationalism in the 1960s, the ability to represent the interests of French and English Canada within national institutions became less important than whether compromises could be reached between the governments of Canada and Quebec.

The modus vivendi that for a couple of cen-turies prevented French–English conflicts from exploding into challenges to the idea of a single Canada seemed to come unstitched during the 1960s. Quebec independence, which previously had been a marginal idea that surfaced only spor-adically in the province's politics, became a serious proposition advocated by many French-speaking intellectuals and supported by a sizable minority of Québécois. The independence option spawned a number of organized political groups during the 1960s. In 1968, most of them threw their sup-port behind the newly formed pro-independence Parti Québécois (PQ). Since then, the debate over whether the province should remain in Canada, and if so on what terms, has been one of the chief dimensions of Quebec political life.

In attempting to understand how great a threat Quebec separatism has posed to the Canadian com-munity, we will consider two aspects of the issue: political violence and public attitudes.

Political Violence

Canadians are not accustomed to the violent reso-lution of political disputes. There have been only two political assassinations since Confederation, the first when D'Arcy McGee was shot down on the muddy streets of Ottawa in 1868 and the second in 1970 when Quebec's Minister of Labour, Pierre

Laporte, was strangled to death by members of the Front de Libération du Québec (FLQ). The Political Terror Scale compiled by several American research-ers ranks Canada well down the list of countries in terms of riots, armed political attacks, deaths from domestic political violence, and government sanctions to repress or eliminate a perceived threat to the state.[23] Non-violent protest has occupied a more prominent place in Canadian politics, as one would expect in any genuine democracy. But even in this regard, protest demonstrations historically have been much rarer in Canada and less likely to be associated with violent outcomes than in many other advanced industrialized democracies.[24]

Violence has not, however, been either absent or unimportant in Canadian politics. Much of that violence has involved labour disputes or workers' protests where the police or military were called in to protect the interests of employers and the cap-italist social order. The violent suppression of the Winnipeg General Strike in 1919 and the use of the Royal Canadian Mounted Police in Regina in 1935 to break up the "On-to-Ottawa Trek" of unem-ployed workers during the depth of the Depression are perhaps the two most noteworthy instances of such violence. The forcible detention of many Japanese, German, and Italian Canadians during World War II is another instance of state political violence. In more recent years a number of anti-globalization protests, as in Quebec City in 2001, Toronto in 2010, and Montreal during the student protests in the spring of 2012, have shown that political violence is not absent from the Canadian scene. But these clashes, which very clearly involve demands for radical change, do not challenge the territorial integrity or idea of Canada. Violence related to French–English relations does, however, have the potential to challenge the Canadian com-munity. Canadian history is punctuated with epi-sodes of such violence, going back to the hanging of the francophone Métis leader Louis Riel in 1885. This provoked denunciations of the Conservative government and Prime Minister John A. Macdonald from many francophone leaders. Although they did not sympathize with the rebellion that Riel led, francophones felt that Ottawa's unwillingness to commute Riel's execution sentence was influenced by anti-French prejudice. Violence broke out again in 1918 in Quebec City over the conscription issue. French Canadians believed that Canada's involvement in World War I was motivated by the colonial attachments that English Canadians still felt for Britain, and they were massively opposed to the imposition of conscription.

Listen to the "2012 Student Protest in Quebec" podcast, available at: www.oupcanada.com/Brooks8e

Violence flared in the streets of Montreal in 1955 when Maurice "Le Rocket" Richard was suspended by the president of the National Hockey League, Clarence Campbell. French-Canadian supporters of Les Canadiens and their star player saw the suspension as more than punishment for a stick-swinging incident. They saw it as yet another example of ethnically motivated discrimination on the part of "les maudits anglais" (the damned English).

The 1960s saw renewed violence, this time a spate of bombings and vandalism directed at symbols of the federal government's authority and anglophone domination in the province of Quebec. This was mainly the work of the FLQ, a very small group of people who achieved national prominence when they kidnapped British trade commissioner James Cross and Quebec cabinet minister Pierre Laporte in October 1970. The federal government reacted by invoking the War Measures Act, under which normal civil liberties were suspended. Almost 500 people were detained under the authority of the Act, 62 of whom were charged with various offences. Laporte's body was found shortly after imposition of the Act. Cross was released by the FLQ a few weeks later in exchange for safe passage out of the country for his captors.

The October Crisis, as the affair came to be called, was unique in Canada's political history. It was the only occasion when the War Measures Act has been invoked during peacetime. The government of Pierre Trudeau, which acted on the urging of the Quebec Liberal government of Robert Bourassa, argued that civil order was teetering on the verge of collapse in Quebec and that a state of "apprehended insurrection" existed. Most commentators argue that Ottawa's reaction was excessive, even in the unfamiliar circumstances of political kidnappings and uncertainty that existed at the time. Excessive

or not, the October Crisis needs to be placed in its proper perspective. The political kidnappings were the work of a tiny band of political extremists whose tactics enjoyed little support among Quebec nationalists. Although there was some sympathy for the goals of the FLQ, this evaporated after their murder of Pierre Laporte.

In recent years political violence has been linked most often to unresolved disputes between groups of Aboriginal Canadians and public authorities. During the summer and autumn of 1990 a group of Mohawk Warriors, protesting the planned expansion of a golf course on land they claimed as their own, barricaded a road leading to the golf course. The confrontation eventually escalated, resulting in the death of one Quebec police officer, a sympathy blockade by Mohawks at Kahnawake of the Mercier Bridge leading into Montreal, an important commuter route for the city, and other sympathy blockades of rail lines and roads by other Indian bands in communities across the country. Eventually, the standoff at Oka, Quebec, led to riots involving the white townspeople and members of the local Mohawk band of Kanesatake, intervention by thousands of Canadian troops, and even United Nations observers.[25] Fears of another Oka were raised in 1995 when small groups of Natives occupied land that they claimed was sacred at Gustafsen Lake, BC, and Ipperwash Provincial Park in Ontario. Violence broke out in both cases and a Native was shot dead at Ipperwash. Many other confrontations have occurred over the past few decades.[26]

Since then a number of violent episodes, but no deaths, have occurred in New Brunswick, Ontario, and Quebec (see Table 2.2). Although the circumstances of each case were unique, they all had one element in common: resistance by Aboriginal Canadians against laws, policies, or property claims based on what they maintained to be their distinct status and rights. In the case of the standoff at Caledonia, Ontario, some spokespersons for the Six Nations Reserve have stated bluntly that the rulings of Canadian courts do not apply to their people. Some non-Aboriginal Canadians agree. Such attitudes, regardless of whether we agree with them, represent a significant challenge to the notion of a single Canadian political community.

Public Attitudes

"Égalité ou indépendance!" ("Equality or independence!") The sentiment is familiar to anyone familiar with the history of Quebec nationalism. The slogan did not originate with the separatist PQ. *Égalité ou indépendence* was the title of a booklet written by Daniel Johnson, leader of the Union Nationale and Premier of Quebec between 1966 and 1968, and served as his party's campaign slogan in the 1966 election. Neither Johnson nor the Union Nationale was committed to separatism. With the birth of the Parti Québécois in 1968, the province acquired a political party whose leader, René Lévesque, and platform were committed to taking Quebec out of Canada. Daniel Johnson's rhetoric and René Lévesque's commitment represented and helped catalyze an important change in Quebec politics. This change involved the idea of Quebec independence. Before the mid-1960s independence was a marginal idea in the province's politics, supported by many Québécois intellectuals but not taken seriously by the main political parties or by the public. Since then, independence has attracted the support of a sizable minority of Québécois.

According to public opinion polls, the level of popular support for Quebec independence has ranged between a low of about 20 per cent to a high of nearly 60 per cent over the last four decades (see Figure 2.1). Without reading too much into the numbers, we may say that there appears to be a durable core of support for the idea of Quebec independence. The level of support varies over time and also depending on what sort of independence is envisaged by the pollster's question. Support is always higher for softer options such as "sovereignty-association"—a term generally understood to mean a politically sovereign Quebec that would be linked to Canada through some sort of commercial union or free trade agreement—than for outright political and economic separation. It is clear that many Québécois are conditional separatists. Indeed, even among PQ supporters there has always been much less enthusiasm for complete separation than for separation with economic association.

When the PQ was first elected to office in 1976, it was clear that Quebec voters were not casting their ballots for separatism. The PQ was committed to holding a referendum on Quebec independence, so that non-separatists and soft separatists were able to vote for the party without fear that a PQ government would necessarily mean Quebec independence. Indeed, a survey conducted during the 1976 campaign revealed that only about half of those intending to vote for the PQ actually favoured independence.[27] When the PQ sought re-election in 1981, following a decisive referendum defeat the previous year, it ran on its record in office rather than on its continued goal of Quebec independence. In fact, the PQ promised not to hold another referendum during its next term. As in 1976, the PQ's 1981 victory could not be interpreted as a vote for separatism. Similarly, in 1998 the PQ won re-election after a campaign in which such issues as unemployment and health-care reform clearly overshadowed the issue of Quebec's future in or out of Canada. At that time, Premier Lucien Bouchard felt constrained to admit that the 43 per cent of votes cast for the PQ, versus 44 per cent for the Quebec Liberal Party, could in no way be viewed as a mandate for independence nor even for another referendum in the near term.

The first direct challenge to the Canadian political community came in May of 1980, when the PQ government held its promised referendum on sovereignty-association. The referendum was very carefully—some said trickily—worded. It stressed that what was being proposed was not a radical break from Canada, but a negotiated political independence for Quebec that would maintain economic ties to Canada.

> The Government of Quebec has made public its proposal to negotiate a new arrangement with the rest of Canada, based on the equality of nations; this arrangement would enable Quebec to acquire the exclusive power to make its laws, administer its taxes and establish relations abroad—in other words, sovereignty—and at the same time to maintain with Canada an economic association including a common currency; no change in political status resulting from these negotiations will be effected without

approval by the people through another referendum; on these terms, do you give the Government of Quebec the mandate to negotiate the proposed agreement between Quebec and Canada? Yes. No.

Despite the PQ's careful strategy, Quebec voters rejected the sovereignty-association option by a vote of 59.6 per cent ("Non") to 40.4 per cent ("Oui"). Even among francophones, a majority voted against Quebec independence.[28] Advocates of Quebec separatism were quick to point out that sovereignty-association was more popular among younger than older voters. Time, they argued, would turn the tide in favour of independence. Others argued that the greater popularity of the "Oui" option among those

who entered adulthood in the nationalist 1960s and early 1970s—Quebec's "baby boomers"—reflected the exceptional politically formative experiences of this generation, and that subsequent generations, not raised in the intensely nationalist ferment that characterized the 1960s in Quebec, would find separatism less appealing.

It does not appear, however, that Quebec separation is less popular among young francophone Québécois than it was among their counterparts in the 1960s and 1970s. Support for separatism remains stronger among younger cohorts of Quebec's francophone electorate than among other voters. Separatist sentiment is especially strong among young, highly educated Québécois, as was also true in the 1960s. Studies of the subsequent

'If a referendum was held today regarding Quebec sovereignty, would you vote for or against Quebec sovereignty?' (percentage in favour)

FIGURE 2.1   Support for Quebec Independence, 1978–2014

*The results for 1980 and 1995 are based on the referendum questions for each of those years.

Note: The columns for each year may not add up to 100 per cent because "don't know" and "no response" are not included.

Sources: Adapted from Simon Langlois, *La société québécoise en tendances, 1960–1990* (Québec: Institut québécois de recherche sur la culture, 1990), 649. Percentages for 1998–2005 and 2014 are based on polls conducted by Léger Marketing. Data for 2008 from *La Presse*/CROP, "Le climat politique au Québec," 14–28 août 2008.

1995 Quebec referendum, which, on a differently worded question, the "Non" side won by the narrowest of margins (49.6 per cent to 48.5 per cent), show that a solid majority of younger francophone voters, between the ages of 20 and 30, voted for independence. Separatists drew the conclusion that support for independence would continue to grow over time, as older cohorts of the electorate were replaced by younger, pro-independence ones. In fact, however, support for separatism across the francophone population of Quebec has not grown over the two decades since the 1995 referendum.

Accustomed to the challenge that Quebec separatism poses to the political community, most Canadians probably were surprised when the Oka crisis revealed the existence of another challenge to the idea of a single Canada. In fact, however, the armed confrontation at Oka had several precedents. Violent confrontations between Natives and whites punctuate Canadian history, going back to before the extermination of the Beothuk Indians of Newfoundland in the 1700s (the last Beothuk died in 1829). Some of the major episodes of violence between Natives and whites are described in Table 2.2.

These violent clashes are linked by a common thread: the struggle between the traditional independence of Aboriginal communities and the authority of, first, European colonial authorities and then that of the Canadian state. Native resistance to the rule of Canadian authorities and the efforts of the authorities to establish their rule and overcome this resistance span over three centuries of Canadian history. But the struggle between Aboriginal aspirations for autonomy and the authority of the majority community has only occasionally produced flashpoints of violence. Long periods of apparent peace have been more characteristic of Aboriginal–non-Aboriginal relations. We say "apparent peace" because even during these periods the conflict between the aspirations of many Aboriginal communities and the demands and restrictions imposed on them by the Canadian state was only dormant, waiting for the catalyst of some issue or incident. The confrontation at Oka turned out to be just such an incident, galvanizing Native groups and throwing into sharp relief the issues of Aboriginal land claims and demands for self-government.

The land claims issue is essentially about who has the right to control territory to which various Aboriginal communities claim a historical right. Treaties signed by Ottawa and First Nations after Confederation, as well as treaties prior to Confederation—which were intended to extinguish Native claims to these territories in exchange for reserves, money, and other benefits—do not cover all of Canada. In fact, enormous areas encompassing much of the North and both the western and eastern extremities of the country were not covered by historic (pre-1975) treaties. Moreover, about 40 per cent of status Indians[29] are not members of bands that have signed treaties with Ottawa. Having never been vanquished militarily or given up their territorial rights through a treaty, they claim that the land their ancestors inhabited still belongs to them. This and other issues related to Canada's Aboriginal population are examined in Chapter 16.

Land claim negotiations progressed at a snail's pace for decades, leading most Aboriginal groups to conclude that Ottawa really had not been serious about settling these claims, many of which related to government misuse and misappropriation of lands that had been reserved for Indians who had signed historic treaties. With the Oka confrontation, when the Mohawk Warriors claimed to be an independent nation with a historical right to the land on which the local municipality planned to extend a golf course, the issue truly became part of the public consciousness. This claim to be a sovereign nation, outside the authority of Canadian law, was more extreme than most Native demands for self-government. And it was a claim that was steadfastly rejected by the federal government and most Canadians. "Native self-government," Prime Minister Brian Mulroney declared at the time, "does not now and cannot ever mean sovereign independence. Mohawk lands are part of Canadian territory, and Canadian law must and does apply."[30] A few years later, Liberal Prime Minister Jean Chrétien also rejected the claims of some Natives that they stand outside the authority of Canadian law. This has been the position of every Canadian government since then.

TABLE 2.2 Major Violent Confrontations between Natives and Non-Natives and/or Political Authorities

Date	Native Group and Location	Event
1700s	Beothuk (Newfoundland)	Many were killed by Europeans.
1763	Seneca, Ojibway, and other tribes (area near Detroit)	Led by Odawa war chief Pontiac, a confederation of tribes rebelled against British rule in several bloody confrontations.
circa 1794	Shawnee and other tribes (Ohio River Valley)	Led by Shawnee war chief Tecumseh, several Indian tribes attempted unsuccessfully to resist white settlement and control of the Ohio Valley.
1803	Nuu'chah'nulth (British Columbia)	Chief Muquinna leads a raid on the trading ship Boston in Nootka Sound, killing all but two of the crew.
1850s–1880s	Kwakwaka'wakw, Gitxsan, and other tribes (British Columbia)	British "gunboat diplomacy" pursued on Pacific coast against unco-operative tribes and miscreant individuals, with Native villages torched and destroyed by British.
1869–70	Métis (Manitoba)	In the Red River Rebellion, Métis fought for provincial status and guaranteed land and cultural rights.
1885	Métis and Plains Indians (Saskatchewan)	In the Northwest Rebellion, a series of battles took place between Métis and Indian forces, on one side, and white militia volunteers and soldiers, on the other.
1990	Mohawk (Quebec)	This armed confrontation at Oka resulted in the death of a Quebec police officer when the police tried to storm a barricade and riots against Natives protesting the expansion of a golf course on land they claimed was theirs by historical right.
1995	Shuswap (British Columbia) Chippewa (Ontario)	Armed confrontations took place at Gustafsen Lake, BC, and Ipperwash Provincial Park in Ontario. In both cases a small group of Natives occupied land they claimed was sacred. Dudley George of the Kettle and Stony Point First Nation was shot and killed by police at Ipperwash.
2000	Mi'kmaq (Burnt Church, NB)	Conflict between Aboriginals and non-Aboriginals over fishing rights flared up in vandalism, boat ramming by federal Fisheries officers, and shots fired.
2004	Mohawk (Quebec)	Anti-police riot took place when 67 Aboriginal officers, authorized by Grand Chief James Gabriel and the Mohawk band council and financed by the federal Solicitor-General, were trapped in the Kanesatake police station for three days by armed protesters from the local Mohawk community.
2006	Six Nations (Ontario)	Police arrests of 16 Six Nations protesters at Caledonia in southern Ontario were responded to by fires and the blockade of a major highway by hundreds of Natives who claimed that land being developed for houses rightfully belonged to them, dating back to the Haldimand Grant of 1784, although an Ontario court decision had ruled otherwise.

Recent land claim settlements that include structures for Aboriginal self-government, notably the creation of Nunavut in the eastern Arctic and the Nisga'a Final Agreement in British Columbia, state explicitly that laws of general application continue to apply to those who inhabit these Native lands and that the Charter of Rights and Freedoms applies to their governments. Nevertheless, a sort of de facto acceptance of separate communities, defined by their Aboriginal ethnicity and heritage, now exists within Canada. This is discussed more fully in Chapter 16.

Freedom

"Live free or die" reads the motto on licence plates in the state of New Hampshire. Individual freedom is said to be part of the American political creed, symbolized in such icons as the Statue of Liberty, Philadelphia's Liberty Bell, the Bill of Rights, and the Declaration of Independence. Canadians, it is usually claimed, are more willing than Americans to limit individual freedom in pursuit of social order or group rights. Is this true?

On the face of it, freedom does indeed appear to occupy a more central place in the American political culture. Not only are many of the country's iconic symbols linked to the idea of personal freedom, the American creation story is about individuals banding together against a repressive state in defence of their freedom. References to freedom are much more common in the American political conversation than in Canada, and the libertarian movement—for which personal freedom trumps all other political values—is far more prominent in the United States than in Canada. Themes of individualism, liberty, and self-reliance, as well as mistrust of the state as the potential enemy of freedom, are woven through the American historical narrative.

For all this, however, the differences between what Canadians and Americans believe when it comes to freedom tend not to be dramatic. Moreover, these differences are almost always narrower than the gap separating the values of Canadians from Western Europeans.

Earlier in this chapter we discussed the concept of path dependency. The greater prominence of freedom in the American historical narrative and contemporary political conversation may be traced to the origins of the United States and Canada. As Lipset and others have observed, the American Revolution launched these two countries on different trajectories in regard to personal freedom and the individual's relationship to the state. Mistrust of the state was, from the beginning, an important theme in American political thinking. The constitutional system of checks and balances and divided governmental power, as well as a constitutionally entrenched Bill of Rights, all reflected this original preoccupation with protecting the individual's rights and freedoms against encroachments by the state.

English Canada was not founded on an ethos of limited government. Nor did the country experience self-government and then independence until

long after the Revolution that Loyalists rejected. Instead of celebrating what Abraham Lincoln, in the Gettysburg Addresss (1863), describes as "a new nation, conceived in liberty and dedicated to the proposition that all men are created equal," most of Canada's leaders celebrated the connection to Great Britain and the conservative idea that "freedom wears a crown"[31] until well into the twentieth century. As Lipset observes, "If [Canada] leans towards communitarianism—the public mobilization of resources to fulfill group objectives—the [United States] sees individualism—private endeavour—as the way an 'unseen hand' produces optimum, socially beneficial results."[32] Canadian writer Pierre Berton made the same point when he maintained that "We've always accepted more governmental control over our lives than . . . [Americans] have—and fewer civil liberties."[33]

Attitudinal data provide a basis for generalizations about the value attached to freedom in the two societies. Using questions that require people to choose between the protection of individual liberty and the defence of social order, a survey conducted in the 1980s found that Americans consistently gave more freedom-oriented responses.[34] This pattern of difference between Canadians and Americans has persisted over time. The 1991 World Values Survey (WVS) found that Americans (75 per cent) were considerably more likely than Canadians (61 per cent) to say that, if required to choose, they would opt for liberty over equality. The 2012 AmericasBarometer survey asked whether respondents believed that those who disagree with the majority represent a threat to the country. Canadians were slightly more likely than Americans to agree (54 per cent vs 45 per cent). The same survey found that Americans are significantly more likely than Canadians to approve of various legal forms of political protest and to agree that persons critical of the national form of government should have such rights as the right to demonstrate, run for office, vote, and make speeches on television. Canadians were found to be less likely, by a significant margin, to say that the authorities should always abide by the law in order to catch a criminal.[35] On questions related to individualism (Figure 2.2), Canadians are hardly differentiated

A. Individuals should take more reponsibility for providing for themselves. (percentage agreeing)

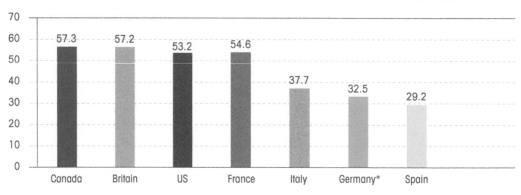

B. In the long run, hard work usually brings a better life. (percentage agreeing)

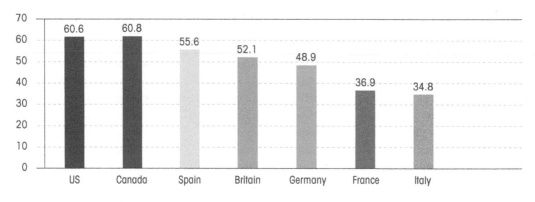

C. Some people feel they have completely free choice and control over their lives, while other people feel that they have no real effect on what happens to them.
(percentage expressing a great deal of freedom)

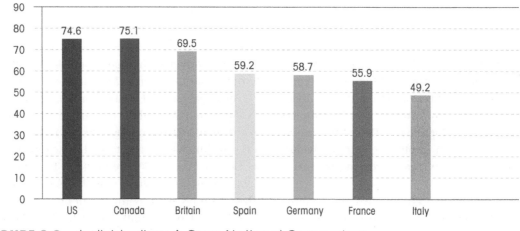

FIGURE 2.2   Individualism: A Cross-National Comparison

D. Why are there people who live in need? (percentage choosing 'because of laziness and lack of will power' as their first choice)

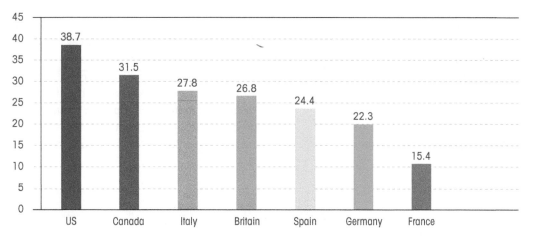

E. Competition is good. It stimulates people to work hard and develop new ideas. (percentage agreeing)

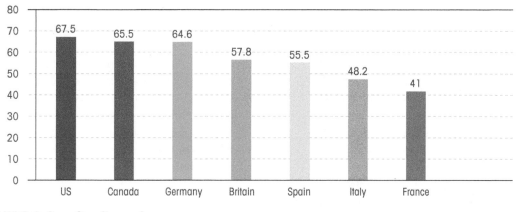

FIGURE 2.2   Continued

Source: Data from the World Values Survey, Wave 5: 2005–9, at: <www.worldvaluessurvey.org>. Reprinted with permission.

from Americans in their belief that people are responsible for their own success and happiness. In the selected European countries (Germany, France, Britain, Italy, and Spain) shown in this figure, there is in most instances somewhat less faith expressed in the "pull yourself up by your own bootstraps" mentality that many North Americans espouse.

Before we conclude that the historic characterization of Americans as more preoccupied with and protective of personal freedom than Canadians continues to be true, we need to consider an important objection. Some people argue that the important difference between Canadians and Americans is that they tend to understand freedom in different ways. Americans are more likely than Canadians to understand freedom as the absence of limitation on individual behaviour, what is sometimes called negative freedom. This, according to critics such as the Canadian philosopher Charles Taylor, actually denies real freedom to many people. Canadians' greater willingness to permit government restrictions on individual behaviour does not mean that they value freedom less. Instead, it means they are more likely than Americans to believe that real freedom often requires that government interfere with individual property rights and economic markets. Moreover, governments should guarantee to all citizens such things as public education and health care in order to help equalize the opportunities available both to the well-off and the less-privileged. Canadians, some argue, have what might be characterized as a positive conception of freedom, one that requires that governments act in ways that empower individuals to make choices rather than get out of the way.

Some support for this idea that Canadians and Americans understand freedom and the conditions that nurture it in different ways is found in the results of a 2009 survey on economic mobility in these two countries. Canadians were more likely than Americans to express the belief that government does more to help people move up the economic ladder (46 per cent of Canadians agreeing, compared to 36 per cent of Americans), whereas

Media Spotlight

BOX 2.3 Is a Society without Guns Less Free?

The Second Amendment to the United States Constitution famously declares that the "right of the people to keep and bear arms, shall not be infringed." Although most Americans agree that some limitations on gun ownership are warranted, surveys show that a majority also believe that individuals should be free to own guns for hunting, sport shooting, or personal defence of their families, homes, and property.

Canadians are much less likely to share this belief. Indeed, issues of personal freedom are almost entirely absent from the Canadian conversation on gun ownership and control. Instead, community safety, rural versus urban lifestyles, and Aboriginal hunting traditions and rights are the concerns most likely to be raised in Canada. If the issue of freedom arises it is much more likely to be expressed as the right of the community and individuals to be free from the danger attendant upon too many guns in too many hands than the freedom of individuals to protect themselves and their families without having to rely on the state to do this for them.

Canadians are very much like the populations of most affluent democracies when it comes to gun ownership. The United States is the outlier. The reason for this involves the circumstances of the American Revolution and the Second Amendment, whose inclusion in the Bill of Rights was directly attributable to armed insurrection against a tyrannical state. No other democracy, Canada included, has such a provision in its constitution. For most of the history of the United States the fact that this right existed was largely inconsequential, governments not being inclined to legislate much in the way of gun control. But when they did, in the last four decades of the twentieth century, the fact that this constitutional provision existed could be and was linked to a historical narrative of freedom, individualism, and self-reliance, not to mention mistrust of the state. Gun ownership became, in the eyes of many Americans, a legitimate and even vital pillar of personal freedom. This did not and could not happen in Canada, whose constitution never included such a provision and whose national story did not include citizens' militias, Minutemen, and rebellion against an armed and tyrannical state.

So does the much greater freedom for persons to own guns in the United States make that society freer than Canada? Few Canadians will think so. Many Americans, on the other hand, will see private gun ownership as an important dimension of personal freedom, where some states have open-carry laws permitting shoppers to carry their loaded assault weapons into Walmart or dine at Burger King while packing heat, an issue that drew wide media attention in 2014. This is certainly one of the issues where Canadian and American ideas of freedom are most likely to clash.

Americans were more likely than Canadians to believe that government did more to hurt mobility (46 per cent vs 39 per cent). This is, admittedly, not a particularly large gap between the beliefs of Canadians and Americans.[36]

In the wake of the terrorist attacks of 11 September 2001, both the American and Canadian governments passed laws that involved greater restrictions on individual rights and freedoms. Public opinion surveys showed that Canadians were considerably less likely than Americans to believe that such restrictions were necessary, but at the same time polls showed that Canadians were about as accepting of security measures that involved some loss of privacy safeguards as were Americans.[37] In 2008 the CBC launched a prime-time drama called *The Border*, which portrayed Americans as more concerned with security and the protection of social order and Canadians as more vigilant in defending individual rights. A sort of role reversal has taken place, argue some, such that Canada is now the society that cares more about freedom and the United States has become the country obsessed with threats to its security.

The evidence for this claim is less than clear. The post-9/11 spike in American support for measures that appeared to purchase security at the cost of reduced freedoms and rights for some has dissipated over time. Moreover, opposition to limitations on freedoms and rights existed in the United States from the moment the Patriot Act was passed in 2001 and this opposition gained strength and won victories in both Congress and the courts as time went on. Although it is arguable that 9/11 produced a short-term gap between Canadian and American attitudes concerning the security/freedom trade-off, it is not at all certain that the core beliefs of Americans became less freedom-oriented as a result of these terrorist attacks.

Equality

A long line of sociologists, political scientists, and historians, going back to Alexis de Tocqueville and other Europeans who visited North America in the nineteenth century, agreed that America's political culture was more egalitarian and Canada's

more hierarchical. To arrive at this conclusion, of course, one had to ignore the existence of slavery in the United States until the end of the Civil War, followed by Jim Crow segregation laws that persisted well into the second half of the twentieth century. Nevertheless, the historical evidence suggests very strongly that Canadian society was somewhat more elitist and socio-economic mobility less than in the United States.[38]

Listen to the "Security and Sovereignty: Perspectives on the World's Longest Undefended Border" podcast, available at: www.oupcanada.com/Brooks8e

In more recent times, however, it has been usual for Canadians to think of their society as the more egalitarian one and for some Americans to agree with them! As Figure 2.3 shows, Canadians appear to value equality *more* than do Americans, at least when it comes to the redistributive aspects of this concept. They are much more likely to support public policies such as a publicly funded health-care system and a guaranteed minimum income, programs intended to narrow the gap between the poor and the well-off. A comparative study of the development of the welfare state in Canada and the US corroborates this difference. Robert Kudrle and Theodore Marmor argue that ideological differences between the two societies are the main reasons for the earlier enactment and more generous character of welfare state policies in Canada, observing that "In every policy area it appears that general public as well as elite opinion . . . [has been] more supportive of state action in Canada than in the United States."[39] At the same time, some observers caution that too much is often attributed to cultural differences in explaining differences between social policies in these countries. Gerard Boychuk argues that the significance of race politics in the United States and of territorial politics in Canada explains more of the difference in the health policies of the two countries than does political culture.[40]

In Canada, egalitarianism has its roots in a more collectivist tradition; in the United States it draws on a more individualistic tradition. But the value differences between the two societies tend to be shaded rather than starkly contrasting, as Figure 2.3 shows. Nevertheless, they help to explain Canadians' apparently greater acceptance—historically at any rate—of state measures targeted at disadvantaged groups and regions. Lipset's conclusion seems a fair one: "Canadians are committed to redistribution egalitarianism, while Americans place more emphasis on meritocratic competition and equality of opportunity."[41]

This difference between the two societies, however, should not be exaggerated. If Americans care more about equality of opportunity and Canadians about equality of condition, then we would expect to find greater acceptance of economic inequalities among Americans. But the evidence is unclear. In 2013 the average CEO of a Fortune 500 company in the United States made 331 times what the average American worker earned, compared to a ratio 30 years earlier of about 48:1. In Canada the gap is not quite as great, the average compensation of a CEO of one of the top 100 companies being 171 times that of the average Canadian worker, a ratio that has about doubled over the past 20 years. Canadians and Americans are, however, almost identical in their beliefs about what would constitute a "fair" ratio of maximum-to-minimum earnings. Respondents from both countries say that it should be about 10 to 1.[42] A survey carried out in 2013 for the Pew Research Center found that almost identical percentages of Canadians (58 per cent) and Americans (61 per cent) agreed that the economic system favours the wealthy.[43] When asked whether they thought it was more important to reduce inequality or to ensure that everyone has a fair chance to improve their economic standing, 71 per cent of Americans and 68 per cent of Canadians chose ensuring a fair chance (see Figure 2.3).[44] If Canadians are truly more oriented towards equality of condition, and if this is an important difference between the values of Canadians and Americans, then one would expect to find a greater gap. Miles Corak observes that "Both Americans and Canadians feel strongly that individual characteristics, like hard work, ambition, and [education], lead to upward economic mobility. In both countries, factors external to the individual, outside of his or her control, rank much lower."[45] Majorities in both countries expressed the view that all of their fellow citizens had a fair chance of moving up the economic ladder. Corak notes that Canadians were about as

likely as Americans to support merit-based differences, including the right of hard workers to make more than others, the limited role of luck, gender, and race in determining one's economic fortunes, and the fairness of inequalities when there is equality of opportunity.

In Canada, more than in the United States, debates over equality historically have been about group rights and equality between different groups in society, and less about equality between individuals. This difference goes back to the founding of the two societies. While the American Constitution made no distinction between groups of citizens, Canada has a long tradition of recognizing group rights, going back to the Quebec Act of 1774, which incorporated protection for religious rights, and the British North America Act of 1867 in which protections for both religious and language rights are included. This history, many have argued, has resulted in greater tolerance of cultural diversity in Canada than one finds in the United States. This is the familiar, if exaggerated, theme of the Canadian "mosaic" versus the American "melting pot." Although the dominant narrative in Canada suggests that non-French, non-British groups have felt less pressure to abandon their language and customs in Canada than have non-English-speaking groups in the United States, rates of cultural assimilation have been high in both societies. Moreover, Canadian governments have shown themselves to be as capable as their American counterparts of discriminating against ethnic and religious communities. For example, in both countries many people of Japanese origin were deprived of their property and kept confined to camps during World War II. The religious practices of Doukhobors, Hutterites, Mennonites, and Jehovah's Witnesses have at various times brought them into conflict with either Ottawa or provincial governments. And in both Canada and the United States immigration policy until the 1960s discriminated against non-white, non-European peoples—although this is no longer characteristic of policy in either country.

Despite evidence that, in Canada, too, tolerance of cultural diversity has known limits, these limits have been less restrictive than in the United States. The treatment of Canada's Aboriginal peoples, for

A. People who get help from government social
   assistance programs are lazy.

B. Government should implement strong policies
   to reduce income inequality.

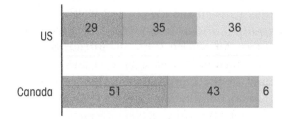

■ Agree (6–7) ■ No clear opinion (3–5) ▨ Disagree (1–2)

C. Universities should set aside openings for
   students from racial/ethnic minorities.

D. Same-sex couples should have the right to marry
   (percentage agreeing*) 8–10 on a 10-point scale
   (10 = strongly agree, 1 = strongly disagree)

■ Agree (6–7) ■ No clear opinion (3–5) ▨ Disagree (1–2)

E. I would not want my child to marry someone of a different race
   (percentage agreeing)

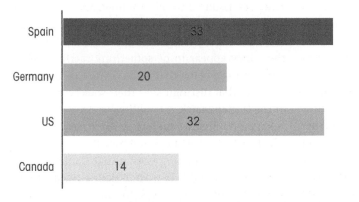

FIGURE 2.3   Some Dimensions of Equality in Canada and the United States

*This is the percentage of white Americans who approve of interracial marriage. The figure for Canada includes people of all races.

Source: Parts A–D are adapted from data reported in the Environics Institute, *AmericasBarometer Canada 2012*; Part E is adapted from data in Association for Canadian Studies, *A Four-Country Survey of Opinions on Racism and Prejudice in 2010: Canada, the United States, Germany and Spain*, 21 January 2011.

example, has been less harsh and less violent than that of America's Native minorities. Moreover, nothing in Canada's history compares to the official discrimination and the physical violence directed against American blacks for much of that country's history. An official policy of **multiculturalism** has existed in Canada since 1971 and was recognized in the Constitution in 1982.[46] Moreover, Canada's Constitution appears to provide a firmer basis for affirmative action programs and other state activities that have as their goal "the amelioration of conditions of disadvantaged individuals or groups including those that are disadvantaged because of race, national or ethnic origin, colour, religion, sex, age or mental or physical disability."[47]

The thesis of the Canadian mosaic versus the American melting pot should not be pushed too hard. Despite the fact that cultural assimilation seems historically to have been part of the American ethos, to the point that it is even expressed in the national motto "E pluribus unum" (from the many, one), a combination of government policies and court decisions in the US has steered that country away from the melting pot and towards a mosaic society. An extensive system of Spanish-language schools has been created in parts of the United States, particularly California, over the last two decades. Public services in many languages, including Spanish of course, but also Korean, Chinese, and Vietnamese, are required by law in many states and cities. American law requires multilingual ballots and poll workers in some circumstances. Affirmative action policies, from university admission quotas to "minority set asides" (minority quotas in the allotment of government contracts), and congressional boundary lines drawn to maximize the proportion of minority voters (referred to as majority-minority districts) began earlier and have been taken further in the United States than in Canada. (Federal and provincial electoral boundary laws allow what are referred to as "communities of interest" to be taken into account in the drawing of these lines. Mainly because electoral boundaries are determined by non-partisan commissioners instead of by politicians, as is common in the US, the process has been less controversial in Canada.) Universities and

other schools in the United States pioneered the concept and practice of minority-oriented curricula (African-American studies, for example), and this dimension of cultural pluralism is well established there, even while some other aspects of multicultural policy appear to be under assault. Indeed, the very intensity of controversy over multiculturalism, affirmative action, and ascription-based policies in the United States is to some degree a reflection of just how successful the mosaic model has been in influencing public life in that society. The backlash attests to the inroads it has made.

At the same time, we should not imagine that the idea of multiculturalism and the programs and structures that seek to implement the mosaic model have gone unchallenged in Canada. Neil Bissoondath's *Selling Illusions: The Cult of Multiculturalism in Canada*,[48] Reginald Bibby's *Mosaic Madness: The Poverty and Potential of Life in Canada*,[49] and Salim Mansur's *Delectable Lie: A Liberal Repudiation of Multiculturalism*[50] are three of the salvoes launched against official multiculturalism (as opposed to tolerance of diversity and pluralism not sponsored and reinforced by the state).

In view of how deeply the distinction between the Canadian mosaic and the American melting pot is embedded in the collective psyche of Canadians, it seems surprising that there has been little effort to test empirically this article of faith. But perhaps this is not so surprising. After all, the thing about articles of *faith* is that they do not require proof. They are assumed to be so self-evidently true that searching examination of the evidence on which they rest is considered a waste of time. Moreover, there may appear to be something sacrilegious in questioning a belief that is so central to Canadians' ideas of what distinguishes their society from that of the United States.

Raymond Breton and Jeffrey Reitz risk this sacrilege in what is the most ambitious and systematic attempt to test the proposition that Canadians are more tolerant of diversity than their allegedly more assimilationist neighbours to the south. In *The Illusion of Difference* they review existing studies of the mosaic versus melting pot thesis and examine a number of comparative surveys and census data from the two countries. They conclude that the differences between Canada and the United States are "more apparent than real." The Canadian style, they argue, "is more low-key than the American; moreover, Canadians have a conscious tradition of 'tolerance' that Americans do not have." These differences in the way multiculturalism and ethnic diversity have been thought of in the two societies "have not produced less pressure towards conformity in Canada, or less propensity to discriminate in employment or housing."[51] Comparing rates of language retention, ethnic group identification, participation in ethnically based social networks, and attitudes and behaviour towards racial minorities, Breton and Reitz make the case that almost no empirical data support Canadians' cherished self-image of their society as being more tolerant and less assimilationist than that of the United States. Their conclusion is supported by a more recent study of language retention based on Statistics Canada's 2002 Ethnic Diversity Study.[52] One out of five persons speaks a foreign language at least some of the time at home in both the United States and Canada, according to each country's most recent census.

Perhaps in response to the public's growing sense that cultural mosaic policies have contributed to national disunity, in late 1998 the federal government proposed changes to the Immigration Act that would require prospective immigrants to Canada, other than those in the family and refugee classes, to know either French or English. This proposal was criticized by some as having the effect, if not the intention, of discriminating against prospective immigrants from countries—mainly less developed countries—where the likelihood of knowing either English or French is relatively low. The Citizenship Act has long required that those applying for Canadian citizenship be able to communicate in one of the official languages, a requirement that was made more stringent in 2012.

Gender equality is another dimension of group rights that has acquired prominence in recent decades. In both Canada and the United States attitudes concerning the appropriate roles and behaviour of men and women have changed sharply in the direction of greater equality. The visible signs of this change are everywhere, including laws on pay equity, easier access to abortion, greater female than male participation and graduation rates in universities, increased female representation in male-dominated professions, how females are portrayed by the media, and greater female participation in the political system.

All of the above are indirect measures of attitudes towards gender equality. Although they do not provide a direct indication of cultural values, we might reasonably infer these values from what we observe in the economy, the educational system, and politics. Comparing Canada to the United States using such measures, we come up with a mixed scorecard. The differences between the two societies tend not to be very large, Canada being "more equal" on some counts, the United States on others.

For example, a 2010 international ranking of women's economic opportunities by The Economic Intelligence Unit determined that Canada did better on some counts and the United States on others.[53] As of 2012, women were better represented on the boards of directors of corporations in the United States (16.6 per cent) than in Canada (10.3 per cent).[54] The percentage of female elected officials in each country's federal legislature is slightly greater in Canada: in 2011 about 25 per cent of members elected to Canada's House of Commons were female, while 18 per cent of those elected to the US House of Representatives and 20 per cent of those elected to the Senate in 2012 were female. According to the data collected by the World Values Survey, public opinion is almost identical in the two countries regarding relations between the sexes and the roles appropriate to each.

As for racial equality and tolerance, however, most Canadians are quite convinced that their society does better on these counts than the United States. There is little doubt that racism and racial tensions have been less prominent in Canadian history. Although it is tempting to infer from the statistics on racial segregation, income differences associated with race, crime and sentencing data, and a host of other measures that Americans tend to be more racist than Canadians, such an inference may not be warranted. To come at this a bit differently, should one conclude from the election of a black American as President of the United States in 2008, while no black has ever been the leader of a Canadian political party, that Americans are more tolerant of racial difference? Does the fact that a much higher percentage of blacks hold public office in the United States than in Canada, or that the number of blacks among the CEOs of the largest 1,000 companies in the United States is greater than for the largest 1,000 companies in Canada, suggest that the United States, not Canada, is the more racially tolerant society? The answer, most would agree, is no. The enormous differences in the historical circumstances shaping race relations in the two societies and the much greater relative size of the black population in the United States will be cited by most as reasons to be wary of drawing such conclusions. The fact is that demography and history ensure that race and racism are far more central to American political life than to politics in Canada.

According to data from the World Values Survey, Canadians and Americans are among the most racially tolerant populations in the world. Under 5 per cent of respondents in both countries choose "people of a different race" from a list of kinds of people they would not want as neighbours. But as may be seen in Figure 2.3, Americans are more than twice as likely as Canadians to say that they would not want their child to marry someone of another race (32 per cent vs 14 per cent; the figures were 33 per cent in Spain and 20 per cent in Germany). On the basis of this question alone we might be inclined to conclude that Canadian society is less racist. But we should keep in mind that the average incomes of black Canadians are about 80 per cent of those for white Canadians, roughly the same as in the United States. The percentage of interracial couples is actually higher in the United States (8.4 per cent) than in Canada (4 per cent). At the same time, however, black–white couples constitute only a small share of all interracial couples in the United States, suggesting that some interracial taboos have not disappeared. The bottom line is this: comparing racial equality in Canada and the United States is not as straightforward and predictable as one might imagine.

In Canada, all citizens' health care is administered via a public system in which a pool of funds provides for medical costs. Those funds are collected via taxation and are managed and paid out by government. During the recent health-care debate in the United States, many protested proposed reforms for a similar universal system, claiming that health-care management should be determined by a private system composed of users, medical providers, and insurers—not governments. The pros and cons of each system continue to be debated in both countries. Right: Republican Michele Bachmann speaks during a rally against the US health-care reform bill in 2009 (CP Images/AP Photo/Alex Brandon); left: Friends of Medicare chairperson Christine Burdett speaks about Alberta's proposed health-care reform in 2001 (The Canadian Press Images/*Edmonton Journal*/Larry Wong).

Citizen Expectations for Government

Canadians, it has often been argued, are more likely than Americans to look to government to meet their needs. They are, moreover, more likely to accept state actions that they dislike, instead of mobilizing against such policies and the governments that institute them. Thomas Jefferson's declaration, "That government is best which governs least," has an oddly foreign tone to Canadians. The mistrust of government and implicit celebration of individualism that inspired Jefferson's aphorism have not resonated in Canada the way they have throughout American history.

The belief that Canadians expect their governments to do more than do Americans, and are more passive in the face of state action, including government policies they may not like, is firmly entrenched. It may once have been an accurate characterization of an important difference between the political cultures of Canada and the United States. The inconvenient reality, however, is that the two countries have converged considerably, such that a sweeping generalization about Canadians being more statist and deferential than Americans is simply not supported by the evidence. Canadian governments have been resistant to the expansion of a private presence in health care and post-secondary education, although this resistance has weakened over the past couple of decades. They own corporations whose activities range from producing electricity to television broadcasting, while American governments have generally been content to regulate privately owned businesses in these same industries. Canadian governments are much more actively involved in promoting particular cultural values, especially those associated with bilingualism and multiculturalism, than are most governments in the United States. In Canada the public sector historically has accounted for a larger share of gross national expenditure than in the United States, although the difference between the two countries is today very small. Similarly, although governments in Canada used to spend a greater share of GDP on social programs, now the

difference between the two countries is quite negligible.[55] One difference that remains involves taxation. Canadian governments collect a somewhat larger share of total national income in taxes than do governments in the United States.[56] All in all, this adds up to a rather mixed picture, but certainly not one that allows us to confidently say that Canada is a more statist society than the United States.

What about the evidence for Canadians' alleged passivity in the face of government actions they dislike? Is it true that Canadians are more deferential to authority, including political authority, than their American counterparts? It was once fairly common to hear Canadian political experts intone that we were a more orderly society. The stability that Canadians experienced through this country's parliamentary system and constitutional monarchy, compared to the rather chaotic "mobocracy" to the south, provided a sort of protective mantle under which citizens were better able to enjoy their democratic rights and freedoms. "We've always accepted more governmental control over our lives than . . . [Americans] have—and fewer civil liberties," argued Pierre Berton, Canada's foremost popular historian. But, he added, "the other side of the coin of liberty is license, sometimes anarchy. It seems to us that . . . Americans have been more willing to suffer violence in . . . [their] lives than we have for the sake of individual freedom."[57]

Canadians' apparent greater faith in government, compared to the more skeptical attitudes of Americans, owes a good deal to a collectivist ethos that sets Canadians and their history apart from the United States. It is this ethos that Canadian nationalists are invoking when they argue that Canada's public health-care system and more generous social programs reflect the "soul" of this country, and that their dismemberment would send Canadians down the allegedly mean-spirited path of American individualism. Some of Canada's most prominent thinkers, including George Grant and Charles Taylor, have argued that the collectivist ethos and greater willingness of Canadians than Americans to use the state to achieve community goals are central to the Canadian political tradition.

In *Lament for a Nation*, Grant argued that the Canadian political tradition was marked by a communitarian spirit that rejected the individualism of American-style liberalism. He traced the roots of this spirit to the influence of conservative ideas and the British connection, which helped to keep alive a benign view of government as an agent for pursuing the common good. This distinctive national character was, Grant believed, doomed to be crushed by the steamroller of American liberalism and technology, homogenizing influences that would ultimately flatten national cultures throughout the capitalist world. Grant's "lament" was in the key of what has been called **red Toryism**. Red Tories are conservatives who believe that government has a responsibility to act as an agent for the collective good and that this responsibility goes far beyond maintaining law and order. In Canada today, since the 2003 merger of the Canadian Alliance and the Progressive Conservative Party to form the federal Conservative Party, some would argue that red Tories are an endangered political species.

Charles Taylor, Canada's most internationally acclaimed philosopher, is firmly on the left of the political spectrum. He agrees with Grant about the importance of collectivism in Canada's political tradition. Taylor has always been extremely critical of what he calls the "atomism" of American liberalism, a value system that he believes cuts people off from the communal relations that nurture human dignity. Like most Canadian nationalists, he believes implicitly in the moral superiority of Canada's more collectivist political tradition.

Taylor is one of the leading thinkers in the contemporary movement known as **communitarianism**. This is based on the belief that real human freedom and dignity are possible only in the context of communal relations that allow for the public recognition of group identities and that are based on equal respect for these different identity-groups. Taylor argues that the key to Canadian unity lies in finding constitutional arrangements that enable different groups of Canadians to feel that they belong to Canada and are recognized as constituent elements of Canadian society. "Nations . . . which have a strong sense of their own identity," says Taylor, "and hence a desire to direct in some ways their common affairs, can only be induced to take part willingly in

multinational states if they are in some ways recognized within them."[58] He calls this the recognition of "deep diversity." The realization of deep diversity would require, at a minimum, official recognition of Quebec as a distinct society and probably constitutional acknowledgement of an Aboriginal right to self-government. To some this might sound like a recipe for dismantling whatever fragile sense of Canadian community already exists. Taylor insists, however, that one-size-fits-all notions of community do not work in the modern world.

The characterization of Canada as a deferential society, or at least one where citizens are less likely to question political and other sources of established authority than in the United States, has been challenged in recent years. In *The Decline of Deference*,[59] Neil Nevitte agrees that Canadians are less deferential today than in the past. He attributes this to the post-materialist values of those born in the post–World War II era. **Post-materialism** attaches comparatively greater importance to human needs for belonging, self-esteem, and personal fulfillment than does **materialism**, which places greater stress on economic security and material well-being. Such issues as employment and incomes matter most to materialists, whereas post-materialists are likely to place higher value on so-called quality-of-life issues such as the environment, human rights, and group equality. Materialists are more likely than post-materialists to have confidence in public institutions and to trust the judgments of elites.

Nevitte shows that Canadians' confidence in government institutions, a category that included the armed forces, police, Parliament, and public service, declined during the 1980s and that high levels of confidence are much less likely to be expressed by those between the ages of 25–54 than among older citizens. He also finds that Canadians are, if anything, slightly more skeptical of government institutions than are Americans—not what one would expect to find if the traditional stereotype of deferential Canadians versus defiant Americans holds true.

We should not be too quick to conclude that the old characterization of Canadians as being more deferential towards political authority and trusting of government than Americans has been flipped on its head. Post-materialist values may indeed be more pervasive in Canada than in the United States. But data from the 2012 AmericasBarometer Survey show that only with respect to the armed forces and the President/Prime Minister do Americans express more confidence than Canadians. Levels of confidence in the police, Parliament/Congress, the public service, and government are not very different in the two countries.[60]

Asking people how much confidence they have in state institutions is one possible measure of deference. But another involves behaviour that requires people to act in a defiant manner towards authority or at least to behave in ways that require them to take a public position on a divisive issue. Signing petitions, joining boycotts, and attending lawful demonstrations are acts that, while not necessarily defiant towards authority, are not characteristic of a deferential population. Figure 2.4 shows that Canadians and Americans are not very different when it comes to such behaviour. The evidence, however, certainly does not support the revisionist claim that Canadians have become less deferential than Americans.

Another angle on citizen expectations for government is provided by what political scientists call **social capital**. This involves the fabric of connections between members of a community. It is made up both of norms, such as trust in one's neighbours,

and of such behaviours as voting and participating in community organizations. The roots of this concept can be found in Alexis de Tocqueville's observations on the propensity of mid-nineteenth-century Americans to join together in voluntary associations to achieve communal goals. Tocqueville believed that these voluntary associations were the connective tissue of American democracy. They reminded citizens in immediate and practical ways of the fact that they belonged to a community and depended on one another.

Many commentators on American society argue that social capital in that country has been in serious decline for years. The evidence for this claim is not, however, rock solid. But what is clear is that Americans continue to be more likely than Canadians and the citizens of other rich democracies to belong to voluntary associations and to participate in their activities. Figure 2.5 shows that a much larger share of the American population devotes some of their time to unpaid work for religious, youth, sports and recreation, educational, and cultural groups. These are activities that, in Canada, are more likely to be the responsibility of state agencies and financed by public revenues. This difference between Canadians and Americans is corroborated by the 2012 AmericasBarometer survey. Using a composite measure of civic engagement (it included attending local meetings, helping solve local problems, following the news daily,

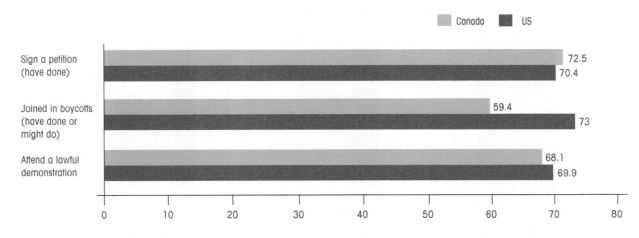

FIGURE 2.4   Engaged Citizen Behaviour, Canada and the United States

Source: Data from the World Values Survey, Wave 5: 2005–9. Reprinted with permission.

participating in demonstrations or protests, signing petitions, sharing political information, and having an interest in politics), it was found that Americans were significantly more likely than Canadians to score high in civic engagement.[61] One might conclude from this difference that Americans are more likely than Canadians to believe that private citizens and the voluntary associations they create—not the state—should be responsible for meeting many of society's needs. Canadians are somewhat more likely to see these activities as the responsibility of government.

Some significant part of the civic and communal engagement of Americans is due to the far greater strength of traditional religious values in the United States compared to Canada. Roughly 4 out of 10 Americans say that religion is very important in their life, compared to about 1 in 5 Canadians.[62] Canada is, quite simply, a more secular society than the United States, though not nearly as secular as some Western European democracies.

Secularization involves a decline in the belief that religion and religious authorities should be looked to for guidance about how to behave and how to evaluate behaviour, and an increase in the social, cultural, and political influence of authority that is not based on religious faith.

For most of their respective histories, Canada and especially French-speaking Canada were generally thought of as being more traditionally religious than the United States. Religious elites certainly appeared to have more influence in Canada, at least until the 1960s. Since then, the process of secularization has advanced more rapidly in Canada and other Western democracies than in the United States. Figure 2.6 shows that on a range of measures Americans tend to be more traditionally religious than Canadians. Spain and Germany are included for purposes of comparison.

The more secular character of Canada's political culture helps to explain why issues with important moral dimensions, such as abortion and stem

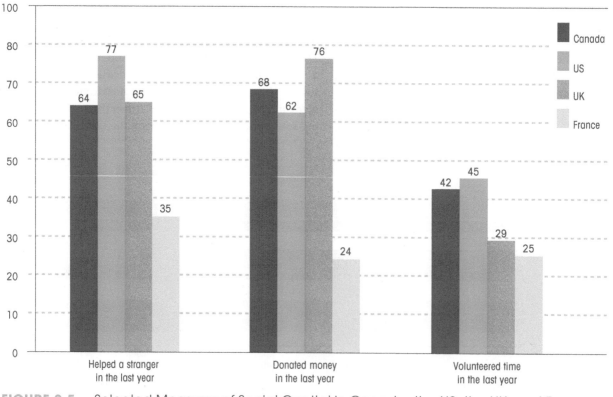

FIGURE 2.5   Selected Measures of Social Capital in Canada, the US, the UK, and France

Source: Based on data reported in Charities Aid Foundation, *World Giving Index 2013*, December 2013.

A. God is very important in my life. (percentage agreeing)

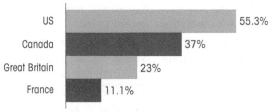

US	55.3%
Canada	37%
Great Britain	23%
France	11.1%

B. I attend religious services at least once per week.

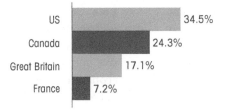

US	34.5%
Canada	24.3%
Great Britain	17.1%
France	7.2%

C. I agree that marriage is an outdated institution. (percentage agreeing)*

US	12.6%
Canada	21.5%
Germany	20.4%
Spain	31.6%

D. It would be better for the country if more people with strong religious beliefs held public office. (percentage agreeing)*

US	39.4%
Canada	21.8%
Germany	18.9%
Spain	12%

E. I take some moments of prayer, meditation or comtemplation.*

US	80.4%
Canada	75.9%
Great Britain	45.4%
France	30%

FIGURE 2.6   Strength of Traditional Religious Values: Canada, the United States, and Selected Western European Countries

*These data are from the 2000 wave of the World Values Survey; these questions were not asked in Wave 5 (2005–9).

Source: World Values Survey, Wave 5: 2005–9. Reprinted with permission.

cell research using human embryo cells, have been more controversial in the United States than in Canada and why Canadian legislation recognizing same-sex marriage was passed in 2005 while in the United States this particular battle rages on despite a 2013 Supreme Court ruling that was widely interpreted as a victory for same-sex couples. The more secular nature of Canadian culture also helps to explain why Canadian politicians, unlike their American counterparts, infrequently invoke religious references or even mention God in their public statements. Being perceived as too religious can even be a liability in Canadian politics. This is seldom true in the United States, except in the most liberal pockets of the country.

How Different Are Canadian and American Values?

The dream of tory origins
Is full of lies and blanks,
Though what remains when it is gone,
To prove that we're not Yanks?
      Dennis Lee, "When I Went Up to Rosedale"

Observing English Canada and the United States about 100 years ago, the French sociologist André Siegfried argued that the differences between them were relatively small and certainly insignificant by European standards. Siegfried was one of the first to weigh in on a question that has been at the centre of the comparative study of political culture in Canada and the United States: which are politically more significant, the similarities or differences in the values and beliefs of these two societies?

One hundred years after Siegfried, Michael Adams[63] and Philip Resnick[64] are among those who argue that these value differences are significant and growing. Adams goes so far as to conclude that Canada and the United States are fundamentally different and maintains that this has always been the case. Resnick is more cautious. He acknowledges the undeniable similarity between Canadian and American culture but argues that, in many important ways, Canadians have more in common with Western Europeans, such as the French, than they do with Americans. Moreover, Resnick believes that

this affinity with Europeans and the gap between Canadians and Americans have been growing in recent years.

Drawing on data from the three rounds of the World Values Survey (1981, 1990, and 2000), Christian Boucher tests the Adams–Resnick hypothesis. Based on 28 measures that have been included in all three waves of the survey, Boucher arrives at the following conclusions:

- Both Canada and the United States have undergone substantial value change over the last two decades, becoming more "progressive and secular regarding some aspects of economic, social, political and moral issues."
- "The values differences between Canada and the United States are small . . . except for religious and moral issues."[65]
- Canadians and Americans are becoming more similar when it comes to some values and more different in regard to others. There is no clear, across-the-board pattern of either convergence or divergence in their value systems.

Data from the latest wave of the World Values Survey provide further confirmation of Boucher's three conclusions. Indeed, the most striking finding is how much more similar Canadian attitudes and beliefs are to those of Americans, compared to the citizens of Western European societies.

As Boucher observes, the widest value difference between Canadians and Americans—indeed, between Americans and almost all other Western populations—involves religion. The 2012 AmericasBarometer survey found that twice as many Americans (39 per cent) as Canadians (19 per cent) said that religion is important in their life. Traditional religiosity is a much greater factor in the United States than in Canada and, consequently, social conservatism is a much more powerful force in that country's politics.

In the end, what may be most significant about this debate over the extent of the value differences between Canada and the United States is that it has gone on so long and continues to generate controversy among those who study Canadian politics.

The differences are relatively small, certainly, compared to those between Canada and most other Western democracies. But this is a debate whose survival does not depend on the reality of large or growing value differences (see Figure 2.7). It is rooted, instead, in the precariousness of the national identity of English-speaking Canada. This identity has always been based on the premise of significant value differences between Canada and the United States, a premise used to explain why these two countries are not united under one constitution and *should not* be so united.

It is probably fair to conclude that the magnitude of these value differences has never been, and is not at present, very great. But neither is it inconsequential. It is also certain that this issue very often becomes embroiled in politics, as politicians, commentators, citizens—and political scientists—allow their preferences to influence their reading of the evidence.

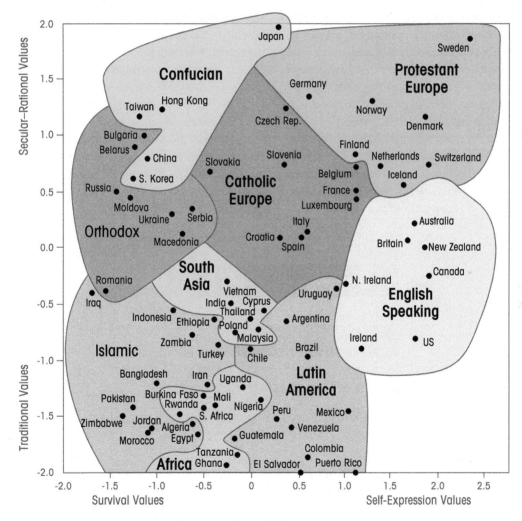

FIGURE 2.7 Inglehart-Welzel Cultural Map of the World

This map shows that many basic values are closely correlated. The scale on the vertical axis represents a continuum from traditional to secular values; the horizontal scale, ranging from survival values to self-expression values, reflects the fact that increasing wealth in many societies since the 1960s has meant that, as Ronald Inglehart puts it, "priorities have shifted from an overwhelming emphasis on economic and physical security toward . . . subjective well-being, self-expression and quality of life."

Source: Adapted from World Values Survey, Wave 5: 2005–9. Reprinted with permission.

Politics in Focus

BOX 2.4 Centre-Left vs Centre-Right Nation

A generation ago the most astute American observer of the Canadian political scene remarked that all three Canadian political parties—the Conservatives, the Liberals, and the NDP—were to the left of the Democratic Party. Seymour Martin Lipset made this comment in 1988 when the Democratic Party's presidential candidate was the governor of Massachusetts, the country's most liberal state! Lipset was making a point that went beyond the party systems of Canada and the United States. Canada's ideological centre of gravity, he argued, was clearly to the left of that in the United States.

This remains the case, although the political value differences between the two societies often are not very great. The 2012 AmericasBarometer survey asked Americans and Canadians to choose which ideological position best described them. Figure 2.8 illustrates the result.

Whereas two-thirds of Canadians placed themselves in the ideological centre of their country's politics, only slightly more than one-third of Americans chose this placement. More Americans (42 per cent) chose "right" as their ideological orientation, twice as many as said "left." This poll was carried out just months before Democratic President Barack Obama's re-election and at a time when the Democrats controlled the Senate.

Not only are Americans much more likely to self-identify on the right, ideologically they are more polarized than Canadians. The main reason for this difference is the significantly greater strength of both social and economic conservatism in the United States than in Canada. Compared to its southern neighbour, Canada is a more left-leaning society, as it was when Lipset made this observation a generation ago.

| Canada | 14 | 68 | 18 |
| USA* | 21 | 37 | 42 |

■ Left (1 to 3)   ■ Middle (4 to 7)   ■ Right (8 to 10)

FIGURE 2.8   General Political Orientation, Canada and the United States

Source: Environics Institute, *AmericasBarometer 2012*, full report, p. 17.

Starting Points for Research

Katherine Fierlbeck, *Political Thought in Canada: An Intellectual History* (Toronto: University of Toronto Press, 2006). Explores the history of political thought over the course of Canadian history, including the forces that have shaped the political ideas of Canadians.

Edward Grabb and James Curtis, *Regions Apart: The Four Societies of Canada and the United States* (Toronto: Oxford University Press, 2010). Written by two sociologists, this book provides an excellent comparison of cultural values in Canada and the United States and the historical factors that have contributed to their differences.

Seymour Martin Lipset, *Continental Divide: The Values and Institutions of the United States and Canada* (Toronto: C.D. Howe Institute, 1989). This remains one of the best surveys of the voluminous work done on the differences and similarities in the political cultures of Canada and the United States, written by one of the most astute observers of political culture in these two countries.

Philip Resnick, *The European Roots of Canadian Identity* (Peterborough, Ont.: Broadview Press, 2005). In this wide-ranging analysis Resnick argues that the fundamental values and beliefs of Canadians are more like those of Western Europeans than of Americans and that the European affinity of Canada became more evident and was reinforced by the war in Iraq.

David Thomas and David Biette, eds, *Canada and the United States: Differences That Count*, 4th edn (Toronto: University of Toronto Press, 2014). This collection includes many useful essays on differences in Canadian and American values, behaviour, institutions, and policies, ranging from health care to crime.

Review Exercises

1. Look at Figure 2.1, Support for Quebec Independence, 1978–2014. Can you suggest some reason(s) for the wide fluctuations in the percentage of Quebecers saying they would vote for Quebec sovereignty? Why was it so high in 1990 and 1995? Based on this data, can we draw any conclusions about the likelihood of Quebecers choosing to separate at some point in the future?

2. Where would you place each of the parties represented in the federal Parliament on a political ideology scale ranging from far left to far right? Where would you place the party that governs your province? Where would you place yourself? In each case, explain why you chose a particular place on the scale for a party or yourself.

3. Choose any three organizations from the following list. From the information included at their websites, decide whether each organization advocates mainly collectivist or individualistic ideas. Explain whether and why, or why not, you think these organizations represent the ideas of significant numbers of Canadians.
   Fraser Institute: <www.fraserinstitute.ca>
   Centre for Social Justice:
     <www.socialjustice.org>
   Canadian Centre for Policy Alternatives:
     <www.policyalternatives.ca>
   Canadian Labour Congress: <www.clc-ctc.ca>
   Ecojustice Canada: <www.ecojustice.ca>
   National Citizens' Coalition:
     <www.nationalcitizens.ca>
   Council of Canadians: <www.canadians.org>

4. A Google search of "Canadian anti-Americanism" will generate no end of entries. Do you think English-speaking Canadians tend to be anti-American? If so, is this because their values are quite different from those of Americans, or are there other reasons? Is anti-Americanism still an influential force in Canadian politics?

3

The Social and Economic Setting

Politics unfolds against a backdrop of social and economic conditions. This chapter focuses on the following aspects of Canadian society:

- Material well-being.
- Equality.
- Discrimination.
- Quality of life.
- Poverty.
- Independence.

Fishing has long been an important industry for Canadians, both economically and culturally. More than one thousand communities across the country rely heavily on fishing as their primary business. Though less than 4 per cent of Canadians work in the fishing industry, Canada is one of the world's largest fish and seafood exporters, with the Arctic, Atlantic, and Pacific Oceans and the Great Lakes giving Canadians a wide fishing diversity. (PraxisPhotography/Getty Images)

As Yogi Berra would have said, it was déjà vu all over again. In the weeks before the 2012 American presidential election, social media were abuzz with posts from Americans claiming that if their candidate did not win, they would be packing their bags and heading to Canada. Among them were Cher, Susan Sarandon, and George Lopez. Many more Democratic supporters than Republican ones made this blustery promise. Several years earlier, after President George W. Bush's 2004 re-election, many Canadians were gratified to read stories claiming that thousands of Americans were inquiring into the possibility of moving to Canada. This seemed to them to be the surest confirmation of their belief—a belief shared by most Canadians—that Canada is superior in important ways to the powerhouse to the south, the benchmark against which we always compare ourselves and our achievements. The Canadian self-image is one of compassion, tolerance, and prosperity. Canadians tend to see themselves as being more compassionate and more tolerant than Americans. Their neighbours may be richer, but most Canadians believe that their country's prosperity is more equally shared. And they believe that this is as it should be.

Canadians are indeed fortunate. But that good fortune is not shared by all Canadians. Roughly three million Canadians fall below what is conventionally called the "poverty line," the low-income point established by Statistics Canada. In recent years, anti-globalization protesters, poverty activists, and spokespersons for the homeless have all been critical of conditions in Canada and the performance of government in this country.

In this chapter we will examine the social and economic setting of Canadian politics. At various points comparisons will be made between Canada and other countries, between regions in Canada, between various points in Canada's history, and between actual conditions and some idealized standards that have been applied to the performance of Canada's political system. Our goal in this chapter is not, however, chiefly to judge. Instead, our main purpose is to understand the societal context that influences, and is influenced by, politics and public policy. In doing so we will be selective, focusing on aspects of Canadian society and the economy that are closely associated with several values that most Canadians consider to be important.

Obviously, such values as material well-being, equality, quality of life, and independence will be interpreted differently by different people. Disagreements aside, these values are of special importance for two related reasons. First, they represent public purposes that most of us expect governments to preserve or promote. Second, political controversies are frequently about one or more of these values—disagreements over how to achieve them; over what value(s) should give way, and by how much, when they conflict; about whether they are being adequately met; and so on. It makes sense, therefore, to focus on these dimensions of the social and economic setting of Canadian politics.

Political issues and outcomes are not determined in any simplistic manner by such things as the extent and nature of inequalities in Canadian society or the level of material well-being, any more than political ideologies and institutions translate directly into political behaviour and public policy. Like ideology and institutions, the social and economic settings of politics establish boundaries to political life. They do so by determining the sorts of problems a society faces, the resources available for coping with these problems, the nature and intensity of divisions within society, and the distribution of politically valuable resources between societal interests.

Material Well-Being

Canada is an affluent society. This simple fact is sometimes obscured by the news of fresh layoffs, plant closings, slipping competitiveness, and pockets of poverty. For much of the late twentieth century, the average real purchasing power of Canadians was the second highest in the world, topped only by that of Americans. In the last couple of decades Canada has slipped significantly. As of 2012, 10 OECD countries ranked ahead of us in terms of average real purchasing power, or **purchasing power parities** (see Figure 3.1). This does not mean that Canadians have become, on average, poorer in any absolute sense. It means, rather, that other countries have grown richer more quickly and leaped ahead of Canada.

On a global scale, however, Canadians remain relatively wealthy. Affluence affects both the opportunities and problems faced by policy-makers. The problem of poverty, for example, assumes a very different character in an affluent society like Canada from that in a poorer society like Mexico or a destitute one like Sudan. Not only does Canada's poverty problem look rather enviable from the standpoint of these other countries, but the means that governments in Canada have available to deal with this problem are far greater than those that can be deployed by the governments of poorer societies. The very definition of what constitute public problems, warranting the attention of government, is also influenced by a society's material conditions. Environmental pollution, a prominent issue on the public agendas of affluent societies, tends to be buried under the weight of other pressing social and economic problems in less affluent societies.

Within the elite club of affluent societies, cultural and institutional differences are probably more important as determinants of the public agenda and government response to them than are their differences in material well-being. But the particular characteristics of a national economy, factors upon which material affluence depends, are significant influences on the politics and public policies of any society. These characteristics include the sectoral and regional distribution of economic activity, the level and distribution of employment, characteristics of a country's labour force, the profile of its trade with the rest of the world, and so on. Despite enjoying one of the highest standards of living in the world, Canadians have seldom been complacent about their affluence. Fears that Canada's material well-being may rest on fragile footings have long been expressed. They have mainly involved anxiety over the outsourcing of jobs and the restructuring of the Canadian economy as well as fears that the country's economic

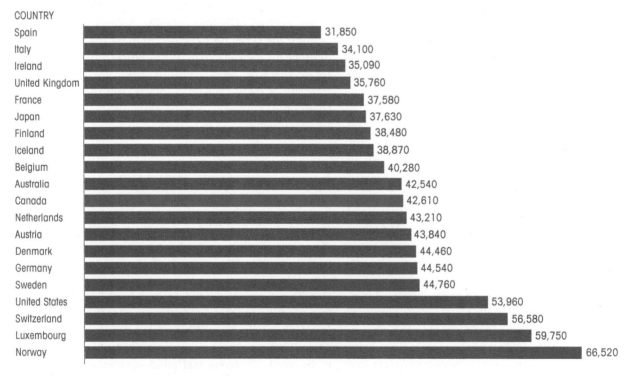

FIGURE 3.1   Per Capita PPPs* ($US) for Richest OECD Countries, 2012

*Purchasing power parities.

Source: World Bank, "Gross national income per capita 2012, PPP," at: <http://databank.worldbank.org/data/download/GNIPC.pdf>.

prosperity may be too dependent on international demand for natural resources.

The economy and unemployment are perennially towards the top of the issues Canadians identify as the most important facing the country. Indeed, since the global financial crisis of 2008 they have been the top two issues.[1] Compared to other advanced industrialized democracies, Canada has done fairly well when it comes to unemployment and job creation. Over the past 30 years the national level of unemployment has fluctuated between a low of 6 per cent (2007) and a high of 13 per cent (1983), averaging about 7–9 per cent during most of this period. In the United States, by comparison, the rate over this same period has fluctuated between a low of 4 per cent (2000) and a high of about 10 per cent (1983 and 2010), averaging about 6 per cent over the last three decades but being somewhat higher than in Canada over the past several years. The long-term unemployment rate in Canada (i.e., the percentage of the unemployed who have been out of work for at least 12 consecutive months) is about half the OECD average and one of the best in the world. The rate of job creation is directly related to the rate of growth in the economy. Since the mid-1990s, Canada has had the highest annual growth rate of any G7 economy, which has translated into the best record of job creation in this elite club of affluent democracies.[2] Indeed, only Australia, which is not a member of the G7, has had a better rate of job growth. Looking at the distribution of employment across sectors of the Canadian economy, one finds that Canada closely resembles the world's other major capitalist economies. Over three-quarters of workers are in service industries (78 per cent), about 10 per cent are employed in the manufacturing sector, roughly 4 per cent work in primary industries like farming, fishing, forestry, and mining, and the remaining 7 per cent work in construction (2011). These shares are similar to those of our major trading partner, the United States, and those of other leading capitalist democracies.[3] Over time, the service sector's share of total employment has grown dramatically, from about 40 per cent in the mid-twentieth century to the current level of about eight in 10 jobs. The shares in the primary and secondary sectors have

obviously declined, more sharply in primary industries than in manufacturing. These employment trends have led many to worry that the Canadian economy is "deindustrializing." But it is not simply Canada where such dramatic change has taken place. Broadly similar changes have occurred in all of the world's major capitalist economies over the last several decades.

The fact that manufacturing jobs are fewer, less secure, and, in many cases, lower-paying than they were in the past has caused much concern in Canada, as in the United States, France, and other wealthy societies whose prosperity, not so long ago, seemed to be based on this sector. Economists, however, are not in agreement on the question of whether a shrinking manufacturing sector and greater reliance on service-sector employment is necessarily a bad thing from the standpoint of incomes and general prosperity. Some, including Harvard economist Michael Spence, argue that globalization is directly responsible for a dearth of jobs in the American and other Western economies. Others, including another Harvard economist, Robert Lawrence, and business writer Richard Katz, maintain that a shortage of jobs and flat incomes have much more to do with government policies and internal factors than with the outsourcing of jobs.[4]

Fears over the export of low-skill manufacturing jobs have been replaced in more recent years by worries that more highly skilled jobs, including those requiring a good deal of education, have been moving abroad to some developing countries. Much of the work in computer programming, financial services, and even legal services has moved to India. An increasing share of the production of machine tools, dies, and moulds for manufacturing has relocated to China. These are more recent forms of **outsourcing**. Unlike the earlier movement of textile, footwear, and repetitive low-skill jobs to developing countries, these newer forms of outsourcing involve the loss of more highly skilled and highly paid jobs. Examples are easy enough to find, from the telephone call that you receive from India on behalf of a Canadian bank or other financial services company trying to sell you new products to the software design that contributed to the latest video game you may be thinking of buying.

These fears may be unfounded. Canada's job creation rate has been one of the best in the developed world for over a decade and virtually all labour economists project that as the country's population continues to age, the supply of workers, including those needed to fill highly skilled and well-paying jobs, will not meet the projected demand (see Box 3.1). But even if it could

Media Spotlight

BOX 3.1 The New Underclass?

In January of 2013, *Maclean's* magazine featured a cover story on what it called "the new underclass." The underclass is a term that came into use in the United States in the 1960s to describe that stratum of American society that was at the very bottom of the socio-economic ladder and whose prospects and hopes for a better life were dimmest. Predominantly black and usually estimated by sociologists to be not more than 1–2 per cent of the total population, the underclass is argued by scholars such as William Julius Wilson to have emerged in large part because of economic restructuring and the disappearance of unskilled manufacturing jobs.

This is not the underclass that *Maclean's* had in mind. The Canadian underclass its cover story examined is "a generation of well-educated, ambitious, smart young Canadians that," the article controversially concluded, "has no future." Leaving aside whether this dismal prediction is even remotely likely, the label "underclass" was surely intended to seize readers' attention. In fact, however, the lives and prospects of those to whom it was applied bear little resemblance to the destitution, violence, and general hopelessness of the American underclass.

The authors of the *Maclean's* article were surely aware of this. But in one limited respect, at least, their use of the term "underclass" may have been apt. What they call the new underclass, many argue, has been created by the dynamics of economic restructuring. "There's been growth at the top—there's more good, white-collar jobs than there used to be," says labour studies professor Wayne Lewchuk, "but we have fewer middle jobs, and more bad jobs. . . . So the problem now is if you get one of those bad jobs, even out of university, there's no middle rung for you to go to. . . . (University graduates are) stuck in that bottom tier and they're just not seeing a path to a better job—ever."

How did this happen? Analyses like the *Maclean's* article acknowledge that uninformed labour market choices by many young Canadians have contributed to the problem of underemployment and low incomes for many with post-secondary degrees. But economic restructuring and corporate cost-cutting, both of which are consequences of globalization, have played their part in what Lewchuk and others call the hollowing out of the middle class. Slightly more than one of four Canadians between the ages of 25 and 29 live with their parents (2011), compared to 11 per cent in 1981, suggesting that a growing number of young Canadians are having to put their independence and their hopes on hold.

Is the picture really as bleak as this? Before you decide that your choice of a degree in something other than engineering, health sciences, or international copyright law was perhaps not such a good idea, or that maybe you should have paid more attention when your high school guidance counsellor was making the case for a career in welding or heavy machinery operation, consider these facts. The likelihood of being unemployed drops significantly with formal education. As of 2011 about 16 per cent of those who dropped out of high school were unemployed, compared to 8 per cent for high school graduates and just under 5 per cent for university graduates.[5] Notwithstanding the gloomy diagnosis of the *Maclean's* article, the proportion of workers with a university degree who held low-skilled jobs (requiring a high school diploma at most) did not change among workers aged 25–34 between 1997 and 2012.[6] You may wish to take heart from the conclusion of a recent study: "(T)he data show that while the number of post-secondary graduates has grown in recent years, the benefits of a degree in terms of more stable employment and higher earnings have not diminished."[7]

be shown that outsourcing has and will continue to result in a hemorrhage of jobs, one could still make the case that sharing employment opportunities with people in less affluent parts of the world is preferable to providing them with foreign aid. If Canadians truly believe that the world's wealth should be shared more equally—which is what they regularly tell pollsters—then they should applaud the redistribution of economic activity from the rich countries of the world to those that aspire to a higher standard of living. But most do not.

Equality

Canadians are not used to thinking of themselves and their society in terms of class. Pressed to self-identify with a particular rung on the class ladder, the majority of Canadians will choose middle class. The 2012 Focus Canada survey found that 56 per cent self-identified as middle class, 19 per cent as lower middle class, and 18 per cent as upper middle class. Only 1 per cent chose the label "upper class" and just 5 per cent chose "lower class."[8] Canada is, at least in terms of how its citizens perceive themselves, a middle-class society.

At the same time, however, Canadians are aware of inequalities based on income. Asked who Canadian politicians defend, the rich, the poor, or both equally, 51 per cent said that they defended the rich, 43 per cent said that they defended the rich and the poor equally, and only 6 per cent said that they defended the poor over the rich. Six out of 10 said that politicians *should* defend the rich and the poor equally, and one out of three said that they should defend the poor over the rich. Slightly more than half of Canadians (51 per cent) said that the government should implement strong policies to reduce income inequality and almost one-third of Canadians said that the way to do this is to increase taxes on the rich.[9]

For various reasons Canadians are probably more aware of inequalities today than they were a few decades ago. Despite this heightened awareness, most Canadians still cling to the belief that their society is predominantly middle class. This belief—which is by no means false—springs from the dominant liberal ideology. Individualism and a belief that opportunities to get ahead in life are open to those with the energy and talent needed to take advantage of them are at the core of this liberal ideology. To say that society is predominantly middle class means, from this ideological perspective, that the barriers to upward mobility are relatively low for the vast majority of people. The fact that some people are extraordinarily wealthy and others are quite destitute needs to be set alongside an even more prominent fact, i.e., that most Canadians occupy a broad middle band in terms of their incomes and lifestyles.

Wealth is unevenly divided in all societies. Few people believe that the sort of levelling implied by Karl Marx's aphorism, "From each according to his abilities, to each according to his needs," is desirable. But many people are disturbed by the jarring contrast between conspicuous luxury and destitution in their society. The gap between rich and poor is not as great in Canada as in some other industrialized democracies. Nevertheless, it is considerable and persistent. Moreover, some groups bear the brunt of poverty much more heavily than others.

In 2011 the wealthiest 20 per cent of the population accounted for about 47 per cent of all income, while the poorest one-fifth accounted for slightly less than 5 per cent.[10] These shares are not dramatically different from what they were a half-century ago. In 1960, the bottom quintile of Canadians accounted for just over 4 per cent of all money income compared to about 41 per cent for the top fifth of income earners. The change over time looks a bit more dramatic if one focuses on the very wealthiest of Canadians. The top 1 per cent of tax filers accounted for just under 10 per cent of income in 1960 and just over 12 per cent in 2010. Perspective is sometimes everything. Before World War II, the top 1 per cent of income earners in Canada accounted for about 18 per cent of income, a share that declined dramatically during the war and then more gradually in the following decades, reaching a low of about 8 per cent in the late 1970s. All of these figures include social transfers such as public pensions, social security payments, and employment insurance. State spending narrows the gap between those at the top and bottom of the income ladder from what it would be in the absence of redistributive policies. In 2011 the lowest quintile of income earners received 29.1 per cent of the value of all federal transfers, compared to 11.4 per cent for those in the highest quintile. At the same time, those at the top of the income ladder account for a greater share of government revenue. In 2010 the top 1 per cent of income earners paid 21.2 per cent of federal, provincial, and territorial income taxes, compared to 13.4 per cent in 1982. The share paid by the other 99 per cent of tax filers in 2010 was 78.8 per cent, down from 86.6 per cent in 1982.

In recent years, news stories and academic studies purporting to show a growing gap between the rich and the poor in Canada have contributed to a widespread belief that inequality has increased. It has, but probably not as much or in the ways that most Canadians imagine. Fortin and her colleagues show that the distribution of both market and disposable income in Canada has grown more unequal since the late 1970s.[11] Most of the increase in inequality occurred during the decade of the 1990s. This trend has flattened in recent years. Both the increase in inequality and the more recent levelling off are due to the share of income going to the very wealthiest Canadians. At the same time, most Canadians

are better off today than they were 30–40 years ago. Figure 3.2 shows that the median incomes of Canadian families and unattached individuals increased in real terms between 1976 and 2010.

Compared to the distribution of income in other advanced capitalist societies, Canada's is fairly typical. The distribution of income is more equal than in some countries, such as the United States, but less equal than in others, including France and the Scandinavian democracies. Income inequality increased significantly during the 1990s but has remained stable since then.[12] Nevertheless, a 2013 survey found that three-quarters of Canadians believed that the gap between the rich and the poor had increased in recent years, and 45 per cent agreed that inequality was a very big problem. But only one out of five Canadians said that addressing income inequality should be the government's main priority, compared to four out of 10 Germans who said that this should be their government's priority notwithstanding that income inequality is less in Germany than in Canada.[13]

The distribution of income is only part of the story in any assessment of equality. The other part involves the extent of poverty. Poverty is to

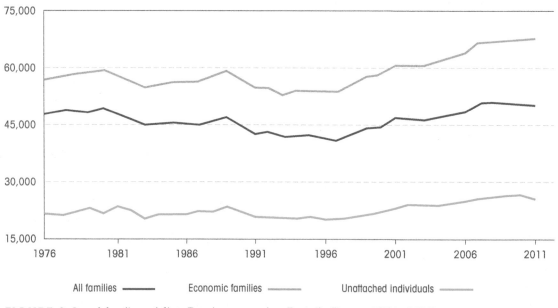

FIGURE 3.2 Median After-Tax Income by Family Type, 1976–2010

Source: Statistics Canada, *Income in Canada, 2006,* Catalogue no. 75-202-X, chart 1, p. 9; Employment and Social Development Canada, at: <www4.hrsdc.gc.ca/.3ndic.1t.4r@-eng.jsp?iid=21>.

some degree a relative concept, meaning something different in an advanced industrialized society like Canada than in a developing country like Nigeria. In Canada, poverty is usually measured using Statistics Canada's definition of what constitutes an income that is so low that an individual or household lives in "straitened circumstances." Statistics Canada's low-income cut-offs (LICOs) are generally referred to by the media, academics, politicians, and others as the **poverty line**. This low-income threshold, with some variation depending on family size, region of the country, and city (or rural) population, is reached by a household that spends over 20 per cent more of their annual family income on the basic necessities of living (food, clothing, and shelter) than does the national average household. To give an example of the variation due to difference costs of living in different parts of the country, the LICO for a family of two adults and two children in 2011 was estimated to be $38,313 in Toronto and $32,693 in rural Quebec.

The term "poverty line" has become an established part of Canada's political vocabulary, evoking images of need and destitution in the minds of many if not most Canadians. There is, however,

nothing magical or inevitable about the particular definition of "low income" used by Statistics Canada or any other agency or expert measuring poverty. The limitations of Statistics Canada's low-income cut-offs have been acknowledged by the agency itself.[14] A study by the National Council of Welfare observes that these limitations include the fact that all poverty lines are relative, they are not absolute measures of need or deprivation; and they are all arbitrary to some degree, based on value judgments about what constitutes poverty in a particular society.[15]

Although the number of Canadians whose incomes fall below the poverty line varies from year to year, the figure has fluctuated over the past few decades between a high of about 16 per cent (1996) and a low of 9–10 per cent in recent years. The likelihood of being poor is not, however, evenly distributed across the population. As Figure 3.3 shows, the likelihood of having a low income is significantly greater for some groups. These figures tell only part of the story. Lone-parent families are much more likely to be headed by women than by men and are also much more likely to fall below the poverty line. The higher poverty rate for off-reserve Aboriginal

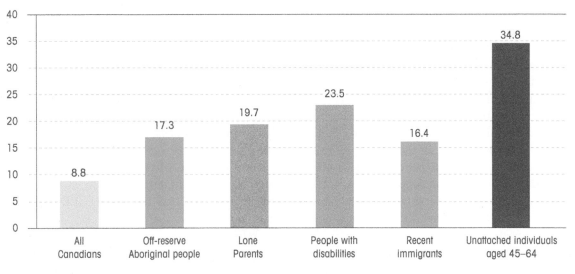

Economic families, two persons or more

FIGURE 3.3   Low-income Rates among Working Age Main Income Recipients, Various Groups, 2010

Source: Employment and Social Development Canada, at: <www4.hrsdc.gc.ca/.3ndic.1t.4r@-eng.jsp?iid=23>.

Canadians is much lower than that for the roughly half-million Natives who live on reserves.

Why are certain groups particularly susceptible to poverty? There is no single or simple answer. A few of the contributing causes are fairly clear, however. In the case of Aboriginal Canadians, individual discrimination no doubt has played a role in explaining their higher jobless rate and lower incomes. Today, however, it is certain that lower levels of education have been and continue to be a factor explaining the employment and income gap between Aboriginal and other Canadians. This begs the question: why are education levels considerably lower among Aboriginal Canadians? They are particularly low among Aboriginal Canadians who live on reserves. This is not accidental. Reserves are, for the most part, small and far from major population centres. Employment opportunities are comparatively few. The conditions that support educational aspirations and opportunities are much less likely to be present than in off-reserve communities. Only 40 per cent of Aboriginal Canadians living on reserves have completed high school, compared to about 60 per cent for those living off-reserve and close to 80 per cent for non-Aboriginal Canadians. The employment rate among those living on reserves is only about 70 per cent that of Aboriginal Canadians living off-reserve and only about 60 per cent that of non-Aboriginal Canadians. Those living on reserves have incomes that, on average, are about 60 per cent of what Aboriginal Canadians off-reserve make, and only 40 per cent of what non-Aboriginals make. Close to 30 per cent of the income of those living on reserves involves government transfers of one sort or another, compared to just under 20 per cent for those living off-reserve and slightly more than 10 per cent for non-Aboriginal Canadians. The conclusion is inescapable: a person who lives on a reserve is far more likely than one who does not, whether Aboriginal or not, to be unemployed and poor.[16]

Inequality also has an important regional dimension in Canada. Income levels and employment rates vary significantly between provinces, as well between regions within provinces. Personal incomes in what have traditionally been among the poorest provinces (Newfoundland and Labrador, New Brunswick, and PEI) are about 85–90 per cent of the Canadian average but only 70–80 per cent of incomes in the wealthiest provinces (Alberta and Saskatchewan). The citizens of these less affluent provinces have been much more dependent on various transfer payments from government for part of their incomes than have Canadians in wealthier provinces. Figure 3.4 shows that interregional variation in average personal incomes has narrowed over the last few decades, although it is still quite wide. The narrowing of the gap has been due mainly to government transfers that provide greater income benefits to the residents of the poorer provinces than to those of the richer ones. In the 2012–13 fiscal year, Ottawa transferred $3,541 per person to residents of PEI, $3,289 to citizens of New Brunswick, but only $1,015 to each Albertan and $1,244 per person in Ontario.[17]

One of the important dimensions of equality, and one of the chief influences on it, is **socio-economic mobility**. This refers to the ability of individuals, families, and groups to move from one social or economic position to another. Socio-economic mobility implies the existence of hierarchically arranged differences in society, such as those that exist between income groups and occupations. These differences exist in all societies to a greater or lesser extent. Where socio-economic mobility is high, movement up and down the social ladder is more common and the barriers to entry into high-paying occupations, prestigious status groups, or powerful elites are relatively low. This is what students of mobility call an open society. In a closed society there is relatively little intergenerational movement on the social ladder and barriers to entry into privileged social and economic groups are high.

Most Canadians believe that theirs is a relatively open society, and compared to most rich countries it is. Miles Corak has examined how closely sons' rankings on their society's income ladder are related to the earnings of their fathers.[18] He reports that intergenerational mobility in Canada is surpassed by that in only a small number of wealthy democracies, and then just marginally (see Figure 3.5). At the same time, however, an abundance of evidence shows that social stratification in Canada remains high and real opportunities

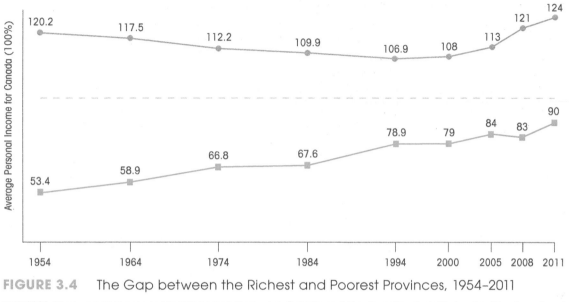

FIGURE 3.4   The Gap between the Richest and Poorest Provinces, 1954–2011

Until 2005, the two provinces used in this comparison were Ontario and Newfoundland and Labrador. Newfoundland and Labrador has continued to have the lowest per capita income in most years since then, but Alberta has been the wealthiest province in most years since 2005.

Source: Statistics Canada, *Provincial Economic Accounts.*

to climb the socio-economic ladder are perhaps lower than the conventional wisdom suggests. The **vertical mosaic** that John Porter analyzed a half-century ago has been opened up, but gender, ethnicity, race, and family background continue to exert a significant downward pull on mobility.

Of these factors, family background appears to be the most important. More specifically, the education, occupation, and income of one's parents—these three factors being highly correlated—have a significant impact on the likelihood that a person's income and class position will be better or worse than that of his or her parents. (Mobility is a two-way street and includes the possibility of slipping down the income ladder between generations, not just climbing it.) Corak reports that the probability of a son born to a father whose income is in the lowest 20 per cent of income earners reaching the upper half of all Canadian income earners is 38 per cent. This compares favourably to the United States, where the probability of someone from this same rung of the income ladder reaching the upper half of income earners is 30 per cent. On the middle rungs of the income ladder the likelihood of

moving up a rung or two (one or two deciles on the income ladder) is about 50 per cent in both countries. But at both the top and the bottom of the income ladder there is a lower probability of mobility in the United States than in Canada.[19]

Income mobility in Canada appears to have remained fairly stable since the 1990s. Table 3.1 compares the movement of persons from one income quintile to another for the five-year periods 1993–7 and 2005–9. The highest level of mobility is observed for those in the lowest income quintile, about four out of 10 of whom moved up the income ladder during each of these periods. Much of the observed movement is the normal and expected result of people reaching different stages in the life cycle, such as leaving school and entering the workforce or retiring and experiencing a decline in income. But as Jason Clemens of the Macdonald-Laurier Institute observes, "67.3 per cent or over two-thirds of the individuals covered by the data found themselves in a higher or lower quintile in 2009 compared to where they started in 2005, which reflects a high degree of income mobility in society."[20]

TABLE 3.1   Moving Up and Down the Income Ladder: Income Mobility in Canada, 1993–7 and 2005–9

	2005–9			1993–7		
	Proportion of Persons Who Moved into a Higher Quintile (%)	Proportion of Persons Who Moved into a Lower Quintile (%)	Total Mobility (%)	Proportion of Persons Who Moved into a Higher Quintile (%)	Proportion of Persons Who Moved into a Lower Quintile (%)	Total Mobility (%)
Lowest Quintile	43	0	43	41	0	41
Second Quintile	41	20	61	38	20	58
Third Quintile	34	29	63	33	27	60
Fourth Quintile	24	38	62	25	34	59
Highest Quintile	0	40	40	0	39	39
Overall Average	28	25	53	27	24	51

Source: Jason Clemens, *Income Inequality: Oversimplifying a Complicated Issue*, Macdonald-Laurier Institute, April 2012, table 2, p. 32, at: <www.macdonaldlaurier.ca/files/pdf/Income-Inequality-April-2012.pdf>. Reprinted with permission.

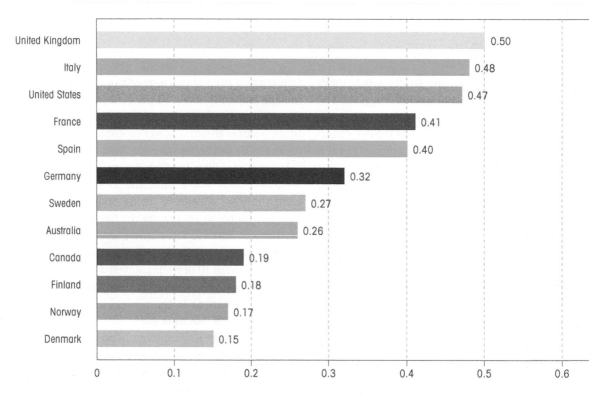

FIGURE 3.5   Intergenerational Elasticity of Earnings between Fathers and Sons, Selected Countries

The higher the intergenerational elasticity of earnings, the more highly correlated one's income is with that of one's parents.

Source: Miles Corak, "Chasing the Same Dream, Climbing Different Ladders: Economic Mobility in the United States and Canada," Economic Mobility Project of the Pew Charitable Trusts, Jan. 2010, at: <www.economicmobility.org/assets/img/EMP_US_Canada_Fig1.jpg>. Reprinted courtesy of The Pew Charitable Trusts.

So the good news is that upward economic mobility in Canada is reasonably high and inter-generational social mobility in Canada appears to be higher than in the United States, Great Britain, France, and some other wealthy democracies.[21] Moreover, Canada does a better job than many other societies in terms of how quickly immigrants and their children are able to climb the socio-economic ladder.[22] Smooth integration into the labour force often does not happen immediately, despite the fact that the Canadian economy has needed highly skilled immigrants for decades. Indeed, a mountain of evidence demonstrates that immigrants' skills are often underutilized, at least for a certain period of time after their arrival in Canada. A 2003 study by Statistics Canada found that six in 10 immigrants were working in different occupational fields in Canada than they had been, or for which they were trained, in their home country.

Immigrants' job prospects do, however, improve over time. The employment rate of those between the ages of 25 and 44, who arrived in Canada between 1991 and 1996, was 61 per cent, but the employment rate for the members of this group increased to 74 per cent by 2001. Although this was still several percentage points below the employment rate for native-born Canadians, it clearly was a significant improvement over a relatively short period of time. Some immigrants simply need to spend some time in school, upgrading, acquiring language skills, or becoming certified in their occupational field. The fact that an increasing number of immigrants in Canada's labour force are non-European and members of what in Canada are called *visible minorities* raises the issue of whether some of the barriers facing immigrant workers are due to discrimination.

It seems likely, however, that problems of assessing foreign credentials, lack of Canadian work experience, and language and cultural barriers are more significant in explaining the underemployment and underutilization of highly skilled and highly educated immigrants. Indeed, in some parts of Canada being an immigrant is about as common as being Canadian-born. According to the 2011 census, the foreign-born comprised about 46 per cent of the population of the Greater Toronto Area, 40 per cent of the population of the Vancouver metropolitan region, and 23 per cent of the population of Montreal. Visible minorities (which, according to the government's definition, do not include Aboriginal peoples) constitute significant shares of the population in these cities: 47 per cent in Toronto, 45 per cent in Vancouver, and 20 per cent in Montreal. Other major Canadian cities, including Calgary, Edmonton, and Ottawa, also have large immigrant and visible minority populations. In such countries as France, the United Kingdom, Germany, and the Netherlands, those who have been born in the country to immigrant parents continue to lag far behind the native-born in education and income. This is not true of Canada. Consider the following findings from a recent Statistics Canada study, based on 2006 census data:

- Second-generation Canadians, both of whose parents were immigrants, are more educated than the Canadian-born whose family roots in Canada go back at least three generations. This is true for both males (21 per cent of the Canadian-born children of immigrants have at least a BA, compared to 14 per cent for "old-stock" Canadians) and females (24 per cent vs 15 per cent).
- The Canadian-born children of immigrant parents are more likely than old-stock Canadians to hold managerial or professional jobs (among males, 38 per cent vs 31 per cent; among females, 37.5 per cent vs 34 per cent).
- Both men and women who were born in Canada to immigrant parents are likely to earn more than old-stock Canadians (among males, $41,490 vs 39,098; among females, $27,127 vs $24,819).
- These patterns apply to all main immigrant communities with the exception of those from Latin America and the Caribbean.[23]

What about the political and economic elites in Canadian society? John Porter argued that they were largely self-perpetuating, recruiting new members chiefly from those groups that already dominated them. Does this continue to be true? Academic and

The Social Fabric

BOX 3.2 Is Canada Still a Vertical Mosaic?

One of the most persistent images that Canadians have of their society is that it has no classes. This image becomes translated into the assertion that Canadians are all relatively equal in their possessions, in the amount of money they earn, and in the opportunities which they and their children have to get on in the world. . . .That there is neither very rich nor very poor in Canada is an important part of the image. There are no barriers to opportunity. Education is free. Therefore, making use of it is largely a question of personal ambition.

John Porter, *The Vertical Mosaic*, 1965

John Porter was a sociologist at the University of Toronto. His 1965 book, *The Vertical Mosaic*, challenged the way Canadians thought about their society and influenced a generation of opinion leaders and policy-makers. Canadians were used to thinking about their society as a pluralistic mixture of ethnicities, languages, and religions even before the notion and policy of multiculturalism came into fashion. So the "mosaic" in the book's title was familiar enough. But they also thought of their society as one that was, by and large, free of class divisions and the sort of structured and persistent inequalities that characterized Western European societies and were challenged by socialist, labour, and communist parties in such countries as the UK, Italy, and France.

Drawing on a wealth of statistical data, Porter demonstrated that in fact the Canadian mosaic was characterized by just the sort of structured and persistent inequalities in representation and opportunity that

Canadians believed were absent from their society. It was, he argued, a *vertical* mosaic in which certain groups dominated and reproduced their dominance from generation to generation, and others were marginalized. Canadians of British ancestry dominated the political, corporate, cultural, and other elites. Those of French ancestry occupied an important place in the political elite and in French-speaking segments of Canada's cultural elites. Other ethnic groups were, by and large, grossly under-represented on the higher rungs of Canada's political, economic, and cultural ladders. Canadians were wrong, Porter argued, to believe that the hallmarks of their society were mobility and opportunity.

The Canada that Porter analyzed existed half a century ago. Nevertheless, many critics argue that structural inequalities of the sort that he described still characterize Canadian society. Canadians are more attuned to the issues of inequality today than they were two generations ago. At the same time, they still believe overwhelmingly that they are middle class and that theirs is a middle-class society. The idea that Canada is a vertical mosaic is no longer a radical and strange notion. But the hammerlock that Canadians of British and French ancestry held on positions of prestige, influence, and high incomes is no longer as tight as it was in Porter's time. Moreover, the explosion in higher education since the 1960s—in 1965 there were about 204,000 students enrolled in Canadian universities compared to about 1,150,000 in 2011—has meant that access to the middle class, while not equal across all ethnic, racial, and other lines in Canada, is certainly greater today than it was in Porter's day.

journalistic writing on Canada's **corporate elite** agrees that this group is highly unrepresentative of the general population and that access to it appears to be much greater for those from certain backgrounds than from others. The most systematic studies of the social characteristics of the corporate elite have been carried out by sociologists John Porter and Wallace Clement. Porter's study was based on data for 1951 and Clement's on data for 1972.[24] They both found that this elite (which they defined as the directors of Canada's dominant corporations) was overwhelmingly male, about a third had attended private schools like Upper Canada College or Ridley, many had upper-class backgrounds (50 per cent in 1951 and 59.4 per cent in 1972), those with non-Anglo-Saxon ethnic origins were under-represented (comprising 13.8 per cent of Clement's 1972 group, compared to 55.3 per cent of the Canadian population), and about half (51.1 per cent in 1972) belonged to one or more of the six most prominent private clubs in Canada. The picture they sketched was one of a self-perpetuating group whose social backgrounds and adult activities set them sharply apart from the general population.

The corporate elite operate as a social network that reproduces itself largely through self-recruitment. Education at elite schools adds to what John Porter called the "social capital" of its members, reinforcing elite ties that are maintained in the adult world of business. Club membership provides a complement to the boardroom, a social setting that is very much part of the personal relations essential in business life. For this reason the question of private club membership became a matter of political controversy during the 1980s. Women's groups especially charged that the exclusively male character of these clubs reinforced men's dominance of the business world by excluding women from its social network.

Using data from 1991, Milan Korac replicated the analysis of Porter and Clement. He reported findings almost identical to those of these two earlier studies. For example, men constituted 92 per cent of the corporate elite; 42 per cent had attended exclusive private schools; those from non-Anglo-Saxon backgrounds were still grossly under-represented (only 22.1 per cent of the economic elite, compared to 74.7 per cent of the population); and well over half of the economic elite belonged to one or more of the Toronto Club, the Mount Royal Club, the Rideau Club, and the St James Club.[25] Almost nothing, it appeared, had changed.

Although the corporate elite today is far from mirroring Canadian society, there are indications that having been born into this elite is somewhat less important in gaining entry than in the past. The Canadian-born still dominate, as may be inferred from the fact that almost all of the corporate directors surveyed for a recent study said that they had English (76.4 per cent) or French (20.3 per cent) as

their mother tongue. German was the first language learned for 2.4 per cent. Language is, of course, a weak proxy for ethnicity, but given the significant change in the ethnic composition of Canadian society over the past four decades, driven mainly by immigration from countries where French and English are not the primary languages, it seems pretty clear that these newer Canadians have yet to crack the corporate elite in large numbers. Fewer than 5 per cent of the directors surveyed self-identified with a visible minority group and 1 per cent self-identified as Aboriginal.[26] The greatest change involved the increased representation of women. Although the corporate elite is still overwhelmingly male, 14 per cent of all directors of Financial Post 500 companies were female in 2012.

Access to the political elite is certainly more open than in the past. Traditionally, Canada's major political parties were dominated by males of either British or French ethnic origins. They still are, but the representation of females and Canadians of non-British, non-French origins has increased sharply over the last couple of decades. The election of Audrey McLaughlin as NDP leader in 1989 marked the first time a woman had been chosen to lead a national political party, followed by the 1993 selection of Kim Campbell as leader of the Conservative Party and of Alexa McDonough as leader of the NDP in 1994. Over the last two decades several of the provinces and all of the territories have had female premiers, and parties led by women have won election in five of the provinces. Several of Canada's major cities have had female mayors, going back to the middle of the last century.

The domination of Canada's political elite by males of British and French ethnic origins is less striking than in the past. Jerome Black's study of the ethno-racial background of members of Parliament elected in 1993, 1997, and 2000 found that about one-quarter of them had minority (non-British, non-French) ancestry and another 10 per cent had mixed majority–minority ancestry. Most of this minority ethnic group membership involved ancestral ties to other European groups. Visible minorities constituted only about 6 per cent of MPs elected over these three elections, which was about half their share of the Canadian population. At the same time, evidence suggests that this segment of the political elite is more diverse today than when Porter documented the overwhelming dominance of males from the two "founding peoples," British and French. About 13 per cent of MPs sitting in 2010 were born outside of Canada, a higher percentage than in any developed democracy with the exception of Australia. A study by the Public Policy Forum reported that just under 10 per cent of MPs elected in 2011 were members of visible minority groups.[27] Women account for just over one in four members of the House of Commons, a figure far below the female share of the population but significantly greater than it was a generation ago.

Why do inequalities like those described in the preceding pages exist? What consequences do they have for Canadian politics and society? These are complex questions that cannot be fully dealt with here. We may, however, suggest some of the elements of their answers. Several factors contribute to inequality, including deliberate discrimination, systemic discrimination, choice, and politics.

Deliberate Discrimination

The prejudice that one person feels towards the members of some other group becomes deliberate discrimination when it is acted upon. For example, the landlord who refuses to rent to someone he suspects of being homosexual is discriminating against that person and by extension against all members of that group. Deliberate discrimination is characterized by the intent to treat the members of some group in an unequal manner. The intent that underlies social prejudice and bigotry is, however, often hard to prove. While this sort of discrimination certainly still exists in Canadian society, and targets the members of some groups more than others, it is probably much less important in explaining inequality than the following three causes.

Systemic Discrimination

This is discrimination without conscious individual intent. It is the discrimination that inheres in

Graeme MacKay/Artizans.com

A person's political concerns and values can be influenced by one's stage of life; many young individuals' concerns shift when they acquire jobs and start families, for example. The political struggles that groups undertake are informed by these shifting values.

traditions, customary practices, rules, and institutions that have the effect of favouring the members of one group over another. For example, in 1999 the British Columbia Human Rights Commission ruled that the section of the province's Highway Act requiring motorcyclists to wear helmets discriminated—albeit unintentionally—against male Sikhs, whose religion requires the wearing of a turban. Another example would be height and/or weight requirements that traditionally have existed for certain jobs. Because women are typically smaller than men, it could be and has been argued before human rights commissions that these requirements are discriminatory unless they can be shown to be legitimately related to the nature of the job. The examples mentioned above merely scratch the surface of **systemic discrimination**. A further example will help to demonstrate just how deeply rooted and even invisible systemic discrimination may be. In our society most people learn that child-rearing is primarily a female function. Despite the significant changes that have occurred in recent decades when it comes to ideas about appropriate gender roles, the assumption of maternal primacy when it comes to the care and nurturing of children is deeply embedded in our culture and social practices. It is even reinforced through the law (how else to explain the fact that 85 per cent of child custody orders in cases of separation and divorce assign sole custody to the mother?). Differences in how males and females are viewed when it comes to the family and children and how they may be treated under the law are influenced by these societal values.

Choice

Individual choice also contributes to inequality. For example, a status Indian who decides to stay on the reserve reduces his or her opportunities of finding a job, and if one does find employment it probably will pay less than a job in the city. Native reserves are usually far from centres of population and economic activity, so an economic cost accompanies the choice of life on the reserve. Likewise, if one decides to live in Cape Breton, northern Ontario, New Brunswick, or many other regions of Canada, there is a greater probability that one will be unemployed or earn less than someone else who went down the road to Toronto or Calgary.

Mobility choices like these are not always easy. A person who grows up in the poverty and deprived environment that characterize most Native reserves may neither perceive nor have much choice about his or her future. Only by applying a rather generous meaning to the word may one conclude that someone from a second-generation welfare family has much individual choice regarding education and future career opportunities. Nevertheless, individuals often can and do find themselves in circumstances where choices are open to them. These choices can be factors that contribute to inequality.

Politics

Debates over equality generally are couched in the rarefied language of rights and justice. The concepts on which they rest may be philosophical and the arguments legalistic. None of this should conceal the fact that these debates are essentially political struggles. Seldom is an individual's or group's claim of unfair or unequal treatment not linked to a demand for action and change. Moreover, the resolution of debates on equality will often be influenced by a sort of pragmatic spirit of compromise. Are there circumstances where some forms of discrimination might be reasonable because they are necessary to protect or promote other values? What forms of inequality should be tolerated and which ones eradicated?

Fairness, justice, and equality are cultural notions. A century ago only a small minority of Canadians regretted that women were without most of the rights taken for granted today. Poverty was once believed to be primarily the fault of the person suffering from it—an explanation that absolved society, the economic system, and governments from blame for the suffering of many whose greatest offence was to be born into the sort of circumstances that make a life of poverty very likely. As values and beliefs change, a society's notions of what is fair may also be transformed.

Value shifts of this sort are almost certain to be accompanied, and influenced, by political struggles. If Canadians are more conscious today of the discrimination that has been practised against the country's Aboriginal peoples it is because of the efforts of Aboriginal groups and their supporters to bring these inequalities to the public's attention and influence government policy. The social policies that redistribute wealth from more affluent to less affluent Canadians did not emerge overnight: they were built up gradually over time in response to struggles between conflicting interests and values. Political parties, interest groups, individuals, and various parts of the state may all be participants in these struggles.

The structure of the state matters too, affecting what sorts of inequalities are dealt with by governments and influencing the opportunities and resources available to different interests. It is likely, for example, that Canadian governments have long targeted more money at regional economic inequalities than have American governments because of the particular division of powers between Ottawa and the provinces under Canada's Constitution and the relatively greater political leverage of provincial governments than of state governments in the United States. To use another example, the entrenchment of the Charter of Rights and Freedoms in the Canadian Constitution has had an enormous impact on the prominence of equality rights issues, the strategies that groups use to achieve their goals, and the treatment of certain groups. The interplay of interests, ideas, and institutions that is politics plays a key role in determining what inequalities get on the public agenda and whose claims succeed.

Quality of Life

The United States, the world's wealthiest society, has one of the world's highest rates of homicide and a drug problem that costs thousands of lives and billions of dollars annually, to say nothing of the enormous misery associated with it. It also has a high rate of alcoholism, many thousands of homeless people, and a high level of marriage breakup (which translates into many single-parent families, usually headed by women, and a high incidence of child poverty), to mention only a few of the social pathologies of that rich society. Racism, urban blight, and the environmental and other costs associated with suburban sprawl are a few of the other dilemmas with which the world's richest country must cope. Canadians often take smug pride in being less afflicted by these problems. But Canada's high standard of living, like that of the United States, is also tarnished by problems that undermine the **quality of life** (QOL) experienced by millions. These problems often become politicized as groups demand that governments take action to deal with them. In some cases government policies are blamed for having caused or contributed to a QOL problem. For example, Native groups and those sympathetic to their demands argue that the appallingly bad quality of life experienced by many Native Canadians is due to unjust and discriminatory policies. While the QOL in Canada is comparatively high, the picture is not uniformly bright for all groups. Aboriginal Canadians, in particular, experience conditions far below what most Canadians would consider decent and acceptable in a society as wealthy as ours.

One way of measuring the QOL in a society is to ask people how happy or satisfied they are. Pollsters have done this for decades. What they find is that Canadians are by and large happy: most of them, most of the time, and in general terms. Interestingly, however, and depending on the survey, they are less likely to say that they are very happy than Colombians or Brazilians, people from countries that are much poorer and where life expectancy is considerably shorter than in Canada or other rich countries.[28] People in comparatively rich countries such as Italy, the United Kingdom, and France report being even less happy with their lives—much less—suggesting that no invariable correlation exists between the happiness of national populations and material well-being.

There is, however, a clear correlation between material well-being and the level of satisfaction with life expressed by a nation's population. Canadians and the citizens of other wealthy countries are more likely to express a high degree of satisfaction with their lives than to say that they are very happy. The 2012 AmericasBarometer survey found that 25 per cent of Canadians said they were very satisfied with their lives, and another 60 per cent said that they were somewhat satisfied. But a persistent and significant minority of Canada's population is not satisfied. Attitudinal data like these tell one nothing about the causes of dissatisfaction or the sorts of problems that actually undermine the QOL in a society. To get at these one must rely on objective measures that may reasonably be construed as reflections of QOL. We will look at mortality, crime, suicide, alcoholism, and destitution.

Compared to other advanced industrialized societies, Canada does relatively well on all of these measures. Its mortality rate of about 8 per 1,000 members of the population and the infant mortality rate of roughly 5 per 1,000 are about average for wealthy democracies. Average life expectancy is about 81 years, 10 years longer than it had been in 1961, at about 79 years for males and 83 years for females.

In terms of violent crime, Canada is unexceptional. Canada's current homicide rate is somewhat below two homicides per 100,000 population, compared to a rate of about five per 100,000 in the United States (2011). Although rates vary marginally

The Social Fabric

BOX 3.3 Why Are Danes the Happiest People in the World?

In April of 2012 the United Nations held the Conference on Happiness, which commissioned the World Happiness Report. The Report concluded that Danes were the happiest people in the world. This was not the first time that Denmark had been ranked the world's happiest place. Among European countries, Denmark has been ranked the happiest by the annual Eurobarometer survey every year since 1973. What is their secret?

The answers vary. Harvard economist Jeffrey Sachs, the director of the 2012 report, says that happiness is produced by a combination of factors. "Political freedom, strong social networks and an absence of corruption," he writes, "are together more important than income in explaining well-being differences. . . . At the individual level, good mental and physical health, someone to count on, job security and stable families are crucial." Political scientist Ronald Ingelhart, director of the World Values Survey, answers the question a bit differently, arguing that Denmark's secret involves a combination of prosperity, democracy, and high levels of social tolerance. Philip Greenspun, a computer science professor at MIT, suggests that one of the key factors is lower material expectations and less of a keeping-up-with-the-Joneses mentality of the sort that characterizes societies where conspicuous consumption leads to greater competitiveness and anxiety.

Before we conclude that the Danes have discovered something we all need to emulate, keep in mind that the populations of countries quite different from Denmark that don't have much in the way of a welfare state or job security, and where political freedom may not be particularly impressive and corruption is common, also score very high in terms of happiness. Mexicans and Colombians always finish towards the top of surveys of national happiness, and neither of these countries has these attributes. It seems, therefore, that there are different pathways to national happiness.

Finally, it may be worth noting that historically the suicide rate in Denmark has been unusually high for an affluent Western country, coming down to about the same rate as in Canada and the United States only in the last several years. Alcohol consumption and abuse, including among teenagers, are higher in Denmark than in most of its European neighbours. Close to half of all Danish marriages end in divorce (a fact that some point to as positively related to happiness, because divorce is very easy and inexpensive in Denmark and females find it easier than in many other countries to combine work and single parenthood). The country's leading film director, Lars von Trier, is a self-confessed depressive whose *oeuvre*, whatever its artistic merits, is quite disturbing. Perhaps, after all, something is rotten in the state of Denmark!

The Social Fabric

BOX 3.4   Is Life Expectancy the Best Indicator for the Health Dimension of Quality of Life?

The life expectancy indicator has sometimes been criticized as placing too much emphasis on quantity of life and not enough on quality of life. To address that issue, the life expectancy report card indicator is complemented by the premature mortality and self-reported health status indicators.

Another indicator often used to account for quality of life is health-adjusted life expectancy, or HALE. HALE is the average number of years a person can expect to live in good health. Instead of considering all years of life as equal, as in the conventional life expectancy indicator, the HALE weights years of life according to health status.

HALE is calculated by subtracting from life expectancy the average number of years in ill-health weighted for severity of the health problem.

In 2007, the most recent year for which HALE data are available, Canada's general life expectancy was 80.7 years, but the average number of years that Canadians could expect to live in full health was 73 years. This means that the average Canadian spends 90.5 per cent of his or her life in good health.

Source: Conference Board of Canada, "How Canada Performs 2012," at: <www.conferenceboard.ca/hcp/details/health/life-expectancy.aspx>. © The Conference Board of Canada

from year to year, the statistics certainly do not support the popular assumption that murders have become more common. Canada's homicide rate has actually declined since the mid-1970s.[29]

Statistics on other violent crimes, such as rape, domestic violence, and assault, are difficult to interpret. This is partly because of changes in reporting procedures that can produce an increase or decrease from one year to the next without there being any real change in the actual incidence of the offence. Changes to the law and public attitudes may also affect crime statistics. For example, rape and domestic assault charges and convictions are dramatically higher today than a generation ago. This increase is mainly due to the greater willingness of victims to come forward, a willingness that results from changed social attitudes and reforms to the law on sexual assault and domestic assault, as well as the use of plea bargains between the Crown and defence whereby those charged agree to plead guilty to at least some charges, receive less severe sentences, and cases do not proceed to the time-consuming and costly (for the state and for the defendant) business of a trial. Comparison between countries is complicated by variations in policing

practices, the definition of offences, and the manner in which crime statistics are collected.

Interpretation problems aside, the data do not suggest that Canada is an exceptionally dangerous place to live. At the same time, the widespread belief that Canada is a much less crime-ridden place than the United States is not supported by the empirical evidence. A 2004 survey of crime victimization in Western democracies found that, with the exception of homicide, victimization rates for other violent offences and crimes against property were not lower in Canada than in the US. (In some cases these rates were even higher in Canada.[30]). The rate of reported burglaries is only slightly lower in Canada than in the United States and is quite a lot higher than in such countries as Japan, Italy, Finland, and Norway.[31] A 2012 survey found that 13 per cent of Canadians and 12 per cent of Americans said that they had been the victim of a crime during the previous year. Canadians and Americans are also about as likely to feel safe in their neighbourhoods, 35 per cent of Canadians and 40 per cent of Americans saying that they felt very safe.[32]

Suicide and alcoholism and other drug abuse are social pathologies that are symptomatic of a low QOL.

Suicide is the tenth leading cause of death among Canadians and the second leading cause of death among young adults, ages 15–34, after accidents and unintentional injuries.[33] As in other countries, the rate of successful suicide is considerably higher among men than women, at about 16 per 100,000 population for men compared to five per 100,000 for women. There is enormous international variation even when levels of national wealth are controlled for, suggesting that suicide is more closely related to culture than level of economic development. For example, Mexico's rate is just over one per 100,000, Italy and the United Kingdom have rates of about five and six per 100,000, respectively, while Japan (20 per 100,000) and Hungary (about 40 per 100,000) have among the highest rates. Canada's rate of about 11 per 100,000 falls in the middle for affluent democracies.

Estimating alcohol and other forms of substance abuse is difficult, but a high level of drug use in a population carries high personal and social costs. The 2004 Canadian Addiction Survey found that 24 per cent of respondents said they had experienced some form of harm from their own alcohol abuse at some point in their lifetime, and 33 per cent said they had experienced some harm during the previous year, ranging from insults and verbal abuse to physical assault, as a result of someone else's alcohol consumption.[34] Alcoholism in Canada is about average for Western industrialized countries and is dramatically lower than in such countries as Hungary, Germany, Italy, and France. Abuse of other non-medical drugs generally is not considered to be a major problem in most of Canadian society, although particular cities, including Vancouver and Toronto, and some isolated Native communities have been well-publicized exceptions. On the whole, the social and economic costs associated with illegal drug use in Canada are probably less than those produced by alcohol and tobacco consumption, although the lack of hard data makes it difficult to reliably assess the costs inflicted on individuals and society by drug abuse.

Advanced industrial societies all have in place a "safety net" of social programs intended to protect individuals and households from destitution. Nevertheless, some people fall between the cracks. When the safety net fails to catch a significant number of those who, for one reason or another, cannot make ends meet, this is surely an indication that the QOL experienced by some people falls below acceptable standards of human decency. Homelessness and the demands placed on food banks are two indicators of holes in the social safety net.

The extent of homelessness is difficult to pin down for the obvious reason that the homeless, unlike those who have a fixed address, cannot be enumerated, telephoned, or otherwise kept track of with any accuracy. Statistics Canada's first attempt to count the homeless came up with the implausibly low figure of 14,145, based on the number of people nationwide sleeping in emergency shelters the night of 15 May 2001. The 2008 Senate report, *Poverty, Housing and Homelessness*, acknowledged the difficulties and did not even attempt to attach a number to this problem. At the other extreme, the Calgary-based Sheldon Chumir Foundation for Ethics in Leadership estimated that in 2005 the number of homeless was somewhere between 200,000 and 300,000, figures widely reported by the media even though their reliability was suspect. Based on various sources of data, a 2013 report of the Canadian Alliance to End Homelessness estimates that about 150,000 persons use homeless shelters each year, a number that does not include street people who do not use shelters, those who use some other shelter such as women's shelters, or the "hidden homeless," who stay with friends or family when they have nowhere else to go.[35] As Canada's largest city, with housing prices that in recent years have been surpassed only by Vancouver, Toronto experiences homelessness on a scale and with a visibility probably greater than elsewhere in Canada. It is not, however, a problem unique to Toronto, Vancouver, or other large cities where the cost of accommodation is relatively high.

The number of Canadians who rely on food banks for part of their needs has also increased. Food Banks Canada estimates that in a typical month in 2012 almost 900,000 persons used food banks in Canada. About half of these users were Ontarians. Only 12 per cent of food bank users were employed. Just over half were on social assistance. Aboriginal Canadians and single-parent families are disproportionately represented among food bank users. There are over 800 food banks in Canada, about 40 per cent of which are run solely by volunteers.[36] Demands on food banks are largely cyclical, increasing during periods of higher than usual unemployment. But a more permanent component to food bank demand appears to have grown in recent years, even when the economy has been expanding and the rate of unemployment has been falling. This component, many argue, is created by the **welfare gap** between the income that social assistance provides and the cost of paying for life's necessities. The width of this gap varies across the country, first, because social assistance benefits are determined by the individual provinces and, second, because of regional variations in the cost of living. But the gap is wide in all provinces (see Figure 3.6). As social assistance benefits fail to keep pace with increases in the cost of living, the demand on food banks inevitably increases. Given the growth in the "normal" use of food banks, an increase in the level of unemployment can push an already strained system to the breaking point.

Homelessness, food banks, and the gap between social assistance and the cost of making ends meet all place the emphasis on neediness and suggest that Canada has a poor record in providing opportunity for those at the lower end of the income scale. Not everyone agrees. Based on Statistics Canada's Longitudinal Administrative Databank, which tracked a cohort of over one million Canadians from 1990 to 2009, Charles Lammam and his colleagues argue that the reality is much more positive than many Canadians believe. "Within the span of a decade," they write, "83 per cent of Canadians initially in the bottom 20 per cent of income earners in 1990 had moved to a higher income group. By 2009 (the last year for which we have data), 87 per cent had moved up. In other words, nearly nine out of 10 Canadians who started in the bottom

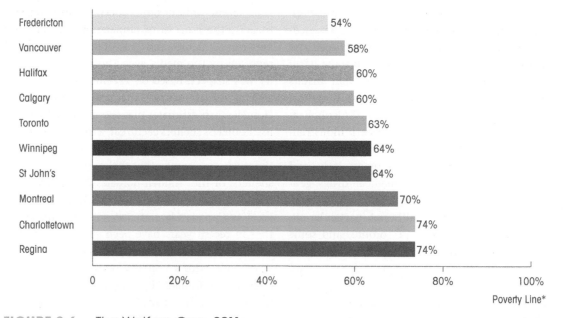

FIGURE 3.6   The Welfare Gap, 2011

*Based on the Market Basket Measure (MBM) used by Statistics Canada and Human Resources and Social Development Canada, for a couple with two children.

Note: The welfare gap is the difference between total welfare income (social assistance benefits, child tax benefits, and federal and provincial sales tax credits) and the Market Basket Measure for each province. It does not take into account the value of welfare benefits such as subsidized accommodation, daycare, dental care, etc. Thus, for example, total welfare income in Vancouver is 58 per cent of the MBM, so that a shortfall of over 40 per cent exists. In Charlottetown it is 74 per cent, with a 26 per cent shortfall.

Source: Based on data from National Council of Welfare, *Welfare Incomes 2011*. Data may be found at: <www.canadiansocialresearch.net/welfare_incomes_2011.htm> and Statistics Canada, at: <www.statcan.gc.ca/pub/75f0002m/2013002/tbl/tbl04-eng.htm>.

20 per cent had moved out of low income 19 years later."[37] As may be seen in Table 3.2, the average income of someone in the lowest quintile in 1990 (in 2009 dollars) was $6,000. This person's income had increased to $38,100 by 2009. The average person in the top quintile in 1990 made $77,200. Twenty years later this person made $94,900. Some people remain stuck at the bottom of the income ladder, of this there is no doubt. But for most, the normal evolution of the life cycle is accompanied by upward mobility. The story that Lammam and his colleagues tell is not one of failure, but of success.

Canada is an affluent society. Its social pathologies are fairly typical of those experienced by other advanced industrial societies. The surrogate measures of the QOL we have examined suggest that the United Nations is certainly right in rating Canada as one of the world's best countries in which to live. But the QOL is sharply lower for one group, namely, Aboriginal Canadians. Consider these facts:

- Life expectancy for Aboriginal Canadians is about seven years less than for the population as a whole. It is particularly low among the Inuit, at 64 years for men and 73 for women, compared to 79 and 83 for all Canadians.[38]
- Infant mortality rates are twice as high among Natives as among non-Natives.
- Native Canadians are three times more likely to die of accidents, violence, or self-inflicted harm than the general population.

- Death due to virtually every major category of disease, including disorders of the circulatory and respiratory systems, infectious and parasitic diseases, and diseases of the digestive system, is more common among Native Canadians—in some cases dramatically so—than in the general population.
- Although less than 4 per cent of the population are Aboriginal Canadians (defined to include Indians, Inuit, and Métis), just under one-quarter of those in prisons are Aboriginal. Native Canadians also comprise almost one-fifth of all murder victims and over one-fifth of all murder suspects in Canada. Aboriginal Canadians are over six times more likely than other Canadians to die as a result of homicide.
- The suicide rate among Aboriginal Canadians is close to three times the Canadian rate. For the Inuit it is about six times the national rate.
- Alcoholism is much more prevalent among Natives than non-Natives. It has been estimated that 50–60 per cent of accidents and deaths among status Indians are alcohol-related.
- Many Aboriginal people live in overcrowded conditions. About one-fifth of Indian dwellings are crowded (defined as more than one person per room), the figure rising to about one-third on reserves. This is several times greater than the Canadian rate.

TABLE 3.2 Average Income of the Same Group of People, 1990 and 2009

		Average Income in 1990 ($2009)	Average Income in 2009 ($2009)	Dollar Increase, 1990 to 2009	Percentage Increase, 1990 to 2009
	Bottom 20%	6,000	44,100	38,100	635
Income	Second	16,500	44,500	28,000	170
group	Third	30,100	47,500	17,400	58
in 1990	Fourth	45,700	60,100	14,400	32
	Top 20%	77,200	94,900	17,700	23

Source: Charles Lammam, Amela Karabegović, and Niels Veldhuis, *Measuring Income Mobility in Canada* (Vancouver: Fraser Institute, 2012), at: <www.fraserinstitute.org/uploadedFiles/fraser-ca/Content/research-news/research/publications/measuring-income-mobility-in-canada.pdf>.

Independence

A democracy requires self-government. This means that public policies affecting the lives of citizens should be taken by people they have elected and who are accountable to them for their actions. The first major step towards self-government in Canada was taken in 1848, when the principle of responsible government was recognized in the colonies of Nova Scotia and the United Canadas (followed by the other British North American colonies soon afterwards). Responsible government meant that the governor, himself chosen by the British Colonial Office, was obliged to select cabinet ministers who were members of the elected legislature. A cabinet without the support of a majority in the legislature would be required to resign.

Self-government advanced another step with Confederation. The British North America Act of 1867 created a new country out of the colonies of Nova Scotia, New Brunswick, and the United Canadas, and transferred to its federal and provincial legislatures the exclusive right to make laws for Canada and its provinces. An enormous step towards self-government was achieved. But this was not the full achievement of self-government because certain powers were withheld from Canadian governments and, therefore, from the voters who elected them. These included:

- *The power to enter into foreign treaties.* Under section 133 of the BNA Act this remained the responsibility of the British government. Treaty-making power was formally transferred to Canada in 1931 by the Statute of Westminster.
- *The power to amend the Constitution.* This also remained in the hands of the British Parliament. The BNA Act that created Canada, and which established the powers of the federal and provincial governments, was a British law. It could only be changed by passing another British law. This situation remained unchanged until 1982, when the BNA Act and all its amendments were patriated and renamed the Constitution Act. Britain's authority to pass laws applying

to Canada was ended and a procedure for amending the Constitution in Canada was established (see Chapter 6).

- *The power to interpret the Constitution.* At Confederation, the highest court for the colonies of British North America was the Judicial Committee of the Privy Council (JCPC). The JCPC was a committee composed of members of the British House of Lords. The BNA Act left intact the JCPC's authority over Canada. This continued until 1949, when the Supreme Court of Canada became the final appellate court for this country and, as such, Canada's constitutional umpire.
- *Citizenship.* Until 1947 there was no Canadian citizenship status that did not involve being a British subject. Residents of Canada who were born in Canada carried a passport that was not identical to the British passport, but that nevertheless declared them to be British subjects. This changed with the passage of the Canadian Citizenship Act, 1947.

Step by step the Canadian state achieved the full powers of self-government that it exercises today. With the passage of the Constitution Act, 1982, the last formal impediment to political sovereignty was removed. But the issue of political sovereignty was not put to rest. Going back to the 1950s and especially the 1960s, Canadian nationalists have argued that the policies and preferences of the United States government have often determined the actions of Canadian governments. Nationalists have also charged that the economic and cultural sovereignty of Canada have often been limited and even violated by American influence. Formal political sovereignty, according to Canadian nationalists, is empty so long as the country's economic and cultural destinies are controlled by others.

In the real world, however, no self-governing democracy is totally independent of external influences. Trade, the movement of people, military alliances and animosities, and contemporary mass media are some of the chief factors that create a web of interdependence between modern societies. Moreover, contemporary thinking on national sovereignty is quite different today, in Canada and in many other societies, from what it was only a few decades ago. Canadians and their political leaders are much more open to the idea of limitations on a country's sovereign right to act as it wishes, limitations that result from participation in treaties and multilateral organizations dealing with climate change, human rights, land mines, the law of the sea, and so on. The question is not, therefore, whether political life in Canada or in any other country is unaffected by influences from outside. Instead, the real question is whether the nature and extent of these external influences are such that they undermine what might be considered a reasonable level of political independence.

If one looks at Canada's economic relations with the rest of the world, both historically and today, there is no denying our enormous dependence on foreign sources of investment capital, imports, and

markets for Canadian exports. Some of the main features of Canada's international economic relations are listed in Box 3.5.

This dependence must, however, be put into perspective. Several advanced industrial democracies, including the Netherlands, Belgium, Sweden, and Germany, and the European Union as a whole, rely on trade for a greater share of their GDP than does Canada. The European Union imposes considerably greater limitations on the policy-makers of its member states than the Canada–United States Free Trade Agreement and the North American Free Trade Agreement (NAFTA) impose on Canadian and American governments. What is unique about Canada is the extent to which our trading relations depend on a single partner, i.e., the United States. Among advanced industrialized economies, only Japan comes close to this level of dependence on a

Governing Realities

BOX 3.5 Canada's Economic Links to the World

Past . . .

- Much of the money used to build the roads, railways, and canals of Canada's early commercial economy was borrowed from foreign, mainly British, investors.
- At Confederation, Canada was already heavily in debt to foreign investors.
- It is estimated that about 450 American companies had established subsidiaries in Canada by 1913.
- By the 1920s, the United States surpassed Britain as the major source of foreign investment in Canada.
- The level of foreign ownership in Canada peaked in 1971 at 37 per cent of corporate non-financial assets. The level was close to 60 per cent for manufacturing industries.

Present . . .

- The Canada–US trade relationship is the largest in the world, involving $742 billion in goods and services in 2012. (China–US trade is next and closing fast, at about $560 billion in 2012.)
- Canada has long been the single largest supplier of energy to the United States. About 90 per cent

of Canadian energy exports are destined for the American market.

- Foreign investors, mainly American, control about one-fifth of corporate non-financial assets in Canada. American ownership is much higher in the oil and gas, mining, and manufacturing sectors. Over half of all American investment in Canada is located in Ontario.
- About one-third of Canada's GDP comes from trade. In 2011, roughly two-thirds of Canadian trade in goods and services was with the United States (about 70 per cent of our export trade and 61 per cent of import trade).
- Canada went from being a net importer of investment capital to a net exporter around 1996. As of 2011, the estimated market value of foreign direct investment in Canada was $607 billion, 54 per cent of which was American investment. The market value of Canadian direct investment abroad was about $684 billion, 40 per cent of which was in the United States. Canada is one of the top 10 sources of foreign investment in the United States economy.[39]

single trading partner.

In terms of investment, Canada remains heavily dependent on foreign capital. But this dependence has weakened over the last couple of decades and American share of all foreign ownership in the Canadian economy has declined. At the same time, Canadian investment abroad—and therefore our penetration of other economies—has increased. Indeed, as a result of the increasing globalization of business and investment, Canada has come to look more and more like several other advanced industrial economies in terms of its level of foreign ownership. Again, however, Canada is rather unique in the degree to which it remains dependent on a single source of foreign investment, i.e., the United States. Whether this matters has long been a controversial subject and is one that is examined in Chapter 17.

Culturally, Canada, especially English-speaking Canada, has always lived in the shadow of the United States (see Box 3.6). Physical proximity, a common language, and shared values have facilitated the flow of cultural products—books, magazines, films and DVDs, television programs, music recordings, computer software—between the two countries. Economics has ensured that this flow has been mostly from the United States to Canada. This is because of the much greater domestic audience/readership available to American producers, which enables them to produce high-quality mass-appeal products that are attractive to advertisers. Advertising revenue is the main or sole source of income for most privately owned media businesses (films, compact discs, DVDs, video games, and books are the chief exceptions). It just makes economic sense for Canadian broadcasters to buy a product that is demonstrably popular with viewers, at a cost that is a fraction of what it would be if the same sort of program, with the same advertising budget, stars, writers, and production team, were to be produced in Canada.

The result has been predictable. American-made films, television programs, video games, popular music, magazines, and social media spill over into Canada's English-language market. In fact, they dominate all of these Canadian markets. American books also do very well in the English-Canadian market, with authors like Danielle Steele, Stephen King, Sophie Kinsella, Dan Brown, and James Patterson featuring on the best-seller lists both north and south of the border. Newspapers, a mass medium that has been in steady decline for years, are the main exception to the rule of American dominance. This is because of provisions in Canada's Income Tax Act that heavily favour Canadian-owned newspapers and because, for most people, daily newspapers are primarily sources of local information.[40]

Let us return to our initial questions. Is Canada's political independence undermined by the country's economic dependence on the United States and by the enormous influence of American mass media in English Canada? In what ways? Is the Canadian predicament so different from that faced by many other industrialized democracies in today's interdependent world?

The answer to the first question is clearly "yes." Canadian policy-makers, at all levels, must be sensitive to the actions and possible reactions of governments in the United States. Moreover, many of the public policy matters they deal with, from transboundary pollution to interest rates, are affected by circumstances in the United States, circumstances over which Canadians and their governments can exert little, if any, control. Canada's economic and cultural linkages with the United States affect us in too many ways to be listed here. That roughly 70 per cent of our export trade is with the United States obviously means our economy will be highly vulnerable to the state of the American economy and to changes in the exchange rate between the Canadian and American dollars. Our heavy diet of Hollywood films and American television and magazines and our reliance on an Internet dominated by American websites certainly affect the images and ideas in our heads. To the extent these American cultural imports erode distinctively Canadian values (whatever these may be, or might have been), one may argue they also erode the cultural basis for a Canadian society and public policies different from those of the United States.

Faced with a challenge from a larger, more powerful economy and from industries of mass culture that lay waste to domestic competition, governments may choose to respond with protectionist policies. They attempt to insulate domestic industries or local culture from foreign competition through import restrictions, subsidies to domestic producers, regulations affecting business practices and cultural industries, and so on. Canadian policy-makers have resorted to all of these measures, as have policy-makers elsewhere. To cite but one example, Canadian broadcasting policy is determined largely by the rules the Canadian Radio-television and Telecommunications Commission (CRTC) imposes on television and radio. The CRTC establishes and enforces a dense thicket of regulations governing Canadian content and these regulations have a very simple bottom line: to ensure that more Canadian music and television programming reaches the airwaves than would be the case if market forces were allowed to operate without restriction.

But the real question is whether the Canadian "dilemma" is so different from that of many other countries. After all, Hollywood's *Transformers: Age of Extinction, X-Men: Days of Future Past, Teenage Mutant Ninja Turtles,* and *Guardians of the Galaxy* were the box office hits of 2014 throughout much of the world, just as they were in North America. All world top-grossing films have been American for about three decades. McDonald's restaurants span the globe, so much so that the standardized cost of a "Big Mac" is used by the respected business newspaper, *The Economist*, as a measure of the cost of living in different countries. At the beginning of 2013 about 5,500 of Starbucks' 18,000 stores were located in just under 50 countries outside of North America. There are over 4,000 KFC locations in China alone, bringing American-style eating habits to the world's most populous country. The US-dominated Internet, direct broadcast satellites, the cable news networks, international credit cards, and the multinational corporations have shrunk the globe, so that no country is free from some other's cultural or economic incursions. Is Canada really such a special case?

The answer to this question will inevitably be

Media Spotlight

BOX 3.6 The Long Shadow of American Culture

- About two-thirds of television viewing time in English Canada is spent watching American programs. This increases to about 90 per cent in the case of drama and comedy viewing time.
- During a fairly typical week in mid-March 2013, 27 of the 30 most-watched television programs in English Canada were American. The exceptions included a *Hockey Night in Canada* telecast, a CTV evening news program, and an episode of the CBC's *Murdoch Mysteries*. In contrast, none of the 30 highest-rated programs in the French-language market for that week were American (www.bbm.ca).
- The Canadian and American cinema markets are, for the most part, treated as one by film producers, distributors, and advertisers.

- Canada's feature film and television production industries depend on a life-support system of government subsidies, channelled through the Income Tax Act and Telefilm Canada, and through the production activities of the Canadian Broadcasting Corporation and National Film Board. These same forms of support are provided by Quebec government agencies to francophone television and film producers in that province. Despite this, few genuinely Canadian films reach the feature film market in English Canada. French-language films produced in Quebec do better in that segment of the Canadian market, but even there the top-grossing films are mainly American.

coloured by one's own values. How much dependence on another economy is too much? Is dependence on what is still the world's leading economy preferable to a more diversified trade profile with other economies? And anyway, this sort of diversification cannot simply be willed into being. It requires policies that may impose domestic costs on some groups and alienate Canada's major trading partner. Has Canada had much choice over its history but to rely on the British economy and then the American economy?

On the cultural front, if most Canadians prefer American films, television programs, magazines, and music over homegrown alternatives, should their governments interfere? It stretches credulity to suggest that protectionist measures like the Canadian content quotas imposed on broadcasters are a response to audience demands. Obviously they are not. And anyway, what are the differences in Canadian culture that policy-makers want to preserve? Does protectionism preserve these values, or just the industries that depend on the state's cultural life-support system?

All countries are subject to external influences that limit the independence of their elected governments. Canada is not unique in this regard. Nevertheless, one may fairly say that these influences are felt somewhat more powerfully in Canada than in most other countries. In the twenty-first century a self-governing democracy does not require, or at least can hardly expect, the freedom from external influence that nationalists argue would be desirable for Canada. If it did, then none of the members of the European Union would qualify! An element of anti-Americanism—a dislike of American culture, institutions, and, especially, public policies—certainly contributes to the Canadian nationalist critique of American influence. These nationalist arguments are based on an outdated ideal of national autonomy that bears increasingly little resemblance to today's world of interdependent states.

Starting Points for Research

Conference Board of Canada, *How Canada Performs,* at: <www.conferenceboard.ca/hcp/default .aspx>. A report card on a wide range of social and economic indicators, based on data mainly from 2000 to 2010.

Julie McMullin, *Understanding Social Inequality: Intersections of Class, Age, Gender, Ethnicity, and Race in Canada,* 3rd edn (Toronto: Oxford University Press, 2014). A widely used textbook that explores the complex relationships among various dimensions of inequality in Canada.

James J. Rice and Michael J. Prince, *Changing Politics of Canadian Social Policy,* 2nd edn (Toronto:

University of Toronto Press, 2013). Places the development of social policy in a historical context, including an understanding of how globalization has affected the role of the state.

Raghubar D. Sharma, *Poverty in Canada* (Toronto: Oxford University Press, 2012). A finely grained analysis of how and why poverty is more prevalent among some groups in Canada than among others.

Statistics Canada, at: <www.statcan.gc.ca/start -debut-eng.html>. Springboard to census and National Household Survey data on various characteristics of Canadian society. Click on headings found under "Browse by subject."

Review Exercises

1. What are the characteristics of the richest 1 per cent of the Canadian population? You may want to start with the information at: <www.cbc.ca/news/canada/who-are-canada-s-top-1-1.1703321>. To what degree do gender, class background, education, and ethnicity affect the likelihood of getting into the top 1 per cent?

2. How much food bank use is there and how many homeless people are in your community? How would you go about finding answers to these questions? (Suggestions: Call a member of your city or town council and ask for the names of persons or organizations that operate food banks and shelters. Alternatively, you might call your local office of the United Way or a religious organization like the Salvation Army to ask about these matters.)

3. How would you define poverty? Calculate a monthly budget for a single person—including expenditures for food, shelter, clothing, transportation, and entertainment—that you think is the minimum necessary to ensure a decent standard of living. What annual income is necessary to maintain this standard of living? Ask a friend or family member to do the same exercise (don't give him or her any hints about your own calculations).

4. Who are the most influential people in your town or city? Make a list of the 10 most influential people. Once you have put together your list, think about why you have included these particular people. Are they politicians? Business people? Journalists? Activists? Labour leaders? In each case, what is the basis for their influence and who is able to hold them accountable for their actions?

4

Diversity and Multiculturalism

Diversity is both a part of the social reality of Canada and one of the leading values associated with Canadian politics. In this chapter we examine the politics of diversity in Canada, paying special attention to issues of multiculturalism and equality. Topics include the following:

- The changing ethnic character of Canadian society.
- Increased awareness of diversity.
- The institutionalization of diversity.
- The political representation of ethnic groups.
- Other models of integration and accommodation.
- The economic integration of immigrants.

Francesco Perilli's "Monument to Multiculturalism" depicts a man aided by doves joining two meridians of the globe. The statue, presented to the city on its sesquicentennial, stands in the square outside Toronto's Union Station. As Canadian society continues to become more diverse, there is a need to reflect the experiences and issues of all Canadians in public institutions such as schools and the political arena nationwide. (© Rudy Sulgan/Corbis)

Over the last generation respect for diversity has joined equality and freedom as one of the core values of Canadian politics. Indeed, many would go so far as to say that it has become *the* pre-eminent Canadian cultural trait, the quality that more than any other defines Canada and how our society and political life are different from those of other countries, but particularly from the United States. Canada is, as former Prime Minister Joe Clark once put it, "a community of communities." Canadians, we are often told, are united by their differences. This claim appears to be at least paradoxical and possibly even contradictory. What it means, however, is that tolerance, respect, the recognition of group rights, and a belief in the equal dignity of different cultures are central to the Canadian ethos. Indeed, the very idea that there is such a thing as a Canadian ethos is comparatively recent, emerging at the same time as this image of Canada as the pluralistic society par excellence and a model of cultural coexistence.

This image of Canada is not without its ironies and skeptics. Foremost among the ironies is the fact that separatist sentiment in Quebec—support for which is far from extinguished—challenges this rosy picture of Canada as a model of cultural coexistence. On the skeptical side, many people maintain that the diversity-centred image of Canada, and policies and institutions based on it, does more to undermine Canadian unity than strengthen it. Others question whether multicultural democracy can work at all, in Canada or elsewhere, except in special circumstances. They note the resurgence of ethnicity-based nationalism in the modern world and the breakup or instability of many countries that combine different cultures within their borders.

Ironies and skepticism aside, there is no denying that the politics of diversity has moved to the centre of Canada's political stage in recent decades. The evidence ranges from official recognition of multiculturalism in the law and under the Constitution to occasional controversy over the impact of recent immigration on Canadian society. While diversity is nothing new in Canada—Canadian society has always been pluralistic and the official recognition of group rights goes back at least as far as the 1774 Quebec Act, under which the British authorities recognized the religious rights of French Canadians—the idea that it should be recognized, protected, and even promoted through the actions and institutions of the state has existed for only the last couple of generations.

In this chapter we will examine the politics of diversity and the policy of multiculturalism in Canada. The issues that will be examined include the following:

- how Canada's population characteristics have changed over time;
- the ways in which diversity politics has been institutionalized in state institutions and policies;
- controversies associated with the Canadian multicultural experience and comparisons to policies in other pluralist democracies.

From Founding Nations to Multiculturalism: The Changing Ethnic Demography of Canada

The Canada we know today was built on two premises: the displacement and marginalization of Aboriginal Canadians and the settlement and development of the land by European immigrants. Not only were the vast majority of the immigrants who settled in Canada during the country's formative years European, they were overwhelmingly of French and British Isles origins. Many of the latter came to Canada via the United States in the wave of Loyalists and non-Loyalists who left America during the three decades after the War of Independence. The languages they established in Canada were mainly French and English. With very few exceptions their religion was Christian, either Roman Catholic or Protestant. For much of Canada's history they would be referred to without hesitation as the founding nations or **charter groups**, the founding partners in the Canadian enterprise. One was French-speaking and Catholic and the other English-speaking and mainly Protestant.

At the time of Confederation the virtual monopoly of those of French and British ancestry on Canadian public life was symbolized in the partnership of John A. Macdonald, the leading English-Canadian advocate of an independent Canada, and George-Étienne Cartier, the major spokesperson for French Canada. The first Canadian government under Macdonald did not include anyone who was *not* a member of these so-called charter groups (not to be confused with today's Charter groups!). This image of Canada as a partnership—albeit an unequal one—of two European charter groups survived well into the twentieth century. It was not until the 1960s and, more specifically, the work of the Royal Commission on Bilingualism and Biculturalism (the B&B Commission) that the two-nations image of Canada experienced any serious competition. Spokespersons for non-French and non-British groups in Canada argued that this image of Canada and the policies that were based on it excluded them from the Canadian picture. These groups were, in the main, also representative of Canadians of European origin. Ukrainian spokespersons, for example, were prominent among those who were critical of the two-nations, bicultural image of Canada. The demands of these dissenting groups stopped well short of equality of status with English and French for their groups and languages. What they demanded and won was official recognition of Canada as a *multicultural society*, not a bicultural one. This was achieved through the 1971 passage of the Multiculturalism Act and the creation of a new federal Ministry of State for Multiculturalism. Today, the role and responsibilities that began in 1971 fall under the rubric of the Department of Canadian Heritage.

The image of Canada as a sort of New World extension of two European peoples and their value systems was being challenged by some Canadian intellectuals during the 1960s. John Porter's influential book, *The Vertical Mosaic*,[1] drew attention to the stratified nature of Canada's pluralistic society, in which English Canadians dominated virtually all of the important elites and controlled the channels of recruitment into them. The picture he painted was of a Canada in which influence, status, and wealth were held disproportionately in the hands of one of Canada's two charter groups and where the members of other groups were largely blocked from access to the opportunities monopolized by Anglo-Canadians. This situation, Porter argued, was inconsistent with the democratic values of openness, socio-economic mobility, and equality preached by Canadian politicians and believed in by the general population. His analysis of the systemic inequality and discrimination that characterized Canadian society would provide much of the inspiration for a generation of social critics who, unlike their predecessors, did not take for granted the domination of the British charter group and the exclusion of increasing numbers of Canadians from an image of Canada as consisting of two peoples, the French and English.

The challenges launched by intellectual critics such as Porter and by the groups that wanted the biculturalism in the B&B Commission to be replaced with multiculturalism would not have had much of an audience or impact had it not been for the changes to Canada's population characteristics that were well underway by the 1960s. These demographic changes have accelerated since then, presenting even greater challenges to older notions of Canadian pluralism than those first launched in the 1960s. To put it simply, the share of Canada's population with neither French nor British Isles ethnic origins has increased quite dramatically. Immigrants from Eastern and Southern Europe became increasingly important within Canada's overall immigration picture between the 1950s and 1970s. They have been joined in recent decades by increasing numbers of non-European immigrants, many of whom come from non-Christian cultures.

Prior to the 1981 census Canadians were asked to indicate a single ethnic origin. The 1871 census, Canada's first, reported that 61 per cent of the population was of British Isles ancestry, 31 per cent of French ancestry, and only 8 per cent of other ancestry, mainly other European countries of origin and Aboriginal Canadians (3 per cent). The 1971 census found that the non-French and non-British European ancestry share of the population had increased significantly to over one-fifth of the population. Those of British and French ancestry continued to dominate, however, at 44 per cent and 29 per cent of the population, respectively. The ethnic ancestry picture is now much more complicated, but also more realistic, now that Canadians are able to report multiple ancestries. In 1991, 28.9 per cent of Canadians reported multiple ancestries, increasing to 42.1 per cent in 2011. Just over half of all Canadians claim British Isles origins as at least one of their ancestries. The proportion claiming French ancestry has fallen to only about one in six Canadians, a much lower figure than the percentage of those who have French as their mother tongue. This may be explained by the fact that many French Canadians, and indeed many Canadians, give simply "Canadian" as their ethnic origin. Indeed, in the 2011 National Household Survey just under one-third of the population gave "Canadian" as their sole ethnic origin or one in combination with some other ancestry. About 15 per cent of Canadians claim an Asian ancestry, alone or in combination with some other ethnic origin.[2]

The changes in Canada's ethnic demography are seen most strikingly in the largest metropolitan areas, magnets for new immigrants. It is here that new Canadians of neither British nor French

ethnic origins have been drawn and where the **visible minority** population has increased significantly in recent years (see Figure 4.1). In fact, Statistics Canada has projected that visible minorities, which already accounted for 47 per cent of the population of the Greater Toronto Area and 45 per cent of Greater Vancouver in 2011, will comprise close to 60 per cent of the population of each of these metropolitan areas by 2031.[3]

Change in the ethnic distribution of Canada's population has been brought about by shifting patterns of immigration. For most of Canada's history the major sources of immigration were Europe and the United States. In recent years the leading sources of immigration have been Asian countries, including China, Pakistan, India, and the Philippines (Statistics Canada includes the Middle East under Asian immigration). Immigration from Africa, the Caribbean, and Latin America has comprised a much greater share of total immigration than was the case before the 1970s. Whereas just under 95 per cent of all immigrants to Canada before 1961 were born in Europe or the United States, that figure was only 22.3 per cent for the period 1991–2001 and fell to about one in five of those who

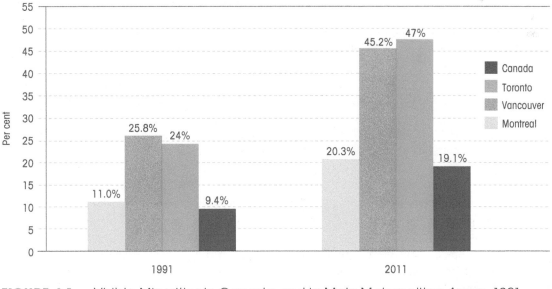

FIGURE 4.1 Visible Minorities in Canada and in Main Metropolitan Areas, 1991 and 2011

Source: Statistics Canada, *Canada's Ethnocultural Portrait: The Changing Mosaic*, Catalogue no. 96F0030XIE2001008; Statistics Canada, *Immigration and Ethnocultural Diversity in Canada*, National Household Survey, 2011.

immigrated between 2001 and 2011. Immigrants from Asia, the Middle East, Africa, Latin America, and the Caribbean, who together accounted for only 5.5 per cent of all immigrants prior to 1961, grew to about 77.5 per cent of all immigration during the 1991–2001 decade and about three-quarters for the years 2001–11. The dramatic change that has taken place in the sources of immigration to Canada may be seen in Figure 4.2.

Canada remains, even after recent waves of immigration from non-European countries, a predominantly Christian society. As Figure 4.3 shows, about two-thirds of Canadians claim an affiliation with either the Catholic Church or a Protestant denomination. This is down from all but a sliver of the population at the time of Confederation and even represents a considerable drop since 1971, about the time the profile of Canadian immigration began to shift away from traditional European sources. This decline in the percentage of the population claiming a Christian religious identification has been due chiefly to a sharp increase over the last generation in the number of people without a religious affiliation. As of 2011, they constituted 24 per cent of the population. People belonging to non-Christian religions continue to constitute a rather small minority, at about 9 per cent of the

population. Their presence in particular cities, however, such as Sikhs and Hindus in Vancouver and Muslims, Hindus, and Buddhists in Toronto, is much greater than it is nationwide.

The growth of the non-European and non-Christian elements of Canadian society has not been entirely free from tensions and unease on the part of some (see Box 4.1). Most people appear to be accepting of the changes taking place in their society, but a 2004 survey of Canadians' attitudes towards cross-cultural and interracial marriage found that a significant minority of the population is uneasy with the idea of their children mixing with members of certain groups.[4] Reservations were greatest in the case of marriage to Muslims, Pakistanis or East Indians, and blacks, in that order. Older Canadians are much more likely to express disapproval of marriage with members of these groups than are younger Canadians. For example, 47 per cent of respondents aged over 60 said that they were not very or not at all comfortable with the idea of their child marrying a Muslim, compared to 24 per cent of those aged 18–29.

Interestingly, the region of the country where disapproval of marriage to Muslims was highest was Quebec, where 43 per cent—compared to the national figure of 35 per cent—said they were

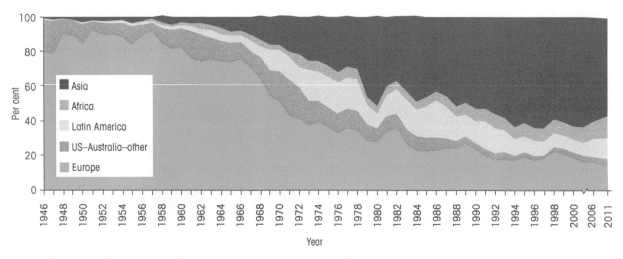

FIGURE 4.2 Place of Birth of Immigrants, 1946–2011

Source: Roderic Beaujot, "Effect of Immigration on Demographic Structure," discussion paper no. 02-09 (Oct. 2002), at <www.sociology.uwo.ca/popstudies/dp/dp02-09.pdf>; Statistics Canada, "Immigration in Canada: A Portrait of the Foreign-born Population, 2006 Census," Figure 2, *Census of Canada,* 2006; and Statistics Canada, *Immigration and Ethnocultural Diversity in Canada,* National Household Survey, 2011.

not very or not at all comfortable with such marriages. Quebecers were also slightly more likely (33 per cent vs 27 per cent) to disapprove of their children marrying Pakistanis. Subsequent surveys have confirmed this difference between Quebec and other provincial populations.[5] These results do not seem to fit with the idea of Quebec as one of the most open and tolerant regions of the country. The explanation may have to do with the perception that these groups are less likely than others to integrate into Quebec's majority francophone society or, perhaps, that these groups are less likely

Governing Realities

BOX 4.1 The Kirpan, Religious Freedom, and Canadian Multiculturalism

Beliefs and behaviours that are unfamiliar may or may not generate controversy. The fact that many Canadians of Ukrainian, Russian, and Serbian ancestry are members of the Orthodox Church and celebrate Christmas and Easter several days after the dates of these statutory holidays is probably unknown to many Canadians. Once known, most people will be indifferent. They might not be indifferent, however, if members of the Orthodox Church demanded forms of public recognition for their religious holidays, such as the right to a paid holiday.

Something of the sort was at issue in 2001 when a young Sikh male attending public school in British Columbia was told that he could not bring his kirpan to school. The kirpan is a metal ceremonial dagger that Sikh males are required to wear at all times after being baptized. It symbolizes religious loyalty. The parents of the boy in question were told by the school authorities that he would be permitted to wear a kirpan made of wood or plastic, some material that would eliminate or at least reduce its capacity to be used as a weapon. His parents refused, arguing that their son's religious freedom, guaranteed by the Charter, was violated by the school board's policy. Eventually the dispute reached the Supreme Court. In March 2006 the Court ruled that the wearing of a kirpan in schools for religious reasons is indeed protected by the Charter.

This case was about both religious freedom and multiculturalism. Indeed, the two values are intertwined, as the court said in its ruling:

Religious tolerance is a very important value of Canadian society. If some students consider it unfair that G may wear his kirpan to school while they are not allowed to have knives in their possession, it is incumbent on the schools to discharge their obligation to instil in their students this value that is at the very foundation of our democracy. A total prohibition against wearing a kirpan to school undermines the value of this religious symbol and sends students the message that some religious practices do not merit the same protection as others. Accommodating G and allowing him to wear his kirpan under certain conditions demonstrates the importance that our society attaches to protecting freedom of religion and to showing respect for its minorities.[6]

Canadians are overwhelmingly supportive of multiculturalism in principle, but in practice their tolerance for accommodating difference has not always matched this support. As noted above and demonstrated in January 2011, this might be especially true in Quebec, where four members of the World Sikh Organization, who had been invited to testify before a legislative committee examining a proposed law on reasonable accommodation of ethnic minorities, were denied entry to Quebec's National Assembly because they wore kirpans. As one of the four, Balpreet Singh, said: "Unfortunately, we weren't allowed to enter because we wear the kirpan, which is a bit ironic because we were here to speak upon the issue of accommodation and we weren't accommodated."[7] Within weeks, the members of Quebec's National Assembly voted unanimously to ban the wearing of the Sikh ceremonial dagger from the province's legislative buildings.

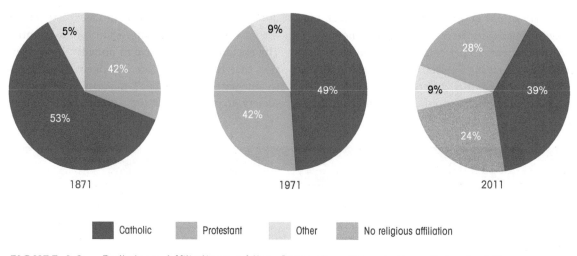

FIGURE 4.3 Religious Affiliations of the Canadian Population, Selected Years

*The "Other" category for 2011 includes other Christians (2.6%), Christian Orthodox (1.6%), Muslim (2%), Jewish (1.1%), Buddhist (1%), Hindu (1%), and Sikh (0.9%).

Source: F.H. Leacy, ed., *Historical Statistics of Canada*, 2nd edn (Ottawa: Minister of Supply and Services Canada, 1983); Statistics Canada, National Household Survey, 2011, Data Tables.

than others to respect the idea of gender equality that Quebecers embrace more firmly than other Canadians.

A 2010 survey found that Quebecers are not more likely than Canadians in Ontario and Alberta, and only slightly more likely than their fellow citizens in Manitoba and Saskatchewan, to be opposed to racially mixed marriages.[8] This

seems to support the argument that religion, in particular Quebecers' greater tendency to believe that Muslims are unlikely to integrate into Quebec society, rather than race explains Quebecers' more likely objection to marriage with Muslims. This explanation is supported by the data in Table 4.1, which shows that Quebecers and French-speaking Canadians, most of whom reside in Quebec, are

TABLE 4.1 Percentage Who Feel That Identity Is Threatened When the Turban, Hijab, or Kippa Is Seen

I feel my identity is threatened when I see people wearing a turban, hijab, or kippa.	Total (n = 1,503)	Regions		Language		
		Quebec (n = 403)	Rest of Canada (n = 1,100)	English (n = 922)	French (n = 402)	Other (n = 168)
Total agree	32%	46%	27%	27%	52%	22%
Strongly agree	15%	23%	12%	12%	25%	11%
Somewhat agree	17%	23%	15%	15%	27%	11%
Total disagree	60%	48%	64%	66%	44%	63%
Somewhat disagree	22%	22%	21%	20%	24%	24%
Strongly disagree	39%	26%	43%	46%	20%	39%
Don't know / Refusal	7%	6%	9%	7%	4%	15%

Source: Association for Canadian Studies, *Soccer & Turbans*, 14 June 2013, at: <www.acs-aec.ca/en/social-research/?limit=10&start =70&csort=&order=#?limit=10&start=0&csort=&order=>.

considerably more likely than other Canadians to say they feel threatened by outward signs of certain cultural differences.

Along with greater diversity in the ethnic, religious, and racial composition of Canada, the demographic picture has become more recognizably varied in other ways, too. These include family composition, sexual orientation, and disability.

Families. Families tend to be smaller today than they were a generation ago and considerably smaller than they were two generations ago. There are many more single-parent families than in the past (today, roughly one out of every six families) and many more couples who choose not to marry (over 10 per cent of all couples nationally, ranging from a low of about 7 per cent in some provinces to 20 per cent in Quebec).[9] Same-sex couples are more numerous than in the past, although precisely how much more so is impossible to say as virtually no data were collected on such matters until recently.

Sexuality. There probably is no reason to assume that the ratio of those who are heterosexual, compared to those who are gay/lesbian, has changed significantly over time. What has changed, however, is the willingness of non-heterosexuals to proclaim openly their sexuality and the readiness of a growing number of Canadians to accept this in many, if not all, circumstances. Consequently, sexual diversity is much more apparent today than was the case when social pressures and the law discouraged all but a small number of non-heterosexuals from "coming out."

Times have changed, as the hundreds of thousands who annually line the streets and march in Toronto's Gay Pride parade attest. Canada has openly gay politicians, some of its churches ordain and marry homosexuals, and human rights codes and court interpretation of the Charter prohibit discrimination based on sexual preference. This is not to imply that this aspect of Canadian diversity is no longer controversial. These matters continue to divide Canadians. The struggle over the legal definition of marriage as excluding same-sex unions was seen by many as the last major legal barrier to the equality of gays and lesbians with heterosexuals. This struggle was waged in the courts and in the court of public opinion. As recently as a decade ago polls showed that only about 25 per cent of Canadians supported same-sex marriage. Court rulings followed by legislation passed by Parliament in 2005 extended full legal status to same-sex marriages. Since then public opinion has changed quite dramatically. Polls taken in the last couple of years show that about 60 per cent of Canadians support same-sex marriage and fewer than 20 per cent disapprove strongly.[10]

Disability. According to statistics, a greater proportion of the population is disabled today than at any point in Canada's history. Health Canada reports that about one in eight Canadians claims to experience either a mental or physical disability. But as in the case of sexuality, it is doubtful whether the actual incidence of Canadians suffering from various forms of disability is greater today than in the past. What has changed, however, is both our society's ideas about what constitute disabilities and the legal definition of what counts as a disability for purposes of pensions, workers' compensation, social assistance, employment, housing, and other matters. The recognition of disabledness has increased and, moreover, has become one of the diversity criteria used by governments in making public policy.

Official Recognition and the Institutionalization of Diversity

Multiculturalism was given its own minister—albeit a minister of state, which is a rung down from a departmental minister—in 1972. But the official recognition of groups of Canadian citizens according to their group characteristics and the institutionalization of diversity go back much further. We have already mentioned that the Quebec Act of 1774 represented the first official confirmation of the status and rights of a particular segment of the population, in this case French-speaking Catholics. But the distinction of "first" probably ought to be conferred upon the Royal Proclamation of 1763. This document recognized the presence and rights of "the several Nations or Tribes of Indians with whom we are connected, and who live under our protection." Aboriginal Canadians were recognized by the Proclamation as distinct rights-bearing peoples under the protection of the British Crown. This relationship continues to the present day—although the Canadian government long ago assumed the obligations that originally belonged to Britain—perpetuated and institutionalized through the Indian Act and s. 35 of the Constitution Act, 1982, which embeds the treaty rights of Aboriginal peoples in Canada.

There is, therefore, a long history of recognizing diversity in Canada. But until the 1960s that recognition extended principally to the French- and English-language communities (s. 133 of the Constitution Act, 1867), the Catholic and Protestant religions for schooling purposes (s. 93 of the Constitution Act, 1867), and Aboriginal Canadians. This changed as a result of the emergence of feminism as a political force in the 1960s and 1970s and the increasing popularity—first among some elites, spreading later to the general population—of multiculturalism and group-oriented thinking about rights.

Leslie Pal argues that the institutionalization of diversity in Canadian public life was leveraged during the late 1960s and throughout the 1970s and 1980s by the activities of a small organization, the Citizenship Branch, within the Department of Secretary of State (SOS).[11] The grants disbursed by the Citizenship Branch through its Official Language Minority Group, Women's Program, and Multiculturalism section helped finance thousands of organizations that, in time, made group-related policy demands on government, raised the profile of diversity issues, and reinforced the idea that government should be protecting and promoting group interests. SOS played a pivotal role in financing diversity advocacy. "Measured in dollars," Pal concludes, "the programs were insignificant. Measured in increased tolerance for minorities and women, they were at best marginally successful."[12] But their enduring significance, Pal argues, was to help reshape the structures of government and the relationship of the state to groups of citizens in ways that institutionalized diversity.

This process of recognizing and promoting diversity did not stop at SOS. Human rights commissions at both the federal and provincial levels have

played an important role in expanding the concept of minorities. The earlier emphasis on language, religion, and ethnic origins has had to compete in recent years with such non-racial and non-cultural forms of minority status as gender, sexual orientation, dependence on alcohol and drugs, and social conditions. Human rights commission officials, as R. Brian Howe and David Johnson argue, have been at the forefront of the movement to extend the recognition of diversity through expanding the number of rights-bearing groups. They write:

> By providing education about rights, and by publicizing the existence of a system of rights protection, human rights programs and institutions politicized Canadian society in the direction of making demands for wider rights. Rights consciousness and awareness of human rights commissions encouraged more and more groups to pressure for more and more rights. The result was a steady expansion of human rights protections, the entrenchment of human rights legislation, and the institutionalization of human rights commissions, embedded in an increasingly politicized society in which rights-conscious human rights interest groups demanded ever-wider rights.[13]

At the federal level, the activities of the Canadian Broadcasting Corporation, including its Aboriginal language broadcasting operations, the National Film Board, and Telefilm Canada all have contributed to the public projection of images of Canadian society that reflect the diversity of the country's population and history. The Department of Canadian Heritage has inherited the functions pioneered by the Citizenship Branch of SOS, providing grants to an enormous array of groups and operating as the leader within government for the promotion of Canadian pluralistic identity. For example, in the 2012–13 fiscal year Canadian Heritage disbursed close to $1 billion to hundreds of groups and projects, ranging from small one-time grants, such as $40,000 over two years for Toronto-based Africa New Music and $34,300 to the Vancouver International Bhangra Celebration towards the cost of a festival, to expensive ongoing grants such as those to the YMCA of Greater Toronto, TV5 Monde (an international French-language broadcaster), and provincial departments and agencies that spend the money on cultural and diversity activities.[14] At the same time, much of what Canadian Heritage supports is not tied to specific ethnic and cultural communities. It provides money for athletic organizations such as the Canadian Soccer Association and cultural activities such as the Canadian Opera Foundation, as well as special events and celebrations such as those associated with the 200th anniversary of the War of 1812. In fact, the balance of spending by Canadian Heritage has clearly shifted in the direction of activities not linked to particular ethnic and cultural communities, representing quite a change from the priorities of its predecessor department, the Department of Multiculturalism and Citizenship (1991–6).

Diversity and Political Representation

The 1878 cabinet of Sir John A. Macdonald had 14 members. All but one were born in Canada. About 80 per cent (11 of 14) had British Isles ethnic origins and the others were of French ancestry. All were either Catholic (4 of 14) or Protestant.

The 2013 cabinet of Stephen Harper was not as different from Sir John A.'s government as one

Ingrid Rice/© Simon Fraser University

Ujjal Dosanjh served as the thirty-third premier of British Columbia from 2000 to 2001 and was a Liberal MP from 2004 to 2011, serving the riding of Vancouver South. His receipt of the Pravasi Bharative Samman, the Expatriate Indian Honour for persons of Indian origin demonstrating excellence across the world, speaks to his achievements in Canada, where visible minorities have not historically been proportionately represented in the political elite.

might have expected. Of its 38 members, only a couple (Bal Gosal and Alice Wong) were born outside of Canada. About three-quarters had French or British ethnic origins and most of the others had European ancestry. The religious affiliation of MPs is today more difficult to ascertain from public records than it was in the past, but only a handful of the members of cabinet may have had a non-Judeo-Christian religious affiliation. It is probable that some had no religious affiliation. On the whole, however, the demographic composition of Harper's 2013 cabinet was arguably more similar to than different from the Macdonald cabinet of 1878, except in one striking respect. The Harper government

Media Spotlight

BOX 4.2 Little Mosque on the Prairie

Canadians who live in the Greater Toronto Area, Vancouver, Montreal, Windsor, or several other larger urban centres are aware that Muslims are part of the Canadian mosaic. Mosques, Islamic schools, traditional Islamic dress, and the controversies that inevitably accompany cultural difference, even in a society with a long history of cultural pluralism, are among the visible signs of this religious community. But a mosque and Muslims in small-town Saskatchewan?

This was the setting for the CBC's weekly situation comedy, *Little Mosque on the Prairie*, which ran between 2007 and 2012. The incongruity of a Muslim community in a small prairie town, which does not appear to have had much experience with visible or religious minorities, gives the locale an edge that multicultural Toronto would not have. The premise of the show was straightforward: Muslims are different in terms of their religious beliefs and practices, and some of these differences spill over into lifestyle differences, but these differences are insignificant compared to the values they share with other Canadians. While these differences provided the grist for the misunderstandings and minor conflicts in each week's episode, in the end everything always worked out. Indeed, the Muslims in this small town seemed remarkably like other Canadians in most important ways. In one episode a Muslim female is shown playfully slapping her husband's bottom, a gesture that most viewers might imagine is frowned on by traditional Muslim standards of female modesty but seems very equality-of-the-sexes. The give-and-take between traditional and more liberal versions of Islam was, in fact, one of the program's leitmotifs.

The program was launched at a time when the issue of what sort of accommodations should be made to cultural minorities, including Muslims, was increasingly part of the public conversation in Canada. It enjoyed considerable popularity during its first season, although the program's ratings slipped subsequently. Nonetheless, the concept caught the attention of television producers in the United States, where Fox Television announced in June 2008 that it would produce an American adaptation of the show. This did not happen. Indeed, a reality program called *All American Muslim*, set in Dearborn, Michigan, and shown on TLC, was cancelled after one season. During its short run the program was at the eye of a storm when a major retailer decided to pull its advertising in response to complaints from the Florida Family Association and other groups. Whether this gave Fox pause about a *Little Mosque* adaptation is not clear.

During its five-year run *Little Mosque on the Prairie* had an impact far beyond what its rather modest ratings might have suggested. It was discussed in the media in countries throughout the world, including the United States, France, Finland, the UK, and South Africa. It has been widely discussed by academics who study diversity and the cultural portrayal of and integration of Muslims into Western societies.[16] Reaction to the program among Muslims in Canada and elsewhere was mixed. In some ways the program was, as many commentators have remarked, simply a Muslim-Canadian version of *The Cosby Show*, using humour to show that cross-cultural differences are not as scary as many imagine and are, in any case, resolvable. This is, of course, a very Canadian message.

included 12 women and one Aboriginal Canadian, whereas Macdonald's included none.

Fifty years ago John Porter remarked that Canada's political elite was still dominated by males from the two charter groups. Members of these groups continue to be disproportionately represented, at least if we define the political elite rather narrowly to include only the federal cabinet. In the late 1950s John Diefenbaker appointed to cabinet Canada's first female minister, Ellen Fairclough, and first non-charter group Canadian, Michael Starr, of Ukrainian origin. Canada's first Jewish member of cabinet was Herb Gray, appointed in 1969. But despite the election of increasing numbers of candidates from non-Judeo-Christian backgrounds over the last couple of decades, relatively few have been promoted to cabinet. People claiming non-European ancestry (although sometimes in combination with Canadian or European ancestry) account for close to one-quarter of the population but continue to be under-represented at this highest level of the federal government.

The situation is not different in the case of the judicial elite and the highest ranks of the federal bureaucracy. If we look at the 83 individuals who have been members of the Supreme Court since its creation, all but a handful have had British or French ethnic origins and all have had Judeo-Christian backgrounds. The same, broadly speaking, is true of the ranks of deputy ministers in Canada. The main change to have occurred in both of these elites is the increased presence of women.

By bringing attention to the continuing dominance of these elites by persons of the French and British ancestry, we are not suggesting that this indicates discrimination against those who come from other backgrounds. A couple of qualifying factors need to be taken into account. First, it takes time for demographic change to work its way through to the top of a political system. Most of the increase in the non-European ancestry share of the Canadian population has occurred since the 1970s. It is rare for one to become a member of one of the elites examined above before the age of 40, and most are in their fifties and sixties. As the size of the pool of Canadians of non-European ancestry with the qualifications and other attributes

necessary to become a member of one of these elites increases, we might expect to see more of these persons selected.

Second, the relevance of ethnicity and our ability to pigeonhole someone in a particular group have become increasingly problematic. Growing numbers of Canadians have mixed ethnic origins and a considerable share of the population now rejects the traditional ethnic identities, preferring to describe their origins as Canadian. Consequently, it may be more accurate to say that the political, judicial, and bureaucratic elites in Canada are dominated by persons of French, British, *and* Canadian origins. Those of non-European ancestry continue to be under-represented, but as their numbers increase in law schools, MBA programs, and professions from which these elites are likely to recruit, there is reason to imagine the gap will close. A recent study from the Greater Toronto Area, Canada's most ethnically diverse metropolitan community, indicates that for visible minorities, at least, progress up this ladder has been slow.[15]

Other Models of Integration and Accommodation

Canada is a very diverse society. But whether it can claim to be the world's most diverse and accommodating society is moot. The percentage of Canada's population born outside the country is greater than that of any other G8 country and surpassed among affluent democracies only by Australia (Figure 4.4). Among the world's major cities, Dubai and Brussels have larger foreign-born populations than either Toronto or Vancouver, although it is fair to point out that in both of these cases most of the foreign-born are there for reasons related to work and have no intention of becoming citizens. Close to six out of 10 residents of Miami were not born in the United States and such cities as New York and Sydney, Australia, are not too far behind Canada's major metropolitan areas in terms of their foreign-born populations.

Measuring diversity is a tricky business. The size of the foreign-born population is, obviously, a rather

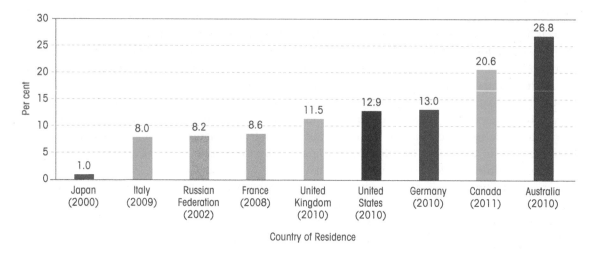

FIGURE 4.4   Foreign-born Population as a Percentage of the Total Population, G8 Countries and Australia

Source: Statistics Canada, *Immigration and Ethnocultural Diversity in Canada*, National Household Survey 2011, 7.

crude measure. One might argue that if almost all of the foreign-born come from countries that share the same language and the same general culture, which is true of the foreign-born Latino population in Miami, that this represents less diversity than a case like Toronto, where there is no single dominant language or cultural community within the city's foreign-born population. Demographers are quick to point out that ethnic diversity is not the same as cultural diversity. But ethnically and culturally, Canada is always towards the top of developed countries in rankings of diversity. The Harvard Institute for Economic Research[17] and the Center for Transnational Studies at the University of Bremen[18] provide confirmation of this.

The Canadian model of multiculturalism represents one possible regime for the accommodation and recognition of the ancestral cultures of minorities, including their languages and religious beliefs. Other models exist and it would probably surprise most Canadians to learn that some Western democracies have taken group recognition and the protection of cultural rights considerably further than in Canada. Table 4.2 shows a range of models for the accommodation and recognition of

Listen to the "Reasonable Accommodation of Cultural Differences" podcast, available at: www.oupcanada.com/Brooks8e

minority cultures. At one end is what we might call *deep diversity multiculturalism*, represented by the Netherlands until about a decade ago. At the other end of the spectrum is *integration without major or official accommodation*, as found in France. Between these extremes fall Canada and the United States. Quebec has its own rather different regime of integration and accommodation that also falls between these extremes. The Canadian version of multiculturalism is towards the middle of this scale in terms of the degree to which the state is obliged to protect and promote minority cultures and identities.

The Dutch Experiment with Deep Diversity Multiculturalism

To understand how multiculturalism is viewed by a particular society and why certain institutions and policies exist, one needs to examine the historical circumstances and demographic conditions of that society. In the case of the Netherlands, increasing wealth and a shortage of unskilled labour led to an increase in immigration during the 1970s. "Guest workers"—immigrants who were not given citizenship rights and who were expected to return to their countries of origin after a certain number of years in the Netherlands—arrived from Morocco and Turkey, along with non-European immigrants from former Dutch colonies. They were followed by refugees from Sri Lanka, Iran, Iraq, and Somalia in the 1980s and 1990s and by the relatives of Moroccan and Turkish workers already living in the Netherlands. This influx of non-European immigrants took place against the historical backdrop of World War II and the Holocaust, and a sense of what has been called "Dutch guilt." This involves a widespread feeling, the Anne Frank story notwithstanding, that the country's population did not do enough to resist the Nazi occupation and the deportation of Dutch Jews. Therefore, the adoption of multiculturalism, mainly in the 1990s, was inspired by a constellation of factors. It was, in a sense, compensation for what was seen as a failure to stand up for minorities during the Nazi occupation. It was also a practical response to a labour market situation where guest workers were expected to return to their countries of origin eventually, so providing them and their children with education and public services in their own languages, and in various ways making it unnecessary for these immigrants to integrate into Dutch society, appeared to make sense. But the policy also accorded with the liberal politics that was ascendant among Western intellectuals and was particularly strong in secular, tolerant Holland.

TABLE 4.2 Models of Cultural Accommodation

	Deep Diversity Multiculturalism	Interculturalism	Official Multiculturalism	De Facto but Contested Multiculturalism	Universalism with Skeptical Acceptance of Some Aspects of Multiculturalism
Characteristics	• Allows and encourages groups to maintain their languages, religions, and identities • Provides public support for schools, religious organizations, community centres	• Advocates the official recognition of minority cultures and state measures to protect their rights and sustain their practices and beliefs	• Allows and even encourages the retention of minority cultural identities through state support for cultural organizations, heritage language instruction, inclusion in state symbols, ceremonies, etc.	• Allows for the retention of minority cultural identities with some state support • Opposed by some as divisive	• Discourages the official recognition of group cultural identities • The public space and state institutions are based on a universal set of values and a single national identity
Guiding principles	• "The larger society is obliged to support the institutions symbolizing and sustaining the identity of the majority."*	• Mutual respect between the cultural majority and minorities and a willingness from both sides to accommodate the other and adapt	• Minority cultures deserve respect and recognition • Based on concept of reasonable accommodation	• Cultural pluralism is positive, but citizens should be encouraged to share a common civic identity	• Pragmatic recognition of culture minorities exists • Cultural minorities should be discouraged from retaining separate identities and should be encouraged to identify with the universal values of the society
Countries	• The Netherlands during the 1990s, until roughly 2004	• Recommended for Quebec by the Bouchard-Taylor Commission, 2008	• Canada	• United States	• France

*Paul Sniderman and Louk Hagendoorn, *When Ways of Life Collide: Multiculturalism and Its Discontents* (Princeton, NJ: Princeton University Press, 2007), 5.

The result was a multicultural regime based on a principle that the Canadian philosopher, Charles Taylor, has called "deep diversity." It involves the idea that in a pluralistic society no single national identity is possible or even desirable without depriving some minority or minorities of equal status, recognition, and dignity. Taylor argues that different communities can belong to a country in different ways and that competing loyalties are not necessarily destabilizing for a society. This ethos underpinned the Dutch experiment with multiculturalism. Paul Sniderman and Louk Hagendoorn summarize the results as follows:

In the Netherlands, as much as can be done on behalf of multiculturalism has been done. Minority groups are provided instruction in their own language and culture; separate radio and television programs; government funding to import religious leaders; and subsidies for a wide range of social and religious organizations; "consultation prerogatives" for community leaders; and publicly financed housing set aside for and specifically designed to meet Muslim requirements for strict separation of "public" and "private" spaces.[19]

In short, Dutch multiculturalism went considerably beyond the Canadian model in the extent to which it supported and promoted minority cultural identities.

Although diagnoses of what went wrong vary, there is a general consensus that the Dutch model failed. The fact that immigrant communities were not integrated into the wider Dutch society—on the contrary, the incomes of Muslims, Turks, and Moroccans remained the lowest in the country—permitted a situation to develop where members of these groups saw themselves, and were seen by the majority group, as being *in* the country without being *of* the country. A 2013 study by the Netherlands Institute for Social Research found that social contact between white native-born Dutch and the country's main immigrant groups had diminished over the preceding 17 years.[20] The strong electoral showing of anti-immigration parties in the 2007 and 2010 Dutch elections led some to dismiss the rejection of the country's multiculturalism regime as the intolerant reaction of the xenophobic right. But this was far from the entire truth. Liberal intellectuals also have become disillusioned with multiculturalism and increasingly question whether their country's large Muslim minority is willing to accept such values as freedom of speech, gender equality, and tolerance of diverse lifestyles that are embraced by the liberal intelligentsia and, indeed, by most of Dutch society.

American Multiculturalism: Contested Institutionalization

Canadians, conditioned as they often are to believe that the United States is an assimilationist melting pot that actively discourages immigrants from retaining their ancestral cultural identities, are likely to be perplexed by the suggestion that there is any sort of multiculturalism regime in that country. In fact, however, the main difference between Canadian and American multiculturalism may be that in Canada it is enshrined in law and the Constitution and has become, since the 1970s, a central aspect of the story that Canadians tell themselves and others about who they are and what they are about culturally. Not coincidentally, this narrative serves the culturally and politically important function of establishing a frontier of difference between Canada and the United States.

What public authorities across the United States do to protect and in some ways even to promote minority cultural identities is not very different from policies and programs in Canada. Laws providing rights to public services in languages other than English—Spanish, for the large Latino population in the United States, but other languages, too—are common across the country. In California, the code governing state services requires that state agencies employ persons who speak minority languages, provide interpreters for non-English-speaking citizens needing state services, and offer information about government services in minority languages. In practice, the minority language usually is Spanish, but the law does not limit this requirement to Spanish and services in many other languages are provided by some agencies. Most states offer driver examinations in foreign languages, many of them in multiple languages. New York is one of many states that provide publicly paid interpreters for all litigants and witnesses in both criminal and civil law proceedings.

When it comes to the incorporation of minority ethnic identities and cultures into their public life, Americans can hardly be said to lag behind Canadians. There may be less celebration of diversity in the institutions and activities of the US federal government than in Canada, but many state and local governments across the United States, as well as community activities that do not depend on government funding and initiatives, extensively recognize and celebrate ethnic diversity. An important difference is that there is less agreement in American society that multiculturalism—which usually is referred to as "diversity"—is a good thing. In Canada the idea of multiculturalism is widely accepted. In the United States it is a hot-button issue that divides liberals from conservatives. Moreover, there has been much more willingness in the United States, from researchers and not just ideological warriors, to consider the possibility that the official recognition of diversity may generate conflict and impede the economic progress of the recognized minorities.[21]

The area of American life where multiculturalism is most evident, institutionalized, and contested involves the country's educational system. Ethnic studies exploded onto American university campuses at the end of the 1960s. Even the most casual perusal of curricula, programs, and research centres in American higher education shows that diversity education is at least as pervasive in that system as in Canada. In words that most Canadian educators would find comforting and familiar, the curricular guidelines created for the National Council for Social Studies state:

> Multicultural education helps students understand and affirm their community cultures and helps to free them from cultural boundaries, allowing them to create and maintain a civic community that works for the common good. Multicultural education

seeks to actualize the idea of *e pluribus unum* within our nation and to create a society that recognizes and respects the cultures of its diverse people. . . . A unified and cohesive democratic society can be created only when the rights of its diverse people are reflected in its institutions, within its national culture, and within its schools, colleges and universities.[22]

On the other hand, in May 2010 the state legislature of Arizona passed a law prohibiting courses in public schools that "advocate ethnic solidarity instead of the treatment of pupils as individuals." Arizona is not alone in having passed such measures. Clearly, the institutionalization of ethnic studies has not gone unchallenged.

Although Americans are less likely to embrace multiculturalism as an idea and see it as a defining characteristic of their society, their attitudes towards cultural minorities and immigrants are not, in some important respects, very different from those of Canadians. A 2011 survey by the German Marshall Fund reported that almost two-thirds of Americans agreed that it would be a very good or somewhat good idea to allow people to immigrate to the United States if they spoke English fluently and had a good chance to fit in smoothly with the country's culture. A majority, 55 per cent, agreed that immigrants enriched the national culture.[23] Canadians may be somewhat warmer to immigration and the contributions that minorities make to the national culture: a 2010 survey found that three-quarters agreed that "Canada's cultural life is enriched by people with different cultural backgrounds than the majority."[24] But it would be a mistake to imagine that Canadians, unlike Americans, do not harbour doubts about the willingness of newcomers to integrate into their society (see Figure 4.5).

France: Where Multiculturalism Exists But Is Not Officially Embraced

When you step out of the exit of Paris's Gare du nord train station you immediately see that the capital of France is a place where races and cultures meet. But they do not always mix. If you take the

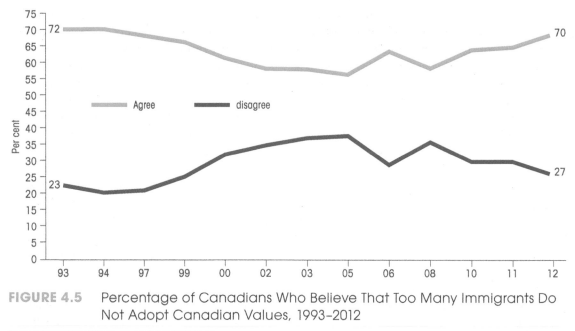

FIGURE 4.5   Percentage of Canadians Who Believe That Too Many Immigrants Do Not Adopt Canadian Values, 1993–2012

Source: Environics Institute, *Focus Canada 2012*, 46.

metro to the city's perimeter, where *les banlieux* (the suburbs) begin, you immediately sense that Paris is a highly segregated place. In Montreuil, for example, at Paris's eastern edge, the vast majority of the population is non-white and a significant portion is Muslim.

What percentage is non-white and what percentage is Muslim? No one knows for sure because French law prohibits state authorities from asking people their race, ethnicity, or religion. This prohibition exists because the official ideology of the French state, enshrined in the constitution, is based on universalist values of *liberté, égalité, et fraternité* (freedom, equality, and social solidarity). These values are at the heart of the French civic identity. Along with the French language they define what it means to be French.

Like many other countries of Western Europe, France has become culturally more diverse as a result of non-European immigration over the last several decades. The most reliable statistics show that just over 10 per cent of the population is foreign-born. Immigrants from France's former colonies in Africa and elsewhere have arrived in large numbers, some originally as guest workers, some as refugees, some because they had a right to residence

and citizenship in France as a result of their colonial relationship to the métropole, and others illegally. Today it is estimated that about one-tenth of the French population is Muslim. The official ideology enforced by the state sees only citizens, regardless of their skin colour, religion, and ethnic ancestry. But the reality of French society is multicultural. And in response to that fact the state has grudgingly and to a limited degree provided some recognition of the existence and importance of minority cultural identities. It has done so within the framework of a classically liberal approach, focusing on cases of discrimination on the basis of ethnic origin, race, religion, and so on. The Haute autorité de lutte contre les discriminations et pour l'égalité is the key institution in this regard, operating much as a human rights commission does in Canada.

Tensions between the evolving multicultural reality of French society and the universalist ideology of the state have been increasingly evident in recent years. In the autumn of 2009 the government of President Nicolas Sarkozy launched what it called *le grand débat sur l'identité nationale*, creating a commission and soliciting input from individuals across the country. The idea that France, of all countries, would create a commission to study the *problem* of national identity would have been unthinkable a couple of decades earlier. Although some dismissed the national identity initiative as a politically motivated attempt to pander to the prejudices of right-of-centre voters, this interpretation ignores the widespread unease, cutting across the French ideological spectrum, regarding what are seen as challenges to the principles of gender equality and secularism in France. The debate about national identity was, in fact, a debate about the compatibility of Islam—or some forms of Islam—and the French civic culture.

Two of the measures taken by the French government, and widely supported by the French public,

included what might be called "citizenship-values contracts" for newcomers (*le contrat d'accueil et d'intégration*) and a ban on the wearing of the burqa and the niqab in public places (schools, government offices, public transportation, etc.). It should be said that France was not alone in enacting such measures. Citizenship-values contracts were also mandated in Germany, the Netherlands, the United Kingdom, and several other Western European democracies and have been advocated by the Parti Québécois for newcomers to Quebec. Likewise, laws banning face veils exist in Belgium and at the regional and local levels in a number of European countries.[25]

CP Images/AP Photo/Bob Edme

For 20 nights beginning on 27 October 2005, civil unrest gripped the suburbs of Paris and other parts of France. In riots that saw the burning of just under 9,000 vehicles and nearly 3,000 arrests, the tensions that had been building among the country's youth population—particularly those from impoverished ethnic neighbourhoods—exploded. Media reported that discrimination against immigrants and French society's negative perception of practising Muslims may have played a role in inciting the riots.

Quebec: Multiculturalism, Interculturalism, or Something Else?

Since the 1960s, when the preference of immigrants for the English language caused Quebec demographers to predict, and nationalist spokespersons to fret, that the French language and distinctive culture of Quebec would be placed under increasing pressure, immigrants have been an important part of the debate about language and cultural policy in Quebec. For decades, Quebec's birth rate has been below the level needed to reproduce the population. Immigration has long been crucial for population and labour market growth, as is also true in the rest of Canada. And as is true of the rest of Canada, the sources of immigration to Quebec have shifted from Europe to other parts of the world. According to the 2011 National Household Survey, about two-thirds of immigrants in Quebec came from countries outside of Europe and the United States. The figure is close to 80 per cent among those who immigrated between 2006 and 2011. Africa, Asia, the Middle East, and the Caribbean have become major sources of immigration to the province.

The debate in Quebec has shifted somewhat from the impact of immigrants on the French language—after all, many of these immigrants come from former French colonies and speak French—to the integration of newcomers into Quebec culture and society. Tensions in the province were crystallized in the highly publicized case of Hérouxville, a small town 180 kilometres north of Montreal, whose local government adopted a declaration of cultural standards that newcomers were expected to respect.[26] These standards were targeted mainly at what the town councillors believed to be typical forms of Muslim behaviour, stating that immigrants were unwelcome in their community of less than 2,000 if they covered their faces, carried weapons to school (a reference to the Sikh kirpan), practised genital mutilation, stoned or burned women to death, and so on. The furor that the publication of this code of behaviour incited—the story was widely covered throughout the world, including in France, Great Britain, and the United States—eventually led the Quebec government to appoint a consultative commission on "reasonable accommodation," under the leadership of philosopher Charles Taylor and sociologist Gérard Bouchard.

In the eyes of some, their report seemed to recommend that the Quebec government and Quebec citizens adopt a form of multiculturalism within the province rather similar to that which has been embraced by the federal government for decades. The report's reception was not enthusiastic. Most French-speaking Quebecers, and not simply the folks in Hérouxville and communities like it, felt that the emphasis in the Bouchard-Taylor report leaned too far in the direction of accommodation and openness to change on the part of old-stock Québécois—sometimes called *les québécois de souche*—and not enough on the need for newcomers to adapt and accept not only the language of the French majority, but their culture and mores as well (see Box 4.3).

What the Bouchard-Taylor report recommended was called **interculturalism**. This was proposed as an alternative to the Canadian multicultural regime, about which Quebecers are more skeptical than their compatriots in the rest of the country. Multiculturalism is about accommodating the different values and practices of minorities. It imposes an obligation of tolerance on the majority, if, in fact, a "majority" even can be identified in such a pluralistic society. Indeed, some would argue that the concept of multiculturalism, as it has evolved over time and as Canada's many minority communities have increased in number and size, does not recognize the idea of the majority but simply many different cultures and peoples. Interculturalism, on the other hand, as explained by the Bouchard-Taylor Commission, is about reconciliation and mutual adaptation on the part of both the dominant majority and minorities: both sides must be prepared to make cultural concessions. Quebec, historically and today, has a clearly identifiable majority population; urban Canada, especially outside Quebec, increasingly does not.

Quebec nationalism has always been uneasy with the Canadian concept of multiculturalism, which is often seen to be in competition with the notion that Canada ought to be viewed as a partnership between two founding peoples, one French-speaking and the other English-speaking. The separatist Parti Québécois argued that the emphasis of interculturalism on compromise and mutual adaptation sidesteps what for most Quebecers is the real problem: the protection and preservation of their French identity. "It is not necessary to be born here to be part of our collective journey," said PQ leader Pauline Marois, "but you have to get on the train."[27] The provincial government distanced itself from the Bouchard-Taylor report and very little has been done to implement its ambitious and extensive recommendations.

As in the case of France, Belgium, and some other Western European countries, Quebec introduced legislation that would deny public employment and government services to women wearing face coverings such as the burqa or the niqab. This policy has the support of the Quebec Council on the Status of Women and the Muslim Canadian Congress, although it is opposed by such Muslim associations as the Canadian Islamic Congress and is clearly contrary to the spirit of the Bouchard-Taylor Commission. "Multiculturalism is not a Quebec value," said Louise Beaudoin, the Parti Québécois's designated spokesperson for secularism. "I think a lot of the onus is being placed on us, telling us how we have to accept this and that. It seems to me a

Politics in Focus

BOX 4.3 The Bouchard-Taylor Report and Its Political Reception

Our deliberations and reflections have firmly convinced us that integration through pluralism, equality and reciprocity is by far the most commendable, reasonable course. Like all democracies in the world, Québec must seek to reach a consensus against a backdrop of growing diversity, renew the social bond, accommodate difference by combating discrimination, and promote an identity, a culture and a memory without creating either exclusion or division.

Source: From *Building the Future: A Time for Reconciliation*, the report of the Bouchard-Taylor Commission on Reasonable Accommodation, p. 241.

Quebec's Premier Jean Charest responded immediately to the report and its recommendations.

No society can succeed by withdrawing or turning in on itself. Our nation and economy can only grow by continuing to welcome others.

Immigration is not a right. Immigrating to Quebec is a privilege. And welcoming immigrants is a responsibility shared by all Quebecers.

There is a line to be drawn between the two. Quebecers have every right to decide the kind of society we want to live in. We have values that are not negotiable, and those values come with responsibilities.

As Premier of Quebec, I assume the supreme responsibility of protecting and promoting the French language. New Quebecers and members of cultural communities must speak it. The language is a meeting point for minorities and the majority.

As citizens, we must also respect the personal convictions of each individual. And for its part, the state, which serves all members of society, must affirm the secular nature of our institutions.

Today, I am announcing that the actions of my government, as inspired by the Bouchard-Taylor Commission, will:

- Reinforce francization prior to the arrival of immigrants.
- Provide for a signed statement by potential immigrants committing to the common values of our society.
- Develop a mechanism to help decision makers handle questions of *accommodation* while respecting the secular character of our institutions.
- I am also asking members of the National Assembly to collaborate in adopting Bill 63, which would amend the Charter of Rights and Freedoms to affirm the equality of men and women.

Source: From a speech by Premier Jean Charest, 22 May 2008, at: <www.premier-ministre.gouv.qc.ca/salle-de-presse/discours/2008/mai/2008-05-22-en.shtml>.

different question should be asked and it should be asked of the people who absolutely insist on wearing either the burqa or the niqab, or the kirpan in the National Assembly."[28]

The issue of accommodation versus adaptation, which is central to the Bouchard-Taylor notion of interculturalism, arose again in 2012–13 in a highly publicized controversy over whether young soccer players should be allowed to wear turbans. A virtually identical controversy had roiled the waters of Quebec politics several years earlier, involving the wearing of the Muslim veil on the soccer pitch. In both cases the attitudes of Quebecers and French-speaking Canadians were quite different from those of Canadians in the rest of Canada and English-speakers. Quebecers and French-speakers were much more likely to support a ban on these forms of dress on the playing field. A Léger Marketing poll taken in the spring of 2013, when the turban controversy was national news, found that 87 per cent of Quebecers agreed that an athlete should not be permitted to modify his or her equipment for religious reasons. The Parti Québécois minority government introduced its controversial Charter of Quebec Values on 10 September 2013, but was defeated in the April 2013 provincial election before the province's National Assembly could vote on it. Despite criticism of the Charter from the Liberal Party of Quebec, after winning the election the Liberals proceeded to introduce quite similar legislation banning Muslim face veils in the public sector, including schools, as well as the chador, which exposes the face. It also proposed to amend the Quebec Charter of Human Rights to include mention of the religious neutrality of the state and to create a hierarchy of rights in which gender equality would take precedence. All in all, the Liberal government's proposals appeared to be quite similar to those of the defeated PQ government.

Immigration and Economic Integration

Immigration has long been a crucial factor contributing to the growth of Canada's population. At various points in the country's history more people have left Canada than have entered, but the balance over time has strongly favoured immigration over emigration (see Table 4.3). As the fertility rate in Canada has fallen over the last several decades to the current rate of about 1.6 (the population replacement rate is 2.1), immigration has become crucial for population maintenance and growth.

We have seen that the sources of immigration to Canada have changed dramatically since the 1970s. This is partly due to the fact that several of the European countries that previously had been major sources of immigration were becoming more affluent. Economics has always been a main driver of population migrations, with people fleeing impoverished circumstances and moving towards places they believed would provide them and their families with a better life and more opportunities. The economic recovery and increasing affluence of Western Europe in the decades following World War II reduced the incentives for people to leave for Canada, the United States, and Australia, all of which were main destinations for European immigrants.

But another factor contributing to the change in the pattern of immigration to Canada was the reform of immigration law. Prior to the 1960s the law had discriminated in favour of European nationals and essentially held the door wide open to immigrants from the United Kingdom. Moreover, immigration policy actively discriminated against certain non-European groups at various points in Canada's history, notably against Chinese immigrants beginning in 1885 through the imposition of a head tax. The tax began at $50 per person but increased 20 years later to $500. The head tax was abolished in 1923 and replaced with a ban on Chinese immigration that was not repealed until 1947.

The Immigration Act, 1967 eliminated racial discrimination and ethnic favouritism and established a points system that has been used since then. Immigrants who apply under the economic category—the law also recognizes family reunification and refugee status as grounds for immigration, as well as business-class immigrants who bring capital and entrepreneurial skills—receive points for their level of proficiency in one or both of Canada's official languages, years of formal education, years of work experience, age (most points are awarded to those between 20 and 50 years of age), having arranged employment in Canada, and adaptability (this includes having family already in Canada and a number of other factors). Canada is not the only country to use such a point system. Australia and New Zealand, countries that like Canada have relatively high levels of immigration, also use this system (see Box 4.4). Immigrants who arrive under the points system are much more likely than family-class immigrants or refugees to have the education, language skills, and job-related qualifications that enable them to integrate more quickly into the labour force and the Canadian middle class (see Figure 4.6). Language proficiency, which is linked

in subtle and not so subtle ways to familiarity with cultural norms in the host society, is a key factor affecting employment prospects and earnings. Immigrants who mainly or always use a language other than French or English at work are essentially trapped in a lifetime of much lower incomes.[29]

In view of the criteria that need to be met to qualify as an economic-class immigrant, it is not surprising that these new Canadians tend to be more educated than Canadian-born citizens of the same age. But education, professional certification, and years of work experience abroad do not necessarily produce easy entry into the Canadian labour force, at least not right away. A longitudinal study of immigrant employment in Canada found that about 90 per cent of prime working-age immigrants (25–44) who arrived in the economic

TABLE 4.3 Net Immigration* and Contribution to Population Growth, Canada, 1851–2011

	Population (at end of period)	Immigration	Average Immigration (% of population)	Emigration	Contribution to Population Growth
1851	2,523,000				
1851–61	3,230,000	352,000	1.22%	170,000	23.0%
1861–71	3,689,000	260,000	0.75%	410,000	–32.6%
1871–81	4,325,000	350,000	0.87%	404,000	–8.5%
1881–91	4,833,000	680,000	1.49%	826,000	–28.7%
1891–1901	5,371,000	250,000	0.49%	380,000	–24.2%
1901–11	7,207,000	1,550,000	2.46%	740,000	44.1%
1911–21	8,788,000	1,400,000	1.75%	1,089,000	19.7%
1921–31	10,376,700	1,200,000	1.25%	970,000	14.5%
1931–41	11,506,700	149,000	0.14%	241,000	–8.1%
1941–51	14,009,400	548,000	0.43%	379,000	7.9%
1951–61	18,238,200	1,543,000	0.96%	463,000	25.5%
1961–71	21,962,082	1,429,000	0.71%	707,000	21.7%
1971–81	24,820,382	1,429,000	0.61%	636,000	28.6%
1981–91	28,030,864	1,381,000	0.52%	490,000	27.7%
1991–2001	31,048,284	1,881,000	0.64%	428,000	48.2%
2001–11	31,613,000	2,456,133		464,765	57%

*Net immigration equals total immigration minus total emigration for each period.

Roderic Beaujot and Deborah Matthews, "Immigration and the Future of Canada's Population," Table 1, 30 Jan. 2000, at: <www.sscl.uwo.ca/sociology/popstudies/dp/dp00-1.pdf>, updated with data from Human Resources and Skills Development Canada, *Canadians in Context—Population Size and Growth*, at: <www4.hrsdc.gc.ca/.3ndic.1t.4r@-eng.jsp?iid=35>.

Governing Realities

BOX 4.4 What Should Determine Who Gets In?

In recent years roughly two-thirds of annual immigration to Canada has been under the economic category, whereby prospective immigrants must score a certain number of points to qualify for entry to Canada. This system for determining who gets in is referred to by economists as a human capital model, emphasizing as it does the attributes of immigrants most likely to contribute positively to the economy and less likely to place a burden on state spending. The system is not without its critics. In the United States, where the human capital model is not used, there has been pressure for its adoption.

The arguments against this model are expressed by the American Immigration Council: "(T)he new point system would put some categories of people at a disadvantage. Specifically, women, people who work in the informal economy (including those who do unpaid work), individuals with family ties to US citizens with insufficient human capital credentials (i.e., formal education and employment history), middle age and older adults, and applicants from less-developed countries."[30]

The point systems used in Canada, Quebec, Australia, and New Zealand are shown in Table 4.4.

TABLE 4.4 Share of Points Allocated by Selection Criteria and by Immigration System

Criteria	Canada	Quebec*	Australia	New Zealand
Education	25%	23–6%	30%	25%
Language	24%	18–21%	13%	Mandatory
Work Experience	21%	7%	5%	23%
Age	10%	13–15%	15%	12%
Arranged Employment	10%	8–9%	10%	23%
Adaptability*	10%	31–6%	27%	19%
Maximum Points	100	107–23	200	265
Pass Mark	67	55–63	120	140

*Minimum pass marks differ in Quebec for single applicants relative to those with spouses/partners.

Source: TD Economics, *Knocking Down Barriers Faced by New Immigrants to Canada: Fitting the Pieces Together*, 7 Feb. 2012, 8, at: <www.td.com/document/PDF/economics/special/ff0212_immigration.pdf>. Reprinted with permission from Craig Alexander.

class found work within their first two years in the country. Roughly half found work in their intended occupation, 40 per cent within their first year in Canada.[31] This means, of course, that about half of these highly educated, highly qualified immigrants were not successfully integrated into the Canadian labour force after two years. Why?

The answer sometimes given is "discrimination," in systemic forms and in subtle and more overt forms. In fact, however, the explanation is far more complex than this and raises the question, "What do we mean by discrimination?" Research by Jeffrey Reitz and others points to four main factors that slow or even block the entry of highly educated, skilled immigrants into the professions they held in their countries of origin. They include the following:

- *Language proficiency.* Being proficient in the official language of one's community of residence and workplace is positively correlated with the likelihood of being employed in one's intended occupation. Not being fluent in one of the official languages—and this can include having an accent that interferes with the ability of clients, patients, or co-workers to understand the speaker—can limit an immigrant's employment prospects. One study of immigrants in the Greater Toronto Area (GTA) found that roughly one-third mentioned language as a barrier they faced in the workforce.[32]

- *Cultural norms.* This is often associated with language proficiency. Communication is not only about understanding the words spoken by someone else. It is also about the unspoken meanings and messages transmitted in everything from a face-to-face conversation to an e-mail message. Not having been raised in the language community and associated culture of the majority may be a disadvantage in terms of communications skills. At any rate, there is little doubt that some Canadian employers will believe this to be the case and may be reluctant to hire an immigrant worker for fear that customers,

clients, or patients may not "connect" with him or her as well as with someone who is more fluent in the mainstream culture.

- *Work experience.* Having worked for 14 years with two employers in Lahore (Pakistan) or for seven years with an employer in Posdan (Poland) may not be viewed seriously by a Canadian employer who has never heard of these places. Even if the places of previous employment are recognized, it would not be surprising if an employer in, say, Calgary placed more confidence in work experience with a company that he or she knows, in Toronto or Victoria, than in a company that he or she has not heard of, in a market far away. The lack of Canadian work experience was cited as a workforce barrier by one-third of immigrants in a GTA study.[33] This Catch-22 situation often is the experience of highly educated, skilled immigrant workers. To get the job in Canada one needs experience. But the experience one has may not be recognized in Canada.

- *Credentials.* Degrees and professional certification are usually required for a professional or other skilled occupation; however,

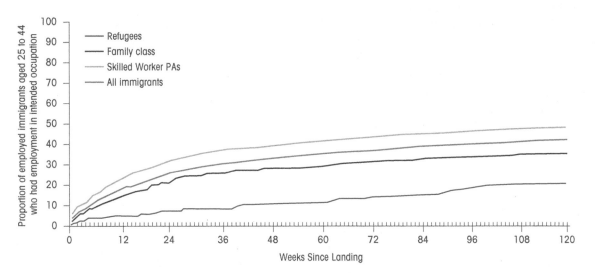

FIGURE 4.6   Economic Integration of Immigrants

Source: Statistics Canada, Longitudinal Survey of Immigrants to Canada: Progress and Challenges of New Immigrants in the Workforce 2003, Chart 2, Catalogue no. 89-615-XwE2005001, Oct. 2005, at: <www.statcan.gc.ca/pub/89-615-x/2005001/4079178-eng.htm>.

degrees and certification earned abroad are often not recognized in Canada (sometimes those earned in one province are not recognized in another!). Once in Canada, a highly educated immigrant may have to return to school to acquire a degree, certification, or training that will qualify him or her for the anticipated job. These barriers to the recognition of foreign degrees and certification are not always, and perhaps not even usually, arbitrary and without reasons associated with the competencies expected of a person in a given profession in this country. But in some cases they may be. Ottawa and the provinces have taken steps in recent years to improve the process whereby degrees and qualifications earned abroad are evaluated.[34]

Do these four factors add up to discrimination? This may depend on what one means by discrimination. If one means norms and rules that have as their consequence the differential treatment of individuals on the basis of characteristics that tend to be associated with a person's country of origin—the likelihood of speaking English or French proficiently; the probability that one will have degrees or work experience that are not as readily acknowledged as those earned in Canada—then this certainly amounts to discrimination. Some might argue, however, that these criteria are relevant to a person's ability to perform a job at a high or even reasonable level of competence or in a manner satisfactory to some customers, clients, or patients. Is it discriminatory, they might ask, to place more confidence in one person over another because one understands him or her better or is familiar with the background and credentials of one person but not at all with those of the other? We make choices on the basis of these sorts of considerations all the time. Indeed, in a world of imperfect information, where we cannot know everything that might be relevant to a decision that we need to make and where the costs of acquiring such information may be high, we necessarily rely on what is familiar to us. Just because a decision is based on what does and does not fall into our comfort zone—the range of what we think we know and that is familiar to us—does that make it discriminatory? Here, the answer will depend in part on ideology—conservative or liberal; individualist or communitarian—and in part on which side of the hiring desk one is seated.

Whatever one concludes about the human capital model used to determine who is permitted into Canada as an economic-class immigrant, and whether or not one believes that even highly educated and well-qualified immigrants face unfair and unreasonable barriers in the Canadian workforce, one thing is certain. The fact that immigration is comparatively uncontroversial in Canada and that the country lacks the sort of immigrant, low-income enclaves found in many Western countries may be ascribed to the Canadian immigration system. Canadians' overwhelming support for multiculturalism and the generally high level of support for current immigration levels that has existed for most of the past couple of decades have surely been influenced by the fact that immigrants tend to integrate into the middle class more rapidly and more often in Canada than in such countries as France, Germany, the Netherlands, the UK, and even the United States.[35]

Starting Points for Research

Neil Bissoondath, *Selling Illusions: The Cult of Multiculturalism in Canada* (Toronto: Penguin, 2002). The author challenges the prevailing belief that official multiculturalism benefits the ethnic, racial, and other minorities that it purports to help.

Raymond Breton and Jeffrey Reitz, *The Illusion of Difference: Realities of Ethnicity in Canada and the United States* (Toronto: C.D. Howe Institute, 1994). This is one of the very few works that actually attempts to test whether the rate of ethnic assimilation is faster in the United States than in Canada. A useful update is Martin Turcotte, "Passing on the Ancestral Language," *Canadian Social Trends* 80 (Spring 2006): 20–6.

Will Kymlicka and Kathryn Walker, eds, *Rooted Cosmopolitanism: Canada and the World* (Vancouver: University of British Columbia Press, 2012). As in Kymlicka's earlier book, *Multicultural Odysseys: Navigating the New International Politics of Diversity* (Toronto: Oxford University Press, 2007), this collection discusses Canadian multiculturalism in relation to global trends in the understanding of citizenship, identity, and belonging.

Jeffrey Reitz et al., *Multiculturalism and Social Cohesion: Potentials and Challenges of Diversity* (New York: Springer, 2009). A critical assessment of multicultural policy in Canada, making extensive use of the 2002 national Ethnic Diversity Survey.

Phil Ryan, *Multicultiphobia* (Toronto: University of Toronto Press, 2010). A lively analysis of Canadian multiculturalism and its critics.

Janice Stein et al., *Uneasy Partners: Multiculturalism and Rights in Canada* (Waterloo, Ont.: Wilfrid Laurier University Press, 2007). Essays by several prominent Canadian writers on some of the debates and tensions that exist around the Charter and Canada's policy and ethos of multiculturalism.

Review Exercises

1. Ethnic and racial profiling involves the practice of singling out people for different and disadvantageous treatment because of their ethnicity or race. Find two or three cases where this has been alleged to be a systematic practice in Canada. You might start by going to the websites of the Canadian Race Relations Foundation <www.crr.ca>, the Canadian Bar Association <www.cba.org>, and the Canadian Civil Liberties Association <www.ccla.org>.

2. Canadians and their leaders usually attribute the comparatively good relations between ethnic communities in Canada to the country's policy of multiculturalism. But some experts on immigration, diversity, and integration argue that Canada's immigration policy, which for several decades has favoured immigrants with higher levels of education and job skills, is the main factor explaining why Canada's pluralist model appears to work better than those in some other democracies. How would you set about testing these claims? Where would you find the data needed to test these propositions?

3. Over the last decade quite a lot of research has been done on the question of whether cultural diversity may, in fact, contribute to lower levels of social trust. One of the major researchers in this field is Harvard's Robert Putnam. Read the article at <www.theguardian.com/society/2007/jul/18/communities.guardiansocietysupplement> and, optionally, listen to the interview with Putnam at the link found at this webpage. Explain the basis for these concerns about a possible negative relationship between diversity and levels of social trust. Do they strike you as well founded?

5 Regionalism and Canadian Politics

Regionalism and regionally based political conflict are enduring aspects of the Canadian political condition. This chapter looks at several important aspects of regionalism in Canadian politics, including the following topics:

- Predictions of the demise of regionalism.
- Reasons for the persistence of regionalism.
- The boundaries of Canada's regions.
- Regional political cultures.
- Regional grievances and western alienation.
- Western versus central Canadian "visions" of the country.

A Canadian Pacific freight train locomotive pulls into Banff station. Canada's transcontinental railway was built at the end of the 19th century, connecting many (but not all) of the varied regions of Canada. Canada's enormous size and diverse regions produce a wide-range of political cultures, and create obstacles and advantages to the workings of the federal government.

(© Neale Clark/Robert Harding World)

"Canada has too much geography," declared the country's longest-serving Prime Minister, Mackenzie King. By this he meant that the vastness of the country and the diversity in the natural endowments and interests of its regions produced conflicts that would either not exist in a more compact country or whose resolution would be less difficult. Canadians have always accepted the truth of King's dictum, believing that the challenges of **regionalism** and inter-regional conflict are a central part of the Canadian story. Indeed, as we noted in Chapter 1, one of the most astute observers of Canadian politics, Donald Smiley, once identified regionalism as one of the three fundamental axes of Canadian politics. It was, he rightly noted, the source of major political divisions and controversies throughout Canada's history. And it continues to be one of the defining features of Canada's political landscape today.

Along with King, most Canadians have viewed regionalism as a problem. Aside from occasional patriotic celebrations of Canada's regional diversity and sheer size, as in the spate of songs that emerged around Canada's centennial year and in the speeches of politicians and after-dinner speakers, few have argued that size and regional diversity are positive attributes in political life. Students of American politics will know, however, that some of the founders of the United States believed these attributes to be positive, perhaps even necessary, characteristics of a political system respectful of freedom. In the *Federalist Papers*, James Madison argued that a larger territory encompassing a greater diversity of regional interests was more likely to provide protection for personal freedoms, group rights, and sectional interests than would a smaller, more homogeneous country. Madison reasoned that as the physical size of a country increased and the scope of its social and especially economic interests was enlarged, the likelihood of any particular group being able to dominate others or of being able to form a coalition with other interests to achieve such domination would decline. Small countries with comparatively homogeneous populations were, he thought, incapable of maintaining respect for individual and minority rights. The majority would inevitably exercise a sort of

tyranny, using their superior numbers to oppress the rights of others. This was less likely to happen in a larger, more diverse country.

Madison's argument has never resonated very positively in Canada, with the exception of some supporters of this view in western Canada. The debates on Confederation contain no echoes of this argument for a vast republic to ensure the protection of rights. The expansion of Canada was seen by most as a necessary pre-emptive action to reduce the possibility of the vast western territories being annexed by a United States where the idea of Manifest Destiny and the fact of territorial expansion were riding high. Surprisingly, perhaps, one of the few Canadians to theorize about the consequences of regionalism in the style of Madison was Pierre Trudeau, usually thought of as being a prime minister with a strong preference for centralized federal power. Trudeau's thoughts on the political virtue of regionalism were, however, formulated before he entered federal politics. Aside from the early Trudeau and some disgruntled westerners, few Canadians have disagreed with Mackenzie King's assessment that regionalism has been primarily a burden on the back of Canadian politics.

The Unexpected Persistence of Regionalism

The last few decades have seen an upsurge in regionalism in Canada, a trend mirrored in many other parts of the world. The signs of this upsurge can be seen in the party system, western alienation, regional economic disparities, and intergovernmental conflict.

The party system. For most of Canada's history the two historically dominant parties, the Liberals and Conservatives, competed with each other across Canada. Although they did not draw equally well from all regional segments of the electorate—the Liberal Party did much better than the Conservatives in Quebec for most of the twentieth century and the Conservative Party tended to be stronger than the Liberals in the West for most of the second half of that century—both were very clearly national political parties with significant support across Canada.

Since the 1993 general election, the character of Canada's party system has appeared to be more regionally than nationally based. This is most obvious in the case of the Bloc Québécois, which only runs candidates in Quebec and which elected more MPs from that province than any other party in 1993, 1997, 2004, 2006, and 2008 before the party's collapse in the 2011 general election. The Canadian Alliance, formerly the **Reform Party**, won almost all its seats west of Ontario and received the greatest share of the popular vote of any party in the combined four western provinces during the 1993, 1997, and 2000 federal elections. The Progressive Conservative Party, long a truly national party in terms of the regional breadth of its support, elected more of its MPs from the Atlantic provinces in these three elections than from any other part of the country. The Alliance and the Progressive Conservatives merged into the Conservative Party of Canada before the 2004 election, a union that delivered less than a handful of seats in Ontario and none from Quebec in that election. Only the

Liberal Party appeared capable of claiming significant support in all regions of the country over these four national elections, although even its regional levels of support were very uneven.

The 2006 and 2008 elections saw a continuation of very weak Liberal support west of Ontario, but a resurgence of Conservative support in Ontario and even in Quebec. Nevertheless, recent elections, including that of 2011, have produced party representation in Parliament that is strikingly fragmented along regional lines.

Regionalism is also apparent when one looks at the provincial party systems across Canada. Unlike in some federal countries, such as the United States and Australia, the parties that compete to form a government at the provincial level in Canada are often different from those that compete for seats from that province in federal elections. Quebec is an obvious case in point, where the Parti Québécois has been one of the two dominant provincial parties since that province's 1970 election. The PQ is a political party that exists only in Quebec. In British Columbia, provincial elections are mainly competitions between the NDP and the province's Liberal Party. Although the Conservative Party does well in federal elections in BC, its provincial counterpart almost disappeared in the 1990s and in recent elections has received only a handful of votes and no seats in provincial elections. In recent years elections in Saskatchewan have been contests between the NDP and the Saskatchewan Party. The provincial Liberal Party has been very weak in recent elections and there is no provincial Conservative Party (instead there is a Progressive Conservative Party that runs candidates in a handful of ridings). In short, there is considerable asymmetry between provincial party systems and the pattern of party competition in federal elections in many of Canada's provinces.

Western alienation. Western grievances against Ottawa and the Ontario–Quebec axis have dominated

Malcolm Mayes/Artizans.com

The historical positions of provinces in relation to one another are always changing. In 2009, Ontario received federal equalization payments for the first time, earning it the label of a "have-not" province; at the same time, Newfoundland and Labrador, previously considered a "have-not" province, experienced a budget surplus.

the national political scene for as long as the western provinces have been part of Canada. But in the 1970s there was a sharp upward ratcheting in the rhetoric associated with these grievances. At this point the term "western alienation" entered the lexicon of Canadian politics. As had always been the case, economics was at the root of this discontent. Spokespersons for the western provinces argued that Ottawa treated the resources with which the West was well endowed, and which formed the basis for western prosperity, differently and less favourably than those located primarily in provinces like Ontario and Quebec. Although Albertans were the most vocal in making this case, politicians and industry leaders in British Columbia and Saskatchewan provided a supportive chorus.

Economic disparities. The gap between the real prosperity of the richest and poorest provinces of Canada has not grown narrower. Indeed, if the federal government transfers intended to narrow this gap are excluded, the disparity has increased between wealthy provinces such as Alberta and Saskatchewan and the less affluent provinces, including New Brunswick and Newfoundland and Labrador. By itself, such disparity does not necessarily mean greater inter-regional conflict if the central government is able to subsidize incomes and public services in the poorer regions and if taxpayers in the wealthier regions are willing to pay for this regional redistribution of wealth.

The last two decades have shown that the political will to maintain these redistributive transfers has become weaker. Part of the reason for this has been the economic decline of Ontario. From the time Ottawa began a policy of redistributing wealth from the more affluent to the less affluent provinces, Ontario was the single largest source of money transferred to recipient provinces. This changed in 2009–10 when Ontario began to receive equalization payments.

Intergovernmental conflict. The pendulum of federal–provincial power has swung from Ottawa to the provinces and back again several times since Confederation. Prime Minister John A. Macdonald's hope that the provincial governments would become little more than "glorified municipalities," deferring to Ottawa on all matters of national importance, was stymied from the beginning by provincial politicians who had other ideas and by judges whose interpretation of the division of powers in Canada's Constitution did not accord with Macdonald's. In recent years intergovernmental conflict has been alive and intense on a number of fronts, including environmental policy, health care, taxation, cities, post-secondary education, and federal procurement decisions. Judging from these conflicts, regionalism continues to mark the Canadian political landscape.

The persistence and even resurgence of regionalism, in Canada and elsewhere, took many by surprise. One of the few points of agreement among most twentieth-century social and political observers was that as the conditions of people's existence became more alike, their values, beliefs, and behaviour would converge. Modern transportation, mass media, public education, and consumer lifestyle habits would break down the barriers that previously separated regional communities and nurtured their distinctiveness, such that regionalism would become a weaker force in social and political life. Those on the left predicted that region, like religion and ethnicity, eventually would be replaced by class as the dominant fault line in the politics of modernized societies. Indeed, some went so far as to argue that only the obfuscations and manipulations of the dominant class, exercised through their control of the mass media and political parties, kept alive the fiction that region, and not class, was more important in shaping the interests and identities of average people.

Contrary to these expectations, and despite the undeniable fact that in many important ways the lives of people across the rich industrialized societies of the world are more alike today than two or three generations ago, regionalism and its even more robust cousin—nationalism—continue to be important forces in political life. This certainly is true in Canada, as the signs of the vitality of regionalism discussed above attest, and as the persistence of a significant nationalist movement in Quebec demonstrates. Three principal factors help to explain the attraction and persistence of regionalism.

First, traditional thinking underestimated the degree to which regionally based states and elites may invest in regionalism—and regionally based nationalism too, as in the case of Quebec—when this investment either serves their own interests or, more charitably, promotes their vision of what is in the best interests of the regional community they purport to represent. During the 1970s Canadian political scientists began to use the term **province-building** to describe the phenomenon of powerful provincial governments using the various constitutional, legal, and taxation levers available to them to increase their control over activities and interests within their provincial borders and, in consequence, their stature vis-à-vis Ottawa. Alberta and Quebec were the two provinces most often cited as illustrations of this drive on the part of provincial state elites to extend the scope of their authority.

Although these two provinces may have been the outstanding examples of province-building in action, the phenomenon was not limited to them. Alan Cairns argued that the strength of regionalism in Canada was, in fact, primarily due to a Constitution that gave Canada's provincial governments considerable law-making and revenue-raising powers, reinforced by what he saw as the natural tendency of those who controlled, worked for, or depended on provincial states to protect and extend their turf. We will have more to say about this later in the chapter.

A second factor not anticipated by those who predicted the demise of regionalism involves the failure of national institutions—political, cultural, and economic—to produce levels of national integration and identity that would overcome regionally based ways of thinking and acting in Canadian politics. To put this a bit differently, many Canadians, particularly in Quebec and in the West, have remained unconvinced that the institutions of the national government and its policies have their best interests in mind. Students of federalism have made a distinction between *inter*-state federalism, where conflict and co-operation are played out between the national and regional governments, and *intra*-state federalism, where these forces are managed and accommodations reached within the institutions of the national state. There certainly has been

no shortage of national structures and policies intended to accommodate regional interests and perspectives. A short list of these, past and present, would include the following:

Structures
- The Senate incorporates the principle of regional representation, with Ontario, Quebec, the four western provinces, and the three Maritime provinces all being assigned the same number of seats.
- The Supreme Court Act requires that at least three of the nine justices be members of the Quebec bar. Moreover, the custom has developed over time whereby it is expected that three of the judges will be from Ontario and at least one from each of the western and eastern regions of the country.
- The federal cabinet has always been at the centre of attempts to ensure regional representation in federal decision-making. Every prime minister has given careful consideration to the representation in cabinet of each region and, insofar as possible, each province.
- Section 36 of the Constitution Act, 1982 commits the federal government to the principle of "making equalization payments to ensure that provincial governments have sufficient revenues to provide reasonably comparable levels of public services at reasonably comparable levels of taxation." Although the practical significance of this constitutional commitment is far from clear, the spirit of it clearly involves a federal obligation to assist the less affluent provincial governments in paying their bills.

Policies
- For about two decades, and in response to criticism that the Canadian media and federal cultural policy were strongly biased towards central Canada, Ottawa has attempted to "regionalize" its cultural activities in various ways. One of these involves regional programming through the Canadian Broadcasting Corporation

and a conscious policy of ensuring that regional points of view are expressed in its national programming, as required by the Broadcasting Act, 1991. Another involves the programs and spending activities of the Department of Canadian Heritage, which, like the CBC, has a mandate to express the diversity of Canada, including its regional diversity and histories.

- Federal support for regional economic development has a long and much-criticized history in Canada. These activities were given an organizational focus and a major spending boost through the 1968 creation of the Department of Regional Economic Expansion, which has morphed into departments and agencies by other names over the years.[1] Today, Ottawa's support for the economies of the less affluent provinces is channelled mainly through five regional development agencies under the Department of Industry.

- When making decisions that have important regional spending and employment implications, from the awarding of contracts to the location of government offices, Ottawa is always sensitive to the probable reactions of citizens and their spokespersons in regions competing for a share of the federal pie.

Although it would be unfair to write off these structures and policies as amounting to a complete and abject failure, they clearly have not succeeded in neutralizing regionalism. It is always possible, of course, that regional grievances and the acrimony that often accompanies intergovernmental relations in Canada might have been worse in the absence of these efforts at intra-state federalism.

A third factor whose importance was overlooked by those who anticipated the decline of regionalism involves the persistence of differences in the economic interests and social characteristics of regions. It is undeniably true that, in many respects, how people in Ontario and Saskatchewan live, the sorts of jobs they are likely to do, the programs they watch on television, and the cultural milieu in

which they live are more alike today than was the case in the mid-twentieth century. But differences persist and their political importance, often fanned by politicians or other regional spokespersons, is considerable. For example, about one-quarter of Alberta's GDP is accounted for by the petrochemical industry, a level of dependence on this particular industry unrivalled in Canada. Ontario's economy is far more dependent than any other province on the automobile industry, with just over 30 per cent of all provincial exports, representing about 11 per cent of Ontario's GDP, accounted for by automotive vehicles and parts. Almost all of this goes to the United States. British Columbia accounts for over half of all Canadian lumber and wood product exports, most of which go to the United States, China, and Japan. As these few examples suggest, the economic issues that will capture the attention of politicians and the public differ considerably among the provinces.

If we shift from economics to demography we also find some significant differences between provinces and regions. On the whole, and with one major exception, the political impact of these demographic differences tends to be considerably less than that of the different economic interests of Canada's regions. The major exception is, of course, Quebec. It is the only majority francophone province, with over 80 per cent of the provincial population claiming French as their mother tongue and a majority having French ancestry. Nunavut, where about 85 per cent of the population is Aboriginal, represents another case of a region whose ethnic character is dramatically different from the rest of Canada. This is not to say that there are not enormous differences in the demographic character of provinces like British Columbia, which has been a magnet in recent decades for non-European immigrants, most of them from Asia, and Nova Scotia, where the predominance of people whose ancestry is from the British Isles has been barely diminished by immigration. But the political significance of these demographic differences is less than in the case of Quebec or Nunavut. The ethnic character of Nova Scotia does not get expressed in Canadian politics in the way that Quebec's francophone character does.

Mapping Regionalism in Canada

How many regions does Canada have? The answer depends on our definition of region. A map with boundaries drawn along economic lines will look different from one drawn along lines of demography or history. Some have argued that the only sensible way to conceive of regions in Canada is along provincial lines, such that each province constitutes a separate region. More commonly, however, political observers have tended to combine certain provinces into the same region, particularly the western and easternmost provinces. But here, too, there are difficulties. The justification for lumping Manitoba and British Columbia into a common region designated the "West" is not obvious. Aside from both being west of Ontario they may appear to have no more in common than Manitoba and Nova Scotia. Difficulties aside, it has been common to speak of four or five main regions in Canada: the West (or British Columbia and the Prairies), Ontario, Quebec, and the Atlantic provinces. From the point of view of both physical and cultural geography, as well as economics, the Canadian North comprises another significant region.

Listen to the "Is It Time to Redraw the Regional Map of Canada?" podcast, available at: www.oupcanada.com/Brooks8e

There are three principal ways of determining the boundaries of regions, all of them useful. They involve economics, values, and identity.

Canada's Economic Regions

Common economic interests, often linked to physical geography, may provide a basis for the classification of regions. Atlantic Canada's greater dependence on fisheries, Ontario and Quebec's greater manufacturing base, and the West's comparatively greater reliance on grain production and natural resources are economic interests that have provided a basis for thinking of these parts of Canada as constituting distinctive regions. As Table 5.1 shows, the economic characteristics of Canada's provinces vary considerably.

The regional variation that exists in Canada's industrial structure has often been at the root of major political conflicts between regions of the country and between Ottawa and the provinces. The Kyoto Protocol on limiting greenhouse gas emissions, which requires policies to reduce the use of carbon-based fuels, pitted Ottawa against Alberta for over a decade. Albertans and their government knew that the environmental gains envisaged by advocates of the Kyoto Protocol would be achieved at the expense of the industry that is central to their province's economic well-being. The federal government was able to point to public opinion polls showing that a clear majority of Canadians favoured the ratification of the Kyoto agreement. As it turned out, the victory of the Conservative Party in the 2006 national election rendered the issue moot, given the party's lack of sympathy for the Kyoto guidelines and different approach to dealing with climate change.

Historically, the federal government's major economic policies have been slanted towards the interests of central Canada. On occasion the discrimination against and even exploitation of other regions of the country, particularly the West, has been egregious. Examples include the following.

Tariffs. For most of Canada's history a cornerstone of economic policy was high tariffs on manufactured imports, the costs and benefits of which were distributed unequally between the country's regions. The cost for western farmers to ship grain by rail to the Fort William railhead (today's Thunder Bay), despite federal subsidies, always seemed greater than it should have been to those in the West, and shipment of eastern manufactures to the West made prices higher than they might have been if trade, protected by the high tariffs of the National Policy beginning in 1879, could have followed more natural north–south lines to contiguous American states and regions. The extensive prime lands controlled by the Canadian Pacific Railway as part of its original agreement with the government in the nineteenth century also rankled western sensitivities.

One study of tariff impacts prior to the 1989 Canada–US Free Trade Agreement concluded that

TABLE 5.1 Selected Economic and Population Characteristics, by Province

Province	Median Family Income (2011)* ($)	Unemployment Rate (average for 2008-12) (%)	Manufacturing Share of GDP (2011) (%)	Key Industries	Population Growth, 2006-11 (%)	Median Government Transfers to Families (2011) ($)
NL	53,000	13.7	3.2	Fishing, mining, oil & gas, newsprint	1.8	12,300
PEI	53,000	11.3	8.7	Agriculture, tourism, fishing	3.2	11,300
NS	60,600	8.8	7.5	Forestry, agriculture, tourism, fishing	0.9	8,400
NB	54,000	9.3	11.3	Forestry, mining, agriculture	2.9	9,700
Que.	58,500	7.9	14.2	Manufacturing, mining, hydroelectric power	4.7	7,900
Ont.	70,600	8.0	12.4	Motor vehicles & parts, manufacturing, finance	5.7	5,900
Man.	67,900	5.1	11.5	Manufacturing, agriculture	5.2	4,600
Sask.	77,700	4.8	6.3	Agriculture, mining	6.7	4,500
Alta	91,300	5.4	6.4	Oil & gas, agriculture	10.8	2,300
BC	67,600	6.8	7.2	Forestry, tourism, mining	7.0	5,200
Canada	68,400	7.4	11.5		5.9	6,000

*Households consisting of a couple living together, with or without children. This is market income, not including government transfers or income tax.

Source: Various online publications of Statistics Canada, at: <www.statcan.ca>.

the per capita benefits for Ontario were about equal to the per capita costs imposed on the West and Atlantic Canada. Quebecers were also net beneficiaries, but the decline of that province's manufacturing base by the 1980s reduced the level of these benefits from what it had been for most of the previous century.[2]

Terms of entry into Confederation. Outside of Alberta and Saskatchewan, few Canadians know, and probably even fewer care, that when these provinces entered Canada in 1905 they did not immediately receive all of the law-making powers held by the other provinces. Specifically, they did not have control over natural resources within provincial borders, a power that sections 92 and 109 of the Constitution Act, 1867 assigns exclusively to the provinces. The reason for this discriminatory treatment involved, quite simply, Ottawa's desire to retain control over the economic development of the Prairies, a part of the country that was being settled rapidly in the early 1900s and whose expansion was essential to the National Policy goal of building a larger domestic market for the manufacturers of Ontario and Quebec.

The National Energy Program (1980). A generation after it was abolished by the Conservative government of Brian Mulroney in 1984, the **National Energy Program** (NEP) remains vivid in the memory of many Albertans. It involved, they quite reasonably believed, an enormous transfer of wealth from Alberta to the rest of Canada, and chiefly to the consumers and industries of Canada's industrial heartland. It was perpetrated by a Liberal government they saw as being hostile to western, and especially Alberta's, interests. The NEP placed a limit on the price that could be charged in Canada for oil and gas from Canadian sources. This price was considerably below the going world price. Canadian producers' ability to export their petroleum at the higher world price was limited by the fact that any energy exports had to be approved by the National Energy Board. Albertans saw the NEP as a thinly disguised subsidy their province was made to pay to

central Canada. These fears were rekindled when the price of oil and gas rose dramatically in 2005, leading to proposals from some eastern Canadian politicians that Alberta's energy "windfall" be shared more equitably with the rest of Canada.[3]

When world oil prices doubled in 2007–8, there was somewhat less talk about the rest of Canada getting a slice of Alberta's growing revenue pie. Part of the reason for this change was probably the fact of a Conservative government in power, holding all 28 of Alberta's seats in the House of Commons and led

Governing Realities

BOX 5.1 Neighbours at Odds over the Northern Gateway

Historically, Alberta and British Columbia have generally been on the same page when it comes to natural resource issues, if only because they found themselves in opposition to policies of the federal government. When bumper stickers reading, "Let the eastern bastards freeze in the dark," proliferated in Alberta after Ottawa's imposition of the NEP, many British Columbians agreed with the underlying premise. Federal policies, including energy policies, seemed to be based on what was good for Ontario and Quebec, with little thought for the interests of the West. The prosperity of Alberta, BC, and Saskatchewan is tied to the export of natural resources, another factor that has usually made them good neighbours when it comes to resource issues.

This changed in 2012–13. The issue was the proposed Northern Gateway oil pipeline that would transport oil from northern Alberta to the inland port at Kitimat, BC, from where it would be shipped by tankers to markets in Asia. Public opinion polls in BC showed that a majority of the province's citizens opposed the pipeline and, moreover, that many more people strongly opposed the pipeline than strongly supported it. Environmental groups and First Nations also opposed the pipeline's construction. Hearings on whether Enbridge, the pipeline proponent, would receive a permit for construction were held before a federal review panel under the authority of the National Energy Board Act and the Canadian Environmental Assessment Act. Shortly after her re-election in May 2013,

BC Premier Christy Clark announced that her government was officially opposed to the pipeline.

For its part, the Conservative government in Ottawa supported the proposal, allying itself with the Alberta government and in opposition to that of BC. The collision of environmental concerns with energy interests has created circumstances that were almost unthinkable a generation ago. Albertans were used to eastern Canadian criticism of the oil sands, which appeared to them to be simply the latest chapter in a long-standing story of eastern Canadian insensitivity to western interests. Criticism and, worse, active opposition from a resource-dependent neighbour were something rather new.

One year later the issue remained unresolved. Ottawa gave its blessing to the Northern Gateway, as expected, but the BC government insisted that all five conditions it had established back in 2012 had to be met before it would issue permits necessary for construction and operation of the pipeline. As of the summer of 2014 only one of these conditions had been met.

Even if these provincial neighbours patch up their differences, the fate of the Northern Gateway is not assured. "It is difficult to imagine the pipeline proceeding in the face of strong and angry First Nations opposition," writes Ken Coates. "The political and logistical challenges—imagine Caledonia times five or 10—would be formidable and the political fallout so substantial that it could easily prove to be destabilizing on a national scale."[4]

by a prime minister from that province. But another part of the explanation was that the issue of energy costs was now framed largely in environmental terms. How to wean consumers and industry from dependence on fossil fuels and reduce CO_2 emissions had become a far more prominent issue than whether the good fortune of some provinces meant that they should be expected to share the wealth.

This shift in how the energy issue, and particularly Alberta oil, was framed did not put an end to inter-regional conflict. Criticisms of Alberta the greedy were replaced by those of Alberta the despoiler of the environment and major source of global warming. Provincial and federal politicians from Quebec were outspokenly critical of the environmental impact of oil sands development, as were such varied activists as rock star Neil Young and South African Archbishop Desmond Tutu.

Canada's Cultural Regions

In what is perhaps the most widely cited—and disputed—study of regional political cultures in Canada, Richard Simeon and David Elkins conclude that "there are strong differences among the citizens of Canadian provinces and those of different language groups in some basic orientations to politics."[5] They go on to argue that these regional variations cannot be totally explained by demographic and socio-economic differences between Canada's regions. The sources of these differences in basic political orientations are, Simeon and Elkins admit, unclear. But their existence, they insist, is undeniable.

Other researchers have arrived at very different conclusions about the nature and extent of regional political cultures in Canada. Indeed, if there is anything approaching a consensus on this question—and it is a shaky consensus at best—it is that regional variations in basic and enduring political values and beliefs are not very great in English-speaking Canada, and while the differences between French-speaking Quebec and the rest of Canada appear to be more significant, they are not enormous.

A large number of surveys support this conclusion. They include the following:

- *Charter values.* A 2002 Environics survey of Canadians' attitudes towards the Charter of Rights and Freedoms found a "lack of any significant regional differences of opinion on the Charter's legitimacy or the relationship between Parliament and the courts."[6] The study's authors observed that there does not appear to be any difference across regions of Canada in support for such Charter principles and values as bilingualism and minority language, education rights, multiculturalism, the appropriateness of "reasonable limits" on freedom of expression, and the rights of the accused. The one outlier, however, was Quebec. While sharing with other Canadian regions support for the Charter and its general principles, Quebecers were considerably more likely to value equality over personal freedom and consistently more likely than their compatriots in other regions to support the extension of equality rights to disadvantaged groups. Asked about restricting police powers to guarantee the legal rights of vulnerable groups, Quebecers were somewhat more likely to support such restrictions. The 2002 Environics survey reported that 71 per cent of Quebecers said the police *should not* be allowed to enter and search a criminal suspect's home or office without a search warrant, compared to 63 per cent in the rest of Canada. Similarly, only 61 per cent of Quebecers expressed the view that the police and courts have to spend too much time worrying about the rights of criminals, compared to 72 per cent of Canadians living outside Quebec. On the matter of the rights of refugee claimants, Quebecers were again more likely than other Canadians to come down on the side of protecting individual rights (85 per cent compared to 75 per cent). These differences between Quebec and the other regions are not enormous, but they are all in the same direction.[7]

- *Trust.* A 2013 survey by Ekos Politics found that, for the most part, only small variations exist between provincial populations in the level of trust they have in various groups and institutions. Respondents were asked to indicate how much trust they had in government, nurses, doctors, teachers, newspapers, journalists, television news, pollsters, social media, and bloggers. If there was any discernible pattern at all, Quebecers appeared to be somewhat more trusting than other provincial populations.[8]

- *Faith and religious authority.* Quebec, once thought to be the most traditionally religious province, now appears to be the least. Variations among other provincial populations are small. A 2012 survey found that Quebecers are less likely than other provincial populations to say that religion is important in their lives, that God exists, that bad deeds are punished, and that a higher power governs the world. The provincial populations, including Quebec, are not very different in levels of trust in people who are very religious or not very religious, but Quebecers are much less trusting of clergy and religious leaders than are Canadians in other provinces.[9]

- *Diversity.* Once again, Quebecers appear to stand apart from the populations of other Canadian regions. While there is widespread support across Canada for the concept of diversity, Quebecers are more likely than other Canadians to express some doubts. A 2011 survey found that Quebecers were more likely to agree that having many ethnic groups weakens the national culture, immigrants should give up their customs and traditions and become more like the majority, and to say they prefer to live in a neighbourhood where most people share their cultural background. They were less likely than other regional populations to agree that the majority should try harder to accept the customs and traditions of cultural and religious groups and that society is strengthened by having many cultural and religious groups.

Differences between the other regional populations tended to be small.[10]

- *Factors contributing to success.* Asked what qualities are needed to get ahead in life, there is broad agreement across the regions, with the exception of Quebec. Quebecers are somewhat less likely than other regional populations to agree that having ambition, working hard, and having a good education are important factors. They are somewhat more likely to say that being corrupt can help one get ahead. This 2009 mail survey was based on a rather small sample (N = 420) and so the regional samples are much smaller than one would like and therefore one needs to be wary about these findings.[11]

- *Ideology.* The conventional wisdom, as found in the media, is that Canada's most left-leaning province is Quebec and the most right-leaning is Alberta. The rest fall somewhere in between. A 2012 survey by Ekos provides only tepid confirmation for this claim. Asked to place themselves on a 7-point scale where 1 was most liberal and 7 was most conservative (respondents were told that the question referred to their political beliefs or ideology, not support for political parties), Quebecers were very clearly the least likely to place themselves towards the conservative end and were more likely than the citizens of other provinces to place themselves at the liberal end of the spectrum, although just barely ahead of citizens in British Columbia. There was quite a lot of variation among the other provincial populations. Those in Saskatchewan and Manitoba—these provinces were combined because of the relatively small sample sizes from each—were the most likely to self-describe as ideologically conservative, more likely than Albertans.[12]

The sample sizes for some of the provinces in the 2012 Ekos study were too small to allow for a high level of confidence that the results were representative of those provincial populations. A 2013 survey conducted for the Manning Centre had somewhat better margins of error and arrived at conclusions slightly different from those of the Ekos survey. Again, a 7-point ideological scale was used. Quebecers scored lowest in conservatism, as they had in the previous year's survey. But the difference between Quebec and the other provinces was quite small. Quebec stood apart, however, when respondents were asked whether they identified with the Conservative Party. It is probably fair to infer that those who identify with the Conservative Party are, for the most part, ideologically more conservative than other Canadians. Only 13 per cent of Quebecers identified with the Conservative Party, compared to 18 per cent in Atlantic Canada, 24 per cent in Ontario, 43 percent in the Prairie provinces, and 25 per cent in BC. A warning: the Manning Centre surveys have found a fair degree of year-to-year variation in Conservative Party identification in the various regions, so this is clearly an imperfect surrogate measure of ideology.[13]

One of the most thorough examinations of political ideology in Canada corroborates the conclusion that, Quebec aside, the regional variations in political culture in the rest of Canada are not very great.[14] Based on a large national survey, Michael Ornstein and Michael Stevenson measured Canadians' support for social programs, redistributive policies, foreign investment, labour unions, and large corporations. Their examination of the variation in the ideological profiles of the provinces reveals that the differences are, for the most part, small and that Quebec stands out as the one province that is clearly to the left of the others. Moreover, contrary to the findings of Simeon and Elkins 20 years earlier, Ornstein and Stevenson do not find any significant variation between the provinces, Quebec included, in levels of political efficacy or political participation. "Not one province," they argue, "differs significantly from the national mean for the measure of efficacy,"[15] and the small provincial variations in participation do not conform to the pattern found by Simeon and Elkins.

The Simeon and Elkins thesis of significant cultural variation between the predominantly English-speaking provinces is not supported by data collected by the 2012 Focus Canada survey, carried out by Environics.[16] Here are some of its findings:

- Levels of trust are fairly high and very similar across the predominantly English-speaking regions. Asked, "If you lost a wallet or purse that contained $200, how likely is it to be returned with the money in it if it was found," 56 per cent of respondents in Atlantic Canada said it would be very likely, as did 52 per cent in Ontario, 50 per cent in the Prairies and 54 per cent in BC. Only 31 per cent of Quebecers thought that it would be very likely.
- In response to the statement, "Most people are better off in a free market economy, even though some people are rich and some are poor," the variation between the predominantly English-speaking regions of the country is not great, the percentages of respondents who completely or mostly agree being 62 (Atlantic), 63 (Ontario), 63 (Prairies), and 60 (BC). In Quebec, 55 per cent of respondents agree.
- There is some variation between the populations of the predominantly English-speaking regions in their response to the question, "How important is multiculturalism to the Canadian identity." In Atlantic Canada 57 per cent say that it is very important, as do 51 per cent in Ontario, 48 per cent in the Prairies, and 63 per cent in BC. But the clear outlier is Quebec, where only 38 per cent say it is very important.
- Huge majorities in all of the predominantly English-speaking regions of the country agree that the health-care system is very important to the national identity: Atlantic (92 per cent), Ontario (89 per cent), Prairies (79 per cent), and BC (86 per cent). In Quebec 66 per cent of respondents said that it was very important to the national identity.

Despite the rather impressive number of studies that fail to corroborate the Simeon and Elkins argument that all of the provinces have distinctive political cultures, researchers continue to test this claim. In a recent study based on survey data from the Comparative Provincial Elections Project, McGrane and Berdahl compare provincial populations across several values that include sense of political efficacy, belief in the honesty of politicians, feeling that government is wasteful, support for free markets, and post-materialism values. They find that the differences between provincial populations are not particularly significant, but that the differences between regions of Canada are more striking. "Overall, the data suggest that Canadian political culture has stronger *inter-regional* variations than *inter-provincial* variations." They add that, "On nearly all of the indices, there do seem to be distinct groupings of Ontario, Quebec, the Prairies and, to a lesser degree, the Atlantic provinces."[17]

The case for the existence of strong regional political cultures in English-speaking Canada is not helped if one looks at how provincial populations view their attachment to Canada and to their own province, and whether they believe that Canadians share the same values. Quebec tends to be the outlier among the provinces when it comes to most of these perceptions. As may be seen in Figure 5.1, the sense of belonging to Canada is very high across the predominantly English-speaking provinces. In Quebec, however, it is comparatively low.

Quebecers are not, as one might expect, more likely than other Canadians to report a strong sense of belonging to their province that compensates for their weaker attachment to Canada. Identities, attachments, and loyalties are not necessarily competitive. This is evident from the fact that citizens in Saskatchewan and in Atlantic Canada tend to have a very strong sense of belonging to Canada and to their own region. They appear to be even more likely than Quebecers to have a strong attachment to their province. Ontarians are the outliers when it comes to the sense of belonging to one's province. They are considerably less likely than Canadians in other provinces to report a strong provincial attachment.

Canadians in all provinces except Quebec believe that they have much in common with their compatriots in other parts of the country. Significant majorities in all of the predominantly English-speaking

provinces strongly agree that, despite differences, Canadians have many things that unite them. As may be seen in Part C of Figure 5.1, Quebecers are dubious. They are also only half as likely as other Canadians to agree that citizens in all provinces have the same values (see Part D).

Cross-Border Regions

An alternative method of mapping regions is suggested by Debora VanNijnatten and her colleagues in their work on **cross-border regions** (CBRs). They define a CBR as a distinct grouping of neighbouring and nearby provinces and states with economic, cultural, and institutional linkages that create commonalities between the members of this binational (Canada–US) grouping and set it apart from other regions. Dense ties of trade and investment between the provinces and states that comprise a CBR are fundamental to such regions. They give rise to physical infrastructure such as roads, rail lines, bridges, tunnels, and shared water routes. They also provide the impetus for cross-border institutions and processes—both public, between subnational governments, and between non-governmental groups—whose functions are to co-ordinate, plan, promote, and resolve conflicts related to the economic linkages between the members of a CBR. A significant degree of shared values and even a sense of regional identity characterize some of the CBRs that span the Canada–US border.

Based on an analysis of the density of economic, institutional, and socio-cultural ties between adjacent and nearby provinces and states, VanNijnatten and her colleagues propose a rather different map of regionalism (see Figure 5.2). It includes the following regions:

- *The West.* This CBR consists of British Columbia, Alberta, Yukon, Alaska, Washington, Idaho, Oregon, and Montana. It is characterized by a feeling of remoteness from the central governments of each country and a strong sense of regional identity, such that residents may be more alike in their values than they are with

A. Personal sense of belonging to Canada (% saying extremely strong*)

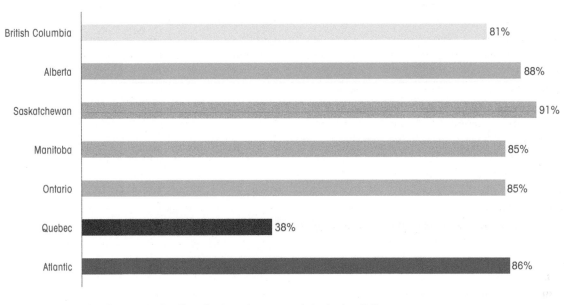

*On a 7 point scale where 7 was the strongest score, respondents who chose 5–7.

B. Personal sense of belonging to your province.

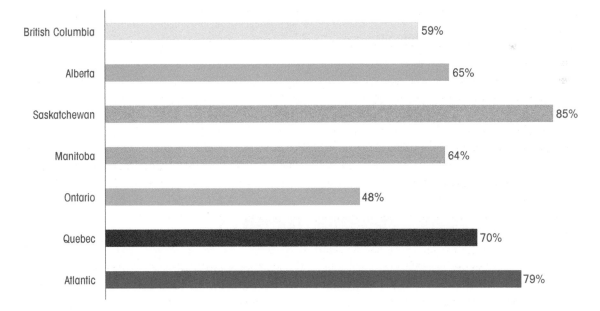

FIGURE 5.1   Regional Perceptions of Belonging and of Shared Canadian Values

Continued

C. Despite differences, we Canadians have many things that "Unite us."**

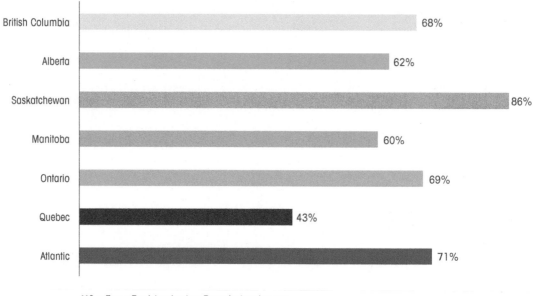

**6 or 7 on a 7 point scale where 7 equals strongly agree.

D. Canadians have the same values regardless of which province they live in.***

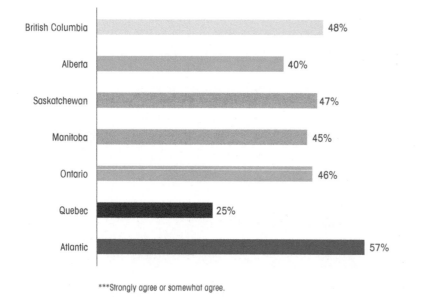

***Strongly agree or somewhat agree.

FIGURE 5.1   Continued

Source: Parts A and B are adapted from data at Ekos Politics, *Looking Backward, Looking Forward: Five Big Forces Shaping Our Society*, 9 Jan. 2013, 37, 38, at: <www.ekos.com/admin/articles/FG-2013-01-09.pdf>; Part C is adapted from data in AmericasBarometer, Canada 2012, 26; Part D is from Environics Institute, *Focus Canada 2012*, 21.

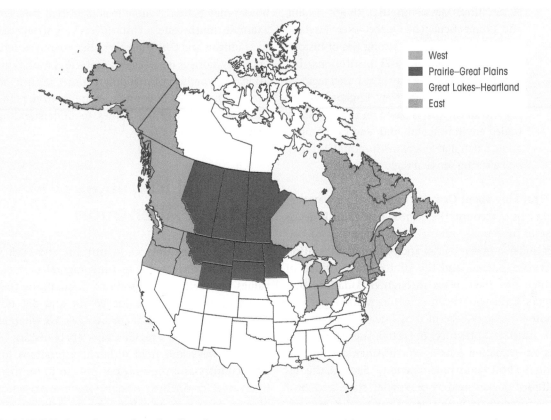

FIGURE 5.2   Cross-Border Regions

Source: Adapted from Debora VanNijnatten, "Canada–US Relations and the Emergence of Cross-Border Regions," Government of Canada, Policy Research Initiatives, 2006, at: <www.policyresearch.gc.ca>.

their compatriots in other regions of their respective countries. A dense network of private and public institutional linkages spans the Canada–US border and more emphasis is placed on shared environmental issues than characterizes other regions.

- *The Prairie–Great Plains*. This CBR includes Alberta, Saskatchewan, and Manitoba on the Canadian side, and Montana, Wyoming, North Dakota, South Dakota, and Minnesota on the US side (Alberta and Montana were identified by the CBR project as belonging to both this CBR and the West). Although the institutional linkages between these relatively sparsely populated and natural resource-dependent provinces and states are less deeply entrenched than is true of the other CBRs, the economic ties between them are extensive and strong

linkages exist based on shared management of common watersheds.

- *The Great Lakes–Heartland*. The shared waters of the Great Lakes and the enormous volume of trade and daily flow of vehicles and people across the Canada–US border are the most obvious features of this CBR. A dense network of cross-border institutions, public and private, links these states and provinces. But unlike the West, there is no strong sense of shared regional identity.
- *The East*. Although Quebec and Canada's Atlantic provinces have some significant trade and institutional linkages, their ties to adjacent and nearby American states are rather different. Quebec is part of a CBR that includes Vermont, Maine, New Hampshire, and New York, while the Atlantic provinces belong to a CBR that includes Maine, New

Hampshire, Massachusetts, Rhode Island, and Connecticut. The Quebec–New England CBR is characterized by strong ties of history, trade, transportation, and institutions, but nothing much in the way of a shared regional identity. The Atlantic–New England grouping within the East is based on ties of history, trade, environmental and energy co-operation, a rich network of institutional linkages, and a strong sense of regional identity.

Thinking about Canadian regions in a way that takes into account these cross-border linkages is useful in various ways. First, it enables us to better understand the causes and nature of integration between Canada and the United States, much of which has taken place through regionalized networks. Canada–US economic integration is perhaps more accurately described as integration between the states and provinces of each of these four CBRs. As VanNijnatten puts it, North American integration is a bottom-up phenomenon.[18] Second, the significant powers held by provincial, state, and local governments on both sides of the border, and the fact that transportation, environmental, security, energy supply and distribution, and many other matters tend to be regional in nature, ensure that these subnational governments and private regional organizations and institutions will be important players in the management of cross-border issues. This is nowhere more apparent than in the case of environmental issues. Several recent studies of the cross-border management of issues, ranging from the regulation of river flows to schemes for the promotion of renewable energy sources for regional electricity grids, highlight the key role played by sub-national governments and organizations.[19]

At the same time, the CBR concept has clear limitations. Some states and provinces are bi-regional in this scheme. Most of New York and Pennsylvania, for example, could be included in the Great Lakes–Heartland region, and Alberta and Montana are inconveniently included in both the West and Prairie–Great Plains regions. Another problem with this scheme is that it seeks to fit entire political jurisdictions into particular regions. But the economic and cultural linkages across the international border may be much more localized than this. For example, southwestern Ontario has very strong ties to Michigan and Ohio, but these ties are not experienced by northern or eastern Ontario. Limitations aside, this method of mapping regions alerts us to the fact that political boundaries are far from being the final word when it comes to understanding regionalism.

Regional Identities and Western Alienation

If, instead of looking for significant and enduring regional differences in fundamental political values and beliefs—the sorts of orientations that Ornstein and Stevenson looked for and did not find, except in the case of Quebec—we ask whether citizens of Canada's regions view their history in different ways and hold different aspirations for their country and their region's role in it, we then find rather compelling evidence for the existence of what deserve to be called regional political cultures. In particular, the West has long been characterized by sentiments of resentment towards and alienation from Ottawa and what westerners perceive to be the political preoccupations of central Canada. These sentiments vary in intensity across the western provinces and also fluctuate in response to specific circumstances and events. Gibbins and Arrison argue that it is reasonable to speak of "national visions" in the West that, in their words, "address not simply the place of the West within the Canadian federal state, but also the nature of *Canada* as a political community."[20] These visions are not merely reactions to citizens' sense of being unfairly treated and marginalized within Canadian politics—the resentment captured in the Reform Party's founding slogan, "The West wants in." Rather, these western visions of Canada are deeply rooted in regional histories and memories that are not the same as those of central and eastern Canada.

Starting in a major way in the 1950s with W.L. Morton, western Canadian historians began to react against what they saw as a narrative of Canadian history told from a central Canadian perspective, with little allowance for the distinctive experiences and cultures of the West. This perspective, said Morton, "fails to take account of regional experience and history and makes coherent Canadian history seem an 'imperialist creed,' an imposition on Maritime, French-Canadian, Western and British Columbian history of an interpretation which distorted local history and confirmed the feeling that union with Canada had been carried out against local sentiment and local interest."[21] Morton and many others have attempted to counter the centralist bias of Canadian history writing, but the belief lives on that the West's stories are not given fair weight by a Canadian academic and cultural establishment whose centre of gravity is in the Toronto–Ottawa–Montreal triangle.

In a broadly similar vein Barry Cooper, a Calgary-based political scientist, argues that a distinctive political tradition exists in western Canada, the roots of which lie in the history of that region. "[D]ualism," he observes, "is not the political issue in the West that it is in central Canada. Moreover, multiculturalism does not mean the same thing to a third or fourth generation non-French, non-British Westerner as it does to someone from the Azores or Calabria living on College Street in Toronto."[22] What is referred to as **western alienation**, Cooper argues, is not in fact a psychological, sociological, or economic condition experienced by those in the West. Rather, it is the awareness that the public realm—whose voices are heard and what counts as legitimate political discourse—belongs to others. These others are the citizens of central Canada and the elites who purport to speak on their behalf.

Of course, the history of the West and the political traditions that have evolved in western Canada are not disconnected from those of the rest of Canada. Likewise, as Gibbins and Arrison observe, "western visions" of the nature of the Canadian political community and that region's place in it are not restricted to the West. They identify a set of core values they believe are more solidly anchored in the West than in other regions of Canada, but the same values also find support among Canadians in other regions, including French-speaking Quebec. The difference is one of degree. Western visions

of Canada are more likely to embrace the *individual* equality of all Canadians, the equal status of all provinces, and a populist style of doing political business.

Regarding the first of these values—individual equality—Gibbins and Arrison rightly note that reservations about the official recognition and even constitutionalization of multiculturalism and a group rights concept of Canada have come largely from such popular western spokespersons as John Diefenbaker and Preston Manning, and, one would add, Stephen Harper. Such visions of Canada are part of what Alberta political scientist Barry Cooper refers to as the "Laurentian Canada" perspective that projects the history, preoccupations, and preferences of Ontario and Quebec onto the rest of the country.[23] The election of ideologically conservative provincial governments in the 1990s and early twenty-first century, such as those of Ralph Klein, followed by Ed Stelmach, in Alberta and Gordon Campbell in British Columbia, and the impressive support in western Canada for Reform/Alliance and then the Conservative Party in federal elections, are factors that appear to corroborate this argument that westerners are more receptive to what might be characterized as a classically American conception of equality. This involves the equal treatment of all individuals, without taking group membership into account, and formal equality of opportunity. On the other hand, little in the way of survey evidence supports the claim that westerners are significantly different from their compatriots in other regions in what they think about equality. Moreover, the quite different histories of the western provinces—compare that of Saskatchewan to neighbouring Alberta, for example—should give pause to anyone who wishes to generalize about a *western* conception of equality. Finally, the more recent crop of western premiers leading what are thought of as ideologically conservative governments, including Christy Clark in BC, Alison Redford in Alberta until March 2014, and Brad Wall in Saskatchewan, have been more moderate than the generation that preceded them.

The second core value of the western vision that Gibbins and Arrison identify is provincial equality. This really has two components. One is

Politics in Focus

BOX 5.2 The West as Canada's Internal Colony

John W. Dafoe was a journalist and editor with the Winnipeg Free Press, back in an era when newspapers were still the dominant medium whereby people learned about public affairs and the Winnipeg Free Press was considered one of Canada's leading dailies. The foundation that bears Dafoe's name annually awards a prize to what it judges to have been the non-fiction book that contributes most to the understanding of Canada. In 2013 the prize went to Mary Janigan's Let the Eastern Bastards Freeze in the Dark: The West Versus the Rest Since Confederation. *As a staunch defender of western interests he believed were regularly ignored by Ottawa, Dafoe most certainly would have approved of this selection. Here is Janigan's summary of the story that she tells:*

> The struggle over resource control twines through the nation's history as vividly as those wrenching debates over language and culture. The political actors who were once larger than life are now forgotten. But the legacy of their fights with the Rest of Canada, which played out in furious time across the decades, lingers in the language and the airy assumptions of today's politicians. Those battles have created an edgy regional identity. Even first-generation Westerners bristle at the mere mention of federal regulatory incursions. Canadians in other provinces still suspect Westerners of abusing the national patrimony—when they would never assert the same control over the hydro resources of Quebec or Newfoundland and Labrador.

These attitudes are bred in the bone, integrated after generations of political struggles between the West and the Rest of Canada. While Quebec struggled to maintain its status as one of the founding peoples of Canada, the West fought for the same constitutional right of resource control that other provinces possessed. The ingredients for trouble were woven into the very founding fabric of the nation. In the late 1860s when Ottawa purchased Western lands and resources from the Hudson's Bay Company, it viewed the West as a colonial space that it could span with a railroad and settle with immigrant farmers. The unexpected resistance of Louis Riel and the Métis to this second-class status was the first in a long line of objections to the West's limited powers and Ottawa's oblivious intrusions. In response, Ottawa and the other provincial governments countered that they had bought the West: the Rest owned the West. The most strident clash occurred on that cusp of time when the Great War ended and the First Ministers gathered to remake their world. By the time that tempers cooled, regional identities had solidified. The narratives of mutual suspicion were set.

This is *not* a regional story. It is the story of Canada. And it is still playing out in real time whenever Canadians ponder the privileges and the challenges of the West's resource wealth.

Source: Excerpt from Janigan, *Let the Eastern Bastards Freeze in the Dark: The West Versus the Rest Since Confederation* (2013). Reprinted with permission from Mary Janigan. http://maryjanigan.ca/

the sense that Canadian federalism would operate more fairly if the West had more influence on decisions taken by Ottawa. The idea of an elected Senate in which each province has an equal number of senators is one that has been spearheaded by western spokespersons since the 1980s. The other component of this core value involves opposition to any arrangement that appears to treat Quebec differently from and more favourably than the western provinces. Opposition to the Charlottetown Accord in the 1992 referendum was significantly higher in the four western provinces than in the rest of English-speaking Canada. Constitutional recognition of Quebec as a distinct society and other provisions that may well have been interpreted as providing special status for Quebec were, of course, among the most controversial sections of the Charlottetown Accord. Observers of the western political scene know that westerners have often felt resentment against Quebec, believing it to be the "spoiled child" of Confederation. The West's enthusiasm for the idea that the provinces are all equal in their rights and powers clashes with Quebecers' preference for a binational vision of the country in which Quebec, as the home of 90 per cent of French-speaking Canadians, and the rest of Canada are equal partners.

The third component of the western vision involves a populist style of politics. **Populism** arose in the American West and Midwest in the late 1800s out of the perception that economic and political elites, often far from where the people affected by their decisions lived, were too powerful and unsympathetic to the people's interests. The western Canadian version of populism was a combination of imported ideas and homegrown conditions that made the American message resonate in a farm and resource-based economy where people were constantly reminded by the railroads, the banks, the tariffs, and the grain elevator companies that they did not control their own destiny.

Populism, in its simplest form, seeks to return power to the common people. It sees elected politicians as delegates of those who elected them and therefore is hostile to party discipline and aspects of parliamentary government that reduce a public official's ability or willingness to be a direct tribune of his or her constituents' preferences. Populists favour recall votes to remove unfaithful public officials from office, plebiscites and referendums to give people a more direct say in the decisions that affect them, short terms of office, and term limits for public officials. In what is probably the best study of referendums in Canada, Patrick Boyer shows that this favoured instrument of populist democracy has been used far more extensively in the West than in other parts of Canada.[24] About 60 per cent of all provincial referendums held since Confederation have been in the four western

provinces. The Reform Party's original platform placed a heavy emphasis on referendums and recall votes, although this became a less prominent feature of the Alliance Party's platform. After Alliance morphed into the Conservative Party the populist proposals that had been distinguishing features of the original Reform message were watered down considerably. They maintain a greater following, however, in western Canada than in the rest of the country.

This may be seen in a number of measures enacted by western provincial governments. British Columbia passed a recall law in the 1990s—the first province to do so—and the British Columbia government of Gordon Campbell held a 2002 referendum on the highly contentious question of Aboriginal land claims and treaty negotiations in the province. BC held another referendum in 2005 and again in 2009 on a proposal to change the province's electoral system, and in 2011 a mail-in referendum asked about changing the province's sales tax. All of the four western legislatures have laws requiring that proposals for constitutional amendment be submitted to the people in a referendum, although Canada's Constitution does not require this. In short, there have been strong indications that populist values are more solidly rooted in the West than in the rest of Canada. On the other hand, however, the Conservative Party, shaped and led by westerners, has distanced itself from egalitarian populism since winning power in 2006.

Indeed, the Conservative Party's string of victories in the 2006, 2008, and 2011 federal elections has seen a sharp decline in western Canadians' belief that their region is unfairly treated by the national government. The Prime Minister is from Alberta, several of his most influential cabinet ministers are from the West, and the Conservative Party has won a majority of seats in the four western provinces in every election since 2006. Is western alienation finally dead?

In a recent analysis of western Canadians' perceptions of their treatment by Ottawa, Loleen Berdahl notes a sharp decline between 2004, when the Liberals were still in power, and 2008 in the percentage of westerners who say that the federal government treats their province worse than the others.

The decline is most dramatic in British Columbia and Alberta. Data from the 2011 Canadian Election Survey confirm that westerners appear to be much less alienated from the federal government than prior to the Conservative victory of 2006 (see Figure 5.3). Berdahl notes that westerners who identify with the Conservative Party are, not surprisingly, most likely to feel that their province is treated fairly by Ottawa, but the decline in the percentage of respondents saying that their province is treated worse than other provinces cuts across political parties.[25]

Having friends in high places certainly appears to take the edge off sentiments of alienation. But another factor that appears to have contributed to the decline in the West's sense of resentment towards the federal government may be immigration. Neil

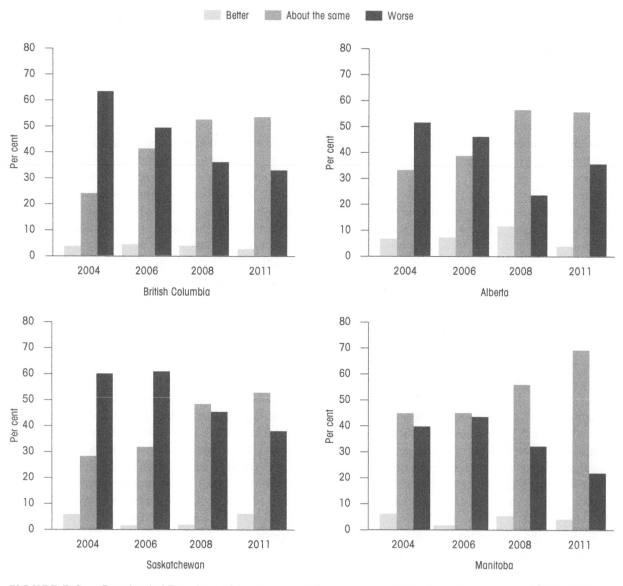

FIGURE 5.3   Provincial Treatment by Federal Government, Western Provinces, 2004, 2006, 2008, 2011

Source: Loleen Berdahl, "Whither Western Alienation? Shifting Patterns of Western Canadian Discontent with the Federal Government" (Calgary: Canada West Foundation, Oct. 2010), 3, with data for 2011 added from the Canadian Election Study.

Nevitte and his colleagues find that immigrants from non-European source countries tend to be "more federally oriented than the local population in their province." British Columbia has been a magnet for many immigrants to Canada, and Alberta to a lesser extent. The historical memory of grievances that has long fuelled western alienation is, of course, less likely to exist among the non-native born,[26] although, as Janigan maintains, even first-generation westerners "bristle" at "federal regulatory incursions" (see Box 5.2). At the same time, Alberta in recent years has received significant migration from other provinces.

Western alienation, however, should not be dismissed as mere history. The sense of regional grievance, with roots reaching back to the nineteenth century, can resurface very quickly and with real political consequences. During the 2012 federal by-election in Calgary Centre, comments by federal Liberals Justin Trudeau and David McGuinty were widely covered and criticized by the local media. In a 2010 interview Trudeau had said that "Canada isn't doing well right now because it's Albertans who control our community and socio-democratic agenda."[27] Along with McGuinty's comment that Alberta MPs were "shills" for the oil industry and his suggestion that they "go home"—as if somehow Canada is not home to Albertans—these reminders of the East/West divide may well have cost the Liberals their chance to win that election. When it appeared the federal government might be open to providing funding for a new hockey arena in Quebec City to attract a National Hockey League franchise, Canadians in Saskatchewan were quick to point out that Ottawa had just turned down Regina's request for federal assistance to build a

Some of the recent growth of Alberta's population can be attributed to migration from the Maritime provinces. Despite Newfoundland and Labrador's recent resource-based growth, the province's population continues to decline and workers continue to migrate from the region elsewhere.

new CFL football stadium. "So will Harper throw money at Quebec," asked the Prince Albert *Daily Herald*, "in the hopes of winning more seats there, but spark Western alienation?"[28] Energy politics, however, is most likely to stir the deep wells of resentment and mistrust that westerners and their governments have towards Ottawa and what they see as the traditional political elite (see Box 5.3).

As Canada's poorest region with its own list of grievances against the federal government and central Canada, one might have expected that the Maritime provinces would have generated an eastern version of western alienation. The easternmost provinces have indeed produced leaders, such as Newfoundland Premiers Joey Smallwood (1949–72), Brian Peckford (1979–89), and Danny Williams (2003–10), who have taken a back seat to none in being outspoken critics of what they saw as unjust treatment of their province by Ottawa. A radical-populist Maritime rights movement— the Antigonish Movement centred at St Francis Xavier University—swept the region in the 1930s, and proposals for Maritime union have existed since before Confederation, continuing to surface as ideas, though with little political support, from time to time. But the dissatisfaction of Maritimers has never produced a major political vehicle for the expression of alienation and resentment, such as

Media Spotlight

BOX 5.3 Rex Murphy Warns Thomas Mulcair on the Dangers of Waking Western Alienation

I find so very puzzling the recent comments (and the pugnacity with which they have been delivered) of . . . the NDP's Thomas Mulcair, on the development of the oil sands. I fail utterly to see what he meant, or could hope to gain, by calling three premiers—Alison Redford of Alberta, Brad Wall of Saskatchewan, and Christy Clark of BC—"Harper's messengers." He's brusquely declared them irrelevant. That'll be news to the voters in those three provinces. . . .

He is vibrating strings best left still. Alberta, in particular, still carries angry memories of the last occasion a "national" framework was placed on its energy development. The Trudeau government's imposition of the National Energy Plan (NEP) burned Alberta deeply, reinforced every negative stereotype—true or false—westerners had about the "eastern establishment." It set up very real strains of what was called at the time "western alienation" and even a few voices calling for separation. That careless policy came close to testing the strength of Confederation.

It's taken more than a couple of decades to exorcise the demon of the NEP from western memories—particularly Albertan ones—and now along comes the freshly minted leader of Her Majesty's Opposition firing both barrels at the oil sands, blasting its pace of development, and— effectively—blaming the economic woes of Ontario, Quebec and New Brunswick on the economic success of the West.

This is raw territory. It seeks collision, not compromise. It is aggressive and impatient. It plays against the preferred strains of our national character, and against the style of leadership that places—when possible—accommodation and understanding ahead of quick confrontation.

It does not do needlessly to provoke any region of Canada, anytime. It certainly does not do to antagonize the West and deplore its latter-day successes with resource development. They have seen that play once already. And they will have no patience whatsoever should Mr. Mulcair or anyone else seek to see it restaged.

Source: *National Post*, "Rex Murphy on Thomas Mulcair: How recklessly unCanadian," May 19, 2012. Material reprinted with the express permission of: National Post, a division of Postmedia Network Inc.

the Progressive movement of the 1920s, the Social Credit Party from the 1930s to the 1970s, and the Reform Party in the late 1980s and 1990s in western Canada. Why not?

The answer is complex, but two elements are certainly crucial. First, the populist values linked to western alienation from its beginnings a century ago have been comparatively weak in the Maritime provinces. The reasons for this involve a combination of demographic and economic differences between the eastern and western regions of Canada, but also differences in the political histories of the two regions. Whereas Alberta and Saskatchewan did not achieve provincial status until 1905—and then, without control of their natural resources for 25 years—Nova Scotia and New Brunswick, despite some loud and articulate anti-Confederation voices in the region, were original members of the Confederation pact, and PEI soon followed. The historically dominant parties have deep roots in the Maritimes, stretching back to Confederation. **Protest parties** have always found it difficult to break through the two-party domination in the East. The Progressives failed to win a single seat from the region even in 1921, when they emerged from the general election as the official opposition. Social Credit and the Reform Party did no better. It was not until 1974 that the NDP won a seat from the region. In more recent years the NDP's fortunes have improved in the Maritimes. But whereas in western Canada NDP provincial governments have been able to capture the deep resentment of their citizens over what they perceive to be unfair and even exploitative treatment—this was true, for example, under the NDP government of Allan Blakeney in Saskatchewan (1971–82)—NDP governments in eastern Canada have not been elected on the basis of this sort of appeal, nor have they expressed this sort of message.

Economically and demographically the Maritimes have been in decline, relative to the rest of Canada, since the late nineteenth century. The region's population as a share of the national population has plummeted since Confederation.

As shown earlier in this chapter, the economies of the eastern provinces are among the weakest in Canada. This remains true despite Newfoundland and Labrador's impressive resource-fuelled growth of recent years. (The province's population has barely changed over the last decade and it continues to lose highly educated and skilled workers to other parts of the country, notwithstanding increases in its provincial GDP and government revenues.) All of the eastern provinces depend on money redistributed by Ottawa from more prosperous regions of the country to pay for public services. This stands in stark contrast to the prosperity that Alberta and British Columbia have experienced during most of the last half-century, and that Saskatchewan now enjoys as a result of higher world prices for natural resources found in the province, and to the dramatic population growth experienced in the two westernmost provinces.

The much more assertive attitude of western than eastern Canadians and their greater willingness to reject the traditional political parties in favour of protest parties surely is linked to confidence in the economic future of their region. "The West wants in," the founding slogan of the Reform Party, was not the plea of a weak and supplicant region. Rather, it was the demand of a region whose population believed that Canadian politics needed to adjust to the reality of their economically powerful and growing provinces. Pollster Darrell Bricker and journalist John Ibbitson argue that the traditional political elites of Ontario and Quebec have failed to recognize this new reality. "The provinces that mattered most don't matter as much anymore," they write. "The country's centre has shifted west, and power has shifted with it."[29] Barry Cooper agrees and takes the argument a step further. "The real divisions in Canada's future are not those of French and English speakers or of Aboriginals and settlers," he argues, "but those between rich and poor regions, declining and growing regions, regions that embrace the past and those that shape the future. And the dividing line is the Ottawa River."[30]

Starting Points for Research

Keith Archer and Lisa Young, eds, *Regionalism and Party Politics in Canada* (Toronto: Oxford University Press, 2002). Although a bit dated, this is an excellent collection of essays on the regional nature of Canada's party system, with a particular emphasis on western Canada.

Christopher Dunn, ed., *Provinces: Canadian Provincial Politics*, 2nd edn (Toronto: University of Toronto Press, 2006). The chapters in this collection offer the best single-volume coverage of political institutions, public administration, public policy, and political attitudes and behaviour in Canada's provinces.

Loleen Berdahl and Roger Gibbins, *Looking West: Regional Transformation and the Future of Canada* (Toronto: University of Toronto Press, 2014). Berdahl and Gibbins's earlier book, *Western Visions, Western Futures*, was the best short survey of the special characteristics of western Canada's political value system and the roots and consequences of western alienation. in *Looking West* they provide an updated picture of western Canada and argue that the future of Canada is powerfully influenced by developments in the West.

Mary Janigan, *Let the Eastern Bastards Freeze in the Dark: The West Versus the Rest Since Confederation* (Toronto: Random House, 2012). Winner of the John W. Dafoe Prize in 2013 for the non-fiction book contributing most to the understanding of Canada.

Nelson Wiseman, *In Search of Canadian Political Culture* (Vancouver: University of British Columbia Press, 2007). Wiseman examines the distinctiveness of regional political cultures and emphasizes their importance in Canadian politics.

Review Exercises

1. Compare media coverage in three different regions of the country. You may do this by consulting hard copies or online versions of three daily papers in three different provinces—one from the West, one from Ontario, and one from an eastern province. Check the front page, the editorial page, and letters to the editor. Do you find any indication of a different news agenda or different perspectives in different provinces?

2. How well do you know other regions of Canada? Make a list of the personal connections that you have outside of your province. Have you lived in or visited other provinces? Which ones? Do you have friends or family members in other provinces? In which ones? Do you know which parties form the governments of other provinces? Can you name their premiers? Their capitals? Have you spent more time travelling or living in the United States or other countries than in other provinces? Do you ever think that you might move to another part of Canada for employment? Where?

3. Who were Amor de Cosmos, Henry Wise Wood, Louis Robichaud, and Joseph Howe? What is the significance of each for his region of the country?

Part III
The Structures of Governance

The root of the word *government* is the Latin verb *gubernare*, meaning to guide or direct. And, indeed, what government does is to provide direction for a society through the management of the public's business. This general function is performed through a number of more specialized institutions, including a country's legislature, head of state and head of government, system of courts, and bureaucracy. Their authority and roles within a country's structure of government will depend in large part on the constitution. Laws are made, implemented, and enforced, and redress is provided to aggrieved citizens on the basis of the written and unwritten rules embodied in a country's constitution. This, at any rate, is the ideal of democratic governance.

Constitutions and structures of government are reflections of the societies in which they are embedded. In the case of Canada, the Constitution adopted in 1867 and the country's parliamentary system of government may be understood as responses to particular societal and historical circumstances. The same is true for the important revisions that took place as a result of the Constitution Act, 1982. But once in place, constitutions and institutions of government tend to have what political scientists call an *independent effect* on political outcomes. In other words, the issues that get onto the political agenda, how they are framed, what voices are listened to, and what ultimately happens are influenced to some degree by the structures of government. Societal factors are important—the environment of ideas and interests that press on those who exercise public authority—but political outcomes will depend on the nature of the constitutional and governmental systems through which they are processed.

One of the most difficult challenges in political analysis is to separate from the influence of *societal factors* the influence that *structural factors*—constitutions and government institutions—have on politics and policy. There is no one-size-fits-all answer to this question. The balance between structural and societal factors depends on the issue in question. But most of the time governmental structures play an important role in the determination of political outcomes.

The Constitution

6

Constitutions are at the heart of democratic politics. This chapter examines key features of the Canadian Constitution. It includes the following topics:

- Functions of a constitution.
- Rights and freedoms.
- Parliamentary government.
- Responsible government.
- Ministerial responsibility.
- Parliamentary and constitutional supremacy.
- Judicial independence.
- The House of Commons and the Senate.
- The biases of British parliamentary government.
- Changing the Constitution.
- Citizen participation in constitutional reform.
- Does Quebec have the right to separate?

Prime Minister Pierre Elliott Trudeau signs the 17 April 1982 constitutional proclamation that patriated Canada's Constitution, giving the country full political independence from the United Kingdom. The Constitution of Canada outlines the country's system of government and the rights of citizens. (Ron Bull/GetStock.com)

Most Canadians have only a vague and often inaccurate idea of what is included in their country's Constitution. A 2012 survey found that only half could identify from a list of choices the date when it came into force (1 July 1867). Barely more than one-quarter could correctly identify the original four provinces (Nova Scotia, New Brunswick, Quebec, and Ontario). One-third could provide some information on the different functions of the executive, the House of Commons, the Senate, and the judiciary. Four out of ten could list some of the rights and freedoms in the Charter of Rights and Freedoms. Fewer than one-third knew that French and English are the official languages of Canada. Only one out of five knew that the federal and provincial governments may act in ways that violate certain rights and freedoms in the Charter.[1]

Perhaps ignorance on this scale does not matter. After all, does knowledge of dusty facts from the nineteenth century make one a better person? Will your ability to earn a living be impaired if you cannot identify Canada's official languages? Are people likely to find you less interesting if you don't know what is in the Charter of Rights and Freedoms, let alone that governments can, in some circumstances, ignore the guarantees in that constitutional document? The answer to all of these questions may well be "no."

What is certain, however, is that you cannot truly claim to understand Canadian politics and government without having some basic knowledge of what is in the Constitution. You may be able to identify the political parties and their leaders (although if you know nothing about the Constitution then it is unlikely that you have this other knowledge); you may have passionate opinions on climate change, seal hunting, and health care; and you may have ideas about who exercises power in society and on what basis. But you will not truly understand why things happen the way they do in Canada's system of government, nor will you know who to hold to account when and for what. This understanding requires a knowledge of the Constitution, in Canada as in any other democracy.

A **constitution** is the fundamental law of a political system. It is fundamental because all other laws must conform to the constitution in terms of *how they are made* and in terms of their *substance*.

A constitution is a necessary condition for democratic politics. Without it there is no civilized way of resolving conflicts and no way of predicting either the powers of government or the rights of citizens.

A constitution is expected to establish order, allowing for the peaceful settlement of differences. Early liberal thinkers like Thomas Hobbes, John Locke, and Jean-Jacques Rousseau all used the concept of the "state of nature" to illustrate the impulse behind constitutional government. The state of nature, wrote Hobbes, was a state of chaos in which no individual could feel secure in the possession of his property or life. This insecurity leads people to demand a constitution where there is none, and to accept the necessity of a constitution even if they find it difficult to agree on its precise components.

In modern societies the alternatives to constitutional government are anarchy—the sort of chaos and civil strife that exists in countries where state authority has broken down—or totalitarianism. Where anarchy reigns, there are no generally accepted rules for resolving the differences between factions of the population. The state does not exist in any meaningful way. Under totalitarianism the state exists. But because its powers are unlimited and all realms of social and economic life are subordinate to it, it makes no sense to talk of a constitution. If the rules of a board game can be changed at will by one of the players then it is nonsense to speak of rules. So, too, with a constitution: if its terms are purely arbitrary it ceases to be a constitution in anything other than name. The rules that make up a constitution deal with two sets of relations. One of these involves the relationship between citizens and the state. A constitution empowers the state to act, to pass laws on behalf of the community. At the same time a democratic constitution will *limit power*. It does this by identifying those freedoms and individual rights, and in some cases group rights, that the state cannot infringe. The other set of relations encompassed by a constitution involves the distribution of functions and powers between different parts of the state. Modern government is, after all, a complex mechanism. This mechanism is often analyzed under three main functional headings: the legislature (making the law); the executive (implementing the law); and the judiciary (interpreting the law). The reality of the modern state is more complicated than this tripartite division of powers suggests. But whatever the degree of complexity is, the rules that govern the relations between the various parts of the state are an important component of the constitution.

In a federal state like Canada, where the Constitution divides law-making powers between a national government and regional governments, the rules governing the relations between these two levels are also part of the Constitution. This third aspect of the Constitution overshadowed the other two for most of Canada's history. Indeed, before 1982, when the Charter of Rights and Freedoms was adopted, the relations between individuals and the state in Canada were defined by the courts mainly in terms of federal and provincial legislative powers.

A constitution, then, is a set of rules that govern political life. These rules may take three forms: written documents, the decisions of courts (called the **common law**), or unwritten conventions. **Constitutional conventions** are those practices that emerge over time and are generally accepted as binding rules of the political system. An example would be the convention that the leader of the party that wins the most seats in a House of Commons election is called on to form a government. This rule is not set down in the written constitution. In Canada the first two components of the Constitution—written documents and the common law—together comprise *constitutional law.* Conventions, while part of the Constitution, do not have the status of constitutional law, at least not in Canada. This distinction was made by the Supreme Court of Canada in a 1981 ruling (see Box 6.1). It should not be interpreted to mean that constitutional law is more important than constitutional conventions. What it does mean, however, is that the rules of constitutional law are enforceable by the courts, whereas constitutional conventions are not.

Constitutional Functions

A constitution does more than provide a basis for non-violent politics. It also performs several more specific functions that include the following.

Representation

All modern democracies are representative democracies, in which politicians make decisions on behalf of those who elect them. But this still leaves enormous room for variation in how the population is represented, who is represented, and how the people's representatives are selected.

A constitution prescribes both the *basis* of political representation and the *method* by which representatives are chosen. The basis of democratic representation may be by population, by territory, or by group. Representation by population is based on the principle of "one person, one vote." Under such a system, all elected members of the legislature should represent approximately the same number of voters. This arrangement is most likely to allow the preferences of a simple majority of the population to be translated into law. Although virtually all modern democracies incorporate some form of "rep by pop" in their constitutions, many temper majority rule by representing regions as well. For example, the American Constitution gives each state the right to two senators, despite the fact that the population of the largest state is about 60 times that of the smallest. Representation in Canada's Senate is also by region: Ontario, Quebec, the western provinces, and the Maritime provinces each have 24 seats; Newfoundland and Labrador has six; and the northern territories are represented by three senators. Federalism is a form of government that embodies the principle of territorial representation. It does so by giving regional governments the exclusive right to pass laws on particular subjects.

A constitution may also accord representation to groups. New Zealand's constitution, for one, guarantees four seats in that country's legislature to representatives of the Maori minority. Singapore has guaranteed seats for official ethnic minority groups. Pakistan reserves 60 seats in the national legislature for women and 10 for non-Muslims. In Canada, suggestions for Senate reform have sometimes included proposals to guarantee seats for women and for the representatives of Aboriginal Canadians. The defeated 1992 Charlottetown Accord would have ensured that Quebec, whose share of Canada's population has been falling steadily, would maintain one-quarter of all seats in the House of Commons. This was, one might argue, a thinly disguised guarantee for francophone group representation. Proposals like that in the Charlottetown Accord and the various guarantees of group representation that exist in some countries are based on premises about democracy that are quite different from those that underpin one person/one vote.

A constitution also establishes the methods by which the holders of public office are selected. Election and appointment are the two basic methods, but each allows for a wide variety of procedures that affect who is represented and how responsive public officials are to the popular will. For example, it is typical for members of the judiciary to be appointed for life, a practice expected to insulate them from popular passions and the partisan preferences of elected governments. An elected legislature is a standard feature of democratic political systems and, for that matter, of non-democratic ones. But many constitutions divide the legislative power between an elected chamber and an appointed one, as in Canada, the United Kingdom, and Germany.

Finally, the electoral process itself has a crucial influence on representation. As we will see in Chapter 11, the single-member constituency system used in Canada discourages political parties from directing their appeals at a narrow segment of the national electorate. Unless that segment happens to be concentrated in a particular region, such a strategy will not pay off in elected members. A system of proportional representation, whereby a party's percentage of the popular votes translates into a corresponding share of seats in the legislature, has a very different effect. It promotes a splintering of the party system and allows for the direct representation of such interests as ardent environmentalists in Germany, orthodox Jews in Israel, and anti-immigration elements in the Netherlands. In a system like Canada's, these groups would have to rely on whatever influence they could achieve within one of the larger political parties or else turn to non-electoral strategies to influence public opinion and government policy.

Power

The simple fact of constitutional government means that the state is empowered to act and that

Governing Realities

BOX 6.1 What Is a Constitutional Convention?

. . . (M)any Canadians would perhaps be surprised to learn that important parts of the Constitution of Canada, with which they are the most familiar because they are directly involved when they exercise their right to vote at federal and provincial elections, are nowhere to be found in the law of the Constitution. For instance it is a fundamental requirement of the Constitution that if the Opposition obtains the majority at the polls, the Government must tender its resignation forthwith. But fundamental as it is, this requirement of the Constitution does not form part of the law of the Constitution. . . .

The main purpose of constitutional conventions is to ensure that the legal framework of the Constitution will be

operated in accordance with the prevailing constitutional values or principles of the period. . . .

The conventional rules of the Constitution present one striking peculiarity. In contradistinction to the laws of the Constitution, they are not enforced by the courts. . . .

It is because the sanctions of convention rest with institutions of government other than courts, such as the Governor General or the Lieutenant-Governor, or the Houses of Parliament, or with public opinion and, ultimately, with the electorate that it is generally said that they are political.

Source: Supreme Court of Canada, *Attorney General of Manitoba et al. v. Attorney General of Canada et al.*, 28 Sept. 1981.

its actions may be backed up by the full weight of public authority. A constitution, therefore, provides the basis for the legitimate exercise of state power. But it also *limits* and *divides* power, at least under a democratic constitution. For example, a constitutional requirement that elections periodically be held restrains state power by making those who wield it accountable to, and removable by, the electorate. The existence of separate branches of government under the constitution, or of two levels of government as in the case of federalism, divides state power between different groups of public officials. How power is divided among the various parts of the state, or between the national and regional governments, is not determined solely by the constitution. But constitutional law and conventions affect both the extent and distribution of state power.

Rights

A right is something that a person is entitled to, like the right to vote or the right not to be held against one's will without a reason being given. Constitutions vary greatly in the particular rights they assign to individuals and to societal groups. At a minimum, a democratic constitution establishes the basic right of citizens to choose their government. But most constitutions go beyond this to guarantee—although not without limit—such rights as the individual's right to free speech, freedom of association, and freedom of religion and conscience, as well as legal rights such as freedom from arbitrary detention and unreasonable search and seizure. These rights limit the state's power vis-à-vis the individual. They do so by making that power dependent on popular consent (democratic rights) or by establishing an individual's right not to be interfered with by the state (personal liberty).

Rights may also empower individuals by requiring the state to either protect or promote their interests. For example, a right to equal treatment under the law provides individuals with a constitutional remedy in cases where they have been discriminated against because of their sex, race, ethnic background, or whatever other basis of discrimination is prohibited by the constitution. The state is obliged to protect their interests. As a practical matter this requires the state to act—to pass a law, create a program, spend money, or in some other way take steps that will provide redress for those who fall into the category of persons who have been judged to experience unequal treatment under the law. The protection of equality may see the state involved in sweeping and ongoing activities like affirmative action or racial desegregation on the grounds that such steps are necessary to alleviate discrimination.

Constitutions may also recognize the special status of particular groups, thereby giving special rights to their members that are not enjoyed by others. For example, Canada's Constitution declares that both French and English are official languages with "equality of status and equal rights and privileges as to their use in all institutions of the Parliament and government of Canada."[2] This is a *positive* right in the sense that it obliges the state to assume particular linguistic characteristics, and, therefore, to protect actively the rights of French- and English-speakers—at least in matters that fall under Ottawa's jurisdiction. A constitution that recognizes the special status of particular religious denominations, as the Israeli constitution recognizes the Jewish religion, the Iranian constitution the religion of Islam, or the British constitution the Church of England, empowers the members of these religious groups to varying degrees by giving them state-protected rights that are not held by other denominations.

Community and Identity

When Pierre Trudeau wrote that "A nation is not more and no less than the entire population of a sovereign state,"[3] he was arguing that a constitution establishes a political community. And in an obvious sense it does. A constitution is the set of fundamental rules that govern political life *in a particular territory*. Its rules are operative within that territory and not elsewhere. Individuals in Rimouski, Quebec, and in Kitimat, British Columbia, are part of the same constitutional system and share a formal political status as Canadians. Even if they perceive their differences to be more important than what they share, this does not diminish the fact that they have legal membership in the same constitutional community.

Carrying the same national passport and being eligible to vote in the same elections may seem a rather weak basis for a *sense of community*, a sentiment that transcends the formal ties of common citizenship. The fact of being citizens of the Soviet Union, for example, did not erase the strongly nationalist sentiments of Ukrainians, Estonians, Latvians, and other ethnic communities within that former country. For these groups the Soviet constitution and the political community it created were things to regret, not to celebrate. Likewise in Canada, a significant minority of the population—Quebec separatists—rejects the Canadian political community and would prefer to live under a different constitution creating an independent Quebec.

A constitution, therefore, may inspire negative or positive feelings among the members of a political community. Or it may leave them feeling indifferent. These feelings may be associated with the political community that a constitution creates, but they may also be associated with the particular institutions, values, and symbols embedded in a constitution. For example, the monarchy and other institutions and symbols redolent of Canada's colonial past have historically been an aspect of the Canadian Constitution dividing Canadians of French and British ancestry.

Official bilingualism and constitutional proposals that would recognize Quebec as a "distinct society" within Canada have been two of the most divisive constitutional issues in modern Canadian history. On the other hand, some features of the Constitution unite, rather than divide, Canadians. There is, for example, overwhelming support among all regions and social groups for the Charter of Rights and Freedoms. In general, we may say that a constitution generates a shared identity among the citizens of a country to the extent that most people have positive feelings towards the political community it creates and the values it embodies. On these counts, Canada's Constitution has had a mixed record of successes and failures.

National Purpose

When the first permanent white settlement was established in 1608 at what today is Quebec City, it operated under a royal charter that proclaimed the Catholic mission of the French colony. Aside from being an outpost of political and economic empire, it was to be a beachhead of Christianity from which Catholicism would spread to the rest of the continent. The constitution of New France was therefore linked to a communal goal, to a sense of purpose and direction for society.[4]

This is not so rare. The constitution of the People's Republic of China starts with a very long preamble that describes the country's path to socialism. The constitutions of the Islamic Republic of Iran and of Pakistan both declare that society should conform to Muslim religious teachings. The most controversial part of the failed Meech Lake reforms to Canada's Constitution, the recognition of Quebec as a "distinct society," would have transformed Quebec nationalism from a political reality to a constitutionally entrenched fact. This was because the Quebec legislature and government would have been constitutionally required to "preserve and promote" the distinct character of the province, which the distinct society proposal made clear was the French-speaking character of Quebec.

The constitutional document that created Canada, the Constitution Act, 1867, also included a number of provisions that embodied a national purpose. This purpose was the building of a new country stretching from the Atlantic to the Pacific oceans and an integrated economy tying together this vast territory. The nation-building goal is evident in the anticipation that other parts of British North America eventually would be admitted into Canada,[5] in the prohibition of barriers to trade between provinces,[6] and even in the constitutional commitment to build the Intercolonial Railway, a project described as "essential to the Consolidation of the Union of British North America, and to the assent thereto of Nova Scotia and New Brunswick."[7] The Constitution Act, 1982 commits Ottawa and the provinces to the promotion of equal opportunities for Canadians and the reduction of economic disparities between regions of the country.[8] Some argue that this represents at least one of Canada's national purposes, namely, the equitable treatment of its citizens regardless of their province of residence. Such declarations of national purpose may be symbolically important, but they do not always have teeth. By way of illustration, the fact that the Constitution Act, 1867 prohibits internal barriers to trade between the provinces has not prevented the proliferation of a dense thicket of provincial protectionist measures, many of which continue to exist today.

Canada's Constitution

As constitutional documents go, Canada's is fairly lengthy. In fact, it is not one document but a series of laws passed between 1867 and 1982. Together they are both longer and more detailed than the United States Constitution. Even so, the written documents of Canada's Constitution provide only a fragmentary and even misleading picture of how the Constitution actually works. Many of the most basic features of the Constitution—including most of those that deal with the democratic accountability of government to the people—are nowhere to be found in these documents. On the other hand, some of what is included in the written Constitution would, if acted on, probably result in a constitutional crisis! For example, the Queen is formally the head of state in Canada and has the constitutional authority to make decisions of fundamental importance, such as when an election will take place and who will be appointed to cabinet. No one expects, however, that she will actually make such decisions.

Canada's Constitution, like all constitutions, embodies values and principles central to the political life of the country. In its 1998 decision on the constitutionality of Quebec separation, the Supreme Court of Canada referred to these values and principles as the "internal architecture" of the Constitution,[9] or what, in an earlier ruling, the Court had called the "basic constitutional structure."[10] These basic principles, although not necessarily part of the written Constitution, "form the very foundation of the Constitution of Canada."[11]

The principles that the Supreme Court identified as making up the internal architecture of Canada's Constitution include federalism, democracy, constitutionalism and the rule of law, and respect for minority rights.

Federalism

"The principle of federalism," declares the Supreme Court, "recognizes the diversity of the component parts of Confederation, and the autonomy of provincial governments to develop their societies within their respective spheres of jurisdiction."[12] In other words, provinces are not constitutionally subordinate to the federal government and Ottawa is not dependent on the provinces for the exercise of those powers assigned to it by the Constitution. The written Constitution distributes law-making and revenue-raising authority between the central and regional governments. This distribution reflects the underlying federal principle that some matters properly belong to provincial societies and their governments to decide, while others are national in scope and properly decided by the Parliament and government in Ottawa. We will explore more fully the nature and development of Canadian federalism in Chapter 8.

Democracy

Democracy has always been one of the fundamental, if unwritten, givens of Canada's constitutional system. A literal reading of Canada's written Constitution before the inclusion of the Charter of Rights and Freedoms in 1982 might well lead someone who knows nothing of Canada's history and culture to draw a very different conclusion. Aside from the fact that periodic elections were required under the Constitution Act, 1867, there were few other explicit indications that the Constitution adopted by the founders was democratic. On the contrary, while the authority of governments was detailed painstakingly, the Constitution was remarkably silent when it came to the rights of citizens. Why was this so?

In explaining the silence of the pre-Charter Constitution, the Supreme Court states that to have declared explicitly that Canada was a democracy, and to have specified what that entailed, would have seemed to the founders "redundant" and even "silly." "The representative and democratic nature of our political institutions," the Court writes, "was simply assumed."[13] This assumption was suggested in the preamble to the Constitution Act, 1867, which states that Canada has adopted "a Constitution similar in Principle to that of the United Kingdom." The very centrality of the democratic principle and the fact that it was simply taken for granted as the baseline against which government would operate explain why the framers of the written Constitution did not perceive the need to state what all assumed to be obvious.

But the precise meaning of the democracy principle, as we saw in Chapter 1, is not obvious and has evolved over time. Women did not have the vote for more than 50 years after Confederation, and only a minority of the population found anything undemocratic in this exclusion. Even when the meaning of democracy is specified in a written constitution, as it was to a very considerable degree in the United States Constitution and the Declaration of Independence that preceded it, expectations and understandings change over time, as they have over the course of American history. What meaning is properly attributed to the democratic principle of Canada's Constitution today?

The Supreme Court's 1998 decision answers this question by distinguishing between process and outcomes. On the process side, the Court observed that majority rule is a basic premise of constitutional democracy in Canada. The fact that Canada has a federal constitution means, however, that "there may be different and equally legitimate majorities in different provinces and territories and at the federal level."[14] In other words, a nationwide majority does not trump a provincial majority if the matter in question belongs constitutionally to the provinces or requires the approval of some number of provincial legislatures (which is true for most constitutional amendments).

In a 1986 Charter decision,[15] the Supreme Court had expressed the view that the democratic principle underlying the Charter and the rest of Canada's Constitution is also linked to substantive goals. Among these are the following:

- respect for the inherent dignity of every person;
- commitment to equality and social justice;
- social and cultural diversity, including respect for the identities of minority groups' social and political institutions that enhance the opportunities for individuals and groups to participate in society.

This view was echoed in the Supreme Court's 1998 ruling. In words directly relevant to the issue of Quebec separation, the Court said that "The consent of the governed is a value that is basic to our understanding of a free and democratic society."[16] Democratic government derives its necessary legitimacy from this consent. Moreover, the legitimacy of laws passed and actions taken by a democratic government rests on "moral values, many of which are imbedded in our constitutional structure."[17] The Supreme Court did not elaborate on what these moral values might be.

Constitutionalism and the Rule of Law

"At its most basic level," declares the Supreme Court, "the rule of law vouchsafes to the citizens and residents of the country a stable, predictable and ordered society in which to conduct their affairs."[18] It guarantees, therefore, that all public authority must ultimately be exercised in accordance with the law and that there will be one law for all persons. When it comes to light that some public official has overstepped the bounds of his or her office, regardless of the office-holder's intentions, or that someone has been accorded preferred treatment under the law because of personal connections, we rightly are offended. Such actions violate the premise of the rule of law, namely, that ours is a government of laws, not of men and women, and that everyone is entitled to equal treatment under the law.

Like the rule of law, the constitutionalism principle involves predictable governance that has its source in written rules rather than in the arbitrary wills of individuals. The constitutionalism principle is expressed in s. 52(1) of the Constitution

Act, 1982, which states that the Constitution is the supreme law of the land and that all government action must be in conformity with the Constitution. Before the Charter was entrenched in the Constitution and the constitutionalism principle was expressly stated, the final authority of the Constitution was less certain. The pre-Charter era was one of **parliamentary supremacy**. This meant that, in essence, so long as one level of government did not trespass onto jurisdictional turf that the Constitution assigned to the other level, it was free to do as it liked. The principle of parliamentary supremacy is captured in the aphoristic statement attributed to the eighteenth-century Swiss-English constitutional theorist, Jean-Louis de Lolme, that "Parliament can do anything except change a man into a woman and a woman into a man." The constitutionalism principle, by contrast, places certain matters relating to rights and freedoms beyond the reach of any government.

Constitutionalism and the rule of law temper and modify the principle of majority rule in a democracy. They do so by ensuring that the mere fact that a majority of citizens—even an overwhelming majority—supports a particular government action does not mean that such an action will be either lawful or constitutional. Together, these principles constitute a sort of bulwark against what Tocqueville called the "tyranny of the majority."

Protection of Minorities

The recognition of group rights has a history in Canada that goes back to the beginnings of British colonial rule. The Royal Proclamation of 1763 includes considerable detail—the meaning of which is a matter of dispute—on the rights of the "several Nations or Tribes of Indians . . . who live under our protection." The Quebec Act of 1774 recognized the rights of Catholics in Quebec and guaranteed the overwhelmingly French-speaking population the enjoyment of their "Property and Possessions, together with all Customs and Usages relative thereto, and all other [of] their Civil Rights," concessions that most historians agree were intended to ensure the support of the Catholic Church authorities in Quebec at a time when rebellion was

simmering in the American colonies. Group rights were recognized again through the "double majority principle" that operated when Canada East (Quebec) and Canada West (Ontario) were joined together through a common legislature during the period 1841–67. Under this principle any bill touching on matters of language or religion in either Canada East or Canada West had to be approved by majorities of legislators from both Canada East—mainly French and Catholic—and Canada West—mainly English and Protestant. In practice this gave a veto to each ethnolinguistic community in regard to legislation affecting minority rights.

The Constitution Act, 1867 entrenched the principle of minority rights through the section 93 guarantee of minority religious education rights and the section 133 declaration that French and English were to have official status in the Parliament of Canada, the legislature of Quebec, and courts created by either of those bodies. "The protection of minority rights," declares the Supreme Court, "was clearly an essential consideration in the design of our constitutional structure even at the time of Confederation."[19] The principle acquired a new level of prominence as a result of the Charter of Rights and Freedoms. The Charter enlarges the scope of official-language minority rights, explicitly recognizes Aboriginal rights, opens the door to a multitude of group rights claims through the equality section of the Charter (s. 15), and provides a basis for a variety of minority rights claims through other sections, including the legal rights and democratic rights provisions of the Charter.

A useful way of analyzing a constitution is to approach it from the angle of each of the relationships governed by constitutional rules. As noted earlier, these relationships include: (1) those between individuals and the state; (2) those between the various institutions of government; and (3) those between the national and regional governments. The first category involves rights and freedoms, the second deals with the machinery and process of government, and the third category is about federalism. A constitution also includes a fourth category of rules that establish what procedures must be followed to bring about constitutional change. Federalism is dealt with in Chapter 8. We turn now to an examination of the other three dimensions of Canada's Constitution.

The Charter of Rights and Freedoms

Since 1982 Canada's Constitution has included formal distinctions between fundamental political freedoms, democratic rights, mobility rights, legal rights, equality rights, and language rights. These are the categories set down in the Charter of Rights and Freedoms. Most of the rights and freedoms enumerated in the Charter were, however, part of Canada's Constitution before 1982. In some cases they can be found in the Constitution Act, 1867. In others, they were established principles of the common law. Some were set down in the Criminal Code. The inclusion of these rights and freedoms in the Charter, however, has made an important difference in Canadian politics. Groups and individuals are far more likely today than in the pre-Charter era to reach for the judicial lever in attempting to protect their rights. Second, these rights have been more secure since the Charter's passage. This has been due to the courts' willingness to strike down laws and practices on the grounds that they contravene the Charter's guarantees of rights and freedoms. Prior to the Charter, Canadian courts were reluctant to strike down a law on the basis that it was an infringement of human rights.

Fundamental Freedoms

Fundamental political freedoms are guaranteed in section 2 of the Charter. These include freedom of religion, belief, expression, the media, assembly, and association. During the pre-Charter era these freedoms, or *political liberties* as they are sometimes called, were part of the common law and of Canada's British parliamentary tradition. Individual freedoms were part of the British constitution and thus became part of Canada's. Even before the Charter, then, political freedoms occupied a place in the Canadian Constitution. Their protection by the courts, however, was rather tenuous. Except in a

few instances, the courts were unwilling to rule that a freedom was beyond the interference of government. Instead, political liberties were defended using the federal division of legislative powers as the basis for striking down a particular government's interference with individual freedom.

Democratic Rights

The basic democratic right is the opportunity to vote in regular elections. This right predated Confederation. It was embodied in the Constitution Act, 1867 through those sections that establish the elective basis of representation in the House of Commons and in provincial legislatures (ss. 37 and 40), through the requirement that the legislature meet at least once a year (ss. 20 and 86), through the right of citizens to vote (s. 41), and through the five-year limit on the life of both the House of Commons and provincial legislatures, thereby guaranteeing regular elections (ss. 50 and 85). All of these sections are now "spent," having been superseded by ss. 3–5 of the Charter.

Mobility Rights

Mobility rights were not explicitly mentioned in Canadian constitutional law before 1982. Section 121 of the Constitution Act, 1867 prohibits the provincial governments from imposing tariffs on commodities coming from other provinces, but there is no mention of restrictions on the movement of people. Such restrictions are now prohibited by section 6 of the Charter. This guarantee of individual mobility rights was prompted by Ottawa's fear that some provincial governments were undermining the idea and practice of Canadian citizenship by discriminating in favour of their own permanent residents in some occupational sectors and by imposing residency requirements as a condition for receiving some social services. The Charter does not, however, categorically ban these types of discrimination. It allows "reasonable residency requirements as a qualification for the receipt of publicly provided social services"[20] and permits affirmative action programs favouring a province's residents "if the rate of employment in that province is below the rate of employment in Canada."[21] The impact of section 6 on provincial practices limiting the mobility of Canadians between provinces has been marginal.

Legal Rights

Most rights-based litigation, both before and since the Charter's passage, has been based on individuals' and corporations' claims that their legal rights have been violated. Legal rights involve mainly procedural aspects of the law, such as the right to a fair trial, the right not to be subjected to unreasonable search and seizure, the right not to be held without a charge being laid, and the right to legal counsel. Before these rights were entrenched in the Constitution through the Charter, they were recognized principles of the common law and constitutional convention. For example, the field of administrative law was based largely on the principles of *natural justice*: hear the other side, and no one should be a judge in his own case. These were accepted parts of Canada's democratic tradition and constitutional tradition even before they were entrenched in section 7 of the Charter. And like political freedoms, democratic rights, and equality rights, these legal rights were included in the Canadian Bill of Rights passed in 1960. In addition, the rights of accused parties were set forth in Canada's Criminal Code.

It is apparent, however, that the constitutional entrenchment of legal rights has made an important difference. The courts have been much bolder in striking down parts of laws and in overturning administrative and police procedures than they were in the pre-Charter era. For example, a successful legal challenge to Canada's abortion law became possible only when the right to "security of the person" was explicitly recognized in section 7 of the Charter.[22] More generally, Charter decisions have expanded the legal rights of the accused, prisoners, and immigrants.

Equality Rights

Equality rights are entrenched in the Constitution through section 15 of the Charter. They embody the **rule of law** principle that everyone should be treated equally under the law. But the Charter extends this principle to expressly prohibit discrimination based on race, national or ethnic origin, colour, religion, sex, age, or mental or physical disability.[23]

The particular headings in this list are important, given that Canadian courts historically have preferred to base their rulings on the precise text of laws and the Constitution. Women's groups and those representing the physically and mentally disabled clearly believed that the wording of the Charter made a difference, and both fought hard—and successfully—to have the original wording of section 15 changed. The 1960 Canadian Bill of Rights, which applied only in areas of federal jurisdiction, did not include age or mental and physical disability in its catalogue of equality rights.

The Charter explicitly declares that affirmative action is constitutional.[24] Thus, the equality rights section of the Canadian Constitution is designed to cut two ways. It provides individuals with grounds for redress if they believe that the law discriminates against them. But it also provides a basis for laws that treat different groups of people differently in order to improve the condition of disadvantaged individuals or groups.

Equality rights also are important features of provincial human rights codes. Between 1962 and 1975 every province adopted such a code. Quebec's is probably the most extensive, including even certain economic and social rights. These rights are administered and enforced by provincial human rights commissions.

Language Rights

At Confederation, the issue of language rights was dealt with in three ways. Section 133 of the Constitution Act, 1867 declares that both English and French are official languages in the Parliament of Canada and in the Quebec legislature, and in any court established by either the national or Quebec government. Section 93 of that same Act declares that rights held by denominational schools when a province became part of Canada cannot be taken away. As a practical matter,

Catholic schools in Manitoba or even Ontario were often French-speaking, and most English-language schools in Quebec were Protestant. Consequently, what were formally denominational rights in section 93 were, in many cases, effectively language rights as well. This did not help when it came to their protection—or non-protection. The third approach—and in practical terms the most important language rights provision of the Constitution Act, 1867—is put forth in section 92. This assigns to the provinces jurisdiction over "all Matters of a merely local or private Nature in the Province" (s. 92.16). Combined with exclusive provincial jurisdiction over education (s. 93), this has given provincial governments the tools to promote or deny, as the case may be, the language rights of their anglophone or francophone minorities.

The Constitution Act, 1982 extends language rights in several ways. These include the following:

- The declaration of the official equality of English and French, found in section 133 of the Constitution Act, 1867, is repeated and broadened to encompass "their use in all institutions of the Parliament and government of Canada" (s. 16.1) and services to the public (s. 20).
- The New Brunswick legislature's earlier decision to declare that province officially bilingual is entrenched in the Constitution Act, 1982. The official status of English in the legislature and courts of Quebec and Manitoba is reaffirmed (s. 21).
- The right of anglophones and francophones to have their children educated in their mother tongue is entrenched, subject to there being sufficient demand to warrant the provision of such services out of public funds (s. 23).

Language rights would have been given an additional twist if the Meech Lake Accord (1987) or Charlottetown Accord (1992) had become constitutional law (see Chapter 8). The most controversial feature of both accords was the recognition of Quebec as a "distinct society." The "distinct society" clause would have obliged Quebec's legislature

and government to "preserve and promote the distinct identity of Quebec." Some critics, including former Prime Minister Pierre Trudeau, argued that this would promote the concentration of French in Quebec, with harmful consequences for the status of the French-speaking minorities in the other provinces and for the English-speaking minority in Quebec.

Aboriginal Rights

Aboriginal rights are also included in Canada's Constitution. Their explicit recognition dates from the passage of the Charter in 1982. Section 25 declares that the rights and freedoms set forth in the Charter "shall not be construed so as to abrogate or derogate" from whatever rights or freedoms the Aboriginal peoples of Canada have as a result of any treaty or land claim settlement. It also entrenches in the Constitution "any rights or freedoms that have been recognized by the Royal Proclamation [of 1763]." Section 35(1) of the Constitution Act, 1982 may appear to limit Aboriginal rights to the status quo that existed in 1982, stating that "The *existing* aboriginal and treaty rights of the aboriginal peoples of Canada are hereby recognized and affirmed" (emphasis added). In fact, however, this has been less a limit than a boost for Aboriginal rights, which have been effectively constitutionalized by the 1982 Constitution Act. We examine this in greater detail in Chapter 16.

Parliamentary Government in Canada

The whole edifice of British parliamentary government rests on a foundation of unwritten traditions and rules. These traditions and rules touch on the most fundamental principles of democracy and on practices that are essential to the orderly functioning of government. Such matters as the selection of the Prime Minister, which party has the right to form a government and when it loses that right, the relationship between the Crown and the government and between the government and the legislature, the rights of the political opposition, and the role of the judicial branch of government cannot be understood from a simple reading of the Constitution. Nevertheless, for all of these matters certain rules are generally agreed upon and are vital parts of the Constitution—so vital, in fact, that when they are challenged the political system faces a crisis.

British parliamentary government was exported to Canada during the nineteenth century. Its main features have remained largely unchanged since then, when the British North American colonies achieved the right to self-government in their domestic affairs. As we have seen, the Constitution Act, 1867 explicitly reaffirms this British parliamentary inheritance. While the declaration that Canada has adopted "a Constitution similar in Principle to that of the United Kingdom" might appear to be somewhat nebulous, Canada's founders understood very clearly what it meant. The Constitution of the United Kingdom was, and remains today, a set of political traditions without a core constitutional document similar to those found in other Western democracies. Those who founded Canada took these traditions as their starting point and grafted onto them certain institutions and procedures—particularly federalism—for which British parliamentary government provided no guide.

Parliament

The distinguishing feature of British-style parliamentary government is the relationship between the various institutions that together comprise Parliament. Parliament consists of the monarch and the legislature. The monarch, currently Queen Elizabeth II, is Canada's head of state. According to the strict letter of the Constitution, the monarch wields formidable powers. These include which party will be called upon to form the government, when Parliament will be dissolved and a new election held, and the requirement that all legislation—federal and provincial—must receive royal assent before it becomes law. In fact, however, these powers are almost entirely symbolic, and the role is essentially a ceremonial one. When the monarch is not in Canada (which is most of the time), her

powers are exercised by the Governor General. At the provincial level, the lieutenant-governors are the Queen's representatives.

The power that resides formally in the monarchy is in reality held by the Crown's advisers, the Privy Council. The **Privy Council** formally includes all members of the present and past cabinets. However, only present members of cabinet exercise the powers of the Privy Council, and these people are usually elected members of the legislature. At the head of the cabinet is the Prime Minister. The structure of Canada's Parliament is shown in Figure 6.1.

Parliament comprises, then, both the *executive* and *legislative* branches of government. Those who actually exercise the executive power are drawn from the legislature. In deciding who among those elected members of Parliament (MPs) and appointed senators will become members of the government, the rule is quite simple. The leader of the political party with the most seats in the elected House of Commons has the right to try to form a government that has the support of a majority of MPs. He or she is the person who chooses members of the cabinet. If at any time the government loses its majority support in the House, tradition requires that it resign. At this point a fresh election would be called or, if another party could put together a government that would be supported by a majority

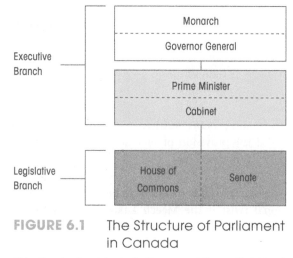

FIGURE 6.1 The Structure of Parliament in Canada

Note: The structure is basically the same at the provincial level, with two differences. The monarch's powers are exercised by a lieutenant-governor and the legislature consists of a single elected chamber.

of MPs, the Governor General could call on the leader of that party to try to form a government.

Responsible Government

In order to govern, therefore, the Prime Minister and cabinet require the confidence of the elected House of Commons. This constitutional principle is called **responsible government**. If a government loses the confidence of the House—through either a defeat on an important piece of legislation (i.e., the annual budget or legislation related to government spending) or on a motion of non-confidence proposed by an opposition party—it loses the right to govern. This may appear to place enormous power in the hands of MPs, capable of making and breaking governments at will. It does not. The reason why the constitutional theory of responsible government does not translate into government tremulous before the legislature is **party discipline**. This is another tradition of British parliamentary government, according to which the MPs of a party generally vote as a unified bloc in the legislature. Few aspects of Canada's system of government are less popular and more poorly understood than party discipline (see Box 6.2).

Of the 41 governments elected between 1867 and 2011 only six fell because of a defeat in the legislature. In all six cases these were *minority governments*: governments that depended on the support of another party's MPs to win votes in the legislature. But even in these apparently precarious circumstances, it was usually the government that finally determined when an election would occur. On only one occasion has a government been defeated in the Commons and then had its request for dissolution of Parliament and a fresh election denied. That was in 1926, and the denial provoked a constitutional crisis over the appropriate role of the Governor General. There was at least the chance of history repeating itself when the Progressive Conservative government's budget

In January 2010, faced with the second prorogation of Parliament since 2008, some Canadians voiced their displeasure at the premature shutdown of government, claiming the decision was politically, rather than practically, motivated.

Politics in Focus

BOX 6.2 Must MPs Be Bobbleheads?

Canadian MPs have been called many unkind things over the years. Prime Minister Pierre Trudeau once referred to them as "nobodies," at least when they stepped off Parliament Hill. They have been called sheep and trained seals for their habit of voting as their party leaders tell them they ought, regardless of what their constituents might prefer or as their own reason might dictate. But perhaps the unkindest cut of all came in the spring of 2013 when the widely respected weekly, *The Economist*, referred to them as bobbleheads. Government party MPs, it wrote, "form an appreciative backdrop to ministers during Question Period, nodding and applauding when required. If given a chance to speak, they diligently parrot the party's talking points. And on all but the most insignificant matters they vote the party line. If they have any original thoughts they keep them to themselves."[25]

The bobblehead characterization was occasioned by Conservative MP Mark Warawa's unsuccessful effort to introduce a motion in the House of Commons that would have condemned sex-selection abortion. Four other Conservative MPs supported him. It is likely that many more were sympathetic to the motion, but the government had made clear its unwillingness to see the abortion debate reopened. In the interest of party solidarity these other MPs swallowed their consciences and toed the party line.

Canadians have long said that they don't like party discipline. A 1983 Gallup Poll found that half of Canadians thought MPs should vote according to the preferences of their constituents and that only 8 per cent said they should vote as their leader requires them to do. The 1991

Citizens' Forum on Canada's Future reported that party discipline was believed by most of those who engaged in this process to be "a major constraint on the effectiveness of elected officials in representing constituents' views and in controlling a government agenda which may be out of touch with citizens' concerns." An Environics poll taken in the spring of 2013, shortly after the Warawa affair, found that seven out of ten Canadians surveyed favoured legal restrictions on the ability of party leaders to control their parties' candidates and MPs.

Party discipline, it seems, has few friends and is widely seen to be undemocratic. So why does it continue to exist? Senator Eugene Forsey, one of Canada's foremost experts on parliamentary government, argues that without it Canadian government would be less accountable. It enables voters to know where each party stands on the issues and to hold the parties accountable at the next election. He contrasts this to the American tradition of weak party discipline, which, he argues, results in legislators and even the President being able to say "I wasn't responsible. I did (or did not) support that law. Blame the others, not me." This may result in lawmakers who are seen to be more responsive to their constituents, but at the cost of voters not being able to hold the parties collectively responsible for policy choices.[26]

Defenders of party discipline argue that abolishing or even significantly relaxing the practice would result in a chain reaction of consequences for Canada's parliamentary system, including the weakening of party leaders. Critics agree, and say that this is precisely why such reform is needed.

was defeated in 1979. The government had been in office a mere nine months and the possibility of a minority Liberal government, supported by the NDP, was not totally outrageous. As it happened, however, Governor General Ed Schreyer granted Prime Minister Clark's request for a new election,

although Schreyer claimed afterwards that he seriously considered asking the leader of the opposition to try to form a government.

The possibility that MPs, and not Canadian voters, might bring about a change in government appeared very real in the late autumn of

2008, just weeks after a federal election produced a Conservative minority government. The three opposition parties reached an agreement to bring down the government and replace it with a Liberal–NDP coalition that would have been led by then Liberal leader Stéphane Dion. The Conservative government cried foul, pointing out that an election had been held only weeks before and that it had won a significantly greater share of the popular vote than any of the opposition parties. Rather than turn over the reins of power to a Liberal–NDP coalition, backed by the Bloc Québécois, the Conservatives would have requested a dissolution of Parliament and fresh elections. The Governor General, Michaëlle Jean, was saved from being a twenty-first-century Lord Byng by the government's decision to prorogue Parliament (see Box 6.3), preventing a vote that could have brought down the government. Opponents of the government now had their opportunity to cry foul, but public opinion showed that most Canadians opposed the idea of a Liberal–NDP coalition propped up with BQ support.

Responsible government is not some dusty constitutional relic. It operates today, but not in the narrow sense of legislatures making and defeating cabinets. Instead, it suffuses the parliamentary process in the form of the *rights of the legislature* and the corresponding *obligations of the government*. The legislature has the right to scrutinize, debate, and vote on policies proposed by the government. To carry out these activities the legislature has the general right to question the government and to demand explanations for its actions and for those of bureaucratic officials

Listen to the "Perspectives on Proroguing" podcast, available at: www.oupcanada.com/Brooks8e

Governing Realities

BOX 6.3 Prorogation: When the Banal Becomes Controversial

Until fairly recently—December of 2008 to be more exact—few Canadians had heard the word "prorogue." It comes from the Latin, *prorogare*, meaning to defer. The procedure it refers to is used by the government to end a session of Parliament. Essentially, the business of the legislature shuts down until Parliament resumes sitting. Whatever legislative business was left unfinished when Parliament is prorogued dies. This business may or may not be reintroduced when the legislature is recalled, but the point is that the new session of Parliament will be a fresh start in terms of legislation, committee business, and other activities.

In some ways it is odd that Canadians were not more familiar with the word and what it involves. Every session of Parliament ends as a result of prorogation or, alternatively, dissolution. Dissolution ends the life of a Parliament and new elections for the House of Commons result. Between 1868 and 2013 Parliament was prorogued 106 times. So it is hardly a rare occurrence.

On most occasions prorogation is used when the government believes it is time to reconfigure its legislative agenda. A new Speech from the Throne, in which the Governor General reads the government's legislative plans for a new session of Parliament, announces this fresh beginning. The use of prorogation has been controversial only when it was perceived by critics to be a way of avoiding politically damaging circumstances in the legislature and thereby of evading the government's accountability to the voters who elected it.

The Harper government was not the first to use prorogation in such circumstances. Canada's first Prime Minister, John A. Macdonald, prorogued Parliament in 1873 to shut down an inquiry into a scandal that was probably the cause of his party's defeat in the election held later that year. The Liberal government of Jean Chrétien prorogued Parliament in 2003, critics charged, to avoid having Parliament receive a damning report from the Auditor General on improprieties and possible illegalities in the spending of public money in Quebec under a federal sponsorship and advertising program. Clearly, prorogation may sometimes be used for partisan advantage. But most of the time its use is far more banal and unnoticed.

who act in the government's name. The government, for its part, has a constitutional obligation to provide opportunities for legislative scrutiny of its policies and to account for its actions before Parliament. These rights and obligations are to a large extent codified in the *standing orders*—the rules that govern parliamentary procedure.

Responsible government, then, is part of the living constitution. But its formal definition bears little resemblance to the reality of modern parliamentary government. Disciplined political parties and dominant prime ministers ensure that cabinets seldom are defeated at the hands of unco-operative legislatures. But if the ultimate sanction that underlies the notion of responsible government has been lost—it really only operated for a brief period in Canadian history, between 1848 and 1864 in the legislature of the United Canadas—the practice of cabinet government that is accountable to the elected legislature remains.

Ministerial Responsibility

The accountability of the government to the legislature is the reason behind another principle of British parliamentary government, that of **ministerial responsibility**. It entails the obligation of a cabinet minister to explain and defend policies and actions carried out in his or her name. This individual accountability of cabinet ministers rests on a combination of constitutional law and parliamentary tradition. Section 54 of the Constitution Act, 1867 gives to cabinet the exclusive right to put before the legislature measures that involve the raising or spending of public revenue. In practice, such measures are introduced by particular members of the government. For example, changes to the tax system are proposed by the Minister of Finance. The Constitution also requires that any legislation that involves raising or spending public money must originate in the elected House of Commons. This reflects the democratic principle of no taxation without representation. Only the people's elected representatives, legislators who can be removed in a subsequent election, should have the right to propose laws that affect voters' pocketbooks. The accountability of ministers is, therefore, to the people's elected representatives.

Two fundamental principles of British parliamentary government, i.e., strong executive authority and democratic accountability, come together in the concept of ministerial responsibility. Strong executive authority is a tradition that dates from an era when the monarch wielded real power and the principle that these powers depended on the consent of the legislature was not yet established. When the legislature finally gained the upper hand in seventeenth-century Britain, the tradition of strong executive power was not rejected. Instead, it was tamed and adapted to the democratic principle that government is based on the consent of the governed. Since then, individual ministers and cabinet as a whole have exercised the powers that, symbolically, continue to be vested in the Crown. But they do so in ways that enable the people's elected representatives to vote on their proposals and to call them to account for their policies (see Figure 6.2).

In recent times the constitutional principle of ministerial responsibility has come under increasing pressure. The enormous volume of decisions taken in a minister's name and the fact that much of the real power to determine government policy has passed into the hands of unelected officials mean that no minister can be well informed about all the policies and actions undertaken in his name. According to some, the solution is to locate accountability where decision-making power really lies. This strategy is reasonable for most actions and decisions. But elected members of the government must remain directly accountable for the general lines of policy and for major decisions; otherwise, a vital link in the chain of accountability that joins the people to those who govern is lost (see Box 6.4).

Parliamentary Supremacy versus Constitutional Supremacy

Another central feature of British parliamentary government is that of **parliamentary supremacy**. In concrete terms, this means that the courts will not second-guess the right of Parliament to pass any sort of law, on any subject. Parliament embodies the popular will, and unpopular laws can always be defeated by changing the government at the next election. In a federal system like Canada's there is one complication. Law-making powers are divided between the national and regional governments. But so long as Ottawa acts within its spheres of constitutional authority, and the provincial governments within theirs, both the federal and provincial parliaments are supreme.

Such was the situation in Canada until 1982. When called on to determine whether a law was constitutional or not, the courts almost always referred to the federal division of powers set down in the Constitution Act, 1867. If a legislature was not intruding onto the constitutional territory of the other level of government, its actions were by definition constitutional. The only exception to this rule was in the case of laws or actions that ran afoul of procedural rules of the common law, like the principles of natural justice. The substance of laws, on the other hand, would not be questioned.

Parliamentary supremacy was dealt a major blow by the Charter. Those who opposed the Charter argued that entrenching rights and freedoms in the written Constitution would result in a transfer of power from legislatures to the courts. This, indeed, is what has happened. Since 1982 the Supreme Court has struck down numerous federal and provincial laws on the grounds that they violate the guarantees set forth in the Charter. The defenders of parliamentary supremacy claim that a system of court-protected rights and freedoms is fundamentally undemocratic. Their reasoning is that it

FIGURE 6.2   The Constitutional Roots of Ministerial Responsibility

substitutes the decisions of non-elected judges for those of the people's elected representatives.

What is beyond doubt is that parliamentary supremacy has been replaced in Canada by **constitutional supremacy**. The Constitution Act, 1982 makes this very clear. Section 32 declares that the Charter applies to both the federal and provincial governments and to all matters under their authority. Section 52(1) is even more categorical. It states that "The Constitution of Canada is the supreme law of Canada, and any law that is inconsistent with the provisions of the Constitution is,

Politics in Focus

BOX 6.4 The Gomery Report on Ministerial Responsibility

I believe that the proposition that Ministers and their political staff have no responsibility for the proper implementation and administration of government programs and policies is an inadequate and incomplete expression of the principle of ministerial responsibility. The Minister should take steps, in consultation with the Deputy Minister, to see that trained personnel are available to administer any new initiatives and to establish proper procedures and oversight mechanisms. The Minister should give sufficient directions to the Deputy Minister so that the latter will be able to properly supervise the actions of the subordinate personnel. *Willful ignorance of administrative inadequacies will not absolve a Minister from responsibility for failures within the department.*

Source: Canada, Commission of Inquiry into the Sponsorship Program and Advertising Activities, *Final Report: Who Is Responsible?* (Ottawa, 1 Feb. 2006), 18–19; emphasis added.

to the extent of the inconsistency, of no force or effect." A vestige of Parliament's former superiority is retained, however, through s. 33 of the Charter. This is the so-called "notwithstanding clause." It enables either Parliament or a provincial legislature to declare that a law shall operate even if it violates the fundamental freedoms, legal rights, or equality rights sections of the Charter. Such a declaration must be renewed after five years; otherwise, the Constitution reasserts its supremacy.

As a footnote, it is perhaps worth noting that even in Westminster, the "mother of parliaments," the principle of parliamentary supremacy has been limited over the past few decades. This began with the UK's entry into the European Union in 1972, making some British legislation subject to decisions made in Brussels. The devolution of some of the British Parliament's powers to the legislatures of Wales and Scotland, the passage of the 1998 Human Rights Act, and the establishment of a Supreme Court for the UK in 2009 (this function was exercised previously by a committee of the House of Lords) have in practice limited parliamentary supremacy.[27]

Judicial Independence and the Separation of Powers

The role of the judicial branch of government is based on constitutional convention rather than law. The Constitution Act, 1867 includes several sections that deal with the system of provincial courts, including how judges shall be selected, how they may be removed, when provincial Superior Court judges must retire (age 75), and who will determine judicial salaries.[28] But there is no mention of the Supreme Court of Canada or of any other federal courts. Instead, section 101 authorizes Parliament to establish a "General Court of Appeal for Canada," which it did in 1875 (the Supreme Court of Canada) and again in 1970 (the Federal Court of Canada).

Canadian constitutional law is silent on the powers, indeed on the very existence and composition, of this country's highest court of appeal. Nor is the relationship between the judicial and other branches of government described in much detail. This stands in sharp contrast to the American Constitution, in which lengthy descriptions of the powers of Congress (the legislative branch) and the President (the executive branch) are followed by Article III on the judicial branch of government. In Canada, however, the role of the judiciary is based largely on constitutional convention and statute law. The fundamental principles that underlie that role are judicial independence and separation of powers.

Judicial independence means that judges are to be free from any and all interference in their decision-making. Former Chief Justice Brian Dickson declared that the core of this principle involves "the complete liberty of individual judges to hear and decide the cases that come before them."[29] It is particularly important that judges be protected from interference by the government. Despite the fact that the principle of judicial independence is deeply embedded in Canada's political culture and enshrined in laws on contempt of court and in guidelines for ministerial conduct, doubts have been raised over whether these protections are adequate. The fact that court budgets are determined by governments represents, in the eyes of some, a potential limitation on judicial autonomy.

The principle of **separation of powers** guarantees the special role of the judiciary. This role is to interpret what the law and the Constitution mean when disputes arise. As in the case of judicial independence, this principle relies more on cultural norms, statute law, and constitutional convention than it does on constitutional law. There is, however, at least one important reference to the role of the judicial branch in the Constitution. This is section 24 of the Constitution Act, 1982, which declares that the enforcement of the Charter shall be through the courts. The perception that the courts represent a check on the powers of Parliament and the provincial legislatures—a perception that has taken hold since the Charter's passage in 1982—involved an Americanizing trend in Canadian politics. The concept of checks and balances between the three branches of government is basic to the American Constitution. It is not, however, part of British parliamentary democracy, although the independence of the judiciary is.

The separation of the judiciary's role from that of Parliament is not watertight. The ability of the federal and provincial governments to refer a resolution or draft legislation to the courts for a decision on its constitutionality—a practice called a "reference"—does not, strictly speaking, respect the principle of separation of powers. These constitutional reference cases enable governments to use the provincial and Canadian supreme courts to receive advisory opinions before acting or to thrust a politically volatile issue into the hands of judges. The separation of powers is also breached when judges step outside their role as interpreters of the law's meaning to advocate some position or reform. Since the mid-1980s the justices of Canada's highest court, in public speeches and interviews, have occasionally weighed in on matters of public controversy, including the funding of bilingualism, gender bias in the law and justice system, multiculturalism, and the appropriate role of the judicial branch in Canada's parliamentary system (see Box 6.5).

Relations between the House of Commons and the Senate

When the founders designed Canada's Parliament, they took the bicameral structure of Britain's legislature as their model. Accordingly, the legislative branch was comprised of two bodies, an elected House of Commons (the lower house) and an appointed Senate (the upper house). A literal reading of the Constitution suggests that their powers are roughly equal. The major difference is that money bills must be introduced in the House of Commons. In fact, however, the superiority of the elected House of Commons has been clear from day one. The unelected character of the Senate has always sat uneasily in Canada's democratic political culture, even when the right to vote was much more limited than it is today. This fact, along with the obvious patronage of most government appointments to the Senate, undermined its legitimacy.

The superiority of the House of Commons over the Senate is reinforced by several constitutional conventions. Probably the most important of these involves the selection of the Prime Minister and other members of the government. Constitutional law does not require that they be drawn from the House of Commons, but it is unthinkable today that the Prime Minister not be an elected MP. Occasionally, one or two senators are appointed to cabinet, but this often has been because the party in power had few (or no) MPs from a particular region of the country. The appointment of Michael Fortier to the Senate after the Conservatives' 2006 election victory (with the promise that he would run for a seat in the House of Commons in the next federal election) was such a case. Fortier was

The Social Fabric

BOX 6.5 Justice Rosalie Abella on Judicial Impartiality and Independence

Weighing values and taking public policy into account does not impair judicial neutrality or impartiality. Pretending we do *not* take them into account, and refusing to confront our personal views and be open in spite of them, may be a bigger risk to impartiality. It is of course fundamental that judges be free from inappropriate or undue influence, independent in fact and appearance, and intellectually willing and able to hear the evidence and arguments with an open mind. But neutrality and impartiality do not and cannot mean that the judge has not prior conceptions, opinions or sensibilities about society's values. It means only that those preconceptions ought not to close his or her mind to the evidence and arguments presented. We must be prepared, when the situation warrants, to experience what Herbert Spencer called The Tragedy of the Murder of a Beautiful Theory by a Gang of Brutal Facts. In other words, there is critical difference between an open mind and an empty one.

Source: "Constitutions and Judges: Changing Roles, Rules and Expectations," lecture given at University College London, 7 July 2011, 9, at: <www.ucl.ac.uk/constitution -unit/events/judicial-independence-events/Justice _Abella_Lecture_to_JIP_07-07-11.pdf>.

an influential lawyer and financier from Montreal, a city in which the Conservatives did not win a seat in 2006, and was immediately appointed to the cabinet position of Minister of Public Works and Government Services. Occasionally, the Prime Minister will appoint to cabinet someone who is neither an MP nor a senator. By tradition, however, this person will very soon afterwards seek election to the House of Commons. The whole system of democratic accountability would crumble if the Prime Minister and other members of the

government were not elected officials, answerable in Question Period and removable by voters in the next election.

Another convention that reinforces the superiority of the House of Commons is found in the legislative process itself. All bills must pass both the Senate and the House of Commons before they become law. Moreover, the stages through which a bill must pass are identical in both houses of Parliament. For most of Canada's history it was generally accepted that the Senate ought not to

Politics in Focus

BOX 6.6 Chief Justice McLachlin Criticizes Government Minister

Are there circumstances when a judge is justified in criticizing the actions of the government? The issue arose when Supreme Court Chief Justice Beverley McLachlin publicly thanked the Canadian Bar Association (CBA) for its stern rebuke of Immigration Minister Jason Kenney. The CBA had accused the minister of failing to respect the independence of the judiciary. Kenney's criticism of the Court basically involved the charge that judges were inappropriately substituting their policy preferences for those of the government. Should the Chief Justice have remained above the fray? You decide.

Canada's Chief Justice of the Supreme Court has joined other members of the legal profession to denounce Immigration Minister Jason Kenney's recent comments regarding the judicial system.

Last February Minister Kenney sparked uproar when he criticized Federal Court judges for not "toeing the line of the Harper government's immigration policies." He accused judges of stalling cases and not doing enough to help the government remove "unwanted" refugees and immigrants with criminal records.

In a stern public response, the Canadian Bar Association president issued a letter defending judges against the remarks, saying that the legal system is not intended to serve government policy, but to remain an impartial and independent judiciary.

This week, Chief Justice Beverley McLachlin brought the issue back to light when speaking to the CBA governing council. She praised CBA president Rod Snow for defending judges who are not able to respond to such public criticisms, and for reminding the minister that the judicial system is not in place to serve political agendas.

"I was certainly—and I think all judges were—very pleased when an issue arose earlier this year when a minister of the Crown seemed to suggest that some judges were insufficiently solicitous to government policy," said McLachlin. "We were very, very gratified to see your president writing a powerful public letter to the minister in question, reminding the minister of the importance of public confidence in an impartial judiciary, that bases its decisions on the law and not on government policy."

She added that the criticisms from the CBA need to be taken seriously by legislators such as Kenney now and in the future, in order to preserve the values of this country.

"It's very important when the Bar speaks out and says this is an important, institutional, democratic value, an independent judiciary, and we need to preserve it. And we're grateful to the CBA for doing that."

Source: Richard Foot, "Chief Justice Supports Criticism of Kenney," *National Post,* 13 Aug. 2011, at: <news.nationalpost .com/2011/08/13/chief-justice-supports-criticism-of-kenney/>. Material reprinted with the express permission of: Postmedia News, a division of Postmedia Network Inc.

obstruct or reject the will of the elected House of Commons. On occasion, the Senate would suggest minor revisions to legislation, sending it back to the House of Commons for reconsideration. However, after the 1984 election of the Progressive Conservative government the Senate—dominated by people appointed during over two decades of almost unbroken Liberal government—became more recalcitrant. On important legislation dealing with such matters as drug patents, government spending, Unemployment Insurance, the Goods and Services Tax, and the Canada–United States Free Trade Agreement the Senate delayed and in some cases rejected bills coming from the House of Commons. Senate unwillingness to pass bills sent to it by the elected House put the two chambers at loggerheads again in 2010. Opposition members of the Senate Finance Committee deleted several sections from an omnibus budget bill that had been passed by the House of Commons. A few days later the bill was passed by the full Senate, but the question remained: Do senators have the right to say no to budget proposals sent to them by the elected House of Commons? Constitutional law does indeed give senators this right; constitutional convention suggests they should not try to exercise it. As is so often the case, however, constitutionalists are not in agreement on this.[30]

The Biases of British Parliamentary Government

Along with people, pop music, and the English language, Westminster-style parliamentary government has been one of Britain's chief exports to that country's former colonies, Canada included. We have described the major features of British parliamentary government, as adapted to Canadian circumstances. Let us consider whether this system tends to favour certain interests and outcomes more than others. In discussing ministerial responsibility we noted that the pre-democratic tradition of strong executive authority never was abandoned under British parliamentary government. Instead, it was adapted to the democratic principle that government is based on the consent of the people, a principle embodied in the powers

of an elected legislature and in the doctrine of responsible government. When we recall that the legislature that embodied the popular will originally was elected by and accountable to only a fraction of the people, i.e., property-owning males, this adaptation does not appear very revolutionary or particularly democratic. Of course, universal male suffrage arrived by the latter half of the 1800s, and females were enfranchised early in the twentieth century, extending participatory rights to all citizens of a certain age and not simply a privileged group of them (except for Aboriginal peoples: Inuit gained the vote in 1950; all status Indians only in 1960). This democratization of citizenship rights, however, did not fundamentally alter the non-participatory biases already embedded in the structure of British parliamentary government.

Following Philip Resnick's arguments in *Parliament vs. People*, we may label these biases *statism*. A statist political tradition is one characterized by a relatively strong political executive and by a population that tends to be deferential towards those in power. The adoption of British parliamentary government, first in the colonial legislatures during the mid-1800s and then through the Constitution Act of 1867, mainly reaffirmed the tradition of centralized executive authority that had existed before the elected legislature's approval was needed to pass laws. This reaffirmation of strong executive power is, Resnick argues, apparent throughout Canada's founding Constitution Act. "What our Founding Fathers were doing," he maintains:

> was consolidating an orderly . . . move from direct colonial rule to House Rule. . . . They had a particular kind of [political] order in mind, the parliamentary system as it had evolved in Britain, combining the interests of monarchs, lords and commoners. If by the latter part of the nineteenth century this system was increasingly responsive to the wishes of an electorate, restricted or enlarged, it was by no means a servant of the electorate.[31]

Some might say, that was then but this is now. Yet, the institutions of government adopted through the

Confederation agreement and, equally important, the expectations of the political elites who controlled the levers of state power reached forward to shape the future course of Canadian politics. Parliament was sovereign, but Parliament was not merely the people. It included the Crown, the traditional seat of state authority whose powers came to be exercised by a prime minister and cabinet with few checks from the legislature. "Parliamentary sovereignty," Resnick argues, "fostered attitudes in the population which were nominally participatory but maximally deferential towards those exercising political power. The mystique of British Crown and Constitution helped make illegitimate all forms of political activity not sanctioned or channeled through parliamentary institutions."[32] This is an important point. Resnick is arguing that the historically more deferential political culture of Canada, as compared to the United States, did not simply happen. It was generated to some degree by parliamentary institutions that discouraged popular participation in politics beyond the rituals of voting and enshrined a sort of top-down philosophy of governance.

The evidence suggests that Resnick is right. Of course, there have been influential currents of participatory politics in Canadian history, particularly coming out of western Canada. But these populist urges have had to struggle against a parliamentary tradition that concentrates political power in the hands of the Prime Minister (or premiers) and cabinet. This style of governance is epitomized in the long tradition of elite deal-making that has characterized federal–provincial relations. But it also surfaces when this country's political leaders reject referendums or constituent assemblies on constitutional change as being "un-Canadian" or foreign to our political tradition. Indeed, the statist political tradition fostered by British parliamentary government is apparent in a multitude of ways, large and small. Many argue that the Canadian state's orchestration of culture, going back to the founding of the CBC, has been a defensive response to the Americanizing pressures from mass media industries centred in the United States. To some degree this is true. But this explanation of state-centred nationalism in Canada does not pay adequate attention to the possibility that the state's efforts may pre-empt those of groups in civil society and encourage a climate of dependence on our governments as, in Resnick's words, "organizers of our civic consciousness."[33] If governments had done less, and private citizens had done more, to construct the identities that are part of Canadian culture, perhaps national unity would have been less fragile throughout much of the country's history.

To the extent that the Charter of Rights and Freedoms modifies British parliamentary government in Canada by replacing parliamentary supremacy with constitutional supremacy and by helping to generate a greater consciousness of rights among members of the public, it has shifted Canadian politics away from its elitist past towards a more participatory model. Indeed, it is now commonplace to claim that the Charter ushered in a new era in Canadian politics characterized by far less deference to elites. There is some truth in this claim, but the impact of the Charter on Canada's political culture is often exaggerated. The British parliamentary system that operates in Canada, albeit modified by the Charter and the principle of constitutional supremacy, continues to concentrate power in the hands of the Prime Minister and cabinet and still provides few opportunities for direct public participation in governance beyond voting in elections. More importantly, the statist culture of governance that Resnick associates with the British parliamentary system is not fundamentally challenged by the fact that, because of the Charter, the courts have become more important venues for resolution of political issues and thus many groups now bypass electoral and legislative politics. Politics waged in the courts is not necessarily more democratic and accessible than these other forms and forums for politics, as many, on both the left and right of the political spectrum, concede.

Back to Resnick's argument: does Canada's constitutional model, involving an adaptation of the British parliamentary system, continue to have statist biases that centralize power and discourage popular participation? The answer is not simple. Other constitutional arrangements in other countries also have been criticized for promoting or, at least, permitting centralized power. The European Union has elaborate and extensive mechanisms for citizen participation in EU governance, under the terms of the Lisbon Treaty. Notwithstanding these strategies, complaints of a "democratic deficit" in EU governance are as loud and frequent as at any time in the past. Resnick is probably right that the parliamentary model adopted in Canada has, throughout most of the country's history, promoted a top-down style of governance and discouraged—even delegitimized—forms of political participation not focused on and channelled through a parliament dominated by the prime minister and cabinet. But institutional arrangements are only part of the story. Even without the undeniable impact that the Charter has had on governance and citizen expectations regarding their relationship to the state, the culture of governance in Canada would almost certainly have become less deferential over the last generation. This has happened in democracies throughout the world, with and without major constitutional changes.

Changing the Constitution

Constitutions are meant to last a very long time, but they seldom do. Among the 47 countries whose independence predates 1900, only about a third have constitutions that date from before 1950. Canada's Constitution Act, 1867 is one of the oldest and most durable. Only the United States (1789), Sweden (1809), the Netherlands (1814), and the United Kingdom (1832, when the Reform Act was passed) have older constitutions.

A *coup d'état* is one way of changing a constitution. More peaceful means may also accomplish dramatic change, including the wholesale replacement of one constitution by a fundamentally different one; but radical alteration of the fundamental rules and structures of government is much less common than is constitutional reform. Reform aims at changing some aspect(s) of the existing constitution, leaving the basic constitutional structure intact. Limited change of this sort is generally accomplished through a formal procedure set down in the constitution. Reforms that result from such a

process are called *constitutional amendments*.

When does constitutional reform become constitutional upheaval? This is difficult to pinpoint, but the line has certainly been crossed when, as a result of change, a constitution is no longer recognizable as what it was. For example, the 1982 Constitution Act did three main things: (1) transformed Canada's written Constitution from a set of British laws into Canadian constitutional laws that could only be changed by Canadians, a process known as patriation; (2) entrenched the Charter of Rights and Freedoms in the Constitution; and (3) established formal mechanisms for changing the Constitution. As important as these changes are, they did not amount to a new Constitution. Most features of parliamentary government and of federalism remained the same. On the other hand, the replacement of parliamentary government by American-style congressional government, the elimination of federalism, or—least far-fetched of all—the political independence of Quebec would in each case represent a radical transformation of Canada's Constitution.

Constitutional change may also come about through the gradual evolution of principles and practices. For example, the principle that the Governor General should accept the advice of the Prime Minister on when Parliament should be dissolved and a new election called was one that emerged imperceptibly as Canada shook off the vestiges of its colonial relationship to Great Britain. It was only when this principle was breached by Governor General Lord Byng in 1926 that it became clear that this relationship between the Prime Minister and the Governor General was part of the Constitution. The clear superiority of the House of Commons over the Senate on matters of legislation is another constitutional convention that became clearer with the passage of time. Those appointed to the Senate in 1867 primarily were prominent politicians from the new provinces. It was during this early period that the Senate became known as the chamber of "sober second thought." Over time, however, the practice of patronage appointments, the emergence of assertive provincial governments as spokespersons for regional interests, and changing ideas about democracy and representation all contributed to the Senate's decline vis-à-vis the Commons.

Amending the Constitution before 1982

The Constitution Act, 1867 gave Ottawa a very modest power to amend the Constitution of Canada regarding matters that concerned only the federal government.[34] In practical terms, all this power amounted to was the ability to change electoral districts and boundary lines. The Act gave the provincial governments a similar power.[35] Canada's founders, however, did not establish an amending procedure that could be used to change the division of powers between Ottawa and the provinces, and all the other important matters could not be changed using the very limited amendment powers conferred by sections 91(1) and 92(1). They did not even discuss such a procedure, a curious oversight in view of the fact that the federal Constitution of the United States—the only federal model that existed at the time—was very clear on the amendment procedures that had to be followed. In Canada, the only clear requirement was that a request would have to be made to the British Parliament to change the Constitution. The reason for this was, of course, that the Canadian Constitution was a British law, originally passed as the British North America Act, 1867.

What was not clear was who would have to agree here in Canada before a resolution could be sent to London. Would all provincial governments have to agree if a proposed amendment affected their powers? Did Quebec or Ontario or any other province enjoy a special right to veto amendments? Just how much provincial consent was needed to change the Constitution? It was not even clear what would happen if all 10 provincial legislatures and the House of Commons agreed to an amendment, but the unelected Senate rejected it. Formally, at least, the Senate appeared to have the power to block constitutional change.

After decades of uncertainty, the issue was decided by the Supreme Court in 1981. The background to this decision was the stalemate in constitutional negotiations between Ottawa and the provinces. The Liberal government of Pierre Elliott Trudeau wanted to patriate the Constitution, entrench in it a Charter of Rights and Freedoms, and establish a formal procedure for future constitutional amendments. Only the governments of Ontario and New Brunswick supported Ottawa's proposal. The conflict ended up in the courts when the governments of Manitoba, Newfoundland, and Quebec each decided to ask their provincial supreme courts whether Ottawa's actions were constitutional. There was some variation in the questions and wording of these provincial references. Nonetheless, they all asked: (1) whether Ottawa's proposed amendments affected provincial powers; and (2) if provincial consent was constitutionally required in order to make such changes. Quebec's reference also asked if that province had a special veto over amendments. These decisions were then appealed to the Supreme Court of Canada.

In its *Reference on the Constitution*[36] the Court made the following points:

- Some level of provincial consent was required for changes affecting provincial powers. This requirement was a constitutional convention, not part of constitutional law. It could not, therefore, be enforced by the courts.
- The level of required provincial consent was not at all clear. It was the Court's view that a majority of the provinces certainly had to agree, but unanimous consent was not necessary.
- In constitutional law, no province had a special right of veto over constitutional change. The Court did not give an opinion on whether such a right existed as a matter of constitutional convention.
- Ottawa did not need provincial consent before requesting the British Parliament to change Canada's Constitution in ways affecting provincial powers. If the federal government chose to act without the consent of the provinces, or with the support of only a few of them, this would be legal—but at the same time unconstitutional!

Both Ottawa and the dissenting provinces claimed victory as a result of the Court's decision.

Legally, the way was clear for Ottawa to act with or without the consent of the provinces. Politically, unilateral action remained a very risky option, particularly in light of the Court's acknowledgement that some level of provincial consent was required by constitutional convention. All 11 governments returned to the bargaining table, each side conscious of the constitutional turf occupied by itself and its opponents. In November of 1981, 10 of them were able to reach agreement on a compromise document that became the Constitution Act, 1982. Only the Parti Québécois government of Quebec rejected the proposed changes. Despite Quebec's refusal to sign the 1981 agreement, the Constitution Act, 1982 is constitutional law in that province just as it is elsewhere in Canada. A 1982 Supreme Court decision confirmed this.[37]

Amending the Constitution since 1982

The uncertainties surrounding constitutional amendment have been largely dispelled by the Constitution Act, 1982. Part V of the Act sets out the amendment procedures. In fact, it establishes four different procedures, each of which applies to certain types of constitutional change. These procedures and when they are used are explained in Table 6.1.

Any of the four amendment procedures may be set in motion by either Ottawa or a provincial government (s. 46[1]). But because intergovernmental agreement is crucial to the success of most amendments, the most likely scenario is that the Prime Minister and the provincial premiers will first reach an agreement that will then be submitted to their respective legislatures. This procedure led to the Meech Lake Accord, the first proposal for constitutional amendment under the 1982 rules. Negotiations and deal-making between governments—the pre-legislative stage of the amendment process—are as crucial now as when the amendment process was governed by convention. The new procedures have not formally expanded the opportunities for public participation, nor have they enlarged the legislature's role in the process.

Not content with the distinction of having four different procedures for amending the Constitution, the 10 governments that agreed to the 1982 Constitution Act included another extraordinary feature in the amendment rules. This is the "opting-out" section (s. 40). Under this section, a provincial government that does not agree to an amendment that transfers powers relating to education or other cultural matters from the provinces to Ottawa is not obliged to give up this power. Moreover, Ottawa is required to provide "reasonable compensation" to any dissenting province. The Meech Lake and Charlottetown Accords would have expanded the opting-out section, guaranteeing a dissenting province the right to reasonable compensation in the case of any transfer of legislative powers from the provinces to Ottawa. In fact, this would only have enshrined in the Constitution as a provincial right and federal obligation a practice that has existed in Canada since 1964.

The first effort at amending the Constitution using the 1982 rules ended in acrimonious failure. The proposed amendment was in fact a group of changes collectively known as the Meech Lake Accord. The Accord was a 1987 agreement between Prime Minister Brian Mulroney and the 10 provincial premiers. It was a response to a series of five demands that the Quebec Liberal government of Robert Bourassa wanted met before it was willing to sign the 1981 agreement that produced the Constitution Act, 1982. The main changes proposed by the Meech Lake Accord included: recognition of Quebec as a distinct society; constitutional recognition of a provincial (i.e., Quebec) right to control its own immigration policy (something Quebec had under a 1978 agreement between Ottawa and Quebec); provincial power to nominate justices for the Supreme Court of Canada; constitutional entrenchment of a provincial right to opt out of federal–provincial shared-cost programs and to be reimbursed for running parallel programs of their own; and certain changes to constitutional amendment procedures and categories (see Table 6.1).

After three years of wrangling marked by both an anti-French backlash in parts of English Canada and a revival of separatist nationalism in Quebec, the Accord expired. The legislatures of Manitoba and Newfoundland failed to ratify it by the 23

TABLE 6.1 Amending the Constitution

Procedure	Requirement	Application
1. General (ss. 38, 42)	• Resolution passed by the House of Commons and the Senate* • Two-thirds of the legislatures of the provinces that together comprise at least half the population of all the provinces	• Reduction or elimination of powers, rights, or privileges of provincial governments or legislatures • Proportionate representation of the provinces in the House of Commons • Senate • Supreme Court of Canada (except its composition) • Extension of existing provinces into the territories • Creation of new provinces
2. Unanimous consent (s. 41)	• Resolution passed by the House of Commons and the Senate* • Resolution passed by every provincial legislature	• Queen • Governor General • Lieutenant-Governors • Right of each province to at least as many seats in the House of Commons as it has in the Senate • Use of the English or French language (except changes that apply only to single province) • Composition of the Supreme Court • Changing the amending procedures of the Constitution
3. Ottawa and one or more provinces (s. 43)	• Resolution passed by the House of Commons and the Senate* • Resolution passed by the legislature of each province where the amendment applies	• Alteration of boundaries between provinces • Use of French or English in a particular province or provinces
4. Ottawa or a province acting alone (ss. 44, 45)	• If Ottawa, a resolution passed by the House of Commons and the Senate* • If a province, a resolution passed by its legislature	• Executive government of Canada, the Senate, and the House of Commons, subject to the limits established by ss. 41 and 42 of the Constitution Act, 1982

*If after 180 days the Senate has not passed a resolution already passed by the House of Commons, Senate approval is not necessary.

June 1990 deadline imposed on the process by the Constitution.

Both the birth and the death of the Accord suggested that not much had changed as a result of formalizing the amendment process. The proposed changes that made up the Accord represented a deal struck by 11 heads of government with no public participation or legislative debate. In fact, the Prime Minister and some of the provincial premiers were very insistent that their agreement could not be altered in any respect. It was submitted to their legislatures for ratification, not for possible modification. Public participation was solicited very late in the process, and then only because the Accord seemed destined for defeat. Indeed, there was little to suggest that any of the governments saw public participation as anything more than a resource to use when convenient. Groups and individuals opposed to the Accord's provisions denounced this process as being undemocratic.

The critics may have been right. But it was also clear that any change to the 1987 first ministers' agreement would have required that a new resolution be submitted to Parliament and all the provincial legislatures, and the ratification process would have to start over again. Debate and popular participation *after* an amendment resolution has been agreed to by governments are almost certain to prolong the amendment process and probably reduce the chances of reaching an agreement.

The death of the Meech Lake Accord seemed to indicate that the political process of constitutional amendment remained largely as it was before 1982. The final several months leading up to the ratification deadline were marked by acrimonious debate and some ad hoc efforts to salvage the Accord, and finally ended with Quebec being largely isolated from the other provinces. There was a sense of déjà vu about the whole affair. Quebec had been similarly isolated in 1971 when the first Bourassa government suddenly withdrew its acceptance of the Victoria Charter amendments, and then again in 1981 when Quebec Premier René Lévesque claimed to have been betrayed by a last-minute deal concocted between the other provinces and Ottawa. In each case agreement ran aground because the Quebec government and some of the governments of English Canada were unable to settle their differences on Quebec's status within Canada. Meech Lake came to grief because of the same obstacle that had blocked previous efforts at constitutional change.

The next two years saw dozens of government-organized public hearings on the Constitution and hundreds of conferences and forums organized by academics, political parties, and interest groups. Ottawa and the provinces were determined to avoid the charges of elitist deal-making that had been levelled at the Meech Lake process. In this they failed. Although there were ample opportunities for citizens and groups to express their views on constitutional reform, the proposals presented to Canadians in the 26 October 1992 referendum were widely viewed as yet another instance of the elites cutting a deal and trying to foist it on the public.

The Charlottetown Accord, as these proposals were called, represented the culmination of what the federal government rather misleadingly called the "Canada round" of constitutional negotiations (the period leading up to Meech Lake having been labelled the "Quebec round"). In fact, however, the desire to get the Quebec government's political agreement to the constitutional changes of 1982 and the worry over the post-Meech Lake resurgence of support for separatism were the chief reasons why the constitutional issue dominated Canadian politics with a vengeance between 1990

The failure of the Meech Lake Accord is a testament to the difficult realities of amending the Constitution.

and 1992. Moreover, the deal ultimately struck at Charlottetown in August 1992 bore a striking resemblance to the Meech Lake Accord in some important respects. Besides certain carry-overs from Meech, such as Quebec's "distinct society" status, Supreme Court nominations, and provinces' ability to opt out of shared-cost programs without financial penalty, the main features included:

- a Canada clause listing the fundamental characteristics of Canadian society;
- entrenchment of the right to Aboriginal self-government;
- an elected Senate with equal representation from the provinces and, eventually, special seats for Aboriginal representatives;
- francophone veto in the Senate regarding bills affecting the French language or culture;
- a guarantee to Quebec of at least 25 per cent of the seats in the House of Commons;
- confirmation of the provinces' exclusive jurisdiction in several policy areas, and some decentralization of powers to the provinces in the areas of immigration and labour policy.

A sense of the potentially far-reaching changes proposed in the Charlottetown Accord is conveyed by the Canada Clause (see Box 6.7). This provision sought to express the fundamental values of Canadians. Had the Accord been passed the Canada Clause would have been included as section 2 of the Constitution Act, 1867 and would have given the courts guidance in their interpretation of the entire Constitution, including the Charter of Rights and Freedoms. It is impossible to know how judges would have interpreted many of the provisions of the Canada Clause. What is certain, however, is that it would have given to the courts a whole new field of opportunity, on top of that already provided by the Charter, to involve themselves in the policy-making process. It requires little imagination to predict that subsection (1)f of the proposed Canada Clause, committing Canadians to "respect for individual and collective human rights and freedoms of all people," could become the legal basis for challenges to social spending cuts, or that subsection (1)b on the Aboriginal peoples of Canada could become the basis for legal claims on tax resources and distinctive legal rights for Aboriginal Canadians. The Canada Clause, whatever its impact on Canadian society would have been, was certainly a constitutional lawyer's paradise.

In the national referendum on the Charlottetown Accord, a majority of Canadians (54.5 per cent) rejected the proposed reforms, including provincial majorities in British Columbia, Alberta, Saskatchewan, Manitoba, Quebec, and Nova Scotia, as well as the Yukon. The result in Ontario was virtually a dead heat. During the impassioned referendum campaign it was clear that many English Canadians said "no" to the Charlottetown Accord because they thought it gave Quebec too much, while many francophone Quebecers rejected the deal because they believed it gave them too little! Indeed, the only serious question asked by members of the Quebec media and the province's politicians during the campaign was "Did Quebec get enough in the Charlottetown Accord?" Although the 1992 agreement provided the Quebec government with more than had been proposed by the Meech Lake Accord, this was not enough in the nationalist political climate that prevailed in the post-Meech years.

On the other hand, a further decentralization of powers to the provinces and special status for Quebec proved to be more than most English Canadians could stomach. While it is always treacherous and somewhat misleading to talk about Quebec or any society as though it has a single set of aspirations, the failure of the Meech Lake and Charlottetown Accords confirmed that a wide gap existed between those of francophone Quebecers and their compatriots in the rest of the country.

Citizen Participation in Constitutional Reform

For most of Canada's history the only direct actors in constitutional reform were governments. This changed during the negotiations and debates that led to the Constitution Act of 1982, when a number of citizens' interest groups played an active role through lobbying government and attempting to influence public opinion. These groups, and many others inspired by the opportunities created by the Charter, were instrumental in bringing about the death of the 1987 Meech Lake Accord, which had been agreed to by the 11 first ministers in the old pre-1982 decision-making style. During the two years of consultation and negotiation that preceded the signing of the 1992 Charlottetown Accord these citizens' interest groups were very much part of the process. Informally, at least, Ottawa and the provincial governments appeared to have conceded the legitimacy and necessity of a more inclusive style of constitution-making.

What they did not concede, however, was a direct role for public participation and consent. Under the old elitist policy-making style, popular consent was mediated by the heads of government. Under the more inclusive policy-making style that emerged in the early 1980s, popular consent was mediated by these heads of government *plus* certain citizens' interest groups claiming to speak on behalf of women, ethnic and racial minorities, Aboriginal Canadians, the disabled, official-language minorities, and so on. But not until the decision was taken in the late summer of 1992 to submit the Charlottetown reforms to the people in a national referendum was the public given a direct role in the constitutional amendment process. This represented a remarkable break from Canada's elitist tradition of constitution-making. With few exceptions, mainly from western Canada, the idea of a referendum to approve constitutional change had been rejected throughout Canada's history. When a formal procedure for constitutional amendment was being debated in the 1930s one of the country's most prominent constitutionalists dismissed the suggestion of a referendum as being inconsistent with cabinet government and a device for "passing the buck."[38] Frank Underhill, expressing the views of most intellectuals, argued that average citizens were generally incompetent to decide matters of constitutional change and that their elected representatives usually held more advanced views on public affairs. Legislatures, not citizens, he argued, should be required to ratify constitutional reforms.[39]

The idea of a referendum on the Meech Lake Accord surfaced from time to time in the English-language media. It was dismissed, however, by Prime Minister Mulroney and most of the provincial premiers as being alien to Canada's political tradition. This view was as likely to be expressed by those on the social democratic left, such as the national New Democratic Party leader Ed Broadbent and Manitoba's NDP Premier Howard Pawley, as by those to the right of the political spectrum.

But in the flood of condemnation that followed the death of the Meech Lake Accord the idea gathered force that popular ratification should be sought in any future attempt to change the Constitution. Quebec's provincial government committed itself to holding a provincial referendum on whatever agreement it reached with Ottawa. British Columbia also passed a law requiring provincial ratification of reform proposals. However, most politicians remained steadfast in their opposition. Ottawa's decision, after much hesitation and obvious reluctance, to introduce legislation enabling Parliament to authorize a referendum (more precisely, a plebiscite, in that the vote would be formally non-binding) reflected practical necessity more than

Governing Realities

BOX 6.7 The Canada Clause of the Proposed Charlottetown Accord

(1) The Constitution of Canada, including the *Canadian Charter of Rights and Freedoms*, shall be interpreted in a manner consistent with the following fundamental characteristics:

a) Canada is a democracy committed to a parliamentary and federal system of government and to the rule of law;

b) the Aboriginal peoples of Canada, being the first peoples to govern this land, have the right to promote their languages, cultures and traditions and to ensure the integrity of their societies, and their governments constitute one of three orders of government in Canada;

c) Quebec constitutes within Canada a distinct society, which includes a French-speaking majority, a unique culture and a civil law tradition;

d) Canadians and their governments are committed to the vitality and development of official language minority communities throughout Canada;

e) Canadians are committed to racial and ethnic equality in a society that includes citizens from many lands who have contributed, and continue to contribute, to the building of a strong Canada that reflects its cultural and racial diversity;

f) Canadians are committed to a respect for individual and collective human rights and freedoms of all people;

g) Canadians are committed to the equality of female and male persons; and,

h) Canadians confirm the principle of the equality of the provinces at the same time as recognizing their diverse characteristics.

principled conviction. The powerful Quebec caucus of the governing Conservative Party opposed such legislation. The Minister of Intergovernmental Affairs, Joe Clark, had often expressed serious reservations about a referendum. But Quebec and British Columbia were committed to holding a referendum and there was a good chance that the reform proposals would be rejected in both provinces. A national referendum campaign and a favourable vote in most regions was a possible way of legitimizing reform proposals in this divisive climate.

The decision to hold a referendum on the Charlottetown Accord and the willingness to abide by what was, legally speaking, a non-binding popular vote, appeared to mark the beginning of a new era in Canadian constitution-making. Most commentators believed so, arguing that governments in the future would find it impossible to ignore the 1992 precedent of a popular ratification vote.

Such predictions may be premature. A country's political culture and ways of conducting politics seldom change abruptly as a result of a single experience. First ministers will continue to be the key players in any future effort at constitutional reform. Both political tradition and the formal amendment procedure ensure their dominance. But a repeat of the Meech Lake process—an accord negotiated and agreed to without public consultation—has become virtually unthinkable. It is fair to say, however, that a process of consultation and opportunities for public participation in some form have become necessary preconditions for any future agreement.

It remains to be seen whether governments will feel obliged to submit future agreements to the electorate for ratification or whether the Charlottetown experience was an aberration that has left no mark on Canada's political culture. In British Columbia and Alberta, where populism runs a bit deeper than in most of the rest of the country, the political pressure for constitutional referendums may be irresistible. In the case of Quebec, the idea that any major change in that province's constitutional status must be approved by the electorate is now firmly established. These provinces are the ones most likely to insist on popular ratification of constitutional reform. If they do, it becomes very awkward

for Ottawa not to concede a role for direct public participation through a national referendum, as happened in 1992.

Does Quebec Have the Constitutional Right to Secede? (and Does It Matter?)

On 20 August 1998 the Supreme Court of Canada handed down its much awaited decision on the constitutionality of Quebec separation. In the eyes of some, the most remarkable aspect of the ruling was that it was made at all. The separation of Quebec, if and when it comes about, is a political matter that will be determined by politicians and the people, not by nine appointed judges in Ottawa. This was certainly the view of most Quebec nationalists and of Quebec's Parti Québécois government, whose disdain for the process was such that it refused to send lawyers to argue the case for the constitutionality of Quebec secession. Indeed, the Supreme Court's involvement in this matter was widely viewed by francophone Quebecers as unwarranted meddling in the internal affairs of the province.

Ottawa's decision to refer the issue of the constitutionality of Quebec secession to the Supreme Court was prompted by the actions of Montreal lawyer Guy Bertrand. A one-time separatist, Bertrand had already begun legal proceedings in Quebec challenging the constitutionality of unilateral secession by Quebec. Ottawa's 1996 decision to refer the question to the Supreme Court of Canada was, in part, due to the simple fact that Bertrand's private action had already released the genie from the bottle. Nonetheless, political risks were associated with Ottawa's involvement in a court challenge to Quebec secession. The Liberal government's decision to push forward, despite these risks, was consistent with what had come to be known as the "Plan B" approach to Quebec separatism. Whereas Plan A had involved efforts to satisfy moderate Quebec nationalists with promises of distinct society status for Quebec and some decentralization of powers to the provinces, Plan B was a hardline approach that relied on convincing Quebecers that separation would carry significant economic costs and that some parts of the territory of Quebec might not fall under the authority of an independent Quebec state (this was the partition threat, made by predominantly anglophone communities and Aboriginal groups in Quebec, and occasionally expressed by Stéphane Dion, the Liberal Minister of Intergovernmental Affairs). The court challenge to Quebec secession became a major component of the Plan B strategy.

In the reference submitted by Ottawa to the Supreme Court, three questions were asked:

- Question 1: Under the Constitution of Canada, can the National Assembly or government of Quebec effect the secession of Quebec from Canada unilaterally?
- Question 2: Does international law give the National Assembly or government of Quebec the right to effect the secession of Quebec from Canada unilaterally? In other words, is there a right to self-determination in international law that applies to Quebec?
- Question 3: If there is a conflict between international law and the Canadian Constitution on the secession of Quebec, which takes precedence?

The Court decided that there is no conflict, and so only the first two questions were addressed.

The Court's answer to the first question was a model of ambiguity that provided both federalists and separatists with congenial arguments. In strictly legal terms, said the Court, the secession of Quebec involves a major change to the Constitution of Canada that "requires an amendment to the Constitution, which perforce requires negotiation."[40] However, the Constitution of Canada consists of more than the Constitution Acts passed between 1867 and 1982. "Underlying constitutional principles," said the Court, "may in certain circumstances give rise to substantive legal obligations . . . which constitute substantive limitation upon government action."[41] These underlying constitutional principles provided the basis for the Court's argument that if a clear majority of Quebecers voted "yes" to an unambiguous question on Quebec separation, this would "confer legitimacy on the efforts of the government of Quebec to initiate the Constitution's amendment process in order to secede by constitutional means"[42] (see Box 6.8). These underlying constitutional principles also impose on Ottawa and the provincial governments outside of Quebec an

Politics in Focus

BOX 6.8 Can Quebecers Vote Their Way Out of Canada?

Although the Constitution does not itself address the use of a referendum procedure, and the results of a referendum have no direct role or legal effect in our constitutional scheme, a referendum undoubtedly may provide a democratic method of ascertaining the views of the electorate on important political questions on a particular occasion. The democratic principle identified above would demand that considerable weight be given to a clear expression by the people of Quebec of their will to secede from Canada, even though a referendum, in itself and without more, has no direct legal effect, and could not in itself bring about unilateral secession. Our political institutions are premised on the democratic principle, and so an expression of the democratic will of the people of a province carries weight, in that it would confer legitimacy on the efforts of the government of Quebec to initiate the Constitution's amendment process in order to secede by constitutional means. In this context, we refer to a "clear" majority as a qualitative evaluation. The referendum result, if it is to be taken as an expression of the democratic will, must be free of ambiguity both in terms of the question asked and in terms of the support it achieves.

Source: Supreme Court of Canada, *Reference re the Secession of Quebec* (1998).

obligation to negotiate the terms of secession, if and when Quebecers and their provincial government express the democratic will to separate.

So who wins on the first question? The answer is that both federalists and separatists found enough in the Supreme Court's ruling to allow them to claim victory. Federalists emphasized that Quebec has no constitutional right to secede unilaterally unless a "clear majority" of Quebecers, on an "unambiguous" question, expressed their will to do so, presumably through a referendum. Separatists—or at least those who were even willing to acknowledge the Court's ruling—emphasized that the Court had agreed that the democratically expressed will of Quebecers was decisive in determining whether unilateral secession was constitutional, and that if Quebecers were to express their clear support for separation the rest of Canada would be constitutionally bound to respect this decision and negotiate the terms of secession.

The Court's answer to the second question—whether international law gives Quebec the right to secede—was both shorter and less ambiguous. The Court said "no." While acknowledging that the right of self-determination of peoples exists in international law, the Supreme Court held that this right did not apply to Quebec.

The Court did not answer the contentious question of whether the Quebec population, or a part of it, constitutes a "people" as understood in international law. It argued that such a determination was unnecessary because, however the Quebec people might be defined, it is clear that Quebecers are neither denied the ability to pursue their "political, economic, social and cultural development within the framework of an existing state,"[43] nor do they constitute a colonial or oppressed people (a claim that is a staple of contemporary Quebec historiography). The Court's pronouncements on these matters are found in Box 6.9.

Does the 1998 Supreme Court ruling make a difference? Probably not, or at least not much of one, as even the Court seemed to acknowledge at various points in its decision. On the issue of what would constitute a "clear majority" and an "unambiguous question" in a referendum on

Quebec independence, the Court admitted that "it will be for the political actors to determine what constitutes a 'clear majority on a clear question'."[44] Likewise, the practical meaning of what the Court said was that the constitutional obligation of the rest of Canada to negotiate the terms of separation with Quebec, if Quebecers express the democratic will to secede, would be for political actors to settle. Finally, in response to the argument that a unilateral declaration of independence by Quebec would be effective regardless of whether the Court's test of a clear majority on a clear question was met, the judges could say only that this might well be true, but the action would be unconstitutional nonetheless. One suspects that separatists would not lose much sleep over the constitutionality of such a declaration, particularly if various countries reacted by recognizing the new Quebec state.

Ottawa's response to the 1998 Supreme Court ruling was to pass the Clarity Act in 2000. This law empowers Parliament to review the wording of any future referendum question to determine whether it complies with the Supreme Court's requirement that such a question be "unambiguously worded." It also empowers Parliament to review the margin of victory for the separatism option in a referendum to ensure that it meets the "clear majority" standard required by the 1998 ruling. Under this law the Parliament of Canada could, conceivably, refuse to enter into negotiations on separatism with Quebec if it determined that one or both of these conditions were not met. "Conceivably" is the key word here. There are strong reasons to think that Ottawa's rejection of a referendum question designed by a sovereignist Quebec government, or of even a fairly narrow margin of victory for those in favour of independence, could well backfire. Such action might play into the hands of separatists who would be quick to accuse the federal government and the rest of Canada of meddling in Quebec's affairs. The aim of the Clarity Act was doubtless to strengthen the federalists' hand in a future Quebec referendum, but the actual result could prove to be quite the opposite.

In the end, the most interesting thing about the Clarity Act is surely the questions it forces us

Politics in Focus

BOX 6.9 International Law and the Self-Determination of Quebec

There is no necessary incompatibility between the maintenance of the territorial integrity of existing states, including Canada, and the right of a "people" to achieve a full measure of self-determination. A state whose government represents the whole of the people or peoples resident within its territory, on a basis of equality and without discrimination, and respects the principles of self-determination in its own internal arrangements, is entitled to the protection under international law of its territorial integrity.

The Quebec people is not the victim of attacks on its physical existence or integrity, or of a massive violation of its fundamental rights. The Quebec people is manifestly not, in the opinion of the *amicus curiae*, an oppressed people.

For close to 40 of the last 50 years, the Prime Minister of Canada has been a Quebecer. During this period, Quebecers have held from time to time all the most important positions in the federal Cabinet. During the 8 years prior to June 1997, the Prime Minister and the Leader of the Official Opposition in the House of Commons were both Quebecers. At present, the Prime Minister of Canada, the Right Honourable Chief Justice and two other members of the Court, the Chief of Staff of the Canadian Armed Forces and the Canadian ambassador to the United States, not to mention the Deputy Secretary-General of the United Nations, are all Quebecers. The international achievements of Quebecers in most fields of human endeavour are too numerous to list. Since the dynamism of the Quebec people has been directed towards the business sector, it has been clearly successful in Quebec, the rest of Canada, and abroad.

The population of Quebec cannot plausibly be said to be denied access to government. Quebecers occupy prominent positions within the government of Canada. Residents of the province freely make political choices and pursue economic, social, and cultural development within Quebec, across Canada, and throughout the world. The population of Quebec is equitably represented in legislative, executive, and judicial institutions. In short, to reflect the phraseology of the international documents that address the right to self-determination of peoples, Canada is a "sovereign and independent state conducting itself in compliance with the principle of equal rights and self-determination of peoples and thus possessed of a government representing the whole people belonging to the territory without distinction."

Source: Supreme Court of Canada, *Reference re the Secession of Quebec* (1998).

to ask about when and how it is politically legitimate to break up a country. The issue came to the fore in early 2013 when a Bloc Québécois MP introduced a private member's bill proposing that the Clarity Act be repealed. This placed the NDP, most of whose Quebec MPs had strong nationalist sympathies, in a bind. If the party supported the bill, it would be seen in the rest of Canada as tight with the separatists. If it opposed the bill, many Quebecers who voted NDP in the 2011 election would be displeased. The party reacted by introducing its own private member's bill that clarified the Clarity Act by stating that a vote of 50 per cent plus 1 in a referendum would constitute the "clear majority" referred to in the 1998 Supreme Court ruling and in the Clarity Act. In fact, not only is this the position of Quebec separatists, it is also the official position of the Quebec Liberal Party. But it is a position that has little support outside of Quebec, among Canadians who believe that a stronger majority ought to be necessary to break up a country.

Starting Points for Research

Alan Cairns, *Constitution, Government, and Society in Canada: Selected Essays* (Toronto: McClelland & Stewart, 1988). Several of Cairns's most insightful and widely cited articles are here, including his 1977 presidential address to the Canadian Political Science Association on the impact of political and bureaucratic self-interest and the Constitution on federalism and intergovernmental conflict.

Peter W. Hogg, *Constitutional Law of Canada* (Scarborough, Ont.: Carswell, 2007). This is perhaps the leading text on Canadian constitutional law, widely used in political science and law courses alike. It is available in a student edition (2013).

Christian Leuprecht and Peter H. Russell, eds, *Essential Readings in Canadian Constitutional Politics* (Toronto: University of Toronto Press, 2011). Classic and contemporary writings on various aspects of the Canadian Constitution.

Peter Russell, *Constitutional Odyssey: Can Canadians Become a Sovereign People?*, 3rd edn (Toronto: University of Toronto Press, 2004). One of Canada's leading constitutional scholars provides an excellent survey of constitutional struggles in Canada.

F.R. Scott, *Essays on the Constitution* (Toronto: University of Toronto Press, 1977). This somewhat dated classic is unsurpassed in the quality of insight that Scott, among Canada's foremost constitutionalists and poets, brings to the analysis of Canada's constitutional history.

Review Exercises

1. What are the pros and cons of the comparatively strict form of party discipline practised in Canada's House of Commons? How do you think our constitutional system would change if all votes in the House of Commons were free votes?

2. Draft a "Canada Clause" to be added at the beginning of the Constitution Act, stating in no more than 100 words the core principles and values that Canada stands for and that should guide interpretation of the Constitution. Compare yours to those drafted by other members of your class and to similar sorts of clauses at the beginning of the United States and French constitutions.

3. The Canadian and American constitutional systems are compared in Chapter 4 of Eugene Forsey's *How Canadians Govern Themselves*, at: <www.parl.gc.ca/about/parliament/senatoreugeneforsey/book/chapter_4-e.html>. What, according to Forsey, are the main differences? Explain why you mainly agree or mainly disagree with his argument about which system is better.

7 Rights and Freedoms

In modern democracies political demands often are expressed in the language of rights and freedoms. This chapter examines some of the controversies associated with rights and freedoms, and discusses the impact of the Canadian Charter of Rights and Freedoms on Canadian politics. Topics discussed include:

- What do "rights" and "freedoms" mean?
- The origins and meanings of rights.
- The pre-Charter era: 1867–1981.
- The Charter and constitutional supremacy.
- The "notwithstanding" clause.
- Applying the Charter.
- Individual rights and freedoms.
- Equality and the Charter.

The Canadian Museum for Human Rights in Winnipeg, the first national museum outside the National Capital Region, opened on 19 September 2014. The museum's eleven interactive galleries present various perspectives on human rights' violations and movements throughout history.

(Photo courtesy of Josel Catindoy.)

Few things unite Canadians more than their support for human rights. At the same time, some of the most profound divisions in Canadian society and politics have to do with rights. This is no coincidence. When we use the language of rights and make an argument about how things ought to be using that language, we fall very easily, almost inevitably, into the realm of moral absolutes. Morality involves our ideas of how things ought to be, grounded on notions having to do with human dignity, worth, and, if we are of a religious turn of mind, the sacred. Absolutes are, of course, just that. They are propositions that are not open to compromise, limitation, or infringement of any sort. When rights are understood as moral absolutes there is no room for compromise. Moral absolutes are, by their nature, non-negotiable. This creates a potential dilemma when different segments of the population do not share the same moral absolutes, or when some people think that an issue ought to be resolved simply on the basis of whatever rights claims might be involved, and others think that non-rights considerations such as national security, economic prosperity, or bureaucratic efficiency should weigh heavily in the balance.

In reality, no right or freedom is absolute. There are two reasons for this. One is that rights and freedoms may and often do come into conflict, necessitating some compromise. For example, should freedom of expression protect the right of an individual to shout "Fire!" when there is none in a crowded theatre? This hypothetical case was used by American Supreme Court Justice Oliver Wendell Holmes to explain when and why limits on free speech are justified. Holmes established the "clear and present danger" test,[1] according to which freedom of speech could legitimately be curtailed when it posed an unmistakable and immediate danger to others. Falsely shouting "Fire!" in a crowded theatre obviously endangers the safety of those in the room. To guarantee an individual's freedom of expression in such circumstances is unreasonable because it could jeopardize the right of other individuals to be protected from danger.

The trade-offs between competing values are seldom as simple as in the preceding example. Should freedom of expression protect people who publicly communicate statements that "willfully promote hatred"[2] against some group distinguished by race, ethnicity, language, or religion? When do national security considerations or society's interest in preventing trafficking in drugs warrant wiretaps and other violations of the individual's right to privacy? How far should the public's interest in minimizing fraudulent claims on the public purse be allowed to justify intrusions into the homes and lives of welfare recipients or of those in public office? Is affirmative action a legitimate means for promoting social equality, or is it reverse discrimination against those who are not members of the groups targeted for special consideration? When does one right or freedom trump another? And who should determine these trade-offs: the courts or the people's elected representatives?

A second reason why no right or freedom can be treated as an absolute is because to do so often would be impractical. If, for example, a constitution guarantees the right of official-language minorities to public education or services in their mother tongue—as Canada's does—does that mean that all government services everywhere in the country should be available in each of the official languages? Does it mean that minority-language education should be provided in a community where only a very few families are demanding a school? Common sense suggests that there are limits to how far, and in what circumstances, the principles of linguistic equality and minority rights should apply.

What about administrative procedures determined by budget and personnel restrictions, but that may impose hardship on individuals and perhaps even limit their rights if these procedures are curtailed? The Supreme Court has addressed this question on a number of occasions when a government whose procedures or rules were challenged on Charter grounds argued that they were necessary for financial reasons. The courts have not been sympathetic to budgetary arguments. "Budgetary considerations in and of themselves cannot justify violating a *Charter* right, although they may be relevant in determining the appropriate degree of deference to governmental choices based on a non-financial objective."[3] Some taxpayers may view the matter differently.

Even in what may appear to be the most straightforward of circumstances, in which no compromise seems possible, the reality is that a balancing act between rights and other values may take place. Consider the case of human life and the measures that should be taken to preserve it. A 30-year-old person who needs a liver transplant to stay alive is more likely to receive this organ than an 80-year-old. Most, but not all of us, may find this preference for the younger person to be entirely reasonable. We might be even more likely to approve it if we learn that the 30-year-old is the mother of two young children and her family's main breadwinner, whereas

the 80-year-old has a history of serious health problems and is considered unlikely to survive very long after a liver transplant operation. For most people, at least, the determination of whether one person's right to life ought to be protected more vigilantly than another's will be influenced by knowledge of surrounding circumstances like these.

Dilemmas await us at every turn. Despite this, and despite the passions unleashed by such controversies, rights and freedoms have had a low profile in Canadian politics for most of this country's history. Reflecting on her time as a law student, Supreme Court Justice Rosalie Abella says that the question of the role of the courts in developing and protecting rights was hardly ever discussed when she graduated in 1970. But since the passage of the

"I'm trying to see you, Albert, in the light of our new Charter of Rights and Freedoms . . ."

No right or freedom is absolute. Questions such as *When should one individual's rights and freedoms be diminished to protect those of others?* and *Should one right or freedom supersede another?* are raised when applying a document such as the Charter to everyday situations.

Charter of Rights and Freedoms in 1982, she says, rights and the role of the courts in their interpretation have been very much at the centre of Canada's political radar screen.[4] The Charter entrenched various rights and freedoms in the Constitution. Moreover, by establishing the principle of constitutional supremacy (sections 32 and 52[1] of the Constitution Act, 1982), the 1982 constitutional reforms placed these rights more or less beyond the interference of governments. "More or less" because section 1 of the Charter states that these rights and freedoms are "subject only to such reasonable limits prescribed by law as can be demonstrably justified in a free and democratic society," and section 33(1) enables either Parliament or a provincial legislature to declare that a particular law or provision of a law shall operate even if it violates rights or freedoms guaranteed in sections 2 or 7 to 15 of the Charter. Together, sections 1 and 33 appear to maintain some measure of parliamentary supremacy over the courts and the Charter.

There is little doubt, as Justice Abella and so many others have observed, that the Charter has decisively changed the face of Canadian politics. The authority of elected legislatures has receded before the authority of the Constitution and the courts. A transformation has taken place in the venues and language of Canadian politics. The discourse of "rights," always a part of the political scene, has assumed much greater prominence since passage of the Charter. Individuals, organized interests, and even governments have turned increasingly to litigation as a means of influencing public policy. During the first decade after the Charter's passage, about 1,000 Charter cases a year were decided by Canadian courts,[5] reflecting the increased importance of the judiciary as a forum for the resolution of political conflict. About 20–30 Charter rulings were handed down by the Supreme Court each year, including many that had major effects on public policy. The pace of such judicial interventions has slowed somewhat in recent years. Between 2008 and 2012 the Supreme Court decided 69 Charter cases, or about 14 per year. Over this same period Charter cases made up about 20 per cent of all cases decided by

the Court.[6] Does the Charter matter? The answer may seem to be obvious. But expert opinion on this matter is not in agreement. Most political scientists argue that the Charter has profoundly transformed Canadian politics and society. But some commentators, including Harry Arthurs, a former dean of Osgoode Hall Law School and one of Canada's most distinguished lawyers, argues that the Charter "has not . . . significantly altered the reality of life in Canada."[7] Which groups (leaving aside lawyers) have won as a result of Charter politics, and which have lost ground? Has Canadian society become more democratic as a result of the unprecedented prominence accorded to rights and freedoms since the Charter's passage?

These are crucial questions on which there is no consensus. To answer them we need a baseline that will enable us to assess developments since the Charter became part of Canada's Constitution. Let us begin by examining the concepts of rights and freedoms. We will then examine the history of rights and freedoms in Canada, pre- and post-Charter.

Coming to Terms: What Do Rights and Freedoms Mean?

Although there is a long tradition in Western constitutional law of distinguishing between rights and freedoms, often the practical distinction is rather blurred. An individual's freedom to believe something or to behave in a particular way may be expressed in terms of a right. "I have a right to picket this employer" (freedom of assembly), or "I have a right to distribute pamphlets explaining that the [you fill in the blank] are responsible for most of the evils that beset the world" (freedom of expression). Likewise, the right to fair and equal treatment by the law is often framed in terms of the conditions necessary to ensure a personal freedom. For example, an accused person's right to be tried within a reasonable time—a right guaranteed by section 11(b) of the Charter—may well be violated if he or she has to spend a year in prison before being tried or "free" but under onerous bail restrictions. Obviously, this individual's personal freedom is seriously compromised in such circumstances. Or consider the case of abortion. Those who argue against legal restrictions on a woman's access to abortion claim that such laws violate a woman's right to control her body, an important dimension of the right to privacy. In this case the right being claimed is nothing less than freedom from interference by the state, or what Alan Borovoy has called the "right to be left alone."[8]

Rights and freedoms are not, therefore, watertight compartments in reality. Nevertheless, constitutional experts usually reserve the term "rights" for those individual and group **entitlements** that "are considered so fundamental to human dignity that they receive special protection under the law and usually under the constitution of a country."[9] Freedoms involve an individual's liberty to do or believe certain things without restraint by government. Whereas the defence of rights often requires some government action, the protection of freedoms requires that government refrain from interfering in certain matters. Under the influence of the United Nations **Universal Declaration of Human Rights** (1948), the term **human rights** has become the commonly used designation for this bundle of rights and freedoms. Included among them are the following:

- *Political rights/fundamental freedoms.* These include freedom of association, assembly, expression, the media, conscience, and religion, and the right to privacy.
- *Democratic rights.* Among these are the rights of all adult persons to vote and stand for public office. Requirements that elections periodically be held and that the law apply equally to those who govern and those who are governed are also important democratic rights.
- *Legal rights.* These are essentially procedural rights intended to ensure the fair and equal treatment of individuals under the law. They include, *among others*, the right to due process of law, freedom from arbitrary arrest, the right to a fair hearing, the right to legal counsel, and the right not to be subjected to cruel or unusual punishment.
- *Economic rights.* Although they usually are not listed as a separate category of entrenched rights, economic rights occupy an important place in all capitalist democracies. They include the right to own property and not to be deprived of it without fair compensation, the right to withhold one's labour, and freedom of contract.
- *Equality rights.* This is the most recent and probably the most controversial category of rights. The American Constitution, the first modern constitution to include an entrenched guarantee of equality rights, refers only to every person's right to "equal protection of the laws."[10] The more recent tendency, however, has been to enumerate the proscribed bases of legal discrimination, such as race, religion, ethnicity, gender, and age. Canada's Charter also includes mental or physical disability and has been interpreted by the courts to prohibit discrimination based on sexual orientation.

These five categories by no means exhaust the rights that may be protected by law. *Language rights* represent an important category of group rights in many societies, Canada included. Other group rights, such as for religious minorities or Indigenous peoples, may also be protected by law. Some argue that *social rights*, or what are sometimes called *entitlements*, including the right to a job, economic security, public education, decent housing, and adequate health care, should also have the status of entrenched constitutional rights. *Environmental rights*, including citizens' rights to clean air and water, to the preservation of wilderness areas, and to the protection of species diversity, are advocated by some groups, including the Canadian Bar Association. Some go even further, calling for the protection of animal rights and the dignity of plant life (see Box 7.1).

In Canada, many of the main categories of human rights are entrenched in the Charter. Table 7.1 identifies the sections of the Charter that correspond to each of them.

Governing Realities

BOX 7.1 Should Trees, Rivers, and Endangered Species Have Constitutionally Protected Rights?

The constitution of Ecuador includes a chapter entitled "The Rights of Nature." It appears to place the welfare and rights of plants, animals, and ecosystems on a par with those of human beings. "Nature," it declares, "where life is reproduced and exists, has the right to exist, persist, maintain and regenerate its vital cycles, structure, functions and its processes in evolution." It goes on to state that "Nature has the right to restoration," and that in cases of severe or permanent environmental damage, including damage caused by the exploitation of natural resources, the state is obliged to adopt "adequate measures to eliminate or mitigate the harmful environmental consequences." The state is also obliged to take steps to prevent "the extinction of species, the destruction of the ecosystems or the permanent alteration of natural cycles." This last provision includes a constitutional ban on the "introduction of organisms and organic and inorganic material that can alter in a definitive way the national genetic patrimony."

Including such protections in a constitution involves a fundamental shift in thinking about rights. Historically, rights have been based on ideas about human dignity and happiness. The notion that non-human life forms should be invested with rights that do not depend on the needs and desires of human beings is radically different. It is based on a rejection of what are referred to by the advocates of plant and animal rights as anthropocentric—human-centred—and species-specific notions of justice that unfairly privilege human beings.

To get a better sense of the reasoning and world view on which such arguments rest (if you don't already share them) visit the website of People for the Ethical Treatment of Animals (www.peta.org).

TABLE 7.1 Human Rights and the Charter

Rights Category	Pre-Charter Protections	Charter Protections
1. Political rights/ fundamental freedoms	Common-law protections implied in the preamble of the Constitution Act, 1867	s. 2
2. Democratic rights	Constitution Act, 1867, ss. 41, 50, 84, 85	ss. 3–5
3. Legal rights	Common law; Criminal Code	ss. 7–14
4. Economic rights	Common-law rights re: contract, property, mobility, etc.	s. 6 (and implied under some other sections)
5. Equality rights	Common law; s. 93 of Constitution Act, 1867, guaranteeing educational rights of religious denominations	ss. 15, 28
6. Language rights	Constitution Act, 1867, s. 133	ss. 16–23
7. Aboriginal rights	Treaties	s. 25, plus s. 35 of Constitution Act, 1982
8. Social rights	None	Although not mentioned directly, some court rulings suggest that some social rights are implied

Media Spotlight

BOX 7.2 Amnesty International on Human Rights Abuses

For several decades Amnesty International has operated as a watchdog for human rights violations in countries throughout the world. Here are some excerpts from its 2012 report on Canada.

Indigenous Peoples' rights

In April, a leaking pipeline spilled an estimated 4.5 million litres of crude oil onto the traditional territory of the Lubicon Cree in northern Alberta, the largest spill in the province since 1975. In August, the province allowed the pipeline to resume operation without meaningful consultation with the Lubicon People. International human rights bodies have long expressed concern over the failure to respect Lubicon land rights.

In August, a federal audit concluded that 39 per cent of water systems in First Nation communities have major deficiencies, with 73 per cent of drinking water systems and 65 per cent of waste water systems constituting medium or high risk to health. . . .

Women's rights

In July, the federal Minister responsible for the Status of Women stated publicly that the government did not intend to establish a national action plan to address the high levels of violence faced by Indigenous women.

In October, in British Columbia a provincial inquiry was opened into the police response to the cases of missing and murdered women, many of whom were Indigenous, in Vancouver. Before the inquiry began, 17 of the 20 organizations granted intervener status withdrew because of concerns over fairness.

Counter-terror and security

Hearings by the Military Police Complaints Commission into concerns that Canadian soldiers transferred prisoners in Afghanistan to the custody of Afghan officials, despite a serious risk they would be tortured, concluded in February. The Commission's report had not been issued by the end of the year. . . .

Omar Khadr, a Canadian citizen apprehended by US forces in Afghanistan in 2002 when he was 15 years old and detained at Guantánamo Bay since October 2002, became eligible to be transferred to serve the remainder of his sentence in Canada on 1 November. He had been sentenced to an eight-year prison term in October 2010 following a plea agreement. The Canadian government had not reached a decision on his transfer application by the end of 2011.

Refugees and asylum-seekers

In June, the government reintroduced proposed legislation that would penalize asylum-seekers arriving in Canada in an irregular manner, such as when a human smuggler arranges their travel in a group by sea. The proposals include lengthy mandatory detention without timely review of the grounds of detention and other measures that violate international norms.

Police and security forces

In April, RCMP officers in Prince George, British Columbia, used a Taser against an 11-year-old boy. The RCMP announced in September that the officers involved would not be disciplined or charged.

In June, the Toronto Police Services released an internal review of policing of the G8 and G20 Summits in 2010, during which more than 1,000 people were arrested. The Toronto Police Services Board's independent civilian review of some aspects of the policing operation was continuing at the end of 2011. The provincial and federal governments rejected calls for a public inquiry.

International justice

In October, the government failed to arrest former US President George W. Bush when he travelled to British Columbia, despite clear evidence that he was responsible for crimes under international law, including torture. Amnesty International, *Amnesty International Report 2012: The State of the World's Human Rights* (2012), 99–100.

Should Amnesty International's report on Canada be cause for concern?

On the Origins and Meanings of Rights

There is no inevitability to either the precise rights recognized by a constitution or the meanings that come to be associated with them. Rights, like a society's notions of justice, are constructed out of concrete historical circumstances. Some of the rights claimed in present-day Canada and the rights discourses that emerge around these claims and counterclaims are quite different from those of even a couple of generations ago. And much of Canadian rights discourse would be unrecognizable in a society like Iran, where very different religious, cultural, and economic forces have contributed to the recognition of and meaning ascribed to rights. There are, therefore, no absolute rights that may be adduced from human history. What may appear to be the most obvious and uncontroversial rights claims—for example, the right to vote or the right to express one's personal beliefs—are denied in many societies.

Rights come from political struggles. A claim made by an individual or a group will be expressed as a right only when it is denied or placed in jeopardy by the words or actions of some other party. For example, the claim that a woman has a right to abort her pregnancy arises because of legal and practical restrictions on access to abortion. The experience of limitations on freedom of speech, religion and conscience, or association produce calls for their constitutional protection. Groups and individuals come to the defence of the right to privacy precisely because they perceive that it is threatened by state actions. Likewise, when a linguistic group claims the protection or promotion of their language as a right, this is an indication that conflict exists between linguistic groups in that society.

Political struggle is a necessary condition for rights claims. It is not, however, a sufficient condition. Only some political conflicts acquire the character of rights issues. To be recognized as legitimate, a rights claim must be successfully linked to one or more of a society's fundamental values. These fundamental values operate as limits on rights discourse.

This may be seen in the case of same-sex marriage. Before the 1970s, sexual relations between persons of the same sex constituted a punishable offence under the Criminal Code. Change began when the Minister of Justice, Pierre Trudeau, famously stated in 1967 that "the view we take here is that there's no place for the state in the bedrooms of the nation. I think that what's done in private between adults doesn't concern the Criminal Code." Although Trudeau certainly was not the first to take the position that consenting adults had a *right* to privacy in their sexual relations, his statement was important in shaping the conversation about homosexuality and helping to shift public opinion from a view that considered homosexuality to be deviant and criminal behaviour, to the idea that this was a matter of personal choice or of inherent orientation that should not be regulated by the state. Trudeau's comment and the legislation he introduced to decriminalize sex between persons of the same sex were important steps in changing the political and cultural conversation and transforming same-sex relations into a rights issue.

Decriminalization was, however, only the first step. Canadian public opinion was still opposed to homosexuality in some circumstances and certainly did not accept the idea that homosexuals should be allowed to be teachers or to have the same rights under family law as heterosexual couples. Surveys showed that the percentage of Canadians saying that two adults of the same sex having sexual relations is always wrong was high until the 1990s (63 per cent in 1975; 62 per cent in 1985; 59 per cent in 1990; and 32 per cent in 2000).[11] At the same time, however, polls showed that by the end of the 1970s a strong majority of Canadians agreed that "homosexuals are entitled to the same rights as other Canadians" (1980, 70 per cent; 1990, 81 per cent; 2000, 71 per cent).[12] But when asked about particular rights, such as the right of homosexuals to marry, Canadian public opinion was a bit slower to change. Polls showed that before the mid- to late 1990s, just over one-third of Canadians supported same-sex marriage. Between 1998 and

2005 public opinion changed from being fairly evenly divided on this issue to being supportive of legal recognition of same-sex unions.[13]

The idea of homosexuality, long relegated to the illegitimate margins of Canadian society and even deemed criminal in some circumstances, was becoming more widely accepted in Canadian society. This opened the way for legislative change, including the decriminalization of same-sex sexual relations and, by the 1970s, the inclusion of prohibitions against discrimination on the basis of sexual preference in provincial human rights codes. Although the Charter did not explicitly mention sexual preference in s. 15 on equality rights, court rulings very soon recognized this as an analogous form of discrimination that, like discrimination based on race, religion, disability, and so on, was proscribed by the Charter. The decline of traditional religiosity in Canada and the boost provided by the Charter to the general conversation on rights combined to produce growing popular receptivity to the argument that recognition of same-sex marriage was a matter of human rights.

The fact that Canadians are much more likely to be receptive to rights arguments today than in the past, finding them normal, appropriate, and often convincing, does not mean that issues must be framed in a manner that draws on the language and conceptual architecture of rights. Indeed, it is often the case that political conflict is over how an issue should be framed and whether it should be thought of as one involving rights or as an issue that pits interests and values against one another. Take the case of immigration. It is possible to frame this issue entirely in the language of economics, demography and social integration, national security, and other concerns. But it is also possible to frame the issue as a matter of human rights. The NDP's official policy platform does this, stating that "Promoting the reunification of families [ought to be] the main priority of the Canadian immigration policy while respecting the diversity of family models according to the Charter of Rights and Freedoms."

Rights talk—framing issues on the language of rights and anchoring the discourse on rights documents, including the Charter—is often difficult to oppose. Who wants to be seen as being "against" or at least unsympathetic to human rights? But as Michael Ignatieff observes, it is not always the appropriate way to view and resolve an issue. "Human rights activism," he writes, "likes to portray itself as an anti-politics, in defense of universal moral claims designed to delegitimize 'political,' i.e., ideological or sectarian, justifications for the abuse of human beings. In practice, impartiality and neutrality are just as impossible as universal and equal concern for everyone's human rights."[14] The advocacy of human rights, Ignatieff argues, often involves a sort of idolatry of human rights. By this he means that rights may be treated as universal moral absolutes, brooking no opposition and permitting no compromise. Ignatieff argues that a pragmatic approach to the defence and advocacy of rights is often more effective politically and appropriate in a world in which ideas of justice and what constitutes a good life vary between cultures. His argument is chiefly against what he sees as a sort of rights imperialism that westerners sometimes engage in when they lecture other societies and cultures about how things ought to be. But what Ignatieff calls the idolatry of human rights, the failure to imagine that any other way of understanding and resolving an issue might be legitimate and helpful, is as likely to exist at home as on the international scene.

Rights and Their Protection

During the 1980–1 debate on constitutional reform, critics of an entrenched charter of rights warned that entrenchment would lead to the Americanization of Canadian politics. Since then, they have lamented that their prediction has come true. The "Americanization" they warned of, and that many still regret, has two main aspects. One involves a more prominent policy role for unelected judges and a related decline in the status of elected legislatures. The other is an increase in recourse to the courts to solve political disputes.

Some of those who opposed entrenched rights argued that rights and freedoms are better protected by elected legislatures, accountable to the electorate for their actions, than by unelected judges. By "better," they meant that the decisions of elected politicians are more likely to correspond with the sentiments of citizens—or at least that if they do not there exists a democratic mechanism, i.e., elections, to hold politicians accountable for their choices. Rights, the opponents of entrenchment argued, should not be interpreted independently of popular opinion. Nor should important political controversies be determined by unelected officials.

What the critics denounced as the undemocratic flaws of entrenchment, advocates of the Charter acclaimed as its virtues. Rights, they argued, should not be subject to the vicissitudes of public opinion as these are reflected in the legislature. The fact that judges are not elected and are virtually immune from removal before the age of 75 serves to protect, not undermine, democracy. What sort of democracy, entrenchment advocates ask, would permit rights and freedoms to depend on shifting popular sentiments and politicians' calculations of political expediency?

The difference between the opponents and advocates of entrenchment is not over the importance of rights. It is not even primarily about the appropriate balance between the rights of individuals and minorities versus those of the majority. As unflinching a civil libertarian as Alan Borovoy initially argued against the entrenchment of rights.[15] The difference between these two positions is over how best to *protect rights*. Those who advocate the American model of entrenched rights prefer to put their faith in the Constitution and the judges who interpret it. Those who prefer the British model of parliamentary supremacy are more dubious about judge-made law and more inclined to place their trust in the prudence and democratic responsiveness of elected governments. (It is perhaps worth noting here that even in the UK the British model has been adapted to the contemporary reality of international law and norms that operate to influence domestic policy and erode the supremacy of elected lawmakers.)

Does the record of rights enforcement in other countries permit us to draw conclusions about whether the American or British model is "best"? Has the Charter made a difference in how well rights are protected in Canada? There are no easy answers to these questions. Rights activists are themselves divided in their assessment of entrenchment's impact. But if definitive answers are elusive, we can at least attempt to understand how rights have been argued and enforced in Canadian politics. The Charter, we will see, represents an important watershed.

The Pre-Charter Era: 1867–1981

There is not a single reference to the subject of rights in R. MacGregor Dawson's *Constitutional Issues in Canada, 1900–1931*, published in 1933.[16] In Dawson's *The Government of Canada* (1947), the first textbook on Canadian government, one finds a mere handful of references to fundamental rights and liberties.[17] J.A. Corry and J.E. Hodgetts's *Democratic Government and Politics* (1946)[18] pays greater attention to rights, devoting an entire chapter to a comparison of civil liberties in Britain, the United States, and Canada. Generally, however, rights issues occupied a distinctly marginal place in Canadian political science and even in legal circles until the middle of the twentieth century.

A couple of factors were responsible for what might appear to be a puzzling silence on questions of rights and their protection in Canada. The most important undoubtedly was federalism. The Constitution Act, 1867 contains very few references to the rights and freedoms of Canadians. It does, however, include a very detailed catalogue of the "rights" of governments, i.e., the legislative and fiscal powers of Ottawa and the provinces. Faithful to the principle of parliamentary supremacy, the courts were unwilling to overrule the authority of elected legislatures. This is why Alan Borovoy, at the time the head of the Canadian Civil Liberties Association, originally opposed the Charter of Rights and Freedoms. "The truth is," he argued, "that we have had far more success [in advancing rights] in the political and legislative arenas than in the judicial. . . . [T]he courts have shown a monumental reluctance to apply the protections for civil liberties that exist in our present Bill of Rights."[19] Borovoy and other civil libertarians lamented the fact that throughout most of Canada's history, issues that clearly involved the protection of rights and freedoms were dealt with by the courts as federalism questions. To have a chance at success, therefore, rights claims had to be packaged in the constitutional categories of federalism. In retrospect, the resulting jurisprudence was bizarre, to say the least. Consider the following cases:

- *Reference re Alberta Statutes* (Alberta Press case, 1938).[20] The law in question was the Accurate News and Information Act, passed by the Alberta legislature in 1937. It imposed censorship restrictions on the province's newspapers, based on the Social Credit government's belief that the press was unfairly critical of its policies. Ottawa referred this and two other pieces of Social Credit legislation to the Supreme Court for a ruling on their constitutionality. The Court was unanimous in striking down the press censorship law. Two of the judgments in this case referred to the "right of free public discussion of public affairs" as being a right fundamental to parliamentary democracy and implied under the preamble to the Constitution Act, 1867, which states that Canada is adopting "a constitution similar in principle to that of the United Kingdom." But both of these judgments, although using somewhat different reasoning, suggested that the federal government possessed the authority to impose restrictions on freedom of the press. The Alberta law was, therefore, struck down essentially on federalism grounds.
- *Saumur v. City of Quebec* (1953).[21] The City of Quebec had passed a bylaw forbidding the distribution in the streets of any printed material without the prior consent of the Chief of Police. Without explicitly singling out any group, this bylaw was intended to curb proselytizing activities by the Jehovah's Witnesses sect, whose activities and teachings strongly

offended Catholic Church authorities. In a five-to-four decision, the Court struck down the bylaw. An analysis of the judges' reasoning reveals how disinclined they were to place the protection of fundamental freedoms over the authority of government. On the majority side, four of the five justices decided that the bylaw was **ultra vires** (i.e., beyond the legal authority of the government in question). The fifth was willing to concede that the regulation fell within provincial jurisdiction, but felt that the right to disseminate religious material was protected by Quebec's Freedom of Worship Act. On the dissenting side, two of the judges argued that the bylaw fell within the province's jurisdiction over civil rights. No one suggested that freedom of religious expression ought to be protected from interference by any and all levels of government.

- *Switzman v. Elbling* (Padlock Case, 1957).[22] In 1937 the Quebec government had passed a law declaring illegal the use of a house for the propagation of Communism, authorizing the Quebec police to put a padlock on premises where such activities were suspected. The Supreme Court of Canada ruled that the impugned Act had the effect of making the propagation of Communism a crime. But criminal law is under the exclusive jurisdiction of Ottawa and so the "Padlock Law" was struck down as being ultra vires. The issue of political censorship was raised by a couple of justices, but this was not the basis for the Court's ruling.
- *Attorney General of Canada and Dupond v. Montreal* (1978).[23] This case involved a Montreal bylaw that restricted freedom of assembly in public places. The bylaw was used during the 1960s to prevent public demonstrations during a period of political turmoil and occasional terrorist incidents. By a five-to-three vote the Supreme Court upheld the constitutionality of this restriction. The majority argued that the impugned bylaw regulated matters of a local or private nature and therefore came under the authority of the

province. Interestingly, the dissenting judges did not focus on the issue of freedom of assembly. Instead, they argued that the Montreal bylaw was ultra vires because it represented a sort of "mini-Criminal Code" and thus intruded upon Ottawa's exclusive authority to make criminal law. As a final note, the judgment in this case was unequivocal in dismissing the relevance of the Canadian Bill of Rights (1960). "None of the freedoms referred to," wrote Justice Beetz, "is so enshrined in the constitution as to be above the reach of competent legislation."[24]

Federalism was not the only factor responsible for the relatively low profile of rights issues until well into the twentieth century. Public opinion was generally sanguine about the treatment of rights and freedoms in Canada. A Gallup Poll taken in 1957 found that 63 per cent of Canadians agreed that "personal rights are being fully protected" and only 19 per cent disagreed. University graduates were as likely as drop-outs to hold this view.[25] The thinking of most informed Canadians was probably that rights were best protected by legislatures, the common law, and a vigilant public: the system that Canada had inherited from the United Kingdom. But increasing doubts about the adequacy of these guarantees were being expressed by civil libertarians during the 1940s and 1950s. These doubts were sown by apparent rights violations like Quebec's infamous "Padlock Law" (1937), the Alberta government's attempt to censor the press (1937), the threatened deportation of Japanese-Canadians in 1945–6, and the arbitrary measures taken during the Gouzenko spy affair of 1946. These constituted, according to political scientist Norman Ward, "disturbing signs of a weakening concern by Dominion and provincial governments for personal rights and liberties."[26] Corry and Hodgetts agreed, arguing that the protections provided under British parliamentary government were not sufficient in a young country facing the challenge of absorbing large numbers of persons of diverse ethnic origins and cultural backgrounds.[27]

This growing concern over civil liberties was shared by some influential groups, including the Canadian Bar Association. The solution, they argued, was a bill of rights that would be entrenched in the Constitution. Canada's participation in the United Nations, and the human rights commitments entered into through the UN, reinforced the voices of those calling for constitutionally entrenched rights. When the Conservative Party came to power in 1957 under the leadership of John Diefenbaker, who had long been an outspoken advocate of entrenched rights, the timing for a Bill of Rights seemed propitious.

But there was a major snag. A constitutional Bill of Rights would affect the powers of both Ottawa and the provinces and, it was believed, would therefore require provincial consent. It was clear that some of the provinces would oppose entrenchment. For this reason the Conservative government chose to introduce the Bill of Rights as a statute, requiring only the approval of the House of Commons and the Senate. The **Canadian Bill of Rights** became law on 10 August 1960.

The Bill of Rights proved to be a major disappointment for civil libertarians. The first Supreme Court decisions on its application were very cautious. In a case involving a challenge to the federal Lord's Day Act, the Court took the position that the Bill of Rights only reaffirmed the rights and freedoms status quo that existed at the time it became law (1960). Speaking for the majority, Justice Ritchie declared that the Canadian Bill of Rights "is not concerned with 'human rights and fundamental freedoms' in any abstract sense, but rather with such 'rights and freedoms' as they existed in Canada immediately before the statute was enacted."[28]

After nearly a decade of judgments that, to paraphrase Saskatchewan former Chief Justice Emmett Hall, whittled away at the Bill of Rights,[29] the Supreme Court suddenly abandoned its cautious approach. The case involved an Indian, Joseph Drybones, who was convicted under section 94(b) of the Indian Act. This provision of the Act made it an offence for an Indian to be intoxicated off a reserve. In challenging this provision, Drybones's lawyer argued that it conflicted with the Canadian Bill of Rights guarantee of "equality before the law," subjecting Indians to criminal sanctions to which other people were not exposed. This was obviously true. But if the Court remained faithful to its earlier interpretation, this would not be sufficient to render the discrimination unconstitutional.

By a five-to-three vote the Supreme Court used the Bill of Rights to strike down section 94 of the Indian Act.[30] This proved, however, to be a one-off decision. Perhaps realizing the Pandora's box they were opening through this more activist interpretation of the Bill of Rights, a majority of the judges retreated from this position after *Drybones*. This became crystal clear a few years later in the *Lavell* case,[31] where the majority upheld the constitutionality of another provision of the Indian Act against a challenge that it denied equality before the law.

Another nail was hammered into the Bill of Rights' coffin by the Court's decision in *Hogan v. The Queen* (1975).[32] In *Hogan*, a person suspected of driving while intoxicated refused to take a breathalyzer test before seeing his lawyer. He ultimately took the test and this evidence proved to be instrumental to his conviction. The question before the Supreme Court was whether evidence should be excluded if it has been obtained in an improper manner. Under the common law, Canadian judges had followed the rule that such evidence would be admitted so long as it was relevant to the case at hand. But the Canadian Bill of Rights included a number of legal rights, including the right of an accused or detained person "to retain and instruct counsel without delay" (s. 2[c][ii]).

The Supreme Court was unwilling to apply the Bill of Rights in this case. It appeared, therefore, that not only could the Bill of Rights not be used to strike down conflicting federal legislation—at least not laws on the books before 1960—it did not take precedence over established rules of the common law. Chief Justice Laskin's dissenting argument that the Bill of Rights should be interpreted as a "quasi-constitutional instrument" was never supported by a majority of his colleagues. The glimmer of hope that the *Drybones* decision had sparked was extinguished during the 1970s, producing renewed calls for constitutionally entrenched rights.

Before passage of the Charter, the only rights entrenched in Canada's Constitution were associated with democratic elections, religion, and language. Section 41 (now spent) of the Constitution Act, 1867 specified who was qualified to vote and

section 50 indicates that no House of Commons may sit for longer than five years (thus ensuring elections). Section 93 of the Constitution Act, 1867 declares that the educational rights of denominational minorities may not be diminished from what they were when a province entered Confederation. Section 133 establishes the equal standing of French and English in Parliament and in federal courts, and in the Quebec legislature and in the courts of that province. Neither of these latter two sections proved to be very effective in protecting minority rights.

The major test of section 93 involved the Manitoba Public Schools Act, passed in 1890. This law eliminated the Catholic and Protestant schools that had existed in the province and replaced them with a single public school system. The Act also eliminated the official status of French in the province. In *Barrett*,[33] the Judicial Committee of the Privy Council decided that this law did not violate the educational rights of the Roman Catholic minority because Catholics, like the members of any religious denomination, were free to set up their own private schools. The fact is, however, that the Manitoba Act, 1870 very clearly guaranteed the rights of Catholic schools, stating that no law could be passed that "prejudicially affects any right or privilege with respect to Denominational Schools [schools operated by churches] which any class of persons have by Law or practice in the Province at the Union."

In two other cases involving section 93, the courts refused to accept the argument that this section also protected the educational rights of language minorities. The argument had at least a ring of plausibility because, historically, the Roman Catholic schools in Manitoba were predominantly francophone and in Ontario they were often francophone, while in Quebec the Protestant schools were anglophone. Thus, when in 1913 the Ontario government issued regulations banning the use of French as a language of instruction in both public and separate (Catholic) schools, this had a negligible impact on public schools but dealt a major blow to the predominantly francophone Catholic schools of eastern Ontario. The issue arose again in the 1970s when the Quebec government passed

Bill 22, restricting access to the province's English-language schools, most of which were under the control of Protestant school boards. In both instances the courts rejected outright the claim that section 93 should be read as a protection for linguistic rights in addition to denominational ones.[34] From the standpoint of promoting bilingualism outside of Quebec, the courts' unwillingness to read language rights into section 93 represented a real setback.

The issue of language rights was at the heart of a pair of Supreme Court decisions handed down in 1978 and 1979. Both of these decisions involved the limited guarantee of bilingualism established by section 133 of the Constitution Act, 1867. In each case the Court declared that this guarantee was beyond the interference of governments, thus repudiating the idea of parliamentary supremacy.

In the first case, *Attorney General of Quebec v. Blaikie*,[35] the Court upheld a Quebec Superior Court decision that had ruled unconstitutional those sections of Quebec's Bill 101 that attempted to make French the sole official language in that province. While Bill 101 did not ban the use of English from the legislature and the province's courts, and the Quebec government continued to print and publish laws and legislative documents in both languages, the law's clear intent was to make French the only official language for all government activities and the dominant language in the province's courts. This, the courts decided, violated the spirit—if not the strict letter—of section 133.

The issue in the second case, *Attorney General of Manitoba v. Forest* (1979),[36] was essentially the same, although the circumstances were quite different. Here, the challenge was against Manitoba's Official Language Act of 1890. Although it twice had been ruled unconstitutional by lower courts, in 1892 and 1909 (in the earlier case, as noted above, the JCPC overruled the lower court decision), the Act had continued in force. When in 1979 the Supreme Court of Canada finally vindicated those who had fought against the elimination of francophone rights in Manitoba, the victory was a hollow one, to say the least. In the words of René Lévesque, Quebec's Premier at the time, the decision came 90 years too late to make a difference for the province's francophone community.

Life under the Charter

It probably is fair to say that the changes generated by the Charter have far exceeded the expectations of all but a few of the politicians and experts who presided at its birth. On a quantitative level, the Charter has been the direct stimulus for explosive growth in the number of rights cases that come before the courts. Hundreds of Charter cases are decided by Canadian courts each year, and in a typical year about two dozen of these have been rulings by the Supreme Court or one of the provincial superior courts. Since its passage in 1982 the Charter has been used to strike down over 80 federal and provincial laws or parts of laws. The Court is, however, more likely to uphold the validity of a challenged law, as it has about two-thirds of the time over the past two decades. In the case of some laws, for example, the Immigration Act, the Income Tax Act, and the Criminal Code, dozens of Charter-based rulings have been handed down by the Supreme Court. An even greater number of provincial laws have been the subject of Supreme Court Charter rulings. Over the last several years about one-fifth of the rulings handed down by the Supreme Court have involved constitutional matters based on the Charter.[37]

In terms of "quality," the change produced by the Charter has been no less pronounced. The previous pattern of deciding rights issues as federalism cases, asking only whether a government was transgressing the jurisdictional turf of the other level of government, has been abandoned. Rights issues are now dealt with head on, argued by litigants and decided by judges on the basis of the Charter. Moreover, the courts have shed most of their traditional reluctance to question the substance of duly enacted laws and regulations. Emboldened by the Charter's unambiguous declarations that the "Constitution is the supreme law of Canada" and that the courts have exclusive authority to interpret and enforce the Charter's guarantees, judges have struck down provisions in several dozen federal and provincial statutes. Although judges are quite aware of the expanded role they play in the political process, most of them insist that there is nothing undemocratic in this and that it is quite incorrect to assert, as some critics do, that judges engage in policy-making from the bench and have too much power. Retired Supreme Court Justice John Major speaks for most of his colleagues on the bench and in the legal profession when he says that "there is no such thing as judicial activism in Canada."[38] Chief Justice Beverley McLachlin has said that "there is no clear demarcation between applying the law, interpreting the law, and making the law."[39] She did not mean this as a criticism of what critics call judicial activism, but instead as an explanation and justification for what critics see as too vast a role for judges.

Reasonable Limits and the Charter

It appears that the courts are invited to exercise self-restraint, commonly called **judicial restraint**, by the opening words of the Charter. Section 1 declares that the guarantees set forth in the Charter shall be "subject only to such reasonable limits prescribed by law as can be demonstrably justified in a free and democratic society." What are these **reasonable limits**? The Supreme Court established a two-part test in the case of *The Queen v. Oakes* (1986).[40] The first part of this test asks whether a government's objective in limiting a right is of sufficient importance to warrant such an encroachment. The second part of the test asks whether the extent of the limitation is proportionate to the importance of the government's objective. In order to satisfy this second criterion, a limitation must meet three conditions: (1) it must be rationally connected to the government's objective; (2) it should impair the right in question as little as is necessary to meet the government's objective; and (3) the harm done to rights by a limitation must not exceed the good that it accomplishes.

In *Oakes*, the Court was called upon to determine whether a "reverse onus" provision in the Narcotic Control Act violated the presumption of innocence set forth in section 11(d) of the Charter. Under that Act, a person found guilty of possessing drugs was automatically considered guilty of trafficking unless he could prove his innocence on this more serious charge. The Court did not question the importance of the objective associated with this provision of the Act, i.e., to prevent drug trafficking. But in applying the second part of the test that they developed in *Oakes*, the justices decided that the means, in this case placing the onus on the accused to prove his innocence, was disproportionate to the end.

The separation of legislative ends, part one of the **Oakes test**, from an assessment of the means used to accomplish them may appear to be a way around the thorny problem of judges second-guessing the decisions of duly elected governments. In fact, however, it is not possible to answer such questions as whether a right is impaired as little as possible in the circumstances, or whether the means are proportionate to the ends, without wandering into the realm of political value judgments. Since *Oakes*, the courts have been reluctant to question the ends associated with laws and regulations limiting

Since the Charter of Rights and Freedoms was entrenched in the Constitution, the Supreme Court of Canada has assumed a much more prominent role in our political system.

rights. But they have not been shy about using the second part of the *Oakes* test to dismiss governments' section 1 justifications.

This was apparent in the Supreme Court's decision in *Ford v. Attorney General of Quebec* (1988).[41] The case involved a challenge to those sections of Quebec's Bill 101 that prohibited commercial advertising in languages other than French. The Quebec government argued that this limitation was necessary in order to preserve the economic value of the French language and the predominantly French character of the province. The Court accepted that this was a perfectly legitimate policy goal (it passed part one of the *Oakes* test), but argued that the Quebec government had not shown that "the requirement of the use of French only is either necessary for the achievement of the legislative objective or proportionate to it."[42] Not content to let matters rest here, the Court suggested what the Quebec government perhaps should have done to accomplish its legislative purpose in a way acceptable under section 1 of the Charter. "French could be required," it suggested, "in addition to any other language or it could be required to have greater visibility than that accorded to other languages."[43]

In fairness to judges, why shouldn't they give legislators an idea of how the law needs to be changed to bring it into line with their interpretation of the Constitution? The point is, however, that means and ends are not neatly separable in the real world of politics. Moreover, a requirement that means be proportional to the ends just begs the question of *who* should determine how much or little is enough? Were the judges who decided the *Ford* case in a better position to know what measures would best protect the economic value of the French language and the francophone character of Quebec? These questions resurfaced with a vengeance when the Supreme Court ruled on 21 September 1995 that the federal ban on tobacco advertising violated the Charter's guarantee of freedom of expression. The total ban did not, in the eyes of the majority of the Court, satisfy the second part of the *Oakes* test. "The government had before it a variety of less intrusive measures when it enacted the total ban on advertising," observed Justice Beverley McLachlin. Commenting on the government's refusal to allow the Court to see documents pertaining to advertising and tobacco consumption, including one on the alternatives to a total ban on advertising, she added, "In the face of this behaviour, one is hard-pressed not to infer that the results of the studies must undercut the government's claim that a less invasive ban would not have produced an equally salutary result."[44] Anti-smoking groups responded to the decision by calling on Ottawa to use the "notwithstanding" clause to override Charter protection for tobacco advertising. Many staunch Charter boosters became skeptics overnight. They were awakened by the tobacco advertising decision to a basic truth of constitutionally entrenched rights: the price of entrenchment is that judges assume a more important role in political life and that one does not always agree with their reasoning.

The "Notwithstanding" Clause: Section 33

"What the Charter gives, the legislature may take away." This appears to be the meaning of section 33 of the Charter, the **"notwithstanding" clause**. It states that either Parliament or a provincial legislature may expressly declare that a law shall operate even if it offends against section 2 or sections 7–15 of the Charter. This clause was not part of Ottawa's original Charter proposal, but was inserted at the insistence of several provinces. Indeed, it appears that federal–provincial agreement on the constitutional deal that produced the Charter would have died without this concession.[45]

Although the "notwithstanding" clause appears to provide governments with a constitutional escape hatch from much of the Charter, it has rarely had this effect. It has been resorted to on only a handful of occasions. In explaining why he believed that governments would be reluctant to use section 33 to pass laws that violated Charter guarantees, civil libertarian Alan Borovoy wrote: "The mere introduction of a bill to oust the application of the Charter would likely spark an enormous controversy. . . . Without solid support in the legislature and the community, a government would be very reluctant to take the heat that such action would invariably generate."[46]

Borovoy's confidence that public support for the Charter and vigilant media would provide adequate protection against government recourse to section 33 was not shared by everyone. Civil liberties groups and the legal profession were, by and large, outspokenly critical of the "notwithstanding" clause, to the point that a court challenge was launched against it immediately after the Charter was proclaimed.[47] The basis of this challenge was that if the Constitution is the supreme law of the land, as the Constitution Act declares, then no part of it should be placed beyond the powers of judicial review. By this reasoning, a legislature's decision to invoke section 33 should itself be reviewable, and therefore able to be overturned by the courts. In a 1985 ruling, the Quebec Court of Appeal agreed. This decision was, however, overruled by the Supreme Court of Canada in *Ford v. Attorney General of Quebec* (1988). The Court pronounced in favour of a literal interpretation of section 33—which also happens to correspond to the intentions of those provincial governments that insisted that the "notwithstanding" clause be included in the Charter—requiring only that a legislature expressly declare its intention to override the Charter.

It is clear, therefore, that there are no serious legal roadblocks in the way of a government using section 33 to circumvent the Charter. But in fact, it has been invoked on only a few occasions—if one does not take into account the PQ's policy, between 1982 and 1985, of inserting the "notwithstanding" clause into all laws passed by the Quebec legislature and retroactively into all existing provincial statutes. (These actions were part of a symbolic and legal strategy against the constitutional reforms of 1982, to which the PQ government had not agreed.) This suggests that there are significant political barriers to its use. Quite simply, governments do not want to give the appearance of denying rights to their citizens. There are, however, circumstances where the denial of rights may inflict little political damage on government and may even produce political dividends.

This was certainly true of the Quebec Liberal government's 1989 decision to use the "notwithstanding" clause to re-pass, with some modifications, the provisions of Bill 101 that had been ruled unconstitutional by the Supreme Court. Public opinion,

the province's francophone media, and the opposition PQ all were strongly supportive of legislative restrictions on the use of languages other than French. While the government's move precipitated the resignation of three anglophone cabinet ministers and drove many English-speaking voters into the arms of the newly formed Equality Party in the next provincial election, there is no doubt that the political costs of not overriding the Charter would have been far greater.

Likewise, the political costs were negligible when Saskatchewan's Conservative government inserted section 33 in a 1986 law passed to force striking public servants back to work. The government feared that, without the "notwithstanding" clause, the courts might rule that back-to-work legislation infringed the freedom of association guaranteed by section 2 of the Charter. Rather than run this risk, it chose to act pre-emptively to override this right. (As it turned out, the Supreme Court later decided that collective bargaining and strike action are not protected by the Charter.) Denying government employees the right to strike is often popular with the public. Some analysts suggested that the Saskatchewan Conservatives' use of section 33 against public servants may even have produced a net gain in votes for the party in the election that followed about a year later.[48]

In 2000 the Alberta legislature invoked the "notwithstanding" clause when it passed the Marriage Amendment Act. This law reasserted the legal definition of marriage as a union between a man and a woman, at a time when pressure to recognize same-sex marriage was increasing and it appeared that the courts might rule that the Charter required a redefinition of marriage. By invoking the "notwithstanding" clause the intention was to protect the traditional definition of marriage in Alberta against a Charter challenge. This was popular with most Albertans at the time. As it happened, however, a subsequent Supreme Court decision ruled that the legal definition of marriage can only be determined by the federal government, so Alberta's law was struck down on that basis.

It is not impossible to imagine circumstances in which politicians and the public might support the use of the "notwithstanding" clause to counter an unpopular Supreme Court decision. In 2005, when

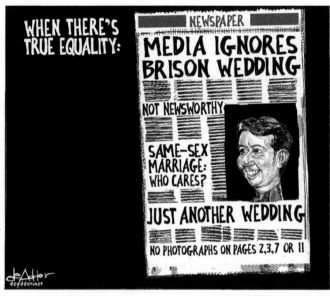

In 2007, Liberal MP Scott Brison became the first federal politician in Canadian history to marry a partner of the same sex. Do you think an event like this would continue to be newsworthy today? Why or why not?

Parliament changed the legal definition of marriage to include same-sex couples, the official position of the Conservative Party, then in opposition, was that as a government it would introduce legislation to re-establish the traditional definition of marriage. Given what the courts had said on the matter, it was clear that such a law would have to include the "notwithstanding" clause to circumvent the equality rights section of the Charter. The Conservatives have formed the government since 2006 and no such law has been introduced. In the meantime public opinion on same-sex marriage is now much more supportive than it was even a decade ago. It would surely take a major disconnect between the values reflected in a Supreme Court ruling and those of the Canadian public or of a provincial population to persuade a government to consider invoking the seldom-used notwithstanding clause.

Applying the Charter

News stories involving the use of the Charter to challenge some law or administrative procedure are today quite routine. During the more than three decades since the Charter's passage hundreds of appeals court rulings have fleshed out the meaning of the rights and freedoms it guarantees. Some of these meanings were established early on and have remained unchanged. Others continue to evolve. The Charter is, as Lord Sankey once said of the Canadian Constitution, "a living tree capable of growth and expansion within its natural limits." How the tree will grow in the future is not entirely clear, but over 30 years of life with the Charter enables us to discern the main tendencies in judicial interpretation of its provisions.

We will focus on three of these tendencies of particular significance. First, how have the courts interpreted the Charter's scope and authority? Second, what difference has the Charter had on the relationship between the state and individuals? Third, what have been the Charter's effects on equality in Canada? The last two issues are, of course, fundamental to our assessment of Canadian democracy.

Scope and Authority

In its first Charter decision, *Law Society of Upper Canada v. Skapinker* (1984), the Supreme Court made clear its position on judicial review of the Charter. In this case, Joel Skapinker, a South African citizen living in Canada, had sought admission to the Ontario bar but had been denied because he was not a Canadian citizen. After an appeal court in Ontario ruled that he had been wrongfully denied on the basis of the mobility rights section of the Charter (s. 6), the case moved on to the Supreme Court, which, taking a cautious approach, ruled against Skapinker. Consciously modelling its position along the lines of *Marbury v. Madison* (1803), the landmark American Supreme Court ruling that established that Court's supervisory role over the US Constitution, the Supreme Court of Canada declared its intention to assume a similar role in applying the Charter. "With the Constitution

Act 1982," wrote Justice Willard Estey, "comes a new dimension, a new yardstick of reconciliation between the individual and the community and their respective rights, a dimension which, like the balance of the Constitution, remains to be interpreted and applied by the Court."[49]

A new dimension, perhaps, but not a revolution. Although the Constitution must be considered the supreme law of the land, judges should interpret it in ways that "enable [the legislature] to perform the high duties assigned to it, in the manner most beneficial to the people."[50] In other words, judges should not be too quick to second-guess elected lawmakers.

Skapinker was more a broad statement of intent than a clear signpost. A year later the Court was given the opportunity to show how activist it was prepared to be in applying the Charter. The case involved a challenge to procedures under Canada's Immigration Act, whereby applicants for political refugee status were not given an automatic right to a hearing. By a 6–0 vote, the Supreme Court decided that this violated fundamental principles of justice. Three of the justices based their ruling on a section of the Canadian Bill of Rights that guarantees the "right to a fair hearing," while the other three went further in arguing that the right to a hearing is implied under section 7 of the Charter, guaranteeing "the right to life, liberty and security of the person and the right not to be deprived thereof except in accordance with the principles of fundamental justice." Justice Bertha Wilson took the most aggressive approach to the Charter, arguing that "the guarantees of the Charter would be illusory if they could be ignored because it was administratively convenient to do so."[51] At least some of the judges, then, demonstrated their willingness to take a hard-line approach to the Charter, whatever the administrative and budgetary effects on government policy might be. As it transpired, the *Singh* decision resulted in thousands of additional cases being added to what was already a huge backlog of refugee claims, and precipitated the introduction of a new law whose intent was to limit refugees' access to Canada.[52]

Singh was followed by a string of 1985 rulings that defined in sharper hues the Supreme Court's approach to the Charter's application. In *The Queen v. Big M Drug Mart* (1985), the Court struck down the federal Lord's Day Act on the grounds that it violated the Charter's guarantee of freedom of religion. From the standpoint of the interpretive rules being developed by judges in applying the Charter (see Boxes 7.4 and 7.5), the most significant feature of the *Big M* case was the willingness of all of the justices to inquire into the purposes associated with the rights and freedoms set forth in the Charter. The Court signalled its readiness to go beyond the simple words of the Charter and the stated intentions of those who drafted it to interpret the historical meaning and social purposes of a concept like, in this particular case, freedom of religion. This approach is the very hallmark of judicial activism.

The issue of what the Charter's drafters actually intended was raised in *Reference re B.C. Motor Vehicle Act* (1985).[53] In this case, British Columbia's Attorney General argued that section 7 protection for the "principles of fundamental justice" was meant by the governments who agreed to the Charter to be a guarantee of procedural fairness (the issue raised in *Singh*). It was not, he argued, intended to enable the courts to assess the fairness of the "substance" of laws. In rejecting the government's argument, the Court quite correctly reasoned that it is not always possible to separate substance and procedure. For example, a law whose substance is the denial of a procedural right associated with the principles of fundamental justice is both procedurally and substantively unfair. The majority was quick to add, however, that judicial review under section 7 should be limited to the criminal law and legal rights, and should not extend to all public policy.

On the question of what the Charter's drafters had intended for section 7, the Court ruled that arguments about intentions could not be binding for two reasons. First, it is not possible to state categorically what legislative bodies intended for the Charter as a whole or for particular provisions of it. Second, if the original intentions were treated as binding on the courts, then "the rights, freedoms and values embodied in the Charter in effect becomes [*sic*] frozen in time to the moment of adoption with little or no possibility of growth, development and adjustment to changing societal needs."[54] This implies, of course, that judges will determine what constitute "changing societal needs" (see Box 7.4).

As reasonable as arguments about the uncertainty surrounding legislative intentions and the need to allow for flexibility in response to changing societal conditions and public opinion may sound, it should be pointed out that the Court has sometimes taken lawmakers' intentions very seriously. This was true in the *Quebec Protestant School Boards* (1984)[55] ruling, where the Court relied on the drafters' intentions for section 23 of the Charter in striking down the education provisions of Quebec's Bill 101. It has also been evident in other decisions, including *Re Public Service Employee Relations Act* (1987).[56] In denying that the right to strike is protected by the Charter, the Court argued that the drafters of the Charter were deliberately silent on economic rights. (The Court changed its mind on this in the 2001 *Dunmore* decision, discussed below.)

The issue of the Charter's scope was the focus of another of the Court's 1985 decisions, *Operation Dismantle v. The Queen*.[57] A coalition of groups opposed to testing the cruise missile in Canada argued that these tests violated the Charter's guarantee of the right to life and security of the person by making nuclear war more probable. The Court rejected this argument on the grounds that the alleged facts in the plaintiff's claim were unprovable speculations. But the other question before the Court was whether cabinet decisions—the decision to allow cruise missile tests was taken by cabinet—and foreign policy and defence issues are reviewable by the courts. The federal government argued that cabinet decisions are "Crown prerogatives" and therefore off limits to the courts. The Supreme Court disagreed. It argued that section 32 of the Charter should be interpreted to apply to all government actions. On the precise question of whether foreign policy and defence issues are inherently political and beyond the reach of judicial review, the Court did not express an opinion. Twenty-five years later, confronted with a somewhat similar question, the Supreme Court ruled that when it comes to foreign policy and defence issues, "the government must have flexibility in deciding how its duties under the royal prerogative

over foreign relations are discharged [but] *the executive is not exempt from constitutional scrutiny*" (emphasis added; see Box 7.3).

An additional feature of the Court's approach to the Charter's scope deserves mention. This involves its insistence that the Charter applies only to relationships between the state and citizens, not to private-sector relationships. Thus, the Charter cannot be used by someone who believes he has been denied a job or an apartment because of his race, or by a person whose private-sector employer requires that she retire at the age of 65. Forms of discrimination like these are pervasive throughout society, but they are not inequalities that can be overcome using the Charter. The Supreme Court has on several occasions articulated this distinction between public (covered by the Charter) and private, as in *Dolphin Delivery* (1986).[58] The Charter, it stated, "was set up to regulate the relationship between the individual and the government. It was intended to restrain government action and to protect the individual."[59] This position is, in fact, faithful to the intentions of those who framed and agreed to the Charter.

The Court's refusal to recognize economic rights is related to this public/private distinction. As noted earlier, the Charter is deliberately silent on economic and property rights, except for the qualified protection it extends to the right to live, work, and be eligible for social benefits in any province. Claims that certain economic rights are implied by provisions of the Charter have generally received a cold reception. For example, the courts have expressly rejected business's arguments that corporations should fall within the ambit of section 7 of the Charter, which guarantees the "right to life, liberty and security of the person." Corporate personhood for purposes of Charter protection has been rejected by Canadian courts, although it is accepted in the United States.[60] The economic rights claims of workers have fared somewhat better at the hands of judges. In a 1987 ruling on whether a right to strike exists, the Supreme Court declared that "The constitutional guarantee of freedom of association . . . does not include, in the case of a trade union, a guarantee of the right to bargain collectively and the right to strike."[61] The right to

Politics in Focus

BOX 7.3 When the Charter and Crown Prerogatives Collide

The case of Omar Khadr is well known in Canada. Khadr is a member of a family that immigrated to Canada from Egypt in 1977. The family had ties to Osama bin Laden and several members fought against the NATO forces in Afghanistan. Omar Khadr was 15 years old when he was captured by American troops after allegedly having killed a soldier with a grenade. After recovering somewhat from severe wounding he suffered in the firefight with NATO forces, Khadr was sent to the Guantánamo Bay detention camp in Cuba, where he remained from 2002 until 2012. During much of this time he was not provided with legal counsel. His demands that the Canadian government intervene on his behalf and request his repatriation to Canada were rejected by successive Canadian governments.

Khadr's case eventually reached the Supreme Court of Canada. Here are some key excerpts from its June 2010 ruling:

Canada actively participated in a process contrary to its international human rights obligations and contributed to K's ongoing detention so as to deprive him of his right to liberty and security of the person, guaranteed by s. 7 of the *Charter*, not in accordance with the principles of fundamental justice . . . . While the US is the primary source of the deprivation, it is reasonable to infer from the uncontradicted evidence before the Court that the statements taken by Canadian officials

are contributing to K's continued detention. The deprivation of K's right to liberty and security of the person is not in accordance with the principles of fundamental justice. The interrogation of a youth detained without access to counsel, to elicit statements about serious criminal charges while knowing that the youth had been subjected to sleep deprivation and while knowing that the fruits of the interrogations would be shared with the prosecutors, offends the most basic Canadian standards about the treatment of detained youth suspects.

K is entitled to a remedy under s. 24(1) of the *Charter*. . . . The appropriate remedy in this case is to declare that K's *Charter* rights were violated, leaving it to the government to decide how best to respond in light of current information, its responsibility over foreign affairs and the *Charter*.[62]

Khadr was awarded costs by the Court, but challenging the government's prerogative to make foreign policy decisions was a step that the justices were unwilling to take. After a plea bargain before an American military tribunal to avoid lifetime imprisonment by the US, Omar Khadr remained incarcerated at Guantánamo until his transfer to Canada in September 2012, to complete the remainder of an eight-year prison sentence.

Source: Judgments of the Supreme Court of Canada: *Canada v. Khadr*, 2010 S.C.C. 3.

bargain collectively and to strike are not, the Court ruled, fundamental rights or freedoms that deserve the constitutional protection of freedom of association under the Charter. "They are," the majority declared, "the creation of legislation, involving a balance of competing interests,"[63] and their scope and limitations are appropriately determined by legislatures. To put it very simply, economic rights were viewed as subordinate to political ones.

It is sometimes said that today's dissent becomes tomorrow's law. This appears to be true in the matter of the Supreme Court's interpretation of freedom of association, guaranteed by section 2(d) of the Charter, and workers' rights. In *Dunmore* (2001),[64] the Court struck down as unconstitutional an Ontario law that excluded agricultural workers from collective bargaining rights available to other groups of workers. In reaching this decision

Governing Realities

BOX 7.4 Some General Principles of Interpretation That Guide the Courts in Charter Cases

The Charter is designed and adopted to guide and serve the Canadian community for a long time. Narrow and technical interpretation, if not modulated by a sense of the unknowns of the future, can stunt growth of the law and hence the community it serves. It is clear that headings were systematically and deliberately included as an integral part of the Charter for whatever purpose. At the very minimum a court must take them into consideration when engaged in the process of discerning the meaning and application of the provisions of the Charter.

The task of expounding a constitution is crucially different from that of construing a statute. A constitution is drafted with an eye to the future. Its function is to provide a continuing framework for the legitimate exercise of governmental power and, when joined by a bill or a charter of rights, for the unremitting protection of individual rights and liberties. It must be capable of growth and development over time to meet new social, political, and historical realities often unimagined by its framers. The judiciary is the guardian of the constitution and must, in interpreting its provisions, not "read the provisions of the Constitution like a last will and testament lest it become one."

Neither before nor after the Charter have the courts been enabled to decide upon the appropriateness of policies underlying legislative enactments. In both instances, however, the courts are empowered, indeed required, to measure the content of legislation against the guarantees of the Constitution.

It was never intended that the Charter could be used to invalidate other provisions of the Constitution, particularly a provision such as s. 93 of the Constitution Act, 1867, which represented a fundamental part of the Confederation compromise.

In *The Queen v. Big M Drug Mart*, Dickson J. elaborated on how the interests that are intended to be protected by a particular Charter right are to be discovered: "in my view this analysis is to be undertaken, and the purpose of the right or freedom in question is to be sought by reference to the character and the larger objects of the Charter itself, to the language chosen to articulate the specific right or freedom, to the historical origins of the concepts enshrined, and where applicable, to the meaning and purpose of the other specific rights and freedoms with which it is associated within the text of the Charter."

A hierarchical approach to rights, which places some over others, must be avoided, both when interpreting the Charter and when developing the common law. When the protected rights of two individuals come into conflict, as can occur in the case of publication bans, Charter principles require a balance to be achieved that fully respects the importance of both sets of rights.

Source: Canada, Department of Justice, *Canadian Charter of Rights Decision Digest*, Appendix A, at: <www.canada.justice.gc.ca/Publications>. Reproduced with the permission of the Minister of Public Works and Government Services Canada, 2006.

the majority borrowed from the reasoning found in the dissent in the 1987 *Re Public Service Employee Relations Act* decision, rejecting the view that the fundamental freedoms in the Charter are intended to protect only political freedoms, but not economic ones. Then, in 2007, the Court did a complete about-face from its 1987 ruling in *Health Services and Support v. British Columbia*, accepting that collective bargaining rights are protected by the Charter's guarantee of freedom of association (see Box 7.5).

Every major Supreme Court ruling on the Charter serves to clarify the scope and authority of judicial review. In focusing on several early Charter decisions the point has been to demonstrate that the Court very quickly abandoned the tradition of judicial deference and assumed, instead, an activist stance in applying the Charter. How far judges go in using the Charter to strike down laws and administrative practices is really up to them. There are, of course, two provisions of the Charter that may be seen as potential brakes on the courts' authority. One is the "reasonable limits" clause (s. 1) and the other is the "notwithstanding" clause (s. 33). In practice, however, neither of these has been very effective in limiting the scope of judicial activism.

Individual Rights and Freedoms

Some individual rights and freedoms are better protected today as a result of the Charter. Court decisions have limited certain police powers, expanded the rights of those accused of crimes and of prisoners, women seeking abortions, and gays and lesbians. On the other hand, Supreme Court decisions upheld the constitutionality of provincial and federal anti-hate laws that, at least according to some critics, place vague and overly broad restrictions on freedom of expression; upheld the constitutionality of mandatory publication bans in certain criminal trials; and upheld restrictions on the ability of

individuals and organizations other than political parties and their candidates to spend money during an election campaign. In cases involving individual rights and freedoms, the courts are called upon to balance these Charter guarantees against such interests as national security and community safety and standards, as well as other democratic and social values.

This balancing act may be seen in the case of *R. v. NS* (2012), in which the issue was whether a person wearing a niqab (a full face veil that reveals only the eyes) for religious reasons should be required to show her face when testifying in a criminal trial. The defendant in this case argued that she should be allowed to wear the niqab when giving testimony against her uncle and cousin in a sexual assault trial. She maintained that her religious beliefs required her to wear the niqab in the presence of male strangers and that this belief ought to be protected by the right to religious freedom in the

Governing Realities

BOX 7.5 On Freedom of Association and Collective Bargaining Activities: The Supreme Court Changes Its Mind

Freedom of association guaranteed by s. 2(*d*) of the *Charter* includes a procedural right to collective bargaining. The grounds advanced in the earlier decisions of this Court for the exclusion of collective bargaining from the s. 2(*d*)'s protection do not withstand principled scrutiny and should be rejected. The general purpose of the *Charter* guarantees and the broad language of s. 2(*d*) are consistent with a measure of protection for collective bargaining. Further, the right to collective bargaining is neither of recent origin nor merely a creature of statute. The history of collective bargaining in Canada reveals that long before the present statutory labour regimes were put in place, collective bargaining was recognized as a fundamental aspect of Canadian society, emerging as the most significant collective activity through which freedom of association is expressed in the labour context. Association for purposes of collective bargaining has long been recognized as a fundamental Canadian right which

predated the *Charter*. The protection enshrined in s. 2(*d*) of the *Charter* may properly be seen as the culmination of a historical movement towards the recognition of a procedural right to collective bargaining. Canada's adherence to international documents recognizing a right to collective bargaining also supports recognition of that right in s. 2(*d*). The *Charter* should be presumed to provide at least as great a level of protection as is found in the international human rights documents that Canada has ratified. Lastly, the protection of collective bargaining under s. 2(*d*) is consistent with and supportive of the values underlying the *Charter* and the purposes of the *Charter* as a whole. Recognizing that workers have the right to bargain collectively as part of their freedom to associate reaffirms the values of dignity, personal autonomy, equality and democracy that are inherent in the *Charter*.

Source: *Health Services and Support v. British Columbia*, (2007) S.C.C. 27.

Charter. The accused persons in this trial argued that their ability to receive a fair trial was undermined by the inability of the judge and jury to see her face while she was giving testimony. In seeking to reconcile these conflicting rights claims, the Court ruled that "A witness who for sincere religious reasons wishes to wear the niqab while testifying in a criminal proceeding will be required to remove it if (a) this is necessary to prevent a serious risk to the fairness of the trial, because reasonably available alternative measures will not prevent the risk; and (b) the salutary effects of requiring her to remove the niqab outweigh the deleterious effects of doing so."[65] The justices' awareness of the larger social context of their ruling may be seen in Box 7.6.

The courts' rulings on legal rights challenges to Canada's criminal law illustrate the generally more liberal treatment of individual rights in the Charter era. Charter decisions have produced many important changes in law enforcement practices, including the following:

- "Reverse onus" provisions, requiring a defendant to prove his innocence of a charge, have been ruled unconstitutional.
- Evidence obtained by inappropriate means, such as confession obtained without informing an accused person of his right

The Social Fabric

BOX 7.6 Multiculturalism, Religious Freedom, and the Justice System

This appeal illustrates the tension and changes caused by the rapid evolution of contemporary Canadian society and by the growing presence in Canada of new cultures, religions, traditions and social practices. This case is not purely one of conflict and reconciliation between a religious right and the protection of the right of the accused to make full answer and defence, but engages basic value of the Canadian criminal justice system. The Charter protects freedom of religion in express words at s. 2(a). But fundamental too are the rights of the accused to a fair trial, to make full answer and defence to the charges brought against him, to benefit from the constitutional presumption of innocence and to avert wrongful convictions. Since cross-examination is a necessary tool for the exercise of the right to make full answer and defence, the consequences of restrictions on that right weigh more heavily on the accused, and the balancing process must work in his or her favour. A defence that is unduly and improperly constrained might impact on the determination of the guilt or innocence of the accused.

The Constitution requires an openness to new differences that appear within Canada, but also an acceptance of the principle that it remains connected with the roots of our contemporary democratic society. A system of open and independent courts is a core component of a democratic state, ruled by law and a fundamental Canadian value. From this broader constitutional perspective, the trial becomes an act of communication with the public at large. The public must be able to see how the justice system works. Wearing a niqab in the courtroom does not facilitate acts of communication. Rather, it shields the witness from interacting fully with the parties, their counsel, the judge and the jurors. Wearing the niqab is also incompatible with the rights of the accused, the nature of the Canadian public adversarial trials, and with the constitutional values of openness and religious neutrality in contemporary democratic, but diverse, Canada. Nor should wearing a niqab be dependent on the nature or importance of the evidence, as this would only add a new layer of complexity to the trial process. A clear rule that niqabs may not be worn at any stage of the criminal trial would be consistent with the principle of public openness of the trial process and would safeguard the integrity of that process as one of communication.

Source: *R. v. N.S.*, 2012 SCC 72, (2012) 3 S.C.R. 726, at: <scc.lexum.org/decisia-scc-csc/scc-csc/scc-csc/ en/12779/1/document.do>, 7–8.

to legal counsel, or evidence gotten from a workplace computer without a warrant cannot be used to help convict that person.

- Writs of assistance, under which the police were able to enter premises at any time without a search warrant, have been ruled unconstitutional.
- Search and seizure powers have been restricted.
- Thousands of persons accused of criminal offences had the charges against them dismissed because of an Ontario Superior Court ruling that lengthy delays in getting them to trial contravened their Charter right "to be tried within a reasonable time."

In striking the balance between individual rights and freedoms and other societal interests and values, the Court has not hesitated to come down on the side of the latter. This may be seen in the Supreme Court's decision to uphold hate speech provisions of Canada's Criminal Code in the case of *R. v. Keegstra* (1990).[66] James Keegstra was an Alberta high school teacher who taught his students that the Holocaust was a hoax and that an international Jewish conspiracy pulled much of the world's political, economic, and cultural strings. He was charged under s. 319(2) of the Criminal Code, which makes it a punishable offence to communicate statements, other than in private conversation, that wilfully promote hatred against any identifiable group. In a 4–3 ruling the majority on Canada's highest court held that the content of speech, in and of itself, could be considered so offensive as to place it outside the protection of s. 2 of the Charter. They reasoned that the "pain suffered by target group members," Canada's "international commitments to eradicate hate propaganda," Canada's "commitment to the values of equality and multiculturalism in ss. 15 and 27 of the Charter," and "our historical knowledge of the potentially catastrophic effects of the promotion of hatred" combined to make section 319(2) of the Criminal Code a reasonable limit on freedom of expression.

The Supreme Court's ruling in *Keegstra* paid virtually no attention to the question of whether the messages communicated by the accused placed anyone or any group of persons in imminent peril. Such a test was considered to be wholly unnecessary. Instead, the majority accepted the argument that some speech is quite simply inconsistent with the sort of society that Canada is or ought to be and therefore should not be tolerated by law and protected by the Constitution. The Court repeated this reasoning in *Saskatchewan (Human Rights Commission) v. Whatcott* (2013), in which it stated that it was not necessary to show a clear connection between speech and harm to the members of the group targeted by that speech. "The difficulty of establishing causality," the Court said, "and the seriousness of the harm to vulnerable groups justifies the imposition of preventive measures that do not require proof of actual harm. The discriminatory effects of hate speech are part of the everyday knowledge and experience of Canadians."[67]

Individual freedom of expression, as guaranteed by section 2 of the Charter, was again the issue in *Harper v. Canada* (2004).[68] The case originated as a challenge brought by Stephen Harper in 2000, when he was president of the National Citizens' Coalition, to legislated restrictions on the right of so-called "third parties"—groups and individuals other than registered political parties and their candidates—to spend money on political advertising during election campaigns. In its 2004 ruling the Supreme Court upheld these restrictions by a 6–3 majority. The decision is particularly interesting because of the conception of democracy that underpins the majority's ruling, one that sees unfettered freedom of speech as a danger to the equality rights of citizens (see Box 7.7).

Four years later the Supreme Court returned to the issue of free speech in the case of *WIC Radio Ltd. v. Simpson* (2008). A radio talk show host and former British Columbia politician, Rafe Mair, compared the ideas of a local conservative activist, Kari Simpson, to those of Hitler and the Ku Klux Klan. Mair made the comparison in a radio broadcast that attacked Simpson's views opposing the use of school materials and lessons that conveyed a positive portrayal of homosexual lifestyles. Simpson claimed that Mair's comments were defamatory and not protected by section 2 of the Charter.

Politics in Focus

BOX 7.7 Does the Ability to Spend Money during an Election Campaign Jeopardize Democracy?

The majority said . . .

In the absence of spending limits, it is possible for the affluent or a number of persons pooling their resources and acting in concert to dominate the political discourse, depriving their opponents of a reasonable opportunity to speak and be heard, and undermining the voter's ability to be adequately informed of all views. Equality in the political discourse is thus necessary for meaningful participation in the electoral process and ultimately enhances the right to vote.

(Third-party advertising spending limits) prevent those who have access to significant financial resources, and are able to purchase unlimited amount of advertising, to dominate the electoral discourse to the detriment of others; they create a balance between the financial resources of each candidate or political party; and they advance the perception that the electoral process is substantively fair as it provides for a reasonable degree of equality between citizens who wish to participate in that process. . . . The limits set out in (the law) allow third parties to inform the electorate of their message in a manner that will not overwhelm candidates, political parties or other third parties while precluding the voices of the wealthy from dominating the political discourse.

The minority said . . .

The effect of third-party limits for spending on advertising is to prevent citizens from effectively communicating their views on issues during an election campaign. The denial of effective communication to citizens violates freedom of expression where it warrants the greatest protection—the sphere of political discourse. Section 350 (of the Canada Elections Act) puts effective radio and television communication beyond the reach of "third party" citizens, preventing citizens from effectively communicating their views on election issues, and restricting them to minor local communication. Effective expression of ideas thus becomes the exclusive right of registered political parties and their candidates.

There is no evidence to support a connection between the limits on citizen spending and electoral fairness, and the legislation does not infringe the right to free expression in a way that is measured and carefully tailored to the goals sought to be achieved. The limits imposed on citizens amount to a virtual ban on their participation in political debate during the election period, except through political parties . . . the Attorney General has not demonstrated that limits this draconian are required to meet the perceived dangers.

Source: *Harper v. Canada* (2004).

Defamation—the impugning of someone's character or actions in a manner that results in real damage being done to that person's reputation, including such consequences as impairment of his or her ability to earn a living—is a private law matter. Like slip-and-fall accidents on private property or odours from a pig barn that a neighbour claims reduce his enjoyment of his property and its market value, such matters do not fall directly under the Charter. They are covered by the common law that emerges from judicial rulings on actual cases. However, as the Supreme Court stated in the *Simpson* decision, "the evolution of the common law is to be informed and guided by Charter values."[69] Mair argued that the doctrine of fair comment protected him against the charge of defamation. The Supreme Court agreed. Its ruling used the Charter values of freedom of expression and freedom of the media to broaden the defence of fair comment and limit the ability of plaintiffs to intimidate those who would make controversial public statements. The result of this 2008 ruling is that it is more difficult for public figures or organizations to successfully sue, arguing that their reputation has been damaged, and therefore less likely that journalists and broadcasters will censor themselves out of fear of incurring such lawsuits.

Is there an identifiable pattern in the Court's interpretation of the individual rights guaranteed by the Charter? Aside from what most commentators characterize as a moderately activist approach, the Court has shown few sharply pronounced tendencies. Moreover, the Court is sometimes sharply divided in its approach to individual rights, as it was in the 1990 *Keegstra* ruling on hate speech (see Box 7.8), in its 1995 ruling on Ottawa's tobacco advertising ban, and in the 2004 *Harper* ruling on election spending by third parties. The Court has also been divided on a number of important cases dealing with legal rights. Some critics accuse it of having been too sympathetic to the protection of individual rights over other values and interests, but others view the Court as too timid in its rulings.[70]

Equality and the Charter

"Does the Charter Matter?" asked a 2005 article by legal scholars Harry Arthurs and Brent Arnold. They conclude: "not much."[71] They "examine the progress of groups that the Charter was intended to benefit (Aboriginal peoples, women, visible minorities, and immigrants)." It is, of course, difficult to determine what independent impact Charter rulings may have had on equality. Public opinion, social activism, legislative action not prompted by the Charter, demographic change, and other factors must also be part of the mix in any such assessment. In fact, it is methodologically impossible to do what Arthurs and Arnold purport to do. The Charter is only one of the factors influencing issues of equality in Canadian society. But to suggest that "the Charter has mattered less than was hoped and expected by its authors"[72] simply misses the point.

Section 15 of the Charter deals explicitly with equality rights. Other sections of the Charter, particularly the section 7 guarantee of life, liberty, and security of the person, section 25 on Aboriginal rights (as well as section 35 in Part II of the Constitution Act, 1982), section 3 on the democratic right to vote, and the minority language rights sections of the Charter have also been important constitutional levers used by groups to advance their equality claims. Those who argue that these sections of the Charter have mattered less than was hoped in overcoming various forms of inequality often point to the fact that the Charter only applies to abuses of governmental power. As constitutional expert Peter Hogg puts it:

> The real threat to civil liberties in Canada comes not from legislative and official action, but from discrimination by private persons—employers, trade unions, landlords, realtors, restaurateurs and other suppliers of goods or services. The economic liberties of freedom of property and contract, which imply a power to deal with whomever one pleases, come into direct conflict with egalitarian values.[73]

Although section 15 cannot be used to fight these private forms of discrimination, provincial human rights codes enforced by commissions do cover private-sector relations.

Those who believe the Charter has not made enough of a difference when it comes to equality also lament the courts' unwillingness to treat equality rights as superior to other rights in the Charter or to other parts of the Constitution. Not only must the courts balance equality rights against the "reasonable limits" provision of the Charter—this is a tightrope they must walk with all of the rights set forth in the Charter—they must also weigh section 15 rights against other rights and freedoms. How to strike this balance was the issue before the Supreme Court in *Re Education Act* (1987),[74] dealing with the constitutionality of an Ontario law extending full public funding to that province's Roman Catholic schools.[75] The Supreme Court ruled that the equality of religion guaranteed by section 15 did not override provincial governments' authority to grant special educational rights to Catholics and Protestants under section 93 of the Constitution Act, 1867. The Supreme Court has stated categorically that the Charter does not establish a hierarchy of rights, to the dismay of those who believe the

Charter should be seen and used as a tool for the advancement of equality.

Nevertheless, in some cases the equality guarantees of the Charter have provided the basis for fairly dramatic and controversial reversals of long-standing public policy. This was true of the Supreme Court's ruling in *M. v. H.* (1999), a case that involved a challenge to the heterosexual definition of spouses in the Family Law Act. In earlier decisions the Court had ruled that discrimination on the basis of sexual orientation is analogous to the enumerated grounds for discrimination proscribed by s. 15 of the Charter (*Egan v. Canada*, 1995). It came as no surprise, therefore, when the Supreme Court decided that the heterosexual definition of a cohabiting couple under the Family Law Act was unconstitutional, because it denied the same status and rights to homosexual couples. The Court determined that the exclusion of same-sex relationships from the spousal support provisions of the Family Law Act was not rationally connected to the objectives of the Family Law Act and thus could not be justified under the reasonable limits section of the Charter. The federal government had already announced its intention to change the law so as to provide same-sex couples with the same status as heterosexual ones. The ruling in *M. v. H.* simply made this job easier.

After a decade and a half of considering equality cases without a systematic and consistent framework for assessing s. 15 claims, the Supreme Court developed just such a framework in *Law v. Minister of Human Resources Development* (1999).[76] At its heart is the question of whether the differential treatment of the members of a group under the law is demeaning to human dignity. The Supreme Court has been very clear and consistent since its first section 15 rulings that the rights and freedoms guaranteed by the Charter should not become tools that the advantaged and wealthy can use to protect their status. In the Charter, especially its equality sections, the Court has suggested what might be described as an "ameliorative" or "progressive" purpose. "In general terms," the Court stated in the *Law* decision, "the purpose of s. 15(1) is to prevent the violation of essential human dignity and freedom through the imposition of disadvantage,

stereotyping, or political or social prejudice, and to promote a society in which all persons enjoy equal recognition at law as human beings or as members of Canadian society, equally capable and equally deserving of concern, respect and consideration."[77] In their interpretation of s. 15 of the Charter, judges have been sensitive to the social and economic context of the inequalities that appear before them as Charter claims. Indeed, many of the major Charter rulings on equality read like sociological or historical treatises. This is precisely what alarms those among the Charter's critics who recoil at what they see as judicial usurpation of the legislature's function.

Judicial sensitivity to the broader societal and historical context of their interpretations of equality rights was very clear in the Supreme Court's 2008 ruling in *R. v. Kapp*. The case involved a group of non-Aboriginal fishermen who were charged with salmon fishing during a 24-hour period reserved under federal law to three Aboriginal bands. The non-Aboriginal fishermen claimed that the law violated their equality rights under the Charter by making legal distinctions based on race. The Supreme Court agreed that this law made such distinctions, but held that they were constitutionally protected by the affirmative action clause, s. 15(2), of the Charter. In arriving at this decision the Court reiterated its long-held view that s. 15 guarantees substantive equality for Canadians, not identical treatment. This decision opens the door to the judicial consideration of evidence and arguments based on history, economics, and sociology. Indeed, the decision in *Kapp* included references to over 50 books, articles, and other publications on equality matters.

Returning to Arthurs and Arnold's conclusion that the Charter has not made much of a difference in equality in Canada, a more accurate way of expressing this might be that it is impossible to determine how much of the change in the direction of equality in such matters as women's reproductive rights, the marriage and other statutory rights of same-sex couples, and more broadly for lesbian, gay, bisexual, and transgender Canadians and for Aboriginal rights would have happened, or happened when it did, in the absence of the

Charter. The Charter's impact, including the influence that the equality rights provisions have had on Canadian society and law, operates in many and diffuse ways. At all levels of government those who draft legislation and guidelines and regulations under the authority of laws are aware of the need for such rules to comply with the Charter and the manner in which the courts have interpreted its equality guarantees. In the conversation on rights that takes place in the courtroom, but also in the classroom, in the media, in faith communities, and throughout Canadian society, the Charter and its equality guarantees have made a difference. Social activists frame their demands and often their political strategies with the Charter and the possibility of judicial rulings in mind.

Has the Charter "Americanized" Canadian Politics?

Early critics of the Charter said that it would "Americanize" Canadian politics. By this they meant that it would do three things they believed were regrettable. First, it would elevate the importance of unelected judges and the courts, giving them a much more prominent role in determining important policy matters. Second, it would undermine the operation of parliamentary government in Canada by diminishing the authority of Parliament to determine the law and to be held accountable to the people, not to the courts, for its decisions. Third, it would generate a more litigious society in which individuals and groups are more likely to base their claims and political arguments on rights, making compromise more difficult and bypassing such political processes as elections and lobbying in preference for the courts. If a victory can be won in court, the critics charged, there will be less need to worry about winning victories in the court of public opinion. The end result of all this, the critics lamented, would be the Americanization of Canadian politics.

For better or for worse—and there are many people on both sides of this divide—much of this prediction has come to pass. Judges are far more prominent in policy-making than they were in the pre-Charter era. Parliamentary supremacy has been replaced by constitutional supremacy, with the Supreme Court as chief arbiter. And important and controversial issues are often decided in the courts or as a result of court decisions pushing governments in a particular direction. Despite these important changes, the Charter has not resulted in a wholesale Americanization of Canadian politics. Judges in Canada have tended to interpret the Charter's guarantees in distinctively Canadian ways, anchored in aspects of Canada's political culture that are different from those of the United States (Box 7.8).

This is demonstrated by the case of hate speech that targets a particular group. In Canada, the law and judicial interpretation of section 2 of the Charter stresses the *content of speech*, whereas in the United States the test of whether hateful speech directed at the members of a group is protected by the First Amendment is the *probability that actual harm may result*. Judges in Canada and the United States have taken significantly different approaches towards hate speech and its relationship to the guarantee of freedom of expression found in the constitutions of their respective countries. That difference boils down to this. In the United States, just because you say something demonstrably false and odious about the members of a group does not mean that you lose the Constitution's protection to speak your mind. If, however, this speech becomes what lawyers call "fighting words," liable to incite violence, then it loses the protection of the First Amendment. But in Canada, some speech is considered to be so nasty that, by its very nature, it promotes hatred and is undeserving of constitutional protection, as is demonstrated by the majority opinion in *Keegstra*. Embedding protection for free speech in Canada's Constitution has not resulted in Canadian judges simply aping the interpretations of their American counterparts, at least not when it comes to hate speech. Moreover, the greater willingness of Canadian courts—as well as legislatures—to restrict hate speech on the grounds that some ideas and their expression contribute nothing to democratic life, and therefore can be restricted without doing any harm to freedom, is

Politics in Focus

BOX 7.8 Is Hate Speech Protected by Free Speech?

Canada

Hate propaganda contributes little to the aspirations of Canadians or Canada in either the quest for truth, the promotion of individual self-development or the protection and fostering of a vibrant democracy where the participation of all individuals is accepted and encouraged. . . . Consequently, the suppression of hate propaganda represents impairment of the individual's freedom of expression which is not of a most serious nature . . . .

Indeed, one may quite plausibly contend that it is through rejecting hate propaganda that the state can best encourage the protection of values central to freedom of expression, while simultaneously demonstrating dislike for the vision forwarded by hate-mongers. In this regard, the reaction to various types of expression by a democratic government (and the criminalization of certain forms of speech) may be perceived as meaningful expression on behalf of the vast majority of citizens.

Source: *R. v. Keegstra*, (1990) 3 S.C.R. 697.

United States

The First Amendment generally prevents government from proscribing speech, or even expressive conduct, because of disapproval of the ideas expressed. Content-based regulations are presumptively invalid. From 1791 to the present, however, our society, like other free but civilized societies, has permitted restrictions upon the content of speech in a few limited areas, which are "of such slight social value as a step to truth that any benefit that may be derived from them is clearly outweighed by the social interest in order and morality."

. . . One must wholeheartedly agree . . . that "it is the responsibility, even the obligation, of diverse communities to confront (hateful) notions in whatever form they appear," but the manner of that confrontation cannot consist of selective limitations upon speech. . . . The point of the First Amendment is that majority preferences must be expressed in some fashion other than silencing speech on the basis of its content.

. . . (T)he reason why fighting words are categorically excluded from the protection of the First Amendment is not that their content communicates any particular idea, but that their content embodies a particularly intolerable (and socially unnecessary) mode of expressing whatever idea the speaker wishes to convey.

Source: *R.A.V. v. St Paul*, 505 U.S. 377 (1992), at: <www.findlaw.com>.

consistent with a cultural difference between these countries that predates the Charter era.

The difference between Canada and the United States in how particular rights are interpreted may also be seen in how their respective courts have dealt with the matter of campaign spending by individuals and groups other than parties and their candidates. In Canada this spending is tightly restricted by law, restrictions that the Supreme Court has said are reasonable limits on free speech because of their importance in helping to level the playing field between those who have plenty of resources to formulate and communicate their point of view and policy preferences, and those who do not. Money distorts access to the marketplace of ideas, said the majority in *Harper*, and this distortion undermines democracy.

In the United States the Supreme Court has expressed an entirely different view on this question. "Premised on mistrust of governmental power," the Supreme Court said in *Citizens United*, "the First Amendment stands against attempts to disfavor certain subjects or viewpoints. Prohibited, too, are restrictions distinguishing among different speakers, allowing speech by some but not others. . . . Speech restrictions based on the identity of the speaker are all too often simply a means to control content."[78] The fact that distortions in the marketplace of ideas may be created or magnified by inequality in resources, some groups and individuals having much more ample means than others, is not seen to be a justification for limiting the free speech rights of those who have more.

On other matters too, including prisoners' democratic rights and the principles to be followed in drawing electoral boundaries, the highest courts of Canada and the United States have followed very different paths.[79] The judicial understanding of the separation of church and state is also quite different in the two countries, a difference that the Charter has perhaps diminished but has not erased.[80] Scholars disagree on whether the rights traditions of Canada and the United States are diverging or converging. It is clear, however, that in some important respects at least, entrenchment of the Charter in Canada's Constitution has not led to the disappearance of important cultural differences between Canada and its southern neighbour.

Starting Points for Research

Alan Cairns, *Disruptions: Constitutional Struggles, from the Charter to Meech Lake* (Toronto: McClelland & Stewart, 1991). These essays of one of Canada's pre-eminent political scientists focus on the consequences of the Charter for Canadian politics and were written between the 1976 election of the Parti Québécois and the 1990 demise of the Meech Lake Accord.

James B. Kelly and Christopher P. Manfredi, eds, *Contested Constitutionalism: Reflections on the Canadian Charter of Rights and Freedoms* (Vancouver: University of British Columbia Press, 2009). Includes contributions from Canada's foremost experts on the Charter.

Christopher Manfredi, *Judicial Power and the Charter: Canada and the Paradox of Liberal Constitutionalism*, 2nd edn (Toronto: Oxford University Press, 2001). Manfredi examines the tension between the political accountability of elected legislatures and the increasing power of the courts in this analysis of Charter decisions.

Kent Roach and Robert J. Sharpe, *The Charter of Rights and Freedoms*, 5th edn (Toronto: Irwin Law, 2013). Written by two law professors, this is a very readable book that focuses on the Supreme Court's Charter rulings.

Review Exercises

1. Find a story in the media that deals with the Charter. Summarize it, covering as many of the following points as are relevant:
   (a) What are the circumstances?
   (b) Who are the people or organizations involved?
   (c) What law/regulation/action/practice is being challenged?
   (d) At what stage is the challenge?
   (e) Are lawyers or other experts interviewed? Who are they?
   (f) What right or freedom of the Charter is at stake in this story?

2. What is the background of a Supreme Court judge? Visit the Supreme Court of Canada website <www.scc-csc.gc.ca>. Click on "About the Court," then, under "Member of the Court," click on the name of a particular judge. In a paragraph or two, provide a profile of one of the current justices. (If you prefer, you may use a recent edition of *Who's Who* to acquire this information.)

3. What are the pros and cons of requiring that at least some judicial nominations—e.g., those for the Supreme Court and perhaps also for provincial appeals courts—should be subject to open public scrutiny? The Conservative government held committee hearings on the 2006 nomination of Justice Marshall Rothstein to the Supreme Court of Canada and again for Justice Marc Nadon (whose nomination was later rejected by the Court on a technicality) in 2013. Is this model an improvement on the process that existed prior to Rothstein's nomination? Would some other model be preferable?

4. Compare the Charter of Rights and Freedoms to some of its counterparts in other democracies (simply type into your search engine the words "constitution" and the countries that you are interested in—for example, France, Germany, and the United States—and you will find websites that provide this information). What are the main similarities between them? Are there any aspects of these other rights documents that you think should be adopted in Canada?

Federalism

8

Canada's Constitution establishes two levels of government—national and provincial—both of which have important law-making and taxation powers. This system of divided jurisdiction is known as federalism. In this chapter some of the major issues associated with federalism are discussed, including the following:

- What is federalism?
- The origins, maintenance, and demise of federal states.
- The origins of Canadian federalism.
- The federal division of powers.
- The courts and federalism.
- Quebec's impact on federalism.
- Centre–periphery relations.
- Intergovernmental relations.
- Financing federalism.
- The federal spending power and national standards.

The ceiling of the Senate Chamber shows the French fleur-de-lys, the English lion, the Irish harp, the Welsh dragon, the Scottish thistle, and Canadian maple leaves, reflecting the nationalities of Canada's early European settlers who were brought together to form the government of Canada.

(© Mark Spowart/Alamy)

When the proposal to create an independent Canada was discussed at Charlottetown (1864) and Quebec (1867), the main subject of debate was the relationship between the new national and regional governments. Two decades of self-government and the constitutional traditions imported from Britain provided the colonies with ready guideposts for most other features of the Constitution. Federalism, by contrast, was uncharted territory. Most of the founders' practical knowledge of the principles and operation of federalism was based on their observation of the United States. The lessons they took from the American experience were mainly negative. Secession of the Confederacy and the bloody Civil War of 1861–5 did not inspire much confidence in the American model. Despite all this, Canada's founders opted for a federal system of government.

What Is Federalism?

In a federal system of government the constitutional authority to make laws and to raise revenue is divided between a national government and some number of regional governments. Neither the national government acting alone nor the regional governments acting together have the authority to alter the powers of the other level of government. They are co-ordinate and independent in their separate constitutional spheres. Citizens in a federal state are members of two political communities, one national and the other coinciding with the boundaries of the province, state, canton (the name given to the regional units of a federal state vary between countries) in which they reside.

Federalism is a legal term and its existence is based on the constitution. If a single government controls all legislative and taxation powers in a country, then no amount of administrative decentralization or variation in the economic, social, or cultural characteristics of its regions will make it a federal state. Federalism is chiefly a property of constitutions, not of societies. Nonetheless, some political scientists refer to "federal-type" societies, a tendency that has been labelled the *sociological approach* to federalism. Its most prominent advocate, American political scientist William S. Livingston, argues that "the

essence of federalism lies not in the constitutional or institutional structure but in the society itself."[1] "Federalism," Livingston declares, "is a function of societies."[2] By this he means that in a society characterized by important ethnic, language, or other cultural divisions, and where different cultural communities tend to predominate in different parts of the country, federalism is likely to be seen as a means of accommodating diversity at the same time as it provides for unity.

Despite the popularity that this idea of federalism has enjoyed, it is fundamentally wrong. It is true enough that some federal political systems, such as those of Canada, Switzerland, and Belgium, exist in societies that conform to Livingston's model of a federal society. But others do not. The United States, which pioneered modern federalism, did not opt for what was an essentially untried political system because of important cultural differences between its founding states.[3] Austria, Germany, and Argentina all have federal constitutions, but they all rank rather low in terms of cultural diversity and none has a large regionally concentrated minority cultural community within its borders. Some of the world's most culturally diverse countries, including ones where a large cultural minority or minorities are concentrated in particular regions of the country, do not have federal constitutions. Indeed, if one looks at the world ranking of countries' ethnic diversity, there is absolutely no correlation between the level of diversity and the likelihood that a country has a federal constitution.

If federalism is understood as a characteristic of societies rather than of their constitutions, then most of the world's countries would seem to qualify. After all, most countries have politically significant ethnic or linguistic minorities that often are concentrated in a particular region of the country. This is true of dozens of countries across Africa, Asia, Eastern Europe, and the Middle East. But only a handful of these countries have adopted federal constitutions. The mere fact that a country is culturally pluralistic and has one or more spatially concentrated cultural minorities surely may be quite important in understanding that country's politics. But it does not make them federal. Cultural diversity can be reflected and managed in a country's politics in many ways. Federal institutions are only one possibility among many. The idea and concept of federalism cannot, therefore, be detached from the institutions of government. A federal constitution institutionalizes regional divisions by associating them with different governments. The regionalism responsible for the adoption of a federal constitution in the first place is reinforced by political and administrative rivalries between the national and regional governments. Regional politics can certainly take place in the absence of a federal constitution. But the political significance of regional differences tends to be elevated under federalism by associating them with different political jurisdictions and the governments that preside over them.

Federalism divides political authority along territorial lines. It is not, however, the only form of government to do so. Important policy-making and administrative powers may be exercised at the regional level even in a unitary state. The extent to which these activities are *decentralized*, i.e., placed in the hands of regional officials, or remain *centralized* at the national level is determined by the particular social, geographic, and political conditions of a country. This is also true of federal states, where the constitution provides only a partial and sometimes very misleading guide to the real division of powers between governments. Political authority is also linked to territory in *confederations* and *economic and military associations*. These are formal groupings of independent states that have agreed to assign certain policy-making and administrative functions to a common institution or set of institutions. All member states have a say—though not necessarily an equal say—in the decision-making of such a body, while at the same time retaining their ultimate sovereignty (see Box 8.1).

Governing Realities

BOX 8.1 Territory and Political Authority

In the *unitary* form of government, even when there is a good measure of administrative or legislative devolution or decentralization, sovereignty or competence resides exclusively with the central government, and regional or local governments are legally and politically subordinate to it. (Examples include France, Japan, China, and Turkey.)

In the *federal* form of government, sovereignty or competence is distributed between central and provincial (or state) governments so that, within a single political system, neither order of government is legally or politically subordinate to the other, and each order of government is elected by and exercises authority directly on the electorate. (Examples include Canada, the United States, Belgium, Australia, and Germany.)

In the *confederal* form of government, even where there is a considerable allocation of responsibilities to central institutions or agencies, the ultimate sovereignty, including the right to withdraw from this form of association, is retained by the member-state governments. Furthermore, the members of the major central institutions are delegates of the constituent state governments. (The most prominent example is the European Union, although it has features that resemble the federal form of government, including a parliament whose members are elected directly by the citizens of the EU countries rather than being selected by member-state governments.)

An *economic or military association*, when it has common organizing institutions, is a confederal type of government in which the functions assigned by the participating states to the common institutions are limited mainly to economic or military co-operation and co-ordination. (Examples include the North American Free Trade Association and the North Atlantic Treaty Organization.)

Source: Adapted from Canada, Task Force on Canadian Unity, *Coming to Terms: The Words of the Debate* (Hull, Que.: Supply and Services Canada, 1979), 21–2; emphasis, updates and examples are added.

The Origins, Maintenance, and Demise of Federal States

Only about two dozen of the 193 member states of the United Nations have a federal system of government. This is an estimate rather than a precise number of federal states because the determination of whether a political system is federal is not an exact science (see Figure 8.1). For example, Mexico, Argentina, and Russia generally are included in the club of federal states, but the central governments of these countries have sometimes interfered with the autonomy of state governments. How many countries actually belong to the federalism club is less important than the fact that the club is a small one, although it does include some of the world's largest and most powerful countries. Unitary government is far more popular, even in countries where regionally based internal divisions are strong.

What are the circumstances that lead to the adoption of a federal political system? Although there is no simple answer, it is possible to identify a general condition present at the birth of all federal states and vital to the continued health of a federal union. This involves agreement among the regional components of the federal state that the benefits of being part of the union exceed whatever costs membership may impose. A federal state is based, therefore, on a *consensus of regions*. Students of international law and federalism disagree over whether any part of a federal state has a legal right to break away from the union. But the political facts are that when a region no longer shares the national consensus on which federalism is based, its separation becomes a real possibility.

"Federalism," declared Pierre Trudeau, "has all along been a product of reason in politics. . . . it is an attempt to find a rational compromise between the divergent interest groups which history has thrown together; but it is a compromise based on the will of the people."[4] This is why federal unions often are referred to as "pacts," "contracts," or "bargains." The key role of consent may be seen in the case of the former Soviet Union. As part of the post-World War II deal between the Soviet Union and the US-led Western democracies, the countries of Estonia, Latvia, and Lithuania were made members of the Soviet "federal" state against their will. Their unwilling entry into the Soviet Union, combined with the fact that Moscow dominated the regional republics through the Communist Party's monopoly on power, exposed the hollowness of the Soviet Union's federal pretensions. But with the 1989 abolition of the Communist Party's legal monopoly on power and the greater autonomy enjoyed by the regional republics, the Soviet Union very quickly fell apart. Without even a minimal consensus on the desirability of maintaining the central government, and without the Communist Party and Red Army to keep them in check, republic after republic declared national independence.

Trudeau's argument that federalism is the product of reason has the support of many who have studied the emergence of federal political systems. It is, however, a bit idealistic and does not tell us very much about the precise reasons why federalism is adopted, much less why it persists. In what he calls a theory of circumstantial causality,[5] Michael Burgess identifies a list of common interest factors and external or internal threats that may contribute to the choice of federalism. The precise mix varies, he argues, across particular cases (see Table 8.1).

Federal democracies originate in compromise. The fact that some regions are more enthusiastic than others about the federal compromise—indeed, some may enter it only in despair at the lack of viable alternatives—does not diminish the voluntary consent of the regions forming the basis of a federal union. Once established, however, a federal state may achieve a new dynamic. The existence of a national government and the idea of national citizenship can be centralizing factors that offset the decentralizing pull of regional interests. Federalism is sustained, then, not simply on the basis of rational calculations on the part of regional populations and politicians. It may indeed be sustained by a *sense of political nationality*. According to Donald Smiley, one of Canada's foremost experts on federalism, political nationality "means that Canadians as such have reciprocal moral and legal claims upon one another that have no precise counterparts in their relations with others, and that Canadians

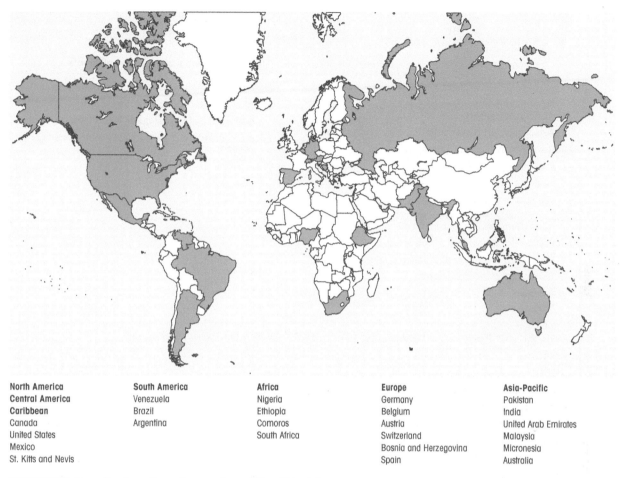

North America	South America	Africa	Europe	Asia-Pacific
Central America	Venezuela	Nigeria	Germany	Pakistan
Caribbean	Brazil	Ethiopia	Belgium	India
Canada	Argentina	Comoros	Austria	United Arab Emirates
United States		South Africa	Switzerland	Malaysia
Mexico			Bosnia and Herzegovina	Micronesia
St. Kitts and Nevis			Spain	Australia

FIGURE 8.1   Federalism throughout the World

Source: Privy Council Office. World Federations. Retrieved from http://www.collectionscanada.gc.ca/webarchives/20071115073849/http://www.pco-bcp.gc.ca/aia/index.asp?lang=eng&page=federationworld © Privy Council Office, 2014.

as such have a continuing determination to carry out a significant number of important common activities together."[6] It is, in short, a sense of political community that transcends regional, ethnic, and linguistic identifications, although it does not replace or necessarily overshadow the other identities citizens may have.

Federalism ultimately is sustained by the sense of political nationality—or community—that develops around the national state. By the same token, the breakup of a federal state is sure to be presaged by the deterioration of this sense of community. Sometimes a sense of political nationality is never solidly established in the first place, as it was not in post-independence Nigeria, whose federal system immediately came under stress and collapsed from within shortly after having been adopted. In other cases a sense of political nationality may be destroyed, or fail to develop, because of a particularly divisive regional conflict, as American federalism was split asunder by the slavery issue. The most stable federal systems are those where regional communities share in a sense of political nationality that dampens the decentralizing tendencies produced by regional differences. Switzerland, the contemporary United States, Germany, and Australia are good examples of such stability. The Swiss case in particular demonstrates that regionally based ethnolinguistic divisions do not necessarily prevent the development of a durable political nationality.

TABLE 8.1 Factors Contributing to the Choice of Federalism	
Common Interests	**External and/or Internal Threats**
Shared political values.	A sense of military insecurity, real or imagined.
Expectations of stronger economic ties and associated benefits.	A sense of economic insecurity, real or imagined.
A multiplicity of ranges of communications and transactions.	A sense of cultural insecurity, real or imagined.
The desire for political independence.	A perceived threat to the stability of the existing political order.
Prior political association.	
Strategic (territorial) considerations.	
Geographical proximity.	
Common cultural and ideological factors, such as nationalism, religion, and inherited traditions and customs.	
Political leadership and a broadening of the political elite.	
Similarity of social and political institutions.	
The appeal of federal models.	
The culmination of historical processes that were founded upon prior political commitments.	

Source: Michael Burgess, *Comparative Federalism: Theory and Practice* (New York: Routledge, 2006), 100.

To say that a weak sense of political nationality is associated with unstable federalism really just begs the question: What determines the strength of political nationality? Why do regional divisions acquire the status of independence movements in some federal states but not in others? Several factors come into play, but the most basic is the politicization of regional inequality. If the citizens of a particular region feel strongly that existing federal structures discriminate against their interests economically and politically, and if this sense of grievance is politicized through a social movement or political party, the federal bargain will come under strain. History seems to indicate, however, that the likelihood of regional grievances threatening the stability of federalism is greatest when they are linked to a nationalist movement. Nationalism usually is accompanied by territorial claims. These claims can range from demands for outright independence to more moderate calls for greater autonomy for the region where members of the national community are concentrated. Nationalism is also likely to be associated with a historical narrative in which the nation is seen to have been unfairly treated by the central government and those who control it.

Flemish nationalists in Belgium, Scottish nationalists, Basque nationalists in Spain, Corsican separatists in France, and Québécois separatists in Canada all share such a narrative. What Smiley called a sense of political community is difficult to sustain when this sort of nationalism is widespread among the members of a spatially concentrated cultural community (see Box 8.2).

The Origins of Canadian Federalism

Canada's federal Constitution was a compromise. Most of the anglophone Fathers of Confederation favoured a unitary system of government under which all power would be in the hands of a new national parliament. They were opposed, however, by two groups. The strongest opposition came from the French-Canadian representatives of Canada East, what today is Quebec. This group, led by George-Étienne Cartier, insisted on constitutional protection for their cultural community. They believed that the most effective way to protect their

Politics in Focus

BOX 8.2 Language, Nationalism, and Federalism

This country has two major language communities that have coexisted, sometimes on uneasy terms, since the country achieved independence in the nineteenth century. One of these communities has a significant nationalist movement that includes a couple of political parties committed to independence for their national community. Many of this country's citizens believe that their language community and region has subsidized public services and incomes in the other community for decades and they feel resentful. This resentment is deepened by historical memories of social and political inequality between the two communities. As of 2015, the prospects for their continued cohabitation seem fair to poor. The country described here is Belgium.

Over the years Belgium has been compared frequently to Canada, facing some rather similar challenges and attempting to manage conflict between its two main language communities, French and Flemish (Belgium also has a very small German-speaking official-language community), through a federal constitution. Unlike Canada, however, the nationalist movement that aspires to break up the country is associated with the wealthier majority community—the Flemish-speaking

north of the country. In the national elections of 2010 and 2014 the most popular political party in the Flemish region of the country was the Flemish Nationalist Party (NVA), a party committed to independence and led by a multilingual historian whose 2010 victory speech began with the words, "Nil volentibus arduum" (For those who have the will, nothing is impossible).

Comparisons between Belgium and Canada can be misleading. Nevertheless, political scientists and constitutionalists from each country have looked to the other to find answers about what does and does not work in managing inter-community relations in a federal state. If recent developments in Belgium hold any lessons for Canada, the main one probably is this: when the ties of identity and shared cultural values that bridge the language gap between communities are weak, and when one group believes that existing state institutions treat it unfairly, federalism is in trouble. The compromise at the heart of federalism's viability ultimately depends on the sentiment of the people or, more precisely, the *peoples* who live together under a federal constitution. This is what the French historian Ernest Renan meant when he said that federalism is a daily referendum of the popular will.

---

interests was through a federal union that gave exclusive jurisdiction over linguistic and cultural matters to the provincial governments. Federalism was also the preferred constitutional option of Maritime politicians. Maritimers had developed strong local identities they were unwilling to see submerged under unitary government. They also realized that their regional interests would be swamped if there were to be a single national legislature in which much more populous Ontario and Quebec would dominate. Besides, in an era when politics and patronage were virtually synonymous it was only reasonable that regional politicians would want to retain control over such important

sources of contracts as roads and public works, as well as bureaucratic sinecures.

Although the anglophone politicians of Ontario and Quebec tended to be much less enthusiastic about federalism, some of them saw merit in the idea of dividing legislative powers between two levels of government. For example, Grit politician George Brown expressed the view that conflict between the English Protestant and French Catholic communities—conflict that had produced government instability and political deadlock in the legislature of the United Canadas and that was one of the reasons behind the Confederation movement—would be reduced by assigning local matters to the provincial legislatures.[7] Ottawa would deal with matters of national interest, like trade and commerce, immigration, defence, and transportation. The presumption that sectional rivalries and local interests would not enter into deliberations on these national issues proved to be naive, to say the least.

The forces pushing the colonies of British North America towards political union required a strong national government. Commercial interests, particularly railroad promoters, wanted unification because their ability to raise investment capital abroad was linked to Canada's creditworthiness. A larger union with a wider revenue base and an integrated national economy was crucial to the railroad promoters' interests and to those of the Canadian financial institutions linked to them. Likewise, a strong central government was needed if British North America was to assume the burden of its own military defence and if expansion into the sparsely populated region between Ontario and British Columbia was to be accomplished. Tugging in the opposite direction were the facts of cultural dualism and the existence of colonial administrations and regional societies that were unwilling to be completely submerged in a unitary state that would inevitably be dominated by Ontario and Quebec. Federalism was a necessary compromise between these contradictory tendencies.

What sort of federal union did the founders envisage? Obviously, politicians had various expectations. Some, such as Canada's first Prime Minister, John A. Macdonald, anticipated that the provincial governments would be little more than glorified municipalities, subordinate to Ottawa. Others, including Oliver Mowat, who as Ontario's Premier led the movement for provincial rights during the 1870s and 1880s, clearly did not share this centralist vision.[8] Individual expectations aside, the agreement the founders reached gave the most important legislative powers and sources of public revenue of the time to the federal government. Ottawa was given authority over trade and commerce, shipping, fisheries, interprovincial transportation, currency and banking, the postal service, and several other areas of endeavour related to managing the economy. Responsibility for immigration and agriculture was divided between the federal and provincial

governments, but in the event of a conflict Ottawa's legislation would prevail. The federal government was assigned the duty to build an intercolonial railway connecting Montreal to Halifax. Together, these powers appeared to establish Ottawa's clear superiority over the provinces in economic matters. When we consider that promoting economic growth and military defence (also a federal responsibility) were two of the chief functions of the nineteenth-century state—maintaining public order was the third, and responsibility for this was divided between Ottawa and the provinces—there is little doubt that Ottawa was assigned the major legislative powers of that era.

Ottawa's superiority also was clear on the taxation front. Donald Smiley notes that customs and excise taxes—indirect forms of taxation—accounted for about three-quarters of colonial revenues prior to Confederation. The Confederation agreement made these the exclusive preserve of the federal government, which could "[raise] Money by any Mode or System of Taxation" (s. 91[3]). The provinces were restricted to the less developed field of "Direct Taxation" (s. 92[2]), as well as royalties on provincially owned natural resources (s. 109). Not only were provincial revenue sources meagre compared to those of the federal government, the Confederation agreement also established the practice of federal money transfers to the provinces (s. 118, repealed in 1950). The dependence of the economically weaker provinces on subsidies from Ottawa began in 1867 and continues to this day (see the discussion later in this chapter).

In addition to all this, the Confederation agreement included several provisions that have been described as *quasi-federal*. They appear to establish a nearly colonial relationship between Ottawa and the provinces by permitting the federal government to disallow laws passed by provincial legislatures. Sections 55, 56, and 90 of the Constitution Act, 1867 give provincial lieutenant-governors, appointees of Ottawa, the authority to reserve approval from any Act passed by a provincial legislature for a period of up to one year, or to disallow the Act at any time within a year of its passage. These were widely used powers during the first few decades after Confederation and were used periodically during the first half of the twentieth century. In most instances Ottawa was reacting to provincial economic policies that challenged its own priorities and jurisdiction. Moreover, section 92(10c) gives the federal government the authority to intervene in a provincial economy by declaring that the construction of a "public work" (this could be anything from a road to an oil field) is in the national interest. This power has been used 470 times, but has not been used since 1961. Finally, section 93(3)(4) actually gives Ottawa the power to pass laws respecting education, an area of provincial jurisdiction. It may do so where education rights that denominational minorities held when a province entered Confederation are abrogated by provincial law. This power has never been used.

Assuming that it is even possible to sort out the founders' intentions, do they really matter? Legally, no. In interpreting the federal division of powers the courts have generally been unreceptive to arguments about what the Fathers of Confederation really had in mind.[9] Indeed, the Supreme Court of Canada's ruling in the 1981 Patriation Reference, *Re Constitution of Canada*, declared flatly that "arguments from history do not lead to any consistent view or any single view of the nature of the British North America Act. So, too, with pronouncements by political figures or persons in other branches of public life. There is little profit in parading them."[10]

Politically, however, arguments about intentions can matter. Politicians and other opinion-makers sometime argue that Canadian federalism ought to be seen as a compact between French and English Canada or, alternatively, a contract among provinces that agreed to give up certain powers to a new national government of their creation. Both the compact and contract theories of federalism maintain that the federal "bargain" cannot be changed without the mutual consent of those who agreed to it. In the case of the compact theory, this means that Quebec—the province in which most francophones reside and the only province in which they are in the majority—should have a veto over any constitutional change that affects either the federal distribution of powers or the relative weight of Quebec in Parliament and on the Supreme Court (where three of the nine justices must be members of the Quebec bar). This argument was rejected by the Supreme Court of Canada in the 1981 Patriation Reference.

Those who argue that federalism is a contract among the provinces claim that each of them has the right to veto constitutional change that affects

The Fathers of Confederation at Charlottetown. Canada's entrance into federalism was far from a unanimous decision; rather, the system of divided jurisdiction was a compromise that made Ottawa the seat of national power to control collective issues such as defence, immigration, and trade, while leaving the provinces to preside over issues of a more local nature, such as culture and education.

George P. Roberts/National Archives of Canada fonds/C-000733 provincial powers or national representation. The contract view of federalism is also the foundation for claims that each province should have equal representation in a reformed Senate. In fact, there are three variants of contract theory.[11] One would restrict the right of veto to the original signatories (Nova Scotia, New Brunswick, Quebec, and Ontario). A second extends it to all provinces, regardless of when they joined Canada. The third takes the position that the unanimous consent of the provinces is not required to change the federal distribution of powers, but that "substantial provincial agreement" is necessary. Like compact theory, none of these variants of contract theory has any legal foundation.

The political importance of these compact/contract theories may be seen in the fact that for nearly 50 years Canadian governments were unable to agree on a formula for amending the Constitution. Between the first serious attempt in 1935 and the 1982 promulgation of the Constitution Act, it proved impossible to get all the provincial governments to agree to an amendment formula. Unanimous provincial consent, based on the contract theory view of federalism, appeared to be a political requirement for enacting such a formula (although if one or two of the smaller provinces had been the only dissenters this "requirement" might have been overcome). Moreover, many constitutionalists and political scientists came to assume—wrongly, it turned out—that unanimity or something close to it was also a legal requirement.

The compact interpretation of Canadian federalism continues to carry political weight. The Quebec government's refusal to agree to the Constitution Act, 1982 was widely viewed as a serious blow to the Constitution's legitimacy. Former Prime Minister Brian Mulroney regularly, if misleadingly, spoke of bringing Quebec into the Constitution. Legally, of course, the 1982 reforms applied right across Canada. But politically the Prime Minister had a point. The government of Quebec, whose claim to speak on behalf of one of the country's two founding nations rests on the fact that the province is home to about 90 per cent of Canadian francophones, did not consent to these far-reaching constitutional changes.

Both of Quebec's major provincial political parties, the Parti Québécois and the Quebec Liberal Party, continue to insist that Canadian federalism must be viewed as a compact between founding nations, a view that enjoys diminishing support in the rest of Canada. The sovereignist position of the PQ has always been that this compact was never respected and is, in any case, not viable. Quebec's Liberal Party and its leaders have agreed that this compact has not always been respected. In his submission to the Supreme Court in the *Reference on Quebec Secession*, former leader of the Quebec Liberal Party, Claude Ryan, wrote, "If the movement in favour of sovereignty was able to put down its roots and develop itself in Quebec it is precisely because more and more Quebecers came to the conclusion that this equality, which had been the dream of many generations, will never be realized with the Canadian federation."[12] This continues to be the official position of the party.[13]

The contract theory of Canada lives on politically, as was seen in the conflict between Ottawa and the provinces over whether provincial approval is needed to reform the Senate. In February 2013 the federal government submitted a reference to the Supreme Court asking whether it had the constitutional authority to proceed unilaterally in reforming the Senate to establish limited terms for senators and eliminate property qualifications for senators, and whether and how much provincial consent might be needed to abolish the Senate. Several of the provinces, supported by some constitutional experts, took the position that provincial consent, and certainly the consent of their province, would be necessary for any reform of the Senate.[14]

The Federal Division of Powers

Whatever the intentions of the founders when they drafted the Constitution Act, 1867, it is clear today that both levels of government exercise wide-ranging legislative and taxation powers. Their ability to do so ultimately rests on the responsibilities assigned to them by the Constitution. Canada's founders took exceptional pains to specify the responsibilities of each level of government. But a literal reading of the division of powers they decided on and of the formal changes that have been made to it since then provide at best a partial and at worst a misleading guide to Canadian federalism. In some cases policy areas were unimagined when the federal division of powers was framed—electronic communications, air transportation, and environmental protection would be examples—and so these legislative powers are not explicitly assigned either to Ottawa or to the provinces. In other cases what were minor responsibilities in the nineteenth and early twentieth centuries have assumed greater importance as a result of economic and societal changes, and of changes in the state itself.

The heart of the federal division of powers is found in sections 91 and 92 of the Constitution Act, 1867. Each of these sections contains a detailed list of enumerated powers that belong exclusively to Parliament (s. 91) or the provincial (s. 92) legislatures. Combined with several other sections that also deal with the division of powers, this is the constitutional foundation of Canadian federalism. An examination of who holds what powers reveals that both Ottawa and the provinces have the capacity to act in most of the major policy fields (see Table 8.2 and Box 8.3).

Some of the constitutional powers listed in Table 8.2 could reasonably have been placed under more than one policy heading. The authority to tax, for example, has been used to promote economic growth, to redistribute income between groups, and to subsidize all sorts of special interests. Unemployment insurance is both an economic policy, tied to manpower retraining and a claimant's job search activities, and a social policy that has the effect of redistributing income to less affluent regions of the country where unemployment is higher. Immigration policy has always been harnessed to the needs of the Canadian economy and has also been tied to cultural policy through citizenship services and language training for immigrants.

At the same time, governments have sometimes found the authority to legislate through powers that are implied, rather than stated, in the Constitution. The most important example of this involves the federal government's spending power. Ottawa spends billions of dollars annually on programs that fall under the jurisdiction of provincial and municipal governments. The feds also provide money to universities (for research and student scholarships) and to school boards (for language instruction), even though these organizations fall under the constitutional authority of the provinces, and to individuals for purposes that might appear to fall under provincial jurisdiction (e.g., tax benefits for child care). Ottawa's constitutional "right" to spend money for any purpose has never been definitely established in the courts.[15] Nevertheless, the spending power today provides the constitutional basis, such as it is, for such major federal grants to the provinces as the Canada Health Transfer (CHT), Canada Social Transfer (CST), and equalization payments.

The Courts and Federalism

Laypersons might imagine that such constitutional terms as "trade and commerce," "property and civil rights," and "direct taxation" have straightforward meanings. This view has not been shared by constitutional lawyers, governments, and the private interests that have challenged federal and provincial laws. For these groups the federal division of powers is a dense thicket of contradictory and contested meanings and opportunities, and the interpretation attached to a particular enumerated power is often a matter to haggle over in the courts. The judicial decisions that have resulted from these disputes have played an important role in shaping the evolution of Canadian federalism. Among the many contentious sections of the Constitution, Ottawa's authority to "make laws for the peace, order, and good government of Canada" (POGG) and the federal government's "trade and commerce" power have been among the most significant in their impact on the division of powers.

TABLE 8.2   The Federal Division of Powers under the Constitution Acts

	Ottawa	Provinces
Public finance	**(1867)** • 91(3): authority to raise money by any "Mode or System of Taxation" • 91(4): authority to borrow money **(1982)** • 36(2): commits Ottawa to the principle of equalizing public revenue levels in the provinces	**(1867)** • 92(2): authorizes direct taxation within the province • 92(3): authority to borrow money • 92A(4): permits provinces to use "any mode or system of taxation" in the case of non-renewable natural resources, forestry resources, and electrical energy
Managing the economy	**(1867)** • 91(2): regulation of trade and commerce • 91(2A): unemployment insurance • 91(5): post office • 91(10, 12): navigation, international waters, and offshore resources • 91(14, 15, 16, 18, 19, 20): national monetary system • 91(17, 22, 23): commercial standards • 92(10.c): authority to intervene in a provincial economy by declaring a public work to be in the national interest • 95: agriculture • 121: prohibits provincial taxes on imports from other provinces, thus reinforcing the concept of a national economic union **(1982)** • 6(2): guarantees the economic mobility of citizens anywhere within Canada, reinforcing the concept of a national economic union	**(1867)** • 92(9): authority to issue commercial licences • 92(10): public works within the province • 92(11): incorporation of companies with provincial objects • 92(13): property and civil rights • 92A: reaffirms provincial authority over natural resources within their borders • 95: agriculture, but federal law takes precedence • 109: establishes provincial ownership of natural resources within their borders **(1982)** • 6(4): permits provinces to favour provincial residents in hiring if the rate of unemployment in that province is above the national average
Social policy and the quality of life	**(1867)** • 91(24): Aboriginal Canadians • 91(26): marriage and divorce • 93(3, 4): authority to protect the educational rights of denominational minorities • 94A: old age pensions, but provincial law prevails • 95: immigration	**(1867)** • 92(7): hospitals • 92(12): solemnization of marriage • 93: education • 94A: public pensions • 95: immigration, but federal law prevails
Cultural policy	**(1867)** • 133: official bilingualism of Parliament **(1982)** • 16(l), 19, 20: establishes official bilingualism in all institutions of the federal government	**(1867)** • 92(16): all matters of a merely local or private nature • 93: education • 133: official bilingualism of Quebec legislature **(1982)** • 16(2), 17(2), 18(2), 19(2), 20(2): establishes official bilingualism in all institutions of the New Brunswick government
Administration and enforcement of law	**(1867)** • 91(27): criminal law • 91(28): penitentiaries • 96: appointment of judges of provincial courts • 100: authority to set judicial salaries • 101: authority to establish a general court of appeal for Canada, and other federal courts	**(1867)** • 92(14): administration of justice and the organization of courts within the province • 92(15): authority to establish penalties for violations of provincial laws
International relations and defence	**(1867)** • 91(7): military and defence • 132: authority to enter foreign treaties and perform obligations under them	**(1867)** • Since the Supreme Court's decision in the *Labour Conventions* case of 1937, it appears that provincial consent is required to implement foreign treaty obligations involving matters of provincial jurisdiction. There is, however, no consensus on this.

TABLE 8.2 Continued		
	Ottawa	**Provinces**
Other legislative authority	(1867) • 91 (preamble): authorizes Parliament to make laws for the "peace, order, and good government" of Canada • 91(29): matters not falling under the enumerated powers of the provinces come under Ottawa's jurisdiction	(1867) • 92(8): municipal institutions • 92(16): all matters of a local or private nature in the province
Environmental policy	(1867) • 91: peace, order, and good government of Canada (this basis for federal power is suggested in the Canada Water Act) • 91(10): navigation and shipping • 91(12): sea coast and inland fisheries • 91(27): criminal law • 95: agriculture • 132: foreign treaties	(1867) • 92(5): management and sale of public lands • 92(10): local works and undertakings • 92(13): property and civil rights • 92(16): matters of a merely local or private nature (1982) • 92A: non-renewable natural resources, forestry resources, and electric energy

Peace, Order, and Good Government

The courts have tended to place a narrow interpretation on the federal Parliament's general authority to make laws for the **"peace, order, and good government of Canada."** This power has been reduced over time to one that may provide the constitutional basis for federal actions in emergency circumstances. It cannot, however, be used to justify federal laws during "normal" times. This narrow interpretation of POGG began with the *Local Prohibition* case (1896). The Judicial Committee of the Privy Council ruled that POGG could not be used by Ottawa to override the enumerated powers of the provinces. The decision also marked the introduction into Canadian constitutional law of the "national dimensions" test. Lord Watson wrote:

> Their Lordships do not doubt that some matters, in their origin local or provincial, might attain such dimensions as to affect the body politic of the Dominion, and to justify the Canadian Parliament in passing laws for their regulation or abolition in the interest of the Dominion.[16]

When does a matter acquire "national dimensions"? This question was dealt with in a series of three decisions handed down in 1922, 1923, and 1925. In *Re Board of Commerce Act and Combines and Fair Prices Act 1919* (1922), the JCPC struck down two federal laws introduced after World War I to prevent monopolistic business practices and hoarding of essential commodities. For the first time the "emergency doctrine" was articulated, according to which Parliament could pass laws under the authority of POGG only in the case of a national emergency. Writing for the majority, Viscount Haldane declared that:

> Circumstances are conceivable, such as those of war or famine, when the peace, order and good Government of the Dominion might be imperilled under conditions so exceptional that they require legislation of a character in reality beyond anything provided for by the enumerated heads in either s. 92 or s. 91.[17]

Essentially, the JCPC ruled that some national crisis must exist before federal laws can be based on POGG. The fact that a matter has acquired "national dimensions" would not, by itself, be sufficient to justify such exceptional legislation.

Despite the JCPC's admission that peacetime circumstances could conceivably warrant Ottawa acting under the authority of POGG, subsequent rulings suggested that POGG was really a wartime power. In the first of these decisions, *Fort Frances Pulp and Power Co. v. Manitoba Free Press* (1923), the JCPC declared that war-related circumstances were sufficient to warrant legislating under POGG. Moreover, Viscount Haldane's opinion in *Fort Frances* indicated that the courts should be reluctant to question Parliament's judgment that a war-related emergency exists. Rulings in 1947 by the JCPC and in 1950 by the Supreme Court of Canada repeated this view.[18]

Governing Realities

BOX 8.3 Who Has Authority over Water?

When the Constitution Act of 1867 came into effect, water was considered to be significant in three main ways. It was important for navigation, as a source of fish, and for irrigating farmland. In fact, the third of these was not yet particularly important in Canada, although the building of dams and the diversion of rivers for irrigation had begun to be a contentious issue in the United States. The supply of fresh water for drinking was taken for granted. Water pollution was not an issue. No one had heard of invasive species. The issues surrounding hydroelectric power did not yet exist. And the idea that Aboriginal rights and interests should be taken into account when it came to water would have been greeted with incredulity.

It is hardly surprising, then, that water is not one of the enumerated legislative powers under sections 91 and 92 of the Constitution Act, 1867. Over time, however, it acquired enormous importance and the question of which level of government held the constitutional authority to regulate its use was asked more often and with greater urgency. Ottawa based its case on a clutch of constitutional provisions, including the "peace, order, and good government" clause, the trade and commerce provision, jurisdiction over coastal and inland fisheries, as well as over navigation and shipping, and its authority to enter into foreign treaties (though not necessarily to implement the terms of such treaties). More recently the federal government's exclusive jurisdiction over criminal law has been advanced as a basis for a federal role in water policy.

The provinces have had their own list of constitutional claims to authority over water. These have included jurisdiction over property and civil rights, municipal institutions, local works and undertakings, the authority conferred by s. 92(5) regarding the management of public lands, and "all matters of a merely local or private nature in the province" (s. 92(16)). Conflict over who has jurisdiction has occasionally led to court battles over pollution, the building of dams, and the management of fisheries.

In the 1960s and 1970s governments in developed economies throughout the world, Canada included, became more active in matters concerning water pollution, passing laws and creating environmental bureaucracies to manage this issue. What Ottawa immediately discovered was that provincial and local governments already claimed responsibility for providing clean water, dealing with sewage, regulating agricultural, industrial, and residential activities that influence water supply and quality, and managing recreational and commercial fishing in their lakes and rivers. Some things, of course, these provincial and local governments could not do, including negotiating water treaties with foreign governments, regulating water that flowed across provincial boundaries, and managing the waters off Canada's coasts. But most of the key regulatory functions related to water supply and quality, which have immediate impacts on Canadians' lives and on their communities, were and continue to be under the control of provincial and local governments.

Some water experts lament the decentralized and divided reality of authority over water in Canada and believe that a more robust federal presence and national standards would be preferable. Whether or not they are right—and it is not obvious that a dominant federal role would produce better water policy, whatever "better" might be understood to mean—the fact is that the constitutional authority to regulate water is divided and overlapping. The "watertight compartments" metaphor of Canadian federalism, proposed by the Judicial Committee of the Privy Council in the 1930s, is never leakier than when applied to water.

In those cases where the courts have rejected POGG as a valid basis for federal legislation, the impugned laws were intended to deal with peacetime circumstances. The first of these was the decision in *Toronto Electric Commissioners v. Snider* (1925). Relying on the "emergency doctrine" it had developed in the *Board of Commerce* case, the JCPC struck down Canada's major industrial relations law, the Industrial Disputes Investigation Act, 1907. The JCPC again rejected peacetime recourse to POGG in the 1937 reference decision on Ottawa's Employment and Social Insurance Act, 1935.[19] The federal government's attempt to justify this law under POGG, on the grounds that unemployment was a matter of national concern and, moreover, that it threatened the well-being of the country, was considered inadequate by the JCPC.

Confronted with broadly similar reasoning in the 1970s, the Supreme Court of Canada found that POGG could be used to justify federal laws during peacetime. The Court was asked to rule on the constitutionality of Ottawa's Anti-Inflation Act, 1975. A majority of the Court accepted the federal government's argument that mounting inflationary pressures constituted an emergency justifying legislation that encroached on provincial jurisdiction. Not only was the "emergency doctrine" liberated from war-related circumstances, the Court also indicated its reluctance to challenge Parliament's judgment on when emergency circumstances exist. The result, according to constitutionalists like Peter Russell, is that Ottawa now appeared to have fairly easy access to emergency powers under this doctrine.[20] Constitutionally, this may be so. Politically, however, any federal government would think twice before legislating in a manner that interferes with provincial constitutional authority and invoking the emergency powers doctrine as the basis for such interference.

The national dimensions test, first expressed in the 1896 *Local Prohibition* case, has come to be the more practically important aspect of POGG. In several cases since the 1950s the federal government has defended legislation that treads upon provincial turf by arguing that the matter in question had national dimensions, thereby justifying federal legislation under the authority of POGG.[21]

The criteria used by the Supreme Court in deciding whether a matter has national dimensions should not be approached by the faint of heart and routinely lead to disagreements between justices of the Court.

Trade and Commerce

On the face of it, Ottawa's authority over the regulation of trade and commerce (s. 91[2])[22] appears rather sweeping. Any economic activity or transaction would seem to fall within its scope. In fact, however, court decisions have construed the trade and commerce power to be much narrower than this, limited largely to interprovincial and international trade. At the same time, provincial jurisdiction over property and civil rights in the provinces (s. 92[13])[23] has been interpreted as the provinces' own version of the "trade and commerce" power. This line of judicial interpretation began with the decision in *Citizens' Insurance Co. v. Parsons* (1881). Based on its view that a broad, literal interpretation of s. 91(2) of the Constitution Act, 1867 would bring any and all aspects of economic life under the authority of Ottawa, leaving the provinces powerless to affect business, the JCPC interpreted "regulation of trade and commerce" to include "political arrangements in regard to trade requiring the sanction of parliament, regulation of trade in matters of interprovincial concern, and it may be that they would include general regulation of trade affecting the whole Dominion."[24] To construe Ottawa's trade and commerce power otherwise, the JCPC argued, would be to deny the "fair and ordinary meaning" of s. 92(13) of the Constitution Act, 1867, which assigns property and civil rights in the provinces to the provincial governments.

The legacy of *Parsons* has been that Ottawa's authority to regulate trade and commerce has been limited to interprovincial trade, international trade, and general trade affecting the whole of Canada. But even this definition of federal jurisdiction has presented problems of interpretation. For example, what about a federal law whose principal goal is to regulate trade that crosses provincial borders, but which has as an incidental effect the regulation of some transactions that occur wholly within a province? Is such a law constitutional under s. 91(2)? Until the 1950s the courts' answer was "no."[25]

But a series of Supreme Court decisions, culminating in *Caloil v. Attorney General of Canada* (1971), signified a broader interpretation of Ottawa's power to regulate interprovincial trade.[26] In *Caloil*, the Court acknowledged that a federal law prohibiting the transportation or sale of imported oil west of the Ottawa Valley interfered with local trade in a province. Nevertheless, the Court upheld the federal law on the grounds that its "true character" was "the control of imports in the furtherance of an extraprovincial trade policy."[27] Ottawa's authority was given an additional boost by a 1971 reference decision of the Supreme Court. In the *"Chicken and Egg" Reference*—no kidding, "Chicken and Egg"— the Court ruled unconstitutional a provincial egg-marketing scheme that restricted imports from other provinces on the grounds that it encroached on Ottawa's trade and commerce power. Justice Bora Laskin, who would later become Chief Justice of the Supreme Court, referred specifically to the trend towards a more balanced interpretation of federal and provincial jurisdiction over trade.[28] Laskin argued that, "to permit each province to seek its own advantage . . . through a figurative sealing of its borders to entry of goods from others would be to deny one of the objects of Confederation . . . namely, to form an economic unit of the whole of Canada."[29] What of the *Parsons* allusion to general trade affecting the whole of Canada? In both *MacDonald v. Vapor Canada Ltd.* (1977) and *Attorney General of Canada v. Canadian National Transportation* (1983), the Court raised the question of when trade affects the whole country and thereby justifies, per *Parsons*, federal regulation under the trade and commerce power. The answer was given in *General Motors of Canada v. City National Leasing* (1989), when the Supreme Court laid down five criteria that must be met before Ottawa may regulate commerce under the "general trade" provision of s. 91(2) of the Constitution. They include the following:

1. the impugned legislation must be part of a general regulatory scheme;
2. the scheme must be monitored by the continuing oversight of a regulatory agency;
3. the legislation must be concerned with trade as a whole rather than with a particular industry;
4. the legislation should be of a nature that the provinces jointly or severally would be constitutionally incapable of enacting; and
5. the failure to include one or more provinces or localities in a legislative scheme would jeopardize the successful operation of the scheme in other parts of the country.[30]

In May 2010 the federal government referred the proposed Canadian Securities Act to the Supreme Court for an advisory opinion on its constitutionality. Prompted by the financial crisis that swept across the United States and other capitalist economies in 2008–10, the Act was intended to strengthen Ottawa's regulatory role in Canadian capital markets. The case was particularly interesting due to the fact that the federal government relied entirely on the trade and commerce power in arguing that it had the constitutional authority to regulate the national securities trading market. In December 2011 the Supreme Court ruled against the federal government. "While the economic importance and pervasive character of the securities market may, in principle, support federal intervention that is qualitatively different from what the provinces can do," said the Court, "they do not justify a wholesale takeover of the regulation of the securities industry which is the ultimate consequence of the proposed federal legislation."[31]

At the same time as Ottawa was experiencing this setback, new rules established by the US Congress to regulate a securities industry that was largely responsible for dragging the global economy to the verge of disaster were being implemented. The irony is that simple words of the United States Constitution—and certainly the founders' intentions—give Congress less scope for the regulation of trade and commerce than the Canadian Constitution appears to give to Parliament. Whereas court rulings in the United States have produced a situation where very few serious obstacles stand in the way of Congress regulating any economic transaction, no matter how local it may appear to be, judicial interpretation in Canada has had the opposite effect. Comparing the evolution of the trade and commerce power in these two countries provides a textbook example of the importance of the courts when it comes to the division of powers under federalism.

The Impact of Judicial Decisions

Court rulings seldom put an end to conflicts between Ottawa and the provinces. Instead, they typically become part of the bargaining process between governments. Consider the following examples:

- *Employment and Social Insurance Act Reference* (1937). The JCPC struck down a federal statute establishing a program to deal with national unemployment. This was followed by negotiations between the federal and provincial governments, leading to a 1940 constitutional amendment that gave Ottawa authority over unemployment insurance.
- *Public Service Board v. Dionne* (1978). The Supreme Court confirmed Ottawa's exclusive jurisdiction to regulate television broadcasting. Immediately after the decision was handed down, the federal Minister of Communications announced Ottawa's willingness to negotiate some division of authority with the provinces.
- *CIGOL v. Government of Saskatchewan* (1978). In *CIGOL*, a provincial tax on natural gas was found to be a direct tax and therefore outside the jurisdiction of the province. When Ottawa and the provinces were negotiating constitutional reform in 1980–1, the issue of provincial control over natural resources was on the table. The result was s. 92A of the Constitution Act. It appears to permit the form of resource taxation that was ruled ultra vires in the *CIGOL* decision.
- *Re Constitution of Canada* (1981). The Supreme Court ruled that Ottawa's proposal to patriate the British North America Act and to change it in ways affecting provincial powers was legal, but that it was unconstitutional in the conventional sense (see Chapter 6). The

decision gave the federal government a legal victory, at the same time as the provinces were given the moral high ground. Within weeks all governments were back at the table trying to find a negotiated solution.

- *Reference re Secession of Quebec* (1998). On the face of it, this appeared to be a victory for Ottawa and federalist forces generally. The Supreme Court ruled that neither the Canadian Constitution nor international law confer on the government and National Assembly of Quebec the right to secede from Canada unilaterally. The Court added, however, that a "clear majority vote in Quebec on a clear question in favour of secession would confer democratic legitimacy on the secession initiative which all of the other participants in Confederation would have to recognize." Thus the Constitution does, in fact, recognize the constitutionality of Quebec secession. So who really won, the separatists or the federalists? As was also true of the Court's ambiguous 1981 pronouncement in the Patriation Reference, both sides were able to claim a victory of sorts. The 1998 ruling did not resolve the issue of Quebec separation—indeed, no one expected this would be its result. Instead, by clarifying some of the constitutional questions associated with Quebec secession, the Court provided all sides in this ongoing political struggle with ammunition for future sniping.
- *Reference Re Securities Act* (2011). In its ruling that Ottawa's proposal to regulate the national securities market was unconstitutional, the Supreme Court indicated what needed to be done to establish a federal regulatory role in this field. Co-operation with the provinces in a joint regulatory regime, the Court indicated, would pass constitutional muster. In its 2013 budget the federal government served notice that it intended to do just that. Most of the provinces continued to object, but the issue clearly had shifted from the courts to the playing field of intergovernmental relations.

Evolving Federalism

It is generally believed that judicial decisions decentralized Canadian federalism in a way that the Fathers of Confederation had not planned, but that this tendency has been attenuated since 1949 when the Supreme Court became Canada's highest court of appeal. Some bemoan the judiciary's decentralizing influence, particularly that of the JCPC during Canada's first half-century. Others maintain that the limits placed on Ottawa's general legislative authority (POGG) and trade and commerce power, and the broad interpretation of provincial authority over property and civil rights, have reflected the political reality of Canada. As Pierre Trudeau observed, "it has long been the custom in English Canada to denounce the [Judicial Committee of the] Privy Council for its provincial bias; but it should perhaps be considered that if the law lords had not leaned in that direction, Quebec separatism might not be a threat today: it might be an accomplished fact."[32]

Judicial review is only one of the factors that have shaped the evolution of federalism. In fact, legal disputes over the division of powers are only symptomatic of underlying tensions at the root of intergovernmental conflict. Over the course of Canadian history these tensions have three main sources: (1) the status of Quebec and the powers of the Quebec state; (2) relations between the more heavily industrialized and populous centre of the country and the outlying western and eastern regions; and (3) the political and administrative needs of governments.

Quebec

"What does Quebec want?" The question has been asked countless times over the years by English Canadians, some of whom genuinely wanted to know and others who asked it out of exasperation, believing all along that the answer would be unacceptable. The complementary question, "What does English Canada want?" has been posed less often. Yet neither question makes sense in isolation from the other. To understand what Quebec wants from Canada it is also necessary to consider what the rest of Canada expects from, and is willing to concede to, Quebec. Quebec's unique role in Canadian federalism derives from two factors. One is its predominantly French-speaking character. Over 80 per cent of the provincial population claims French as their mother tongue and about 90 per cent of all Canadian francophones reside in Quebec. The second factor is Quebec's size. At Confederation it was the second most populous province and Montreal was the hub of Canada's commercial and financial industries. Although its weight relative to the rest of Canada is much less today, Quebec is still Canada's second most populous province, accounting for slightly less than one-quarter of Canada's population. Neither Ontario nor Quebec is as economically dominant as in the past, but as a centre for finance and manufacturing Quebec continues to be surpassed only by Ontario.

Quebec's distinctive social and cultural fabric explains why it has made special demands on Canadian federalism. Because it is a large province with the second largest bloc of seats in the federal Parliament and because francophones have always been able to control Quebec's provincial legislature, the demands of Quebec have had a significant impact on the evolution of Canadian federalism. This impact has been experienced on two main fronts: 1) the Constitution, and 2) the financial and administrative practices of federalism. We will examine Quebec's impact on the financial and administrative dimensions of federalism later in this chapter.

Quebec's influence on the Constitution predates the Confederation agreement. Between 1848 and 1867 Ontario and Quebec formed the United Canadas, governed by a single legislature in which the two colonies held equal representation. This was Canada's first experience with the federal principle of regional representation. Predominantly francophone Quebec and predominantly anglophone Ontario were joined in a legislative partnership that required the agreement of both regional communities. It turned out to be a failure. Quebec's influence on the Constitution was also strongly evident in the Confederation agreement. Its representatives were the most insistent on a federal constitution for Canada, under which the provincial government would have authority over those matters considered vital to the preservation of the language, religion, and social institutions of Quebec. The clerical and political leaders of French Canada were unanimous in viewing Canadian federalism as a pact between two peoples. "Canadian Confederation," declared Henri Bourassa in 1902, "is the result of a contract between the two races in Canada, French and English, based on equality and recognizing equal rights and reciprocal duties. Canadian Confederation will last only as long as this equality of rights is recognized as the basis of the public right in Canada, from Halifax to Vancouver."[33]

The equality Bourassa had in mind did not last very long. It had already been violated in Manitoba, where the status of French in the provincial legislature and the educational rights of francophone Catholics were swept away a couple of decades after that province entered Confederation. It was also violated in Ontario, where Regulation 17 (1913) banned French instruction from the province's public schools. These developments contributed to the identification of French Canada with Quebec, the only province in which francophones were in the majority and where they could effectively defend their rights and preserve their culture.

The constitutional consequences of limiting French Canada to the boundaries of Quebec became apparent by the middle of the twentieth century. As Ottawa became increasingly involved in areas of provincial jurisdiction, particularly through its spending power but also by monopolizing the field of direct taxation between 1947 and 1954 under a tax rental agreement with the provinces, the Quebec government became more and more protective of what it argued were exclusive provincial powers under the Constitution. Indeed, the Quebec government of Maurice Duplessis was the first among the provinces to reject Ottawa's exclusive occupation of the personal income tax field, imposing its own provincial income tax in 1954. But not until the Quiet Revolution of the 1960s, marking the eclipse of the conservative anti-statist nationalism that had dominated Quebec politics for more than a century, was Quebec's resentment towards Ottawa's encroachment onto provincial territory

matched by aggressive constitutional demands. The first major indication of this occurred during the federal–provincial negotiations on a public old-age pension scheme (1963–5). Quebec Premier Jean Lesage stated that his government would only agree to a constitutional amendment giving Ottawa the authority to pass pension legislation if Quebec were able to opt out of the federal plan. Ottawa agreed, and thus was born the Canadian practice of provinces being able to opt out of a federal shared-cost program without suffering any financial loss.

Quebec's constitutional demands appeared to become even more ambitious a few years later. The 1966 provincial election saw the Union Nationale party run on the slogan "Québec d'abord!" (Quebec first!) The party's leader, Daniel Johnson, had authored the book *Egalité ou indépendance* and in the election campaign the Union Nationale called for major constitutional reform that included the transfer of virtually all social and cultural matters to the province, constitutional recognition of Canada's binational character, and exclusive provincial control over the major tax fields then shared with Ottawa. In fact, however, these demands were not pursued with much vigour during the party's five years in power (1966–70). The one constitutional issue on which the Union Nationale government did confront Ottawa was that of international representation for Quebec. But as Kenneth McRoberts observes:

> In purely symbolic terms Quebec's demands seemed very significant; Quebec was seeking to assume what many regarded as the trappings of sovereignty. Yet . . . these demands did not directly attack the real distribution of power and responsibilities to the extent that various Lesage demands, such as a separate Quebec Pension Plan, had.[34]

Despite the lack of substantive change in Quebec's constitutional status and powers during this period, the province's nationalist undercurrent was gaining momentum. The creation of the Parti Québécois (PQ) in 1968, under the leadership of René Lévesque, brought under one roof most of the major groups committed to the political independence of Quebec. The Liberal Party of Quebec remained federalist, but advocated what amounted to special status for Quebec within Canadian federalism. "Un fédéralisme rentable" (profitable federalism) was the passionless way in which Liberal leader Robert Bourassa explained Quebec's commitment to Canada.

Constitutional negotiations between Ottawa and the provinces had been ongoing since 1968. The 1970 election of a Liberal government in Quebec appeared to provide an opportunity to bring these talks to a successful conclusion. But when the 11 governments got together at Victoria in 1971, it became apparent that Quebec's price for agreeing to a constitutional amendment formula and a charter of rights was higher than Ottawa was willing to pay.[35] The impasse was over social policy. Quebec demanded constitutional supremacy in an area in which Ottawa operated several major programs, including family allowances, unemployment insurance, manpower training, and old-age pensions. Moreover, the Quebec government wanted the fiscal means to pay for provincial policies in these fields. Ottawa went some way towards meeting these demands. The Trudeau government refused, however, to concede the principle of provincial supremacy over social policy and would not provide a constitutional guarantee that provinces would receive financial compensation for operating their own programs in these areas. The federal–provincial compromise reached in Victoria fell apart days later in Quebec, where the deal was widely seen as constitutional entrenchment of an unacceptable status quo.

After Quebec's rejection of the Victoria Charter, the Bourassa government adopted a piecemeal strategy for changing federalism, negotiating with Ottawa on single issues like family allowances, social security, and telecommunications. It was unsuccessful, however, in extracting any major concessions from a federal government that believed provincial powers were already too great, and that was staunchly opposed to special status for Quebec.

A rather different strategy was followed by the PQ government of René Lévesque after it came to power in 1976. The PQ was committed to holding a provincial referendum on its option of political

sovereignty for Quebec, combined with some form of economic association with the rest of Canada. But instead of simple confrontation with Ottawa, the Lévesque government pursued an *étapiste* (gradualist) strategy of providing "good government"—which required some degree of co-operation with Ottawa because of the intricate network of intergovernmental programs and agreements—while attempting to convince the Quebec population that its best interests lay in **sovereignty-association**. The two governments co-operated on dozens of new capital spending projects, on management of the economy, and on immigration policy. The PQ government even participated in federal–provincial talks on constitutional reform in 1978–9. All of this occurred against the background of the looming referendum on the PQ's separatist option.

Sovereignty-association was rejected by Quebec voters in May 1980. But they re-elected the PQ to office in 1981. It was thus a PQ government that participated in the constitutional negotiations towards "renewed federalism" that the federal Liberal government had initiated after the Quebec referendum. But it was also a PQ government that refused to sign the final product of these talks, the November 1981 accord that became the Constitution Act, 1982. The PQ's refusal was hardly surprising in light of the fact that none of the demands that Quebec governments had made since the 1960s were included in the 1981 constitutional accord. Indeed, the province's Liberal opposition also found the accord to be unacceptable. The Constitution had undergone its most dramatic reform since its passage in 1867, but the provincial government of the country's second largest province and home to 90 per cent of Canada's francophones had not agreed to these changes. Although the legality of the Constitution Act, 1982 was not in doubt, its political legitimacy was.

This was the situation when Robert Bourassa and the provincial Liberals were returned to power in 1985. Their election appeared to reflect the muted tenor of Quebec nationalism in the post-referendum era. Change had also taken place in Ottawa. Prime Minister Brian Mulroney, elected in 1984, did not share Pierre Trudeau's view that the provinces were already too powerful for the good of the national economy and political unity. Nor was he viscerally opposed to some form of special status for Quebec, as Trudeau was. Conditions seemed propitious, therefore, for a new arrangement that Quebec would accept.

It was not to be. The Quebec government put forward a package of five demands that had to be met before it would agree to the constitutional reforms passed in 1982. These proposals were agreed to by Ottawa and all of the provincial premiers on 30 April 1987, forming the basis for what became known as the Meech Lake Accord. As we have seen in Chapter 6, these constitutional proposals died on the drawing board, and two years later, in 1992, the Charlottetown proposals for constitutional reform, which offered Quebec even more and also brought Aboriginal Canadians to the table, were defeated in a national referendum.

In the wake of the Charlottetown Accord's rejection, politicians of all stripes fled from the constitutional issue. It was not an issue in the 1993 federal election campaign, at least not outside Quebec. In Quebec, however, these matters were kept before the voters by the Bloc Québécois, under the leadership of a former Progressive Conservative Party cabinet minister, Lucien Bouchard. The Bloc's raison d'être was, of course, to achieve political independence for Quebec. Their success in capturing 54 of Quebec's 75 seats in the 1993 general election may not have been a surrogate vote for separation, but it certainly demonstrated the depth of Quebec voters' dissatisfaction with the federal government and existing constitutional arrangements.

Despite their obvious wish to avoid the constitutional quagmire, the Liberals were forced to confront the issue as a result of the 1994 election of the PQ in Quebec. The PQ was committed to holding a referendum on Quebec independence within a year of their election. When the referendum campaign began in September 1995, the *indépendantiste* side got off to a sputtering start. There appeared to be little enthusiasm among Québécois for the PQ's separatist vision, and the early polls showed the "no" side to be leading by a margin of as much as 20 percentage points. The federalist campaign relied on messages intended to convince Quebecers they would suffer economically if the province voted "yes." Federal Minister

of Finance Paul Martin and prominent business spokespersons warned Quebec voters that the days after separation would be dark ones.

About halfway through the campaign, however, leadership of the "yes" side passed from Quebec Premier Jacques Parizeau to Bloc Québécois leader Lucien Bouchard. Support for independence took off, due in large measure to Bouchard's charismatic style and unsurpassed ability to connect emotionally with francophone Quebecers, but also because of what in retrospect can be seen to have been a terribly uninspired campaign by the federalists. Prime Minister Jean Chrétien chose to stay on the sidelines until the last couple of weeks of the campaign, when polls showed the "yes" side to be leading. His previous refusal to make any concrete constitutional offer to Quebec wavered during the period before the vote, when he suggested that he supported constitutional recognition of Quebec as a distinct society and a Quebec veto over any future constitutional reform. On 30 October 1995, the "no" side emerged with the narrowest of victories: 49.6 per cent against independence, 48.5 per cent for, with spoiled ballots accounting for the rest.

The federal government's reluctance to deal with the issue of constitutional reform and with Quebec's demands before the 1995 referendum forced its hand was due in great measure to its realization that Canadians' reactions to the constitutional issue tended to range from indifference to deep hostility. But as their uncertain performance in the referendum campaign showed, the Liberals' silence may also have been due to their inability to formulate a positive response to the sovereignty option proposed by Quebec nationalists.

This inability can be traced to the Liberal model of federalism that took shape during the Trudeau era. Although not centralist in any absolute sense— Canada has surely been among the least centralized federal systems in the world in recent decades— it assumes that a strong central government is essential to the maintenance of Canadian unity. Moreover, this model is in general opposed to what is called "asymmetrical federalism," i.e., the constitutional recognition of differences in the status and powers of provincial governments; in particular, it is against constitutional entrenchment of special status for Quebec. The Constitution Act of 1982, particularly the Charter and the denial of a right of constitutional veto to any single province, embodies this vision of federalism.

This model is, of course, hotly contested. The main challenge comes from Quebec nationalists, not only from separatists but also from Quebec's nationalist-federalists. This latter group, which includes the Liberal Party of Quebec, maintains that constitutional reforms, including, at a minimum, recognition of Quebec's special responsibility for the protection and promotion of the French language in Canada and a Quebec veto over constitutional change, are necessary to keep Quebecers interested in Canadian federalism. The federal Liberals, since Trudeau stepped down as party leader in 1984, have shown a willingness to concede much of what the nationalist-federalists demand, as seen in the party's support for the Meech Lake and Charlottetown Accords and in some pronouncements made by its recent leaders, Michael Ignatieff and Justin Trudeau.[36] However, their enthusiasm for these constitutional reforms has been tempered by a realization that they receive mixed reviews among voters in Ontario and generate downright hostility in western Canada, and by a loyalty among some Liberals to Trudeau's brand of no-special-status-for-Quebec federalism.

In the wake of the close call experienced by federalists in the 1995 Quebec referendum, where a clear majority of francophones voted for the sovereignty option, the federal Liberal Party showed that it was ready to cut the cord connecting it to the Trudeau era. Only weeks after the referendum the Liberal government introduced a motion recognizing Quebec as a distinct society, assigning the province a veto over constitutional change, and transferring to Quebec some authority for job training. Ontario and British Columbia also were assigned veto power, as were the Prairie and Atlantic regions if at least two provinces representing more than 50 per cent of the regional population opposed a proposed amendment. The first two of this trio of reforms have clear constitutional implications. The federal motion did not, of course, change the written Constitution. However, to the extent that Ottawa allows its behaviour to be governed by what the Liberal government of the time characterized as a constitutional offer to Quebecers, it does change the constitutional rules in an informal way. Likewise, the resolution introduced by the Conservative government and passed by the House of Commons in 2006, recognizing Quebec as a nation within a united Canada, does not change the constitutional status of Quebec in any formal way. But it may be argued to confer a

left: CP Images/The Canadian Press/Tom Hanson;
right: CP Images/The Canadian Press/Jacques Boissinot

"Oui" supporters rally on the floor of the Palais des congrès in Montreal as they wait for the results of the 1995 referendum vote (left); "Non" supporters react to poll results as the pro-Canada vote inches up to 50 per cent en route to a slim victory in the 1995 sovereignty referendum (right).

sort of de facto special status on Quebec in matters of constitutional reform.

These federal actions marked a return to a tradition of flexibility in Canadian federalism that predates Pierre Trudeau's entry into federal politics. It is a tradition familiar to those who know the history of intergovernmental relations in Canada. Instead of "big bang" changes to the Constitution—the Charter and the other reforms of 1982 having been the only change of this sort—the rules and arrangements governing relations between Ottawa and the provinces would evolve in a piecemeal and gradual manner, without fanfare and without recourse to formal constitutional amendment.

Centre–Periphery Relations

Canada spans five and a half time zones and occupies the second largest land mass of any country. Despite this vastness, the narrow belt that runs between Windsor and Montreal—the "industrial heartland" of Canada as it has long been called—is home to over 55 per cent of Canada's population and generates about 60 per cent of national income and production. Ontario and Quebec together account for just under 60 per cent of the 308 seats in the House of Commons. No national political party can hope to form a government without considerable support from the voters of at least one, and usually both, of these provinces. They comprise Canada's centre, in terms of their political and economic power.

Predictably, the provincial governments of Ontario and Quebec carry greater weight in Canadian federalism than do those of the other provinces. The other eight provincial governments preside over regions whose interests, throughout most of the country's history, have been subordinated by Ottawa to those of central Canada. In this sense these other provinces constitute Canada's *peripheries*, situated on the edge—sometimes precariously so—of national politics. Resentment towards central Canada and the federal government has deep roots in the politics of these provinces, particularly in the West. Their litany of historical grievances includes, to mention only a few: tariff policy that for a century protected manufacturing jobs

and corporate profits in Ontario and Quebec; the perceived insensitivity of the country's Toronto- and Montreal-based financial institutions when it came to western interests; Ottawa's treatment of the petroleum resources concentrated in the West; investment and spending decisions by the federal government; official bilingualism and what westerners in particular perceive to be Ottawa's favouritism towards Quebec's interests. No one can seriously doubt that the peripheral provinces have a case. As Donald Smiley has written, "there are dangers that Canadian problems will be resolved almost entirely within the framework of the heartland of the country with the progressive alienation from national affairs of those who live on the peripheries."[37]

The federal principle of regional representation is embodied in the Canadian Senate, in which Ontario, Quebec, and the western provinces each have 24 senators, and the four Atlantic provinces have 30, despite very significant differences in the populations of these regions. Much more importantly, regional representation has always been a foremost consideration when prime ministers select cabinet ministers and in making certain other federal appointments. Over the years Ottawa has created, disbanded, and recreated various departments and agencies whose activities were ostensibly to promote economic development in various regions of the country, thereby further institutionalizing the significance of regions in the structure of the federal state. Yet all of this, taken together, has not provided these regions with what they believe to be an adequate voice in national politics. **Intrastate federalism**—the representation and accommodation of regional interests within national political institutions—has failed to overcome the belief that Ontario and Quebec are always at the head of the line. Deprived of what they deem to be fair and adequate influence in Ottawa, the peripheral regions of the country have tended to rely on their provincial governments for the protection and promotion of their interests.

The fact that more MPs are elected from Ontario and Quebec than from all the other provinces combined has always been the root cause of Ottawa's tendency to favour central Canadian interests. This political factor has been reinforced by the ideological bias of Canadian politics, a bias that has tended to interpret Canadian history and identity in terms of experiences more germane to central Canada than to the peripheral regions. The very concept of "Canada" has been associated with a counter-revolutionary or Loyalist tradition based on a rejection of the values and political institutions of the United States and on the cultural dualism so important to the political history of central Canada. Neither of these experiences is central to the identity and political consciousness of western Canadians.[38] In the East, too, the national myths, symbols, and identities associated with "Canada" often have had little relationship to the experience of Maritimers.[39] "Canadians have never shared the same myth," states fifth-generation Albertan and political scientist Barry Cooper. "Not in the past, however far back you wish to go, and not today either."[40]

The dominance of Ontario and Quebec in national politics and the subordinate status of the interests and cultural values of the peripheral regions of the country have been reflected in what often were strained relations between Ottawa and the provincial governments of the peripheries. For example, although Ottawa has exercised its constitutional power to disallow provincial laws 112 times, only a few of these were laws passed by Ontario or Quebec.[41] When Manitoba joined Confederation in 1870 it did so without control over public lands situated in the province.[42] Ottawa retained control in order to promote its own nation-building strategy relating to railway construction and western settlement. Similarly, Ottawa kept these powers when Saskatchewan and Alberta became provinces in 1905,[43] using the argument that this was necessary to accomplish its immigration and settlement objectives for western Canada. All of these provinces received subsidies from Ottawa as compensation for the revenue they were deprived of by not controlling public lands and, in Alberta and Saskatchewan, natural resources. Their governments did not consider this to be adequate recompense for the quasi-colonial status imposed on them by Ottawa.

There is nothing subtle about the disallowance power, or about denying some provinces constitutional powers possessed by other provincial governments. In recent decades the list of grievances against Ottawa has comprised less blatant forms of policy discrimination against the interests of the peripheries. Among the items perennially on this list are claims that Ottawa does too little to support prairie grain farmers or the east coast fishing industry, and that the federal government's spending decisions unfairly favour Ontario and Quebec. Even in provinces like Alberta, British Columbia, and Saskatchewan, which are wealthy by Canadian standards, a sense of powerlessness in the face of central Canadian dominance has been a major component of their provincial politics. "The West," observes Alberta historian Doug Owram, "has never felt in control of its own destiny. None of the wealth of recent years has eased this feeling. In fact, the tremendous wealth of the region merely sharpens the contrast with the political powerlessness that exists on the national level."[44] Although the fact of having an Albertan, Stephen Harper, as Prime Minister has taken the edge off this sentiment, it has not disappeared entirely. The outrage of Albertans, several weeks after the 2008 election, when the opposition parties attempted to dislodge the Conservatives from power and replace them with a coalition government supported by the Bloc Québécois, showed that the region was still very conscious of the long decades when it was on the outside of federal politics, looking in. In a study commissioned by the Canada West Foundation, Loleen Berdahl argues that although western dissatisfaction with Ottawa has declined under the Conservative government, long-standing sentiments of resentment and mistrust could be reawakened by a change in political circumstances.[45]

This mismatch between the economic strength and political weakness of the West is more likely to sharpen than diminish in the future. Between 1996 and 2009 British Columbia's population grew by about 600,000 persons, Alberta's by roughly 859,000, but Quebec's by only about 506,000. During the five years from 2006 to 2011, the combined population increase of Alberta, British Columbia, and Saskatchewan was twice that of Quebec (706,701 vs 356,870) and as great as the increase in Ontario's population (691,593). The three westernmost provinces have for many years been among Canada's fastest-growing. The combined population of Alberta and BC is now larger than that of Quebec, but together they have 64 seats in the House of Commons, compared to Quebec's 75 seats. Moreover, the economic muscle of these western provinces has increased in recent years. About one-third of the 100 largest industrial firms in Canada have their head offices in the four western provinces, most of them resources companies. At the level of major cities, the economic prosperity and buoyant growth that have characterized Vancouver and Calgary for most of the last two decades contrasts sharply with the relative economic decline of Montreal, the hub of Quebec's economy.

Aware of their region's economic strength and its growing population, and with friends in high places since the Conservative Party won power in the 2006 election, western Canadians have expected that their voice in national politics will be heard. Part of this expectation is that Ottawa will not impose policies on their provincial governments or treat their provincial governments as junior partners in the Canadian enterprise, as many westerners believed was the case under years of Liberal rule. Under Prime Minister Stephen Harper, the Conservative government has embraced a policy that it calls "open federalism," intended to satisfy what have often been seen as the mutually exclusive viewpoints and interests of Quebec and the West. As Box 8.4 explains, the policy is not without its critics.

State Interests and Intergovernmental Conflict

The fact that Quebec is overwhelmingly francophone, while the other provinces are not, gives it a special set of interests that any Quebec government feels bound to defend. Likewise, grain farming and resource extraction in Saskatchewan, petroleum in Alberta, the automotive industry in Ontario, and forestry in British Columbia shape the positions taken by the governments of these provinces on taxation, trade, and other policies affecting these interests. Each province comprises a particular constellation of economic, social, and cultural interests that together influence the demands its provincial government makes on federalism. Intergovernmental conflict, then, is to some extent the clash of conflicting regional interests.

This is, however, only part of the explanation. Governments do not simply reflect societal interests. They actively shape these interests through their policies, sometimes deliberately and other times inadvertently. Moreover, governments have their own political and administrative interests, the pursuit of which may have nothing to do with the interests of those they represent. "Canadian federalism," Alan Cairns has argued, "is about governments, governments that are possessed of massive human and financial resources, that are driven by purposes fashioned by elites, and that accord high priority to their own long-term institutional self-interest."[46] This state-centred interpretation of federalism maintains that conflicts between governments are likely to be generated, or at least influenced, by the "institutional self-interest" of politicians and bureaucrats.

The evidence in support of this view is overwhelming. Intergovernmental turf wars, over their respective shares of particular tax fields and over which level will have jurisdiction over what policy areas, often seem remote from the concerns of Canadian citizens. For example, in its 2013 budget, Ottawa proposed the creation of a Canada Job Grant program for the unemployed. The program would provide unemployed workers with money to pay for training courses for highly skilled jobs. Provincial governments and employers would have to match the federal contribution to this program. The provincial governments reacted with a solid wall of opposition, demanding that their own job training programs not be replaced by this new shared-cost program and also that they have the right to opt out of the Canada Job Grant program with compensation to pay for their own provincial programs.[47] One suspects that unemployed workers who would be eligible to receive retraining money probably don't care very much, or at all, about who runs the program or who provides the money. But looked at from the state's point of view, how revenue sources and legislative competence are divided between levels of governments affects the ability of

Politics in Focus

BOX 8.4   "Open Federalism": Ideology, the Constitution, and Intergovernmental Style

In 2004, while he was the leader of the opposition in the House of Commons, Stephen Harper wrote an article published in the *Toronto Star* in which he explained what he called "open federalism." This was not the first time a party and its leader had attached a label to what was promised to be a new style and direction in federal–provincial relations. Soon after Confederation the *provincial rights* movement emerged, spearheaded by the Ontario government of Oliver Mowat. It was a reaction to what was perceived to be Ottawa's centralist designs for Canadian federalism. The term *co-operative federalism* was used by the Liberal Party and the NDP. It involved a growing role for Ottawa, in co-operation with the provincial governments, building and financing the Canadian welfare state. In the 1979 election campaign, Progressive Conservative Party leader Joe Clark memorably characterized Canada as a "community of communities." The term was not intended to refer to the multicultural aspects of Canadian society, but to Canada as a partnership of provincial communities in which people "live on a local scale." Clark's characterization was in response to the belief held by some Canadians, particularly in the West, that the style and direction of federalism under Pierre Trudeau's Liberal Party was too centralist. *Asymmetrical federalism* is another model of intergovernmental relations that basically involves a willingness to see different provinces exercise different powers and have a variety of relationships, both financial and in terms of legislative powers, to the federal government. The term has been used more often by political scientists than by politicians and it usually implies a special status for Quebec within Canadian federalism.

Open federalism, as advocated by Harper, borrows elements of the provincial rights movement, Joe Clark's vision of Canada as a community of communities, and asymmetrical federalism, without being reducible to any one of these models of federalism. What open federalism most assuredly rejects are the notions of a dominant role for Ottawa and a more centralized style of federalism.

The Conservative Party's 2005 policy declaration identified several features of open federalism. These included a shift in the federal–provincial balance towards the provinces, greater respect for what the Constitution says about the division of powers, reining in the federal spending power, a commitment to redressing the fiscal imbalance between Ottawa and the provinces, and willingness to accept special arrangements for Quebec (this last feature is inferred rather than stated outright). According to some critics, the real goal is smaller government, which is expected to be achieved by limiting and even reducing Ottawa's legislative and spending powers. Open federalism, they claim, is a flimsy cover for a hidden agenda of less federal involvement in social policy and retreat from environmental matters on the pretext that these are mainly in the provinces' domain.

This attribution of deceitful cleverness could be correct. But it may also be far off the mark. The Prime Minister and many of his closest and most trusted advisers are westerners who have long resented what they believed to be a sort of father-knows-best style of federalism. Westerners have never accepted the vision of themselves as junior partners in Canadian federalism, bound to defer to a national government whose priorities and agenda have most often favoured Ontario and Quebec. Those who airily dismiss the case for open federalism as an ideological smokescreen ignore a long history of opposition to centralizing visions of federalism in Canada going back to the early years of the country and John A. Macdonald's expectation and hope that the provincial governments would be mere "glorified municipalities." Much of this opposition—perhaps even most of it—has had little to do with the issues of left versus right, but a lot to do with whether regional or national interests and values should prevail.

politicians to pursue their interests in re-election, career advancement, and personal prestige, and their own conception of the public interest. So, too, in the case of bureaucratic officials, we may assume that they, also, are not indifferent towards matters that influence the future of the organizations and programs to which their personal careers, fortunes, and ambitions, and their own conception of the public interest, are tied.

During the 1970s and 1980s it became popular to speak of *province-building*. This involves the process of developing larger and more sophisticated provincial states, whose governments are more assertive in their relations with Ottawa. The concept is premised on Cairns's argument that elected governments and their bureaucracies, possessed of significant legislative and revenue-raising powers under the Constitution and supported by province-oriented economic interests, will attempt to shape economic and social development in their province in accordance with their own preferences and needs. Historically, province-building has been associated mainly with the provincial governments of Quebec and Alberta. For their different reasons—a nationalist agenda in the case of Quebec and conflict with Ottawa over the management of petroleum resources in the case of Alberta—these provinces were more likely than others to aggressively pursue greater control over their respective economies and provincial societies.[47]

One might have expected that Ontario would be at the forefront of province-building, given the size and competence of its provincial state and the fact that it presides over the country's most important provincial economy. Ontario's sheer weight in Canadian politics has meant that it generally has been able to count on a sympathetic hearing in Ottawa. With the exception of the NDP government of Bob Rae (1990–5) and more recent complaining during the Liberal government of Dalton McGuinty (2003–13) about the **fiscal imbalance** between what Ontario contributes to federal coffers and what it receives back in federal transfers and spending, aggressive and persistent "fed-bashing" has not been a popular blood sport among that province's politicians. In other respects, however, Ontario governments have not lagged behind their more aggressive counterparts, and frequently have been at the forefront in expanding the political and administrative reach of the provincial state.

Intergovernmental Relations

The Constitution, we have seen, does not establish a neat division of legislative and taxation powers between Ottawa and the provinces. All of the chief sources of public revenue—personal and corporate income taxes, payroll taxes, sales taxes, royalties on natural resources and public-sector borrowing—are shared between the two levels of government. Likewise, both the federal and provincial governments are involved in all the major policy fields. Defence and monetary policy come closest to being exclusive federal terrain, although provincial governments do not hesitate to express their views on such issues as the location of armed forces bases, major defence purchases, and interest rates. On the provincial side, snow removal, refuse collection, and sidewalk maintenance are the sorts of local activities that supposedly are free from federal involvement. But not entirely: the money that Ottawa transfers annually to the provinces affects the amounts that provincial governments pay to their municipalities, thereby having an impact on municipalities' ability to carry out these local functions.

Divided jurisdiction has given rise to a sprawling and complicated network of relations linking the federal and provincial governments. This network has often been compared to an iceberg, only a small part of which is visible to the eye. The "visible" tip of intergovernmental relations involves meetings of the Prime Minister and provincial premiers (first ministers' conferences) and meetings of provincial premiers. These meetings, which have become less frequent in recent years, always generate considerable media attention and some part of their proceedings usually takes place before the television cameras (see Figure 8.2). Less publicized, but far more frequent, are the hundreds of annual meetings between federal and provincial cabinet ministers and bureaucrats. Many of these meetings take place in the context of ongoing federal–provincial structures like the Continuing Committee on Economic and Fiscal Matters, established in 1955, and the Economic and Regional Development Agreements negotiated between Ottawa and the less affluent provinces. Others are generated by the wide range of shared-cost activities that link the two levels of government, from major spending programs such as the Canada Health Transfer and Canada Social Transfer to smaller federal subsidies such as for official minority-language education. In 2013, 79 federal–provincial meetings took place at the level of ministers, deputy ministers, and other senior officials.[48]

Executive federalism is a term sometimes used to describe the relations between cabinet ministers and other high-ranking officials of the two levels of government. The negotiations between them and the agreements they reach are usually undertaken with minimal, if any, input from either legislatures or the public. The lack of transparency character-istic of this decision-making process, combined with the fact that the distinction between federal and provincial responsibilities is often blurred by the deals it produces, has generated charges that

executive federalism is undemocratic. It is undemo-cratic because it undermines the role of elected legislatures whose role, if they have one at all, is usually limited to ratifying *faits accomplis*. Second, an agreement to finance jointly the cost of a pro-gram or to share a particular tax field or legislative power makes it difficult for citizens to determine which level of government should be held respon-sible for what policies. Third, executive federalism provides no meaningful opportunities for public debate of intergovernmental issues that affect the standard of health-care services, environmental conditions, post-secondary education, energy and natural resources, and other matters of real concern to citizens. Political parties, interest groups, and individual Canadians generally are excluded from a decision-making process dominated by cabinet ministers and intergovernmental affairs specialists of the two levels of government.

In addition to these indictments of executive fed-eralism, Donald Smiley lists three others.[49]

- It distorts the political agenda. Executive federalism has a territorial bias. It reinforces the significance of territorially concentrated

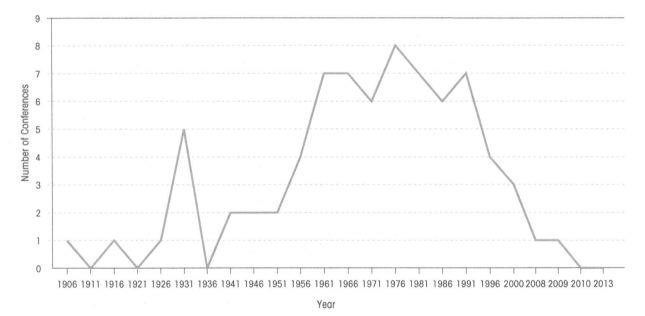

FIGURE 8.2   First Ministers' Conferences, 1906–2013

Source: Adapted with author updates from Canadian Intergovernmental Conference Secretariat, "First Ministers' Conferences, 1906–2004," at <www.scics.gc.ca/CMFiles/fmp_e.pdf>.

interests and of the provincial governments that represent them, at the same time as it undervalues the importance of other interests that cut across provincial boundaries.

- It fuels government expansion. Competitive relations between Ottawa and the provinces have produced inefficient duplication, as each level of government has its own programs and bureaucracies to pursue similar goals.
- It perpetuates intergovernmental conflict. The increasing sophistication of executive federalism, conducted through specialized bureaus staffed by intergovernmental affairs specialists, reduces the likelihood of resolving federal–provincial disputes. This is because specialized intergovernmental affairs bureaus, which exist in all provinces and at the federal level, and the experts who staff them tend to perceive issues in terms of the powers and jurisdiction of their particular government. Intergovernmental conflict is in a sense institutionalized by the fact that what is perceived to be at stake are the power, resources, and prestige of one's government.

With all due respect to Professor Smiley, it is hard to imagine how intergovernmental affairs could operate in Canada without the architecture and processes of executive federalism. Overlapping authority is an unavoidable fact of life under Canada's federal Constitution. In light of this, is it realistic to imagine that complex administrative and financial agreements can be negotiated in public forums? And besides, much of policy-making is carried on in a closed fashion, dominated by cabinet ministers and bureaucratic elites. Why condemn executive federalism for traits that are deeply embedded in Canadian policy-making generally? Still, the characteristics of executive federalism are out of sync with the expectations many Canadians have about how governance should be conducted. Transparency and opportunities for participation are more likely to be insisted on today than during the decades of the 1960s and 1970s when executive federalism became the hallmark of intergovernmental relations. Governments will continue to

conduct much of their negotiations behind closed doors and the constitutional division of powers will continue to be characterized by overlap, competition, and ambiguity. But public acceptance of this and other elitist forms of policy-making is today much weaker than in decades past.

The fact that meetings of the Prime Minister and premiers have virtually disappeared warrants some comment. These were once an annual occurrence that would be televised live and that often provided moments of drama, particularly when Prime Minister Trudeau and Premier Lévesque were at the table! Prime Minister Harper's critics charge that he avoids these meetings because of a decision-making style averse to circumstances he is unable to control. This may be true. The Prime Minister's spokespersons present the matter rather differently. They point out that Harper had more than 250 face-to-face meetings and telephone conversations with premiers between his election in 2006 and the summer of 2013. They say that the Prime Minister prefers this one-on-one style because it fits with his belief that, by and large, the provinces should be left to manage their own affairs without federal interference and because history shows that first ministers' meetings too often resulted in a wall of provincial demands for more money from Ottawa.[50]

Financing Federalism

From the very beginning, money has been at the centre of intergovernmental relations. The Confederation agreement included an annual per capita subsidy that Ottawa would pay to all provincial governments.[51] Moreover, the new federal government agreed to assume liability for the debts of the provinces as they stood in 1867.[52] Taxation powers were divided between the two levels of government, with Ottawa receiving what were at the time the major sources of public revenue.

These financial arrangements have never been adequate. The provinces' legislative responsibilities proved to be much more extensive and expensive than the founders had anticipated. This has been referred to as the *fiscal gap*. Provincial governments attempted to fill this gap between their revenues and their expenditure requirements through an increasing array of provincial taxes. Licence fees, succession duties, and personal and corporate income taxes all were used to increase provincial revenues. In addition, the provinces pressed Ottawa for more money. Indeed, only two years after Confederation the federal subsidy paid to Nova Scotia was increased. An important precedent was thereby established: federal–provincial financial relations are determined by governments, not by the Constitution.

Today, combined provincial and local revenues and expenditures surpass those of Ottawa. This was not always the case. In 1950 combined provincial and local revenues were about half those of the federal government. Sixty years later, combined provincial and local own-source revenues—excluding transfers from Ottawa—exceed those of the federal government by about 20 per cent.[53] The revenue position of the provinces improved steadily between the 1950s and the 1970s, as Ottawa conceded *tax room*—i.e., an increasing share of particular revenue sources like the personal income tax—to aggressive provincial governments. But at the same time, provincial dependence on subsidies from Ottawa remains high in several provinces. In the case of the poorest provinces, money from Ottawa currently accounts for about half of their total revenue. Part of this dependence has been encouraged by Ottawa through **shared-cost programs**, provincially administered programs where Ottawa's financial contribution is geared to the amount that a province spends. In the 1960s, when many of these programs were being put in place, it was common for Ottawa to match provincial spending dollar for dollar.

Created in 1966 from what previously had been a number of separate spending programs, the major shared-cost program in Canada was the Canada Assistance Plan (CAP), which financed welfare and other provincial social services. Beginning in 1991 Ottawa placed a cap on the annual increase in its contribution to provinces under this plan. Four years later the federal government replaced CAP with the Canada Health and Social Transfer to the provinces, the amount of which was not geared to provincial spending. Federal grants for health care

and post-secondary education also were launched on a shared-cost basis, but were converted by Ottawa into **block funding** programs through the Federal–Provincial Fiscal Arrangements Act of 1977. The federal government argued, reasonably enough, that the shared-cost formula did not encourage the provinces to control program costs. Under block funding, Ottawa's financial contribution is geared to the previous year's subsidy plus an amount calculated on the basis of growth in the recipient province's gross product. Ottawa is not obliged to match provincial spending; indeed, the effect of the switch to block funding was to transfer an increasing share of the burden of health care and post-secondary education costs onto the shoulders of the provinces.

But perhaps this is where the burden belongs. After all, these social programs fall under the constitutional jurisdiction of the provinces. For their part the provincial governments argued that Ottawa encouraged them to spend more on social services by offering to share program costs on a matching basis. It was unfair, they claimed, for the federal government to try to back out of financing policy areas whose growth it encouraged. In fact, the government of British Columbia launched a court challenge in response to Ottawa's 1991 cap on the annual increase in federal transfers for social assistance. The Supreme Court ruled, however, that Ottawa acted within its constitutional authority.[54] The provinces' second complaint was that their ability to increase their own-source revenues to compensate for reduced federal transfer payments is limited because they share all of the major tax fields with Ottawa. Unless the federal government is willing to give up some tax room (i.e., some of its share of total tax revenue from a particular source) to the provinces, provincial governments face the hard choice of increasing the total tax burden on their citizens, charging or increasing user fees (e.g., tuition fees), or cutting back on program expenditures. A third grievance came from the less affluent provinces. They argued that any reduction in Ottawa's commitment to financing provincial social services hurts the poorer provinces more than it does the wealthier ones. The Maritime provinces in particular have been and continue to be dependent on federal transfers in order to offer a level of social services comparable to that in other provinces. Figure 8.3 shows federal transfers to the provinces in 2012–13 as a percentage of provincial gross revenues.

Some of the money Ottawa transfers to the provinces carries conditions as to how it must be spent. These are called conditional grants. Transfers with no strings attached are called unconditional grants. Important examples of both include the following:

- Provincial social assistance programs must be based exclusively on need, and must not make previous residency in the province a condition for receiving benefits.
- The block transfers that Ottawa makes to the provinces under the Canada Health Transfer (CHT) and the Canada Social Transfer (CST) must be spent on health care and post-secondary education, and social services previously covered under CAP.

- The Canada Health Act, 1984 includes a provision that reduces Ottawa's payment to provincial governments that permit physicians to extra-bill their patients. The terms of the CHT and CST also specify that provinces must respect the principles of the Canada Health Act, 1965 (portability of coverage between provinces, comprehensiveness of provincial plans, universality, public funding, and public administration). Ottawa's contribution to provincial health-care spending is, therefore, subject to some conditions.
- Equalization grants are paid to provincial governments whose per capita tax revenues (according to a complex formula negotiated between Ottawa and the provinces) fall below the average of the two most affluent provinces. **Equalization** accounts for about one-quarter of all federal cash transfers to the provinces and about one-fifth of the total revenue of the least affluent

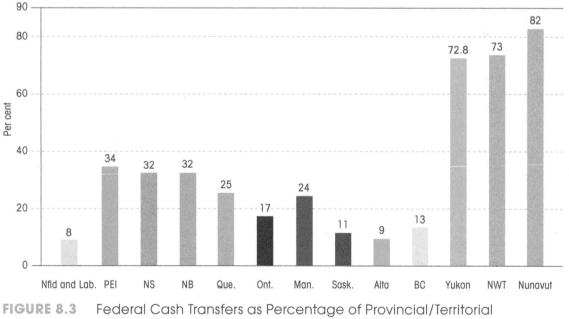

FIGURE 8.3   Federal Cash Transfers as Percentage of Provincial/Territorial Government Revenues, 2012–13

The fact that federal transfers as a share of provincial revenue are lowest in the case of Newfoundland and Labrador is due to the 1985 Atlantic Accord, under which the oil and gas reserves off the coast of the province, which the federal government owns, may be taxed by the province. In exchange for this the province's equalization transfer, which used to constitute a very large share of provincial revenue, has been phased out. The per capita non-equalization cash transfers that Newfoundland and Labrador receives from Ottawa continue to be higher than those of any other province.

Source: Canada, Department of Finance, *Federal Support to Provinces and Territories*, at: <www.fin.gc.ca/access/fedprov-eng.asp>. Reproduced with the permission of the Minister of Finance Canada, 2014.

TABLE 8.3 Federal Transfers to Provinces and Territories, 2005–15

Major Transfers	(millions of dollars)									
	2005–6	2006–7	2007–8	2008–9	2009–10	2010–11	2011–12	2012–13	2013–14	2014–15
Canada Health Transfer	20,310	20,140	21,729	22,768	24,476	25,672	26,952	28,569	30,283	32,114
Canada Social Transfer	8,415	8,500	9,607	10,552	10,857	11,179	11,514	11,859	12,215	12,582
Equalization	10,907	11,535	12,925	13,462	14,185	14,372	14,659	15,423	16,105	16,669
Offshore Accords	219	386	563	663	645	869	787	443	350	203
Territorial Formula Financing	2,058	2,118	2,279	2,313	2,498	2,664	2,876	3,111	3,288	3,469
Other Payments					74	525	952	680	56	
Total Federal Support	41,909	42,680	47,102	49,758	52,736	55,281	57,539	60,085	62,297	65,037
Change from 2005–6		+.771	+5,193	+7,849	+10,827	+13,372	+15,830	+18,176	+20,389	+23,128
Per Capita Allocation (dollars)	1,301	1,312	1,434	1,499	1,570	1,628	1,683	1,731	1,774	1,831

Source: Department of Finance, *Federal Support to Provinces and Territories*, at: <www.fin.gc.ca/access/fedprov-eng.asp>. Reproduced with the permission of the Minister of Finance Canada, 2014.

provincial governments. It carries no conditions as to how it must be spent. Table 8.3 provides a breakdown of federal transfers to the provinces.

The adequacy of federal transfers is not the only issue that has set Ottawa against the provincial governments. Another long-standing complaint of the provinces is that shared-cost programs distort provincial spending priorities because of the enticement of matching federal grants. Ottawa's spending power, they argue, permits undue federal interference in matters of provincial jurisdiction. Over the years the government of Quebec has been most insistent about this. Indeed, during the 1950s the provincial government of Maurice Duplessis refused to accept federal money for the construction of Quebec's portion of the Trans-Canada Highway and for universities, and was not even compensated for the fact that Canadian taxpayers

residing in Quebec were paying for these programs in the other provinces. In 1965 the Quebec government of Jean Lesage opted out of the newly created Canada Assistance Plan (although Quebec has never been freed from the fairly minimal program standards that Ottawa sets) and some other conditional grant programs, receiving compensation in the form of tax room surrendered by Ottawa to the province. Both the Meech Lake and Charlottetown Accords included a provision that would have obligated Ottawa to provide "reasonable compensation" to any provincial government choosing not to participate in a new national shared-cost program, so long as the province's own program was "compatible with the national objectives." Critics argued that this opened the door for an erosion of **national standards** in social policy. Defenders claimed that this particular section just constitutionalized a long-standing practice in Canadian federalism.

Politics in Focus

BOX 8.5 Two Former Premiers and Two Views on Federal Transfers

For . . .

No Canadian should have his or her life chances determined solely by geography. Canadians enjoy a political culture much like a family; we are all responsible for each other. These principles, enshrined in our Constitution, differentiate us from our friends in the United States where no such program exists. The vehicle for leveling the national playing field is the country's equalization program. Because of equalization, the gap between richer and poorer provinces has been reduced. The Canadian people understand the principle. (Polls demonstrate) that overwhelming majorities in each province support equalization.

Still, ideological opponents of equalization argue that such a program is wrong; they claim that it interferes with the operation of market forces and perpetuates poverty in some regions of the country. These claims are demonstrably wrong. Equalization has never prevented provinces from developing their own natural resources. Saskatchewan's oil and natural gas industries were developed even though that province's equalization payments declined as a result. Equalization did not obstruct the mining of potash in Saskatchewan, nickel in Manitoba, and hydroelectric development in Quebec, Manitoba, and Newfoundland and Labrador. There is no reason for it to be otherwise in the future. Furthermore, Ontario has always supported equalization, recognizing as it does that a strong Canada also strengthens that province.

Source: Excerpt from Howard Pawley, former Premier of Manitoba (1981–8) and Adjunct Professor, University of Windsor, in *Opinion Canada 7*, 10 (17 Mar. 2005).

Against . . .

I think it was Karl Marx who once said that religion is the opiate of the masses. Well, I can tell you that federal dependency is the opiate of this region, Atlantic Canada. Dependency—unemployment insurance, welfare cheques, transfer payments—have all become a narcotic to us to which we have become addicted. And there is not a person in this room that can tell you and me that we have not been influenced and affected, and had our behaviour modified by being part of that culture, because it shaped everything that we are. We know it to be true. We know it better than anybody else in Canada.

Looking at experience from all over the world, I can tell you that those jurisdictions which establish low and predictable corporate tax regimes end up resulting in much better growth, and long-term growth, and a much better environment for business to prosper.

What we need to do is get rid of all of the make-work projects and the money we spend transferring people to federal unemployment. We need to get rid of all those programs and either get rid of the taxes low income people pay or offer income supplementation so they are always better off working in a job. If we do that, if we change that incentive system, it will have a powerful impact on Atlantic Canada.

I despise the people who whine and snivel about their lot in life within this country. People who tell us that, unless they get their lighthouses saved, they're going to separate from Canada, have no time in my book. We may not like base closures in Atlantic Canada, and we certainly don't like transfer payment cuts . . . but we will not—we will not—consider that an act of alienation or humiliation.

Source: Excerpt from Frank McKenna, former Premier of New Brunswick (1987–97), in a speech to the Atlantic Vision Conference of Atlantic Canadian Premiers in Moncton, NB, 9 Oct. 1997.

The Federal Spending Power, National Standards, and the Social Union

In the 1990s it became popular to vilify certain provincial governments, particularly the Conservative governments of Ralph Klein in Alberta and Mike Harris in Ontario, for having undermined national standards in social programs. In fact, however, one of the major threats to national standards came from Ottawa's shrinking financial commitment to provincially administered social programs. Federal transfers as a share of provincial program spending fell from 21 per cent in 1986–7 to 16 per cent in 1996–7.[55] The wealthier provinces, including Ontario, Alberta, and British Columbia, faced the largest burden of these federal cuts, starting with Ottawa's 1990 decision to limit the annual increase in Canada Assistance Plan payments to these provinces to 5 per cent.

Ottawa's retreat from financing provincial social programs became unmistakable with the 1995 federal budget. Described as a "new vision of confederation" by Liberal Finance Minister Paul Martin, the 1995 budget replaced the shared-cost programs that paid for welfare and social services under the CAP and EPF funding for health and post-secondary education with a single block transfer called the Canada Health and Social Transfer (CHST). The CHST institutionalized the ad hoc freezes and caps on transfers that both Liberal and Tory governments imposed from the early 1980s. It did so, in Ottawa's words, by ensuring that "the amounts transferred will not be determined by provincial spending decisions (as under cost-sharing)."[56] Caps and freezes also had this effect, the difference being that Ottawa could always excuse what were effectively transfer cuts by citing their "temporary" nature. The CHST appeared to put the decisive nail in the coffin of shared-cost programs and thus to mark a retreat from Ottawa's commitment to maintaining national standards in social policy, a commitment that has always depended on the federal spending power. In 2004 the CHST

was divided into the Canada Health Transfer and the Canada Social Transfer, a change that provided greater transparency in identifying how much money was being transferred for what provincial spending purposes.

The appearance may, however, be deceptive. The Liberals' determination to rein in federal transfers to the provinces was not matched by a corresponding rhetoric of decentralization. On the contrary, the Liberal government refused to concede ground on the issue of national standards, particularly in regard to the health-care system (see Box 8.6). Their message to the provinces was this: we will give you fewer and fewer dollars with which to pay for your health-care services, but we will continue to set conditions on how those services must operate.

The Liberals' resolve was put to the test by the Conservative government of Alberta, which allowed the establishment of private clinics for certain health services like cataract operations, where patients, for a price, can jump the queue they would otherwise face in the publicly funded system. At the end of the day, however, all Ottawa could do was withhold some of the health-care dollars Alberta received from the feds. For a wealthy province like Alberta, where federal cash transfers amount to less than 10 per cent of the provincial health-care budget, this is a penalty without much sting.

In explaining the advantages of the CHST, the 1995 budget documents stated that it would "end the intrusiveness of previous cost-sharing arrangements."[57] More specifically, the transition to block funding under the CHST was argued to have the following beneficial effects:

- Provinces will no longer be subject to rules stipulating which expenditures are eligible for cost-sharing or not.
- Provinces will be free to pursue their own innovative approaches to social security reform.
- The expense of administering cost-sharing will be eliminated.
- Federal expenditures will no longer be driven by provincial decisions on how, and to whom, to provide social assistance and social services.[58]

Provinces would not, however, be free to do whatever they pleased under the new fiscal arrangements. The Liberal budget mentioned health care and social assistance as two areas where national standards would be maintained. In the case of social assistance this amounted only to an interdiction on minimum residency requirements. In regard to health care, the Liberals insisted that provinces would have to respect the principles of the Canada Health Act. But even if Ottawa was able to enforce national standards on the provinces, critics noted that the lumping together of Ottawa's transfer for health care, social assistance, and post-secondary education under the CHST would permit provinces greater room to redistribute their spending between politically unpopular welfare programs and more popular health-care and education spending.

Ottawa's retreat from its financial commitment to provincially administered social programs—a retreat motivated more by the Liberal government's desire to reduce its budget deficit rather than by what Finance Minister Martin grandly called a "new vision of federalism"—was not received well by provincial governments. Ottawa's success in transforming its own budget deficits into surpluses was largely due to cuts in transfers to the provinces, the use of Employment Insurance fund surpluses as general revenue, and increased federal tax revenues during the economic boom of the mid- to late 1990s. Very little of the turnaround in federal finances was due to cuts in Ottawa's program spending, although the Liberal government certainly conveyed this impression. From the provinces' point of view, Ottawa's deficit-cutting strategy was at their expense, leaving provincial governments with the politically difficult choices between raising taxes or cutting services or doing a bit of both. Moreover, the Liberal government's insistence that national standards for health care and welfare would have to be respected was particularly galling, ignoring the old adage that he who pays the piper calls the tune.

Graeme MacKay/Artizans.com

Ottawa's contributions to health care will keep pace with provincial spending until 2016–17, after which Ottawa's total share of health-care spending may begin to fall. As a result, the provinces will need to introduce cost-saving measures. In this cartoon, the artist suggests that one such "creative cost-saving measure" might be to revert to nineteenth-century forms of treatment.

This was the background to the idea of a Canadian *social union*, a concept that emerged in the wake of the transfer cuts announced in Ottawa's 1995 budget. Although the meaning attributed to the term depended on who was defining it, it is fair to say that the social union involved some new set of arrangements for funding and determining program standards in the areas of health, welfare, and post-secondary education. Some provincial governments viewed the social union as a commitment to national standards in social policy that are not federally imposed standards, but that instead are negotiated between the provinces and Ottawa in a spirit that respects each province's constitutional authority in matters of social policy. This was a decentralized version of the social union, under which the balance of control over and money to fund social programs would shift to the provinces. Ottawa and some of the more transfer-dependent provinces viewed the social union differently, insisting on a central role for the feds in maintaining the

Governing Realities

BOX 8.6 Health Care and Federalism: Canada's Second Longest-Running Soap Opera

After the issue of Quebec's constitutional status, health care has a reasonable claim to being Canadian federalism's second longest-running soap opera. Elements of intrigue, betrayal, good, and evil intermingle in a story that reveals much about the nature of intergovernmental relations.

It may seem odd that there is a story to be told, given the frequent claim that health is an area of exclusive provincial jurisdiction under the Constitution. But the reality is much more complicated. As the Supreme Court observed in a 1982 ruling, "'health' is not a matter which is subject to specific constitutional assignment but instead is an amorphous topic which can be addressed by valid federal or provincial legislation, depending on the circumstances of each case on the nature or scope of the health problem in question."[59] Although the provinces reject the Court's reasoning, Ottawa has been able to enter the field of health care through its spending power, its authority over criminal law, POGG, and several other constitutional levers that include authority with respect to Aboriginal affairs,

patents, some aspects of the environment, and sports and fitness.[60]

A "soap opera digest" summary of how the story has unfolded might go something like this. Ottawa and the provincial governments co-operated during the 1960s to create a national health-care system that would be administered by the provinces, but where they would share the costs with the federal government. Ottawa, flush with revenue in the 1960s and disposed to encourage provinces to spend money on social programs under provincial jurisdiction, agreed to match provincial spending on health care, a formula that provided little incentive for the provinces to control costs. The feds began to back away from this open-ended commitment to health care in the late 1970s. Over the next 20 years the federal contribution to health care, as a share of total public spending on health, would drop dramatically from about 50 per cent to 20 per cent.

Provincial cries of betrayal were met with federal accusations of provincial treachery, as Ottawa accused

interprovincial uniformity of social program standards, limiting provincial barriers against citizens from other provinces when it comes to social services, and continuing a strong federal role in financing social programs. The Quebec government kept its distance from the formal social union negotiations, insisting on a principle that has long been defended by provincial governments of various party stripes in Quebec, namely, that neither Ottawa nor the other provinces have any constitutional authority to interfere with Quebec's autonomy in setting its standards for social policy.[63]

Ideology was never very far from the surface of debates on the social union. To the degree that the social union was associated with a redistribution of power and money away from Ottawa and towards the provinces, it was often characterized as being part of a market-oriented agenda that was hostile

to entitlements and the welfare state. This characterization, however, was always overly simplistic and misleading. It is certainly true that the ideologically conservative governments of Ontario and Alberta in the later 1990s preferred a version of the social union that would increase their autonomy in determining standards in provincial social policy and that, as a consequence, would weaken Ottawa's ability to set and enforce national standards. But it is also the case that the NDP government in British Columbia and the PQ government in Quebec—neither of which were ideological soulmates of their Ontario and Alberta counterparts—also supported more provincial autonomy.

On 4 February 1999, Prime Minister Chrétien and nine of the 10 provincial premiers agreed to the Social Union Framework Agreement (SUFA). Quebec's separatist Premier Lucien Bouchard was some of the provinces of allowing creeping privatization and the importation of "American-style" health care. No one could agree on the numbers. Ottawa protested that its contribution was much greater than the provinces claimed, if the mysterious phenomenon of "tax points" were included. Ottawa threatened to withhold dollars from Alberta in a struggle characterized by some as nothing short of good, compassionate Canadianism versus evil individualistic conservatism.

By the end of the 1990s Ottawa and several of the provinces launched major studies of the health-care system, producing duelling reports on what was wrong and what to do about it. Alberta's Mazankowski Report recommended greater room for private elements to operate alongside the public health-care system. Ottawa's Romanow Report recommended more spending—much more spending—as a major part of the solution to the system's woes. In early 2004, Ottawa and the provinces agreed to a deal whereby $41.3 billion in new health-care funding would be transferred to the provinces over the following 10 years. This ensured that the federal contribution to provincial health-care spending did not decline during the period of the agreement and, to

some degree, reduced the intergovernmental tension associated with health-care spending.[61]

But not entirely. Well into its fourth decade, there is little likelihood that the Canadian health-care soap opera will disappear from the prime-time schedule anytime soon. It became an important campaign issue in the 2004 and 2006 federal elections. In 2012 the Parliamentary Budget Officer, Kevin Page, issued a report in which he stated that Ottawa's contributions to health care would keep pace with provincial spending until 2016–17, after which they would be tied to the rate of economic growth.[62] Assuming that increases in health-care spending continue to outstrip the rate of increase in the economy, which has been the case for years, this means that Ottawa's share of total health-care spending will begin to fall. This will be good for Ottawa, Page notes, giving it more leeway to cut taxes and pay down its debt, but will leave the provinces with harder choices about cutting spending, increasing taxes, or both.

If there is a federalism lesson to be learned from the last 30 years of intergovernmental conflict over health care it is this: sharing the costs of an expensive policy area is a prescription for political and bureaucratic rivalry, muddied accountability, and mutual recriminations.

present but refused to sign the agreement, maintaining that Ottawa's retention of the right to set national standards in social policy and penalize provinces that refused to conform to those standards represented an unconstitutional intrusion into matters of provincial jurisdiction. In taking this stand Premier Bouchard remained faithful to a position that all Quebec governments, separatist and non-separatist, have insisted on since the 1960s.

The willingness of Alberta, Ontario, and British Columbia to agree to such a social union pact, with Ottawa formally retaining its right to withhold money from any province that, in its view, violated the principles of the social union and to initiate new federal programs in the area of social policy, was probably due to money. Ottawa promised all of the provinces more money—about $2.5

billion per year in new health-care funding—which, according to critics, really amounted to a reinstatement of federal transfers that had been cut over the previous few years. Only Quebec, for political reasons, was able to reject this enticement. The Quebec government was alone in insisting that the SUFA include the right of a province to get out of new national social programs with financial compensation to operate its own programs free of federal standards. Ottawa insisted that the social union pact is binding on Quebec, despite that province's unwillingness to sign it. In this case "binding" meant that the Quebec government received some new health-care funding, just like the other provinces, but beyond this Ottawa lacked any serious levers to compel an unco-operative Quebec government into complying with the other provisions of the deal.

Current Challenges of Fiscal Federalism

The idea of a Canadian social union has moved to the margins of the conversation on Canadian inter-governmental relations. The federal Conservative government, committed to the notion of open federalism, is not inclined to talk very much about national standards in social programs and certainly not to talk about imposing such standards on provincial governments. In its place the issue of fiscal disparities between the provinces has assumed centre stage. This has long been an issue in Canadian federalism. Ontario, Alberta, and British Columbia, over most of the last several decades, have contributed more to federal coffers than they received back in transfers. These "have" provinces provided the revenue redistributed to "have-not" provinces, enabling the latter to finance a level of social services they otherwise would not have been able to afford. In recent years, however, the fiscal disparities issue has assumed a rather different character. "Fiscal disparities in Canada," writes Matthew Mendelsohn, "are increasingly driven by commodities, yet our fiscal arrangements do not redistribute commodity wealth. This places Ontario in a unique situation, lacking the natural resources of the oil and gas provinces, but also significantly more prosperous than the traditional Equalization-receiving provinces."[64] Alberta, Saskatchewan, and Newfoundland and Labrador, with significant natural resources wealth from which they derive much of their provincial revenue capacity, are now the leading "have" provinces in Canada's system of fiscal federalism. Ontario, the country's largest province, has received equalization payments since 2009. But at the same time, Ontario's citizens and businesses contribute more to federal coffers than the province receives back in federal transfers. Thus the rather bizarre situation exists whereby the province that continues to pay the single largest share of the redistribution of wealth between Canadian provinces is officially a "have-not" province and is likely to remain so as long as the world price for oil and gas and some other natural resources—the basis of the superior revenue capacity of Alberta, Saskatchewan, and Newfoundland and

Labrador—remains high. Mendelsohn and others argue that this undermines Ontario's ability to pay for its own services, which already are financed at levels lower than in most other provinces, and to invest in provincial economic development.

Aside from Ontario politicians and some experts on fiscal federalism, few people share a sense of urgency when it comes to the new face of fiscal disparities. The provinces whose wealth and revenue capacity are based on natural resources are unmoved by Ontario's dilemma. One might imagine that the Atlantic provinces would see that a poorer Ontario is, ultimately, to their disadvantage. Alberta and Saskatchewan are wealthy, but they are not large enough to replace Ontario as the motor for the redistribution of wealth in Canada. Roughly 40 per cent of federal revenue is collected in Ontario, compared to about 15 per cent in Alberta.

On top of this problem of fiscal disparity between the provinces is the even older problem of the fiscal gap, i.e., the difference between the revenue-generating capacity of provinces and the cost of their policy responsibilities. The nature of the problem is described by Thomas Courchene:

> [T]he provinces are facing progressively insatiable demands for greater spending in those areas that are not only demand-driven but as well have powerful political constituencies—medical practitioners, hospitals, and pharmacare among others. While those delivering the health services typically embody high-level human capital and embrace state-of-the art technology, the reality is that the services themselves tend to be consumption oriented. Under the pressures of an aging population these expenditures will be, and already are, crowding out provincial spending in areas that are investment-related such as human-capital development and research areas essential for success in the information era.[65]

Finding a solution to this problem is almost certainly more difficult than resolving that of Ontario's anomalous role as both equalization recipient and major source of the money used to redistribute wealth between Canada's provinces.

Starting Points for Research

Herman Bakvis and Grace Skogstad, eds, *Canadian Federalism: Performance, Effectiveness, and Legitimacy*, 3rd edn (Toronto: Oxford University Press, 2012). This is the best recent reader on Canadian federalism and intergovernmental relations.

Alan Cairns, *Charter versus Federalism: The Dilemmas of Constitutional Reform* (Montreal and Kingston: McGill-Queen's University Press, 1992). The essays in this collection examine the demise of the older elite accommodation-style politics and the dominance of federalism issues, and the ascendance of what Cairns calls "Charter Canadians," whose identities and demands on government are powerfully influenced by the Charter.

Richard Simeon, *Political Science and Federalism: Seven Decades of Scholarly Engagement* (Kingston, Ont.: Institute of Intergovernmental Relations, Queen's University, 2002). This is a highly readable survey of the study of federalism in Canada since the Great Depression.

David E. Smith, *Federalism and the Constitution of Canada* (Toronto: University of Toronto Press, 2010). A marvellous history of Canadian federalism from its origins by one of Canada's foremost experts on the subject.

Pierre Elliott Trudeau, *Federalism and the French Canadians* (Toronto: Macmillan, 1968). In these classic essays, written before he became Prime Minister, Trudeau considered the meaning and significance of Canadian federalism, the protection of French language rights, the role of Quebec in Canadian federalism, and the development of nationalism in French Canada.

Review Exercises

1. What is the Council of the Federation? Do you think that it plays an important role in intergovernmental relations? Should its role be strengthened and perhaps even included in the Constitution? Why or why not?

2. Visit the website for one of the provincial or territorial governments (go to www.cic.gc.ca/ENGLISH/newcomers/before-provincial-gov.asp and then click on a province, or enter the name of the province and the words "provincial government" in a Google search). Make a list of the main public issues discussed at the site. What information is provided about the relationship of the province's/territory's finances and programs to Ottawa?

3. Draw up a list of issues that would have to be resolved if Quebec were to separate from the rest of Canada. Attach a level of difficulty to each, ranging from 1 (very easily resolvable) to 10 (almost impossible to resolve).

4. Does it matter which level of government pays for what share of health-care costs and which government or governments set the rules for health policy? In answering this question be sure to address the issues of constitutionality, political accountability, Canadian values, and taxpayer interests.

9

The Machinery of Government

Modern government is a vast and complicated affair. This chapter examines the key components of the machinery of government, including the following topics:

- The monarch and Governor General.
- The Prime Minister and cabinet.
- Central agencies.
- The legislature.
- The influence and activities of MPs.
- A democratic deficit?
- The courts.
- How a law is passed.

The Rotunda, also known as Confederation Hall, is located in the Centre Block of Parliament. It functions as the midpoint of the hallway between the House of Commons and the Senate, the two parts of Canada's legislature. (Krzysztof Dydynski/Getty Images)

According to many commentators, Canada's machinery of government is broken, or at least in need of a serious overhaul. Several of the country's most respected political scientists and journalists have complained that power has become too concentrated in the hands of the Prime Minister and his closest advisers. This, they say, undermines democratic accountability. Some critics charge that the courts have become too powerful, going well beyond their traditional role in interpreting the law to significantly influence policy. It seems that everyone, to one degree or another, agrees that Parliament is dysfunctional. Proposals to reform Question Period, revamp the committee system, loosen party discipline, and make the Senate elected or abolish it entirely are among the many solutions that have been proposed for what are seen to be the legislature's shortcomings. Talk of a democratic deficit has been ongoing for many years, much of this linked to what are believed to be the broken or worn out parts of the machinery of government.

Before we can judge whether these claims have merit, we need to understand how Canada's system of government operates. The formal organization of the government of Canada is shown in Figure 9.1. Portrayed this way, the structure appears to be quite simple—deceptively simple, as it turns out! The three branches of government coincide with three major functions of democratic governance: the legislature makes the laws; the executive branch implements the laws; and the judicial branch interprets the laws.

In reality, however, these compartments are not watertight. The legislature does indeed debate and pass laws, but these laws typically originate in the executive branch as bills that are seldom expected to change much, if at all, as they make their way through the legislative mill. The legislature, in fact, is dominated by a small group of its members—the Prime Minister and cabinet—who oversee the executive branch. The judicial branch of government does not, strictly speaking, involve itself in the making of laws. In recent times, however, Canadian courts have played a major role in the determination of policy on such matters as Sunday shopping, abortion, Aboriginal landownership, the collective bargaining rights of workers, and same-sex benefits such as pension rights for gays and lesbians and the legal definition of marriage. The courts may truly be said to have made policy, or at least shaped it in decisive ways, on many important public issues. As we saw in Chapter 7, critics of the courts argue

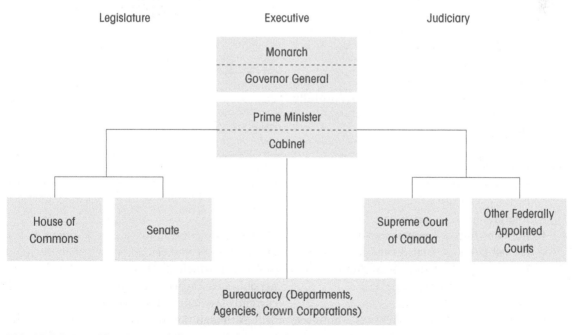

FIGURE 9.1 The Formal Organization of Canadian Government

that through their responsibility for interpreting the law judges become involved in what amounts to policy-making. The bureaucrats whose job it is to implement the laws passed by Parliament often have enormous discretion in determining the actual meaning of legislation that provides them with only very general guidelines about what they are expected to do. When elected officials delegate discretion to non-elected bureaucrats are they not also delegating part of their law-making function?

While the actual operations of the machinery of Canadian government are more complex than its formal organization in Figure 9.1 suggests, nevertheless, the respective roles of the legislative, executive, and judicial branches are significantly different and their differences are rooted in our expectations for democratic government. These expectations can be briefly summarized as follows:

The legislative branch shall . . .
- represent the people and be accountable to them through periodic elections;
- debate public issues and provide a forum for competition between political parties;
- make laws.

The executive branch shall . . .
- implement the laws;
- ensure that the public's business is carried out efficiently, accountably, and in accordance with the law;
- be non-partisan at the bureaucratic level, such that non-elected officials faithfully carry out the policies of whatever party forms the government of the day.

The judicial branch shall . . .
- be non-partisan and free from interference by the government;
- interpret the law's meaning;
- not substitute its preferences for those of elected public officials in matters of public policy, as distinct from legal and constitutional interpretation.

Democratic expectations are not, however, immutable. Today, many people expect that the bureaucracy should be representative of the population it serves, an expectation that may affect bureaucratic recruitment and promotion policies. Some argue that it is neither realistic nor desirable to expect non-elected officials to be politically neutral and that accountability for policy (as distinct from its implementation) should be shared between politicians and bureaucrats. The elevated status of Canadian courts in the political process since the Charter of Rights and Freedoms was passed in 1982 has been welcomed by those who see judges as more likely than politicians to protect rights and promote democracy. Others lament that the courts have come to trespass on turf that properly belongs to the people's elected and accountable representatives. The courts are also expected by many to be representative, instead of being dominated by white males. The under-representation of women and minorities on the bench, these critics say, undermines the courts' ability to reflect the diverse interests and values of Canadians.

Expectations for our institutions of government are not chiselled in stone. In this chapter we will discuss the main characteristics and roles of the institutions that comprise the machinery of Canadian government, including the changes that have taken place in their roles and the controversies associated with these changes.

The Executive Branch

The Monarch and Governor General

Canada is a constitutional monarchy. The monarch, currently Queen Elizabeth II, embodies the authority of the Canadian state. Any action of the government of Canada is taken in the Queen's name.[1] The monarch is responsible for appointing the Prime Minister and for deciding when Parliament will be dissolved and a new election held. When she is not in Canada, which is, of course, most of the time, her duties are carried out by the Governor General, currently David Johnston, a former university president. Although the strict letter of the Constitution suggests that the role of the monarch in Canada's system of government is a formidable one, most Canadians realize that the Queen and Governor General perform mainly symbolic functions. The real decision-making powers of the executive are exercised by the Prime Minister, who is the head of government, and cabinet.

In matters such as the selection of the Prime Minister and the dissolution of Parliament, constitutional convention is infinitely more important than the discretion of the monarch. For example, when one party wins a majority of the seats in an election, the choice of Prime Minister is automatic. Even when no party has a majority, it is understood that the leader of the party with the most seats will be given the first opportunity to try to form a government that has the support of a majority in the legislature. If, however, it is clear that the members of the other parties will not support a government led by this person, the monarch's representative may turn directly to the leader of another party. This happened in Ontario after the 1985 provincial election. Whatever the legislative scenarios appear to be, it is understood that a newly elected legislature must at least be given the opportunity to meet. The monarch's representative cannot simply decide that there is no point in convening the legislature and that a new election should be held straightaway.

Likewise in the case of dissolving Parliament, the monarch's discretion is limited by constitutional conventions that have developed over time. Normally, the Prime Minister's request that Parliament be dissolved and a new election held will be granted automatically. It is remotely conceivable, although highly improbable, that in circumstances of minority government the monarch's representative could refuse such a request and instead ask the leader of another party to try to form a government. The last time this happened was in 1926, when Governor General Lord Byng refused Prime Minister Mackenzie King's request for a new election. This refusal provoked a minor constitutional crisis. Since then, the view of most constitutional experts has been that the monarch's representative is required to accept the "advice" given by the Prime Minister.

The Byng precedent suddenly and rather unexpectedly became relevant several weeks after the federal election of 2008, which produced a Conservative minority government. Although the factors that precipitated the affair are a matter of dispute—some claim that the opposition parties were outraged at what they saw as the government's failure to pay proper attention to the economy in the Minister of Finance's economic statement, while others argued that the Conservatives' proposal to eliminate public funding for political parties was the real trigger for the unexpected unity among the opposition parties—the opposition parties agreed to bring down the government on a motion of non-confidence in the House of Commons. They also agreed to a pact whereby the Liberals and NDP would form a coalition government for a period of at least two years, supported by the BQ. But before they could replace the Conservatives as the government, the Governor General would have to refuse Prime Minister Harper's request for a new election, instead calling on Liberal leader Stéphane Dion to form a government. Constitutional experts were divided on the question of whether the Governor General would be breaking an important unwritten rule of the Constitution in turning down such a request for new elections. In the end, the question became moot when Prime Minister Harper decided to request a prorogation of Parliament until late January 2009, when the government planned to introduce a budget.

The monarch and Governor General play no significant role in setting the government's policy agenda or in the subsequent decision-making process. Royal assent to legislation is virtually automatic. It has never been withheld from a law passed by Parliament. On the occasions when the monarch's provincial representatives, the lieutenant-governors, used the disallowance and reservation powers, this was almost always at the behest of the elected government in Ottawa.[2]

What role, then, does the monarchy play in Canada's system of government? We have said that the monarch's role today is primarily a symbolic one. This does not mean that the functions performed by the Queen and Governor General—and lieutenant-governors at the provincial level—are

Listen to the "Who Is Canada's Head of State? (and Does It Matter?)" podcast, available at: www.oupcanada.com/Brooks8e

unimportant. The ceremonial duties that are part of government must be performed by someone, and it may be that assigning them to a head of state who is above the partisan fray reduces the possibility of too close an association between the political system itself—the state—and the leadership of particular political factions within it. As James Mallory argues, "[the monarchy] denies to political leaders the full splendor of their power and the excessive aggrandizement of their persons which come from the undisturbed occupancy of the centre of the stage."[3] Perhaps, but it must be admitted that these state functions are performed by an elected president in countries such as the United States and France without there being much evidence that this has imperilled those democracies. On the other hand, both the American and French political systems have legislative checks on executive power that do not exist in a British parliamentary system. Mallory may be correct, therefore, in his belief that a non-elected head of state serves as a buffer against the self-aggrandizing tendencies of elected politicians. Paradoxically, then, a non-democratic institution, i.e., an unelected head of state, may contribute to the protection of a democratic social order.

But the monarchy has not always been an uncontroversial pillar of stability in Canadian politics. Despite the constitutional fact that the monarch's status in Canada's system of government is that of the King or Queen of Canada, not of the United Kingdom, the institution of monarchy has been perceived by some as an irritating reminder of Canada's colonial ties to Britain and of the historical dominance of Anglo-Canadians in this country's politics. This was particularly true during the 1960s, when royal visits to Quebec acted as lightning rods for the anti-federalist grievances of Quebec nationalists. Ancient memories of English domination and French subordination have faded, but they have not disappeared. The failure of the Meech Lake Accord in 1990 led many francophone politicians to call for the cancellation of the Queen's scheduled visit to Montreal. When French–English tensions run high, the issue

Listen to the "Who Should Represent Canada and Why?" podcast, available at: www.oupcanada.com/Brooks8e

of which groups in Canada are symbolically represented by the monarch resurfaces.

Despite occasional imbroglios over royal visits, we should not exaggerate the institution's contribution to national disunity. The summer 2010 tour of Canada by Queen Elizabeth II avoided Quebec entirely. This may have been due to competing demands on her time. But the decision not to visit Quebec might also have been influenced by the fact that the November 2009 visit to Montreal of Prince Charles and Lady Camilla Parker-Bowles occasioned egg-throwing, chants of "le Québéc pour les québécois," and several arrests of demonstrators who were mainly associated with the ultra-nationalist/leftist Réseau de résistance du québécois. The incident suggested that the institution of the monarchy has not entirely lost its power to excite passions in Canada.

A new sort of controversy was associated with the position of Governor General during the tenure of Adrienne Clarkson (1999–2005). Clarkson's spouse, John Ralston Saul, is a well-known philosopher-historian and author. Saul's writing and public pronouncements on contemporary issues, as when he was critical of the American reaction to the terrorist attacks of 11 September 2001 and expressed skepticism about George W. Bush's competence as a world leader, focused attention on the question of whether his relationship to the Governor General ought to have limited his forays into political matters. While his defenders noted that he was a private citizen, entitled to the same freedom of speech to which any other citizen is entitled, this was somewhat disingenuous. Like Governor General Clarkson, Saul was referred to as "His Excellency" and made use of the publicly financed staff and other facilities that are part of the office of Governor General. Whether this reality ought to have limited his participation in the more controversial side of public life was a matter on which there was disagreement.

Perhaps more importantly, Governor General Clarkson showed occasional signs of wanting to reshape the boundaries of the office's role in public life. For example, in 2001 she sent a message of congratulations to a gay couple in Ontario who were wed in Toronto's Metropolitan Community Church. This occurred at a time when there was much public controversy over the legal definition of marriage. Critics charged that as a non-elected and non-partisan head of state, Clarkson should not have expressed views that could have been construed as critical of existing law and therefore politically divisive. Michaëlle Jean, Clarkson's successor as Governor General, also was not averse to wading into potentially controversial waters (see Box 9.1).

The Prime Minister and Cabinet

In contrast to the passive and principally symbolic roles of the monarch and Governor General, the Prime Minister (PM) and cabinet are at the centre of the policy-making process. One of the PM's first duties is to select the people who will be cabinet ministers. In the vast majority of cases these will be other elected members of the House of Commons. It has occasionally happened that a senator or two has been appointed to cabinet to give the government representation from a region where the governing party had elected few or no members, or because of the special abilities of a senator. In the British parliamentary tradition, cabinet members always are drawn from the same political party as the PM (but see Box 9.2). In recent decades the size of the federal cabinet has ranged from a low of 20 to a high of almost 40 members. Provincial cabinets are somewhat smaller.

The power of the PM and cabinet rests on a combination of factors. One of these is the written Constitution. Section 11 of the Constitution Act, 1867 states that "There shall be a Council to aid and advise in the Government of Canada, to be styled the Queen's Privy Council for Canada." Section 13 of that Act goes even further to specify that the actions of the monarch's representative in Canada, the Governor General, shall be undertaken "by and with the Advice of the Queen's Privy Council for Canada." The Privy Council is, of course, the cabinet, under the leadership of the PM. Although, formally, anyone who has ever been a member of cabinet retains the title of privy councillor after leaving government, only those who are active members of the government exercise the powers referred to in the Constitution.

Politics in Focus

BOX 9.1 The Governor General Urges Alberta's Legislature to Share the Wealth

The pioneer spirit of independence and resourcefulness in this province is legendary. And yet your deserved reputation for fierce individualism and economic self-reliance belies another lesser-known aspect of Alberta's character: your people are among the most generous of Canadians. Eighty-five per cent of you make financial contributions to charitable and non-profit organizations. Combined with those who volunteer their time, 94 per cent of your citizens believe in giving back.

Alberta's tremendous prosperity affords you the opportunity to make the most of this attitude of sharing. Surely a prime benefit to be derived from such communal wealth is the ability it gives us: to ensure that no one is left behind, and that each among us has a voice.

The health and prosperity of every society is compromised by the people within it who suffer from poverty, who are disadvantaged by birth, who fight against discrimination of all kinds.

Here in this House, at a time of unprecedented prosperity in your province, you have a golden opportunity to continue this tradition. Your capacity to make a difference in the lives of others through your actions and decisions is limitless.

Source: From "Her Excellency the Right Honourable Michaëlle Jean, Speech on the Occasion of the Official Welcoming Ceremony at the Legislative Assembly," 4 May 2006, at: <http://www.gg.ca/document.aspx?id=12150>. Office of the Secretary to the Governor General of Canada 2006.Reproduced with the permission of the Minister of Public Works and Government Services 2006.

These powers include control over the budget. Section 54 of the Constitution Act, 1867 requires that any legislation or other measure that involves the raising or spending of public revenue must be introduced by cabinet. In fact, cabinet dominates the entire legislative agenda of Parliament, not just money matters. MPs who are not members of the cabinet do have the right to introduce private members' bills. But the meagre time allocated to considering these bills and the operation of party discipline combine to kill the prospects of most of these initiatives.

More important than these written provisions of the Constitution, however, are constitutional conventions relating to the PM and cabinet. Although the position of Prime Minister is not even mentioned in the written Constitution, it is understood that the person who leads the dominant party in the House of Commons has the power to decide the following matters:

- who will be appointed to, or removed from, cabinet;

- when a new election will be held;
- the administrative structure and decision-making process of government;
- the selection of persons to a wide array of appointive positions, including deputy ministers, judges of all federal and provincial courts, senators, members of federal regulatory agencies and of the boards of directors of federal Crown corporations, ambassadors, etc.

These are formidable powers. They help to explain why the PM is always the pre-eminent figure in Canadian government, even when his or her decision-making style is a collegial one that encourages the participation of other members of cabinet. The PM's pre-eminence is reinforced by constitutional conventions on accountability. Although individual cabinet ministers are separately accountable to Parliament for the actions of their departments and the entire cabinet is collectively accountable for government policy, the PM cannot avoid personal accountability for the overall performance of government and for all major policies. The opposition

Governing Realities

BOX 9.2 Adapting Parliamentary Tradition to New Realities

The 2010 British election produced no clear winner. It did, however, produce a clear loser. Gordon Brown's Labour Party went from forming the government with 349 of the 650 seats in the House of Commons to a second-place finish with 258 seats and only 29 per cent of the popular vote. The Conservative Party, led by David Cameron, won 307 seats based on 36.1 per cent of the vote, and the Liberal-Democratic Party of Nick Clegg won 57 seats and 23 per cent of the vote.

In the past these might have been seen as the ingredients for minority government. Instead, Conservative leader Cameron did something that few had expected. He entered an agreement with Liberal-Democrat leader Clegg to form a coalition government in which the Lib-Dems would be given seats in cabinet. This is a true coalition government of the sort that is common across much of Western Europe. It marked a dramatic break from the British

parliamentary tradition of single-party rule. And perhaps the most remarkable fact associated with this sharp break with tradition was how little fuss it generated. Citizens and political commentators, for the most part, took it in stride.

If this sort of change is possible in the "mother of parliaments," could it happen in Canada? Possibly. It would require particular circumstances, including an election that produces no clear winner and the willingness of two parties, with enough seats between them to command a majority in the legislature, to share the reins of power. This second condition is more elusive than it might appear, particularly in the case of a historically dominant party that might see such co-operation as carrying risks for its future election prospects. But as the British case shows, it is not out of the question; indeed, the British precedent can now be invoked in support of such a departure from parliamentary tradition.

parties and the media ensure that the PM takes the heat for these matters.

Responsible government is another constitutional convention that strengthens the power of the PM and cabinet. As we noted in Chapter 6, responsible government encourages party discipline. This means that the elected members of a party will tend to act as a unified bloc on most matters, particularly when voting on budget measures and important government legislation. If the members of the governing party break ranks, the government will fall. Party discipline, therefore, ensures that members of the governing party will normally be docile in their support of the government's policies. And when the government has a majority in both the House of Commons and the Senate, the automatic backing of the government party's backbenchers (i.e., MPs who are not cabinet ministers) enables the PM and cabinet to move their legislative agenda through Parliament without serious impediment. Cabinet dominance may be attenuated, however, during periods of minority government and when different parties control the House of Commons and the Senate. In such circumstances the PM and cabinet must necessarily be more sensitive to the preferences and manoeuvres of the opposition parties, given the greater risk of being defeated on a vote in the House or having legislation stymied by Senate opposition.

The weakness of Canada's political party organizations is another factor that reinforces the dominance of the PM and cabinet. Parties, particularly the Liberal and Conservative parties, are geared primarily towards fighting election campaigns. Neither the Conservative Party nor the Liberal Party is what one would consider a social movement party with extensive ties to and dependence on organizations and groups in civil society. These parties are much more concerned with raising money, selecting candidates, and contesting elections than they are with formulating policy. They usually have little influence on the policies adopted by the party leadership when it forms the government. There are two main reasons for this emphasis on elections. One is the parties' efforts to attract a broad base of support. This requires that the party's leadership be allowed a large margin to manoeuvre

in communicating the party's policies to different groups. A second reason involves the absence, except in the case of the NDP, of formal affiliations between the parties and organized interests. Since 1961 the NDP has been formally affiliated with the Canadian Labour Congress. Formal affiliations usually have the effect of narrowing a party's electoral appeal and increasing the weight in a party's internal affairs—including leadership selection and policy-making—of the affiliated group(s). Some, including prominent labour activist Buzz Hargrove, argue that it also has the effect of limiting organized labour's influence with other political parties that are more likely to win in particular constituencies or to form a government, and that labour should abandon its formal ties to the NDP in favour of strategic support for candidates and parties.[4] In any case, history shows that when in power, NDP provincial governments have not been willing to tie themselves rigidly to the party's platform and have occasionally been willing to incur the ire of their union backers.

Statute law is not an important source of prime ministerial power. It provides, however, a significant legal basis for the authority and responsibilities of individual cabinet ministers. The statute under which a government department, agency, or Crown corporation operates will always specify which minister is responsible for the organization's actions. Legislation may also assign to a particular minister special powers over a part of the bureaucracy, such as a right of approval or veto of all or some category of the organization's decisions, or the right to order an agency or Crown corporation to base its decisions on particular guidelines or to act in a specific way. In fact, however, this sort of intervention is more likely to come from the PM and cabinet acting collectively rather than being the initiative of an individual minister.

The constitutional and statutory foundations of prime ministerial and cabinet powers are reinforced by the relationship between the political executive and the media. This relationship is close and mutually dependent. The PM and members of cabinet regularly speak "directly" to the people or to targeted publics via the media. Even when presenting or defending the government's policies in the House of Commons, they are aware of the wider audience to whom their words and behaviour are communicated by television cameras and the parliamentary press corps. For their part, journalists typically turn first to the PM and the responsible ministers when reporting on politics. In doing so, the media contribute to the personalization of politics and, more particularly, to the popular identification of government with the PM and cabinet. These tendencies are reinforced by the visual character of television—the medium that most Canadians depend on for national news—and modern electioneering techniques that focus on the party leaders.

The reality of direct communications between the PM and cabinet and the public has undermined the role of the legislature and political parties. When public sentiment can be gauged through public opinion polls and when the PM and cabinet ministers can speak to either the general public or targeted groups via the media and personal appearances, the government is unlikely to feel the need to rely on its MPs and the party organization to communicate its message. The result is that Parliament often seems to be little more than a procedural sideshow. This infuriates some constitutional purists, for whom Parliament is the proper conduit between the state and society. They argue that the practice of responsible government, the bedrock of the British parliamentary system, is subverted by direct communications between the government and the people. MPs, they argue, should be the linchpin between Parliament and the people. This rather old-fashioned sounding argument is joined by another that has a more contemporary ring. PMs and governments that bypass Parliament and MPs and, instead, communicate directly with the people are thereby contributing to an excessive and dangerous concentration of power. Canada's system of parliamentary government already concentrates power in the hands of the PM. Anything that allows him or her to sidestep accountability in Parliament simply adds to the aggrandizement of his role and weakens parliamentary checks on the government's power.

The communications role of the PM and cabinet is related to their representative functions. From the beginnings of self-government in Canada, cabinet formation has been guided by the principle that politically important interests should, whenever possible, be "represented" by particular cabinet ministers. Adequate representation of different regions and even particular provinces has always been considered important, as has representation of francophones (see Figure 9.2).

The numerical dominance of anglophones has always ensured that they would be well represented in any government. Representation from the business community—the Minister of Finance has often been a person with professional connections to either the Toronto or Montreal corporate elite—and the inclusion of ministers perceived to be spokespersons for particular economic interests, particularly agriculture and occasionally labour, have also been significant factors in making appointments to particular cabinet positions. Some representational concerns, such

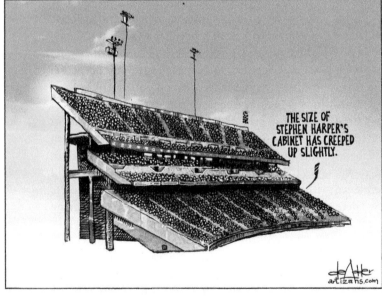

THE SIZE OF STEPHEN HARPER'S CABINET HAS CREEPED UP SLIGHTLY.

Michael de Adder/Artizons.com

Creating a cabinet that adequately represents all of the country's regions is a formidable challenge for any prime minister. Following the 2011 election, the number of cabinet ministers swelled from 32 to 39, an action that drew criticism from some.

as an adequate balance of Catholics and Protestants, have disappeared while others, such as the representation of women and non-French, non-British Canadians, have become increasingly significant.

Representational concerns also surface in the case of the PM. These concerns are particularly important when a party is choosing its leader. Candidates are looked at, by party members and the media, in terms of their likely ability to draw support from politically important regions and groups. At a minimum, an aspiring leader of a national political party cannot be associated too closely with the interests of a single region of the country. Moreover, he or she must be at least minimally competent in French. In practical terms, this means being able to

read parts of speeches in French and answer questions in French. Given the numerical superiority of anglophone voters, it goes without saying that any serious leadership candidate must be able to communicate well in English.

Being the leader of a national political party or even PM does not automatically elevate a politician above the factional strife of politics. Conservative Prime Minister John Diefenbaker (1957–63) was never perceived as being particularly sensitive to Quebec's interests, despite the fact that his party held a majority of that province's seats in the House of Commons between 1958 and 1962. Liberal Prime Minister Pierre Elliott Trudeau (1968–79, 1980–4) was never able to convince western Canada—not

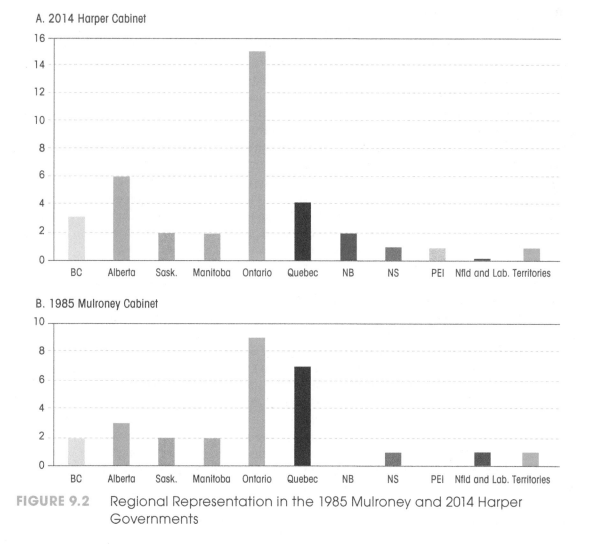

FIGURE 9.2 Regional Representation in the 1985 Mulroney and 2014 Harper Governments

that he always tried very hard—that he shared their perspectives on Canadian politics. For westerners, Trudeau and the Liberals represented the dominance of "the East" and favouritism towards Quebec. Conservative Prime Minister Brian Mulroney was more successful than Trudeau in drawing support from all regions of the country. But he, too, came under attack, particularly from the West, for allegedly neglecting western interests in favour of those of central Canada, especially Quebec. Liberal Prime Minister Jean Chrétien was widely perceived as being more successful than his predecessors in attracting the support of both French and English Canadians. In fact, however, under Chrétien's leadership the Liberal Party did less well in Quebec than during the Trudeau years—the Liberals were outpolled by the Bloc Québécois in both 1993 and 1997, and in 2000, while the Liberals gained 44.2 per cent of the vote to the BQ's 39.8 per cent, the BQ garnered 38 seats to 36 for the Liberals. The Liberals ran a distant second to the Reform Party/ Canadian Alliance west of Manitoba in 1993, 1997, and 2000. Chrétien's popularity and the success of the Liberal Party under his leadership rested largely on Liberal strength in Ontario and on the fact that the right-of-centre vote was divided between the Reform/Alliance and Conservative parties.

A prime minister whose party's representation in the House of Commons from a key region is relatively weak can attempt to convey a message of inclusion by appointing a high-profile cabinet minister from that region. This is precisely what Conservative Prime Minister Stephen Harper did after the 2006 election. His party won only 10 of Quebec's 75 seats, but he moved immediately to appoint to the Senate and to cabinet Quebec's Michael Fortier. Fortier had been the co-chair of the 2005–6 Conservative federal election campaign and had run unsuccessfully as a Tory candidate in Quebec. He was made Minister of Public Works, the government department at the heart of the advertising scandal in Quebec that arguably led to the Liberals' downfall in the election. At the same time, Harper appointed four newly elected MPs from Quebec to his cabinet, three of these to the perennially important portfolios of Industry, Labour, and Transport.

Under Harper's leadership the Conservative Party has managed to win successive elections, including a majority in 2011, with very weak support in Quebec. This marks an important departure from the history of Canadian elections, in which some significant support from both French and English Canada was always needed to form a majority government. This change has come about because of Quebec's declining share of the national population and the increasing share in western Canada, a population shift that ends up being reflected in the distribution of seats in the House of Commons because of the decennial redistribution that takes place based on the latest census. In 1949, the first federal election in which Canada had 10 provinces, Quebec had 28 per cent of the seats in the House. As of the next federal election it will have 23 per cent. Alberta and BC combined will have 22 per cent, just two seats fewer than Quebec, and the four western provinces will have 31 per cent of all seats in the House. The ability to cobble together sufficient support from different regions of the country will always be important in Canada. But aside from Ontario, it may now be the case that no region's support is a necessary condition for a party to form a majority government.

Representation is about power. The PM and cabinet wield considerable power over the machinery of government, which is why representation in the inner circle of government is valued by regional and other interests. This power is based on the agenda-setting role of the PM and cabinet and on their authority within the decision-making process of the state.

Each new session of Parliament begins with the Speech from the Throne, in which the Governor General reads a statement explaining the government's legislative priorities. This formal procedure is required by the Constitution.[5] Although a typical Throne Speech will be packed with generalities, it will also contain some specific indications of the agenda that Parliament will deal with over the ensuing months. For example, the 2013 Throne Speech included, among others, the following goals and promises:

- Freeze the overall federal operating budget.

- Complete negotiations on an economic and trade agreement with the European Union and continue trade agreement negotiations with Japan, South Korea, and India.
- Consult with provincial governments towards the goal of a co-operative regulatory system for securities and capital markets.
- Reform sentencing provisions of the Criminal Code to end the practice of automatic early release for serious repeat offenders and sentencing discounts for child sex offenders.
- Continue to defend the seal hunt on the grounds that it is an important source of food and income for coastal and Inuit communities.

Budgets represent a second way in which the PM and cabinet define the policy agenda. Every winter, usually around late February, the Minister of Finance tables the **estimates** in the House of Commons. This is what students of public finance call the *expenditure budget*.[6] It represents the government's spending plans for the forthcoming fiscal year (1 April–31 March). Given that most public policies involve spending, changes in the allocation of public money provide an indication of the government's shifting priorities. The government can also use the expenditure budget to signal its overall fiscal stance. Increased spending may be part of an expansionary fiscal policy. Spending restraint and cutbacks, as during the 1990s, may signal the government's concern that the total level of public spending and the size of the public-sector deficit are damaging the economy.

From time to time, usually every two years, the Minister of Finance will present in Parliament a **revenue budget**. Sometimes this is referred to as an *economic statement*. It outlines the government's forecast for the economy and plans to change the tax system and introduce other changes intended to influence growth, employment, investment, and competitiveness. Revenue budgets are major opportunities for the government to shape the economic policy agenda.

Even when the bills and budget proposals of government have not originated in cabinet—they often have been generated within some part of

the bureaucracy—or when they appear to be simple reactions to politically or economically pressing circumstances, these initiatives must still be accepted and sponsored by the government. In deciding which initiatives will be placed before Parliament, the priorities among them, and the strategies for manoeuvring policies through the legislature and communicating them to the public, the government influences the policy agenda. As Figure 9.3 shows, cabinet and cabinet committees, particularly the Treasury Board, are central players in the annual expenditure budget process.

Agenda-setting is part of the decision-making process in government. It is a crucial part, being that early stage during which public issues are defined and policy responses are proposed. The role of the PM and cabinet at this and other stages of the policy process is institutionalized through the formal structure of cabinet decision-making. Between 1968 and 1993 the key committee of cabinet in terms of establishing the government's policy and budget priorities was the Priorities and Planning (P&P) Committee. It was chaired by the Prime Minister and included only the most influential members of cabinet. This formal distinction between a sort of inner and outer cabinet was abolished under Prime Minister Kim Campbell (1993). Gone, too, is the elaborate system of formal committees created during the Trudeau years. The structure of cabinet decision-making was streamlined under the Chrétien Liberals to include only five permanent subcommittees of cabinet: Economic Union, Social Union, Treasury Board, the Special Committee of Council, and Government Communications. Under Stephen Harper, the Committee on Priorities and Planning, chaired by the Prime Minister, has been reinstituted. There are five additional committees: Operations (day-to-day co-ordination of the government's agenda and issue management); Social Affairs; Economic Prosperity and Sustainable Growth; Treasury Board; and Foreign Affairs and Defence.

The formal structure of cabinet decision-making, including its committee structure, has never been more than an imperfect guide to who has influence over what within the government of the day. Under Pierre Trudeau, the Priorities and Planning

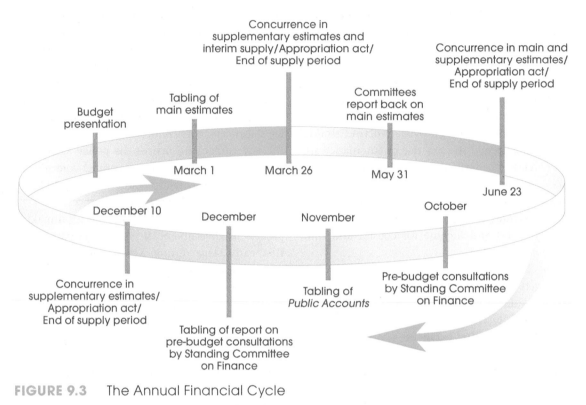

FIGURE 9.3   The Annual Financial Cycle

Source: Parliament of Canada, *House of Commons Procedure and Practice*, 2nd edn (2009), Figure 18.1, at: <www.parl.gc.ca/procedure-book-livre/Document.aspx?Language=E&Mode=1&sbdid=F26EB116-B0B6-490C-B410-33D985BC9B6B&sbpid=FDA208A7-CAA9-40B7-9A42-3F3C5BB83CC7>.

Committee was a true inner cabinet with final decision-making authority. But its membership ranged from about 15 to 20 cabinet ministers, not all of whom could be placed in the Marc Lalonde or Donald Macdonald category of government heavyweight. Under Stephen Harper, Priorities and Planning has 16 members, in addition to the PM. Jason Kenney, one of the government's most influential ministers, was not a member of this committee (2014). No one imagined, however, that his voice in government was less important than those of several ministers who sat on Priorities and Planning.

The one reliable rule of thumb is this: ministers are influential to the degree that the Prime Minister allows them to be influential and supports their favoured projects and initiatives. A minister who has a reputation for having the PM's ear and being part of his inner circle acquires enhanced status among his or her colleagues in Parliament and in the eyes of the media. Other factors may also contribute to a minister's influence, such as having a base of support within the party or being in charge of a powerful part of the bureaucracy. Nevertheless, the personal relationship between the PM and a minister is always a significant determinant of a minister's influence. The decision-making process in cabinet does not occur only through formal committee meetings. One-on-one conversations in the corridors of the Langevin Building (the location of the Privy Council Office), in the PM's office in the West Block, over the phone, or however and wherever they may take place have always been crucial in the decision-making process. No organization chart can capture this informal but crucial aspect of ministerial influence. Nor can it convey the extent to which the Prime Minister is the dominant player in this decision-making process. Political observers have long characterized the PM's status in cabinet as *primus inter pares*—first among equals.

But as Donald Savoie notes, there is no longer any *inter* or *pares*. There is only *primus*, the PM, when it comes to setting the government's agenda and taking major decisions.[7]

Ministerial control over the bureaucracy is another dimension of cabinet's decision-making authority. The word "control" should be used carefully, however. Ministers are virtually never involved in the day-to-day running of the departments that fall under their nominal control. Moreover, policy initiatives are more likely to be generated within the bureaucracy, often in dialogue with interests with whom they interact in the course of administering their programs, than to spring from the fertile imagination of the responsible minister. There are, of course, exceptions. Stéphane Dion, when he was the federal Minister of Intergovernmental Affairs, was the principal author of the 2000 **Clarity Act**, an idea he had championed from the time of the 1995 Quebec referendum. Under the Conservative government of Stephen Harper, it appears that unelected advisers in and around the Prime Minister's Office have played a greater role than in the past in shaping the government's policy agenda. At the same time, the role of the permanent bureaucracy, which some argue is mistrusted by the Conservatives as too liberal, has been weaker than is usually the case. In 1990 Donald Savoie wrote a book entitled *The Politics of Public Spending*, in which he argued that, as a general rule, most ministers, most of the time, act as cabinet advocates for the interests of their department, its budget and programs, and the groups that depend on them. More than 20 years later he has revised this conclusion, arguing that ministers often rely more heavily on advisers outside of the state than on senior bureaucrats in deciding policy.[8]

Central Agencies

Cabinet has always been a decision-making body. But when John A. Macdonald and the first cabinet met in 1867, they dealt with a workload that was only a fraction of that facing government today. There were only a handful of departments and no publicly owned corporations or regulatory agencies.

Moreover, federal–provincial relations were still relatively uncomplicated (although this would not last long!). The scope and complexity of contemporary government are much greater. To deal with the sheer volume of information that comes before cabinet and the hundreds of separate decisions that it takes annually, cabinet needs help. This help is provided by central agencies.

Central agencies are parts of the bureaucracy whose main or only purpose is to support the decision-making activities of cabinet. More concretely, this means they perform such functions as providing cabinet with needed information, applying cabinet decisions in dealing with other parts of the bureaucracy, and communicating cabinet decisions and their implications to the public, provincial governments, or other organizations within the federal state. The general character of their policy role, their direct involvement in cabinet decision-making, and their ability to intervene in the affairs of departments led political scientists Colin Campbell and George Szablowski to refer to the senior officials of central agencies as "superbureaucrats."[9] This was three decades ago. Donald Savoie may well be correct in his assessment that senior officials across the federal bureaucracy have lost influence in recent times, such that these erstwhile superbureaucrats are no longer quite so super. Nevertheless, those in the central agencies occupy the crucial space where, in the words of one official interviewed by Savoie, "the rubber meets the road, where the public service meets politics, and all . . . that means."[10]

The main organizations usually considered to have central agency status are the Department of Finance, the Privy Council Office (PCO), the Treasury Board Secretariat, and the Prime Minister's Office.

Department of Finance

The Department of Finance plays the leading role in the formulation of economic policy. Its formal authority is found in the Department of Finance Act, 1869, the Financial Administration Act, and several other statutes. The authority that the law confers on Finance is reinforced by the department's informal reputation within the state.

Although comparatively small—it employs about 750 persons (2012)—Finance has always been a magnet for "the best and the brightest" within the public service because of its unrivalled status in all aspects of economic policy-making.

The Finance Department has what amounts to almost exclusive authority over the preparation of the revenue budget, budget speeches, and economic statements delivered in Parliament by the Finance Minister. Whatever input other parts of the bureaucracy and interests outside of government have is at the discretion of the Minister of Finance and the department. New initiatives in taxation and trade policy and in managing the level of government spending and debt will often be generated within Finance. Even when a new policy idea originates elsewhere, it is unlikely to reach the legislation stage if Finance is steadfastly opposed.

Finance officials are able to influence the entire spectrum of government policy through their role in the annual formulation of the expenditure budget. They are involved at the very beginning of the expenditure budget process, providing projections on the future state of the economy and the fiscal framework within which spending choices will have to be made. A Finance forecast of weak economic activity and lean taxation revenues will impose across-the-board restraint on departments jostling for scarce funds. But in addition to this macro-level influence on policy, Finance officials may also be involved in micro-level decisions about programs and in setting the policy agenda. In the words of one senior federal bureaucrat:

> Budget cutting tends not to be "take 10 percent off your budget and do what you will." The Department of Finance tends to say "you will take so much off such-and-such a program in such-and-such a way, in such-and-such a time frame, and once they've said all of those things, you really have a fairly small box to start playing in. . . . The Speech from the Throne might be a Speech from the Throne, but I can tell you that there is an awful lot of Finance finger in the pie . . . [and t]here's nothing in there that they haven't figured out how to finance.[11]

The dominant status of Finance was reinforced during the 1990s when deficit reduction and debt management became Ottawa's overriding priorities. Once Ottawa turned the corner on the deficit issue and began to accumulate considerable budget surpluses during the late 1990s, many believed that Finance's stranglehold on the government's agenda would loosen under pressure from those who believed that Ottawa could afford to restore spending on some of the programs that had been cut during the mid-1990s. In fact, however, Finance lost none of its authority at the centre of the policy-making universe. As Donald Savoie observes:

> the budget has come to dominate policy and decision-making in Ottawa as never before. This holds significant advantages for the centre of government. It enables the prime minister and the minister of finance to introduce new measures and policies under the cover of budget secrecy and avoid debate in Cabinet—and perhaps, more importantly, long interdepartmental consultations and attempts to define a consensus.[12]

In other words, the unrivalled status of Finance within the federal bureaucracy is one of the factors that effectively reinforces the power of the PM, who, along with his or her Minister of Finance, is the only member of the government to be intimately involved in the process that leads up to the making of a budget or economic statement in the House of Commons. The point is made in a rather understated way by a Library of Parliament analysis of the Minister of Finance's role: "the minister of Finance's control over the allocation of spending makes him or her one of the most powerful ministers in Cabinet."[13] Indeed!

Finance has only a handful of programs for which the department is directly responsible, but they are important, big-ticket ones. One of these is *fiscal equalization*, under which unconditional payments are made to provincial governments whose revenues fall below a level agreed to by Ottawa and the provinces. These payments amount to over $16 billion per year (2014). Finance oversees the entirety of federal transfers to the provinces, of which equalization is a part, including the Canada Health Transfer and Canada Social Transfer. Combined CHT and CST cash transfers to the provinces were worth about $42.5 billion in 2013–14, with another $24.2 billion in tax room ceded by Ottawa to the provinces (2013). Changes in the conditions under which these and other transfers are made and in the size of the transfer, all of which are negotiated periodically with the provinces, do not happen without the close involvement of Finance.

The Privy Council Office

The Privy Council Office is the cabinet's secretariat and a principal source of policy advice to the Prime Minister. It employs about 800 persons (2012) but, as is also true of Finance and the PMO, the PCO's

influence cannot be gauged from its size. Donald Savoie characterizes it as "the nerve centre of the federal public service."[14] The PCO was formally created by Order-in-Council in 1940. The position of Chief Clerk of the Privy Council, the foremost bureaucrat in the federal government, was put on a statutory basis in 1974 without any specification of the duties associated with this position. The authority of this person and the influence of the PCO derive mainly from their intimate and daily involvement in cabinet decision-making.

In the first comprehensive study of central agencies, Campbell and Szablowski argued that the PCO is the lead agency for "strategic planning and formulation of substantive policy."[15] The PCO's role is "strategic," they argued, because it is situated at the confluence of all the various policy issues

The reading of a new budget is a ceremonial affair in Ottawa, and though no one knows its origin, there is a long-standing tradition of the Finance Minister purchasing and wearing a new pair of shoes for the occasion. Finance Minister Jim Flaherty always wore new shoes.

CP Images/The Canadian Press/Nathan Denette

and decisions that come before cabinet. This has not changed:

> The PCO does not have formal authority over line departments, but its roles in assisting the prime minister and Cabinet give it substantial influence. Line departments must consider the advice of the PCO very carefully because the advice generally reflects the wishes of the prime minister or Cabinet. In addition, because the PCO acts as a gatekeeper for the information that is made available to Cabinet, departments must ensure that their submissions reflect the PCO's guidance. The PCO often filters or summarizes information provided by departments to ensure that the prime minister and Cabinet have adequate supporting information to make informed decisions.[16]

In terms of its organization, the PCO is divided into a number of secretariats that provide support services for the various committees of cabinet. These services range from such mundane functions as scheduling and keeping the minutes of committee meetings to activities that carry the potential for real influence, such as providing policy advice and dealing directly with government departments. Perhaps more than any other single component of the bureaucracy, the PCO is capable of seeing "the big picture" of government policy. This picture embraces policy *and* political concerns. A former head of the PCO, Gordon Robertson, once summarized the different roles of the PCO and the Prime Minister's Office in the following way: "The Prime Minister's Office is partisan, politically oriented, yet operationally sensitive. The Privy Council Office is non-partisan, operationally oriented, yet politically sensitive."[17] Although Robertson's characterization of the different roles of the PCO and PMO was made four decades ago, it continues to be apt. As Donald Savoie observes, "the office briefs the prime minister on any issue it wishes, controls the flow of papers to Cabinet, reports back to departments on the decisions taken, or not taken, by Cabinet, advises the prime minister on the selection of deputy ministers . . . on

federal–provincial relations and on all issues of governmental organization and ministerial mandates."[18] If the government of Canada is a railway, the PCO is Grand Central Station.

Savoie argues that the title "Clerk of the Privy Council" is in some ways a misnomer as this most senior member of the federal bureaucracy in fact serves and reports to the PM, not to cabinet as a whole. Along with the PM's chief of staff in the PMO, the Clerk of the PCO is the only official who meets almost daily with the PM when he is in Ottawa. "The clerk," Savoie observes, "has direct access to the prime minister as needed."[19] The Clerk of the Privy Council is, effectively, a sort of deputy minister to the Prime Minister, and as such is always one of the most influential persons in the federal government. Savoie argues that in recent years this intimacy has, to some degree, undermined the partisan neutrality of the PCO. The Clerk and other senior officials, he maintains, have become too close to the PM and his senior staffers.[20]

The Treasury Board Secretariat

The Treasury Board Secretariat (TBS) supports the functions of the Treasury Board. The Treasury Board is the only cabinet committee that has a statutory basis, going back to 1869. The Treasury Board is, in a sense, guardian of the purse strings, but it performs this function in more of a micro fashion compared to Finance's macro authority in relation to spending matters. The Treasury Board is also the government's voice on employment and personnel matters and on administrative policy within the federal government. Its authority is, in a word, extensive. But although the responsibilities of the TBS are wide-ranging and important, it occupies the shadows of the policy-making and agenda-setting process when compared to Finance and the PCO. Donald Savoie quotes a senior federal official who compares the roles of Finance, the PCO, and the TBS this way: "PCO looks after the broad picture and resolves conflicts between ministers and departments. Finance looks after the big economic and budgeting decisions. The Treasury Board looks after the little decisions."[21]

"Little," however, should not be confused with "unimportant." Particularly from the standpoint of program managers within the federal bureaucracy, the activities and decisions of the Treasury Board and TBS are quite significant. The TBS includes the Office of the Comptroller General of Canada (OCG), whose functions include departmental audits, establishing and enforcing accounting standards in government, and the evaluation of particular programs. As government employer, the Treasury Board negotiates with federal public-sector unions, establishes the rules for recruitment and promotion, is involved in implementing the terms of the Official Languages Act relating to the representation of francophones in the public service and the availability of services to the public in both official languages, and is responsible for equity matters, including setting rules for increasing the representation of women, visible minorities, disabled persons, and Aboriginal people in the Canadian public service. These clearly are important functions.

TBS officials formulate the expenditure outlook that, along with the economic outlook and fiscal framework developed by Finance, is the starting point in the annual expenditure budget exercise. The expenditure forecasts provided by TBS are used by cabinet in making decisions on the allocation of financial resources between competing programs. The involvement of TBS officials does not stop here. Along with the spending committees of cabinet, they assess the spending proposals and plans that departments are required to submit each year. Preparation of the main estimates, the detailed spending plans that the government tables in the House of Commons each winter, is the responsibility of the Treasury Board. Given the range of its activities it is not surprising that TBS is the largest of the central agencies, with almost 2,000 employees. Because the TBS has the deepest ongoing knowledge of government spending programs of all central agencies, it is often turned to by the PCO and Finance—its more muscular and glamorous cousins—for information and advice.[22]

The Prime Minister's Office

Unlike the other central agencies, the Prime Minister's Office (PMO) is staffed chiefly by partisan appointees rather than by career public servants. These officials are the Prime Minister's personal staff, performing functions that range from handling the PM's correspondence and schedule to speech-writing, media relations, liaison with ministers, caucus, and the party, and providing advice on appointments and policy. Gordon Robertson's observation that the PMO is "partisan, politically oriented, yet operationally sensitive"[23] captures well the role of this central agency. In its relations with other parts of the federal government the PMO serves as the PM's political eyes and ears, and has the added distinction of being able to speak on behalf of the PM. The PMO is headed by the PM's chief of staff. No other non-elected official is in such regular contact with the PM.

Since the expansion in the PMO that took place under Pierre Trudeau nearly four decades ago, the size of the Prime Minister's staff has varied enormously. Trudeau more than doubled the staff from the 40 persons who worked in the PMO under Prime Minister Pearson. Under Prime Minister Mulroney the staff reached just under 200. Today the PMO employs about 100 persons. This may seem to be a rather large number of people to serve the needs of one person, even a very important person such as the Prime Minister. But the demands on the Prime Minister's time are enormous and the process of coordinating his activities, providing him or her with briefing and advice, and dealing with the volume of communication that flows into and from the Prime Minister's Office are daunting, to say the least. The bottom line for all staffers in the PMO, from the chief of staff to those who answer the phones, is summed up by a former PMO staff member in these words: "Our job is quite simple really, we make the PM look good."[24] This can, of course, be a challenge.

To give but one example of how PMO officials perform this job, let us consider the preparation that takes place before Question Period in the House of Commons. In Canada the Prime Minister is expected to attend Question Period, held shortly after 2:00 p.m. on Monday through Thursday and in the late morning on Fridays, when the House is sitting and when he or she is in Ottawa. Moreover, the Prime Minister is expected to remain in the House for all of Question Period. The PM is the star of the show and Question Period occupies the central place in media coverage of Parliament and in Canadians' idea about the process of government because of this understanding that the Prime Minister should be present to answer questions about the activities and policies of his or her government.

Question Period is, potentially, a political minefield, a fact attested to by the presence of journalists in the gallery, few of whom ever bother to be physically present for any of the debates or committee proceedings that take up most of Parliament's working day. Given the stakes, preparation of the PM and his or her ministers is crucial. Within the PMO a handful of staffers arrive each day before sunrise to begin the process of sifting through the day's newspapers and web and broadcast media coverage from the previous day and that morning, identifying those issues that the opposition parties are most likely to pounce on during Question Period. But their job does not stop there. They also craft responses to the anticipated questions, a process that involves considerable partisan and tactical thinking. The most successful response to an opposition member's question is, of course, one that turns the tables and puts the opposition on the defensive or in some way embarrasses the questioner and his or her party. Staffers in the PMO have done their job well when they provide their boss with the ammunition for just such a response.

Although the PMO is clearly the most partisan of the central agencies, it would be quite wrong to think of the PMO as being unconcerned with policy matters. Protecting the Prime Minister and making him look good necessarily involve PMO officials in issues of policy, large and small. "Senior PMO staff," says Savoie, "will get involved in whatever issue they and the prime minister think they should."[25] It simply is not possible to draw a line between the drafting of a speech for the Prime Minister, a function that typically will take place in the PMO, and providing policy advice. Moreover, officials in the PMO work regularly and closely with those in the PCO to push forward the PM's agenda. But how involved PMO officials are in the shaping of policy and what their influence is vis-à-vis other central agency officials and departmental managers will, as always, depend on the Prime Minister. Ultimately, the Prime Minister decides from whom to seek advice and who will be a player on any particular issue.

Prime Ministerial Government

For decades various commentators on the Canadian political scene have asked whether Canadian prime ministers were becoming more "presidential" in their stature and power. The question, however, was always based on the false premise that an American President is more powerful in relation to the country's legislation and his own party than is a Canadian Prime Minister. In fact, there have always been fewer checks on the behaviour of a Canadian Prime Minister than on an American President, and any occupant of the White House would envy the sort of constitutional latitude enjoyed by the leader of the Canadian government. Canadian commentators who purported to see creeping presidentialization occurring in Canada's system of government were, in fact, mistakenly attributing to the American head of state powers beyond those actually held by the US President, but which Canadian prime ministers have always had.

In recent years this ill-informed debate has come to a close. Indeed, it is now widely recognized that the Canadian Prime Minister has far more clout within the Canadian system of government than the President has in the American system and, moreover, that power has become increasingly centralized in the hands of the PM and those around him. These days, if one looks for counterweights to the PM's power they are more plausibly found in the courts, the media, and in some of the provincial capitals than in Parliament. This centralization of power has advanced to such a degree that some of Canada's most astute political commentators now characterize Canada's system of government as *prime ministerial* rather than *parliamentary* government.[26] Donald Savoie and Jeffrey Simpson are among those who argue that not only has the influence of Parliament been effectively eclipsed by the growth of **prime ministerial government**, but cabinet, too, has been left on the margins of the policy-making process, "a kind of focus group for the prime minister," in the words of a recent Liberal cabinet minister,[27] or what Jeffrey Simpson calls a "mini-sounding board"[28] where decisions already approved by the PM and his advisers in key central agencies are rubber-stamped.

The greater influence of the Prime Minister within the Canadian system of government than the President in the American system is due to structural differences between these two governmental systems. But the high degree of centralization of power that commentators such as Savoie and Simpson argue has occurred under recent prime ministers—a trend that began before Prime Minister Harper came to power—may be explained by a combination of personal style and the political incentives to choose more rather than less centralization. The individuals who occupy the role of Prime Minister all have their own preferences when it comes to decision-making. Some prefer a more participatory process, as was true of Lester Pearson (1963–8) and Pierre Trudeau (1968–79, 1980–4), at least during Trudeau's earlier years. Marc Lalonde, one of the most influential ministers during the Trudeau era, has described cabinet meetings under Trudeau as resembling university seminars during which the Prime Minister often remained silent for much of the time while the members of his government expressed their views. This is the decision-making style, as noted earlier, in which the Prime Minister has been depicted as "first among equals." The historical evidence from politicians' memoirs and journalistic accounts, however, suggests that the collegial style may have been less common than is sometimes believed. In an analysis of prime ministers' decision-making styles, Savoie points out that even Trudeau bypassed the formal process of cabinet decision-making in the case of all of the major policy initiatives taken during his last four years as PM. Likewise, Brian Mulroney and Jean Chrétien did the same when it came to some of the signature policies launched during their respective periods as Prime Minister.[29] Nevertheless, there is little doubt that a more centralized decision-making style is a feature of contemporary Canadian government, where priorities are effectively set and decisions are made by the Prime Minister and a relatively small group of advisers, only some of whom may be cabinet ministers.

It is tempting to locate the roots of prime ministerial government in the personalities of such leaders as Brian Mulroney, Jean Chrétien, and Stephen Harper. But it is also worth asking what a prime minister would gain by choosing a more participatory decision-making style characterized by greater opportunities for involvement and influence on the part of all members of cabinet and more delegation of policy-making responsibility to individual cabinet ministers. The pluses seem nebulous and hard to pinpoint. They might include the gratitude of the cabinet ministers empowered by the *primus inter pares* style and the plaudits of old-school purists who believe this is the decision-making ideal that all prime ministers should strive to achieve. But the various risks a prime minister would take by adopting a significantly more decentralized and collegial approach are fairly easy to identify. They include the following:

- The decisions or publicly expressed views of individual cabinet ministers might be perceived to be in conflict with other government actions, promises, or policies and thus cause embarrassment to the government.
- Ministers will often have their own strongly held preferences on issues, but it is also well known that most ministers soon see their role at the cabinet table as that of defender of "their" department, programs, budget allocation, etc. The *primus inter pares* style of collective cabinet decision-making probably has a built-in bias towards protection of the status quo and against change that appears to threaten the programs, prestige, and budget interests of a significant number of ministers.
- A collegial cabinet decision-making style is more likely to allow for the emergence of powerful, high-profile cabinet ministers who may be seen by the media, within the governing party, and by the public as rivals to the Prime Minister.

The Legislature

The legislature is a study in contrasts. Its physical setting is soberly impressive, yet the behaviour of its members, particularly during Question Period, is often thought to be unfit for the schoolyard. Its constitutional powers appear to be formidable, yet

THEY'VE REPLACED THE SLIP COVERS ON THE LOUNGE CUSHIONS!

SENATE REFORM

8·24 WWW.GRAHAMHARROP.COM

Graham Harrop/© Simon Fraser University

En route to taking office in 2006, Stephen Harper's Conservative government expressed the intent to introduce legislation on Senate reform. Their proposed overhauls of the Senate process included an eight-year limit on the term of Senate service and, eventually, the requirement that senators be elected to their seats rather than appointed. In an April 2014 ruling the Supreme Court of Canada determined that no significant reform of the Senate may take place without provincial consent.

modern state. Representation, accountability to the people, and choice are the cornerstones of liberal democratic theory. An elected legislature that represents the population either on the basis of population or by region—or both—and party competition are the means by which these democratic goals are to be accomplished. But the modern state is also characterized by a vast bureaucratic apparatus that is not easily controlled by elected politicians. Moreover, while the Prime Minister's power has always been vastly greater than that of other members of Parliament, the concentration of power in and around the office of the Prime Minister appears to have reached unprecedented levels. As the scale and influence of the non-elected parts of the state have grown and prime ministerial government has been consolidated, the inadequacies of traditional democratic theory—centred on the role of the legislature—have become increasingly apparent.

If the legislature is less able to perform the functions associated with it in democratic theory, one solution may be to look elsewhere for representation and accountability. If power has drifted to non-elected officials, then perhaps ensuring that the bureaucracy is representative of the population may be a way to increase the likelihood that they will be democratically responsive. If the legislature is no longer able to control or effectively monitor the activities of the government, perhaps the answer lies in creating independent parliamentary officers. Many such officers have been empowered at both the federal and provincial levels including, federally, the Office of the Auditor General, the Office of the Privacy Commissioner, the Commissioner of the Environment and Sustainable Development, and the Parliamentary Budget Officer. Critics charge that their proliferation—an estimated 80 such officers are employed at the federal, provincial, and territorial levels—is both a symptom of

its actual influence on policy usually is much less than that of the cabinet and the bureaucracy. All major policies, including all laws, must be approved by the legislature, but the legislature's approval often seems a foregone conclusion and a mere formality. One of the two chambers of the legislature, the House of Commons, is democratically elected. The other, the Senate, has long had an unenviable reputation as a sinecure for party hacks and other appointed unworthies.

The contradictions of the legislature have their source in the tension between traditional ideas about political democracy and the character of the

Parliament's decline and a contributing factor to the delegitimization of the legislature. "A veritable accountability industry," says David Pond, "is being created outside the walls of Parliament and the provincial legislatures."[30] But as long as the job of holding government accountable is getting done, does it matter if elected legislators are doing it? Some argue that there is no substitute for an elected legislature that is able to hold government accountable for its actions (see Box 9.3).

Canada's legislature has two parts, the House of Commons and the Senate. Representation in the elected House of Commons is roughly according to population—roughly, because some MPs represent as few as 26,000 constituents (Labrador),

while others represent close to 180,000 (Brampton West). Each of the 308 members of the House of Commons is the sole representative for a constituency, also known as a "riding."

Senators are appointed by the government of the day as vacancies occur. They do not have set terms of office and may hold their seats until age 75. Representation in the Senate is on the basis of regions. Each of the four main regions (Ontario, Quebec, the four western provinces, and the Maritimes) has 24 seats. Newfoundland has six, and there is one from each of the Yukon, Northwest Territories, and Nunavut for a total of 105 seats. Eight temporary seats were added by the Mulroney government in 1988 to overcome Liberal

Politics in Focus

BOX 9.3 Is There No Substitute for Parliament?

Michael Chong, Conservative MP for Wellington-Halton Hills, argues that Parliament risks falling into irrelevance. Here are some excerpts from an article he contributed to Policy Options in 2010.

In the (2008) federal election, 59 percent of Canadians turned out to vote, the lowest turnout since Confederation. The fact that more than four out of ten voters stayed away from the ballot box is evidence of a growing gap between Canadians and their Parliament.

This growing gap undermines the centrality of Parliament to public debate. The increasing irrelevance of Parliament to many Canadians is forcing these debates into other forums, such as the courts, the Internet and civil society. While each of these various forums plays an important role in public debate, they cannot represent the democratic will of the Canadian people. Only the 308 Members of Parliament, duly elected by their constituents, can do that. If Parliament is becoming increasingly irrelevant to Canadians and is not central to public debate in Canada, then public policy will be determined in an increasingly nondemocratic fashion.[31]

The solution, Chong argues, starts with the reform of Question Period. He has described it as "a testosterone-laden, anger-filled screaming match, characterized by aggressive body language and by those who can yell the loudest." For decades, he says, it has emphasized partisanship and hyperbole at the expense of substance, MPs have behaved rudely in ways that bring discredit to the House of Commons, most MPs are relegated to the role of spectators or cheering sections for their respective parties, and it eats up an inordinate amount of time and resources for ministers and their staffs. Chong submitted a motion that would have seen sweeping reforms to Question Period and that, he believes, would cause Canadians to have more respect for Parliament and confidence in government.

Whether Chong's diagnosis is correct and his solution the right one, Canadians won't know anytime soon. On 6 October 2010 the House of Commons overwhelmingly approved Chong's motion. No action was taken and the motion subsequently died when Parliament was dissolved for the 2011 elections.

opposition in the Senate to the Goods and Services Tax (GST), thus temporarily raising the total number of senators to 112.[32] In recent years there have been suggestions that senators be elected, that they serve limited terms, and some have proposed that a certain number of Senate seats be reserved for women and Aboriginal Canadians.

In law, the powers of the House of Commons and Senate are roughly equal, and all bills must pass through identical stages in both bodies before becoming law (see the Appendix at the end of this chapter). But despite the similarity of their formal powers, the superiority of the House of Commons is well established. For most of its history, the Senate generally deferred to the will of the Commons on all but relatively minor matters. This changed after the 1984 election of a Progressive Conservative majority in the House of Commons. On several occasions the Liberal-dominated Senate obstructed bills that had already been passed by the Commons. When the Senate balked at passage of the politically unpopular GST the government decided it had had enough. Using a largely unknown constitutional power it appointed eight new Conservative senators, thereby giving the Conservative Party a slender majority. Under the Chrétien government the partisan balance in the Senate shifted back to a Liberal majority. The squabbles that often occurred after 1984, when the House of Commons was controlled by one party and the Senate by another, became increasingly rare during the years 1993–2006, when the Liberals formed the government and re-established a Liberal majority in the Senate through the filling of vacancies.

This Liberal majority posed a problem for the minority Conservative government elected in 2006, blocking and delaying several pieces of legislation sent to it from the House of Commons. Instead of filling Senate seats with Conservative Party loyalists as vacancies occurred, Harper allowed these vacancies to accumulate before appointing 18 new senators in December 2008. The government explained this delay as having been due to its commitment to Senate reform and, in particular, the election of senators. It was, however, unable to win enough support in the House of Commons for such reform and, in any case, it was not clear that

direct election and term limits for senators could be accomplished without changing the Constitution.

The legislature performs a number of functions basic to political democracy. The most fundamental of these is the passage of laws by the people's elected representatives. Budget proposals and new policy initiatives must be placed before Parliament for its approval. The operation of party discipline ensures that bills tabled in the legislature are seldom modified in major ways during the law-passing process. This does not mean, however, that Parliament's approval of the government's legislative agenda is an empty formality. The rules under which the legislature operates ensure that the opposition parties have opportunities to debate and criticize the government's proposals.

Writing a generation ago, Robert Jackson and Michael Atkinson argued that those involved in the pre-parliamentary stages of policy-making anticipate the probable reactions of the legislature and of the government party caucus before a bill or budget is tabled in Parliament.[33] While this may have been true in the past, it no longer appears that those who actually take policy decisions and draft legislation lose much sleep over what they think will be the reaction of backbench MPs. On the influence of **caucus**, Savoie states that government party MPs "report that they are rarely, if ever, in a position to launch a new initiative, and worse, that they are rarely effective in getting the government to change course. They also do not consider themselves to be an effective check on prime ministerial power."[34] In the words of one government party MP, "We simply respond to what Cabinet does, and there are limits to what you can do when you are always reacting."[35] Interviews conducted with MPs in 2010 found that the chance to express one's point of view in the privacy of caucus was a source of satisfaction for many legislators. At the same time, however, many MPs acknowledged that they were frustrated by having to vote on the floor of the House as their party directed them, suggesting that caucus may be more about catharsis than influence.[36] Little evidence from recent years suggests that the Prime Minister and those around him involved in making policy pay much attention to the preferences of those in the legislature, on either the government or opposition side of the aisle. They are, however, very likely to pay serious attention to the results of opinion polls and focus groups that have been commissioned to gauge public reaction to a policy.

Although the legislature may often, indeed usually, play second fiddle to more direct means used by government to take the public pulse on issues, it is far from being irrelevant in the policy-making process. Functions performed by the legislature include scrutiny of government performance, constituency representation, debate of issues, and legitimation of the political system.

Oversight of Government Performance

Various regular opportunities exist for the legislature to prod, question, and criticize the government. These include the daily Question Period, the set-piece debates that follow the Speech from the Throne and the introduction of a new budget, and Opposition Days, when the opposition parties determine the topic of debate. Committee hearings and special parliamentary task forces also provide opportunities for legislative oversight of government actions and performance, although the subjects that these bodies deal with are mainly determined by the government. Party discipline is a key factor that limits the critical tendencies of parliamentary committees, particularly during periods of majority government.

Earlier we said that Question Period, for better or for worse, has become both the centrepiece of Parliament's day and the chief activity shaping the ideas that most Canadians have of what goes on in Parliament. The introduction of television cameras into the legislature in the late 1970s has reinforced the stature of Question Period as the primary forum through which the opposition can scrutinize and criticize the government on matters big and small. This is the opposition parties' main chance to influence the issues that will be discussed in the media and the way the government will be portrayed by the press.

In fact, however, the dynamic of Question Period involves reciprocal influences between the media

and opposition parties. It has often been said that this morning's *Globe and Mail* or *National Post* headline becomes this afternoon's leading volley in Question Period, but things are not this simple. Journalists also react—although not always in the way that opposition parties may like—to the questions and lines of attack that opposition parties launch against the government. For example, during the spring of 2013 the opposition parties carried out a sustained assault on the government and, in particular, a couple of prominent Conservative senators. Every day brought a fresh round of questions and accusations concerning expenses that these senators had claimed, but that opposition critics charged were fraudulent. This was clearly an opposition campaign to generate as much negative publicity for the Harper government as possible and create a public perception of the government as corrupt. To what degree this issue was media-driven as opposed to opposition party-driven is impossible to say. What is clear is that this sort of critical scrutiny of the government serves the interests of both the opposition parties, who wish to see the government embarrassed and its popular support drop, and the media, who know that controversy and the scent of wrongdoing attract more readers and viewers than do reports that all is well with the world.

Committees of the House of Commons, whose membership is generally limited to about 20 MPs, may appear to be a forum where the leash of party discipline can be loosened and backbench MPs may acquire some expertise in particular policy areas that will enable them to assess the merits of legislation in a more informed and less partisan manner. Students of American politics know that congressional committees are where the real action is in Congress, and that what enters one end of the committee sausage-grinder may not bear much resemblance to what emerges from the other end, if it emerges at all. In Canada's Parliament, however, committees seldom

Listen to the "It's Not as Bad as You Think: Political Corruption in Canada" podcast, available at: www.oupcanada.com/Brooks8e

modify in more than marginal ways what is placed before them and virtually never derail any bill the government has introduced in the House. Far from being a source of opportunity and satisfaction for MPs who wish to see themselves as being truly engaged in the law-making process, much evidence suggests that committees are a source of frustration for many MPs and that they do not provide a serious vehicle through which the legislature can scrutinize the activities of government and call it to account for its actions. In his study of MPs' behaviour and perceptions of their jobs, David Docherty states that "several rookie Liberals indicated that the failure of their own executive to treat committee work and reports seriously was the single most frustrating (and unexpected) aspect of their job as an MP."[37] Docherty found that frustration with House committees was not limited to government party members. Opposition MPs also expressed disappointment with the inability of committees to make more than a marginal and occasional difference. On the other hand, a 2010 study based on interviews with MPs found they were more likely to express satisfaction with their committee work, and to see it as constructive and relatively non-partisan, than with any other aspect of their job.[38]

It may well be, as this 2010 study concludes, that committee work is not a source of frustration for all or even most MPs. It remains the case, however, that their work typically does not make much of a difference. "People will tell you," said one MP interviewed for the 2010 study, 'I've done great work on a committee.' But you really have to say, 'You did good work. You travelled. You studied this and that. But what did you accomplish? Show us where the legislation changed and what you did.'"[39] Despite some tinkering over the last couple of decades, the ostensible goal of which was to increase the independence of committees and thereby augment the influence of the legislature, the fact that party discipline operates in committees just as it does on the floor of the House of Commons undoes all of these reforms. Moreover, all but a small fraction of what committees do is reactive—responding to a bill tabled in Parliament by the government, examining spending proposals submitted by the government, or pursuing some investigative task assigned to a committee by the government. Within this straitjacket there can be little wiggle room for non-partisan accounting of the government's record and proposals.

Listen to the "Who Should Represent Canada and Why?" podcast, available at: www.oupcanada.com/Brooks8e

Senators argue that life is different in the red chamber. They point to the Senate's long string of committee and task force studies on topics ranging from corporate concentration in Canada's media industries to the decriminalization of marijuana possession. Being appointed to serve until the age of 75, most of them argue, loosens the constraint of party discipline. Not having to worry about whether their party leader will sign their nomination papers at some future election and being unconcerned with how their actions will affect their prospect of being appointed someday to cabinet, senators can behave with far greater independence than their House of Commons colleagues (see Box 9.4).

This argument, while not totally false, is both naive and self-serving. It is naive in that it ignores the palpable reality that most senators have demonstrated pretty firm and unswerving loyalty to the party, and especially the Prime Minister, that appointed them. This is not surprising when one looks at who becomes a senator and why. Most are people who have served their party long and well, and it would be more than a bit unusual if they were suddenly, after appointment to the Senate, to change the patterns of loyalty that got them there in the first place. That there are mavericks and "characters" in Canada's Senate whose idiosyncrasies and speechifying in that chamber would not be tolerated by their party in the House is beyond question. But how many Canadians know or care about this? The truth is that the media seldom report the excellent work done by many exceptional people who serve in Canada's Senate. Few are paying attention except the senators themselves.

The self-serving nature of senators' claim that their greater independence enables them to scrutinize and criticize the government to a degree not permitted in the House of Commons is pointed out by Jeffrey Simpson.[40] Simpson notes that senators routinely point to their many committee reports on important policy matters, undertaken at arm's length from the government, as proof of the significant role the unelected Senate performs in Canada's system of government. This is, Simpson rightly observes, a sort of *faute de mieux* argument.

Politics in Focus

BOX 9.4 Edmund Burke and the Canadian Senate

Edmund Burke was a member of the British House of Commons in the late 1700s. In his famous "Letter to the Sheriffs of Bristol," Burke explains why a member of the legislature—even one elected by the people—should not be overly concerned to ascertain and reflect the ideas and preferences of his constituents. Lawmakers should see themselves as trustees, he argued, not as the mere servants of public opinion. "Your representative owes you, not his industry only, but his judgment," said Burke, "and he betrays, instead of serving you, if he sacrifices it to your opinion." The lawmaker's role and responsibility were to rise above popular passions, narrow interests, and political expediency in order to formulate what Jean-Jacques Rousseau—a contemporary of Burke's, though not particularly a soulmate in matters of governance—called the general will. Lawmakers who thought of themselves as delegates of the people were, Burke felt, merely pandering to the mood of the moment. Their real duty was to their conscience and to an idea of the national interest that

was not determined by simply adding those in support of a proposal, subtracting those against it, then acting based on the result.

Burke's trustee lives on in the Canadian Senate, many of whose members are quite proud to acknowledge that they feel beholden to no one and to nothing except their conscience and their own ideas about what is in the best interests of the country. Notwithstanding the caricature of senators as lazy party hacks, many if not most of them are intelligent, thoughtful men and women who care deeply about Canada and who take their responsibilities very seriously. But do these qualities buy them a pass from the sort of accountability that most people expect in a modern democracy? Although a handful of other Western democracies have non-elected upper houses as part of their legislatures, only Canada does not set term limits on its non-elected senators. Edmund Burke at least had to explain himself to the citizens of Bristol and persuade them that his self-image as a trustee was worthy of their votes.

Lacking other plausible justifications for the existence of an unelected Senate stuffed with people whose appointments represent a form of patronage bestowed by the present Prime Minister and his/her predecessors, senators point to their committee work and its products. Certainly, their reports have often influenced the contours of public debate on an issue and the independence often associated with them could not have occurred in the House. But there is no reason to believe that only the Senate as currently constituted could make such a contribution to the process of scrutinizing government policy, investigating important issues, and proposing legislative change. Indeed, the committee work that senators point to as their proudest accomplishment and chief raison d'être usually just covers the same ground that think-tanks,

academic studies, and government-commissioned studies have mapped.

The legislature's oversight function also operates through the Office of the Auditor General. Created in 1878, the modern history of the office dates from 1977 when the Auditor General Act broadened its responsibilities from what were essentially auditing and accounting functions to examining how well programs and governments were being managed. This has proven to be a wide-ranging mandate. The Auditor General reports to the House of Commons and is authorized to issue up to three reports per year in addition to an annual report (Box 9.5). The first annual reports of the Auditor General tended to focus rather narrowly on the question of whether money appropriated by Parliament was spent in authorized ways

Politics in Focus

BOX 9.5   Casting a Spotlight on Government Mismanagement

The Office of the Auditor General's reports seldom produce more than temporary discomfort for the government of the day. There have been exceptions, the most significant in recent years being the sponsorship scandal, involving millions of dollars in advertising government sponsorship contracts in Quebec for services that were not provided or were at grossly inflated prices. Auditor General Sheila Fraser blew the whistle on this pattern of misspending in her February 2004 report. A Royal Commission, headed by Justice John Gomery, was created to examine the affair and charges were laid.

More typically, however, the Auditor General's reports highlight mismanagement, inefficiency, and ineptitude, not criminality. For example, the 2008 annual report was critical of the Canada Border Services Agency for failing to keep track of the whereabouts of 41,000 people who had been ordered to leave the country. In 2010 some squirming among politicians occurred when the Auditor

General revealed that MPs had refused her request to audit about $533 million in annual parliamentary spending. Faced with a barrage of public and media criticism, MPs relented. In his 2012 report, Auditor General Michael Ferguson charged that the Department of National Defence had failed to inform Parliament of the full cost of purchasing F-35 fighter planes and essentially made the decision to purchase this particular fighter plane without following proper purchasing rules.

But the effectiveness of the Office of the Auditor General cannot be measured by the number of "gotcha!" cases it reports or the amount of embarrassment it creates for the government. Knowing that the Auditor General performs an ongoing oversight function and that program inefficiencies and mismanagement may be brought to light in his or her reports is already a serious incentive for senior managers to do what they can to avoid being caught in the crosshairs of a negative audit.

and followed required accountability guidelines. Since passage of the 1977 Act, the concept of "value for money" has been part of the Auditor General's terms of reference. In 1995 the Auditor General Act was changed again, creating the position of Commissioner of the Environment and Sustainable Development within the Office of the Auditor General, thereby broadening its mandate to include the environmental audit of government programs and institutions. The statute also allows the Auditor General wide discretion in the selection of particular aspects of government spending for special scrutiny.

The result of all this has been that the Office of the Auditor General is today much larger and does much more than was the case several decades ago. Its annual reports and special studies often generate extensive and unfavourable media coverage of particular aspects of government performance.

But even more often this spotlight goes out rather quickly. This is less the fault of the Auditor General than a commentary on a media system that has a short attention span, in which few stories have a shelf life of more than a week or two.

Representation

Whatever shortcomings it may have, the House of Commons is an important point of contact between citizens and government. Symbolically, the elected House embodies the principle of government by popular consent. The partisan divisions within it, between government and opposition parties, have the additional effect of affirming for most citizens their belief in the competitive character of politics—excessively competitive, many believe! At a practical level, citizens often turn to their elected representatives when they experience problems with bureaucracy or when they want to express their views on government policy.

Unlike the elected Commons, the Senate does not perform a significant representational role in Canadian politics. This is despite the fact that senators are appointed to represent the various provinces and regions of Canada. The unelected character of Canada's upper house and the blatantly partisan criteria that prime ministers have usually relied on in filling Senate vacancies have undermined whatever legitimacy senators might otherwise have achieved as spokespersons for the regions. Provincial governments, regional spokespersons in the federal cabinet, and regional blocs of MPs within the party caucuses are, in about that order of importance, vastly more significant in representing regional interests.

Debate

The image that most Canadians have of Parliament is of the heated exchanges that take place across the aisle that separates the government and opposition parties. Parliamentary procedure and even the physical layout of the legislature are based on the adversarial principle of "them versus us." This principle is most clearly seen in the daily Question Period and the set-piece debates that follow the Speech from the Throne and the introduction of a new budget. At its best, the thrust and riposte of partisan debate can provide a very public forum for the discussion of national issues, as well as highlight the policy differences between the parties. Unfortunately for the quality of political discourse in Canada, parliamentary debate is more often dragged down by the wooden reading of prepared remarks, heckling and personal invective, and occasional blatant abuses of either the government's majority or the opposition's opportunities to hold up the business of Parliament.

It is a mistake to imagine that the purpose of parliamentary debate is to allow for a searching discussion of issues in a spirit of open-mindedness. Generally, MPs' minds are made up when a measure is first tabled in Parliament. Or if their minds are not made up on a bill, they know that, in most cases, they will be under enormous pressure to vote

as their party leadership directs. So if debate is really theatre, what is the point of the long hours spent criticizing and defending legislative proposals and the government's record, all at taxpayers' expense?

Legislative debate is important for two reasons. First, outcomes are not always predictable. Even when the government party holds a commanding majority in Parliament, or when the policy differences between government and opposition are not significant, the dynamic of debate on an issue is not entirely controllable by the government or by Parliament. Media coverage of the issue, reporting of public opinion polls, the interventions of organized interests, other governments, and even individuals who have credibility in the eyes of the media and the public all will have a bearing on the trajectory of parliamentary debate.

Parliamentary debate is also important because it reinforces the popular belief in the open and competitive qualities of Canadian democracy. "[T]he challenging of the 'noble lies' of the state," writes C.E.S. Franks, "through the institutionalization of doubt in question period and debate is one of the unusual and underappreciated virtues of the parliamentary system."[41] The stylized conflict between government and opposition parties, which is the essence of the British parliamentary system, emphasizes disagreements and differences. At the same time, however, adversarial politics obscures the fact that these partisan disagreements often take place within a fairly narrow band of consensus on basic values. The words and deeds of the opposition, when it holds power, have frequently borne a strong resemblance to the government that preceded it.

What Franks describes as an "underappreciated virtue" of the parliamentary system is, in fact, seen to be an indecorous shouting match by many, if not most, Canadians. They are more likely to view this give and take—Question Period at least, which is the only activity in Parliament a significant share of the population has seen either in person or, more commonly, on television—as dysfunctional rather than virtuous. As we saw earlier in this chapter, some critics, including some MPs, believe the partisan spectacle of Question Period actually undermines respect for government and dampens citizen engagement. This may or may not be true. What is clear, however, is that the blame for this situation does not belong entirely to the parties and their MPs. "Partisan attacks and political jousting," observes Andrea Ulrich, "result in exciting exchanges that are deemed [by the media to be] newsworthy, and the public eagerly watches the battles, all the while complaining about the behaviour of those they elected for just those qualities that hold their attention."[42]

Legitimation

Parliament is both a legislative and a legitimizing institution. Laws must pass through the parliamentary mill before being approved, and thus Parliament performs a crucial legislative function. But it also performs a legitimizing function because most of the mechanisms of democratic accountability are embodied in the structure and procedures of Parliament. It represents the people. It scrutinizes the actions of government. And it debates public issues. Along with elections and judicial review of the Constitution, Parliament appears to be one of the chief bulwarks against the danger that government will abuse its powers.

Listen to the "Who Should Represent Canada and Why?" podcast, available at: www.oupcanada.com/Brooks8e

How well Parliament performs its democratic functions is another matter. But the structures and procedures of the legislature are built around the ideas of open government and popular consent, and the constitutional requirement that the actions of government must be approved by Parliament. These factors help to legitimize the political system and the policies it produces. If most people held the view that the legislature is a farce, then its contribution to the perceived legitimacy of Canadian government would be undermined. Canadians do not hold this view. Their cynicism about the integrity of politicians and their disdain for parties do not appear to undermine their faith in parliamentary institutions.

Although the concentration of power in and around the Prime Minister has reached unprecedented levels, the legislature is not quite the helpless pawn of the government that some believe it to be. Using the rules of parliamentary procedure, opposition parties are able to prod, question, and castigate the government all in front of the parliamentary press gallery and the television cameras in the House of Commons. The opposition's behaviour is usually reactive, responding to the government's proposals and policies. Nevertheless, the legislature's function as a talking shop—the *parler* in "parliament"—enables it to draw attention to controversial aspects of the government's performance. MPs are not quite the "nobodies" that Pierre Trudeau once labelled them. But they are far from having the policy influence of their American counterparts, who, because of much looser party discipline and very different rules governing the law-making process, are very definitely "somebodies" when it comes to law-making and who, for this reason, are often assiduously courted by interest groups and the President himself.

Earlier, we said that caucus, the body of elected MPs belonging to a particular party, generally does not have much influence on the party leadership, at least not in the government party. When Parliament is in session, it is usual for a party's caucus to meet at least weekly. Caucus is not, however, considered unimportant by party leaders. The Prime Minister regularly attends caucus meetings, as do members of his or her cabinet when they are in Ottawa. These meetings often amount to little more than what one MP describes as "bitching sessions," but almost never do MPs challenge the Prime Minister behind the closed doors of the party's weekly meeting.[43]

Some insiders argue, however, that the government caucus provides a real opportunity for backbench members to influence government policy through frank debate away from the eyes and ears of the media and the opposition. A recent study of the government caucus under Prime Ministers Chrétien, Martin, and Harper concludes that many backbench MPs believe their voices are, in fact, taken seriously by the party leadership during the party's weekly closed-door meetings. "[T]he degree of influence exerted by backbenchers appears to be shaped by several factors, perhaps the greatest of which is the party leader's tolerance for dissent, which in turn is shaped by the political context facing a party."[44] Other things being equal, the circumstances of minority government require tighter party discipline and are less conducive to the expression of dissent than when the governing party has a majority in the House of Commons. This generalization does not, however, cover all cases. If a policy is a high priority of the government, the prospect that a caucus revolt will defeat or substantially change it is extremely remote. This may be true even when the policy is a very unpopular one, as was the GST, introduced by the Conservative government in 1990.The leadership's willingness to tolerate dissent in caucus may also be less in the case of divisive issues the government believes may cause it considerable embarrassment in the media and potentially a loss of voter support. This was certainly true of the abortion issue in the spring of 2013. A group of Conservative MPs, led by Mark Warawa, supported a non-binding motion that would have condemned sex-selective abortions. In this case it appears that the Conservative MPs who supported this motion had their opportunity to make their case in caucus. In the end, however, the government was not willing to allow a vote on the motion.

MPs who fail to toe the line once an issue has been aired in caucus are likely to experience the fate of those Liberals who voted against the Chrétien government's gun law in 1995: the loss of committee assignments. Expulsion from caucus is another sanction that may be used to punish recalcitrant backbenchers. It needs to be kept in mind that the caucus of the governing party—as is true of the legislature as a whole—usually enters the policy-making process late, after much study, consultation, and negotiation have already taken place. Embedded in the legislation that the members of the government party caucus are asked to vote for is a complex fabric of compromises and accommodations between government and interest groups, different agencies of government, or even Ottawa and the provinces. It is unlikely that the government will be willing to see this fabric come unravelled because of caucus opposition.

Following the prorogation of Parliament in December 2009, many Canadians used social media (such as Facebook) to express their disappointment in the government. Does the prorogation of Parliament represent a democratic deficit? Why or why not?

Graeme MacKay/Artizans.com

What Does an MP Do?

Many Canadians believe that their politicians are overpaid, underworked, and liable to line their own pockets at public expense. Stories of "gold-clad" MPs' pensions and of senators guilty of ethically questionable billing practices help to fuel this widespread but generally unfair charge. Most backbench MPs work very long hours, whether in Ottawa or at home in their constituencies (see Box 9.6). The demands on their time ratchet upward in the case of members of the government and party leaders, all of whom are required to travel extensively in carrying out their jobs. But what does a typical MP do? For most MPs, the single largest block of their working day is devoted to taking care of constituency business. David Docherty reports that the MPs he surveyed from the thirty-fourth (1988–93) and thirty-fifth (1993–7) parliaments claimed to devote just over 40 per cent of their working time to constituency affairs. The second largest block of time was spent on legislative work, such as committee assignments and attending Question Period and debates. These activities run a fairly distant second, however, to constituency work, as shown in Figure 9.4.

In performing their functions, all MPs are provided with a budget that enables them to hire staff in Ottawa and in their riding office. How they allocate these resources is up to them, but most MPs opt to have two staffers in Ottawa and two in the constituency office. MPs are also provided with public funds to maintain their constituency office and are allowed an unlimited regular mail budget and four mass mailings to constituents—known as "householders"—per year. Although these resources are paltry compared to those at the disposal of US congressional representatives and senators, they are superior to those of legislators in the United Kingdom, Belgium, France, and many other democracies. And while they may be adequate to enable an MP to carry out his or her constituency duties, they are not sufficient to pay for high-powered policy analysts and other research staff.

Docherty found that MPs who were new to Parliament tended to spend more time on constituency work than those who had been in the legislature for a longer period of time. "[T]he longer members serve in office," he observes, "the less time they will devote to constituency work."[45] This shift from constituency to policy-oriented work

does not, however, mean that a veteran MP's constituents are less well served than those of an MP who is new to Parliament. Docherty found that the Ottawa staffs of veteran MPs tended to make up the difference, spending more of their time on constituency business as their MPs' focus shifted to policy concerns. "No matter what stage of their career," Docherty states, "members of parliament see helping individuals as their most crucial duty."[46] In this, MPs show themselves to be realistic about the limits on their ability to be lawmakers.

The Democratic Deficit?

During the 1990s it became increasingly popular to speak about a **democratic deficit** in Canadian politics. This resulted, it was said, from what critics believed to be the excessive centralization of power in and around the Prime Minister and cabinet and the marginalization of the legislature to little more than an occasionally entertaining, more often embarrassing, but almost always irrelevant sideshow. Jeffrey Simpson's book, *The Friendly Dictatorship*, made the case for significant reform of the way in which Parliament conducts its business, as did many other political commentators.

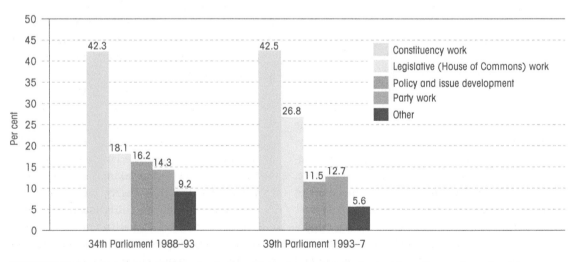

FIGURE 9.4   How an MP Spends the Day (per cent of working time devoted to different tasks)

Source: This figure is reprinted with permission of the Publisher from *Mr. Smith Goes to Ottawa: Life in the House of Commons* by David Docherty © University of British Columbia Press 1997. All rights reserved by the Publisher.

Prime Minister Harper's prorogation of Parliament in November 2008 and December 2009, each time in circumstances where it appeared likely that the government was on the brink of being defeated in the House, fuelled charges that the democratic deficit was deeper than ever.

Is there a democratic deficit in Canada? Those who think the Prime Minister should have a relatively unfettered hand in shaping the legislative agenda and moving it through Parliament will not think so. On the other hand, criticisms such as those made by Keith Martin (Box 9.6), Jeffrey Simpson, Donald Savoie, and others insist that the deficit is large and perhaps growing larger. A recent book on the democratic deficit in Canada and the United States, edited by Patti Tamara Lenard and Richard Simeon, suggests several factors that may have contributed to a growing disconnect between the people and those who govern them and to what is believed to be an unhealthy concentration of political power. The impotence of the Canadian legislature and the emergence of prime ministerial government are only part of the picture they describe.[47]

In considering whether there is a democratic deficit a baseline first must be established. A deficit compared to what? Is political power concentrated in fewer hands today than in the heyday of the so-called "mandarins," the cabal of senior public servants who effectively ran the federal government in the post-World War II era and whose ties to the Liberal Party, which formed the government most of the time, were very intimate? Perhaps we have more democratic and participatory expectations as a result of cultural changes that have swept across the Western world. Europeans have talked for many years about a democratic deficit in EU politics, so we are certainly not alone, nor are we the first to wring our hands about unresponsive political elites and broken institutions of accountability. There is little doubt that "democratic deficit" sometimes is merely a slogan when used by some critics who do not like the ideological coloration or policy direction of a particular government or the sort of outcomes produced by the electoral or legislative system. At the same time, however, the term performs the very useful function of causing us to think about how well our political institutions achieve the goals we associate with democracy. And if we find they do not provide the transparency, accountability, and responsiveness to the popular will that we expect, then this indeed is a democratic deficit.

The Courts

Responsibility for Canada's judicial system is divided between Ottawa and the provinces. While the Constitution gives the federal government the exclusive right to make criminal law, it assigns responsibility for the administration of justice and for law enforcement to the provinces. Consequently, all provinces have established their own systems of courts that interpret and apply both federal and provincial laws.

The Constitution also gives Ottawa the authority to create courts. This authority was used in 1875 to create the Supreme Court of Canada. Since 1949 the Supreme Court has been Canada's highest court of appeal. Ottawa again used this constitutional power in 1971 to create the Federal Court of Canada. It has jurisdiction over civil claims involving the federal government, cases arising from the decisions of federally appointed administrative bodies like the Immigration Appeal Board, and matters relating to federal income tax, copyrights, and maritime law—all of which fall under the legislative authority of Ottawa. The structure of Canada's court system is shown in Figure 9.5.

Courts apply and interpret the law. They perform this role in matters ranging from contested driving offences and squabbles over wills to disputes over the most fundamental principles of the Constitution. The decisions of judges often have profound implications for the rights and status of individuals and groups, for the balance of social and economic power, and for the federal division of powers. It is, therefore, crucial that we understand the political significance of the judicial process and the methods of interpretation typically used by the courts.

The independence of judges is the cornerstone of the Canadian judicial system. Judges are appointed

Politics in Focus

BOX 9.6 Parliament: An MP's View

There really is no such thing as a typical day in the life of an MP: they work in Ottawa when Parliament is in session; they travel back and forth to their constituencies and to conferences and meetings of various kinds; and they work in their constituencies. For some MPs, such as Dr Keith Martin from British Columbia, who served from 1993 to 2011, the job is gratifying but increasingly frustrating because of the extent to which party discipline and partisanship have created a democratic deficit whereby members must "toe the party line" or risk ostracism.

Canada's Parliament is a child of the British Westminster system where the party in power tries to implement their agenda while opposition parties hold the government to account. Canada is supposed to be a democracy yet fundamental democratic principles and rights, such as the right to freedom of speech, are consistently violated in the nation's senior governing body. As a result the ability of our citizenry to have their wishes expressed in Parliament by the MPs they elect has been dramatically compromised over the last 30 years and especially over the last eight.

Today, MPs are expected to parrot what is given to them by the leader of their party regardless of what their constituents want. The position a party takes is made by its leader and a small number of advisers who are not elected by the people and thus are not accountable to them. MPs have little or no say in what a party does. Their role is to represent their party to the people and not their constituents to Parliament.

MPs who advocate for the will of their constituents over that of the party will be penalized by the party. They will not be allowed to speak in Parliament. They will be removed from any position they hold, and can be banished from caucus and forced to sit as independents (see the cases of MPs Michael Chong and Bill Casey). This significantly harms an MP's ability to represent his or her constituents and produces very difficult ethical dilemmas for the member. Do you support the will of the people over that of the leadership of your party and weaken your influence within your party, or do you buckle under, go against the will of the citizens you represent but maintain whatever influence you may have within your party?

No democratically elected leader in the West has as much power as a Canadian Prime Minister. This role was described by Quebec Supreme Court Justice John Gomery as "one-man government."

Against this backdrop is the press, which in Canada has become concentrated in very few hands. Fighting for a shrinking advertising dollar, the media have resolved to increase their readership or viewership by focusing on "infotainment." Reality TV and *People* magazine trump news and informative documentaries.

Into this milieu enters the member of Parliament, a person who has chosen to seek and successfully attained public office to better his or her community and the country as a whole. What a shock it is when that person enters the hallowed halls of the House of Commons.

When they are in Ottawa, MPs' day-to-day work in Parliament revolves around the House of Commons and committees. Time spent in the House of Commons (House duty), where they listen to speeches, give

by governments. But once appointed they hold office "during good behaviour"[48]—or to age 75. What constitutes a lapse from "good behaviour"? A criminal or a serious moral offence could provide grounds for removal, as could decisions of such incompetence that they undermine public respect for the law and the judiciary. This test of judicial misconduct was set down more clearly in the 1990 Nova Scotia Court of Appeal inquiry into the exoneration of Donald Marshall Jr following his having spent 11 years in prison for a murder he did not commit: "Is the conduct alleged so manifestly and speeches, and ask questions about legislation, is poorly attended. There are usually fewer than 15 MPs, out of 308, sitting in the House at any one time and fewer people sit in the public galleries. The debates, however, are televised.

Most speeches are written by the party for their MPs, who stand up and read them. Their speeches toe the party line with a heavy emphasis on criticizing other parties for real or imagined failures. Personally, I write my own speeches and use them to advance new solutions on the subject under debate.

MPs also spend four to six hours per week on committees that they are appointed to sit on. Committees used to be a place where partisanship was kept to a minimum and discussions revolved around important issues of the day. Today, Parliament's committees are highly dysfunctional and are simply an extension of the partisan bickering found in the House of Commons. Studies are done, but rarely does anyone pay any attention to them. Committees are a colossal waste of time and money and are meant to keep MPs busy and unproductive. The rest of the time members meet with groups who wish to lobby them on an issue.

MPs generally work 10 hours a day Monday to Thursday when Parliament is in session. They travel back to their home ridings Thursday night and work Friday, Saturday, and Sunday in their ridings, where they attend community functions and deal with constituency problems. If an MP tries to create and implement solutions to problems, then the workload can easily reach 80 hours a week or more.

When an MP comes to Parliament, he or she has some decisions to make. If MPs want to advance up the ladder within their own party they should do exactly what they are told to do and engage in rabid, partisan attacks against other parties. An MP should not think independently and work collaboratively with MPs from other parties in order to move ideas forward. To do so is to run the risk of being labelled a maverick or not being seen as a team player. This is unfortunate, as failing to engage in the independent, critical analysis of problems weakens our political system, and fails the nation.

A tough road, but one that is very gratifying, is for the MP to have an agenda of initiatives to pursue and build partnerships with citizens, NGOs, activists, the private sector, and other MPs to implement these solutions. Building coalitions, advancing ideas, and leading is the purview of an MP. This approach will make the individual MP run afoul of the party leadership, but, in the end, why have this job unless you are willing to take chances and be courageous in the pursuit of solutions that will make our world a better place to live?

Parliament can change, but it will require courage. Leaders will have to stare down the status quo and champion the innovations that will address the big challenges we face.

Democracy and party discipline make strange bedfellows. Enforcing oppressive discipline over MPs in the manner that is done today corrodes our democracy by severing the will of the people from being exercised in Parliament. In this environment an MP faces difficult challenges, but he or she was elected by the people, and for the people. They must do what they have to do to live with themselves and be able to look into the eyes of the people they represent with a clear conscience.

Dr Keith Martin, MD, PC, was the member of Parliament for Esquimalt-Juan de Fuca in British Columbia. First elected to office in 1993 as a member of the Reform Party of Canada, he sat as a Liberal from 2004 to 2011, when he chose not to stand for re-election.

profoundly destructive of the concept of impartiality, integrity and independence of the judicial role, that public confidence would be sufficiently undermined to render the judge incapable of executing judicial office?"[49] In such circumstances the appointing government may launch removal proceedings against a judge. In fact, however, this has seldom happened. Formal proceedings have rarely been initiated and have very seldom been prosecuted to their ultimate conclusion, i.e., the actual removal of a judge by resolution of Parliament or a provincial legislature.[50] Indeed, no federal judge has ever been removed from office through this process. Judicial independence is also protected by the fact that judges' salaries and conditions of service are established by law. Consequently, governments cannot single out any individual judge for special reward or punishment.

But as Ralph Miliband puts it, to say that judges are "independent" begs the question, "Independent of what?" As members of the societies in which they live—usually successful members of the middle and upper-middle classes—they cannot be neutral in the values they bring to their task. Judges, observes Miliband, "are by no means, and cannot be, independent of the multitude of influences, notably of class origin, education, class situation and professional tendency, which contribute as much to the formation of their view of the world as they do in the case of other men."[51] Thus, when one says that the judiciary is "independent" this should be understood as a description of its formal separation from the executive and legislative branches of

the state. When it comes to the dominant value system of their society, judges are no more independent than are the members of any other part of the state elite. Leaving aside the socio-economically unrepresentative character of the legal profession and the effects of formal training in the law, in Canada, as in the vast majority of democracies, all judges are appointed by governments.[52] One would hardly expect these governments to appoint radical critics of society, even supposing that a significant number of such individuals existed within the more respected ranks of the legal profession from which judges are selected. Moreover, governments control promotion within the system of courts—who will be promoted from a district court to a superior court, and so on. This may also exert a chilling effect on unconventional judicial behaviour.

The socio-economic background of judges and the process by which they are selected have been argued by some to introduce certain biases into the judiciary. In recent years the legal profession from

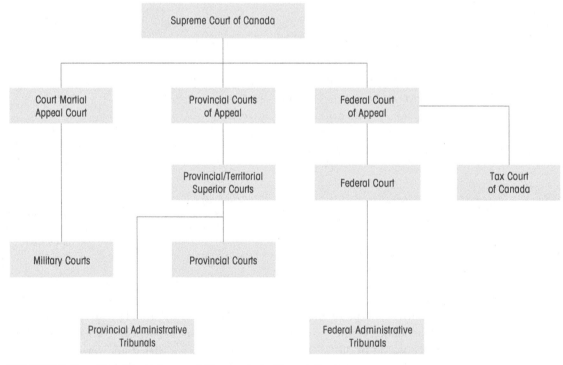

FIGURE 9.5   The Structure of Canada's Court System

Source: *Canada's Court System*, Figure: Outline of Canada's Court System, page 3. http://www.justice.gc.ca/eng/csj-sjc/css-ajc/page3 .html. Department of Justice Canada, 2005. Reproduced with the permission of the Department of Justice Canada, 2014.

which judges are selected has become more representative than it was through most of Canada's history. The process of representation starts with who is admitted to law school. For a profession that prides itself on what it believes to be its sensitivity to issues of fairness and social justice, there is frustratingly little and at best only scattered information on this subject. Law schools and the legal profession have collected data on gender and racial representation among their student bodies and practitioners, but there is not much in the way of systematically collected data on the socio-economic background of those who get into law school, enter the legal profession, and subsequently become part of the pool from which judges are selected. One of the few useful studies, carried out by sociologist Michael Ornstein and based on an examination of the legal profession in Ontario, found that the representation of visible minorities has increased steadily. It is highest among younger members of the profession and increased from about 2 per cent of lawyers between the ages of 25 and 34 in 1981 to 17 per cent in 2001. For Canada as a whole, and across all age groups, it was about 14 per cent in 2001. The representation of non-white Canadians in the legal profession was, Ornstein found, significantly lower than in most other professions including medicine, engineering, university professors, and business managers.[53] According to a 2012 study by Ryerson University's Diversity Institute, visible minority judges constituted under 3 per cent of all federally appointed judges.[54]

Women have much greater representation in the legal profession than a generation ago. In 1971 they comprised only about 5 per cent of the legal profession. Today they constitute close to 40 per cent of all lawyers. Females also represent about one-third of judges in Canada. The main argument for the increased representation of women on the courts has been that they bring important perspectives on the law and on society that have been less likely to be embraced by male judges.[55] The same argument is made for the increased representation of some other under-represented groups, including visible minorities.

Less studied, but surely no less significant, is the over-representation in the legal profession and among judges of persons from the higher rungs of the socio-economic ladder. Data from the United States confirm the dramatic class bias in the legal profession, particularly in the more prestigious and influential legal circles and among judges, that begins with the selection process at law schools.[56] Most of the evidence for Canada, however, is hardly more than anecdotal. Of course, a class bias already exists when it comes to who is more likely to attend university. This bias becomes more pronounced in the case of who is likely to be accepted into and graduate from professional programs. There may be no reason to imagine that such bias is greater in the case of law schools than, say, MBA programs or medical schools. Nonetheless, life experiences and socio-economic background, as Miliband has suggested, certainly have some influence on how one views the world and, in this case, interprets the law.

At the same time, it is simplistic and incorrect to assume any sort of automatic correspondence between a judge's ethnicity, gender, or socio-economic background and the likelihood that he or she will decide cases in a particular way. The judicial profession in Canada—still mainly male, white, and from middle- and upper-class origins—is much more liberal today than it was 40 or 50 years ago. It used to be argued that the judiciary had a conservative impact on the law and its interpretation because of the background characteristics of judges and the nature of law and of the judicial function. We are used to thinking of the law as simply "the rules made by governments" that "apply to everybody in society."[57] But the law is more than this. It represents values that have accumulated over a long period of time. The concepts, meanings, precedents, and interpretive rules that shape judicial decision-making tend to inhibit sharp breaks with the past. Legal reasoning in Anglo-American judicial systems is based on the concept of *stare decisis*. This means that in deciding a case judges should be guided by decisions in previous cases where the circumstances and issues were similar, and also that lower courts are bound by the rulings of higher courts.

Recent history has shown, however, that Canadian judges are quite prepared to depart from established precedents when they think the circumstances warrant this and, moreover, that they have sometimes shown a willingness to be ahead of public opinion on some issues. Particularly at the highest levels of the judicial system, judges are generally quite aware of the socio-economic and political consequences of their decisions. In a 1989 decision the Supreme Court rejected the traditional liberal notion of equality as identical treatment before the law in favour of what is sometimes called **substantive equality**. This requires that individuals be looked at in terms of their group characteristics and the possible advantages or disadvantages they may have experienced as a result of these attributes. It is likely that the Court was ahead of public opinion on this matter. Canadian courts were surely ahead of public opinion when it came to same-sex marriage. The Charter has been a decisive factor in this matter of judges being more willing to depart from legal precedents. In one of the earliest Charter decisions, *R. v. Big M Drug Mart Ltd* (1985), the Supreme Court stated that the Charter "does not simply 'recognize and declare' existing rights as they were circumscribed by legislation current at the time of the Charter's entrenchment." The Charter has enabled Canadian judges to look at familiar issues through a different lens and arrive at very different rulings, thus weakening the conservative tug of *stare decisis*. Some critics disagree. "The Charter's potentially radical and liberatory principles of equality, freedom, and democracy," argues Joel Bakan, "are administered by a fundamentally conservative institution—the legal system—and operate in social conditions that routinely undermine their realization."[58] By his account, judges are for the most part incapable of escaping from certain conservative understandings of the Charter and of rights—particularly an unwillingness to recognize social rights—and from conservative conceptions that prevent them from playing a transformative role in Canadian society. Of course, this just leads us to wonder what Canadians want or expect from judges! Those who argue that the courts should play a transformative role were deeply disappointed in September 2013 when the Ontario Superior Court refused to hear a case involving homelessness. Advocates for the homeless argued that sections 7 and 15 of the Charter should be interpreted as providing a right to housing and that the existence of homelessness involves a Charter violation. The governments of Ontario and Canada opposed this interpretation, insisting that the courts had no authority to decide such matters. The Ontario Superior Court agreed.

As we saw in Chapter 7, some argue that recourse to the courts to achieve ends that cannot be accomplished through the political process is fundamentally undemocratic. It is simply wrong, however, to conceive of the courts as being outside the political process. Even before the Charter, the courts were very much a part of politics and policy-making in Canada. Their rulings on the federal–provincial division of powers and on all manner of policy questions have always been part of Canadian politics. Quebec nationalists have long complained that the Supreme Court of Canada has a pro-federal bias, a claim that—true or not—reflects the inescapable involvement of the Court in the politics of federalism. The fact that by law three of the Supreme Court's nine judges must be members of the Quebec bar, and that by tradition three should be from Ontario, two from the West, and one from Atlantic Canada, shows that the essentially political issue of regional representation has been considered important for the judicial branch, just as it is important in the executive and legislative branches of government.

In recent years the issue of representation on the bench, particularly on the Supreme Court, has become even more politically charged. The 1998 retirement of Justice John Sopinka unleashed an unprecedented flurry of behind-the-scenes lobbying and public advocacy on behalf of particular candidates for this vacancy on Canada's highest court. The retirement of Justice Peter Cory in 1999 likewise was preceded by active lobbying in legal circles, particularly on behalf of female candidates for the job. Gender and judicial ideology appear to have become more prominent criteria in the Supreme Court selection process, at least in the eyes of many advocacy and rights-oriented groups (see Box 9.7). Many critics argue that the judicial selection process is mired in partisanship and a lack of transparency and should be reformed.[59]

If we accept, then, that the courts are unavoidably part of the political process, is there any basis for the claim that recourse to the courts may be undemocratic? The short answer is "yes." Several decades before the Charter, James Mallory argued that business interests cynically exploited the federal division of powers in the British North America Act to oppose increased state interference in their affairs, regardless of which level of government was doing the interfering.[60] Respect for democratic principles and the Constitution was the cloak behind which business attempted to conceal its self-interest.

In the Charter era similar criticisms have been expressed. Charter critics like Ted Morton and Rainer Knopff argue that recourse to the courts by abortion rights advocates, gay and lesbian rights groups, and Aboriginals, among others, have produced rulings that often elevate the preferences of special interests over more broadly held values.

The Social Fabric

BOX 9.7 Is the Supreme Court "Representative" of Canada?

When the Conservatives came to power in 2006, the Supreme Court consisted of five men and four women. With the retirement of Justice Morris Fish in 2013, the gender balance on the Court was five men and three women. This became an issue as a number of individuals and groups argued that the next appointee needed to be a woman in order to re-establish a fair gender balance on the Court. The issue arose during the confirmation hearing for Marc Nadon, a Federal Court of Appeal judge, as a result of a question from Irwin Cotler, constitutionalist and internationally known human rights lawyer.

Irwin Cotler, MP for Mount Royal: Some hoped that this nomination in particular would preserve gender parity on the Court. In your opinion, what element of diversity do you contribute to the bench and why would that be desirable?

Marc Nadon, nominee to the Supreme Court: I have a hard time saying why I add to diversity. . . . I have a specific background, as does each one of you. I have my own life journey, for better or for worse. I have a legal vision. I had the career I've described to you. As a judge, I've heard hundreds if not thousands of cases on just about every topic under the sun. I've learned a lot, I've heard many arguments, I've had many opportunities to reflect on all of these topics that concern not just those affected by a case, but those that concern society, Charter issues. . . .

I've had 20 years to reflect on that and the law doesn't operate in a vacuum; many things must be understood to be a good judge. For example, history, sociology, and this isn't to toot my own horn, but for 20 years one of the things I've appreciated as a judge is that I've had the opportunity, as opposed to practising law, being a judge gives us the freedom, there's no excuse for not understanding or trying to understand all the major issues of a society.

Am I the ethnic candidate that fits perfectly? Well, I can't answer that. I'll let others answer that question.

Some people answered in the negative. The day after Nadon's appearance before the House of Commons committee, a CBC news story began with the headline, "A noticeable trend to less diversity, women on the country's top courts." Fewer women, perhaps. But less diversity? No one asked Nadon about the class circumstances of his upbringing or what in his life might make him more or less sensitive to class inequalities. No one seemed to think the fact that the highest Court has never included a non-white person was worth mentioning. Nor was it raised by anyone on the committee that the Court has never included someone from outside the Judeo-Christian tradition. It seems that some forms of diversity matter more, to some, than do others.

Source: House of Commons, Ad hoc Committee on Supreme Court Nominees, 2 October 2013; my transcript from the video-recorded proceedings.

More importantly, from the standpoint of our examination of the machinery of government, they agree with Andrew Petter's argument that the Charter era has brought about the "legalization" of Canadian politics.[61] "The legalisation of politics," Petter writes, "has increased the stature and authority of lawyers and legal discourse within Canadian society and has diminished the importance and influence of politicians and democratic engagement."[62] This process is far more pervasive than the occasional overturning of a statute might suggest. Petter notes that it operates throughout the bureaucracy, federally and provincially, as public servants regularly anticipate and are guided by their understanding of what the Charter requires and how it will affect policies and guidelines they are drafting.

Emboldened by the entrenchment of rights in the Constitution and the declaration of constitutional supremacy in section 52 of the Constitution Act, 1982, judges have been less deferential to governments and legislatures than in the past. Moreover, a network of rights-oriented advocacy groups, law professors, lawyers, journalists, and bureaucrats working within the rights apparatus of the state (from human rights commissions to the ubiquitous equity officers found throughout the public sector) has emerged, which, in the words of Morton and Knopff, "prefers the policy-making power of the less obviously democratic governmental institutions."[63] The institutions they are referring to are the courts and quasi-judicial rights commissions and tribunals.

The era of judges deferring to the will of elected officials is over. The Charter was the catalyst for what both critics and supporters see as an enormous increase in the policy role of the courts. While acknowledging that the courts now play a vastly greater role in the policy process, including matters of social policy, Chief Justice Beverley McLachlin argues that judges do so in a spirit of impartiality (see Box 9.8). She is, of course, correct that judges are not political in the sense of being representatives of one or another party and its agenda. But with all due respect to the Chief Justice and her colleagues on the bench, it is disingenuous or at least naive to suggest that judges are impartial in the sense of being apolitical, i.e., without

political beliefs, values, and preferences. We are back to Ralph Miliband's observation that judges are no more independent of the value system of their society than any other part of the state elite. We expect them to be independent of party influence, but until the law contains its own self-evident meanings—in which case we would have no need for courts—judges will not be politically impartial.

Appendix: How a Law Is Passed

The law takes various forms. A statute passed by the House of Commons and the Senate, and given royal assent by the Governor General, is clearly a law. But decisions taken by cabinet that have not been approved in the legislature also have the force of law. These are called "Orders-in-Council." Thousands of them are issued each year, and they are published in the *Canada Gazette*. The decisions of agencies, boards, and commissions that receive their regulatory powers from a statute also have the force of law. Finally, there are the regulations and guidelines issued and enforced by the departmental bureaucracy in accordance with the discretionary powers delegated to them under a statute. These also have the force of law.

In a strictly numerical sense the statutes passed annually by Parliament represent only the tip of the iceberg of laws promulgated each year. Nevertheless, virtually all major policy decisions—including budget measures and the laws that assign discretionary power to the bureaucracy—come before the legislature. The only exception has been when the normal process of government was suspended by passage of the War Measures Act. This happened during World War I, again during World War II, and briefly in 1970 when Ottawa proclaimed the War Measures Act after two political kidnappings in Quebec by the Front de libération du Québec. The War Measures Act was replaced by the Emergencies Act in 1988.

During normal times the law-making process involves several stages and opportunities for debate and amendment. The steps from the introduction

Governing Realities

BOX 9.8 Chief Justice McLachlin Defends the Court's Involvement with Questions of Social Policy

The fact that judges rule on social questions that affect large numbers of people does not, however, mean that judges are political. There is much confusion on this point in the popular press. Judges are said to be acting politically, to have descended (or perhaps ascended) into the political arena. Judges, on this view, are simply politicians who do not need to stand for election and can never be removed.

This misapprehension confuses outcome with process. Many judicial decisions on important social issues—say affirmative action, or abortion, or gay rights—will be political in the sense that they will satisfy some political factions at the expense of others. But the term "political" is used in the context to describe an outcome, not a process. While the outcomes of cases are inevitably political in some broad sense of the term, it is important—critical, even—that the process be impartial. It is inescapable that judges' decisions will have political ramifications. But it is essential that they not be partisan. In their final form, judgments on social policy questions are often not all that different from legislation. It is the process by which the judgments are arrived at that distinguishes them. Legislation is often the product of compromise or conflict between various

political factions, each faction pushing its own agenda. The judicial arena does not, and should not, provide simply another forum for the same kind of contests. Judges must *maintain the appearance and reality of impartiality*. It is impartiality that distinguishes us from the other branches of government, and impartiality that gives us our legitimacy.

. . . (Our) changing society affects the work of judges. The nature of the questions they decide, and the public expectation that they will decide them fairly and well, place new demands on judges. It no longer suffices to be a competent legal scholar and a fair arbiter. To perform their modern role well, judges must be sensitive to a broad range of social concerns. They must possess a keen appreciation of the importance of individual and group interests and rights. And they must be in touch with the society in which they work, understanding its values and its tensions. The ivory tower no longer suffices as the residence of choice for judges.

Source: Excerpt from remarks of the Right Honourable Beverley McLachlin, PC, Chief Justice of Canada, on "The Role of Judges in Modern Society," given at the 4th Worldwide Common Law Judiciary Conference in Vancouver, BC, 5 May 2001. At: <www.scc-csc.gc.ca/aboutcourt/judges/speeches/role-of-judges_e.html>.

of a bill in parliament to the final proclamation of a statute are set out in Figure 9.6.

There are two types of bills: private members' bills and government bills. Private members' bills originate from any individual MP, but unless they get the backing of government they have little chance of passing. Government bills dominate parliament's legislative agenda. When major legislation is being proposed, a bill is sometimes preceded by a *white paper*. This is a report for discussion, based on research by the bureaucracy (and sometimes the legislature as well), and serves as a statement of the government's legislative intentions. Major legislation may also follow from the recommendations of a Royal Commission, a task force, or some other

consultative body created by the government to study and make recommendations on an issue.

Once a bill has been drafted by government, it is introduced into the Senate, or more usually, into the House of Commons. Here, it is given *first reading*, which is just a formality and involves no debate. Then the bill goes to *second reading*, when the main principles of the bill are debated and a vote is taken. If the bill passes second reading it is sent to a smaller legislative committee, where the details of the bill are considered clause by clause. At this committee stage, amendments can be made but the principle of the bill cannot be altered. The bill is then reported back to the House, where all aspects, including any amendments, are debated.

At this *report stage* new amendments also can be introduced. If a bill passes this hurdle it then goes to *third reading* where a final vote is taken, sometimes after further debate. Once a bill has been passed in the House, it is then sent to the Senate where a virtually identical process takes place. If a bill was first introduced in the Senate, then it would now be sent to the House. Finally, a bill that has been passed in both the House and the Senate can be given royal assent and become law.

FIGURE 9.6   From Bill to Statute

Starting Points for Research

Peter Aucoin, Mark Jarvis, and Lori Turnbull, *Democratizing the Constitution: Reforming Responsible Government* (Toronto: Emond Montgomery Publications, 2010). This book won the Donner Prize in 2011, given for excellence in public policy writing by Canadians. The authors argue that "the lack of a shared basic understanding of the 'unwritten rules' of the Canadian constitution has undermined the functioning of responsible government."

David Docherty, *Mr. Smith Goes to Ottawa: Life in the House of Commons* (Vancouver: University of British Columbia Press, 1997). This excellent analysis of legislative behaviour and influence in the House of Commons is based largely on surveys of MPs.

Lydia Miljan, *Public Policy in Canada*, 6th edn (Toronto: Oxford University Press, 2012). This text examines the forces that shape Canadian public policy and surveys several policy fields, including health, Aboriginal, social, economic, family, and environmental policy.

Donald Savoie, *Governing from the Centre: The Concentration of Power in Canadian Politics* (Toronto: University of Toronto Press, 1999). Here Savoie makes the case that the concentration of power in and around the Prime Minister's Office has reached unprecedented and undemocratic levels. This "must read" for those interested in the inner workings of the machinery of government should be followed by Savoie's *Court Government and the Collapse of Accountability in Canada and the United Kingdom* (Toronto: University of Toronto Press, 2008).

Review Exercises

1. Who is the current Chief of Staff to the Prime Minister? Who is the current Clerk of the Privy Council? What are their backgrounds (education, professional experience, partisan involvement, etc.). Find a story in the media that discusses the influence of one of these individuals.

2. Put together a list of the various governmental organizations (federal, provincial, municipal) you have been in contact with during your life and the reasons for the contact(s). Think hard—the list is probably longer than you imagine at first.

3. Go to the website for the Cable Public Affairs Channel (www.cpac.ca/en/). You may view live hearings from the Supreme Court, parliamentary committees, or debates/Question Period from the floor of the House of Commons. Watch 30 minutes of hearings from the Supreme Court or from a parliamentary committee and summarize your observations in no more than 200 words.

10 The Administrative State

For policies to have an impact they must be implemented. This is the role of the bureaucracy. Implementation, however, is not an automatic process of converting laws into actions. Unelected officials often wield enormous discretion in applying laws and administering programs. Moreover, their influence is felt at numerous points in the decision-making process preceding the actual introduction of a bill in Parliament. This chapter examines the federal bureaucracy, focusing on the following topics:

- The development of the administrative state.
- Professionalization of the public service in Canada.
- The political rights of public servants.
- The functions of the bureaucracy.
- Departments.
- Public enterprise.
- Regulatory agencies.

Canada Post Corporation, along with the Canadian Broadcasting Corporation (CBC), the Bank of Canada, Canada Revenue Agency, Export Development Canada, Parks Canada, and a whole host of other government institutions, make up the federal bureaucracy and are responsible for carrying out the policies set by the government of Canada. Reporting falling profits, Canada Post announced in 2014 that it would phase out door-to-door mail delivery. (ThinkStock/©bukharova)

During the first year after Confederation, the government of Canada spent about $14 million. Its revenues were about the same. It is uncertain how many employees worked for the federal government. Apparently no one thought it worthwhile to keep track of this information before 1900, when it was found that the Canadian government had 12,000 employees. The organization of the federal government was fairly simple in the years after Confederation, with 10 major departments and four main agencies by 1873.[1]

This uncomplicated structure did not last. By 1960 federal spending had reached $5.7 billion. The federal government consisted of 92 major departments and agencies employing about 200,000 persons. The need for an organization chart to help keep track of this growing complexity was keenly felt and, indeed, the Financial Administration Act had been passed in 1951, providing a legal framework to make sense of the variety of structures that had emerged in a mainly ad hoc and uncoordinated manner over the years. How to keep on top of the leviathan that modern government had become was, by the 1960s, an important concern of those who studied Canadian government and **bureaucracy**. It has been so ever since.

Today, federal spending is approaching $300 billion. The list of federal departments and agencies runs into the hundreds.[2] Roughly 263,000 people work for these organizations, a total that does not include the Canadian military or the Royal Canadian Mounted Police. The size of government is even larger and its complexity much greater if one includes provincial and local governments. Indeed, the activities of these other levels of government affect the lives of most Canadians in ways that may appear to be more direct and significant than those of the federal government. Hospitals, doctors' services, schools, rubbish collection and disposal, water treatment, public housing, police, roads, and urban mass transit: these are all primarily the responsibilities of provincial and local governments. Together, these governments outspend and out-tax the federal government.[3]

Statistics like these, however, tell only part of the story. When the American writer Henry David Thoreau visited Canada in 1850 he was struck by the statist culture: "In Canada you are reminded of the government every day. It parades itself before you. It is not content to be the servant but will be the master."[4] For Thoreau, remnants of the British aristocratic system and of the French feudal system gave to Canada an Old World character where hierarchy, distinction, and deference were woven through the culture. Although the state was not large in terms of its resources, its influence was more pervasive and the awe—understood as a combination of deference and respect—that it elicited from citizens was greater than in the United States. So Thoreau believed from his travels through what is today Quebec.

A statist mentality may have existed in nineteenth-century Canada, although the testimony of Thoreau needs to be placed alongside that of others, such as fellow writer Susanna Moodie. She believed that the arrival of the "lower orders" in the New World caused them to abandon the proper deference they owed their social superiors and adopt an "I'm as good as you, Jack" mentality.[5] But whether Thoreau or Moodie comes closer to the mark in characterizing the mentality of the times, the state in Canada was puny. It employed comparatively few people, accounted for but a small share of the country's economy, and did many fewer things than it does today.

It was different from the contemporary state in another important way. Today we take for granted that most state officials will be bureaucrats who are hired and promoted according to job-relevant criteria and who keep their positions regardless of which party controls the government. In other words, we expect that **patronage**—the practice of making decisions about the distribution of public resources based on friendship, family, loyalty, or in exchange for benefits of various sorts—will be very limited. It may still be all right if the Prime Minister appoints a loyal friend and partisan ally to a position in the PMO, but we would find it unacceptable if he stuffed the bureaucracy, the courts, the higher rungs of the military, or the RCMP with such people. And, indeed, laws and staffing rules limit the possibility of such practices occurring. Nor would most of us consider appropriate the awarding of public contracts based on political favouritism. Patronage continues to exist, but the point is that in the nineteenth century such practices were both common and believed by many to be normal and acceptable. The gears of the state were lubricated with generous amounts of patronage to a degree and in circumstances that today would be considered unethical and sometimes even illegal.

Professionalization of the Public Service

The **merit principle**, whereby hiring and promotion decisions were expected to be based on such qualifications as relevant experience, academic degrees, professional credentials and certification, and other attributes deemed to be relevant to the competent performance of the job, was introduced by the Civil Service Amendment Act, 1908. Prior to this reform, the practice of patronage-based appointments was rampant, as was also true in most other democracies and certainly in the United States, where pressures for public service reform also were building. The Royal Commission to Enquire into and Report on the Operation of the Civil Service Act and Kindred Legislation stated that "patronage seems to run more or less through every department of the public service. It was the universal feeling among the officials who gave evidence before the Commissioners that this patronage evil was the curse of the public service."[6]

But the reforms instituted by the 1908 law were quite limited, extending the merit principle in hiring only to what was called the "inside service" in Ottawa but not to the thousands of federal civil service positions elsewhere in the country. This changed 10 years later when the Conservative government of Robert Borden passed the Civil Service Act, 1918, extending merit principle hiring and the authority of the non-partisan Civil Service Commission (today called the Public Service Commission of Canada) to federal positions outside of Ottawa.

The merit principle was a key part of a larger process of professionalization of the public service. Another reform involved various prohibitions on the political activities of unelected state officials. The reasoning was quite simple. Bureaucrats should be able to serve whatever party formed the government, uninfluenced by their own political beliefs and partisan preferences. A politically neutral public service was considered essential to a modern, professional bureaucracy. This reasoning was premised on the **politics–administration dichotomy** that was an important aspect of progressive thought about the democratic state in the late nineteenth and early twentieth centuries. It held that only elected politicians should make choices between competing values and interests, choices that would be embodied in the laws. The proper function of non-elected state officials was to implement these choices without regard for their personal views and preferences. Even some of those who supported the politics–administration dichotomy worried about what would eventually be seen as the dehumanizing and even totalitarian implications of viewing state bureaucrats as, in Max Weber's words, "specialists without spirit, sensualists without heart."[7]

In any case, the 1908 and 1918 reforms placed strict limits on the rights of public servants to participate in politics beyond voting. They could not contribute money to a party or a candidate for public office and, although the law was not entirely clear on these matters, it appeared they could not put campaign signs on their lawns, make public speeches or publish articles in newspapers or elsewhere in which they expressed their political views, or even belong to a party and attend its meetings.

This would not change until 1967 when the Public Service Employment Act was passed. The Act specifically omitted attending political meetings and contributing money from the political activities that were off limits to public servants. It also gave to the Public Service Commission the authority to grant unpaid leaves of absence to public servants running for office. Increasingly, however, the inherent tension between the obligation of political neutrality imposed on public servants and their political rights as citizens was viewed as a problem, at least by those whose right to participate in the political process was restricted on account of their employment status. Their demands for the same rights enjoyed by other citizens were part of the broader movement towards the expansion and recognition of rights that produced human rights codes in the 1960s and 1970s and the Charter of Rights and Freedoms in 1982. Armed with the Charter, public servants have gone to court to challenge what they believed to be unconstitutional limitations on their political rights. Here is what the courts have said in three of these cases.

Fraser v. PSSRB

Neil Fraser was a public servant with Revenue Canada's Kingston office. He was outspoken and even vitriolic in his criticism of the federal government's adoption of the metric system and also of the Charter of Rights and Freedoms. After repeated warnings and suspensions by his employer, Fraser was dismissed from his job. In challenging his dismissal, Fraser did not argue that his right to free speech under the Charter had been violated (not only would this have been hugely ironic, but the Charter was not part of the Constitution when his dismissal occurred). Instead, he argued that federal law concerning the dismissal of employees made a crucial distinction between job-related and non-job-related criticism and that a public servant ought to be as free as any private citizen to criticize policies unrelated to his or her job or department. The government responded that public criticism by an employee of any government policy may have the effect of undermining the actual and perceived neutrality and impartiality of the public service.

The Supreme Court, in its 1985 ruling, agreed with Fraser's contention that public servants should be allowed non-job-related criticism of government policy. But it held that, in this case, his criticisms crossed the line and could, in fact, be considered job-related. Here is the key section of the Court's ruling:

> . . . As a general rule, federal public servants should be loyal to their employer, the Government of Canada. The loyalty owed is to the Government of Canada, not the political party in power at any one time. . . . In some circumstances a public servant may actively and publicly express opposition

to the policies of a government . . . if, for example the Government were engaged in illegal acts, or if its policies jeopardized the life, health or safety of the public servant or others, or if the public servant's criticisms had no impact on his or her ability to perform effectively the duties of a public servant or on the public perception of that ability. But, having stated these qualifications . . . it is my view that a public servant . . . must not engage, as the appellant did in the present case, in sustained and highly visible attacks on major Government policies.[8]

Osborne v. Canada (Treasury Board)

Bryan Osborne was a public servant working in the Actuarial Branch of the Department of Insurance within the Treasury Board. He was elected by his Liberal Party riding association to serve as a delegate at the party's 1984 leadership convention. Osborne resigned as a delegate after his employer warned him that he would face disciplinary action if he failed to do so. But subsequently, when a by-election was called in his riding, Osborne requested and received a leave of absence from his job to stand as a candidate for the Liberal Party nomination. He admitted that he did this to be free to attend the party's leadership convention, after which Osborne withdrew from the nomination race and requested that he be reinstated in his job. His political leave was terminated and Osborne did, in fact, return to his job.

Other public servants were also involved in this case, but the issue was the same: did s. 33(1) of the Public Service Employment Act, which prohibits public servants from engaging in work for or against a candidate, violate their Charter rights? Osborne and the other public servants in this case argued that their rights of free speech and freedom of association were infringed. In a 1991 judgment, the Supreme Court agreed. It ruled that these prohibitions were "over-inclusive and went beyond what is necessary to achieve the objective of an impartial and loyal civil service." The government's argument that these were reasonable limits on

Charter rights was rejected. Only the requirement that a public servant must take an unpaid leave to stand as a candidate and the restrictions on the political activities of deputy ministers were upheld by the Court.[9]

Haydon v. Canada (Treasury Board)

Dr Margaret Haydon was a veterinarian with Health Canada. In 2001 she was given a 10-day suspension after having told a *Globe and Mail* reporter that a ban imposed by the Canadian government on imports of Brazilian beef was motivated more by political factors than genuine health concerns. Prior to this incident Dr Haydon had been publicly critical of government health policies on two occasions, one of which resulted in a warning from her employer.

This case involved issues similar to those in *Fraser*. In the 2004 *Haydon* ruling, the Federal Court of Canada reiterated what the Supreme Court had said in that earlier decision on the employee's duty of loyalty and the reasons for this duty. It then elaborated on the balance between a public servant's free speech rights and his or her duty of loyalty:

> The following factors are relevant in determining whether a public servant in speaking out has breached his loyalty duty: the employee's level within the hierarchy; nature and content of the expression; visibility of the expression; sensitivity of the issue; truth of the statement made; steps taken to determine the facts prior to speaking; efforts to raise concerns with the employer; extent of damage to employer's reputation and impact upon employer's ability to conduct business.
>
> Where disciplinary action is taken against a public servant, the employer must demonstrate that the comments were inappropriate and harmful. . . .
>
> The duty of loyalty constitutes a reasonable limit on freedom of expression. . . .[10]

If Dr Haydon had been engaged in what is called **whistleblowing**—bringing public attention to government actions or policies that she believed endangered public health or safety, based on her careful examination of the facts—the balance between her right to free speech and her duty of loyalty would have tipped in favour of the former. But that was not what she was doing, the Court decided.

Efficiency and Accountability

When the state was small and its functions many fewer than today, the need for expertise was felt less strongly. Some positions required special skills and training, such as government surveyors, statisticians with the Dominion Bureau of Statistics (rechristened Statistics Canada in 1971), and accountants working for the Treasury Board. But most positions in the bureaucracy did not require much, if anything, in the way of higher education, specialized credentials, and professional certification. The long struggle for adoption of the merit principle in public-sector hiring and promotion was largely a response to the obvious inefficiencies likely to result from staffing decisions based on friendship, family, and partisan connections. But it was also related to an important shift taking place by the late nineteenth century in ideas about the state, its proper functions, and its potential.

These ideas are sometimes referred to as the **positive state**: a state that is active in attempting to shape society and influence its direction. It was championed by liberal intellectuals such as John Dewey in the United States (*The Public and Its Problems*, 1927), socialist thinkers in the United Kingdom, most prominently the members of the Fabian Society, and in Canada by Progressive movement intellectuals such as Adam Shortt, a University of Chicago-educated economic historian at Queen's University and an original member of the Civil Service Commission. Shortt expressed the intellectual spirit of his times when he wrote, "One does not attempt fine work through the instrumentality of a mob. . . . It is through a select, active minority that the most effective and progressive ideas as to political and social welfare must be introduced."[11] The state, thinkers like Shortt believed, needed to be staffed by people with expert training to meet the challenges of a modern society in which policy problems were typically complex and not capable of being understood, let alone solved, by non-experts.

One of the first of such experts to make an important mark on the federal public service was Oscar Douglas Skelton. Like Shortt, he had been educated at the University of Chicago and taught at Queen's University. It is part of the lore of Canadian intellectual history that Skelton's *Socialism: A Critical Appraisal* (1911) received the backhanded compliment of being referred to by Lenin as a sophisticated embodiment of intellectual power in the service of capitalism. Skelton's insistence that Canadian foreign policy should be determined independently of the British Empire, and that Canada's most important external relationship was with the United States, coincided with the views of the Liberal Prime Minister, Mackenzie King. In 1925 Skelton was appointed by King as Under-Secretary of State for External Affairs. Until his death in 1941, Skelton was beyond doubt the most influential figure in the determination of Canada's foreign policy, an influence acknowledged by King in several passages from his diaries. Indeed, J.L. Granatstein dates the beginning of the modern civil service in Canada from Skelton's entry into the Ottawa bureaucracy. Skelton recruited into External Affairs several highly educated individuals, many of whom had done post-graduate work at Oxford or at an American university. In addition, he was the director of research for the Royal Commission on Dominion–Provincial Relations (1937).

Another professor from Queen's, the economist W.C. Clark, was appointed in 1932 as Deputy Minister of Finance. Clark's role as one of the key architects of Keynesian economic policy after World War II is well known. He was at the centre of a group of Queen's economists who were prominent members of the bureaucratic elite through their positions in the Department of Finance and the Bank of Canada. This group included W.A. Mackintosh and John Deutsch, both of whom served as Deputy Minister of Finance and ultimately became Principal of Queen's. Indeed, Queen's developed a reputation as a recruiting ground for the senior levels of the bureaucracy.

The links between the federal bureaucracy and academe during this period when the administrative state was being consolidated have been examined by John Porter. He found that in 1953 just under a fifth of the bureaucratic elite (composed of the 243 senior officials of federal government departments, agencies, and Crown corporations) had taught in a university at some point, and an even greater proportion of the highest-ranking bureaucrats (9 out of 40 at the deputy minister level) were former university teachers.[12] The unrivalled dominance of the Department of Finance in economic policy and in the developing field of social policy meant that this group, and the economics profession generally, had a relationship to public policy and the state not enjoyed by other social scientists. This certainly was evident in the formation and activities of the Royal Commission on Canada's Economic Prospects (Gordon Commission, 1956). In the words of one commentator, "The Gordon Commission was like a vast wind tunnel with the door accidentally left open: it sucked up practically every available economist in the country."[13]

The special relationship of economics to public policy and the state already had begun to take shape in the 1930s. The recruitment of university-trained economists for the Department of Finance and the research department of the Bank of Canada, created in 1935, as well as for the economic studies commissioned for the Nova Scotia Royal Commission on the Economy (1934), the National Employment Commission (1936), and the Royal Commission on Dominion–Provincial Relations (1937–40), provided the institutional opportunities for the increasing integration of the economics profession into the state. Even before John Maynard Keynes's ideas on the manipulation of aggregate demand by government became the orthodox view among economists and policy-makers, providing what appeared to be an irrefutable intellectual foundation for the positive state, widespread skepticism clearly existed about what had been thought to be the self-correcting markets of classical economic theory. Likewise, governments were willing to rely on trained professionals for advice on how to influence macroeconomic activity.

World War II saw state planning on a level never previously experienced in Canada, with increasing recruitment of university economists into such government bodies as the Department of Finance and the Wartime Prices and Trade Board. They formed the core of what Mackenzie King referred to as the "intelligentsia," a group of experts for whom wartime planning provided opportunities to influence policy from within the state. Their influence and the special relationship of the economics profession to public policy were consolidated by the federal government's formal acceptance of Keynesian economic policy in the White Paper on Employment and Income (1945) and in the governing Liberal Party's 1945 election platform.

These decades stretching from the 1925 appointment of Skelton as Under-Secretary of State for External Affairs to the 1950s saw the rise of what historian Doug Owram has called "the government generation."[14] Trained in the modern social sciences, often holding graduate degrees from American universities, they represented a new breed of senior bureaucrat for whom government was viewed as the necessary instrument for maintaining economic prosperity and solving social problems. They were, in an important sense, the architects of the positive state in Canada, a state characterized by professionalism and an increasingly influential role for the bureaucracy.

By the end of the 1950s some were of the opinion that the senior bureaucracy had become, in fact, too influential. The election of the Progressive Conservative Party in 1957 under John Diefenbaker, after 22 uninterrupted years of Liberal government, presented a challenge to the model of an impartial and politically neutral bureaucracy. Would senior bureaucrats, who had worked with Liberal politicians for almost a generation developing the modern Canadian state, be willing and able to transfer their loyalty to a new set of political masters and to whatever changes in policy they might insist upon? It is well known that Prime Minister Diefenbaker and some of his cabinet ministers mistrusted the bureaucracy, suspecting many senior officials of Liberal sympathies and of being subtly unco-operative with the Conservative government and its policies. In *Lament for a Nation*, the philosopher George Grant famously accused the senior Ottawa bureaucrats of being complicit with the Liberal Party and the representatives of American capital in a continentalist vision of the Canada–United States relationship that Diefenbaker rejected.

Ironically, soon after the 1963 defeat of Diefenbaker and the return to power of the Liberal Party, the power of the **"Ottawa mandarins"** whom Diefenbaker so mistrusted began to decline. The Canadian administrative state was entering a new phase in its development, characterized by dramatic growth in revenue, expenditure, personnel, and programs. Between 1965 and 1975, the number of federal public servants increased by 50 per cent, from 203,419 to 307,390.[15] The growth was greatest in the Department of Health and Welfare, National Revenue, and the Unemployment Insurance Commission, but also took place because of the creation of new departments, each with its own raft of programs to administer. These included Communications (1970), Consumer and Corporate Affairs (1968), the Environment (1972), Regional Economic Expansion (1970), and Science and Technology (1973). Federal revenue increased between 1965 and 1975 by almost 400 per cent, from $9.3 billion to $34.7 billion. Expenditures grew from $8.6 billion to $36.8 billion. Spending increased most rapidly on social services, including health, social welfare, and education. Much of this increase in social spending took the form of transfer payments to the provinces, whose expenditures were growing even more rapidly than Ottawa's. As the administrative state grew in size and complexity, the influence of the so-called mandarins declined. Influence within the state became more diffuse and, in a sense, impersonal. Of course, some officials would continue to be found at the top of the administrative food chain, including the deputy ministers of Finance and Justice, the governor of the Bank of Canada, and the chief clerk of the Privy Council. But the days when the bureaucratic power-brokers could be gathered around a medium-sized table in the dining room of the Château Laurier were definitely over.

The 1970s marked the beginning of what some social and political commentators, particularly on the left, began to call the **crisis of the state**. This referred to what appeared to be the inability or unwillingness of governments to finance the welfare state policies put in place over the preceding four decades. The Keynesian consensus—the belief that governments could and should manage their economies by using a repertoire of fiscal policy measures, notably taxation and government spending—was increasingly challenged in the economics and policy-making communities and was largely discredited in many Western democracies by the 1980s. The reason had to do largely with a rapid and dramatic increase in accumulated public-sector debt. Federal deficits increased during the 1970s and 1980s, a trend that was not reversed until the late 1990s. Year after year of deficit spending, financed through borrowing, necessarily produced an increase in the stockpile of government debt. Public debt charges that amounted to $1.9 billion in 1970, or about 13 per cent of total federal expenditures, reached $30 billion, or 16 per cent of total spending, in 1980 and about $41 billion (27 per cent of total spending) in 1990, peaking at 30 per cent of total federal expenditure in 1997.

Although it was generally agreed that something had to be done in response to the Canadian economy's slide into recession in late 2008, different ways of "doing something" about the problem were proposed. In the above cartoon, the Liberal opposition of the time is shown to have held different positions on spending before and after the announcement of the recession deficit.

The term "crisis" is often used too casually and often for ideological purposes. Whether there was a crisis of the state during these decades depends on what one means by crisis. What is certain, however, is that the confidence associated with the Keynesian welfare state declined and government spending increasingly was seen to be a problem. But state spending in Canada as a share of GDP did not decline until the late 1990s (see Figure 10.1), nor was there any significant slashing of government programs and regulation during this same period. Healthy economic growth in Canada over most of the past quarter-century has produced significant growth in government revenues. This, rather than spending cuts, has been the key factor that transformed years of government deficits into surpluses starting in 1997, ending only in 2008 when the Canadian economy followed the American and other Western economies into recession.

The last couple of decades, perhaps even extending as far back as the late 1970s, might be characterized as an era of diminished expectations for the Canadian state. It is difficult to imagine that, in the years before then, proposals for a guaranteed annual income and full employment that would be guaranteed by the state were talked about quite seriously by policy-makers and commentators who were not dismissed as "radical." Nor was the idea of governments "fine-tuning" their economies through a judicious spending increase here or a timely tax measure there likely to be greeted with skepticism and even derision. The neo-liberal ideology of smaller government, less regulation, and a greater reliance on markets, according to many observers, has replaced the Keynesian welfare state consensus of the post-World War II era.

But this claim is not entirely true. To begin with, not everyone shares in the diminished expectations for the state that have become more prevalent

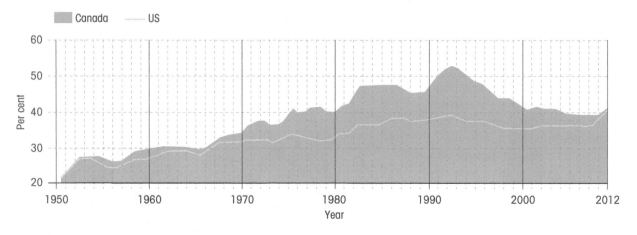

FIGURE 10.1 State Spending as Share of GDP, Canada and the US, 1950–2012

Source: © National Post/Niels Veldhuis and Jason Clemens, "Canada's Advantage," *Financial Post*, 28 Apr. 2009, based on data from *OECD Economic Outlook*, Statistics Canada, and the US Department of Commerce; updated to 2012 from International Monetary Fund, *World Economic Outlook Database*, October 2012. At: <www.network.nationalpost.com/np/blogs/fpcomment/archive/tags/Jason+Clemens/default.aspx>.

over the past few decades. The NDP, labour unions, the Council of Canadians, much of the social sciences and social services community, a significant number of those in the media, the environmental movement, and many others remain optimistic, to varying degrees and depending on the circumstances, about the ability of the state to solve problems. Moreover, they see the state as a necessary instrument for the promotion of social justice, environmental protection and improvement, and economic prosperity, the benefits of which do not accrue mainly to a few. It is simply incorrect to argue that a consensus about an activist state has been replaced by the view that a diminished state is preferable. The mood of lesser expectations for the state surely has had the upper hand in recent decades, but it has been vigorously contested.

Finally, it is also not the case that the administrative state has been downsized significantly over this same period of time. The public sector's share of the Canadian labour force today is about as large as it was in 1980, with about one in five workers employed either directly or indirectly by the state.[16] Although some of Canada's most prominent public enterprises have been sold to private investors since the 1980s, including Petro-Canada, Air Canada, and Canadian National, the role of the federal and provincial governments in the Canadian economy, through direct ownership but more significantly

through regulation, taxation, and purchasing, remains very important. Human rights codes, pay equity rulings, and environmental laws have made the state more rather than less intrusive in some ways over the past couple of decades. So is the downsized neo-liberal state in Canada a myth or reality?

It may be a bit of both. Despite widespread public skepticism about bureaucracy and the effectiveness of government, most people continue to demand that government "do something" when a perceived problem arises. When the Canadian economy slid into recession in late 2008, the reaction of most Canadians was not that the government should stand back and let market forces take their course. On the contrary, most expected the government to act—to spend money, pass laws, bail out industries, and protect jobs. Although there was no agreement about what industries should be helped and whose jobs should be protected, there appeared to be a widespread sense that government actions were needed. And when the economy is doing well, even ideologically conservative governments, such as the Conservative government of Stephen Harper, produce a long "to do" list that the Governor General reads in the Speech from the Throne. In other words, they see themselves and the state apparatus over which they preside as being in the problem-solving business.

Globalization and the State

The administrative state arose over time in response to changes in the nature of society and the economy. It is unrealistic to assume that its particular form will remain fixed as conditions around it change. Foremost among these changes has been the process of globalization. It has affected the Canadian state in regard to the capacity, structure, and idea of the state.

State Capacity

For the administrative state to carry out its many functions it must have the resources to do so. In turn, this requires an adequate stream of revenue to cover the cost of paying bureaucrats' salaries and benefits, building and maintaining roads, funding for schools and hospitals, paying those on state pensions and social assistance, and all the other expenditures of government. This is part of what is meant by state capacity. It has been affected by the unprecedented ease and speed of capital movements between countries, provinces and states, and even between cities.

The consequences have been twofold. Governments have become more sensitive to the demands of businesses whose activities create jobs and thereby contribute to state revenues in various ways, from the payroll taxes (i.e., Employment Insurance and Canada Pension Plan premiums) paid by employers and employees to the sales taxes paid when workers and their families make purchases. They are also more sensitive to the expectations of investors, a category that often includes foreign governments and institutional investors such as large pension funds, who buy their bonds. It is possible to exaggerate the degree of this sensitivity. Governments in Canada and elsewhere obviously have not scrapped all of those laws and regulations that are unpopular with various parts of the business and investment community. The mobility of capital, while greater during the last few decades than at any other time in history, is limited by a number of factors. These include the economic costs associated with relocating production facilities or services. Such costs involve more than mothballing existing facilities and opening new ones. Even more significant, in some cases, may be the cultural friction that results when services, such as customer services in communications and banking, are moved to another country where labour may be cheap, but proficiency in the language of clients and understanding of the myriad cultural nuances that contribute to satisfactory service may be weaker than in the country where these services were originally based. Moreover, the state is not always as defenceless in the face of capital movements and investors' preferences as is often suggested. "There are many good reasons for doubting the theoretical and empirical basis of claims that states are being eclipsed by contemporary patterns of globalization," argue David Held and Anthony McGrew. "[A]ny assessment of the cumulative impacts of globalization," they write, "must acknowledge their highly differentiated character since it is not experienced uniformly by all states."[17]

A second consequence of the unprecedented ease with which capital and jobs move around the globe is that, to maintain state capacity, governments have become less dependent on revenue generated by the direct taxation of businesses and more dependent on revenue from the taxation of individuals. Income taxes, sales taxes, payroll taxes, and user fees all have become more important as sources of state revenue. The personal income tax accounts for close to half of all federal government revenue, up from about one-third of total revenue in the late 1960s. Corporate income taxes in 2012 accounted for about 12–13 per cent of total government revenues, but this can vary significantly from year to year. Since 1966 they have accounted for as little as 5.7 per cent of total revenue to as much as 19.2 per cent. Most of the remaining revenue collected by Ottawa is paid by individuals in one form or another (mainly workers' share of payroll taxes and the GST). At the provincial level, the personal income tax is typically two to three times more important than corporation taxes as a source of revenue.

State Structure

It is often said that globalization has contributed to the downsizing of the state, but this is too

Governing Realities

BOX 10.1   Globalization and the Transformation of the State

Contemporary globalization is associated with a transformation of state power as the roles and functions of states are re-articulated, reconstituted and re-embedded at the intersection of globalizing and regionalizing networks and systems. The metaphors of the loss, diminution or erosion of state power can misrepresent this reconfiguration. For whilst globalization is engendering, for instance, a reconfiguration of state–market relations in the economic domain, states and international public authorities are deeply implicated in this very process. Economic globalization by no means necessarily translates into a diminution of state power; rather, it is transforming the conditions under which state power is exercised. Moreover, in other domains, such as the environmental, states have adopted a more activist posture whilst in the political domain they

have been central to the explosive growth and institutionalization of regional and global governance. These are not developments which can be explained convincingly through the language of the decline, erosion or loss of state power per se. For such metaphors (mistakenly) presume that state power was much greater in previous epochs; and, on almost every conceivable measure, states, especially in the developed world, are far more powerful than their antecedents. But so too are the demands placed upon them. The apparent simultaneous weakening and expansion in the power of states under conditions of contemporary globalization is symptomatic of an underlying structural transformation.

Source: David Held and Anthony McGrew, "Globalization," *The Oxford Companion to Politics.*

simplistic and rather misleading. Certainly, the privatization of some services and the sale of some state enterprises to private investors have occurred in Canada, as in many other countries, as the state searches for infusions of money or seeks to offload costs. And in some cases privatization very clearly has been motivated by ideology. The outsourcing of certain functions also may be a way of reducing the influence of public-sector unions, which, in turn, is expected to reduce costs. All of these policy shifts involve changes to the structure of the state and are aimed at making it leaner, whether motivated by considerations of costs or ideology, or both.

Nevertheless, the state has hardly withered away. In 1991 total public-sector employment in Canada was 2.7 million. In 2013 it was 3.6 million, or just under one in four jobs, which is about the share of public-sector employment 20 years ago. But the structure of the state has changed and some functions that used to be carried out directly by government have been outsourced.

At the same time, globalization has contributed to the state taking on new or expanded functions or legitimizing its actions based on ideas

and institutions that have been generated by this process. Although we tend to associate globalization with economics, this is only part of what it involves. Fundamentally, globalization is about interdependence and the various ways in which the world has become a "smaller" place. One of these ways involves the development of an international architecture of policy-making and globalized networks of interests and ideas that influence domestic state officials and civil society. Human rights commissions and courts in Canada regularly refer to international agreements and developments concerning rights. Canadian state officials involved with matters of Arctic sovereignty and economic development participate in negotiations with other Arctic states, sometimes bilaterally and other times in multilateral forums. Energy and environment officials in Canada are very aware that they do not operate in isolation from the rest of the world when it comes to oil sands development, climate change measures, species at risk, and so on. Officials in the Department of Defence and Canada's intelligence services are influenced by their participation in international missions, organizations, and policy communities. The same may be said of officials in health care, education, immigration, and other fields.

The Structure of Canadian Bureaucracy

The federal public sector employs roughly 529,000 people working in close to 400 different organizations (all figures as of 2011). Just over half of them work directly for government departments and agencies. They are public servants, in the narrow legal sense of this term. Their employer is the Treasury Board and the organizations they work for fall directly under the authority of a cabinet minister. Close to 20 per cent are employed by federally owned Crown corporations and the remainder work in some capacity in the Canadian Forces, the RCMP, or some other federal agency. The organizations they work for receive all or part of their funding from the federal government and are subject to rules that it sets, but these organizations operate with some degree of autonomy.

Public-sector employment is even greater at the provincial, territorial, and local levels. In 2011, the combined employment of these governments came to about 964,000 persons. This figure does not include hospitals and other health-care facilities, schools, or enterprises owned by these levels of government, which together add another 2,136,000 employees to the public-sector total. If we define the public sector broadly to include those organizations that receive all or a major part of their operating revenues from one or more levels of government, then more than one in five Canadian workers fall within this sector. It includes nurses, teachers, firefighters and police officers, workers for Children's Aid Societies and at some women's shelters, and so on.

Despite frequently heard claims that the welfare state has been replaced by a new reality of downsized government, the public sector remains quite extensive. That part of it often labelled the "bureaucracy" may be divided into three main components: the public service (chiefly departments); independent and semi-independent agencies and tribunals; and Crown corporations.

Public service. About half of the federal public sector falls under this category. It includes all statutory departments and other organizations whose members are appointed by the Public Service Commission (PSC) and are employees of the Treasury Board. This is the part of the bureaucracy most directly under the authority of cabinet.

Agencies and tribunals. These organizations perform a wide variety of regulatory, research, and advisory functions. Among the most widely known federal regulatory agencies are the Canadian Radio-television and Telecommunications Commission (CRTC, which regulates communications and broadcasting), the National Transportation Agency (air, water, and rail transportation), and the National Energy Board (energy when it crosses provincial and international boundaries). Many important areas of regulation, including trucking, public utilities within provincial boundaries, and most labour relations, are controlled by provincial governments.

These organizations have a greater degree of independence from government than those that fall under the public service. With few exceptions their members are not appointed by the PSC, nor are they employees of the Treasury Board. The precise degree of autonomy enjoyed by an agency or tribunal varies, but in some cases it is almost total.

Crown corporations. These organizations, in most cases, perform commercial functions and typically operate at "arm's length" from the government of the day. As of 2013 there were 49 such corporations. They hire their own employees, determine their own internal administrative structures, and in many instances behave much like privately owned businesses. Over the last few decades some of the largest of these corporations, notably Atomic Energy of Canada Limited, Air Canada, Canadian National Railway, and Petro-Canada, have been privatized.

These three categories do not cover the entire federal bureaucracy. Some relatively small but important parts of that bureaucracy, including the Auditor General's Office (discussed in Chapter 9) and the Commissioner of Official Languages, are independent of cabinet, reporting directly to Parliament. The

Royal Canadian Mounted Police also has a distinct legal status, as does the Canadian Forces.

Together, this vast administrative apparatus has responsibility for implementing public policy. At the most prosaic level—the level where virtually all of us have made personal contact with the state—officials deal with passport applications, meat inspections, taxation queries, processing Employment Insurance benefits, dealing with job seekers at Canada Employment centres, and a vast number of similarly routine administrative tasks. But at the top of the bureaucratic pyramid are women and men whose relationship to public policy is much more active. Senior officials within the departmental bureaucracy, particularly deputy ministers and assistant deputy ministers, interact frequently with cabinet ministers and senior officials in central agencies. They are called on to testify before committees of the legislature. These officials often deal directly with the representatives of organized interests. They are universally acknowledged to have influence in shaping public policy, although the extent of their influence is a matter of debate.

The bureaucracy is not a uniform structure. One can identify several different functions performed by organizations within the administrative system. These include:

- the provision and administration of services to the public, often to narrow economic, social, or cultural clientele groups;
- the provision of services to other parts of the bureaucracy;
- the integration of policy in a particular field, or the generation of policy advice;
- the adjudication of applications and/or the development and application of regulations (such as food, product, or hazardous waste safety standards, issuing of broadcast licences, licensing pilots and flight engineers, and literally hundreds upon hundreds of similar activities);
- the disbursement of funds to groups or individuals, as with the grants to artists and cultural organizations administered by the Canada Council;

- the production of a good or the operation of a service that is sold to buyers.

These functions are not mutually exclusive. A large and organizationally complex department like the federal Department of Transport is involved in service delivery, the regulation of transport standards, and the development of policy. Almost all government departments, regardless of their primary orientation, have a policy development capacity. During the 1970s this was formalized—although not necessarily enhanced—with the creation of policy analysis units, usually at the assistant deputy minister level. An informal policy advisory capacity, however, has always existed at the level of senior officials. This role is based on their expert familiarity with the programs administered by the department and on the fact that, typically, they remain within a particular policy field longer than their nominal superiors in cabinet. The turnover rate for deputy ministers and other senior bureaucrats has increased since the era of the Ottawa mandarins, from the 1940s to the 1960s, when a coterie of top officials whose careers were associated with particular parts of the bureaucracy exercised an extraordinary influence on the direction of federal policy. The more recent emphasis has been on senior officials as managers, whose management skills are transferable across policy fields. This emphasis, combined with the more rapid turnover of deputy ministers since the early 1980s, may have contributed to a decline in the policy influence of senior bureaucrats.

In fact, it would be more accurate to say that power in the bureaucracy has become more diffuse. The days when a mere handful of key deputy ministers could dominate the policy-making process are gone. Today, bureaucratic influence is distributed more widely, in large part because of the increased importance of central agencies like the Privy Council Office and the Treasury Board Secretariat, but also because it is rare for a deputy minister to remain in charge of a particular department for more than a few years. Nevertheless, there is little doubt that senior bureaucrats continue to be key players in policy-making.

The passing of the era of the Ottawa mandarins and the emergence of central agencies as an alternative source of expert policy advice to cabinet have not undermined the fundamental basis of bureaucratic influence on policy. This influence rests on the following factors:

- Departments are repositories for a vast amount of information about current and past programs and about the day-to-day details of their administration. Cabinet ministers continue to depend on the permanent bureaucracy for advice on policy. Senior bureaucrats occupy strategic positions in the policy process because of their ability to shape the information and recommendations reaching the minister.
- The relationship of a department to the social or economic interests that benefit from the programs it administers is a source of departmental influence on policy. Departmental officials clearly are not indifferent in their sympathies towards conflicting societal interests. Moreover, the bureaucracy is an important target for professional lobbyists and interest group representatives who wish to influence policy.
- "Ministers," observes Donald Savoie, "do not manage."[18] Their deputy ministers perform this job. Given the competing pressures on a minister's time, the deputy minister inevitably assumes the job of senior manager of the department over which a cabinet minister nominally presides. In many instances the chief responsibility for policy direction also will be assumed by the deputy minister.
- Most laws contain provisions delegating to bureaucrats the authority to interpret the general terms of the law in its application to actual cases (see Box 10.2). This is also true of other statutory instruments with the force of law (for example, the thousands of Orders-in-Council that issue from cabinet each year). The task of implementation—applying the law to actual cases—is not a neutral one. In some cases this discretion is exercised at a low level in the bureaucratic hierarchy (for example, decisions by a border officer on whether a person re-entering Canada with

certain goods, or goods of a certain value, should be required to pay duties).

To summarize, the bureaucracy enters the policy process both early and late. Bureaucrats are the people who actually administer the programs established by law. In doing so they regularly exercise considerable discretion, a fact that often leads special interests to focus at least part of their attention on the bureaucracy. Departmental officials are also involved in the early stages of the policy process because of the intimate knowledge they have of existing programs and the daily contact between bureaucrats and the groups directly affected by the programs they administer. Moreover, the annual expenditure budget, which provides a fairly reasonable indication of a government's policy priorities, is based largely on the information provided by departments. New legislation is invariably influenced, to a greater or lesser degree, by the input of senior permanent officials. These officials are both managers and policy advisers, and they are very clearly part of the inner circle of policy-making that extends outward from cabinet. They may not be as close to the inner circle of power as was once the case, but they clearly remain key players in the state elite.

Representative Bureaucracy

On top of all the other expectations held for bureaucracy in democratic societies, it is also expected to "represent" the population. This means that the composition of the bureaucracy should reflect in fair proportion certain demographic characteristics of society. Affirmative action programs and quota hiring and promotion are the tools used in pursuit of this goal. The basic reasoning behind arguments for **representative bureaucracy** is twofold. It is argued that such a bureaucracy will have greater popular legitimacy than one that does not reflect the nation's demography (e.g., women and men, ethnic groups, Aboriginal peoples, the disabled). Second, it is claimed that its representative character will help ensure that the advice bureaucrats give to politicians and the services they provide to their clienteles are sensitive to the values and aspirations of the governed.

As reasonable as this may sound, the idea and implementation of representative bureaucracy have always been problematic. Which groups should be singled out for representation? What constitutes "fair proportion"? To what extent, if at all, are other values like efficient performance and equal rights for all compromised by such a policy? Can the idea of a representative bureaucracy be squared with that of a politically neutral one?

Problems aside, a grossly unrepresentative bureaucracy certainly can pose problems. Comparatively few French Canadians were found

Media Spotlight

BOX 10.2 The Delegation of Discretion

The Broadcasting Act is the key law regulating television, radio, and telecommunications in Canada. Like many laws it delegates to non-elected officials the power to make rules that flesh out the very general terms of the statute they implement. For example, officials with the Canadian Broadcasting Corporation, a Crown corporation, and with the Canadian Radio-television and Telecommunications Commission, the regulatory agency that licenses broadcasters, must determine the meaning of the following vague objectives set down in the Broadcasting Act:

3. (1) It is hereby declared as the broadcasting policy for Canada that . . .

    (d) the Canadian broadcasting system should

      (i) serve to safeguard, enrich and strengthen the cultural, political, social and economic fabric of Canada,

      (ii) encourage the development of Canadian expression by providing a wide range of programming that reflects Canadian attitudes, opinions, ideas, values and artistic creativity, by displaying Canadian talent in entertainment programming and by offering information and analysis concerning Canada and other countries from a Canadian point of view,

      (iii) through its programming and the employment opportunities arising out of its operations, serve the needs and interests, and reflect the circumstances and aspirations, of Canadian men, women and children, including equal rights, the linguistic duality and multicultural and multiracial nature of Canadian society and the special place of aboriginal peoples within that society, and

    (iv) be readily adaptable to scientific and technological change; . . .

And moreover,

    (l) the Canadian Broadcasting Corporation, as the national public broadcaster, should provide radio and television services incorporating a wide range of programming that informs, enlightens and entertains;

    (m) the programming provided by the Corporation should

      (i) be predominantly and distinctly Canadian,

      (ii) reflect Canada and its regions to national and regional audiences, while serving the special needs of those regions,

      (iii) actively contribute to the flow and exchange of cultural expression,

      (iv) be in English and in French, reflecting the different needs and circumstances of each official language community, including the particular needs and circumstances of English and French linguistic minorities,

      (v) strive to be of equivalent quality in English and in French,

      (vi) contribute to shared national consciousness and identity,

      (vii) be made available throughout Canada by the most appropriate and efficient means and as resources become available for the purpose, and

      (viii) reflect the multicultural and multiracial nature of Canada. . . .

Source: Broadcasting Act, Chapter B-9.01, section 3 (1991).

at the senior levels of the federal bureaucracy in the 1940s, 1950s, and 1960s, and this led to major public service reforms and Canada's first policy of representative bureaucracy under Lester B. Pearson and Pierre Elliott Trudeau. On the other hand, most students of British bureaucracy agree that the strongly upper-class character of that country's public service did not prevent it from co-operating with the post-World War II Labour government in implementing reforms opposed by the upper class. Nor has the unrepresentative and elitist character of the French bureaucracy been considered an obstacle to policies favoured by the left.

One thing is certain: governments that have instituted policies of affirmative action and quota hiring, what they call setting targets, have done so chiefly for political reasons.

In recent years, a number of Crown corporations have faced budgetary cutbacks and restrictions. In 2014, it was announced that Canada Post would be reducing up to 8,000 positions—primarily mail carrier positions—over five years, prompting a range of reactions from the public.

Among the most important political reasons is national unity. In Canada it has long been recognized that the merit principle, which ignores the ascriptive characteristics of individuals and looks only at their job-related achievements and skills, should not interfere with what one writer called "a tactful balance of national elements."[19] Until fairly recently, this balancing act chiefly involved ensuring adequate francophone representation in the management ranks of the bureaucracy. Indeed, it is fair to say that until the 1970s this was the only serious representational factor taken into account in public service recruitment and promotion. John Porter's analysis of the senior federal bureaucracy during the 1950s showed that only the British, French, and Jewish ethnic groups were significantly represented, and those of British origin were clearly dominant.[20] Women and visible minorities were almost completely absent from the senior levels of the public service.

As the ethnic composition of Canadian society has changed—people of non-British, non-French ancestry now comprise over 30 per cent of the population[21]—and especially as the discourse of collective rights and group identities has achieved greater prominence, the old concern with "fair" linguistic representation has been joined by efforts to recruit and promote women, visible minorities, Aboriginal Canadians, and the disabled. Affirmative action programs are required by the federal Employment Equity Act, established by the Treasury Board, and monitored by the Public Service Commission. Since the 1980s these programs have relied mainly on a system of employment targets rather than on mandatory quotas for group representation. Ottawa and the provincial governments continue to use targets and incentives to encourage senior managers to hire and promote members of designated groups. In 2002 the federal government, through the Treasury Board, issued an employment directive to departmental managers that required them to increase the proportions of visible minorities—defined by the Treasury Board as someone other than an Aboriginal person who is non-white—on their staffs to 20 per cent and that one out of every five appointments to the executive category of the public service be from visible minorities by 2005. In more recent years the Treasury Board has based its representation targets on the labour force availability of persons falling within each of the four designated groups under the Employment Equity Act. Setting targets is one thing, but achieving them is another, as explained in Box 10.3.

The line separating targets from quotas is always a matter of debate, as is the determination of what groups should be represented in what proportion.

The Social Fabric

BOX 10.3 Elusive Targets: Diversifying Personnel in the Canadian Forces

Military officials are preparing to scale back targets related to the number of women and visible minorities in uniform because they say the current goals are "unattainable," according to a defence department audit. . . .

Despite an end to combat operations in Afghanistan and deep budget cuts, officials say the military needs more than 4,000 new recruits each year to offset attrition and keep 68,000 full-time troops in uniform.

As part of that, the Canadian Forces, like all federal government departments and agencies, is required by law to work towards increasing the number of women, visible minorities, aboriginals and people with disabilities within its workforce. . . .

As part of this, a complex calculation has been used to establish targets for diversifying the Canadian Forces, while dozens of initiatives have been launched to help meet these goals.

The targets were last updated in 2010 and aimed to have 25.1 per cent of the military represented by women, 11.8 per cent by visible minorities, and 3.4 per cent by Aboriginal Peoples.

Yet in an audit conducted last year and only recently made public, defence officials complained the revised goal for women "is unattainable without the imposition of significant measures."

They added the new goal was "unrealistically high" because of the "flawed" calculation used to establish the target.

While auditors found the percentage of new recruits enrolled in basic training each year who were women has fallen from 15.58 per cent to 12.67 per cent between 2008 and 2011, women's overall representation in the military grew from 13.59 per cent to 13.68 per cent.

Progress on increasing the representation of visible minorities also "falls well short," defence officials reported, even though the number has increased steadily from 2.83 per cent in 2008 to 3.86 per cent in 2011.

The defence officials complained that the targets were "imposed" on the Canadian Forces, and though new initiatives to diversify the military's representation are in development, so too are efforts to develop "more realistic" goals.

Officials said they were hoping to establish "revised" goals for women and visible minority representation by March 2017.

Royal Military College professor Christian Leuprecht, who specializes in diversity within the Canadian military, was aghast that defence officials were moving to slash the targets for women and visible minorities.

He said doing so would create a sort of self-fulfilling prophecy by reducing the pressure to recruit more of each, which he felt was necessary if the military wants to ensure it represents Canada's changing culture and population.

"This is not just spreadsheets of multiculturalism and you fill in the numbers and hope to meet the targets," he said.

Adding more women and visible minorities will be increasingly essential if the military is to remain at its current strength, Leuprecht added, given that its "traditional" recruiting pool—young, white men from rural communities—is shrinking.

Officials justified their decision to reduce the goals by noting that the representation of women and visible minorities in the Canadian Forces is about the same as in the Australian military and higher than in the British military, though it lags the United States.

Source: Lee Berthiaume, "Canadian Forces to reduce 'unattainable targets' for the recruitment of women, visible minorities," *National Post*, 18 August 2013. Material reprinted with the express permission of: Postmedia News, a division of Postmedia Network Inc.

In 2013 this issue landed at the centre of New Brunswick's political radar when groups representing English-speakers and French-speakers took opposing positions on what constituted fair linguistic representation in that province's public service. Anglophones outnumber francophones by a 2:1 ratio in New Brunswick. French-speaking groups advocated that 50 per cent of the public service should be bilingual—the current share is about 40 per cent—while English-speaking groups complained that unilingual but otherwise qualified anglophones would be unfairly overlooked by such a policy.[22]

Some interpret fair representation as a proportion of the bureaucracy equal to a group's share of the population. This premise underpinned private member's bill C-473, An Act to Amend the Financial Administration Act, tabled and debated in the House of Commons in the spring of 2013. This bill would have required quotas to increase female representation on the boards of directors of federal Crown corporations. Males and females would have to have equal representation on these boards within six years of the law coming into effect. Anne-Marie Day, the bill's NDP sponsor, argued that Canada should follow the example of such countries as Norway in legislating this sort of numerical equality, otherwise the imbalance between males and females would persist. Those opposed to the bill, including the government's spokesperson, Michelle Rempel, rejected the logic and fairness of legislated quotas. "Any type of advancement that I achieve in my career, I want to be measured on merit and not on gender," she said. "If one were to talk to many of my colleagues in this place, this could be fundamentally described as the next wave of feminism in this country. Equality means equality in performance and merit. That is why I have an issue with this bill. I think it suggests that women cannot get there on their own."[23] Their very different positions on this issue of representation in an important part of the Canadian bureaucracy mirror an important split in Canadian public opinion on what equity involves and how best to achieve it. The bill died before being referred to committee.

Starting Points for Research

Christopher Dunn, ed., *The Handbook of Canadian Public Administration*, 2nd edn (Toronto: Oxford University Press, 2010). Virtually all key aspects of the structures and processes of Canadian public administration are covered in this fine collection, with contributions from some of the foremost students of Canadian bureaucracy and policy-making.

David Good, *The Politics of Public Money* (Toronto: University of Toronto Press, 2007). A worthy successor to the spenders and guardians analysis found in Donald Savoie's 1990 book, *The Politics of Public Spending in Canada*.

David Johnson, *Thinking Government: Public Sector Management in Canada*, 3rd edn (Toronto: University of Toronto Press, 2011). An excellent textbook on public administration in Canada.

Donald Savoie, *Breaking the Bargain: Public Servants, Ministers and Parliament* (Toronto: University of Toronto Press, 2003). Arguably Canada's foremost scholar of bureaucracy and governance explores, in his own words, "the territory between elected and permanent government officials—a kind of no man's land."

Part IV
Participation in Politics

Politics does not stop at the doors of Parliament. It spills out onto the streets and into community halls and corporate boardrooms, involving citizens, organized interests, and the media. What is sometimes referred to as *civil society* both acts on and in turn is acted on by the institutions of the state, making demands, organizing resistance, and providing support in various ways.

The participation of groups in civil society assumes many forms. Individual citizens play a role as voters and collectively through what is described as public opinion. Some of them are involved in more active ways, belonging to and working for political parties or participating in groups that attempt to shape the political conversation and government policy. Organized interests often attempt to influence the actions of government, through a range of techniques that include lobbying, legal action, and attempting to influence public opinion. The media's specialized function involves reporting and framing the political conversation. Most of what we know about the political world is mediated by those whose job involves selecting information (i.e., news) for print and broadcast and then interpreting it.

In the following three chapters we will examine some of the most important forms of participation in Canadian politics. The focus is on parties, elections, and voters, organized interests, and the media. In any democracy these elements of civil society must be largely independent of the state. Indeed, the extent to which they are able to act autonomously, setting their own agendas and behaving free of direct control or indirect manipulation by the state, is one of the tests of any democracy. At the same time, we need to be alert to the possibility that concentrated power in civil society can pose the same sort of danger to democracy that government by the few and mainly for the few can represent.

Parties and Elections

11

Political parties and elections are essential features of modern democracy. This chapter examines the characteristics and influence of these institutions in Canadian political life. The following topics are covered:

- The origins and evolution of Canada's party system.
- Brokerage politics.
- The role of minor parties.
- Recent elections.
- Is the party system undergoing fundamental realignment?
- Party leadership selection.
- The electoral system and its consequences.
- Voting behaviour.
- Party finances and special interests.

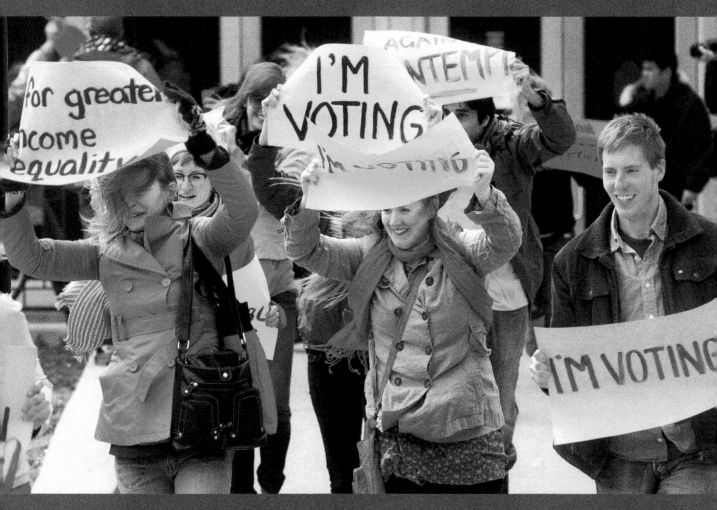

Students at Carleton University demonstrate their commitment to voting in a series of vote mobs that took place during the 2011 election. Despite these campaigns, fewer than 40 per cent of voters under 30 voted in the 2011 election, while 75% of voters aged 65-74 were at the polls. Turnout by age group is lowest among 18–24 year olds in all provinces, but steadily increases by age brackets. (Wayne Cuddington/ Ottawa Citizen. Reprinted by Permission.)

Elections and the political parties that contest them represent the main contact points between most citizens and their political system. Most adult citizens vote at least some of the time, although perhaps not in every election and probably more often federally than in provincial and local elections. This may be, in fact, the extent of their participation in politics: short bursts of attention to candidates and their messages and occasional visits to the polls, interspersed between lengthier periods of inattention and political inactivity. Only about six of 10 eligible voters actually cast their ballots in the last few federal elections, but even among those who did not vote we can probably assume that most were at least aware that an election was taking place.

Elections remind us that we live in a democracy in which those who wish to govern must win the support of the governed—or of some considerable number of the governed. Elections are the cornerstone of democratic governance, yet many believe they have become meaningless and even farcical affairs in which political parties and their candidates serve up sound bites instead of sound policy in campaigns orchestrated by the same people who put together marketing campaigns for cars and deodorants. Political parties have for years ranked among the lowest of social institutions in public esteem. It would seem, therefore, that democracy's cornerstone suffers from some worrisome cracks.

Doubts about the democratic qualities of democracy's showpiece are not new. One of the oldest fears is that those with money are more likely than those without it to be able to influence voter behaviour. In the nineteenth century the influence of money often took such petty forms as candidates buying beer or whisky for voters, a practice facilitated by the fact that voters cast their ballots in public. But the role of money also assumed more dramatic forms, as when Hugh Allan essentially bankrolled the Conservative Party leading up to the 1874 federal election in exchange for a promise from John A. Macdonald that Allan would be made president of the railroad company chartered to build the Canadian Pacific Railway. Over a century ago Liberal cabinet minister Israël Tarte remarked that "Elections are not won with prayers," a fact of political life that has become even truer in the age of television campaigning. But fact of life or not, if parties and votes can be purchased by those with deep pockets, this surely undermines the democratic credibility of the electoral process.

Money is not the only factor that stands accused of defiling democracy's temple. Political parties and candidates have often been criticized for avoiding important issues and framing electoral discourse in ways that deflect attention from major divisions in society, oversimplifying the issues, or trivializing politics by substituting style and image for substance. The "dumbing down" of public life has been facilitated—some would argue necessitated—by the fact that modern elections are fought largely through the medium of television, a medium that by its very nature elevates images over ideas. But the claims that parties and candidates avoid certain divisive issues and attempt to frame electoral discourse in ways that privilege certain interests while marginalizing others predate the rise of television campaigning. The criticisms occasionally levelled at parties and elections in Canada may appear petty when viewed alongside the problems of one-party states and the practices of ballot fraud, voter intimidation, and bribery that are routine in many countries where elections are held. But Canadians are not used to comparing their democratic institutions and processes to those of Côte d'Ivoire, Zimbabwe, Russia, or Egypt. We place the bar higher than this and measure the performance of our political parties and our electoral system against ideas of equality and participation that have evolved out of our liberal democratic tradition. Judged against these values, the Canadian experience is not perfect, although critics differ over the nature and extent of its shortcomings.

Parties: Definition and Functions

Political parties may be defined as organizations that offer slates of candidates to voters at election time. To this end they recruit and select party candidates, raise money to pay for their campaigns, develop policies that express the ideas and goals for which their candidates campaign, and attempt to persuade citizens to vote for their candidates. In a democracy parties are not created by the state, nor are they agents of the state. They are, in Eugene Forsey's words, "voluntary associations of people who hold broadly similar opinions on public questions."[1]

It is usual to give as one of the distinguishing characteristics of political parties their attempt to "elect governmental office-holders."[2] This can, however, be somewhat misleading. While most parties hope to elect candidates to office, and some even have a realistic prospect of electing enough candidates to form a government, other parties may contest elections chiefly to get their ideas onto the public stage, without any expectation of garnering more than a small fraction of the vote. This would seem to be true of the Marijuana Party, whose stated mission is the decriminalization of cannabis, and the Marxist-Leninist Party, whose quixotic advocacy of global revolution by the proletariat remains largely unchanged from Karl Marx and Friedrich Engels's *Communist Manifesto* of 1848. The Rhinoceros Party ran candidates in many Canadian ridings during the 1970s and 1980s and again in 2011, injecting welcome humour into elections—the party stood for the repeal of the law of gravity, among other things—without any serious expectation of electing candidates to office.

John Meisel, one of Canada's foremost experts on parties and elections, identifies seven functions that political parties play in a democracy.[3]

1. *Integrating citizens into the political system.* Historically, parties have served as important linkages between citizens and the governmental system. Through voting for parties and thinking about public affairs in terms of policies and ideologies represented by parties, citizens develop attachments to the political system more generally. This connection, Meisel argues, has weakened as political parties have fallen in public esteem and have come to be perceived by many as simply another unresponsive and unaccountable institution in a political system characterized by alienating institutions.

2. *Developing policy.* In many democracies different parties represent clear ideological and policy options. Moreover, party members and their deliberations are important sources of the policies that a party will advocate during election campaigns and seek to implement when in power. Canada's historically dominant Liberal and Conservative parties have seldom been sharply different from one another in ideological terms or in their behaviour when in power. They have occasionally stood for significantly different policies during election campaigns, as was true in 1988 when the Liberals opposed the Canada–United States Free Trade Agreement negotiated by the Conservative government, and in 2008 when the Liberals proposed a carbon tax, a policy condemned by the Conservatives. Neither party, once in office, has felt tied to the policy platforms developed by the extra-parliamentary wing of the party—witness the Liberal government's refusal to scrap or reform the GST after winning the 1993 election, despite what was generally perceived to be a firm commitment to do so in the party's "Red Book" of election promises. Before coming to power in 2006 the Conservative Party promised to make all votes in the House of Commons, except for budget matters, free votes where MPs would not be bound to vote the party line. This and other platform promises dealing with the operation of Parliament have been abandoned since the party won power.

The federal New Democrats—and the Reform Party before it morphed into the present Conservative Party—have provided voters with clearer policy choices than have the historically dominant parties. The NDP has also been, of all Canada's national parties, the one characterized by the greatest involvement of the party's extra-parliamentary membership in policy development. Of course, if the NDP were to form a government it might well distance itself from policy promises in ways similar to the Conservatives and Liberals in power. This certainly was the experience of the NDP when it was elected to govern in Ontario (1990–5) and instituted policies never contemplated by the party when it was in opposition.

3. *Elite recruitment.* With rare exceptions, those elected to federal and provincial office in Canada are associated with a political party and run as the official candidates of their parties. Parties choose

their candidates and their leaders, and in doing so they determine the pool of persons from whom elected public officials, including members of the government, will be drawn. In most democracies the bar to participation in the selection of party leaders is fairly low, requiring interest and personal motivation as much as anything else. The fact of the matter is, however, that in virtually all democracies those with more formal education, higher incomes, and jobs that carry greater social status are much more likely than their fellow citizens to participate in the selection of party candidates and leaders, and are also more likely to stand for and be chosen as party candidates.

4. *Organization of government.* Governing parties propose; opposition parties oppose. This somewhat oversimplified formula expresses an important fact about the role that parties play within the system of government. They provide a partisan structure to the process of law-making and the debate of public affairs. Under the British parliamentary system that exists in Canada, this partisan structure is by design an adversarial one. The principle of "us versus them" is reflected in the physical layout of the legislature, in which the government benches face those of the opposition parties (separated by a distance said to be that of two sword lengths!), and in the traditions and procedures observed in conducting the business of Parliament.

5. *Structuring the vote.* Just as parties lend structure to the activities of the legislature and allow for the identification of the government with a particular party (or coalition of parties in some democratic systems), they also serve to structure the vote in elections. Only a handful of political parties are serious contenders for citizens' votes, which simplifies enormously the information-gathering task facing voters. Instead of having to determine what every individual candidate stands for they can—and most people do—rely on party labels as a sort of shorthand for the ideas and policies that a candidate represents. Each party represents, in a sense, a particular selection on a limited menu. The parties will differ from one another in their voter appeal with different segments of the population, and most voters can be said to have most-favoured and least-favoured political parties. These partisan

leanings, at the weak end, or loyalties and identifications, at the strong end, provide a degree of continuity in voting behaviour. This continuity can, however, be quickly shattered. This happened in 1993, when the federal Conservative vote collapsed and two new parties, the Bloc Québécois and the Reform Party, suddenly emerged to win second and third place in the election. The 2011 election witnessed a similarly impressive seismic shift in voter choice, the Liberals' support falling to the lowest level in the party's history and the NDP catapulting to second place in the popular vote and first place among Quebecers. Until the 1993 election it had been common to characterize Canada as having a two and one-half party system. The Liberal and Conservative parties both had a realistic chance of forming a government, and between them usually accounted for about 85 per cent of the popular vote. The NDP accounted for the balance. This fairly stable structure to the vote and to the parliamentary status of the parties dissolved in 1993, for reasons discussed later in this chapter.

6. *Organizing public opinion.* Parties are often characterized as right-wing or left-wing. They may be described as moderate or extremist. The labels "liberal," "conservative," and "socialist"—or some other descriptors—may be used to signify that they occupy particular places on the ideological map. Parties reflect, but may also help create or at least reinforce, divisions within society. They do so through the issues they identify as important, the way they frame these issues, and the policies they propose.

Canada's two historically dominant political parties have largely avoided ideological appeals in favour of a flexible centrist style of politics often labelled **brokerage politics**. They have not talked to voters using the language of class politics—rich vs poor, bosses vs workers, corporations vs unions, the 1 per cent vs the 99 per cent—and have attempted to accommodate the preferences of major interests, regions, and communities through a flexible policy style. Of course, politics has to be about something, and even the most centrist and waffling of parties cannot avoid taking positions on some divisive issues. Historically, language, religion, and region have been among the key issues distinguishing the Liberals from the Conservatives, the Liberals doing better among francophones, Catholics, and in the provinces east of Manitoba, and the Conservatives doing better among Protestants and western Canadians. These differences have helped to organize Canadian public opinion on religious (in the past), linguistic, and territorial lines. The NDP and its predecessor, the **Co-operative Commonwealth Federation** (CCF), have been the only significant parties presenting voters with a class-based definition of Canadian politics. In recent decades the ability of the historically dominant parties to organize public opinion in ways that preserved their dominance, by bridging major divisions in Canadian politics, was challenged by parties of protest. The Reform Party/Canadian Alliance emerged out of westerners' dissatisfaction with the older parties. Likewise the Bloc Québécois, which enjoyed strong support in Quebec from 1993 to 2008, emerged from the failure of brokerage politics to accommodate Quebec nationalism.

7. Interest aggregation. Organizations that represent secondary school teachers, gays, or advocates for wetlands preservation may be influential in politics. However, the narrowness of their respective agendas and the fact that each represents only a small segment of the population mean that they could not hope to elect a Teachers' Party, Gay Rights Party, or Save-the-Ducks Party to power. Parties, especially parties that hope to form a government, must aggregate different interests. This requires that they be willing to reach compromises on issues, bringing together under the party's tent

Len Norris/© Simon Fraser University

"Then it's settled. We model ourselves on Canada and use a four-party system."

There are advantages and disadvantages to Canada's multi-party approach to politics. One clear advantage is that it provides more opportunities for disparate viewpoints to be heard, as evidenced by issues brought forward by parties such as the Reform/Alliance, NDP, Bloc Québécois, and Green Party. Disadvantages of a multi-party state are discussed later in the chapter.

a coalition of different interests sufficiently broad to win election.

To be electorally successful it is not necessary that a party bring all major groups or regions under its tent. The Liberal Party, the most successful of Canada's national parties during the twentieth century, often formed a government with little representation from western Canada. In recent years the Conservative Party has managed to win elections and form a government with relatively little support from voters in Quebec. History shows that it is rare for a party to do well in all regional segments of the electorate. Interest aggregation, and therefore a message that bridges divisions between important groups in the electorate, is necessary to win an election. But the result is not always national unity.

The Origins and Evolution of Canada's Party System[4]

The Nature of Brokerage Politics

The origins of Canada's two historically dominant political parties—the Conservatives and the Liberals—can be traced back to the shifting coalitions and alignments in the United Province of Canada in the 1840s and 1850s. Although these groups were much more amorphous and unstable than modern political parties and would not really coalesce into cohesive organizations until the 1880s, they did represent distinct political tendencies. On the one hand was the governing coalition of Liberal-Conservatives (which would eventually drop the "Liberal" from its official name) under the leadership of John A. Macdonald in Canada West and his French-Canadian counterpart, George-Étienne Cartier, in Canada East. This disparate organization encompassed a number of distinct groups: moderate Reformers from what was to become Ontario, moderate Conservatives (the *bleus*) from Canada East (Quebec), the commercial and industrial interests of English-speaking Quebec, and the remnants of the old ruling oligarchies in Upper and Lower Canada, the Family Compact and the Château Clique. Many of these groups had potentially conflicting interests (Catholics and Protestants, French and English, urban and rural elements), but the organization was held together largely by the political dexterity of Macdonald and by the gradual development of a unifying vision, one based on the nation-building program eventually enshrined in the **National Policy** of 1878–9. The key elements of this program were the implementation of a protective tariff designed to promote the growth of manufacturing in Ontario and Quebec, the encouragement of western settlement to open up a market for the products of central Canadian industry and to protect this territory from American encroachment, and the creation of a transcontinental railroad to ship the manufactured goods of the centre to the newly opened western territories.

On the other hand was an even looser opposition coalition, comprising the Clear Grits of Canada West and the *rouges* of Canada East. Both of these groups shared a common admiration for the republican and individualist ideas of the United States and both advocated free trade with the Americans. They also shared a deep hostility to the commercial and banking interests linked to Macdonald's governing party. But the two groups made for rather uneasy partners, since the Grits were outspokenly critical of the Roman Catholic Church. So were the *rouges*, for that matter (and their anti-clericalism placed serious obstacles in the path of electoral success in their home province of Quebec), but there was nonetheless considerable ethnic and religious tension between the two groups. It was only when Wilfrid Laurier assumed the leadership of the Liberal Party in 1887 that these diverse elements were moulded into a relatively cohesive political organization.

It would be a mistake to make too much of the differences in ideas and policies that separated the Liberals and Conservatives during the formative years of the Canadian party system (roughly 1880 to 1920). Admittedly, the Liberals were identified with free trade and provincial rights, and after 1885 (when Louis Riel was hanged for treason following the failed Northwest Rebellion) they appeared to be "more sensitive to the interests of French Canada" than the Tories.[5] They were also more sympathetic to the plight of the farmer than were the Conservatives. The latter, meanwhile, were generally thought of as the party of the British connection, the party of privilege—in the sense that its leading spokesmen claimed that all healthy and stable societies are ruled by a *natural* governing elite—the party of centralization and economic protection. But these ideological differences, far from constituting fundamental clashes of world outlooks on which the two sides sought to mobilize their supporters, were almost always subordinated to the central preoccupation of Canadian politics: *patronage.*

The scramble to control the distribution of government largesse was undoubtedly the dominant feature of Canadian politics during the 1860s and 1870s, when a number of provisions in our electoral law helped to force political life into that mould. In particular, the use of the open ballot, whereby voters simply declared their choice at the polls in the presence of a government official (and anybody else who happened to be in the room at the time!), provided numerous opportunities for bribery, coercion, and intimidation, and made it difficult for anybody whose livelihood depended on government contracts to vote against candidates supported by the ruling cabinet (see Box 11.1).

Non-simultaneous or staggered elections permitted the government to call elections in safe ridings before having to work its way into more doubtful territory. The governing Conservatives stretched the voting period over three months in the 1872 election. This practice encouraged candidates in many ridings to be *ministerialists*, so called because their "politics were not to support a party but a ministry and any ministry would do."[6] This was the surest way to provide for a steady flow of government patronage into the successful candidate's **constituency**.

The elimination of the open ballot and staggered elections by the mid-1870s, along with the gradual standardization of electoral regulations across the different provinces, did not reduce the importance of patronage in federal politics—far from it. Despite the removal of some of the crasser forms of electoral corruption by the 1880s, the two federal parties still operated in a political environment characterized by the absence of civil service reform (the merit principle), a highly restricted franchise, and a weak working class (there were plenty of workers, but they tended to be unorganized and did not share a collective political identity). All of these factors, it has been suggested, predispose political parties to appeal to potential supporters through networks of

Politics in Focus

BOX 11.1 The Open Ballot

The Liberals, for reasons that are not hard to discern, favoured the secret ballot, and every year after 1869 saw a Liberal motion for the adoption of the ballot fall by the wayside. The opportunities for bribery of voters, the coercion of employees by their superiors and of civil servants by the Conservatives, and the open interference of the clergy in Quebec all were cited as arguments by the Liberals. The Conservatives tacitly admitted the justice of the opposition's case, but yielded nothing. One staunch party man went so far on one occasion as to observe with commendable frankness that, after all, elections could not

be carried on without money, and "under an open system of voting, you can readily ascertain whether the voter has deceived you." The Prime Minister thought the (secret) ballot "un-British." Another was critical of it on the ground that it would let a dishonest elector sell his vote to two or three different parties, instead of just one. With these and other cogent reasons for preserving electoral purity, the open system of voting was allowed to last until 1874.

Source: Norman Ward, *The Canadian House of Commons*, (Toronto: University of Toronto Press, 1950), 158. Reprinted with permission of the publisher.

patron–client relations (where votes are exchanged for certain "favours") rather than on the basis of collectivist appeals and class-based ideologies.[7]

This is precisely the situation described by the French political sociologist, André Siegfried, when he visited Canada in 1898 and again in 1904. Siegfried complained that the preoccupation with questions of "material interest" and "public works" tended to "lower the general level of political life" in Canada. He also noted that Canadian politics was hardly lacking in substantive issues—rivalries between Catholics and Protestants, French and English, for example—that could have been addressed by the two major parties, but that the party leaders "prefer that they should not be talked about. The subjects which remain available for discussion are not numerous. In addition, the parties borrow one another's policies periodically, displaying a coolness in this process that would disconcert us Europeans."[8]

Siegfried's comments on the nature of party competition in Canada are still remarkably relevant (see Box 11.2). If Siegfried were somehow transported to present-day Canada, he would probably conclude that there have been few substantive changes in our party system since he published his analysis of Canadian society and politics in 1906. The emphasis on accommodating the diverse interests—regional, linguistic, ethnic, class, religious—of the electorate through the prudent employment of "public works" and individual material incentives is still a prominent feature of federal and provincial politics. Elections are usually preceded by a barrage of new government programs and spending initiatives in various parts of the country—ill-disguised attempts by the party in power to purchase electoral support in key ridings. As well, the nonchalant borrowing of elements of one party's program by another party, which Siegfried found so disconcerting, has been practised with gusto in recent decades. Among the more flagrant modern examples of this habit we might mention the 1974, 1984, 1993, and 2006 federal elections. In the first case, Pierre Trudeau's Liberal government implemented wage-and-price controls in an attempt to cure inflation, only a few months after an election in which the Liberals had castigated the Conservatives and their leader, Robert Stanfield, for proposing just such a policy. In 1984, the new leader of the Conservatives, Brian Mulroney, is widely thought to have scored a decisive win in the television debate with his Liberal counterpart, John Turner, on the issue of patronage appointments. Voters were seemingly impressed by the Tory leader's display of moral outrage at Turner's feeble attempt during a televised debate to justify appointing a raft of Liberals to plum positions at the tail end of the Trudeau dynasty. But not long after the election, the Tories themselves were practising pork-barrel politics on a scale that made their predecessors look like rank amateurs.

During the 1993 election campaign the Liberal Party under Jean Chrétien promised to eliminate the despised GST and reopen negotiations with the Americans on the Free Trade Agreement (FTA), both of which were part of the Conservatives' legacy. To no one's surprise the Americans indicated that they were not interested in renegotiating the FTA, and the Liberals retreated from their campaign bravado. In the case of the GST, after two years in power it became apparent that what the Liberals really meant by elimination of the GST was the harmonization of this tax with its provincial counterparts into a single sales tax. This was very far from what voters had been led to believe. In the campaign leading up to the 2006 election, the Conservatives promised that if elected they would not tax income trusts.[9] Within a year the Conservative government reversed itself on this issue, offering justifications that apparently had been unknown to it during the election campaign. These kinds of flip-flops by the older parties on key issues—and many more examples could be cited—only serve to fuel the electorate's cynicism about politics in general and their distrust of politicians in particular.

The electoral opportunism exhibited over the years by both the Liberals and the Conservatives should not to be taken to mean that the two older parties have no principles or ideological commitments whatsoever. As was also the case when Siegfried was studying the Canadian party system, in more recent times Canada's oldest parties have represented somewhat distinct traditions, particularly on matters concerning federalism

Politics in Focus

BOX 11.2 An Early Illustration of the Brokerage Theory of Canadian Politics

The fact that in the Dominion parties exist apart from their programs, or even without a program at all, frequently deprives the electoral consultations of the people of their true meaning. In the absence of ideas or doctrines to divide the voters, there remain only questions of material interest, collective or individual. Against their pressure the candidate cannot maintain his integrity, for he knows that his opponent will not show the same self-restraint. The result is that the same promises are made on both sides, following an absolutely identical conception of the meaning of power. Posed in this way, the issue of an election manifestly changes. Whoever may be the winner, everyone knows that the country will be administered in the same way, or almost the same. The only difference will be in the personnel of the government. This is the prevailing conception of politics—except when some great wave of opinion sweeps over the whole country, covering under its waters all the political pygmies. . . .

The reason for this . . . is easy to understand. Canada, we know, is a country of violent oppositions. English and French, Protestant and Catholic, are jealous of each

other and fear each other. The lack of ideas, programs, convictions, is only apparent. Let a question of race or religion be raised, and you will immediately see most of the sordid preoccupations of patronage or connection disappear below the surface. The elections will become struggles of political principle, sincere and passionate. Now this is exactly what is feared by the prudent and far-sighted men who have been given the responsibility of maintaining the national equilibrium. Aware of the sharpness of certain rivalries, they know that if these are let loose without any counter-balance, the unity of the Dominion may be endangered. That is why they persistently apply themselves to prevent the formation of homogeneous parties, divided according to race, religion, or class—a French party, for instance, or a Catholic party, or a Labour party. The clarity of political life suffers from this, but perhaps the existence of the federation can be preserved only at this price.

Source: André Siegfried, *The Race Question in Canada*, ed. and trans. Frank Underhill (Toronto: McClelland & Stewart, Carleton Library edition, 1966 (originally published in French, 1906)), 113–14.

and Canada–US relations. With the accession of Pierre Trudeau to the party leadership in 1968, the Liberals became identified in the minds of most Canadian voters with a strong central state (hence the ongoing battles between Ottawa and the provinces over control of natural resource revenues), with economic nationalism (Petro-Canada, the National Energy Program, the Foreign Investment Review Agency [FIRA]), and with "French power." The Tories, meanwhile, came increasingly to be associated with political decentralization: Joe Clark, when he was leader of the party and briefly Prime Minister in the late 1970s, described Canadian federalism as a "community of communities," which Trudeau sarcastically rejected as "shopping-mall" federalism. The Conservatives also came to embrace the notion of free trade with the United States; this

represented a reversal of the party positions on the subject in the late nineteenth and early twentieth centuries, when the Liberals strongly advocated continentalist economic policies. Finally, the neo-conservatism of the 1980s, spearheaded by British Prime Minister Margaret Thatcher and US President Ronald Reagan, found its most receptive audience among the Conservatives during the Mulroney years.

In recent years the federal Liberal Party has been associated with a somewhat more centralist vision of federal–provincial relations and a brand of mild to occasionally hotter anti-Americanism, while the Conservatives have branded themselves as a more decentralist party and more sympathetic to Washington than their Liberal rivals. The two historically dominant parties have also taken significantly different positions on climate change and energy policy.

Despite these apparent differences in the policy orientations of the two older parties in recent times, Siegfried's central contention about the Canadian party system remains indisputable. Our historically dominant parties have continued to be much more flexible, opportunistic, and wary of ideological appeals to the electorate than those in most European nations. The nature of our electoral system and the norms that govern party competition in this country are such that the Liberals and Conservatives can usually fight elections without having to worry too much about keeping their principles intact or consistent. Many observers of the Canadian party system have attached a specific label to this type of flexible, non-ideological party system: it is a *brokerage* party system. That is, the two older parties at the federal level act as "brokers of ideas . . . middlemen who select from all the ideas pressing for recognition as public policy those they think can be shaped to have the widest appeal."[10] Each of the parties attempts to cobble together a winning coalition of voters at election time; the voting support for the two major parties, therefore, does not come from stable, well-defined social groups, as is the case in many Western European countries. Most importantly, politics in Canada lacks an obvious *class* dimension. Conflicts between the working class and capitalists over the political and economic rights of workers, and over the distribution of national wealth, take a back seat to other issues—those arising out of linguistic and regional rivalries, for instance, or divisions that are not obviously linked to social class such as age, gender, environmental views, or attitudes towards the United States.

This aspect of Canadian politics led some observers to describe the Canadian party system as less developed or less modern than those of most other industrial nations. Robert Alford, for example, declared in his classic study of voting behaviour in four Anglo-American democracies (the United States, Canada, Great Britain, and Australia) that Canada had the lowest level of class voting among the nations he examined.[11] Alford's explanation of this situation echoed the one advanced by Siegfried

almost 60 years earlier: "Class voting is low in Canada because the political parties are identified as representatives of regional, religious, and ethnic groupings rather than as representatives of national class interests, and this, in turn, is due to a relative lack of national integration."[12] Class divisions and antagonisms are certainly not absent in Canada, Alford observed, and he predicted that once the issue of national unity had been resolved, class voting would increase and Canada would come to resemble other modern democracies—Great Britain, for instance (see Box 11.3).

In the 50 years since Alford's book was written, it should be noted, his prediction has simply not come true: issues related to class and the language of class conflict are still rare occurrences in Canadian politics. The two older parties do not normally appeal to specific class constituencies and still avoid class issues when possible. Moreover, the self-described left-wing party in Canada, the NDP, historically has received nowhere near a majority of the votes of blue-collar workers or even of all unionized workers. This was even true in the 2011 election, when the NDP received the second largest share of the popular vote at almost 31 per cent.

Brokerage theory, then, makes two fundamental claims about Canada's two historically dominant political parties: first, they do not appeal to specific socio-economic groupings, and they lack cohesive ideological visions (especially those based on class interests and identity); second, the parties are flexible and opportunistic because this sort of behaviour is necessary to preserve the fragile unity of the nation. This brings to mind Siegfried's observation that there are all kinds of pressing issues in Canadian politics, but that the prudent and cautious leaders of the two main parties do not want them to be discussed, for fear of inflaming group jealousies and thereby jeopardizing the stability of the country.

An alternative explanation of the absence of class politics in Canada is advanced by Janine Brodie and Jane Jenson in *Crisis, Challenge, and Change*.[13] They argue that brokerage theory tends to view political parties as more or less passive transmission belts for societal demands. In the vocabulary of empirical social science, brokerage theorists consider parties

Politics in Focus

BOX 11.3   Revisiting Robert Alford on Class Voting

Robert Alford's analysis of class-based voting in Anglo-American democracies was written towards the end of a period during which the prevailing belief among social scientists was that modernization led to a decline in the social and political significance of non-class divisions and identities such as religion and ethnicity and to an increase in the importance of class. This idea goes back to the late nineteenth century when socialist movements and parties emerged on the scene in Western Europe. Material interests, it was believed, would inevitably lead increasing numbers of voters to align themselves with parties they viewed as defenders of their class interests. "The leftist parties represent themselves as instruments of social change in the direction of equality," wrote Seymour Martin Lipset; "the lower-income groups will support them in order to become economically better off, whereas the higher-income groups will oppose them in order to maintain their economic advantages."[14] Canada, Alford argued, was lagging behind the other Anglo-American democracies in developing a modern party system based on class voting.

Rather than Canada moving towards the class-based politics predicted by Alford and most others of his generation, however, it appears that much of the rest of the democratic world has been moving towards the Canadian model of parties and voting that are not strongly anchored to class. Post-materialists explain this by arguing that younger cohorts of citizens entering the electorate in affluent Western democracies have been less responsive to the politics of material self-interest and therefore class appeals. By the 1990s Lipset had changed his mind about the inevitability of increased class-based voting, noting that "(it) has declined in every country for which data are available."[15]

Political scientists continue to debate whether and why class-based voting has declined. But in Canada, at least, class remains a much weaker predictor of how citizens are likely to vote than region, language, religion, and whether one is married.

to be *dependent variables*: their behaviour is shaped by the divisions that exist in society—in Canada's case, the most important divisions being those of language, ethnicity, region, and religion. Brodie and Jenson call for a more nuanced view of parties, one that treats them simultaneously as *dependent* (influenced by society) and *independent* (actively shaping societal demands) variables. The most important aspect of the independent, creative function of political parties in liberal democracies like Canada is their role in creating a *definition of politics*. "From a myriad of social tensions," they write, "the definition of politics identifies and selects those susceptible to 'political' solutions. Political parties, in other words, by defining the political, contribute to the organization and disorganization of groups in the electorate."[16]

Class identities and conflicts were not part of how the historically dominant parties defined the Canadian political condition. Without such cues and with issues framed by the older parties in a language that did not recognize the relevance or often the existence of class divisions, voters grew used to thinking about Canadian politics in terms of regional and ethnolinguistic divisions, leadership and sound management of public affairs, Canada–US relations and other non-class issues.

Brodie and Jenson argue that in the period immediately following Confederation, class, religion, language, and other social differences competed with each other—more or less equally—as potential support bases for the two federal parties. Since both of these parties drew the bulk of their support from the same social group—property-owning males—they tended to avoid the issue of class in their competition for votes. As a strategy for differentiating their "product" from that of the governing Conservatives, the Liberals gradually seized on the issue of ethnic, religious, and linguistic differences and "became the party of French Quebec (and later of other ethnic minorities) while the Conservatives solidified their base among Anglophone Canadians."[17] In later years, the authors claim, the two traditional parties would frequently try to avoid discussing class issues such as the rights and place of workers in Canadian society by redefining them as regional or cultural concerns. The NDP, they contend, has not been able or willing to challenge the prevailing definition of politics in Canada, and therefore is forced to compete with the Liberals and Conservatives under conditions that permanently handicap it and leave a significant portion of the Canadian electorate effectively disenfranchised.

Brodie and Jenson's explanation of the non-class nature of the Canadian party system is an important contribution to our understanding of politics in this country. Nevertheless, it does seem somewhat overdrawn, since it appears to downplay or minimize the pre-eminence of religious and ethnic divisions in Canadian society in the late nineteenth century and to exaggerate the extent to which the parties have been able to play up the issues of language and culture for their own electoral advantage. One important reason that class identity came so slowly and unevenly to Canadian workers was precisely the role played by religious institutions—the Catholic Church and the Orange Order, most notably—in organizing the working class. The Orange Order appealed to workers as Scottish or Irish Protestants, while the Catholic Church stressed the spiritual mission of French-Canadian workers and was reluctant to define society in terms of antagonistic classes (as socialists did). All of this helped to ensure that for large numbers of Canadian workers, their class identity was intermingled with their ethnic and religious allegiance. A large part of the explanation of the relative unimportance of class issues in Canadian politics, therefore, must be found in the social organization of the working class itself, and not simply attributed to the major parties' manipulation of the definition of politics.

The Role of Minor Parties in the Brokerage System: The Case of the Reform Party

Only the Conservative and Liberal parties have formed the government in Ottawa, but several other parties have, from time to time and for shorter or longer periods, played an important role on the federal scene. These minor parties, as they are often called, have occasionally won enough seats to form the official opposition in Parliament and have sometimes held the balance of power during periods of minority government. They have also influenced the political conversation and have sometimes had an important impact on the policies of the governing party. One such party was the Reform Party, of which the current Conservative Prime Minister, Stephen Harper, was a founding member.

Under the leadership of Preston Manning, the son of the former Social Credit Premier of Alberta, Ernest Manning, the Reform Party was founded in late 1987 primarily as a vehicle for western discontent. The Reform Party, which became the Canadian Alliance in 2000, was the latest in a string of western protest movements—its most successful predecessors having been the Progressives in the 1920s, Social Credit and the CCF in the 1930s and 1940s, and the Western Canada Concept in the early 1980s—that have tapped into the powerful feelings of economic and political alienation in the western provinces. These feelings originate in the firm conviction that the West is getting the short end of the stick, economically speaking. For most of Canada's history, many westerners have believed that federal policies, reinforced by the practices of the banks and the railroads, have enabled Ontario and Quebec to siphon off the resource wealth of the West to fuel growth and prosperity in the centre. The two major parties have been seen as co-conspirators in this vicious circle of exploitation, since they were beholden to the powerful economic interests in the metropolitan areas and therefore compelled to enact policies that favoured those regions where the bulk of the seats are to be won in a federal election.

This deep-seated suspicion among westerners of central Canada and national political institutions was briefly dispelled by the 1984 federal election.

Although the new Prime Minister, Brian Mulroney, was himself a bilingual Quebecer, for the first time since the Diefenbaker interlude of the 1950s a large number of prominent westerners were placed in key cabinet positions. Western voters seemed to believe their concerns would get positive response from Ottawa. Gradually, however, their guarded optimism gave way to a shattering disillusionment, as the Conservative government made a number of policy decisions that were viewed as detrimental to western interests. Without a doubt the most publicized instance of "biased" government decision-making was Ottawa's awarding of a multi-million dollar maintenance contract for the CF-18 fighter aircraft to a Quebec-based firm, despite the fact that Bristol Aerospace of Winnipeg had presented what federal officials acknowledged was a technically superior bid. "This enraged not only Manitobans, but most westerners, and the CF-18 decision quickly joined the National Energy Program as a symbol of regional resentment and injustice."[18] Many westerners drew the conclusion from this affair that no matter how many representatives they sent to the House of Commons, the system itself—especially the "national" parties—was biased against the West. A new voice, therefore, that of a regionally based protest party like the Reform Party, was necessary to extract favourable policies from Ottawa.

Although the Reform Party began its life as a strictly regional organization—its constitution originally included a prohibition on fielding candidates east of Manitoba—it quickly capitalized on the public's growing disenchantment with so-called "traditional" political parties to make inroads into Ontario, the bastion of central Canadian power. The percentage of Canadians expressing "a great deal" or "quite a lot" of confidence in political parties had dropped from 30 per cent in 1979 to only 7 per cent in 1991.[19] Reform attacked existing political institutions as being unresponsive, unaccountable, and elitist, and attempted to portray itself as a populist movement rather than a political party. Rigid party discipline—which various governments have promised to relax, without much noticeable effect—was singled out by both voters and the Reform Party as one of the biggest culprits in driving a wedge between the individual citizen and the political

system. Under the Mulroney Conservatives, two Tory backbenchers who were publicly critical of the GST found themselves expelled from the party's caucus. Likewise, and despite Jean Chrétien's promise to relax party discipline, those Liberal MPs who opposed the government's 1995 gun control law were stripped of their parliamentary committee assignments. Such incidents reminded voters that under the traditional parties those they elect to Parliament are expected to vote as the party brass decides, even if this collides with the strongly held desires of their constituents.

There was also a generalized suspicion, fuelled by occasional sordid conflict-of-interest scandals that befell governments in Ottawa and in many of the provincial capitals as well, that politicians had become overly concerned with furthering their own careers or lining their pockets at the expense of their primary duty of representing the wishes and interests of their constituents. The issue of MPs' pensions was and continues to be a lightning rod for this popular sentiment. The Reform Party made much of its commitment to opt out of what it considered to be the unfairly generous terms of MPs' pensions, and in 1995 all but one of the party's MPs chose not to participate in the pension plan. Finally, there was declining tolerance among voters for the kind of closed-door, elitist decision-making that traditionally had characterized Canadian politics under Liberal and Conservative governments.

Responding to the widely held demands among the electorate for greater accountability and a more democratic political structure, the Reform Party and then the Canadian Alliance followed in the path of their populist predecessors, the Progressives and Social Credit, and called for the implementation of a number of institutional reforms that would increase the individual citizen's control over his or her representatives. The Alliance advocated greater use of referendums and citizen initiatives; the right of constituents to recall their MPs, should they be deviating too obviously from their wishes; and relaxation of party discipline, so that most votes in Parliament would be "free" votes. The Reform/Alliance ideology was both populist and conservative, and it regularly found itself alone as the sole political party advocating radical change to the policy status quo. For example, during the 1993 election campaign it was the only party to advocate a major reduction in Canada's annual intake of immigrants during times when the economy was weak. It was also the only party to insist that deficit reduction, to be achieved mainly through spending cuts, should be Ottawa's top priority (a policy the Liberal government subsequently embraced). Reform Party MPs were the main critics in Parliament of the 1995 gun control law requiring the registration of all firearms. The party also stood alone in its opposition to official multiculturalism and bilingualism.

Although the Conservatives, Liberals, and NDP all initially tried to ignore or downplay the significance of the Reform Party, by the summer of 1991—when the report of the Citizens' Forum on National Unity (the Spicer Commission) documented the deep dissatisfaction of many Canadians with the functioning of their traditional democratic institutions, especially the political parties—this protest movement was simply too powerful to be casually dismissed as a sort of political chinook. If the Conservatives and the New Democrats hoped to hold onto at least some of their traditional electoral strongholds in the Prairies, they had to respond to the policy concerns raised by Preston Manning's organization, no matter how distasteful or "populist" they considered them to be. This is exactly what happened during previous cycles of regional protest: the major parties were eventually compelled to head off the electoral challenge of a nascent protest movement (whether it was the Progressives, the CCF, or Social Credit) by endorsing policies that appealed to the new party's supporters. In the case of the Progressives, for instance, the party was opposed to the National Policy tariff (which kept the price of central Canada's manufactured goods relatively high and drove up the costs of farming) and to the discriminatory freight rates charged by the CPR (which made it cheaper to ship manufactured goods from central Canada to the West than to send grain eastward). After the Progressives' meteoric rise to prominence in the 1921 federal election, however, the protest they represented was gradually dissipated by the skilful manoeuvring of the Liberal Prime Minister,

Mackenzie King. King made relatively minor changes in the tariff and in freight rate policy and managed to buy off some of the Progressive leaders with offers of cabinet posts in his government. This was largely the fate of the Co-operative Commonwealth Federation as well: Mackenzie King sought to take the wind out of the socialist party's sails by implementing a number of social welfare policies that its supporters were advocating, including old-age pensions and unemployment insurance.

"Minor" parties like Reform/Alliance perform an important function in our brokerage party system: they provide a much-needed source of policy innovation, goading the major parties into acting on the concerns of regions, classes, or significant social groups they have traditionally ignored or underestimated. Walter Young, in his history of the national CCF, describes the contribution of third parties to the Canadian political system:

> By providing . . . the kind of ideological confrontation which is typically absent in contests between the two major parties, [minor parties] have served to stimulate the older parties and reactivate their previously dormant philosophies. . . . Two parties alone cannot successfully represent all the interests or act as a broker—honest or otherwise. Attempts to represent a national consensus have been usually based on the assessment of a few with limited access to the attitudes of the whole. The result has been that the national consensus has in fact been the view of the most dominant voices in the old parties. And these are the voices at the centre; historically, the voices of the elite or the establishment.[20]

The 1993 and 1997 Elections: The End of Brokerage Politics?

Before the 1993 election it was common to speak of Canada's "two and one-half" party system. The Liberals and Progressive Conservatives were the parties with a realistic chance of forming a government, while the NDP was a stable minority party on

KRIEGER©1997
The Province

Bob Krieger/© Simon Fraser University

Preston Manning, who founded and led the Reform Party of Canada from 1987 to 2000, helped to "fan the flames" on western regional and social conservative issues, forcing the country's dominant parties into ideological debates that would not have surfaced otherwise.

which guarantees the opportunity to speak in the House during Question Period as well as automatic funding for research staff. On the other hand, the Reform Party jumped from one seat that had been won in a by-election to 52 seats. The Bloc Québécois (BQ), created in 1990 by the defections of several Tory and Liberal MPs, went from seven seats to 54. Not since 1921, when the Progressives came second to the Liberals, had voters given the national party system such a jolt.

With the Conservatives and NDP reduced to near irrelevance in the Commons and two new opposition parties, each with strong regional support and neither signalling an interest in brokerage-style politics, it was natural that political analysts should ask whether a realignment was taking place in Canada's national party system. Realignment suggests a durable change, not one caused by transient and unusual factors. Those who interpreted the 1993 election results as evidence of a realignment based this reading on what they saw as voters' dissatisfaction with brokerage-style politics, the weakness of party loyalties among voters, and erosion of the NDP's support across the country. This interpretation was greeted skeptically or even rejected by others. Critics of the realignment argument pointed to such factors as the monumental unpopularity of former Progressive Conservative Prime Minister Brian Mulroney, the erosion of NDP support in Ontario where an unpopular NDP government was in power, a wave of western disaffection with the major parties, and the unusual and presumably passing phenomenon of the Bloc Québécois, spawned in the bitter wake of the 1990 defeat of the Meech Lake Accord.

The case for a realignment was not, however, entirely implausible. Indeed, several of the elements for such a durable restructuring of the vote

the federal scene, regularly winning 15–20 per cent of the popular vote and occasionally holding the balance of power during a period of **minority government**. The distinction commonly made between major and minor parties was rooted in the realities of electoral competition.

The old certainties were shattered by the 1993 election results. The Liberals won a solid majority, taking 177 of the 295 seats in the House of Commons and 41.3 per cent of the popular vote. Neither the Conservatives nor the NDP elected enough MPs to qualify for official party status, and the party system appeared to exist. One of these involved the low esteem in which parties and politicians were—and continue to be—held by voters. In the words of the 1991 Royal Commission on Electoral Reform and Party Financing:

> Canadians appear to distrust their political leaders, the political process and political institutions. Parties themselves may be contributing to the malaise of voters. . . . whatever the cause, there is little doubt that Canadian political parties are held in low public esteem, and that their standing has declined steadily over the past decade. They are under attack from citizens for failing to achieve a variety of goals deemed important by significant groups within society.[21]

The wave of cynicism building in the Canadian electorate weakened attachments to the traditional parties. This opened the door for newcomers on the party scene, the votes won by BQ and Reform candidates having gone mainly to Liberals and Conservatives before 1993.

A second element that seemed to presage a realignment of the party system involved what might be described as the shrinking centre in Canadian politics. The traditional dominance of the centrist Liberals and Progressive Conservatives depended on the existence of a broad popular consensus on the role of government and on the older parties' ability to keep political debate within the familiar confines of language, regionalism, and leadership. This popular consensus had become frayed and the traditionally dominant parties' ability to keep political conflict within "safe" boundaries was diminished.

The political consensus that developed during the post-World War II era was based on the welfare state, an active economic management role for government, and official bilingualism. The Liberals and Conservatives, but particularly the Liberal Party in its role as the government for most of this era, were the architects of the policies that were the practical expressions of this consensus. On constitutional issues, too, the traditional parties were capable of broad agreement. This was evident in the support that all three parties gave to both the Meech Lake Accord and the Charlottetown Accord, a unanimity that certainly was not found in the Canadian population.

Popular consensus on the Keynesian welfare state and activist government was unravelling during the 1980s. Issues like deficit reduction, welfare reform, and lower taxes became the rallying points for dissent from the post-war consensus. Opposition to what is perceived to be state-sponsored pluralism through official multiculturalism and to bilingualism provided another pole for this dissent. In broadening its organization from the West to include Ontario and eastern Canada, the Reform Party was clearly attempting to provide a voice for this dissent that many voters believed was not being provided by the Progressive Conservative Party. Reform's second-place finish in Ontario in the 1993 election, capturing 20 per cent of the popular vote, cannot be explained in terms of "western alienation." These Ontario voters defected mainly from the Conservatives in search of a party that defined the issues in a way they believed responded to the country's true problems. At the provincial level this dissent contributed to the election of the Conservatives under Ralph Klein in Alberta and Mike Harris in Ontario, provincial Progressive Conservative governments that were much closer to the outlook of the Reform Party than they were to the national Progressive Conservative Party under Jean Charest (1993–8) and Joe Clark (1998–2003).

Only the Liberal Party succeeded in practising the old brokerage-style politics. It emerged from the 1993 election as the only truly national party, electing members from every province and territory and receiving no less than one-quarter of the votes cast in any province. The Liberals did only slightly less well in 1997, failing to elect a member only in Nova Scotia and Yukon. In the 2000 election Liberal support ranged from a low of 20.7 per cent of the popular vote in Saskatchewan to a high of 51.5 per cent in Ontario. The party won seats in every province and territory, no other party coming close to this accomplishment. The lesson some drew was that enough space no longer existed in the centre of the Canadian electorate to support two centrist brokerage parties. It became increasingly evident that the

Progressive Conservative Party would have to reposition itself ideologically if it wanted to regain the votes that Reform/Canadian Alliance siphoned off in the 1993, 1997, and 2000 elections. It could not afford to remain a near-clone of the Liberal Party, especially since the Liberals in power created some distance between themselves and the Keynesian welfare state they were instrumental in building. The electoral success of right-leaning Conservatives in Alberta and Ontario suggested that the future of the national party was in this direction.

The 1997 general election was a replay of 1993 in several important respects. The Liberals swept all but one of Ontario's 103 seats. The Reform Party dominated in the West, taking 57 of the 74 seats in Saskatchewan, Alberta, and British Columbia. The Reform share of the vote in Ontario remained stable at slightly less than 20 per cent, but the Conservative share of the Ontario vote recovered to almost equal that of Reform. The Bloc Québécois continued to be the most popular party in Quebec, but it lost some ground in both share of the vote and seats to the Liberals.

More significant than these nuanced changes were the election results in the Atlantic provinces. Twenty-one of the 32 seats in the four Atlantic provinces were won by the NDP and the Conservatives. Indeed, the Conservative Party emerged from the 1997 election appearing to be almost as much an Atlantic Canada party as Reform appeared to be a western Canadian party. Thirteen of the PC's 20 seats were won in Newfoundland, Nova Scotia, and New Brunswick. The NDP, which historically had achieved only minor inroads in Atlantic Canada, won eight seats in the region, representing about 40 per cent of the party's caucus in Parliament. The loss of several Liberal seats and the ascendance of the Conservatives and the NDP in the region were almost certainly due to voters' unhappiness with federal spending cuts, particularly in transfers to provincial governments, which were felt more deeply in their region than in more affluent parts of Canada. The message of fiscal conservatism the Liberals preached, particularly after the 1995 federal budget, was an unnerving one in provinces where job markets and public services have long been sustained by a life-support system of federal assistance.

The rise of the Reform Party in the West and of the Bloc Québécois in Quebec in the 1993 and 1997 elections tells us that the party loyalties of many Canadian voters are not very durable. The Reform Party, joined by some elements from the national and provincial Conservative parties, sought to capitalize on the apparent softness of party loyalties through a movement to create the United Alternative. Formally launched in 1998, the roots of the United Alternative go back to the 1993 election. The Liberals won a strong majority on the strength of only 41.3 per cent of the popular vote. Combined popular support for the PCs and Reform came to 34.7 per cent. While not all Reform voters were disaffected Conservatives, it is safe to conclude that most were. Those on the right of Canada's political spectrum were quick to lament the division of the conservative vote, a situation that enabled the Liberal Party to win seats it probably would not have won, particularly in many Ontario ridings. The combined popular vote of the Conservative and Reform parties in 1997 came to 38.2 per cent, just a fraction less than the Liberals' 38.5 per cent of the vote.

At this point the talk of the need for a "unite the right" movement to defeat the Liberals became more persistent. Spearheaded intellectually by conservative political writer David Frum and organized by the Reform Party, the United Alternative (UA) was created in 1998 and held its first national convention in February of 1999. The convention certainly gave the appearance of inter-party cooperation to unite conservative political forces against the governing Liberal Party. An Ontario cabinet minister, Tony Clement, was the convention co-chair. Conservative Premier Ralph Klein gave the keynote address. Prominent Quebecer and former Liberal Jean Allaire spoke to the convention. The fly in the ointment, from the standpoint of the UA and its goal of realigning Canada's national party system, was that with the exception of only a couple of Conservative MPs, the national Progressive Conservative Party kept its distance from the UA. Conservative leader Joe Clark repeatedly refused to respond to Preston Manning's public invitations to join forces in a new party. This was not surprising in light of Clark's long history as a product and practitioner of brokerage politics.

TABLE 11.1 Summary of Election Results, 1940–2011

A. Percentage of Vote* and Candidates Elected by Political Party at Canadian General Elections, 1940–2011

Party	1940	1945	1949	1953	1957	1958	1962	1963
Liberal	54.9% 181	41.4% 127	50.1% 193	50.0% 172	42.3% 106	33.8% 48	37.4% 99	41.7% 128
PC	30.6% 40	27.7% 68	29.7% 41	31.0% 51	39.0% 112	53.7% 208	37.3% 116	32.8% 95
CCF/NDP	8.5% 8	15.7% 28	13.4% 13	11.3% 23	10.8% 25	9.5% 8	13.4% 19	13.1% 17
Social Credit	2.7% 10	4.1% 13	3.9% 10	5.4% 15	6.6% 19	2.6% —	11.7% 30	— —
Bloc Populaire	— —	3.7% 5	0.8% 0	7.6% 15	5.0% 11	4.6% 6	1.7% 0	11.9% 24
Others	3.3% 6	7.8% 7	2.9% 5	2.3% 4	1.3% 3	0.4% 1	0.2% 1	0.4% 1
Total valid votes Total seats	4,620,260 245	5,246,130 245	5,848,971 262	5,641,272 265	6,605,980 265	7,287,297 265	7,690,134 265	7,894,076 265

Party	1965	1968	1972	1974	1979	1980	1984	1988
Liberal	40.2% 131	45.5% 155	38.5% 109	43.2% 141	40.1% 114	44.3% 147	28.0% 40	31.9% 83
PC	32.4% 97	31.4% 72	34.9% 107	35.4% 95	35.9% 136	32.5% 103	50.0% 211	43.0% 169
NDP	17.9% 21	17.0% 22	17.7% 31	15.4% 16	17.9% 26	19.8% 32	18.8% 30	20.4% 43
Créditistes	4.6% 9	4.4% 14	— —	— —	— —	— —	— —	— —
Social Credit	3.7% 5	0.8% 0	7.6% 15	5.0% 11	4.6% 6	1.7% 0	0.1% 0	*** 0
Reform/Alliance	— —	— —	— —	— —	— —	— —	— —	2.1% 0
Others	1.2% 2	0.9% 1	1.2% 2	0.9% 1	1.5% 1	1.7% 0	3.0% 1	2.6% 0
Total valid votes Total seats	7,713,316 265	8,125,996 264	9,667,489 264	9,505,908 264	11,455,702 282	10,947,914 282	12,548,721 282	13,175,599 295

Party	1993	1997	2000	2004	2006	2008	2011	
Liberal	41.3% 177	38.5% 155	40.8% 172	36.7% 135	30.2% 103	26.2% 77	18.9% 34	
PC/Conservative**	16.0% 2	18.8% 20	12.2% 12	29.6% 99	36.3% 124	37.6% 143	39.6% 166	
NDP	6.9% 9	11.0% 21	8.5% 13	15.7% 19	17.5% 29	18.2% 37	30.6% 103	
Bloc Québécois	13.5% 54	10.7% 44	10.7% 38	12.4% 54	10.5% 51	10% 49	6.0% 4	
Reform/Alliance	18.7% 52	19.4% 60	25.5% 66	— —	— —	— —	— —	
Green Party	— —	— —	— —	4.3% 0	4.5% 0	6.8% 0	3.9% 1	
Others	3.6% 1	1.6% 1	2.2% 0	0.3% 1	1.0% 1	1.1% 2	1.0% 0	
Total valid votes Total seats	13,667,671 295	12,985,964 301	12,857,774 301	13,489,559 308	14,815,680 308	13,832,972 308	14,720,580 308	

*Columns may not add up to 100 per cent due to rounding.

The election of 1945 was the first in which the name Progressive Conservative was used. The New Democratic Party first participated in the election of 1962.

**In 2003 the Progressive Conservative and Canadian Alliance parties merged to form the Conservative Party. The 2004, 2006, 2008, and 2011 election results for this party are reported at this line.

***Less than 0.1 per cent.

Continued

TABLE 11.1   Continued

B. Percentage of Vote* and Candidates Elected by Party and Province, 2011

Province	Liberal	Conservative	NDP	Green Party	Bloc Québécois	Others	Totals Province
NL	37.9 4	28.4 1	32.6 2	0.9 0	—	—	215,874 7
NS	28.9 4	36.7 4	30.3 3	4.0 0	—	—	451,330 11
NB	22.6 1	43.9 8	29.8 1	3.2 0	—	—	388,437 10
PEI	41.0 3	41.2 1	15.4 0	2.4 0	—	—	79,048 4
Que.	14.2 7	16.5 5	42.9 59	2.1 0	23.4 4	—	3,798,430 75
Ont.	25.3 11	44.4 73	25.6 22	3.8 0	—	—	5,531,288 106
Man.	16.6 1	53.5 11	25.8 2	3.6 0	—	—	491,225 14
Sask.	8.6 1	56.3 13	32.3 0	2.7 0	—	—	455,053 14
Alta.	9.3 0	66.8 27	16.8 1	5.3 0	—	—	1,397,346 28
BC	13.4 2	45.5 21	32.5 12	7.7 1	—	—	1,871,665 36
Yukon, NWT, and Nunavut	26.4 0	36.4 2	27.7 1	9.2 0	—	—	39,881 3
Totals, Party	2,783,175 34	5,832,401 166	4,508,474 103	576,221 1	889,788 4	130,521 0	14,720,580 308

*Rows may not add up to 100 per cent due to rounding and the omission of candidates other than those of these five parties.

Clark clearly nurtured the vision of re-establishing the Progressive Conservative Party's status as Canada's other brokerage party.

The 2000 Election: Alliance Stalled?

It is generally conceded by all but the most loyal supporters of Jean Chrétien that the 2000 election was called for no better reason than what appeared to be its winnability. The main opposition party, the Canadian Alliance, had just gone through a fairly divisive leadership race that resulted in the defeat of the party's founder, Preston Manning, and his replacement by another Alberta politician,

Stockwell Day. The Alliance's new leader was a born-again Christian with a reputation for social conservatism. The Liberals could have continued in power for almost two more years before calling an election. But Day appeared vulnerable and so an election was called.

The rest, as they say, is history. The Liberals were re-elected with a larger majority than they held before the election. The Alliance failed to make its much desired breakthrough in Ontario and so continued to be seen as a party of western protest. Stockwell Day's performance in the campaign was generally seen as ineffective, leaving him open to criticism within his own party. This criticism continued to build during the year after the election until the pressure on Day to resign became irresistible. Day stepped down as leader and ran as a candidate in a new leadership race held less than two years after he had defeated Preston Manning. This time Day lost to Stephen Harper, another Albertan but one who was born and raised in Ontario and whose conservatism was perceived to be mainly of the fiscal rather than the social variety.

What makes the story of the 2000 election and Stockwell Day's subsequent loss of the Alliance leadership strange are the following facts, virtually ignored by most members of the media and academic commentators:

- Alliance's share of the popular vote increased from 19.4 per cent in 1997 to 25.5 per cent in 2000.
- The party's share of the popular vote in Ontario increased from 19.1 per cent in 1997 to 23.6 per cent in 2000.
- Alliance increased its seats in the House of Commons from 60 to 66.
- Alliance's share of the popular vote in Ontario exceeded that of the NDP and Progressive Conservative Party combined.

Given these facts, the obvious question is why the 2000 election was widely interpreted as a setback for the Canadian Alliance and a personal defeat for its leader, Stockwell Day.

The answer to this question reveals much about Canadian politics. What an outsider, viewing the Canadian electoral scene for the first time, might interpret as clear progress by the Alliance Party was viewed as a setback by most of the country's opinion-makers because of Alliance's failure to pick up seats in Ontario. Winning only two out of Ontario's 103 seats, and nothing in the eastern reaches of Canada, seemed to reconfirm the party's image as just the latest in a line of western protest parties. Of course, the distortions created by Canada's electoral system (about which more will be said below) were largely responsible for this image of Reform/Alliance. Nevertheless, the bar had been set at an Ontario breakthrough. When this did not happen, due to the Alliance and the Conservative parties splitting the right-of-centre vote, it appeared that the Alliance was stalled. Three successive elections had left it pretty much where it began in 1993.

Why the blame for this should come to rest largely on the shoulders of Stockwell Day provides another insight into Canadian politics. During the election campaign *Maclean's* magazine ran an issue with Day's picture on the cover and the question, "Are Canadians right to fear this man?" The cover story focused on the Alliance leader's religious beliefs and social conservatism, and included claims that Day believed in the literal truth of the book of Genesis and thus rejected evolutionary theory and evidence that the Earth is older than 5,000 years. The fundamental questions posed by the piece were, one, whether Day's ideas were significantly out of sync with those of most Canadians and, two, if he became Prime Minister, whether Day could be trusted not to try to foist an agenda of social conservatism onto Canadian society.

Most Canadians do not read *Maclean's* and it is probably a fair bet that among those who do, support for the Alliance was not very high to begin with. But the *Maclean's* story was only part of a broader pattern of media questioning of Day's religious beliefs and what the political implications of these might be. Questions like these are reasonable enough, but they were not asked in connection with any of the other party leaders. Day may have been singled out for scrutiny because his born-again Christianity placed him further from the safe centre of Canadian spiritual life than the other leaders. But this merely illustrates the point: the constituency for social conservatism is far from being large enough in Canada to elect a party led by someone whose faith is seen to be culturally marginal and of a sort that would lead him or her to champion social policies opposed by most Canadians. Whether a majority of Canadians consider such a leader to be "scary" may be an open question, but there is not much doubt that most of their opinion leaders do and that they believe Canadians should as well. Once the social conservative label was stuck to him, Day was no longer considered viable in Ontario. For Alliance to eventually make its breakthrough beyond the comfortable confines of the West it needed a leader who could not be portrayed, by innuendo or otherwise, as a religious nut.

In terms of the more general implications of the 2000 election, it remained unclear whether the

Former Liberal Party leader Michael Ignatieff proved unable to shake the polarizing narrative that the Conservatives had worked to instill in the minds of Canadians from the beginning of his stint as leader. Perceived as too strongly opinionated on key issues and too close to Americans, Ignatieff lost his own seat in the 2011 federal election and resigned as party leader shortly thereafter.

party *dealignment* that began in 1993 had been succeeded by a reasonably durable realignment of the national party system and voter support. The odds appeared to be against it. The Bloc Québécois continued to capture a significant share of the Quebec electorate—about four of 10 voters—and support for both the NDP and the Progressive Conservatives remained weak. Indeed, the Conservative Party appeared to have become a party of Atlantic Canada, winning about one of every three votes in the four Atlantic provinces and nine of their 12 seats from this region. This was achieved by positioning the party *to the left* of the Liberals in Atlantic Canada, criticizing the Chrétien government's spending cuts and their negative impact on the region. The idea that the Progressive Conservative Party could re-establish itself nationally by outflanking the

Liberals on the left was pretty far-fetched. Emerging from the 2000 election with the smallest share of the popular vote in its history on the national political stage, the PCs and their leadership seemed to be clinging pathetically to the hope that the Alliance would somehow implode and wayward Alliance MPs and voters would return to their proper home in the Progressive Conservative Party.

As for the NDP, 2000 marked the third consecutive election in which the party's national support was in the single digits. The long-simmering debate over whether the way out of marginal status in national politics could be found in moving the party further to the left or in recapturing the centrist orientation it had under former leaders Ed Broadbent and David Lewis eventually led to the resignation of NDP leader Alexa McDonough.

The ensuing leadership race pitted a strongly left-wing Toronto city councillor, Jack Layton, against a less strident long-time Winnipeg MP, Bill Blaikie. Layton's victory suggested that the party was pinning its hopes on a shift to the left and on improving its fortunes in urban Canada.

The 2004, 2006, and 2008 Elections: A Divided Electorate

The 2003 merger of the Canadian Alliance and Progressive Conservative Party eliminated what many considered to be the conditions for permanent Liberal government in Canada. The right was now united and the prospect of making inroads in the Liberal stronghold of Ontario seemed within reach. When the 2004 election was called there were reasons for the opposition parties to feel optimistic. The federal Auditor General, Sheila Fraser, had focused attention in her annual report on what appeared to be inappropriate and probably unlawful misallocation of public dollars on advertising in Quebec. Money had gone to individuals and ad companies with little—and in some cases nothing—provided in exchange. A network of shady dealings and favouritism to Liberal operatives in Quebec was exposed. The Adscam scandal, as this affair was known, resulted in a sharp drop in Liberal support in Quebec and a corresponding boost in the popularity of the BQ. The recently chosen leader of the Liberal Party, Prime Minister Paul Martin, attempted to distance himself from the scandal, but it clearly cast a shadow over what many had expected would be the Liberals' fairly effortless march to another majority government.

The new Conservative Party and the NDP were also going into the 2004 election with new leaders. The stakes were different for these parties. In the case of the Conservatives, a breakthrough in Ontario was the goal. For the NDP, emergence from its near irrelevance since the 1993 election was the objective. Both parties achieved their goals, but neither to the degree that its leader and supporters had hoped for in an election that produced Canada's first minority government in a quarter of a century.

Halfway through the campaign public opinion polls were showing a steady deterioration in Liberal support in English Canada. It appeared that the Conservatives were on the cusp of being swept into power with a minority government on the strength of gains in Ontario. At this point the Liberal campaign went heavily negative with a barrage of attack ads on television and radio. These ads targeted a number of fears about the Conservatives and their leader that many voters clearly held. The Conservatives had a "hidden agenda," it was claimed. This agenda involved the privatization of health care, chipping away at abortion rights, dragging Canada into American-led military adventures, scrapping the Kyoto Accord and other environmental protections, and, in sum, transforming Canada into a northern extension of the United States.

The Liberal strategy appeared to work. The party's share of the national popular vote fell by about four percentage points but it held on to power with a minority government. The Conservatives made gains in Ontario, winning 24 of the province's 106 seats, but this was still far from what it needed to defeat the Liberals. The BQ and NDP both experienced significant gains in their respective shares of the popular vote and number of MPs. It was clear that this was a Parliament unlikely to last more than a year or two.

The 2004 election was a reminder that campaigns do matter. What had appeared to be a probable Conservative victory evaporated in the last weeks of the campaign and, according to some analysts, even in the last few days when the Liberal advertising assault appeared to produce its intended effect in Ontario. Going into the 2006 campaign the polls placed the Liberals comfortably ahead of the Conservatives but the undecided share of the electorate was large, ensuring that this, too, would be a campaign that would matter.

And matter it did. Like the French defending the Maginot Line at the start of World War II, the Liberals attempted to use a familiar strategy that in the end proved ill-suited to the times. The Liberal campaign relied on attack ads from the beginning and tried to portray the Conservatives and their leader very much as they had done in 2004. The Conservatives countered with a strategy of introducing a new policy promise each day. This placed the Liberals on the defensive, responding to such Conservative promises as a reduction in the GST, providing parents with a child-care allowance, improving government accountability, and so on. The Conservatives were able to dominate the issue agenda and, of at least equal importance, avoid the sorts of embarrassing and potentially damaging statements from candidates that had been used against them in previous campaigns. The disciplined and focused character of the Conservative campaign contrasted with the uncharacteristically bumbling and increasingly desperate one waged by the Liberals as that party saw its lead in the polls slip away.

The final result was a Conservative minority government, achieved on the strength of significant gains in the party's popular vote and seat total in Ontario, but also, and surprisingly, because of a breakthrough in Quebec. The Conservatives won almost one-quarter of the popular vote in that province—more than the Liberals—and 10 seats. To consolidate these gains Prime Minister Harper moved quickly to appoint five Quebecers to cabinet, including to such important posts as Transport, Industry, and Labour.

The Conservative victory in 2006 was widely interpreted as a rightward shift in Canadian politics. This may have been so, but the magnitude of the shift was not very great and its staying power was uncertain. Barely more than 36 per cent of the electorate voted for Conservative candidates in an election where Stephen Harper and his party were careful not to rely on ideologically polarizing language or messages. The Liberals continued to be handicapped by the lingering effects of the Adscam scandal, as well as by the perception of many voters that they had become arrogant in power. The NDP

Politics in Focus

BOX 11.4 Unite the Left?

"The lady doth protest too much, methinks." So says the Queen in Shakespeare's *Hamlet*, suggesting that the repeated protestations of an actor whose performance she has just witnessed may in fact conceal exactly what she so insistently denies. Canadian politics is hardly the tragic psychodrama that is *Hamlet*. But when former Ontario NDP leader and current Liberal MP Bob Rae was asked in June 2010 about rumours of high-level talks concerning a possible merger of the national NDP and Liberal Party, his categorical dismissal of such rumours sounded a bit like the Queen's protests.

Whether or not party heavyweights had sat down in the same room to discuss the idea of a unite-the-left merger of the national Liberal Party and the NDP, the idea of such a marriage had been circulating since the 2006 election of the Conservative minority government. Former Liberal cabinet minister Lloyd Axworthy publicly advocated such a merger after the 2008 election, arguing that it was necessary to defeat the Conservative Party of Stephen Harper. Several former NDP politicians, including Roy Romanow, Ed Broadbent, and Lorne Calvert, have spoken in support of the merger concept. No less a figure than former Liberal Prime Minister Jean Chrétien admitted in June 2010 to having had informal discussions with former NDP leader Ed Broadbent about ways of uniting the centre-left vote to defeat the Conservatives. The Liberals and the NDP, with the support of the BQ, signed a formal agreement in 2008 to bring down the Conservative government on a confidence vote and support a Liberal government for an agreed period of time. Such an agreement was far from a merger, but it showed how desperate the parties were to find a way to dislodge the Conservatives from power, something that neither the Liberals nor the NDP appeared capable of doing on their own at the polls.

increased its share of the popular vote and number of MPs back to levels that it had typically enjoyed before the party's collapse in the 1993 election. It was far from clear, therefore, that the Conservative victory signified a move to the right in Canadian politics. Such a judgment would have to wait until the next federal election, which, given the fragmented party standings in the legislature, appeared to be no more than a couple of years away.

The 2008 election failed to confirm this rightward shift. The Conservatives managed to increase their share of the popular vote by a couple of percentage points, mainly at the expense of sagging national support for the Liberal Party under the uncertain leadership of Stéphane Dion. The Bloc Québécois held onto its status as the dominant federal party in Quebec, denying the Liberals one of the pillars they had long counted on to win national elections and preventing the Conservatives from capturing the

seats they needed to form a majority government. The centre-left of Canadian politics appeared to be undiminished in strength. But unlike the years before the 1993 election, the votes on the centre-left of the spectrum were now distributed between four parties—the Liberals, the NDP, the Bloc, and the Green Party—instead of being divided between the Liberal Party and the NDP. The Conservative Party controlled the centre-right of the political spectrum, but it was not clear there were enough votes in this electoral space to deliver the party a majority government.

The years between the 1993 and 2008 elections, which produced such dramatic changes in the parties' representation in the House of Commons, were not accompanied by the sorts of shifts in party support generally associated with a period of realignment. A **realignment election**, or series of elections, produces a durable change in the parties'

On the face of it, the unite-the-left idea may appear to make sense. Axworthy, Broadbent, and others tirelessly point out that the Conservatives have governed since 2006 even though about six in 10 voters cast their ballots for candidates of parties that are to the left of that party. The bold and unpredicted decision of the British Conservative and Liberal-Democratic parties to enter a coalition government after that country's May 2010 election seemed to make the idea of an inter-party merger in Canada a bit more credible, at least in the eyes of some.

So why don't the parties just merge? There are many reasons why such a step would be difficult to accomplish and would not necessarily achieve the goals of those who advocate it. Here are three big ones:

- Some supporters of both the NDP and the Liberal Party hate the idea. Many NDP activists argue that it would pull their party away from what should be its proper left-wing agenda. From the Liberal side, not all activists and certainly not all Liberal voters are left of centre. Many are more comfortable with the ideas

and policies of the Conservatives than they are with those of the NDP.

- A merger of the parties cannot be achieved just because some leaders want it to happen. The parties operate under constitutions that require that their respective memberships be given a say in the matter, as happened in 2003 when the Canadian Alliance and Progressive Conservative parties merged to form the Conservative Party of Canada.
- Egos are at stake. Who would lead this new party? How would the career and leadership prospects of politicians and officials in the two parties be affected by a merger? Is their desire to defeat the Conservatives powerful enough for them to risk losing position and influence within their own party?

None of this means that a merger of the NDP and Liberal Party is impossible, and over the past several years some important people in the parties have talked seriously about it. But the obstacles are huge and, even if overcome, there is no guarantee that the result would be the one that unite-the-left advocates would hope to see.

bases of support. Perhaps the classic illustration of this was the emergence of the New Deal coalition in American politics during the 1930s, when blue-collar workers, Catholics, black Americans, and southerners lined up solidly behind the Democratic Party, ensuring its domination of Congress for the following several decades. In Canada the 1896 election comes closest to deserving the realignment label, as French-Canadian Catholics, a voting bloc that had leaned towards the Conservative Party, shifted to the Liberals after the execution of the Métis leader Louis Riel and the selection of the francophone Wilfrid Laurier as the Liberal leader. The huge vote swings that occurred in 1958 and 1984, when Quebecers massively shifted their support to the Progressive Conservative Party, proved not to be durable.

The most significant and enduring shift that took place beginning with the 1993 election was that a large share of the Quebec electorate voted for the separatist Bloc Québécois in six consecutive elections. Although the demise of the BQ and the re-absorption of most of its supporters into the Liberal Party vote column were confidently predicted at various points, this did not happen. The 1993 election brought about a temporary realignment in Quebec that lasted until 2011. In the rest of Canada, the 2003 merger of the Canadian Alliance and the Progressive Conservative Party appeared to re-establish business as usual. The two historically dominant parties competed to form a national government, with the NDP back in its familiar role as a third party capable of tipping the balance between the larger parties and exercising leverage over a minority government. But business as usual ended with the 2011 election.

The 2011 Election: A 60/40 Country?

Canadian elections have often produced a change in government, but only occasionally have the results redrawn the party map. The election of 1921 was one such case, when the Progressive Party, which had no seats in the House of Commons prior to the election, became the official opposition. By the 1926 election things were back to normal and the Liberal–Conservative duopoly in Canadian party politics had been re-established. The election of 1993, when the Conservative Party's support collapsed and the Bloc Québécois and Reform Party surged into second and third place, respectively, in the House of Commons standings was another case where the party map was redrawn in dramatic fashion.

No such surprises were expected when, on 26 March 2011, the 40th Parliament was dissolved and an election was called. The conventional wisdom was that not very much was likely to change in the party standings. Most of the speculation involved whether the governing Conservative Party would manage to eke out a narrow majority this time. In the absence of a clear issue dividing the parties and galvanizing voters, what excitement existed was generated in large part by the prospect of yet another Conservative minority government. It was widely expected that if this were to happen, the opposition parties would take the first opportunity to defeat the Conservatives in the House and install a coalition government of the sort they had contemplated in 2008 and again in 2009.

And then the unexpected happened. The election of 2011 was a jolting reminder that campaigns matter. No one predicted at the outset that the once mighty Liberal Party, Canada's "natural governing party," as it came to be known in the latter half of the twentieth century, would fall to third place with the support of fewer than one out of five voters. Nor did anyone imagine that the NDP would vault into second place, winning more than twice as many seats as its previous election high of 43 in 1988 and doubling its share of the popular vote. These would have been surprises enough for one election. But perhaps the greatest surprise in this election full of startling results was the almost total collapse of the BQ in Quebec—a party that was comfortably in the lead in that province when the election was called—and the emergence of the NDP as Quebec's leading party. In its entire history the NDP, going back to its original incarnation as the CCF, had elected only two MPs from Quebec. On 2 May 2011, the party captured 59 of the province's 75 seats.

Explanations for these seismic changes in Canadian party politics focused on two major factors: leadership and what was believed to be Quebecers' fatigue with the sovereignists and their goal of Quebec independence. The NDP leader, Jack Layton, was said to have caught the imagination of Canadians, including Quebecers, appearing confident, compassionate, and articulate. Of course, some voters thought that he already showed these leadership qualities in 2004, 2006, and 2008. Layton's death in August of 2011 demonstrated the breadth and depth of the admiration that many Canadians, including those who did not share his social democratic ideology, felt for him. Not since the death of Pierre Trudeau in 2000 had the passing of a public figure provoked such an outpouring of grief and tributes. Layton's rivals for the centre-left vote in the 2011 election, the Liberals' Michael Ignatieff and the BQ's Gilles Duceppe, failed to connect with many of their respective parties' usual supporters. The reasons were different in each case. Ignatieff proved unable to shake the narrative that the Conservatives had done so much to instill in the minds of Canadians from the time of his selection as Liberal leader in 2009. He seemed, according to the critics, aloof and uninspiring after his 35 years spent outside of Canada. In the case of Gilles Duceppe, it was not that his style or personal story—a story that Quebecers knew very well and seemed to approve of in the five previous elections—alienated voters. Rather, his message no longer seemed to resonate with *les québécois*. Ideologically, in terms of such issues as taxation, social spending, the environment, and Canadian troops abroad, the BQ and the NDP were not very different. From its inception in the wake of the failed Meech Lake Accord, the BQ's competitive advantage was its special relationship to Quebec nationalism. That advantage no longer seemed to matter to voters in 2011.

Over the years Quebecers have shown themselves to be capable of dramatic change in how they cast their votes. In 1958 they abandoned the Liberal Party in droves for the Conservatives—a party that had done poorly in the province since the end of the nineteenth century—only to return to the Liberals in the next election. With a Conservative victory imminent in 1984, Quebec voters again swung their allegiance from the Liberals to the Conservatives. But only nine years later the Conservatives could not elect a single member from Quebec and the BQ, which had existed for only a couple of years, won most of the seats from the province and received close to half of the popular vote. Support for the BQ was widely seen as a means whereby nationalist Quebec voters could leverage their province's influence within the House of Commons without having to make the compromises with English-speaking Canada that were necessary in the Liberal and Conservative parties. These dramatic swings in Quebecers' party preferences have been interpreted by many as evidence of strategic voting in a province whose citizens recognize that it is *pas comme les autres*.

Listen to "The 60/40 Country?" podcast, available at: www.oupcanada.com/Brooks8e

The fact that four out of 10 Quebec voters cast a ballot for the NDP in 2011 was seen as the latest instance of this putative tendency towards strategic voting. When the NDP edged closer to the Liberals in the polls and then appeared to be about level with them just after the midpoint of the campaign, media speculation on the possibility of a coalition government led by the NDP became rampant. We cannot know for certain whether a significant number of voters who usually would have voted either Liberal or BQ decided to vote for the NDP for strategic reasons, thinking that Jack Layton's party might actually head a coalition government. We do know, however, that polls in Quebec showed Layton to be more popular than the other party leaders. If strategic reasoning was an important part of the mix of factors that contributed to the massive shift in Quebecers' party preferences in 2011, the gamble did not pay off. The Conservatives won a clear majority nationally and the possibility of an NDP-led coalition melted away along with the last snow in the province of Quebec.

The 2011 election appeared to be all about change and, indeed, the changes were significant. But buried underneath the focus on the NDP surge, the BQ collapse, and the Liberals' worst showing in the party's history were two important elements of continuity. First, issues appeared to take a back seat to the leaders and their perceived strengths and shortcomings. As we saw earlier in this chapter, this is something that André Siegfried remarked upon over 100 years ago: the tendency for Canadian elections to be contests between the parties' leaders rather than struggles between rival ideas and ideologies. This is only partly correct, however. It is not that ideas do not matter in Canadian elections, but rather that they become associated with and absorbed into images that voters have of the party leaders and, in the process, lose some of their independent force. The electoral conversation is not bereft of policy ideas and promises. But these are refracted through perceptions of the party leaders. Leadership becomes the pre-eminent issue and this necessarily focuses attention on what are believed to be the personal attributes of the men and women who lead the parties.

Second, the election results demonstrate that Canada is a 60/40 country. The Conservative Party, the only party with a centre-right platform, won with about 40 per cent of the popular vote. The four centre-left parties, the Liberals being the most centrist of this group, together accounted for about 60 per cent of the vote. This has been the pattern for the past three decades, with the exception of 1984 when the Conservative Party won 50 per cent of the popular vote. Otherwise the electorate has tended to divide ideologically on a 60/40 basis, centre-left parties receiving the majority of the votes cast in these elections. Of course, we can quibble about whether the Liberal Party became a more right-leaning than left-leaning party during the mid- to late 1990s, when Paul Martin was Minister of Finance and leaner government appeared to be the priority. But ideological characterizations are relative and the Liberal brand, as most commentators agree, has always been a bit to the left of the Conservative brand on the Canadian ideological spectrum. In the eight elections from 1988 to 2011 the percentage of the vote received by centre-right parties (a category that includes the Progressive Conservative Party, the Reform Party, the Canadian Alliance, and the Conservative Party of Canada) has ranged between 29.6 per cent (2004) and 43 per cent (1988), averaging just over 37 per cent.

Canada is a country in which the balance of the electorate leans towards the centre-left of the Canadian political spectrum. History will show whether the 2011 election results and the surge of the NDP is a one-off affair or the harbinger of realignment in the party system. Some believe that victory for the left in Canada now requires that the centre-left parties unite, as the right united in the 2003 merger of the Canadian Alliance and the Progressive Conservative Party (see Box 11.4). What is overlooked in this scenario is that some of those who run for office as Liberals and who vote for that party would find life more congenial under the Conservative Party banner than in a centre-left party that includes and might be dominated by activists and supporters of the NDP. Some prominent members of both the Liberal Party and the NDP have talked openly about what they see as the need to unite the left to take electoral advantage of the fact that most Canadians appear to cluster around the centre-left of the ideological spectrum. But as the dust settled after the 2011 election, it did not appear that a merger of any sort was imminent.

Selecting Party Leaders in Canada

When Wilfrid Laurier was chosen as the first French-Canadian leader of the Liberal Party in 1887, about 80 men did the choosing. They were the Liberal MPs in Canada's Sixth Parliament. Laurier's candidacy was promoted by Edward Blake, then leader of the party, after Blake's poor showing in the 1887 general election. Some prominent members of the Liberal Party opposed Laurier as leader, but in the end he had no serious opposition for the post. The rules followed in this leadership selection process were not written down in any formal document. It was simply understood that, following the British parliamentary tradition, it was the prerogative of caucus to choose who among its members would be the party leader.

When the Liberal Party of Canada chose Stéphane Dion as its new leader on 3 December 2006, 4,605 delegates cast ballots in Montreal's Palais des Congrès. About 850 of them were *ex officio delegates*, men and women who because of their positions in the Liberal Party—including elected MPs and provincial legislators, senators, and party officials—automatically had the right to attend and vote at the party's leadership convention. All of these delegates cast their ballots on the final day of a five-day party convention covered on live television, choosing among a field of eight candidates. It took four ballots to select the party's new leader, following formal rules laid down in the 23-page Rules of Procedure for the 2006 Leadership and Biennial Convention.

Shortly before the Liberals' 2006 leadership convention Jeffrey Simpson wrote a column entitled "It's tough to be ahead." And, indeed, in the wake of Michael Ignatieff's defeat and Stéphane Dion's unpredicted victory the conventional wisdom quickly became that there are serious drawbacks to being the frontrunner. The scrutiny is more intense, the analysis and criticism of every word and action more unforgiving. Being an underdog, on the other hand—but not too much of an underdog!—has the advantage of freeing a candidate from this unremitting media spotlight and, potentially, enabling him or her to profit from an "anybody-but-frontrunner-X" movement on the convention floor.

As plausible as all this sounds, it is also incorrect. If one looks at all the Conservative, Liberal, and NDP leadership conventions that required more than one ballot to choose the leader—16 in total—13 were won by the candidate who led on the first ballot. The only exceptions were the Progressive Conservative Party conventions of 1976 (Joe Clark was third on the first ballot and won on the fourth) and 1983 (Brian Mulroney was second on the first ballot and won on the fourth) and the Liberal convention of 2006 (Dion was third on the first ballot and won on the fourth). If there is a lesson to be drawn from the history of leadership conventions in Canada it is that there is a huge advantage to being the frontrunner heading into the convention vote.

In particular circumstances, however, this frontrunner advantage may be absent, as was true in the case of the 2006 Liberal convention. Looking back on the three frontrunners who failed to hang onto their leads (Claude Wagner at the Conservative convention of 1976; Joe Clark at the Conservative convention of 1983; and Michael Ignatieff at the Liberal convention of 2006), the fact that stands out is *not* the wide distribution of initial delegate support between several candidates or the relatively small share of total votes received by the frontrunner on the first ballot. Joe Clark, for example, received 36.5 per cent of first ballot votes in 1983 and eventually lost, whereas Robert Stanfield received only 23.3 per cent in 1967 and Pierre Trudeau received 31.5 per cent in 1968, and the latter two ultimately won. Michael Ignatieff captured 29.3 per cent on the first ballot but was unable to build sufficiently on this initial delegate support.

What does stand out as the common factor running through the failed candidacies of Wagner, Clark, and Ignatieff was the polarizing nature of each man's candidacy. Wagner was a French Canadian running for the leadership of a party that had never had a leader from French Canada. By itself, this fact may not have been decisive. Nevertheless, media accounts at the time suggested that many English-speaking delegates, particularly from the West, resented the idea of choosing a French-Canadian leader from Quebec. Wagner's somewhat tenuous connection to the Progressive Conservative Party—he had been a long-time member of Quebec's Union Nationale—simply reinforced many delegates' perception of him as something of an outsider who did not truly represent the party and its values.

Joe Clark, the candidate who eventually defeated Wagner by a narrow margin on the fourth ballot, was in turn the polarizing candidate at the party's 1983 convention. That convention had been called as a result of Clark's insistence that anything less than an overwhelming endorsement of his leadership at the party's biennial conference in December 1982 would be tantamount to a vote of non-confidence in his leadership. He received the endorsement of only two-thirds of delegates at that 1983 Winnipeg convention, about the same level of support that he had received two years earlier at the party's Ottawa convention. Clark's leadership had been under fire by some within the party since the unexpected fall of his minority government in December 1979 and their subsequent defeat by the Liberals in the 1980 general election. A selection of his frontbench MPs, people who had served under him during his short-lived government, ran against him for the leadership. Many in the party and in the media saw Clark as a weak leader who lacked the ability to defeat the Liberals. An "Anybody but Clark" ("ABC") movement developed during the campaign and continued onto the convention floor, where strategic voting benefited two of Clark's rivals, John Crosbie and Brian Mulroney, until Mulroney finally emerged victorious on the fourth ballot.

The defeat of Michael Ignatieff on the fourth ballot of the 2006 Liberal convention, as in the case of both Wagner and Clark, may be attributed to the polarizing nature of his candidacy. Ignatieff had lived outside of Canada for most of his adult life, in some of his writings he had expressed himself as though he were American, and he had returned to Canada and joined the Liberal Party only a couple of years before running for its leadership, but these were probably not the main reasons for the anti-Ignatieff sentiment that became increasingly apparent as the convention approached. More serious were the ideas and policies he represented.

As an academic, documentarist, and public intellectual of considerable reputation, Ignatieff had left an extensive paper trail. His views on such controversial matters as the decision to depose Saddam Hussein in Iraq (he had supported it), rethinking post-Geneva Convention

Listen to the "Who Is Michael Ignatieff? What Our Leaders' Stories Say about Canadian Politics" podcast, available at www.oupcanada.com/Brooks8e

ideas about torture (like his erstwhile Harvard colleague, Alan Dershowitz, he was open to this), and maintaining a Canadian combat presence in Afghanistan (he was for this) put him on the wrong side of important issues in the eyes of many Liberal convention delegates. Related to all of these issues was a sense that Ignatieff was a bit too close to Americans, or at least not convincing enough in his Canadian nationalism (which inevitably requires distance between Canada and the United States and, usually, staking out an anti-American stand on key issues). Ignatieff was aware of this sentiment and even included a video on his campaign website in which he was critical of anti-Americanism.

In the end, however, Ignatieff's candidacy had too little potential for growth over a multi-ballot convention. Figure 11.1 shows that his vote total increased only gradually after the first ballot and that Stéphane Dion clearly was the chief beneficiary of the movement that took place once some delegates' preferred candidates dropped off the ballot. It is often said that governments lose elections; their opponents don't win them. The same may be said of at least some leadership races where the frontrunner's candidacy polarizes delegates. The 2006 Liberal convention was such a case. While it is indeed true that Stéphane Dion won the party's leadership, the story of his victory was, in an important sense, the story of Ignatieff's loss. It was, as well, a consequence of the fact that Ignatieff was not the only leading candidate carrying "anyone-but"

FIGURE 11.1 The Dynamic of the 2006 Liberal Convention Vote baggage. In second place through the first two ballots was Bob Rae, who normally might have been expected to capitalize from the negative attitudes of some delegates towards Ignatieff, his old college roommate. But Rae, as a former NDP Premier of Ontario and former NDP MP, also had turned to the Liberal Party for a run at the brass ring. His past NDP affiliation was a problem, to be sure, and he was an unacceptable alternative to many delegates who remembered unfavourably his term as Ontario Premier during the recession of the early 1990s.

The poor performance of the Liberals under the leadership of Stéphane Dion in 2008 led to Dion's early resignation, the announcement that another leadership convention would be held in May 2009, and the selection by the party's caucus of Ignatieff as the party's interim leader. This decision was somewhat unusual given that someone viewed as a major contender for the party's leadership would not normally be chosen for this role in the lead-up to a leadership convention. When Bob Rae, the only other high-profile candidate for the Liberal leadership, declined to enter the race, it was clear that Ignatieff would not have any opposition at the forthcoming leadership convention. His leadership was ratified by 97 per cent of the delegates at the convention, but the Liberals had essentially selected a leader using the caucus method, a process they had not employed since the selection of Laurier in the late nineteenth century.

The most recent party leadership races were studies in contrast. After a bruising campaign, Thomas Mulcair was elected leader of the NDP in 2012 on the fourth ballot of voting at the party's Toronto convention. Justin Trudeau, elected leader of the Liberals at the party's 2013 convention in Ottawa, won easily in the first round of voting after a campaign that featured many candidates, most of whom withdrew before the actual convention, but little real interest or suspense about who would ultimately win. About 59,000 party members voted in the NDP leadership race and roughly 31,000 in the Liberal race. Most of these votes were cast via the Internet. By historical standards these numbers may seem impressive, but given the low bar to become an eligible voter—anyone who joined the Liberal Party as a member or supporter at least 41

days before the convention and who paid a modest fee could vote; dues-paying members of the NDP, who were members at least 34 days before the convention, could vote—they were not particularly high. About 131,000 Canadians were eligible to vote in the NDP leadership contest but fewer than half of them did so.

Three Models for Selecting Party Leaders

The 2006 Liberal leadership convention involved a method for choosing party leaders that began in Canada in 1919. That year marked the transition from the *caucus model*, where party leaders were chosen by other elected MPs of their party, to the *convention model* (see Table 11.2). In some ways this transition was a simple product of circumstances. Wilfrid Laurier had called a national convention of the Liberal Party in 1919 to discuss policy at a time when the party was reduced to mainly Quebec representation in the House of Commons. Laurier died soon after the convention was called and the party's national executive decided to use the Ottawa meeting as an opportunity to choose his successor. In doing so they were breaking new ground. In no other British parliamentary democracy were party leaders chosen in this manner. Presidential candidates in the United States were, of course, selected at conventions that brought together state delegations. In adopting the convention model for their party—a model that would be followed by other Canadian parties—Liberals were aware of the American practice. But the Canadian convention model has always been different from the American one in important ways, from the process used to choose convention delegates to procedures on the convention floor.

Criticisms that the convention model was elitist and too easily dominated by money and backroom deal-making were heard with increasing frequency after the 1960s. When the Reform Party began to choose its leaders through a direct vote of all party members the pressure on other parties to follow suit was difficult to resist. In 1997 the Bloc Québécois chose Gilles Duceppe as its leader using the one-member, one-vote (OMOV) model. The Progressive

TABLE 11.2 Three Models of Leadership Selection

Model 1	Model 2	Model 3
Party Caucus	Party Activists (narrow)	Party Activists (broad)
Few and closed ——————————————————————————————————— Many and open		
Participants		
Elected members of the party (i.e., MPs)	Party members elected by members of their riding associations to serve as delegates at the leadership convention, plus ex officio delegates*	Party members
Procedures		
Selection takes place behind closed doors, often without competition between rival candidates	Selection takes place at a party leadership convention, often after several months of campaigning	Selection takes place through votes cast by party members: some voting may take place at a fixed convention site but most votes are cast electronically by party members who are elsewhere
Examples		
Liberal Party: Mackenzie, 1873; Blake, 1880; Laurier, 1887; Ignatieff, 2008	King, 1919; St Laurent, 1948; Pearson, 1958; Trudeau, 1968; Turner, 1984; Chrétien, 1990; Martin, 2003; Dion, 2006	Justin Trudeau, 2013
Conservative Party: Macdonald, 1867; Abbott, 1891; Thompson, 1892; Bowell, 1894; Tupper, 1896; Borden, 1901; Meighen, 1920; Gutherie, 1926; Meighen, 1941	Bennett, 1927; Manion, 1938; Bracken, 1942; Drew, 1948; Diefenbaker, 1956; Stanfield, 1967; Clark, 1976; Mulroney, 1983; Campbell, 1993; Charest, 1995	Clark, 1998; Harper, 2004
CCF-NDP:	Woodsworth, 1933; Caldwell, 1942; Argue, 1960; Douglas, 1961; Lewis, 1971; Broadbent, 1975; McLaughlin, 1989; McDonough, 1995; McDonough, 2001	Layton, 2003; Mulcair, 2012
Bloc Québécois: Bouchard, 1990	Bouchard, 1991	Duceppe, 1997

*An ex officio delegate is one whose formal position entitles him or her to a vote in the choice of party leader. Elected MPs and party office-holders are examples.

Conservative Party followed in 1998, choosing Joe Clark as its leader using the OMOV model, and today all of the parties use some variant of the OMOV model.

Whether this model produces better results than the caucus or convention models depends on what one means by "better." The argument for OMOV is that it democratizes the leadership selection process, broadening the scope of participation and thereby reducing the influence of elites within the party. Combined with limitations that all of the parties place on leadership campaign spending (they were set at $950,000 in the 2013 Liberal race and $500,000 in the 2012 NDP contest) and the contribution limits and reporting requirements that have existed under Canadian law since 2004, this is expected to make leadership races more open, less about who has the most dollars and more about who has the most supporters within the rank and file of the party. It is hard to argue against such aims. At the same time, however, it is not yet clear that these reforms to the leadership selection process produce leaders who are more likely to be successful at winning elections and holding together the different elements that exist within any political party.

The Electoral System and Its Consequences

Many Canadians were shocked when George W. Bush was elected President of the United States in 2000, even though he received about one-half million fewer votes than Al Gore. What they did not realize is that such an outcome can and has happened in Canada. In 1979 the Liberal Party received about 4 per cent more of the popular vote than the Conservatives, but the Conservatives won 22 more seats and formed the government. In the 1998 provincial election in Quebec, the Quebec Liberal Party won 43.7 per cent of the popular vote compared to 42.7 per cent for the Parti Québécois. Despite this the PQ won a strong majority of seats in Quebec's National Assembly. It occasionally happens that the party that wins a provincial or federal election in Canada is not the party that wins in the popular vote. Even more common, however, is the situation where the governing party is elected on the strength of only 38–40 per cent of the popular vote. Canadians who were scandalized by George W. Bush's victory in 2000 would do well to consider that Bush won a larger share of the eligible electorate than did Jean Chrétien's Liberal Party in the Canadian election of that same year. But no one seriously contested the legitimacy of Chrétien's victory.

Canada's electoral system does not reward parties in proportion to their share of the popular vote. The Conservative Party, whose candidates garnered just under 40 per cent of the popular vote in the 2011 election, won 54.2 per cent of all seats in the House of Commons. On the other hand, the 12 per cent of the popular vote that the Conservatives received in the Greater Montreal area translated into none of the 34 seats from that metropolitan region. The Liberals received 18.9 per cent of the national popular vote but only 11 per cent of the seats in the Commons while the NDP, for the first time in its history, was over-rewarded by the electoral system, winning 30.6 per cent of the popular vote but electing 33.1 per cent of all MPs. But the prize for apparent injustice was taken by the Green Party, whose 3.9 per cent of the popular vote produced only one seat in the House of Commons, and by

the Bloc Québécois, whose 6 per cent of the popular vote translated into 1.3 per cent of all seats in the House of Commons.

To understand what has happened in recent elections, we must first describe the Canadian electoral system, whose principal features are the same at both the federal and provincial levels. It is based on the **single-member constituency**: one person is elected to represent the citizens of a particular geographic area called a constituency or riding. The candidate who receives the most votes in a constituency election becomes the member of Parliament (or provincial legislator) for that constituency. This is called a **plurality electoral system**. A majority of votes is not necessary to be elected and, given the fragmentation of votes between the three main parties, is the exception rather than the rule.

A political party's representation in the House of Commons will depend, therefore, on how well its candidates fare in the 308 constituency races that take place on election day across Canada (the number of constituencies increased to 338 in April 2014, in time for an election some time in 2015). The advocates of the single-member, simple plurality electoral system point to its ability to produce majority governments as the system's chief virtue. It manages, they claim, to transform something less than a majority of votes for a party into a majority of seats, thereby delivering stable majority government. In fact, however, the system's performance on this count has been rather mediocre. Nine of the 19 general elections from 1957 to 2011 produced minority governments. The chief alternative to the single-member, plurality electoral system is some form of **proportional representation** (PR). Under a PR system, the number of members elected by each party about coincides with its share of the popular vote. This sounds eminently fair, but PR has its critics. Detractors criticize it on three main counts. First, they claim it promotes a splintering of the party system, encouraging the creation of minor parties that represent very narrow interests and undermining the development of broad-based national parties capable of bridging sectional rivalries and the differences between special interests. Second, proportional representation is said to produce unstable government. The unlikelihood that any party will have a majority of seats and, therefore, the need to cobble together and maintain a coalition government result in more frequent elections. And even between elections, the inter-party deals necessary to maintain a coalition government may paralyze cabinet decision-making. Countries such as Italy and Belgium, where governments seldom lasted longer than a year or two during much of the post-World War II era, are said to illustrate the horrors of PR (curiously, proportional systems with a relatively low level of executive turnover, such as the Netherlands and Germany, are seldom mentioned by the critics).

A third standard criticism of PR systems is that they encourage ideological polarity and enable extremist parties to achieve representation in the legislature. There is no doubt that countries having proportional electoral systems do tend to have more political parties represented in their legislatures than those with plurality systems, and the ideological distance between the extreme ends of the party spectrum will inevitably be greater than that separating Canada's major parties, or Democrats and Republicans in the United States (another plurality electoral system). In fact, however, the ideological distance between those parties in proportional systems that are likely to be the senior partner in any coalition government tends to be no greater than between, say, the Conservative Party and the NDP in Canada. Moreover, not everyone would agree that more, rather than less, ideological dispersion between parties is a bad thing. One might argue that it improves voters' ability to distinguish between parties on the basis of the values and policies they represent. The prospect that extremist parties will infiltrate the legislature through a proportional system is also less worrisome than is claimed by detractors. Both theory and experience suggest that the closer a party gets to membership in a governing coalition, the more moderate its behaviour will be.[22]

The "winner-take-all" electoral system that exists in Canada is not without its own detractors. In a classic analysis, Alan Cairns identifies several consequences for Canada's party system and national unity that flow from the single-member, simple plurality system.[23]

- It tends to produce more seats than votes for the strongest major party and for minor parties whose support is regionally concentrated.
- It gives the impression that some parties have little or no support in certain regions, when in fact their candidates may regularly account for 15–30 per cent of the popular vote.
- The parliamentary composition of a party will be less representative of the different regions of the country than is that party's electoral support.
- Minor parties whose appeal is to interests that are distributed widely across the country will receive a smaller percentage of seats than votes.

Cairns concludes that the overall impact of Canada's electoral system has been negative. The system has, he argues, exacerbated regional and ethnolinguistic divisions in Canadian political life by shutting out the Conservative Party in Quebec for most of the last century and giving the impression that the Liberal Party was the only national party with support in French Canada. Cairns's article on the electoral system's effects was written in the late 1960s. If it were written today it would also mention, among other consequences, the gross under-representation of the Liberals in western Canada over the last couple of decades, despite their receiving between one-quarter and one-third of western votes in most elections, and the failure of the Reform Party to elect a single member from Ontario in 1997 and Alliance's election of a mere two Ontario MPs in 2000, despite receiving more votes in that province than in the three westernmost provinces combined. As William Irvine observes, "the electoral system confers a spurious image of unanimity on provinces. By magnifying the success of the provincial vote leader, the electoral system ensures that party caucuses will over-represent any party's 'best' province."[24] And this is not the only quirk of our electoral system.

Along with the distortions that Canada's electoral system produces, another argument for reform is that the present system leaves many voters feeling disempowered and contributes to low levels of voter turnout. Critics also charge that this sense of being disempowered may lead to "strategic voting," whereby a voter in a particular riding will cast his or her ballot not for the party or candidate of choice but for the party or candidate with the greatest likelihood of defeating the projected front-runner in that riding. Such a phenomenon might be a reasonably compelling argument for reform of the electoral system, but little evidence beyond the anecdotal suggests that it exists. Those who study voting behaviour have been unable to find evidence that any significant number of Canadians vote strategically—on the contrary, there appear to be many cases where labour groups have advocated such voting, without any indication that this has had the desired effect—although there is stronger evidence that voter disillusionment with the choices on offer may cause some to stay home on election day.

Voter turnout in federal elections declined over the last several elections until 2006, reaching bottom at about 58 per cent of the eligible electorate in 2004 before rebounding to 65 per cent in 2006. It fell off again to only 59 per cent in 2008 and then increased marginally to 61.5 per cent in 2011. However, this overall decline in voter participation could be caused by other factors, such as a generalized dissatisfaction with parties and politics, independent of any sense that one's vote may be futile because of the electoral system. There is absolutely no definitive proof that voters' perceptions of the electoral system's impact on the probable consequences of each person's vote influences the likelihood that they will go to the polls on election day.

Historically, the party that has stood to gain most from the replacement of Canada's electoral system by some form of proportional representation has been the CCF-NDP. It received a smaller percentage of total seats in the Commons than its share of the national vote in every general election until 2011. Irvine's point about the tendency of the electoral system to magnify the success of the most popular party in a province and punish those parties whose share of the vote does not achieve some critical mass has certainly been borne out by recent election results. Reform received 20 per cent of the Ontario vote in 1993, coming in second behind the Liberals' 53 per cent, but was rewarded with only one seat to

the Liberals' 98. Reform's share of the Ontario vote dropped by only one percentage point in 1997, but it failed to elect a single member from the province. In the 2000 election Alliance candidates captured almost one-quarter of the votes cast in Ontario, good enough for almost 2 per cent of the province's seats! This helped fuel the misperception of Alliance as being merely a western party, when in fact over one million votes, representing about one-third of all votes cast for the Alliance Party, were received in Ontario. Given the realities of political life, however, there is no reason to imagine that either the Liberal or Conservative Party is likely to champion electoral reform, let alone adopt proportional representation. Their dominance would almost certainly be eroded by such a system. Another electoral disaster on the scale of that experienced by the party in 2011 might, however, cause the Liberals to think differently about PR (see Box 11.5).

Voting Behaviour

Few generalizations regarding Canadians' voting behaviour withstand the test of time, dating back to the execution of Riel and the selection, two years later, of Laurier as Liberal leader. Regionally, the Conservative Party began its long association with western voters in 1957 with the election of the Diefenbaker government. Conservative candidates outpolled Liberals and the party elected more MPs from the four westernmost provinces in most elections after 1957. This tendency was accentuated after the 1972 election. The Liberal Party's fortunes in the West sank dramatically under the leadership of Pierre Trudeau and the region became thought of as mainly Conservative and NDP turf. The Reform Party, we have seen, was the vehicle for this anti-Liberal resentment after many western voters became disappointed with the behaviour in office of the Conservative government of Brian Mulroney. A pox on both your houses, westerners seemed to say.

Quebec appeared to be an electoral stronghold for the Liberal Party over most of the last century. But this association was weakened with the emergence of the Bloc Québécois. The BQ outpolled

Politics in Focus

BOX 11.5 Who's for PR?

Historically, the NDP was the only party that talked regularly and positively about introducing a proportional representation electoral system in Canada. This was not surprising, given that the NDP and its predecessor, the CCF, were under-rewarded in every federal election they contested until 2011. Today, PR has support from prominent individuals within a number of parties, although this support is often qualified and cautious.

Former Liberal Party leader Stéphane Dion supports what he has called a "moderate" form of proportional representation. In a 2012 speech, Dion explained his proposal:

> We would elect five MPs by riding, or perhaps four or three when a low population density warrants it. There would be some exceptions—such as for the territories, which, for practical reasons, would remain one-member districts. But the standard would be five-member districts. The number of seats would remain the same; what would be reduced is the number of ridings.
>
> This would give Canada a type of proportional representation that would reduce the artificially amplified regional concentration of seats won by the various parties. Indeed, any party obtaining

the most votes in a given riding would be unlikely to win more than three out of five, or two out of three seats. Thus, seats would be truly up for grabs in all ridings, even in the most Conservative ones in Alberta and the most Liberal ones in Toronto and Montreal.

True, larger ridings would comprise several communities and not only one. But it is also true that with the current system, not every community has its own riding. In fact, all too often, the boundaries of our small ridings split our communities into two or three parts. Every time the electoral map is revised, I have to fight to make sure this does not happen in Saint-Laurent or Cartierville, the two communities that form my riding. With larger ridings, it would be easier to guarantee that each community remains intact within the same riding.

True, this means that individual MPs would no longer hold a monopoly position in their ridings: they would have to co-exist with the four other MPs in the riding. But this can only benefit their constituents. Today, voters have no recourse when they are stuck for four years with a lazy, incompetent or absentee MP. Under the new system, constituents

the Liberals in six of the seven general elections between 1993 and 2011. In 2006 a resurgent Conservative Party received more votes in Quebec than the Liberals and only two percentage points fewer in 2008, although winning fewer seats in both elections.

In regard to social class, differences between voters for the Liberal and Conservative parties have never been very great and certainly have been less important than regional and ethnolinguistic differences. The NDP's formal affiliation to organized labour might have been expected to reflect a preference among working-class Canadians for

that party. But as we have seen, class identity has never been particularly strong for most Canadians. Electoral studies carried out since the 1960s have shown that although NDP support generally is stronger among voters who belong to unions than among most other segments of the electorate, it has never been the case that a majority of working-class voters (whether this is defined by voter self-identification or by some objective measure of class such as occupation) have opted for NDP candidates.

Studies of voter choice in Canada, the United States, and other Western democracies suggest that the decision to vote for a particular party or would be able to deal with a different elected official. Healthy competition among the five MPs in a given riding would provide Canadians with better territorial representation.

A House of Commons elected this way would likely be more representative of women and cultural diversity, as the parties would have an incentive to diversify their offering of candidates in each riding.

Also true, the proportional representation resulting from five-member ridings would be less likely to elect one-party majority governments. We would probably have coalition governments made up of two or three nation-wide parties.[25]

Dion may call this "moderate," but in fact it would involve a rather dramatic restructuring of Canada's electoral system and, as he acknowledges, would almost certainly move Canada from the orbit of one-party government characteristic of Anglo-American democracies to the coalition government model common across much of Western Europe. The current leader of Dion's party, Justin Trudeau, made clear during his leadership campaign that he is not interested in PR: "I do not support proportional representation because I believe deeply that every member of Parliament should represent actual Canadians and Canadian communities, not just political parties."[26] Of course, under Dion's

proposal MPs would continue to represent Canadian communities, although Canadians would no longer be able to point to a single MP as their own.

Since its breakthrough in the 2011 election the NDP has toned down its enthusiasm for PR, although it remains officially committed to reform of Canada's electoral system. Party leader Thomas Mulcair has said that he favours a mixed proportional representation system of the sort that exists in some countries, under which some MPs would continue to be elected on the basis of the current system and others on the basis of how well the parties do in the national popular vote. Mulcair has said that before any such reforms occur he believes there needs to be a national consultative process of some sort and perhaps even a referendum asking citizens whether they support such changes.[27]

The support that Mulcair and Dion have given to PR is featured at the website of the National Advisory Board of Fair Vote Canada, the main advocacy organization in support of PR. Prominent Canadians associated with all the main parties are included on this board, including Bob Rae and Lloyd Axworthy (Liberals), Ed Broadbent and Lorne Nystrom (NDP), and even Conservative Senator Hugh Segal, former Conservative MP Patrick Boyer, and Rick Anderson of the conservative Manning Centre. PR is, however, far from the centre of the political radar in Canada and the prospects that the electoral system will be reformed in the near future are quite remote.

candidate associated with a party is the result of a complex set of interrelated factors. These factors, and the causal relationships between them, may be seen in Figure 11.2. This is a revised version of Cameron Anderson and Laura Stephenson's funnel of causality model. It traces the path leading from socio-demographic characteristics of voters through their partisan identification and ideological leaning, which in turn affect the information universe that shapes how they view candidates, issues, and parties at a particular point in time (most crucially during an election campaign), leading ultimately to voter choice.

Partisan identification was long believed to be a key factor influencing voter choice. Researchers tended to distinguish between what were characterized as "durable" and "flexible" partisans, the former being more likely to report the same party choice in election after election and, moreover, to have the same party identification as their family, especially that of the father. But as Figure 11.3 shows, the likelihood of voters claiming to identify with a particular political party is less today than it was a couple of generations ago. Moreover, dramatic shifts in voter support for particular parties—major cases in point include the collapse

Politics in Focus

BOX 11.6 The French Run-off System

Electoral systems are vitally connected to constitutions. Those who propose significant reforms to a country's system of electing politicians need to be aware that such changes may, and probably will, produce important domino effects throughout their system of government. Proportional representation, if adopted, would almost certainly guarantee that Canada would regularly have coalition governments, partnerships between two or more political parties that would divide cabinet representation between them. This would produce important changes in the dynamic of party relations in the legislature, in government accountability, and possibly even in election campaigning.

Another reform that may appear attractive, but that would also produce far-reaching changes, is the French run-off system. Along with several other countries, France elects its President separately from the members of its legislature, the elections taking place at different times. Moreover, to ensure that the President has the support of most people, French presidential elections involve two stages. The first is a run-off election in which several parties' candidates are on the ballot, although it is usually the case that only a couple of them receive more than about 20–30 per cent of the popular vote apiece. The two candidates receiving the most votes move on two weeks later to the decisive presidential election that will produce a majority for one of them. And thus does *la république française* elect a leader who has the support of a majority of the people.

There is something obviously appealing to the idea of a system guaranteed to produce majority support for the country's foremost leader in elections where voters are given the chance to vote directly for the person they want to lead the country. Other things being equal, it appears to confer on him or her much greater legitimacy than a leader of a party that won only 35–40 per cent of the popular vote, the percentage often received by the governing party in Canada. But such a system also requires that the head of government or head of state (in France, the President is the head of state and the Prime Minister, appointed by the President, is head of government, but the President is clearly the national leader) be elected separately from the legislature. Decoupling the executive from the legislative branch in this manner would involve a profound change in Canada's system of government. It might even seem to lead towards an American-style system of separation of powers. But this need not be so. The French preserve an important accountability and policy-making linkage between these branches of government by giving the President the authority to select the Prime Minister and other members of the government, who are elected members of the legislature.

As matters currently stand in Canada, only those who reside in the riding for which the Prime Minister is the member of Parliament have directly voted for (or against) him or her. And in choosing their MP, Canadian voters must weigh what they think about the local candidates against who they would like to be leader of the country. Would the greater Cartesian clarity of the French be an improvement, or might it produce its own set of problems?

---

of the Progressive Conservative Party vote in 1993 and the more gradual but very significant drop in the Liberal Party's share of the popular vote in the 2008 and 2011 elections—alert us to the fact that party identification is easily abandoned by many voters. It continues, however, to be a significant predictor of how one is likely to vote.

One is not born, of course, with a party identification, any more than one is born with an ideological disposition or any other political value, belief, or world view. The factors influencing the likelihood of acquiring a particular partisan identification or ideological leaning that may be associated with voter choice have been widely studied in Canada

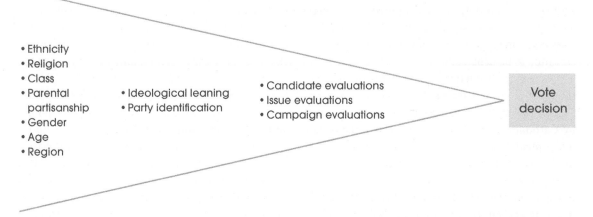

FIGURE 11.2   The Funnel of Causality Model of Voter Choice

Source: Adapted from Cameron D. Anderson and Laura B. Stephenson, eds, *Voting Behaviour in Canada* (Vancouver: University of British Columbia Press, 2010), 4, Figure 1.1.

since the first Canadian Election Study carried out in 1965. Some of the main socio-demographic factors thought to influence voting behaviour are indicated in the left-hand column of Figure 11.2.

Class continues to exert only a weak impact on partisan identification and voting behaviour. This is particularly true if objective measures of social class, such as occupation, education, and income, are used. Class appears to be a stronger predictor if it is measured subjectively, according to how individual voters perceive their class membership and ideological leanings. But, as Elisabeth Gidengil

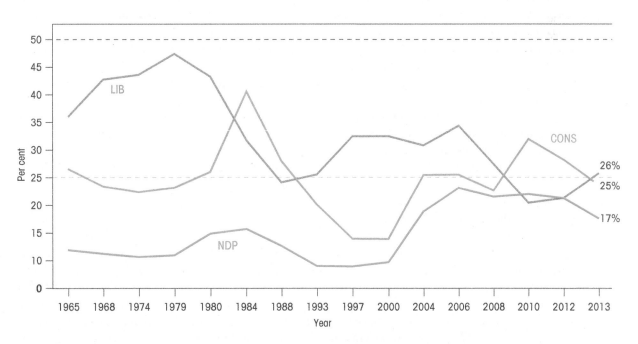

FIGURE 11.3   Party Identification in Canada, 1965–2013

Source: Manning Centre, *2013 Manning Barometer* (slides), at: <manningcentre.ca/wp-content/uploads/2013/12/2103-Manning-Barometer-Slides_sm.pdf>.

observes, "there is only a loose connection in Canada between objective class position and class ideology."[28] The reasons for the weak impact of class position on partisan identification and voting continue to be debated.

Whereas the influence of class on voting is weak, that of religion continues to be significant. As mentioned earlier, the overwhelming support given by Catholics to the Liberal Party was a major factor contributing to that party's electoral success in the twentieth century. Support for the Liberals collapsed across the board in 2011, but even before that election the Catholic pillar of Liberal Party support was weakening. Data from the 2008 Canadian Election Study show that about 42 per cent of Catholics outside of Quebec claim to have voted for Liberal candidates, compared to 36 per cent for the Conservatives and 21 per cent for the NDP. If instead of denominational affiliation we look at religiosity, measured by the percentage of respondents who agree with the statement, "Religion is very important in my life," we find a strong correlation among voters outside of Quebec. In 2008, 54 per cent of these respondents claimed to have voted for the Conservative Party, compared to 28 per cent who voted Liberal and about 18 per cent for the NDP.

The impact of ethnicity on partisanship and voting behaviour has operated mainly through the fact that those of French ancestry, and particularly those whose mother tongue is French, have been very likely to support the Liberal Party. This relationship has not been particularly strong since the election of 1993. Most Canadians of French ancestry and about 90 per cent of Canadian francophones reside in Quebec. In only one federal election between 1993 and 2011 did the Liberal Party receive more votes in Quebec than any other political party. Outside of Quebec, the correlation between French ancestry and language and voting for the Liberal Party appears to remain strong. In 2008, for example, almost half of francophones appear to have voted for Liberal Party candidates, compared to about 23 per cent for the Conservatives and 30 per cent for the NDP. (These numbers need to be viewed with caution because, of the 1,158 respondents outside Quebec surveyed for the 2008 election study, only 66 self-identified as francophones.)

A gender gap between male and female voting patterns has been observed in both Canadian and American elections. In American presidential elections (the pattern is less clear in congressional and state elections), the Democratic Party's candidate has received more votes from women than has the Republican candidate in every election since 1992. The explanation usually advanced is that female and male voters tend to differ to some degree in the importance they assign to certain issues and their preferences on these issues. The values more likely to be found among women than men result in female voters being more likely than males to vote for parties of the left. This is also true in Canada. The Conservative Party receives a larger share of its popular vote from men than from women. The NDP, on the other hand, has received a larger share of its vote from women than from men, at least in recent elections. The combined share of the female popular vote received by the Liberal Party and the NDP is always somewhat greater than their combined share of the male popular vote. The picture is complicated somewhat by the existence of what Wilson and Lusztig call a "marriage gap." Married voters, including women, are more likely than unmarried voters to prefer an ideologically conservative party.[29]

Immigration has been an important component of Canadian population growth and, therefore, a significant proportion of the Canadian electorate consists of people born outside the country, which has attracted the attention of those who study voting behaviour. Data from the Canadian Election Studies, going back to the 1960s, show that the Liberal Party has been the most popular party among voters born outside of Canada. The Liberals have received a larger share of the votes of the foreign-born than of those born in Canada, while the reverse has been true for the Conservative Party (and its predecessors, the Progressive Conservative Party, the Reform Party, and the Canadian Alliance Party). In the case of the NDP, the difference between foreign- and Canadian-born voters has tended to be small. The difference, however, is quite significant in the case of the BQ, with foreign-born voters being much less likely than Canadian-born voters to support this party.

Recent elections suggest this picture of strong immigrant support for the Liberal Party may be changing. In the 2008 election the Conservatives did almost as well as the Liberals among voters born outside of Canada and in 2011 non-Canadian born voters were somewhat more likely to vote for the Conservative Party than for the Liberals. It may be too early to speak confidently of a durable shift in the voting tendencies of immigrants, but it is clear that the Liberal hammerlock on majority-immigrant constituencies has been broken. In 2004 the Liberals held all 18 of the majority-immigrant constituencies in the GTA. In 2011 they were reduced to five of these ridings. The Conservatives won 10 of these seats and the NDP won three.[30]

Over the years, few socio-demographic factors have been as strongly correlated with voting behaviour as the region where voters live. The likelihood that a voter will support the Conservative Party is much greater if that voter lives in one of the four western provinces than in Ontario, and even greater than if that voter lives in the Atlantic provinces. But it is tricky making sense of the independent impact of region—i.e., the causal effect that the region of the country in which a voter lives has, once the effects of other factors such as class, ethnicity, religion, and country of birth are controlled for. Some argue that the independent effect of region on voting operates through the existence of different regional political cultures. But as we saw in Chapter 5, there is no agreement among Canadian political scientists that, with the exception of Quebec, these interprovincial differences are particularly significant. There is, however, a consensus that region provides a context for voting and for the evaluation of the parties, their leaders, and the issues. Exactly what that context involves is a matter of dispute.

Political Participation

Today Canadians are less likely to vote than at almost any time since Confederation. Indeed, in recent years they have been less likely to vote in some national elections than have Americans in that country's presidential elections. But Canadians are not alone in staying away from the ballot box. Voter turnout has been slipping in Western democracies generally, a trend that has generated a good deal of hand-wringing about the health of democracies and various explanations for this decline in participation.

Two facts are clear, in Canada and elsewhere. Younger citizens are considerably less likely to vote than their older compatriots. Second, they vote at a lower rate than people their age did in the past. "We know that age is the best predictor of voting," write André Blais and his colleagues on the Canadian Election Study team; "the older one is, the more likely one is to vote. The challenge is to unravel the meaning of that relationship, to ascertain whether this reflects a life cycle effect . . . , a generation effect . . . or both."[31] The life cycle effect refers to the fact that people become more likely to vote as they grow older, a phenomenon generally attributed to changes in their life circumstances (entering a permanent relationship, having children, buying a home, establishing roots in a community) that cause them to feel more invested in their community and to recognize the relevance of government decisions to their own lives. The generation effect refers to the possibility that the members of a particular generation may be less likely than those of preceding ones to vote. This could be caused by various factors, such as a society-wide increase in cynicism about politics or a drop in those non-age factors known to be linked to the likelihood of voting, including years of formal education and political interest and knowledge.

Based on voter surveys between 1968 and 2000, Blais and his colleagues arrive at a number of conclusions with regard to declining voter turnout:

- There are important life cycle effects. For example, a person who is 30 is about 8–11 percentage points more likely to vote than someone 20 years old. The likelihood of voting increases by about 15 percentage points from age 20 to age 50.[32]
- There is a clear generational effect. Comparing voters in the same age cohort but belonging to different generations (for example, a 25-year-old baby boomer surveyed for the 1974 election study and a 25-year-old surveyed for the 2000 study), the generation

effect on declining voter turnout is at least as significant as life cycle effects: "age being held constant, the propensity to vote decreases by more than 20 points from the oldest to the most recent cohort."[33]

- Blais and his colleagues note that "younger generations view the act of voting differently" from previous generations.[34] They are less likely to see it as important and less likely to view it as a civic duty.
- The generational difference is not found among the university-educated. Controlling for age, voters with a university degree who are post-baby boomers are as likely to vote as their boomer predecessors. But among those in other educational cohorts there is a sizable generational gap in the likelihood of voting.

Of course, all of this just begs the question—two questions, really. Why are the members of more recent generations less likely to be interested in politics and less likely to believe that they have a moral responsibility to vote? Second, does declining turnout matter?

The answer to the first question is unlikely to involve a single factor; two rather different clusters of causes have been identified by researchers. One involves a lower level of deference towards authority and established institutions among post-baby boomers and a greater tendency to embrace values and beliefs associated with what has been called post-materialism (see Chapter 2). The weaker belief that voting is a civic duty is said to reflect the less deferential character of the more recent generation of voters. This explanation does not help to explain, however, why university-educated members of recent generations vote at about the same rate as earlier generations of voters with similar levels of education.

A second cluster of causes focuses on what are argued to be the failings of parties and politicians. Those who have entered the electorate during the last couple of decades are more likely than those who entered earlier to feel alienated from conventional politics, including parties and elections, and cynical about politicians and their craft. This alienation and cynicism has been produced, at least in

part, by a failure of parties and politicians to convince these newer members of the electorate that what they do is relevant to the lives of citizens or that any meaningful change can be effected by participating in the electoral process. This explanation focuses less on the generational characteristics of young voters than on the shortcomings of the political system they encounter when they enter the electorate. But if parties and politicians are doing a poorer job than in the past in connecting with voters, we still need to explain why younger voters more than older ones react by disengaging from traditional political processes. A possible answer is provided by Henry Milner and others.[35] Milner argues that political literacy and interest among younger voters is lower than used to be the case. They are less likely to read newspapers, follow politics in the media, or be able to correctly identify political figures, institutions, and events than members of previous generations. They have less interest and less knowledge about politics, contributing to a reduced propensity to vote. Milner and most other commentators believe that the quality of democracy will suffer as more of society's members choose to abstain from voting.

But will society really suffer and are the non-voters truly abstaining from political participation? It is understandable that parties and voting are seen by most of us to be the essential linchpins in the relationship between the population and government. The struggle for universal voting rights was long and arduous and its achievement is only a few generations old. Quebec was the last province to grant women the right to vote in 1940 and Aboriginal Canadians, if they maintained their Indian status, did not have the right to vote until 1960. That the self-disenfranchisement of millions of citizens who choose seldom or never to vote might be treated with indifference is shocking to many.

But as important as voting is, it is not the only form of political engagement. A 2003 survey carried out by Statistics Canada[36] asked respondents whether they had engaged in any of the following political activities during the previous year:

- signing a petition;
- searching for political information;

- attending a public meeting;
- boycotting/choosing a product for ethical reasons;
- contacting a newspaper or politician;
- participating in a demonstration or march;
- volunteering for a political party.

The bad news is that almost half of all Canadians, 45 per cent, said they did not participate in any of these non-voting activities. The good news is that this Statistics Canada survey found no evidence that younger Canadians were less likely than their older compatriots to participate in political activities. Just under six in 10 respondents between the ages of 15 and 24 said that they had participated in at least one of these non-voting activities in the previous year, the same rate of participation found for those in the 25–44 and 45–64 age groups. Participation among the oldest Canadians—those 65 years of age and older—dropped off to about four in 10.[37]

It appears, then, that although younger Canadians are much less likely to vote than their older fellow citizens, they are as likely to participate in politics in other ways. Is boycotting or choosing a product on ethical grounds or signing a petition a less significant political act than voting in an election? Reasonable people will disagree on this matter. But perhaps we should at least be open to the possibility that declining voter turnout, particularly among the young, is not necessarily evidence that they are disengaged politically or that the health of democracy is imperilled by this decline.

This conclusion is supported by recent work on the civic engagement of younger Canadians carried out in connection with Apathy Is Boring, a national organization whose aim is to increase youth understanding of democracy. Based on surveys of a non-random and admittedly unrepresentative sample of thousands of young people who attended various cultural events over several years, Larry Leduc and his colleagues assemble a picture of non-traditional

forms of engagement among those often described as millennials or Generation Y (born between the early 1980s and the early 2000s). They find that volunteering is a more universal activity among this group than is voting.

As many or more of our respondents indicated in response to the "community problem" question that they would be willing to sign a petition as we would expect to vote in an election. The availability and widespread use of new media have made alternative forms of engagement both more accessible and potentially more effective. When a respondent says that, in response to a problem, s/he would blog or tweet about it, it is not obvious how engagement of this kind should be thought of in relation to more traditional acts such as voting or signing a formal petition.[38]

Traditional thinking and models of civic participation have no place for tweeting, Facebooking, and other recent and widespread forms of social networking. These are forms of engagement that do not rely on parties or politicians and that may be dismissed

Volunteering and other non-electoral forms of civic engagement are more frequent among millennials than voting. How should politicians react to this and how might they better connect with younger citizens?

Rodrigo de Matos/Artizans.com

as less demanding and less valid than voting, joining a party, attending a political meeting, and similar traditional forms of political participation. It is not obvious, however, that they are less valid or important as expressions of democratic engagement.

Party Finances and Special Interests

Throughout most of their history, the Liberal and Conservative parties relied heavily on corporate contributors to finance their activities. The NDP, by contrast, depended mainly on contributions from individuals and on the financial support of affiliated trade unions. Corporate donations to the national NDP were minuscule.

It is difficult to attach precise numbers to party finances before 1974, for the simple reason that parties were not legally required to disclose their sources of revenue. A study done by Khayyam Paltiel for the federally appointed Committee on Election Expenses (1966) estimated that, before the 1974 reforms, the older parties were dependent on business contributions for between 75 and 90 per cent of their incomes,[39] a figure that did not even include the value of services in kind that they received from businesses, particularly from advertising and polling firms during election campaigns.[40] Not only were the Liberals and Conservatives dependent on business for all but a small share of their revenue, but most of this corporate money was collected from big businesses in Toronto and Montreal.[41] Other experts on party finances have confirmed this historical pattern of dependence on big financial and industrial capital.[42]

Passage of the **Election Expenses Act, 1974** marked a watershed in Canadian party finance. The Act included spending limits for individual candidates and political parties during election campaigns and a requirement that parties and candidates disclose the name of any contributor donating at least $100. A system of public subsidies was introduced, whereby candidates would be reimbursed for half of their expenses, as long as they stayed within the spending limit set by law, if they received at least

15 per cent of the popular vote. The idea behind this particular reform was to weaken parties' financial dependence on special interests. The Income Tax Act was changed to permit the deduction of political contributions. Changes to the Broadcasting Act also were passed, requiring radio and television stations to make available to the parties represented in the House of Commons both paid and free broadcast time during election campaigns.[43]

Tax credits for political contributions and public disclosure requirements for candidates and political parties were intended to reduce the role of money in party politics and elections. The Income Tax Act allows individuals to deduct from their taxable income a percentage of their donation to a registered political party or candidate, up to a maximum tax credit of $650. As of 2014, the maximum amount an individual may donate to a political party or candidate is $1,200. The maximum tax credit of $650 is reached once a donor has given $1,275 in total contributions during a single taxation year. With regard to disclosure, parties and candidates are required to provide the chief electoral officer with a list of all donors who have contributed $200 or more in money or services in kind, as well as an itemized account of their expenditures. Before the 2004 revisions to the Canada Elections Act, parties were not required to disclose how much they spent on important activities such as fundraising and polling between elections, although evidence has long suggested that these were very expensive functions.[44] Since 2004, the law requires much more transparency in the parties' reporting of their annual and election campaign expenditures.

Perhaps the most striking consequence of the 1974 reforms was the dramatic increase in the importance of donations by individuals. These contributions were always the mainstay of NDP finances. Spurred by the tax credit for political donations and the older parties' adoption of sophisticated direct-mail techniques of fundraising, first developed in the United States,[45] contributions by individuals became a major source of income for all three political parties. In fact, contributions from individuals exceeded business contributions to both the PC and Liberal parties in many of the years after the tax credit came into effect. The same was true of candidates' revenue. NDP candidates received very little from corporate donors, but depended on trade union contributions and donations from individuals. The Reform Party/Canadian Alliance relied overwhelmingly on contributions from individuals, as did the Bloc Québécois. Figure 11.4 shows the chief sources of revenue for the five parties represented in the House of Commons in 2003, the last year before the party financing rules were changed, in 2004, the first year after the ban on corporate and union contributions and the introduction of public financing, and in 2011.

The Liberal and Conservative parties' traditional financial dependence on business appeared to have been diluted under the post-1974 model for party and election financing. Nonetheless, corporate donations continued to be a tremendously important source of revenue for the older parties. They continued to account for close to half of total contributions during election years and roughly 40–50 per cent between elections until the 2004 reforms. Moreover, very large corporate contributions represented a sizable share of the older parties' total revenues. If we define a large corporate donation as being at least $10,000, we find that these contributions accounted for about 15 to 30 per cent of total contributions for both the Liberal and Progressive Conservative parties over the 30-year period from the introduction of the 1974 Canada Elections Act to its overhaul in 2004. In 2003, the last year under which the old party financing rules applied, the 10 largest contributions to each of the Liberal, Progressive Conservative and Canadian Alliance (the latter two parties and their finances were merged towards the end of 2003), and New Democratic parties accounted for 16 per cent, 16 per cent, and 39 per cent of total party revenues, respectively. All of the leading 10 contributions to the Liberal and Conservative parties were from corporate donors and all 10 of the NDP's biggest donors were trade unions.

The most important consequence of special-interest contributions to parties and individual politicians was almost certainly the access it bought to policy-makers. Although cases of influence-peddling came to light from time to time, it was usually erroneous to think of political contributions as payments offered in the expectation of receiving

some particular favour. There were, no doubt, instances where firms that relied on government contracts for some part of their revenue, or hoped to receive government business in the future, found it prudent to donate money to parties or candidates. But for most corporate contributors, and certainly for large donors like the banks and those leading industrial firms that were perennial contributors to the two older parties, there was no expectation of a specific quid pro quo.

So why did they bother? One explanation is that corporate political donations represented a sort of insurance premium. As the late Conservative strategist and political adviser Dalton Camp put it:

> For the wise donor, the financing of the political system may very well be a duty and an obligation to the system, but it is, as well, insurance against the unlikely—such as the ascendancy of socialism—or against occasional political aberration, a Walter Gordon budget, say, or a Carter report on tax reform [both perceived to be anti-business policies]. When such contingencies arise, the price for access is modest indeed.[46]

What Camp called a "duty and an obligation to the system" might also be described as an investment in two-party dominance. Business interests were often at loggerheads with both Liberal and Conservative governments over specific policies. But generally speaking, both of the two older parties were, and continue to be, congenial towards corporate enterprise. Business can live with either a Liberal or Conservative government and has a material interest in supporting the centrist politics that characterize the Canadian political system and in avoiding the polarization of party politics between the right and the left.

In addition to helping finance a party system that is generally congenial to business interests, it was long understood that donations helped buy access. Again, the words of Dalton Camp: "Toronto money merely maintains access to the parties, keeping open essential lines of communication, corporate hotlines, so to speak, to the right ears at appropriate times."[47] In many cases the sheer size and

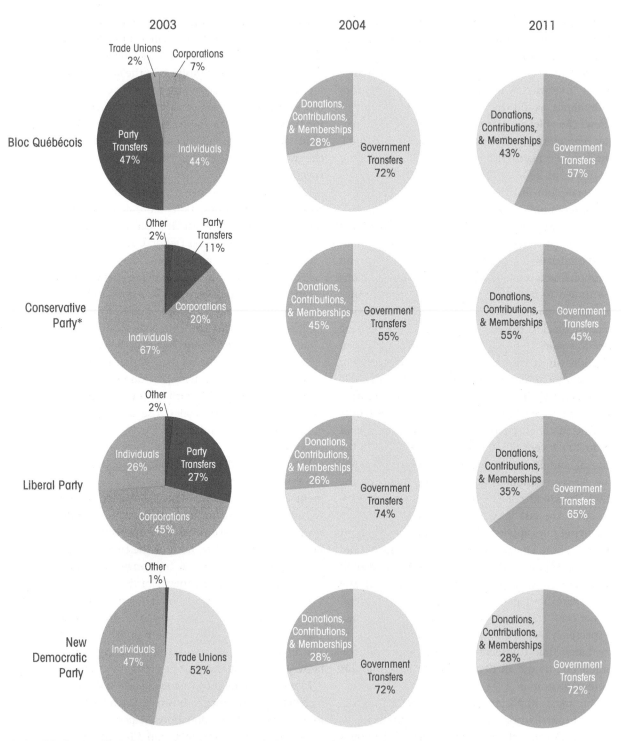

FIGURE 11.4 The Changing Sources of Revenue for the Four Main Parties, before and after the 2004 Reforms, and for 2011

*The Progressive Conservative Party and the Canadian Alliance Party formally merged to form the Conservative Party of Canada on 7 December 2003. Their 2003 financial statements have been combined in this chart.

Source: Data provided by Elections Canada, at: <www.elections.ca>.

importance of a corporation would be sufficient to ensure a hearing when the corporation's owners or managers felt its interests were at stake. In any given year about half of the largest 100 industrial firms in Canada did not even contribute to either of the two older parties. It would be ridiculous to conclude that their lack of generosity cut them off from direct access to political decision-makers. But all things being equal, contributions probably opened the door a bit wider.

The link between party contributions and access became more controversial with the increasing prominence of **paid access opportunities**. These are fundraising events such as dinners and cocktail parties where, for an admission price that could range up to several thousand dollars, donors received the opportunity to rub shoulders and exchange views with party leaders who, if the party was in power, were also members of the government. Money obviously acts as a filter in determining who is likely to participate in such events, as does the party's invitation list. These events were supplemented by an American invention—special clubs for large contributors. Both the Republican and Democratic parties have operated such clubs since the 1980s. For an individual contribution of thousands of dollars (higher for a corporate membership), the donor receives the chance to meet with important politicians, such as congressional committee chairpersons. The Progressive Conservative Party was the first to establish this sort of exclusive donor network in Canada, the "500 Club," which has been succeeded by the Conservative Party's Leader's Circle. Membership costs $1,000. The national Liberal Party also has this sort of paid-admission elite network through its Laurier Club. Admission to the club costs $1,200—half that amount for those under 45. Donations buy the privilege of invitations to exclusive meetings with party leaders, opportunities that are particularly valuable when the party in question forms the government and the party leader is the Prime Minister. It must be said, however, that the entry bar was set much higher before the limitations on political contributions brought in by the 2004 reforms to the Canada Elections Act. The parties cannot charge a membership fee of more than $1,200, given that this is the maximum annual contribution that an individual can make to a party and its candidates. These special donor clubs are now less exclusive than they were when the price of admission was several thousand dollars.

In the eyes of some, paid access opportunities such as these, regardless of whether the price of admission is high or very high, raise an ethical question: at what point does the ability to pay for special access to political decision-makers subvert the democratic process by favouring those with the money to make their views known directly? Defenders argue that parties need funds to carry out their activities and that, even with a tax credit for political contributions, only a small portion of all Canadian taxpayers contribute money directly to parties or candidates. Unless parties and elections are to be financed entirely by public subsidies, the money to pay for advertising, polling, the campaign bus, hall rentals, and so on needs to come from somewhere. Some will argue that donating money is a form of political engagement and expression not unlike devoting time. Some people have more time than money and may prefer to knock on doors, make phone calls, or in other ways contribute their time in the hope of electing a candidate or party. Others may have more money than time and prefer to make a donation. In most Western European democracies, public subsidies cover most and in some cases almost all party expenses, freeing them from what had once been their dependence on contributions from special interests. Canada adopted this public subsidy model in 2004, albeit with room for some private funding. The major elements of the post-2004 model for party and campaign financing in Canada include the following:

- Donations by special interests, including corporations and trade unions, are banned.
- Individuals may donate up to $1,200 in any year to a registered political party or candidate.
- Beginning in 2004, parties received an annual subsidy of $1.75 for every vote they received in the previous election. This was reduced to $1.53 in 2012 and is scheduled to be eliminated entirely by 2015.

- Third parties—organizations and individuals other than registered political parties and their candidates—may spend no more than $200,100 in total, and no more than $4,002 in any single electoral district (as of 2014), on political advertising during an election campaign, effectively preventing them from having any significant impact on the national campaign.
- Candidates for the leadership of registered political parties must provide information on the identity of those who donate to their campaigns. No individual may contribute more than $1,200 in total to the contestants for the leadership of a particular political party. The amount that leadership candidates may spend on their campaigns is set by the parties, not by Canadian law.

No restrictions are placed on spending by political parties, groups, or individuals during periods other than elections. As a result, considerable money is spent on fundraising, polling, consultants, and pre-campaign advertising before an election is called. A clear example of such non-election advertising was the extensive negative ad campaign that the Conservatives launched as soon as Stéphane Dion was chosen as the Liberal leader in 2006, portraying Dion as indecisive and without leadership qualities. The Conservatives did the same when Michael Ignatieff was chosen as the Liberal leader in 2008 and then again, on a more limited scale, when Justin Trudeau became Liberal leader in 2013. Some argue that this type of pre-campaign spending, intended to shape the public's image of a leader or party or to frame issues in particular ways, undermines the intent of the 2004 reforms. Others maintain that the ability to spend money in order to craft a political message and communicate it to citizens is a basic democratic right that is already unjustifiably limited by these reforms. Whether legislation restricting spending on political communications between election campaigns would be upheld by the courts is difficult to say. But as we saw in Chapter 7 in regard to the Supreme Court's ruling in *Harper v. Canada* (2004), the majority of Canada's top justices took the view that unequal spending power undermines the equality of citizens and skews the political conversation towards the interests and values of those with deep pockets.

Regardless of what one thinks about the rights implications of the 2004 *Harper* ruling, a party, candidate, private organization, or individual with a lot of money clearly is able to purchase more media advertising time or space than one with only a little (and is better able to afford the services that are usually necessary to produce high-quality, effective advertising). In recognition of this potential for unequal access to the media, some believe that governments need to regulate who may purchase political advertising, when they may do so, and how much they may spend.

In some European democracies, including France and Germany, paid political advertising on television and radio is banned, as is campaign advertising by private organizations that might be construed as supporting or opposing a party or candidate. In the United Kingdom, the law regulates the permissible length of television ads—they must run for at least 2 minutes and 40 seconds and up to 4 minutes and 40 seconds—based on the apparent belief that longer ads are more likely to communicate information and address issues in less manipulative ways than is the case with the 15–30-second spot ads that are the norm in Canada and the United States. At the other extreme is the United States, where that country's courts have taken a dim view of legislative efforts to limit campaign spending on advertising on the grounds that this would violate the First Amendment's guarantee of free speech.

Canada falls between these positions. Since the mid-1970s Canadian law has empowered the CRTC, Canada's telecommunications regulator, to require television and radio broadcasters to provide a certain amount of air time to registered political parties for their ads during election campaigns. As explained above, campaign spending by so-called "third parties" is sharply limited by Canadian election law. Federal law also limits the amount of money that registered political parties and their candidates may spend during campaigns, thus placing a ceiling on the amount of advertising a party can purchase. The communication activities of political parties via the Internet and social media remain, so far, unregulated (though not for want of desire or effort from many quarters, including Elections Canada).

Starting Points for Research

Cameron D. Anderson and Laura B. Stephenson, eds, *Voting Behaviour in Canada* (Vancouver: University of British Columbia Press, 2010). This book brings together contributions from several of Canada's leading experts on voting.

Canadian Election Study, at: <ces-eec.org/pagesE/home.html>. A large number of publications based on the most recent and past Canadian election studies may be found at this website.

R. Kenneth Carty and Munroe Eagles, *Politics Is Local: National Politics at the Grassroots* (Toronto: Oxford University Press, 2005). The authors examine the local dimension of Canadian party politics, including their finances, organization, candidate selection, campaigns, and media coverage.

Elisabeth Gidengil, Neil Nevitte, André Blais, Joanna Everitt, and Patrick Fournier, *Dominance and Decline: Making Sense of Recent Canadian Elections* (Toronto: University of Toronto Press, 2012). Based on Canadian voting surveys from 2000 through 2008, this book examines a number of theories about voting in light of these data.

Mebs Kanji, Antoine Bilodeau, and Thomas J. Scotto, eds, *The Canadian Election Studies: Assessing Four Decades of Influence* (Vancouver: University of British Columbia Press, 2012). This volume includes contributions from researchers who have been involved in Canadian election studies over the years and provides fascinating perspectives on how the understanding of voter choice has evolved over the past four decades.

Lisa Young and Harold J. Jansen, eds, *Money, Politics and Democracy: Canada's Party Finance Reforms* (Vancouver: University of British Columbia Press, 2012). A collection of essays written by some of Canada's foremost experts on party finance.

Review Exercises

1. Using data available at the website of the Chief Electoral Officer of Canada <www.elections.ca>, determine the following:
   (a) the number of seats each party would have received in the last general election under a straight proportional representation system;
   (b) the number of votes and percentage of the vote received by each candidate in your constituency during the last federal election; and
   (c) the money spent by both the party that won the last election and the winning candidate in your constituency.

2. Visit the websites of two of the political parties represented in the House of Commons. Compare the depth and breadth of information provided about each party's history, current leader, and present policies.

3. How do Canadian political parties select their candidates? For information on this, visit the websites of a couple of the national political parties. Click on the party's constitution, looking for the rules on candidate selection.

4. Televised leaders' debates have been a fixture of Canadian election campaigns since 1968. Compare the debates of 1968 to that of 2011, identifying any important changes that may have taken place. The debates may be found at the CBC's digital archives: <www.cbc.ca/archives/categories/politics/elections/leaders-debates-1968-2011-highlights/leaders-debates-1968-2011-highlights.html>.

12

Interest Groups

Politics does not stop between election campaigns. Much of the effort to influence the actions of government is channelled through interest groups. This chapter examines their characteristics and the role they play in Canadian politics. Topics include the following:

- How many groups, representing what interests?
- The bias of the interest group system.
- Perspectives on interest groups.
- Factors in interest group success.
- The impact of federalism on interest groups.
- Strategies for influence.
- Advocacy advertising.
- Lobbying and lobbyists.

Every interest imaginable is represented by groups who work to influence various levels of government as a way to achieve their goals. This protester is part of Greenpeace's 2012 campaign to protect the Arctic in both Russia and Canada from oil companies and industrial fisheries. (CP Images/AP Photo/Jeff Chiu)

Elections are democracy's showpiece. Important as they are, however, the influence of elections on what governments do is usually rather blunt and indirect. Policies are far more likely to be determined by forces generated within the state and by the actions of organized groups outside of it than by the latest election results. Indeed, it may often seem that special interests dominate the policy-making process in democracies. Their attempts to influence government are unremitting. The resources they marshal often are impressive. And their access to policy-makers is, in the case of some organized interests, privileged. Compared to this, the role of elections and the influence of voters may appear feeble.

Interest groups or pressure groups—the terms can be used interchangeably—have been defined as "private associations . . . [that] promote their interests by attempting to influence government rather than by nominating candidates and seeking responsibility for the management of government."[1] They arise from a very basic fact of social life, the reality of diversity in the interests and values of human beings. This diversity, in turn, gives rise to what James Madison called **political factions**: groups of citizens whose goals and behaviour are contrary to those of other groups or to the interests of the community as a whole.[2] If these factions, or special interests as we are apt to call them today, appear to overshadow the public interest in democracies, there is a simple explanation for this. The tug of one's personal interests—as an automotive worker, teacher, farmer, or postal worker—tend to be felt more keenly than the rather nebulous concept of the public interest. Arguments that appeal to such general interests as consumer benefits or economic efficiency are unlikely to convince the farmer whose income is protected by the production quotas and price floors set by a marketing board. But economic interests are not the only basis for factionalism in politics. Group characteristics like ethnicity, language, religion, race, and gender or the sharing of similar values may also provide the basis for the political organization of interests.

Economically based or not, interest groups are distinguished by the fact that they seek to promote goals not shared by all members of society. Paradoxically, however, their success in achieving these goals often depends on their ability to associate their efforts with the broader public interest. "What is good for General Motors is good for America"[3] may or may not be true. Nevertheless, the slogan makes good sense as a strategy for promoting the interests of GM, North American automobile producers, and business interests generally.

Charting the Territory

The world of interest groups is both vast and characterized by enormous variety. Although no unified reliable list of interest groups exists for Canada or any other democracy, some idea of the sheer number of groups may be had from the directory, *Associations Canada*.[4] Its 2013 edition lists 19,681 organizations, not all of which would meet the criterion of attempting to influence government action. Many groups focus exclusively on non-political activities like providing services and information to their members, but several thousand perform political functions for their members on a regular or occasional basis.

Almost every imaginable interest is represented. There are several hundred women's associations across Canada, close to 1,000 environmental groups, over 2,000 business associations, perhaps 500 organizations representing agricultural interests, about 200 that focus on Aboriginal issues[5]—the range of organized interests and the sheer number of groups within each general category of interests are enormous. Impressive as these figures may seem, they do not provide a complete map of Canada's associational system. They do not, for example, include those transitory groups that emerge briefly around a single issue and then disappear from the scene. Nor do they include international organizations that may attempt to influence the actions of Canadian governments. However we draw its boundaries, the universe of organized interests is vast.

While it is impossible to say exactly how many of these associations qualify as interest groups, no doubt a large number of them are politically active. One way to get a sense of this activity is to look at the list of groups that make representations to a legislative body or a government-sponsored commission considering some issue. For example, well over 1,000 groups made representations and submitted briefs to the Royal Commission on Aboriginal Peoples during its six months of public hearings (1993). The Commission on the Future of Health Care in Canada received submissions from 429 groups and associations during the public consultation phase of its work (2001). In Quebec, the Commission on Accommodation Practices Related to Cultural Differences (2008) received more than 900 briefs and heard testimony from 241 groups and individuals. Even a government inquiry that deals with a rather narrow matter will often generate considerable interest group activity. The 2012 Cohen Commission on the decline of sockeye salmon stocks in the Fraser River granted intervenor status to two governments, one government agency, one union, four corporations and business associations, seven conservation groups, six organizations representing fishers, and about 20 Native groups.

The amount of representation and activity in a single sector can be remarkable. Robert Wolfe reports that over 100 agriculture and food-processing groups participated in the Next Generation consultations organized in 2007 by Agriculture and Agri-Food Canada and that over 60 Canadian agri-food groups participated in at least one, and often several, of the WTO meetings on agricultural trade policy between 1996 and 2006.[6] Alternatively, one may look at the composition of some politically active organizations. The Canadian Labour Congress is the umbrella organization for hundreds of unions, including provincial and national federations of labour and 137 district labour councils that together represent about 3 million workers. The Canadian Chamber of Commerce, one of whose main functions is to influence government policies, represents over 500 community and provincial chambers of commerce and boards of trade; as well, close to 100 trade and professional associations and many international organizations are located in Canada.

The Bias of the Interest Group System

The notion that the pressure system is automatically representative of the whole community is a myth. . . . The system is skewed, loaded and unbalanced in favor of a fraction of a minority.[7]

Obviously, some interest groups are more influential than others. Determining why some groups are more influential and the circumstances, resources, strategies, and tactics that contribute to interest group influence have long interested students of politics and policy. Many have concluded, as E.E. Schattschneider argued 50 years ago, that the interest group system is biased "in favor of a fraction of a minority." Are they right?

Schattschneider argues that the interest group system—he calls it the pressure system—has a business and upper-class bias. Writing about American politics in the early 1960s, he observed that business associations comprised the single largest group of organized interests in American society; they were far more likely than other interests to lobby government and they tended to spend much more money on attempting to influence policymakers than did other interest groups. Moreover, Schattschneider cites impressive evidence demonstrating that "even non-business organizations reflect an upper-class tendency."[8] Persons with higher than average incomes and/or years of formal education are more likely to belong to organized groups than those lower down the socio-economic ladder. He explains the business and upper-class bias of interest group politics as being a product both of superior resources and of the relatively limited size and exclusive character of these special interests. "Special-interest organizations," he argues, "are most easily formed when they deal with small numbers of individuals [or corporations] who are acutely aware of their exclusive interests."[9] This awareness of special interests that are vital to one's material well-being or the well-being of one's organization is characteristic of trade associations like the Canadian Association of Petroleum

Producers, the Canadian Bankers' Association, or a more broadly based business organization like the Canadian Manufacturers & Exporters (formerly the Canadian Manufacturers Association and the Canadian Exporters Association), and also characterizes producer and occupational groups such as the Quebec Dairy Association and the Ontario Medical Association. It is less likely to characterize organizations that represent more general interests.

Most social scientists and political journalists agree with Schattschneider. Charles Lindblom argues that business occupies a "privileged position" in the politics of capitalist societies. In his book *Politics and Markets*,[10] Lindblom attributes this pre-eminence to business's superior financial resources and lobbying organization, greater access than other groups to government officials, and, most importantly, propagandistic activities that—directly through political advertising and indirectly through commercial advertising—reinforce the ideological dominance of business values in society.

One of the key factors most often cited by those who argue that business interests are politically more influential than other organized groups is the **mobility of capital**. Investors enjoy a wide although not absolute freedom to shift their capital between sectors of the economy and from one national economy to another. The epitome of this mobility is found in the transnational corporation—an enterprise whose activities span a number of national economies and whose international character often is used as a lever in dealing with the government of a particular country. In addition to being territorially mobile, investment capital also has the capacity to expand and contract in response to investors' perceptions of the political-economic climate for business. Governments cannot force business and private investors to invest, and what punitive measures they might use to prevent businesses from sitting on earnings—high tax rates on savings or dividends, for example—could easily backfire. Governments in all capitalist societies are concerned with levels of business confidence and are reluctant to take actions that carry a high risk of causing a cutback in investment. The consequences of such a cutback are felt politically

by governments. Weak economic activity tends to translate into popular dissatisfaction and a loss of political support.[11]

The mobility of capital gives rise, in turn, to concern with *business confidence*. Politicians need to care about business confidence because of the very real possibility that they will not be re-elected if business's unwillingness to invest causes unemployment and falling incomes. But another factor that gives pause even to governments that can count on strong popular backing is the state's financial dependence on business. A decline in the levels of investment or profit soon will be felt as a drop in government revenues from the taxation of corporate and employment income, payroll taxes, and the taxation of consumption. The problem of falling revenues is almost certain to be compounded by an increase in state expenditures on social programs whose costs are sensitive to changes in the level of economic activity. Borrowing on the public credit is only a temporary solution to this dilemma, and experience has shown this to be both costly and subject to the limits of international investor confidence.

Neither Lindblom nor anyone else would argue that business interests "win" all of the time, or even that powerful business groups cannot experience major defeats. Instead, they maintain that systemic characteristics of capitalist societies tend to favour business interests over others. This is one of the few propositions about politics that manages to cut across the ideological spectrum, attracting support from the left and right alike (if rather more heavily from the left). There are, however, dissenters.

Those who teach or write for a business school audience, for example, are more likely to view business interests as being simply one set of interests in a sea of competing interest groups making claims on government.[12] Business historian Michael Bliss argues that whatever privileged access business people may have enjoyed in the corridors of political power and whatever superiority business interests may have had in relation to rival claims on government had largely disappeared by the 1980s. "Groups with powerful vested interests," he writes, "including trade unions, civil servants, tenured academics, and courtesanal cultural producers, perpetuated a hostility toward business enterprise rooted in their own fear of competition on open markets."[13]

Bliss's skepticism on the matter of business enjoying a privileged position in Canada's interest group system was expressed after two decades of increasing government regulation and a series of major policy setbacks experienced by certain industries. Geoffrey Hale, the author of the standard textbook on business–government relations in Canada, does not go as far in writing off business power. "The extent of business influence varies widely," he writes, ". . . depending on the relative influence of other stakeholders and the capacity of political or bureaucratic decision-makers to control the policy process and to mobilize public opinion in favour of their initiatives."[14]

In his rebuttal to Lindblom's "privileged position" thesis, David Vogel argues that, on balance, "business is more affected by broad political and economic trends than it is able to affect them."[15] Although Vogel focuses on the United States, he develops a more general argument about the political power of business interests in capitalist democracies. Popular opinion and the sophistication of interest group organization are, he maintains, the keys to understanding the political successes and failures of business and other interest groups. Vogel argues that business's ability to influence public policy is greatest when the public is worried about the long-term strength of the economy and weakest when the economy's ability to produce jobs and to increase incomes is taken for granted.

The political organization of business interests is the second key to understanding the ebb and flow of business influence. Vogel maintains that the victories of environmental, consumer, and other public interest groups in the 1960s and 1970s were largely due to their ability to read the Washington map and work the levers of congressional and media politics. Business interests, by comparison, were poorly organized and amateurish. Since then, however, the political mobilization of business has been without equal. But despite its organizational prowess, divisions within the business community have generally served to check its influence on public policy.

In a subsequent study of business influence in the United States, the United Kingdom, Germany, and Japan, Vogel concludes that "most of the factors that affect the relative political strength of business are beyond the control of business."[16] Business's resources, organization, and personal connections to policy-makers are less important in determining whether business interests win or lose on a particular issue, he argues, than is the nature of the opposition it faces and the openness of the political system to non-business interests. In *The Conspicuous Corporation*, Neil Mitchell makes a broadly similar argument. He agrees that business generally enjoys a privileged position in the politics of capitalist democracies, but that its influence can be seriously impaired if its actions and positions come to be seen as violating important community standards and values, thus weakening public confidence in business or in a particular industry and undermining the legitimacy of business's demands.[17]

Another factor that prevents business interests from dominating politics in all cases is what James Q. Wilson has called "entrepreneurial politics."[18] This involves the ability of politicians and interest groups to identify issues around which popular support can be mobilized in opposition to business interests. The opportunities for entrepreneurial politics are fewer in Canada than in the United States because of the tighter party discipline in Canada's legislature. Entrepreneurial politics is, however, practised outside the legislature by many non-business interest groups, including environmental, Aboriginal, human rights, animal rights, and labour groups, to mention only a handful. Astute use of the media and adept packaging of a group's message to generate public awareness and support for its goals are essential to entrepreneurial politics.

So are business interests perched securely atop the heap of the interest group system in capitalist societies, or do business groups have to slug it out in the political trenches just like other groups and with no more likelihood of victory? Perhaps neither position is correct. This, at any rate, is the conclusion suggested by much of the work on Canadian interest groups. Paul Pross calls this rather agnostic approach *post-pluralism* and others have called it a *neo-institutionalist* approach.

This approach is based on a simple observable fact: policy-making generally involves the participation of a relatively limited set of state and societal actors, a **policy community** centred around a sub-government, i.e., that set of state institutions and interest groups usually involved in making and implementing policy in some field. We will have more to say about the approach later in the chapter. For now, the point is simply that groups representing business interests may or may not be members of a sub-government or policy community. Whether they are and how influential they may be depends on the policy field in question and on the particular configuration of interests active in the policy community. Moreover, neo-institutionalists tend to emphasize the capacity of state actors to act independently of the pressures and demands placed on them by societal interests. This capacity will vary across policy sectors. But the bottom line of the neo-institutionalist approach is that state actors in some policy communities may be quite capable of resisting pressures coming from highly organized, well-heeled business interests—or from any societal interests, for that matter.

Analytical Perspectives on Interest Groups

Pluralism

Pluralism or group theory may be defined as an explanation of politics that sees organized interests as the central fact of political life. It is a societal explanation of politics in that it locates the main causes of government action in the efforts and activities of voluntary associations—trade associations, labour unions, churches, PTAs, etc.—outside the state. When it turns its attention to the role and character of the state in democratic societies, pluralist theory draws two main conclusions. First, the state itself is viewed as a sort of group interest or, more precisely, as an assortment of different interests associated with various components of the state. Second, despite the possibility that the state may have interests of its own, its chief political function is to ratify the balance of group interests in society and to enforce the policies that embody this balance of power. As Earl Latham graphically

put it: "The legislature referees the group struggle, ratifies the victories of the successful coalition, and records the terms of the surrenders, compromises, and conquests in the form of statutes."[19]

The purest embodiment of group theory is found in the work of Arthur Bentley. Society, Bentley argues, can be understood only in terms of the groups that comprise it. He views government as simply a process of "groups pressing one another, forming one another, and pushing out new groups and group representatives (the organs or agencies of government) to mediate the adjustments."[20] This is an extremely reductionist approach. Pluralists after Bentley, figures like David Truman, Robert Dahl, and John Kenneth Galbraith,[21] have certainly been aware of the danger of trying to squeeze too much explanation out of a single cause. But they have remained faithful to two basic elements of pluralist theory, one empirical and the other normative. The empirical element is the claim that politics is a competitive process where power is widely distributed, there is no single ruling elite or dominant class, and the interaction of organized interests outside the state is the chief driver behind the actions of government. The normative element suggests that the outcome of this competitive struggle among groups represents the public interest and, indeed, that this is the only reasonable way of understanding the public interest in a democracy.

Pluralism begat *neo-pluralism*. The neo-pluralist assault took issue with both the empirical and normative claims of group theory. Writers like E.E. Schattschneider, Theodore Lowi, and Charles Lindblom had little difficulty in showing that the interest group system was much less open and competitive than the earlier pluralists had argued. Regarding pluralism's normative features, Lowi took aim at its equation of the public interest with the outcome of struggles between special interests. He argued that the special interest state—what Lowi called interest group liberalism—actually trivializes the public interest and ends up undermining it by pretending that it is no more than the latest set of deals struck between the powerful through the intermediary offices of government.[22]

As if these indictments were not enough, pluralism also stands accused of misunderstanding the true character of political power. By focusing on group competition, their critics argue, pluralists are inclined to see political life as relatively open and competitive because they focus on struggles between groups and the choices of governments. But as Bachrach and Baratz suggest, "power may be, and often is, exercised by confining the scope of decision-making to relatively 'safe' issues."[23] Non-decision-making—the ability to keep issues unformulated and off the public agenda—is a form of power. Having to defend your position against others is an indication of weakness. In fact, however, and as we have already seen, neo-pluralists such as Schattschneider are well aware of the power reflected in what Bachrach and Baratz call non-decisions.

Class Analysis

Viewed through the prism of class analysis, interest groups do not disappear, but their edges become blurred and they take a back seat to the class interests these groups are argued to represent. Some of the major works of contemporary Marxist scholarship do not even mention such terms as "interest group," "pressure group," or "social group."[24] In Canada the class analysis approach is generally referred to as "political economy."[25] Interest groups have been given scant attention in most of the work in the Canadian political economy tradition and are sometimes ignored entirely in preference for such categories as class factions within subordinate and dominant classes.

This is not to say that the reality of organized interests in politics is either denied or ignored by class analysis. Ralph Miliband observes:

> Democratic and pluralist theory could not have achieved the degree of ascendancy which it enjoys in advanced capitalist society had it not at least been based on one

CP Images/Photo by Ray Tang/Rex Features

PETA is known for evocative protests designed to mobilize popular public support. In this July 2010 protest a protester is covered in red body paint to represent the blood shed by baby seals during Canada's annual cull in the Arctic.

plainly accurate observation about them, namely that they permit and even encourage a multitude of groups and associations to organize openly and freely and to compete with each other for the advancement of such purposes as their members may wish.[26]

Miliband's *The State in Capitalist Society* devotes an entire chapter to the role of organized interests in an attempt to refute the pluralist model. Some of the Canadian political economy literature includes examples of how class analysis can coexist with a careful analysis of interest groups. Wallace Clement's *The Challenge of Class Analysis*[27] and Rianne Mahon's study of Canada's textile industry fall into this category. Clement examines the complex network of unions, co-operatives, and associations in Canada's coastal fisheries to, in his words, "lend understanding to the material basis of class struggle."[28] In *The Politics of Industrial Restructuring*, Mahon develops a very sophisticated analysis of trade associations and labour unions in the textile sector, in terms of the fundamental class interests they represent, the organizational capacity of these interests, and their ideological characteristics.[29]

But interest groups, from the perspective of class analysis, are not the basic units of society and political life. Classes are. Thus, organized groups are seen as the bearers of more fundamental interests and ideologies, namely those of classes and their factions. This enables one to acknowledge the uniqueness of individual groups and associations while focusing on larger collective interests represented by individual groups. An association like the Canadian Council of Chief Executives, which represents 150 of the largest private-sector corporations in Canada, would be seen as a representative of "monopoly capital." The Canadian Manufacturers & Exporters, although it represents over 3,000 corporations spanning virtually all manufacturing industries and ranging in size from thousands of employees to a handful, is viewed as an organizational voice for the manufacturing faction of the capitalist class. In fact, some class analyses characterize this organization as an instrument of the oligopolistic, American-oriented faction of the capitalist class. Labour unions, of course, are

viewed from this perspective as representative of subordinate class interests and ideologies, as are groups representing women, Aboriginal peoples, and ethnic and racial minorities.

"[T]he policy process," observes Peter John, "far from being a rational weighing up of alternatives, is driven by powerful socio-economic forces that set the agenda, structure decision-makers' choices, constrain implementation, and ensure that the interests of the most powerful (or of the system as a whole) determine the outputs and the outcomes of the political system."[30] Viewed through this lens, associations of corporations, environmental groups, labour unions, and Aboriginal groups, for example, are properly understood in their relationship to broader forces of class struggle. Failure to view them in this context results in a misunderstanding of how political struggle really operates and what is at stake.

Corporatism

Corporatism is a political structure characterized by the direct participation of organizations representing business and labour in public policy-making. "In its core," states Jurg Steiner, "corporatism in a modern democracy deals with the interactions among organized business, organized labor, and the state bureaucracy. These three actors co-operate at the national level in the pursuit of the public good."[31] Such structures are associated to varying degrees with several of the capitalist democracies of Western Europe, including Sweden, Austria, the Netherlands, Germany, and Switzerland.

The distinctiveness of corporatism as an interest group system is based on three characteristics. One is the existence of *peak associations* for business and labour. These are organizations that can credibly claim to represent all significant interests within the business and labour communities, respectively, and have the ability to negotiate on behalf of the interests they represent. A second characteristic of a corporatist interest group system is the formal integration of business and labour into structures of state authority. Under corporatism, these interests do not simply have privileged access to state policy-makers, they have *institutionalized access*. A third characteristic of corporatism is its ideology of social partnership. As William Coleman says of corporatist ideology in Austria, "There is a commitment to allow class conflict to grow only so far before it is internalized and addressed in ways judged a 'fair' compromise."[32] Compared to pluralism, which is characterized by an intensely competitive interest group system that stands outside the state, a corporatist system is more consensus-oriented and obliterates the barriers between the state and the societal interests represented through corporatist decision-making structures.

One might well ask what possible relevance the corporatist model has to an understanding of interest groups in Canada. The peak associations of business and labour necessary to make corporatism work do not exist in Canada. The most inclusive of Canadian business associations, the Canadian Chamber of Commerce (CCC), is just a loose federation of provincial and local chambers, individual corporations, and trade associations. The national organization exercises no control over its members, and the sheer range of interests represented within the CCC obliges it to focus mainly on very general issues—lower corporate taxation, cutting the level of government spending, reducing the amount of government regulation of business—where there is broad consensus among business people.[33] On labour's side, the ability of an association to claim to represent Canadian workers is weakened by the fact that only three of 10 members of the labour force belong to a union. The Canadian Labour Congress (CLC) is the largest of Canada's labour associations, with close to 100 affiliated unions that represent about 2 million workers. This is only about 15 per cent of the total labour force. Moreover, the CLC cannot claim to represent workers in Quebec. Since 1993 the Fédération des travailleurs et travailleuses du Québec, the largest labour organization in Quebec, has operated independently from the CLC. The province's second largest labour body, the Confédération des syndicats nationaux, is also independent of the CLC.

The two other requirements for corporatism—tripartite decision-making structures bringing together the state, business, and labour and an ideology of social partnership between business and labour—are absent from the Canadian scene. Indeed, Gerhard Lehmbruch, one of the leading students of corporatism, places Canada in the group of countries having the fewest characteristics of corporatism.[34] Canadian political scientist William Coleman agrees with this assessment, although he notes that corporatist policy-making networks are found in the agricultural sector of the Canadian economy.[35] This is due, however, to the decades-old policies and structure in parts of that industry—particularly in the eastern provinces and in the dairy and poultry sectors—rather than having much at all to do with culture and broader patterns of industrial relations.

Some observers have claimed to detect elements of corporatism in various tripartite consensus-building efforts launched over the years by governments in Canada, and in the practice of labour and business organizations being invited to appoint representatives to various public boards and tribunals. Past examples have included the Economic Council of Canada and the Canadian Labour Market and Productivity Centre (both of which are now defunct) and task forces on industrial restructuring orchestrated by Ottawa between 1975 and 1978. Some of the provinces, particularly Quebec, have experimented with tripartite consensus-building, and the periodic "economic summits" organized by Ottawa and several of the provinces from time to time have been interpreted by some as signs of incipient corporatism.[36] None of these produced any fundamental change in the process of economic policy-making. Indeed, Alan Siaroff's study of 24 industrial democracies places Canada among those with the fewest features of corporatism.[37] The obstacles to corporatism in Canada are enormous, including such factors as British parliamentary structures that centralize power in the hands of the Prime Minister and cabinet, a political culture unfavourable to the interventionist planning associated with corporatism, the decentralization of authority that exists in both the business and labour communities, and the division of economic powers between Ottawa and the provinces. Whether or not corporatist-style interest mediation is desirable or not is a different question.[38]

Neo-Institutionalism

Neo-institutionalism is a perspective on policy-making that emphasizes the impact of structures and rules, formal and informal, on political outcomes. "[T]he preferences and rules of policy actors," argue Coleman and Grace Skogstad, "are shaped fundamentally by their structural position. Institutions are conceived as structuring political reality and as defining the terms and nature of political discourse."[39] What does this mean and how does it help us understand the behaviour and influence of interest groups?

First, what has been called neo-institutionalism or the new institutionalism is not so much a model of politics and policy-making as a theoretical premise shared by an otherwise diverse group of perspectives. The premise, quite simply, is that institutions—their structural characteristics, formal rules, and informal norms—play a central role in shaping the actions of individuals and the organizations to which they belong. This "insight" is neither very new nor very surprising. The founders of modern sociology knew very well the importance of institutions in determining behaviour, a relationship most pithily expressed in Robert Michels's aphorism, "He who says organization, says oligarchy."[40] Moreover, few of us would blink at the rather bland assertion that "where you stand depends on where you sit." So where is the "neo" in "neo-institutionalism," and what special contribution can it make to understanding interest groups? Let us begin by examining the diverse roots of the neo-institutionalist approach.

Economics

Rational choice theory forms the bedrock of modern economics. Beginning in the 1950s and 1960s, economists began to systematically apply the concepts of individual (limited) rationality and market behaviour to the study of elections, political parties, interest groups, bureaucracy, and other political phenomena.[41] The economic theory of politics developed from this work emphasizes the role played by rules, formal and informal, in shaping individual choices and policy outcomes. Viewed from this perspective, "institutions are bundles of rules that make collective action possible."[42]

Organization Theory

Appropriately enough, organization theory has been an important source of inspiration and ideas for the neo-institutionalist approach. One of the first political scientists to apply the behavioural insights of organization theory to Canadian politics was Alan Cairns. His 1977 presidential address to the Canadian Political Science Association relied heavily on organization theory. He argued that Canadian federalism is influenced mainly by state actors, the "needs" of the organizations they belong to, and the constitutional rules within which they operate.[43] James March, Herbert Simon, and Johan Olsen are among the organization theorists frequently cited by neo-institutionalists.[44] The spirit of the organizational perspective is captured in Charles Perrow's declaration that "The formal structure of the organization is the single most important key to its functioning."[45]

Society-Centred Analysis

The rising popularity of neo-institutional analysis can be attributed in part to a reaction against explanations of politics and policy-making that emphasize the role of such societal factors as interest groups, voters, political culture, and social classes. This reaction has produced an enormous outpouring of work on the autonomy, or relative autonomy, of the state, i.e., the ability of state actors to act on their own preferences and to actively shape societal demands and interest configurations rather than simply responding to and mediating societal interests. Neo-institutionalism, which focuses on the structural characteristics of and relationships between political actors, has been inspired by this same reaction. This is not to say that neo-institutionalism is a state-centred explanation of politics. But in ascribing a key role to institutions—structures and rules—it inevitably takes seriously the structural characteristics of the state.

Neo-institutionalism deals intensively with what might be called the interior lives of interest groups: the factors responsible for their creation, maintenance, and capacity for concerted political action. James Q. Wilson identifies four categories of incentives that underlie the interior dynamics of interest groups:[46]

- *material incentives*—tangible rewards that include money and other material benefits that clearly have a monetary value;
- *specific solidarity incentives*—intangible rewards like honours, official deference, and recognition that are scarce, i.e., they have value precisely because some people are excluded from their enjoyment;
- *collective solidarity incentives*—intangible rewards created by the act of associating together in an organized group and enjoyed by all members of the group, such as a collective sense of group esteem or affirmation;
- *purposive incentives*—"intangible rewards that derive from the sense of satisfaction of having contributed to the attainment of a worthwhile cause."

Economists also have attempted to explain what Mancur Olson first called the logic of collective action, including how the interior character of a group affects its capacity for political influence.

Neo-institutionalism tends to agnosticism when it comes to the old debate on whether societal or state forces are more important determinants of political outcomes. Such concepts as *policy communities*—the constellation of actors in a particular policy field—or **policy networks**[47]—the nature of the relationships between the key actors in a policy community—are the building blocks of the neo-institutional approach. Embedded in them is the irrefutable claim that "the state" is in fact a fragmented structure when it comes to actual policy-making. So, too, is society. The interests that are active and influential on the issue of international trade or securities market regulation, for example, are very different from those who are part of the official-language policy community. What Coleman and Skogstad describe as the "diversity in arrangements between civil society and the state"[48] inspires this spirit of openness on the state-versus-society debate. The reality is that the relative strength of state and societal actors and the characteristics of policy networks vary between policy communities in the same society and, moreover, the line between state and society often is not very distinct. Paul Pross's visual depiction of what a policy community looks like conveys a good sense of the complexity and potential for fluidity in the relations between interest groups and the state (see Figure 12.1).

A group's capacity for influence within a policy community will depend on its internal characteristics and its external relationships to the larger political system and the state. Philippe Schmitter and Wolfgang Streeck call these the logics of membership and influence, respectively.[49] We have already mentioned some of the factors that may be relevant to understanding a group's interior life. On the logic of influence, Coleman and Skogstad argue that the key determinant of a group's influence is "the structure of the state itself at the sectoral level,"[50] i.e., within a particular policy community. Perhaps. But *macro*-political factors like political culture, the dominant ideology, and the state system's more general characteristics also are important to understanding the political influence of organized interests. Policy communities are perhaps best viewed as solar systems that are themselves influenced by the gravitational tug of cultural and institutional forces emanating from the centre of the larger galaxy in which they move. The diversity of state–society relations between policy communities can be reconciled with larger generalizations about the interest group system, including Lindblom's claim that business interests occupy a privileged position within this system.

The Ingredients of Interest Group Success

There is no magic recipe for group influence. Successful strategies and appropriate targets depend on the issue, the resources and actions of other groups, the state of public opinion, and the characteristics of the political system. But although there is no single formula for influence, it is possible to

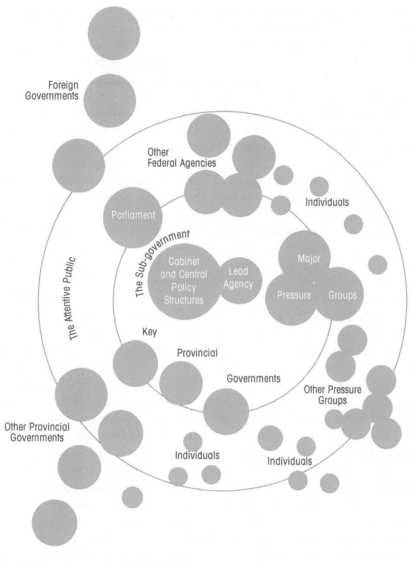

FIGURE 12.1   Policy Community "Bubble Diagram"

Source: Whittington/Williams. *Canadian Politics in the 1990s*, 4E. © 1995 Nelson Education Ltd. Reproduced by permission. www.cengage.com/permissions.

generalize about the factors associated with powerful interest groups. As we will see, these factors are more likely to characterize business groups and their dealings with government than any other set of societal interests.

Organization

It may seem a trite observation, but organized interests are usually more influential than unorganized

ones and are always better equipped to apply sustained pressure on policy-makers. A lone person who writes a letter to the Prime Minister demanding that the government act in a particular way is unlikely to have much impact, even if that person is someone of national stature. Tens of thousands of people writing to the Prime Minister and taking to the streets in front of television and cellphone cameras that bring their demonstrations to the screens viewed by millions of others are more likely to get the Prime Minister's attention. Their impact will be even greater if their demand is channelled through an organization or organizations that can credibly claim to speak on behalf of these thousands of like-minded people, especially if the organizations are skilled at media and government relations. The unco-ordinated efforts of individuals and the fury of a spontaneous protest can have an impact on policy-makers. But this impact is unlikely to be sustained without organization.

Paul Pross, one of Canada's most distinguished experts on interest groups, points to the character of modern government and the policy-making process in explaining why organization is crucial. Modern government, he observes, is a sprawling, highly bureaucratized affair in which the power to influence policy is widely diffused. When government was smaller, the number of policies and programs affecting societal interests were fewer, and power was concentrated in the hands of a small group of senior bureaucratic officials and cabinet. Groups did not require sophisticated organizational structures to manage their dealings with government. This was the era of the "mandarins," the tightly knit group of deputy ministers who dominated the policy process.[51] Pathways to influence were relatively uncomplicated. A conversation with the minister or deputy minister in the restaurant of the Château Laurier or at the Five Lakes Fishing Club was the preferred method of communicating a group's views. Access at this rarefied level, however, was restricted to members of the corporate elite and those representing their interests.

This era began to pass into history during the 1960s. The more complex interventionist state that emerged was not as amenable to the informal, discreet style of influence that powerful economic interests had grown used to during the 1940s and 1950s. As the scope of state intervention widened and its regulation of economic and social matters deepened, it became increasingly necessary that groups have the ongoing capacity to monitor government and deal with it at those levels where power resided. Inevitably, a large, intrusive state means that power is more widely diffused throughout the administrative apparatus of government. It resides in officials who draw up regulatory guidelines and

who interpret and administer technical matters delegated to them under the authority of vaguely worded statutes, and in those who provide advice on programs and policies to the Prime Minister and cabinet.

To deal with the reality of the modern administrative state, groups need to organize. And organize they have. A veritable explosion of associations representing business interests, environmental concerns, consumer interests, women, ethnic groups, official-language minorities, and other interests has taken place during the last few decades. Although most of this expansion in the interest group system has been due to the efforts of those who saw the need and advantage of organization in dealing with government and in order to influence policy and public opinion, some of it has been invited and even orchestrated by the state. The active role of government in promoting the creation of associations that would in turn represent and articulate the interests of their group interests is well documented. It is a phenomenon that appears to have begun in World War I, when the federal Department of Trade and Commerce encouraged the creation of trade associations to represent corporations in the same industry.[52] During the 1960s and 1970s, the Department of Secretary of State was instrumental in the creation and proliferation of a large number of organizations representing women, ethnic groups, and official-language minorities, particularly through the provision of core funding to finance the activities of these groups.[53] If the motivation of the state agencies that encouraged the creation of interest groups was not self-serving, the consequences were. They were helping to organize the interests that depended on their programs and budgets and thereby created constituencies whose support could be useful to the bureaucracy in protecting its policy and budgetary turf.[54]

This practice of state funding for organized groups has continued in recent years, although some of it has been scaled back under the Conservative government. For example, Canadian Parents for French, a group active in promoting French-language schools in English-speaking Canada, receives a large part of its budget from the Official Languages Support Programs Branch of the Department of Canadian

Heritage. The Multiculturalism Program, formerly administered by the Department of Canadian Heritage, involves a wide array of ethnic, racial, religious, and cultural organizations in Canada, many of which lobbied government officials or attempted to influence public opinion on matters of concern to them. (This program has been moved to Citizenship and Immigration Canada and now focuses on integrating groups into Canadian society.[55]) Many Aboriginal and human rights groups receive a significant part of their funding from the Canadian government. The Court Challenges Program provided funding for almost 25 years to organizations representing "members of historically disadvantaged groups" or official-language minorities. The Women's Legal Education and Action Fund (LEAF), a regular and prominent intervenor in Charter cases involving alleged sexual discrimination, often received funding under this program, usually between $35,000 and $50,000 per case.[56] The Conservative government disbanded the Court Challenges Program in 2006 but resurrected part of it in 2008, through the Program to Support Linguistic Rights.

Sophisticated organization has become a *sine qua non* for sustained group influence. Paul Pross uses the term **institutional groups** to describe those interests that possess the highest level of organization. These groups have the following characteristics:

- organizational continuity and cohesion;
- extensive knowledge of those sectors of government that affect their clients and easy communications with those sectors;
- stable memberships;
- concrete and immediate objectives;
- overall goals of more importance than any particular objective.[57]

While many different types of groups can claim to have these characteristics, business associations doubtless are more likely to conform to Pross's criteria for institutionalized groups than those representing other interests. Indeed, associations like the Canadian Council of Chief Executives, Canadian Manufacturers & Exporters, the Canadian Chamber of Commerce, the Conseil du Patronat du Québec, the Canadian Federation of Agriculture, the Canadian Federation of Independent Business, and many of the major trade associations in Canada are among the most organizationally sophisticated interest groups in this country.

Resources

Money is no guarantee of interest group success—but it usually doesn't hurt. It is no accident that the most organizationally sophisticated groups, which enjoy easy access to policy-makers and have the best track records of success in protecting and promoting the interests they represent, tend also to be well-heeled. Money is necessary to pay for the services that are vital to interest group success. A permanent staff costs money—a good deal of money if it includes lawyers, economists, accountants, researchers, public relations specialists, and others whose services are needed to monitor the government scene and communicate both with the group's membership and with policy-makers. The services of public relations firms, polling companies, and professional lobbyists are costly and certainly beyond the reach of many interest groups.

Interest groups representing business tend to have more affluent and stable financial footings than other groups. Their closest rivals are major labour associations; some occupational groups, such as physicians, dentists, lawyers, university professors, and teachers; and some agricultural producer groups. The budgets and personnel of some non-economic groups may also appear to be considerable. For example, in 2012 Ecojustice, one of the foremost environmental groups in Canada, had a budget of about $4.8 million and a staff of 75 distributed across seven offices. Inuit Tapiriit Kanatami, representing Canada's Inuit population, had a 2012 budget of $7.6 million and a staff of 36. These budgets are small, however, alongside those of such groups as the Canadian Bankers' Association, the Canadian Federation of Independent Business, and the Canadian Medical Association, all of which have annual spending budgets in excess of $25 million. The size of an association's staff is not always a reliable indicator of its probable influence with decision-makers—for example, the Canadian Council of Chief Executives (CCCE), whose president is former Liberal cabinet minister John Manley, has a full-time staff of only 14—but these more affluent interest groups tend also to have larger staffs with more specialized personnel. The Canadian Medical Association, for example, employs about 165 persons, the Canadian Bankers' Association about 75, and the Canadian Association of Petroleum Producers about 50. Moreover, there are three important differences between the monetary resources of the major business interest groups and those of other organized interests.

First, the members of business interest groups typically do not rely on their collective associations for political influence to the extent that the members of other interest groups do. Large corporations usually have their own public affairs departments that, among other functions, manage the organization's relations with government. Moreover, corporations will often act on their own in employing the services of a professional lobbying firm or other service that is expected to help them influence policy-makers. Indeed, the clientele lists of such firms as Hill+Knowlton Strategies, Earnscliffe Strategy Group, and the Capital Hill Group read like a "Who's Who" of the Canadian corporate elite (with many non-Canadian corporate clients into the bargain). Corporations have traditionally been major contributors to the Liberal and Conservative parties—business associations seldom donated at all—and annual contributions in the $50,000–$100,000 range were not unusual before the 2004 overhaul of Canada's election and party finance legislation. This kind of contribution was another channel of influence—purchasing access is a better way of describing it—that could be afforded by the individual members of business associations but seldom by the members of other types of interest groups.

The second important difference in the monetary resources of business and non-business associations relates to stability. Simply put, business groups rest on more secure financial footings. They are less subject to the vicissitudes of economic recession and because they do not depend on government or charitable foundation funding they are not exposed to the vagaries of cutbacks and budgetary shuffles. Many other groups cannot make this claim. "It's been painful," said the head of BC's Sierra Club in December 2008, as the Canadian economy slid more deeply into recession. Their annual budget for 2009 was about 60 per cent of what it had been in 2007, leading to significant cuts in staff and activity.[58] A 2009 survey by the Ontario Trillium Foundation reported that about two-thirds of non-profit groups, including social, cultural, and environmental organizations, said their funding had decreased compared to the previous year.[59] Ecojustice experienced a decline of about one-third in its foundation grants in 2009, from $1.25 million to $779,627, a story that could be told by social advocacy and environmental groups across the country.

A third difference involves the ability of business and non-business groups to raise money to deal with a "crisis" issue. The issue of free trade in the federal election campaign of 1988 is a case in point. Although hard numbers do not exist, no one seriously denies that business associations in favour of the Canada–US Free Trade Agreement outspent their opponents by a wide margin in an attempt to influence public opinion on the deal and thereby ensure the election of the Conservatives, the only party that supported the FTA. Much of the pro-FTA money was spent through the Canadian Alliance for Trade and Job Opportunities, an ad hoc association financed by 112 Canadian-based corporations. Most of the major contributors were members of the elite Business Council on National Issues, now known as the Canadian Council of Chief Executives. The Alliance spent a good deal of money, probably at least $2 million, purchasing television and newspaper ads in the year before the election.[60] When a Conservative victory seemed in doubt, the Alliance financed a media blitz during the last three weeks of the 1988 campaign. But deep pockets will not always get the job done (see Box 12.1). During the late 1990s the Canadian corporate elite and its lead association, the CCCE, lobbied hard for the Multilateral Agreement on Investment (MAI). The MAI was a proposed treaty among the wealthy industrialized countries that would have imposed serious restrictions on governments' ability to discriminate against foreign investors through, for example, requirements that they source materials locally or meet other conditions for investing in a nation's economy. In the end, opposition to the MAI from labour unions and anti-globalization groups in Canada and abroad led the governments who were championing the MAI to abandon their efforts. The superior resources of the corporate backers of the MAI were not enough to win this particular battle.

Money is not the only useful resource in promoting an interest group's objectives. John Kingdon identifies several other resources that enable a group to influence what gets on (or stays off) the policy agenda and the alternatives considered by policy-makers. These include electoral influence, the capacity to affect the economy negatively, and group cohesion.[61]

Electoral Influence

The perceived ability to swing a significant bloc of votes is an important group resource. While all interest group leaders claim to speak on behalf of

Media Spotlight

BOX 12.1   Money Doesn't Guarantee That You'll Win: Reforming Telecommunications Regulations

"Canada ranks among the ten most expensive countries within the OECD in virtually every category and among the three most expensive countries for several standard data only plans." This observation was made by Dr Michael Geist, the holder of the Canada Research Chair in Internet and E-commerce Law at the University of Ottawa, in reaction to the July 2013 publication of an OECD study on telecommunications rates in the organization's 34 member countries. The study was issued at the same time as the federal government was the target of a no-holds-barred public relations campaign called "Fair for Canada," financed by Rogers, Telus, and Bell Canada Enterprises. These three companies control about 90 per cent of the Canadian wireless communications industry. In full-page newspaper ads and radio ads across the country, these three dominant players claimed that reforms favoured by Ottawa would result in lost jobs and a foreign takeover of the industry, an industry, they added, whose infrastructure they built and paid for.

When dominant corporations in an oligopolistic industry go public in this way, it is a sure sign that their traditional and preferred methods of influencing policy have failed. Big corporations and industry associations generally prefer lobbying over court battles and PR campaigns. The fact that they had to take their argument public did not

mean, however, that they had given up on these other channels of influence. A report published in *The Hill Times* stated that as of the summer of 2013, Rogers, Telus, and BCE had 15 registered lobbyists who reported 86 communications with public officials in August alone.

It is not often that a Canadian government locks horns with corporations as dominant as these three have been in the Canadian wireless industry. It appears that the federal government had hoped that a large American carrier, Verizon, would enter the Canadian industry and in doing so create more competition that would put downward pressure on rates. Verizon declined the opportunity to enter the Canadian market. Ottawa did not give up on its goal of reducing rates in the industry. The 2013 Speech from the Throne included what was called a "Consumer First Agenda," targeting mobile phone service providers with new regulations aimed at reducing their ability to charge the rates and contract termination penalties that earned the Canadian industry its low ranking in the 2013 OECD study. The Throne Speech also took aim at pricing practices in the airlines and credit card industries. For a government generally thought of as pro-business and anti-regulation, such measures might appear odd. But even pro-business governments require voters in order to get re-elected.

the group's membership, politicians know that the claim is more credible in some cases than in others. The sheer size of a group's membership can be an important resource, as can the status or wealth of its members and their geographic distribution. The distribution factor can cut two ways. In political systems like Canada's, characterized by the election of a single member from each constituency, the concentration of a group's members in a particular region, other things being equal, will increase the political influence of that group. Candidates and parties are likely to see the advantage of proposing policies that are attractive to such a regionally concentrated group, whose votes are crucial in order to win the seats in that region. On the other hand, geographic dispersion of a group's membership may also be advantageous, even under an electoral system like Canada's. A group's claim to speak on behalf of members who are found across the country, and who can be mobilized to vote in a particular way, can be an impressive electoral resource. It is, for example, an argument regularly used by the Canadian Federation of Independent Business, which has about 100,000 members across Canada.

Capacity to Inflict Damage on the Economy

The ability to "down tools," close businesses, scale back investment plans, refuse to purchase government bonds, or in some other way inflict harm on the economy or public finances (or both!) can be a powerful group resource. It is a resource possessed mainly by business groups. Unions and such other occupational groups as physicians or agricultural producers have a more difficult time using "economic blackmail" to influence policy-makers. There are two reasons for this. First, when a group such as nurses, teachers, dockworkers, postal workers, truckers, or doctors attempts to tie up the economy or some important public service by withholding their labour, the linkage between the behaviour of such a group and the social or economic consequences of their actions is extremely visible. Regardless of the factors that led to their action, the general public is likely to perceive the situation as one where the *special* interests of such a group stands in sharp contrast to the *public* interest. A union or other occupational group that attempts to use the threat of economic or social chaos to back up its demands should not count on favourable public opinion. On the contrary, public support for or indifference towards a group's demands is likely to change to hostility in such circumstances. In the case of unions, they suffer from the additional disadvantage of being held in rather low esteem by Canadians. Surveys regularly show that public confidence in labour unions is lower than for most other major social institutions.

A second reason why business interests are better able than other economic interest groups to successfully use the threat of economic damage in pursuing their objectives has to do with culture. In a capitalist society like ours, the fundamental values that underpin the strength of business interests—the belief in private property, the importance of profits, and faith in markets as the best mechanism for generating and distributing wealth—lend legitimacy to the general interests of business. Particular industries or corporations may be perceived as being greedy or socially irresponsible, but the values generally associated with a capitalist economy enjoy widespread support. When workers lay down their tools to apply pressure in support of their demands there is a good chance their action will be interpreted as irresponsible. But if a business refuses to invest in new plant and machinery, lays off workers, or relocates, the reactions of policy-makers and the public are likely to be quite different. Most of us accept that business is about making a profit. The damage that a failure of business confidence may do to an economy may be regrettable, but business people are less likely to be accused of being irresponsible because they are seen to be acting in accordance with the rules of a system that most of us accept.

Group Cohesion

"United we stand, divided we fall" has always been an accepted rule of interest group influence. Other things being equal, an association's hand will be strengthened if it is able to convince policy-makers that it speaks with a single voice and genuinely represents the views of its membership. This is not always easy. We have already noted that both labour and business interests are highly fragmented in Canada and are represented by a large number of associations, not one of which can credibly claim to speak on behalf of all labour or business interests.

The same is true for many other collective interests in Canadian society. Hundreds of organizations represent different groups of agricultural and food producers. Native Canadians are represented by many associations, the largest of which is the Assembly of First Nations. The AFN's ability to speak on behalf of all Aboriginal groups is limited, however, by the fact that it does not speak for Métis and non-status Indians (who are represented, respectively, by the Métis National Council and the Congress of Aboriginal Peoples) or for the Inuit (represented by the Inuit Tapiriit Kanatami). Cohesion once appeared to be greatest in the women's movement. Founded in 1972 and originally financed entirely by the federal government, the National Action Committee on the Status of Women (NAC) was for many years the major umbrella association that at its peak represented about 700 smaller women's organizations. This appearance, however, was somewhat deceiving. By the late 1980s NAC was increasingly beset by internal divisions, and the confrontational style its leadership favoured was not supported by some groups within the women's movement. By 2004 NAC was insolvent and any claim it had to be the major organizational voice for Canadian women's groups was no longer credible. Today it exists in name only.

Group cohesion typically becomes less problematic as the number of members represented by an organization grows fewer and the similarity between members increases. But what is gained in cohesion may, of course, be lost as a result of the perception that an association represents a narrow special interest. As well, it is easier to present a united front when an association is speaking on behalf of just one group. Alliances with associations representing other group interests, however, may be politically useful. The downside, again, is the problem of submerging group differences in such a common front.

A rather different problem of cohesion involves the relationship between a group's leaders and its membership. Evidence of a gap between the goals of leaders and those they purport to represent will

undermine an association's credibility in the eyes of policy-makers. A variation of this problem exists when an interest group claims to speak on behalf of a collectivity that is largely unorganized, or where there are good reasons for doubting that the group actually expresses the views of those they claim to represent. Labour unions' claims to speak on behalf of Canadian workers are weakened, in the eyes of some, because they represent fewer than four out of every 10 workers. The legitimacy of the AFN as the voice of status Indians in treaty negotiations with Ottawa has been challenged in recent times by influential Aboriginal groups that prefer to speak on their own behalf. "Whatever meetings and decisions are made at that meeting at AFN (in Whitehorse), for the record . . . [the AFN] do not speak on behalf of Onion Lake Cree Nation people, period," said Chief Wallace Fox, referring to the matter of treaty negotiations. "Our people speak for themselves."[62]

The dynamics of group cohesion tend to favour certain types of interests more than others. As is also true of the other group resources we have examined, the winners are mainly business interest groups. To understand why this is the case, consider two widely accepted propositions about interest group cohesion.[63] First, as the number of members in an organization increases, the likelihood that some individuals will believe they can reap the benefits of the organization's actions without having to contribute to it also increases. This is called the **free-rider problem**. Other things being equal, smaller groups are more cohesive than larger ones. Second, groups able to offer exclusive benefits to their members, i.e., benefits only available to members of the organization, will be more cohesive and more capable of concerted political pressure than those that rely on collective benefits, i.e., benefits that will accrue to society as a whole. A corollary of this second proposition is that organizations relying on material incentives to attract and retain members, and that therefore can motivate members with the prospect of shared material benefits, will be more cohesive than groups that rely on non-material incentives.[64]

When we examine the actual interest group system, we find that business groups tend to have smaller memberships. Indeed, some are quite small, particularly those that represent companies in oligopolistic industries. For example, the Canadian Vehicle Manufacturers Association represents only four companies, the Forest Products Association of Canada has only 18 members, and the Canadian Bankers' Association has 51 member organizations. Even an industry association with a larger membership such as the Canadian Association of Petroleum Producers, which has about 100 producer members and roughly 150 members in supplier and other allied industries, is more cohesive in terms of member interests than most non-business groups. Some business associations, such as Chambers of Commerce, the Canadian Federation of Independent Business, and Canadian Manufacturers & Exporters, have large memberships. But these organizations represent more general interests of the business community, while the more specific interests of corporations are represented through trade associations that have smaller memberships.

Business groups are not the only ones to rely on exclusive benefits and material incentives to attract, maintain, and motivate members. Labour unions, agricultural producer groups, and professional associations do as well. But one needs to remember that cohesion is only one group resource. Farmers' groups or labour unions may be as cohesive as business associations but still inferior to business in terms of the other resources at their disposal.

Safety in the Shadows

Placard-carrying animal rights activists, a blue-suited spokesperson for an organization presenting a brief to a parliamentary committee, a full-page newspaper ad promoting a particular policy, or a social media campaign aimed at mobilizing public opinion on an issue are all highly visible manifestations of interest groups in action. They are not, however, necessarily the most effective pathways of group influence. Often it is what does not happen—the absence of visible signs of groups exerting themselves to influence policy—that tells us most about the strength of organized interests. In the jungle that is the interest group system, some seek safety in the shadows.

The status, privileges, or interests of some groups are not matters of public debate, and this tells us something about the power of these groups. As E.E. Schattschneider writes, "The very expression 'pressure politics' invites us to misconceive the role of special-interest groups in politics."[65] "Private conflicts," he argues, "are taken into the public arena precisely because someone wants to make certain that the power ratio among the private interests most immediately involved shall not prevail."[66] On reflection, the point is obvious and yet profoundly important. Society's most powerful interests would prefer to avoid the public arena where they have to justify themselves and respond to those who advocate changes that would affect their interests. They are safe in the shadows. But when the light of public debate is shone on them they become prey to attacks from other groups and they lose their security. Conflict, Schattschneider notes, always includes an element of unpredictability. Consequently, even private interests with impressive group resources may suffer losses in their status and privileges, depending on what alliances form against them, the direction of public opinion, and the behaviour of political parties. Indeed, when previously unquestioned interests have reached the public agenda and are recognized as group interests, this registers a loss of influence on the part of such a group.

When the security of the shadows is lost, the relative safety of a fairly closed policy community may be a decent substitute. In the United States, the concept of an **iron triangle** has been used to describe the closed system of relations between an interest group and the administrative agencies and congressional committees with which it routinely deals. Most commentators agree that the "iron triangles" that may have characterized policy-making in the United States have become less rigid over the last few decades. Moreover, because one of the corners in these triangular relationships involved Congress and its powerful committees, the "iron triangle" concept never travelled very well beyond the United States. The terms "sub-governments," "policy communities," and "policy networks" are now more commonly used in both the United States and elsewhere to describe the reality of relatively exclusive constellations of state and societal actors who dominate routine policy-making in a particular field. Indeed, the ability to maintain the routine nature of policy-making is vital to preserving the privileged status of the dominant actors in a policy community.[67]

The Impact of Federalism on Interest Groups

Hardly a corner of Canadian political life is unaffected by federalism, the interest group system included. Because the Constitution divides political authority between two levels of government, one of the first challenges facing an interest group is to determine where jurisdiction lies or, as is often the case, how it is divided between the national and provincial governments. An extensive literature has developed on federalism and interest groups in Canada.[68] We will examine three of the more general propositions that emerge from this body of work.

The first has been labelled the *multiple crack hypothesis*.[69] According to this understanding of federalism's impact, the existence of two levels of government, each of which is equipped with a range of taxing, spending, and regulatory powers, provides interest groups with opportunities to seek from one government what they cannot get from the other. Business groups have been the ones most likely to exploit the constitutional division of powers, and in many well-documented cases they have done so successfully.[70] In the special case of Quebec, where state actors since the 1960s have sought to acquire greater control over areas of social, labour, and economic policy within the province, the provincial state has often encouraged interest groups to organize themselves and look first to the provincial government.[71]

A second interpretation of federalism's impact on interest groups argues that a federal constitution tends to weaken group influence by reducing the internal cohesion of organized interests. According to this argument, divided authority to make policy on matters that affect a group's interests will

encourage it to adopt a federal form of organization.[72] Although this may seem a politically prudent response to the realities of divided legislative authority, it may reduce the ability of groups to speak with a single voice and to persuade governments that they have the capacity for collective action to back up their demands. A group's influence may be weakened even further when the two levels of government are in serious conflict, a situation that may spill over to create division within the group itself (for example, along regional lines) and between its representative associations.[73]

A third proposition about federalism and interest groups involves what might be called the statist interpretation of federalism's impact. According to this view, governments and their sprawling bureaucracies increasingly dominate the policy-making scene, particularly when jurisdictional issues are involved. Societal groups, even those with considerable resources, may be largely frozen out of the process of intergovernmental relations. Alan Cairns implies as much in arguing that modern Canadian federalism is mainly about conflicts between governments and their competing political and organizational goals.[74] Leslie Pal draws similar conclusions—although he is careful not to over-generalize his findings—from his study of the historical development of Canada's Unemployment Insurance program. Pal finds that the impact of societal groups on the original form of UI and on subsequent changes to the program was minor compared to the role played by bureaucratic and intergovernmental factors.[75] Unlike the "federalism as opportunity" view, this interpretation sees federalism—at least the modern federalism of large, bureaucratic state structures at both the national and regional levels—as a constraint on the influence of business and other societal interests.

The "federalism as opportunity" and "federalism as constraint" views are best thought of as representing the two ends of a continuum along which actual cases fall. Examples can be found to support either of these interpretations. Between them are other instances (probably the majority) where the federal division of powers and the intergovernmental rivalry that it allows provide opportunities for interest groups (the "multiple cracks" referred to earlier), but also place limits on their influence. Opportunity or constraint, federalism does have some influence on how interests organize for political action, the strategies they adopt when trying to influence policy, and the likelihood of their success.

Strategies for Influence

There are three basic strategies open to interest groups. One is to target policy-makers directly, through personal meetings with officials, briefs, and exchanges of information. This is the *lobbying option*. Another strategy is to target *public opinion* in the expectation that policy-makers will respond to indications of considerable popular support for a group's position. The media play a crucial role here, because they are the channel by which a group's message will be communicated to the wider public. A variation of the public opinion option involves alliance-building. By building visible bridges with other groups on some issue, a group may hope to persuade policy-makers that its position has broad support. A third strategy involves *judicial action*. This confrontational strategy involves a very public challenge and an outcome that is likely to leave one side a winner and the other a loser. For some groups it tends to be an option of last resort, used after other strategies have failed. But for other groups, such as the Women's Legal Education and Action Fund (LEAF), Equality for Gays and Lesbians Everywhere (EGALE), Ecojustice, and the Canadian Civil Liberties Association, litigation is a basic weapon in their arsenal of pressure tactics (see Box 12.2).

These strategies are not mutually exclusive. A group may use more than one of them at once or switch from one strategy to another. Nor can one draw firm conclusions about the relative effectiveness of different influence strategies. Much depends on the nature of the issue and the character of the policy community within which a group's actions reverberate. Despite the contingent quality of group influence, a few generalizations are possible. They include the following:

- Everyone recognizes that one of the keys to influence is being involved early in the policy-making process, when ideas are just being considered and legislation has not yet been drafted. Lobbying is the generally preferred strategy at this stage of the policy process. Confrontation and visibility are relatively low, and the importance of thorough preparation and credible technical information is high.
- Groups that are well-established members of a policy community, routinely consulted by government officials, will tend to prefer a lobbying strategy. More public and confrontational strategies involve the risk of bringing unpredictable elements into the policy-making process and will be used only as measures of last resort.
- Groups not well established within a policy community are more likely to rely on confrontation, media campaigns, and other public strategies to get policy-makers to pay attention and respond to the interests they represent.
- Where a group's interests are significantly affected by regulation, lobbying strategies that rely on research and technical information supplied to the bureaucratic officials doing the regulating will be most successful.
- The era of vested interests relying on lobbying strategies has passed. Lobbying remains a very important influence strategy, but even groups enjoying regular high-level access to policy-makers now often find that lobbying is not enough.
- A successful influence strategy is usually quite expensive. This is true whether one is talking about lobbying (which often involves hiring a professional government relations firm), aiming to influence public opinion (which may involve the use of paid advertisements and the services of public relations and polling experts), or going to court. Business groups tend to be better able to pay for these expensive strategies than other groups.

Just what *is* the price of influence? It varies, but a legal challenge that makes its way to the Supreme

Politics in Focus

BOX 12.2 Influence through Litigation

Ecojustice, for many years known as the Sierra Legal Defence Fund, maintains a robust staff that includes lawyers and scientists. The group's *2013 Victories Report* (www.ecojustice.ca/publications/annual-reports/2013 -victories-report/attachment) lists 56 clients from virtually every region of Canada and highlights several cases where the organization partnered with clients in lawsuits or proceedings before a human rights tribunal. LEAF's website lists over 150 cases where the organization intervened in legal proceedings between 1985 and 2010. In 2013 alone, the Canadian Civil Liberties Association was involved in over two dozen cases either as an intervenor or a direct litigant. EGALE has had intervenor status in every case dealing with sexual equality rights since *Egan v. Canada* in 1995. For these groups and others, litigation is a key tool in their efforts to influence public policy and shape the direction of Canadian society. Their impact goes far beyond the individual cases in which they become involved. If these cases are the battles, the war is the wider and longer-term effort to shape the interpretation of the law and the context of public opinion in which policy decisions are made. This is clearly expressed on the website of Ecojustice (www .ecojustice.ca):

> Ecojustice provides legal services free-of-charge to charities and citizens on the front lines of the environmental movement, helping ensure equitable access to environmental justice nationwide. We advocate for effective laws, use the courts to

make sure they are implemented and enforced, and give a voice to Canadians in decisions that affect the air, water and land we all depend on.

> Ecojustice holds governments and corporations accountable to nature. Going to court is never a sure thing. It is expensive, time-consuming and the outcome uncertain. Litigation is a final and powerful option when all other alternatives have been exhausted.

> Our work also extends outside the courtroom. For more than two decades, Ecojustice outreach campaigns, workshops, investigations and reports have strengthened the work of conservationists in Canada and abroad.

LEAF's website includes a similar statement of strategy and tactics:

> LEAF litigates and educates to strengthen the substantive equality rights of women and girls, as guaranteed by the Charter of Rights and Freedoms. Year after year LEAF is working to gain intervener status at the Supreme Court of Canada. Our history includes intervention on hundreds of cases where interpretation of the law promises to increase or decrease the substantive equality of women and girls. LEAF also advances public understanding of women's equality rights through education programs administered by its branches and through its speakers' bureau.

Court can certainly cost millions of dollars in legal bills. If much of the legal work has been contributed on a pro bono basis, as has often been true of sexual equality, same-sex discrimination, and environmental cases, the costs may be considerably less. Large business corporations and industry associations have the financial means to go to

court in defence of their interests. For other groups, it is often necessary for a litigation-oriented advocacy group such as Ecojustice or LEAF to take on the burden of their representation. A recent and fairly typical example of this involved the 2013 intervention of Ecojustice on behalf of a community environmental group, Wellington Water Watchers,

Rodrigo de Matos/Artizans.com

In this cartoon, interest groups (represented by the extended arm holding out birdseed) and the media (represented by the paper birds) are being critiqued together. What do you think the cartoonist is saying about the relationship between these two forces in Canadian politics? Is this criticism fair?

to challenge regulations allowing Nestlé to pump water from a natural source (water that ends up bottled and sold in stores across Ontario) during a period of drought.[76] A campaign directed at influencing public opinion can also be costly. We have already mentioned the multi-million dollar campaign waged by the pro-FTA Canadian Alliance for Trade and Job Opportunities—probably over $2 million spent even before the final blitz during the 1988 federal election campaign. Although this case is almost three decades old and the amount of money may sound rather paltry by today's standards, its importance lies in the fact that it became the catalyst for reform of the law on third-party spending during election campaigns. But business groups are not the only ones to spend lavishly in an effort to shape public opinion. A few years after the flurry of spending on free trade ads, Quebec's Cree Indians spent an estimated $500,000 on paid advertisements and the services of a New York public relations firm in an effort to stop the construction of the Great Whale hydroelectric project in Quebec. The public opinion they were targeting was

in New York, the people who would be the consumers of power generated by Great Whale and exported to the United States, and in 2002 the provincial government dropped its plans for the Great Whale portion of the massive hydroelectric developments in northern Quebec.

In recent years Alberta's oil sands have generated an enormous amount of spending in an effort to influence public opinion, mainly outside of Canada. In February 2009 an anti-oil sands ad was placed in *USA Today*, paid for by the Cree and Chipewyan communities of Alberta. A year later, San Francisco-based Corporate Ethics International (CEI) launched what it called its "Rethink Alberta" anti-tourism campaign with billboards in Denver, Portland, Seattle, and Minneapolis. The billboards cost about $50,000, but were only the beginning of a much larger campaign whose costs were expected to reach hundreds of thousands of dollars. "We're running flash and banner ads on major tourist websites," said Michael Marx, CEI's executive director. "[They] start with images of Banff and then morph into images of the tar sands."[77] In 2013, an American billionaire investor, Tom Steyer, announced that he planned to spend $1 million on ads opposing construction of the Keystone XL pipeline that would transport oil from Alberta to refineries on the Gulf of Mexico.[78] These sums, however, pale alongside the tens of millions of dollars the Alberta and Canadian governments have spent in recent years to tell Canadians, Americans, and others their side of the oil sands story (see Box 12.3). Similarly, following the massive oil spill in the Gulf of Mexico in the spring of 2010, the oil giant BP reported spending $93 million from April through July on advertising to "polish the corporate image" in an attempt to convince customers (and perhaps, especially, investors) it was committed to stopping the wellhead blowout and that it cared about the environment and the communities affected.[79] BP has since spent many more millions on refurbishing its corporate image and in an effort to convince the public, and their politicians, that platform drilling in the Gulf and other offshore locations is safe.

It is usually extremely difficult to pinpoint the resources devoted to an advertising campaign that aims to influence public opinion. Walmart is just one of many companies that has invested a significant amount of money over the years in television and other ads intended to convey the message that the company is a socially responsible and valued member of the communities where its stores are located. The beer and liquor industries have likewise invested large amounts of money in advertising that aims to create a favourable public image of them, as distinct from their products, presumably to preclude the sort of regulation and product advertising limits that have been imposed on the tobacco industry. Labour unions have also resorted to the airwaves and to social media in their efforts to create a more favourable climate of opinion. A recent example was the "Stand up for fairness" television and social media ad campaign launched by CUPE in 2013.[80] None of this spending is related to election campaigns, and therefore does not fall under the rules set by the Canada Elections Act. Indeed, it is certain that the severe limits placed on interest group spending in election campaigns, going back to 2000, and the 2004 ban on corporate and union contributions to parties and candidates have had the effect of increasing the importance of group money spent between elections.

The purchase of newspaper/magazine/billboard space, broadcast time, or the use of social media to convey a political message is called **advocacy advertising**. As the Great Whale, CUPE, and Alberta oil sands cases show, business interest groups are not the only ones to buy advertising in an effort

ForestEthics teamed up with the Mikisew Cree and Athabasca Chipewyan First Nations to place this full-page ad in *USA Today*.

Politics in Focus

BOX 12.3 Lobbyists-in-Chief?

Lobbying is generally thought to be an activity engaged in by corporations, business associations, labour unions, and other groups to influence government action. This portrayal is correct, most of the time. It does happen, however, that governments lobby other governments, using the same strategies and tactics and sometimes employing the same government consulting firms and marketing companies used by private interest groups.

In recent years a major case in point has involved the efforts of the Alberta and Canadian governments to persuade lawmakers in Washington, DC, to approve the Keystone XL pipeline. This $7 billion project would carry oil from northern Alberta across five states to refineries on the Gulf of Mexico. The United States is by far the main customer for Canadian oil and gas, importing $104 billion worth in 2012. Finding a market for Alberta's future oil sands production is crucial for that province's prosperity. Securing that market has not proved easy.

As early as 2005 the government of Alberta was purchasing ad space in subways and other locations in Washington and financing an Alberta pavilion that summer in the US capital, in an attempt to raise the awareness of those in the US government sector of the importance of Alberta in meeting American energy demand. At that time the Keystone XL project was still at the planning stage. A few years later, however, it had become a firm proposal. Opposition from environmentalists, some Aboriginal groups, and politicians on both sides of the border, but most crucially in the US, had crystallized. The 2008 election of Barack Obama and his re-election in 2012 gave these groups reason to hope that the pipeline project could be stopped.

The early investment the government of Alberta made in trying to generate goodwill towards the province's oil exports has been multiplied many times over during the last several years. A complete accounting does not exist of how much has been spent on ads placed in US newspapers, fees paid to lobbying firms in an attempt to influence public opinion. Nevertheless, among societal groups, business uses advocacy advertising most extensively and surely spends more money than non-business groups in taking the public pulse and on ad campaigns (unlike governments, businesses and other private groups are not required by law to disclose what they spend on advertising). The crucial question raised by any form of advertising that carries a political message is whether the ability to pay for media time/space should determine what views get expressed. The critics of advocacy advertising were quick to denounce the blitz of pro-free trade advertising by business during the 1988 election campaign. They argued that the deep pockets of the corporate interests ranged behind free trade made a sham of the democratic political process and totally undermined the intention of the statutory limits on election spending by political parties. The Royal Commission on Elections agreed. Its 1992 report recommended that spending by organizations other than registered political parties be limited during elections. Such restrictions were passed by the federal government in 2000 and their constitutionality was upheld by the Supreme Court of Canada in 2004.

The defenders of advocacy advertising claim that it is a way for business to overcome the anti-business bias of the media and to bridge the "credibility gap" that often exists between business and the public. Mobil Oil, one of the pioneers of this advertising technique, responded to early criticism of such advertising by calling it a "new form of public disclosure,"[82] thereby associating it with freedom of information. Business and economic issues are complex. Advocacy advertising, business spokespersons argue, provides an opportunity for business to explain its actions and to counter public misconceptions. They also point out that the to arrange interviews for Alberta's Premier on American news and public affairs programs, multiple trips to Washington and New York by Alberta government officials to represent the province's case on Keystone XL, financing conferences held in the US, and so on. There is little doubt that it would come to hundreds of thousands of dollars and probably much more. Alberta's PR spending in the United States has, however, been dwarfed by Ottawa's. The federal government has paid for ads on both sides of the border—spending about $9 million in 2012 and three times that in 2013–14—including a series of four ads in 2013 focusing on climate change, energy, security, and trade, respectively. The contract for the federal ad campaign in the US was given to the Canadian affiliate of New York-based FleishmanHillard.

But these governments did not limit themselves to the power of public persuasion. In the spring of 2013 Prime Minister Harper spoke about the Keystone XL pipeline to the influential Council on Foreign Relations in Washington. Alberta Premier Alison Redford spoke at the Brookings Institution that spring. A few weeks later, federal Natural Resources Minister Joe Oliver spoke at the Center for Strategic and International Studies. The Prime

Minister also spoke to President Obama about the pipeline at the G8 Summit in June of 2013. Meetings between Canadian officials and congressional lawmakers during 2012 and 2013 were frequent.

This lobbying full-court press by Canadian governments was almost certainly beyond any that had been seen in the past. Government to government lobbying is not, however, something new. Prime ministers and premiers, and lesser government officials, have often met with American officials, from the President on down, making arguments on behalf of Canadian industries and other interests. Indeed, they did this for about 20 years during the long-standing softwood lumber dispute between Canada and the US. Foreign governments regularly hire professional lobbyists to make their case with congressional lawmakers and officials in the executive branch. It was the visibility and the unfamiliar aggressiveness of Canada's PR and lobbying campaign for Keystone XL that caused eyebrows to be raised. "This new (Canadian) posture," said Jason Grumet of the DC-based Bipartisan Policy Center, "indicates that our neighbors may not smile and say thank you regardless of outcome."[81]

biggest spender on advocacy advertising is government, whose justification for this spending is essentially the same as that of business.[83]

There is no doubt that strategies aimed at influencing public opinion have become increasingly important to interest groups. In fact, in discussing advocacy advertising we have only scratched the surface of these strategies (see Box 12.4).[84] Important as they are, however, strategies that target public opinion usually take a back seat to those that target policy-makers directly. These are lobbying strategies.

Lobbying may be defined as any form of direct or indirect communication with government that is designed to influence public policy.[85] Although the term conjures up images of smoke-filled rooms, "old boy networks," and sleazy deal-making, this is a somewhat unfair caricature of lobbying on two counts. First, lobbying is a basic democratic right.

When a group of citizens organizes to demand a traffic light at a dangerous neighbourhood corner and meets with their local city councillor to express their concerns, this is lobbying. When the president of a powerful business association arranges a lunch rendezvous with an official in the Prime Minister's Office with whom she went to law school, this, too, is lobbying. Simply because lobbying is often associated in the minds of the public and journalists with unfair privilege and even corruption should not obscure the fact that it is not limited to organizations representing the powerful or that, in principle, there is nothing undemocratic about lobbying.

A second way in which the "sleaze" caricature of lobbying conveys a rather inaccurate and certainly outdated impression is by associating it with practices that constitute only a small part of what lobbyists actually do. Direct meetings with influential

Politics in Focus

BOX 12.4 Think-Tanks and Interest Group Influence

A think-tank is an organization that carries out research on some matter of public importance and seeks to communicate its findings and recommendations for government policy to a wider audience that may range from citizens to policy-makers at the highest levels. Its goals tend to be broader and its influence strategies rather different from those of interest groups. Think-tanks are in the business of influencing the climate of ideas within which policy choices are discussed, as well as the particular options considered in dealing with an issue. Some of them are not anchored to an ideological agenda and seldom, if ever, advocate a particular policy option. But others resemble broad-based interest groups like the Canadian Labour Congress and the Canadian Chamber of Commerce in that they have a clear ideological orientation—for example, market-oriented in the case of the Fraser Institute and the Frontier Centre for Public Policy, or left-of-centre and anti-globalization in the case of the Centre for Social Justice and the Caledon Institute—and attempt to nudge public policy in a specific direction.

Many of the world's most prominent think-tanks, particularly in the United States where most such organizations are found, were created by donors in the expectation that they would work to influence the policy conversation in ways favourable to their benefactors. In Canada, the Fraser Institute was created in 1974 at a time when, in the organization's own words, "the intellectual consensus was that government action was the best means of meeting the economic and social aspirations of Canadians." The Institute was originally funded by corporate donations, and from its inception has had a strong business presence on its board of directors.

The Caledon Institute for Social Policy has a very different world view from that of the Fraser Institute. Created in 1992, it is funded mainly by the Maytree Foundation, a philanthropic organization headed by businessman and philanthropist Alan Broadbent. The Canadian Centre for Policy Alternatives was created in 1980. It shares the same ideological space as the Caledon Institute and, in its own words, is "concerned with issues of social, economic and environmental justice." The Centre's original funding came from trade unions and individual members.

public officials are certainly an important aspect of lobbying. Likewise, there is no shortage of evidence that ethically dubious relations occasionally exist between lobbyists and policy-makers (see Box 12.5). But lobbying involves a much wider set of activities than simply buttonholing cabinet ministers or their senior officials. Most professional lobbyists, whether they work for a company or interest group, or for a government relations firm that sells its lobbying expertise to clients, spend the better part of their time collecting and communicating information on behalf of the interests they represent. They monitor the political scene as it affects their client's interests. An effective lobbyist does not simply react, but instead is like an early warning system, providing information about policy when it is still in its formative stages and tracking public opinion on the issues vital to a client's interests. Lobbyists provide information about how and where to access the policy-making system and strategies for influencing policies or winning contracts. They may also provide advice and professional assistance in putting together briefs, press releases, speeches, and other communications, as well as public relations services such as identifying and targeting those segments of public opinion that influence policy-makers on some issue (see Box 12.6). Helping to build strategic coalitions with other groups is another function that lobbyists may perform.

Governing Realities

BOX 12.5 The Potential Influence of Foreign Money, Hospitality, and Lobbying

In June of 2010 the director of the Canadian Security Intelligence Service, Richard Fadden, testified before a parliamentary committee. What he said came as a shock to many Canadians. Their public officials, he said, were being targeted by foreign nationals who hoped to buy political goodwill and policy influence in Canada. One of the main ways this is done is through foreign corporations, governments, or associations funded by foreign governments paying for trips to visit their country. Canadian politicians at all levels of government frequently take such trips, often described as "fact-finding missions," the ostensible goal of which is to nurture contacts and identify business possibilities. The hospitality is often lavish and spouses are frequently invited.

Such trips are not the equivalent of bribes. There is seldom an expectation of a specific quid pro quo. But the foreign government or organization footing the bill does so in the expectation that, at a minimum, it is buying goodwill that will ultimately translate into influence in Canadian political decision-making.

Foreign influence may operate in other ways. For example, three of the 10 member companies of the Canadian Energy Pipelines Association (CEPA) are foreign-owned. In November 2012 lobbyists for CEPA met with 30 Conservative MPs, including two cabinet ministers, six deputy ministers, and a dozen other senior bureaucrats. Foreign companies, including France's Total and China's Sinopec, have supported at parliamentary hearings the Northern Gateway pipeline proposal to transport bitumen from near Edmonton to Kitimat on the BC coast. Although foreign nationals and governments are not allowed to contribute money to Canadian political parties or candidates, or spend money on advertising during a Canadian election campaign, no law prevents them from employing lobbyists or in other ways trying to influence public policy in Canada. Should there be?

Most interest groups lobby government on their own. But for those who can afford it, the services of a professional lobbying firm may also be purchased. There are many such businesses. The *Hill Times* 2013 list of Canada's top 100 lobbyists includes individuals representing 18 government consultant lobbying firms. Some of these businesses employ dozens of professional staff and have annual billings in the tens of millions of dollars; others are small operations that employ a handful of persons. In addition, many law firms and accounting companies, including such prominent ones as Osler, Fraser, Milner Casgrain LLP, MacMillan LLP, and Stikeman Elliot, do lobbying work. The line between legal representation and lobbying is often non-existent, a fact attested to by the presence of many law firms on the public registry of lobbyists.

Since 1989, those who are paid to lobby federal public office-holders have been required to register with a federal agency. The Lobbyists Registration Act provides for three categories of lobbyists:

- *Consultant lobbyists* are those who, for a fee, work for various clients. As of July 2013, there were 783 such individuals registered as active consultant lobbyists.
- *Corporate in-house lobbyists* are those who work for a single corporation and who lobby federal officials as a significant part of their duties. As of July 2013, there were 1,861 individuals registered as in-house corporate lobbyists.
- *Organization in-house lobbyists* are the senior paid officers and other employees of organizations—business, labour, environmental, charitable, etc.—whose activities would include lobbying federal officials. As of July 2013, there were 2,612 in-house organization lobbyists registered with the Lobbyists Registration Branch of Industry Canada.

The majority of active consultant and in-house organization lobbyists represent corporations and business associations (as do the in-house corporate lobbyists). The clientele lists of Canada's leading government relations firms include major players in the Canadian and international corporate world.

Earnscliffe Strategy Group, for example, boasts that it represents such clients as Microsoft, DeBeers, Novartis Pharmaceutical, Chevron, General Motors

Politics in Focus

BOX 12.6 The Revolving Door

For those familiar with Canadian politics, a casual perusal of the names of executives, principals, and senior consultants with Canada's leading government relations firms inspires a sensation of déjà vu. Many of these people were, in previous lives, politicians, senior bureaucrats, leading political party officials, or high-level advisers to prime ministers and cabinet members. Often they have worn more than one of these hats before entering the world of government consulting. Those who study politics have long referred to this as "the revolving door," a term that originated in the United States. The Washington-based public interest group, Open Secrets, describes the phenomenon this way:

> (There is)a door—a revolving door that shuffles former federal employees into jobs as lobbyists, consultants and strategists just as the door pulls former hired guns into government careers. While officials in the executive branch, Congress and senior congressional staffers spin in and out of the private and public sectors, so too does privilege, power, access and, of course, money.

This door also exists in Canada, although movement from the world of lobbying into politics and the public sector is less common in Canada than in the United States. But in both countries, and in other democracies, part of what lobbyists market to clients is the expectation of access to influential public officials. This expectation is more likely to exist and to be realized when the lobbyist comes from a background where he or she has been part of the government sector and acquired personal contacts and knowledge that may open doors for one's clients.

Ian Brodie, the Prime Minister's chief of staff from 2006 to 2008, joined Hill+Knowlton about a half-year after his departure from the PMO. His successor, Guy Giorno, had previously been with one of the most influential business law firms in the country, to which he returned after leaving the PMO in 2010. He was succeeded by Nigel Wright, an executive with Onex, a Toronto-based equity investment firm, who rejoined Onex in their London office in 2014. A Quebec adviser in the PMO, André Bachand, left to join the Earnscliffe Strategy Group as a principal and strategic adviser in 2013. The chief of staff to former Finance Minister Jim Flaherty, Kevin McCarthy, left that same year to become a director at Scotiabank.

Since the passage of the Federal Accountability Act in 2008, former government officials, elected or unelected, are prohibited from lobbying government officials for a period of five years after leaving the public sector. But matters are not as simple as they may seem. Former public officials are permitted to lobby on behalf of their new employer or clients as long as this does not "*constitute a significant part of the individual's work on its behalf*" (Lobbyists Registration Act, Section 10.11 (1) (c)). Moreover, the limits on a former politician, senior staff member, or high-ranking bureaucrat providing "strategic advice" to clients or to colleagues that may indeed contribute to more successful lobbying of government officials appear to be flexible.

These limits, however, may be broken. A former senior adviser to Prime Minister Harper, Keith Beardsley, discovered this in 2009 when the Commissioner of Lobbying determined that Beardsley, who after leaving the PMO joined True North Public Affairs as a principal, had contacted his former employer on behalf of a client and in violation of the Lobbyists Registration Act. It was the Prime Minister's chief of staff, Guy Giorno, who had blown the whistle on Beardsley, reporting a phone call in which Beardsley attempted to arrange a meeting on behalf of a client.[86]

Canada, and McDonald's Canada (www.earnscliffe.ca/clients.php). Box 12.7 lists some of Canada's most prominent consultant lobbyists and some of the clients for whom they work.

As the scope and process of governance have changed, so, too, has the character of lobbying. What was once a rather shadowy activity undertaken by well-connected individuals, who often worked for major law firms that relatively few Canadians had heard of, became increasingly complicated and characterized by a broader range of influence strategies and tools. The old model of lobbying as personal communications to a cabinet minister or high-ranking bureaucrat on behalf of a client morphed into an activity more akin to

Sherpas guiding their climbers towards a destination. Personal contacts with key policy-makers continue to be a large part of what lobbying firms sell, but this is reinforced by extensive knowledge and intensive analysis of the policy matters of concern to clients. Under the leadership of Allan Gregg during the 1980s, Decima Research played an important role in this transformation. It offered clients analysis of the public opinion environment in which their activities were situated and that affected the achievement of their goals. The *Decima Quarterly* provided clients with confidential and up-to-date information on public opinion. When Hill + Knowlton, already a world leader in the lobbying industry, acquired Decima the fusion

Politics in Focus

BOX 12.7 Influential Consultant Lobbyists* and Some of Their Clients

Lobbyist	Company	Clients
André Albinati	Earnscliffe Strategy Group	CIBC
		Eli Lilly Canada
		Nexen Hoffman-La Roche
David Angus	Capital Hill Group	Police Association of Ontario
		Molson Canada
		Hewlett Packard Canada
		CHC Helicopters
		MBDA Missile Systems
		Nishnawbe Aski Nation
Peter Clark	Grey, Clark, Shih	Chicken Farmers of Canada
		Dairy Farmers of Canada
		US Lumber Coalition
		Methanex (multinational methanol producer)
Michael Coates	Hill+Knowlton	Bell Canada Enterprises
		Blackberry
		CNOOC (Hong Kong-based petroleum company)
		SNC-Lavalin

*These four lobbyists were selected from the *Hill Times* 2013 list of Canada's 100 top lobbyists.

Source: Industry Canada, Lobbyists Registration System, online public registry, at: <www.ocl-cal.gc.ca>.

of public opinion expertise, marketing skills, policy analysis, and personal access to government officials was achieved. A sort of one-stop-shopping model for public affairs advice and strategic communication became the new standard and has continued to this day.

This remains the model in Canada, as practised by the heavyweights of the lobbying establishment. Most of the activities engaged in by these lobbyists on behalf of their clients involve economic affairs. The Lobbyists Registration Act requires that lobbyists identify the general subject matter of their activities as well as the government departments and agencies that they contact on behalf of those they represent. From the beginning of the registration system, "industry," "international trade," and "taxation and finance" have been the most frequent subjects on which lobbyists have plied their trade. "Environment" has moved steadily up the list and was ranked fourth in 2013, reflecting the increasing importance of environmental laws and regulations for corporations and business associations. Matters relating to health policy also have been among the most frequent subjects of lobbying in recent years. Lobbyists are required to indicate the government institutions they contact or expect to contact and, since 2006, the particular public officials they lobby. The departments of Finance, Industry, and Foreign Affairs and International Trade, as well as the PCO and the PMO, are perennially among the most targeted institutions. MPs and senators, who were seldom targeted by lobbyists a decade ago, have become among the most frequently contacted of public officials.[87]

Starting Points for Research

Robert Campbell, Michael Howlett, and Leslie Pal, *The Real Worlds of Canadian Politics*, 4th edn (Peterborough, Ont.: Broadview Press, 2004). This book provides rich accounts of the policy-making process in Canada, including the behaviour and influence of interest groups.

William D. Coleman, *Business and Politics: A Study of Collective Action* (Montreal and Kingston: McGill-Queen's University Press, 1988). This remains one of the leading empirical contributions to the study of interest groups in Canada.

Geoffrey Hale, *Uneasy Partnership: The Politics of Business and Government* (Toronto: University of Toronto Press, 2006). This leading textbook on business–government relations in Canada provides a solid introduction to the factors that contribute to and limit the political influence of business interests.

Leslie A. Pal, *Interests of State: The Politics of Language, Multiculturalism and Feminism in Canada* (Montreal and Kingston: McGill-Queen's University Press, 1993). Testing various models of interest group influence, Pal explains the complex interaction between group interests and identity formation, and the interests and goals of public officials.

Donley T. Studlar, *Tobacco Control: Comparative Politics in the United States and Canada* (Toronto: University of Toronto Press, 2002). This work presents an excellent comparative analysis of the actions and influence of the tobacco lobby in Canada and the United States.

Review Exercises

1. Go to the issues page at the website of the Canadian Taxpayers Federation (www.taxpayer.com/campaign-and-issues/). Click on "Petitions." Identify three petition issues and the arguments made by the Federation.

2. How many organized groups do you or have you belonged to or contributed to in some way? Make a list. Which of these do you think attempt to influence public opinion or policy? If you are having trouble coming up with a list, just think about jobs that you may have had (were they unionized?), churches, clubs, or associations that you may have belonged to, causes to which you might have donated money, petitions (online or traditional) you may have signed, etc.

3. Make a list of the various political activities engaged in by interest groups. Which activities do you consider to be strongly democratic, somewhat democratic, and undemocratic? Explain your reasons.

4. When politicians or civil servants leave government to work for lobbying firms or interest groups that they had dealings with while they were in the public sector, the potential for unethical conduct exists. Examine the rules that apply to these circumstances at: <www.parl.gc.ca/ciec-ccie/en/default.asp>. Do you think that these regulations go far enough or too far, or are they about right? Why?

The Media

Media impact on modern political life is profound. In this chapter the following aspects of media influence on politics are examined:

- Shaping the political agenda.
- What do the media produce?
- What determines the mass media product?
- The economic filter.
- The technological filter.
- The legal-regulatory filter.
- The organizational filter.
- The ideological filter.
- The media and democracy.

The media scrum figures prominently in Canadian political life. Shown here is Toronto Police Chief Bill Blair surrounded by reporters at police headquarters after city councillor Doug Ford called for his resignation. Media scrums are also held daily in the hallway outside of the House of Commons, where journalists can obtain unprepared (and potentially controversial) comments from politicians.

(Carlos Osorio/GetStock.com)

Few readers of this book will have met the Prime Minister of Canada. Even fewer will have met the President of the United States. However, virtually all readers will have ideas about these two leaders and many will have strongly held views on their character, abilities, and performance, despite never having exchanged a word with them. What most of us know and believe about presidents and prime ministers, the facts upon which we form our ideas and judgments concerning them, is based on third-hand information, at best. The same may be said, of course, about how we acquire our knowledge and beliefs about most of the world outside of our own neighbourhoods. We rely on the edited images and information offered on the screens of our tablets, smartphones, computers, and televisions, over the radio waves, and via other media in our information-saturated societies. Indeed, some people even rely on newspapers, magazines, and books!

The fact that our ideas are based largely on third-hand information means that we should pay careful attention to the character of the "hands" that communicate this information. Think for a moment about the typical political story that you might find at a news organization's website or watch on the evening television news. It may involve about 30–90 seconds of images of the Prime Minister, other cabinet ministers, and opposition leaders and critics, probably in the House of Commons during Question Period or in the foyer near the entrance to the Commons, where journalists and cameras await their daily feeding by politicians exiting Question Period. The story may include brief segments featuring politicians, experts, and interest group spokespersons commenting on the Prime Minister's remarks. Some portion of the story will consist of the reporter's narration of what is happening and what it means. The news clip has involved a large number of choices by those who assign stories to be covered and those who edit and package the story. This is why the information is described as third-hand. The viewer is not personally a witness to the action or occurrence covered in the story. The reporter's account of what happened is shaped by the decisions of others who have been involved in packaging the story for the television news. Consequently, what the viewer

ultimately sees has been influenced by a number of people whose choices contribute to what we call "the news."

Most citizens have always depended on the media for many of their ideas and information about the world they live in. What is more recent is our awareness of the possibilities for selection, distortion, and manipulation in the process of reporting the news. Long-standing fears that media might have a partisan or ideological bias, or that propaganda might subvert democratic politics by depriving citizens of independent sources of information and varied perspectives on their societies, have been joined in recent years by worries that the biases of the media are more deeply rooted and insidious than ever before. The "seductions of language," says media expert Neil Postman, are trivial compared to the seductions and manipulative powers of the image-based media.[1]

This might not matter so much if it were not the case that the media are crucial to the health of democracy. The founders of the American republic knew this, which is why freedom of the press, along with freedom of speech, religion, and assembly, was specifically mentioned in the First Amendment to the United States Constitution. Freedom of the press was, in fact, already enshrined in several of the state constitutions. For example, Virginia's 1776 Bill of Rights stated "That the freedom of the press is one of the great bulwarks of liberty, and can never be restrained but by despotick government."[2] Canada's founders devoted little attention to freedom of the press, or other freedoms for that matter, assuming that these would be adequately respected under the system of parliamentary government they adopted from Britain and that a democratic society had no need to inscribe on tablets of stone the principles it lived by. (Some of the American founders were of the same view. In the *Federalist Papers*, no. 84, Alexander Hamilton argued that freedom of the press ultimately depended on public opinion and "the general spirit of the people and of the government," and that no explicit constitutional guarantee would be able to protect this or any other freedom in a hostile political culture.)

The ability of those in the media to report on public affairs as they see fit—within the limits of defamation law and recognizing that the public disclosure of some government information could be prejudicial to legitimate national security or policy-making interests that state officials are expected to protect—is crucial to democracy. If broadcasters, Internet sites, social media, or print outlets can be shut down, censored, or punished because public officials do not like the information they convey, the free discussion of public issues is diminished and democracy suffers. Likewise, when governments get into the business of broadcasting, publishing, and advertising, fears are often expressed that public dollars may be spent on partisan and propagandistic purposes. This too may threaten democracy.

At the same time, all countries regulate the media system in some way. This is particularly true of broadcasting, where the airwaves have been defined as public property throughout the world and where there have been technological reasons for restricting the number of broadcasters in order to protect the quality of the television or radio signals reaching consumers. But even this traditional argument for regulation has been challenged by newer technologies that rely on cables and satellites, which have produced an explosion in the quantity of messages that can be sent and received at any time. The proliferation of websites and blogs on the Internet and the explosion of social media have produced a globalized media universe in which more information and a more diverse range of perspectives are available to more people than at any time in human history. In addition, this flood of information has meant that state regulation of information has become increasingly difficult.

But state regulation of the media is not, in the eyes of some critics, the only or even the main threat to freedom of the press and the health of democracy. A more serious threat than state control and censorship, critics argue, is the economic censorship that may result when too few owners control too many media organs that account for too great a share of the market. Moreover, they point to the dependence of most mass media organs on advertising as a key factor that operates to filter out certain forms of controversial, critical, and non-mainstream coverage of political, economic, and social affairs. Whether censorship results from governmental *diktat* or from the working of capitalist markets, they insist, it is censorship just the same.

The relationship of the media to politics is a subject that generates enormous controversy. Before we attempt to make sense of this relationship, let us begin by examining the mass media's role in social learning and the chief characteristics of Canada's media system.

"The Pictures in Our Heads"

The media are creators and purveyors of images and information. As such, they play a role in social learning—the process of acquiring knowledge, values, and beliefs about the world and ourselves. This is a role the media share with other agents of social learning: the family, schools, peer groups, and various formal and informal organizations to which one belongs.

While the family and other agents of social learning all contribute to what Walter Lippmann called "the pictures in our heads," none of them rival the media in their impact on the ideas and information we have about political life. Lippmann wrote, "The only feeling that anyone can have about an event that he does not experience is the feeling aroused by his mental image of that event."[3] The contours of modern political discourse are largely determined by the mass media as they process and report on "reality." Moreover, when it comes to matters remote from one's personal experience and daily life—political turmoil in the countries of the Middle East, the latest battle in the United States Congress, or news from Parliament Hill in Ottawa—the media provide the main source of images and information about the events, issues, and personalities involved. Politicians and generals realize the media's importance, which is why one of the first steps taken in any serious *coup d'état* is to seize control of broadcasting and either shut down or muzzle any newspapers, websites, and other media outlets not sympathetic to the new regime.

It has often been remarked that the media do

not determine *what we think* so much as *what we think about*. Of course, their ability to do so is neither complete nor unrivalled. Other agents of social learning also influence what we think about and what we believe. Unlike these other agents of social learning, however, the special role of the media is the communication of information about the world around us. Indeed, in eighteenth-century Britain the term *fourth estate* was added to the traditional three—the nobility, the clergy, and the common people—to signify the power of the press. British essayist Thomas Carlyle quotes Edmund Burke as having said that, "Whoever can speak, speaking now to the whole nation, becomes a power, a branch of government, with inalienable weight in lawmaking, in all acts of authority."[4]

In this political cartoon, the artist is arguing that the media can be distracted from the central issues of a cause by celebrity activists. Do you follow celebrities on Twitter or other social media, and have they influenced your thinking on an issue?

John Larter/Artizans.com

Such power implies an enormous responsibility. A "free press" has been viewed as a necessary ingredient of democratic politics since the American Revolution. The reasoning is that all other groups and individuals—political parties, candidates for public office, corporations, labour unions, government officials, and so on—are self-interested. They cannot be counted on to give an objective assessment of their goals and actions. Too often their interests will be best served through concealment, deception, and manipulation—by **propaganda** that espouses a particular ideology or policy through the public dissemination of selected information and/or misinformation. Only the media, so the argument goes, have an interest in presenting the facts. They may perform this function imperfectly, and particular media organs may have political biases that reflect the views of their owners, the values of their editors, producers, and journalists, or the prejudices of their readership/viewership. But competition ensures that all significant points of view reach the public.

Is this an accurate picture of the media's role in political democracies? How well do the media cover all significant points of view? Who determines

"the facts," or are they self-evident? Regardless of what the intentions of those in the media might be, what are the actual consequences for politics of their publishing or broadcasting particular stories in particular ways? Let us start by considering the "products" of the mass media.

What Do the Media Produce?

Only a small portion of television and radio time is devoted to public affairs. Most programming, including during the prime-time periods when people are most likely to be watching or listening, aims to entertain rather than inform. Despite the existence of a hard-core minority who tune in mainly or exclusively for news and public affairs, television and radio are essentially entertainment media. Most television viewing and radio listening time is spent watching drama, comedy, game and talk shows, and sports, and listening to music. In the English segment of the television and radio market, most of this viewing and listening involves

American programs and music. The overwhelming domination of American programming in the English-Canadian market has always existed (see Figure 13.1) and may be seen by perusing the top-ranked programs for any given week as recorded by the Bureau of Broadcast Measurement.[5]

The pattern is similar for radio. Private broadcasters account for about 90 per cent of the market, and most of what they offer is music. Although the Canadian Radio-television and Telecommunications Commission (CRTC), the industry's regulatory watchdog, requires all radio stations to carry news, only the largest privately owned stations generate any significant amount of news themselves. Most rely on information supplied by websites, wire services, newspapers, and local sports and weather to meet their news quota. Only stations affiliated with the state-owned Canadian Broadcasting Corporation and Radio-Canada, its French-language counterpart, broadcast a significant amount of national and international public affairs programming generated by their own staff.

Like most radio stations, newspapers are geared primarily to the local market. Although all dailies carry national and international news, much of their space is devoted to community affairs. Studies going back to one carried out in 1981 for the Royal Commission on Newspapers have shown that newspapers are considered to be better than either television or radio as a source of community information, while television is believed to be the best source of information for international, national, and even provincial news. Television is also judged to be most up-to-date, fair and unbiased, believable, influential, and essential to the country. A 2007 survey conducted for the Information Technology Association of Canada confirmed this preference for television as the most important and trustworthy medium.[6] Newspapers were relied on by most readers chiefly as a source of local information.

A handful of Canadian dailies, including the Toronto-based *Globe and Mail* and the *National Post*, do not conform to this community paper model. They also are distinguished by having the greatest national circulations among Canadian newspapers. The emphasis on national and international news is greater in the *Globe and Mail* and the *National Post*

than in other dailies, although such papers as the *Toronto Star*, *Montreal Gazette*, *Ottawa Citizen*, and *Vancouver Sun* also include more of such coverage than is typical of most dailies. The *Globe*'s daily "Report on Business" section and the "Financial Post" section of the *Post* also distinguish them from community-oriented papers; some of the other leading papers, including the *Toronto Star* and the *Montreal Gazette*, also provide much more extensive reporting on business and economics than is typical of Canadian dailies. The *Globe*'s long-standing reputation as English Canada's "national" newspaper—a reputation the *Post* has attempted to challenge since it began publication in 1998—has been acquired in part because of high-calibre journalism. The political columnists and editorial writers of both the *Globe* and the *National Post* are influential players in defining the country's political agenda. Montreal-based *Le Devoir* plays a similar role in Quebec.

For several decades, certainly going back to the 1981 Royal Commission on Newspapers, critics of Canadian newspapers have focused on a number of specific concerns relating to industry structure. Concentrated ownership was seen to be a factor that limited the range of ideas and information that reached the public. Others argued that weak competition had less impact on the range of media information than did the need to make profits and the organizational structure of news-gathering and reporting. Another criticism is that newspapers were and continue to be part of larger corporate networks that usually include non-media interests, and for this reason they have been reluctant to cover stories and interpret events in ways that put their owners' other interests in a bad light. Edward Herman and Noam Chomsky have argued that it is too simplistic to look for direct correlations between ownership and whether and how *particular* issues or stories are reported by a newspaper or other media outlet that is part of a conglomerate. Instead, they maintain, owners exercise their influence more diffusely through "establishing the general aims of the company and choosing its top management."[7]

These concerns about the impact of newspaper industry structure on what is reported and how stories are framed have been rendered much less pressing than they may have been in the past because many fewer people rely on newspapers for information about their country and the world. Newspapers no longer dominate public affairs reporting as they did in the past when a handful or two of prominent journalists set the news agenda not only for the newspaper industry as a whole, but for all of Canada's media system. They included such figures as John Dafoe, Bruce Hutchison, Grattan O'Leary, Claude Ryan, Charles Lynch, June Callwood, Douglas Fisher, Lise Bissonette, and Allan Fotheringham. Together with some of their counterparts from television, particularly from the CBC and Radio-Canada, these journalists formed a sort of epicentre from which stories and interpretations radiated outward to less prestigious media outlets throughout the country. They have been succeeded by a newer generation of journalists, some of whom are quite influential. But many fewer people read or listen to what they have to say about public affairs than was true only a generation ago.

A 2011 survey by Angus Reid Public Opinion found that newspapers were ranked fifth in importance as a source of news and information. Newspapers did much better, however, when Canadians were asked how trustworthy they found various media, although they were not considered to be more reliable than television, online news sources, or radio. All were believed to be reliable or very reliable by about nine in 10 Canadians.[8] At the same time, when Canadians are asked how much they trust businesses in various industries to do what is right, the media industry ranks towards the bottom with only about half of respondents saying that they could be trusted.[9] Traditional media, including newspapers and television, were not spared this harsh assessment. Questions of trust aside, the number of Canadians who read newspapers has declined precipitously over the past two generations, as is the case in many Western democracies. In 1950 there were as many paid newspaper subscriptions as households in Canada. By 2010 this had declined to fewer than one for every three households. Most of this decline occurred by the 1990s.[10] Since then the drop in newspaper readership has been much more gradual, but newspapers

have been faced with a new dilemma. Increasing numbers of readers prefer to read online and many expect to be able to do so without having to pay for what they read. A 2010 survey found that television was still the medium relied on by more Canadians than any other as their main source of news (46.6 per cent), with radio second (21.6 per cent), the Internet third (17.5 per cent), and newspapers last (14.3 per cent).[11]

A growing number of Canadians, especially younger Canadians, prefer to get their news via their laptops, tablets, and smartphones. This does not mean that they abandon traditional media, although some do. For most of those who follow public affairs, however, a mixed diet of media sources has become the new normal. Much of the content found at websites and blogs and circulated via social media continues to come from traditional media sources, including newspapers.

At the same time, however, the way in which traditional news-gatherers and reporters do their jobs has changed rather significantly, influenced by challenges from non-traditional news sources and by the changing technology of mass media. Almost all Canadian journalists now use social media. A 2013 study found that over 90 per cent of them used Twitter, over half maintained a personal blog, and about one-quarter had a personal Google Plus page.[12] Their counterparts across the Western world reported similar reliance on social media. Journalists said that in sourcing stories they trusted readers of their blogs more than they did politicians! According to this same study, blogs with which journalists are familiar have become one of their main sources for stories as well as a means of verifying news reports. Unique visits to their blogs and digital articles have become the gold standard by which Canadian journalists evaluate the success of their work, 86 per cent of them saying this is the single most important measure of their success. This is higher than in any other Western democracy (US, 68 per cent; Sweden, 58 per cent; Spain, 58 per cent; UK, 45 per cent).

Magazines have faced the same challenges confronted by newspapers in recent years. Subscriptions have been falling in an industry that only a couple of decades ago included dozens of magazines that

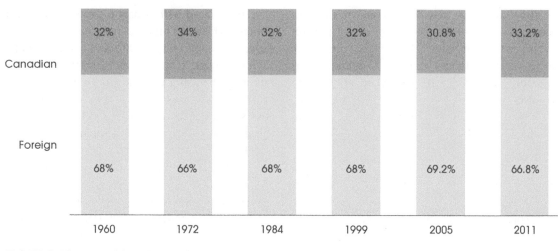

FIGURE 13.1 TV Viewing in English Canada, 1960–2011

Source: Barry Kiefl, Canadian Media Research, "Trends in TV Audiences and Public Opinion, 1996–2006," 14 Mar. 2007, at: <www.friends .ca/files/PDF/HeritComm07mar14.ppt>; Barry Kiefl, Canadian Media Research, "Trends in TV and Internet Use: The Impact of Internet TV on Canadian Programming," July 2011, at: <www.omdc.on.ca/Assets/Research/Research+Reports/Trends+in+TV+and+Internet+Use/ Trends+in+TV+and+Internet+Use_en.pdf>.

had monthly subscriptions of 100,000 or more. Today only about 10 in the English-language market have paid circulations above this mark. Most of the best-selling magazines, including *Chatelaine, Canadian Living, Reader's Digest*, and *Canadian Geographic*, do not cover much in the way of public affairs. The one exception is *Maclean's*. As is also true of newspapers, *Maclean's* has been forced to adapt to the reality of consumers who expect to receive their news immediately, and not just once a week, and on the screen of their smartphone or computer, through a digital edition that features constantly updated content and journalists who blog and tweet.

Compared to the media we have discussed so far, the political significance of film may appear relatively insignificant. As is true of people throughout the world, Canadians usually turn to films for diversion and entertainment, rather than to be informed about public affairs. The average Canadian goes to the cinema only about four or five times per year (more often among those who live in major cities). But some of the time he or she spends in front of the television or computer is spent watching films. Cable television, direct broadcast satellites, pay-TV, VCR/DVD players, tablets, and smartphones

have increased the market penetration of films, freeing the film industry from the movie theatre and bringing its product directly into the home of the consumer. In a sense, this technology has produced a new "golden age" for the film industry, enabling it to recapture some of the prominence it held between the 1930s and the 1950s, before the television set became a standard feature of most households. Whether the quality of what the industry produces these days is better or worse than during the era of Hitchcock, Ford, and Capra is another matter.

Film is at the centre of the modern imagination. If a person has not read the book, he or she probably has seen its film adaptation. Blockbusters such as the *Batman* and *Star Wars* films, the adventures of *Indiana Jones, Spider-Man, Titanic, Avatar*, the Harry Potter films, and the *Lord of the Rings* trilogy are familiar to most of us. The stories they tell, the characters they contain, and the stereotypes they convey both shape and reflect our popular culture. They also shape viewers' world views and reflect and reinforce the dominant ideology. An argument could be made that Bruce Willis, Sylvester Stallone, and the like have had a greater impact on how North Americans (and Europeans to a lesser extent) view the world and react to it—and have affected it—than has any political leader in the Western world over the last half-century. The archetypes and icons of popular culture are more likely to be associated with movies than with any other mass medium.

What does the film industry offer the viewing public? With hundreds of new releases every year from the studios of Hollywood and thousands more from independents in the US, Canada, and elsewhere, one might assume that the industry produces a richly varied product. It does. But only a narrow band of the entire range of film production is backed by the marketing resources of the studios that produce them. This band represents the commercial feature film. The genre may vary, but what distinguishes such a film is that it must appeal to a large mass audience to recoup the millions of dollars—often running to hundreds of millions of dollars—spent on its production and marketing. (*Spider-Man 3*, *Tangled*, and *Pirates of the Caribbean: At World's End* are thought to be the most expensive movies ever produced, each coming in at a cost of close to US$300 million.) Documentary and artistic films generally cost much less to make, but they also generate smaller revenues. They usually are made by small independent film companies or by state-owned filmmakers like Canada's National Film Board. The advent of low-cost direct streaming through Netflix and its competitors has made non-mainstream film more accessible, but little money is spent on marketing these alternatives to what Hollywood and the major television producers offer. The images and stories purveyed by the commercial film industry are often disturbing and occasionally critical of "the system." They may challenge prevailing notions and prejudices, as was true of *To Kill a Mockingbird* (1962), *Guess Who's Coming to Dinner?* (1967), and *Milk* (2008), or confront powerful interests, as in *Wall Street* (1987) and *Erin Brockovich* (2000). Indeed, one of the most enduring motifs of popular film has long been the lone good man—almost always a man—versus the bad system. On balance, commercial film does much more to reinforce dominant values and institutions than it does to challenge them. The

economics of the industry make this inevitable, as explained later in this chapter.

Advertisements are another important part of the media product. Most of us are exposed to hundreds of ads each day. Television and radio are heavily laced with them. Newspapers and magazines are layered with them. Films are vehicles for advertising, with companies willing to pay thousands of dollars for fleeting glimpses of their product in a favourable context. Billboards, storefront signs, pamphlets, flyers, Internet banners and pop-ups, mobile ads that appear on our phones . . . there is no escape. The estimated amount spent on mass media advertising worldwide exceeds the value of Canada's gross national product (GNP). The advertising assault is so massive and unremitting that the vast majority of it fails to pierce our consciousness. Advertisers have long been aware of this and search continually for ways to capture the attention of the viewers, listeners, or readers to whom they want to sell something. Whether we pay attention or tune out, advertising constitutes a continuous "buzz" in the background of our daily lives. What is it telling us?

In the case of most advertising, the intended message is "buy this." We say "most" because some advertising aims to persuade people to vote or to think in particular ways, or simply provides them with useful information (much public service advertising by governments would fall into this last category). The vast majority of advertising, however, aims to affect our behaviour as consumers.

Commercial advertising conveys much more than the intended message, "buy product X." We are urged to buy, period. The high-consumption capitalist economy is sustained by the frenetic materialism that pervades our culture. This materialism, in turn, is reinforced by the mass media through advertising and entertainment programming. When the message "buy this" is hurled at us hundreds of times a day from the time we are quite young, the cumulative impact is to instill and sustain a high-consumption mindset.

Consumerism is only one of the incidental messages communicated through commercial advertising. Gender stereotyping and the use of sexual imagery and innuendo are rampant. The youthful, the slender, the muscular, the large-breasted, the extroverted, the materially successful, and the "cool" are far more likely to appear in advertising than are those who appear to be deficient in these qualities (even when the product being advertised is something as unglamorous as adult diapers, the people who appear in the ads invariably appear to be more energetic, youthful, and attractive than we might imagine would be the case). Who and what are excluded from visual advertising—and the same holds true for all visual media—are as important as who and what are included. The silences and blind spots of advertising and of all mass media include to varying degrees the poor, visible minorities, men and women who do not conform to fairly traditional stereotypes, the physically unattractive, and the socially non-conforming (as this is defined by the marketers of popular culture: a rebellious look may sell, but off-putting difference is avoided). There are, of course, exceptions. But in general, advertisers find it more profitable to appeal to conventional beliefs and prejudices and to very basic emotional needs and insecurities. This

aspect of commercial advertising has not changed since the birth of Madison Avenue (see Box 13.1).

What Determines the Mass Media Product?

The facts of modern life do not spontaneously take a shape in which they can be known. They must be given a shape by somebody.[13] No one except the naive and those with a professional interest in self-deception believes that the mass media simply mirror reality. Confronted with more information than can possibly be conveyed to their readerships and audiences, those who produce the media product must choose what stories, images, and "facts" to communicate. What ultimately is offered to the media consumer is a selective pastiche, a partial and inevitably somewhat distorted version of a "reality" that is constructed in the process of being communicated.

The choices made by reporters, editors, producers, and others who contribute to the media product are

Media Spotlight

BOX 13.1 The Art of Selling

The principles underlying this (commercial advertising) are extremely simple. Find some common desire, some widespread unconscious fear or anxiety; think out some way to relate this wish or fear to the product you have to sell; then build a bridge of verbal or pictorial symbols over which your customer can pass from fact to compensatory dream, and from the dream to the illusion that your product, when purchased, will make the dream come true. "We no longer buy oranges, we buy vitality. We do not buy just an auto, we buy prestige." And so with all the rest. In toothpaste, for example, we buy, not a mere cleanser and antiseptic, but release from the fear of being sexually repulsive. . . . In every case the motivation analyst has found some deep-seated wish or fear, whose energy can be used to move the consumer to part with cash and so, indirectly, to turn the wheels of industry. Stored in the minds and bodies of countless individuals, this potential energy is released by, and transmitted along, a line of symbols carefully laid out so as to bypass rationality and obscure the real issue.

not random. Several factors influence how reality is processed and how politics and public affairs are reported by the media. These factors may be understood as a series of filters that are more likely to let through certain information and images than others. On the whole, and with important exceptions, information and images that threaten the privileges of dominant social and economic groups are less likely to make it through these media filters than those that are fairly orthodox and non-menacing. This claim will strike many readers as absurd, conditioned as most of us are to believe that the media are independent and frequently critical of the powerful. On balance, however, the media do much more to support the status quo, including the distribution of power in society and the economy, than they do to erode it.

The Economic Filter

Most media organs are privately owned, and as such they are subject to the iron law of the marketplace. That law is very simple: they must be able to sell a product that will attract enough subscribers, advertisers, buyers, or patrons—the exact source of revenue depends on the media product—to cover production costs and, usually, earn a competitive return on invested capital. Given the costs involved in producing a daily newspaper, a slick magazine, a high-quality website, a television series, or a feature film, profitability requires a mass market. No media organ needs to appeal to everyone in order to survive, and none tries. But particularly when a marketplace is competitive, there will be a tendency to avoid programming or content that seems likely to have limited appeal in favour of that which will hold onto, or even increase, sales.

State ownership alters, but does not eliminate, the economic pressures to which the mass media are exposed. Publicly owned broadcasters must be sensitive to charges of elitism. This is particularly true of television broadcasting, where the costs of producing high-quality entertainment programming are great. Few politicians will be willing to risk the loss of votes in order to subsidize broadcasting that attracts a tiny audience. Market influences become even greater when a publicly owned broadcaster is required to raise some part of its revenues from advertising or viewer/corporate support.

Economic pressures have an important impact on what the mass media produce. They cannot, however, explain all media behaviour. What finally is offered to viewers, readers, and listeners also is affected by regulatory requirements, the legal system, and the cultural norms of society.

The economic filter operates mainly through the influence that advertising and industry structure have on the media product. Without advertising dollars, privately owned and even (to a lesser degree) publicly owned media companies are not economically viable. These media companies are in competition for the advertising patronage of business.

Rick Mercer holds his award for the *Rick Mercer Report*'s win in the Best Comedy Program or Series category at the 24th Annual Gemini Awards in November 2009. Mercer's satirical news program is part of a growing phenomenon of shows, including Jon Stewart's *Daily Show* and Stephen Colbert's *The Colbert Report* in the US, that offer an alternative viewpoint on current events while ostensibly poking fun at the formats of the infotainment or "soft news" channels.

CP Images/The Canadian Press/Larry Macdougal

It follows, then, that they will be sensitive to their patrons' needs and will tend to avoid reporting or programming that reduces their attractiveness in the eyes of advertisers. In the classic formulation of an American network executive, television "is an advertising-supported medium, and to the extent that support falls out, programming will change."[14] The advertising base of a newspaper or radio broadcaster is typically more local than that of a television network, but the maxim still holds: advertisers' preferences cannot be ignored by an ad-dependent media system.

The commercial imperatives to which most media are subject are politically relevant in a couple of ways. First, dependence on advertising may reduce the likelihood that powerful economic interests will be portrayed in a negative light. This is not to imply that advertisers hold a power of economic blackmail over the heads of media organs. There have been occasions, however, when particular programs were boycotted by corporate sponsors or where their broadcast was followed by advertiser reprisals. In some instances, the anticipated reaction of corporate advertisers is enough to either kill a story or moderate its tone. But the influence of advertising is much more subtle and pervasive than these occasional incidents might suggest. When a 30-second commercial spot during a popular prime-time program on a major American network costs roughly US$300,000–$400,000 (closer to US$600,000 if it is Sunday Night Football and US$4 million for 30 seconds in the case of the 2014 Super Bowl), the economic costs of broadcasting material that offends powerful corporate advertisers obviously are great. Those who make programming decisions certainly are aware of this.

Little evidence supports the occasionally expressed view that news reporting is "censored" or slanted as a result of advertiser interference. In *News from Nowhere*, Edward Epstein declares that none of the hundreds of correspondents and production personnel he interviewed for his study could recall an incident of sponsor interference in a network news broadcast. On the contrary, Epstein observes that stories in direct conflict with the interests of major sponsors were not uncommon.[15] The fear that advertisers may withhold their business, he

argues, has little impact on the content of national news programming, although it may occasionally affect news documentaries and other public affairs programs. Self-censorship, where journalists and producers avoid certain stories or soften their tone in covering them, is certainly much more common and more of a problem than advertiser blackmail.[16]

The influence of advertising operates in a second, less blatant but also more powerful way. Most television broadcasting and most viewing time are devoted to entertainment programming. Naturally, the most lucrative advertising slots are associated with this sort of programming. Therefore, an economic pressure is placed on ad-dependent broadcasters to maximize the amount of high audience-appeal programming during prime-time hours. Most public affairs programming does not have the draw of a popular sitcom, "reality" program, or drama, and consequently is subject to pressures that it be marginalized (relegated to off-peak viewing times, or left up to state-owned or viewer-supported broadcasters) or that it adopt an entertainment format. The emergence of what is often called **infotainment** or "soft news"—news that is packaged using an entertainment, celebrity journalist format—is the norm in the United States. Infotainment is clearly linked to the high price fetched by advertising spots during popular viewing hours. The Canadian industry may not have gone as far in breaking down the traditional barriers between entertainment and public affairs programming, although the local news programming model developed by Rogers Media's *CityNews* channel, which lasted only from 2011 to 2013, was essentially the same as the soft news format pioneered in the United States. As in the United States, the economics of broadcasting in Canada work against the viability of programming that does not attract a mass audience and so the pressures to adopt the infotainment/celebrity newsreader format remain great.

State-owned media organs like the CBC, TV Ontario, and Radio-Québec in Canada and the viewer-supported Public Broadcasting System (PBS) network in the United States are not immune from the influence of advertising. Both the CBC and Radio-Québec rely on advertising for a significant portion of their revenue. In the case of the CBC, advertising income accounts for about one-third of its annual budget. Viewer-supported broadcasters like the American PBS rely on state subsidies (directly and through the tax system) and on foundation and corporate sponsorship of programs for part of their revenue needs. Some critics have argued that corporate sponsorship, like advertising, tends to filter out socially divisive and controversial programming, including criticism of powerful economic interests and the capitalist system. This claim, however, is rather dubious or at least exaggerated. One need only peruse some of the programming on PBS's *Frontline* and *American Experience* programs, among others, to find evidence that refutes this charge.

Dependence on state subsidies does not necessarily remove all constraints on media content. Public broadcasters must constantly be sensitive to charges of bias and ideological favouritism. Over the years CBC television programs like *This Hour Has Seven Days*, *the fifth estate*, *Marketplace*, *The Passionate Eye,* and the various programs hosted by environmentalist David Suzuki, notably *The Nature of Things,* have been accused of having a leftist political bias and of being anti-business. In response to such charges the CBC has long had in place a system of in-house monitoring of its programming and an ombudsman for both its English- and French-language divisions. Much of this monitoring, as during election campaigns, is intended to ensure that the CBC is even-handed in its treatment of the major political parties and their leaders. But monitoring also focuses on the portrayal and coverage of social and economic groups, including business. In the world of public broadcasting, culturecrats' and politicians' aversion to controversy may substitute for the check that dependence on advertising imposes on private broadcasters.

Industry structure is the second component of the economic filter. Fears have long been expressed that as the number of daily newspapers in Canadian urban markets declined and as fewer owners controlled more of the market, the range of information and perspectives would suffer. These fears peaked in the early 1980s when the federal government created the Royal Commission on Newspapers.[17]

It reported that in 1930, 99 publishers owned 116 daily newspapers across the country. In 1980, however, 12 owners controlled 89 dailies and two of these publishers together controlled over half of the Canadian newspaper market. Chain ownership of most newspapers had become a feature of both the French- and English-language newspaper markets. Moreover, the firms that controlled most of the country's dailies also had investments in other sectors of the economy, leading to fears that these other corporate interests might influence whether certain stories were reported and how they might be reported. Cross-media ownership, where a conglomerate might control companies in different sectors of a media market, also became an important concern among critics and industry regulators.

Today the daily newspaper industry in Canada (as in the United States) is characterized by local monopoly. In only eight Canadian cities (Quebec City, Montreal, Ottawa, Toronto, Winnipeg, Calgary, Edmonton, and Vancouver) is there competition between same-language, mass-circulation dailies that have different owners. Most daily newspaper circulation in English Canada is controlled by the Postmedia Network and Quebecor/Sun Media group. Torstar Corporation papers also have a significant market share and Woodbridge, the investment holding company of the Thomson family, owns the influential *Globe and Mail*. In French-speaking Quebec all but a tiny share of the daily newspaper market is controlled by Quebecor and Power Corporation. The influential Montreal-based daily, *Le Devoir*, is independently owned.

Although Canadian newspaper ownership is more concentrated than at any time in history, newspaper circulations have been declining in absolute terms since the 1990s and very sharply in relationship to the number of households over that same period. The early challenge to newspapers' pre-eminent role in coverage of public affairs and, presumably, as an influence on public perceptions of politics came from television. But in more recent years it has come from the ascendant digital media of websites, blogs, and social media. Canadian media analyst Ken Goldstein argues that the fretting about concentrated ownership in the newspaper industry and declining newspaper readerships may be beside the point. "[W]e may come to view the current debates about 'plurality' and 'concentration,'" he says, "as wasteful diversions from a far more fundamental issue for media and democracy—fragmentation of audiences. New technology may have conquered the scarcity of channels, but that is increasingly yielding fragmented audiences based on far more choices and more narrowly-defined interests." Fragmented audiences represent more than a challenge for those who want to make money from producing a media product. "How will a modern democracy function," Goldstein asks, "if we all have less in common?"[18]

This fragmentation has become increasingly characteristic of the television and radio markets, and has always been a feature of the Internet. The days are long past when a handful of American broadcasters, plus the CBC, dominated television broadcasting. Cable and satellite technology and the development of the Internet have created unprecedented opportunities for niche programming targeted at more limited audiences than the traditional broadcasters require to ensure profitability. The economics of electronic media are significantly different from those of print media, such that concentrated ownership is not as prominent an issue in broadcasting as in newspaper markets.

Instead, the ownership issue in broadcasting and newer media like the Internet is framed chiefly as an issue of American penetration into Canadian markets. Canadian viewers may indeed have access to hundreds of television stations through direct broadcast satellite (DBS), cable technology, or Internet streaming, but the fact remains that the most popular ones either originate in the United States or rely to a great extent on programming, often heavily promoted through advertising, produced in the United States. Issues of ownership in the United States and internationally are thereby imported into Canada.

One of these issues involves the new corporate convergence in mass media, particularly in electronic media industries. Multinational media giants control companies that produce content as well as firms in the business of distributing that content. Disney is a prominent example. Best known for producing films and running theme parks throughout the world, Disney also owns the American television broadcaster ABC, as well as several cable networks, animation studios, and television content production businesses. A world in which such multinationals as Disney, Time Warner, Comcast, Sony, Viacom, Apple, and Google dominate the electronic media food chain, from the production of the entertainment and information products through the means for distributing and receiving them, is not likely to provide much opportunity for the expression of distinctively Canadian values, perspectives, and stories. More Canadian programming is produced and available today than ever before (consumption of this home-grown product is, however, another matter). This has been largely due to government regulation and subsidies, to which we now turn.

The Legal/Regulatory Filter

Print media in Canada and in most other democracies are basically free from direct regulation by government. Unlike radio and television broadcasters and satellite, cable, and wireless companies, they do not require a special licence to do business. Newspapers and magazines essentially regulate themselves through press councils created and operated by the members of their respective industries. These councils receive and investigate complaints; they do not systematically monitor performance. Calls for greater state regulation of their behaviour invariably provoke cries of censorship from those in the newspaper and magazine business.

A number of indirect forms of regulation, however, may affect content in the print media. Most of these involve measures whose ostensible aim is to promote Canadian values through newspapers and magazines. For example, the federal Income Tax Act permits advertisers to deduct from their taxable income only the cost of ads placed in newspapers or magazines that are at least 75 per cent Canadian-owned. This explains why foreign ownership of Canadian newspapers has never been an issue, despite the fact that for most of its history the industry has been extremely profitable and might therefore have been expected to attract foreign capital.

It is doubtful, however, whether the provisions of the Income Tax Act favouring Canadian-owned publications has much of an impact on newspaper content. With the chief exceptions of the *Globe and Mail*, the *National Post*, and *Le Devoir*, newspapers are geared mainly to local markets. Community news and local advertising account for a large share of these papers. Their profitability depends on a large local readership that they can "sell" to local advertisers. This, and not the nationality of their owners, will influence newspaper content.

One might argue, however, that the owner's nationality could influence the way a newspaper covers national and international news, as well as sports and comics—two of a paper's most read sections. Canadian-owned papers already depend heavily on news that they purchase from foreign news agencies like the Associated Press wire service, particularly for international news and sports, so foreign ownership probably wouldn't result in much of a change in content. The economics of news-gathering, not the nationality of the owners, is responsible for this dependence on foreign sources of news. In the end, the Income Tax Act almost certainly does more to ensure Canadian ownership than it does to promote Canadian culture.

The situation in the magazine industry is quite different. Canadian ownership provisions of the Income Tax Act also apply to magazines, but the English-Canadian market was long dominated by American magazines and, for a short time, **split-run publications**, where the magazine was based outside of Canada, most of its editorial and other production costs were incurred outside of Canada, and most of its circulation was non-Canadian. A split-run edition of such a magazine could be produced at a very low cost by importing the American version via satellite and adding a few pages of Canadian content, thereby qualifying for the lower Canadian advertising rates that Canadian magazines could offer to advertisers. This was done in 1993 by Time Warner's immensely popular *Sports Illustrated*, which in turn triggered changes in Canadian tax law to halt the practice. By the summer of 1999, following an earlier World Trade Organization ruling against Canada and a revised and punitive Canadian law, a compromise of sorts was negotiated, requiring that split-run editions include a majority of Canadian content in order to sell advertising space at the lower Canadian rate. In recent years this issue has largely dropped from public and government attention.

The split-run issue encapsulates the essential regulatory dilemma for Canadian policy-makers grappling to preserve Canadian culture and promote domestic cultural industries. It boils down to this: the much larger American market enables US magazine publishers to produce a glossier product and pay better rates for articles at a lower per unit cost than their small-market Canadian counterparts. Moreover, Canadians have shown over the years that they like what American magazines offer. US-based publications account for about 60 per cent of total magazine sales in Canada. Availability of Canadian magazines is not the problem. According to the Canadian magazine industry's own figures there are roughly 1,200 magazines published in Canada. But with low cultural barriers between English Canada and the United States, no language barrier, and a high level of consumer and media integration between the two societies, American magazines do not seem to be foreign in the way that British or other English-language ones do.

State regulation is much more intrusive in the case of the electronic media. The original reason for treating broadcasting differently from print media was the need to prevent chaos on overcrowded airwaves. Controlling entry in a market through the licensing of broadcasters seemed the only practical solution to this potential problem. At the same time, however, broadcasting policy has always been based on the assumption that only extensive state intervention can prevent complete American domination of the Canadian market.[19]

The American "threat" is a matter of simple economics, and content regulations for both radio and television constitute one of the pillars of Canadian broadcasting policy. The CRTC establishes and enforces a complicated set of content guidelines that all licensed broadcasters must observe. The idea behind them is to ensure that more **Canadian content** reaches the airwaves than would be available without regulation (see Box 13.2).

Whether or not the system works depends on what one means by "Canadian content." If this signifies that some of the major people involved in the production of a television program or piece of music are Canadian, then the policy has been a success. But if Canadian content is taken to mean the subjects, values, and ideas conveyed through these media, then the verdict may be rather different. Over two decades ago the *Report* of the Task Force on Broadcasting (1986) characterized the content system applied to television broadcasters as "regulatory tokenism." Many of the programs that qualify as Canadian content, it observed, "could be mistaken for American productions and seem to have been made on the assumption that references to their Canadian origin would hurt their appeal to audiences outside Canada, particularly in the United States."[20] This may be true in many instances, but the popularity over the years of such recognizably Canadian programs as *Traders*, *Corner Gas*, *Little Mosque on the Prairie*, and *The Border* shows that the American clone programming format complained of by the Task Force has not always been the recipe for success in Canadian television.

Nevertheless, the pressures to produce programming whose "Canadian-ness" is not apparent have never been greater. Streamed video through Netflix and its competitors is not subject to Canadian content requirements. "Netflix is not a part of the Canadian broadcast ecosystem," complains Scott Moore, CEO of Rogers Media. "They have no Canadian-content requirements. They don't have to spend money on Canadian producers."[21] Short of imposing the sort of Internet censorship practised by such governments as those of China and Iran, it seems certain that new media will undermine whatever effectiveness remains for Canadian television content guidelines.

As in television, the economics of the recording industry encourage products that are marketable outside of Canada. Radio stations typically deal with Canadian content requirements by relying heavily on recordings by performers like Drake, Michael Bublé, Barenaked Ladies, Nelly Furtado, Avril Lavigne, and Justin Bieber, whose music seems as at home in Boston as Toronto, and, to the degree that regulations permit, by marginalizing much of their Canadian content to off-peak hours. The advent of satellite radio has presented Canadian regulators with a new version of the old challenge of Canadians' apparent appetite for American products over homegrown competitors.

Governments also affect the content of the electronic mass media through subsidies paid to Canadian film and television producers and through their direct participation in the industry as broadcasters and filmmakers. The Canadian content quotas established by the CRTC are, in the case of television, met largely through sports, news, and public affairs programming. But most viewing time is spent watching entertainment programs. Very few of these programs are Canadian, again, simply because it makes economic sense to purchase an American-made product for a fraction of its production costs—a product that, moreover, benefits from the inevitable spillover into Canada of advertising that American networks use to promote audience interest. In English-speaking Canada only the CBC broadcasts a significant amount of Canadian-made entertainment programming.

To compensate for the unfavourable economics of domestic production, Ottawa offers subsidies. This is done chiefly through Telefilm Canada, which helps to finance the production of Canadian-made feature films (over 200 of them since 1986), television programs (roughly 2,000 television programs and series since 1968), documentary films, and animation. Telefilm Canada also invests in international co-productions. If you look closely at the credits that scroll across the screen at the end of a Canadian-made television documentary, dramatic series, or children's program, chances are good that you will see that it was subsidized by Telefilm Canada. Most provincial governments also operate media funds. The most ambitious and well-funded of these is Quebec's Société de développement des entreprises culturelles.

While the publicly owned CBC, Radio-Canada, TV Ontario, and Radio-Québec have been among the major recipients of money provided through Telefilm Canada over the years, private television and film producers have also drawn on this source of public money. Fears have long been expressed that private producers typically use these subsidies

Media Spotlight

BOX 13.2 What Is Canadian Content?

Radio

According to the Canadian Radio-television and Tele-communications Commission (CRTC), a musical selection qualifies as Canadian content if it meets any two of the following criteria:

- The music is composed entirely by a Canadian.
- The music is, or the lyrics are, performed principally by a Canadian.
- The musical selection consists of a live performance that is recorded wholly in Canada, or performed wholly in Canada and broadcast live in Canada.
- The lyrics are written entirely by a Canadian.

For AM radio, at least 35 per cent of all music aired must meet this definition of Canadian content. In recognition of FM radio's diversity of formats (and the corresponding supply of appropriate Canadian content recordings), the CRTC allows different levels of required Canadian music content. The quota is as low as 7 per cent in the case of ethnic radio stations.

In the case of French-language radio stations, at least 65 per cent of the music played must have French vocals, a quota that drops to 55 per cent between 6:00 a.m. and 6:00 p.m.

Television

To be considered Canadian, a television program must have a Canadian producer and must earn a minimum six of a possible 10 points based on key creative positions. The CRTC awards points when the duties of these positions are performed by Canadians. There are additional criteria regarding financial and creative control for programs involving foreign production partners. The CRTC requires that Canadian programs be used to fill at least 60 per cent of the overall schedules of both public and private television broadcasters. Moreover, Canadian content must fill at least 50 per cent of evening programming hours for private broadcasters and 60 per cent for public broadcasters.

In fact, the Canadian content guidelines are considerably more complex than this. At the same time, since their introduction amid much controversy by CRTC chairman Pierre Juneau back in 1970, they have never mattered less. As more and more Canadians listen to radio and watch television through online streaming, which is not subject to Canadian content regulation, these guidelines appear to be increasingly futile. This is recognized by the regulators themselves. The CRTC vice-chairman, Peter Menzies, acknowledges that the CRTC "can no longer define ourselves as gatekeepers in a world in which there may be no gates." Instead, he says, it needs to find ways to "act as an enabler of Canadian expression, rather than as a protector."[22]

Source: Based on CRTC documents at: <www.crtc.gc.ca/eng/info_sht/r1.htm> and <www.crtc.gc.ca/eng/archive/1999/PB99-205.HTM#archived>.

to produce films and television programs as unrecognizably Canadian as possible so as not to alienate potential American audiences—the copycat generic productions that the 1986 Task Force on Broadcasting warned against. Again, the profit imperative in broadcasting and film works against the goal of producing and promoting distinctively Canadian cultural products. Even with the maximum level of public support that Telefilm Canada is allowed to provide, the typically low licence fees paid by Canadian broadcasters still leave a production company with a significant share of production costs uncovered. There are, therefore, economic pressures to turn out an exportable product in order to recoup costs through foreign (this will usually mean American) sales. In the case of feature films the problem is largely that the sole major distribution chain, Cineplex, which as of 2013 controlled about three-quarters of all cinemas in the country, does little to promote Canadian-made films. Nor do the companies producing these films have the resources to advertise widely to generate audience interest.

Despite the unfavourable economics of producing recognizably Canadian programs, a situation that subsidies appear not to correct, such programs do get produced. In the end it falls to public broadcasters and the National Film Board to carry most of the burden of showing Canadians what is distinctive about their society and culture. Indeed, this is what these organizations were intended to do. Under the Broadcasting Act the CBC is required to be "a balanced service of information, enlightenment and entertainment for people of different ages, interests and tastes covering the whole range of programming in fair proportion." The CBC, through its English- and French-language divisions, has done far more to Canadianize the airwaves than any other broadcaster, particularly when it comes to dramatic programming and during prime viewing hours. Its ability to do so, however, is threatened by budget cuts that began in the late 1970s. The CBC has responded by increasing its dependence on advertising. This places Canada's main public broadcaster between a rock and a hard place. On the one hand, the CBC is required to rely on Canadian programming. On the other hand, it is increasingly dependent on the revenues from the sale of advertising time, which requires that the CBC's programming achieve audience ratings that will attract and retain advertisers. Most of the CBC's advertising revenue is generated during its sports and news programs. *Hockey Night in Canada* alone has accounted for about 40 per cent of the broadcaster's revenue, and the exclusive right to this valuable property was lost to Rogers Communications at the end of 2013, although for the first four years of the Rogers agreement with the National Hockey League, beginning in 2014–15, the CBC will still broadcast a Saturday night game under the "Hockey Night in Canada" brand.

The NFB's mandate is to "interpret Canada to Canadians and the rest of the world" (Film Act). For over 70 years the NFB has done this to critical and international acclaim, turning out documentaries and serious drama that the private sector has been unwilling to produce. There is, of course, a very simple reason why private companies have not invested in these sorts of productions: the major theatre chains do not want to show them and ad-dependent television stations do not want to broadcast them. Their lack of interest in these productions, made in and about Canada, is due to their belief that they will be unprofitable. Without significantly large advertising budgets and deprived of access to commercial distribution, these films and documentaries live a sort of fugitive life in "art house cinemas," on public broadcasting stations, and through DVDs.

Media content also is affected through federal and provincial laws dealing with obscenity, pornography, and what is called hate speech. None of these terms is defined very precisely in Canadian law, but the federal Criminal Code and the Customs Act, as well as provincial statutes dealing with hate speech, restrict the sorts of printed matter and films that may enter Canada or be distributed here, as well as the media products that individuals may possess. This last restriction became extremely controversial in January 1999 when a British Columbia Supreme Court judge ruled that a 1993 federal law prohibiting the possession of child pornography violated the right to individual privacy guaranteed under the Charter. A firestorm of protest greeted the ruling, which ultimately was upheld by the Supreme Court of Canada. Civil liberties groups were critical of the law for being too general.

The issue of when and how to restrict media content raises issues of censorship, individual privacy, freedom of expression, public morality, and the safety of certain groups, such as the children who become fodder for pornographic films, magazines, and Internet sites. These issues have become increasingly complex and traditional methods used to regulate media content have been challenged by the newer media of wireless communications and the Internet. Proposals to regulate media content on the Internet have ranged from making service providers responsible for the content of the websites and e-mail carried over their networks, to a law that would require the labelling of all online information, identifying the degree of adult content. To this point, however, regulation of the Internet remains relatively light in Canada and other democracies. In 2011 Parliament passed the Act Respecting the Mandatory Reporting of Internet Child Pornography by Persons Who Provide an Internet Service. The law makes Internet service providers legally responsible to report the use of their system for purposes of child pornography to the Canadian Centre for Child Protection. Service providers are not obliged under the law to actively monitor what is communicated through their service or, in the words of the law, "seek out child pornography." The CRTC does not regulate content on the Internet.

The Technological Filter

Few things date more quickly than news. The technology of broadcasting and Internet and wireless communications is instantaneous. Even newspapers and magazines, because of their digital editions and blogging journalists, report and are expected to report events as they unfold. It seems that fewer and fewer people want day-old news, let alone news about what happened a week ago. New media are capable of providing their audiences with developments as they are happening, and this is what news audiences have come to expect.

Militating against reporting that embeds the "now" in a broader context are the limits of time, space, and the manner in which we interact with various media. When print was king, the likelihood that such context would be part of the story was greater than at present. But even then a reporter had only so many words or column inches in which to tell the story. Space to report on any particular story was scarce, given the competition with other news items, advertising, and photos that made up a newspaper or magazine.

Television, we have already noted, continues to be the medium relied on by most people for their knowledge of national and international events. The visual character of this medium lends itself to the personalization of reality—an emphasis on individuals and personalities at the expense of ideas and broad social forces that cannot be related or captured by a camera. Television and any other image-based media have a built-in predisposition towards the personal, the immediate, and the

concrete. "Reality" is conveyed as a constantly shifting pastiche of images that evoke certain feelings and generate certain associations in the minds of viewers. Critics of television and of television news reporting have long complained that those who produce the news assume that the average viewer has an attention span that lasts a minute or two at best.

Industry people are doubtless right when they claim that many viewers are easily bored and that a rapid pace and frequent jolts—scenes of action, confrontation, titillation, people and things in motion, changing venues and speakers—are necessary to capture and hold their attention. But it may also be true that viewers have been conditioned to expect what media critic Morris Wolfe has called high jolts per minute (**JPM**) television and other video. "[A] steady diet of nothing but high JPM television," Wolfe argues, "tends to condition viewers' nervous systems to respond only to certain kinds of stimulation. Their boredom thresholds are frequently so low that TV viewers find it difficult to enjoy anything that isn't fast-paced."[23] Some psychologists argue that the explosive growth in what is labelled attention deficit disorder is, in fact, a result of the impact of television and video games on the central nervous systems of children.[24] The celebration by many of infants as young as a year old being able to play games on tablets and smartphones had led the American Academy of Pediatrics, among others, to warn that early exposure to this sort of stimulation may actually damage language acquisition and learning.[25] Whatever the cause of limited attention spans might be—and they surely existed before the onslaught of new media, although perhaps not on the scale that one observes today—they surely help to explain why the average length of a televised news story is considerably shorter today than it was a generation or two ago. Politicians and others who regularly come before the eye of a camera have long understood the biases of the visual media. Photo opportunities and highly structured, controllable events are among their ways of using television's need for the immediate, the personal, and the visual to their own advantage. Television has had an enormous impact on how elections are fought, how special interests attempt to influence public policy, and how public officials communicate with the people. One of the masters of the medium, the American social activist Jesse Jackson, remarked over three decades ago on the importance of speaking in short memorable sentences—"sound bites" as they are called today. They conform to the needs of television technology; long, rambling, or complex statements do not (see Box 13.3).

Those who produce television programs, including the news, operate on the assumption that action and motion are far more likely to hold viewer attention than are "talking heads." There is, therefore, an exaggerated emphasis on action, and particularly on two-sided conflict. As Edward Jay Epstein explains:

> the high value placed on action footage by executives leads to a three-step distillation of news happenings by correspondents, cameramen and editors, all of whom seek the moment of highest action. Through this process, the action in a news event, which in fact may account for only a fraction of the time, is concentrated together and becomes the central feature of the happening. This helps explain why news on television tends willy-nilly to focus on activity.[26]

The visual character of television produces or at least exaggerates other biases as well. These include a dependence on stereotypes and an emphasis on confrontation.

Dependence on a repertory of stereotypes. Writing over 80 years ago, Walter Lippmann argued that newspaper reporting consisted largely of fitting current news to a **"repertory of stereotypes."** There are cultural reasons for this that we will discuss later. But in the case of a visual medium, there are also technological reasons for this dependence. "Viewers' interest," observes Epstein, "is most likely to be maintained through easily recognizable and palpable images, and conversely, most likely to be distracted by unfamiliar or confusing images."[27]

Emphasis on confrontation. From the standpoint of a visual medium, confrontation has two virtues. First, it involves action—things and people in

Media Spotlight

BOX 13.3 The Philosophy behind the 30-Second TV News Story

Because the television commercial is the single most voluminous form of public communication in our society, it was inevitable that Americans would accommodate themselves to the philosophy of television commercials. By "accommodate," I mean that we accept them as a normal and plausible form of discourse. By "philosophy," I mean that the television commercial has embedded in it certain assumptions about the nature of communication that run counter to those of other media, especially the printed word. For one thing, the commercial insists on an unprecedented brevity of expression. One may even say, instancy. A sixty-second commercial is prolix; thirty seconds is longer than most; fifteen to twenty seconds is about average. This is a brash and startling structure for communication since, as I remarked earlier,

the commercial always addresses itself to the psychological needs of the viewer. Thus, it is not merely therapy. It is instant therapy. Indeed, it puts forward a psychological theory of unique axioms: The commercial asks us to believe that all problems are solvable, that they are solvable fast, and that they are solvable fast through the interventions of technology, techniques, and chemistry. This is, of course, a preposterous theory about the roots of discontent, and would appear so to anyone hearing or reading it. But the commercial disdains exposition, for that takes time and invites argument.

motion—and therefore is stimulating to the eyes. Second, conflict helps to present a story in a way that viewers can easily grasp. Epstein notes that "Situations are thus sought out in network news in which there is a high potential for violence, but a low potential for audience confusion."[28] When the events themselves do not include the necessary visual drama—there is perhaps too little of it, it is too ambiguous, or it takes place over too long a period of time—this can always be provided through the use of video that has been previously recorded: action in the can and ready to go!

Marshall McLuhan's adage, "the medium is the message," reminds us of the unintended or at least not obvious consequences that the technology of communications has on the message and how it is received. Morris Wolfe, Edward Jay Epstein, and Neil Postman are among those who have taken McLuhan's insight to heart. Walter Lippmann, decades earlier, reflected this understanding with his concept of "the pictures in our heads." Their warnings about the biases of visual media were made before the ascendance of social media. It is likely that we are living through a new chapter in the evolution of communications technology with potentially profound consequences for how politics and the news are reported and how we perceive them (see Box 13.4).

Television spot ads—usually only 20–30 seconds long—are one of the major vehicles for political communication. Some worry that the medium debases the message, dumbing down the political conversation. What is the cartoonist suggesting here about Conservative spot ads critiquing Justin Trudeau?

Media Spotlight

BOX 13.4 Technology, Cognition, and How We Perceive the World

The year 2012 may be remembered as a watershed in the technology of communications. The social networking site Facebook recorded 1 billion users or about one out of seven people on the planet. A couple of years earlier Apple launched its iPad, combining several functions in a medium that is something between a laptop and a cellphone. Twitter, which began in 2008 as a social network, had acquired features of a news medium, a transition that may have dated from the Iranian elections of 2009 when Twitter was used by protesters to communicate news about their opposition to the fraud perpetrated by the regime.

The Pew Internet and American Life Project reported that the Internet had surpassed newspapers as a source for news. National and local television stations remained the top two sources of news. But changes appeared to be underway. One-third of cellphone users said that they use the medium to get news and over one-third of those with Internet access claim to have contributed to the news food chain by commenting on a story or disseminating one via Twitter or Facebook. Nicholas Carr's *The Shallows: What the Internet Is Doing to Our Brains* argues that "Whereas the Internet scatters our attention, the book focuses it. Unlike the screen, the page promotes contemplation."[29] Online media, Carr argues, may make us dumber in certain ways, reducing our capacity for creativity and the ability to make cognitive connections, on which intelligence largely rests.

Clearly, technology has transformed the processes by which news is gathered, reported, distributed, and consumed. But as the Pew Project for Excellence in Journalism observes in its 2010 annual report,[30] the impacts are neither simple nor quite what many people believe. The Pew Report identifies several trends driven by changing technology, including the following:

- "Online consumers are not seeking out news organizations for their full news agenda. They are hunting the news by topic and by event and grazing across multiple outlets."
- Old and new media are tied together. New media still have a limited capacity to generate content and rely on traditional media sources for reporting capacity.
- Reportorial journalism—what newspapers and other traditional news outlets do—is shrinking, but commentary and discussion in the media—what cable, radio, social media, blogs, and websites do—is growing.
- "Technology is shifting power to newsmakers, and the newest way is through their ability to control the initial accounts of events." The potential for the manipulation of public opinion through carefully crafted news management may be greater than ever.
- Ease of entry into the blogosphere, social networks, and Internet-based sites has produced enormous growth in the number and ideological range of those reporting, interpreting, and commenting on the news and vying for audiences.

What are we to make of all this? It appears that, for our information about and interpretation of the world, we increasingly rely on media that discourage reflection and contemplation. In turn, these new media rely for most of their content on old media that have fewer resources than in the past for reporting the news. Commentary, interpretation, and opinion comprise an increasingly large share of news coverage communicated through the new media. And the possibilities for news management may be greater today than ever before, as those who make the news are able to get their message framed and communicated directly to audiences via Twitter, Facebook, blogs, and cellphone messages that do not depend on intermediaries. Of course, it is also easier than ever before for people to participate directly in the news system rather than depending on the top-down technologies of the past. So, should we worry about technological change and its consequences or welcome them?

The Organizational Filter

News-gathering and reporting are carried out by organizations. The needs and routine procedures of these organizations influence the content of the news: both what is reported and how it is covered. The organization's dilemma is that news developments are not entirely predictable, and it does not have the resources to be everywhere news might break or to cover all stories equally well. News organizations rely on various strategies to deal with this reality.

In the case of television, several criteria help to impose predictability on the news. Those who have a reputation for being influential or who occupy an official position of some power are more likely to make the news than those whose public profile is lower or whose position does not, in the eyes of news gatherers, automatically confer on them a mantle of credibility. Prime ministers, premiers, and the leaders of opposition parties are assumed to be newsworthy, as are mayors and leading councillors when the news item is local. Spokespersons for what are considered to be important and representative organizations—the Canadian Council of Chief Executives, the Canadian Labour Congress, Equality for Gays and Lesbians Everywhere (EGALE), the Catholic Church, and so on—are also considered to be newsworthy and can count on being sought out when an issue falls into their sphere of concern.

Government officials and powerful private interests understand that news organizations operate within a system of routines and requirements including, for example, the need to have the evening news video recorded by a certain hour to allow time for editing and the rest of the production process. Accommodating the media's needs through well-timed press conferences, photo opportunities, news releases, and staged events—what sociologist Daniel Boorstin once labelled "pseudo-events"—is simple prudence from the standpoint of groups that want to affect public opinion. This practice has been called **news management**. Obviously, governments and the public affairs/media relations bureaucracies of the powerful are not able to control the news agenda. But they are able to influence news reporting and they certainly try. Indeed, part of what government consulting firms are often hired to do is to manage the media strategy of a client.

Publicly acknowledged experts also are sought out by the media. Affiliation with a respectable institution is one of the key determinants of this status. Specialists who are associated with an established institution like the C.D. Howe Institute, the Canadian Centre for Policy Alternatives, the Fraser Institute, or a university—particularly a university located in a city where a media organization has production facilities, although the use of Skype has reduced the importance of proximity to video facilities—are those most likely to be considered newsworthy. The point here is not that only the usual voices will be heard on an issue, but that spokespersons for mainstream views are almost certain to receive a hearing because their institutional affiliation confers on them the status of "acknowledged expert." Spokespersons for marginal groups and unconventional views are much less likely to be deemed newsworthy.

The mass media's demand for the ideas and information generated by experts is based on a combination of factors. One of these is the media's self-image as dispenser of the news and reporter of the facts. Fulfillment of this role requires access to sources of information whose credibility is sound and whose claim to objectivity is generally accepted. Related to this is a second factor: the media's need for low-cost information and instant analysis. To conduct their own analysis would be expensive and time-consuming. Moreover, most journalists are not professionally trained as economists, epidemiologists, constitutional lawyers, political scientists, or whatever other field of expertise a story may call for. It makes economic sense to tap the knowledge of those whose training, reputation, and/or institutional affiliation confer on them the social standing of expert. Third, to protect themselves against charges of bias and lawsuits, media organizations and reporters need information whose accuracy can be reasonably assumed or, and this may amount to the same thing, where an effort has been made to acquire such information. Expert knowledge meets this criterion, and that provided by those with socially respected professional or institutional credentials is particularly useful.

The authority of conventional journalists is today challenged by blog sites and bloggers. The debate over whether bloggers deserve to be considered journalists has been ongoing for more than a decade. In some ways the question may seem to be ridiculous, given that all but a small minority of professional journalists blog, tweet, and maintain the same sort of social media presence as those whose journalistic credibility they disdain. In fact, however, bloggers have won investigative reporting awards and many of the most followed and influential blog sites have editors.[31] Blogging and tweeting have very definitely affected the way mainstream journalists and their employers work, such that when it comes to reporting, the old distinction between "old" and "new" media is no longer particularly useful. As more and more of the news-gathering and reporting enterprise migrates to cyberspace, the organizational filter affects the coverage of politics and public affairs in new ways. Content, as a quick perusal of news stories at Yahoo.ca shows, still comes chiefly from newspapers, press agencies like AP and Reuters, and traditional broadcasters. But as more and more people come to rely for their news about the country and the world on Facebook, Twitter, WordPress, and other social media sites, the dominant role of traditional news organizations will continue to be under pressure. Another challenge comes from what the Pew Center says is a continuing decline in news reporting resources at newspapers, magazines, and television broadcasters. "For news organizations," concludes Pew's 2013 report on the State of the Media, "distinguishing between high-quality information of public value and agenda-driven news has become an increasingly complicated task" (see Box 13.5). The Pew Center's unsettling observations are based on developments in the American media system. Can Canada be far behind?

The Ideological Filter

Those who report the news are often accused by conservatives and business people of having liberal-left and anti-business biases. They are more likely, it is argued, to favour stories and groups that challenge established authority. The CBC in general and some of its programs in particular have occasionally been accused of ideological bias against conservatism and big business (especially American business). Similar charges have been heard in the United States, where Republicans, conservatives, some religious groups, and business interests have often accused the major networks, and journalists generally, of having liberal biases.

The evidence for this claim is mixed. Studies done in the United States a generation ago found that media respondents typically gave more liberal responses to such statements as "Government should substantially reduce the income gap between rich and poor."[32] The researchers concluded that "leading journalists seem to inhabit a symbolic universe which is quite different from that of businessmen, with implications for the manner in which they report the news to the general public."[33] Several recent American studies have confirmed that those in the media, particularly the electronic media, tend to be much more liberal than members of the general population.[34] A somewhat dated study of CBC radio, directed by Barry Cooper, concluded that "on the whole, [the CBC] adopted a left-wing, rather than right-wing critical stance."[35] His study of CBC television news coverage arrives at a similar conclusion, although Cooper expresses it rather differently. "The CBC," he argues, "like all modern media, has directed its energies towards the production of a specific configuration of opinion—namely progressive opinion—and not toward the provision of reliable information about the world."[36]

This conclusion is reinforced by what is probably the most systematic study of Canadian journalists' values and beliefs to date.[37] Based on a survey of 270 electronic and print journalists and a sample of the general public (804 respondents), Cooper and Lydia Miljan draw two main conclusions. First, English-Canadian journalists tend to be more left-of-centre than the general public, a finding that corroborates Cooper's earlier studies. Second, the left-leaning proclivities of journalists affect the way news stories are reported, a finding that may appear unsurprising but does not exactly square with the media's credo of objectivity. Among the ways in

Media Spotlight

BOX 13.5 What Are the Consequences of Media Industry Restructuring?

Signs of the shrinking reporting power are documented throughout (our 2013) report. Estimates for newspaper newsroom cutbacks in 2012 put the industry down 30 per cent since 2000 and below 40,000 full-time professional employees for the first time since 1978. In local TV, our special content report reveals, sports, weather and traffic now account on average for 40 per cent of the content produced on the newscasts studied while story lengths shrink. On CNN, the cable channel that has branded itself around deep reporting, produced story packages were cut nearly in half from 2007 to 2012. Across the three cable channels, coverage of live events and live reports during the day, which often require a crew and correspondent, fell 30 per cent from 2007 to 2012 while interview segments, which tend to take fewer resources and can be scheduled in advance, were up 31 per cent. *Time* magazine, the only major print news weekly left standing, cut roughly 5 per cent of its staff in early 2013 as a part of broader company layoffs. And in African-American news media, the *Chicago Defender* has winnowed its editorial staff to just four while *The Afro* cut back the number of pages in its papers from 28–32 in 2008 to around 16–20 in 2012. A growing list of media outlets, such as *Forbes* magazine, use technology by a company called Narrative Science to produce content by way of algorithm, no human reporting necessary. And some of the newer non-profit entrants into the industry,

such as the Chicago News Cooperative, have, after launching with much fanfare, shut their doors.

This adds up to a news industry that is more undermanned and unprepared to uncover stories, dig deep into emerging ones or to question information put into its hands. And findings from our new public opinion survey released in this report reveal that the public is taking notice. Nearly one-third of the respondents (31 per cent) have deserted a news outlet because it no longer provides the news and information they had grown accustomed to.

At the same time, newsmakers and others with information they want to put into the public arena have become more adept at using digital technology and social media to do so on their own, without any filter by the traditional media. They are also seeing more success in getting their message into the traditional media narrative. . . .

Efforts by political and corporate entities to get their messages into news coverage are nothing new. What is different now—adding up the data and industry developments—is that news organizations are less equipped to question what is coming to them or to uncover the stories themselves, and interest groups are better equipped and have more technological tools than ever.

Source: Pew Research Center.
State of the News Media report for 2013,
http://stateofthemedia.org/2013/overview-5/

which English-Canadian journalists differ from their audiences and readerships are the following:

- Journalists are less religious than the public, 57 per cent saying that they did not espouse a particular religious faith and 32 per cent saying that they definitely believed in God compared to 39 per cent (no religious affiliation) and 56 per cent (definitely believe in God) for the university-educated public.

- Although the ideas of private-sector journalists on the desirability of capitalism, free markets, and private property are broadly the same as those of the general public, the views of the public-sector CBC journalists are significantly to the left.
- The public is more conservative on social issues than those in the media. For example, journalists are more likely than the general public to believe that abortion should

Carlos Osorio/GetStock.com

Was the introduction of new personalities such as outspoken entrepreneur and venture capitalist Kevin O'Leary one of CBC's strategies to combat critics claiming it has an ideological bias against conservatism and big business? Known for his philosophy "Greed is good," O'Leary co-hosted the *Lang and O'Leary Exchange* on CBC Newsworld and sat on the investors' panel on CBC television's *Dragon's Den* until he left the CBC to join CTV in 2014.

be considered a moral and legal right and a much greater share of the public than journalists believes that gay and lesbian issues receive too much media attention.

- Journalists are considerably more likely than the general public to vote for the NDP, the highest level of NDP support by far being among CBC radio journalists.

Miljan and Cooper also note that French-Canadian journalists are closer to their audience/readership in their political and social views than are English-Canadian journalists to theirs.

On the other hand, recent studies by researchers at McGill University found no evidence of a left-leaning partisan bias in the case of Canadian newspapers. Based on their analysis of campaign coverage in 2004 and 2006 in seven major dailies (*Globe and Mail, National Post, Calgary Herald, Vancouver Sun, Toronto Star, La Presse,* and *Le Devoir*), they found that reporting tended to be quite neutral between the parties and, on the whole,

negative towards all of them. Editorial coverage, however, was characterized by partisan favouritism. The party most likely to be on the receiving end of positive editorial coverage was the Conservative Party, hardly the result one would expect to find if those in the media have a left-of-centre bias. In 2006 and 2008 all of the country's leading newspapers, with the exception of the *Toronto Star*, endorsed the Conservative Party.[38] When Aboriginal protests associated with the Idle No More movement dominated the Canadian media landscape in early 2013, many opinion leaders in the Aboriginal community and critics on the left charged that the Canadian media, including major newspapers and several of the country's most prominent journalists, were guilty of conservative, anti-Native biases. Clearly, not everyone agrees with the claim that the sympathies of Canada's media system are on the left.

But even if left-of-centre political and social views are more often found among those in the media than in Canadian society as a whole, this ideological gap needs to be understood in the context of what "left" and "right" mean in Canadian society. "Left" does not mean fundamental opposition to the basic institutions of the capitalist economy. To be on the left in the predominantly liberal societies of Canada and the United States has always meant to be ambivalent about business—to distrust excessive concentrations of economic power and to believe that business must be regulated, while accepting the superiority (in most circumstances) of private property and the market system of allocation. This is the ambivalence of family members who do not see eye to eye on all matters at all times.

News and public affairs reporting focuses on conflict and controversy, often that involving government officials and powerful private interests, which naturally gives the impression that those in the media are anti-establishment critics. The impression is somewhat misleading. Only a minority of those in the mass media—albeit a few colourful and occasionally influential ones—have strong left-wing or right-wing commitments. Those on the right, such as David Frum, Ezra Levant, and Mark Steyn, and those on the left, such as Linda McQuaig, David Suzuki, and Naomi Klein, are the exceptions rather than the rule in Canadian journalism. Most journalists occupy locations towards the middle of the ideological spectrum and generally experience little difficulty in accommodating themselves to the needs of the organization within which they work, their employer's sensitivities, and the values and beliefs of those who consume what they write and say.

It bears repeating that most of what the mass media produce does not fall into the categories of news and public affairs. It should not be assumed, however, that the entertainment and information products of the media industry carry no political messages or ideological biases. They do, both through the images, themes, and interpretations they communicate and through their silences. If the mass media are "more important in confirming or reinforcing existing opinions than they are in changing opinions,"[39] as studies generally suggest, this is partly due to the ideological orthodoxy of most writers, producers, editors, and others who have an influence on the media product.

This is not to suggest there is no place in the mass media for people whose political views lie outside the safer familiar mainstream. The proliferation of blogs in the media system has made such views more accessible than in the past. The point is, however, that those who work in media industries cluster mainly in the familiar centre of the political spectrum. For these cultural workers the other four filters affecting media content are largely beside the point. The conformity of their value systems with that of society's dominant ideology ensures that they seldom, if ever, test the limits of what the system will allow.

In his website on journalism and democracy, *PressThink*, Jay Rosen argues that instead of thinking of those in the media as tilting the political playing field to the left or the right, their more important ideological function is "to place certain people, causes and ideas within the deviant sphere" and therefore to deny them a place in the cultural and political conversation.[40] If these deviant ideas and their promoters are acknowledged at all, they are likely to be framed in a narrative that characterizes them as "dangerous," "fanatical," "hateful," and "extreme"—in short, illegitimate. This treatment was once the fate of communist ideas and thinkers, particularly in the United States during the Cold War.

We should not imagine that members of the media do not perform this ideological function in Canada or in any other democracy, helping to reinforce a sphere of consensus. This does not mean that points of view that fall outside of this ideological consensus will not be heard. But their spokespersons, Rosen says, will "experience the press as an opponent in the struggle for recognition."[41] Spokespersons for "deviant" points of view may nevertheless find a forum for their ideas via the Internet, where all manner of marginal and socially unrespectable ideas manage to thrive.

The Media and Democracy

In regard to propaganda the early advocates of universal literacy and a free press envisaged only two possibilities: the propaganda might be true, or it might be false. They did not foresee what in fact has happened, above all in our Western capitalist democracies—the development of a vast mass communications industry, concerned in the main with neither the true nor the false, but with the unreal, the more or less totally irrelevant. In a word, they failed to take into account man's almost infinite appetite for distractions.[42]

The media, it often appears, have few friends except themselves. Only about one in three Canadians expresses a high degree of trust in journalists.[43] Politicians, business people, and those on the right of the political spectrum regularly accuse the media of having liberal-left biases, of irresponsible scandal-mongering, and of being inherently and unfairly opposed to established authority. Those on the political left, however, are no less critical of the media. They are apt to view the media as the servile handmaidens of powerful interests, particularly economic ones. Both ideological camps, right and left, accuse the media of having strongly anti-democratic tendencies. Conservatives argue that those in the media tend to be more liberal-left than society as a whole, but that they foist their interests and perspectives on the public behind a smokescreen of journalistic detachment and objectivity. Left-wing critics of the media claim that the media are **"manufacturing consent"**[44] for a social system—including political and economic structures—that operates mainly in the interests of a privileged minority. What the mass media foist on the public, leftist critics charge,

are less their own ideological biases than the false consciousness of the dominant ideology.

In this chapter we have argued that the behaviour of the mass media is shaped by a number of filters. These filters cumulatively determine the sort of "product" likely to reach the consuming public. Our conclusion is that the products of the mass media are generally supportive of established values and institutions. Thus, the media tend to reinforce the power of those groups whose interests are best served by the status quo. In order to play this role it is not necessary that the media avoid all criticism of powerful interests. This would be a ludicrous claim. All that is necessary is that an overwhelming preponderance of what appears on the page and screen and over the airwaves conforms to mainstream values. This test is amply met.

On the other hand, the gains made in recent years by socially marginal, politically weak interests,

Media Spotlight

BOX 13.6 "Bye-bye Japan" and "Canada is already full": How Can Citizens Know Who and What to Believe?

David Suzuki is known to most Canadians. Indeed, in separate polls conducted in 2013, Suzuki was found to be the most admired and the most trusted person in the country. His CBC program, *The Nature of Things*, has been watched by millions of Canadians since it began in 1960. Suzuki has hosted it since 1979. If Canadians have a go-to person for the truth, especially scientific and environmental truth, it is likely to be David Suzuki.

And so it may have been particularly disturbing to hear his pronouncement in October 2013 on the imminent disaster that awaits Japan and people living on the west coast of North America as a result of the Fukushima nuclear reactor. Seriously damaged by a tsunami that hit Japan in 2011, the reactor is in the process of being decommissioned by the Japanese. But the process is too slow and risky and the perilous state of the damaged reactor is being hidden by the Japanese authorities and

a complicit media, said Suzuki to an audience at the University of Alberta. "(I)f there's another earthquake of a seven or above that, that building will go and then all hell breaks loose," he warned. "And the probability of a seven or above earthquake in the next three years is over 95 per cent." If and when this happens, Suzuki continued, it will be "bye-bye Japan" and, he said, the west coast of North America should be evacuated.

This is an apocalyptic prediction. Suzuki was once a practising scientist, although not a nuclear physicist or engineer. His dire warnings are shared by many anti-nuclear activists, but not by most scientists.[45] Canadians, or at least many of them, tend to find Suzuki credible on issues involving science and the environment. Should those on the British Columbia coast get ready to move to Alberta?

Only a couple of months before Suzuki's warning about an imminent Fukushima disaster, he told the such as Aboriginal Canadians, LGBT persons, and environmental activists, have been in large measure due to media coverage of their demands and spokespersons (see Box 13.6). This, in turn, has raised public consciousness of the issues and discourse—"Aboriginal self-government," "social justice," "sustainable development"—associated with their demands. Moreover, it can hardly be denied that the media usually do a better job of scrutinizing and criticizing government actions, to say nothing of those of powerful societal groups, than do the opposition parties in Parliament. Indeed, it is precisely the critical and even irreverent tenor of much public affairs journalism that contributes to the widespread belief in the mass media's independent and anti-establishment character.

On balance, the media do an uneven job of providing Canadians with the information needed to make informed judgments about their society and its political issues. The biases of the mass media are towards familiar images and stories—what Lippmann called a "repertory of stereotypes"—oversimplified conflict, the personalization of events, drama and action, and reliance on established opinion leaders. These biases are much more supportive than threatening of the status quo. At the same time, citizens cannot avoid shouldering some of the responsibility for whatever information deficit they experience and ill-founded views they hold. For all the problems surrounding the quality of what may be found via the Internet, there is also no doubt that it has put within the reach of almost everyone an unprecedentedly vast range of information and points of view. If you don't like what you find on the CBC or in the pages of the *Globe and Mail*, go online and get your information elsewhere. Reliance on the same old sources of news and public affairs is a choice, not an inevitability.

French news magazine *L'Express* that, like Australia, "Canada is also full! Even though it is the second largest country in the world," he said, "our useable land surface has been reduced. And our immigration policy is disgusting. We pillage the countries of the southern hemisphere depriving them of their future professionals, and we want to increase our population so as to favour economic growth. It's crazy!"[46] Polls show that most Canadians think the current level of immigration is just fine and that immigration is important for economic growth. Most economists agree with them. Who should Canadians believe, David Suzuki or those experts and policy-makers, including many who admire Suzuki, who disagree with him on immigration, population growth, and the economy?

Democracies rely on the open exchange of information and opinion. The media constitute the major source of this information and opinion, relied on by citizens in forming, confirming, and challenging their ideas about matters from their neighbourhood to the other side of the world. What is a non-expert to do when someone as respected as David Suzuki expresses views that, if they came from someone less known and less esteemed, might be ignored or viewed skeptically?

Whether Suzuki is right or wrong about these particular issues, his is a voice that is listened to by many. Oftentimes we judge the truth or at least the probability of what we hear or read on the basis of the source, in this case the person expressing a particular view. There is a constant and unavoidable danger that, as citizens who necessarily rely on the media for information on which we base our own views, we will selectively tune in certain voices and tune out others. But even the highly admired and respected are not always right.

Starting Points for Research

Barry Cooper and Lydia Miljan, *Hidden Agendas: How Journalists Influence the News* (Vancouver: University of British Columbia Press, 2003). This is one of the few empirical studies of the nature and causes of media bias, and probably the best.

Paul Nesbitt-Larking, *Politics, Society, and the Media: Canadian Perspectives*, 2nd edn (Toronto: University of Toronto Press, 2007). Nesbitt-Larking offers a comprehensive and critical examination of the characteristics and political and social impacts of Canada's media system.

Florian Sauvageau, David Taras, and David Schneiderman, *The Last Word: Media Coverage of the Supreme Court of Canada* (Vancouver: University of British Columbia Press, 2005). An analysis of media coverage, in French and English Canada, of a handful of major Supreme Court rulings.

Stuart Soroka, *Agenda-Setting Dynamics in Canada* (Vancouver: University of British Columbia Press, 2002). Following eight separate policy issues, this book examines the interaction of the media, public opinion, and policy-makers in setting and shaping the policy agenda.

Review Exercises

1. Keep a two-day record of your media consumption, being sure to write down all the television programs and films you watch, the amount and sorts of radio programming you listen to, the newspapers, magazines, and books you read, and your social media and Internet activity. Try not to change what would be your normal pattern of viewing/listening/reading/surfing. Based on this record, answer the following questions:
    (a) What proportion of your daily media consumption is normally devoted to entertainment? News and public affairs? Other purposes?
    (b) Which medium (or media) do you most rely on for news about your local community, your country, the international scene?
    (c) If and when you pick up a newspaper, which section do you read first? What else do you look at in the newspaper? What about the Internet? How often do you click on news stories? Do you rely on blogs, social media, or particular websites to keep you informed? Are they Canadian?

2. Watch the late-evening television news broadcast of one of the main Canadian broadcasters (CBC, CTV, or Global). Make a list of those stories where experts are interviewed, quoted, or referred to (for example, "A study by the C.D. Howe Institute . . ."). Record the positions and, if possible, affiliations of the experts (e.g., professors, government officials, think-tank researchers, activists, etc.). Can you suggest other sorts of experts or organizations that could have been contacted for any of these stories?

3. Visit the websites of *The Guardian* <www.guardianunlimited.co.uk>, National Public Radio <www.npr.org>, the British Broadcasting Corporation's World Service <www.bbc.co.uk>, the *Western Standard* <www.westernstandard.ca>, <www.ipolitics.ca>, <www.adbusters.org>, and <www.motherjones.com>. Have you ever used any of these websites? Do you think many Canadians are aware of them? Do you think they provide perspectives or coverage of national or world affairs that is different from what is offered by the media outlets relied on by most people?

Part V
Contemporary Issues in Canadian Political Life

The complex interplay of ideas, institutions, and processes is best understood through the examination of particular issues that roil the political waters. For example, the long-standing conflict between French and English Canadians, a conflict historically rooted in language, ethnicity, values, and an imbalance in power, has been played out within the framework of particular institutions and managed through certain processes that have evolved over the more than 250 years that French- and English-speakers have lived under the same political roof in what today is Canada. These institutions and processes have affected the relationship between the two communities, at the same time as the values and demographic characteristics and circumstances of these communities have also shaped the laws, constitutional changes, and processes that influence their relations. Case studies of particular issues enable us to untangle the complex web of cause and effect that exists between ideas, institutions, and processes in the real world of politics.

The next four chapters will focus on several important issues in Canadian politics, all of which are crucial to an understanding of what might be described as the Canadian condition. The first involves language politics and Quebec, home to about nine out of 10 French-speaking Canadians. This is the oldest continuing conflict in Canadian politics. The second issue involves women and politics, including the developments that have taken place in laws, attitudes, and social conditions pertaining to women and their participation in politics. The third issue, which in many ways is just as old as the French–English conflict, although it was pushed below the surface of Canadian politics for most of the time Canada has been a country, involves Aboriginal Canadians and their relationship to other citizens and governments in Canada. The final chapter examines Canada's relations with the rest of the world, with a particular emphasis on Canada–US relations. Together, the study of these issues helps us to understand the Canadian political condition as it has evolved over time and as it exists today.

14

Language Politics

Conflict over language has always been a central feature of Canadian politics. This chapter explains why language and the status of Quebec are such prominent issues in Canada. It also examines the chief aspects of federal and Quebec language policies. Topics include the following:

- The demographics of language politics.
- The shift from French-Canadian nationalism to Quebec nationalism.
- The Quiet Revolution and its legacy.
- Language policy in Quebec.
- Federal language policy.
- Is Quebec a distinct society?

St Jean Baptiste Day is a national holiday in Quebec held annually on 24 June. The crowd here is assembled for the annual show on the Plains of Abraham. The holiday was originally a religious festival, but has become more politicized (and sometimes violent) in Canada in the years since the Quiet Revolution. (© Robert Wagenhoffer/Corbis)

For almost half a century Quebec has had a political party, the Parti Québécois, whose first principle is the independence of Quebec. Since its first victory in Quebec's 1976 election, the PQ has governed the province for just about half of the last 40 years. Another separatist party, the Bloc Québécois, emerged onto the federal scene in 1990, becoming the official opposition in the House of Commons after the 1993 election. The BQ was the most successful federal party in Quebec between 1993 and the 2011 election. Public opinion polls taken since the creation of the PQ show that support for Quebec independence is never lower than about one-quarter of the population and, most of the time, the percentage has been closer to 40 per cent. Two referendums have been held on the question.

Well before the possibility of Quebec separating from Canada arose, tensions, misunderstandings, and occasional ill will between French- and English-speaking Canadians existed. Indeed, they go back to the British military conquest of New France, when French-speaking Catholic colonists suddenly found themselves ruled by a minority who did not share their language or their religion. After the 1837 rebellions in Upper and Lower Canada, the British authorities sent the Earl of Durham to the Canadian colonies to report on the causes of political unrest. Lord Durham's report is best remembered for his observation that he found "two nations warring in the bosom of a single state." French and English Canadians would find themselves on opposing sides of many issues in the decades that followed Confederation, including Canada's participation in the Boer War, World War I, conscription for military service in World War I and II, and French-language educational rights in Ontario and Manitoba, to mention only some of the conflicts that divided them. "The Two Solitudes,"[1] the title of Hugh MacLennan's 1945 novel of two families, one French and one English, became shorthand for the distance separating Canada's two ethnolinguistic communities.

At the same time, the story of relations between French and English Canada, and between predominantly French-speaking Quebec and the rest of Canada, has not been one of unmitigated and continuous conflict. French and English Canadians have often voted for the same leaders, liking such politicians as Wilfrid Laurier, Mackenzie King, Louis St-Laurent, Pierre Trudeau, and Jean Chrétien, albeit to varying degrees. They have celebrated many of the same successes, particularly when it comes to international hockey and the Winter Olympics (sports seems to be a great if transient unifier in many divided societies). And it cannot go unremarked that they are still living under the same constitution and sending politicians to the same Parliament almost 150 years after Confederation. Few political systems can boast such longevity. But the conflicts remain important, and no account of Canadian politics, past and present, is complete without an understanding of the language issue and Quebec nationalism.

The Demographics of Language Politics

When New France was formally placed under British control in 1763, francophones outnumbered anglophones by about eight to one in the territory that would become Canada. Forty years later, the two groups were of roughly equal size. From the late 1700s through the mid-1800s the English language gained ground on the French because of the wave of immigrants from the United States and then the British Isles, so that by the 1871 census—Canada's first—Canadians of French origin comprised about one-third of the population.[2] The exceptionally high birth rate among French-Canadian women enabled francophones to hold their own until the end of the 1950s against an English-speaking population that was buoyed by immigration. Regardless of their ancestry and native language, immigrants overwhelmingly adopted English as their new language. Since then, birth rates have dropped precipitously in Quebec, where the vast majority of francophones reside, and the francophone share of Canada's population has nudged down to its present all-time low of about 22 per cent (see Figure 14.1).

The end of *la revanche des berceaux*—the high birth rate that for close to a century enabled French

Canada to maintain its numerical strength against English Canada—coupled with the fact that the vast majority of immigrants have chosen English as their adopted language, finally led to a decline in the francophone share of the Canadian population by the early 1960s. More worrisome from the standpoint of Quebec governments was that demographers began to predict a fall in the francophone share of that province's population, particularly in Montreal where most new immigrants chose to establish themselves. Montreal, which proudly called itself the second largest French-speaking city in the world (after Paris), was expected to be about equally divided between anglophones and francophones by the early twenty-first century.[3] The possibility that francophones would become a minority in Quebec was often raised by Quebec nationalists, although serious demographers like Jacques Henripin argued that this possibility was quite remote.[4] Nevertheless, this decline provided the impetus for provincial language laws intended to stem this tide.

The key factor in shifting the linguistic balance of Quebec, it should be emphasized, was immigration. Given that the province's anglophones were no more fecund than francophones, the language

choices of allophones—Canadian demographers' term for those whose native language is neither English nor French—would be crucial in shaping the linguistic landscape of Quebec. Immigration became the sole contributor to provincial population growth by the 1960s, given that the provincial fertility rate had fallen below the replacement level (i.e., the average number of births per female needed to offset the mortality rate).

With the exception of the relatively few immigrants whose native tongue was French, all other groups overwhelmingly adopted English for themselves and their children. As of the 1961 census, 46 per cent of foreign-born residents of Quebec spoke only English, another 25 per cent spoke English and French, and only 17 per cent spoke only French. Despite provincial language laws that require immigrants to send their children to French schools, make French the sole official language for provincial public services, and promote the use of French in the Quebec economy, evidence indicates that many allophones still opt for English. Figure 14.2 shows that the percentage of Quebecers claiming French as their mother tongue is almost identical to the percentage who speak mainly French in the home. But the percentage

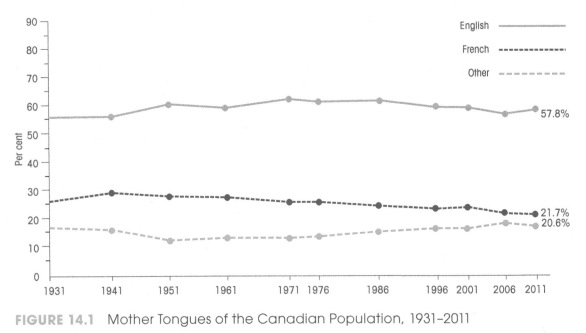

FIGURE 14.1 Mother Tongues of the Canadian Population, 1931–2011

Source: F.H. Leacy, ed., *Historical Statistics of Canada*, 2nd edn, Series A185–237 (Ottawa: Minister of Supply and Services Canada, 1983); *Canada Year Book* (1990), 2–25; Statistics Canada, *2011 Census of Population*, at: <www.statcan.ca/>.

speaking English in the home is greater than that which claims English as its mother tongue. The gains made by the English-speaking community can only be explained by the linguistic choices of those whose mother tongue is neither French nor English. New Quebecers have continued to find English an attractive choice, although less often than before the existing provincial language laws were put into place.

Inside Quebec, the current demographic picture includes the following characteristics.

- French is spoken at home by about 80 per cent of the population (2011 census).

- Contrary to projections made in the 1960s and early 1970s, Quebec has not become less francophone. The 80 per cent of the population speaking French at home compares to 80 per cent in 1901 and 81 per cent in 1961.
- Most of the province's population increase is due to immigration and consequently the linguistic choices made by newcomers to Quebec are crucial to the language balance in the province. According to the 2011 census, about 40 per cent of allophones say they speak French at home most of the time or regularly compared to 30 per cent who speak English at home most of the time or

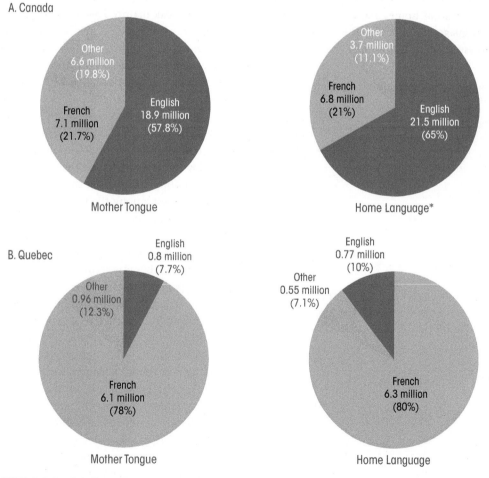

FIGURE 14.2   Mother Tongue and Language Spoken at Home, 2011

*Percentages may not total 100 because those answering English and French, English or French and a non-official language, or English and French and a non-official language are not included.

Source: Statistics Canada, *Census of Canada*, 2011.

regularly. About 30 per cent say they speak their native non-official language at home.

- Quebec's share of Canada's total population has fallen over the last two decades, from 28 per cent in 1971 to about 23 per cent in 2013.

Outside Quebec the language picture looks very different. With the exceptions of New Brunswick and Ontario, the francophone populations of the other provinces are tiny. In fact, in certain provinces and in all but a handful of Canada's major metropolitan areas outside Quebec, some of the non-official-language communities are considerably larger than the French-speaking minority. For example, in Vancouver the number of people who speak French at home, mainly or along with another language, is about 29,000. Those who speak Chinese at home outnumber them by about a 10:1 ratio. Those who speak Punjabi at home outnumber those who speak French by a 4:1 ratio. In Toronto those who speak Chinese at home outnumber those who speak mainly French or French along with another language. Those who speak French at home are also outnumbered by those who speak Urdu, Punjabi, Tamil, Tagalog, and Spanish.

In all provinces except Quebec, the French-language community continuously loses some of its members to the English majority. This may be seen from the difference between the number of people for whom French is their mother tongue compared to the number for whom it is their home language. The difference represents the rate of language transfer to the dominant language group (see Table 14.1). Only in Quebec, where the number of people who speak mainly French at home exceeds the number who have French as their mother tongue, and in New Brunswick is the rate of French-language retention high. By contrast, the rate of language retention among native English-speakers is high everywhere in Canada.

This is not a recent development. In *Languages in Conflict*, Richard Joy carefully documented the trend towards the assimilation of francophones outside Quebec. Joy was the first to make what today seems an obvious point, namely, that the rate of language transfer is greatest among the younger generations. For example, using data from the 1961 census he found that the transfer rate from French to English in the four western provinces was 25 per cent among those aged 45–54, but was 60 per cent for those aged 5–14 and 67 per cent among infants aged 0–4.[5] Only in what Joy called the **bilingual belt**, the narrow region running from Moncton, New Brunswick, in the east, to Sault Ste Marie, Ontario, in the west, was the rate of assimilation among all generations significantly lower. The reason, of course, was the ability to shop, work, go to church, and do the other things that keep a language alive. Outside the bilingual belt, this supportive milieu was seldom encountered. Indeed, the 2001 census showed that the francophone population in every province except Quebec and New Brunswick was older than in Canada as a whole, confirming Joy's prediction that the failure to retain young francophones would contribute to the steady erosion of the community's base.

TABLE 14.1 Percentage and Number of Those Whose Mother Tongue is French and Whose Main Language Spoken at Home is French: Canada, Provinces, Territories, and Canada Less Quebec, 2011

Province	Percentage	Number
NL	47.5	1,435
PEI	48.6	2,765
NS	52.2	18,055
NB	90.0	216,055
Que.	103.5*	6,450,370
Ont.	60.6	340,295
Man.	45.2	21,550
Sask.	29.3	5,550
Alta	39.9	32,390
BC	34.9	24,445
Yukon	60.0	945
NWT	52.4	610
Nunavut	56.7	255

*More people speak French most often at home than have French as their mother tongue.

Source: Statistics Canada, *Census of Canada*, 2011.

At this point some readers may protest that the gloomy picture Joy drew three decades ago is no longer accurate. They will point to statistics that suggest bilingualism outside of Quebec has been increasing in recent years. Indeed, it is today highest among the young, the very group that Joy argued was most likely to transfer to the dominant language group. The rapid expansion of French immersion schools since the 1980s, particularly in Ontario, which accounts for over half of all immersion students in Canada, is responsible for most of this increase. The future of French outside Quebec, they argue, is assured.

What is one to conclude from the fact that while the francophone share of Canada's population outside of Quebec has been declining, the proportion of the population claiming to be bilingual has been increasing? Does this represent a reprieve for French-language minorities? Or are they, as René Lévesque once said, "dead ducks," or as Quebec writer Yves Beauchemin characterized them, "des morts vivantes" ("warm corpses" would be a reasonable translation)?

The pressures of assimilation continue to be intense throughout most of the predominantly English-speaking provinces. A 1990 study by Roger Bernard of the University of Ottawa concluded that a combination of aging populations, low birth rates, marriage to non-francophones, and the general lack of supportive social and economic milieux for French speakers was leading to the collapse of many francophone communities outside Quebec.[6] The 2001 census found that about 50 per cent of married francophones living outside Quebec and New Brunswick had anglophone spouses. Generally, English becomes the lingua franca and the language of the children in such families, even if the children go to French-language or immersion schools. It appears, however, that the fate of larger francophone communities in northern and eastern Ontario and in New Brunswick may be less bleak.

BEFORE... APRÈS...

In 2013, an Italian restaurant in Montreal was cited for using the Italian language on its menu. The portrayal of Quebec's language laws in English Canada is usually extremely critical; usually, the enforcement of these laws is represented with police or military figures, as above.

Graeme MacKay/Artizans.com

Already in 1988, Jacques Henripin cautiously suggested that official bilingualism in New Brunswick and the extension of French-language services and education in Ontario may have slowed the assimilationist tide in those provinces.[7]

As for the increasing level of bilingualism in Canada, which in fact has levelled off in recent years (Table 14.2), we should not be too quick to conclude that the prospects for living in French outside of Quebec have improved. The census question that measures bilingualism ("Can you carry on a conversation in the other official language?") does not provide a measure of languages in use. The fact that increasing numbers of those whose mother tongue is English claim to be functionally fluent in French does not mean that French will be used more often in the home, the workplace, at the pub, and wherever else communication takes place. Indeed, a good deal of evidence suggests that three decades of French immersion education[8] have produced a wave of **receptive bilinguals**— people who are capable of responding to French

TABLE 14.2   Bilingualism in Canada, 1961, 2001, 2011

	1961		2001		2011	
	thousands	%	thousands	%	thousands	%
Canada	2,231.2	12.2	5,231.6	17.7	5,795.6	17.5
Newfoundland and Labrador	5.3	1.2	20.9	4.1	23.5	4.6
Prince Edward Island	7.9	7.6	16.0	12.0	17.0	12.3
Nova Scotia	45.0	6.1	90.3	10.1	93.4	10.3
New Brunswick	113.5	19.0	245.9	34.2	245.9	33.2
Quebec	1,338.9	25.5	2,907.7	40.8	3,328.7	42.6
Ontario	493.3	7.9	1,319.7	11.7	1,395.8	11.0
Manitoba	68.4	7.4	102.8	9.3	103.1	8.6
Saskatchewan	42.1	4.5	49.0	5.1	46.6	4.6
Alberta	56.9	4.3	202.9	6.9	235.6	6.5
British Columbia	57.5	3.5	269.4	7.0	296.7	6.8
Yukon	0.8	5.6	2.9	10.2	4.4	13.1
Northwest Territories including Nunavut	1.6	7.0	4.1	6.5	4.9	6.8
Northwest Territories	n.a.	n.a.	3.1	8.4	3.7	9.1
Nunavut	n.a.	n.a.	1.0	3.8	1.2	3.8
Canada excluding Quebec	892.3	6.9	2,323.9	10.3	2,466.8	9.7

n.a. = not applicable

Source: Jean-François Lepage and Jean-Pierre Corbeil, "The Evolution of English-French Bilingualism in Canada from 1961 to 2011," Statistics Canada (May 2013), at: <www.statcan.gc.ca/pub/75-006-x/2013001/article/11795-eng.pdf>.

communications but do not themselves initiate conversations in French, consume French-language media, or seek out opportunities to live in their acquired second language. A recent study by Statistics Canada notes that bilingualism peaks during school years among anglophones but then drops off over the years as a result of lack of continued exposure to French. In Quebec, however, both francophones and anglophones are more likely to remain bilingual over their life cycle due to greater second-language exposure in that province than elsewhere in Canada.[9] None of this is an argument against bilingual education anywhere in Canada. But claims that four decades of immersion education in Canada have contributed significantly to the greater use of French in the workplace, the home, and public spaces outside Quebec should be viewed with a certain amount of caution.

Moreover, despite 40 years of immersion education in Canada, the rate of functional bilingualism is still relatively low outside of Quebec, at 9.7 per cent in 2011.[10] Almost 60 per cent of all bilingual Canadians reside in Quebec, where the rate of bilingualism is about four times greater than in Ontario. The increase in the level of bilingualism in Quebec since the 1960s has been greater than in the rest of Canada. This is simply to say that Canadian bilingualism is to a considerable degree a predominantly Quebec phenomenon. In fact, the most recent census found that the level of bilingualism among anglophones outside Quebec has declined in recent years.

The bottom line is that the social and economic milieux outside Quebec have not become more supportive for francophones. While provincial government services for the francophone communities of

Ontario have improved since the mid-1980s, and those in New Brunswick are quite good, few people outside the "bilingual belt" can manage to shop, work, and do the other daily social activities in French that help keep a language alive. Even francophone schools in predominantly English-speaking communities experience the pressures of language erosion. René Lévesque's characterization of francophones outside Quebec as "dead ducks" is somewhat overstated. Lame ducks might be closer to the truth.

The Trajectory of Nationalism

French-Canadian nationalism, Pierre Trudeau writes, was originally a system of self-defence. This was certainly true. Conquered by arms, the French-speaking people of New France found themselves subordinated to an anglophone minority about one-eighth their size. English was the language of the new political and commercial elites. The **Conquest of 1759** left French a second-class language within Quebec, and francophones were largely excluded from the colony's structures of power.

Why did francophones not succumb to assimilationist pressures, as they did in Louisiana after it, too, passed from French control? The answer is complex, but three chief factors can be identified. One involved the policies of the British colonial authorities in New France. By the terms of the Quebec Act, 1774, they granted formal protection to the status of the Roman Catholic religion and the *code civil*, the basis of civil law in New France.[11] Faced with rebellion in the Thirteen Colonies, which two years later successfully declared their independence from Britain, this recognition for the rights of the French-Canadian population may have been motivated chiefly by the desire to ensure the allegiance of the clerical and civil leaders of that population. Regardless, it involved official recognition of the rights of the francophone Catholic majority and reinforced the leadership role of that community's clerical elite.

A second factor that explained the different fates of the French language and culture in Louisiana compared to Quebec was demography. French-speakers in the south of the United States were very quickly swamped by a rapidly growing anglophone population. But as we observed earlier in this chapter, although immigration from the United States and then the British Isles tipped the linguistic balance in Canada towards English by the early nineteenth century, the high fertility rate among French Canadians enabled them to hold their ground at about one-third of Canada's population between Confederation and the 1950s.

The defensive posture that Trudeau argues was characteristic of French-Canadian nationalism is the third factor that explains the ability of French Canada to resist the pressures of assimilation. Under the guidance of a clerical elite whose leading social role was strengthened when anglophones occupied the political and commercial elites of the colony, French Canada met the challenge of English domination by remaining loyal to traditional values and institutions. The nationalist ideology that developed in French Canada after the Conquest is summed up in a famous passage from *Maria Chapdelaine*, the classic novel of traditional French Canada:

> Round about us strangers have come, whom we are wont to call barbarians; they have seized almost all the power; they have acquired almost all the money, but in the country of Quebec nothing has changed. . . . [W]e have held our own, so that, it may be, after several centuries more, the world will turn to us and say: these people are of a race that knows not how to perish . . . . In the country of Quebec, nothing shall die, and nothing shall be changed.[12]

Traditional French-Canadian nationalism was guided by the idea of *la survivance*—survival, against the pressures of a dominant culture that was anglicizing, Protestant, materialistic, liberal democratic, and business-oriented. In other words, this dominant anglophone culture was all the things that French Canada, according to the spokespersons for this ideology, was not and should not become. The main ideas expressed in the writings and public pronouncements of the exponents of the traditional nationalism may be summarized briefly:

- French Canada comprised a distinct nation, whose chief characteristics were the Catholic religion and the French language. Preservation of the French language and the Catholic religion were considered inseparable, as the title of Henri Bourassa's book *La langue, guardienne de la foi*[13] explicitly declared. "The preservation of language," Bourassa wrote, "is absolutely necessary for the preservation of a race, its spirit, character and temperament."[14]
- French Canada had a mission, a special vocation as a people. The mission was to remain faithful to its roots, and to resist the lure of materialistic, English, Protestant pressures. The democratic belief in the separation of church and state was seen to be a lamentable heresy spawned by the French Revolution, the American Constitution, and liberalism generally.
- The character of the French-Canadian people was most secure in the province of Quebec, but French Canada was not restricted to the boundaries of that province. In other words, French Canada was defined by sociocultural characteristics, not by the territory of Quebec.

While these were the chief characteristics of the nationalist ideology that became dominant in French Canada during the nineteenth century, a dominance that it maintained until the middle of the twentieth century, there were voices of dissent. In fact, sociologist Marcel Rioux argues that the idea of the French-Canadian nation was first developed by the secular elites of Quebec who espoused liberal and often aggressively anti-clerical views.[15] Political scientist Denis Monière concurs, noting that the authority of the Church was much weaker before and in the decades immediately following the Conquest than is usually believed (especially by English-Canadian historians).[16] He maintains that the "victory" of the conservative

traditional nationalism became assured only after the defeat of Louis-Joseph Papineau's liberal forces in the Lower Canada Rebellion of 1837. Even after the ideological dominance of the Church and the voices of traditional rationalism were firmly established, however, liberal voices of dissent were occasionally heard.[17]

The traditional nationalism came under mounting pressure during the middle of the twentieth century. Its chief tenets were increasingly at odds with the economic and social reality of Quebec. The emigration of hundreds of thousands of French-speaking Quebecers to the northeastern United States during the 1800s demonstrated more clearly than anything else the weakness of the traditional nationalism's hymn to the pastoral vocation of French Canadians. There simply was not enough arable land to support the rural parish lifestyle that the ideologues of the traditional nationalism clung to so tenaciously. The urban population of Quebec surpassed the rural population in the 1921 census (56 per cent to 44 per cent). Between 1926 and 1950 the number of people employed in Quebec's manufacturing sector increased by about 220 per cent, slightly higher than the rate of increase for Canada as a whole (210 per cent), but significantly higher than the rate for the rest of the country if Ontario— where most new investment in manufacturing was located—is omitted from the picture.[18] By mid-century manufacturing workers outnumbered farm workers in Quebec by a large margin.[19] In short, by the early twentieth century the "typical" Québécois lived in a city or town, worked in a factory, store, or office, and had family members who had left the province in search of employment opportunities. It was no longer the rural, agrarian society idealized by the traditional nationalism.

Quebec was following the path of modernization. The urbanization and industrialization that this involved also produced a political side effect of enormous importance. This was the increasing realization that francophones, despite accounting for about four-fifths of the Quebec population, were largely shut out of the centres of economic decision-making and controlled relatively little of the province's wealth. "Is there any inherent or unavoidable reason why," asked Abbé Lionel Groulx in 1934, "with 2,500,000 French Canadians in Quebec, all big business, all high finance, all the public utilities, all our water rights, forests and mines, should belong to a minority of 300,000?"[20] Although the question was not new—Édouard Montpetit, Errol Bouchette, Étienne Parent, and others had raised basically the same issue in arguing that educated francophones needed to rid themselves of their apparent distaste for careers in industry and finance—it was being asked with increasing frequency between the 1930s and the 1950s.[21]

These decades saw the emergence of the first serious challenge to the conservative ideology since the crushed rebellion of 1837. It brought together a diverse group of university professors and students, journalists, union activists, liberal politicians, and even some elements within the Catholic Church (particularly Action catholique). They were united by their opposition to the so-called **"unholy alliance"** of the Catholic Church, anglophone capital, and the Union Nationale party of Maurice Duplessis—and, of course, to the conservative nationalism that seemed unconcerned with French Canadians' marginal economic status. Marcel Rioux calls this anti-establishment challenge the ideology of contestation and recoupment.[22] It contested the traditional elites' monopoly over power in the province and what was argued to be their backward characterization of French-Canadian society and culture. Its goal was to recoup lost ground; to bring Quebec's society, economy, and government up to date, a goal that became known in Quebec as **rattrapage** (catching up).

The nerve centre of this challenge to the conservative establishment and ideology included the Faculty of Social Sciences at Laval University; the intellectual revue **Cité libre**, founded by such figures as Pierre Trudeau and Gérard Pelletier; and the provincial Liberal Party. As the political party attempting to defeat Duplessis, it was natural that the Quebec Liberal Party would attract the energies of those who saw the Union Nationale under *le chef* as one of the principal obstacles to reform.

The traditional ideology and the interests it defended were doomed by their failure to adapt to a changing environment. As Marcel Rioux observes, "[T]he ideology and old power structure in Quebec were becoming anachronistic in the face of the demographic, economic, and social changes that Quebec was experiencing."[23] They managed to hold on until the 1960s largely because of the tight web of patronage politics that Maurice Duplessis used to keep the ideologically conservative Union Nationale in power for most of the period from 1936 until his death in 1959. His death was followed by disorder within the governing Union Nationale. Paul Sauvé, who succeeded Duplessis as Premier, died suddenly within a year. The Union Nationale went into the 1960 provincial election under a leader, Antonio Barrette, who was opposed by many powerful members of the party. The Liberal Party's election victory probably owed as much to disorder within the Union Nationale as to popular support for change. Regardless, the opportunity for reform had come.

The Quiet Revolution and Its Legacy

The first several years of the 1960s are justly considered a turning point in the history of Quebec. Duplessis's death in 1959 and the election of the provincial Liberals under Jean Lesage in 1960 opened the way for the political reforms and social changes referred to as the **Quiet Revolution**. At the heart of these reforms lay an increased role for the Quebec state. It replaced the authority of the Catholic Church in the areas of social services and education, and also acquired a vastly broader range of economic functions. The provincial state was seen as the *moteur principal* of Quebec's attempt to modernize social and political institutions that were ill-suited to the urbanized, industrialized society that Quebec had become. The state, traditionally viewed as a second-class institution in a province where most social services were controlled by the Church and where government was associated with crass patronage, became the focus of nationalist energies.

The nationalism that emerged in the crucible of the Quiet Revolution marked a sharp break with the past. The traditional nationalism had emphasized preservation of the *patrimoine*—the language, the faith, the mores of a community whose roots went back to New France. Although some of its chief spokespersons, such as Abbé Lionel Groulx, associated this community with the region of the St Lawrence River and even with the vision of a Laurentian state whose territory would include what is today the southern region of the province, the essential elements of the traditional nationalism were not defined by either the territory or the powers of the Quebec state.

Rioux has characterized the traditional nationalism as an ideology of conservation. Its goals were the preservation of the traditional values and social structures of French Canada, including the leading role played by the Church in articulating these values and controlling these structures (i.e., the schools, hospitals, labour unions, etc.). The modern welfare state necessarily threatens the dominant social role of the Church and was generally rejected by spokespersons for the traditional nationalism. Although they insisted on constitutional protections for the province's exclusive right to make education policy and put limits on Ottawa's ability to interfere with social affairs in the province, they did not expect that the Quebec state would actively occupy these fields. The traditional nationalism attached no particular value to the Quebec state, except insofar as its powers could be used to ward off federal intrusions that challenged the status of conservative values and the power of the traditional elites—the clergy, anglophone business leaders, and provincial politicians.

Boris Spremo/GetStock.com

A man paints a fleur-de-lys—a symbol of Quebec—on a building under the words "We know what we want" at the time of the 1980 referendum, which sought a mandate for the provincial government to negotiate with the rest of Canada a new status for Quebecers. The new nationalism that arose during the Quiet Revolution was—and still is—felt keenly by supporters of a sovereign Quebec.

Nationalism is always based on some concept of the nation: who belongs to it and who does not. The traditional nationalism did not identify *la nation canadienne-française* with *la société française du Québec*. The boundaries of *la nation* extended beyond Quebec to embrace French Canadians throughout Canada. There were two reasons for this. First, Catholicism and the role of the Church were important elements of the traditional nationalism. Obviously, neither of these stopped at the Quebec border. Second, the anti-statist quality of the traditional nationalism prevented it from associating the French-Canadian nation with the Quebec state.

History had shown that assimilationist pressures and unsympathetic governments faced francophones outside of Quebec. Nevertheless, to identify *the nation* with the Quebec state would have challenged the dominant social role of the Church. The survival of the nation did not depend, according to the traditional nationalism, on the activities of the Quebec state. Instead, it depended primarily on those institutions that were crucial to the continuation from generation to generation of the French language and the Catholic religion—family, school, and parish. Family and parish obviously fell outside the state's authority. And although the schools were under the constitutional jurisdiction of the provincial state, their control was mainly left in the hands of the Church. This did not change until the early 1960s.

The central elements of the traditional nationalism were located outside of the state. This would not be true of the new nationalism that both spurred and was influenced by the Quiet Revolution. Instead of defining *la nation* in terms of language and religion, the ascendant nationalism of the 1960s developed an understanding of Quebec's history, its economy, and its social structure that was based on language and dependency. The dependency perspective portrayed Quebec as a society whose evolution had been shaped and distorted by the economic and political domination of English Canadians.

This secularized version of French-Canadian history, and more particularly of francophone Quebec, cast an entirely different light on the future of the Quebec nation and its relationship to English Canada. If the problem was that Québécois were dominated economically and politically, then the solution required that they take control of their economic and political destiny. To do so, they would have to use the Quebec state. All of the major reforms of the Quiet Revolution—the establishment of a provincial ministry of education, the nationalization of privately owned hydroelectric companies, the creation of Crown corporations like la Caisse de dépôt et placement and la Société générale de financement, and passage of the Quebec Pension Plan—involved using the Quebec state in a newly assertive way.

The replacement of the traditional nationalism by the state-centred nationalism of the Quiet Revolution was not as abrupt as history might suggest, nor was this new nationalism unchallenged. The traditional social order and its values had been crumbling at the edges for at least a couple of decades before the deaths of Duplessis and then of Sauvé finally provided the opportunity for opposition groups to gain power. Once the doors were opened to reform, it quickly became apparent that the anti-Duplessis forces shared little more than a common antipathy towards the old order. They were divided on at least three main levels.

First, there was a split between the federalists and those who advocated either special status or independence for Quebec. The federalists included such prominent figures as Pierre Elliott Trudeau, Jean Marchand, and Gérard Pelletier, all of whom entered federal politics through the Liberal Party in 1965. Leadership of the Quebec autonomy side would fall on René Lévesque, formerly a popular television journalist who had masterminded the nationalization of the hydroelectric industry as a minister in the Lesage government and who became the first leader of the Parti Québécois in 1968.

The second division concerned the size and functions of the Quebec state. Even within the reformist Liberal government of Jean Lesage, sharp differences existed over such major policies as the nationalization of the hydroelectricity industry and the role of the province's investment agency, la Caisse de dépôt et placement. Agreement that the provincial state should play a larger role in Quebec society was not matched by consensus on what that role should be.

Finally, Quebec separatists were divided on ideological lines. Those who came to form the leadership of the *indépendantiste* Parti Québécois, such individuals as René Lévesque, Jacques Parizeau, and Claude Morin, were ideologically liberal. But there were others, within the PQ and in other pro-independence organizations, for whom Quebec independence was inseparably linked to the overthrow of what they argued was a capitalist state. PQ members Pierre Bourgault and Robert Burns, for example, wanted the end of *la domination anglaise* of the Quebec economy but also a radical redistribution of economic power between classes in the province. Although the electoral strength of these left-wing groups never amounted to much, they managed to have a significant impact on political discourse in Quebec, particularly through the province's universities and labour unions and in the extra-parliamentary wing of the PQ.

In view of these divisions, two developments justify the claim that a state-centred nationalism emerged out of the Quiet Revolution. First, the identification of French Canada with the territory of Quebec was a view shared by most nationalists. Indeed, the entry of Trudeau and his fellow federalists into national politics was chiefly a reaction to this Quebec-oriented nationalism. The provincial Liberals' 1962 campaign slogan, **Maîtres chez nous**—masters in our own house—captured a nationalist consensus that ever since has been an accepted tenet of Quebec politics. Second, key institutional reforms of the Quiet Revolution, including the Caisse de dépôt et placement, Hydro-Québec, and the jurisdictional terrain that the Quebec government wrested from Ottawa in the areas of social policy, immigration, and taxation, have left an important mark on Quebec nationalism. They constitute the key institutions and policies of the provincial state upon which the aspirations summed up in the phrase *Maîtres chez nous* depend.

The Unilingual Approach of Quebec

We are Québécois. . . . At the core of this personality is the fact that we speak French. Everything else depends on this essential element and follows from it or leads us infallibly back to it.[24]

The origins of present-day language policy in Canada lie in developments in Quebec during the 1960s. With the election of the Quebec Liberal Party in 1960, the political obstacles to change were largely removed and the outdated character of the traditional ideology was exposed. It was replaced by an emphasis on catching up with the level of social and economic development elsewhere. As many commentators have observed, the construction of the Manicouagan dam in northern Quebec and the development of long-distance lines to transmit electrical power to southern markets—engineered and built by Québécois—became a popular symbol for the new confidence in the ability of French-speaking Quebecers to cope with a modern world and to compete economically. The state, traditionally viewed as a second-class institution in a province in which most social services were controlled by the Church and government was associated with crass patronage, became the focus of nationalist energies. The fact that the new nationalism of the Quiet Revolution turned to the provincial state, in which French-speaking Quebecers were unquestionably in the majority, reinforced the identification of French Canada with the territory of Quebec.

The ideology of *rattrapage* and the identification of French Canada with Quebec had important consequences for language policy in that province. As the instrument for economic and social development, the Quebec state assumed functions previously administered by the Church authorities and also expanded the scope of its economic activities. In doing so it provided career opportunities for the growing number of educated francophones graduating from the province's universities. Access to high-paying managerial and technical jobs in the private sector, however, remained blocked by anglophone domination of the Quebec economy. The relative exclusion of francophones from positions of authority above that of foreman and the concentration of francophone businesses in the *petites et moyennes enterprises* sector of the economy had long been known.[25] This situation ran directly counter to the expectations of the Quiet

Revolution and became an important political issue when the capacity of the public sector to absorb the increasing ranks of highly educated francophones became strained.

Demographic trends comprised an additional factor that shaped provincial language policy in Quebec. Immigrants to the province overwhelmingly adopted the English language. This fact, combined with the dramatic reduction in the birth rate among francophones, lent credibility to a scenario where francophones might eventually become a minority within Quebec. Along with evidence of the exclusion of francophones from much of the province's economic structure, these trends formed the basis for the policy recommendations of the Quebec Royal Commission of Inquiry on the Position of the French Language and on Language Rights in Quebec (the Gendron Commission, 1972). The Commission recommended that the provincial government take legislative action to promote the use of French in business and in the schools. These recommendations were translated into law under the Quebec Liberal government that introduced the Official Language Act[26] and in the Charte de la langue française[27]—or **Bill 101** as it was more commonly known outside Quebec—passed under the subsequent Parti Québécois government.

The principal features of Bill 101—principles that continue to guide language policy in Quebec—include the following.

1. French is established as the sole official language in Quebec, subject to the bilingual requirements imposed on Quebec courts and the province's legislature by s. 133 of the Constitution Act, 1867. In the public services, including the working language of provincial and municipal institutions and of public utilities, as well as the language of communication between these organizations and Quebec citizens, French is the only official language. Certain recognized bodies and institutions, including school boards, municipalities, and hospitals, where those served are mainly non-francophones, may be allowed to provide services in English, but they must also "ensure that their services to the public are available in the official language."[28]

2. Through the requirement that businesses with 50 or more employees receive a *francisation* certificate as a condition of doing business in the province, the Quebec government seeks to increase the use of French as a working language of business in the province. The Charter of the French Language does not establish linguistic quotas for corporations. Instead, it leaves the conditions of certification a matter for individual negotiations between a firm and the Office de la langue française. Despite some initial resistance from the anglophone business community, symbolized by the immediate move of Sun Life's head office from Montreal to Toronto in 1977, this section of Quebec's language law has generally been accepted by employers. More controversial have been the provisions requiring that public signs and advertisements be in French only. A 1988 decision of the Supreme Court ruled that this ban violated the freedom of expression guaranteed in the Charter of Rights and Freedoms.[29] The signage provisions of Quebec's language law were modified in 1989 through Bill 178, which required that exterior commercial signs be in French only, but allowed bilingual interior signs so long as the French language was more prominently displayed. These provisions were amended again in 1993 through Bill 86, which states that the rules governing when signs must be unilingual French and when other languages are allowed shall be established by government regulations—a more flexible approach than enshrining the rules in the statute.[30]

3. The provisions of Bill 101 that initially excited the most controversy were those restricting access to English-language schools in Quebec. Under this law, children could enrol in an English school if one of the following conditions was met: their parents had been educated in English in Quebec; they had a sibling already going to an English school; their parents were educated in English outside of Quebec but were living in the province when the law was passed (1977); they were already enrolled in an English school when the law came into effect. The intent, obviously, was to reverse the overwhelming preference of immigrants for the English language, a preference that demographers predicted would eventually change the linguistic balance in the province, and even more dramatically in Montreal, which attracted the vast majority

of immigrants. In one of the first Supreme Court decisions on the Charter of Rights and Freedoms, the Court held that the requirement that at least one of a child's parents must have been educated in English in Quebec violated section 23 of the Charter, a section that clearly had been drafted with Bill 101 in mind. The practical importance of this ruling is small, given the low level of migration to Quebec from other Canadian provinces. More significant is the fact that the Supreme Court was unwilling to accept the Quebec government's argument that the demographic threat to the position of the French language justified this restriction on language rights under the "reasonable limits" section of the Charter. In 1993 the education provisions of Bill 101 were brought into conformity with s. 23 of the Charter.[31]

Despite some setbacks in the courts, the principles on which Quebec's language policy rests have remained substantially unchanged since the passage of Bill 101. Controversy over the application of the Charter of the French Language erupts from time to time, often over the alleged non-compliance of small businesses with regulations made under the law (see Box 14.1). The dramatic decline in the English-language school system—the number of students enrolled in these schools has dropped by about 150,000 since the 1970s—is another factor that upsets the province's English-language minority. This decline is, of course, a measure of the success of the Charter of the French Language. Indeed, the province's language policy has achieved its two main objectives, namely, increasing the use of the French language in the Quebec economy and stemming the decline in the francophone share of the provincial population.

Language policy in Quebec has been shaped by the idea that the survival of French Canada depends mainly on what happens within the boundaries of that province. The Office de la langue française and the law it administers build on an approach to language promotion that can be traced back to the early 1960s. The Liberal government of Jean Lesage set out to increase francophone participation in the economy through such provincial institutions as la Société générale de financement, la Caisse de dépôt et placement, Sidérurgie québécoise, and an expanded Hydro-Québec.[32] Subsequent governments, Liberal and Parti Québécois alike, built on the foundation laid during the Quiet Revolution. The common denominator since then has been the use of the provincial state as an instrument for the promotion of the French language and the socio-economic advancement of francophones.

The Bilingual Approach of Ottawa

A very different approach to language policy—one based on a conception of French and English Canada that cuts across provincial borders—has been pursued by successive federal governments since the 1960s. Responding to the new assertive nationalism of the Quiet Revolution, the signs of which ranged from Quebec's demands for greater taxation powers and less interference by Ottawa in areas of provincial constitutional responsibility to bombs placed in mailboxes and at public monuments, the Liberal government of Lester Pearson established the **Royal Commission on Bilingualism and Biculturalism**. As Eric Waddell writes, "The federal government was facing a legitimacy crisis in the 1960s and 1970s and had the immediate task of proposing a Canadian alternative to Quebec nationalism."[33] The B&B Commission was a first step towards the adoption by Ottawa of a policy of official bilingualism. This policy was to some degree intended to defuse the *indépendantiste* sentiment building in Quebec, especially among young francophones, by opening Ottawa as a field of career opportunities to rival the Quebec public service.

The alternative Ottawa offered, and that was expressed in the federalist philosophy of Pierre Trudeau, was of a Canada in which language rights would be guaranteed to the individual and protected by national institutions. In practical terms this meant changing the overwhelmingly anglophone character of the federal state so that francophones would not have grounds to view it as an "alien" level of government from which they were largely excluded. These changes have been carried out on two main fronts.

First, what Raymond Breton refers to as the "Canadian symbolic order" has been transformed since the 1960s.[34] Through a new flag, the proclamation of "O Canada" as the official national anthem, new designs for stamps and currency, and the neutralizing of language in the names of some federal institutions, documents, and celebrations (for example, Trans-Canada Airlines became Air Canada, the BNA Act is now officially titled the Constitution Act, 1867, and what was once officially known as Dominion Day is now called Canada Day), a deliberate attempt has been made to create symbols that do not evoke Canada's colonial past and British domination.

Second, the passage of the Official Languages Act (1969) gave statutory expression to the policy of bilingualism that had been set in motion under Lester Pearson. This Act established the Office of the Commissioner of Official Languages as a "watchdog" agency to monitor the three main components of language equality set forth in the Act: (1) the public's right to be served by the federal government in the official language of their choice; (2) the equitable representation of francophones and anglophones in the federal public service; and (3) the ability of public servants of both

Media Spotlight

BOX 14.1 Do "Pasta" and "Fish and Chips" Threaten the French Language in Quebec?

Quebec's language watchdog is backtracking after demanding a chic Montreal Italian restaurant change its menu because Italian words such as "pasta" were too predominant. The Office québécois de la langue française (OQLF) said it may have been over-zealous in its attempt to promote French language in public places. "The office will consider this restaurant's particular situation while taking into account exceptions relating to foreign specialties," said the OQLF in a release late Wednesday.

Massimo Lecas, owner of Buonanotte, said he was contacted by the OQLF on Valentine's Day. He said he was told the menu contains too much Italian. Lecas said he wants his menu to retain a certain Italian flavour, but he says authorities told him words such as *botiglia*, *pasta*, and *antipasto* should all have a French translation written next to them.

Earlier in the day, Martin Bergeron, a spokesman for the OQLF, said the language watchdog is not splitting hairs. While he said he cannot discuss the specifics of the case, Bergeron said the law is clear. "Other languages can be on the menu," he said. "The thing is they must not be predominant over French."

Brit & Chips, a fish and chip restaurant in the Côte-des-Neiges neighbourhood, also received a letter asking it to comply with the language police's guidelines. The OQLF demanded that the owner, Toby Lyle, add the word "restaurant" predominantly above the eatery's name. The province's language watchdog also asked him to change the signs on the washrooms and reduce the size of the English lettering on its "take away" sign. "That's no problem," said Lyle. "We're going to comply with that."

Lyle said he takes issue with the OQLF's order to translate the restaurant's main dish to "poisson frit et frites." He said removing "fish and chips" from the window will push customers away. "If it's going to negatively impact business—a small business in Quebec—then it's obviously a misapplication of the law," he said.

Late Wednesday, OQLF spokesman Martin Bergeron said officials may have misinterpreted the law. "If it's only the name of the dish, if it's an exotic name in the language of origin, that won't be a problem," he said. He said the exception would likely include the exotic dish of fish and chips.

Source: CBC News, "Quebec Language Police Target Restaurants over Language Use," 20 February 2013, at: <www.cbc.ca/news/canada/montreal/is-pasta-french-enough-for-quebec-1.1301918>.

language groups to work in the language of their choice. The situation that the Official Languages Act was intended to redress was one where francophone representation in the federal state was less than their share of the national population. Francophone under-representation was greatest in managerial, scientific, and technical job categories (see Figure 14.3). Moreover, the language of the public service—the language that officials worked in and, in most parts of the country, the language in which citizens could realistically be expected to be served—was English. In view of these circumstances, Ottawa's claim to "represent" the interests of francophones lacked credibility.

Among the main actions taken to increase the bilingual character of the federal bureaucracy have been language training for public servants, the designation of an increasing share of positions as bilingual, and the creation of the National Capital Region as the office blocks of the federal state spread across the Ottawa River into Hull (now Gatineau), Quebec, during the 1970s. Language training for public servants was perhaps the most controversial of these measures. In his annual report for 1984 the Commissioner of Official Languages, D'Iberville Fortier, noted that a relatively small proportion of public servants in positions designated bilingual appeared to have acquired their second-language skills as a result of taxpayer-funded language training. This led Fortier to question the extent to which language training was capable of making public servants effectively bilingual, particularly anglophones who were the main consumers of federal language courses.[35] Fortier's successors occasionally have expressed similar reservations, and over the last couple of decades the focus has shifted away from training current public servants in the other official language to recruiting people who already have the language skills needed for particular positions.

In view of the fact that two of the objectives of the Official Languages Act have been to increase the number of francophones recruited into the public service and to improve francophones' opportunities for upward mobility within it, the designation of positions according to their linguistic requirements probably has been the most significant feature of Ottawa's language policy.

As of 2012, 45 per cent of positions in the federal public service were designated either bilingual or French, about two-thirds of these at a superior proficiency level. Bilingualism is most likely to be required for public service positions in the National Capital Region (Ottawa–Gatineau), Quebec, and outside Canada, at 67 per cent, 66 per cent, and 99 per cent, respectively.

Evidence on recruitment to the federal public service and upward mobility within it demonstrate that the linguistic designation of positions *has* worked to the advantage of francophones. In recent years close to one-third of new appointments to the federal public service have gone to those who claim French as their mother tongue, a level significantly higher than the approximately 22 per cent of the Canadian population comprised of native French speakers. A clear majority of appointments to bilingual positions are filled by francophones. This is true for both new appointments to the public service and for reappointments within the federal bureaucracy, about 70 per cent of each going to francophones. But as the Commissioner of Official Languages regularly observes, increased representation of francophones should not be taken as an indication that French and English are approaching greater equality as *languages of work* in the federal state. Outside of federal departments and agencies located in Quebec, the language of work remains predominantly English. Surveys carried out by the Commissioner of Official Languages between 2005 and 2011 found that francophone public servants were regularly required by their workplace circumstances to communicate in their second official language. And inside Quebec, the ability of anglophone public servants to work in English was often limited.[36]

According to the current Commissioner of Official Languages, Graham Fraser, not enough has changed since this indictment of federal government inaction on one of the major objectives of the Official Languages Act. "Managers don't realize," he states in his 2009 annual report, "that maintaining a work culture that, in many cases, is totally unilingual hinders the public service's efforts to offer quality bilingual services to the public. The domination of English as the lingua franca of the bureaucracy persists even in the National Capital Region."[37] This has led some critics to conclude that French has become a valuable attribute from the standpoint of career advancement, without becoming a working language on a par with English. This may be a fair assessment of the situation, at least outside Quebec.

The policy of designating federal public service positions by their linguistic requirements and increasing the number of positions requiring proficiency in both official languages has certainly increased the bilingual character of Canada's public service as a whole. At the same time, however, most of this bilingualism has been concentrated in the federal bureaucracies of the National Capital Region (66 per cent bilingual), Quebec (67 per cent), and New Brunswick (54 per cent). In the rest of

Canada the percentage of federal public servants who are required to be bilingual is quite low. It is 11 per cent in Ontario outside of the National Capital Region and under 5 per cent in most other provinces. The linguistic polarization of the federal public service on regional lines has been lamented by some Commissioners of Official Languages. It is, however, a not very surprising consequence of the rather small size of francophone minorities in all provinces except Ontario and New Brunswick.

Ottawa's language policy acquired two additional thrusts in the 1970s. The first of these has involved financial assistance to organizations and individuals seeking to defend or expand the rights of official-language minorities and to local francophone cultural organizations outside of Quebec. Most significant in terms of results has been

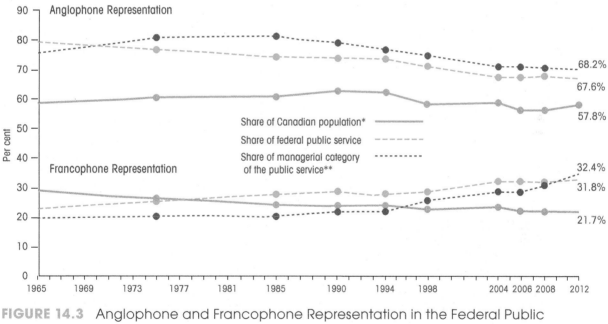

FIGURE 14.3 Anglophone and Francophone Representation in the Federal Public Service as a Whole, in the Management Category of the Public Service, and in the Canadian Population, 1965–2012

*Data for the representation of French- and English-language groups in the Canadian population are taken from the censuses for various years. The question refers to mother tongue, and therefore the figures do not add up to 100 per cent. The most recent census was conducted in 2011.

**The 1965 survey used to determine the language of those in the management category asked respondents to indicate their mother tongue; 5.2 per cent indicated a language other than English or French.

Source: Figures provided in various annual reports of the Commissioner of Official Languages, the *Canada Year Book, the Report of the Royal Commission on Bilingualism and Biculturalism*, volume 3A (Ottawa: Queen's Printer, 1969), 215, table 50, and Treasury Board of Canada Secretariat, *Annual Report on Official Languages*, at: <www.tbs-sct.gc.ca/reports-rapports/ol-lo/11-12/arol-ralo/arol-ralo06-eng.asp#sec6>.

Politics in Focus

BOX 14.2 Another Model for Language Rights: The Case of Belgium

Canada and Belgium have often been compared in regard to language politics. Both countries have two main linguistic communities, English and French in Canada and French and Flemish in Belgium. In each country these languages have official and equal status under the constitution (German is also an official language in Belgium, but the German-speaking minority is less than 1 per cent of the population). Both countries have a history of unequal and sometimes tense relations between their major language communities, English being the dominant community in Canada and the French dominating in Belgium, despite being outnumbered by the Flemish until the late 1960s. Finally, both countries have federal constitutions and they both have separatist movements.

Given these similarities, comparison comes naturally. But Belgium has adopted a model of language rights quite different from Canada's. The Canadian model, we know, is based on the premise that every citizen, anglophone or francophone, has certain language rights that must be recognized anywhere in Canada and that French and English have equal constitutional status in national affairs across the country. The Belgian model is based on the idea that one's language rights depend on where a person lives. This is a *territorial* model of language rights, unlike the Canadian *personal* model.

Here is how the Belgian model works. In Flanders, the Flemish-speaking northern region of the country, public education, government services, election ballots, and signage on roads, at train stations, and for buses are in Flemish only. In Wallonia, the southern French-speaking region, French is the only official language. Brussels, the

financial support for court challenges to provincial laws respecting language rights. These challenges have included Supreme Court decisions in 1979 and 1985 that established the official status of French in the province of Manitoba[38] and successful challenges to the restrictions on education and public signs and advertising contained in Quebec's Bill 101.[39] Until 1985, language rights cases were the only ones supported by Ottawa under its Court Challenges Program. Funding for the Program was temporarily discontinued in 2006 and restored in 2008, but only for language rights cases.

A second thrust of federal policy to promote bilingualism in Canadian society has been through financial assistance for second-language instruction and minority-language schools controlled by the provinces, including French immersion schools and support for summer immersion programs. The immersion phenomenon has seen the proliferation of French immersion schools in cities throughout English Canada. In 2012, about 341,000 students were enrolled in French immersion elementary and secondary schools outside Quebec, compared to roughly 75,000 in 1980. More than half of all French immersion schools and about half of all immersion students in Canada are in Ontario.[40]

The popularity of French immersion education has grown steadily over the last two decades, fuelled by non-francophone parents' perception that bilingualism will give their children an edge in the future competition for good jobs. This perception of greater opportunities for bilinguals, at least in the private sector, remains to be substantiated. Two decades ago, a study of bilingual job opportunities by the Commissioner of Languages answered the question, "Do immersion graduates make good use of their French after high school?" with "Yes, they do—in Ottawa."[41] The 2006 census found that 4.1 per cent of anglophone Canadians claimed to use French most often or regularly at work. But half of these workers are anglophones in Quebec, the percentage being 2.1 for anglophones national capital, is officially bilingual, although French speakers outnumber Flemish speakers by a very wide margin. Citizens vote in national, regional, and local elections, as in Canada. But unlike Canada, there are no national political parties in Belgium. There is a Flemish socialist party and a French one, a Flemish Green party and a French one, and so on. Consequently, the party system cannot be counted on to help bridge the gap between the linguistic communities and their respective regions.

Over the years many Quebec nationalists have pointed to Belgium as a model to be emulated. But Canadian and Quebec federalists from Pierre Trudeau to the present day have always argued that the territorial model, instead of providing a better recipe for coexistence between the linguistic communities, would lead to greater division and ultimately to separation.

The federalists may be right. Although *indépendantisme* is far from dead in Quebec, a certain modus

vivendi seems to have existed in Canada since the 1995 referendum. In Belgium, on the other hand, conflict over language rights in the linguistically mixed periphery of Brussels is a continuous fact of political life. In 2010 and again in 2014 the Flemish Nationalist Party, under the leadership of a multilingual avowed separatist, won more seats than any other party in the Belgian legislature. Suddenly moderate Belgians were talking seriously about the possibility of separatism, although no one believed that it would happen tomorrow.

Belgians have sometimes looked to Canada for lessons in how to make language relations work, and Canadians have returned the gaze. But it is clear that there is no one-size-fits-all formula for peace between language communities. The particulars of a country's history and demography are crucial determinants of whether a certain language rights model will satisfy a country's linguistic communities. They may often prefer an occasionally uneasy cohabitation to divorce.

outside Quebec. Only among francophones did workers report that they often used the other official language—English—in the workplace: close to one-third of francophones in Quebec said that they used English most often or regularly and two-thirds of francophones outside Quebec reported using English most often at work. This hardly supports the picture of a Canadian work world in which the opportunities to use French are great, at least outside Quebec.[42] The 2013 annual report of the Commissioner of Official Languages quotes approvingly from a *Maclean's* article in which the author states that bilingual graduates are in greater demand than ever before and that, on average, they make more money than unilingual graduates. The fact that they make higher incomes may, of course, simply confirm the self-selection class bias that influences who goes to a French immersion school.[43] As for the claim that bilingual graduates are in great demand, the article relies on Commissioner Graham Fraser's statement that, "the

federal government is Canada's largest employer, and it needs bilingual employees." No evidence is provided to show that, outside Quebec, bilingual graduates are very likely to use both languages at work in the private sector.[44] None of this is an argument against immersion education and other public investments in the promotion of bilingualism. It is simply a caution against uncritical acceptance of some of the grand claims made for such programs.

A Distinct Society?

Does Quebec comprise a **distinct society**? Is Quebec more distinct from the other nine provinces than any one of those other provinces is from the rest? What is the basis for Quebec's claim to be distinct? Even if Quebecers' claim to distinctiveness is valid, should distinct society status be entrenched in the Constitution? Is this necessary? Is it desirable?

Few Canadians had heard of "distinct society" before the late 1980s, when the Meech Lake Accord came to grief over the proposal to recognize Quebec as a distinct society within Canada. It is also reasonable to assume that most Canadians are today no wiser about what "distinct society" means. This, it should be added, is despite the fact that in 1995 the House of Commons passed a resolution stating that "Quebec is a distinct society within Canada," and another in 2006 that declares, "the Québécois form a nation within a united Canada." Average Canadians perhaps may be forgiven whatever confusion they have over the distinct society issue. Constitutional experts, political scientists, journalists, and politicians have not been able to agree on what it means!

© Étienne Chaput

The band Les Cowboys Fringants enjoys wild popularity in Quebec and is an important part of the Québécois néo-trad genre (modernized Quebec folk music with a rock sound). While Les Cowboys have garnered a following in France and French-speaking Belgium and Switzerland, they remain relatively unknown to anglophones in the rest of Canada. Is such a cultural factor an indicator of Quebec's distinct nature or does it have little political relevance?

The demand for constitutional recognition of Quebec as a distinct society has been a non-negotiable item on the agenda of Quebec's political elite since the late 1980s. At the same time, the issue excites a popular emotional response both inside Quebec and in the rest of Canada that other constitutional proposals—reforming the Senate, tinkering with the Supreme Court, changing the amendment process, and so on—do not. Let us try to understand the controversy over a distinct society clause by addressing the questions posed at the beginning of this section.

Whether or not Quebec is a distinct society depends on what criteria we use in comparing Quebec to the other provinces. In terms of how people in Quebec make their living, the films they watch, the video games they play, how and where they spend their vacations, and in most other aspects of their lifestyle they are not remarkably different from Canadians in other regions of the country. In fact, if material and lifestyle criteria are used, there is a good case for arguing that Quebec and Ontario are no more different than, say, Ontario and Newfoundland and Labrador.

Not everyone agrees. And it is true that one can point to several important social characteristics of the Quebec population that distinguish it from those of the other provinces. Québécois marry less often and later than other Canadians; the percentage of couples living in common-law relationships is about twice the national average and higher than in any other province; a greater percentage of children (about half of first births) are born outside of marriage than in other provinces; and a higher percentage of Quebecers than other Canadians report single ethnic origins (in 2011, about 72 per cent, compared to 58 per cent for all of Canada and 57 per cent in Ontario). Whereas English-Canadian television viewers prefer American-produced programs during prime time, French-speaking Quebecers are likely to be watching Quebec-made dramas and sitcoms. But to base an argument for constitutional recognition of Quebec as a distinct society on such social characteristics may trivialize the meaning of distinct society. Many of these phenomena have no political relevance. Moreover, in some cases the differences between Quebec and the rest of Canada are too slight to warrant reading much significance into them.

Another possibility is that the beliefs and values of the Québécois set them apart from other Canadians. As we saw in Chapter 5, the evidence for this claim is mixed. Several early studies on regional variations in political culture concluded that Canada, in fact, is comprised of several distinctive regional political cultures. Richard Simeon and David Elkins found that levels of political trust, efficacy, interest in politics, and participation varied significantly between provinces and that this variation persisted even after eliminating the impact of socio-economic factors (i.e., levels of education and income) known to influence these attitudes/behaviours.[45] The implication is, of course, that while Quebec may be a "special case" in terms of its politically relevant values, it is not the only regional special case.

Conversely, other studies of regionalism conclude that no significant attitudinal differences exist between citizens in different parts of the country. Either way, whether Quebec's political culture is argued to be broadly similar to that in the rest of Canada or if one takes the position that several distinct regional cultures exist in Canada, among them Quebec, the argument for constitutional entrenchment of distinct society status for Quebec is weakened.

Nonetheless, one's conclusions may depend on the questions asked and the values they tap. Surveys that ask Canadians whether they think of themselves as Canadians first or as citizens of their province reveal that those in Quebec are most likely to see their primary attachment as provincial. However, regional identity among Newfoundlanders is just about as strong and Prince Edward Islanders are not terribly far behind. Anyway, this evidence of strong provincial loyalty may not matter very much because numerous surveys have shown that Quebecers and other provincial populations are capable of maintaining provincial and Canadian loyalties at the same time. In one of the most rigorous empirical investigations of regional variations in political ideology, Michael Ornstein concludes that "the extent of ideological differentiation in English Canada is very small" and that "the ideological difference between Quebec and English Canada is greater than the internal variation

within English Canada."[46] Ornstein shows that ideological values in Quebec are considerably to the left of those in the other provinces.[47]

On the other hand, a recent study of regional variation in political culture concludes that interprovincial variation is less significant than differences between regions within provinces and that characterization of Quebec as more left wing than the other provinces is unsubstantiated.[48]

In view of these apparently contradictory findings can we conclude that Quebec comprises a distinct society in terms of the values and beliefs of its citizens? Possibly not. What is beyond doubt, however, is that differences between Quebec and the rest of Canada are wide on attitudes relating to language. A 1991 Gallup poll found that 78 per cent of Montrealers, compared to 28 per cent of Torontonians, thought that English-language rights were well protected in Quebec. Asked about the protection of French-language rights outside Quebec, 87 per cent of Torontonians thought they were well protected, compared to only 25 per cent of Montrealers. The two solitudes were perfectly balanced in their mutual mistrust! A 2008 Ipsos-Reid survey found that whereas 63 per cent of Quebecers agreed that the French language needed more protection in Canada, only 11 per cent of Canadians outside Quebec believed that more protection was necessary.[49] On other political issues, differences are often slight or non-existent. Even if we concur with those, like Ornstein, who argue that Quebec is more different attitudinally from the rest of Canada than the predominantly English-speaking provinces are from one another, it may not follow that this difference warrants constitutional recognition of special status. Values and beliefs are not set in stone, as any student of changes in Quebec society and French-Canadian nationalism over the last half-century knows.

A third possible argument for Quebec's distinctiveness relies on history. The outline of such an argument goes as follows. French-Canadian society dates to the seventeenth century when the first immigrants came from France. Most French Canadians actually are descended from those who were already settled in New France at the time of the Conquest. Current generations of French Canadians are heirs to centuries of tradition and resistance against assimilating pressures. This continuity can be seen in the distinctive French spoken in Quebec (and, for that matter, in the dialects spoken in the French-speaking communities outside of Quebec); in Quebec folksongs, popular music, films, and literature; in such social institutions as Quebec's distinctive system of civil law (based on the French Civil Code rather than on English common law); and in the history that children in Quebec learn in school—a history that has always told a rather different story from that learned by students in English schools across Canada.[50] It is this unique history as one of Canada's two "founding peoples" that justifies distinct society status for Quebec. Moreover, history has demonstrated that only in Quebec, where francophones have always formed the majority and have been able to control the levers of provincial government, are the distinctive language and traditions of French Canadians secure against anglicizing pressures and discrimination.

Variations on this basic argument are standard features of Quebec government documents on the Constitution and in the literature of both the Quebec Liberal Party and the Parti Québécois. It is a view widely shared by francophones in Quebec. The unique history argument has been an important part of the case for constitutional recognition of Quebec as a distinct society. These arguments have also been used to make the case for a Quebec veto over constitutional amendments, as indicated in the 1991 *Report* of the Commission on the Political and Constitutional Future of Quebec:

> At its origin, Canada's federal system was founded, from Quebec's point of view, on Canadian duality [French/English] and the autonomy of the provinces. Canadian duality, which rests on the relationship between the French-Canadian and English-Canadian peoples, is seen as the founding principle of the federal system. The federal union is thus conceived of as a pact between these two peoples, that may only be changed with the consent of each of these parties.[51]

This reasoning was expressed in unequivocal terms in An Act Respecting the Fundamental Rights and Prerogatives of the Quebec People and the Quebec State (2000), the Quebec legislature's response to the Clarity Act passed by Parliament in 2000. All parties in Quebec's National Assembly agreed that the Québécois constitute a nation with a right to self-determination and, moreover, that only the citizens and legislature of Quebec have a legitimate voice in the determination of whether the province will become an independent state. "[T]he Québec people," declares this Quebec law, "in the majority French-speaking, possesses specific characteristics and a deep-rooted historical continuity in a territory over which it exercises its rights through a modern national state, having a government, a national assembly and impartial and independent courts of justice." The problem with the historical case for constitutional recognition of Quebec as a distinct society is not that it is based on incorrect or flimsy evidence. Indeed, the historical record speaks for itself. But some of the other provinces claim that their regional histories are equally distinct. Western Canadians and their governments are unimpressed by arguments that Quebec's history is somehow more distinctive than their own. Newfoundlanders are unlikely to be convinced. The unsympathetic reception that spokespersons for the predominantly English-speaking provinces give to the historical argument for Quebec as a distinct society has recently been joined by that of Aboriginal Canadians. They argue that if any community (or communities) has a historical right to distinct society status it is theirs. After all, their languages and traditions had been established for centuries and even millennia before the arrival of Canada's European "founders." No discussion of "founding peoples" or "distinct societies" is complete, they argue, without recognition of the historical status and rights of Aboriginal Canadians.

The final and most persuasive grounds for arguing Quebec's right to distinct society status is the province's linguistic character. As noted earlier, about four out of five Quebecers have French as their mother tongue and an equal percentage report speaking French at home. No other province comes close to this level of French-language dominance; indeed, in no other province do francophones comprise a majority of the population. Roughly

90 per cent of all Canadian francophones reside in Quebec. It was no accident that the Commission on the Political and Constitutional Future of Quebec, established by the Quebec Liberal government of Robert Bourassa after the failure of the Meech Lake Accord, emphasized the distinctive linguistic character of Quebec as the first point in the section of its *Report* on Quebec's *identité proper* (special or unique identity).[52] Moreover, the distinct society clauses proposed by the Meech Lake Accord and the Charlottetown Accord, and more recently in the motion passed by Parliament in 1995 and in the **Calgary Declaration** of 1997, were explicit in declaring that what is distinct about Quebec society is primarily its linguistic character (see Appendix to this chapter).

This argument cannot be refuted. Of course, each province has its own distinctive linguistic character, but the unique linguistic character of Quebec within Canada and, for that matter, in all of North America is undeniable. In no other jurisdiction, provincial or state, is English not the language regularly spoken by a clear majority of the population.

But if the distinct society clauses of Meech Lake and Charlottetown were merely statements of demographic reality, why was there so much fuss? There are a couple of reasons. One is that some people will readily acknowledge Quebec's distinctive linguistic character, but deny that this warrants constitutional recognition of Quebec as a distinct society any more than, say, Newfoundland and Labrador deserves to be recognized as a distinct society because of its special economy, history, and demographic character. Why, they ask, should language be elevated above other social characteristics in determining which provincial societies are distinct and which are not?

A second and probably more important reason why some provincial governments and most English-speaking Canadians resist what might appear to be a compelling linguistic argument for a distinct society clause involves the consequences they believe would follow from entrenching this recognition in the Constitution. Many English Canadians believe this would give to Quebec legislative powers not possessed by other provinces. Some worry that minority rights—those of non-francophones in Quebec and those of francophones outside the province—would

suffer from constitutional recognition of Quebec as a predominantly French-speaking society and of the rest of Canada as predominantly English-speaking. Former Prime Minister Pierre Trudeau argued precisely this, so it is not surprising if rank-and-file Canadians believe this might be the result of such recognition. Fears also have been expressed that a distinct society clause could undermine Charter guarantees of rights and freedoms in Quebec.

Above all, however, what probably bothers English-speaking Canadians outside of Quebec more than anything else is their gut sense that distinct society status for Quebec challenges their idea of Canada. A **two-nations theory** of Canada, while enjoying some popularity in certain political parties and among anglophone political scientists, has never been very popular with the English-Canadian public. In a largely unarticulated way they sense that distinct society recognition for Quebec is a sort of Trojan horse for a two-nations conception of Canada. This offends against a particular understanding of equality that—again, while usually inarticulate—rejects the idea of categories of Canadians instead of Canadians, period. Although many of Canada's national political elite have for years denied that the "one Canada" aspirations of most English Canadians conflict with the recognition of Quebec as a distinct society, Québécois political leaders suffer from no illusions on this count. The *Report* of the Commission on the Political and Constitutional Future of Quebec made this very clear. The *Report* argued that the "one Canada" and "dual societies" conceptions have become increasingly irreconcilable since the passage of the Charter and the other constitutional reforms of 1982. This is because, the *Report* argues, the Constitution Act of 1982 is based on three principles that, while popular outside of Quebec, are fundamentally opposed to the recognition of Quebec as a distinct society. These principles are:

- The equality of all Canadian citizens, from one ocean to the other, and the unity of the society in which they live.
- The equality of all cultures and cultural origins in Canada.
- The equality of the 10 provinces of Canada.

Whatever a distinct society clause in the Constitution might mean in practice—and, notwithstanding the confident pontificating of many politicians and constitutional experts, we should have learned from the experience with the Charter that it is often impossible to predict how Canadian judges will interpret important sections of the Constitution—there can be no doubt that the Quebec elites who insist on it expect it to make a difference. They reject the "one Canada" vision that they argue is represented in the Charter and in the current procedure for amending the Constitution (whereby Quebec does not have a constitutionally entrenched veto). Distinct society is, in their eyes, a corrective against the centralizing implications of the Charter and, moreover, represents a return to the founding spirit of Canada.

Distinct society status and a veto over constitutional change may no longer be enough. Several weeks after the narrow defeat of the separatist option in the 1995 Quebec referendum, the House of Commons passed a motion recognizing Quebec as a distinct society and giving the province (as well as British Columbia, the Prairie provinces, Ontario, and the Atlantic provinces) a veto over constitutional reform. The PQ government in Quebec, the Bloc Québécois in Ottawa, and Quebec's French-language media were not particularly impressed by Ottawa's action. Even the Quebec Liberal Party argued that Ottawa's proposals—which did not change the Constitution—did not go far enough. Ottawa's hope, of course, was to satisfy the demands of enough "soft nationalists" to undercut the support for separatism. For its part, the PQ has been determined to shift the debate away from distinct society and constitutional vetoes, terms that imply a federalism framework, and onto a different plane. That plane involves political independence and economic association.

Quebec citizens, according to some commentators, have grown weary of decades-old debates over political independence, distinct society status, and constitutional reform. Public opinion polls taken throughout 2001–2 showed that about six in 10 Quebecers were opposed to the idea of another referendum on Quebec sovereignty. The rise in popularity of a new provincial party, Action Démocratique du Québec (ADQ), a right-of-centre populist party

that was nationalist but not secessionist, was interpreted by many as a sign of Quebecers' dissatisfaction with the tired dialogue of the PQ and the Quebec Liberal Party. Independence and constitutional reform, according to what quickly became the conventional wisdom, was yesterday's political agenda. Many went as far as pronouncing that Quebec separatism was dead when the ADQ became the official opposition, pushing the Parti Québécois to third place in the political pecking order in the 2007 Quebec election. A 2010 survey conducted for the pro-federalism think-tank, The Federal Idea, reported that 58 per cent of Quebecers believed that the sovereignty debate was over, compared to only 26 per cent who said that it was more relevant than ever. The survey also found that 47 per cent of respondents said there were fewer reasons to become independent than there were when the 1980 referendum was held, compared to 41 per cent who said that there continue to be at least as many reasons.[53]

This obituary is premature, to say the least. The same poll that caused The Federal Idea think-tank to proclaim Quebec sovereignty "outmoded" found that Quebecers were dissatisfied with the functioning of Canadian federalism. Fifty-six per cent said that federalism generally did not produce satisfactory agreements between Quebec and the rest of Canada, versus only 26 per cent who said that it did, and 57 per cent of respondents expressed the view that the French language was less secure in Quebec than it was 30 years earlier. At the federal level, the separatist Bloc Québécois saw its support collapse in the 2011 election, as a wave of NDP support swept across Quebec for the first time in that province's history. However, many (if not most) of the NDP MPs elected from Quebec had separatist backgrounds. The PQ experienced a strong comeback in the 2012 provincial elections, forming a minority government under its leader, Pauline Marois. A poll taken in early 2013, several months after the election of the PQ, found that 42 per cent of Quebec anglophones claimed to have thought about leaving Quebec in the wake of the PQ's victory.[54] If they did, however, perhaps they needn't have, at least not in the immediate term. In April 2014, the PQ and Marois personally suffered a stunning defeat in a provincial election that ushered in a majority Liberal government. The campaign had been fought largely over the PQ promise of another referendum and Marois's insistence on a "charter of secular values" that would ban the wearing of religious symbols by public workers.[55]

Those who thought that the rejection of the PQ by Quebec voters also meant the death of the controversial Charter of Quebec Values did not understand the nature of Quebec nationalism. Within months of assuming office the new Liberal government introduced proposals quite similar to those of the defeated PQ government. In so doing it was responding to polls showing that a strong majority of francophone Quebecers support a ban on public servants, including teachers, wearing religious symbols. The anglicization that is audible in the centre of Montreal has been a simmering issue for several years and is not likely to go away. Quebecers may have said no to the prospect of another referendum when they voted in 2014, but they did not say no to Quebec nationalism.

The fact remains that Quebec is a province *pas comme les autres*, and one that continues to attract special attention from federal politicians. One of the politically significant ways in which Quebec's difference may be seen is in French-speaking Quebecers' weaker attachment to Canada, particularly among younger citizens. A 2006 survey found that only 19 per cent of francophone Quebecers between the ages of 18 and 30 said that they felt "very attached to Canada," compared to 71 per cent among anglophone Quebecers and 45 per cent among allophones. Young francophones also were far less likely than anglophones to believe that Quebec's economic situation would be harmed by independence (29 per cent versus 72 per cent). It comes as no surprise, therefore, that young French-speaking Quebecers were found to be strongly in support of Quebec assuming the status of a country (59 per cent) while support was very weak among young English-speakers (9 per cent) and allophones (30 per cent).[56]

History should teach us that complacency about Quebec's relationship to the rest of Canada is far from being warranted by the enduring facts of the situation, despite sudden shifts in the electoral winds such as the failure of the Bloc Québécois in the 2011 federal election and the defeat of the PQ in the 2014 provincial election. Foremost among these facts is the gap that continues to separate the one-Canada, equality of the provinces, and multicultural visions of the country, which dominate outside Quebec, from the insistence by Quebec's politicians and opinion leaders—federalists and separatists alike—that Quebec must be considered a society whose language, culture, and history make it distinct from the rest of Canada. The art of national unity involves finding ways to bridge this gap.

Listen to the "The Death of Quebec Separatism?" podcast, available at: www.oupcanada.com/Brooks8e

Appendix: Proposals for a Distinct Society Clause

Version I: Meech Lake Accord (1987)

1. The Constitution Act, 1867, is amended by adding thereto, immediately after Section 1 thereof, the following section:
2. (1) The Constitution of Canada shall be interpreted in a manner consistent with: (a) The recognition that the existence of French-speaking Canadians, centred in Quebec but also present elsewhere in Canada, and English-speaking Canadians, concentrated outside Quebec but also present in Quebec, constitutes a fundamental characteristic of Canada; and, (b) The recognition that Quebec constitutes within Canada a distinct society;

    (2) The role of the Parliament of Canada and the provincial legislatures to preserve the fundamental characteristic of Canada referred to in paragraph (1)(a) is affirmed;

    (3) The role of the Legislature and Government of Quebec to preserve and promote the distinct identity of Quebec referred to in paragraph (1)(b) is affirmed;

    (4) Nothing in this section derogates from the powers, rights or privileges of Parliament or the Government of Canada, or of the legislatures or governments of the provinces, including any powers, rights or privileges relating to language.

Version II: Charlottetown Accord (1992)

The Constitution Act, 1867 is amended by adding thereto, immediately after Section 1 thereof, the following section:

2. (1) The Constitution of Canada, including the Canadian Charter of Rights and Freedoms, shall be interpreted in a manner consistent with the following fundamental characteristics:

. . .

(c) Quebec constitutes within Canada a distinct society, which includes a French-speaking majority, a unique culture and a civil law tradition;

. . .

(2) The role of the legislature and Government of Quebec to preserve and promote the distinct society of Quebec is affirmed.

Version III: Motion Passed by Parliament (1995)

THAT

Whereas the people of Quebec have expressed the desire for recognition of Quebec's distinct society;

(1) the House recognize that Quebec is a distinct society within Canada;

(2) the House recognize that Quebec's distinct society includes its French-speaking majority, unique culture and civil law tradition;

(3) the House undertake to be guided by this reality;

(4) the House encourage all components of the legislative and executive branches of government to take note of this recognition and be guided in their conduct accordingly.

Version IV: The Calgary Declaration (1997)

(Adopted by all provincial governments except that of Quebec)

In Canada's federal system, where respect for diversity and equality underlines unity, the unique character of Quebec society, including its French-speaking majority, its culture and its tradition of civil law, is fundamental to the wellbeing of Canada. Consequently, the legislature and the Government of Quebec have a role to protect and develop the unique character of Quebec society within Canada.

Version V: The 2006 House of Commons Resolution

That this House recognize that the Québécois form a nation within a united Canada.

Starting Points for Research

Ramsay Cook, ed., *French Canadian Nationalism: An Anthology* (Toronto: Macmillan, 1969). This collection contains a wide selection of writings from French-Canadian nationalists and about French-Canadian and Quebec nationalists, from the mid-nineteenth century to the Quiet Revolution.

Ramsay Cook, *Watching Quebec: Selected Essays* (Montreal and Kingston: McGill-Queen's University Press, 2005). Essays from one of the most astute observers of Quebec history and politics.

Alain-G. Gagnon, ed., *Quebec: State and Society*, 3rd edn (Toronto: University of Toronto Press, 2004). A comprehensive reader, this collection includes contributions from many of Canada's leading students of Quebec politics.

Alain-G. Gagnon and Raffaele Iacovino, *Federalism, Citizenship, and Quebec* (Toronto: University of Toronto Press, 2007). A challenging book that examines the impact of Quebec nationalism on Canadian politics and proposes a multinational model for the future of the Canadian federation.

Chantal Hébert, *The Morning After: The 1995 Quebec Referendum and the Day That Almost Was* **(Toronto: Knopf, 2014).** A journalist well known as a regular commentator on English-language television, Hébert reflects on the near breakup of Canada in 1995 and the consequences that might have followed had a majority of Quebecers voted yes.

Kenneth McRoberts, *Quebec: Social Change and Political Crisis*, **3rd edn (Toronto: Oxford University Press, 1999).** McRoberts provides an excellent account of Quebec's historical and political evolution.

Charles Taylor, *Reconciling the Solitudes: Essays on Canadian Federalism and Nationalism* **(Montreal and Kingston: McGill-Queen's University Press, 1993).** Written by Canada's most internationally renowned philosopher, several of the pieces in this collection deal with Quebec and Quebec nationalism.

Review Exercises

1. If you are bilingual, this exercise is for you. Watch the videoclip entitled, "Frenglish: Bilingual Montrealers," at <www.youtube.com/watch?v=-yYPD6JJtDM>. Based on what you now know about Quebec after having read Chapter 14, what is your reaction to journalist Ann Marie Withenshaw's views on bilingualism in Quebec and Canada? Do you think that what she says mainly supports those who worry about the anglicization of Montreal or those who believe that bilingualism is the glue that holds Canada together?

2. How bilingual is your community? Make an inventory of the indications that French (or English, if you are in Quebec) language rights are protected and the French language promoted. It might look something like this:
   A. Schools
      French schools
      • Monseigneur Jean Noël
      • Ste-Thérèse
      • Lajeunesse
      Immersion schools
      • Bellewood
   B. Media
      Newspapers
      • Le Rempart
      Radio
      • Radio-Canada (Is there local production?)
      Television
      • Radio-Canada (Is there local production?)
      • TFO (19, cable)

   • TVA (69, cable)
   • TVO (70, cable)
   C. Signs
      • stores
      • traffic signs
      • billboards
      • product labels
      • government office
   D. Churches
      Catholic
      • St-Jérôme
      • Ste-Anne
      • St-Joseph
   E. Clubs, Bars, Community Centres
      • Club Alouette
      • Place Concorde
   F. Employment
      Teaching jobs in French (or English in Quebec); businesses that require French-speaking employees; government agencies that hire French-speaking workers
   G. Public services
      Can you communicate with officials of government agencies in both French and English? Which levels of government?

3. What would be the consequences of Quebec independence for official bilingualism in the rest of Canada? Move past the immediate emotion and backlash to consider what possible consequences separation might have for schools, political parties, government services, business, and the Constitution.

Women and Politics

15

In 1928 the Supreme Court of Canada, in the *Persons* case, addressed the question of whether women had the status of persons under certain laws, including those determining who could be a judge. The Supreme Court said they were not. Common sense and justice prevailed in 1929, however, when the ruling was reversed by the Judicial Committee of the Privy Council, at the time the highest appellate court for Canada. Today, three of the nine justices of the Supreme Court are women. Gender equality was a major issue in Canadian politics from the 1970s to the 1990s. Although the issue may not appear to be as controversial today, this is because of legislative and court victories and important changes in public opinion. Topics in this chapter include the following:

- The extent and causes of female under-representation in politics.
- Early feminism.
- Contemporary feminism.
- Organization.
- Strategies.
- Achievements.
- Attitudes regarding gender.

Louise McKinney

CANADA postage postes 17

Louise McKinney was elected to the Legislative Assembly of Alberta in 1917, the first woman to sit in any legislature in the British Empire, after years of activism for women's right to vote, prohibition, and a bill that would allow women to prevent the sale of their homes without their knowledge. She is one of the "Famous Five" women who challenged the Supreme Court of Canada to acknowledge women as legal persons. (© Canada Post Corporation (1981))

The Social Construction of Gender Differences

Men and women are biologically different. Although obvious, the social implications of this have been the subject of enormous controversy. Until the 1960s and 1970s, there was widespread agreement that the biological attributes of the sexes played a major role in the determination of their respective personality traits, intellectual aptitudes, general abilities, and social roles. Males were considered to be more aggressive, rational, analytical, adventurous, and active than females—and more fitted to leadership roles. Females were generally believed to be more nurturing, emotional, intuitive, cautious, and passive. Nature, not nurture, was considered to be the primary reason for the behavioural and attitudinal differences between males and females and for the social superiority of men over women. This was not only the conventional wisdom, believed and expressed by average men and women. It was also widely subscribed to by health-care professionals, including psychologists.[1]

This view was even shared by the first wave of the women's movement. Beginning in the late 1800s, the objectives of this movement focused on extending voting rights to women and on legal and social reforms geared towards the protection of the family and traditional values. The arguments used to support these demands emphasized fairness and morality. Extending voting rights to women and eliminating some of the grosser forms of legal discrimination against them—such as the common law's ambiguity about whether a woman was a person in law, or the law's failure to ensure a woman's right to property acquired during the course of married life—were matters of fundamental justice based on the equal humanity of the sexes. This argument, however, did not challenge the conventional wisdom on the biological determination of gender differences.

Suffragists often allied themselves with organizations promoting such causes as temperance, educational reform, child labour laws, and public service reform (to eliminate corruption). These causes were central to the character of the early women's movement. Groups like the Woman's Christian Temperance Union (WCTU), the National Council of Women of Canada (NCWC), and the Women's Institutes comprised the movement's organizational hub. These organizations supported female suffrage on the grounds that women voters would inject a morally uplifting element into the grubby business of politics. It was in a woman's nature, they argued, to care more about life and the conditions that nurtured it. Extending full democratic rights to women would immediately elevate the prominence of those issues that most concerned the women's movement, including mothers' pensions, minimum wage laws for women, better industrial health and safety standards, prison and family law reform, and more public spending on education. Women were the morally superior sex, and their participation in politics would make the world a better, more civilized place.

These arguments formed the basis of what has come to be called *social feminism* or *maternal feminism*. Far from challenging the notion that gender role differences are the inevitable product of biology, maternal feminists accepted this assumption wholeheartedly. But they turned it from an argument against political rights for women into the basis of their case for political equality. Some of the leaders of the feminist movement, such as Nellie McClung, in fact used both contemporary-sounding and maternal feminism arguments in demanding the vote and social reforms.[2] The mainstream of this first wave of the women's movement, however, was dominated by the more moderate arguments of social feminism and by traditional family and Christian values. Indeed, looking back on women's struggle to achieve political rights, the wonder is that female suffrage was resisted so vigorously and for so long. Although it challenged men's monopoly on public life, the early women's movement did not threaten the social and economic pillars of male dominance.

But the second wave of feminism did. Simone de Beauvoir's declaration that "One is not born, but rather becomes, a woman"[3] suggests that gender role differences are not inherent. They are socially constructed—passed on and relearned from generation to generation. This is the basic premise of the second wave of the women's movement.

If the real roots of gender inequality lie in the institutionalized practices and cultural norms of society, then the solution must go beyond the formal political equality of the sexes. Anything that promotes stereotyped gender roles that are not based on inherent differences between males and females restricts individual freedom. If one learns that certain careers are not for the members of one's sex, or that child-rearing and homemaking are primarily female responsibilities, this limits one's freedom to choose and to act. Moreover, because many of these stereotyped differences are linked to power relations between men and women, their existence undermines human equality.

©Yousuf Karsh, Yousuf Karsh fonds, Library and Archives Canada/R613-3-0-E.

Agnes Macphail was elected to the House of Commons for the riding of Grey Southeast in the 1921 federal election, making her the first female MP in Canada. Throughout her political career, Macphail advocated for rural issues, penal reform, and seniors' and workers' rights. Macphail founded the Elizabeth Fry Society of Canada to work on the behalf of women and girls in the criminal justice system, and was the first woman delegate to the League of Nations in Geneva, Switzerland.

This is not the place to wade deeply into the turbulent waters of the nature versus nurture controversy. It is clear, however, that the inherent differences between males and females are much less significant than were once believed. In one of the most frequently cited studies on the subject, Maccoby and Jacklin claim that scientific research provides firm support for only four non-physiological differences between the sexes.[4] Three of these differences involve cognitive skills: verbal ability (females better), mathematical ability (males better), and visual-spatial ability (males better). The fourth involves personality: males are more aggressive than females. In the case of both verbal and mathematical ability, differences between the sexes only appear during adolescence, suggesting that social learning may play a role in the development of these skills. All of the four differences claimed by Maccoby and Jacklin are matters of tendency only: for example, males tend to be more aggressive than females and females are more likely than males to excel in verbal ability. A good deal of recent research, however, points to the impact of hormonal changes on the development of male and female brains and suggests that the tendencies identified by Maccoby and Jacklin may be more rooted in biology than in social learning.[5]

The debate continues. One of its most controversial aspects involves the relationship of males and females to children. In virtually all societies throughout recorded history women have assumed primary responsibility for raising children. Are females more nurturing and child-oriented by nature? Or is this gender role difference a product of social learning?

The evidence is inconclusive. One of the great anthropologists of the twentieth century, Margaret Mead, is cited by both sides of this debate. Based on her study of three primitive societies in New Guinea, the "early" Mead argued that:

> Many, if not all, of the personality traits which we have called masculine or feminine are as lightly linked to sex as are the clothing, the manners, and the form of headdress that a society at a given period assigns to either sex. . . . the evidence is overwhelmingly in favor of the strength of social conditioning.[6]

But the "later" Mead had this to say on the subject:

> The mother's nurturing tie to her child is apparently so deeply rooted in the actual biological conditions of conception and gestation, birth and suckling, that only fairly complicated social arrangements can break it down entirely. . . . women may be said to be mothers unless they are taught to deny the child-bearing qualities. Society must distort their sense of themselves, pervert their inherent growth-patterns, perpetrate a series of learning-outrages upon them, before they will cease to want to provide, at least for a few years, for the child they have already nourished for nine months within the safe circle of their own bodies.[7]

The different roles played by men and women in the family and the social learning that prepares them for these roles contribute to the under-representation of women in public life. The question is, are the duties and roles associated with motherhood and homemaking mainly the products of what Mead calls the "inherent growth-patterns" of females or are they chiefly determined by social learning?

This is an old question. In the late nineteenth century, John Stuart Mill commented on the hypocrisy of society's attitudes towards women. Stripped of its moral pretensions, this attitude, Mill argued, could be summarized as follows: "It is necessary to society that women should marry and produce children. They will not do so unless they are compelled. Therefore it is necessary to compel them."[8] Mill was not suggesting that women did not have biological impulses or nurturing tendencies that, perhaps in most cases, would cause them to assume a disproportionate share of child-rearing and household tasks. His argument was simply that the weight of the law and social convention left them with no choice.

Mill's explanation had two parts. He argued that the subservient condition of a married woman—her lack of rights, standing, and personhood in relation to a husband whom the law and society treated as her master—would not be voluntarily chosen by many women, and certainly not by women capable of doing something else. But at the same time, this form of legalized "slavery" or "impressment"—the analogies are Mill's—provided men with a free source of domestic labour. Rather than pay women the "honest value of their labour,"[9] male-dominated society chose to institutionalize this sexual exploitation, at the same time claiming that woman's condition was naturally and even divinely ordained.

According to Mill, men wanted to deny women equal recognition and fair compensation for their domestic labour, simply because most men preferred the status and privileges of master, even if their mastery was limited to the confines of their home. This, argued Mill, was an egotism that inflicted costs on society. By depriving women of opportunities outside of marriage and the home, male-dominated society deprived itself of the talents, intelligence, and contributions of half the population.

Mill's arguments on the social construction of gender differences and the subordination of women were in the tradition of liberal utilitarianism. A rather different angle on women, the family, and power was provided at about the same time by Karl Marx's collaborator, Friedrich Engels.[10]

Engels sought to show that the subservience of women to men within the family and, by extension, in society is based on economic foundations. He argued that the free domestic labour provided by women subsidized capitalist production by reducing the wages that employers had to pay to attract the services of male employers. The male breadwinner/female homemaker family served the interests of the capitalist class because it ensured the reproduction of the working class at low cost. Marxists ever since have pointed out that the values associated with the traditional family also perform an ideological function, helping to ensure the acceptance by subordinate classes and by women of a social system that ensures their subordination. The state actively promoted the sexual exploitation of women within the family through laws restricting the legal and property rights and opportunities of females.

Within the institution of marriage, Engels contended, the relationship between man and woman was analogous to that between the bourgeoisie and the proletariat in society. The property relations that provided the basis for inequalities in power between social classes were mirrored in the relations between husband and wife. It followed from this, he argued, that the emancipation of women required their full integration into society and the economy in order to eliminate their dependence on male wage earners. Women cannot be dependent and equal at the same time, an argument that became an important part of second-wave feminism.

The Under-representation of Women in Canadian Public Life

Women constitute just over 50 per cent of the Canadian population and a slightly larger percentage of the electorate. Despite this and notwithstanding significant gains made over the past couple of decades in the number of women elected to public

office, their representation in politics continues to be far below their share of the population. As of 2012, women comprised just over one in five parliamentarians, federal and provincial. Just under 30 per cent of all candidates in the 2011 federal election, running for the five parties represented in the House of Commons, were women. Only one of the party leaders, Elizabeth May of the Green Party, is female. About one-quarter of municipal councillors across Canada are female. At the same time, however, in 2013 five of 10 provincial premiers, representing 85 per cent of the country's population, were women (this number had fallen to two—BC's Christy Clark and Ontario's Kathleen Wynne—by mid-2014). Moreover, women are more likely to vote than their male counterparts in every age cohort except the oldest voters, over the age of 65.

A similar pattern is found in the case of unelected public officials. Before the 1982 appointment of Justice Bertha Wilson, no woman had ever been a member of the Supreme Court of Canada. Since then Justice Claire L'Heureux-Dubé (1987), Justice

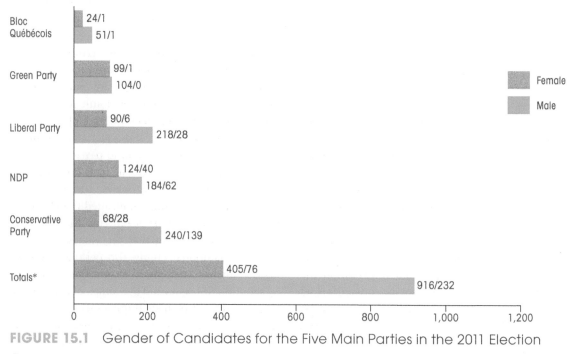

FIGURE 15.1   Gender of Candidates for the Five Main Parties in the 2011 Election

*These totals include only the candidates of these five registered parties in the 2011 election.

Note: The number of male and female candidates for each party is indicated to the right of each bar, followed by the number of male or female candidates actually elected.

Source: Based on data provided in the Report of the Chief Electoral Officer of Canada, 41st General Election (2011).

Beverley McLachlin (1989), Justice Louise Arbour (1999), Justice Marie Deschamps (2002), Justice Rosalie Abella (2004), and Justice Louise Charron (2004) have been appointed to the Supreme Court. Currently, three of the nine Supreme Court justices—Abella, Charron, and Chief Justice McLachlin—and about 31 per cent of all federally appointed judges (364 of 1,180 as of 2013) are women. Significant inroads also have been cut into the senior ranks of the bureaucracy. Women account for about 30 per cent of senior management personnel in the federal public service and about 45 per cent of all executive positions in the federal public service. It is no longer uncommon for women to be appointed to the boards of directors of Crown corporations and to hold leading management roles in these companies. As of 2012, 27 per cent of the senior officers of federal Crowns and about 30 per cent of those on their boards of directors were female.[11]

The gains made by women over the past few decades are significant and undeniable. At the same time, the gap between the participation of males and females in Canadian public life is wide. Why this is the case and why it may matter are questions that continue to be asked. Let us begin with explanations for the continued under-representation of women in public life.

Why Aren't More Women Involved in Public Life?

At a superficial level, the riddle of women's under-representation in public life once appeared to be straightforward: they tended to be less interested in politics and government than were men. Countless studies in Canada, the United States, and the UK have documented the existence of a gender gap in political knowledge, from which it has been inferred that females tend to be less interested in politics than men.[12] Nevertheless, female participation levels have long been about the same as men's for political activities like voting and campaigning. They have, however, been much lower for more demanding activities, such as holding office in a political party and running for office. **"The higher, the fewer"** is how Sylvia Bashevkin

describes this political participation gap between males and females.[13] This gap has narrowed over time, but it continues to exist.

If interest is one of the key determinants of participation at levels above voting, what explains different levels of interest? The answer lies in social learning. Traditionally, females learned from the world around them that politics was a predominantly male occupation. The signals were unmistakable. The Prime Minister/President was a man. So, too, were all but a handful of cabinet ministers and elected representatives. More subtle than the evident maleness of the political profession, but probably more important in discouraging most females from seeing themselves in political roles beyond those of voter and perhaps member of the women's auxiliary of Party X, was the sheer weight of social customs and expectations, communicated in the family, in school, in churches, and through the media. Leadership and an active involvement in the world beyond the family and neighbourhood were associated with masculinity. If females were not actively discouraged from developing an interest in politics, they generally were not encouraged to apply their energies and time to such matters.

The influence of social learning was reinforced by the sexual division of labour in society, particularly in the family but also, and relatedly, in the workplace. The traditional male breadwinner/female homemaker family and the more contemporary two breadwinner/female homemaker household are universally acknowledged by feminists as important sources of female subordination to males, including their under-representation in public life. This operates on two main levels.

1. Psychological. Child-rearing and housework are useful and necessary activities. Society's attitude towards them, however, has been ambivalent. Because they are forms of unpaid labour, at least when carried out by a household member, no objective yardstick exists for determining their value. And so they tend to be undervalued, particularly in comparison to paid work outside of the home. A good deal of evidence suggests that society's general failure to recognize the value of domestic work, or to praise it while historically labelling it "woman's work," has generated frustration and lower self-esteem among many women.[14] Moreover, the traditional roles of mother and homemaker have often operated to limit women *spatially* (tied to the physical demands of the domestic routine), *cognitively* (the relevant world and its activities are more likely to centre on the family and household than in the case of men), and *emotionally* (expressive, nurturing, caring functions are associated with the homemaker, while instrumental, active, and rational qualities are associated with the breadwinner). In brief, the consciousness likely to be produced by the traditional roles of mother and homemaker is not likely to generate the motivations, interests, and personal resources for political activism.

2. Status and professional achievements. Traditionally, women have been under-represented in precisely those occupations from which political office-holders tend to be drawn: law, business, and the liberal professions. In the past, their formal educational attainments tended to be less than those of men, and even today they are under-represented in fields like finance, economics, and engineering, which are important professional backgrounds for many senior positions in the public service. But even when women have made what were and (in some cases like engineering) still are viewed as non-traditional career choices, the likelihood has been great that they have had to take time out from their career and/or not pursue opportunities that would make greater demands on their time or require them to uproot their families. The expectation that the nurturing of children and household duties will fall primarily to women is corroborated by data on the amount of time spent on child-rearing by males and females. Females who work full-time continue to spend about twice as much time caring for children as do men.[15]

The sexual division of labour within the household, therefore, has worked to reduce women's opportunities to achieve the sorts of experience and professional status that often provide the basis for recruitment into parties and other political organizations. If, however, a woman has the motivation and the status achievements to break into public life, there is still a good chance that the competing pressures of household responsibilities will limit the scope of her aspirations. It is certainly true that males are less likely to feel the constraining tug of these responsibilities than females. The 2010 National Household Survey found that among those with children under the age of 15, females spent on average twice as many hours per week on domestic work than did males.[16]

The male breadwinner/female homemaker family is, of course, much less common than it used to be. About 63 per cent of Canadian women over the age of 15 are in the workforce, and for women 25–44 years old the participation rate climbs to roughly 82 per cent (2012). These rates are higher than in most affluent democracies. The labour force participation rate for married women with children under six years old is about two-thirds, compared to barely more than one-quarter in 1971. Whereas 65 per cent of Canadian families were one-earner/male-breadwinner families in 1961, barely more than 10 per cent conform to this model today.

Because women are more likely than men to take time away from their career for child-rearing and to make other career decisions such as not searching for or accepting promotions or new employment opportunities that might reduce the amount of time and energy available for children and domestic tasks, the wage gap between men and women persists.[17] The average female income for full-time workers is about 83 per cent of what men make (2011), up from about 58 per cent in 1967. The proportion of women in relatively high-status professions such as law, medicine, accounting, and university teaching, and in middle management positions in both the private and public sectors, has increased significantly during the last generation. But the highest ranks of the income ladder continue to be dominated by men. Four out of five of Canada's top income earners, those in the highest 1 per cent of all income earners, are male. Labour market experience and time spent with a particular employer are often pointed to as two factors that explain much of the gap between the pay of males and females holding similar jobs.

The domestic division of labour is less unequal than in past generations, particularly among younger families, and the participation of women in the workforce is much greater, including in higher-paying and higher-status professions, than in the past. Nevertheless, the gender differences that persist continue to place limits on women's opportunities for political participation that men are less likely to experience. Other factors are important, too. Among them, researchers have pointed to what some have argued is a hostile media climate that undermines the candidacies of some female candidates,[18] the over-representation of rural Canada, where women are less likely to be candidates and less likely to win seats in the federal and provincial legislatures,[19] and the impact of the electoral system on the likelihood that women will

be elected.[20] Sylvia Bashevkin argues that both men and women often experience an unacknowledged discomfort at the idea of female political leaders.[21] We will return to Bashevkin's argument later in this chapter.

Women in Politics

Women were active in politics before being entitled to vote and run for office. Much of this activity was aimed at achieving full citizenship rights for women. But this was far from being the sole concern

In recent years, more and more women have attained the position of provincial premier. In 2013, five out of 10 provincial premiers were women. This represents a significant shift in representation, but it also represents a need to shift expectations. As the above cartoon suggests, the activities we might think of as "appropriate" for politicians' spouses have historically been gendered as stereotypically feminine.

of women's groups during the pre-suffrage era. They were also active in demanding a long list of social reforms ranging from pensions for widowed mothers to non-militaristic policies in international relations. By contemporary standards, however, the early women's movement was small and politically weak. Moreover, its demands and values—although radical in the context of the times—today appear to have been quite moderate and in some cases even quite conservative.

Although the women's movement of today looks and sounds very different from early versions, elements of continuity span the movement's history. In tracing the history of women's political involvement in Canada, we will focus on the social and ideological forces that have influenced the women's movement, as well as the issues, organizations, strategies, and accomplishments that have characterized the movement at different points in time.

Phase One: The Contradictions of Democracy and Industrialization

Feminist writings and occasional incidents of women mobilizing around particular events or issues before the nineteenth century were quite rare. The democratic impulses released by the overthrow of absolute monarchy in Britain (1688) and by the American (1776) and French revolutions (1789) generated some agitation for equality of political rights, but their consequences in regard to social change were negligible. One early feminist, Olympe de Gouges in France, argued in *Declaration of the Rights of Woman and the Female Citizen* (1791) that patriarchy was the source of society's ills. Her challenge to the patriarchal assumptions that prevailed at the time earned de Gouges the equality of the guillotine during the 1793 Reign of Terror.[22] Although married women did have the right to vote in some societies, they were expected to follow the lead of their husbands—particularly during an era before the secret ballot. In matters of law and property, a woman was subsumed under the person of her father and, after marriage, her husband. This state of affairs had been the focus of calls for reform by late eighteenth-century feminists such as de Gouges and England's Mary Wollstonecraft.

The origins of the women's movement as social action, as opposed to the ideas of a handful of visionary women like de Gouges and Wollstonecraft, usually are located in the mid-nineteenth century. As Sheila Rowbotham writes, "Feminism came, like socialism, out of the tangled, confused response of men and women to capitalism."[23] The progress of capitalism produced both affluence and misery. As more and more people crowded into the cities whose growth was spawned by factory production, a new set of social problems arose. Working-class women, girls, and children were employed in many industries. In fact, their cheap labour provided the basis for the profitability of such industries as textiles, clothing, footwear, and cigar-making. As historian Terry Copp observes of working-class Montreal in the early twentieth century:

> Large numbers of working class women were "emancipated" from the bondage of unpaid labour at home long before their middle class counterparts won entry into male-dominated high income occupations. There was no need to struggle against an exclusionist policy, since employers were only too happy to provide opportunities for women in the factories, shops, and garment lofts of the city.[24]

Hard numbers on female participation in the workforce do not exist before twentieth-century census-takers began to keep track of such things. It has been estimated, however, that women comprised about 20 per cent of the labour force in Montreal during the 1890s. There is no reason to think that the percentage was lower in other cities in which textile mills and footwear and clothing factories were major employers. The low wages put downward pressure on the wages of all unskilled working people.

Working conditions in most manufacturing establishments were hard, to say the least. There were no laws regulating the hours of work, minimum wages, or safety and sanitation in the workplace. A disabling injury on the job usually meant personal financial disaster. While both men and women suffered under these conditions, the exposure of women—usually single—to the harsh environment of the factory and sweatshop was considered more serious because of the era's views on femininity. A woman's natural place was considered to be the home, and her participation in the wage economy was believed, by conservatives and social reformers alike, to be "one of the sad novelties of the modern world . . . a true social heresy."[25]

Early industrialization took its toll on women in other ways as well. The brutal grind and crushing squalor that characterized the lives of many working people could be numbed through drink. And in an era before heavy "sin taxes," beer and spirits were very cheap. Alcohol abuse, although by no means restricted to the working class, was one of the side effects of the long hours of work, inadequate wages, and sordid workplace conditions characteristic of workers' lives. It not only contributed to the ruin of individuals, but to the suffering of their families. Poor sanitation, overcrowding in improperly ventilated housing, and improper diet combined to produce low life expectancy—average life expectancy was about 45–50 years in the last decades of the nineteenth century and tuberculosis was a major killer among the urban working class—and high infant mortality.

The harshness of early industrialization was experienced by both men and women. Its manifestations—child labour, poverty, alcohol abuse—became central issues in the early women's movement because of their perceived impact on the family and on prevailing standards of decency. The Woman's Christian Temperance Union, the Young Women's Christian Association, and the Women's Institutes that sprang up in cities across Canada starting in the late nineteenth century were keenly aware of the clash between the material conditions of working-class women and prevailing notions of femininity and family. The social reforms they urged on government were intended to protect women and the family from what they saw as the corrosive influences of industrial life.

Early feminism, however, was not merely a response to the contradictions that industrialization created for women. The achievement of democracy was also full of contradictions. If democracy was a system of government based on the will of the people, and that recognized the equal

humanity and dignity of human beings, half of the population could not be denied the rights and status enjoyed by the other half.

As John Stuart Mill observed in his essay *On the Subjection of Women*, arguments against the political and legal equality of the sexes took several forms. The principal arguments, and Mill's refutations (*in italic*), included the following:

- Unlike the slavery of one race by another, or the subordination of a defeated nation by its military conqueror, the subjection of women to men is natural. *When hasn't the subordination of one category of the human race by another been labelled "natural" by members of the dominant group? What is said to be natural turns out to be, on closer examination, merely customary and convenient for those who enslave others.*

- Unlike other forms of domination, the rule of men over women is accepted voluntarily by the female population. *This is not true. Some women do not accept the subordinate lot of their sex. And if a majority appear to acquiesce in their second-class status, this should surprise no one. From their earliest years women are trained in the habits of submission and learn what male-dominated society expects of them.*

- Granting equal rights to women will not promote the interests of society. *What this means, in fact, is that equality will not promote the interests of male society. It is a mere argument of convenience and self-interest.*

- What good could possibly come from extending full political and legal rights to women? *Leaving aside the good that this would produce for women—for their character, dignity, and material conditions—all society would benefit from a situation where the competition for any particular vocation is determined by interest and capabilities. Society loses when any group is barred from contributing its talents to humanity. Finally, equality for women would improve the character of men, who would no longer enjoy the sense of being superior to one-half of the human race because of an accident of birth, rather than to any merit or earned distinction on their part.*

Despite Mill's compelling arguments for equality, men who would have been shocked at the imputation that they were anything but democratic continued to ignore and resist demands that women be treated as full citizens. The arguments used to deny political rights for women were intellectually flabby and often amounted to nothing more than "nice women do not want the vote" or "my wife doesn't want the vote."[26] But the logic of democratic rights is universal, and the exclusion of the female half of the population from the enjoyment of these rights was one of the major contradictions of most democracies until well into the twentieth century (see Table 15.1).

The early women's movement focused mainly on three sets of issues: political rights, legal rights, and social reform. Anti-militarism was a fourth, but less prominent, issue on the political agenda of feminists. The social feminism mainstream of the movement was concerned chiefly with what it perceived as threats to the security of women and the family and to the traditional values associated with them. The demands made by organizations like the WCTU and YWCA and by prominent feminists like Nellie McClung were based solidly on the middle-class morality of the times.

The dominant middle-class morality could, and eventually did, accommodate itself to political rights for women. "Respectable" feminists were those who consented to play by the rules of the game as they found it. Political rights for women were expected to make the political parties and government more sensitive to issues of concern to women, such as working conditions for females, child labour, alcohol abuse, and pensions for widowed mothers. Legal rights enabling a married woman to own property in her own name or protecting her from disinheritance in the event of her husband's death were demanded in order to provide more economic security for women and their dependent children. Such social reforms as the prohibition of alcohol sales, family allowances, more humane conditions in women's prisons, and labour legislation dealing with women and children were expected to produce a more civilized, compassionate society. Finally, peace issues within the women's movement were tied directly to the image of woman as the giver and nurturer of life, to what were believed to be the maternal instincts of women.

The mainstream organizations of the women's movement were politically moderate in terms of their goals and their strategies for attaining them. Indeed, it would be fair to say that the goals of social feminism were fundamentally conservative, aimed at protecting women and the family from the corrosive influences of the industrial age. Even Nellie McClung, considered a firebrand of the movement, did not in the least suggest that the social roles of man the provider and woman the nurturer be changed. Instead, McClung and most other leaders of the early women's movement wanted to put women's role on a more secure material footing.

The political tactics employed by mainstream women's groups hardly ever strayed beyond the familiar bounds of accepted practice. Unlike their sisters in Great Britain and the United States, Canadian **suffragists** did not resort to such confrontational methods as chaining themselves to the fences surrounding Parliament, physically resisting the police, or hunger strikes. Instead, they relied

TABLE 15.1 Women's Suffrage

Year	Number of countries where men and women could vote in national elections on equal terms
1900	1
1910	3
1920	15
1930	21
1940	30
1950	69
1960	92
1970	127
1975	129
2013	All*

*Elections are held in all but a handful of the world's countries. Among these countries, Saudi Arabia was the last, in 2011, to grant women the right to vote.

The Guardian, "A Timeline of Women's Right to Vote," at: <www.theguardian.com/global-development/interactive/2011/jul/06/un-women-vote-timeline-interactive>.

on petitions to government and efforts to persuade public opinion.

After about 40 years of campaigning, the first success came in Manitoba in 1916. The other three western provinces and Ontario followed suit within about a year. In the Maritimes, where the suffrage movement was comparatively weak, the achievement of political rights for women was preceded by much less agitation than in the West. Nova Scotia (1918), New Brunswick (1919), PEI (1922), and Newfoundland (1925) extended political rights to women, although in the case of New Brunswick, women were granted only voting rights. They could not hold provincial public office until 1934. Quebec was the straggler among Canada's provinces. Opposition from the Catholic Church blocked political rights for women until 1940.

Nationally, women became citizens between 1917 and 1919. The Wartime Elections Act of 1917 extended federal voting rights to the relatively small number of women serving in the military and to the much larger pool of females whose male relatives were in military service. This was broadened in 1918 to include all women aged 21 years and over. The right to hold office in the House of Commons followed a year later, although women appeared to be barred from entry into the non-elected Senate and from holding other appointive public offices, such as judgeships, by virtue of not qualifying as "persons," as this term was understood in law.

Absurd though it may seem, the personhood of women was considered to be dubious in the years following their enfranchisement.[27] Two prime ministers rejected calls for the appointment of a woman to the Senate on the grounds that women, not being persons as understood in law, were not eligible. The right of females to sit as judges was challenged in the handful of cases where they were appointed to the bench. After a couple of provincial rulings in their favour, the question was placed before the Supreme Court of Canada in 1927. Feminists were shocked when the Court ruled that the legal meaning of "persons" excluded females.

This decision was reversed on appeal by the Judicial Committee of the Privy Council. Its ruling was blunt: "The exclusion of women from all public offices is a relic of days more barbarous than

Library and Archives Canada/Cairine Reay Wilson fonds/C-008408

Cairine Wilson became Canada's first woman senator after her appointment by Prime Minister William Lyon Mackenzie King in February 1930, four months after the 1929 ruling in the case initiated by the Famous Five declared women persons under the law, thereby making them eligible to sit in the Senate. She served until her death in 1962.

ours . . . and to ask why the word [person] should include females, the obvious answer is, why should it not?"[28] While logic and justice won the day in this particular legal battle, women have lost a number of others in the courts. Indeed, some contemporary feminists express strong doubts about the courts and law as vehicles for achieving the movement's goals. Voting rights for women and formal access to the male world of politics and the professions did not change the fact that society still viewed a woman's place as being in the home. Social feminists never really challenged this belief.

Political rights for women might have provided the basis for the reforms envisaged by early feminists if two conditions had existed: (1) a sufficient number of voters were prepared to cast their ballots for candidates and parties who supported the reforms advocated by the women's movement; and (2) a political vehicle existed to articulate the movement's agenda and provide a feminist alternative in electoral politics. Indeed, it appears to have been the belief of many in the women's suffrage movement that the major political parties either would crumble when a flood of independent candidates was elected or would tremble submissively before the demands of reform-minded female voters. But in fact the parties continued to set the agenda of electoral politics along the familiar lines that had long served them so well. That the parties felt no need to respond to the agenda of the women's movement or to recruit more women as candidates showed how slight was the impact of feminism on public consciousness.

The major parties' indifference to the demands of the women's movement was matched by the movement's distrust of the party system. Early feminists were reluctant to rely on the established political parties as vehicles for reform. There were two main reasons for this. One involved the attitude of those who controlled the parties. It was not simply that the Liberal and Conservative parties showed little enthusiasm for the goals of the women's movement, including political rights for women; they were often dismissive and even hostile towards women's concerns and those expressing them. So after achieving the same formal political rights as men, women found that little of substance had changed. They were marginalized within parties dominated by men who, in the words of Canada's first female MP, Agnes Macphail, "Want to Hog Everything."[29] This was not surprising. The parties reflected the dominant beliefs of the time, beliefs that made women in public life—or in any of what were traditionally male preserves—appear an oddity. Even the more egalitarian of Canada's male politicians were not immune from sexism when it came to women in politics. J.S. Woodsworth, at the time a Labour MP from Winnipeg, probably summed up male politicians' grudging acceptance of women in *their* game when he said, "I still don't think a woman has any place in politics."[30]

A second reason why early feminists were reluctant to work within the framework of the party system was that their movement, like the farmers' movement of the same era, was issue-based. The organizations that formed the core of the movement took hard, uncompromising positions on issues like prohibition, political rights for women, and social reform. Political parties, the two major ones at least, were based on principles that rejected the issue-based approach. One of these principles was partisan loyalty, the chief manifestation of which was the sheep-like obedience of elected members to the policy positions established by their party's leaders. Feminists wanted to be able to take positions based on their perception of what was in the interests of women without having to compromise the movement's goals. This concept of direct representation was shared by the farmers' movement of the time but was discouraged by the partisan norms of British parliamentary government.

The anti-party inclinations of feminists were reinforced by the parties' tendency to avoid if possible, and fudge, if avoidance was not possible, issue stances that might alienate important groups of voters. This has been called "brokerage politics" (see Chapter 11). It is an approach that had no appeal to single-issue groups like prohibitionists and suffragists, or to the reform-minded women's movement more generally.

Working outside the established party system and the legislature, in an era when the media were less effective channels for political influence than they are today, carried heavy costs. A legislator who sits as an independent is marginalized in British parliamentary government, not sharing in the opportunities for participation available to the members of political parties. Moreover, the organizational and financial resources of the parties are important advantages that their candidates have over independents. It very quickly became apparent that non-partyism favoured by leaders of the early feminist movement faced insurmountable obstacles.

Phase Two: After the Vote, What?

"Is Women's Suffrage a Fizzle?" asked a 1928 article in *Maclean's*. The question reflected the disillusionment experienced by many in the women's movement only years after having won the vote. Little, it seemed, had changed. Men still dominated the political process. The issues that interested women's groups, with the exception of prohibition, were no more prominent than before women's suffrage. And despite having the same formal political rights as men, women were still viewed as intruders in a world that belonged to men.

Part of the disappointment felt by feminists was due to their unrealistic expectations. Those who spearheaded the fight for women's suffrage believed—wrongly as it turned out—the vote would be the tool that women would use to change the world. As Nellie McClung put it, "Women have cleaned up things since time began; and if women ever get into politics there will be a cleaning out of pigeon-holes and forgotten corners, on which the dust of years has fallen, and the sound of the political carpet-beater will be heard in the land."[31] When the millennial expectations of social feminists were not met, worse than this, when hardly anything appeared to have changed after the victory that was supposed to change so much, frustration and gloom were natural reactions.

It is usual to treat the period from suffrage to the

"I don't object to women running for prime minister . . . as long as it's just to kiss him."

One significant obstacle for women's participation in politics has been overcoming traditional thinking about gender roles.

Len Norris/© Simon Fraser University

new feminism that gained momentum in the 1960s as one long hiatus in the women's movement.[32] A small number of women did run for public office, and an even smaller number won election. Of those elected or appointed to public office, some achieved national prominence. Among them were Ottawa mayor Charlotte Whitton, five-term MP and two-term Ontario MPP Agnes Macphail, British Columbia judges Emily Murphy and Helen Gregory MacGill, and Conservative cabinet minister Ellen Louise Fairclough. But the distinction of being the first woman to enter what had been an exclusive preserve of men, or to achieve recognition for one's talents and capabilities, had little impact on the political and social status of women more generally. The breakthroughs and accomplishments of a few stood in sharp contrast to the unchanged status of the many. A number of plausible reasons help to explain this lack of change. Chief among them are the nature of early feminism, the party system, and societal attitudes.

The nature of early feminism. The mainstream of the women's movement was essentially conservative. Far from wanting to break down traditional **gender roles**, social feminists wanted to protect the social values and family structure on which they rested. Early feminists tended to believe that the political subordination of women was based on their inferior political and legal rights. What they failed to see was that traditional gender roles in the family, the workplace, and other social settings prevented women from participating more fully and effectively in public life.

The party system. We have already explained how the anti-party stance of feminist reformers proved difficult to maintain once they became part of a parliamentary process that was based on partisanship. This was not, however, the only impact that the party system had on women's political involvement. Within the two traditional parties, as well as the CCF-NDP, women's involvement was organized around support services. The women's auxiliary or club was the symbol of the complementary role that women were encouraged to play in political parties dominated by men. These separate organizations for women actually predated women's suffrage by a few years.[33] By the 1960s, this segregation

of active male roles from supportive female roles—essentially an extension of the gender relations that existed within the family and society—was increasingly seen as an impediment to the equal and effective participation of women in politics.

Societal attitudes. Feminism failed to make a greater mark on social attitudes in part because the social feminist mainstream of the women's movement did not challenge conventional ways of thinking about appropriate gender roles. Outside of the mainstream was a more radical feminist fringe, what William O'Neill calls "hard-core feminists,"[34] who were not satisfied with the political rights and the social reforms that constituted the agenda of social feminism. Hard-core feminists such as Flora MacDonald Denison demanded the legal emancipation of women and sexual equality in education, employment, the family: in short, wherever women were systematically subordinated to men.[35] Their ideas were not, however, considered to be "respectable."

If mainstream feminism was a weak force in Canadian politics, which it was, hard-core feminism barely scratched the surface of public life and political discourse. Its more radical critique of female subordination was marginalized in left-wing political organizations, which themselves were on the near-irrelevant periphery of Canadian politics. Even within the CCF, the only left-wing political organization that managed to occupy an important place in Canadian politics, hard-core feminism ran up against some intransigent barriers. As historian Joan Sangster writes:

> [E]vidence indicates that women were channelled into [the CCF's] social committees; that women's feminine character was often described as emotional and sensitive, implying a female inability to cope with the "rational" world of politics; and that women were seen as more apathetic and politically backward than men. Perhaps most important of all, because women's primary responsibility for the family was never questioned, an essential barrier to women's wholehearted participation in politics remained unchallenged and unchanged.[36]

But this raises the question of why social attitudes about gender roles were slow in changing. It is a complex issue that cannot be reduced to a single explanation. An important part of the explanation, however, involved limits on the ability of women to exert some greater degree of control over their reproductive role. Fairly reliable contraceptive devices became widely available and used during the 1950s (mainly condoms and diaphragms) and the 1960s (the birth control pill). It was no coincidence that women began to have fewer children. Smaller families and the ability to be sexually active without fear of becoming pregnant provided the opportunity for women to stay in school longer or participate in the workforce for more years of their reproductive lives. Choice in the realm of reproduction was a crucial material condition for **women's liberation** in other aspects of life.

The pill made it possible, but not inevitable. We still need to understand why the second wave of feminism that became a political force in the 1960s—it already was something of an intellectual force, influenced by writers like Margaret Mead and Simone de Beauvoir—was more critical and more effective than the early women's movement. The explanation has three parts: sexuality, secularism, and economics.

Sexuality had been the deafening silence of the first wave of feminism. The entire topic of sexuality was shrouded in mystery and taboo before the 1960s. The decades since then have been marked by a much greater willingness to talk about sexuality and acknowledge its importance in social relationships. This was a necessary step that opened the way for public debate on such matters as reproductive rights and women's control of their bodies, pornography's possible impact on violence against women, and sexual stereotyping in education and the media.

Sexuality was not entirely in the closet before the 1960s. The subject had received considerable attention from intellectuals since Sigmund Freud based the totality of human experience on males' and females' different struggles to resolve the conflict between their libidinal drives (sexual energy) and the demands of the super-ego (society's expectations and taboos on behaviour). It is no accident that virtually every major intellectual leader of feminism's second wave took direct aim at Freud and what they saw as the patriarchal bias of twentieth-century psychology.[37] They argued that Freudian psychology was phallocentric, and that concepts like the "castration complex," "penis envy," and "masculinity complex" were pseudo-scientific justifications for male dominance, not biologically rooted facts of the human condition.

Once conventional beliefs about sexuality were challenged, this opened the door to a re-examination of traditional gender roles and stereotypes throughout society. The position taken by modern feminists was that these roles and their accompanying stereotypes were mainly social constructions rather than facts of nature. This was the reasoning that underlay the movement's slogan, **"The personal is political."** Conventional beliefs about female passivity, maternal instincts, and domesticity were argued to be the ideological foundations of women's political subordination. The traditional division of labour in the home, workplace, church, and other supposedly non-political settings was argued to be the structural foundation of their subordination. Differences that had been largely accepted and even promoted by women who espoused **maternal feminism** earlier in the century were flatly rejected by the new feminism of the sixties.

Secularism was a second factor that contributed to the changed character of second-wave feminism. Many of the leading individuals in the first wave of feminism had been women of strong religious conviction and even fervour. As well, some of the key organizations in the suffrage and social feminism movements, such as the WCTU, the Imperial Order of the Daughters of the Empire, and the National Council of Women of Canada, had either direct links or an affinity of views with some of the Protestant churches. Early feminism had strong ties to the social gospel movement of the period between the 1890s and the 1930s, a movement that "attempt[ed] to apply Christianity to the collective ills of an industrializing society."[38] Those in the social gospel movement, in common with the early feminist leaders, believed that a New Jerusalem could be created on earth through social reforms.

Their Christianity had a strong secular aspect insofar as it focused on changing conditions in the here and now. But their vision of reform was inspired by traditional Christian ideals.[39]

The second wave of the women's movement was secular in both its goals and inspiration. Its worldly character was broadly in tune with the changed social climate of the post-fifties world, where the traditional moral authority of religion was weaker than previously. In fact, traditional religious values regarding the family, procreation, and appropriate behaviour for males and females, as well as the patriarchal authority structures of most churches, were targets of feminist criticism. While some of the women's movement's earlier leaders, for example, Nellie McClung,[40] had been outspokenly critical of certain church teachings and practices, they had generally embraced traditional moral values, not seeing them as impediments to equality for women.

Economic change was a third factor that influenced the second wave of the women's movement. Women had long constituted an important part of the labour force. Single women in particular provided a pool of very cheap labour in some manufacturing and service industries. The unpaid domestic work of women helped to subsidize the private economy by reducing the price that employers would otherwise have had to pay to male employees. Moreover, women constituted what has been called a "reserve army" of labour that could be mobilized in unusual circumstances, as during the two world wars. Their participation in the wage economy was limited, however, by two conventional beliefs: women should not take jobs that could be held by men, and outside employment was fine for single women but should stop after marriage.

These constraints began to weaken during the 1950s and 1960s. The labour force participation rate of women (i.e., the percentage of working-age women who hold jobs or are looking for jobs outside the home) increased dramatically between 1951 and 1981, from about 25 per cent to half of all women. The increase was greatest among married females with children. Their participation rate increased over 400 per cent over these 30 years. Women's share of the total labour force also increased sharply and today (2013) stands at about 48 per cent.

A number of explanations have been offered for this sharp increase in female labour force participation since the 1960s. Economists have favoured three main arguments:

- Falling real family incomes have compelled women to enter the workforce to maintain the household's purchasing power. (This explanation is more plausible for the period since the 1980s. Real incomes for individual workers increased between the 1950s and the 1970s, the period during which the greatest increase in female labour force participation occurred.)
- Labour-saving household appliances and higher female educational attainment have produced feelings of boredom and dissatisfaction in the home, leading more and more women to seek outside employment.
- As the real wages associated with some "female" jobs increased, outside employment appeared increasingly attractive to women.

There is doubtless some truth in each of these explanations. But it may be that they all miss the mark by ignoring the obvious. Women had become increasingly restive with their traditional role. "[C]hained to these pursuits," wrote Betty Friedan, "she is stunted at a lower level of living, blocked from the realization of her higher human needs." Friedan called this "the problem that has no name."[41] Although difficult to label and express in a culture that told women they should feel fulfilled in the home, the problem amounted to this: "I want something more than my husband and my children and my home."[42] A paying job and greater participation in the world outside of the home were often seen to be that "something more."

Yet another factor, however, should not be ignored. Most of the new jobs created in advanced industrial economies since World War II have been in service industries. Many of these jobs have been relatively low-paying ones that have been traditionally viewed as female occupations. Expansion of the service economy thus produced an increase in the demand for clerical, secretarial, retail sales, cashier/teller, and food service workers. All of these occupations were dominated by females. Many economists have a difficult time dealing with this factor because their model of the economic world says that if the demand for something increases, in this case secretaries and so on, the price should also increase. This did not happen—underpaid "female" occupations remained underpaid—because of conventional beliefs that undervalued the work performed by women, seeing it as temporary or merely a supplement to the main (male) breadwinner's income. Not surprisingly, the world of work and the norms that determined why some jobs were seen as female and other as male, and that influenced compensation levels, became a central part of modern feminism's reform agenda.

Of course, the exploitation of female workers had been an important concern of social feminists, but they never questioned the belief that a married woman's proper place was in the home and that marriage was the most desirable estate for a woman. By the 1960s, the material basis of these conventional views had become shaky. The economic forces that caused a growing number of married women to seek wage employment, combined with the psychological impetus for women to seek fulfillment beyond their homemaker role, changed the nature of women's involvement in the economy. The reality of their segregation into low-pay, low-prestige occupations[43] became less and less palatable to women as their participation in the wage economy increased.

Phase Three: The Personal Is Political

The decade of the fifties was like the quiet before the storm. Post-war economic growth and the "baby boom" combined to reinforce traditional gender roles and stereotypes. Television sitcoms, films, and popular magazines almost unfailingly portrayed the male breadwinner/female homemaker family as the pinnacle of human happiness. Once women had achieved political rights, it seemed that equality was no longer an issue.

This complacence did not last long. By the early sixties voices of discontent were being increasingly heard. Women were challenging the deep-seated beliefs and social structures that limited their participation in the male-dominated world. The "problem that has no name" was being named, and the name was **sexism**. This word is not found in dictionaries before the 1970s, a fact that reflected the unconscious acceptance by most people of gender role differences as natural and even desirable. "Sexism" was coined in the 1960s as a label for behaviour that treated males and females unequally for no better reason than their sexuality. Sexism in its numerous forms and wherever it took place was the target of the women's movement that emerged during these years.

The revival of the women's movement was the result of several factors. Intellectually, writers like Simone de Beauvoir in France, Germaine Greer in Britain, and Betty Friedan and Gloria Steinem in the United States were developing a powerful analysis of women's subordination to men. Their critique went far beyond matters of political and legal rights and social reform, the chief concerns of earlier feminists. Instead, they exposed the social, cultural, and economic roots of inequality. Friedan's approach was typical in its range. In *The Feminine Mystique* (1963) she traced the causes of female subordination to the family, the social sciences (particularly psychology, sociology, and anthropology), education, advertising and the media, mass consumption capitalism, and sexual mores.

Anti-establishment ideas always face an uphill struggle and rarely triumph by their intellectual weight alone. What saved the feminist critiques of Beauvoir, Friedan, and company from the fate of many interesting but ultimately ineffectual intellectual movements were the supportive material conditions and social climate of the 1960s. With about one out of every three women of working age employed outside the home, including about one out of five married women (1961), and increasing numbers of women enrolled in post-secondary education,[44] sexual double standards were increasingly apparent to more women than ever before. Articles on the dilemmas facing the "new woman," telling her how to juggle family, romance, and job, became standard fare in women's magazines like

Chatelaine and *Redbook*. Terms such as "women's lib" and "women's libbers" were more frequently said derisively than not, and most women (and men) probably would not have recognized the names of people like Betty Friedan and Germaine Greer. Nevertheless, modern feminism's argument that the personal is political, that the fight for gender equality had to be waged in the workplace, the media, the schools, and over women's bodies, struck a responsive chord with many.

What the lived experience of women confirmed, the social climate of the 1960s encouraged. This was the era of the civil rights movement in the United States, mounting opposition to American military involvement in Vietnam, the Paris riots of 1968, and anti-establishment political causes generally. Attacks on the "establishment" and its values were common. Student radicalism, protest marches, sit-ins, and occasional violence were the visible signs of a reaction against the status quo. Although the feminist movement did not spearhead the protest movements of the 1960s, it profited from the tendency of these movements to see all established power relations as unjust.

The protest politics of the 1960s affected the women's movement in a second, more enduring way as well. Civil rights advocates in the United States argued that **affirmative action** programs were necessary to provide real equality of opportunity for blacks. Quotas and preferential hiring policies for targeted minorities were justified, they reasoned, because these groups were the victims of forms of systemic discrimination that ensured that few of them would acquire the formal qualifications—degrees, professional school admission scores, job-relevant experience—needed to compete with the members of more advantaged groups. The opponents of affirmative action—reverse discrimination as they were more likely to call it—charged that such a policy just shifted the burden of injustice onto the shoulders of the qualified members of advantaged groups who were not personally responsible for the plight of the minority groups targeted for special treatment. But despite considerable opposition, affirmative action policies were widely adopted by governments and educational institutions in the United States.

The arguments and demands made by the North American women's movement in the 1960s and 1970s bore a strong resemblance to those that emerged during the struggle to advance the rights of American blacks. The discourse accompanying affirmative action for women borrowed arguments and policy measures pioneered in the struggle to increase the economic and social status of blacks in the United States.

Although Canada had no first-hand experience with group-based affirmative action policies before this era—with the exception of some preferential hiring for veterans after World War II—the concept and practice were not totally imported. Language policies adopted in Quebec during the 1970s aimed to increase the representation of francophones in the managerial ranks of that province's economy through agreements negotiated between the government and private companies. At the federal level, the period from the early 1970s saw an increasing number of administrative positions designated officially bilingual. This policy had the practical effect of favouring francophones who, more often than anglophones, had bilingual skills. During the 1980s, Ottawa began the practice of setting "targets"—the word "quotas" was and continues to be rejected—for the representation of particular groups in specified categories of the public service, and eventually of linking the performance evaluation of senior bureaucrats to their success in hitting these targets. The logic of affirmative action was not, therefore, foreign to Canada. Not only was the discourse of group rights already familiar in Canada, largely because of the struggles over language policies and Quebec's constitutional status, but the logic and machinery of targeting groups for preferred treatment were already embedded in the Canadian state.

Contemporary feminism is different from the first wave of the women's movement in more than its analysis and aims. The organizational network of women's groups became much more developed than when female suffrage and social reform were the key issues. Moreover, the movement's strategies have distinguished it from its predecessor. We turn now to an examination of the organizations, strategies, and achievements of modern feminism.

Organizing for Influence

Women have long been active in Canadian politics. As may be seen in Appendix 1 to this chapter, several important women's organizations date from the pre-suffrage era. Moreover, the political parties provided a channel—though not a very effective one—for women's participation in political life. Over the last several decades these organizations have been joined by hundreds more, as the organizational network of the women's movement has proliferated. This proliferation has generated, in response, new state structures to deal with "women's issues" and the groups expressing them.

While the network of women's groups has become denser, some argue that a focus on formal organizations and the structures of women's political involvement is misleading. Historian Anne Firor Scott suggests that there has been a long but "invisible" history of women's struggles against practices and conditions they wanted changed.[45] Many Canadian feminists agree.[46] They maintain that a female political culture operates through contacts and consciousness at the community level—based around issues that affect women in their daily lives—and that it does not rely on the formal political institutions and decision-making processes dominated by men. These grassroots activities tend to be overlooked and undervalued because the dominant political culture "puts a premium on formal, institutionalized political processes, predictable and regulated levels and types of participation and both bureaucratic and hierarchical structures."[47] Some argue that women's influence diminishes and their perspective on issues becomes blunted when they play by the rules of a political game established by men.

Although it is common to refer to the women's or feminist movement, such a label conceals the often profound divisions that exist between women's groups on matters ranging from ideology to political tactics. Just as there is an enormous range of perspectives within feminism, the real world of women's organizations reflects diversity rather than a monolithic bloc. Perhaps the most prominent division within the Canadian women's movement in recent decades has been between the predominantly white middle-class feminists, who led the movement since the 1960s, and non-white feminists whose ties are to less privileged ethnic groups and classes. This second group emphasizes race and class as central themes of their feminist vision. In the words of prominent Canadian feminist and social activist Judy Rebick, "an organization like [the National Action Committee], which has been dominated by white middle class women, must transform almost everything we do to respond to the needs of doubly oppressed women."[48] At the extreme, some have argued that white middle-class feminists are incapable of truly understanding and representing the circumstances and aspirations of women who are black, Aboriginal, poor, or from some other historically oppressed group.

This claim has generated considerable controversy within the feminist movement and in particular organizations such as the now defunct **National Action Committee on the Status of Women** (NAC) and the Women's Legal Education and Action Fund (LEAF). After Judy Rebick's departure in 1993, the NAC's presidents were members of visible minorities and the orientation of the organization very definitely shifted towards an emphasis on the special problems of poor women from such groups. Whether this was a laudable and overdue change of direction is not the point. What is clear, however, is that the NAC's redefinition of the feminist project and division among feminists themselves made it easier for governments to question whether the organization truly represented the concerns and values of a majority of Canadian women. By 2004, what had once been Canada's most prominent organizational voice for feminist concerns no longer had enough money to staff a permanent office and answer its phones.

The decline of the NAC is sometimes seen as indicative of a more widespread decline in the organizational power of women. Indeed, over the past two decades some writers and intellectuals within the women's movement have parted company with their liberal and radical sisters to become what has been called a "third wave," with an emphasis on individual empowerment and on personally claiming the gains of the second wave rather than continuing to repeat what they see as the self-defeating narrative of "victimhood."[49] Nonetheless, consolidating and extending the achievements of the second wave is the central task of a number of vibrant organizations today. Important groups including LEAF, la Fédération des Femmes du Québec, and the National Association of Women and the Law continue to exist and to be active in politics. But even more significantly, women's issues and representation have been institutionalized in many labour unions, professional associations, and departments and agencies of the state at all levels. Although some will disagree, it may simply be that an umbrella organization like the NAC is no longer necessary. Many of the battles it fought and that provided its raison d'être have been won or have seen significant progress. Moreover, the organizational voice of women is today far more pervasive and entrenched in institutions across Canadian society than was true only a generation ago.

Strategies

"There are fifty-six whooping cranes in Canada and one female federal politician."[50] So began a 1971 article by Barbara Frum in *Chatelaine*. Half a century after winning the same political rights as men, the inroads made by women in Canada's political parties were pitifully small. Their participation was still channelled mainly into the activities of women's auxiliaries, whose role was to provide support services for their respective political parties. Although vital to the parties, these activities—social, administrative, fundraising, and campaigning—had low prestige and were remote from their policy- and strategy-oriented structures and roles. Separate women's associations were singled out by the 1970 Royal Commission on the Status of Women as a serious barrier to the full participation of women in party politics. The Commission recommended that they be abolished.

Support-oriented women's associations within the parties mirrored the sexual division of labour that modern feminism condemned. They have long been eliminated at the national and provincial levels in all of the major parties. The trend since the late 1960s has been to replace the traditional women's associations with new women's groups dedicated to increasing women's representation and policy influence. As Sylvia Bashevkin notes, this transition was not been frictionless.[51] Nevertheless, if men still dominate within Canada's political parties—which they do—and if aspects of the feminist political agenda are still resisted, the internal structures of the parties are no longer to blame.

Attempting to increase the representation and influence of women in parties that aspire to govern is a rather blunt strategy for achieving feminist goals. Parties in power, or even within sight of being elected to govern, are disinclined to alienate those voters and organized interests who object to such elements of the feminist agenda as the elimination of legal restrictions on abortion, affirmative action in hiring, and a national program of publicly subsidized daycare. Consequently, the women's movement has sought influence by other means.

One of these means has been the courts. Litigation in support of sexual equality claims has a long history in Canada, going back to the turn of the century when women challenged barriers to their entry into certain professions. But with the notable exception of the 1929 **Persons case**, in which the JCPC overruled Canadian courts in determining that women were persons in law, most of the pre-Charter litigation on sexual equality resulted in defeats for women's claims.[52] Given this dismal track record in the courts, plus the high cost of litigation—several of the pre-Charter cases reached the Supreme Court only because certain lawyers were willing to freely donate their time[53]—it comes as no surprise that this strategy was seldom chosen by women.

The Charter was expected to change all this. Indeed, women's groups fought hard and successfully for the inclusion of section 28 of the Charter, which states that "the rights and freedoms referred to in [the Charter] are guaranteed equally to male and female persons." Their efforts had already ensured that the equality section of the Charter (s. 15) proscribed discrimination based on sex. With sections 15 and 28 in hand, it appeared likely that women's groups would turn to the courts as never before.

They have, but with mixed results. In the first four years after the equality section came into effect (1985–9), 44 cases of sexual discrimination under section 15 were decided by the courts. Most of these cases were instigated by or on behalf of men. In only nine cases were equality claims made by women. Despite victories in some of these cases, feminist legal scholars quickly became dubious about the usefulness of section 15. Michael Mandel uses the term "equality with a vengeance" to describe the early tendency of courts, and of governments responding to court decisions, to interpret the Charter's equality provisions in ways that can backfire against women.[54]

Feminists have argued that the sexual equality guarantees of the Charter are sometimes undermined by two aspects of judicial interpretation. One is the courts' unwillingness to elevate equality rights over other rights and freedoms guaranteed in the Charter. For example, in *Casagrande v. Hinton Roman Catholic Separate School District* (1987),[55] a Catholic school board's decision to fire an unmarried pregnant teacher was upheld on the grounds that section 15 equality rights did not take precedence over the rights of "denominational, separate or dissentient schools" that are also guaranteed by the Constitution. Second, and more serious according to feminists, was the fear that judges would interpret equality in terms of **formal equality** rather than **substantive** equality, being satisfied that no discrimination has occurred if laws treat identically persons who are similarly situated. This is an "equality before the law" approach that, according to feminists, fails to understand the real mechanisms through which discrimination occurs. Systemic discrimination—the inequality created and maintained through social practices and beliefs—cannot be overcome if, in interpreting the law, judges are blind to the sex or other group characteristic of a section 15 claimant. Substantive equality, they argue, requires that judges determine whether a claimant belongs to a disadvantaged group and, second, "whether the impugned law, policy or practice is operating to the detriment of [that disadvantaged group]."[56]

Graeme MacKay/Artizans.com

Women's groups have criticized the government's inaction on issues of representation. The artist of the above cartoon is critiquing electoral candidates for not taking seriously the question of women's representation in public office. How would you answer the moderator's question?

In fact, however, this fear proved unfounded. As early as 1984 the Supreme Court of Canada declared its intention to look beyond the formal words of Charter sections to consider the interests they were meant to protect.[57] In *Edwards Books* (1986),[58] the majority expressed the view that "the courts must be cautious to ensure that [the Charter] does not simply become an instrument of better situated individuals to roll back legislation which has as its object the improvement of the condition of less advantaged persons."[59] A year later, Justices Dickson and Wilson argued that one of the important purposes of the Charter was to assist social and economic "underdogs."[60] These intimations of judicial activism were acted on in the *Morgentaler* abortion decision (1988), where the majority was willing to look at the actual effects of Canada's abortion law to determine whether it violated the "liberty" and "security of the person" guarantees in section 7 of the Charter.

Then, in *Law Society of British Columbia v. Andrews and Kinersley* (1989),[61] which dealt with a resident non-citizen having been rejected for admission to the British Columbia bar because of BC statutory law, Canada's highest court very decisively embraced the concept of substantive equality in interpreting section 15 of the Charter. Although this case did not directly relate to the rights holders enumerated in s. 15, a number of these groups, including LEAF, presented interventions.[62] The Supreme Court argued that the Charter's equality section prohibits laws that have had a discriminatory impact on the members of some group or groups. The decisions written by Justices Wilson and McIntyre both cited approvingly an American Supreme Court precedent that identified "discrete and insular minorities" as groups requiring the protection of constitutional equality guarantees. In fact, the formal equality test so maligned by feminist legal scholars was explicitly rejected by all of the Supreme Court justices.[63] The substantive equality test is now routinely used by the courts in applying s. 15 of the Charter (see Box 15.1).

Before the equality rights section of the Charter took effect, activist and writer Penney Kome identified several political strategies, of which legal action was only one, that were open to women's groups. They ranged from grassroots organizing to deal with emergencies (e.g., a rash of sexual assaults in a neighbourhood) or chronic local problems (e.g., inadequate public transportation or pollution), representations through official channels, lobbying campaigns directed at decision-makers and potential supporters, to media strategies.[64] Lacking the financial resources and the personal access to decision-makers possessed by many business and professional interest groups, the women's movement has made extensive use of all of these political action strategies.

Jacquetta Newman and Linda White distinguish between what they call *insider* and *outsider* influence strategies that have been used by women's groups.[65] Using the court system has been one of the more effective of the insider strategies. But lobbying, presentations to royal commissions, task forces, and other government inquiries, pressure applied within political parties, and media strategies have also been part of the repertoire of strategies used to influence the political conversation and policies. These are insider strategies insofar as they operate within the familiar confines of politics and are focused on influencing state action.

Outsider strategies involve mobilization outside the state that is not focused directly on influencing the actions of government officials. Examples include women-centred services such as rape crisis centres and hotlines, shelters for abused women, and various other women's and family services not directly linked to the state. In most instances, however, the state is an important—sometimes the most important—source of funding for such organizations. This dependence can create tensions in the relationship between the state and the women's organizations that turn to it for money, creating an ever-present possibility that these organizations may be co-opted and their activities influenced by government agencies that provide some portion of their finances. Activism, including take-back-the-night marches and protests and mobilization on university campuses, in front of legislatures, or elsewhere, is another feature of outsider strategies. The effectiveness of such action varies, as Cheryl Collier has shown in a study of the impact of women's movement activism on child care and anti-violence policies.[66]

Achievements

The achievements of modern feminists can be grouped into three types: legislative reform; changes in the structure and process of state decision-making; and improvements in the material/social conditions of women. On some fronts progress towards equality has been undeniable. On others there is disagreement over both the significance of the inequalities that continue to exist and the reasons for their persistence.

Let us begin with changes to the law. Some of the most celebrated achievements of the women's movement have been on this front. Sex was not one of the proscribed grounds of discrimination in the draft Charter proposed by the Liberal government in 1981. It became part of the Charter after the vigorous representations made by women's groups before the Special Parliamentary Committee on the Constitution. Likewise, the section 28 guarantee of legal equality for men and women was a direct product of intense lobbying by women's groups.[67] And in perhaps the most publicized of court decisions on the Charter, the Supreme Court of Canada struck down the section of the Criminal Code dealing with abortion, a decision greeted as a major victory for the women's movement. Several other rulings by Canada's courts have also been generally received as victories by the women's movement. Among these are:

- *Blainey* (1986), a decision that opened boys' sports leagues to girls;
- *Daigle* (1989), in which the Supreme Court ruled that a potential father does not have the right to veto a woman's decision to have an abortion;
- a 1998 Canadian Human Rights Tribunal decision that found the federal government liable for roughly $5 billion in back pay owed primarily to female public servants under pay equity legislation;
- *Ewanchuk* (1999), where the Supreme Court ruled that no defence of implied consent to sexual assault exists under Canadian law;
- *Falkiner v. Ontario* (2002), in which the Ontario Court of Appeal struck down the

"spouse in the house" rule for social assistance recipients on the grounds that it discriminated against women;
- *D.B.S. v. S.R.G.* (2006), in which the Supreme Court ruled that the payers of child support, predominantly males, are required to pay increased child support when their income has increased;
- *Watson* (2008), in which legislation banning protests within a certain distance of abortion clinics was upheld.

There have also been rulings that have been greeted with disappointment by some women's organizations, including *Lesiuk v. Canada* (2003), in which the Supreme Court refused to hear an appeal of a lower court decision that upheld Employment Insurance eligibility rules preventing part-time workers, most of whom are female, from applying for benefits; and *R. v. Ryan* (2013), where the Supreme Court rejected the defence of extreme duress in a case where a woman sought to engage another person to murder her husband.[68]

Legislative reforms advocated by women's groups have also been numerous. Among them are the maternity leave provisions written into the Canada

Governing Realities

BOX 15.1 When Is a Sexual Double Standard Protected by the Charter?

Note: This case involved a male prisoner who objected to cross-sex frisk searches and the presence of female guards when being strip-searched. Male searches of female prisoners were already prohibited. A detailed explanation of the guidelines used by the court in the interpretation of s. 15 is found in Law v. Canada (Minister of Employment and Immigration), (1999) 1 S.C.R. 497.

The jurisprudence of this court is clear: equality does not necessarily connote identical treatment and, in fact, different treatment may be called for in certain cases to promote equality. Given the historical, biological and sociological differences between men and women,

equality does not demand that practices which are forbidden where male officers guard female inmates must also be banned where female officers guard male inmates. The reality of the relationship between the sexes is such that the historical trend of violence perpetrated by men against women is not matched by a comparable trend pursuant to which men are the victims and women the aggressors. . . . Viewed in this light, it becomes clear that the effect of cross-gender searching is different and more threatening for women than for men. The different treatment to which the appellant objects thus may not be discrimination at all.

Conway v. Canada (Attorney General) (1993), 83 C.C.C. (3d) 1.

Labour Code in 1970; the 1983 amendment to the Unemployment Insurance Act that eliminated discrimination against pregnant women; and pay equity laws passed by Ottawa and the provinces. Human rights codes and commissions to enforce them exist nationally and in all of the provinces. They have provided opportunities for women and women's organizations to challenge discriminatory employment and commercial practices in the private sector that the courts have deemed to fall outside the ambit of the Charter.

So have the main legal barriers to sexual equality been eliminated? Not nearly, claim many advocates for women's rights. They point to inaction or what they believe to be the inadequate response of Ottawa and many provincial governments on such issues as daycare, affirmative action, female and child poverty, the persistent pay gap between males and females, and family violence. Critics argue that a popular backlash has enabled governments to roll back some of the gains made in the past or at least to stall progress towards further equality. There may well be instances where this is true. Nevertheless, the progress made as a result of legislation and court rulings over the past three decades is vast and undeniable. A second measure of feminism's achievements involves the decision-making structures of the state. Among the striking characteristics of the modern women's movement are the institutionalization of women's issues in the structures and processes of government, a development often referred to as state feminism, and the movement's financial dependence on government. The 1970 *Report* of the Royal Commission on the Status of Women was followed by the creation of the Canadian Advisory Council on the Status of Women, now called Status of Women Canada (SWC), and the creation of a women's portfolio in the federal cabinet. Similar advisory councils have been created by all provinces, and some have also established special cabinet positions. Within government departments and agencies it is now common to have special divisions devoted to "women's issues" or affirmative action for women and other designated groups. For example, the Public Service Commission of Canada has an Equity and Diversity Directorate that monitors the representation of women, Indigenous Canadians, disabled persons, and visible minorities in the federal bureaucracy. The Treasury Board Secretariat has a Diversity and Equity Employment department within its Human Resources Division. As Penney Kome observes, the creation of status of women councils in the 1970s was followed by a "deluge of equal-opportunity officers, women's directorates, grant officers, labour specialists, and other women's advocates attached to various branches of government."[69] Since 1995 the federal government has required that all of its departments and agencies apply a gender-based analysis to new policies and legislation to identify any gender-specific and potentially inequitable consequences that might result.[70]

Critics have argued that state feminism involves co-optation of feminists and de-radicalization of the demands of the women's movement, as well as favouring a middle-class and professional feminist agenda.[71] On the other hand, some researchers maintain that state feminism has been responsible for significant progress towards equality, particularly when left-of-centre parties form the government. Even when such parties are not in power, state feminism can serve to keep women's issues on the policy agenda and maintain important links between women's groups and state decision-makers.[72]

Financially, much of the women's movement has depended on government money. This dependence has operated through two main channels. One is the budget of the Secretary of State for the Status of Women, within Heritage Canada, which has responsibility for SWC. Similar public funding is also available from provincial governments. The second channel involves federal social spending, part of which takes the form of transfers from Ottawa to provincial governments. Much of the money that ultimately reaches the hands of rape crisis centres, women's counselling services, halfway houses for battered women, and the vast network of services geared to meeting women's needs, as well as women's research and information organizations, is buried in the budgets of the Canada Health Transfer and Canada Social Transfer to the provinces. When Ottawa has cut back on transfers to the provinces, and to social spending generally, this has had the effect of squeezing the financial lifeline of grassroots women's groups that depend on public money.

Those on the left of the women's movement have often criticized the organizational and financial ties between women's groups and the state. They argue that such ties have the effect of co-opting feminists into the state. The demands of these women's groups, critics charge, will perforce be more moderate and their influence strategies less confrontational—and perhaps less effective—than if they resisted the siren call of money and a seat at the table. On the other hand, the independent resources available to voluntary associations are often meagre and so the temptation to seek and accept state support is strong. Likewise, direct representation on a government body provides an opportunity to be part of the process and to express women's perspectives from inside the state.

In fact, despite the financial dependence of women's groups on government, little evidence suggests this has made them more "polite" towards the hand that feeds. Based on his examination of the Secretary of State's support for voluntary groups since the 1960s, Leslie Pal concludes that that these groups have not been co-opted into an agenda set by the bureaucrats and politicians. On the contrary, he argues, women's groups in particular did not hesitate to criticize and embarrass the governments that provided them with the means to publicize the alleged failures of government policy.[73] Sylvia Bashevkin's study of the NAC's strong opposition to the free trade initiative of the Mulroney Conservative government confirms this view. Bashevkin argues that the depth of Ottawa's cuts in funding for the NAC was certainly influenced by its vigorous opposition to free trade, in alliance with other critics of the Conservative government.[74] Janine Brodie argues that although the voices of feminist criticism inside and outside the Canadian state are more muted today than in the late twentieth century, it is incorrect to conclude that gender politics and identities have been erased by neo-liberal ideology.[75]

What about the social conditions of women? Has the women's movement managed to improve the material circumstances of women or change social attitudes regarding gender roles and expectations? Reforming the law and the state is fine, but do contemporary women believe they have achieved equality? For that matter, does everyone understand equality to mean the same thing?

Here, the record of achievement is mixed. There is no doubt that social attitudes regarding appropriate roles and behaviour for males and females have changed over the last two generations. For example, the vast majority of Canadians believe that a woman could run most businesses as well as a man. Most Canadians claim that the sex of a political party leader does not influence the likelihood of their voting for that party (a tiny minority say that a female leader would make them less inclined to support the party, but a considerably larger minority say that a woman at the helm would make them more likely to support such a party). On such issues as abortion and equality of job opportunities for men and women, there is a little evidence of a significant gender gap. As shown in Table 15.2, Canadians' attitudes towards gender equality are more progressive than those of the populations of most other affluent democracies.

Alongside the evidence of changed attitudes are signs that more traditional patterns of behaviour and ideas persist. This may be seen in some of the gender characterizations found in commercial advertising and entertainment programming, in the child-rearing practices of many couples and the unequal division of domestic responsibilities between men and women, and in the relative infrequency of women's career choices taking precedence over men's even in this age of two-earner households. Changed attitudes towards gender roles need to be weighed against the empirical evidence of persistent inequality.

When one turns to the material conditions of women the record is mixed and shows evidence of a significant class divide. Today there are more women lawyers, professors, accountants, and even engineers than in the past, and females are more likely than males to attend university. About one-third of Canadian women between the ages of 24 and 35 have at least a bachelor's degree, compared to only one-quarter of males in this age cohort. Indeed, in 2010 the widely respected public affairs and culture magazine, *The Atlantic*, included a feature article analyzing gender accomplishments and current trends entitled, "The End of Men: How Women Are Taking Control of Everything." Such an analysis, and its conclusion that the gender equality pendulum now swings in favour of females in affluent democracies such as the United States and Canada, would have been unimaginable 20 years ago. Today, however, such stories are commonplace. Over one-third of Canadian dentists are females, roughly four in 10 family and specialized physicians are women, over 40 per cent of lawyers are female, and even in engineering, long a male bastion, women constitute about one in eight engineers. These percentages are higher, in some cases much higher, if we look only at those aged 25 to 34 within each of these professions.[76]

At the same time, evidence indicates that even among professionals, a gender pay gap persists. Based on data for 1,574 MBA graduates in Canada between 1996 and 2007, a recent study found that female graduates earned $8,167 per year less than their male counterparts in their first jobs.[77] The study also found, however, that females were considerably less likely than males to accept first jobs that involved work abroad or extensive international travel, and that they were more than twice as likely as males to accept a job in the public sector or for a non-profit organization. To what degree these differences might have been due to differences between male and female MBAs in their career preferences is impossible to say from this particular study.

The breakthroughs made by middle-class and professional women have not been matched by their less privileged sisters. Consider the following facts:

- Close to two-thirds of all employed women continue to be found in what traditionally have been predominantly female occupations. These include teaching, nursing and other health occupations, clerical or administrative positions, or sales and service occupations. This compares with roughly one-third of employed men who work in these occupations. Pay levels tend to be lower in some of these female-dominated occupations, particularly clerical, administrative, and sales

TABLE 15.2 Attitudes towards Gender Equality, Selected Countries

Country	"When jobs are scarce, men should have more right to a job than women." (% who disagree)	"On the whole, men make better leaders than women." (% who agree)	"A woman wants to have a child as a single parent but she doesn't want to have a stable relationship with a man." (% who approve)*	"I believe men are better suited to lead a company."**
Australia	64.1	24.3	38.7	32
Britain	74.1	17.8	31.2	34
Canada	77.2	17.5	45.1	31
France	73.6	20.7	61.4	27
Germany	65.1	17.8	34.7	32
Italy	57.7	18	35.5	33
Japan	17.1	30	20.5	52
Sweden	93.4	7.7	47.2	23
US	65.9	24.2	51	37

*In some countries, the percentage of those who answered "It depends" was as high as one-third.

**In only one of these countries, Italy, did the percentage of those saying they would rather have a female manager exceed the percentage saying that they would rather have a male manager.

Source: Adapted from data at the website for the World Values Survey, Wave 5: 2005–2009, and Randstad, "Women in Leadership: Still a Tough Battle," *Randstad Monitor*, Mar. 2013 and service positions, which account for close to 60 per cent of working women.

- The average income of a full-time female worker in 2013 was 82.4 per cent of what the average male earned.[78] This represents progress when one considers that the figure was below 60 per cent in the mid-1970s. Most of this difference is accounted for by three factors: the continued segregation of women into lower-paying occupations; more women than men having part-time jobs (when both full- and part-time workers are taken into account, the average income of female workers falls to about 68 per cent of males); and the greater seniority of male employees.

- Women are more likely to be poor than men. Approximately 60 per cent of those below the poverty lines established by Statistics Canada are women. Over time, poverty has assumed an increasingly feminine aspect. For example, in 1961 only about 15 per cent of low-income families (i.e., families with incomes below the poverty line) were headed by women. Today the share is over one-third, as higher levels of marital breakdown and childbirth outside of marriage have produced many more female single-parent households. Single-parent families headed by women constitute the most poverty-prone group in Canada, with close to one-quarter of them living below the poverty line. This is over twice the poverty level for the population as a whole.

The *Financial Post* annually publishes "The Financial Post 500," a survey of the leading companies in the Canadian economy. Five women made the 2013 list of the CEOs of the top 100 companies. Twenty-seven of the leading 500 companies had female CEOs. A 2011 study by the consulting firm Catalyst found that just under 15 per cent of all directorships on the boards of directors of Financial Post 500 companies in Canada were held by women, but that about 40 per cent of these companies had no female directors whatsoever.[79] By whatever measure one cares to use, women are rare

at the highest rungs of the business ladder. Moya Greene, appointed CEO of Canada Post in 2007 (she left in May 2010 to become the CEO of the Royal Mail in the UK), points to two factors that she believes are key to understanding what is often referred to as a "glass ceiling" for women in the corporate world. One is that ambition continues to be seen as more of a masculine than feminine trait, admired when it is associated with men and often looked at askance when displayed by women. The other factor is that of balancing the demands of a high-powered job with family commitments. "It is simply not possible to commit to a major leadership job and be the kind of mother my mother was," Greene observes, adding that this ideal of balance—which is not generally expected of or by male CEOs—is not realistic (see Box 15.2).[80]

The continuing under-representation of women in Canada's corporate elite, at the same time as their participation in the political elite has been increasing, may thwart some of the gains achieved by the women's movement. As economies become internationalized, domestic politics matters less and business matters more. Increasingly, decisions with major social implications are taken by the corporate elite, from which women are still largely excluded. The general opposition of the women's movement to globalization, though it cannot be explained by this factor alone, certainly is influenced by the realization that a relative decline in the power of states and an increase in that of transnational corporations and markets tend to reduce the political clout of women's groups. The feminist criticism of the under-representation of women in the corporate elite is premised in large part on a belief that more women CEOs would make a difference in the sorts of decisions taken by major corporations. This may well be a false premise.

Critics argue that there is still far to go and much unfinished business before a just and fair balance between males and females in Canada is reached. It is perhaps worth noting, however, that the condition of women in Canada is seen as being comparatively good by some international observers. Indeed, a 2012 international survey of 370 gender experts (a category that included experts

Media Spotlight

BOX 15.2 Understanding the Glass Ceiling

A study of high-powered business school graduates from the University of Chicago found that males and females made similar incomes after graduation. But 15 years later the average income of a female graduate was 75 per cent of what a male earned. This was not true, however, in the case of females who did not have children. Their incomes were about the same as those of their male counterparts 15 years after graduation. Daniel Indiviglio asks, "(Is this) really something that should concern us, or just a symptom of the choices we make as a society?" Here's his answer:

> (L)et's redefine the disparity that the studies point out. Imagine there was no classification of men or women, just primary caregivers and primary professionals. Each family with children has one of each. Would anyone really care if primary caregivers didn't climb the corporate ladder as quickly as primary professionals if gender weren't involved? Wouldn't that just make logical sense? If men more often take on the primary professional role, consequently working more intensely and taking fewer vacations than women, then they *should be* promoted more aggressively.
>
> In this case, gender is actually coincidental to the issue outlined above. Imagine if society developed differently instead. What if men regularly took paternity leave, while women returned immediately to work without significant time off? What if men chose to work part-time to make sure they were at the house when the kids arrived home from school, while women preferred to work full-time? What if men drove the children to soccer practice, while women worked late on the presentation for tomorrow's board meeting?
>
> Certainly, there are households where the couple takes on these non-traditional gender roles today—but they're the exception rather than the norm. Should we lament that society hasn't embraced such progress towards equality? Maybe. But there's also a possibility that most men and women in traditional gender roles are perfectly content with the current arrangement. After all, if they aren't, then it's often within their power to live their lives differently.[81]

To be sure, such a perspective as that expressed by Indiviglio must make feminists of all political stripes cringe (except, perhaps, for libertarian third-wave feminists such as Camille Paglia), and to suggest that individuals and couples *often* have the "power to live their lives differently" certainly is debatable. Is it more a question of "damned if you do and damned if you don't"? And what middle-class assumptions are built into this analysis? What do you think?

from United Nations Women, the International Rescue Committee, Plan International, Amnesty USA, Oxfam International, prominent academics, and representatives of faith-based organizations) ranked Canada the best country in the world in which to be a woman.[82] At the same time, Canada does not do quite so well on the UN's gender-related human development index, placing eighteenth in the world in 2012 (eleventh in the world on the overall human development index).[83] Weighing everything in the balance, however, it is undeniable that women have made enormous gains in Canadian society over the past couple of generations.

Appendix 1: Selected Women's Organizations in Canada

Year Established	Name
1870	Young Women's Christian Association (YWCA)
1874	Woman's Christian Temperance Union (WCTU)
1893	National Council of Women of Canada
1897	Federated Women's Institutes of Canada
	National Council of Jewish Women
1908	Canadian Nurses' Association
1918	Federation of Women Teachers Association of Canada
1919	Canadian Federation of University Women
1920	Canadian Teachers' Federation
1930	Canadian Federation of Business and Professional Women's Clubs
1939	Canadian Association of Elizabeth Fry Societies
1960	Voice of Women
1967	Fédération des Femmes du Québec
1971	Women for Political Action
1972	National Action Committee on the Status of Women (NAC)
	Canadian Congress for Learning Opportunities for Women
1974	Canadian Abortion Rights Action League (CARAL)
	National Association of Women and the Law
1976	Canadian Research Institute for the Advancement of Women
1983	REAL Women (Realistic, Equal, and Active for Life)
1985	Women's Legal Education and Action Fund (LEAF)
2001	Equal Voice

Appendix 2: Selected Dates in Women's Progress towards Legal and Political Equality

Year	Event
1916	Alberta, Saskatchewan, Manitoba give vote to women.
1918	Women given franchise in federal elections.
1921	Agnes Macphail first woman elected to Parliament.
1928	Supreme Court rules women are not "persons" and cannot be appointed to Senate.
1929	Judicial Committee of the British Privy Council overturns Supreme Court decision in the Persons case.
1930	Cairine Wilson first woman appointed to the Senate.
1940	Quebec gives vote to women.
1947	Married women restricted from holding federal public service jobs.
1955	Restrictions on married women in federal public service removed.
1957	Ellen Fairclough sworn in as first female federal cabinet minister.
1967	Royal Commission on Status of Women established.
1971	Canada Labour Code amended to allow women 17 weeks' maternity leave.
	About one-third of university graduates are female.
1973	Supreme Court upholds section of Indian Act depriving Aboriginal women of their rights.
	Supreme Court denies Irene Murdoch right to share in family property.
1977	Canadian Human Rights Act passed, forbidding discrimination on basis of sex.
1981	Canada ratifies UN Convention on the Elimination of All Forms of Discrimination against Women.
	Just under half of university graduates are female.
1982	Bertha Wilson becomes the first woman appointed to the Supreme Court of Canada.
1983	Affirmative action programs mandatory in the federal public service.
1984	Twenty-seven women elected to Parliament, six appointed to cabinet.
1985	Section 15 of Charter of Rights and Freedoms comes into effect.
	Employment Equity legislation passed.
	Indian Act amended to remove discrimination against Aboriginal women.
1988	Morgentaler decision strikes down Canada's abortion law.
1989	Andrews decision introduces the concept of "substantive equality" in applying section 15 of the Charter.
	Audrey McLaughlin chosen to lead the national NDP.
1991	Ontario passes pay equity law that applies to the private sector (repealed in 1995).
1993	Kim Campbell becomes Canada's first female Prime Minister.
1995	Alexa McDonough chosen to lead the national NDP.
1997	Sixty-one women elected to House of Commons, eight appointed to cabinet.
2000	Right Honourable Beverley McLachlin appointed Chief Justice of the Supreme Court of Canada.
2001	Just under 60 per cent of university graduates are female.
2002	Justice Marie Deschamps appointed to the Supreme Court of Canada.
2004	Justices Rosalie Abella and Louise Charron appointed to the Supreme Court of Canada, bringing the number of female judges on the nine-person court to four.
2008	Sixty-nine women elected to the House of Commons; seven appointed to cabinet.
2011	Seventy-six women elected to the House of Commons; 10 of 39 cabinet ministers are women.
2013	Five of Canada's 10 provincial premiers, including those of the four most populous provinces, are female.

Source: CACSW, "Progress toward Equality for Women in Canada" (Feb. 1987), 15, with author's additions.

Starting Points for Research

Sylvia Bashevkin, *Women, Power, Politics: The Hidden Story of Canada's Unfinished Democracy* (Toronto: Oxford University Press, 2009). This engaging book, written by one of Canada's foremost feminist scholars, argues that women's progress in Canadian politics has stalled in recent years.

Jacquetta Newman and Linda White, *Women, Politics, and Public Policy: The Political Struggles of Canadian Women*, 2nd edn. (Toronto: Oxford University Press, 2012). This book provides a feminist analysis of the history of the women's movement in Canada and the gender dimensions of public policy.

Joan Sangster, *Through Feminist Eyes: Essays on Canadian Women's History* (Edmonton: Athabasca University Press, 2011). Collection of essays written by one of Canada's most prominent feminist historians.

Linda Trimble, Jane Arscott, and Manon Tremblay, eds, *Stalled: The Representation of Women in Canadian Governments* (Vancouver: University of British Columbia Press, 2013). Covering every province, the territories, and the federal and municipal levels of government, this collection provides an unmatched survey of female representation in Canadian politics.

Review Exercises

1. How many women hold public office in your community? Make a list of elected office-holders on your local city, town, or township council, your mayor, your MP, and your provincial representative. Don't forget judges, if there are courts in your community, and also senior administrators with your local government. What about university and community college presidents, the CEOs of hospitals, and the heads of public utilities? You can find all this information by going to websites and with a little bit of resourcefulness.

2. Read the first three sections of the document entitled "Gender-based Analysis Plus Framework" at <www.swc-cfc.gc.ca/gba-acs/framework-cadre-eng.html> and respond to the following questions:
   (a) Is this an appropriate approach to analyzing and making policy recommendations? Why or why not?

   (b) How influential would this approach be if applied to issues like trade, national security, agriculture, fisheries, and economic growth? Why?
   (c) On what sorts of issues might this approach be most influential? Why?

3. Some European countries have passed laws requiring that a minimum percentage of the directors of publicly traded companies be female. This is a policy supported by some groups in Canada and the United States. Based on the information from Catalyst, at: <www.catalyst.org/catalyst-accord-women-corporate-boards-canada>, explain in 300–500 words why you think mandatory rules for gender representation in the corporate world are or are not a good idea.

Aboriginal Politics

16

For most of Canada's history Aboriginal affairs were relegated to the dim corners of public life. Politicians and most Canadians paid them little attention. This has changed. Native groups have become much more sophisticated in their political strategies and tactics, and the issues that concern them, from landownership to abuse and discrimination, have become important parts of the political conversation in Canada. In this chapter we will examine the following topics:

- Aboriginal demographics.
- The language of Aboriginal politics.
- Who is an Indian?
- The reserve system.
- Assimilation, integration, self-determination.
- The White Paper of 1969.
- The Royal Commission on Aboriginal Peoples.

- Organizing for political influence.
- Sovereignty, landownership, and Aboriginal rights.
- The institutionalization of Aboriginal affairs.
- The way forward.

Idle No More demonstrators block a rail line near Portage La Prairie, Manitoba. The movement, which began in opposition to Bill C-45, opposes legislation that would weaken protections for development in forests and waterways in First Nations territory. (CP Images/The Canadian Press/John Woods)

The Museum of Civilization sits on the edge of the Ottawa River in Gatineau, Quebec, across from the Parliament buildings. Its sinuous curves and striking vistas are the creation of Douglas Cardinal, a Métis and one of Canada's foremost architects. Visitors to the museum start their tour in the Grand Hall, where several totem poles tower over them in an atmosphere of quiet grandeur.

In 2013 and 2014, three human rights groups, two of them from the United Nations, visited Canada to examine living conditions in Aboriginal communities and to investigate whether Canadian authorities have been doing enough to deal with the extraordinary number of Aboriginal women who have been murdered or gone missing. This was not the first time the state of Canada's Aboriginal peoples has been the subject of critical inquiry. A spate of youth suicides in 1993 among the Innu of Davis Inlet and stories of rampant substance abuse among the Innu of Sheshatshiu, Labrador, in 2004—including gas sniffing by teenagers and children as young as six—generated headlines in Canada and abroad. Suicide rates among Canada's Inuit youth are about 11 times the national average and rates among Aboriginal Canadians more broadly are almost six times the national average.

The contrast between the incorporation and celebration of Aboriginal symbols and culture in the official life of Canada and the bleak reality that characterizes the lives of many who live in Native communities is jarring. Canadians are often puzzled by circumstances like those at Sheshatshiu. After all, government expenditures per Aboriginal person in Canada are estimated to be roughly twice the average for non-Aboriginal Canadians.[1] Canadians also are sometimes perplexed by news stories showing the continuing tensions that occasionally have produced outbreaks of violence between Aboriginal communities and their neighbours or the state authorities. Why, they wonder, after years of treaties, legislation, government programs, inquiries, restitution, and financial settlements, does it appear that so much remains unresolved in relations between Aboriginal Canadians and the rest of the country?

Aboriginal Demographics: Who and How Many?

Aboriginal Canadians are those who can trace their ancestry back to before the arrival and permanent settlement of Europeans in what would become Canada. The actual size of this population has been a matter of some controversy over the last couple of decades. Some estimates place the number at 2–3 million, or about 7 to 9 per cent of the national population, while others estimate that the actual number is closer to one-third to one-half of this. Professional demographers are inclined to accept the lower figures, while some Aboriginal spokespersons and politicians maintain that the higher figures are the true ones. Using a definition of "Aboriginal" that comprises those persons who report identification with at least one Aboriginal group—North American Indian, Métis, or Inuit—Statistics Canada provides the following numbers from the 2011 census and the 2011 National Household Survey.

- 1,836,035 people, or about 5.5 per cent of the national population, gave as their ethnic origins North American Indian, Métis, Inuit, or a combination of one of these with some other ethnic origin.
- 1,400,685 people, representing 4.3 per cent of the Canadian population, reported identifying with an Aboriginal group. This was up from 3.3 per cent in the 2001 census.
- 637,660, or just under 2 per cent of the population, are status Indians, i.e., those to whom the Indian Act applies. Just under half of these persons live on reserves.

The regional distribution of those who identify themselves as Aboriginal Canadians is shown in Figure 16.1.

As we saw in Chapter 3, the social and economic conditions of Aboriginal Canadians tend to be considerably less favourable than those of the general population. Aboriginal Canadians are

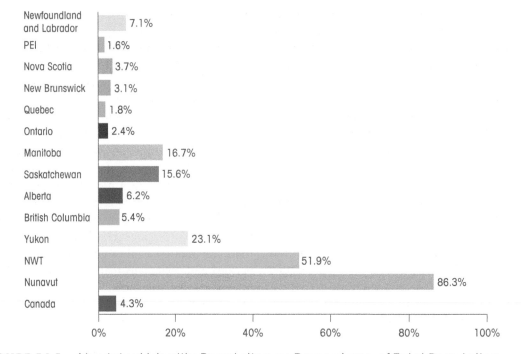

FIGURE 16.1   Aboriginal Identity Population as Percentage of Total Population, Provinces and Territories, 2011

Source: Statistics Canada, National Household Survey, *Aboriginal Peoples in Canada: First Nations Peoples, Métis and Inuit,* Table 2, at: <www12.statcan.gc.ca/nhs-enm/2011/as-sa/99-011-x/99-011-x2011001-eng.cfm#a3>.

twice as likely as other Canadians to be unemployed; status Indians living on reserves are four times more likely to be unemployed. On average, Aboriginal Canadians earn about one-third less than non-Aboriginal Canadians. Government transfer payments make up about one-fifth of Aboriginal income, compared to about one-tenth of income for non-Aboriginal Canadians. The likelihood of falling below the Statistics Canada low-income line is twice as great for the non-reserve Aboriginal population as for the non-Aboriginal population, and considerably higher than this for those living on reserves. Over four out of 10 Aboriginal Canadians have not completed high school, a figure that rises to about six of 10 for those who live on reserves, compared to just over two out of 10 for the non-Aboriginal population. Non-Aboriginal Canadians are about three times more likely than Aboriginal Canadians to have graduated from university.[2]

The Language of Aboriginal Politics

The words used to describe those who trace their ancestry back to the period before the arrival of Europeans in North America provide a useful starting point for understanding the politics of Aboriginality. For most of Canada's history these people and their communities were acknowledged in only a marginal way in the official life of the country and were barely visible in mainstream interpretations of Canadian history and society. The terms "Indians," "Métis," and "Eskimos" were used to describe various segments of the Aboriginal population. The legal meanings and implications of these terms were sometimes contested in the courts, as in the case of the 1939 Supreme Court ruling that the people known as Eskimos did not fall under the meaning of "Indians" as set down in the Indian Act of 1876. On the whole, however, there was little controversy over the terms used to characterize the Aboriginal population of Canada and virtually no sense that the words applied to these communities made a significant difference.

This began to change by the 1960s. Labels that previously had been considered appropriate and unobjectionable, and the concepts and assumptions associated with them, were increasingly brought into question. These challenges resulted from an important change that was underway in Western thought. *Communitarianism*—the belief that communities and communal identities are essential to individual dignity and the maintenance of truly democratic societies—was gaining ground among intellectuals. At the street level this belief was embodied in those elements of the black civil rights movement that called for greater awareness of black identity as something separate and apart from that of American society's white majority. There were echoes of this in the Quebec nationalism of that era, from Pierre Vallières's polemic *Les Nègres blancs d'Amérique* to René Lévesque's insistence that Quebecers needed their own independent state in order to form a free and democratic society.

These years saw the emergence of black, ethnic, and women's studies at universities across North America, a development that would gain momentum in the 1970s. The intellectual premises underlying these programs proved to be far-reaching in their practical implications. One of these premises was that the members of groups, and in particular minority groups that experienced a history of oppression, achieved dignity through their identity with the group and the recognition of that identity by society and the state. A related premise was that treating persons identically, without regard for their group membership and the historical conditions experienced by members of their group, did not produce genuine equality. On the contrary, equality required that these group identities and historical differences be recognized and taken into account by the law. Virtually all calls for greater group self-awareness and demands for official recognition of this collective identity were linked to an analysis and historical narrative of discrimination,

exploitation, and unjust treatment—in brief, inequality—in relations between the group in question and the state. Much of the intellectual impetus for this new analysis came from the writings of such colonial and post-colonial authors as Edward Said and Frantz Fanon as the European imperial colonies in Africa, the Middle East, and Asia disintegrated in the two decades following World War II.

This was a full frontal challenge to what had been thought of as progressive liberal thinking in the decades after World War II. Liberal opinion leaders during this era trained their sights on the eradication of poverty, socio-economic inequality, and discrimination, but believed that achieving these goals involved the full and equal integration of all people, as individuals, into society and the dismantlement of laws, norms, and practices that treated people differently on the basis of skin colour, ethnicity, or religion. The idea that the path to progress could be found in official recognition and institutionalization of difference represented a radical change in thinking.

In the case of Native Canadians, the first step involved rejection of the language of integration and liberal notions of equality that prevailed in the mid-twentieth century. Whatever the motives behind such proposals, their consequences were said to be assimilation and even cultural genocide. The term "Indian" was not immediately rejected by Aboriginal leaders, despite the historical fact of this being an obvious misnomer applied by the early European explorers to those who live in the lands that they mistakenly assumed to be the Far East. Indeed, the label "Indian" continues to be regularly used by the members of some of these communities and their leaders.

By the late 1970s and certainly by the 1980s, "Indian" had lost favour to preference for "Native," "Aboriginal," and "First Nations," a shift that was both intellectual and political. Intellectually, the change in language reflected a reappropriation of the identities and histories of those to whom the descriptions applied. Whereas the word "Indian" inevitably carried historical baggage of conquest, displacement, and subordination, in addition to the fundamental fact of having one's identity named by others, these more recent terms did not. Politically, the terms **"First Nations"** and "First Nations peoples" carried connotations of communal status and rights as well as prior claims. The language of nationalism and the claims of nations—particularly nations that had been colonized by foreign powers—were familiar and powerful in the post–World War II era. The dismantlement of the colonial empires of the European powers and the 1960 United Nations Declaration on the Granting of Independence to Colonial Countries and Peoples both reflected and reinforced nationalist claims and the idea that, in the words of the UN Declaration, "All peoples have the right to self-determination."

Quebec nationalist intellectuals were enthusiastic supporters of this doctrine of national self-determination. They argued that the Québécois constituted a nation or people within any reasonable meaning of these terms and, moreover, that the Quebec nation had experienced "alien subjugation, domination and exploitation [constituting] a denial of fundamental human rights," in contravention of the 1960 UN Declaration.

Mi'kmaq woman making a basket, Nova Scotia, *circa* 1845 (attributed to Mary R. McKie). In Canada, naming convention begins with the collective term used to describe the original people of North America and their descendants (e.g., Aboriginal peoples), then moves to a specific group within that collective (e.g., First Nations, Métis, Inuit), then specifies community (e.g., Mi'kmaq, Woodland Cree, Algonquin, etc.).

If such claims could be made on behalf of the Quebec nation or people, then surely they applied in the case of Aboriginal Canadians. This, at any rate, was the reasoning of many Aboriginal leaders and intellectuals sympathetic to their demands. Indeed, it is difficult to argue that Aboriginal peoples are somehow less deserving of nation status than the Québécois. They certainly can make a more compelling case for having experienced "alien subjugation" and "domination" within the plain meaning of these words in the UN Declaration.

The question of whether Aboriginal communities are nations is not one on which everyone agrees. But the same may be said of the question of whether there is such a thing as the Québécois nation. More important than the judgments of philosophers and other scholars, however, is whether the language used to describe Aboriginal communities has practical consequences. There can be no doubt that the widespread acceptance of the terms "First Nations," "First Nations peoples," "original peoples," and "Indigenous peoples" has had important consequences through the greater perceived legitimacy that such terms confer on a group's claims.

Grown accustomed to hearing Aboriginal groups in Canada referred to by public officials, journalists, and academics as First Nations, many Canadians probably assume that there is some obvious inevitability to this description. But there is not. In fact, the terms "First Nations" and "Aboriginals" are seldom used in the United States, where "Native Americans" and "Indians" are commonly used to designate the members of these groups. In Australia the words "Native" and "Aboriginal," used as nouns, are widely considered to be offensive and derogatory. Even "Aborigines" is rejected by many on the grounds that it has inevitable associations with colonialism. "Indigenous Australians," for the last couple of decades, has been the generally accepted description for those whose ancestry in Australia predates the arrival of European settlers.

The term "Eskimo"—a Native American word that, by popular account, meant "eaters of raw meat"—was long used to refer to the Indigenous peoples who inhabit the Arctic coasts of Canada, Alaska, Russia, and Greenland. It has been pushed aside, in Canada at least, to preference for **Inuit**. But the Indigenous peoples of Alaska and Russia prefer to be called "Yupik" or "Eskimo," again demonstrating that there is no inevitability to the terms used in the conversation on Aboriginal politics.

Relations between Aboriginal communities and the Canadian state were long about treaty obligations and reserves, at least for those groups under treaty. Those who had never signed treaties with the British or Canadian government, such as the Inuit of the Far North and the Innu of Labrador, were often ignored. The language of treaty obligations continues to be important and reserves still exist, but several other terms and the issues associated with them have become part of the policy conversation on Aboriginal affairs. These include "sovereignty," "self-government," "self-determination," and "nation-to-nation." These additions to the vocabulary of Aboriginal politics in Canada reflect the enormous change that has taken place over the last four decades in the scope and nature of Native demands.

The importance of language was demonstrated in the reaction of many Native groups to the Conservative government's 2012 decision to rename the Department of Indian Affairs and Northern Development, the Department of *Aboriginal* Affairs and Northern Development. The government explained that this change was intended to be more inclusive, the word "Aboriginal" embracing not just Indians but all the other Native groups that fall within the meaning of this word. Moreover, "aboriginal" is used in s. 35 of the Constitution Act, 1982, where it is stated that the term applies to the Indian, Inuit, and Métis people of Canada. These explanations did not convince many in the Native community, particularly groups representing status and non-status Indians. The word "Aboriginal," declared the Chiefs of Ontario, "fails to acknowledge the distinct cultures, histories, and rights of First Nations, Inuit, and Métis Peoples." They went on to say that "'Aboriginal' is dismissive of the sacred relationship and obligations which were clearly established in the Treaties between First Nations and the Crown. Using the term 'Aboriginal' reveals indifference towards First Nations' right to self-determination."[3]

Who Is an Indian?

While it has become unfashionable to use the word "Indian" when speaking of the descendants of those who occupied North America before the arrival of Europeans, there are practical reasons for not banning the word "Indian" from a discussion of government policies towards Aboriginal peoples. Under Canada's Indian Act, which has been on the statute books since 1876, a person who qualifies as an Indian under the law has certain entitlements that do not apply to non-Indians. Moreover, those Indian bands that live on land referred to in law as Indian **reserves** are subject to special legal provisions concerning such matters as individual landownership and transfer, a prohibition against mortgages on reserve land, and numerous restrictions on permissible economic activities. Until the Indian Act and the legal status of "Indian" are abolished, any analysis of Aboriginal policies cannot avoid using these terms.

In law, an Indian or status Indian is anyone who has been registered or is entitled to be registered under the Indian Act, including those who belong to communities covered by treaties. The defining characteristics are both biological and social. Indeed, the courts long recognized that a person's "associations, habits, modes of life, and surroundings" may weigh more heavily in the balance than the ethnicity of one's forebears in determining legal status as an Indian.[4] Writing in 1972, Cumming and Mickenberg observed that "The questions of how much Indian blood a person must have, and of how closely an individual must be associated with a native community before he will be considered a 'native person,' have not been answered."[5] The Indian Act of 1876 stipulated that an Indian was any male person of Indian blood who belonged to a band recognized by the federal government, and any child of such a person or a woman married to such a person. Thus, a woman could acquire Indian status as a result of marriage. This was, however, a one-way street. An Indian woman who married a non-Indian lost her legal status as an Indian and the entitlements associated with that status.

This changed in 1985. In response to pressure from Aboriginal women, Canada's obligations under the United Nations International Covenant on Civil and Political Rights, and, most importantly, the sexual equality provisions of the Charter of Rights and Freedoms (sections 15 and 28), the federal government eliminated this obviously discriminatory section of the Indian Act. Legislation passed in 1985 provided women who lost their Indian status as a result of marrying a non-Indian, and any children of such unions, with the right to apply for Indian status. The law also eliminated the possibility of males or females acquiring Indian status as a result of marriage.

Under the Indian Act the federal government sets the rules that determine who is an Indian, but Native bands, the communities that are linked to particular reserves, determine within certain limits set by the law who is entitled to be a band member and therefore live on the reserve. Their right to determine who may be a member of the band has been seen as an important aspect of Native self-government. There have been cases where band membership rules and unwillingness to grant membership to status Indians have been met with charges of discrimination. From the perspectives of the bands, however, their reluctance to admit new members has often been justified on the grounds that they have limited land and other resources and that without guarantees from the federal government that they will receive more, they are reluctant to allow their reserve community to grow.

Canadian law also recognizes the Métis and Inuit as two other categories of Aboriginal peoples of Canada. Although the Constitution Act, 1867 speaks only of "Indians, and Lands reserved for Indians" (s. 91[24]), a 1939 decision of the Supreme Court of Canada pronounced the Inuit to be Indians within the meaning of the Constitution,[6] which meant that the federal government had a paternalistic responsibility for the welfare of these people. They are excluded, however, from the provisions of the Indian Act. **Métis**, a term originally understood to be limited to the mixed-blood descendants of unions between Indian women and Scots or French-speaking traders and settlers in the Red River region of Manitoba, may also be considered Indians under the law if they are the descendants of Métis who were part of Indian communities that fell under treaties. Descendants of Métis who received scrip (certificates that could be used to purchase land) or lands from the federal government are excluded from the provisions of the Indian Act. Nevertheless, Métis are considered to be Aboriginal people within the meaning of the Constitution, and so Ottawa has the authority to pass laws concerning the members of this group. Although there is not much in the way of such legislation, an example is the Legal Studies for Aboriginal Peoples Program, under which the Department of Justice provides financial assistance for Métis and other non-status Indian law students. The Inuit and Métis are grouped with the Indian people of Canada by section 35 of the Constitution Act, 1982, which recognizes and affirms the "existing aboriginal and treaty rights of the aboriginal peoples of Canada."

Today, for largely political, legal, and economic reasons, some people of mixed Aboriginal and European ancestry, such as the Labrador Métis Nation (now called the NunatuKavut Community Council), have appropriated the term "Métis" although their origins are not related to the early western fur trade and their lifestyle, arguably, is not so different from that of many non-Aboriginal people. (The Labrador Métis, or Inuit-Métis, are an interesting case. These are people of mixed Inuit–European heritage living in central and southern Labrador who, for reasons of geography and birthplace, did not qualify as beneficiaries of the Nunatsiavut land claim agreement in northern Labrador.)[7] Between 1996 and 2006 the number of persons self-identifying as Métis doubled to about 400,000 and as of the 2011 census totalled about 460,000 or 1.4 per cent of the Canadian population. A 2013 decision of the Federal Court of Canada ruled that Métis persons, as well as non-status Indians (those who are not on the Indian registry, estimated to number about 200,000), must be treated the same as status Indians under Canadian law.[8] In addition to being the latest wrinkle in the long and complicated story of what "Indian-ness" means under the law, this court ruling appeared to open the door to these groups being able to claim health and education benefits that Ottawa provides to status Indians, as well as an exemption from certain forms of taxation. It is also expected to provide incentives for individuals to discover and claim what may well be their Métis ancestry, thus contributing to a significant increase in the size of Canada's Métis population. The Federal Court ruling stated very clearly that "[this] Court is not asked to determine that there is a duty [on the part of the federal government] to do or not do anything," and that "[t]he Court is not prepared to make some general statement concerning fiduciary duty" towards Métis and non-status Indians, but it is very likely that this expanded legal definition of who is an Indian within the meaning of the Constitution will have financial and other consequences. This certainly has proved to be the case in Newfoundland. In 2013 Ottawa tried to backtrack on a 2008 agreement it made to establish the non-reserve-based Qalipu Mi'kmaq First Nation after more than 100,000 people came forward to register as having the distant Mi'kmaq ancestry and Newfoundland connection required to become a band member (and qualify for federal payments for post-secondary education and non-insured health benefits such as dental and eye care).[9]

The Reserve System

Indian reserves have been called by some Canada's own system of apartheid. Indeed, a South African delegation came to Canada early in the twentieth century to study the pass system then used on Canadian reserves as a means of social control.[10] On the face of it the apartheid label seems a fair one. Average life expectancy and incomes of those who live on reserves are significantly lower than the Canadian norms. Rates of suicide, alcoholism, violent death, unemployment, crowded housing conditions, and infant mortality are all higher than the Canadian average, in some cases dramatically higher. Moreover, although being of Aboriginal descent is not a necessary condition for residence on a reserve, the reserve system was created to provide small, fixed homelands for Indians—mostly in remote areas at or beyond the agricultural fringe—and the vast majority of those residing on reserves today are status Indians. This combination of enormous disparity between life on reserves compared to the mainstream of society and the racial basis for the physical segregation of Indians does sound a lot like apartheid. (This was especially true under the pass system that lasted on some reserves in the Prairie provinces into the 1940s, when Indians were not allowed to leave their home reserve without the written permission of the Indian agent.) Non-Aboriginal Canadians who have seen first-hand the squalor and obvious destitution that characterize many of this country's reserves often wonder how such a system has been allowed to survive in a country that prides itself on being a compassionate democracy and an affluent society.

But when the Liberal government's 1969 White Paper proposed the abolition of reserves along with all the other legal structures that have treated Indians differently from other Canadians, the leadership of Canada's Native communities responded with a vehement "No." They rejected these reforms at the same time as they, and virtually everyone else, acknowledged that the reserves involved a system of paternalistic control by Ottawa over the lives of Indians. This paternalistic, racially based system, whose origins in Canada appear to go back to New France, continues today, as does Native resistance to its abolition. If the system is truly as ill-conceived and broken as its many critics have charged, why is it not rejected outright by the very people who are its "victims"?

The answer is complex. To understand how a racially based system of segregation manages to survive in a liberal democratic society one must examine the origins and operation of Indian reserves in Canada. We also need to consider the goals of today's Aboriginal leaders, many of whom are opposed to the dismantling of the reserve system.

The Indian Act of 1876 defines reserves in the following way:

> The term "reserve" means any tract or tracts of land set apart by treaty or otherwise for the use or benefit of or granted to a particular band of Indians, of which the legal title is in the Crown, but which is unsurrendered, and includes all the trees, wood, timber, soil, stone, minerals, metals, or other valuables thereon or therein.

At the heart of this definition and central to the quandary of the reserve system is the guardianship relationship established between the federal government and Indians living on reserves. The legal ownership of reserve land belongs to the Crown, but the land and all the resources appertaining to it must be managed for the "use or benefit" of the people residing there. In practice this has meant that virtually no legal or commercial transaction of consequence could be undertaken by those living on a reserve without the permission of the federal Department of Indian Affairs, although in recent years these restrictions have been eased somewhat. This is what critics are referring to when they speak of the Indian Act's paternalism. For example:

- Band members may not sell any part of the reserve.
- The federal government retains the ultimate authority to grant timber-cutting licences and to establish their terms.
- Reserve land may not be used as security for loans.

There are over 2,300 Indian reserves in Canada, about two-thirds of them—and of a considerably smaller size—in British Columbia. Together they comprise about 28,000 square kilometres, an area roughly half the size of Nova Scotia.[11] About three-quarters of all reserves are uninhabited. Many bands have leased their reserve land to non-Indians for purposes that include resource exploitation, rights of way, farming, and recreational uses. Reserve populations vary from a handful of persons to just under 20,000 (the Six Nations Reserve in southern Ontario), and most inhabited reserves have populations of fewer than 1,000 people. Roughly 400,000 Indians live on reserves—it is impossible to arrive at a more precise number because census enumerations of the population have not been permitted on many reserves over the last couple of decades, including on some of the larger ones. Although there are reserves in all regions of the country, most reserves and the vast majority of those living on them are located in rural and remote areas and often cannot be reached by road. This has important social and economic consequences. Job opportunities are fewer, those residing on reserves are generally required to leave home to acquire secondary and post-secondary education, and physical isolation impedes the integration of reserve populations into the rest of society. This last effect is not considered to be a bad thing by many in the Indian community. As Harvey McCue explains:

> To many Indians, reserves represent the last visible evidence that they were the original people of this country. The reserve nurtures a community of "Indianness" and reinforces spiritual unity among Indians. Despite the manifest poverty, ill health, poor housing and lack of services, the life-style on reserves, traditional values, kinship affiliations and the land itself all contribute to an Indian's identity and psychological well-being. The relative isolation of most reserves enables Indians to socialize their children to values important to their culture: reticence and non-interference, consensus decision-making and non-verbal communication. Reserves, since they are set apart both physically and legally, help Indians to maintain an ethnic identity within Canada.[12]

McCue's explanation of the role that reserves can play in the retention of Native culture is echoed by Cole Harris: "Native lives were still being lived. There were still joys as well as sorrows in Native households. There were still Native people taking charge of their own lives and getting along in the different world that had overtaken them. . . . Their identities were still Native."[13]

The pressures on Aboriginal Canadians to assimilate to the dominant culture are weaker on reserves and in Nunavut, where most of the population is Inuit. But for most Aboriginal Canadians the retention of Native culture is a challenge, to say the least. This may be seen in the case of Aboriginal languages, the loss of one's mother tongue being an obvious and important aspect of assimilation. Only three of Canada's roughly 53 Aboriginal languages—Cree (83,475), Inuktitut (34,110), and Ojibway (19,275)—continue to be spoken by significant numbers of Aboriginal people. Slightly more than half of those

for whom Cree is their mother tongue say that this is the language they speak most often at home. For those whose mother tongue is Inuktitut, the figure is almost 80 per cent and for Ojibway speakers it is somewhat more than one-third.[14] Recognizing the importance of their language to how they understand themselves and the world, some Aboriginal groups are making impressive attempts at language learning and retention within their communities.[15]

Assimilation, Integration, Self-Determination

Although some of the major components of present-day Aboriginal policy were in place prior to Confederation, the principles underlying federal policy have undergone important transformations. Under French colonial rule there was no official recognition of any Aboriginal title to, or other proprietary interest in, the lands they had long occupied and used before European settlement. France laid claim to territory in the New World by right of discovery and conquest. As G.F.G. Stanley writes:

> The French settler occupied his lands in Canada without any thought of compensating the native. There were no formal surrenders from the Indians, no negotiations, and no treaties such as marked the Indian policy of the British period. . . . Whatever rights the Indians acquired flowed not from a theoretical aboriginal title but from clemency of the crown or the charity of individuals.[16]

Conversion of the Native population to Christianity was a central objective of French colonial policy, implemented through the missionary work of the Jesuits and the Recollets. While clearly based on the premise that Indians were uncivilized, economically backward, and morally inferior to Europeans, French policy did not consider the Native population to be subhuman and beyond redemption. On the contrary, the 1627 Charter of the Company of One Hundred Associates declared that a converted Native had the status and rights of a naturalized

French citizen. Assimilation and non-recognition of any Native proprietary interest in the lands claimed by France were, therefore, the two key principles underlying Aboriginal policy in New France.

With the transfer of French territories in Canada to the British, the foundation was laid for Aboriginal policies that would span the next two centuries. The **Royal Proclamation of 1763** and the treaties entered into between the colonial authorities and Indian tribes very clearly were based on the assumption that Aboriginal peoples had fallen under the protective stewardship of the British state. A proprietary Aboriginal interest in the land was acknowledged, but within the broader context of British sovereignty and the colonial authorities' expectations that European settlement would continue to expand onto land traditionally occupied by Native peoples. Moreover, as both the Royal Proclamation and early dealings between the British and Indians show, the British believed that they were required to compensate the Native population for land that was formally alienated through treaties and purchase agreements. This was an important departure from colonial policy under the French regime.

Efforts at assimilating the Native population were much less rigorous under the British than under the French. There is some truth in Francis Parkman's observation that "Spanish civilization crushed the Indian; English civilization scorned and neglected him; French civilization embraced and cherished him."[17] The British colonial authorities were much less concerned with the state of Natives' souls than with ensuring that the Indigenous population did not impede the growth and development of the colonies they administered. To this end the policy of reserving certain lands for occupation and use by Indians was practised by the British. The policy of establishing Indian reserves was continued after Confederation.

Under the British North America Act (now called the Constitution Act, 1867), Ottawa was assigned exclusive legislative authority over Indian affairs, and within a decade of Confederation the federal government passed the Indian Act, a sweeping piece of legislation that consolidated the dependency relationship that already had been developing between Aboriginal peoples and the state. Under the

Act, Indians living on reserves were placed under the almost total control of the Superintendent-General of Indian Affairs, whose god-like powers would be exercised by federal bureaucrats in Ottawa and by officials in the field referred to as Indian agents. Little of importance could be done by status Indians without the authorization of the Indian agent. All money paid by the federal government to members of a reserve or generated from economic activities on reserve lands was controlled by the federal authorities. To give an idea of how this system operated, if a licence to cut timber on reserve land was issued to a company, that licence could be granted by Ottawa only upon the recommendation of the Indian agent in whose agency the reserve was located, after which payments from the timber company would be received by the federal authorities in trust for the Indian residents of the reserve. The Indian Act made it impossible for Indians living on reserves to assume responsibility and control over their social and economic development.

The extremely limited powers of self-government assigned by the Act to reserve bands (powers that were always subject to approval by Ottawa) were to be exercised through band councils and chiefs elected for three-year terms (see sections 61–63 of the Act). This method for selecting chiefs reflects the assimilationist thinking of the time, whereby democratic practices of European origin were expected to replace Native traditions of governance that involved traditional and inherited leadership. The goal of assimilation is even more apparent in those sections of the Indian Act dealing with enfranchisement. The Act laid out a procedure whereby an Indian could request to become a full and equal Canadian citizen. While enfranchisement was automatic for Indians who acquired a certain social rank, including those with university degrees, lawyers, ordained ministers, and physicians, there was no automatic right to Canadian citizenship for status Indians before 1960, when an amendment to the Act extended Canadian citizenship and the right to vote to all Aboriginal people.

Until well into the latter half of the twentieth century it was widely assumed that Aboriginal Canadians would gradually abandon their language, customs, and lifestyles and be absorbed into

Euro-Canadian society. Speaking in 1950, Minister of Indian Affairs Walter Harris expressed this view. "The ultimate goal of our Indian policy," he said, "is the integration of the Indians into the general life and economy of the country. It is recognized, however, that during a temporary transition period special treatment and legislation are necessary."[18] Integration progressed slowly, however, despite various prohibitions and inducements intended to eradicate what were considered to be backward practices and to reward bands that behaved in what were deemed to be suitable ways. The 1884 ban on the potlatch ceremony (repeated and clarified in 1895) and on religious ceremonies that involved dances (e.g., the sun dance or thirst dance) exemplifies the sanctions used to stamp out Native traditions. The prohibition on using Native languages in the residential schools operated under the authority of the federal government was another method of assimilating Aboriginal people into the mainstream of Canadian society. The Indian Advancement Act, also passed in 1884, whereby much more extensive powers could be delegated to a band by Ottawa, was an example of the carrot approach to encouraging compliant Native leadership and advancing the goal of integration. The extension of voting rights in 1960 brought their political status closer to that of other Canadians, but their legal and social status, and their civil rights, remained quite distinct. Moreover, instead of disappearing from the scene as the early architects of Canada's Indian policy doubtless hoped and expected, Indian reserves continued to exist as islands of shame within an affluent and democratic society.

The government of Pierre Trudeau set out to change this. Within a year of taking office Trudeau's Minister of Indian Affairs, Jean Chrétien, introduced the 1969 **White Paper** on Aboriginal reform. It proposed the total dismantling of the Indian Affairs bureaucracy, an end to the reserve system, the abolition of different status for Indians under the law, and the transfer of responsibility for the education, health care, and social needs of Native citizens to the provinces, which provide these services for all other citizens.

The background to these dramatic proposals involved an elevated awareness of social inequality and discrimination during the 1960s. The black civil rights movement in the United States and the student activism that arose during those years took aim at the exclusion of minority groups from the rights and opportunities available to the majority, as did the rising of the radical American Indian Movement in Minnesota in the late sixties, which possibly served as an impetus for the White Paper. The remedy that many mainstream social activists and civil libertarians proposed was integration, whereby barriers to the full economic, social, and political participation of historically disadvantaged minorities would be abolished. Integration was, in fact, the banner under which the civil rights movement marched in the 1950s and 1960s. It was not believed to be synonymous with assimilation, much less with "cultural genocide" and "extermination" that some critics have since equated with the liberal integrationist vision.

The reaction to the 1969 White Paper from Canada's Aboriginal leadership was swift and overwhelmingly negative. "Now, at a time when our fellow Canadians consider the promise of the Just Society, once more the Indians of Canada are betrayed by a programme which offers nothing better than cultural genocide" was the verdict of Chief Harold Cardinal of the National Indian Brotherhood. "For the Indian to survive," he said, "the government [says] he must become a good little brown white man."[19]

While much in the White Paper proved to be controversial, nothing galvanized Aboriginal opposition more than its proposals concerning treaty obligations and land claims. The government acknowledged that the lawful obligations of the Canadian government must be respected. However, it went on to argue that a "plain reading of the words used in the treaties reveals the limited and minimal promises which were included in them" and that they should not be expected to define in perpetuity the relationship between First Nations and the government of Canada. Moreover, the very concept of a treaty between one part of society and the government of all the people was morally and philosophically repugnant to Pierre Trudeau and the vision of inclusive integration laid out in the White Paper.

Ingrid Rice/© Simon Fraser University

NATIVES FINALLY GET RESULTS FROM THE ROYAL COMMISSION ON ABORIGINAL PEOPLES

Expressing a vision for self-government rooted in the idea of Aboriginal sovereignty, the *Report* of the Royal Commission on Aboriginal Peoples has not moved the federal government to implement the constitutional changes proposed by the Commission.

This vision and the premises on which it was based survive today as a minority point of view among Canada's political and intellectual elites. They have been refuted by numerous court decisions on treaty rights and Aboriginal land claims. Indeed, the trajectory of government policy since the ill-fated 1969 White Paper has been in the direction of recognizing, in the law and in the Constitution, the separate and distinct status of Aboriginal communities within Canadian society. Self-government, a concept that was almost unheard of a couple of generations ago, is endorsed by the Assembly of First Nations, Canada's leading Aboriginal organization, and accepted as both fair and desirable by many Canadians—although most have little idea of what it might involve in practice.

This newer vision for Aboriginal Canadians was set forth in the 1996 *Report* of the **Royal Commission on Aboriginal Peoples**. The Commission started from the premise that Aboriginal Canadians constitute First Peoples whose sovereignty should be respected by the government of Canada. Its *Report* called for the creation

of an Aboriginal third order of government whose existence would be based on the acknowledgement by Ottawa and the provinces that the inherent right to self-government is a treaty right guaranteed by the Constitution of Canada. A form of dual citizenship for Aboriginal Canadians, who would be both Canadian citizens and citizens of Aboriginal communities, was proposed by the Commission. The philosophical premises and policy proposals of the Royal Commission could hardly have been further from those of the 1969 White Paper. Among the most prominent of the Commission's 440 recommendations were the following:

- The government should issue an official admission of the wrongs done to Aboriginal people.
- The inherent right of Aboriginal self-government should be recognized by all governments as a right that exists under the Constitution.
- Natives should hold dual citizenship, as Canadians and as citizens of Aboriginal

communities. The *Report* proposed, instead of the hundreds of Indian reserves and bands and over 1,000 Aboriginal communities in the country, that about 60–80 self-governing groups be created through the political merger of these communities.

- An Aboriginal parliament should be established with an advisory role concerning all legislation affecting Aboriginal Canadians.
- The government should negotiate with Métis representatives on self-government and the allocation to the Métis people of an adequate land base.
- Aboriginal representatives should be participants in all future talks on constitutional reform, with a veto over any changes that affect Aboriginal rights.
- Much more money should be spent on Aboriginal programs.

Running through all of the RCAP *Report* was a simple and fundamental premise: the original sovereignty of Native peoples and their ownership of the land to which they lay historical claim must be acknowledged and their continuing right to a land base and self-government must be embedded in the Constitution. Moreover, the survival and development of Aboriginal cultures can only be achieved through policies that recognize Aboriginal people as distinct communities with special rights and powers. The problem with federal policies for over a century is not, according to this view, that they have treated Indians differently from other Canadians. It is that these policies have not provided the Aboriginal population with either the decision-making autonomy or financial resources to take control over their lives and escape the cycle of dependency that the Indian Act and the reserve system have perpetuated (see Box 16.1).

Politics in Focus

BOX 16.1 Manitoba Grand Chief Derek Nepinak on the Indian Act

On Monday, July 15th, 2013, I threw my Certificate of Indian Status in the garbage during a presentation I was making to my indigenous relatives at the Onion Lake First Nation during our National Treaty Gathering. My gesture demonstrates my commitment to move towards emancipation and my effort to begin the transition from prescriptive identification under the Indian Act, to an empowered identity as a sovereign Indigenous Anishinaabe from my ancestral lands in modern day Manitoba.

"The Indian Act" and the "Certificate of Indian Status" are products of a highly controlled bureaucratic infrastructure that is designed to manage and limit the potential of indigenous people living in the Canadian nation state. The Certificate itself is designed to create and prescribe a legal fiction known as the "status Indian," which is defined under the Indian Act of Canada. The acquisition of the Certificate is an arbitrary and prescriptive process tied to historically racist policies that were developed to create social and family divisions

amongst indigenous people and to limit the scope of obligations of federal governments with respect to historical land agreements. . . .

As indigenous peoples, we must decolonize our experience and reclaim our identities. This necessarily involves a retreat from our current position of allowing government bureaucracies to apply racist policies in determining our eligibility to belong to our communities. More importantly, we must come to the realization and understanding that our treaty agreements have nothing to do with the administration of the Indian Act. If we are ever planning to decolonize our communities, our political organizations and re-establish our nationhood and sovereignty, we must begin by decolonizing ourselves and emancipating ourselves from the Indian Act, one sovereign indigenous person at a time.

Assembly of Manitoba Chiefs, "Statement from the Assembly of Manitoba Grand Chief Derek Nepinak regarding the 'Certificate of Indian Status,'" 17 July 2013.

Some of the Commission's recommendations have been acted on. Steps towards various forms of self-government for many Native communities—though not a one-size-fits-all model enshrined in the Constitution—were already underway before the RCAP made its recommendations. The creation of Nunavut in 1998, with its own legislative assembly and premier and a population that is 85 per cent Inuit, represents a form of self-government under which the Aboriginal population effectively exercises powers similar to those of provinces. Many other and more limited forms of self-government have been negotiated since the RCAP made its recommendations.[20] Reparations have been paid to thousands of Aboriginal survivors who experienced mistreatment and abuse in the residential schools that operated from the late nineteenth century until 1996 when the last residential school, in Saskatchewan, was closed. In June 2008 Prime Minister Stephen Harper issued a formal apology to the victims of these schools on behalf of the Canadian government (see Box 16.2). But no federal government has been willing to embrace the concept of divided sovereignty that was at the heart of the RCAP's approach to Aboriginal reform. The notion of self-government it proposed was premised on the idea that Aboriginal sovereignty must exist alongside and be in no way inferior to the sovereignty that Ottawa and the provinces enjoy under the Constitution.

Organizing for Political Influence

Between 1867 and 2011 only 31 Aboriginal Canadians were elected to the House of Commons. That represents slightly more than half of 1 per cent of all MPs elected since Confederation. The picture is about the same in the Senate, where 15 Aboriginal members have sat, or 1.5 per cent of all senators over the course of Canadian history. Only a handful of Aboriginal parliamentarians have been members of cabinet, including two in the Conservative government that took office in 2011. The Charlottetown Accord on constitutional reform would have guaranteed an unspecified number of Aboriginal members of the Senate, somewhat along the lines of the representation that has been guaranteed since 1867 to the Maori minority in New Zealand's parliament. Of course, the Charlottetown Accord was rejected by the Canadian people—and by a large majority of Aboriginal people—in a 1992 referendum, and the parliamentary path to Aboriginal influence remains weak.

Parliament, however, is only one of the venues where Aboriginal issues are debated and decisions are taken. The mere fact that Aboriginal Canadians have had little direct representation in Parliament is not conclusive evidence of anything. Influence may be exercised in other ways and through other forums. This has certainly been the case for Canada's Aboriginal peoples, whose ability to affect policy has depended far more on their use of the courts, on public opinion, and on what might be called the institutionalization of Aboriginal rights and issues in the structures of the state.

The reaction to the federal government's 1969 White Paper on Indian Policy marked the real beginning of the politicization of the Native movement in Canada, although earlier efforts had been made by Aboriginal leaders to create pan-Canadian and provincial Indian organizations to lobby for their rights (see Box 16.3). Before the dramatic mobilization of opposition to the White Paper, Canada's Aboriginal communities were represented by a small number of ineffective organizations that had difficulty co-operating with one another and in managing their internal divisions. In fact, the federal government, through the control that the Indian agents exercised over spending by Indigenous communities, had long discouraged the political organization of Aboriginal Canadians beyond the band or tribal level. Nevertheless, some efforts at broader political organization were made throughout the twentieth century, leading to the formation of the Assembly of First Nations in 1982.

Media Spotlight

BOX 16.2 The Lasting Legacy of Assimilation

Ottawa's apology to the victims of the residential schools and the roughly $2 billion earmarked for reparations did not cover all of those who were victimized by a policy of assimilation. The article below describes the ongoing case of several Inuit who were selected for what the architects of this particular program doubtless would have described as a beneficial experience.

Inuit who as children were taken south as part of Ottawa's so-called "Eskimo experiment" are suing the federal government, demanding compensation and an apology.

Seven Inuit children were used as "guinea pigs" in the 1950s and 1960s when the government brought them from the Arctic to live with families from Alberta to Nova Scotia.

There they attended southern schools, without a chance to speak Inuktitut, learn traditional practices and eat country food.

"If you just said to the government 'You used us as an experiment, I think you should pay us for that,'" said Peter Ittinuar, who lived with a family in suburban Ottawa. "'You used us unwittingly, you didn't ask our parents, you just took us and in official documents you employed us as experimentees to determine how policy would be written about educating Inuit kids in Canada.'"

Statements of claim filed in the Nunavut Court of Justice allege Canada denied the seven former students the right to communicate with their famil(ies) for long periods.

The court documents allege the seven Inuit were forbidden from practicing their culture, and were "taught that their native language, cultural practices, customs and spiritual beliefs were inferior, wrong, sinful and shameful."

That led to "a loss of cultural identity and sense of belonging within their own community and within Canadian culture," and "a loss of Inuit skills that are necessary to traditional living in the North."

One of the plaintiffs, Zebedee Nungak, described in a 2000 article in *Inuktitut Magazine* his life in suburban Ottawa as growing up alongside "textbook Dicks, Janes and Sallys" while taking part in judo and swimming, playing in rock bands and going to the cottage on summer weekends.

"Here we were, literate Eskimos, able to read and write English, and relate to the works of Shakespeare, yet no longer able to cut snow blocks with a pana (snow knife)," Nungak wrote. "Well versed in calculus, we didn't know how to remove the sungaq (bile sac) from a seal's liver."

Nungak wrote this "cultural starvation" crippled his "sense of identity."

"These scars are hidden from the eye, but cut deep into our souls."

The seven plaintiffs are seeking a total of $350,000 each in damages. More importantly, Ittinuar said, they're looking for an apology, much like former residential school students, who received cash payouts and, last month, an apology from the federal government.

"I think we deserve no less," Ittinuar said.

Source: Chris Windeyer, "'Eskimo Experiment' Claimants Seek Cash, Apology," first published July 4, 2008 in *Nunatsiaq News.*

The "Eskimo experiment," was, in fact, the tip of an iceberg of a deliberate policy of removing Aboriginal children from their families and communities and placing them with non-Native families. In 2013 an Ontario court gave the green light to a class action lawsuit on behalf of thousands of Aboriginal Canadians who experienced such displacement during the 1960s and 1970s, and whose claim is based on loss of cultural identity. The federal government, the defendant in this case, has argued that loss of cultural identity is not a concept recognized by law.

Governing Realities

BOX 16.3 Major Organizations Representing Native Canadians

1870–1938   *Grand General Indian Council of Ontario.* Created by missionaries' efforts to organize the Ojibwa tribes, the Council was conciliatory in its dealings with the Indian Affairs bureaucracy.

1915–27   *Allied Tribes of British Columbia.* An organization of BC bands, one of whose chiefs had travelled to England in 1906 to petition King Edward VII concerning a land claim, the Allied Tribes took up this cause and others, petitioning the Canadian government and Prime Minister Laurier and Britain's Judicial Committee of the Privy Council in the hope of gaining Aboriginal rights and more and larger reserves. They did not succeed.

1918   *League of Indians.* Spearheaded by Frederick Ogilvie Loft, a Mohawk veteran of World War I, this was the first real attempt to establish a national political organization representing Native Canadians. Loft's efforts were actively opposed by the Department of Indian Affairs, which had him under police surveillance, and after some initial organizing success in western Canada the League had failed by the early 1940s.

1945   *North American Indian Brotherhood.* Created by Andrew Paull, a BC Native leader, the Brotherhood advocated the extension of voting rights to Indians without the loss of their status rights under the Indian Act (something Fred Loft had sought), an end to intoxication offences under the Indian Act, and better income support programs for Natives. It never achieved national support among Aboriginal Canadians and was disbanded by the early 1950s.

1961–8   *National Indian Advisory Council.* This was a classic example of the state creating an interest group in the expectation of being able to channel and to some degree control the demands it made. Although the stated goal of the Council was to promote "unity among all First Nations people," it soon fell apart because of statutory differences among the three groups that it brought together: status Indians, non-status Indians, and Métis. The Council did not purport to represent the Inuit.

1968–82   *National Indian Brotherhood.* The breakup of the NIAC was followed by the creation of the National Indian Brotherhood, representing status Indians, and the Congress of Aboriginal Peoples, which represented non-status Indians and the Métis. Despite the fact that it did not speak for all Aboriginal Canadians of Amerindian heritage, the NIB was the first national Aboriginal organization to achieve high public visibility and to be recognized by the Canadian state as the principal voice on Indian affairs. But the NIB had problems of internal cohesion, as was apparent when the organization split over the Canadian government's 1980 proposal to patriate the Constitution.

1968   *Congress of Aboriginal Peoples.* The 1968 breakup of the NIAC led to the formation of the Canadian Métis Society, which a year later was renamed the Native Council of Canada. The NCC brought together organizations representing Métis and non-status Indians. When the Métis National Council emerged in 1983 as a separate voice for the Métis, the NCC adjusted its focus and in 1993 it was rechristened the Congress of Aboriginal Peoples. CAP is a confederation of provincial and territorial organizations that seeks to represent Canada's urban Aboriginal population. In recent years CAP has had something of a rivalry with the

Assembly of First Nations over which group best represents Aboriginal Canadians, with CAP taking a more conciliatory stance on some issues, as reflected by the fact that its National Chief, Patrick Brazeau, was appointed as a Conservative senator by the Harper government in 2009.

1971   *Inuit Tapiriit Kanatami.* Until the 1999 creation of Nunavut, Inuit Tapiriit (originally named Inuit Tapirisat of Canada) was the leading organizational voice for the Inuit. Its origins go back to the mid-1960s when the Indian and Eskimo Association was formed. When Inuit Tapiriit was founded, its initial funding was provided through the federal Secretary of State. Its efforts led to the creation of the territory of Nunavut in the eastern Arctic.

1974   *Native Women's Association of Canada.* This organization, which speaks nationally for 13 regional Native women's groups, has as its mandate the promotion and enhancement of the political, economic, social, and cultural well-being of First Nations and Métis women. The NWAC, currently led by Michèle Audette, has been an important voice in seeking respect for Aboriginal communities, families, and women.

1982   *Assembly of First Nations.* Since its creation the AFN has been the country's foremost interlocutor with government on Aboriginal issues. Its leaders have included several of Canada's most prominent Native spokespersons, including Georges Erasmus, Ovide Mercredi, Matthew Coon Come, and Phil Fontaine. The most recent National Chief, first elected in 2009, was Shawn A-in-chut Atleo, a hereditary chief from Vancouver Island with a background in education and community activism. Atleo stepped down in May 2014 because of a lack of support from some leaders and the grassroots linked to his championing of the federal government's proposed First Nations Control of First Nations Education Act and his seemingly close relationship with the Prime Minister. Perry Bellegarde was elected the new National Chief of the AFN in December 2014. In addition to being regularly consulted by government officials, the AFN has often been an intervenor in court cases involving Aboriginal rights.

1983   *Métis National Council.* Dissatisfied with being represented by the Congress of Aboriginal Peoples, the MNC was created to provide a more focused voice for Canada's Métis population. It is an umbrella organization that brings together the provincial Métis associations of British Columbia, Alberta, Saskatchewan, Manitoba, and Ontario.

2013   *National Treaty Alliance.* In July 2013 a group of about 85 chiefs and band councillors met at Onion Lake, Saskatchewan, at the same time as the annual gathering of the AFN was taking place in Whitehorse, Yukon. Led by Manitoba Grand Chief Derek Nepinak, the assembly at Onion Lake produced a new organization, the National Treaty Alliance, which challenged the view that the AFN should take the lead in treaty negotiations with the federal government.

In addition, many provincial organizations represent Native communities.

Source: Based on information provided in *The Canadian Encyclopedia* (Edmonton: Hurtig, 1988); <www.afn.ca>; <www.nwac-hq.org/>; <www.metisnation.ca>; and <www.itk.ca>.

Sovereignty, Landownership, and Aboriginal Rights: The Battle in the Courts

It has always been our belief that when God created this whole world he gave pieces of land to all races of people throughout this world, the Chinese people, Germans and you name them, including Indians. So at one time our land was this whole continent right from the tip of South America to the North Pole. . . . It has always been our belief that God gave us the land . . . and we say that no one can take our title away except He who gave it to us to begin with.[21]

Disputes over land—who owns it, who has the right to live on it, to benefit from it, and to make laws that apply to those within the boundaries of a particular territory—are among the most intractable. Only recently have more than a small minority of non-Aboriginal Canadians come to realize that the crux of Native demands involves land. Phrases like "self-government for Canada's Aboriginal peoples" have inoffensive and even positive associations until they are linked to exclusive Aboriginal ownership of land and political sovereignty over territory that the majority of Canadians assume to be part of Canada. The words of James Gosnell, quoted above, have been repeated in one form or another by many Aboriginal leaders, from Louis Riel to many of the current generation. Their message is simple: the land belonged to us, much of it was never lawfully surrendered by us, and much of what was surrendered under the terms of treaties was little more than a swindle of major proportions.

Ownership and control over lands to which Aboriginal peoples claim a historic right are argued to be necessary for the survival of Aboriginal culture. In highlighting what are said to be the chief differences between Aboriginal and European-based cultures, nothing is invoked more often than how these respective cultures view the land and their relationship to it. Clearly, the land was crucial to the traditional lifestyles of Native peoples. For this reason such matters as Native hunting and fishing rights were recognized in the treaties entered into between Aboriginal peoples and the governments of European settlers. However, these rights were often restricted or ignored by federal and provincial governments and private citizens.

More controversial and hugely significant in terms of financial implications are Native claims to control mineral or other resources, the exploitation of which, according to some, has little or no relationship to traditional Aboriginal cultures and to the concept of Indianness. This is a very complicated issue that the courts have dealt with since the 1997 *Delgamuukw* decision, where Chief Justice Antonio Lamer wrote that Aboriginal title does not include uses that are "irreconcilable with the nature of the occupation of that land and the relationship that the particular group has had with the land which together have given rise to aboriginal title in the first place."[22] For example, if land is claimed on the grounds that it was a traditional hunting ground, it could not be used in a manner that would destroy its value for this use. But in that same ruling Chief Justice Lamer also said the following: "[A]boriginal title also encompasses mineral rights, and lands held pursuant to aboriginal title should be capable of exploitation in the same way, which is certainly not a traditional use for those lands."[23] The Supreme Court's 2014 ruling in *Tsilhqot'in Nation v. British Columbia* provides the clearest statement yet of the meaning of Aboriginal title and has a great deal of relevance for mineral exploitation, pipelines, electrical transmission corridors, and other infrastructure. These cases are discussed in greater detail below.

Landownership is one thing. Sovereignty is another. The fact that a person or group of persons owns a particular parcel of land, regardless of its size and other characteristics, does not exempt them from the obligation to obey the law of the sovereign country within which their land is located. But many leaders within Canada's Aboriginal communities deny the sovereignty of the Canadian state over them and their land. Former AFN National Chief Ovide Mercredi's comment is fairly typical: "We will not allow some other society to decide what we can do and determine the limits of our authority."[24] Bargaining rhetoric and bottom lines are not always the same, of course. It needs to be said that while virtually all spokespersons for Aboriginal groups express support for the principles of **Aboriginal self-government** and rights, most advocate some form of self-determination that would be realized within the context of the Canadian state. The nature of such an arrangement, however, is the subject of much dispute.

The issues of sovereignty and landownership are obviously intertwined. These matters have been contested and determined largely through the courts, based on the interpretation of treaties. Indeed, it is usual for those who make the case for Aboriginal sovereignty to begin with the Royal Proclamation of 1763. The Proclamation dealt with the North American territories that were formally surrendered by France to England under the terms of the Treaty of Paris. It included detailed provisions regarding relations between the British and the Native inhabitants of these territories (see Box 16.4).

Aboriginal leaders generally view the Royal Proclamation as an affirmation of their existing right to the lands they occupied. Georges Erasmus, a former National Chief of the Assembly of First Nations (1985–91) and co-chair of the Royal Commission on Aboriginal Peoples, argues that "by virtue of that Proclamation, it can be said that First Nations became protected states of the British, while being recognized as sovereign nations competent to maintain the relations of peace and war and capable of governing themselves under this protection."[25] Regarding the treaties subsequently entered into between Aboriginal communities and the British and then Canadian authorities, Erasmus writes, "First Nations did not perceive the treaties as being a surrender of authority."[26]

In fact, however, it is not entirely clear that the Royal Proclamation of 1763—which was formally incorporated into the Canadian Constitution through section 25 of the Charter of Rights and Freedoms—recognizes Aboriginal sovereignty. What is clear, however, is that the Proclamation speaks of the "Sovereignty, Protection, and Dominion" of the Crown in relation to the Native

inhabitants who "live under our protection." That the Royal Proclamation recognizes Aboriginal rights is indisputable.

In the case of *St Catherine's Milling and Lumber Company v. The Queen*, decided by the Judicial Committee of the Privy Council in 1888, the Proclamation was interpreted as establishing for Indians "a personal and usufructuary right, dependent on the good will of the sovereign." In other words, according to this early interpretation the Proclamation neither established nor recognized Indian sovereignty over their traditional lands, but quite clearly referred to the sovereignty of the British Crown over these lands. While one might wish on various grounds to question the legitimacy of this assertion of British sovereignty, the point is simply that there was no explicit recognition of Indian sovereignty, at least according to this ruling of the JCPC.

But perhaps there is an implicit recognition of Aboriginal sovereignty in the Proclamation. This seems to be the argument of those who characterize the Aboriginal–Crown relationship as a nation-to-nation arrangement, a characterization that seems to receive some support from the Proclamation's use of the words "the several Nations or Tribes of Indians," and also from the fact that the Proclamation states clearly that certain lands are reserved for the use of Indians and may not be purchased by private individuals or organizations, but only by the Crown. This restriction on the alienation of what the Proclamation refers to as "Lands of the Indians" might be interpreted as an acknowledgement of Aboriginal sovereignty. At the very least it seems to establish an Indian right to compensation for land transferred by them to the Crown.

The legal case for Aboriginal sovereignty, which today is often expressed in the form of demands that the inherent right of self-government should be recognized in the Constitution, and for Native landownership draws significant inspiration from a case that was not even decided by a court with jurisdiction over Canadian affairs. The 1832 decision of the United States Supreme Court in *Worcester v. Georgia* is often cited approvingly by advocates for Aboriginal sovereignty. Although this case has

Governing Realities

BOX 16.4 From the Royal Proclamation of 1763

And whereas it is just and reasonable, and essential to our Interest, and the security of our Colonies, that the several Nations or Tribes of Indians with whom We are connected, and who live under our protection, should not be molested or disturbed in the Possession of such Parts of Our Dominions and Territories as, not having been ceded to or purchased by Us, are reserved to them or any of them, as their Hunting Grounds—We do therefore, with the Advice of our Privy Council, declare it to be our Royal Will and Pleasure, that no Governor or Commander in Chief in any of our Colonies of Quebec, East Florida, or West Florida, do presume, upon any Pretence whatever, to grant Warrants of Survey, or pass any Patents for Lands beyond the Bounds of their respective Governments, as described in their Commissions; as also that no Governor or Commander in Chief in any of our other Colonies or Plantations in America do presume for the present, and until our further Pleasure be Known, to grant Warrants of Survey, or pass Patents for any Lands beyond the Heads or Sources of any of the Rivers which fall into the Atlantic Ocean from the West and North West, or upon any Lands whatever, which, not having been ceded to or purchased by Us as aforesaid, are reserved to the said Indians, or any of them.

And We do further declare it to be Our Royal Will and Pleasure, for the present as aforesaid, to reserve under our Sovereignty, Protection, and Dominion, for the use of the said Indians, all the Lands and Territories not included within the Limits of Our Said Three New Governments, or within the Limits of the Territory granted to the Hudson's Bay Company, as also all the Lands and Territories lying to the Westward of the Sources of the Rivers which fall into the Sea from the West and North West as aforesaid;

And We do hereby strictly forbid, on Pain of our Displeasure, all our loving Subjects from making any Purchases or Settlements whatever, or taking Possession of any of the Lands above reserved, without our especial leave and Licence for the Purpose first obtained.

And, We do further strictly enjoin and require all Persons whatever who have either wilfully or inadvertently seated themselves upon any lands within the Countries above described, or upon any other Lands which, not having been ceded to or purchased by Us, are still reserved to the said Indians as aforesaid, forthwith to remove themselves from such Settlements.

And Whereas Great Frauds and Abuses have been committed in purchasing Lands of the Indians, to the Great Prejudice of our Interests, and to the Great Dissatisfaction of the said Indians; In order, therefore, to prevent such Irregularities for the future, and to the End that the Indians may be convinced of our justice and determined Resolution to remove all reasonable Cause of Discontent, We do, with the Advice of our Privy Council strictly enjoin and require, that no private Person do presume to make any Purchase from the said Indians of any Lands reserved to the said Indians, within those parts of our Colonies where, We have thought proper to allow Settlement; but that, if at any Time any of the said Indians should be inclined to dispose of the said Lands, the same shall be Purchased only for Us, in our Name, at some public Meeting or Assembly of the said Indians, to be held for the Purpose by the Governor or Commander in Chief of our Colony respectively within which they shall lie; and in case they shall lie within the limits of any Proprietary Government, they shall be purchased only for the Use and in the name of such Proprietaries, conformable to such Directions and Instructions as We or they shall think proper to give for the Purpose. . . .

no official standing in Canadian jurisprudence it nevertheless has been influential in a number of important Canadian decisions on Native rights.

Writing for the majority in *Worcester v. Georgia*, Chief Justice John Marshall distinguished between the right of discovery and possession that European powers could enforce against one another in the New World and the right of historical occupancy enjoyed by the Aboriginal populations that already inhabited land "discovered" and claimed by

Europeans. The right of discovery and possession, said Marshall:

> gave to the nation making the discovery, as its inevitable consequence, the sole right of acquiring the soil and of making settlements on it. It was an exclusive principle, which shut out the right of competition among those who had agreed to it; not one which could annul the previous rights of those who had not agreed to it. It regulated the right given by discovery among the European discoverers; but could not affect the right of those already in possession, either as aboriginal occupants, or as occupants by virtue of a discovery made before the memory of man. It gave exclusive right to purchase, but did not found that right on a denial of the right of the possessor to sell.[27]

Marshall's pronouncement on the prior right of occupancy enjoyed by Aboriginal populations is generally construed as an argument supportive of Native land claims and even sovereignty. But the Chief Justice also had this to say:

> In the establishment of [relations between whites and Natives] the rights of the original inhabitants were, in no instance, entirely disregarded; but were, necessarily, to a considerable extent, impaired. They were admitted to be the rightful occupants of the soil, with a legal as well as a just claim to retain possession of it, and to use it according to their own discretion; but their rights to complete sovereignty, as independent nations, were necessarily diminished, and their power to dispose of the soil, at their own will, to whomsoever they pleased, was denied by the original fundamental principle, that discovery gave exclusive title to those who made it.[28]

This part of *Worcester v. Georgia* is, at the very least, inconvenient for those who purport to find a legal basis for Aboriginal claims to unrestricted landownership and sovereignty in that judicial decision. The legal principles that emerge from this much-cited ruling may be summarized as follows:

- Aboriginal peoples enjoy a right of occupancy and land use that predates the arrival of Europeans.
- Legal title to New World territory claimed by a European power belongs to the discovering nation.
- Aboriginal rights of occupancy and land use are not unrestricted, but rather are limited by the fact that discovery and possession gave the European authorities legal title to and sovereignty over these lands.

Marshall went on to say that the alienation of Indian land could be only to the state or Crown, and that Indian title to lands they claimed by historic right of occupancy and use could be extinguished by either conquest or legal purchase. The Chief Justice made specific reference to the Royal Proclamation of 1763, which, as we have seen, sets down precisely these conditions for the alienation of Indian lands.

The land title issue was centre stage in the 1973 case of *Calder et al. v. Attorney General of British Columbia*. Although the Nisga'a claim to have unfettered legal title to land that they had occupied before the arrival of Europeans was dismissed on procedural grounds, the Court did express itself on the matter of Aboriginal title. One judge denied that it existed; three others recognized original Aboriginal title that, they argued, had been extinguished; and three others argued that Aboriginal title continued to exist. So while six of the seven judges recognized the concept of Aboriginal title, the majority determined that it did not exist in the case of the Nisga'a.

Because the *Calder* decision is so often cited as the legal basis for a right of Aboriginal landownership, it is worth quoting from the two sets of arguments given in this case. "[W]hatever property right may have existed," said Mr Justice Judson for the majority, "it had been extinguished by properly constituted authorities in the exercise of their sovereign powers." In case there was any doubt regarding the Court's meaning, he went on to say that:

[Crown] Proclamations and Ordinances reveal a unity of intention to exercise, and the legislative exercising of, absolute sovereignty over all the lands of British Columbia and such exercise of sovereignty is inconsistent with any conflicting interests, including one as to "aboriginal title."[29]

Since the *Calder* ruling successive governments in Ottawa and Victoria have preferred to emphasize the arguments of the three judges who maintained that Aboriginal title still existed. Their reasons for doing so probably involved a combination of factors. Most importantly, of course, six of the seven Supreme Court justices recognized the concept of Aboriginal title. Also, a shift in elite and public opinion towards greater sympathy for the territorial claims of Aboriginal Canadians was encouraged during the 1970s by the high-profile northern gas pipeline inquiry (1974–7) headed by Justice Thomas Berger of the British Columbia Supreme Court. Justice Berger had been chief counsel for the Nisga'a in the *Calder* case. The arguments he had made to the court in that case, and that were subsequently popularized by extensive national media coverage of the Mackenzie Valley Pipeline Inquiry he chaired, were expressed by Mr Justice Emmett Hall in the Nisga'a ruling:

> This aboriginal title does not depend on treaty, executive order or legislative enactment but flows from the fact that the owners of the interest have from time immemorial occupied the areas in question and have established a pre-existing right of possession. In the absence of an [explicit] indication that the sovereign intends to extinguish that right the aboriginal title continues.[30]

In view of the fact that no treaty or other legal instrument specifically extinguished the Nisga'a title in the land they claimed, it continued to be theirs. The practical ramifications of such a legal opinion, expressed by a minority on the Court, were potentially enormous given that virtually none of British Columbia, except for a small portion of Vancouver Island, was covered by treaties between the Crown and First Nations. Subsequent court rulings alluded to the Nisga'a decision and gave governments little choice but to acknowledge the new reality of a stronger legal basis for Aboriginal land claims.

The issue of Aboriginal title has been addressed in a number of cases since *Calder*. In *Hamlet of Baker Lake et al. v. Minister of Indian Affairs* (1980), the Federal Court of Canada appeared to accept the spirit and reasoning of the minority in *Calder*, arguing that "The law of Canada recognizes the existence of an aboriginal title independent of the Royal Proclamation of 1763 or any other prerogative Act or legislation. It arises at common law." While acknowledging, as has every other court decision on the issue, that the Crown exercises sovereign authority over Native lands, the *Baker Lake* ruling repeated the view that Aboriginal title continued to exist until explicitly extinguished by legislation passed by Parliament.

A decade later, in *Regina v. Sparrow* (1990), the Supreme Court of Canada again addressed the issue of Aboriginal rights, including property rights. This decision continued the line of reasoning found in the *Calder* dissent and the *Baker Lake* ruling, holding that Aboriginal rights are pre-existing rights that are not created by government legislation and that such rights continue to exist until such time as they are explicitly extinguished. "Historical policy on the part of the Crown," said the Court, "can neither extinguish the existing aboriginal right without clear intention nor, in itself, delineate that right. The nature of government regulations cannot be determinative of the content and scope of an existing aboriginal right. Government policy can, however, regulate the exercise of that right but such regulation must be in keeping with s. 35(1) [of the Constitution Act, 1982]."[31]

The specific issue in *Sparrow* was whether the right to fish was an inherent Aboriginal right. Buried in the Supreme Court's ruling was a warning that common-law notions of property are not always appropriate in cases involving Aboriginal rights. "Courts must be careful to avoid the application of traditional common law concepts of property as they develop their understanding of the 'sui generis' nature of aboriginal rights."[32] What does this mean? It could, one might argue, be interpreted as an argument against an unrestricted right of use and sale of a resource like fish or timber, if that use were to be inconsistent with the traditional practices and values of a Native community.

Calder, *Baker Lake*, and *Sparrow* were, in a sense, preliminaries to the main event that took place in the courts from 1987 to 1997. In *Delgamuukw v. British Columbia* the issue of Aboriginal title was addressed head on. A group of Gitksan and Wet'suwet'en chiefs argued that they owned an area in British Columbia roughly the size of the province of Nova Scotia. In their Statement of Claim they asked the Court to make three specific findings:

- The Gitksan and Wet'suwet'en owned the territory in question.
- They had the right to establish their own laws for this territory, and these laws would supersede those of the province.
- They were entitled to compensation for all the resources exploited and removed from the territory since 1858.

The stakes could hardly have been greater, nor the issues of Aboriginal title and the inherent right to self-government more squarely put.

Following rejection of these claims by the British Columbia Supreme Court in 1991 and the subsequent upholding of this judgment in the BC Court of Appeal, the Supreme Court of Canada in 1997 ruled in a unanimous decision that the Gitksan and Wet'suwet'en are the owners of the land to which they claim a historic right of occupancy and use. Where Aboriginal title to land has not been extinguished by the terms of a treaty—and this would include most of British Columbia as well as parts of Atlantic Canada—Aboriginal communities able to prove that they historically occupied and used the land continue to have property rights. Did this mean that non-Aboriginal families living in the Okanagan Valley on pieces of land they thought they owned were in fact illegal squatters? Would a flurry of eviction notices hit residents of Vancouver? Did forestry companies now have to renegotiate leases that were signed with the BC government and that covered land rightfully owned by its original occupants?

In fact, the decision generated more questions than answers. What was clear from the *Delgamuukw* decision, however, was that Aboriginal communities like the Gitksan and Wet'suwet'en have a right to compensation for land determined to be theirs by historical right. The ruling strengthened the hand of Aboriginal groups who previously entered negotiations with governments armed with a rather nebulous concept of Aboriginal title, but who now could say they have a constitutionally protected right of ownership that can only be extinguished through the terms of a treaty with the Crown. Landownership issues aside, the Supreme Court's 1997 decision did not establish a constitutional right to self-government for Aboriginal communities. It did, however, establish that the oral historical accounts of a people are admissible in court as proof of land occupancy and use, something the lower courts had refused to accept.

An even more momentous decision was delivered by the Supreme Court in 2014. In *Tsilhqot'in Nation v. British Columbia* the meaning of Aboriginal title to lands was established with unprecedented clarity. The case arose out of a legal challenge by Chief Roger William of the Xeni Gwet'in Indian Band on behalf of the Tsilhqot'in, who argued that the government of British Columbia, without consultation or compensation, had illegally granted logging rights on territory historically occupied and owned by the Tsilhqot'in. The Court found that the plaintiffs had legal title to an area of about 1,700 square kilometres in the interior of British Columbia, which their ancestors had occupied before the arrival of Europeans, despite the assertion of sovereignty over this territory by, first, the British Crown and then the governments of Canada and British Columbia. A test for determining whether an Aboriginal group has title to a particular territory was established and the rights and limitations associated with that title were clarified.

This decision was greeted as a major victory for Aboriginal groups, which it was. But the nature of the victory and what the ruling means for future relations between Aboriginal groups who claim a historical right of occupancy and ownership of land and the governments and private corporations that may wish to pursue economic development projects on that land are rather complex. The two features of the ruling that deserve to be described as clear wins for Aboriginal groups are, first, the Court's recognition that ownership is not site-specific. In other words, it is not limited to specific villages that were occupied or land that was cultivated by members of an Aboriginal group. "To sufficiently occupy the land for purposes of title," wrote Chief Justice McLachlin, "the Aboriginal group in question must show that it has historically acted in a way that would communicate to third parties that it held the land for its own purposes."[33] The second win involved the Court's ruling that development on land owned by an Aboriginal group may not take place without Aboriginal consent. "[G]overnments and others seeking to use the land must obtain the consent of the Aboriginal title holders."[34] Moreover, this requirement to consult and seek consent exists even if Aboriginal title has not been definitively established. Knowledge that there is a potential Aboriginal claim of ownership over territory where some development is contemplated is sufficient to establish this obligation to consult.

The implications for such projects as the Northern Gateway pipeline that would carry oil from northern Alberta to the BC coast, crossing land claimed by several Aboriginal groups, are clear. What is not clear is whether, after consultation and if an agreement between the Aboriginal group that has or is claiming title and the government is not reached, a pipeline or other development project may not proceed. In other words, do the Aboriginal owners of land have an absolute right of veto over how it is used? Governments and corporations took some solace from the fact that the *Tsilhqot'in* decision referred approvingly to what had been said in *Delgamuukw* regarding incursions on Aboriginal title. "In my opinion," wrote Chief Justice Lamer, "the development of agriculture, forestry, mining, and hydroelectric power, the general economic development of the interior of British Columbia, protection of the environment or endangered species, the building of infrastructure and the settlement of foreign populations to support those aims, are the kinds of objectives that are consistent with this purpose and, in principle, can justify the infringement of Aboriginal title."[35] Does a pipeline such as the Northern Gateway qualify under "general economic development" and, therefore, as a justifiable infringement on Aboriginal title? This cannot be known in advance. What is known is that the Crown may act without the consent of the Aboriginal owners of land only if it has discharged its obligation to consult, its actions serve a "compelling and substantial objective" of the sorts listed above, and these actions do not "substantially deprive future generations [of Aboriginal owners] of the benefit of the land."[36]

The *Tsilhqot'in* ruling is likely to ensure that, in the future, no major economic development project that takes place on or crosses Aboriginal land, even if title has not yet been definitively established, will proceed without very substantial Aboriginal involvement. The bar justifying infringements on that title has been set quite high. Governments, corporations, and Aboriginal groups are likely to find, as they have for many years even before this decision, that negotiations, agreement, and revenue-sharing are preferable to the high-stakes drama and unpredictability of public opinion wars and protracted battles in the courts.

The essential character of treaties between Aboriginal peoples and the Crown is another matter that has arisen in the courts. Some argue that the treaties and other agreements between Aboriginal peoples and the Crown are tantamount to international treaties. If this is so, then it would seem to follow that these Aboriginal peoples have been recognized as sovereign nations capable of entering into agreements with other nations on a basis of legal equality. The Supreme Court of Canada has, on a number of occasions, expressly rejected this view of treaties.[37]

Despite the courts' lack of sympathy for the interpretation of Indian treaties as international agreements, Native spokespersons and some governments have insisted that treaties be viewed in this light. Speaking of those Aboriginal people who agreed to treaties with European powers, Georges Erasmus and Joe Sanders state, "The way [our people] dealt with the Europeans is ample proof of their capacity to enter into relations with foreign powers."[38] On the same subject they write:

Our people understood what the non-native people were after when they came amongst our people and wanted to treaty with them, because they had done that many times amongst themselves. They recognized that a nation-to-nation agreement, defining the specific terms of peaceful coexistence, was being arranged.[39]

Not only are treaties agreements between sovereign nations, according to this view, they are emphatically not real estate transactions comparable to, say, the US purchase of Alaska from Russia. This point is crucial, because the position taken by the courts and most governments in Canada has been that any Aboriginal right to ownership of the land covered by the terms of a treaty is *extinguished* by such an agreement. The nation-to-nation view of treaties denies that any extinguishment occurred, on the grounds that this was not how treaties were understood by the Aboriginal peoples who agreed to them. That non-Natives understood these agreements differently does not, Aboriginal leaders argue, mean that their view, rather than that of Aboriginal people, should be considered the correct one.

On a number of occasions courts have interpreted Indian treaties as contractual agreements. They certainly resemble contracts in that they typically include a rather detailed enumeration of mutually binding obligations. The courts have recognized, however, that Indian treaties constitute a rather unique sort of contractual agreement. This may be seen in the courts' tendency to interpret any ambiguous terms of treaties in favour of Aboriginal rights. As the British Columbia Supreme Court said in *Regina v. Cooper* (1969), "The document embodying this larcenous arrangement must have been drawn by or on behalf of the Hudson's Bay Company and so any ambiguity must be construed in favour of the exploited Chiefs."[40] The Supreme Court of Canada repeated and expanded

Protest is not the only way in which groups and individuals can exercise their political agency in the real world. Here, Hayden King, who is Pottawatomi and Ojibwe from Beausoleil First Nation on Gchimnissing in Huronia, Ontario, takes part in a teach-in on the Indian Act, the 1969 White Paper, and government policies on Aboriginal rights in Toronto in 2013.

on this rule of treaty interpretation in a 1983 decision. The Court declared that "Indian treaties must be construed, not according to the technical meaning of their words, but in a sense in which they would naturally be understood by the Indians."[41]

The question of how treaties negotiated centuries ago should be interpreted today does not provide easy answers. After all, the treaties were negotiated in very different circumstances, by parties of very unequal power and resources who spoke different languages and operated from very different cultural premises, and they were written in the language of only one of the parties. In *R. v. Marshall* (1999), a case involving the claimed right of a Mi'kmaq Indian, Donald Marshall Jr, to fish in contravention of federal fishery regulations, the Supreme Court said that "extrinsic evidence of the historical and cultural context of a treaty may be received even if the treaty document purports to contain all of the terms and even absent any ambiguity on the face of the treaty." The majority added that "where a treaty was concluded orally and afterwards written up by representatives of the Crown"—a practice that was common—"it would be unconscionable for the

Crown to ignore the oral terms while relying on the written ones."[42]

The issue of Aboriginal title to lands and the conditions necessary to satisfy such title to ownership was revisited in *R. v. Marshall* (2005). In this case, Stephen Marshall (not related to Donald Marshall Jr) and 34 other Mi'kmaq Indians were charged with cutting timber on Crown lands without a licence to do so. They argued that they held title to the land and therefore did not require authorization to log it and sell the timber. They also argued that commercial logging represented a natural evolution in the trading activities that their forebears engaged in at the time (1760–1) the treaties in question were entered into.

The Supreme Court rejected both claims. While acknowledging, per the *Delgamuukw* decision, that both European common law and Aboriginal perspectives must be considered in assessing a claim of Aboriginal title and that "evidence of oral history is admissible, provided it meets the requisite standards of usefulness and reasonable reliability," the majority found that the Mi'kmaq claim to having exercised exclusive occupation of the land in question before the arrival of Europeans was unsubstantiated.

On the separate issue of whether modern commercial logging represents a logical evolution of the trading practices the Mi'kmaq engaged in over 200 years ago, the Supreme Court acknowledged that "ancestral trading activities are not frozen in time." But these treaty-guaranteed trading rights did not, it decided, extend to commercial logging. This was not surprising in view of what the Court had said on this question in previous cases. "[T]reaty rights are limited to securing 'necessaries' (which should be construed in the modern context as equivalent to a moderate livelihood), and do not extend to the open-ended accumulation of wealth."[43]

The Institutionalization of Aboriginal Affairs

Treaties and the federal Indian bureaucracy that has existed since before the 1876 passage of the Indian Act ensured that Aboriginal affairs were embedded in the activities of the Canadian state. Government transfers to Aboriginal communities under the terms of treaties, which were administered through the Indian agents, and transfers to individual Natives through welfare spending (Aboriginal Canadians living off-reserve are about three times more likely than other Canadians to receive social assistance) created a web of financial dependency on the state that continues to exist. Historically, the institutionalization of Aboriginal affairs into the structure and activities of the Canadian state has also involved the creation and perpetuation of dependency relations. This continues to be the case, despite some important reforms whose ostensible goal is to break this cycle of dependence.

Sally Weaver has examined Ottawa's funding of the National Indian Brotherhood after the failure of the 1969 White Paper and the institutionalization (unsuccessful, as it turned out) of relations between the federal government and the NIB through procedures of joint consultation and decision-making.[44] A former Liberal Minister of Indian Affairs, Hugh Faulkner, has argued that the motive behind his government's deliberate policy of funding selected interest groups, including Native organizations, was progressive and intended to strengthen the political voice of such groups.[45] Others have been more skeptical. Noel Starblanket, a former president of the National Indian Brotherhood, accused Ottawa of using money as part of a divide-and-conquer strategy for dealing with Native groups.[46] Roger Gibbins and Rick Ponting agree that the potential for the co-optation and control of Native organizations certainly existed as Ottawa became increasingly involved in the funding of these groups. "[T]he provision of money is deemed to carry the right to specify how, for what, and by whom it will be spent," they write. "Other rights deemed to accompany the provision of money are the right to demand proof that the funds have been spent in accordance with the stipulations just cited, and the right to withdraw or terminate the funds."[47] Gibbins and Ponting provide examples of money being used as a lever to control the behaviour of Native groups.

In more recent years this issue of whether and when state funding and other forms of privileged recognition may, by design or simply by consequence, divide Aboriginal groups and perhaps weaken the influence of those whose demands the government finds to be least acceptable, has been much discussed. In January 2013 the AFN and the federal government agreed to work towards negotiations on treaty obligations. Many of the tribal groups represented by the AFN objected to this approach, claiming that the AFN had no authority to negotiate treaty matters on their behalf. The issue came to a head in July 2013 when some provincial chiefs attended the National Treaty Gathering at Onion Lake, Saskatchewan, instead of the annual meeting of the AFN held at the same time in Whitehorse, Yukon. "These are people in the same house who have different views on what the future looks like," said Aboriginal policy expert Ken Coates.[48] The Onion Lake gathering produced the National Treaty Alliance. Some critics claim that this division between Aboriginal leaders was orchestrated by the Conservative government, but the explanation provided by Coates seems more plausible. Different groups have different views on what needs to be reformed and on the future of relations between the Canadian state and their communities.

The leading organizational voices for Aboriginal Canadians continue to depend on public funding provided mainly through the budget of Aboriginal Affairs and Northern Development Canada. There is not much evidence to suggest, however, that this dependence has muted their criticism of government policies or co-opted them into anyone else's agenda. Indeed, over the last couple of decades the criticisms from various leaders of the Assembly of First Nations and other groups have frequently been scathing. These attacks have often been made at international forums, ensuring that the shame factor would be magnified. Moreover, money spent on legal proceedings against the Canadian state, on retaining the services of some of Canada's most high-powered lobbying firms, and on advertising campaigns to influence public opinion in order to change government policy has come, at least in part, from state funding.

The issue of Aboriginal group dependence on public funding was part of the indictment made by the chiefs who gathered at Onion Lake in 2013. "Every dime that runs [the AFN]," said Chief Derek Nepinak, "is at the goodwill of bureaucrats and the Minister of Indian Affairs." Chief Isadore Day of the Serpent River First Nation declared, "It's very easy to negotiate with a thirsty man if you're going to offer him water. That's the situation that has played out; even more so now that the AFN is being gutted of its core funding. It's quite clear that the concessions that have been made by this National Chief [Shawn Atleo] have essentially come back to bite him."[49] A reduction of about one-third in funding to the AFN was announced a short time later in the government's October 2013 budget. Whether the charges of co-optation of the AFN leadership are justified in this particular case, the risk that this may occur is always present when a group depends on state funding. In this instance, however, the charges appeared to have some legs when National Chief Shawn Atleo suddenly resigned in May 2014 after strong criticism from some chiefs and the rank and file, apparently over his support of the government's proposed Bill 33 to revamp First Nations control of education.

The institutionalization of Aboriginal affairs and identity within the Canadian state has also occurred through broadcasting. The early beginnings go back to 1960 when the CBC Northern Service broadcast the first Aboriginal-language program from its Montreal studios. This was followed by some Aboriginal programming through the CBC Northern Television Service, established in 1972, and by $40 million earmarked for Aboriginal-language television and radio programming in the Far North for the period 1983–7. Many other radio and television broadcasting initiatives were launched between 1960 and the mid-1990s, but the consensus is that the major impact of broadcasting to the North, where most viewers and listeners were Aboriginal Canadians, was to "accelerate the process of cultural and language loss, particularly among the young."[50]

The last few decades have seen greater state involvement in support of Aboriginal broadcasting. An official policy of support for Aboriginal-language broadcasting was declared in public notices issued by the CRTC in 1985 and 1990, and in revisions to the Broadcasting Act passed in 1991. No major steps in this direction were taken, however, until the *Report* of the RCAP strongly emphasized the importance of such services to the cultural survival of Native communities. Telefilm Canada began to fund Aboriginal-language television productions in 1996. Since then, about 70 per cent of this funding has gone to documentary programs. The Aboriginal Peoples Television Network, carried by all cable and satellite television providers in Canada, began operation in 1999. Most of its employees are Aboriginal and close to one-third of its programming is in Aboriginal languages. The fact that cable and satellite television providers must carry APTN provides the network with a secure financial basis from subscriber revenues. The Nunavut Film Commission is another source of money for Aboriginal television productions. Ottawa also provides funding for the Aboriginal Peoples Television Network, launched in 1999, for radio broadcasters that serve the Arctic, including CBC Radio North, and for Aboriginal-language broadcasting in southern regions of Canada. The amount of Aboriginal-language programming broadcast by these networks and local stations varies considerably, but even the Inuit Broadcasting Corporation, whose programming is entirely in Inuktitut, offers only a few hours of television programming per day. The airwaves in Aboriginal communities continue to be dominated by English programming and, as discussed earlier in this chapter, the use of Aboriginal languages continues to decline.

A third way in which Aboriginal concerns and issues have been institutionalized through the Canadian state involves employment. Aboriginal representation in the federal public service, negligible for most of Canada's history, today is about proportional to the size of the Aboriginal identity population of the country. Aboriginal Canadians comprise about 4.5 per cent of the federal public service and 2.5 per cent of all those in the executive category of the bureaucracy. In the National Capital Region the figure is about 3 per cent, but Aboriginal employees represent closer to one-quarter of federal bureaucrats in the combined territories of Yukon, the Northwest Territories, and Nunavut. About 40 per cent of all Aboriginal federal employees work

in the North or in the provinces west of Ontario. The largest employer of Native Canadians is Aboriginal Affairs and Northern Development Canada (formerly Indian and Northern Affairs Canada). Almost one-third of its employees are Aboriginal, ensuring that the organizational culture of AANDC is sensitive to the values and backgrounds of those it serves. Since 1994 the department has had an official target of 50 per cent Aboriginal employment. As of 2012, slightly less than 30 per cent of the department's employees were Aboriginal.[51]

The Way Forward

In January 2013, when the Idle No More protests were front-page news across Canada, the *National Post*'s letters editor asked readers to "solve Canada's Native issue, in 75 words or less." One reader's comment seems apt: "We will have to stop using inane, simplified, and misleading phrases like 'the native issue.'"[52] There is, as we have seen, no single issue when it comes to the conditions and demands of Aboriginal communities. These communities are quite diverse. They are represented by many different organizations and their perspectives and preferences, when it comes to their relationship with the Canadian state and the rest of Canadian society, vary quite significantly.

The Idle No More protests, as was also true of the Oka crisis in 1990, the Ipperwash stand-off in 1995, the occupation of a housing project at Caledonia, Ontario, in 2006 (which is unresolved as of 2014), and lesser confrontations between Aboriginal protesters and state authorities, give the impression that little progress has been made in resolving the many and complex issues that lead to conflict. This impression is reinforced by regular stories of ill-housed Aboriginal people living in communities with sanitation and services that one might expect to find in developing countries, but not in one of the world's wealthiest societies. Aboriginal leaders frequently bemoan what they argue is the lack of real progress on these issues and just as frequently impugn the goodwill of the state officials with whom they negotiate. A 2003 survey of off-reserve Aboriginal Canadians carried out by Ekos found that just under six in 10 claimed to have experienced racism over the previous two years.

At the same time, however, the Ekos study found that about two-thirds of those surveyed said that their quality of life was good (only 7 per cent said it was bad) and two-thirds expected that their quality of life would improve over the next year.[53] Conflict, rancour, stalemate, and dire living conditions capture the headlines, but relations between Aboriginal communities and the state are not entirely devoid of progress, even if much of it took a long time to accomplish. Among these positive developments are the creation of Nunavut in 1999, the federal government's formal apology in 2008 for the abuse experienced by generations of Aboriginal children in residential schools and financial compensation for victims, the recent land transfer agreements between the Cree and the government of Quebec, and steps towards the reform and perhaps dismantlement of the Indian Act. The 1997 *Delgamuukw* decision of the Supreme Court, which stated that the Gitksan and Wet'suwet'en have a historic right to their traditional lands, and the Court's 2014 *Tsilhqot'in Nation* decision, which determined that Aboriginal communities have a legal right to veto any development on land to which they hold Aboriginal title, provided a much firmer basis for claims of Aboriginal landownership than previously existed. The sum total of these achievements should not be satisfied complacency, but neither should they be dismissed as inconsequential.

Much of the progress made in recent years has involved agreements reached between Native communities and private-sector companies. Brian Lee Crowley and Ken Coates cite as examples the 2012 agreement between Pinehouse First Nation and uranium companies Cameco and Ariva in northern Saskatchewan. They note that half of Cameco's workforce is Aboriginal and that the company contracts 70 per cent of its supply work to firms that, under federal guidelines, qualify as Indigenous-owned. Two of the major players in the Alberta oil sands, Syncrude and Suncor, have similar agreements with Native groups. Crowley and Coates point to Inuit participation in the Baffinland (Mary River) iron ore mine as a model for further business–Aboriginal co-operation.[54]

These impact and benefit agreements obviously cannot solve all of the problems that beset Aboriginal Canadians. They offer no help to urban Aboriginals, for example, nor are they particularly relevant for those Native communities whose ancestral lands or current reserves do not sit on natural resource wealth. But they do represent an important model that recognizes Aboriginal land claims and provide what Crowley and Coates call an opportunity-driven model for Aboriginal development, instead of the traditional government-transfer model. Making Aboriginal communities direct stakeholders in resource projects and providing training and employment opportunities of the sort that exist at Cameco and Mary River are the pillars of this model.

More relevant to the lives of Canada's reserve and off-reserve Indian populations is reform of the Indian Act. Virtually everyone now agrees that this legislation must be reformed and perhaps even abolished. In 2012 the Conservative government announced its support for Bill C-428, the Indian Act Amendment and Replacement Act, a private member's bill tabled by Manitoba MP Rob Clarke. The bill was passed by the House of Commons in November 2013, after the House's Standing Committee on Aboriginal Affairs and Northern Development heard from many Native leaders. In its preamble, the bill quite rightly describes the Indian Act, which has gone largely unreformed since its passage in 1876, as "an outdated colonial statute." Unlike the White Paper proposals of 1969, this bill did not propose the repeal of the Indian Act. "[M]ost of the proposed amendments under Bill C-428," said the Canadian Bar Association in its submission to the House committee, "are properly characterized as historical housekeeping of archaic and little used provisions of the Indian Act.[55]

Aboriginal groups were divided on the proposed legislation. Manitoba Chief Derek Nepinak spoke for many Native leaders in arguing that:

> Imposing legislation on first nations people pursuant to the Indian Act in this manner perpetuates the federal government's unilateral interpretation of first nations self-government. This approach is inconsistent with our inherent rights, international law,

and declarations endorsed by Canada. . . . [Bill C-428] is another piece of federal government-owned legislation that perpetuates Canada's self-proclaimed authority over indigenous people.[56]

The Assembly of First Nations was more supportive. In its submission to the House committee the AFN agreed with the general aims of Bill C-428, but proposed a number of concrete changes.[57]

Several years before the introduction of Bill C-428, the federal government began what is known as the First Nations Property Ownership (FNPO) initiative.[58] It is intended to address what has always been one of the most criticized aspects of the Indian Act, the inability of First Nations communities to hold legal title to reserve land and to transfer ownership to individuals without losing jurisdiction over transferred land. The initiative—as of early 2014 it had not yet been tabled in Parliament as a bill—has been criticized by some as involving the privatization of reserve lands. Leaving aside the question of why "privatization" should be thought to be an obviously bad thing, the FNPO would be voluntary. Each First Nation reserve community would decide whether or not to adopt it in whole or in part. Some First Nations support the FNPO, while others oppose it.[59]

It is not surprising that reform of the Indian Act raises a red flag for so many people. Despite the fact that virtually everyone is critical of the Act's paternalistic premises and truly archaic provisions, the shadow of the 1969 White Paper, including the claims of cultural genocide that were hurled by such Native leaders as Harold Cardinal, falls over any discussion of reform. But unlike that earlier proposal to abolish the Indian Act and the Indian Affairs bureaucracy of the federal government, recent steps in the direction of reform do not involve the elimination of the concept and recognition of Indianness. Legal recognition of the distinct status of Aboriginal people is something that all major Aboriginal groups insist must remain. At the same time, and although it is seldom acknowledged, the Indian Act has become less relevant to the lives of an increasing number of Aboriginal Canadians. As Ken Coates observes:

The dominance of the Department of [Aboriginal] Affairs in the lives of First Nations communities recedes further each year. Already [in 2008] more than 80 per cent of the funds spent on status Indians are managed by band or tribal governments. . . . Recent northern land claims agreements and agreements in principle signed in British Columbia in 2006 have revolutionized Aboriginal governments and removed most of the authority and relevance of the Indian Act, as the Nisga'a and Yukon First Nations have experienced.

Equally, the Government of Canada has been moving in other ways beyond the limits of the Indian Act in recent years. Ottawa has been working more closely with Métis communities and with urban Aboriginal populations, groups who argued their needs were not being met under the Indian Act, with its emphasis on status Indians and reserve governments. These efforts have challenged the central role of reserve-based band governments created under the Indian Act and have broadened the federal government's programming for Indigenous people in Canada. Put simply, the Indian Act no longer dominates Aboriginal–government relations and no longer provides a singular focus for the management of status Indian affairs.[60]

The way forward, it turns out, is likely to look neither like the integrationist vision of the 1969 White Paper nor the grand "People to people, nation to nation" vision expressed in the *Report* of the RCAP in 1996. It is, however, likely to include some elements of both of these visions and, moreover, to emphasize ways of breaking down the ties of paternalism and dependency that have been the hallmarks of relations between Aboriginal communities and the Canadian state. As has been true over the past four decades, there will not be one path towards reform. It will take place through the courts, Parliament, and the impact and benefit agreements that private resource companies make with Aboriginal communities.

Starting Points for Research

Michael Asch, *On Being Here to Stay: Treaties and Aboriginal Rights in Canada* (Toronto: University of Toronto Press, 2014). Writing from a perspective sympathetic to Aboriginal land claims and sovereignty, Asch examines Canadian history through the lens of relations between Native peoples and European settlers in Canada.

Yale D. Belanger, *Aboriginal Self-Government in Canada: Current Trends and Issues*, 3rd edn (Saskatoon: Purich Publishing, 2008). An excellent collection of contributions on various theoretical, legal, and practical aspects of Aboriginal self-government.

Ken Coates, *A Global History of Indigenous Peoples: Struggle and Survival* (London: Palgrave Macmillan, 2004). A fine account of indigenous civilizations throughout the world, providing very useful context for the understanding of Aboriginal conditions and politics in Canada.

Olive Patricia Dickason, with David T. McNab, *Canada's First Nations: A History of Founding Peoples from Earliest Times*, 4th edn (Toronto: Oxford University Press, 2009). Dickason, one of Canada's leading Aboriginal scholars for many years, draws on research in political science, anthropology, archaeology, biology, and sociology in this history spanning the first peopling of the Americas to contemporary land claim settlements and conflicts.

James S. Frideres, *First Nations in the Twenty-First Century* (Toronto: Oxford University Press, 2011). Frideres, a sociologist and one of Canada's leading scholars on Indigenous peoples and ethnicity, examines the various aspects of government–First Nations relations within a framework of epistemology, Aboriginal languages, and the residential schools and the intergenerational trauma the schools caused.

Review Exercises

1. How do the status and conditions of Aboriginal Canadians compare to those of their counterparts in the United States or Australia? You may find it useful to consult the data in United Nations, Department of Economic and Social Affairs, *State of the World's Indigenous Peoples* (2009), at: <www.un.org/esa/socdev/unpfii/documents/SOWIP_web.pdf>.

2. Should the Charter of Rights and Freedoms apply to all Aboriginal communities in all respects and at all times? Or should Aboriginal rights and the concept of self-government be construed so that they take precedence over the Charter in some circumstances? Formulate an argument on one side of this issue.

3. Identify an Aboriginal community that operates its own justice system, including law enforcement and Native sentencing. Explain how this system operates.

4. In the report entitled *First Nations Representation on Ontario Juries* (February 2013), former Supreme Court Justice Frank Iacobucci states that systemic discrimination is responsible for the under-representation of Aboriginal Canadians on Ontario juries. What evidence does he provide? Focus on pages 53–62 of this report at: <www.firstnationsandjuriesreview.ca/pdf/English_FullReport.pdf>.

Canada in the World

Canadian politics has always played out within the context of issues that transcend national boundaries, and this is especially true today. In this chapter we examine Canada's place in the world, focusing on the possibilities and limits available to Canadian policy-makers as they navigate a turbulent and fast-changing international scene. Topics include the following:

- How Canadians view their place in the world.
- How the world sees Canada and Canadians.
- The meaning of globalization.
- Arguments made about the consequences of globalization.
- Globalization and the intensification of Canadian–American relations.
- The asymmetrical relationship between Canada and the United States.
- Is more integration with the US the answer?
- Multilateralism versus the tug of continentalism.
- Canadian and American views of world affairs.

The Spirit of Haida Gwaii is a sculpture by artist Bill Reid that sits outside the Canadian Embassy in Washington, D.C. The characters of the boat travel together and depend on one another, despite their **differences.** (© Chris Cheadle/Alamy)

"The twentieth century will belong to Canada." This was the bold prediction of Sir Wilfrid Laurier, Liberal Prime Minister of Canada from 1896 to 1911. Laurier's forecast of greatness for Canada was made against the backdrop of the enormous growth that had occurred in the United States over the previous century, when Canada's southern neighbour went from being a cluster of states hugging the Atlantic seaboard to a continent-wide power with the world's largest economy. In the heady years of the early 1900s, as the nation-building strategy launched by Sir John A. Macdonald in 1879 appeared to be fulfilling its promise and about 200,000 immigrants arrived in Canada each year, Laurier's prediction that Canada was destined for greatness probably struck many as more than the usual political rhetoric.

Over 100 years later it is clear that the twentieth century did not "belong" to Canada. The friends and foes of the United States would probably agree that it was the American century, for better or worse. By century's end the economic, cultural, and military dominance of the US was such that, in the eyes of many, comparisons to previous empires understated the sheer scale of America's global influence. The term "hyperpower"—a single country whose global dominance was economic, military, and cultural—entered the modern lexicon.

Notwithstanding the continuing but perhaps declining global power of the United States,[1] some Canadians believe their country has achieved the greatness predicted by Laurier, though in a form that Canada's first French-Canadian Prime Minister did not imagine. "For generations," says philosopher Mark Kingwell, "we have been busy creating, in [the shadow of the United States], a model of citizenship that is inclusive, diverse, open-ended and transnational. It is dedicated to far-reaching social justice and the rule of international law. And we're successfully exporting it around the world . . . by seeing [the UN] for the flawed but necessary agency it is."[2] Canada is, according to many of its opinion leaders, the cosmopolitan, multicultural, equality-oriented, internationalist face of the future. John Ralston Saul, one of Canada's most prominent public intellectuals, argues that "Canada is above all an idea of what a country could be, a place of the imagination . . . it is very much its own invention."[3]

Canada is, he has argued, a successful model of accommodation and flexible ways of thinking about citizenship. The Canadian model, as it has come to be thought of by such intellectuals as Kingwell and Saul, is the real achievement of the last century and the one that is most likely to shape the direction of history in the twenty-first century.

Perhaps so, although Canadians might be surprised to learn that when the world's thoughts turn to the future of democracy, the evolving new world order, or the trajectory of world history, few people other than Canadians mention this country as charting the course. A survey of books written in recent years by leading Western intellectuals on democracy—excluding those written by Canadians—turns up very few references to Canada and certainly no sense that the rest of the world is watching, much less emulating, whatever the Canadian model might involve. Indeed, we are used to hearing that Canada is loved and admired by the rest of the world—Canada regularly is ranked first or close to the top in international assessments of best countries to live in the world[4] and as likely as almost any other country to be viewed as having a positive influence in the world[5]—and that we are often looked to for wise counsel and assistance on troublesome issues far from our shores. It may, therefore, come as something of a surprise to learn that not only our American neighbours, but other national populations as well, appear to know hardly anything about us. As Canadian-born historian Alex Smith observes, "British people are aware that Canadians dislike being confused with Americans. That's the one thing they know about Canada."[6] Politicians' claims that Canada's health-care system is the envy of the world or that we are seen by others as a nation of peacekeepers run up against the fact that very few non-Canadians, outside of the relatively few foreigners who study Canada, have what could be called a finely grained knowledge of the country and its history. They are no more likely than Americans to be able to name Canada's Prime Minister or to know that Canadian troops played an important combat role in the NATO mission in Afghanistan.

In a public lecture at Carleton University in February 2003,[7] Michael Ignatieff challenged his undermining the UN and global co-operation." Further, they declare, "Where Canada was once strong, it is now weak; where we were once prudent, we are now hostile to much of what the UN does and represents."[9]

Former Conservative Prime Minister Joe Clark joined the chorus of critics with his book, *How We Lead: Canada in a Century of Change*. Lamenting what he argues to be the abandonment of a Canadian tradition of middle-power leadership in the world, Clark calls for a return to the emphasis on diplomacy and multilateralism that enabled Canada to command respect on the world stage out of proportion to its size and hard-power attributes. "Co-operation is a Canadian practice and instinct, it is the way we have often met challenges, at home and abroad," he writes. "That mentality is even more relevant in this present period," Clark says, "where the power of persuasion is often more potent than the power of arms."[10]

Not all commentators agree with Clark and the other critics of recent Canadian foreign policy. Prominent historian Jack Granatstein, for one, argues that the idea of Canada as a sort of moral superpower that punched above its weight in global affairs was never particularly credible and is not a viable option in contemporary geopolitics. Instead, he argues, Canada has assumed the role of "a principled, responsible ally [of the US and within NATO] ready to play a credible security role in the world."[11] Critics such as Clark and defenders such as Granatstein base their judgments on what they believe to be Canada's proper aims when it comes to world affairs and on their assessment of how well government policies are adapted to the achievement of these aims. Their differences are due, in part, to the evidence they examine, but even more importantly to the world views they bring to bear in assessing that evidence.

In the study of international relations these world views or theoretical frameworks are referred to as *idealism* and *realism*. For the so-called realists, the world of geopolitics is a tameable but largely ungovernable space in which the self-interests of state and non-state actors compete and where violent conflict and war are inevitable. Realists stress the importance of what is often called hard power, including military capacity and economic sanctions, as means for the protection of national security and the advancement of national interests abroad. The idealist framework—sometimes called the liberal or constructivist model—is much less pessimistic about the prospects for the eradication of conflict and the achievement of peace that does not depend on a balance of military might. Idealists are much more likely than realists to emphasize what they believe to be the potential for diplomacy, multilateral co-operation, and structures of international governance to control and resolve international conflict and protect the security of nations. They stress the importance of what is often called **soft power**, influence that relies on the attractiveness of a nation's values, processes, and structures for representation, negotiation, and co-operation, and a leadership style that relies on example, persuasion, and engagement instead of threats and isolation. Realists are more skeptical of these tools and structures and more likely to place their faith in the nation-state, more limited strategic alliances, and the retention of hard-power capabilities as the best means for protecting and advancing a country's interests.

The realism versus idealism debate is important for an understanding of analyses and assessments of Canada's role in the world. So, too, is the nationalism versus continentalism debate. This debate goes back to the end of World War II when the United States emerged as the world's foremost economic power. It was also one of two military superpowers, the other being the Soviet Union. During the nearly half-century known as the Cold War, which ended with the fall of the Berlin Wall in 1989 and the breakup of the Soviet Union in 1991, the United States was the acknowledged leader among Western capitalist nations. American dominance operated through its leadership in NATO and other regional military alliances, and its unrivalled economic power. No country felt the gravitational pull of American military and economic power more than Canada, its next-door neighbour. Between the end of World War II and the mid-1970s, economic and military integration between these two countries reached levels that generated a nationalist backlash in Canada. Nationalists argued that the advocates and architects of integration were complicit in a continentalist agenda of American domination of Canada. Canadian political sovereignty, cultural distinctiveness, and economic independence were all undermined, they argued, by this continentalist drift.

These two debates, realism versus idealism and nationalism versus continentalism, overlap. Realists are likely to lean towards a continentalist understanding of how best to protect and promote Canada's economic and security interests. Idealists are more likely to be nationalists and therefore wary of Canada being tied too closely to the United States. On such issues as energy policy, missile defence, border security, and trade, realists are more likely to take positions sympathetic to maintaining or even deepening Canada–US integration. Idealists tend to believe that this integration has already gone too far and that a policy of building counterweights to American influence and strengthening international institutions is in Canada's best interests.

The Meaning and Consequences of Globalization for Canada

When the definitive history of the era from the 1970s to the first decade of the twenty-first century is written it will surely best be characterized by the word *globalization*. The 1970s saw the rising economic power of Japan and Germany, as well as the new wealth and influence of the Middle East's oil-rich states; from the end of the 1990s into the early twenty-first century the dramatic rise of the emerging economies of the BRIC countries—Brazil, Russia, India, and especially China—dramatically altered the international economic landscape. Hardly a corner of the globe escaped the consequences. For some countries, including Canada, the impact of the intensification of relations—particularly but not exclusively economic relations—with the rest of the world has been enormously significant.

Some historical perspective is necessary. Canada's economic condition has, in fact, always been dependent on markets outside its borders (see Appendix at the end of this chapter). From the arrival more than 500 years ago of European fishermen who trolled the cod-rich waters off the coast of Newfoundland until the middle of the twentieth century, the economic prosperity of the northern reaches of North America depended on the exploitation and export of a succession of natural resources—fish, fur, timber, and wheat—to markets abroad, and on the import of people, capital, and finished goods. From

Erin Combs/GetStock.com

Canadians pride themselves on the maple leaf being a "passport of goodwill"—that is, a symbol representing characteristics such as tolerance, compassion, prosperity, and politeness, making Canadians the envy of, and welcome all around, the world. Just how accurate is that self-perception?

Media Spotlight

BOX 17.1 Canada's Image Abroad

As national "brands" go, Canada's is a good one. The Anholt-GfK Nation Brands Index annually surveys citizens in 20 countries, asking them questions about exports, governance, culture, people, tourism, immigration, and investment for 50 countries. Canada's international image is always towards the top of the table. In 2012 Canada ranked fifth, surpassed by the United States, Germany, the UK, and France, in that order. When it comes to immigration and investment, Canada came in second, surpassed only by the United States.[12]

The warm feelings that foreigners generally have towards Canada are not matched, however, by much in the way of knowledge about the country or its people. Focus groups organized by Canada's Department of Foreign Affairs in 2003 found that many Parisians had no idea why French was widely spoken in Canada! For their part, Americans, as historian John Bartlet Brebner famously said, are "benevolently uninformed" when it comes to Canada. Canadians tend to resent this. But they are quite wrong to assume that the rest of the world is either better informed about or more interested in their country than are Americans.

The truth is that, like most middle-sized countries throughout the world, Canada is seldom on the radar screen when it comes to media coverage in other societies, including those with which it has close economic, diplomatic, and cultural ties. During eight months spent in France I recall only two occasions when Canada was the subject of a story on the evening news: the deaths in Quebec due to buildings that collapsed under the heavy snowfalls of 2008 and Governor General Michaëlle Jean's visit to Paris in May of that same year. Those of my French students who believed they knew something about Canadian health care and the country's social safety net had learned it from Michael Moore's films, *Sicko* and *Bowling for Columbine*.

When Canada does appear on the international radar screen, the coverage is seldom as positive as many Canadians may imagine. For many years the annual seal hunt on the ice floes off the coast of Newfoundland generated stories critical of Canada, leading to the EU's 2010 decision to ban seal furs and other seal products. More recently, Alberta's oil sands have been in the crosshairs of much of the Western media. A 2012–13 survey of newspaper coverage of the oil sands—usually referred to as the tar sands outside of Canada—in the United States, the UK, and Australia found that this was by far the main issue that gave Canada international visibility. The visibility was not particularly positive. Although balanced or neutral stories predominated in the newspapers of these countries, negative stories outnumbered positive stories by a wide margin in the case of virtually every newspaper with the exception of *The Australian* and American papers based in natural resource-dependent states. Three of the most influential newspapers in the English-speaking world, the *New York Times, The Guardian*, and *The Washington Post*, carried many more stories with a negative than positive tone.[13] The antics of Toronto mayor Rob Ford, from smoking crack cocaine and public drunkenness to racist and lewd remarks, generated a spike in international coverage of Canada during 2013, even producing a bastardized verb form, as in "I Rob Forded like crazy last night, and I can't remember any of it." Few people saw this coverage as being particularly helpful for Canada's image abroad.

Whether a country's image abroad matters very much, and in what circumstances, is an open question. The advocates of cultural diplomacy, soft power, and "smart power"[14] believe so. At the same time as Canada was taking a drubbing in the European press over the oil sands, the Canadian government successfully negotiated a free trade treaty with the EU Commission (2013). Perhaps the negotiations would have gone more quickly and the deal would have been different had this backdrop of negative coverage not existed. Or perhaps the "noise" that accompanies such a relationship does not always matter very much.

the time Europeans began to be seriously interested in what would become Canada by sending ships, settlers, and goods, the Canadian economy was integrated into greater patterns of trade and shaped by forces far from its shores.

At some point, however, a hope and even an expectation developed that Canada would shake off this dependence and become the master of its economic destiny. One sees this already in Sir John A. Macdonald's ambitious National Policy of 1879, the first and only coherent and explicit economic development strategy that Canada had known before the decision to embrace free trade in the late 1980s. One sees it also in Sir Wilfrid Laurier's optimistic prediction that the twentieth century would belong to Canada. And one sees it in the rise of economic nationalism in Canada, particularly from the 1950s to the early 1980s, the path of which was marked by a series of policies and institutions designed to limit American influence in the Canadian economy and promote indigenous capital.

Some of these nationalistic hopes still survive, although they have come to appear increasingly atavistic in a world characterized by unprecedented levels of economic interdependence and global communication. Moreover, Canadians believe the clock cannot be turned back to the time before the Canada–US Free Trade Agreement (1989) and the North American Free Trade Agreement (1994). A 2013 survey carried out by Ekos found that 80 per cent of Canadians believe there should be free trade between Canada, the US, and Mexico. Virtually the same percentage said "yes" when asked whether there should be free trade between Canada and the US. As Figure 17.2 shows, Canadians are the most pro-free trade of the three NAFTA populations.

Today, the serious debate is not about whether the forces of globalization can be rolled back, but how and in what instances they can and should be controlled. In Canada the question of globalization is inseparable from that of Canada's relationship to the United States. Globalization has meant an intensification in economic and other ties to what

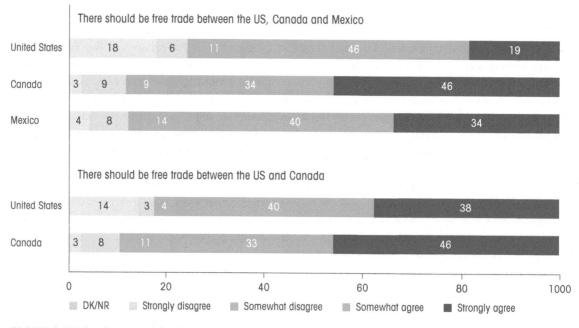

FIGURE 17.2 Support for Free Trade Agreements in Canada, the US, and Mexico, 1983–2013

Source: Frank Graves, Robert Pastor, and Miguel Basáñez, "The NAFTA Promise and the North American Reality," presentation to the Center for North American Studies, American University, Washington, DC, 31 October 2013, at: <www.american.edu/sis/cnas/upload/North-America-October-30-1255-pm-FULL-VERSION.pdf>.

is still the world's largest economy and whose dollar continues to serve as the reserve currency of the world. At the same time, however, it has also involved a larger and more complicated relationship with China and greater exposure to developments throughout the world.

What Is Globalization?

In some ways, globalization may appear to be a very old phenomenon. The Spice Road that snaked from the ports of the eastern Mediterranean across the Middle East and Asia to China 2,000 years ago was an early precursor of the massive flow of goods and services that today knits together all corners of the globe. A characteristic of today's globalized world that usually is thought to distinguish it from international trade in earlier times is the unprecedented volume and speed of the economic exchanges in the contemporary global economy. The World Bank estimates that the percentage of global GDP generated by trade increased from about 7 per cent in 1960 to about 30 per cent today. The value of foreign direct investment worldwide has also increased by a factor of five or six times over this same period.[15] The Zurich-based Swiss Federal Institute of Technology produces an index of globalization for all of the world's countries. It is a highly sophisticated measure that includes economic, social, and political components. Canada ranked thirteenth in the world in overall level of globalization in 2013, placing thirty-fourth in economic globalization, eighth in social globalization, and twelfth in political globalization. Among G8 countries only the UK measured higher, and just slightly, in overall globalization.[16]

Economists point to two chief factors that have driven globalization in recent decades. One is technology. Developments in transportation, telecommunications, and manufacturing have made it profitable to assemble in Mexico appliances designed in Canada or the United States, with parts and component systems from perhaps several different countries, and destined for sale in many different national markets. The global integration of goods production was accompanied by increased transnational flows of investment capital, leading inevitably to a greater integration of financial markets as banks, investment funds, and companies increasingly realized that their activities and opportunities spilled across national borders. Since the end of World War II, policy-makers in the developed countries have generally favoured a more open trading environment that has encouraged this process. Although the world economy is still far from the level playing field that free trade boosters often talk about, there can be no doubt that protectionist barriers have declined over the last several decades, through bilateral agreements like the **Canada–US Free Trade Agreement** (FTA) and several other bilateral agreements negotiated more recently, regional free trade such as that created under NAFTA and in the European Union, and more comprehensive trade liberalization that took place under the aegis of the General Agreement on Tariffs and Trade (1948–94), leading to the 1995 creation of the more formalized and institutionalized World Trade Organization (WTO). National subsidies and protectionism in various guises are still practised to varying degrees by all governments, but the overall trajectory of trade policy in Canada, as elsewhere, has been in the direction of more open markets.

The fact that free or at least freer trade has become the fashionable norm among the developed countries does not mean that doubt has been silenced or dissent squelched. The 1999 Seattle meeting of the WTO, the 2001 Organization of American States (OAS) Summit of the Americas in Quebec City, the G8 meetings in Genoa in 2001 and in Rostock, Germany, in 2007, and the 2010 G20 meetings in Toronto all were accompanied by violent clashes between anti-globalization protesters and police. The Occupy Wall Street movement that began in 2011 and spread across Canada and much of the world (only to sputter out within a couple of years) was inspired by an anti-globalization ethos. Protesters in the streets have been complemented by various other forms of anti-globalization that range from intellectual attacks to political parties, social movements, and interest groups for whom the critique of globalization is a central ideological principle, or even *the* central principle. In Canada these forces include many—very likely most—of those who teach in the social sciences, a significant part of the country's media elite, much of the leadership of the labour movement, the NDP, many religious organizations, environmental groups, and nationalist groups like the Council of Canadians. Their criticisms of globalization receive considerable coverage, from the television screen to the classroom. Indeed, the critique of globalization is probably better known to most Canadians and, for that matter, citizens in other wealthy countries than is its defence.

But globalization is not simply about economics and trade. It also involves the unprecedented movement of people between countries of the world, exchange in cultural values, the more rapid and widespread diffusion of diseases across the world, new security concerns that reach across borders, the introduction of animal and plant species in parts of the world that did not previously know them, and the emergence of the virtual global village made possible by modern telecommunications technology. Again, some of these phenomena are not new. When the Romans conquered and ruled over far-flung parts of their empire, they also introduced and left a legacy of cultural values. The migration of peoples between different territories is a story as old as human history. When Europeans arrived in the New World they brought with them diseases for which the Indigenous peoples lacked immunities, leading to the decimation of many of these populations. And the spread of species between distant parts of the world has a long history. The horse was introduced in the Americas by the Spanish in the sixteenth century and the potato was brought to Europe by them from South America. As in the case of trade, however, all of these flows have increased in volume, reach, and, in many instances, in their consequences for the people and natural environments affected by them. What we today call **"globalization"** may be defined as the historically unprecedented speed and scope of exchanges between different societies and regions of the world. Its consequences continue to be the subject of enormous debate.

The Anti-Globalization Indictment

In many ways the anti-globalization movement and the analysis that underpins it represent the latest edge of a tradition whose origins go back to the critique of capitalism developed by Karl Marx in the middle of the nineteenth century. Marx made several claims that sound familiar today:

- Market economies necessarily create competitive and mutually exclusive interests, most importantly between those who control the means of producing and distributing wealth—the capitalist class—and those who must sell their time, talents, or skills to make a living—the working class.
- As capitalism achieves ever higher stages of development, an increasing polarization of class interests occurs and the gap separating the rich from the poor grows.
- The saturation of domestic market opportunities drives capitalists in search of opportunities abroad, and thus other countries and populations are drawn into the cycle of exploitation, of both workers and resources, upon which advanced capitalism depends.
- Governments in the capitalist world—and this would include international organizations like the WTO, the International Monetary Fund (IMF), the World Bank, and the G8 and G20—are essentially and unavoidably instruments for the repression of subordinate class interests and the protection of capitalism and capitalists.

With only some minor tweaking this is, of course, pretty much the core of the modern condemnation of globalization. Globalization is blamed by its critics for exacerbating the income gap between the affluent and the poor in developed societies, widening the divide between standards of living in the developed and underdeveloped world, undermining indigenous cultures, weakening the ability of governments everywhere to regulate business in the public interest, and reducing governments' willingness and ability to finance social programs. To this list may be added such additional sins as degradation of ecosystems across the globe, child labour and forced labour in parts of the world, international conflict in regions of the world such as the Gulf War of 1991 and the Iraq War of 2003, and the rise of global terrorism. Some of these claims are more plausible than others. Some involve the spurious attribution to globalization of consequences that are due to other causes. Almost all of them are difficult to prove with any certainty.

The pros and cons of globalization cannot be sorted here. Nevertheless, because these issues are hotly debated in Canadian politics, and because the broader consequences of globalization are related to its effects in Canada and affect the international system of which Canada is a part, we need to at least consider the evidence for these various claims. Moreover, a fair assessment of globalization's impact on Canada and throughout the world should also be open to the possibility that globalization has been, on balance, a good thing, or at least that the balance sheet is not entirely red.

Some critics, such as the artist of this political cartoon, argue that the promises of globalization are empty—and that we are just beginning to find out.

John Larter/Artizans.com

Let us review the charges made concerning the general consequences of globalization and the specific impacts alleged by some to have been experienced in Canada.

1. *Inequality between the rich and the poor in Canada and the number of people living in poverty have increased due to globalization.*

Contrary to the conventional wisdom purveyed by probably most academics and journalists, and many politicians, these claims are not self-evidently true. First of all, the distribution of income in Canada is not more unequal today than it was 30 years ago, at least if one compares the share of national income received by those in the top quintile of all families to that received by those in the bottom quintile. There are, granted, various ways of measuring the distribution of income. By some of these measures it appears that income inequality has increased over time. For example, if we focus on the share of income and wealth accounted for by the very highest income earners—say, the top 1 to 5 per cent of all earners—there is no doubt that this fraction of the population accounts for a greater share of all income than was true a couple of generations ago. Other measures, however, tell a different story. And in any case, the causal linkage between globalization and developments in the distribution of income is not as clear as many contend. Income inequality may change or remain the same in response to numerous factors, including government policies, shifting demographic patterns, economic restructuring caused by factors other than globalization, and so on. Globalization may be part of an explanation, but ideology more than analysis often elevates it to the status of the primary cause of income inequality.

What about poverty? The argument is often made that globalization has increased the ranks of the marginalized, producing more who are unable to afford a decent standard of living. Child poverty, the phenomenon of the working poor, and an apparent increase in visible destitution—homelessness, begging, reliance on food banks, etc.—are argued by some to be at least partially due to economic globalization.

There are at least two problems with such claims. The first is the familiar one of wrongly attributed causality. As in the case of the distribution of income, change may be the result of a number of factors that have little or nothing to do with economic globalization. For example, it is demonstrably true and known to all serious students of family policy that the sharp increase over the last generation in the number of single-parent households—usually headed by women—has been a major factor driving the increase in child poverty. As a group, single mothers tend to have lower-than-average incomes. Consequently, they and their dependent children are at a greatly elevated risk of falling below the poverty line, however that line is defined. This has a lot to do with ideas about marriage, divorce laws, and income supports for single parents, but not much to do with globalization.

The other problem involves the very claim that poverty has increased. The truth of this claim is at least open to dispute. Using Statistics Canada's definition of what constitutes a low income, a smaller share of the population falls below what is often called the "poverty line" at present than was the case 40 years ago. Moreover, claims about the extent of poverty are often confused with developments in the distribution of income, so that greater inequality in income is assumed—mistakenly—to signify an increase in poverty. Increased inequality within the society may increase the self-perception of poverty for those less well-off, but it does not mean that a greater proportion of the population is in dire straits. Although poverty is an undeniable problem in a rich country like Canada, it requires a rather imaginative and contestable definition to conclude that the scale of poverty has increased.

2. Economic globalization has increased the income gap between the rich and poor countries of the world.
The conventional wisdom holds that the income gap between developed and developing countries is increasing. This raises two questions. First, is this claim true? Second, if it is true, is globalization to blame?

The answer is mixed. Increased trade between such countries as China, India, Brazil, Mexico, Malaysia, the Philippines, Vietnam, and the developed world has contributed to rising incomes in these countries and the growth of a middle class that, while small

by Western standards, is usually thought to be a crucial ingredient if a society is to acquire democratic institutions. The increased participation of these and other developing countries in the global economy has actually contributed to a significant reduction in global poverty and a narrowing in the gap between richer and poorer countries.[17] At the same time, however, such countries as Bangladesh, Pakistan, and virtually all of Africa remain desperately poor, but the examples of the countries where living standards have improved suggest that it is not economic globalization that causes countries to remain mired in destitution. Indeed, virtually all of the world's poorest countries are ranked towards the bottom of the table in the Zurich-based index of economic globalization, mentioned earlier.[18] Some argue that the loan conditions of the IMF and the World Bank and the subsidies that rich countries often provide to domestic industries—especially agriculture and natural resources—which might otherwise be export opportunities for developing countries, are among the reasons for the large and even widening gap between the rich and poor countries of the world. Even assuming some truth to these claims, increasing participation in the world economy has generated higher average standards of living in many countries that, until a couple of decades ago, were miserably poor.

3. Globalization undermines indigenous cultures, producing broadly homogeneous Western values and lifestyles in societies across the world.
The coffee chain Starbucks has roughly 20,000 locations in 60 countries throughout the world. KFC, based in Louisville, Kentucky, has about as many locations in 120 countries. Facebook, Twitter, Instagram, and other social media have users throughout the world. Almost all of the world's most valuable brands, as annually measured by brand management company Interbrand, are Western (defining "Western" to include Japanese and South Korean companies and products, for the simple reason that companies like Toyota, Samsung, and Hyundai have long been totally integrated into the global market).[19] The experience of travelling abroad and switching on CNN International in hotel rooms across the world,

seeing Western products and corporate logos virtually everywhere, and being able to carry on with one's work and life through an Internet system dominated by Western- and especially American-based sites certainly seems to corroborate the claim that globalization has swamped local cultures in its wake. And at the level of general populations, there can be no doubt that some significant convergence has taken place in the music people listen to, the films they watch, the clothing styles they favour, and the food they eat.

These signs of cultural convergence in the direction of a Western norm are not merely superficial. But at the same time they are probably not nearly as profound or, for that matter, as insidious as critics claim. If one examines social and political institutions from the family to structures of local and national governance, there is little evidence that globalization has eroded differences and pushed different societies and cultures towards a common norm. On the contrary, students of contemporary nationalism and of the continuing importance of religious identities in many parts of the world argue that the persistence and even resurgence of these communal identities is, in fact, a reaction to cultural homogenization. In other words, economic integration and the cultural consequences that inevitably accompany it may actually generate an affirmation of distinctive cultural identities. This affirmation is often virulently anti-western/anti-American and sometimes accompanied by violence. National and regional communities—and especially their elites—may be motivated to resist the displacement of their languages, values, and institutions by those of the dominant global culture. At the same time, however, this resilience in the face of westernizing influences may reflect the inherent, and often underestimated, strength of local customs and institutions. This is the conclusion of, among others, Pippa Norris and Ronald Inglehart. They argue that cultural "firewalls" exist that tend to "limit the capacity of [westernizing] media to alter enduring values and attitudes."[20]

4. *Globalization has undermined the resolve and the ability of governments to regulate business in the public interest, to finance social safety nets, and,* *generally, to act as a counterweight to markets and rampant individualism.*

Despite being widely believed, little solid evidence supports any of these related claims. Taking the case of Canada as an example, the size of government, as measured by the share of GDP accounted for by the public sector, is about 40 per cent today, compared to about 45 per cent 25 years ago. Public spending on health care, education, and income maintenance programs (public pensions, employment insurance, social assistance, disability payments, etc.) accounts for as great a share of all program expenditures today as it did a generation ago. While it is true that no new "big ticket" social spending programs have been added over the last couple of decades, none of the major ones have been eliminated (though some, such as unemployment insurance and mothers' benefits for children, have been significantly overhauled). The decline in the government share of GDP is largely due to the fact that the growth of the economy has outpaced the increase in public spending. Overall levels of individual taxation have increased in Canada over this period, as they have in most affluent countries. And despite the privatizations and deregulation that have taken place in some sectors, if the sheer volume of health, consumer, and workplace safety and environmental and rights-based regulation is examined, as well as the number of regulatory bodies, one would be hard-pressed to conclude that the state's regulatory function is in decline. Indeed, many argue that regulation, rather than direct spending, has become increasingly popular as policy-makers' instrument of choice in dealing with policy problems.

A 2001 report carried out by the United Nations concludes that economic globalization has not produced, across the board, a decline in what the report calls **state capacity**.[21] On the contrary, the UN report argues that, among developed countries, the state's capacity to maintain social safety nets and pursue such non-market goals as protection of the environment remains solid. The report argues that, notwithstanding what has become the conventional wisdom, "there is no evidence that globalization weakens the State. On the contrary, increased globalization goes hand in hand with higher [public] expenditure."[22]

The story is quite different in the case of many developing countries, but the authors of this report do not point the finger of blame at globalization. Rather, they blame "state capacity deficit" in these countries—ineffective public administration characterized by low levels of professionalism, high levels of corruption, inadequate technology, and weak social policies—for their failure to take advantage of the economic opportunities that globalization offers. A very large literature supports this conclusion. The relationship between state capacity and poverty is to some considerable degree cyclical: desperately poor countries find it difficult to overcome the endemic and systemic problems that contribute to inadequate state capacity. But the point is that the fundamental problem besetting many developing countries is inadequate governance, not economic globalization.

5. *Globalization has increased the exposure of national economies, including Canada's, to developments abroad, thereby rendering the competitiveness of industries and the well-being of communities and workers more precarious than in the past.*

It is hard to refute the claims made by this last indictment of globalization. It is a simple matter to point to jobs, corporations, indeed entire industries that have relocated in search of cheaper labour, laxer environmental and workplace standards, and lower taxation. In the 1970s and even the 1980s, the merchandise on the shelves of Sears, Walmart, or other major retailers was produced mainly in North America. This has not been true for quite some time. A bumper sticker popular in more heavily unionized, automotive communities reads, "Out of work yet? Keep buying foreign." This, it seems, is the trump card in the hands of the anti-globalization movement.

But matters are not that straightforward. The outsourcing of production and even some services has contributed to lower costs for many products. Unskilled and lower-skilled workers in affluent democracies have been among the losers created by economic globalization, but consumers in general have benefited. Most economists argue that the migration of lower-skilled jobs to low-wage economies has encouraged workers in affluent

economies to acquire education and skills that make them employable in industries where production and services are not easily outsourced. Moreover, in recent years we appear to have seen that outsourcing has limits that are reached when wages and other factors of production in developing economies increase to a level where it makes sense for businesses to relocate closer to the markets for what they are producing. "Reshoring," the return of manufacturing jobs that had been outsourced to production facilities in developing countries, is hardly a tidal wave. But there is evidence that the exodus of manufacturing jobs in the United States—Canada and Western Europe have not, to this point, experienced the reshoring phenomenon—has been staunched and a modest uptick in employment has been taking place.

"Out of work yet? Keep buying foreign" may be a catchy slogan that seems to encapsulate the problem of economic globalization. In fact, however, it is premised on the idea that the rather short period in world history—really not more than half a century—during which time low-skilled manufacturing jobs could command relatively high wages and provide these workers and their families with a middle class lifestyle was sustainable. Perhaps it was, if protectionist trade barriers that impeded the growth of incomes and of a middle class in developing countries had been maintained. The cost, however, would very likely have been levels of international tension even greater than those the world has known over the past few decades. Countries that trade with each other are, other things being equal, less likely to go to war with one another.

Globalization and Canada–US Relations

Toyota and Honda are thought to be foreign automakers. But several of their most popular models, driven by millions of Canadians and Americans, have much more Canada–US content than certain models produced by the so-called Detroit Three. The Honda Accord and Civic and the Toyota Camry and Avalon all include between 70 and

80 per cent North American content. Compare this to the Ford Fusion (20 per cent), Ford F-series trucks (60 per cent), and Buick Lacrosse (57 per cent). General Motors' Chevrolet Equinox, assembled in Ingersoll, Ontario, has an engine from China (the engine for the Sport model is produced in the US), a transmission produced in Japan, and an estimated 60–65 per cent Canada–US content.

Globalized production, sourcing, and investment have forced us to rethink what were, until fairly recently, firmly established ideas about what is Canadian. The case of the automotive industry is merely one example—though a particularly important one in terms of its employment and income implications—of the globalized economic realities that characterize much of the Canadian economy. Products exported from companies operating in Canada routinely include foreign content, and imported products will often include content produced in Canada. Moreover, most of Canada's provincial economies, including all of the largest ones, do more business with economies outside of Canada than with all of the other provinces combined.[23] Thus, not only is the old idea of a made-in-Canada product cast in doubt, but the very notion of a Canadian economy seems a bit outdated given the reality of this country's enormous dependence on international trade.

Some developed economies, including those of Italy, the UK, and France, are about as dependent on foreign trade as Canada, and some, including Germany and the Netherlands, depend on trade for an even larger share of their GDP than does the Canadian economy. But none of these other economies is as dependent on trade with a single trading partner as Canada is with the United States. The numbers speak for themselves. The total value of Canada–US trade in merchandise, services, and investment makes this the largest bilateral trading relationship in the world (although the China–US relationship is poised to surpass it in the near future). Over 70 per cent of Canadian exports of goods and services go to the United States, accounting for roughly one-fifth of Canada's total GDP. A somewhat lower share of Canada's substantial import trade comes from the United States, at slightly more than 60 per cent of total imports

of goods and services. This is down from about three-quarters of total imports around 1999–2001, a decline due largely to the increased importance of imports from China and a drop in cross-border automotive vehicle and parts trade. Canada has been the major export market for American goods for over half a century and is today the leading export market for about three-quarters of all US state economies. The United States has long been the largest source of foreign investment in Canada, currently accounting for close to two-thirds of all foreign investment, and is the location for about half of all Canadian direct investment abroad.

This bilateral trading relationship has a long history, but in recent years it has achieved an unprecedented level of intimacy. The real value of trade between the Canadian and American economies has more than doubled since the FTA took effect in 1989, increasing gradually at first and then more dramatically since NAFTA came into effect in 1994. The value of both exports to and imports from the United States, and as a share of total Canadian exports and imports, declined somewhat after 2001. This was due to a combination of reasons, including exchange rates, the increasing importance of China as a source of Canadian imports, and weakened demand in the recession-buffeted US economy in 2008–10. Trade with the US has rebounded in recent years, as may be seen in Figures 17.3 and 17.4. This relationship has never been one of equals and is not more so today than in the past. Revealingly, when the Canadian media were full of stories about the imposition of American duties on Canadian softwood lumber imports in 2005, there was barely any attention to the issue in the American media. Nor did the 2006 agreement that ended this long-standing dispute receive more than passing notice on the US side, whereas it was hugely controversial in Canada. Canada–US trade disputes that lead the national news in Canada are lucky if they receive a mention in the American press, particularly outside border states that might be more immediately affected. The trading relationship is not only huge; it is hugely asymmetrical, affecting Canada's vital interests far more than it does those of the United States (see Table 17.1).

Politics in Focus

BOX 17.2 Globalization's Soft Spot?

The argument that globalization has increased the exposure of the economies of developed countries to events far beyond their borders appeared to be confirmed in 2008. But it was not conflict in the oil-rich Middle East or political upheaval in China that sent the economies of the developed world into a downward spiral. Rather, it was the financial sector meltdown triggered by the billions in dollars of bad loans made by American banks and other lenders in what became known as the "sub-prime crisis." The crisis began in the United States, as millions of homeowners in a soft economy found themselves in default on their mortgages and housing prices plummeted, resulting in worthless loans on the books of financial companies. It was compounded when these same companies, fearful that others in their industry were teetering on the verge of insolvency or were already there, refused to loan to each other, strangling the supply of credit in the economy.

The crisis quickly spread to other economies in Western Europe, Japan, Russia, and China. Stock values tumbled, some banks and commercial investors had to be bailed out by their governments, and the belief that the health of these economies had been "decoupled" from events in the United States—a belief that had recently become the conventional wisdom—was shown to be very far from the truth. Talk of a depression on the scale of the Great Depression of the 1930s was heard on both sides of the ocean.

Although Canada's financial sector did not experience the high-profile bank closings and bailouts seen in Europe and the United States, Canadians were not untouched by the crisis. As the world economy slowed dramatically, demand for some of the natural resources that had powered the growth of the Canadian economy over the previous several years and produced an increase in the value of the Canadian dollar softened and prices went down. Moreover, the drop in consumer

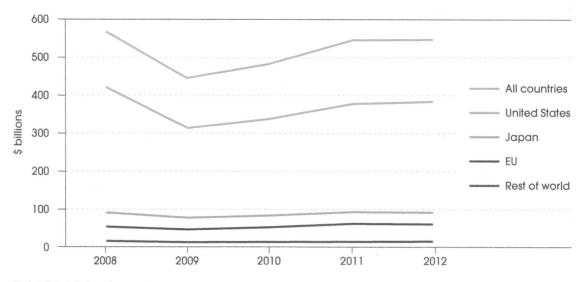

FIGURE 17.3   Canadian Exports of Goods and Services by Major Region, 2008–12

Source: Canada, Department of Foreign Affairs and International Trade, *Canada's State of Trade—Trade and Investment Update—2013*, Figure 4.1, at: <www.international.gc.ca/economist-economiste/performance/state-point/state_2013_point/index.aspx?lang=eng>. Reproduced with permission of the Department of Foreign Affairs, Trade and Development Canada, Ottawa, 2015.

demand in the United States, Canada's major export market, resulted in the further weakening of an already enfeebled manufacturing sector in Ontario and Quebec.

On the face of it this crisis resembled that of the stock market crash of 1929 and the Great Depression of the 1930s. Over-exuberant growth and unrealistically inflated values were followed by a financial sector collapse and a dramatic decline in consumer demand and business investment. But this latest crisis was different in important ways, both of which are linked to globalization. First, the impact of the financial meltdown in the United States on foreign financial markets, and ultimately on the economies of these countries, was faster and more far-reaching than in the 1930s. The world's financial markets are much more integrated and mutually dependent now than they were earlier in the century. Second, the possibility of governments being able to deal with the crisis appeared to be greater than during the decade of the Great Depression. The architecture of international co-operation among governments, as inadequate as it doubtless is in important respects, simply did not exist two and three generations ago. Canada, the United States, Great Britain, the European

Central Bank, and a handful of other national banks agreed in October 2008 to implement a co-ordinated cut in interest rates across these national economies. This was an unprecedented instance of globalized policy-making—albeit crisis policy-making—in response to an economic situation whose scope and depth were also linked to globalization.

The prospects of another global financial crisis on the scale of 2008 may have receded, but they have not disappeared. As first Greece, then Ireland, Italy, Portugal, and Spain teetered on the brink of insolvency between 2010 and 2012, bank bailouts, financial reforms, and austerity measures were implemented across much of the EU during what became known as the Eurozone crisis. Prime Minister Harper and the Obama administration weighed in on the crisis and participated at meetings of the G8 and G20 where reforms to the European financial system were discussed. In a 2011 report entitled *Future Global Shocks*, the OECD identified the world financial system, characterized by unprecedented levels of interdependence between national economies, as a continuing risk to global stability and prosperity.[24] It may be that this is economic globalization's most serious soft spot.

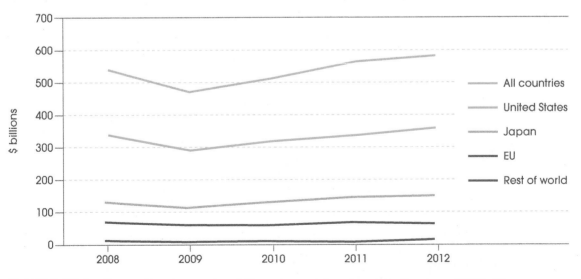

FIGURE 17.4   Canadian Imports of Goods and Services by Region, 2008–12

Source: Canada, Department of Foreign Affairs and International Trade, *Canada's State of Trade—Trade and Investment Update—2013*, Figure 4.2, at: <www.international.gc.ca/economist-economiste/performance/state-point/state_2013_point/index.aspx?lang=eng>. Reproduced with permission of the Department of Foreign Affairs, Trade and Development Canada, Ottawa, 2015.

It would be an overstatement to say that Canada has no leverage in this relationship. After all, Canada is the single largest source of energy imports to the US and is the destination for over half the value of all US automotive exports. The Canadian economy is extremely important, and even strategically important, to the United States. Canada is the major source of foreign imports for 35 of the 50 American states and for many years has been the single largest foreign supplier of energy to the United States. But the influence this might otherwise give Canadian negotiators in trade disputes with Washington is diluted by Canada's far greater across-the-board dependence on the American economy. To give but two examples, an end to petroleum exports from Alberta to the United States would bring Alberta's economy to its knees and would produce an immediate drop of about 3–4 per cent in Canada's GDP, but this would represent only a drop of about 7 per cent in the total supply of petroleum consumed in the United States. Likewise, if the American border were to be closed to automotive vehicles and parts from Canada this would represent an immediate loss of about 10 per cent of Ontario's GDP. State economies like those of Michigan and Ohio would experience serious losses from the end of automotive trade with Canada, but the impact on the overall American economy would amount to less than 1 per cent of American GDP.

This enormous imbalance in the Canada–US trade relationship was one of the chief arguments put forward in the 1980s by the Canadian advocates of free trade. The federal government's official policy of reducing Canada's reliance on trade and investment with the United States—a policy called the Third Option, adopted in 1972—had proven about as effective as a statute repealing the law of gravity. A decade later, Canada was even more dependent on the American economy as a destination for exports and a source of imports. Canada's major manufacturers, but also important exporters of natural resources such as wood products, oil and gas, and hydroelectricity, recognized that their growth prospects depended on access to the American market. The Canadian Manufacturers' Association,[25] which began life a century earlier calling for protectionist tariffs, became a convert to and a politically weighty advocate of a Canada–US free trade agreement. A growing wave of protectionist sentiment in the American Congress during the 1980s seemed to lend urgency to Canadian free traders' case, helped by the pro-free trade recommendations of the 1981–5 Royal Commission on the Economic Union and Development Prospects for Canada. Canada's best economic hope, big business and the country's leading economic experts agreed, was in tighter formal economic integration with the United States. Even among many of those who were dubious about some of the economic claims made for free trade, the political argument that this would help shield Canadian industries from Congress's protectionist moods was persuasive.

TABLE 17.1 An Asymmetrical Economic Relationship, 2012

		Canada (%)	United States (%)
1.	Exports to the other country as a share of total GDP	22	2
2.	Investment from the other country as a share of total stock of foreign investment	52 (1st)	8 (4th)
3.	Share of total exports going to the other country	75	19
4.	Share of total imports coming from the other country	51	14

Source: *CIA Fact Book*, at: <www.cia.gov/cia/publications/factbooks/geos/us/html>; Organization for International Investment, *Foreign Direct Investment in the United States: 2013 Report*, at: <www.ofii.org/sites/default/files/FDIUS_2013_Report.pdf>; Canada, Department of Foreign Affairs and International Trade, *Canada's State of Trade—Trade and Investment Update—2013*, at: <www.international.gc.ca/economist-economiste/performance/state-point/state_2013_point/index.aspx?lang=eng>.

The Canada–US Free Trade Agreement took effect on 1 January 1989. It was followed in 1994 by the **North American Free Trade Agreement**, bringing Canada, the United States, and Mexico together into a free trade zone that encompasses most industries and forms of investment. Both agreements created an architecture of dispute settlement rules, agencies, and monitoring requirements that have not taken the politics out of trade disputes, but provide administrative forums for their resolution. Experience has demonstrated that these new forums do not replace other methods of making trade policy. The older forums and channels still matter, as does the World Trade Organization. But on the whole it is fair to say that the rules and the dispute settlement mechanisms created under the FTA and NAFTA make it more difficult for the member governments to pursue trade policies that favour their domestic interests. They may still do so, but they run the risk of eventually having to pay the cost of sanctions if their policies are found to be in violation of these agreements.

The asymmetry in the Canada–US economic relationship is not helped, from Canada's point of view, by the fact that Americans—from policy-makers to average citizens—often have little awareness of the scale of these relations or, perhaps worse, harbour misconceptions about them. In recent years virtually every survey that has asked Americans to identify their country's major trading partner finds that China is the country most likely to be mentioned. A 2013 poll found that Canada came in fourth, after China, Japan, and Mexico, when Americans were asked which two countries were the most important markets for American exports.[26] Before China's economic ascendance, Japan and Mexico were often more likely to be thought of by Americans as their country's major trading partners, even though the value of Canada–US trade far exceeded that of either of these other trade relationships. Relatively few Americans know that Canada is their country's leading foreign supplier of energy. At the same time, and even though many Americans are unaware of the scale and nature of the Canada–US economic relationship, American public opinion towards Canada is positive when it comes to trade. Americans are far more likely to say that they would

support Canadian ownership of natural resource companies in the US than ownership by nationals of any other country.[27]

Lack of information coupled with goodwill towards Canada may not, in the end, be much of a liability when it comes to Canada's relations with the United States. What American policy-makers and opinion leaders think about Canada will usually be more important than the beliefs and attitudes of average Americans. A study of what members of the United States Congress said about Canada during floor and committee proceedings during the years 2001–10 concludes that, "contrary to popular belief, many American politicians are informed about Canadian domestic matters and aware of what is happening in Canada."[28] On matters of trade, energy, and defence, members of the Senate and the House, both Democrats and Republicans, tended to be positive towards Canada. The picture was mixed, however, when the subject involved border security or health care (see Table 17.2).

Attracting the attention of American policy-makers is not always a good thing. In recent years China and Mexico, the United States' two leading trading partners after Canada, have received far more attention from members of Congress than has Canada. Most of that attention has been critical. Given the general goodwill that exists in Congress and in the United States more generally towards Canada, the challenge is not so much reversing ideas that American policy-makers have about Canada and US–Canada relations as getting them to pay attention when it matters. As Allan Gotlieb, Canada's ambassador to the United States from 1981 to 1989, has observed, a major part of Canada's problem in its trade relations with the United States has always been getting the attention of those who matter in Washington.[29] He argues, however, that the answer may not lie in government-financed media blitzes designed to let Americans know how important we are to them. Nor does he put much stock in Canadian efforts to lobby US interests, such as home builders' associations or Chambers of Commerce, in the hope that they will pressure Congress and administrative officials in ways congruent with Canadian trade interests. "Like it or not," Gotlieb says, "in the US political system a foreign country is just another special interest. And not a very special one at that. It lacks the clout of a domestic special interest because it cannot contribute to political campaigns or deliver votes." What, if anything, can Canadian policy-makers do to make their voices heard?

Gotlieb's answer has two parts. "First and foremost," he argues, "influence must be aimed at the highest level of the US political system, the presidency, the top personal advisors to the President and the key cabinet secretaries." Gotlieb places special importance on the personal relationship

TABLE 17.2 Percentage of Comments about Canada That Were Positive, Neutral, and Negative, by Issue and Party, 107th–111th Congresses, 2001–10

Part I: House of Representatives

	Positive (%)	Neutral (%)	Negative (%)
Trade and Commerce			
Democrat	61	8	31
Republican	65	13	22
Health Care			
Democrat	83	16	1
Republican	19	1	80
Energy and Environment			
Democrat	49	44	11
Republican	89	7	7
Borders and Security			
Democrat	38	24	38
Republican	24	18	58
Defence and Foreign Affairs			
Democrat	100	0	0
Republican	82	0	18

Part II: Senate

	Positive (%)	Neutral (%)	Negative (%)
Trade and Commerce			
Democrat	54	12	34
Republican	55	14	31
Health Care			
Democrat	77	17	6
Republican	9	2	89
Energy and Environment			
Democrat	62	18	21
Republican	67	27	7
Borders and Security			
Democrat	43	18	40
Republican	58	20	22
Defence and Foreign Affairs			
Democrat	90	0	10
Republican	86	0	14

Source: Adapted from Alexander Moens and Nachum Gabler, *What Congress Thinks of Canada*, May 2011, Fraser Institute, p. 48, at: <www.fraserinstitute.org/uploadedFiles/fraser-ca/Content/research-news/research/publications/whatcongressthinksofcanada.pdf>.

between Prime Minister and President, complemented, ideally, by a good rapport between the Canadian Foreign Minister and the US Secretary of State. The personal relationship factor tends to be dismissed as irrelevant or of distinctly minor importance by many political scientists. Gotlieb's own experience in Washington, however, leads him to believe that "[i]f a matter is on the President's personal agenda, there is far better chance of a favourable outcome. If the President is concerned, word goes down to many hundreds of top loyal political appointees."

Second, Gotlieb argues that tighter formal integration between the two countries would help protect Canadian economic and border security interests from the political vicissitudes that arise in American politics and that can roil the waters of Canada–US relations. "It is possible," he maintains, "that a single market or customs union would enhance our interests." Moreover, Gotlieb notes that Canadian governments may well have more leverage in economic matters than is often believed if they are willing to offer trade-offs on border control, terrorism, and defence issues. To be sure, this is a rather large "if." His conclusion extends the logic that led the Canadian government to embrace the free trade option in the 1980s. "Canada," Gotlieb states, "should look to a broader and deeper economic and security zone in which the rules of engagement would be less arbitrary, more predictable and provide greater common security." He advocates a "grand bargain" with the United States, establishing a North American community of law.[30] This, he believes, is the best hope for overcoming the unavoidable and lopsided asymmetry—both political and economic—in the Canada–US relationship.

Gotlieb's proposal for a "grand bargain" that would establish a North American community of law—really something along the lines of the

POLITICAL ROLLER COASTER

Michael de Adder/Artizans.com

The proposed cross-border Keystone XL pipeline expansion, which, if approved, would extend from Hardisty, Alberta, as far south as Houston, Texas, is characterized in the cartoon above as a political roller coaster. Regardless of the specific outcome, the Keystone XL expansion and the debates surrounding it will impact Canada–US relations.

institutional and policy integration that exists under the European Union—is echoed in business writer Diane Francis's 2013 book, *Merger of the Century: Why Canada and America Should Become One Country*.[31] Indeed, there is a long tradition, going back to Goldwin Smith's 1891 book, *Canada and the Canadian Question*, of arguments for going beyond economic integration between Canada and the United States to some form of political integration. In 2005 the prestigious Council on Foreign Relations brought together representatives from Canada, the United States, and Mexico to propose such a course for the three NAFTA partners.[32] Such ideas remain political non-starters in Canada and the United States.

There appears to be significant support on both sides of the border, however, for smaller steps towards greater Canada–US integration. In 2010 the Canadian International Council, led by then Research In Motion's CEO, Jim Balsillie, issued a report entitled *Open Canada: A Global Positioning Strategy for a Networked Age*. Its analysis of the Canada–US relationship was broadly simi-lar to those of Gotlieb and the Council on Foreign Relations. "Nothing [we have considered] imperils Canada's vital national interests more than obstacles to a free-flowing Canada–US border," states the report.[33] But instead of the "Big Bang" approach that Gotlieb proposed and that Diane Francis calls for, the Council recommended a "series of little bangs, a steady drumbeat of small gains that build confidence and momentum toward a more ambi-tious plan at a more propitious date."[34] The Council rejected what it characterized as an ideologically driven and false dichotomy between multilateral-ism and closer integration with the United States. In words guaranteed to send Canadian nation-alists reaching for the nearest defibrillator, the Council declared:

> To insulate ourselves from US political capri-ciousness or border hardening, we need to become America's indispensable ally. That may sound subservient to some Canadians, but it falls within the best traditions of independent Canadian internationalism. The relative decline of American influence means it has to reach out to trusted allies. Canada does not need to play little brother to the US to stay in the family—just the opposite. Still, progress will require mature bipartisan leadership. Any attempt to exploit this for political gain will scupper a deep-ening of Canada's national interest.[35]

Critics of such a view argue that it makes no sense to tie Canada even more tightly to an American economy they believe to be in decline. Indeed, the Conservative government of Stephen Harper, generally thought to be quite sympathetic to argu-ments for greater Canada–US integration, negoti-ated a formal trade agreement with the European Union (2013) and free trade agreements with sev-eral other countries. These agreements have not, however, been framed as attempts to decouple Canada from its dependence on trade with the United States. Instead, the Conservative govern-ment's rhetoric on trade insists upon the primacy of the Canada–US relationship and portrays these

other free trade agreements as steps towards open-ing new markets for Canadian business rather than weakening ties to the United States. In fact, this familiar dichotomy between greater integration with the United States or diversification in trade and investment in order to find counterweights to **dependence** on Canada's much larger neigh-bour is now rather stale and in some ways a false opposition. There is little to no prospect of Canada becoming significantly less dependent on trade with the United States, at least for many years. This means that issues of border security and the movement of goods and people will continue to be hugely important, for Canadians even more than for Americans. At the same time, it makes sense to seek out new and expanded trade and investment opportunities, particularly in emerging markets. Finding the right balance between the competing pulls of integration and independence has always been the challenge for Canadian foreign policy, no less so today than in the past.

Integration and Independence: Finding the Right Balance

Former Canadian Prime Minister and Nobel Peace Prize winner Lester B. Pearson was one of the chief architects of Canadian foreign policy in the post-World War II era. In his memoirs Pearson wrote that American dominance in the world and Canada's particular dependence on the United States were among the key hard realities confronting Canadian policy-makers.[36] These realities, Pearson observed, "brought us anxiety as well as assurance."

This continues to be the Canadian condition when it comes to the possibilities open to this country in world affairs. The asymmetrical eco-nomic relationship between Canada and the United States, overlain by structures of policy inte-gration that operate through the Canada–US Free Trade Agreement and NAFTA—and before these comprehensive trade agreements, through sectoral treaties including the Auto Pact and the Canada–US Defence Production Sharing Agreement—leave Canada with little room to throw its weight around in conflicts with its American neighbour. As discussed above, Canada's economic prosperity continues to be highly dependent on trade with the United States. The policy implications of this dependence can hardly be overstated.

For several decades the response of successive Canadian governments—the Progressive Conservative government of Brian Mulroney (1984–93) excluded—has been to search for and support counterweights to American dominance. Chief among these have been the United Nations and multilateral institutions more generally. **Multilateralism** involves the resolution of international differences and conflicts through structures and processes that represent many states and give all of them a voice, though not necessarily an equal voice, in decision-making. The United Nations has been the most prominent structure for multilateralism in the post-World War II era. There are, however, many other international organizations to which Canada belongs, including the North Atlantic Treaty Organization (NATO), the World Bank, the Organisation for Economic Co-operation and Development (OECD), the World Trade Organization (WTO), the Organization of American States (OAS), the Commonwealth, and la Francophonie.

Some of these multilateral organizations are dominated by the United States and therefore can hardly be said to serve as counterweights to its might. NATO, for example, has almost never blocked the will or modified the military objectives of American administrations, the 2003 refusal of several of its members to guarantee the alliance's support for Turkey in the event of an attack by Iraq being the chief exception to this rule. Influence in the International Monetary Fund's decision-making is weighted, based on the size of member-state contributions, and the United States is its major contributor. Multilateralism does not, therefore, necessarily dilute American influence. It can, in fact, magnify this influence by providing greater political legitimacy to American goals through their association with other countries and structures of multilateral decision-making. On the whole, however, multilateralism clearly holds out the possibility of allowing for the representation of

interests and points of view that might dilute the dominance of the United States.

"One of the great foreign policy challenges facing Canada," observes Michael Ignatieff, "is staying independent in an age of [American] empire."[37] This is a large part of the explanation for multilateralism's attractiveness in the eyes of many Canadians and those who govern them. Multilateralism, when it is not a convenient cover for the ambitions and interests of a single member state, as the Warsaw Pact clearly was for the former Soviet Union or as the IMF and World Bank are alleged to be by critics of America's global economic power, implies that states are willing to accept some limitations on their national sovereignty. Canada's governing elites and opinion leaders, like their counterparts in Europe, "have a vision of a multilateral world in which . . . sovereignty is not unconditional, but limited and bound by human rights agreements, or multilateral engagements which limit and constrain the sovereignty of states in the name of collective social goods."[38] It would be an overstatement to say that all Canadians accept this multilateral vision of the world, but recent history suggests it has broad popular support. The problem for Canada—a problem also experienced by many other allies of the United States, though less acutely—is that multilateralism has not been embraced as enthusiastically by its major trading partner and has sometimes produced outcomes setting Canada at odds with the United States.

There are, as there have long been, limits to how far and in what circumstances Canadian foreign policy can depart from that of the United States. In the case of Canada's refusal in 2003 to support the war on Iraq, this did not damage the security interests and military goals of the United States. The fact that the United Kingdom, Spain, over a dozen other European governments, Japan, Australia, and an assortment of other countries lent their support to this military action made the absence of Canadian support virtually unnoticed in the United States. Indeed, it was only noticed when some American media outlets reported the booing of the American national anthem at a hockey game in Montreal! The Liberal government's 2004 decision to reject participation in an American-led missile defence system—a system agreed to by governments in Britain, Australia, Japan, Germany, Italy, Israel, the Czech Republic, Denmark, Netherlands, Spain, Turkey, and Romania—did not produce any noticeable costs in the Canada–US relationship. In the case of the "war on terrorism," launched after the terrorist attacks of 11 September 2001, the space available for Canada to ignore American preferences has been considerably less. This is because the policy actions taken by the American government have involved border security, air travel, and immigration, matters that directly affect Canada. With about $1.5 billion per day in trade crossing the border between the two countries, and given the enormous number of jobs and investments in Canada that depend on the smooth flow of goods and people across this border, the Canadian government has had little choice but to co-ordinate its policies with those of the American government. This co-ordination, however, has stopped short of Canadian acceptance of the idea of a common security perimeter around Canada and the United States, a concept that would require that Canadian immigration policy be brought into line with American policy.

Canadians have often felt a certain degree of unease in the face of their country's obvious and extensive dependence on the United States. They have been aware that the relationship between the two countries is not one of equals and that Canada will usually, but not always, have less leverage than its superpower neighbour.[39] "Close, but not too close" captures the ambivalence that many Canadians feel when they contemplate a relationship that has known moments of friction (see Box 17.3). These moments have been vastly overshadowed by a dense and complex web of co-operation and shared values and interests that ensure, in President John F. Kennedy's words, that "what unites us is far greater than what divides us."[40]

Kennedy spoke these words over 50 years ago. Since then Canada–US relations have deepened in virtually every respect except in terms of the cross-border movement of people. Pulling in the other direction, however, are three developments viewed by some as having the potential to loosen the ties between Canada and the United States.

One of these developments is globalization. Canada is less dependent today on trade with the United States—at least on the import side of the ledger and in terms of foreign direct investment—than at any time in the last half-century. A significant part of this apparent diversification in Canada's trade involves the rise of China as a manufacturing powerhouse and source of merchandise imports. China has also become a significant source of investment capital, in Canada as elsewhere in the world. On the export side, although the share of total Canadian exports accounted for by the American market has declined since the all-time high reached in 2001 (83 per cent), recent levels of about 70–75 per cent are more or less the average over the past four decades. Moreover, although Canadian investment abroad has increased significantly since the 1980s, most of it has been in the United States. Globalization has meant some loosening in Canada's economic dependence on the United States, but with the exception of significantly increased imports of merchandise and capital from China, it has not produced the level of trade diversification often claimed.

A second and not unrelated development involves what many believe to be American decline. This is, it needs to be said, a highly contested characterization of the role and influence of the United States in the world. The safest observation is that a relative decline of American power, certainly economically, has occurred over the last decade, due principally to the rise of China. If American economic power truly is on the wane and growth prospects seem brighter in emerging economies, perhaps a policy of trade diversification makes sense for Canada. This appears to be the logic behind a series of initiatives undertaken by the Canadian government in recent years, such as free trade negotiations and agreements with South Korea, the European Union, India, and several South American countries, as well as the willingness to look to China as a market for Canadian oil in the event that the Keystone XL pipeline is not approved.

A final potential source of loosening in the Canada–US relationship involves border security. It is simply a fact that crossing the border is a more time-consuming and frustrating affair since the terrorist attacks on the United States of 11 September 2001. Almost all of this "thickening" of the border has been due to security concerns on the American side. These concerns have created some amount of pressure for the Canadian government to harmonize certain aspects of its immigration screening policy with that of the United States, most notably through the 2011 Canada–US Perimeter Security Agreement. This agreement was a step towards the Immigration Information Sharing Treaty, which, beginning in late 2013, permitted much greater sharing of biographic and biometric information on all travellers entering the two countries and crossing the border between them. Still, there are political limits on how far any Canadian government can move towards this sort of policy harmonization without paying a price with voters who see this as an unacceptable sacrifice of Canadian sovereignty. Despite the extensive co-operation that has taken place between the two governments and their agencies since 9/11, security is likely to remain a factor that makes the border less rather than more permeable.

The Social Fabric

BOX 17.3 The World Looks Different, Depending on Your Side of the Border

Canadians and Americans are more alike in their values and beliefs than either is to other national populations. When it comes to their views on world affairs, however, they do not always see eye to eye. To begin with, Americans are about twice as likely as Canadians to say that their country's influence in the world is positive (in 2008, 64 per cent to 34 per cent). In fact, Canadians are less likely than almost any other Western population to believe the global influence of the United States is positive. Canadians are also much less likely than Americans to agree that "Under some conditions war is necessary to obtain justice" (48 per cent to 74 per cent). Canadians fall about halfway between Americans and the average for most Western societies when it comes to their belief that justice may sometimes require going to war. Perhaps not surprisingly, given that the attacks of 9/11 happened on American soil, Americans are much more likely than Canadians to believe that a terrorist attack over the next year is a real possibility (85 per cent to 48 per cent).

On other matters, however, the differences between Canadians and Americans are small to non-existent. They are about equally likely to support economic sanctions against states that behave badly in the world or that treat their own people badly (81 per cent of Canadians and 78 per cent of Americans). Both agree that their country has a responsibility to be a moral leader in the world (86 per cent of Canadians and 79 per cent of Americans). Canadians are only slightly more likely than Americans to support humanitarian aid (80 per cent to 74 per cent) and developmental assistance (65 per cent to 57 per cent).

In regard to bilateral issues, Canadians and Americans agree on some issues and disagree on others. Large majorities in both countries agree that it is important "to work together to develop an integrated energy policy to remove any dependence on Middle East oil" (84 per cent of Americans and 78 per cent of Canadians). They are also fairly close in their support for greater and closer co-operation on border security (69 per cent of Americans and 62 per cent of Canadians). But when asked whether they support greater bilateral co-operation on matters of national security (64 per cent of Americans and 45 per cent of Canadians) and anti-terrorism measures (76 per cent of Americans and 58 per cent of Canadians), a significant gap opens between the two populations.

Sources: British Council, *Transatlantic Network 2020*, at: <www.britishcouncil.org/market_research_-_pdfv.3.pdf>; IPSOS, Halifax International Security Forum, *Global @dvisor*, Nov. 2013, at: <www.ipsos-na.com/download/pr.aspx?id=13255>; Environics Institute, *Focus Canada 2012*, <www.environicsinstitute.org/uploads/institute-projects/environics%20institute%20-%20focus%20canada%202012%20final%20report.pdf>; Nanos-UB North American Monitor, *Tracking Perceptions on US–Canada Relations, 2005–2013*, at: <www.niagarareport.buffalo.edu/documents/2013Dataand9yearsummary.pdf>.

The world's longest undefended border, as it has long been described, is a metaphor for the extraordinary intimacy of the Canada–US relationship. As metaphors go, it may not be as apt as it was during the twentieth century. Border officers on the Canadian side now carry guns, as their American counterparts have for many years, and American drones patrol much of the airspace between the two countries. Nevertheless, the intimacy of this relationship continues to be remarkable. The ties of culture, economics, security, and geography that President Kennedy remarked upon when he visited Ottawa in 1961 ensure that the United States will continue for many years to be Canada's most important bilateral relationship, far overshadowing all others.

Conclusion

The boundary separating Canadian politics from developments in the rest of the world has always been porous, and never more so than today. This fundamental truth of life in an inescapably globalized world was brought home to Canadians, and to people throughout the world, by the attacks on the United States of 11 September 2001, the global financial crisis that began in 2008, and by popular uprisings against dictatorships in the Arab world, starting in Tunisia in 2011 and spreading to Egypt, Libya, and Syria. As in Iran, after the regime stole the election of 2009 from those who opposed the rule of the mullahs, social media—Facebook, Twitter, and video captured and sent from cellphones—were crucial in organizing popular resistance to autocratic rule and equally crucial in getting the story to the outside world. Canadians watched on their video screens as the drama of what appeared to be democratic revolts unfolded thousands of kilometres from home.

Listen to the "Who Owns the Arctic?" podcast, available at: www.oupcanada.com/Brooks8e

Few matters of consequence in Canadian public life do not have an international dimension. Canada's claim to sovereignty in the Arctic is disputed by many countries, although the Canadian discovery in September 2014 on the seabed of Queen Maud Gulf of one of the two ships from the disastrous mid-nineteenth-century Franklin expedition in search of a Northwest Passage is expected by some to shore up the Canadian claim. Energy policy and, in particular, the development of the oil sands in Alberta have brought Canada into the crosshairs of global attention. The country's economic prospects are so obviously linked to decisions and developments outside Canadian borders that any conversation about economic policy that fails to account for the global context of government projections for spending and revenue cannot be taken seriously. Domestic policy conversations on human rights, immigration, Aboriginal affairs, the environment, and social inequality are all nested in larger transnational conversations on these matters.

Given these realities, it is perhaps disheartening and even worrisome that many Canadians know so little about their world. This was brought home in a rather striking way when a sociology professor at Memorial University made headlines with her story of how much difficulty her students had in correctly identifying oceans and continents on a map.[41] This demonstrates, of course, what is perhaps the great irony of our times. More information is available, from a wider variety of sources, at the click of a mouse or the touch of a screen, than at any point in human history. We may all have seen YouTube clips of gassed civilians in Syria or a collapsed textile factory in Bangladesh, but for many people these are images without a context. Democracy depends on citizens being able to contextualize the images and information they consume. Without this context, which requires knowledge and the analytical tools necessary to make sense of it, we cannot truly understand our world and our country's place in it.

Appendix: Timeline of Canada in the World

late 1400s–early 1500s	Fishing by Basque, English, Portuguese, French, and Spanish ships on the Grand Banks off the east coast of Newfoundland, and whaling, especially by the Basques, off the Labrador coast and in the Strait of Belle Isle, the first economic exploitation of Canadian resources by Europeans.
Late 1500s	Trade in beaver pelts and other furs begins, providing the basis for the eventual extension of trading routes from Quebec all the way to the north of Saskatchewan and Alberta.
1603–8	Samuel de Champlain makes two visits to Canada, establishing the city of Quebec in 1608 on his second voyage; European colonization of Canada begins.
1759–63	The war between Britain and France spills over into a rivalry in the New World, British troops defeating French forces at Quebec in 1759. The formal transfer of New France to Britain takes place in 1763 under the Treaty of Paris.
Early 1800s	Canada becomes a major supplier of white pine for British ships.
1812–14	The War of 1812 between Britain and the United States produces many battles on Canadian territory and the shared waters of the Great Lakes.
1820s	In an effort to dilute the influence of American-born residents of Canada the colonial authorities encourage immigration from the British Isles. The arrival of tens of thousands of immigrants from Ireland during the Potato Famine of the 1840s marks the significant beginning of ethnic pluralism that went beyond the French and English ethnic communities.
1854	The first Reciprocity Treaty with the United States is signed, abrogated by the US government in 1865.
1867	The creation of Canada as a sovereign state—in most respects, but with some important limitations—is prompted by fears that the United States might have designs on parts of British North America and by Britain's unwillingness to continue to pay for the defence of Canadian territory.
1870–1	The vast territories controlled by the Hudson's Bay Company are transferred by Britain to Canada in 1870 and British Columbia becomes the fifth province in 1871, after which Canada stretches from the Atlantic to the Pacific oceans.
1879	The National Policy is adopted by the Conservative government. It includes a sharp increase in tariffs on manufactured goods, a policy intended to protect fledgling Canadian producers from American competition but which also has the effect of encouraging US-based companies to set up operations in Canada, leading to very high levels of foreign ownership and lower levels of productivity in Canadian industry as a result of foreign-owned corporations that produce only for the small Canadian market.
1903	Resolution of the Alaskan Boundary Dispute: the lone British commissioner on a six-person joint commission sides with the three American commissioners, giving to the United States a long strip of coastal land that Canadian authorities claimed ought to be part of British Columbia.
1909	The International Boundary Waters Treaty between the United States and Canada takes effect, creating the International Joint Commission, with equal representation from both countries (see 2009, below).

1911	The Canadian general election is fought largely on the issue of reciprocity in trade with the United States. The pro-reciprocity government of Wilfrid Laurier is defeated.
1914–18	World War I: Canada is a junior partner in the alliance against Germany, Canadian troops falling under the command of British officers. Over 63,000 Canadian soldiers died in the war.
1919	Canada becomes a founding member of the League of Nations.
1920	Canada passes from the economic orbit of Great Britain into that of the United States: American investment now officially exceeds the value of British investment.
1921	Canada's Prime Minister, Mackenzie King, sees multilateralism as a way to assert Canada's independence from Great Britain in international affairs.
1931	Under the Statute of Westminster, Canada acquires the authority to negotiate and sign foreign treaties in its own right, a power that Great Britain had exercised on Canada's behalf.
1939–45	Canada participates in World War II, but no longer as a subordinate of Great Britain. Canada emerges from the war as one of the world's leading economies. About 47,000 Canadian soldiers died in the war.
1945	Canada becomes a founding member of the United Nations. The UN and multilateralism generally are seen as counterweights to the influence of the United States on Canadian foreign policy.
1947	Canada is a founding member of the General Agreement on Tariffs and Trade (GATT) and the North Atlantic Treaty Organization (NATO).
1950–3	Canada participates in the Korean War under the umbrella of a UN Security Council resolution. The official figure is that 516 Canadian soldiers died in this conflict.
1956	Suez crisis: Canada sides with the United States against the Franco–British invasion of Egypt, and Canadian Foreign Minister Lester Pearson, who brokers a settlement to end the crisis, is awarded the Nobel Peace Prize.
1957	The North American Air Defense Command (NORAD) is created, a partnership of Canada and the United States against the possibility of a Soviet missile attack. Early warning radar stations are established on Canadian territory: the Pinetree Line across southern Canada in 1954, and the Mid-Canada Line, at the 55th parallel, and the Distant Early Warning (DEW) Line, along the 70th parallel, in 1957.
1960s	Under Lester Pearson, the Canadian government becomes critical of US involvement in the Vietnam War, although Canadian companies continue to profit from the production of defence-related exports used in that war. Under Quebec Premier Daniel Johnson, that province becomes more assertive in its demands for representation and an independent voice abroad. Canadian dependence on the United States becomes a prominent political issue as the level of American ownership in key resource and manufacturing sectors of the Canadian economy reaches unprecedented levels.
1962	The Kennedy administration's request that the Canadian government permit nuclear warheads on missiles located on Canadian territory, which the American administration argued was required by Canada's obligations under NORAD and NATO, is refused by the Diefenbaker government, creating a major rift in Canada–US relations. The Liberal government elected in 1963 complies with the request.
1972	The Liberal government of Pierre Trudeau announces the "Third Option" policy of diversifying Canadian trade and thus reducing Canada's economic dependence on the United States. By the end of the decade the percentage of total export and import trade tied to the American economy is at an all-time high.

1976	The G7, the annual meeting of the leaders of the world's seven largest capitalist democracies, is created when Canada joins the G6 countries of Britain, France, Italy, Japan, the United States, and West Germany.
1985	The Macdonald Royal Commission on the Economic Union and Development Prospects for Canada, created by the Trudeau government in 1982, makes free trade with the United States its major recommendation. The Conservative government of Brian Mulroney approaches the Reagan administration in 1985 to open free trade talks.
1989	The Canada–US Free Trade Agreement takes effect.
1994	The North American Free Trade Agreement (NAFTA) among Canada, Mexico, and the United States takes effect.
1997	Canada signs the Kyoto Accord, later ratified in 2002. A decade after signing, Canada's CO_2 emissions exceed the targets agreed to in the accord by about 25 per cent.
2000	Over 80 per cent of Canada's imports and exports are tied to the United States and about one-third of Canada's GDP depends on trade with the United States.
2001	After the terrorist attacks of 11 September 2001, movement across the Canada–US border becomes a major issue in the bilateral relations between these two countries. As a member of NATO, Canada supports the American-led invasion of Afghanistan to replace the Taliban regime. Eventually, Canada becomes a major contributor of combat forces in Afghanistan.
2003	The Liberal government of Jean Chrétien decides not to join the Anglo-American alliance that invades Iraq to overthrow the Saddam Hussein regime. Massive opposition to the war in Quebec, and within the Liberal Party's Quebec caucus, is an important factor in the government's decision to withhold any significant support.
Early 2000s	Canada's claim to full sovereignty in the waters of the High Arctic is not accepted by other nations with a direct Arctic presence, including the United States, Russia, Denmark, and Norway. As the possibility of a shipping passage through the Arctic increases and the prospects for natural resource exploitation in the High Arctic also become greater, the issue of Arctic sovereignty assumes greater urgency.
2005	Canada, Mexico, and the United States agree to the Security and Prosperity Partnership, an agreement that appears to pave the way towards greater policy co-ordination among the three countries. The first formal summit of the SPP is held in Montebello, Quebec, in 2007.
2008	Canada has roughly 2,500 troops stationed in Afghanistan and plays a major combat role within the NATO mission fighting the resurgent Taliban. Canadian public opinion remains divided on Canada's involvement as the number of Canadians killed in combat and on patrols exceeds 100.
2009	The 100th anniversary of the Boundary Waters Treaty between Canada and the United States, creating the IJC. Despite some high expectations associated with the IJC when it was created, most policy experts agree that the complex and important web of transboundary environmental governance between the countries now operates largely through agreements and networks of sub-national governments.
	Barack Obama assumes the presidency of the United States and Prime Minister Harper's office announces that the President's first official visit outside the US will be to Canada. Canadians have high expectations for the new President and his foreign policies.
2010	In March the Conservative government announces that Canadian troops in Afghanistan will be withdrawn in 2011, in compliance with a motion passed in the House of Commons

in 2008; 157 Canadian troops and four civilians were killed during the course of this NATO mission.

2010	Canada's bid for a two-year non-permanent seat on the UN Security Council fails.
2013	Canada assumes the position of chair of the Arctic Council for a two-year term, enabling it to shape the agenda of issues affecting circumpolar nations, including claims of Canadian sovereignty over the continental shelf in the Arctic, but also social, economic, and health issues related to Native populations in the region.
2013	Canada and the European Union conclude a free trade agreement. FTAs had already been negotiated over the previous few years with Panama, Jordan, Peru, and Colombia, and negotiations were ongoing with South Korea, India, Japan, and other countries.
2013	Nine hundred Canadian soldiers leave for Afghanistan as part of Operation Attention. Their mission is to train Afghan soldiers and police officers.
2014	Canada joins in the western sanctions directed against Russia for its annexation of Crimea and support for the pro-Russian separatists in eastern Ukraine. Financial support is provided for various forms of training related to governance and civil society in Ukraine, as well as military transportation of non-combat supplies.
2014	In August, Prime Minister Stephen Harper makes his ninth straight annual visit to Canada's Arctic regions to "show the flag." This time he returns to announce a remarkable discovery related to Canada's Arctic sovereignty and its status as a northern nation: a team of Canadian oceanographers and archaeologists has found one of the two ships from the ill-fated Franklin expedition of the 1840s on the ocean floor of Queen Maud Gulf, south of King William Island.

Starting Points for Research

Robert Bothwell and Jean Daudelin, eds, *Canada Among Nations 2008: 100 Years of Canadian Foreign Policy* (Montreal and Kingston: McGill-Queen's University Press, 2008). Published as part of the *Canada Among Nations* series, this collection provides an excellent overview of various aspects of Canadian foreign policy over the country's first 100 years.

Brian Bow, *The Politics of Linkage: Power, Interdependence, and Ideas in Canada–US Relations* (Vancouver: University of British Columbia Press, 2009). Bow examines four cases of conflict (nuclear weapons, 1959–63; Canadian claims to sovereignty in Arctic waters, 1969–71; the National Energy Program, 1980–3; invasion of Iraq, 2002–4) between the Canadian and American governments and explains why Canada did not experience hard-power punishment despite its refusal to go along with American government preferences.

Paul Cellucci, *Unquiet Diplomacy* (Toronto: Key Porter, 2007). This memoir of a former US ambassador to Canada provides an interesting perspective on Canada–US relations during the years that included 9/11, the invasion of Afghanistan, and the Canadian government's decision not to participate in continental missile defence.

W. Andy Knight and Tom Keating, *Global Politics* (Toronto: Oxford University Press, 2010). An excellent introduction to globalization and its consequences for national and international politics.

Stephen Randall and John Herd Thompson, *Canada and the United States: Ambivalent Allies*, 4th edn (Montreal and Kingston: McGill-Queen's University Press, 2008). Quite simply the best history of the Canada–US relationship.

Review Exercises

1. Canada participates in a large number of international organizations. For each of the following organizations explain what it does, the nature of Canada's participation, and the leading issues faced by the organization in recent years.
   - Organization of American States
   - North Atlantic Treaty Organization
   - World Trade Organization
   - International Criminal Court

2. How dependent is your community on international trade? To find out, identify the five or six leading employers in your area. You can do this by contacting your local Chamber of Commerce or the economic development office of city hall. Contact these companies and ask for information about how much of their goods or services they export, to what countries, and how many people they employ. What other aspects of globalization can be observed in your community?

3. In December of 2012 the Canadian government formally withdrew from the Kyoto Accord on climate change. What reasons were given by the government? What have critics said about this decision? On balance, do you think this decision was the right or wrong thing to do? Why?

Glossary

Aboriginal self-government A concept premised on the idea that Native communities should be viewed as possessing at least some of the attributes of sovereign peoples and that, therefore, they have a right to be self-governing. Various models and degrees of self-government have been implemented over the last couple of decades, one of the most ambitious being the territory of Nunavut.

Advocacy advertising The purchase of newspaper/magazine space, signs or billboards, or broadcast time to convey a political message.

Affirmative action Measures intended to increase the representation of a targeted group or groups beyond what it would be without special intervention. These measures may include hiring and promotion practices, school admission policies, selection rules for committees, and so on.

Authority A form of power based on the recognition by the person or persons who obey that the person or organization issuing a command or making a rule has a legitimate right to do so and should be obeyed.

Bilingual belt A term coined by Richard Joy in *Languages in Conflict* that refers to the narrow region running from Moncton, New Brunswick, in the east to Sault Ste Marie, Ontario, in the west, in which is found the vast majority of Canada's francophone population and where the rate of francophone assimilation is lower than elsewhere in Canada.

Bill 101 Quebec's Charte de la langue française, the first piece of legislation passed by Quebec's National Assembly in 1977, soon after the Parti Québécois came to power. It made French the sole official language in Quebec for purposes of provincial public administration, restricted access to English-language schools, and imposed French-language requirements on business in Quebec. Despite some setbacks in the courts over the years, Quebec's language policy continues to be based on the principles set forth in Bill 101.

Block funding A formula under which Ottawa's financial contribution to a provincially administered program or policy field is not geared to the level of provincial spending. The Federal–Provincial Fiscal Arrangements Act of 1977 began this practice of replacing the *shared-cost program* model with block funding. The Canada Health Transfer and Canada Social Transfer are the major block funding transfers from Ottawa to the provinces.

Brokerage politics Style of politics that stresses the ability of parties to accommodate diverse interests, a feat that requires flexibility in policy positions and ideological stance. Brokerage politics is often characterized as non-ideological, a characterization that is somewhat misleading because the claim of brokerage-style parties to be non-ideological simply means they represent the dominant ideology accepted uncritically by most members of society. The Liberal and Conservative parties have been the main practitioners of brokerage politics

on Canada's national stage, the Liberal Party being the more successful of the two over the last century.

Bureaucracy Word (*bureaucracie*) coined by the French writer Vincent de Gournay in the mid-1700s to refer to rule by unelected officials. Today, the term "bureaucracy" encompasses all of the unelected officials of the public service whose employment is within the central administration of a government and who may wield power on behalf of that government.

Calgary Declaration A statement agreed to in 1997 by all of the provincial premiers except Quebec's Lucien Bouchard. It stopped short of endorsing the recognition of Quebec as a distinct society, instead referring to the "unique character of Quebec society."

Canada–US Free Trade Agreement (FTA) A wide-ranging trade agreement between Canada and the United States that has been in effect since January 1989. The FTA reversed the historical pattern of Canadian protectionism enshrined in the National Policy of 1878–9 but that had been steadily eroded after World War II, and created an architecture of dispute settlement rules, agencies, and monitoring requirements. The FTA was largely subsumed under the *North American Free Trade Agreement* in 1994.

Canadian Bill of Rights Human rights legislation passed by the Canadian Parliament in 1960 that includes many of the same rights and freedoms guaranteed by the Charter. However, the Bill of Rights is a statute and does not have the status of constitutional law.

Canadian content Media content that is demonstrably Canadian according to various criteria related to writers and composers, performers (musicians, actors, etc.), producers, and place of production. Regulations developed and enforced by the Canadian Radio-television and Telecommunications Commission require television and radio broadcasters and cable companies to ensure that a specified share of their programming satisfies the criteria of Canadian content.

Caucus The elected members of a particular political party in the legislature. When Parliament is sitting, each party's caucus usually will meet at least once per week, during which time matters of policy and political strategy may be discussed.

Central agencies Parts of the bureaucracy whose main or only purpose is to support the decision-making activities of cabinet. The five organizations usually considered to have central agency status are the Privy Council Office, the Prime Minister's Office, the Department of Finance, the Treasury Board Secretariat, and the Intergovernmental Affairs Office within the PCO.

Charter groups (old and new) Until a generation ago it was common in Canada to speak of French and British Canadians as Canada's two founding peoples or "charter groups." With the 1982 passage of the Charter of Rights and Freedoms and the explosion of Charter-based litigation, the term "Charter groups" has come to be associated with rights-seeking organizations representing such groups as women, gays and lesbians, disabled persons, and Aboriginal Canadians. Another reason for the eclipse of the older meaning of the term is that it is thought by many to ignore the original pre-European inhabitants of what would become Canada.

Cité libre The intellectual review founded in the 1950s by such prominent Quebecers as Pierre Trudeau and Gérard Pelletier, which was one of the key centres for opposition to the so-called *unholy alliance* of the Church, anglophone capital, and the Union Nationale under Maurice Duplessis.

Clarity Act A federal law passed in 2000 that empowers Parliament to review any future referendum question on Quebec independence to determine whether it is unambiguously worded. This, according to a 1998 Supreme Court ruling, is one of the requirements that a question must satisfy if the outcome of a referendum is to be considered constitutional.

Class analysis A perspective on politics that insists on the overriding importance of social classes based on their relationship to the means of producing and distributing wealth.

Coercion A form of power based on the use or threat of force (e.g., fines, imprisonment).

Common law In Anglo-American legal systems such as Canada's, the component of the law based on the decisions of courts. Like statute law, passed by legislatures, common-law rules are enforceable in the courts.

Communitarianism Those belief systems, like socialism, based on the premise that real human freedom and dignity are only possible in the context of communal relations that allow for the public recognition of group identities and that are based on equal respect for these different group identities.

Conquest of 1759 The military victory of the British forces led by Wolfe over Montcalm in what was New France, but which subsequently became British territory under the Treaty of Paris of 1763. The Conquest has always been a symbol in French Canada, particularly in Quebec, of subjugation to the English community and the loss of communal autonomy.

Conservatism Historically, an ideology based on the importance of tradition that accepted human inequality and the organization of society into hierarchically arranged groups as part of the natural order of things. Today, conservatism in Canada and the United States is associated with the defence of private property rights and free trade, individualism, opposition to the welfare state, and, in the case of social conservatives, emphasis on the traditional family, religion, and what are sometimes referred to as "traditional values."

Constituency Also known as a riding, the territory represented by a member of Parliament. As of the 2015 federal election there will be 338 constituencies, up from 308, the populations of which range from a low of about 20,000 to a high of roughly 200,000 constituents.

Constitution The fundamental law of a political system. In Canada it includes written components—chiefly the Constitution Acts—and unwritten conventions that are more or less established, such as the understanding that the calling of an election is the Prime Minister's prerogative.

Constitutional conventions Practices that emerge over time and are generally accepted as binding rules of the political system, such as the convention that the leader of the political party with the most seats in the House of Commons after an election shall be called upon to try to form a government with majority support in the House. Unlike the written Constitution, conventions are not enforceable in the courts.

Constitutional supremacy Section 52(1) of the Constitution Act, 1982 declares that "The Constitution of Canada is the supreme law of Canada, and any law that is inconsistent with the provisions of the Constitution is, to the extent of the inconsistency, of no force or effect." This means that the laws of all governments and their agencies must conform to the Constitution. Before the Constitution Act, 1982 came into force, Parliament and provincial legislatures were supreme so long as each acted within its own sphere of legislative competence. This was known as *parliamentary supremacy*.

Co-operative Commonwealth Federation (CCF) Predecessor to the New Democratic Party, the CCF was created in 1932 as an alliance of three main elements: disgruntled farmers, chiefly from western Canada, central Canadian intellectuals, and labour activists. The party first ran candidates in the 1935 federal election. Its founding policy document, the Regina Manifesto, called for extensive state planning and control of the economy, a steeply progressive income tax, and the creation of a welfare state.

Corporate elite Those who control the dominant corporations and investment firms in an economy. John Porter defined the term in *The Vertical Mosaic* (1965) to include the directors of Canada's dominant corporations, a usage that was followed by Wallace Clement and Milan Korac in their later studies of this elite. All of these researchers concluded that the Canadian corporate elite is a largely self-perpetuating group whose exclusive social backgrounds and activities set them apart from the general population.

Corporatism A political structure characterized by the direct participation of organizations representing business and labour in public policy-making.

Crisis of the state Marxist scholars began in the 1970s to talk about various sorts of crises said to afflict the capitalist state, including the fiscal crisis of the state. The central idea is that during the 1970s and 1980s the rate of capitalist expansion was slowing compared to the decades of the 1950s and 1960s and pressures on state spending were increasing. This led to increased deficit spending but also to pressure on capitalist governments to cut back on their spending and reduce the size of government.

Cross-border regions (CBRs) Distinct groupings of neighbouring and nearby Canadian provinces and American states whose economic, cultural, and institutional linkages create commonalities between the members of these binational groupings and set each such region apart from other regions.

Cultural hegemony According to Marxists and some elements within contemporary feminism, the values and beliefs of the dominant class or of males, respectively, are accepted as normal and inevitable by society as a whole, despite the fact that they are contrary to the true interests of subordinate classes or females.

Democracy A political system based on the formal equality of all citizens, in which there is a realistic possibility that voters can replace the government, and in which certain basic rights and freedoms are protected.

Democratic deficit A term signifying the gap that critics argue exists between the principles and aspirations embodied in Canada's democratic political culture—including accountability, participation, and openness—and the actual practices and institutions of governance.

Dependence The limitations on a country's autonomy that may arise from its economic, cultural, or military ties to another country or countries. During the 1960s and 1970s it was popular on the left of Canadian politics to characterize Canada as a dependent satellite within the orbit of the United States. The ties between these two countries have not weakened since then, but it is now more common to view Canada's dependent condition within the broader framework of economic and cultural globalization.

Distinct society The view that Quebec is unique and distinct from the other provinces. The Meech Lake Accord of 1987 proposed the amendment of the Constitution to recognize Quebec as a distinct society. In both the Meech Lake and Charlottetown (1992) Accords the distinct society clause was explicitly linked to the fact that Quebec is the only province in which a majority of the population is francophone and would have required the Quebec government to protect and promote the French language. In 1995 Parliament passed a resolution recognizing Quebec as a distinct society. It does not, however, have the force of constitutional law.

Election Expenses Act, 1974 Before 1974 party and candidate spending on election campaign activities was essentially unregulated and there were no legal requirements that revenues and expenditures be publicly disclosed. The Election Expenses Act places spending limits on registered political parties and their candidates during election campaigns, allows for the reimbursement for part of the expenses of candidates who receive at least 15 per cent of the vote, and requires the public disclosure of all contributions of $100 or more to parties and candidates.

"End of ideology" A thesis advanced by American sociologist Daniel Bell in the 1960s, which argued that traditional right/left ideological thinking had become irrelevant and outmoded as a consequence of a developing consensus on the desirability of the welfare state, government regulation of business, and political pluralism.

Entitlements What might be called social rights of citizenship, such as public education, pensions, welfare, and various forms of assistance for those in need. It is a concept associated with the welfare state and a redistributive ethic in public life.

Equalization Transfers made by Ottawa to provincial governments whose per capita tax revenues (according to a complex formula negotiated between Ottawa and the provinces) fall below the average of the two most affluent provinces. Equalization is the second largest federal transfer to the provinces, after the Canada Health Transfer and Canada Social Transfer.

Estimates Sometimes referred to as the expenditure budget. Every year towards the end of February the government will table its spending estimates for the forthcoming fiscal year (1 April to 31 March) in the House of Commons.

Executive federalism A term often used to describe the relations between the Prime Minister and premiers and cabinet ministers of the two levels of government. The negotiations between them and the agreements they reach have often been undertaken with minimal, if any, input from their legislatures or the public.

False consciousness A Marxist concept describing the inability of subordinate social classes to see where their real interests lie and their acceptance of cultural values and beliefs that justify their exploitation by the dominant class.

Feminism A framework for interpreting and explaining politics and society that sees gender as the fundamental basis of conflict in society and associates politics, in all its forms, with the systemic domination of males over females.

First Nations A term commonly used in Canada to refer to communities descended from those who inhabited North America before the arrival of Europeans. This term is not generally used in several other countries that have Aboriginal, pre-contact minorities.

Fiscal imbalance A term used to describe two aspects of public intergovernmental finance in Canada. It has been used since the 1930s to refer to the shortfall between the spending requirements of provincial governments and their revenues, while the federal government had revenues sufficient to pay for its program requirements and to transfer revenue to the provinces. This was described as the "fiscal gap" until fairly recently. The other meaning involves the gap that exists between what citizens and corporations in the wealthier provinces, particularly Alberta and Ontario, contribute to the federal government in various forms of taxation and what they and their provincial governments receive back in federal program spending and transfers. As of 2009, the fiscal imbalance for Ontario was estimated by the Mowat Centre at the University of Toronto to be roughly $11 billion.

Formal equality One of two different standards, the other being *substantive equality*, that may be applied by the courts to the Charter's equality guarantees. The formal equality standard requires that all individuals be treated the same under the law, regardless of the fact that the life circumstances of members of different groups may be significantly different and may affect the likelihood of their achieving constitutional guarantees of equality.

Fragment theory Theory proposed by American historian Louis Hartz, which maintains that the ideological development of New World societies such as Canada, settled by European colonization, was strongly determined by the social characteristics and cultural values of their early immigrants. Such societies were fragments of the Old World because their creation coincided with a particular ideological epoch in the Old World from which the founding immigrants came.

Free-rider problem The likelihood that some members will believe they can reap the benefits of an organization's actions without having to contribute to it as the number of members in the organization increases.

Gender roles The belief that male and female genders are socially constructed, one of the fundamental premises of much of contemporary feminism. As Simone de Beauvoir put it, "One is not born, but rather becomes, a woman." This premise provides the intellectual basis for attacks on many of the traditional roles and expectations associated with males and females. A spirited debate exists between those who argue that gender roles are fundamentally socially constructed and those who maintain that biological differences between the sexes provide the basis for many of the important differences in male and female behaviour, aptitudes, and preferences.

Globalization The increasing interdependence of states, economies, and societies throughout the world, a phenomenon characterized by, among other things, dramatically higher levels of international trade and capital mobility than in the past, the increased mobility and migration of peoples, cultural convergence in terms of consumer tastes between societies, particularly in the developed countries of the world, and the emergence of international institutions for the development and enforcement of economic and human rights standards.

Government The elected individuals and political party controlling the state at a particular point in time.

"higher, the fewer, The" Canadian political scientist Sylvia Bashevkin's characterization of the fact that, although female participation levels in politics are about the same as men's for activities like voting and campaigning, the proportion of women tends to decrease as the political activity becomes more demanding, such as holding office in a political party or being a candidate for public office.

Human rights All the basic rights and freedoms of citizens. Also called "civil liberties" or "civil rights," these include political rights, democratic rights, legal rights, economic rights, and equality rights. Other human rights can include language rights, social entitlements, and environmental rights.

Ideology A set of interrelated beliefs about how society is organized and how it ought to function.

Influence A form of power that depends on the ability of a person or group of persons to persuade others that it is reasonable and/or in their self-interest to behave in a particular way (e.g., to vote for a particular candidate or party).

Infotainment A hybrid television form that packages news and public affairs reporting in an entertainment format that typically includes a "celebrity journalist/host," short analysis that emphasizes action, confrontation, and controversy, and relatively little historical and background information. It is sometimes called "soft news."

Institutional groups Interest groups characterized by a high degree of organizational sophistication, the distinguishing features of which include organizational continuity, stable membership, extensive knowledge of sectors of government that affect their members and easy access to public officials in these sectors, concrete and immediate objectives, and overall organizational goals that are more important than any specific objective.

Interculturalism A Quebec variant of *multiculturalism*. As explained by Quebec's Consultation Commission on Accommodation Practices Related to Cultural Differences (the Bouchard-Taylor Commission, 2008), interculturalism involves a policy of reconciliation and mutual adaptation on the part of both the dominant majority and minorities: both sides must be prepared to make cultural concessions. This is rather different from the more pluralistic concept of multiculturalism, which does not assume a majority group as part of the equation or an explicit need for concession.

Intrastate federalism The representation and accommodation of regional interests within national political institutions such as the Senate. In Canada, federalism has operated mainly through intergovernmental relations. Intrastate federalism, while often argued to be a means of overcoming decentralist tendencies in Canada, has not achieved much success.

Inuit Aboriginal people who comprise the vast majority of those living in the Canadian Arctic, including in Nunavut, Nunavik (Arctic Quebec), Nunatsiavut (northern Labrador), and the Inuvialuit Settlement Region in the western Arctic (Northwest Territories). The forebears of the Inuit migrated from northeast Asia to North America thousands of years later than most other Aboriginal peoples migrated to the Americas.

Iron triangle An American term used to describe the closed system of relations between an interest group and the administrative or regulatory agencies and congressional committees with which the group normally deals.

JPM Acronym for "jolts per minute," a term coined by Canadian media analyst Morris Wolfe to refer to what he calls The First Law of Commercial Television: "Thou shalt give them enough jolts per minute or thou shalt lose them."

Judicial independence The principle according to which judges should be free from any and all interference in their decision-making. It is particularly important that they be free from interference by the government to ensure that the courts are seen to be independent and non-partisan. One of the key protections for judicial independence is the fact that once judges are appointed they cannot be removed from office before retirement age, usually 75, except for serious cause (such as criminal behaviour or serious incompetence).

Judicial restraint The practice of judges deferring to the will of elected governments when their laws and actions are challenged as being unconstitutional. Before the Charter was passed in 1982, it was extremely rare for Canadian courts to declare duly passed laws unconstitutional, unless they were *ultra vires*. Section 1 of the Charter, the reasonable limits clause, provides the courts with the opportunity to defer to elected public officials. However, many critics charge that the tradition of judicial restraint has been replaced by American-style judicial activism.

Legitimacy The acceptance by most people that the rules and institutions comprising the state are fair and should be obeyed. It is closely related to the concept of consent in democracies.

Liberalism Historically, an individualistic ideology associated with freedom of religious choice and practice, free enterprise and free trade, and freedom of expression and association in politics. During the latter half of the twentieth century in Canada and the United States, liberalism came to be associated with support for the welfare state, the protection of minority rights, and the regulation of business.

Libertarians Those who believe that individuals should be allowed the largest possible margin of freedom in all realms of life, including those that involve moral choices. Although they are often thought of as ideologically conservative, libertarians are more likely to align themselves with people and groups thought of as left-leaning on such issues as abortion, homosexual rights, and banning prayer from public schools.

Lobbying Any form of direct or indirect communication with public officials that is intended to influence public policy. Although often associated in the public mind with unfair privilege and corruption, lobbying is not limited to organizations representing the powerful and is not inherently undemocratic.

Loyalism The value system associated with the Loyalists, those who opposed the American Revolution and who migrated north to the British colonies after the defeat of the British in the American War of Independence. Their ideological beliefs have been the subject of much debate, but there is a consensus that they brought to Canada a loyalty to the British Crown and to that which was deemed "British" and a rejection of the developing American identity.

Maîtres chez nous The Quebec Liberal Party's 1962 election campaign slogan, meaning "masters in our own house." It captured the new spirit of Quebec nationalism that emerged during the period of the Quiet Revolution.

"Manufacturing consent" Phrase originally used by Walter Lippmann to refer to government's use of propagandistic techniques to cultivate popular acceptance of its rule. It is also the title of a 1988 book by Noam Chomsky and Edward Herman, in which they argue that the privately owned and oligopolistic media system in the United States—and, according to like-minded critics, in Canada as well—fosters popular consent for a social system that operates mainly in the interests of a privileged minority.

Marxism A framework for interpreting and explaining politics and society that sees class divisions as the fundamental basis of conflict in society and associates politics with a pervasive pattern of domination by those who own and control the means of creating and distributing wealth over those who do not.

Materialism The belief that economic security, material well-being, and acquisition are of primary importance in human relations. Consequently, from a materialist perspective, incomes and employment are of greater concern than human rights or the environment, for example.

Maternal feminism Also called "social feminism," a description of the early women's movement from the late 1800s to the early twentieth century. Maternal feminism accepted the assumption that the biological differences between men and women provided the basis for their different social roles, women being by nature more caring about life and the conditions that nurture it. Maternal feminists fought for legal and political reforms that they expected would improve the conditions of women and their families. The temperance movement was clearly allied to maternal feminism, for the simple reason that alcohol was widely seen as one of the chief threats to the security of women and their families.

Merit principle The practice of making hiring and promotion decisions based on such qualifications as experience, academic degrees, professional credentials and certification, and other attributes deemed to be relevant to the competent performance of the job. This policy was first adopted by the federal government with the passage of the Civil Service Amendment Act, 1908.

Métis Originally, the mixed-blood descendants of unions between Indian women and Scots or French-speaking traders and settlers in the Red River region of Manitoba; more recently, the term has been applied to and appropriated by other groups in Canada of mixed Aboriginal and European ancestry.

Ministerial responsibility The obligation of a cabinet minister to explain and defend in the legislature—and, ultimately, to be responsible for—the policies and actions of his or her department.

Minority government A situation where no single political party controls a majority of seats in the House of Commons. In such circumstances the party with the largest number of seats will require the support of at least some members of one or more other parties in order to win votes in the House of Commons and govern. Majority government, when one party controls a majority of the seats in the House, has been more common in Canada, although the elections of 2004, 2006, and 2008 produced minority governments.

Mobility of capital The movement of operations or investments between sectors of the economy and from one national economy to another. This mobility of capital is a major reason why governments must be concerned with business confidence and will often be reluctant to take measures that, while politically popular, may offend important business interests.

Multiculturalism A value system based on the premise that ethnic and cultural identities and traditions are important to human happiness and dignity and that public policy ought to recognize, support, and promote the retention of these identities and traditions. In Canada an official policy of multiculturalism has existed since 1971. The Charter of Rights and Freedoms acknowledges the "multicultural heritage of Canadians" and the Multiculturalism Act, 1988 commits the Canadian government to a policy of promoting multiculturalism. This is done largely through the Department of Canadian Heritage.

Multilateralism An approach to the resolution of problems that relies on collective decision-making through international organizations such as the UN, the International Criminal Court, NATO, and the WTO. It is based on an assumption that member states should be willing to give up some national sovereignty and accept the decisions of multilateral organizations to which they belong.

Nation A group of people who share a sense of being a community based on religion, language, ethnicity, a shared history, or some combination of these. See also Box 1.7.

National Action Committee on the Status of Women An umbrella organization that represented roughly 700 women's organizations across Canada. During the 1980s the NAC was generally viewed by the media and government as the major organizational voice for the women's movement, and most of the group's revenue came from the federal government. The organization fell on hard financial times by the late 1990s and ceased to operate by 2003.

National Energy Program (NEP) Nationalist economic policy introduced in 1980 that limited the price that could be charged in Canada for oil and gas from Canadian sources and provided preferential tax treatment for Canadian-owned companies investing in the petroleum sector. It was viewed by Alberta as a thinly disguised subsidy that their province—Canada's leading petroleum producer—was made to pay to the petroleum-consuming populations and industries of central Canada. The NEP was opposed by multinational petroleum companies and the American government as discriminating against foreign investors.

National Policy The Conservative Party's nation-building strategy and election platform in 1878 that began to be implemented in 1879. Its three components included a significant increase in protective tariffs to promote manufacturing in Ontario and Quebec, construction of a transcontinental railroad, and encouragement of western settlement to expand the market for the manufactured products of central Canada and to protect this territory from American encroachment.

National standards Rules established by the federal government that apply to areas of provincial jurisdiction, particularly health care and social assistance. For example, the Canada Health Act, 1984 prohibits extra-billing by doctors and imposes financial penalties on provinces that allow the practice. The enforcement of national standards depends primarily on the fact that Ottawa transfers money to the provinces to pay for certain social programs.

Neo-institutionalism A perspective on policy-making that emphasizes the impact of formal and informal structures and

rules on political outcomes. The roots of this perspective lie in economics, organization theory, and a reaction to society-centred approaches to understanding politics and policy.

News management The practice of organizing press conferences, photo opportunities, and other planned events in ways that accommodate the media's need for images and information that are available by newspaper/broadcaster deadlines and in a form likely to be attractive to news editors and to readers or viewers.

North American Free Trade Agreement (NAFTA) A treaty signed by Canada, Mexico, and the United States, under which most duties on goods and services traded between these economies are eliminated and the treatment of each country's investors is, with some limited exceptions, the same as that of domestic investors. The treaty took effect on 1 January 1994.

"Notwithstanding" clause Section 33 of the Charter of Rights and Freedoms, which states that either Parliament or a provincial legislature may expressly declare that a law shall operate even if it contravenes the fundamental freedoms (s. 2), legal rights (ss. 7–14), or equality rights (s. 15) in the Charter. This clause has been invoked rarely, most controversially by the Quebec government in 1989.

Oakes **test** Established by the Supreme Court of Canada, a test that the courts apply in determining whether a law or government action that contravenes a right or freedom guaranteed by the Charter is nevertheless constitutional under the "*reasonable limits*" section of the Charter (s. 1). To be considered "reasonable," a limitation must be based on an important public policy goal and must be proportionate to the importance of this goal.

Operationalize To define a concept in terms of the method or methods used to measure it. For example, democracy might be defined as a political system in which all adults have the legal right to vote and more than one political party competes to form the government. Both of these criteria can be measured.

"Ottawa mandarins" The coterie of top officials, particularly deputy ministers and the governor of the Bank of Canada, who dominated federal policy-making during the period of the 1940s to the 1960s; from "mandarins," the term given to high officials in the ancient Chinese empire.

Outsourcing The movement by transnational corporations of jobs and material inputs for production to less developed countries where labour and inputs cost less.

Paid access opportunities Fundraising events, i.e., dinners and cocktail parties, where, for a donation that can range up to several thousand dollars, donors received the opportunity to meet and exchange views with party leaders or cabinet ministers.

Parliamentary supremacy When Parliament's authority is superior to that of all other institutions of government. In concrete terms this means that the courts will not second-guess the right of the legislature to pass any law, on any subject, as long as it does not involve a matter that, under the Constitution, is properly legislated on by another level of government. Parliamentary supremacy was effectively replaced by *constitutional supremacy* as a result of the Constitution Act, 1982.

Party discipline The practice of MPs belonging to the same party voting as a unified bloc as directed by their leader. This practice is based on a combination of reasons, the foremost being the understanding that the government is required to resign if it loses an important vote in the House of Commons. The Prime Minister and other party leaders control various levers that can be used to maintain party discipline, including expulsion of a member from party caucus, withholding promotion or other rewards from an MP, or refusing to allow him or her to run as the party's candidate in the next election.

Path dependency models Explanatory framework, as in *fragment theory* or formative events explanation, that emphasizes the impact of key historical events and conditions on the trajectory that will be followed by a society, a value system, or an economy.

Patronage The awarding of favours, such as contracts, jobs, or public spending in a community, in exchange for political support. This was the central preoccupation of Canadian politics during the first several decades after Confederation. It continues to be an important practice in Canada and other democracies, although when the exchange of support for government largesse is too obvious this is seen by many to border on corruption.

"Peace, order, and good government of Canada" (POGG) The preamble to section 91 of the Constitution Act, 1867 includes this phrase, which has been interpreted by some as a general grant of legislative power to the federal government. Over time, however, court rulings reduced POGG to an emergency power that can only provide the constitutional basis for federal actions in special circumstances. In a 1977 decision, the Supreme Court indicated that it would not be quick to question Parliament's judgment that special circumstances, warranting legislation under the authority of POGG, exist.

"personal is political, The" The slogan of the modern feminist movement that emerged in the 1960s. "The personal is political" expresses the feminist view that the roots of gender inequality are found in structured male–female relations throughout society and that therefore the achievement of equality for women requires that attitudes and practices in the home, school, workplace, media, and elsewhere must be changed.

***Persons* case** In this 1929 decision of the Judicial Committee of the Privy Council, the JCPC overturned a Supreme Court of Canada ruling that women were not considered persons for purposes of holding certain public offices.

Pluralism An explanation of politics that sees organized interests as the central fact of political life and explains politics chiefly in terms of the activities of groups.

Plurality electoral system An electoral system in which the candidate with the most votes is elected by a simple plurality; in multi-party states such as Canada, in most instances those who are elected do not receive a majority of the votes.

Policy community The constellation of state and societal actors active in a particular policy field.

Policy networks The nature of relations among the actors in a *policy community*.

Political factions Groups of citizens whose goals and behaviour are contrary to those of other groups or to the interests of the community as a whole.

Political identities An identity is a state of mind, a sense of belonging to a community that is defined by its language, ethnic origins, religion, regional location, gender, or some other social or cultural characteristics. Identities become political when those who share them make demands on the state or when the state recognizes a group identity as a reason for treating a group's members in a special way.

Politics The activity by which rival claims are settled by public authorities. See also Box 1.1.

Politics–administration dichotomy Advocated by progressive reformers beginning in the late nineteenth century, a concept that involves an ideal of governance whereby only elected politicians should make choices between competing values and interests, choices that would be embodied in the laws. The proper function of non-elected state officials is to implement these choices without regard for their personal views and preferences.

Populism A vision of politics based on the premise that the general population should have as many opportunities as possible to participate directly in political decision-making and that those elected to govern ought to view themselves as delegates of the people and therefore obliged to reflect their preferences. Populists favour recall votes to remove unfaithful public officials, plebiscites and referendums, short terms of office and term limits for public officials, and citizen initiatives to force action on an issue or policy proposal. They oppose party discipline.

Positive state A state that is active in attempting to shape society and influence its direction. It was championed by liberal intellectuals such as John Dewey in the United States (*The Public and Its Problems*, 1927), socialist thinkers in the United Kingdom, most prominently the members of the Fabian Society, and in Canada by Progressive movement intellectuals early in the twentieth century.

Post-materialism Emphasizes human needs for belonging, self-esteem, and personal fulfillment; consequently, high value is placed on quality-of-life issues such as the environment, group equality, and human rights.

Postmodernism A world view that rejects absolute truths of any kind and conceives of state–society relations as contingent and relative but of the state as nonetheless oppressive, whereby oppression may be targeted at groups based on their race, gender, ethnicity, sexual preference, or some other trait that places them outside the dominant group in control of the levers of state power.

Poverty lines "Low-income cut-offs" (LICOs) established by Statistics Canada that are routinely referred to by journalists, politicians, academics, and others as "poverty lines." These cut-offs or poverty lines represent a relative measure of low income, currently defined to mean that more than 63 per cent of income (20 percentage points above the national average) is spent on food, clothing, and shelter.

Power The ability to influence what happens. It may assume various forms, including *coercion, influence* (persuasion), and *authority*.

Prime ministerial government The argument made in recent years by commentators such as Jeffrey Simpson and Donald Savoie that the concentration of power in the hands of the Prime Minister and his advisers has reached unprecedented levels and that both Parliament and cabinet have been relegated to the margins of the policy-making process. While both Simpson and Savoie suggest that the development of prime ministerial government was partly due to the leadership style of Liberal Prime Minister Jean Chrétien, they argue that there are more fundamental and enduring factors that have contributed to this concentration of power.

Privy Council Essentially the cabinet, under the leadership of the Prime Minister. Formally, anyone who has ever been a member of cabinet retains the title of privy councillor, but only those who are members of the government of the day exercise the constitutional and legal powers associated with the Privy Council.

Propaganda The promotion of a particular ideology or view on public policy by the public media dissemination of selected information and/or misinformation. Although propaganda is commonly understood to be a tool used by non-democratic governments to mislead and deceive the populace, powerful economic interests and governments in democratic societies use the media system for what are essentially propagandistic purposes.

Proportional representation A system whereby the number of seats that a party receives in the legislature is based roughly on the share of the popular vote cast for that party. Variants of proportional representation exist in many European countries.

Protest parties Political parties that have arisen out of dissatisfaction with the operation of brokerage politics in Canada and what has been seen, particularly in western Canada, as the inability of the Liberal and Conservative parties to represent certain regional interests. The *Reform Party*, created in 1987, was the most recent of these parties. Others have included the Progressives, Social Credit, the Western Canada Concept, and the early *Co-operative Commonwealth Federation*.

Province-building The phenomenon of powerful provincial governments creating large and competent bureaucracies and using the various constitutional, legal, taxation, and public opinion levers available to them to increase their control over activities and interests within their provincial borders and, in consequence, vis-à-vis Ottawa. Province-building is most often associated with Alberta in the 1970s and Quebec during the 1960s and 1970s, but is observed more generally in several provinces at various points in time.

Public agenda The issues, concepts, and ideas current in a society's politics at any point in time. The capacity to get an issue onto the agenda or framed in a particular way may be an indication of political influence, but the ability to keep an issue from being formulated as a matter on which most people think government should act may also be a sign of a group's influence.

Purchasing power parities (PPPs) A measure of average real purchasing power that takes into account both average nominal incomes and what a standardized currency unit can purchase in a country. Although average nominal incomes are much higher in many countries than in Canada, if PPPs are used to measure standardized purchasing power Canadians are among the most affluent people in the world.

Quality of life (QOL) A concept that refers to the level of satisfaction with life that members of a society experience, their material well-being, their level of health, the state of their environment, the level of equality between groups, or some combination of these. The United Nations annually ranks countries according to its "human development index," which combines various factors, including literacy, infant mortality, average life expectancy, average income, and average years of formal education. This UN index is accepted by some as a measure of QOL.

Québécois de souche Quebecers, and more specifically francophone Quebecers, whose roots in the province go back many generations. The term is used to distinguish what in English might be called old-stock Quebecers from more recent arrivals whose first language usually is not French and whose cultural heritage is not French Canadian. A similar term is *"Québécois pure laine"* (pure-wool Quebecers). This distinction between old-stock Quebecers and others is objected to by some as being fundamentally discriminatory, but others maintain that the attachment of immigrants to the French language and Quebec's distinctive culture has often been weak.

Quiet Revolution The early 1960s in Quebec when the provincial Liberal government of Jean Lesage reorganized and developed the Quebec state to take control of important institutions such as education and the economy. During the Lesage years (1960–6) the conservative traditional nationalism was swept away by a more aggressive Quebec nationalism that turned to the Quebec state as the chief instrument for the modernization of Quebec society and the advancement of francophone interests.

Rattrapage French for "catching up"; one of the key goals of the anti-establishment challenge to the conservative ideology and elites that dominated Quebec during the 1940s and 1950s. *Rattrapage* involved bringing Quebec's society, economy, and government up to the level of development that existed in the rest of Canada, a goal that required a larger and more interventionist provincial government.

Realignment election An election (or series of elections) that produces a durable change in the political parties' bases of support within a region or regions of a country.

Reasonable limits Section 1 of the Charter of Rights and Freedoms states that the rights and freedoms guaranteed by the Charter are subject to "such reasonable limits prescribed by law as can be demonstrably justified in a free and democratic society." See also *Oakes test*.

Receptive bilinguals People who are capable of responding to French communication but do not themselves initiate conversations in French, consume French-language media, or seek out opportunities to live in their acquired second language.

Red Toryism The belief system associated with Canadian conservatives who believe that government has a responsibility to act as an agent for the collective good and that this responsibility goes far beyond maintaining law and order. Red Tories have supported the creation of public enterprises to achieve a range of cultural and economic goals and are generally supportive of Canadian nationalism.

Reform Party Political party founded in 1987 under the slogan "The West wants in" that became the Canadian Alliance Party in 2000. The Reform Party emerged out of the feelings of alienation that peaked in western Canada during the 1980s, triggered by the Conservative government's 1987 decision to award a major defence contract to Quebec instead of Manitoba and the widespread view that whether the Liberal or Progressive Conservative Party was in power federally, western interests would continue to be sacrificed to those of central Canada.

Regionalism A political identity based on a shared sense of place. It may be linked to a variety of cultural, economic, institutional, and historical factors that tend to distinguish the inhabitants of one region of a country from those of other regions.

"Repertory of stereotypes" A term coined by Walter Lippmann that refers to the media's tendency to fit current news to a limited number of stereotypes that make news stories more easily understandable for audiences/readers, but that also sacrifice nuance and even distort the news by squeezing it into a familiar package.

Representative bureaucracy The practice of hiring and promotion so that the composition of the bureaucracy reflects in fair proportion the representation of demographic characteristics in society. In Canada, the concept and practice of representative bureaucracy were first applied to increase the share of francophones in the public service. Since the 1980s it has been expanded to include women, Aboriginal people, visible minorities, and disabled persons.

Representative democracy A form of democracy in which citizens delegate law-making authority to elected representatives, holding them responsible for their actions through periodic elections.

Reserves Territories set aside under treaties between the federal government and Indian communities for the members of such communities; the vast majority of those residing on reserves are status Indians.

Responsible government The constitutional principle according to which the Prime Minister and cabinet require the support of a majority of members in the House of Commons in order to govern. If the government can no longer maintain majority support in the House, in other words, if it loses the confidence of the House, it is compelled by constitutional convention to resign.

Revanche des berceaux French for "revenge of the cradles," a term that referred to the high birth rate that enabled French Canada to maintain its numerical strength vis-à-vis English Canada from Confederation until the 1960s. Since then the birth rate in predominantly francophone Quebec has fallen to one of the lowest provincial rates in Canada. This, combined with non-francophone immigration to Canada and the assimilation of francophones outside Quebec, has contributed to a gradual decline in the francophone share of Canada's population.

Revenue budget A taxation budget presented from time to time in Parliament, announcing changes to the taxation system. Whereas the expenditure budget (*estimates*) is tied to a regular cycle of decision-making, a new revenue budget may be tabled at any time as, in the government's view, conditions require.

Revolutionary origins and counter-revolutionary origins American sociologist Seymour Martin Lipset argues in *Revolution and Counter-Revolution* (1960) that the political histories and ideological development of the United States and Canada have been significantly marked by the American Revolution of 1776. The political values, symbols, and institutions of the United States have been based on the liberal ideas of the Revolution while, historically, those in Canada have been based on a rejection of what the Revolution stood for.

Right, left, and centre Labels that signify a range of ideological beliefs from collectivist (left) at one end of the spectrum to individualistic (right) at the other, with those in the middle ground (centre) embracing elements from both extremes.

Royal Commission on Aboriginal Peoples Commission established by the federal government in 1991 and chaired by Georges Erasmus and René Dussault. Its 1996 *Report* included about 440 recommendations for the reform of Aboriginal policy. The fundamental premise of the *Report* was that the original sovereignty of Aboriginal peoples and their ownership of the land to which they laid historic claim should be acknowledged and their right to self-government should be embedded in the Constitution.

Royal Commission on Bilingualism and Biculturalism Federal Royal Commission created in 1963 in response to the new assertive nationalism of the Quiet Revolution. The B&B Commission recommended numerous reforms aimed at protecting the rights of the francophone minority outside Quebec and transforming the federal government into a more bilingual institution. The Official Languages Act of 1969 embodied some of the recommendations made by the B&B Commission, as did the federal policy of *multiculturalism* announced in 1971.

Royal Proclamation of 1763 Declaration of the British Crown regarding the North American territories formally surrendered by France to England under the terms of the Treaty of Paris. The Proclamation included detailed provisions about relations between the British and the Native inhabitants of these territories, whereby unsettled lands were reserved for the Indians and could be alienated only by the Crown, as occurred in much of Canada through the treaty process in the last half of the nineteenth century and in the first decades of the twentieth century.

Rule of law A vital principle of democratic government, which means that the actions of governments and their agents must be based on the authority of law and that all persons, the governed and those who govern, are subject to the same laws.

Secularization A trend observable throughout the developed world whereby people place greater value on materialism and less value on the spiritual or eternal dimension of life.

Separation of powers A constitutional principle, supported by s. 24 of the Charter, that guarantees the special role of the judiciary, without interference from the legislature or the executive, to interpret what the law and the Constitution mean when disputes arise.

Sexism Term coined during the 1960s as a label for behaviour that treats males and females unequally for no other reason than the fact of being male or female.

Shared-cost programs Provincially administered programs, such as those in the field of health care, to which Ottawa contributes money earmarked for a particular purpose. During the 1960s and 1970s it was common for Ottawa's contribution to be determined by how much a province spent on such a program. Since the late 1970s successive federal governments have abandoned this model in favour of *block funding*.

Single-member constituency A voting system under which each member of the legislature is elected to represent a particular constituency or riding, receiving this right when he or she receives more votes than any other single candidate in the election held in that constituency. It is not necessary to receive a majority of the votes cast in a constituency, and under Canada's multi-party system most successful candidates do not.

Social capital A concept that refers to norms of interpersonal trust, a sense of civic duty, and a belief that one's political participation matters. Contemporary theorists like Robert Putnam argue that the successful functioning of democracies depends on a high level of social capital among the general population. Social capital reflects the power within society that the individual derives from attachment to social networks, such as work, church groups, community associations, clubs, and the like.

Socialism An ideology based on the principle of equality of condition. Historically, socialists led the fight for a greater state role in managing the economy, better working conditions and rights for workers, and the egalitarian and redistributive policies associated with the welfare state. Modern socialists, or social democrats, often temper their advocacy of an egalitarian society with an acceptance of capitalism and the inequalities that inevitably are generated by a market economy.

Socio-economic mobility The ability of individuals, families, and groups to move from one social or economic position to another. Where socio-economic mobility is high, movement up and down the social ladder is relatively common and the barriers to entry into high-paying occupations, prestigious status groups, or powerful elites are relatively low.

Soft power Term coined by American scholar Joseph Nye to describe forms of international influence based on culture, values, and the perceived legitimacy of a nation's international aims, rather than on armaments, sanctions, and coercion. Soft power is associated with *multilateralism* and support for international structures of governance and problem resolution such as the UN and the International Criminal Court.

Sovereignty-association A term generally understood to mean that a politically sovereign (independent) Quebec would continue to be linked to Canada through some sort of commercial union, free trade agreement, and shared currency. Sovereignty-association was the option proposed to Quebecers in the 1980 referendum.

Split-run publications American magazines, such as *Time* and *Sports Illustrated*, that published a Canadian edition at low cost by importing the American version via satellite, adding some pages of Canadian content, and thereby qualifying for the same advertising rates that apply to Canadian-based magazines.

State The structures through which public authority is exercised, including the legislature, bureaucracy, courts, police, armed forces, and other publicly owned or controlled institutions, such as schools and hospitals. See also Box 1.2.

State capacity A term used in a 2002 UN report on globalization to refer to a state's ability to maintain social safety nets and pursue non-market goals such as protection of the environment and promotion of equality. This report suggested that a "deficit" in state capacity, resulting from low levels of training and professionalism, inadequate technology, and corruption, impedes the ability of many developing countries to take advantage of economic opportunities presented by globalization.

Substantive equality An approach to the interpretation of equality rights and s. 15 of the Charter premised on the idea that individuals may experience advantages or disadvantages as a result of belonging to a particular group and that their equality rights claims should be judged against the reality of these group-based inequalities in society. This approach rejects the concept of *formal equality* that treating all individuals identically under the law can guarantee equality.

Suffragists Advocates of the right to vote for women. Many of the early suffragists supported female enfranchisement on the grounds that women voters would inject a morally uplifting element into politics. Nellie McClung was Canada's best-known suffragist.

Survivance, la French for "survival." *La survivance* captures the conservative character of traditional French-Canadian nationalism, focused as it was on preserving the religious and linguistic heritage of French Canada in the face of assimilationist pressures.

Systemic discrimination Discrimination without conscious individual intent. Systemic discrimination inheres in traditions, customary practices, rules, laws, and institutions that have the effect of placing the members of one or more ascriptive groups at a disadvantage compared to other groups.

Totalitarianism A system of government that suppresses all dissent in the name of some supreme goal.

Two-nations theory Canada, viewed from this perspective, is fundamentally a partnership between two ethnolinguistic communities or nations, one French-speaking and the other English-speaking. This premise underlies such constitutional proposals as a Quebec right of veto over constitutional reform and recognition of Quebec as a distinct society. Although the two-nations theory continues to enjoy popularity among French-Canadian nationalists and some English-Canadian intellectuals, it appears to have much less public support in English-speaking Canada.

Tyranny of the majority Term used by Alexis de Tocqueville in *Democracy in America* (1835) to refer to the danger that majoritarian democracy might oppress the rights of minorities.

Ultra vires From the Latin, meaning "beyond its strength." A judicial ruling of ultra vires means that a legislative act is beyond or outside the constitutional power or authority of that legislature; in contrast, an "intra vires" judicial ruling means that a legislature has acted within its constitutional competence.

"Unholy alliance" The term that critics sometimes applied to the three pillars of the conservative Quebec establishment during the 1940s and 1950s: the Catholic Church, anglophone capital, and the Union Nationale under the leadership of *le chef*, Maurice Duplessis.

Universal Declaration of Human Rights A declaration passed by the United Nations in 1948 that provides the basis for various international covenants to which Canada is a signatory, such as the International Covenant on Civil and Political Rights and the International Covenant on Economic, Social and Cultural Rights.

Vertical mosaic The title of a 1965 book by Canadian sociologist John Porter in which he argued that Canadian society was characterized by a vertical mosaic of patterned inequality between different ethnic and religious groups. See also *corporate elite*.

Visible minority A term that refers to people who belong to a minority that is non-white in colour or race, but that does not include Aboriginal Canadians. This is the definition used in the federal Employment Equity Act and by Statistics Canada and the Census of Canada. The term entered the Canadian political lexicon in the 1980s. It is not commonly used in the United States or France to refer to non-white minorities.

Welfare gap The difference between total welfare income (social assistance benefits, child tax benefits, and federal and provincial sales tax credits) and the low-income cut-offs established by Statistics Canada. See Figure 3.6.

Western alienation A belief held by many in western Canada, but particularly in Alberta and British Columbia, that Ottawa and the mainstream political parties are by and large insensitive to the interests and preferences of western Canadians. The roots of this sentiment go back to the high tariff policies and freight rates of the federal government from the late nineteenth century. Regional parties of protest such as the Progressives after World War I and, more recently, the *Reform Party* have emerged from this sense of regional grievance. This sentiment has subsided in recent years.

Whistleblowing When a public servant brings attention to government actions or policies that he or she believes endanger public health or safety. Such actions are protected by law, but in deciding to go public with information acquired in the course of his or her job, a public servant must be mindful of his or her duty of loyalty to the government and take care to get the facts right.

White Paper An ambitious set of reforms to Aboriginal policy proposed in 1969 by the Liberal government. The White Paper, titled *Statement of the Government of Canada on Indian Policy*, would have ended the system of Indian reserves and abolished different status for Indians under law. It was strongly opposed by most Native spokespersons and was soon abandoned.

Women's liberation A term that came into widespread use during the 1960s to refer to the struggle for equal rights for women. Feminist intellectuals such as Betty Friedan, Germaine Greer, and Gloria Steinem were among the leaders of the women's liberation movement. The character and demands of the movement were to some degree influenced by the black civil rights movement in the United States, feminist leaders drawing parallels between the systematic oppression and subordination of blacks and what they argued was the rather similar treatment of women.

Notes

Part I Introduction

1 An Introduction to Political Life

1. *Reader's Digest Canada*, May 2013, at: <www.readersdigest .ca/magazine/2013-trust-poll/job-fair-most-trusted-and -most-distrusted-professions>.
2. World Values Survey, 2000.
3. Wislawa Szymborska, "Children of Our Era," *Miracle Fair: Selected Poems of Wislawa Szymborska* (New York: Norton & Company, 2002), 44.
4. Charles Merriam, *Public and Private Government* (New Haven, CT: Yale University Press, 1944).
5. Jill Vickers, *Reinventing Political Science* (Halifax: Fernwood, 1997), 113–14.
6. See the full exchange online at <archives.cbc.ca/IDC-1-71 -101-610/conflict_war/october_crisis/clip6>.
7. The two most prominent cases include the so-called "Toronto 18" who were arrested in 2006 for planning bombings and hostage takings and the 2013 plot to derail a VIA Rail train. In both cases there were links to Al Qaeda.
8. Leo Panitch, "State," in *The Canadian Encyclopedia*, 2nd edn (Edmonton: Hurtig, 1988), vol. 4, 2071.
9. Quoted in Vickers, *Reinventing Political Science*, 42.
10. CBC, "20 Arrested at Climate Protest on Parliament Hill," 7 Dec. 2009, at: <www.cbc.ca/news/canada/ottawa/story/ 2009/12/07/greenpeace-parliament-protest.html>.
11. NPR, Democracy Now, "48 Arrested at Keystone Pipeline Protest as Sierra Club Lifts 120-Year Ban on Civil Disobedience," 14 Feb. 2013, at: <www.democracynow .org/2013/2/14/8_arrested_at_keystone_pipeline_ protest>.
12. Allison Jones, "Idle No More: Judge Slams Ontario Police for Not Ending First Nations Protest near Kingston," 7 Jan. 2013, at: <www.ctvnews.ca/canada/judge-slams -ontario-police-for-not-ending-first-nations-rail -blockade-1.1103669>.
13. Howard Zinn, *Declarations of Independence: Cross-Examining American Ideology* (New York: Harper Perennial, 1991).
14. Noam Chomsky and Edward S. Herman, *Manufacturing Consent: The Political Economy of the Mass Media* (New York: Pantheon Books, 1988).
15. Victor Davis Hanson, talk at Woodrow Wilson Center, 2 June 2005, Washington, DC.
16. C.B. Macpherson, *The Real World of Democracy* (Toronto: CBC Enterprises, 1965).
17. Vali Nasr, "The Rise of 'Muslim Democracy'," *Journal of Democracy* 16, 2 (2005): 15.
18. Gabriel A. Almond and Sidney Verba, *The Civic Culture* (Princeton, NJ: Princeton University Press, 1963).
19. The Legatum Institute, *The 2012 Legatum Prosperity Index*, at: <webapi.prosperity.com/download/pdf/PI2012 _MethodologyV4.pdf>, 26–7.
20. Amy Crawford, "For the People, by the People," *Slate*, 22 May 2013, at: <www.slate.com/articles/news_and_politics/ politics/2013/05/new_england_town_halls_these _experiments_in_direct_democracy_do_a_far_better .html>.
21. Quoted in Henry Steele Commager, *Living Ideas in America* (New York: Harper, 1951), 556.
22. Neil Postman, *Amusing Ourselves to Death* (New York: Viking, 1985), 107.
23. *The Economist*, "Ballot Measures: A Liberal Drift," 10 Nov. 2012, at: <www.economist.com/news/united -states/21565972-local-votes-suggest-more-tolerant -countrybut-not-more-left-wing-one-liberal-drift>.
24. Eugene Forsey, *How Canadians Govern Themselves*, 8th edn (Ottawa: Library of Parliament, Public Information Office, 2012), 30.
25. Robert B. Reich, *Supercapitalism: The Transformation of Business, Democracy and Everyday Life* (New York: Knopf, 2007), 18.
26. See <www.worldvaluessurvey.org>.
27. Centre for Social Justice, at: <www.socialjustice.org/ index.php?page=economic-inequality>.

Part II The Societal Context of Politics

2 Political Culture

1. "In Search of the Canadian Dream," *The Atlantic* (Dec. 2004).
2. Russell Kirk, *The Conservative Mind* (London: Faber & Faber, 1953).
3. Daniel Bell, *The End of Ideology* (New York: Free Press, 1962), 402–3.
4. David Bell and Lorne Tepperman, *The Roots of Disunity* (Toronto: McClelland & Stewart, 1979), 23.
5. Fernand Ouellet, *Histoire économique et sociale du Québec, 1760–1850* (Paris: Fides, 1966).
6. Bell and Tepperman note that the estimated number of anglophones in what are now the Maritimes, Quebec, and Ontario at the time of the American Revolution was about 15,000. Between 30,000 and 60,000 Loyalists immigrated to these British colonies in the years immediately after 1776, and a steady stream of "late Loyalists," perhaps attracted by British offers of free

land, immigrated north to Upper Canada over the next few decades. See *The Roots of Disunity*, 45, 80–1.

7. William Christian and Colin Campbell, *Political Parties and Ideologies in Canada*, 2nd edn (Toronto: McGraw-Hill Ryerson, 1982), 23–5; Gad Horowitz, "Conservatism, Liberalism, and Socialism in Canada: An Interpretation," *Canadian Journal of Economics and Political Science* 32 (1966): 143–71.

8. Kenneth McRae, "The Structure of Canadian History," in Louis Hartz, ed., *The Founding of New Societies* (New York: Harcourt, Brace & World, 1964), 235.

9. Bell and Tepperman, *The Roots of Disunity*, 76–7.

10. Horowitz, "Conservatism, Liberalism, and Socialism."

11. Seymour Martin Lipset, *Continental Divide* (Montreal: C.D. Howe Institute, 1989), 1.

12. Bell and Tepperman, *The Roots of Disunity*, 61–2.

13. James Mahoney, "Path Dependence in Historical Sociology," *Theory and Society* 29 (2000): 507–8.

14. Reg Whitaker, "Images of the State in Canada," in Leo Panitch, ed., *The Canadian State* (Toronto: University of Toronto Press, 1977), 30.

15. Patricia Marchak, *Ideological Perspectives on Canada* (Toronto: McGraw-Hill Ryerson, 1975), 115.

16. Pierre Trudeau, "Some Obstacles to Democracy in Quebec," in Trudeau, *Federalism and the French Canadians* (Toronto: Macmillan, 1968).

17. In 1951, 80 per cent of Quebec's workforce was in secondary industries (manufacturing and construction) and the service sector, a percentage that was higher than for Canada as a whole (78 per cent).

18. See Kenneth McRoberts, *Quebec: Social Change and Political Crisis*, 3rd edn (Toronto: McClelland & Stewart, 1988), 90–100.

19. Margaret Atwood, *Survival* (Toronto: House of Anansi Press, 1972), 33.

20. Will Kymlicka, "Being Canadian," *Government & Opposition* 38, 3 (2003): 385.

21. W.L. Morton, "The Dualism of Culture and the Federalism of Power," in Richard Abbott, ed., *A New Concept of Confederation*, Proceedings of the Seventh Seminar of the Canadian Union of Students (Ottawa, 1965), 121.

22. Donald Smiley, *The Canadian Political Nationality* (Toronto: Methuen, 1967).

23. Political Terror Scale, at: <www.politicalterrorscale.org>.

24. Judith Torrance, *Public Violence in Canada 1867–1982* (Toronto: University of Toronto Press, 1986), 57–66.

25. See the analysis of Oka in Robert Campbell and Leslie Pal, "Feather and Gun," *The Real Worlds of Canadian Politics*, 2nd edn (Peterborough, Ont.: Broadview Press, 1991), 267–345.

26. A good summary of these cases is provided in Edward J. Hedican, "Policing Aboriginal Protests and Confrontations: Some Policy Recommendations," *International Indigenous Policy Journal* 3, 2 (2012), at: <ir .lib.uwo.ca/iipj/vol3/iss2/1>.

27. McRoberts, *Quebec*, 239.

28. En collaboration, *Québec: Un pays incertain: Réflexions sur le Québec post-référendaire* (Montréal: Québec/Amérique, 1980), 170–2.

29. Status Indians are those registered under the Indian Act.

30. *Globe and Mail*, 26 Sept. 1990.

31. This is the title of a 1957 book by John Farthing, a Canadian conservative, who argued that in a world divided between American-style democracy and the Marxist models represented by the Soviet Union and Communist China, Canada and the other Commonwealth democracies represented a preferable political model.

32. Lipset, *Continental Divide*, 136.

33. Pierre Berton, *Why We Act Like Canadians* (Toronto: McClelland & Stewart, 1982), 16.

34. Paul M. Sniderman et al., *Liberty, Authority, and Community: Civil Liberties and the Canadian Political Culture* (Berkeley: Survey Research Center, University of California, 1988), Figures 9A–9D.

35. Environics Institute, *AmericasBarometer: Canada 2012*, pp. 38–9, 47, at: <www.vanderbilt.edu/lapop/canada/ Canada-2012-Report.pdf>.

36. Miles Corak, "Chasing the Same Dream, Climbing Different Ladders: Economic Mobility in the United States and Canada," Economic Mobility Project of the Pew Charitable Trusts, Jan. 2010, at: <www.economicmobility.org>.

37. Frank Graves, "The Shifting Public Outlook on Risk and Security," in Karlyn Bowman and Frank Graves, *Threat Perceptions in the United States and Canada: Assessing the Public's Attitudes toward Risk and Security*, One Issue, Two Voices Series, Issue Four (Washington: Canada Institute, Woodrow Wilson Center, Oct. 2005), 10–15.

38. S.D. Clark, *The Canadian Community* (Toronto: University of Toronto Press, 1962); Seymour Martin Lipset, "The Value Patterns of Democracy: A Case Study in Comparative Analysis," *American Sociological Review* 28, 4 (1963): 515–31.

39. Robert Kudrle and Theodore Marmor, "The Development of Welfare States in North America," in Peter Flora and Arnold J. Heidersheimer, eds, *The Development of Welfare States in Europe and America* (New Brunswick, NJ: Transaction Books, 1981), 110.

40. Gerard Boychuk, "National Health Insurance in Canada and the United States: Race, Territorial Integration and the Roots of Difference," paper presented at the annual meeting of the Canadian Political Science Association, Vancouver, June 2008.

41. Lipset, *Continental Divide*, 156.

42. The CEO pay differential data comes from Lawrence Mishel, Jared Bernstein, and Sylvia Allegretto, *The State of Working America 2004/2005* (Ithaca, NY: Cornell University Press, 2005); the data on attitudes is found in Lars Osberg and Timothy Smeeding, "Fair Inequality? An International Comparison of Attitudes toward Pay Differentials," working paper, Russell Sage Foundation, 2005, 31, at: <www.russellsage.org/programs/main/ inequality/workingpapers/051025.267178/>.

43. Pew Research Center, *Economies of Emerging Markets Better Rated during Difficult Times*, 23 May 2013, at: <www.pewglobal.org/files/2013/05/Pew-Global-Attitudes-Economic-Report-FINAL-May-23-20131.pdf>.

44. Corak, "Chasing the Same Dream," 3.

45. Ibid., 14.

46. Constitution Act, 1982, s. 27.

47. Constitution Act, 1982, s. 15(2).

48. Neil Bissoondath, *Selling Illusions: The Cult of Multiculturalism in Canada* (Toronto: Penguin Books, 1994).

49. Reginald Bibby, *Mosaic Madness: The Poverty and Potential of Life in Canada* (Toronto: Stoddart, 1990).

50. Salim Mansur, *Delectable Lie: A Liberal Repudiation of Multiculturalism* (Brantford, Ont.: Mantua Books, 2011).

51. Raymond Breton and Jeffrey Reitz, *The Illusion of Difference* (Toronto: C.D. Howe Institute, 1994), 133.

52. Martin Turcotte, "Passing on the Ancestral Language," *Canadian Social Trends* no. 80 (Spring 2006): 20–7.

53. The Economist Intelligence Unit, *Women's Economic Opportunity*, June 2010, at: <graphics.eiu.com/upload/WEO_report_June_2010.pdf>.

54. Catalyst, "Women on Boards," 31 May 2013, at: <www.catalyst.org/knowledge/women-boards>.

55. OECD, at: <stats.oecd.org/Index.aspx?QueryId=4549>.

56. OECD, at: <www.oecd.org/ctp/tax-policy/revenuestatisticstaxratioschangesbetween2007and2011.htm>.

57. Berton, *Why We Act Like Canadians*, 16–17.

58. Charles Taylor, "Deep Diversity and the Future of Canada," at: <www.uni.ca/taylor.html>.

59. Neil Nevitte, *The Decline of Deference: Canadian Value Change in Cross-National Perspective* (Peterborough, Ont.: Broadview Press, 1996).

60. Environics Institute, AmericasBarometer, *Canada 2012*, 24, at: <www.vanderbilt.edu/lapop/canada/Canada-2012-Report.pdf>.

61. Ibid., 12.

62. Ibid., 63.

63. Michael Adams, *Fire and Ice: The United States, Canada and the Myth of Converging Values* (Toronto: Penguin, 2003). Adams's argument is softened somewhat in his chapter, "Canadian and American Values Divergences: The Narcissism of Small Differences?" in David Thomas and Barbara Boyle Torrey, eds, *Canada and the United States: Differences that Count*, 3rd edition (Toronto: University of Toronto Press, 2008), 45–60.

64. Philip Resnick, *The European Roots of Canadian Identity* (Peterborough, Ont.: Broadview Press, 2005).

65. Christian Boucher, "Canada–U.S. Values: Distinct, Inevitably Carbon Copy, or Narcissism of Small Differences?" *Horizons* 7, 1 (2004): 46.

3   The Social and Economic Setting

1. Environics Institute, *Focus Canada 2012*, p. 10, at: <www.environicsinstitute.org/uploads/institute-projects/environics%20institute%20-%20focus%20canada%202012%20final%20report.pdf>.

2. OECD, at: <www.oecd-ilibrary.org/sites/factbook-2013-en/07/02/02/ltunemp_g1.html?contentType=&itemId=/content/chapter/factbook-2013-58-en&containerItemId=/content/serial/18147364&accessItemIds=&mimeType=text/html>.

3. United States Department of Labor, Bureau of Labor Statistics, "Sectoral Employment Shifts around the World," 6 July6 2012, at: <www.bls.gov/opub/ted/2012/ted_20120706.htm>.

4. This debate is taken up in Michael Spence, "Globalization and Unemployment," *Foreign Affairs* (July–Aug. 2011), at: <www.foreignaffairs.com/articles/67874/michael-spence/globalization-and-unemployment>, and Richard Katz and Robert Lawrence, "Manufacturing Globalization," *Foreign Affairs* (Nov.–Dec. 2011), at: <www.foreignaffairs.com/articles/136594/richard-katz-robert-z-lawrence-michael-spence/manufacturing-globalization#>.

5. Statistics Canada, *Labour Force Survey*.

6. Statistics Canada, "What Has Changed for Young People in Canada?" July 2013, p. 8, Table 2, at: <www.statcan.gc.ca/pub/75-006-x/2013001/article/11847-eng.pdf>.

7. Joseph Berger and Andrew Parkin, *The Value of a Degree: Education, Employment and Earnings in Canada*, p. 7, at: <contactpoint.ca/wp-content/uploads/2013/01/pokvol4_ch1_e.pdf>.

8. Environics Institute, *Focus Canada 2012*, 14.

9. Ibid., 53, 55, 56.

10. All of the figures in this paragraph are based on the most recent data from Statistics Canada.

11. Nicole M. Fortin et al., "Canadian Inequality: Recent Developments and Policy Options," *Canadian Public Policy* 38, 2 (2012): 121–45.

12. Conference Board of Canada, *How Canada Performs: A Report Card on Canada*, at: <www.conferenceboard.ca/hcp/details/society/income-inequality.aspx>.

13. Pew Research Center, *Economies of Emerging Markets Better Rated during Difficult Times*, 23 May 2013, at: <www.pewglobal.org/files/2013/05/Pew-Global-Attitudes-Economic-Report-FINAL-May-23-2013.pdf>.

14. M.C. Wolfson, J.M. Evans, and OECD, "Statistics Canada's Low Income Cutoffs: Methodological Concerns and Possibilities," Statistics Canada discussion paper, 1989.

15. National Council of Welfare, *A New Poverty Line: Yes, No or Maybe?* (Ottawa: Minister of Public Works and Government Services Canada, 1999), 1.

16. National Aboriginal Economic Development Board, *The Aboriginal Economic Benchmarking Report*, June 2012, at: <www.naedb-cndea.com/wp-content/uploads/TheAboriginalEconomicBenchmarkingReport2.pdf>.

17. Finance Canada, at: <www.fin.gc.ca/fedprov/mtp-eng.asp>.

18. Corak explains that the data and literature available on the relationship between daughters' income rankings and their parents' earnings are still too meagre and incomplete to allow for the same sort of analysis. See Miles Corak, "Chasing the Same Dream, Climbing

Different Ladders: Economic Mobility in the United States and Canada," Economic Mobility Project of the Pew Charitable Trusts, Jan. 2010, at: <www.economicmobility .org>.

19. Ibid., Figures 2 and 3.

20. Jason Clemens, *Income Inequality: Oversimplifying a Complicated Issue*, Macdonald-Laurier Institute, April 2012, 33.

21. Jo Blanden, Paul Gregg, and Stephen Machin, *Intergenerational Mobility in Europe and North America* (London: Sutton Trust, Apr. 2005).

22. Miles Corak, *Intergenerational Earnings Mobility among the Children of Canadian Immigrants* (Bonn: Institute for the Study of Labor, 2006).

23. Abdurrahman Aydemir, Wen-Hao Chen, and Miles Corak, *Intergenerational Earnings Mobility among the Children of Canadian Immigrants*, Statistics Canada Catalogue no. 11F0019MIE, no. 267 (Ottawa: Minister of Industry, 2005). See also Statistics Canada, *Educational and Economic Outcomes for Second-Generation Canadians: The Children of Immigrants*, at: <www.statcan.gc.ca/pub/ 11f0019m/2008319/s9-eng.htm>.

24. John Porter, *The Vertical Mosaic* (Toronto: University of Toronto Press, 1965); Wallace Clement, *The Canadian Corporate Elite* (Toronto: McClelland & Stewart, 1975).

25. Milan Korac, "Corporate Concentration and the Canadian Corporate Elite: Change and Continuity," MA thesis (University of Windsor, 1992).

26. Canadian Board Diversity Council, *Annual Report Card 2012*, at: <www.boarddiversity.ca/sites/default/files/CBDC -Annual-Report-Card-2012-ENG.pdf>.

27. Public Policy Forum, *Edging toward Diversity: A Statistical Breakdown of Canada's 41st Parliament, with Comparisons to the 40th Parliament*, June 2011, at: <www.ppforum.ca/ sites/default/files/edging_towards_diversity_final.pdf>.

28. *WIN-Gallup International Global Index of Happiness*, table B1, at: <www.wingia.com/web/files/news/38/file/38.pdf>.

29. Conference Board of Canada, *How Canada Performs 2012*.

30. Jan van Dijk et al., *Criminal Victimisation in International Perspective* (Tilburg, Netherlands: Tilburg University and United Nations Office on Drugs and Crime, 2007), 132, Figure 28.

31. Conference Board of Canada, *How Canada Performs 2012*.

32. Environics Institute, AmericasBarometer, *Canada Report 2012*, 48, 50.

33. Statistics Canada, at: <www.statcan.gc.ca/daily-quotidien/ 111101/t111101b1-eng.htm>, and Canadian Association for Suicide Prevention, at: <www.suicideprevention.ca/ about-suicide/>.

34. Health Canada, *Canadian Addiction Survey 2004*, Mar. 2005, pp. 43, 45, at: <www.ccsa.ca/2005%20CCSA% 20Documents/ccsa-004028-2005.pdf>.

35. Canadian Alliance to End Homelessness, *The State of Homelessness in Canada 2013*, at: <www.homelesshub .ca/ResourceFiles/SOHC2103.pdf>.

36. Food Banks Canada, *Hunger Count 2012*, at: <www .foodbankscanada.ca/getmedia/3b946e67-fbe2-490e -90dc-4a313dfb97e5/HungerCount2012.pdf.aspx?ext= .pdf>.

37. Charles Lammam, Amela Karabegović, and Niels Veld-huis, *Measuring Income Mobility in Canada* (Vancouver: Fraser Institute, 2012), at: <www.fraserinstitute.org/ uploadedFiles/fraser-ca/Content/research-news/research/ publications/measuring-income-mobility-in-canada.pdf>.

38. Most of the health statistics in this list may be found in Health Canada, *First Nations & Inuit Health*, at: <www .hc-sc.gc.ca/fniah-spnia/pubs/aborig-autoch/stats-profil -atlant/index-eng.php#taba11>.

39. Statistics Canada and Department of Foreign Affairs and International Trade, State of Trade 2012, at: <www. international.gc.ca/economist-economiste/assets/pdfs/ performance/SoT_2012/SoT_CIdC_2012_Intro-ENG .pdf>.

40. The Canadian Journalism Project, 3 Apr. 2013, at: <j-source .ca/article/8-10-canadians-read-newspapers-weekly -nadbank-report>.

4   Diversity and Multiculturalism

1. John Porter, *The Vertical Mosaic* (Toronto: University of Toronto Press, 1965).

2. Statistics Canada, 2011 National Household Survey, data tables.

3. Statistics Canada, "Study: Projections of the Diversity of the Canadian Population," *The Daily*, 9 Mar. 2010, at: <www.statcan.gc.ca/daily-quotidien/100309/dq100309a -eng.htm>.

4. Environics Poll conducted for the Department of Canadian Heritage, 29 Mar.–18 Apr. 2004.

5. Association for Canadian Studies, *Groups and Intergroup Relations: Canadian Perceptions*, Oct. 2011, slide 5.

6. *Multani v. Commission scolaire Marguerite-Bourgeoys*, [2006] 1 S.C.R. 256.

7. CBC News, "Sikhs with Kirpan Not Allowed in Que. Legisla-ture," 18 Jan. 2011, at: <www.cbc.ca/canada/montreal/story/ 2011/01/18/sikhs-denied-entry-nat-ass-quebec.html>.

8. Association for Canadian Studies, *A Four-Country Survey of Opinion on Racism and Prejudice*, 21 Jan. 2011, p. 21, at: <www.acs-aec.ca/pdf/polls/racismandprejudice-2010 .pdf>.

9. Statistics Canada, *Fifty Years of Families in Canada: 1961 to 2011*, at: <www12.statcan.gc.ca/census-recensement/ 2011/as-sa/98-312-x/98-312-x2011003_1-eng.cfm>.

10. Jenkins Research Blog, "An Historic Evolution of Public Opinion: A Look Back at Same-Sex Marriage in Canada," at: <jenkinsresearch.wordpress.com/>.

11. Leslie A. Pal, *Interests of State: The Politics of Language, Multiculturalism, and Feminism in Canada* (Montreal and Kingston: McGill-Queen's University Press, 1993).

12. Ibid., 281.

13. R. Brian Howe and David Johnson, *Restraining Equality: Human Rights Commissions in Canada* (Toronto: University of Toronto Press, 2000), 35.

14. Department of Canadian Heritage, "Disclosure of Grants and Contributions over $25,000," at: <www.pch.gc.ca/pc-ch/dp-pd/sc-gc/lst-eng.cfm?sDate=2013-01-01&eDate=2013-03-31>.

15. Myer Siemiatycki, *The Diversity Gap: The Electoral Under-representation of Visible Minorities*, Nov. 2011, at: <diversecitytoronto.ca/wp-content/uploads/Final-Report.pdf>.

16. See, for example, Aliaa Dakroury, "Toward Media Reconstruction of the Muslim Imaginary in Canada: The Case of the CBC's Sitcom *Little Mosque on the Prairie*," in Jasmine Zine, ed., *Islam in the Hinterlands: Exploring Muslim Cultural Politics in Canada* (Vancouver: University of British Columbia Press, 2012), 161–82.

17. <www.washingtonpost.com/blogs/worldviews/wp/2013/05/16/a-revealing-map-of-the-worlds-most-and-least-ethnically-diverse-countries/>.

18. <www.pewresearch.org/fact-tank/2013/07/18/the-most-and-least-culturally-diverse-countries-in-the-world/>.

19. Paul Sniderman and Louk Hagendoorn, *When Ways of Life Collide: Multiculturalism and Its Discontents* (Princeton, NJ: Princeton University Press, 2007), 15.

20. Willem Huijnk and Jaco Dagevos, *Closer Together? The Socio-cultural position of Non-Western Migrants in the Netherlands*, 20 Dec. 2012, at: <www.scp.nl/english/Publications/Summaries_by_year/Summaries_2012/Closer_together>.

21. Peter Skerry, "Beyond Sushiology: Does Diversity Work?" *Brookings Review* 20 (Winter 2002): 20–3.

22. James Banks, Professor of Diversity Studies at the University of Washington, for the National Council for Social Studies, at: <www.socialstudies.org/positions/multicultural>.

23. German Marshall Fund, *Transatlantic Trends*, 2011, pp. 20, 30, at: <trends.gmfus.org/files/2011/12/TTI2011_Topline_final1.pdf>.

24. Association for Canadian Studies, "Is There a Common Canadian culture?" 2 June 2010, at: <www.acs-aec.ca/pdf/polls/12754873512518.doc>.

25. BBC, "The Islamic Veil across Europe," 1 July 2014, at: <www.bbc.com/news/world-europe-13038095>.

26. See <municipalite.herouxville.qc.ca/Standards.pdf>.

27. CBC News, "Minority Report 'Misses the Point' PQ Says," 23 May 2008, at: <www.cbc.ca>.

28. Alexander Panetta, "PQ: Multiculturalism Is Not a Quebec Value," 19 Jan. 2011, at: <ipolitics.ca/2011/01/19/pq-multiculturalism-not-a-quebec-value/>.

29. Derrick Thomas, "The Impact of Working in a Non-Official Language on the Occupations and Earnings of Immigrants in Canada," *Canadian Social Trends* (2009), Statistics Canada, at: <www.statcan.gc.ca/pub/11-008-x/2009001/article/10771-eng.htm>.

30. Immigration Policy Center, "Defining 'Desirable' Immigrants: What Lies Beneath the Proposed Merit-Based Point System?" at: <www.immigrationpolicy.org/just-facts/defining-desirable-immigrants-what-lies-beneath-proposed-merit-based-point-system>.

31. Statistics Canada, *Longitudinal Survey of Immigrants to Canada: Progress and Challenges of New Immigrants in the Workforce* (Ottawa, 2003), at: <www.statcan.gc.ca/pub/89-615-x/2005001/4079178-eng.htm>. For detailed comparative analyses of contemporary immigration to Canada and the United States, see Carlos Teixeira, Wei Li, and Audrey Kobayashi, eds, *Immigrant Geographies of North American Cities* (Don Mills, Ont.: Oxford University Press, 2011).

32. TD Economics, *Knocking Down Barriers Faced by New Immigrants to Canada: Fitting the Pieces Together*, 7 Feb. 2012, p. 13, at: <www.td.com/document/PDF/economics/special/ff0212_immigration.pdf>.

33. Ibid.

34. See Canadian Information Centre for International Credentials, at: <www.cicic.ca/en/index.aspx>.

35. Jeffrey Reitz, "Economic Opportunity, Multiculturalism, and the Roots of Popular Support for High Immigration in Canada," 2013, at: <munkschool.utoronto.ca/ethnicstudies/files/2013/02/Reitz-Economic-Opportunity-Multiculturalism-and-the-Roots-of-Popular-Support-CISAN-UNAM-Mexico-City-2012.pdf>.

5   Regionalism and Canadian Politics

1. A good survey of this organizational evolution is provided by Jean Dupuis in *Federal Regional Economic Development Organizations*, 17 Mar. 2011, at: <www.parl.gc.ca/content/lop/researchpublications/2011-05-e.htm>.

2. Cited in *The Economist, special survey of Canada*, 15 Feb. 1986, 16.

3. Pierre Fortin, "Tout à l'Alberta, rien pour les autres?" *L'Actualité*, 5 oct. 2005, 50–2.

4. Ken Coates, "First Nations Hold the Key to Northern Gateway Pipeline," *Globe and Mail*, 17 June 2014.

5. Richard Simeon and David Elkins, "Regional Political Cultures in Canada," *Canadian Journal of Political Science* 7, 3 (1974): 397–437.

6. Centre for Research and Information on Canada, *The Charter: Dividing or Uniting Canadians?* (Apr. 2002), 30. At: <www.cric.ca>.

7. Ibid., 31.

8. Frank Graves, "The Trust Deficit: What Does It Mean?" *Ekos Politics*, 14 May 2013, at: <www.ekospolitics.ca>.

9. "In God We Canadians Trust?" survey conducted by Léger Marketing for the Association for Canadian Studies, Apr. 2012, at: <www.acs-aec.ca/pdf/polls/In%20God%20Canadians%20Trust%20II.pdf>.

10. Association of Canadian Studies, "Multiculturalists with Concerns," 8 Oct. 2011, at: <www.acs-aec.ca>.

11. Association of Canadian Studies, "Getting Ahead in Canada: Rightly or Wrongly, Canadians Believe Their Society Is Egalitarian," June 2010, at: <www.acs-aec.ca>.

12. Ekos Politics, *Looking Backward, Looking Forward: Five Big Forces Shaping Our Society*, 9 Jan. 2013, p. 31, at: <www.ekos.com/admin/articles/FG-2013-01-09.pdf>.

13. Manning Centre for Building Democracy, *2013 Manning Barometer*, at: <manningcentre.ca/2013poll>.

14. Michael Ornstein and Michael Stevenson, *Politics and Ideology in Canada* (Montreal and Kingston: McGill-Queen's University Press, 1999), ch. 5.

15. Ibid., 206.

16. Environics Institute, *Focus Canada 2012*, at: <www.environicsinstitute.org/uploads/institute-projects/environics%20institute%20-%20focus%20canada%202012%20final%20report.pdf>.

17. David McGrane and Loleen Berdahl, "'Small Worlds' No More: Reconsidering Provincial Political Cultures in Canada," *Regional and Federal Studies* (2013): 9, at: <dx.doi.org/10.1080/13597566.2013.794415>.

18. Debora VanNijnatten, "Canada–US Relations and the Emergence of Cross-Border Regions," 4, Briefing Notes, Government of Canada, Policy Research Initiatives, 2006, at: <www.policyresearch.gc.ca>.

19. [Stephen Brooks and Barry Rabe, eds,] *Environmental Governance on the 49th Parallel: New Century, New Approaches* (Washington: Woodrow Wilson Center, Feb. 2010), at: <www.wilsoncenter.org/sites/default/files/IJCFinal.pdf>.

20. Roger Gibbins and Sonia Arrison, *Western Visions: Perspectives on the West in Canada*, 2nd edn (Toronto: University of Toronto Press, 2003), 45.

21. W.L. Morton, "The Bias of Prairie Politics," *Transactions of the Royal Society of Canada* series 3, 49 (June 1955): 66.

22. Barry Cooper, "Western Political Consciousness," in Stephen Brooks, ed., *Political Thought in Canada: Contemporary Perspectives* (Toronto: Irwin, 1984), 230.

23. Barry Cooper, "Fresh News from Laurentian Canada," *Reviews from the Frontier* No. 2 (Apr. 2013), Frontier Centre for Public Policy, 7, at: <www.fcpp.org/files/1/RW02Laurentian_AP22F1.pdf>.

24. Patrick Boyer, *Direct Democracy in Canada: The History and Future of Referendums* (Toronto: Dundurn Press, 1992).

25. Loleen Berdahl, "Whither Western Alienation? Shifting Patterns of Western Canadian Discontent with the Federal Government" (Calgary: Canada West Foundation, Oct. 2010), 3-6.

26. Antoine Bilodeau, Stephen White, and Neil Nevitte, "The Development of Dual Loyalties: Immigrants' Integration to Canadian Regional Dynamics," *Canadian Journal of Political Science* 43, 3 (Sept. 2010): 515–44

27. CBC, "Trudeau Campaign Forced to Address 2010 Comments on Alberta," 22 Nov. 2012, at: <www.cbc.ca/news/canada/story/2012/11/22/pol-trudeau-tele-quebec-comments-alberta-quebec.html>.

28. "A Stadium and Western Alienation," *Prince Albert Daily Herald*, 2 Mar. 2011.

29. Darrell Bricker and John Ibbitson, *The Big Shift* (Toronto: HarperCollins, 2013).

30. Barry Cooper, "Fresh News from Laurentian Canada," 2.

Part III The Structures of Governance

6   The Constitution

1. Abacus Data Poll, "Public Opinion and Knowledge of Canada's Constitution," commissioned by the Canadian Constitutional Foundation, Mar. 2012, at: <constitutionday.ca/wp-content/uploads/2012/03/Detailed-National-Survey-Results.pdf>.

2. Constitution Act, 1982, s. 16(1).

3. Pierre Trudeau, *Federalism and the French Canadians* (Toronto: Macmillan, 1968), 187.

4. *Commissions des gouverneurs et intendants du Canada, 1612*, at: <eco.canadiana.ca/view/oocihm.40524/34?r=0&s=1>.

5. Constitution Act, 1867, preamble.

6. Ibid., s. 121.

7. Ibid., s. 145 (repealed in 1893).

8. Constitution Act, 1982, s. 36.

9. *Reference re Secession of Quebec*, Aug. 1998, at p. 18 of online decisions.

10. *OPSEU v. A.G. of Ontario*, [1987] 2 S.C.R. 2, S7.

11. *Reference re Secession of Quebec*, 19.

12. Ibid., 20.

13. Ibid., 21.

14. Ibid., 22.

15. *R. v. Oakes*, [1986] 1 S.C.R. 103, 136.

16. *Reference re Secession of Quebec*, 22.

17. Ibid., 23.

18. Ibid.

19. Ibid., 25.

20. Constitution Act, 1982, s. 6(3)(6).

21. Ibid., s. 6(4).

22. *Morgentaler, Smoling and Scott v. The Queen* (1988), 37 C.C.C. (3rd) 449.

23. Constitution Act, 1982, s. 15(1).

24. Ibid., s. 15(2).

25. *The Economist*, "Revolt of the Bobbleheads," 8 Apr. 2013, accessed online at: <www.economist.com>.

26. Eugene Forsey, *How Canadians Govern Themselves*, 8th edn, at: <www.parl.gc.ca/about/parliament/senatoreugeneforsey/book/assets/pdf/How_Canadians_Govern_Themselves8.pdf>.

27. See the discussion at <www.parliament.uk/about/how/sovereignty/>.

28. Constitution Act, 1867, ss. 96–100.

29. *The Queen v. Beauregard,* [1986] 2 S.C.R. 56. This was the basis of a 1986 court action brought against the Quebec government by several Provincial Court judges and the Chief Justice of the Quebec Superior Court.

30. See C.E.S. Franks, "Omnibus Bills Subvert Our Legislative Process," *Globe and Mail*, 14 July 2010.

31. Philip Resnick, *Parliament vs. People* (Vancouver: New Star Books, 1984), 19.

32. Ibid., 25.

33. Ibid., 38.
34. Section 91(1). Repealed by the Constitution Act, 1982.
35. Section 92(1). Repealed by the Constitution Act, 1982.
36. *Re Constitution of Canada* (1981), 125 D.L.R. (3rd) 1.
37. *Re Attorney General of Quebec and Attorney General of Canada* (1982), 140 D.L.R. (3rd) 385.
38. Cited in Paul Gérin-Lajoie, *Constitutional Amendment in Canada* (Toronto: University of Toronto Press, 1950), 241.
39. Cited ibid., 234.
40. *Reference re Secession of Quebec*, 26.
41. Ibid., 19.
42. Ibid., 27.
43. Ibid., 35.
44. Ibid., 4.

7   Rights and Freedoms

1. *Schenck v. United States*, 249 U.S. 47 (1919).
2. These are the words used in the "anti-hate" section of Canada's Criminal Code.
3. *Nova Scotia (Workers' Compensation Board) v. Martin; Nova Scotia (Workers' Compensation Board) v. Laseur*, [2003] 2 S.C.R. 504, 2003 SCC 54.
4. Justice Rosalie Abella, "Constitutions and Judges: Changing Roles, Rules and Expectations," lecture delivered at University College London, 7 July 2011, at: <www.ucl.ac.uk/constitution-unit/events/judicial-independence-events/Justice_Abella_Lecture_to_JIP_07-07-11.pdf>.
5. University of Calgary, *Charter Database*.
6. These statistics are reported in the constitutional cases overview published annually by Osgoode Hall Law School.
7. Harry Arthurs and Brent Arnold, "Does the Charter Matter?" *Review of Constitutional Studies* 1, 1 (2005): 38.
8. Alan Borovoy, *When Freedoms Collide: The Case for Our Civil Liberties* (Toronto: Lester & Orpen Dennys, 1988), 24.
9. Walter S. Tarnopolsky, "Human Rights," in *The Canadian Encyclopedia*, 2nd edn (Edmonton: Hurtig, 1988), vol. 2, 1024.
10. United States Constitution, 14th amendment, 1868.
11. Reginald Bibby, "Ethos versus Ethics: Canada, the U.S. and Homosexuality," paper presented at the annual meeting of the Pacific Sociological Association, San Francisco, Apr. 2004, 9.
12. Reginald Bibby, "Homosexuality in Canada: A National Reading," 13 May 2002, 2, at: <www.reginaldbibby.com/images/PCReleaseHomosexualityMay02.pdf>.
13. "The Dynamics of Gay Marriage Support," at: <jenkinsresearch.files.wordpress.com/2013/03/gay-marriage-trends.png>.
14. Michael Ignatieff, *Human Rights as Politics, Human Rights as Idolatry*, The Tanner Lectures on Human Values, Princeton University, 4–7 Apr. 2000.
15. Borovoy, *When Freedoms Collide*, ch. 10.
16. R. MacGregor Dawson, *Constitutional Issues in Canada, 1900–1931* (London: Oxford University Press, 1933).
17. R. MacGregor Dawson, *The Government of Canada* (Toronto: University of Toronto Press, 1947).
18. J.A. Corry and J.E. Hodgetts, *Democratic Government and Politics* (Toronto: University of Toronto Press, 1946).
19. Richard Gwyn, "Bill of Rights No Simple Issue," *Ottawa Citizen*, 9 Oct. 1980, 12.
20. *Reference re Alberta Statutes*, [1938] S.C.R. 100.
21. *Saumur v. Quebec and Attorney General of Quebec*, [1953] 2 S.C.R. 299.
22. *Switzman v. Elbing and Attorney General of Quebec*, [1957] S.C.R. 285.
23. *Attorney General of Canada and Dupond v. Montreal*, [1978] 2 S.C.R. 770.
24. Quoted in Peter H. Russell, *Leading Constitutional Decisions*, 4th edn (Ottawa: Carleton Library Series, 1987), 390.
25. Diefenbaker Canada Centre, "Voter Concern for Personal Liberties Declines in Decade but One in Five Still Feels Civil Rights are Endangered," at: <www.usask.ca/diefenbaker/galleries/virtual_exhibit/bill_of_rights/sanders_letter_to_dief.php>.
26. Norman Ward, *The Government of Canada* (Toronto: University of Toronto Press, 1987), 84.
27. Corry and Hodgetts, *Democratic Government and Politics*, 462.
28. *Robertson and Rosetanni v. The Queen* (1963), quoted in Russell, *Leading Constitutional Decisions*, 399.
29. Quoted in Walter S. Tarnopolsky, *The Canadian Bill of Rights*, 2nd edn (Toronto: McClelland & Stewart, 1975), 132.
30. *R. v. Drybones*, [1970] S.C.R. 282.
31. *Attorney General of Canada v. Lavell*, [1974] S.C.R. 1349.
32. *Hogan v. The Queen*, [1975] 2 S.C.R. 574.
33. *City of Winnipeg v. Barrett*, [1892] A.C. 445.
34. *Ottawa Roman Catholic Separate School Trustees v. Mackell*, [1917] A.C. 62; *Protestant School Board of Greater Montreal v. Minister of Education of Quebec* (1978), 83 D.L.R. (3d) 645.
35. *Attorney General of Quebec v. Blaikie*, [1979] 2 S.C.R. 1016.
36. *Attorney General of Manitoba v. Forest* (1979), 101 D.L.R. (3d) 385.
37. A summary of statistics on the Supreme Court and Charter rulings, as well as other constitutional rulings, is published annually by Osgoode Hall Law School's Research Paper Series. See <ssrn.com/abstract=2179010>.
38. Quoted in Sanjeev Anand, "The Truth about Canadian Judicial Activism," *Constitutional Forum constitutionnel* 15, 2 (2006): 87.
39. Beverley McLachlin, "Respecting Democratic Roles," *Constitutional Forum constitutionnel*, 14, 3 (2005): 19.
40. *R. v. Oakes* (1986), 26 D.L.R. (4th) 20.
41. *Ford v. Attorney General of Quebec*, [1988] 2 S.C.R. 712.
42. Quoted in F.L. Morton, Rainer Knopff, and Peter Russell, *Federalism and the Charter* (Ottawa: Carleton University Press, 1989), 578.
43. Ibid., 579.
44. Quoted in "Tobacco Ad Ban Struck Down," *Globe and Mail*, 22 Sept. 1995, A1, A11.

45. Roy Romanow et al., *Canada . . . Notwithstanding: The Making of the Constitution 1976–1982* (Toronto: Carswell, 1984), 211.

46. Borovoy, *When Freedoms Collide*, 211–12.

47. *Alliance des Professeurs de Montréal et al. v. Attorney General of Quebec* (1983), 9 C.C.C. (3d) 268.

48. F.L. Morton, "The Political Impact of the Canadian Charter of Rights and Freedoms," *Canadian Journal of Political Science* 20, 1 (Mar. 1987): 47.

49. Morton, Knopff, and Russell, *Federalism and the Charter*, 446.

50. Ibid., 389.

51. *Singh v. Minister of Employment and Immigration* (1985), 17 D.L.R. (4th) 469.

52. Morton, Knopff, and Russell, *Federalism and the Charter*, 446.

53. *Reference re Section 94(2) of the Motor Vehicle Act (B.C.)*, [1985] S.C.R. 486.

54. *Hunter et al. v. Southam Inc.*, [1984] 2 S.C.R. 145.

55. *Attorney General of Quebec v. Quebec Protestant School Boards* (1984), 10 D.L.R. (4th) 321.

56. *Reference re Public Service Employee Relations Act, Labour Relations Act and Police Officers Collective Bargaining Act* (1987), 38 D.L.R. (4th) 161.

57. *Operation Dismantle Inc. et al. v. The Queen* (1985), 18 D.L.R. (4th) 481.

58. *Retail, Wholesale & Department Store Union, Local 580 et al. v. Dolphin Delivery Ltd.* (1986), 33 D.L.R. (4th) 174.

59. Quoted in Michael Mandel, *The Charter of Rights and the Legalization of Politics in Canada*, 2nd edn (Toronto: Thompson Educational Publishing, 1994), 204.

60. *Citizens United v. Federal Election Commission*, 558 U.S. 310 (2010).

61. *Reference re Public Service Employees Relations Act (Alberta)*, quoted in Morton, Knopff, and Russell, *Federalism and the Charter*, 496.

62. *Canada v. Khadr*, 2010 SCC 3.

63. Quoted in Mandel, *The Charter of Rights*, 193.

64. *Dunmore et al. v. Attorney General for Ontario and Fleming Chicks*, 2001 SCC 94.

65. *R. v. N.S.*, 2012 SCC 72, [2012] 3 S.C.R. 726, at: <scc.lexum.org/decisia-scc-csc/scc-csc/scc-csc/en/12779/1/document.do>, p. 4.

66. *R. v. Keegstra*, [1990] 3 S.C.R. 697.

67. *Saskatchewan (Human Rights Commission) v. Whatcott*, [2013] 1 S.C.R. 467.

68. *Harper v. Canada*, [2004] 1 S.C.R. 827.

69. *WIC Radio Ltd. v. Simpson*, 2008 SCC 40.

70. Kirk Makin, "Supreme Court Becoming 'Charter Averse,' Expert Says," *Globe and Mail*, 12 Apr. 2013, accessed online.

71. Harry Arthurs and Brent Arnold, "Does the Charter Matter?" *Review of Constitutional Studies*, 1, 1 (2005): 37–117.

72. Ibid., 117.

73. Peter Hogg, *Constitutional Law of Canada*, 2nd edn (Toronto: Carswell, 1988), 786.

74. *Reference Re An Act to Amend the Education Act (Ontario)* (1987), 40 D.L.R. (4th) 18.

75. Before the law was passed, provincial support to Roman Catholic schools ended after Grade 10.

76. *Law v. Minister of Human Resources Development*, [1999] 1 S.C.R. 497.

77. Ibid.

78. *Citizens United v. Federal Election Commission*, 558 U.S. 310 (2010).

79. Christopher Manfredi and Mark Rush, "Electoral Jurisprudence in the Canadian and U.S. Supreme Courts: Evolution and Convergence," *McGill Law Journal* 52 (2007): 460–1.

80. Christopher L. Eisgruber and Mariah Zeisberg, "Religious Freedom in Canada and the United States," at: <www-personal.umich.edu/~zeisberg/Eisgruber_Zeisberg.pdf>.

8   Federalism

1. William S. Livingston, *Federalism and Constitutional Change* (Oxford: Clarendon Press, 1956), 2.

2. Ibid., 4.

3. In *Democracy in America*, Alexis de Tocqueville states that the cultural differences between communities separated by very short distances in Europe were far greater than any that he observed between the different states of the United States. As *The Federalist Papers* and the deliberations of the American founders at the Philadelphia convention of 1787 make clear, accommodating cultural diversity was not an important factor in the decision to choose a federal constitution.

4. Pierre Elliott Trudeau, "Federalism, Nationalism and Reason," in Trudeau, *Federalism and the French Canadians* (Toronto: Macmillan, 1968), 195.

5. Michael Burgess, *Comparative Federalism: Theory and Practice* (New York: Routledge, 2006), 97.

6. Donald Smiley, *The Canadian Political Identity* (Toronto: Methuen, 1967), 30–1.

7. Peter Waite, *The Life and Times of Confederation 1864–1867* (Toronto: University of Toronto Press, 1962), 96.

8. The diversity of expectations was reflected in newspaper accounts of the Confederation agreement. See ibid., 111.

9. There are some exceptions. In *Citizens Insurance Co. v. Parsons; Queen Insurance Co. v. Parsons* (1881), the Judicial Committee of the Privy Council ruled that Ottawa's trade and commerce power did not take pre-eminence over enumerated provincial powers. In explaining why, Sir Montague Smith stated that the founders "could not have intended that the powers exclusively assigned to the provincial legislature should be absorbed in those given to the dominion parliament." Reproduced in Peter H. Russell, ed., *Leading Constitutional Decisions*, 4th edn (Ottawa: Carleton University Press, 1987), 35.

10. Ibid., 527, *Re Constitution of Canada* (1981).

11. Edwin Black, *Divided Loyalties: Canadian Concepts of Federalism* (Montreal and Kingston: McGill-Queen's University Press, 1975), 17.

12. Amicus curiae concerning Certain Questions Relating to the Secession of Quebec, 31 Jan. 1998.

13. See *Liberal Values in Contemporary Quebec*, pp. 75–9, on the party's website at: <www.plq.org/doc/liberal_values.pdf>.

14. Jordan Press, "Provinces Insist Consent Required," *Regina Leader-Post*, 3 Aug. 2013, at: <www.leaderpost.com/news/Provinces+insist+consent+required/8745421/story.html>.

15. Hamish Telford, "The Federal Spending Power in Canada: Nation-Building or Nation-Destroying?" Institute for Intergovernmental Relations, Queen's University, Working Paper Series, 1999 (4), at: <www.queensu.ca/iigr/WorkingPapers/Archive/1999/1999-4HamishTelford.pdf>.

16. *Attorney General of Ontario v. Attorney General of Canada* (Local Prohibition case), 1896, in Russell, ed., *Leading Constitutional Decisions*, 59.

17. *Re Board of Commerce Act and Combines and Fair Prices Act*, 1919, 1922, ibid., 75.

18. *Co-operative Committee on Japanese Canadians v. A. G. Canada*, [1947] A.C. 87; *Reference re Validity of Wartime Leasehold Regulations*, [1950] S.C.R. 124.

19. *Attorney General of Canada v. Attorney General of Ontario* (Employment and Social Insurance Act Reference), 1937.

20. See Peter Russell, "The Anti-Inflation Case: The Anatomy of a Constitutional Decision," *Canadian Public Administration* 10, 4 (Winter 1977).

21. *Johannesson v. West St. Paul*, [1952] 1 S.C.R. 292, [1951] 4 D.L.R. 609; *Munro v. National Capital Commission*, [1966] S.C.R. 663, 57 D.L.R. (3d) 753; *R. v. Crown Zellerbach Can. Ltd.*, [1988] 1 S.C.R. 401.

22. Constitution Act, 1867, s. 91(2).

23. Ibid., s. 92(13).

24. Russell, ed., *Leading Constitutional Decisions*, 39.

25. *The King v. Eastern Terminal Elevator Co.*, [1925] S.C.R. 434; *A.G. of British Columbia v. A.G. of Canada* (Natural Products Marketing Reference), [1937] A.C. 377; *Canadian Federation of Agriculture v. A.G. of Quebec* (Margarine Reference), [1951], A.C. 179.

26. *Ontario Farm Products Marketing Reference*, [1957] S.C.R. 198; *R. v. Klassen* (1959), 20 D.L.R. (2nd) 406 (Manitoba Court of Appeal); *Caloil v. A.G. of Canada*, [1971] S.C.R. 543.

27. *Caloil*, 551.

28. Russell, ed., *Leading Constitutional Decisions*, 194.

29. Ibid., 199.

30. *General Motors of Canada Ltd. v. City National Leasing*, [1989] 1 S.C.R. 641.

31. *Reference Re Securities Act*, 2011 SCC 66.

32. Trudeau, "Federalism, Nationalism and Reason," 198.

33. Henri Bourassa, "The French Language and the Future of Our Race," in Ramsay Cook, ed., *French Canadian Nationalism* (Toronto: Macmillan, 1969), 141.

34. Kenneth McRoberts, *Quebec: Social Change and Political Crisis*, 3rd edn (Toronto: McClelland & Stewart, 1988), 214.

35. See Richard Simeon, *Federal–Provincial Diplomacy* (Toronto: University of Toronto Press, 1972), 115–22.

36. Canadian Press, "Ignatieff's Quote on Quebec Separation Sparks Strong Reaction," 24 Apr. 2012, at: <www.cbc.ca/news/politics/story/2012/04/24/pol-ignatieff-quebec-bbc-charest-poll.html>; Laura Payton, "Trudeau Says Sovereignty Less of a Bogeyman Now," 14 Feb. 2012, at: <www.cbc.ca/news/politics/story/2012/02/14/pol-justin-trudeau-quebec-sovereignty.html>.

37. Quoted in George Woodcock, *Confederation Betrayed!* (Vancouver: Harbour Publishing, 1981), 8.

38. This argument is developed by Barry Cooper in "Western Political Consciousness," in Stephen Brooks, ed., *Political Thought in Canada* (Toronto: Irwin, 1984), 213–38.

39. James Bickerton, *Nova Scotia, Ottawa, and the Politics of Regional Development* (Toronto: University of Toronto Press, 1990).

40. Barry Cooper, "Fresh News from Laurentian Canada," *Reviews from the Frontier* No. 2 (Apr. 2013), Frontier Centre for Public Policy, 8, at: <www.fcpp.org/files/1/RW02Laurentian_AP22F1.pdf>.

41. G.V. LaForest, *Disallowance and Reservation of Provincial Legislation* (Ottawa, 1955).

41. Ottawa ceded control to Manitoba in 1930.

42. Alberta and Saskatchewan also acquired these powers in 1930.

43. Doug Owram, "Reluctant Hinterland," in Larry Pratt and Garth Stevenson, eds, *Western Separatism* (Edmonton: Hurtig, 1981), 61.

44. Loleen Berdahl, "Whither Western Alienation? Shifting Patterns of Western Canadian Discontent with the Federal Government," Canada West Foundation, Oct. 2010, 9, at: <cwf.ca/pdf-docs/publications/Whither-Western-Alienation.pdf>.

45. Alan Cairns, "The Governments and Societies of Canadian Federalism," in Cairns, *Constitution, Government, and Society in Canada* (Toronto: McClelland & Stewart, 1988), 153–4.

46. John Ibbitson, "Premiers to Face Off against Ottawa over 'Flawed' Job Program," *Globe and Mail*, 21 July 2013, at: <www.theglobeandmail.com/news/politics/premiers-to-face-off-against-ottawa-over-job-program/article13337953/>.

47. See R.A. Young, Philippe Faucher, and André Blais, "The Concept of Province-Building: A Critique," *Canadian Journal of Political Science* 17, 4 (Dec. 1984): 785. Two of the major works using this concept are John Richards and Larry Pratt, *Prairie Capitalism* (Toronto: McClelland & Stewart, 1979), and McRoberts, *Quebec*.

48. Privy Council Office, Canadian Intergovernmental Conference Secretariat, at: <www.scics.gc.ca/english/conferences.asp?t=q&y=2013&m=8>.

49. Donald Smiley, "An Outsider's Observations of Federal–Provincial Relations," in R.D. Olling and W.M. Westmacott, eds, *Perspectives on Canadian Federalism* (Scarborough, Ont.: Prentice-Hall Canada, 1988).

50. Jason Fekete, "Why Prime Minister Stephen Harper Steers Clear of Premiers' Meetings," Postmedia, 24 July

2013, at: <o.canada.com/2013/07/24/premiers-meetings-rarely-include-prime-minister-stephen-harper/>.

51. Constitution Act, 1867, s. 118.
52. Ibid., s. 111.
53. Based on data from Canada, Department of Finance, *Fiscal Reference Tables, 2011*, and Statistics Canada, *Canadian Economic Observer*, Historical Statistical Supplement 1994–95, Catalogue no. 11-210.
54. *Reference re Canada Assistance Plan* (B.C.), [1991] 2 S.C.R. 525.
55. Paul Boothe and Derek Hermourtz, "Paying for ACCESS: Province by Province," paper delivered before the Political Economy Research Group, University of Western Ontario, 24 Oct. 1997, Figure 3b.
56. Department of Finance Canada, *Budget 1995: Key Actions and Impacts*, unpaginated.
57. Ibid.
58. Ibid.
59. *Schneider v. The Queen*, [1982] 2 S.C.R. 112.
60. Marlisa Teidemann, "The Federal Role in Health and Health Care," 20 Oct. 2008, Parliament of Canada, at: <www.parl.gc.ca/Content/LOP/ResearchPublications/prb0858-e.htm>.
61. See<www.cbc.ca/news/politics/story/2012/01/12/pol-cp-pbo-health-transfers-cut.html>.
62. Office of the Parliament Budget Office, *Renewing the Canada Health Transfer: Implications for Federal and Provincial–Territorial Fiscal Sustainability*, 12 Oct. 2012, at: <www.pbo-dpb.gc.ca/files/files/Publications/Renewing_CHT.pdf>.
63. Joseph Facal, "Social Policy and Intergovernmental Relations in Canada," Saskatchewan Institute of Public Policy, Apr. 2005, at: <www.uregina.ca/sipp/documents/pdf/PPP32_Facal.pdf>.
64. Matthew Mendelsohn, *Back to Basics: The Future of the Fiscal Arrangements*, Mowat Centre, Dec. 2012, p. 5, at: <www.mowatcentre.ca/pdfs/mowatResearch/75.pdf>.
65. Thomas Courchene, *Surplus Recycling and the Canadian Federation: Reassessing the Allocation of Federal Money and Power*, Institute for Intergovernmental Relations, Apr. 2013, at: <www.queensu.ca/iigr/WorkingPapers/NewWorkingPapersSeries/WorkingPaperCourcheneSURPLUSRECYCLINGFINAL.pdf>.

9   The Machinery of Government

1. "The Executive Government and Authority of and over Canada is hereby declared to continue and be vested in the Queen." Constitution Act, 1867, s. 9.
2. In the provinces, the Crown's authority is exercised through the lieutenant-governors, who are appointed by the Governor General to serve five-year terms.
3. James R. Mallory, *The Structure of Canadian Government*, rev. edn (Toronto: Gage, 1984), 42–3.
4. As head of the Canadian Auto Workers, one of Canada's major unions, Buzz Hargrove advocated what came to be called "tactical voting" by union members, whereby they should vote for the Liberal or NDP candidate who appeared to be most likely to defeat a Conservative Party candidate. In 1999 the CAW, under Hargrove's leadership, did not officially endorse the Ontario NDP, the first time in the history of the union that it broke with the NDP during an election campaign.
5. Constitution Act, 1867, s. 54.
6. A good explanation of the annual budget cycle is found in Alex Smith, "A Guide to the Estimates," Library of Parliament, at: <www.parl.gc.ca/Content/LOP/ResearchPublications/prb0925-e.htm>.
7. Donald Savoie, *Governing from the Centre: The Concentration of Power in Canadian Politics* (Toronto: University of Toronto Press, 1999), ch. 4. See also Savoie, *Power: Where Is It?* (Montreal and Kingston: McGill-Queen's University Press, 2010), ch. 6.
8. Donald Savoie, *Whatever Happened to the Music Teacher? How Government Decides and Why* (Montreal and Kingston: McGill-Queen's University Press, 2013).
9. Colin Campbell and George Szablowski, *The Super-Bureaucrats: Structure and Behaviour in Central Agencies* (Toronto: Macmillan, 1979).
10. Savoie, *Governing from the Centre*, 4.
11. Leslie Pal, *Beyond Policy Analysis* (Toronto: Nelson Canada, 1998), 92.
12. Savoie, *Governing from the Centre*, 189.
13. Alex Smith, "The Roles and Responsibilities of Central Agencies," Library of Parliament, 23 Apr. 2009, at: <www.parl.gc.ca/content/lop/researchpublications/prb0901-e.htm#a20>.
14. Savoie, *Governing from the Centre*, 109.
15. Campbell and Szablowski, *The Super-Bureaucrats*, 29.
16. Smith, "The Roles and Responsibilities of Central Agencies."
17. Gordon Robertson, "The Changing Role of the Privy Council Office," *Canadian Public Administration* 14 (Winter 1971): 506.
18. Savoie, *Governing from the Centre*, 109.
19. Ibid., 121.
20. Donald J. Savoie, *Court Government and the Collapse of Accountability in Canada and the United Kingdom* (Toronto: University of Toronto Press, 2008).
21. Ibid., 195.
22. Ibid.
23. Robertson, "The Changing Role of the Privy Council Office," 506.
24. Savoie, *Governing from the Centre*, 101.
25. Ibid., 103.
26. Donald Savoie, in *Governing from the Centre* and *Court Government and the Collapse of Accountability*, and Jeffrey Simpson in *The Friendly Dictatorship* (Toronto: McClelland & Stewart, 2001), make this argument.
27. Savoie, *Governing from the Centre*, 260.
28. Simpson, *The Friendly Dictatorship*, 248.
29. Donald Savoie, "The Federal Cabinet: Revisiting Court Government in Canada," in Luc Bernier, Keith Brownsey,

and Michael Howlett, eds, *Executive Styles in Canada: Cabinet Structures and Leadership Practices in Canadian Government* (Toronto: University of Toronto Press, 2005), 17–46.

30. David Pond, "The Impact of Parliamentary Officers on Canadian Parliamentary Democracy: A Study of the Commissioner of the Environment and Sustainable Development and the Environmental Commissioner of Ontario," Canadian Study of Parliament Group, p. 3, at: <www.studyparliament.ca/English/pdf/PondPaperFinal-2010-e.pdf>.

31. Michael Chong, "The Increasing Disconnect between Canadians and Their Parliament," *Policy Options* (Sept. 2010), 24–7.

32. The total number of Senate seats rose from 104 to 105 with the creation of the new territory of Nunavut on 1 April 1999.

33. Robert J. Jackson and Michael A. Atkinson, *The Canadian Legislative System*, 2nd edn (Toronto: Gage, 1980), 22.

34. Savoie, *Governing from the Centre*, 91.

35. Ibid., 92.

36. Samara, *It's My Party: Parliamentary Dysfunction Reconsidered*, 2010, pp. 12–13, at: <www2.samaracanada.com/downloads/ItsMyParty.pdf>.

37. David C. Docherty, *Mr. Smith Goes to Ottawa: Life in the House of Commons* (Vancouver: University of British Columbia Press, 1998), 234.

38. Samara, "MP Exit Interviews," 2010, at: <www.samaracanada.com/What-We-Do/MP-Exit-Interviews>.

39. Samara, *It's My Party: Parliamentary Dysfunction Reconsidered*, 12.

40. Simpson, *The Friendly Dictatorship*, 23.

41. C.E.S. Franks, "Debate and Question Period," in *The Parliament of Canada* (Toronto: University of Toronto Press, 1987), 156.

42. Andrea Ulrich, "A Question of Accountability: Is Question Period in Canada Working?" *Queen's Policy Review* 2, 2 (Fall 2011): 1–16.

43. Patti Tamara Lenard and Richard Simeon, eds, *Imperfect Democracies: The Democratic Deficit in Canada and the United States* (Vancouver: University of British Columbia Press, 2013).

44. Jane Hilderman and Paul Thomas, "Climbing the Ladder of Dissent: Backbench Influence in the Canadian House of Commons," paper presented at the annual meeting of the Canadian Political Science Association, University of Victoria, 4–6 June 2013, 17.

45. Docherty, *Mr. Smith Goes to Ottawa*, 204.

46. Ibid., 206.

47. Lenard and Simeon, eds, *Imperfect Democracies*.

48. See the Constitution Act, 1867, s. 99(1). This phrase, or reference to "misbehaviour," is found in the federal and provincial statutes that govern the removal of judges.

49. Allan McEachern, "Report to the Canadian Judicial Council of the Inquiry Committee Established Pursuant to Subsection 63(1) of the Judges Act at the Request of the Attorney General of Nova Scotia," 1990.

50. Nova Scotia Family Court judge Raymond Bartlett was removed for judicial misconduct in 1987 after an investigation by the provincial Judicial Council.

51. Ralph Miliband, *The State in Capitalist Society* (London: Quartet Books, 1973), 124.

52. Judges of county courts and all higher courts are appointed by Ottawa. Provincial court judges are appointed by the provinces. See Figure 9.5 in the text.

53. Michael Ornstein, *The Changing Face of the Ontario Legal Profession*, Report to the Law Society of Upper Canada, Oct. 2004, at: <rc.lsuc.on.ca/pdf/equity/ornsteinReport.pdf>.

54. Wendy Cukier, *Improving Representation in the Judiciary: A Diversity Strategy*, Ryerson University, Diversity Institute, 27 June 2012. See also Kirk Makin, "Of 100 New Federally Appointed Judges 98 Are White, Globe Finds," *Globe and Mail*, 17 Apr. 2012.

55. See Marie-Claire Belleau and Rebecca Johnson, "Les femmes juges feront-elles véritablement une différence? Réflexions sur leur présence depuis vingt ans à la Cour suprême du Canada," *Canadian Journal of Women and the Law* 17, 1 (2005): 27–39.

56. Richard H. Sander, "Class in American Legal Education," *Denver University Law Review*, 88, 4 (2011): 631–82.

57. Canada, Department of Justice, *Canada's System of Justice* (Ottawa: Supply and Services Canada, 1988), 7.

58. Joel Bakan, *Just Words: Constitutional Rights and Social Wrongs* (Toronto: University of Toronto Press, 1997), 3.

59. See, for example, Cristin Schmitz, "Political Patronage a 'Huge Problem' in Appointing Judges Says Former Premier," *Ottawa Citizen*, 25 Sept. 2005; Jennie Russell, "Appointment of Judges Politically Biased in Alberta, Critics Say," CBC News, 25 July 2013, at: <www.cbc.ca/news/canada/edmonton/story/2013/07/24/edmonton-political-base-judicial-appointment.html>.

60. James Mallory, *Social Credit and the Federal Power* (Toronto: University of Toronto Press, 1954).

61. Andrew Petter, "Legalise This: The Chartering of Canadian Politics," in James B. Kelly and Christopher P. Manfredi, eds, *Contested Constitutionalism: Reflections on the Canadian Charter of Rights and Freedoms* (Vancouver: University of British Columbia Press, 2009), 33–49.

62. Ibid., 33.

63. Rainer Knopff and Ted Morton, *Charter Politics* (Toronto: Nelson Canada, 1992), 79.

10 The Administrative State

1. These figures are from Jacques DesRoches, "The Evolution of the Organization of Federal Government in Canada," *Canadian Public Administration* 5, 4 (1962): 408–27.

2. A list of these organizations may be found at <www.canada.gc.ca/depts/major/depind-eng.html>.

3. Readers wanting a good overview of the structural characteristics and activities of these other levels of government will find this in Andrew Sancton, *Canadian Local Government* (Don Mills, Ont.: Oxford University Press,

2011), and Christopher Dunn, ed., *Provincial Politics* (Toronto: University of Toronto Press, 2006).

4. Henry David Thoreau, "A Yankee in Canada" (1850), p. 38, at: <www.thoreau-online.org>.

5. Susanna Moodie, *Roughing It in the Bush* (1852).

6. Royal Commission to Enquire into and Report on the Operation of the Civil Service Act and Kindred Legislation, *1908—Report of the Commissioners*, p. 13, at: <www.psc-cfp.gc.ca/plcy-pltq/rprt/impart/chapter4 -chapitre4-eng.htm>.

7. Max Weber, *The Protestant Ethic and the Spirit of Capitalism* (New York: Charles Scribner, 1958 [1904–5]), 182.

8. *Fraser v. PSSRB*, [1985] 2 S.C.R. 455, para. 41.

9. *Osborne v. Canada (Treasury Board)*, [1991] 2 S.C.R. 69.

10. *Haydon v. Canada (Treasury Board)*, [2004] FC 749. See Office of the Commissioner for Federal Judicial Affairs Canada, at: <reports.fja.gc.ca/eng/2005/2004fc749.html>. Reproduced with the permission of the Minister of Public Works and Government Services Canada, 2011.

11. Quoted in Carl Berger, *The Writing of Canadian History*, 2nd edn (Toronto: University of Toronto Press, 1986), 24.

12. John Porter, *The Vertical Mosaic* (Toronto: University of Toronto Press, 1965), 611.

13. Ibid., 435.

14. Doug Owram, *The Government Generation: Canadian Intellectuals and the State*, 1900–1945 (Toronto: University of Toronto Press, 1986).

15. All figures in this section are based on F.H. Leacy, ed., *Historical Statistics of Canada*, 2nd edn (Ottawa: Statistics Canada, 1983).

16. This includes teachers, hospital workers, police officers, firefighters, public transit workers, social workers, and others whose salaries derive mainly or entirely from the budget of one or more levels of government. See ENAP, "Canadian Governments Compared: Public Employment," at: <etatscanadienscanadiangovernments .enap.ca/en/nav.aspx?sortcode=2.0.2.0>.

17. David Held and Anthony McGrew, "Globalization," in Joel Krieger, ed., *The Oxford Companion to Politics of the World*, 2nd edn (New York: Oxford University Press, 2001), 324–27.

18. Donald Savoie, *Governing from the Centre: The Concentration of Power in Canadian Politics* (Toronto: University of Toronto Press, 1999), 248.

19. Alexander Brady, *Democracy in the Dominions* (Toronto: University of Toronto Press, 1947), 82.

20. Porter, *The Vertical Mosaic*.

21. Precise figures on the ethnic origins of the Canadian population are impossible to come by because of intermarriage between members of different ethnic groups and because Statistics Canada, in the census, now allows multiple responses to the ethnic origin question as well as "Canadian" ethnic origin as a response.

22. CBC News, "Duelling Language Petitions Ignite Debate over Hiring," 31 July 2013, at: <www.cbc.ca/news/canada/ new-brunswick/story/2013/07/31/nb-official-language -petitions-725.html>.

23. Hansard, *House of Commons Debates*, 17 June 2013, at: <www.parl.gc.ca/HousePublications/Publication.aspx ?Mode=1&DocId=6239224&Language=E>.

Part IV Participation in Politics

11 Parties and Elections

1. Eugene A. Forsey, *How Canadians Govern Themselves* (Ottawa: Supply and Services Canada, 1982), 32.

2. Leon Epstein, *Political Parties in Western Democracies* (New Brunswick, NJ: Transaction Books, 1980 [1967]), 9.

3. John Meisel, "Decline of Party in Canada," in Hugh G. Thorburn, ed., *Party Politics in Canada*, 4th edn (Scarborough, Ont.: Prentice-Hall, 1979).

4. This section was co-authored by Professor A. Brian Tanguay, Wilfrid Laurier University.

5. George M. Hougham, "The Background and Development of National Parties," in Hugh G. Thorburn, ed., *Party Politics in Canada* (Toronto: Prentice-Hall, 1963), 13.

6. Escott Reid, "The Rise of National Parties in Canada," in Hugh G. Thorburn, ed., *Party Politics in Canada*, 5th edn (Scarborough, Ont.: Prentice-Hall, 1985), 12. See also Norman Ward, *The Canadian House of Commons* (Toronto: University of Toronto Press, 1950), 157–62.

7. See, in particular, Martin Shefter, "Party and Patronage: Germany, England, and Italy," *Politics and Society* 7, 4 (1977): 403–51; Epstein, *Political Parties in Western Democracies*, ch. 5.

8. André Siegfried, *The Race Question in Canada* (Toronto: McClelland & Stewart, Carleton Library Edition, 1966 [English translation first published 1907]), 114.

9. An income trust is an investment vehicle that, prior to the change in the law that took effect in 2011, enabled investors to receive profits earned by a corporation before the corporation's income was taxed.

10. J.A. Corry, *Democratic Government and Politics*, 2nd edn (Toronto: University of Toronto Press, 1951), 22. Variations on this theme can be found in R.M. Dawson and Norman Ward, *The Government of Canada*, 5th edn (Toronto: University of Toronto Press, 1987), 430–3, and Hugh G. Thorburn, "Interpretations of the Canadian Party System," in Thorburn, ed., *Party Politics in Canada*, 5th edn (Scarborough, Ont.: Prentice-Hall, 1985), 20–40. For a critique of the adequacy of brokerage theory, see Janine Brodie and Jane Jenson, *Crisis, Challenge and Change: Party and Class Revisited* (Ottawa: Carleton University Press, 1988), ch. 1.

11. Robert Alford, *Party and Society* (Westport, CT: Greenwood Press, 1963), 250–1. Alford computed his index of class voting by subtracting the percentage of non-manual workers voting for left parties (in Canada,

the Liberals and the NDP, according to Alford) from the percentage of manual workers voting for the left parties, on the assumption that a party of the left should receive the bulk of its support from the traditional blue-collar (manual) occupations. Obviously, Alford's index leaves a great deal to be desired and has been subjected to substantial criticism over the years. In particular, his classification of the Liberal Party of Canada as a party of the "left" is objected to by many critics.

12. Ibid., 251.

13. Brodie and Jenson, *Crisis, Challenge and Change*.

14. Seymour Martin Lipset, P.F. Lazarsfeld, A.H. Barton, and J. Linz, "The Psychology of Voting: An Analysis of Political Behavior," in G. Lindzey, ed., *Handbook of Social Psychology* (Cambridge, MA: Addison-Wesley, 1954), 1136.

15. T.N. Clark and S.M. Lipset, "Are Social Classes Dying?" *International Sociology* 8 (1991): 403.

16. Janine Brodie and Jane Jenson, "Piercing the Smoke-screen: Brokerage Parties and Class Politics," in Alain G. Gagnon and A. Brian Tanguay, eds, *Canadian Parties in Transition: Discourse, Organization, and Representation* (Scarborough, Ont.: Nelson, 1989), 28.

17. Brodie and Jenson, *Crisis, Challenge and Change*, 34.

18. Robert M. Campbell and Leslie A. Pal, *The Real Worlds of Canadian Politics* (Peterborough, Ont.: Broadview Press, 1989), 5.

19. Canadian Institute of Public Opinion, *The Gallup Report*, "Confidence in Political Parties Declines," 1 Feb. 1989, and "Government Increasingly Becoming Object of Scorn among Canadians," 20 Feb. 1991.

20. Walter Young, *The Anatomy of a Party: The National CCF, 1932–61* (Toronto: University of Toronto Press, 1969), 298, 300.

21. Canada, Royal Commission on Electoral Reform and Party Financing, *Reforming Electoral Democracy*, vol. 7 (Ottawa: Supply and Services Canada, 1991), 221.

22. William P. Irvine, *Does Canada Need a New Electoral System?* (Kingston, Ont.: Institute of Intergovernmental Relations, Queen's University, 1979), 46–7.

23. Alan Cairns, "The Electoral System and the Party System in Canada, 1921–1965," *Canadian Journal of Political Science* 1, 1 (Mar. 1968): 55–80.

24. Irvine, *Does Canada Need a New Electoral System?*, 14.

25. Stéphane Dion, "A Voting System for Canada," 18 Aug. 2012, at: <stephanedion.liberal.ca/en/articles-en/p3-voting-system-canada-2/>.

26. Leslie MacKinnon, "Some Liberals Join NDP in Push for 'Fairer' Voting System," CBC News, 20 Sept. 2013, at: <www.cbc.ca/news/politics/some-liberals-join-ndp-in-push-for-fairer-voting-system-1.1862550>.

27. Ibid.

28. Elisabeth Gidengil, "An Overview of the Social Dimension of Vote Choice," in Mebs Kanji, Antoine Bilodeau, and Thomas J. Scotto, eds, *The Canadian Election Studies: Assessing Four Decades of Influence* (Vancouver: University of British Columbia Press, 2012), 104.

29. J. Matthew Wilson and Michael Lusztig, "The Spouse in the House: What Explains the Marriage Gap in Canada?" *Canadian Journal of Political Science* 37, 4 (2004): 979–96.

30. Zack Taylor, Phil Triadafilopoulos, and Christopher Cochrane, "On the Backs of Immigrants? Conservative Politics and New Canadian Voters," paper presented at the annual meeting of the Canadian Political Science Association, Edmonton, 2012, 11, Table 2.

31. André Blais et al., "Where Does Turnout Decline Come From?" *European Journal of Political Research* 43 (2004): 221–2.

32. Ibid., 224.

33. Ibid., 225.

34. Ibid., 227.

35. Henry Milner, *Civic Literacy: How Informed Citizens Make Democracy Work* (Boston: Tufts University Press, 2002); Milner, *The Informed Political Participation of Young Canadians and Americans*, May 2008, at: <www.civicyouth.org/PopUps/WorkingPapers/WP60Milner.pdf>.

36. Statistics Canada, 2003 *General Social Survey on Social Engagement: An Overview of Findings*, Catalogue no. 89-598-XIE (Ottawa, 2004).

37. These non-electoral forms of civic engagement are discussed in Paul Howe, *Citizens Adrift: The Democratic Disengagement of Young Canadians* (Vancouver: University of British Columbia Press, 2010), ch. 2.

38. Larry Leduc et al., "Youth, Democracy and Civic Engagement: The 'Apathy Is Boring' Surveys," p. 20, at: <www.cpsa-acsp.ca/papers-2012/Leduc.pdf>.

39. See Khayyam Paltiel, *Political Party Financing in Canada* (Toronto: McGraw-Hill Ryerson, 1970), 19–75.

40. These services are discussed by Reg Whitaker, *The Government Party: Organizing and Financing the Liberal Party of Canada, 1930–1958* (Toronto: University of Toronto Press, 1977), 204–6, 216–63.

41. According to Khayyam Paltiel, "For the 1972 [national] election half the funds raised in Ontario by the Liberal Party were collected personally by the chairman of the party's Treasury Committee from 90 large corporations." Paltiel, "Campaign Financing in Canada and Its Reform," in Howard R. Penniman, ed., *Canada at the Polls: The General Election of 1974* (Washington: American Enterprise Institute, 1975), 182.

42. See A.B. Stevenson, *Canadian Election Reform: Dialogue on Issues and Effects* (Toronto: Ontario Commission on Election Contributions and Expenses, 1982); Whitaker, *The Government Party*.

43. The number of hours per network and the division of time between the parties are determined by the CRTC. In deciding how much time each party receives the CRTC is guided by a formula weighted according to each party's share of the seats and popular vote in the previous election.

44. Khayyam Paltiel, "Political Marketing, Party Finance, and the Decline of Political Parties," in Gagnon and Tanguay, eds, *Canadian Parties in Transition*, 342.

45. See Larry Sabato, *The Rise of Political Consultants* (New York: Basic Books, 1981), especially ch. 4.

46. Dalton Camp, *Points of Departure* (Toronto: Deneau and Greenberg, 1979), 91.

47. Ibid.

12 Interest Groups

1. V.O. Key, *Politics, Parties, and Pressure Groups*, 4th edn (New York, 1958), 23.

2. James Madison, *The Federalist Papers*, no. 10 (New York: New American Library, 1961 [1787]).

3. This slogan is attributed to Thomas Sloan, a chairman of GM during the 1920s.

4. *Associations Canada* (Toronto: Grey House Publishing, 2013).

5. Estimates based on ibid.

6. Robert Wolfe, "Trade Policy Begins at Home: Information and Consultation in the Trade Policy Process," in Mark Halle and Robert Wolfe, eds, *Process Matters: Sustainable Development and Domestic Trade Transparency* (Winnipeg: International Institute for Sustainable Development, 2009).

7. E.E. Schattschneider, *The Semi-Sovereign People* (New York: Holt, Rinehart and Winston, 1960), 35.

8. Ibid.

9. Ibid.

10. Charles E. Lindblom, *Politics and Markets* (New York: Basic Books, 1977), especially chs 13–16.

11. Bruno S. Frey, *Modern Political Economy* (New York: John Wiley & Sons, 1978), ch. 11.

12. See, for example, W.T. Stanbury, *Business–Government Relations in Canada: Grappling with Leviathan* (Toronto: Methuen, 1986), and James Brander, *Government Policy toward Business*, 4th edn (Toronto: John Wiley & Sons, 2005).

13. Michael Bliss, *Northern Enterprise: Five Centuries of Canadian Business* (Toronto: McClelland & Stewart, 1987), 578.

14. Geoffrey Hale, *Uneasy Partnership: The Politics of Business and Government in Canada* (Toronto: University of Toronto Press, 2006), 94.

15. David Vogel, *Fluctuating Fortunes: The Political Power of Business in America* (New York: Basic Books, 1989), 193.

16. David Vogel, *Kindred Strangers: The Uneasy Relationship between Politics and Business in America* (Princeton, NJ: Princeton University Press, 1996).

17. Neil J. Mitchell, *The Conspicuous Corporation: Business, Public Policy, and Representative Democracy* (Ann Arbor: University of Michigan Press, 1997).

18. James Q. Wilson, "The Politics of Regulation," in Wilson, ed., *The Politics of Regulation* (New York: Basic Books, 1980), 370.

19. Earl Latham, *The Group Basis of Politics* (New York: Octagon Books, 1965), 35.

20. Arthur F. Bentley, *The Process of Government* (Evanston, Ill., 1935), 208.

21. David B. Truman, *The Governmental Process* (New York: Alfred Knopf, 1951); Robert Dahl, *Who Governs?* (New Haven, CT: Yale University Press, 1961); John

Kenneth Galbraith, *American Capitalism: The Concept of Countervailing Power* (Boston: Houghton Mifflin, 1952).

22. Theodore Lowi, *The End of Liberalism* (New York: W.W. Norton, 1969).

23. P. Bachrach and M. Baratz, "Two Faces of Power," *American Political Science Review* 56, 4 (1962): 948.

24. This is true of Nicos Poulantzas, *Political Power and Social Classes* (London: New Left Books, 1973); Fred Block, *Revising State Theory* (Philadelphia: Temple University Press, 1987); Bob Jessop, *The Capitalist State* (New York: New York University Press, 1982). Interest groups are given some passing mention in James O'Connor, *The Fiscal Crisis of the State* (New York: St Martin's Press, 1973); Claus Offe, *Contradictions of the Welfare State* (Cambridge, MA: MIT Press, 1984). Among the leading Marxist intellectuals, it is perhaps fair to say that only Ralph Miliband has very much to say on interest groups; see Miliband, *The State in Capitalist Society* (London: Quartet Books, 1973).

25. The term "political economy" includes three separate streams or meanings today: the Canadian tradition of political economy, which, after Harold Innis's early work, moved squarely to the left; the political economy in the Downs–Buchanan tradition, with a centre of gravity in the United States and a pro-market orientation; and the political economy work among those in international relations, whose focus is globalization and its discontents and whose orientation is more often than not on the left.

26. Miliband, *The State in Capitalist Society*, 131.

27. Wallace Clement, *The Challenge of Class Analysis* (Ottawa: Carleton University Press, 1988), chs 7 and 8.

28. Ibid., 132.

29. Rianne Mahon, *The Politics of Industrial Restructuring: Canadian Textiles* (Toronto: University of Toronto Press, 1984).

30. Peter John, *Analysing Public Policy*, 2nd edn (New York: Routledge, 2012), 92.

31. Jurg Steiner, *European Democracies* (New York: Longman, 1986), 221.

32. William D. Coleman, *Business and Politics: A Study of Collective Action* (Montreal and Kingston: McGill-Queen's University Press, 1988), 224.

33. It occasionally happens, however, that the CCC is capable of taking a firm position on issues that are more divisive in the business community. Its support for the Canada–US Free Trade Agreement was an example of this.

34. Gerhard Lehmbruch, "Concertation and the Structure of Corporatist Networks," in John Goldthorpe, ed., *Order and Conflict in Contemporary Capitalism* (Oxford: Clarendon, 1984), 65–6.

35. Coleman, *Business and Politics*, ch. 6.

36. These tripartite initiatives are discussed in detail in Pierre Fournier, "Consensus Building in Canada: Case Studies and Prospects," in Keith Banting, research coordinator, *The State and Economic Interests*, vol. 32 of the research studies for the Royal Commission on the Economic Union and Development Prospects for Canada (Ottawa: Supply and Services Canada, 1986), 291–335.

37. A. Siaroff, "Corporatism in 24 Industrial Democracies: Meaning and Measurement," *European Journal of Political Research* 36 (1999): 175–205.

38. William Coleman is among those who have argued that such structures would benefit Canada economically. See Coleman, *Business and Politics*, ch. 13.

39. William D. Coleman and Grace Skogstad, "Introduction," in Coleman and Skogstad, eds, *Policy Communities and Public Policy in Canada* (Toronto: Copp Clark Pitman, 1990), 2.

40. Michels's argument was that the specialization of function that accompanies organization inevitably results in domination of the organization by a minority and, therefore, creates the likelihood that the goals pursued by the organization will more closely reflect those of its leadership than its membership. Robert Michels, *Political Parties* (London: Jarrold, 1915).

41. Some of the classics of this literature include Anthony Downs, *An Economic Theory of Democracy* (New York: Harper and Row, 1957); Mancur Olson, *The Logic of Collective Action* (Cambridge, MA: Harvard University Press, 1965); James M. Buchanan and Gordon Tullock, *The Calculus of Consent* (Ann Arbor: University of Michigan Press, 1965); Anthony Downs, *Inside Bureaucracy* (Boston: Little, Brown and Company, 1967).

42. Michael Atkinson, "How Do Institutions Constrain Policy?" paper delivered at the conference "Governing Canada: Political Institutions and Public Policy," McMaster University, 25 Oct. 1991, 8. A good introduction to this approach and its application to politics is provided by Queen's University economist Dan Usher in *Political Economy* (London: Blackwell, 2003).

43. Alan Cairns, "The Governments and Societies of Canadian Federalism," *Canadian Journal of Political Science* 10, 4 (1977): 695–725.

44. These works include James G. March and Herbert Simon, *Organizations* (New York: John Wiley, 1958); James G. March, *Decisions and Organizations* (Oxford: Blackwell, 1988); James G. March and Johan P. Olsen, "The New Institutionalism: Organizational Factors in Political Life," *American Political Science Review* 78 (1984): 734–49; James G. March and Johan P. Olsen, *Rediscovering Institutions: The Organizational Basis of Politics* (New York: Free Press, 1989).

45. Charles Perrow, *Complex Organizations: A Critical Essay*, 3rd edn (New York: Random House, 1986), 260.

46. James Q. Wilson, *Political Organizations* (New York: Basic Books, 1973), 3–4.

47. These definitions are the ones used in Coleman and Skogstad, "Introduction." They are not, however, agreed upon by everyone who mines this vein.

48. Coleman and Skogstad, "Introduction," 25.

49. Ibid., 23.

50. Ibid., 24.

51. J.L. Granatstein, *The Ottawa Men* (Toronto: Oxford University Press, 1982).

52. O. Mary Hill, *Canada's Salesman to the World: The Department of Trade and Commerce, 1892–1939* (Montreal and Kingston: McGill-Queen's University Press, 1977), 172.

53. Leslie A. Pal, *Interests of State* (Montreal and Kingston: McGill-Queen's University Press, 1992), ch. 6.

54. A. Paul Pross, *Group Politics and Public Policy* (Toronto: University of Toronto Press, 1986), 68–9.

55. See Table 3-2, "Crosswalk between Old and New Multicultural Program Objectives," in Citizenship and Immigration Canada, *Evaluation of the Multicultural Program*, Mar. 2012, pp. 20–1, at: <www.cic.gc.ca/english/pdf/research-stats/multiculturalism.pdf>.

56. Voices-voix, "Women's Legal Education and Action Fund," 15 Nov. 2012, at: <voices-voix.ca/en/facts/profile/womens-legal-education-and-action-fund-leaf>.

57. Pross, *Group Politics and Public Policy*, 114–16.

58. Larry Pynn, "Recession Hits Environmental Organizations as Funding Slides," *Vancouver Sun*, 18 Dec. 2008, at: <www.sierraclub.bc.ca/.../recession-hits-environmental-organizations-as-funding-slides>.

59. Ontario Trillium Foundation, "Recession Not Over, Not-for-Profits Still Struggling," at: <www.trilliumfoundation.org>.

60. G. Bruce Doern and Brian W. Tomlin, *Fear and Faith: The Free Trade Story* (Toronto: Stoddart, 1991), 219.

61. John W. Kingdon, *Agendas, Alternatives, and Public Policies* (Boston: Little, Brown and Company, 1984), 54–7.

62. Michael Woods, "Assembly of First Nations Head Shawn Atleo Calls for Aboriginal Unity as Challenge to Authority Mounts," *Postmedia News*, 16 July 2013, accessed online.

63. Olson, *The Logic of Collective Action*.

64. Wilson, *Political Organizations*, 36–8.

65. Schattschneider, *The Semi-Sovereign People*, 37.

66. Ibid., 38.

67. Good analyses of several Canadian policy communities are found in Coleman and Skogstad, eds, *Policy Communities and Public Policy in Canada*.

68. This literature was brought together in Hugh G. Thorburn, *Interest Groups in the Canadian Federal System*, vol. 69 of the research studies for the Royal Commission on the Economic Union and Development Prospects for Canada (Ottawa: Supply and Services Canada, 1985). A more recent review of this literature is found in Robert Boatright, "The Place of Quebec in Canadian Interest Group Politics," *American Review of Canadian Studies* 41, 1 (2011): 2–19.

69. Richard J. Schultz, *Federalism, Bureaucracy and Public Policy: The Politics of Highway Transport Regulation* (Montreal and Kingston: McGill-Queen's University Press, 1980), 148.

70. See, for example, M.W. Bucovetsky, "The Mining Industry and the Great Tax Reform Debate," in A. Paul Pross, ed., *Pressure Group Behaviour in Canadian Politics* (Toronto: McGraw-Hill Ryerson, 1975), 89–114.

71. Boatright, "The Place of Quebec in Canadian Interest Group Politics."

72. The long-accepted claim that Canada's federal Constitution has led most associations to adopt a federal form of organization is not supported by the facts—at least not in the case of business associations. A survey by William Coleman finds that about three-quarters

of business associations have unitary structures. Coleman's conclusion is that Canada's industrial structure has a far greater impact on how business associations organize themselves than does the Constitution. See Coleman, *Business and Politics*, 260.

73. See Schultz, *Federalism, Bureaucracy and Public Policy*, especially ch. 8.
74. Alan Cairns, "The Governments and Societies of Canadian Federalism," in Cairns, *Constitution, Government, and Society in Canada* (Toronto: McClelland & Stewart, 1988), 167.
75. Leslie A. Pal, *State, Class, and Bureaucracy* (Montreal and Kingston: McGill-Queen's University Press, 1988).
76. Wellington Water Watchers, at: <www.wellingtonwaterwatchers.ca/2013/05/latest-on-nestle-legal-battle-to-keep-drought-time-water-pumping-restrictions-in-place/>.
77. CBC News, "Anti-Oil Sands Ads Target Alberta Tourism," 14 July 2010, at: <www.cbc.ca/money.story/2010/07/14/con-oilsand-tourism.html>.
78. Laura Litvan, "Lobbyists Cash in as Keystone XL Pipeline Slugfest Enters Sixth Year," *Financial Post*, 17 Sept. 2013.
79. CBS News, "BP Spent $93M on Advertising after Gulf Spill," 1 Sept. 2010, at: <www.cbsnews.com/stories/2010/09/01/national/main6827683.shtml>.
80. CUPE, "New TV Ad Marks Next Phase of CUPE Campaign," at: <www.cupe.on.ca/s359/new-marks-next-phase>.
81. Amy Harder, "Meet Canada, Keystone's Marquee Lobbyist," *National Journal Daily*, 15 July 2013, at: <www.nationaljournal.com/columns/power-play/meet-canada-keystone-s-marquee-lobbyist-20130714>.
82. Quoted in Duncan McDowall, ed., *Advocacy Advertising: Propaganda or Democratic Right?* (Ottawa: Conference Board of Canada, 1982), v.
83. For example, a former federal Minister of Justice defended his government's advertising on proposed constitutional reforms by saying, "Government is too complex nowadays to rely on policy by press release. Programs must be explained—not by reporters but by people who created them." Ibid., 7. On the subject of government advertising, see Jonathan Rose, *Making "Pictures in Our Heads": Government Advertising in Canada* (Westport, CT: Greenwood Publishing Group, 2000).
84. See, for example, Kenneth Kollman, *Outside Lobbying: Public Opinion and Interest Group Strategies* (Princeton, NJ: Princeton University Press, 1998).
85. A fascinating though somewhat dated account of lobbying in Canada is John Sawatsky, *The Insiders: Government, Business, and the Lobbyists* (Toronto: McClelland & Stewart, 1987).
86. Office of the Commissioner of Lobbying of Canada, "Report on Investigation: The Lobbying Activities of Keith Beardsley," at: <ocl-cal.gc.ca/eic/site/012.nsf/eng/h_00619.html#ToC>.
87. All of this data may be found under "Lobbying Statistics" at the website of the Office of the Commissioner of Lobbying of Canada, at: <ocl-cal.gc.ca>.

13 The Media

1. Neil Postman, *Amusing Ourselves to Death: Public Discourse in the Age of Show Business* (New York: Penguin, 1985).
2. Henry Commager, ed., *Documents of American History*, 8th edn (New York: Appleton, Century, Crofts, 1968), 104.
3. Walter Lippmann, *Public Opinion* (New York: Harcourt, Brace and Company, 1922), 13.
4. Thomas Carlyle, *On Heroes and Hero-Worship in History*, "Lecture V. The Hero as a Man of Letters: Johnson, Rousseau, Burns," 19 May 1840, at: <www.gutenberg.org/files/1091/1091-h/1091-h.htm#link2H_4_0006>.
5. See Bureau of Broadcast Measurement data, at: <www.bbm.ca/en/top_programs.html>.
6. "ITAC Media Choice & Trust Poll," at: <www.itac.ca>.
7. Edward Herman and Noam Chomsky, *Manufacturing Consent* (New York: Pantheon, 1988), 8.
8. Canadian Media Research, "Even in the Digital Era, Canadians Have Confidence in Mainstream News Media," 11 May 2011, at: <journalism.ubc.ca/files/2011/05/CMRC_Trust_Report_11_May.pdf>.
9. Canada Results: 2013 Edelman Trust Barometer, slides 11 and 14, at: <fr.slideshare.net/EdelmanInsights/canada-results-2013-edelman-trust-barometer>.
10. Communications Management Inc., Sixty Years of Daily Newspaper Circulation Trends: Canada, United States, United Kingdom, 6 May 2011, pp. 6, 9, at: <media-cmi.com/downloads/Sixty_Years_Daily_Newspaper_Circulation_Trends_050611.pdf>.
11. Canadian Media Research, Trends in TV and Internet Use, July 2011, p. 13, at: <www.omdc.on.ca/Assets/Research/Research+Reports/Trends+in+TV+and+Internet+Use/Trends+in+TV+and+Internet+Use_en.pdf>.
12. This and all other data reported in this paragraph are found in Oriella PR Network, *Global Digital Journalism Study* 2013, at:<www.oriellaprnetwork.com/sites/default/files/research/Brands2Life_ODJS_v4.pdf>.
13. Lippmann, *Public Opinion*, 345.
14. Quoted in Todd Gitlin, *Inside Prime Time* (New York: Pantheon, 1983), 253.
15. Edward Jay Epstein, *News from Nowhere: Television and the News* (New York: Random House, 1973).
16. See "Self Censorship: How Often and Why," Pew Center for the People and the Press, 30 Apr. 2000, at: <www.people-press.org/2000/04/30/self-censorship-how-often-and-why/>.
17. Canada, *Royal Commission on Newspapers, Report* (1981).
18. Ken Goldstein, "Don't Blame the Papers: The Declining Political Influence of the Printed Press," 20 June 2011, at: <www.opendemocracy.net>.
19. See the discussions in Frank Peers, *The Politics of Broadcasting 1920–1951* (Toronto: University of Toronto Press, 1969); Marc Raboy, *Missed Opportunities: The Story of Canada's Broadcasting Policy* (Montreal and Kingston: McGill-Queen's University Press, 1990).
20. Task Force on Broadcasting, *Report*, 433.
21. Marsha Lederman, "TV's New Equation: Content

Bonanza Meets Revenue Crisis," *Globe and Mail*, 15 June 2013, accessed online.

22. Laura Payton, "One-third of Canadians Watch TV Online, CRTC Says," CBC News, 26 Sept. 2013, accessed online.

23. Morris Wolfe, *Jolts: The TV Wasteland and the Canadian Oasis* (Toronto: James Lorimer, 1985), 18.

24. Richard DeGrandpre, *Ritalin Nation: Rapid-fire Culture and the Transformation of Human Consciousness* (New York: W.W. Norton, 1999). Other researchers, beginning with the French otolaryngologist Alfred Tomatis and his patient and later colleague, Guy Bérard, have shown that ADD and similar problems are related to a hearing deficit in frequency. See especially Guy Bérard and Sally Brockett, *Hearing Equals Behavior: Expanded and Updated* (Manchester Center, VT: Shires Press, 2011); Laurna Tallman, *Hemispheric Integration and the Ears: A Scientific and Inclusive Paradigm of Human Behaviour including the Mild and Severe Forms of Mental Illness* (Marmora, Ont.: Northern Light Books, 2011).

25. American Academy of Pediatrics, at: <pediatrics .aappublications.org/content/128/5/1040.full>.

26. Epstein, *News from Nowhere*, 263.

27. Ibid., 262.

28. Ibid.

29. Nicholas Carr, "Is Google Making Us Stupid? What the Internet Is Doing to Our Brains," *The Atlantic* (July–Aug. 2008). See also Nicholas Carr, *The Shallows: What the Internet Is Doing to Our Brains* (New York: W.W. Norton, 2010).

30. Pew Project for Excellence in Journalism, 2010 report, at: <www.stateofthemedia.org>.

31. Mark Glaser, "Distinction between Bloggers, Journalists Blurring More Than Ever," 28 Feb. 2008, at: <www.pbs .org; http://www.pbs.org/mediashift/2008/02/distinction -between-bloggers-journalists-blurring-more-than -ever059/>.

32. Stanley Rothman and S. Robert Lichter, "Personality, Ideology and World View: A Comparison of Media and Business Elites," *British Journal of Political Science* 15, 1 (1984): 36.

33. Ibid., 46. See also S. Robert Lichter, *The Media Elite* (New York: Hastings House, 1990).

34. Pew Research Center Project for Excellence in Journalism, *The State of the News Media 2008: Journalists Report* (Washington: Pew Research Center, 2008), 18–19, at: <www.stateofthemedia.org/files/2011/01/Journalist -report-2008.pdf>.

35. Barry Cooper, *Sins of Omission: Shaping the News at CBC TV* (Toronto: University of Toronto Press, 1994), xi.

36. Ibid., 227.

37. Lydia Miljan and Barry Cooper, *Hidden Agendas: How the Beliefs of Canadian Journalists Influence the News* (Vancouver: University of British Columbia Press, 2003).

38. Blake Andrew, Antonia Maioni, and Stuart Soroka, "Just When You Thought It Was Out, Policy Is Pulled Back In," *Policy Options* (Mar. 2006): 74–9.

39. Leon Epstein, *Political Parties in Western Democracies* (New York: Praeger, 1967), 237.

40. Jay Rosen, "Audience Atomization Overcome: Why the Internet Weakens the Authority of the Press," at *Jay Rosen's PressThink*: <pressthink.org/2009/01/audience -atomization-overcome-why-the-internet-weakens-the -authority-of-the-press/>.

41. Ibid.

42. Aldous Huxley, *Brave New World Revisited* (New York: Harper & Brothers, 1958), 44.

43. Ipsos Reid poll conducted between 14–19 December 2011 and 28 May–4 June 2012, on behalf of Postmedia News and Global Television.

44. The term is used by Herman and Chomsky in their analysis of the political role of the American media. They, in turn, borrow it from Walter Lippmann, who had in mind, however, government's use of propagandistic techniques to cultivate popular acceptance of their rule.

45. A more typical assessment is that of Jeremy Hsu in a 2013 issue of *Scientific American*: <www.scientific- american.com/article.cfm?id=radioactive-water-leaks -from-fukushima>.

46. L'Express, 1 July 2013, at: <www.lexpress.fr/emploi -carriere/emploi/david-suzuki-le-rechauffement -climatique-rend-le-canada-vulnerable_1259426 .html#qlKX0FBTKUo4KM4U.99> (my translation).

Part V Contemporary Issues in Canadian Political Life

14 Language Politics

1. Hugh MacLennan, *Two Solitudes* (Toronto: New Canadian Library, 2008 [1945]).

2. Information on mother tongue was first collected with the census of 1931. Before then, the census only asked about ethnic origin. Demographer Jacques Henripin suggests that French ethnic origin was probably a good surrogate measure for language group at the time of Confederation.

3. In fact, Jacques Henripin predicted that over 40 per cent of Montrealers would be anglophone by 2001. This prediction was based on census data from 1971. See *L'Immigration et le déséquilibre linguistique* (Ottawa: Main d'oeuvre et immigration, 1974), 31, tableau 4.7.

4. Henripin estimated that at the rate of decline experienced in the early 1970s, Quebec would still be 77 per cent French-speaking by 2001.

5. Richard Joy, *Languages in Conflict* (Toronto: McClelland & Stewart, 1972), 58, Table 25.

6. Roger Bernard, *Le choc des nombres* (Ottawa: Université d'Ottawa, 1990).

7. Jacques Henripin, "The 1986 Census: Some Enduring Trends Abate," *Language and Society* 24 (Fall 1988): 8–9.

8. The first experience with immersion education was in 1975 in St Lambert, Quebec.

9. Jean-François Lepage and Jean-Pierre Corbeil, "The Evolution of English–French Bilingualism in Canada from 1961 to 2011," Statistics Canada (May 2013), at: <www.statcan.gc.ca/pub/75-006-x/2013001/article/11795-eng.pdf>.

10. All of the statistics in this paragraph are from ibid.

11. See Peter C. Waite, *Pre-Confederation* (Toronto: Prentice-Hall, 1965), 54–5.

12. Louis Hemon, *Maria Chapdelaine*, trans. Sir Andrew Macphail (Toronto: Oxford University Press, 1921), 212–13.

13. Henri Bourassa, *La langue, guardienne de la foi* (Montréal: Bibliothèque de l'action française, 1918).

14. Henri Bourassa, "The French Language and the Future of Our Race," in Ramsay Cook, ed., *French Canadian Nationalism* (Toronto: Macmillan, 1969), 133.

15. Marcel Rioux, "Sur l'evolution des ideologies au Quebec," English translation in Richard Schultz et al., eds, *The Canadian Political Process*, 3rd edn (Toronto: Holt, Rinehart and Winston, 1979), 99–102.

16. Denis Monière, *Ideologies in Quebec* (Toronto: University of Toronto Press, 1981), esp. ch. 2.

17. These voices included such figures as Gonzalve Doutre, Errol Bouchette, and Olivar Asselin, and the activities of the Institut Canadien.

18. F.H. Leacy, ed., *Historical Statistics of Canada* (Ottawa: Supply and Services Canada, 1983), R1–22, R81–97.

19. The numbers were about 390,000 in manufacturing compared to 249,000 in agriculture. The figure for the agricultural labour force counts only males.

20. Quoted by Pierre Trudeau in "Quebec on the Eve of the Asbestos Strike," in Cook, ed., *French Canadian Nationalism*, 35–6.

21. Victor Barbeau, *Mesure de notre taille* (1936); Barbeau, *Avenir de notre bourgeoisie* (Montréal: Editions de l'action canadienne française, 1939); Jacques Melançon, "Retard de croissance de l'entreprise canadienne-francaise," *L'actualité économique* (jan.–mars 1956): 503–22.

22. Rioux, "Sur l'évolution," 105–8.

23. Ibid., 105.

24. René Lévesque, *An Option for Quebec* (Toronto: McClelland & Stewart, 1968), 14.

25. See Melançon, "Retard de croissance."

26. Lois du Quebec, 1974, c. 6.

27. Lois du Quebec, 1977, c. 5.

28. See sections 23–29.1 of the Charter of the French Language, at: <www2.publicationsduquebec.gouv.qc.ca/dynamicSearch/telecharge.php?type=2&file=/C_11/C11_A.html>.

29. *Ford v. Attorney General of Quebec*, [1988] 2 S.C.R. 712.

30. Charter of the French Language, s. 58.

31. Charter of the French Language, s. 73.

32. See the discussion of these economic initiatives in Kenneth McRoberts, *Quebec: Social Change and Political Crisis*, 3rd edn (Toronto: McClelland & Stewart, 1988), 132–5.

33. Eric Waddell, "State, Language and Society: The Vicissitudes of French in Quebec and Canada," in Alan Cairns and Cynthia Williams, eds, *The Politics of Gender, Ethnicity and Language in Canada*, vol. 34 of the research studies for the Royal Commission on the Economic Union and Development Prospects for Canada (Toronto: University of Toronto Press, 1985), 97.

34. Raymond Breton, "The Production and Allocation of Symbolic Resources: An Analysis of the Linguistic and Ethnocultural Fields in Canada," *Canadian Review of Sociology and Anthropology* 21, 2 (1984): 129.

35. Commissioner of Official Languages, *Annual Report 1985* (Ottawa: Supply and Services Canada, 1986), 50.

36. Office of the Commissioner of Official Languages, *Making it Real: Promoting Respectful Co-Existence of the Two Official Languages at Work*, Apr. 2005, at: <www.ocol-clo.gc.ca/html/stu_etu_042005_e.php>; Office of the Commissioner of Official Languages, Annual Report, 2012–2013, section 2, at: <www.ocol-clo.gc.ca/html/ar_ra_2012_13_e.php#section_2>.

37. Commissioner of Official Languages, *Annual Report 2009–10*, at: <www.ocol-clo.gc.ca/html/ar_ra_2009_10_e.ph>.

38. *Attorney General of Manitoba v. Forest* (1979), 101 D.L.R. (3d) 385; *Reference re Language Rights under the Manitoba Act, 1870* (No. 1) (1985), 19 D.L.R. (4th) 1.

39. *Attorney General of Quebec v. Quebec Protestant School Boards* (1984), 10 D.L.R. (4th) 321; *Ford v. Attorney General of Quebec*.

40. These figures are from the annual reports of Commissioner of Official Languages.

41. Commissioner of Official Languages, *Annual Report 1985*, 172.

42. Statistics Canada, *Use of English and French at Work*, Catalogue no. 96F0030XIE2001011 (Ottawa, Feb. 2003).

43. Waddell, "State, Language and Society," 101; Sharon Lapkin, ed., *French as Second Language Education in Canada: Recent Empirical Studies* (Toronto: University of Toronto Press, 1998); Sheryl Ubelacher, "Few Chances to Use French Immersion Skills," *Toronto Star*, 4 Dec. 2007.

44. Commissioner of Official Languages, *Annual Report, 2012–2013*, s. 4.2.

45. Richard Simeon and David Elkins, "Regional Political Cultures in Canada," *Canadian Journal of Political Science* 7, 3 (1974): 397–437.

46. Michael Ornstein, "Regionalism and Canadian Political Ideology," in Robert Brym, ed., *Regionalism in Canada* (Toronto: Irwin, 1986), 78.

47. Ibid., 66, Table 2.

48. David McGrane and Loleen Berdahl, "'Small Worlds' No More: Reconsidering Provincial Political Cultures in Canada," *Regional and Federal Studies* 23, 4 (2013): 479–93.

49. Ipsos, 3 July 2008, at: <www.ipsos-na.com/news-polls/pressrelease.aspx?id=3989>.

50. See <www.uni.ca/curriculum.html>. Also "Whose History for Whose Future?" Sixth Biennial Conference on the Teaching and Learning of History, Quebec City, 24–6 Oct. 2008.

51. Québec, Commission sur l'avenir politique et constitutionnel du Québec, *Rapport* (Québec, 1991), 17.

52. Ibid.

53. "Survey: 30 Years after the 1980 Referendum, Quebeckers Believe That Issue Is Outmoded," 18 May 2010, at: <www.ideefederal.ca>.

54. CBC News, "Anglophones Wary of PQ Government, Poll Suggests," 18 Feb. 2013.

55. David Olive, "Good Reasons Marois's Parti Quebecois Was Hurled from Office: Olive," *Toronto Star*, 7 Apr. 2014, at: <www.thestar.com/business/2014/04/07/good_reasons_pauline_maroiss_parti_quebecois_was_hurled_from_office_olive/html>.

56. CRIC Quebec Youth Survey.

15 Women and Politics

1. See Kristina Zosuls et al., "Gender Development Research in Sex Roles: Historical Trends and Future Directions," *Sex Roles: A Journal of Research* 64, 11–12 (June 2011): 826–42.

2. Nellie McClung, "Hardy Perennials," in McClung, *In Times Like These* (Toronto: University of Toronto Press, 1972), 43–58.

3. Simone de Beauvoir, *The Second Sex*, trans. H.M. Parshley (London: Jonathan Cape, 1970), 273.

4. E.E. Maccoby and C.N. Jacklin, *The Psychology of Sex Differences* (Stanford, CA: Stanford University Press, 1974).

5. *Scientific American Mind*, "Special Issue: Male vs. Female Brains," May–June 2010, at: <bama.ua.edu/~sprentic/101%20SAMind%202010-May-June%20issue.pdf>.

6. Margaret Mead, *Sex and Temperament in Three Primitive Societies* (New York: Dell, 1969 [1935]), 260.

7. Margaret Mead, *Male and Female* (New York: William Morrow, 1950), 191–2.

8. John Stuart Mill, *On the Subjugation of Women* (1869), at: <www.fordham.edu/halsall/mod/jsmill-women.html>.

9. Ibid.

10. Friedrich Engels, *The Origin of Family, Private Property and the State* (1884), at: <www.marxists.org/archive/marx/works/1884/origin-family/index.htm#intro>.

11. 2012 Catalyst Census of Women Corporate Officers and Top Earners of the FP500 in Canada (Toronto: Catalyst Canada, Feb. 2013).

12. An interesting cross-national study is Emily Guynan, "The Gender Gap in Political Knowledge: A Comparison of Political Knowledge Levels In the United States, Canada, and Great Britain," MA thesis, Louisiana State University, 2004, at: <etd.lsu.edu/docs/available/etd-04082004-150047/unrestricted/Guynan_thesis.pdf>.

13. Sylvia Bashevkin, *Toeing the Lines* (Toronto: University of Toronto Press, 1985).

14. See the literature review in Pat Armstrong and Hugh Armstrong, *The Double Ghetto: Canadian Women and Their Segregated Work*, 3rd edn (Toronto: McClelland & Stewart, 1994), 182–9.

15. Statistics Canada, *Families, Living Arrangements and Unpaid Work*, "Time Spent on Unpaid Care of a Child in the Household, by Working Arrangement and Age of Youngest Child, 2010," Dec. 2011, Table 6, at: <www.statcan.gc.ca/pub/89-503-x/2010001/article/11546/c-g/c-g007-eng.htm>.

16. Ibid, "Average Number of Hours per Week of Domestic Work, by Age of Youngest Child in the Household, 2010," Chart 7.

17. Marie Drolet, "Why Has the Gender Wage Gap Narrowed?" Statistics Canada, *Perspectives on Labour and Income*, Spring 2011, at: <www.statcan.gc.ca/pub/75-001-x/2011001/pdf/11394-eng.pdf>.

18. Elizabeth Goodyear-Grant, "Crafting a Public Image: Women MPs and the Dynamics of Media Coverage," in Sylvia Baskevkin, ed., *Are Doors Opening Wider? Studies of Women's Political Engagement in Canada* (Vancouver: University of British Columbia Press, 2009), 147–66.

19. Louise Carbert, "Are Cities More Congenial? Tracking the Rural Deficit of Women in the House of Commons," in Sylvia Baskevkin, ed., *Are Doors Opening Wider? Studies of Women's Political Engagement in Canada* (Vancouver: University of British Columbia Press, 2009), 70–90.

20. Sylvia Bashevkin, "When Do Outsiders Break In? Institutional Circumstances of Party Leadership Victories by Women in Canada," *Commonwealth and Comparative Politics* 48, 1 (2010): 72–90.

21. Sylvia Bashevkin, *Women, Power, Politics: The Hidden Story of Canada's Unfinished Democracy* (Don Mills, Ont.: Oxford University Press, 2009).

22. See Anthony Thomson, *The Making of Social Theory: Order, Reason, and Desire*, 2nd edn (Don Mills, Ont.: Oxford University Press, 2010), 54–5.

23. Sheila Rowbotham, *Hidden from History* (London: Pluto Press, 1974), 47.

24. Terry Copp, *Anatomy of Poverty* (Toronto: McClelland & Stewart, 1974), 43.

25. The statement was made by Montreal's Chief Inspector of Factories in the late 1800s. Quoted ibid., 49.

26. Nellie McClung, "Hardy Perennials," in McClung, *In Times Like These* (Toronto: University of Toronto Press, 1972), 56.

27. See the discussion in Penney Kome, *Women of Influence* (Toronto: Doubleday Canada, 1985), ch. 2.

28. Quoted ibid., 32.

29. This was the title of a retrospective article that Macphail wrote in 1949, after having served five terms as an MP for Ontario's South Grey constituency.

30. Quoted in Bashevkin, *Toeing the Lines*, 16.

31. McClung, "Hardy Perennials," 48.

32. See, for example, Bashevkin, *Toeing the Lines*, 20–3.

33. Catherine L. Cleverdon, *The Woman Suffrage Movement in Canada* (Toronto: University of Toronto Press, 1974), 98, 114, 204.

34. The terms "hard-core" and "soft-core" feminism were first used by William O'Neill in *Everyone Was Brave: A History of Feminism in America* (New York: Quadrangle, 1971).

35. Deborah Gorhan, "Flora MacDonald Denison: Canadian Feminist," in Linda Kealey, ed., *A Not Unreasonable*

Claim: Women and Reform in Canada (Toronto: Women's Press, 1979), 47–70.

36. Joan Sangster, "The Role of Women in the Early CCF," in Linda Kealey and Joan Sangster, eds, *Beyond the Vote: Canadian Women and Politics* (Toronto: University of Toronto Press, 1989), 127.

37. Beauvoir, *The Second Sex*, ch. 2; Germaine Greer, *The Female Eunuch* (Nylesbury, UK: Hazel Watson and Viney, 1970); Betty Friedan, *The Feminine Mystique* (New York: Norton, 1963), ch. 5; Kate Millett, *Sexual Politics* (Garden City, NY: Doubleday, 1970).

38. A. Richard Allen, "Social Gospel," in *The Canadian Encyclopedia*, 2nd edn (Edmonton: Hurtig, 1988), vol. 3, 2026.

39. See Richard Allen, *The Social Passion* (Toronto: University of Toronto Press, 1971).

40. Nellie McClung, "Women and the Church," in McClung, *In Times Like These*, 67–79.

41. Friedan, *The Feminine Mystique*.

42. Ibid., 32.

43. Armstrong and Armstrong, *The Double Ghetto*, 42–3.

44. The ratio of males to females in universities was 5:1 in 1920, 3.1:1 in 1960, and 1.8:1 in 1970. Today, more females than males are enrolled in university undergraduate programs.

45. Anne Firor Scott, *Making the Invisible Woman Visible* (Urbana: University of Illinois Press, 1984).

46. See Kealey and Sangster, eds, *Beyond the Vote*.

47. Ibid.

48. Judy Rebick, "Fighting Racism," *Feminist Action* 6, 2 (June 1992).

49. See Leslie Grimard, "The Feminine Mystique at Fifty: Time for a New Feminism," *Public Discourse*, 7 Mar. 2013, at: <www.thepublicdiscourse.com/2013/03/9230/>.

50. Barbara Frum, "Why There Are So Few Women in Ottawa," *Chatelaine* 44 (Oct. 1971): 33, 110.

51. Bashevkin, *Toeing the Lines*, 110–19.

52. See the summaries of landmark judgments in National Action Committee on the Status of Women, *Women and Legal Action* (Oct. 1984), 8–27.

53. This was true in *Murdoch* (1973), *Canard* (1975), and *Bliss* (1979).

54. Michael Mandel, *The Charter of Rights and the Legalization of Politics in Canada* (Toronto: Wall and Thompson, 1995), 389–99.

55. *Re Casagrande and Hinton Roman Catholic Separate School District* (1987), 38 D.L.R. (4th) 382.

56. Canadian Advisory Council on the Status of Women, *Canadian Charter and Equality Rights for Women: One Step Forward or Two Steps Back?* (Sept. 1989), 19.

57. *Hunter v. Southam* (1984); *R. v. Big M Drug Mart* (1985).

58. *Edwards Books and Art Ltd. et al. v. The Queen* (1986), 30 C.C.C. (3d) 385.

59. Quoted in F.L. Morton, Rainer Knopff, and Peter Russell, *Federalism and the Charter* (Ottawa: Carleton University Press, 1989), 483.

60. *Alberta Labour Reference* (1987).

61. *Law Society of British Columbia v. Andrews and Kinersley*, [1989] 1 S.C.R. 143.

62. Christopher P. Manfredi, *Judicial Power and the Charter: Canada and the Paradox of Liberal Constitutionalism*, 2nd edn (Don Mills, Ont.: Oxford University Press, 2001), 123–4.

63. See the abridged text of the ruling in Morton et al., *Federalism and the Charter*, 582–603.

64. Penney Kome, *The Taking of Twenty-Eight: Women Challenge the Constitution* (Toronto: Women's Press, 1983).

65. Jacquetta Newman and Linda Smith, *Women, Politics and Public Policy* (Don Mills, Ont.: Oxford University Press, 2006), 133–44.

66. Cheryl Collier, "Neo-liberalism and Violence against Women: Can Retrenchment Convergence Explain the Path of Provincial Anti-Violence Policy, 1985–2005?" *Canadian Journal of Political Science* 41, 1 (2008): 19–42.

67. Kome, *The Taking of Twenty-Eight*.

68. A list and summaries of cases involving women's rights may be found at the website of LEAF: <leaf.ca/legal-issues-cases-and-law-reform/search-cases/>.

69. Kome, *Women of Influence*, 93.

70. Status of Women Canada, "A Brief History of GBA+," at: <www.swc-cfc.gc.ca/gba-acs/history-histoire-eng.html>.

71. Sue Findlay, "Facing the State: The Politics of the Women's Movement Reconsidered," in Heather Jon Maroney and Meg Luxton, eds, *Feminism and Political Economy: Women's Work, Women's Struggles* (Toronto: Methuen, 1987); Sandra Burt, "Organized Women's Groups and the State," in William D. Coleman and Grace Skogstad, eds, *Policy Communities and Public Policy in Canada: A Structural Approach* (Toronto: Copp Clark Pitman, 1990).

72. Dorothy McBride Stetson, ed., *Abortion Politics, Women's Movements and the Democratic State: A Comparative Study of State Feminism* (Oxford: Oxford University Press, 2001); Alexandra Dobrowolsky, *The Politics of Pragmatism: Women, Representation and Constitutionalism in Canada* (Don Mills, Ont.: Oxford University Press, 2000).

73. Pal, *Interests of State*, ch. 10.

74. Sylvia Bashevkin, "Free Trade and Canadian Feminism: The Case of the National Action Committee on the Status of Women," *Canadian Public Policy* 15, 4 (1989): 363–75.

75. Janine Brodie, "We Are All Equal Now: Contemporary Gender Politics in Canada," *Feminist Theory* 9, 2 (2008): 145–64.

76. TD Economics, "An Overview of Canada's Labour Market from the NHS," 5 July 2013, at: <www.td.com/document/PDF/economics/special/OverviewOfCanadasLabourMarket.pdf>.

77. Catalyst, "Canada's 'Best and Brightest' Women Face Gaps in Pay, Opportunity, New Catalyst Report Finds," 3 Dec. 2013.

78. Statistics Canada, "Table 282-0072: Labour Force Survey Estimates (LFS), Wages of Employees by Type of Work, North American Industry Classification System (NAICS), Sex and Age Group," CANSIM (2014).

79. Catalyst, "Women on Corporate Boards in Canada," at: <www.catalyst.org/catalyst-accord-women-corporate-boards-canada>.

80. Moya Greene, "Remarks for the HSBC Women of Influence Luncheon Series," *Metro Toronto Convention Centre*, 28 Sept. 2007.

81. Daniel Indiviglio, "Why Working Mothers Fall Behind," *The Atlantic* (online edition), 4 Aug. 2010.

82. Thomson Reuters Foundation, "Canada Best G20 Country To Be a Woman, India Worst—TrustLaw Poll," 13 June 2012, at: <www.trust.org/item/?map=poll-canada-best-g20-country-to-be-a-woman-india-worst/>.

83. United Nations, UNdata, at: <data.un.org/DocumentData.aspx?q=HDI+&id=332>.

16 Aboriginal Politics

1. The National Aboriginal Economic Development Board, *The Aboriginal Economic Benchmarking Report*, June 2012, p. 16, at: <www.naedb-cndea.com/wp-content/uploads/TheAboriginalEconomicBenchmarkingReport2.pdf>.

2. All of these statistics are from ibid. or from Employment and Social Development Canada, *Indicators of Well-Being in Canada*, at: <www4.hrsdc.gc.ca/.3ndic.1t.4r@-eng.jsp?iid=23>.

3. Chiefs of Ontario, "Disconcerting Use of the Term 'Aboriginal' Unveiled in Announcement of New Federal Cabinet," at: <www.chiefs-of-ontario.org/node/189>.

4. *Regina v. Howson* (1894), 1 Terr. L.R. 492 N.W.T. S.C. 494.

5. Peter A. Cumming and Neil H. Mickenberg, eds, *Native Rights in Canada* (Toronto: General Publishing, 1972), 9.

6. *Reference whether "Indians" includes "Eskimo,"* [1939] S.C.R. 104.

7. See John C. Kennedy, ed., *History and Renewal of Labrador's Inuit-Métis* (St. John's: ISER Books, 2014), esp. 1–37.

8. *Daniels v. Canada*, 2013 FC 6.

9. Sandro Contenta, "In Newfoundland, Too Many Want Recognition as Mi'kmaq Indians, Federal Government Says," *Toronto Star*, 5 May 2013, at: <www.thestar.com/news/insight/2013/05/05/in_newfoundland_too_many_want_recognition_as_mikmaq_indians_federal_government_says/html>.

10. Olive Patricia Dickason, with David T. McNab, *Canada's First Nations: A History of Founding Peoples from Earliest Times*, 4th edn (Don Mills, Ont.: Oxford University Press, 2009), 517, n. 27.

11. Indian and Northern Affairs Canada, *Resolving Aboriginal Claims*, 2003, p. 2, at: <www.aadnc-aandc.gc.ca/DAM/DAM-INTER-HQ/STAGING/texte-text/rul_1100100014175_eng.pdf>.

12. Harvey McCue, "Indian Reserve," *The Canadian Encyclopedia*, 2nd edn (Edmonton: Hurtig, 1988), vol. 2, 1056.

13. Cole Harris, *Making Native Space: Colonialism, Resistance, and Reserves in British Columbia* (Vancouver: University of British Columbia Press, 2002), 291–2.

14. Statistics Canada, *Aboriginal Languages in Canada*, Figure 2, at: <www12.statcan.gc.ca/census-recensement/2011/as-sa/98-314-x/98-314-x2011003_3-eng.cfm>.

15. For a valuable discussion of Aboriginal languages in contemporary Canada, see James S. Frideres, *First Nations in the Twenty-First Century* (Don Mills, Ont.: Oxford University Press, 2011), ch. 6.

16. G.F.G. Stanley, « The First Indian 'Reserves' in Canada, » *Revue d'histoire de l'Amérique française* (1950): 168, 209–10.

17. Francis Parkman, *The Jesuits in North America in the Seventeenth Century* (Toronto: George N. Morang, 1907 [1867]), 131.

18. Quoted in Royal Commission on Aboriginal Peoples, *Report*, vol. 2, *Restructuring the Relationship* (Ottawa, 1996), 531–2.

19. Harold Cardinal, *The Unjust Society* (Edmonton: Hurtig, 1969), 1.

20. Mary Hurley, "Aboriginal Self-Government," 15 Dec. 2009, at: <www.parl.gc.ca/content/lop/researchpublications/prb0923-e.htm>.

21. Indian leader James Gosnell, quoted in Michael Asch, *Home and Native Land: Aboriginal Rights and the Canadian Constitution* (Vancouver: University of British Columbia Press, 1993), 29.

22. *Delgamuukw v. British Columbia*, [1997] 3 S.C.R. 1010 at para. 128.

23. Ibid., para. 122.

24. Quoted in Melvin H. Smith, *Our Home or Native Land?* (Toronto: Stoddart, 1995), 143.

25. Georges Erasmus and Joe Sanders, "Canadian History: An Aboriginal Perspective," in Diane Engelstad and John Bird, eds, *Nation to Nation: Aboriginal Sovereignty and the Future of Canada* (Concord, Ont.: House of Anansi Press, 1992), 6.

26. Ibid., 8.

27. Quoted in Cumming and Mickenberg, eds, *Native Rights in Canada*, 17.

28. Ibid., 18.

29. Quoted in David De Brou and Bill Waiser, eds, *Documenting Canada: A History of Modern Canada in Documents* (Saskatoon: Fifth House Publishers, 1992), 572.

30. Ibid.

31. Ibid., 665.

32. Ibid., 666.

33. *Tsilhqot'in Nation v. British Columbia*, 2014 SCC 44 at para. 38.

34. Ibid., para. 76.

35. *Delgamuukw v. British Columbia*, para. 83.

36. Ibid., para. 86.

37. Cumming and Mickenberg, eds, *Native Rights in Canada*, 55.

38. Erasmus and Sanders, "Canadian History," 3.

39. Ibid., 4.

40. Quoted in Cumming and Mickenberg, eds, *Native Rights in Canada*, 61–2.

41. *Nowegijick v. The Queen*, [1983] 1 S.C.R. 29.

42. *R. v. Marshall*, [1999] 3 S.C.R. 456.

43. *R. v. Marshall*, 2005 SCC 43 (case no. 30063).

44. Sally Weaver, "The Joint Cabinet/National Indian Brotherhood Committee: A Unique Experiment in

Pressure Group Politics," *Canadian Public Administration* 25 (Summer 1982): 211–39.

45. J. Hugh Faulkner, "Pressuring the Executive," *Canadian Public Administration* 25 (Summer 1982): 248.

46. Ninth annual presidential address to the National Indian Brotherhood, Fredericton, New Brunswick, Sept. 1978.

47. Rick Ponting and Roger Gibbins, *Out of Irrelevance: A Socio-Political Introduction to Indian Affairs in Canada* (Toronto: Butterworths, 1980), 124.

48. Canadian Press, "Rival Meetings Hint at Aboriginal Divisions," 15 July 2013, at: <www.ipolitics.ca/2013/07/15/rival-meetings-hint-at-aboriginal-divisions/>.

49. Michael Woods, "Assembly of First Nations 'Does Not Have the Authority' to Negotiate Treaties with Government, Rival Group Charges," *National Post*, 11 July 2013, at: <news.nationalpost.com/2013/07/11/assembly-of-first-nations-does-not-have-the-authority-to-negotiate-treaties-with-government-rival-group-charges/>.

50. Gary Granzberg et al., "New Magic for Old: TV in Cree Culture," *Journal of Communication* 27, 4 (1977): 155–77; Gary Granzberg, "Television as Storyteller: The Algonkian Indians of Central Canada," *Journal of Communication* 32, 1 (1982): 43–52.

51. Treasury Board Secretariat of Canada, *Employment Equity in the Public Service of Canada, 2011–12*, Appendix A, Table 1, at: <www.tbs-sct.gc.ca/reports-rapports/ee/2011-2012/ee04-eng.asp#tocAppA>.

52. "Today's Letters: Ideas for Solving the 'Native Issue'," *National Post*, 14 Jan. 2013, at: <fullcomment.nationalpost.com/2013/01/14/todays-letters-ideas-for-solving-the-native-issue/>.

53. Ekos, *Survey of First Nations People Living Off-Reserve, Métis and Inuit*, conducted for Indian and Northern Affairs Canada, Oct. 2006, at: <knet.ca/documents/OFF_RESERVE_SURVEY_E1.pdf>.

54. Brian Lee Crowley and Ken Coates, "Rage and Rebirth: The Way Forward for First Nations," *iPolitics*, 19 Dec. 2012, at: <www.macdonaldlaurier.ca/mli%E2%80%99s-brian-lee-crowley-and-ken-coates-in-ipolitics-%E2%80%93-rage-and-rebirth-the-way-forward-for-first-nations/>.

55. Canadian Bar Association, National Aboriginal Law Section, Submission to the House of Commons Standing Committee on Aboriginal Affairs and Northern Development, Apr. 2013, p. 12, at: <www.cba.org/cba/sections_abor/PDF/13_21_eng.pdf>.

56. Testifying before the House of Commons Standing Committee on Aboriginal Affairs and Northern Development, 19 Nov. 2013, at: <www.parl.gc.ca/HousePublications/Publication.aspx?DocId=6309043&Language=E&Mode=1>.

57. AFN, Presentation to the House of Commons Standing Committee on Aboriginal Affairs and Northern Development, 18 Apr. 2013, at: <www.afn.ca/uploads/files/13-04-18_rc_jwr_remarks_to_aano_on_c-428.pdf>.

58. First Nations Property Ownership Initiative, at: <fnpo.ca/Proposal.aspx>.

59. A vigorous defence of these proposed reforms is offered by Chief Shane Gottfriedson, Commissioner of the FNPO Initiative, in his response to an editorial in *The Walrus*, "Losing the Land Again," at: <fnpo.ca/cmsuploads/2013-01-30_ltr_walrus.pdf>.

60. Ken Coates, *The Indian Act and the Future of Aboriginal Government in Canada*, Research Paper for the National Centre for First Nations Governance, May 2008, pp. 30–1, at: <fngovernance.org/ncfng_research/coates.pdf>.

17   Canada in the World

1. The idea that America and in particular its influence abroad are in decline has been popular over the past decade. Not everyone agrees. A summary of some of this debate may be found in Stephen Brooks, *American Exceptionalism in the Age of Obama* (New York: Routledge, 2013), ch. 1.

2. Mark Kingwell, "What Distinguishes Us from the Americans," *National Post*, 5 Mar. 2003, A16.

3. John Ralston Saul, *Reflections on a Siamese Twin: Canada at the End of the Twentieth Century* (Toronto: Penguin, 1997), 171.

4. One of these annual surveys is carried out by the New York-based consultancy firm, Reputation Institute, at: <www.reputationinstitute.com/thought-leadership/country-reptrak>.

5. BBC World Service Poll, "Views of China, India Slide While UK's Ratings Climb: Global Poll," at: <www.globescan.com/images/images/pressreleases/bbc2013_country_ratings/2013_country_rating_poll_bbc_globescan.pdf>.

6. CBC News, "How the World Sees Canada," 1 July 2012, at: <www.cbc.ca/news/canada/how-the-world-sees-canada-1.1130319>.

7. Published as Michael Ignatieff, "Canada in the Age of Terror: Multilateralism Meets a Moment of Truth," *Policy Options* (Feb. 2003), at: <www.irpp.org>.

8. Andrew Nikiforuk, "Oh Canada: How America's Friendly Northern Neighbor Became a Rogue, Reckless Petrostate," *Foreign Policy*, 1 July 2013, at: <www.foreignpolicy.com/articles/2013/06/24/oh_canada#sthash.bsh2C8NO.dpbs>.

9. John Trent, ed., *The United Nations and Canada: What Canada Has Done and Should Be Doing at the United Nations* (Ottawa: World Federalist Movement, 2013), 2, at: <www.worldfederalistscanada.org/documents/CanadaUNEng.pdf>.

10. Joe Clark, *How We Lead: Canada in a Century of Change* (Toronto: Random House, 2013), 23–4.

11. Jack Granatstein, "Harper's Foreign Policies have Made Canada a World Player," *National Post*, 30 Jan. 2012, at: <fullcomment.nationalpost.com/2012/01/30/jack-granatstein-harpers-foreign-policies-have-made-canada-a-world-player/>.

12. Anholt-GfK Nation Brands, Press Release, 14 Nov. 2013, at: <www.gfk.com/documents/press-releases/2013/20131114_nation-brand-index-2013.pdf>.

13. Cormex Media Lab, "Analysis of Global, English-language Newspaper Coverage of Canada's Bitumen Sands Resource for the Twelve Months Ending 31 March 2013," 30 Apr. 2013, at: <www.cormex.com/cormex/medialab_reports/Cormex_MediaLAB_APR2013_Oil_v_Tarsands.pdf>.

14. Coined by Harvard's Joseph Nye in 2003, "smart power" refers to a combination of hard- and soft-power strategies that does not eschew military power, but emphasizes institutions and processes, including national image-building, that are expected to give a country's policies more legitimacy in the eyes of others.

15. Pankaj Ghemawat with Steven A. Altman, *DHL Global Connectedness Index 2012*, Nov. 2012, at: <www.dhl.com/content/dam/flash/g0/gci_2012/download/dhl_gci_2012_complete_study.pdf>.

17. Swiss Federal Institute of Technology Zurich, KOF Index of Globalization, at: <globalization.kof.ethz.ch/>.

18. Robert Hunter, "Is Globalization Reducing Poverty and Inequality?" *World Development* 32, 4 (2004): 567–89; World Bank, *The State of the Poor: Where Are the Poor and Where Are They Poorest?* Apr. 2013, at: <www.worldbank.org/content/dam/Worldbank/document/State_of_the_poor_paper_April17.pdf>.

19. 2013 KOF Index of Globalization, at: <globalization.kof.ethz.ch/media/filer_public/2013/03/25/rankings_2013.pdf>.

20. Interbrand, List of most valuable global brands for 2013, at:<www.interbrand.com/en/best-global-brands/2013/Best-Global-Brands-2013-Brand-View.aspx>.

21. Pippa Norris and Ronald Inglehart, eds, *Cosmopolitan Communications: Cultural Diversity in a Globalized World* (Cambridge: Cambridge University Press, 2009), 5.

22. United Nations, Department of Economic and Social Affairs, *World Public Sector Report: Globalization and the State* (New York: UN, 2001).

23. Ibid., ch. 3.

24. British Columbia, BC Stats, "Exports and Imports–Data," at: <www.bcstats.gov.bc.ca/StatisticsBySubject/ExportsImports/Data.aspx>.

25. OECD, *Future Global Shocks: Improving Risk Governance* (Paris 2011), at: <www.oecd.org/governance/48256382.pdf>.

26. Renamed the Alliance of Manufacturers & Exporters Canada in 1996 and Canadian Manufacturers & Exporters in 2000.

27. Center for North American Studies, American University, *The NAFTA Promise and the North American Reality*, 31 Oct. 2013, slide 15, at: <www.american.edu/sis/cnas/upload/North-America-October-30-1255-pm-FULL-VERSION.pdf>.

28. Canadian-American Business Council, *Beyond the Canadian-American Border*, 20 Nov. 2012, p. 11, Figure 4.1, at: <abacusdata.ca/wp-content/uploads/2012/11/Can-AM_Report_CABC_Nov2012_FINAL.pdf>.

29. Alexander Moens and Nachum Gabler, *What Congress Thinks of Canada*, May 2011, Fraser Institute, pp. 1–2, at: <www.fraserinstitute.org/uploadedFiles/fraser-ca/Content/research-news/research/publications/whatcongressthinksofcanada.pdf>.

30. Allan Gotlieb, "Getting Attention," *National Post*, 17 May 2002, A17.

31. Allan Gotlieb, "A Grand Bargain with the U.S.," *National Post*, 5 Mar. 2003, A16.

32. Diane Francis, *Merger of the Century: Why Canada and America Should Become One Country* (Toronto: HarperCollins, 2013).

33. Council on Foreign Relations, *Building a North American Community* (New York: Council on Foreign Relations, 2005). This report was preceded by Robert Pastor's *Toward a North American Community: Lessons from the Old World for the New* (Washington: Peterson Institute, 2001).

34. Canadian International Council, *Open Canada: A Global Positioning Strategy for a Networked Age?* (Toronto: CIC, 2010), 18, at: <www.onlinecic.org/opencanada>.

35. Ibid., 21.

36. Ibid., 20.

36. For an interesting revisionist view of the Pearson legacy in foreign affairs, which takes to task those on the right (see Box 17.3) and those on the left for using Lester Pearson in support of their ideological stances, see Mark Neufeld, "'Happy Is the Land That Needs No Hero': The Pearsonian Tradition and the Canadian Intervention in Afghanistan," in J. Marshall Beier and Lana Wylie, eds, *Canadian Foreign Policy in Critical Perspective* (Don Mills, Ont.: Oxford University Press, 2010), 126–38.

37. Ignatieff, "Canada in the Age of Terror."

38. Ibid.

39. In *The Politics of Linkage: Power, Interdependence, and Ideas in Canada–US Relations* (Vancouver: University of British Columbia Press, 2009), Brian Bow examines four cases of conflict between the Canadian and American governments, explaining why, despite Canadian refusal to comply with the preferences of the US administration, Canada did not experience hard-power punishment.

40. President John F. Kennedy, "Speech to the Canadian Parliament," 17 May 1961, at: <www.presidency.ucsb.edu/ws/index.php?pid=8136>.

41. CBC News, "Professor Says Students Can't Identify Continents on Map," 15 Jan. 2013, at:<www.cbc.ca/news/canada/newfoundland-labrador/professor-says-students-can-t-identify-continents-on-map-1.1324022>.

The 2015 Canadian Election
Change and Continuity

In many ways, the 2015 Canadian election was quite remarkable. The party that began the campaign in first place in the public opinion polls, the NDP, finished a distant third. Its support in Quebec plunged almost as dramatically as it had risen in the 2011 election. The Liberal Party, whose performance in the 2011 election was weaker than at any point since Confederation, doubled its share of the popular vote and quadrupled its number of MPs to form a majority government. In the four Atlantic provinces, the Liberals won more than half the vote and every seat. The 78-day official election campaign—campaigning had in reality started long before the election was called—was about twice as long as usual and saw each of the three parties leading the polls at one point or another (see Figure 1). Just days before the election, most pollsters acknowledged that the outcome was still in doubt. Finally, so-called "strategic voting," where voters are encouraged to vote for the candidate who they think is most likely to be able

to defeat the candidate of the party that they absolutely do not want to win, was much discussed and, according to some accounts, more common than usual in the 2015 election.

In other respects, however, the election of 2015 was anything but remarkable. The victorious Liberal Party won a majority of seats on the strength of just under 40 per cent of the popular vote, as the Conservative Party had done in 2011. Indeed, 38 to 43 per cent of the popular vote has been enough for a party to form a majority government on eight occasions since the two-party duopoly of the Liberals and the Conservatives was broken in 1935.[1] The NDP returned to third-party status and won just under 20 per cent of the popular vote, numbers that have been fairly typical of its performance in federal elections for most of the past 50 years. The Liberals were once again the most successful party in Quebec, a status that the party has enjoyed in the vast majority of elections since 1896. The Conservative

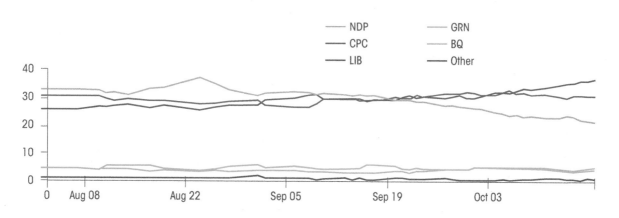

FIGURE 1 Poll Averages during the 2015 Canadian Election Campaign

Source: Adapted from Éric Grenier, "Éric Grenier's Poll Tracker" (Canadian Broadcasting Corporation, 18 Oct. 2015), at <http://www.cbc.ca/news2/interactives/poll-tracker/2015/>

Party's greatest strength was in western Canada, where it won 54 of its 99 seats, although its support in Manitoba and British Columbia was somewhat weaker than it had been in the last several elections.

So although the results of the 2015 election were described by the New York Times as a "stunning rout" in favour of the Liberals, and by Maclean's as an "epic victory" for the Liberal Party, in some important ways the election was a return to business as usual in Canadian party politics. At the same time, however, it was an election about change. Indeed, change was the overarching theme of the campaign, with the NDP and the Liberal Party promising to deliver both policies and a style of government different from those of the Conservatives under Prime Minister Harper, while the Conservatives argued that Canadians would be better off ignoring the siren song of change, particularly as the economy headed into turbulent waters. The fact that 218,787 fewer people voted for the Conservative Party in 2015 than in 2011, and that 4,160,101 more voted for the Liberals in 2015 than in 2011, seemed to indicate that the taste for change was more powerful than the Conservatives' message of trusted, proven leadership.

At some level, of course, elections are always about change versus more of the same. A governing party wants to hold onto power, and opposition parties want to defeat the governing party. The dynamic of the status quo versus change is built into this equation. But the changes proposed by the victorious Liberal Party were more sweeping than has often or even usually been the case in electoral contests between Canada's two historically dominant political parties. Indeed, it is arguable that the contrast between the Conservatives and the Liberals had not been as stark since the 1988 election, when the Conservatives supported the Canada–US Free Trade Agreement and the Liberal Party opposed it. On climate change, taxation and public finances, relations with Canada's Aboriginal communities, and national security, the Liberal Party took positions sharply different from those of the governing Conservatives and even outflanked the NDP on the left on the issues of taxation and government deficits. Moreover, the Liberal Party promised to replace Canada's single-member, simple plurality electoral system with some form of proportional representation, a commitment that Justin Trudeau had stuck to from his election as party leader.

As is usually the case in federal elections, the campaign was really two overlapping campaigns, one in Quebec and the other in the rest of Canada. This is not just a matter of the dominant language of the campaigning and media coverage being French in Quebec and English in the rest of the country. Nationalist sentiment in Quebec always ensures that the issues and how they are discussed will be rather different in that province. What appeared to be the possibility of a resurgent Bloc Québécois and the return of its former leader Gilles Duceppe reinforced this provincial difference. (For more on the campaign in Quebec and how it was distinctive, watch the interview with Dr Emmanuelle Richez that is part of this 2015 election update.)

The Results

The Liberal Party won 39.5 per cent of the popular vote and 184 of the seats in the expanded 338-seat House of Commons. As may be seen in Table 1, the Liberal Party was massively over-rewarded by Canada's single member, simple plurality electoral system in Atlantic Canada; it was also over-rewarded in Quebec, Ontario, Manitoba, and British Columbia. Other representations of the 2015 election results may be found on the very fine website maintained by Dr Andrew Heard of Simon Fraser University (https://www.sfu.ca/~aheard/elections/index.htm) and also on the website of Elections Canada (http://elections.ca/content.aspx?section=ele&document=index&dir=pas/42ge&lang=e).

The collapse of the NDP, which went into the election campaign as the official opposition and leading in the polls, was chiefly due to the erosion of the party's support in Quebec (see the interview with Dr Richez). The NDP went from 59 to 16 seats in Quebec. In the rest of Canada, the NDP's loss was considerably less. It fell from 44 seats outside Quebec in the 2011 election to 28 in 2015, almost all of this decline accounted for by a swing in the centre-left vote to the Liberals in Atlantic Canada and Ontario. The NDP's leader, Thomas Mulcair, held onto his own seat in the Montreal riding of Outremont and stayed on as the party's leader as the 42nd Parliament began.

Mulcair's Conservative Party counterpart, former prime minister Stephen Harper, also was victorious in his riding of Calgary Heritage. Unlike Mulcair, however, Harper immediately resigned as party leader and

TABLE 1 Percentage of Votes and Candidates Elected by Party and Province or Territory, 2015

Province	Liberal	Conservative	NDP	Green Party	Bloc Québécois	Others	Totals Province
NL	64.5	10.3	21.0	1.1	—	—	256,091
	7	0	0	0			7
NS	61.9	17.9	16.4	3.4	—	—	523,179
	11	0	0	0			11
NB	51.6	25.3	18.3	4.6	—	—	442,519
	10	0	0	0			10
PEI	58.3	19.3	16.0	6.0	—	—	87,468
	4	0	0	0			4
Que.	35.7	16.7	25.4	2.3	19.3	—	4,233,693
	40	12	16	0	10		78
Ont.	44.8	35.0	16.6	2.9	—	—	6,532,714
	80	33	8	0			121
Man.	44.6	37.3	13.8	3.2	—	—	601,024
	7	5	2	0			14
Sask.	23.9	48.5	25.1	2.1	—	—	551,914
	1	10	3	0			14
Alta.	24.6	59.5	11.6	2.5	—	—	1,929,197
	4	29	1	0			34
BC	35.2	30.0	25.9	8.2	—	—	2,350,701
	17	10	14	1			42
Yukon, NWT, and Nunavut	50.2	22.2	25.2	2.4	—	—	51,192
	3	0	0	0			3
Totals, Party	6,943,276	5,613,614	3,470,350	602,944	821,144	141,450	17,592,778
	184	99	44	1	10	0	338

*Rows may not add up to 100 per cent because of rounding and the omission of candidates other than those of the five parties listed in the table.
Source: Based on data from Elections Canada, "October 19, 2015: Election Results," at <http://enr.elections.ca/Provinces.aspx?lang=e>.

was soon replaced as interim leader of the Conservative Party by another Albertan, Rona Ambrose. In this role Ambrose was assisted by Denis Lebel, the party's deputy leader and its principal spokesperson in Quebec. Conservative support was weaker in every province in 2015 compared to the 2011 election. But most worrying for the Conservative Party, perhaps, was its dismal performance in the seat-rich region of the Greater Toronto Area (GTA). It won only 3 of the 47 seats in the GTA, the other 44 going to the Liberals. It also lost seats in the metropolitan areas of Ottawa and Vancouver, and even in its urban strongholds of Calgary and Edmonton.

The Bloc Québécois, which went into the 2015 election with only two MPs in the House of Commons, regained a bit of the ground that it had lost in 2011. It won 10 seats, compared to 4 in 2011, despite the fact

that its share of the popular vote actually fell a few percentage points. The BQ's leader, Gilles Duceppe, failed to win in his own riding and once again resigned.

Although most attention was focused on seat and vote totals in 2015, there was another statistic that was noteworthy. Voter turnout was up significantly from the 2011 election and was, in fact, higher than at any time since 1993 (see Figure 2). Whether this represents the beginning of a reversal in a decades-old trend of declining voter turnout, only time will tell. Much of the decline that has taken place over the past couple of decades has been due to lower rates of voting among younger voters, particularly those under the age of 30, compared to the rates for this age cohort in previous generations.[2] According to Elections Canada, turnout among first time voters was about 3 percentage points higher in 2015 than in 2011. Voter turnout was up among all age groups in 2015 compared to 2011, but most sharply among those aged 18–24 years (from about 39 per cent to roughly 57 per cent) and those aged 25–34 years (from 45 per cent to 57 per cent).

Why Did the Liberals Win, the Conservatives Lose, and the NDP Return to Third-Party Status?

Explanations for the outcome of the 2015 election are many and diverse. It was very clearly an election in which the campaign made a difference. All three main parties saw their poll numbers move up and down over the 78 days of the official campaign. Issues ranging from the state of the economy to how many Syrian refugees Canada should accept and how soon were addressed by the parties and were on the minds of voters. The leaders' performances in the televised debates may have made a difference—although the research on the impact of such debates suggests that they mainly reinforce pre-existing party preferences—and television advertising and social media, but particularly the former, surely had impacts on voters' perceptions of the

parties and their leaders.

The difficult part is determining which issues, ads, leaders' statements, social media interventions, or other features of the campaign made a difference. The mere fact that journalists, bloggers, popular tweeters, or other opinion leaders opined that a particular issue, ad, or leader's performance had an impact on voter support is, by itself, proof of nothing. This is why the Canadian Election Study (CES) exists! Since the first such study of the 1968 election, under the direction of Queen's University political scientist John Meisel, teams of researchers have carried out surveys of Canadian voters in an effort to better understand the factors that explain the political choices of individuals and the results of particular elections. The current research team consists of Patrick Fournier (Université de Montréal), Fred Cutler (University of British Columbia), Stuart Soroka (University of Michigan), and Dietlind Stolle (McGill University), with collaborators at several other universities in Canada and the United States (http://ces-eec.arts. ubc.ca/english-section/the-team/). The 2015 CES survey of a representative sample of Canadians is available online at https://ces-eec.arts.ubc.ca/english-section/surveys/.

In the meantime, some of Canada's most astute political scientists, pollsters, and journalists have provided their assessments of the campaign and the results in an online publication of the University of British

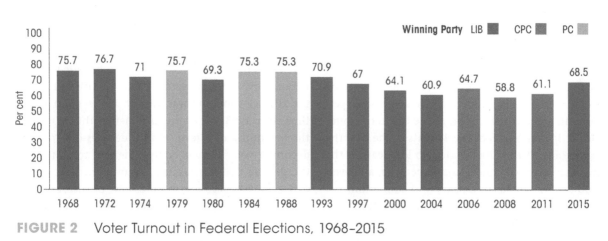

FIGURE 2   Voter Turnout in Federal Elections, 1968–2015

Source: Based on data from Elections Canada, "Voter Turnout at Federal Elections and Referendums," at <http://www.elections.ca/content. aspx?dir=turn&document=index&lang=e&section=ele>

Columbia Press that appeared just three weeks after the 19 October election: *Canadian Election Analysis 2015: Communication, Strategy, and Democracy*, edited by Alex Marland and Thierry Giasson (http://www.ubcpress.ca/CanadianElectionAnalysis2015). And if you are interested in my analysis of the 2015 election results, you can find it in the 15 November 2015 podcast "Economic Angst and Voting for Change in 2015," available on the companion website for your textbook (http://www.oupcanada.com/higher_education/companion/politics/9780199011155/student_resources.html).

Notes

1 I am not counting the 1921 federal election that saw the Progressive Party run candidates and emerge as the official opposition in the House of Commons, a rather unusual exception to the pre-1935 party system.

2 See Figure 2 in Andre Barnes and Erin Virgint, "Youth Voter Turnout in Canada: 1. Trends and Issues," Parliament of Canada, Legal and Legislative Affairs Division, 7 April 2010, revised 9 August 2013, at http://www.lop.parl.gc.ca/content/lop/researchpublications/2010-19-e.htm#a5.

The 2016 US Election
President Trump and the Future of Canada–US Relations

"Oh my God!" This was the headline on the front page of *Le Journal de Québec* the day after Donald Trump was rather surprisingly elected as the 45th president of the United States. Similar reactions were common around the world. "¡A temblar!" (Start Trembling) was the headline on the front page of Mexico City's *Excélsior*. "Er?!" (Him?!) was blazoned across the front of Vienna's *Kurier*. But the most creative combination of surprise and dismay may have appeared on the front page of a UK tabloid, *The Daily Mail*, which read, "Trumpquake."

The world's reaction to the widely unexpected election of Donald Trump was not universally negative. It was, however, overwhelmingly so. Much of this negativity was generated by Trump's words: his promise to build a wall along the US–Mexico border; his musings about barring Muslims from entering the United States; his description of NATO as obsolete and his statement that many of its members, as well as Japan, need to start paying for more of their own defense; and his promise to "tear up NAFTA" and walk away from the Trans-Pacific Partnership trade agreement. Some of the world's jittery and even fearful reactions to Trump's victory were due to his unorthodox style. "Diplomatic," "conciliatory," and "statesman-like" were words conspicuously absent from virtually all commentary on Trump's style and character until his rather measured victory speech in the wee hours of 9 November 2016 and his meeting with President Obama a day later.

More than most populations around the world, Canadians appeared to have reason to worry about a Trump presidency. During the campaign, Trump characterized NAFTA as "the worst trade deal in history." When asked about NAFTA two days after Trump's election, Prime Minister Trudeau described the trade agreement as "the longest and best trade deal in the history of the world." During his run for the White House, Trump had promised that, once sworn in as president, he would immediately begin the process of renegotiating better terms for the United States. If renegotiating did not quickly produce a better deal for the United States, Trump declared, he would kill NAFTA by invoking the article that enables a party to withdraw after six months notice. Experts were divided on whether President Trump would be able to withdraw without congressional approval.

Regardless of how the process would unfold, the consequences of an end to NAFTA would be enormous for Canada. Exports to the United States account for a large share of most provinces' GDP. The automotive and manufacturing industries of Ontario are joined at the hip with those of the American Midwest. The prosperity of British Columbia's lumber industry depends on exports to the American market. Every provincial economy has important trade ties to the United States and would experience both employment and public revenue consequences if the largely tariff-free regime that NAFTA created were to end.

It was not just trade agreements that caused some Canadians to lose sleep. Trump's fossil fuel-friendly policies guaranteed that the Keystone XL pipeline, blocked by the Obama administration, would be back on the table. Some Canadians looked forward to this while others saw it as a step backward. President Trump's promise to cancel US participation in the Paris Agreement on climate change was sharply at odds with the position of the Trudeau government and the views of most Canadians.

Policy differences aside, there was also the question of whether the general values and style of the Trump administration would damage Canada–US relations. The Liberal Party's 2015 victory ushered in what Prime Minister Trudeau described as a "bromance" between himself and President Obama. Most Canadians did not expect the same chemistry to exist between Prime Minister Trudeau and President Trump. "I'd be curious to know," said New Democratic Party MP Nathan Cullen in a 9 November 2016 interview, "what values President Trump and Prime Minister Trudeau share." Cullen added, "This is not anyone we've seen before in Canada–US relations. . . . He's a bully."

This begs the question of whether or not personal relationships between presidents and prime ministers matter when it comes to getting things done. Almost all of what has been written on this subject is not much better than anecdotal. Two days after Donald Trump's election victory, Prime Minister Trudeau was in Sydney, Nova Scotia, where he was asked how he would deal with a president who the questioner described as "racist, misogynist, and a bigot." Trudeau deftly avoided responding to this characterization of the man who received the votes of almost 60 million Americans by noting that the Canada–US relationship is much bigger and more longstanding than any person on either side of the border.

Trudeau was certainly right about this. Moreover, when candidate Trump railed against trade deals that were bad for America, he almost always mentioned China, Mexico, and Japan, in that order. Nevertheless, Canada was caught up in the wave of anti-trade sentiment that swept across the United States during the 2016 election cycle. Trump was not the only candidate to ride this wave. Bernie Sanders' remarkable run for the Democratic nomination for president made opposition to free trade one of the centrepieces of his campaign, and even Hillary Clinton felt compelled to distance herself from trade deals that she had supported before Sanders' unexpectedly vigorous challenge for the Democratic Party's presidential nomination. Protectionism was in fashion on both the right and the left during the 2016 US election campaign.

This was not unprecedented. Protectionist sentiment was running strong in the United States in the early 1980s, which was a key factor behind the decision of the Conservative government of Brian Mulroney to seek a free trade deal with the United States. During the 2008 primary campaign, both Hillary Clinton and Barack Obama promised to end NAFTA if it could not be renegotiated to better serve the interests of American workers and companies. "I think we should use the hammer of a potential opt-out as leverage," said then Senator Obama, "to ensure that we actually get labour and environmental standards that are enforced."

Threats to walk away from NAFTA, or at least to insist on major reforms, have also come from the Canadian side of the border. In the 1993 federal election campaign, the Liberal Party leader Jean Chrétien promised that, under his government, NAFTA, which had not yet been ratified, would be renegotiated to better serve Canadian interests. As was true of Clinton and Obama's threats and promises in 2008, nothing came of this campaign rhetoric.

"America First" was the campaign slogan that Donald Trump embraced when he laid out his foreign policy goals in April 2016. Whether the wave of protectionism that he encouraged and endorsed during his successful presidential campaign will result in a major reversal of the tide of trade liberalization—a hallmark of globalization—is doubtful. There are too many powerful economic interests in the United States and abroad that depend on a world in which national barriers to the movement of capital and jobs have come down. At the same time, however, national governments and political leaders ignore at their peril the votes of those who have been left behind by free trade. These votes help to explain Donald Trump's 2016 victory, Britain's decision to leave the European Union, and the rise of populist resentment toward political elites across much of the democratic world.

Canadians are not mere bystanders to these developments. A 2016 Angus Reid poll found that about only one-quarter of Canadians agreed that NAFTA is good for the country and about one-third supported its renegotiation. Prime Minister Trudeau appears to recognize that Canadians are ambivalent about free trade, which may explain why, only two days after Donald Trump's election, Trudeau stated, "If Americans want to talk about NAFTA, I'm happy to talk about it." It is hard to imagine that the results of such talks would lead to less economic integration between the world's two most integrated economies.

Index